BFI FILM AND TELEVISION HANDBOOK 2002

www.bfi.org.uk/handbook

 British Film Institute

Editor: Eddie Dyja

Project Manager: David Sharp
Deputy Editor: Linda Wood
Production: Tom Cabot

Information Services
Statistics Manager: Peter Todd
Statistics Research: Erinna Mettler, Phil Wickham
Statistics Tabulation: Ian O'Sullivan

Additional Research/Editorial Assistance
Sean Delaney, Allen Eyles, Liz Heasman, Louise
Johnston, Les Roberts, David Sharp
Database Consultant: Lavinia Orton
Marketing: Rebecca Watts, Sarah Prosser
Cover Design: ketchup

Advertising Consultant: Ronnie Hackston

Website: www.bfi.org.uk/handbook

With many thanks to those who assisted with
photographs: BBC, *bfi* Collections, Buena Vista
International, Carlton, Channel 4 Television, Columbia
TriStar, Entertainment Film Distributors, FilmFour
Distributors, Granada, Icon, Miramax, Pathé
Distribution, Twentieth Century Fox, Universal Pictures
International, United International Pictures (UK), The
Walt Disney Company, Warner Bros, Yash Raj, Yorkshire
Television

The views expressed in this book are those of the
author, and do not necessarily reflect *bfi* policy in any
given area.

Printed in Great Britain by Bath Press, Bath

A catalogue record for this book is available from the
British Library.

ISBN 0 85170 9044

Price: £20.00

Front Cover images (clockwise)

Captain Corelli's Mandolin © Universal Pictures/UIP
Bridget Jones's Diary © Universal Pictures/UIP
Ali G Amanda Searle/© Channel 4
Anne Robinson © BBC 2001
Lara Croft Tomb Raider © Paramount/UIP

Contents

CHOICE

THE OPTIONS YOU WANT, THE QUALITY YOU EXPECT

Kodak Vision 800T film 7289/5289
Tungsten-800 EI Daylight-500* EI

The world's fastest tungsten-balanced stock. Offers the sharpness and grain structure you would expect only in slower products. Allows for increased creative flexibility in low light, fast action, anamorphic, super 35mm and other filming conditions, where systems speed is vitally important.

Kodak Vision 500T film 7279/5279
Tungsten-500 EI Daylight-320* EI

With improved grain and sharpness, this high speed tungsten balanced stock offers rich colours and excellent detail in low and very low light conditions.

Kodak Vision 250D film 7246/5246
Daylight-250 EI Tungsten-64**EI

A high speed daylight balanced film stock providing the highest image quality for its speed. It delivers a rich reproduction of blacks in natural and mixed lighting conditions.

Eastman EXR 100T film 7248/5248
Tungsten-100 EI Daylight-64*EI

A medium speed tungsten balanced stock with wide exposure latitude. Very good grain and saturation producing excellent highlights and shadow detail.

Kodak Vision Expression 500T film 7284/5284
Tungsten-500 EI Daylight-320* EI

This high speed stock combines lower contrast, for smooth, pleasing skintone and softer overall look, with very wide exposure latitude - for fine image detail, especially in the shadows. Natural colour reproduction and a neutral tone scale make this stock an excellent choice for shooting in minimal, variable and mixed lighting conditions.

Kodak Vision 320T film 7277/5277
Tungsten-320 EI Daylight-200* EI

This unique tungsten balanced stock offers a less saturated look with slightly lower contrast whilst providing superb shadow detail as well as clean, white highlights.

Kodak Vision 200T film 7274/5274
Tungsten-200 EI Daylight-125* EI

A higher speed tungsten balanced stock with fine grain and outstanding sharpness, offering a wide exposure latitude and excellent colour reproduction. A very good all round stock that works very well in almost any lighting condition.

Eastman EXR 50D film 7245/5245
Daylight-50 EI Tungsten-12**EI

A daylight balanced stock, extremely sharp and virtually grain free. This film offers a wide exposure latitude with rich, natural colours. An excellent choice for bright exteriors.

Contact Numbers
To order film stock telephone the Order Services Department direct on **01442 845945**, or fax us on **01442 844458**. Your order will be handled by Julie Jackson, Julie Carrington or Anne-Marie Masson.

www.kodak.com/go/motion

there's more to the story™

ACKNOWLEDGMENTS

Fort Handbook can be a pretty desolate place at times. Happily, I have been fortunate to have found many willing helpers who have been quick on the draw and kept me posted with the various changes that have taken place within the industry. My sincere thanks to all those who have supported and contributed to the *bfi Film and Television Handbook* throughout the year.

Up in the hills that lone pioneer, old Tom Cabot, ensured that the Handbook was produced to its usual high standard.

When I most needed it the Seventh Cavalry arrived in the form of Linda Wood, who with boundless dexterity, tirelessly rounded up the stragglers from the directory.

Passing the tumbleweeds and heading into Dodge City I am indebted to the pony express led by Peter Todd and his team in the Information Service of the *bfi* – Phil Wickham, Erinna Mettler and Ian O'Sullivan for supplying the statistics. And a special big whip-crack-away to Phil and Erinna for their extra contributions to the overview.

Entering into the saloon bar I encountered the good, the bad and the ugly. I pick out the good – Sean Delaney, Allen Eyles, Nicole Fries, Liz Heasman, Ronnie Hackston, Michael Henry, Louise Johnston, Tina McFarling, David Sharp, Ian Thomson – and tip my Stetson to them.

I also pay my respects to the Sheriff's Office who kept law and order – Sophie Contento, Andrew Lockett, Sarah Prosser and Rebbeca Watts – and saw that all was done by the book.

A special word of thanks this year goes to Danny Birchall, Ruth Stevens and Matt Ker who have sent the *Handbook* out online via smoke signals.

For a few dollars more, I salute some other high plains drifters who have supported me up to the hour of high noon – Karen Aniola, Tyrone Blackford, Melissa Bromley, Maureen Brown, Linda Briggs, Christophe Dupin, Eugene Finn, Alan Gregory, Lucia Hadjiconstanti, Alex Hogg, Adrian Hughes, Matt Ker, Ed Lawrenson, Jonathan Morris, Lavinia Orton, Markku Salmi, Sara Squire and Tise Vahimagi.

Screen Finance, Screen International and *Screen Digest* acted like the Western Union and provided us with the necessary information so that we could compile the statistical sections and their continued support and co-operation is deeply appreciated.

Thanks also go to those fellow travellers on the stagecoach, including the following organisations and individuals: The BBC, The British Film Commission (BFC), British Screen Finance, British Videogram Association (BVA), Central Statistical Office (CSO), Cinema Advertising Association (CAA), Entertainment Data Inc. (EDI), The Department for Culture, Media and Sport (DCMS), The Film Council, Independent Television Commission (ITC), Tim Adler, Roger Bennett at ELPSA, Lavinia Carey, Patrick Frater, Allan Hardy, Barrie MacDonald and Steve Perrin.

Eddie Dyja, Handbook Editor, September 2001

2001/02

MONSTERS, INC.

THE SHIPPING NEWS

RETURN TO NEVERLAND

KATE & LEOPOLD

LILO & STITCH

Buena Vista International (UK) Ltd, 3 Queen Caroline Street, Hammersmith, London W6 9PE

www.thefilmfactory.co.uk

FOREWORD

by Joan Bakewell CBE,
Chair of the British Film Institute

I have just completed my first year as Chair of the *bfi* and I'm delighted to report that the past year has been one of solid achievement. Since the fundamental restructuring of government film support in 2000 that changed our whole landscape, we have moved rapidly and purposefully to implement the *bfi*'s new strategy. That strategy makes education our priority: we now have in place an impressive range of opportunities for young people, in schools, clubs and colleges to enjoy and appreciate the richness of film culture.

We are making more films available in more places across the country. New collaborations secured this year with UCI and Odeon have brought access to *bfi* material to 40 cinemas, complementing the work of our film booking services to regional film theatres, independent cinemas, specialist exhibitors and film societies. We will not stop there. We want to bring the wealth of cinema to as many people as possible. Indeed, we would like everyone who loves film to find themselves within reach of the collections which we hold in trust for the nation. In London the National Film Theatre has refocussed its programming to improve access to world cinema and our collections. The Regus London Film Festival and the Lesbian and Gay Film Festival have attracted more films and bigger audiences than ever before.

Plans for a major new Film Centre on London's South Bank are now more than a distant dream. The outstanding British architect David Chipperfield recently won a high profile competition to design the building and Lord Puttnam is leading our appeal. Hopes are high for a purpose-built centre where our library, museum, cinemas and offices will all find a home.

The *bfi*'s Film and Television Handbook is but one of the many things we do well. It has become an essential reference work throughout the industry and a valuable resource for anyone new to the medium. I am delighted to commend the latest edition to you.

INTRODUCTION

by Jon Teckman,
Director of the British Film Institute

2002 is an important year for the British Film Institute as it marks the 50th anniversary of our National Film Theatre (NFT). Throughout this period, the NFT has remained one of the places to see the world's biggest and best choice of films. To celebrate this achievement we will be hosting a number of events during the year starting with a season devoted to the works of Akira Kurosawa who was one of the first directors featured when the NFT opened in 1952. The actual anniversary itself, in October 2002, will be marked by a retrospective of the works of the great British film and television actor, Sir Alec Guinness.

During the coming year we will also be developing a range of other initiatives to take forward our commitment to increasing access to our collections and vast databases of information about film and television. This wonderfully informative Film and Television Handbook is just one

manifestation of the many ways in which we try to share our knowledge and expertise with the film and television worlds and the general public.

Some of the new offerings which are either available now or will be developed in 2002 include:

Improved remote access to *bfi* resources
The *bfi* National Library's book catalogue, with more than 42,000 records, is now available on the Internet, allowing users everywhere to research our vast collection of books on film and television. As well as reference books, the database lists pamphlets, bibliographies, PhD theses, directories, yearbooks, annual reports, encyclopedias, filmographies and published scripts. Searches may now be made by film title, personality, subject and keyword, as well as book title and author. More details are available at **www.bfi.org.uk/library/olib**

New theatrical, DVD and Video releases
Theatrical releases planned for 2002 include: *To Sleep with Anger* (Burnett, US 1990), *Brighton Rock* (Boulting, GB 1947), *Saturday Night and Sunday Morning* (Reisz, GB 1960), *The Loneliness of the Long Distance Runner* (Richardson, GB 1962), *If...* (Anderson, GB 1968), *Freaks* (Browning, US, 1932), *High Society* (Walters, US 1956)

The library's online catalogue – finger clicking good

Saturday Night and Sunday Morning to be re-released in 2002

and *Sunset Boulevard* (Wilder, US 1950). We also plan to release up to 16 DVD/Video titles including: *A Taste of Honey* (Richardson, GB, 1961), *The Loneliness of the Long Distance Runner* (Richardson, UK, 1962), *British Avant-Garde Vols 3 and 4, Chaplin at Essanay, Stray Dog* (Kurosawa, Jp, 1949) and *Voyage to Italy* (Rossellini, Italy, 1953).

A new TV Archive strand

Until now, access to our collections of classic television material has been limited to research and monthly cinema screenings at the NFT. We have therefore launched a new Archive TV strand which will release classic TV productions and make them available on video and DVD. The first titles to be released are Ken Russell's elegant and moving *Delius; Song of Summer* (1968), based on Eric Fenby's memoir of the composer Delius, *The Stone Tape* (1972), a cult ghost story written by Nigel Kneale of Quatermass fame which has not been seen since 1973, and Jonathan Miller's acclaimed adaptation of the classic M R James ghost story *Whistle and I'll Come to You* (1968) starring Michael Hordern. Plans for future titles include a companion piece to *Song of Summer*, Ken Russell's *Elgar* (1962), and two stunning interpretations of war: *Culloden* (1964) and *The War Game* (1966). For more detailed information, please visit our website at **www.bfi.org.uk/archivetv**

bfi presents 'ImagineAsia'

Our commitment to promoting public access to film relating to the UK's many and diverse cultures and communities is progressing well with the launch of the ImagineAsia project. – an eight month UK-wide celebration of the cinema cultures of India, Sri Lanka, Bangladesh and Pakistan, including British-Asian, work which will reach major cities throughout England, Wales,

Northern Ireland and Scotland. The project plan includes the world's first Indian cinema education pack for schools and colleges, major seasons of films and talks at the NFT and other cinemas UK-wide, video and DVD releases, a major international conference, and the publication of books on celebrated filmmaker Yash Chopra and Nurjehan. Eminent film personalities like Aamir Khan, Shyam Benegal, Shekhar Kapur and Meera Syal have agreed to be patrons of the event.

bfi Touring Exhibition

The two year tour will be launched early in 2002 and aims to provide an abbreviated showcase of *bfi* activities reaching audiences in Sheffield, Birmingham, Bristol, Manchester and London. We are also planning to reach audiences in Scotland and Northern Ireland. The exhibition will have broad audience appeal, specifically targeting family audiences and children aged 7-16 years, as part of our efforts to engage and invest in our future generations. The exhibition looks forward to the development of a new museum within our planned new Film Centre on London's South Bank. The exhibition will also pilot new innovations in service delivery which, if successful, may become permanent features in the new museum. Prime exhibits on tour are likely to include Marilyn Monroe's dress from *Some Like It Hot*, Charlie Chaplin's hat and cane, Russell Crowe's costume from *Gladiator* and the *Big Brother* chair. Educational workshops will also be made available at venues. The touring exhibition will be the first phase of a longer term touring exhibition programme which the *bfi* is currently developing in our efforts to reach new audiences.

First titles on video/DVD from Archive TV strand

bfi's two main festivals go on tour in 2002

Film touring programmes

The touring programmes for our two main festivals, the Regus London Film Festival and the London Lesbian and Gay Festival, will continue in 2002. In addition to this a number of tours are planned which include: programmes to coincide with the ImagineAsia project; the Sheffield International Documentary Film Festival on Tour, Studio Ghibli (a Barbican touring programme, at selected venues), and showcases celebrating the works of directors, Akira Kurosawa and Kon Ichikawa.

Digitisation of *bfi* collections – *bfi* Online

Harnessing the latest information and communications technologies to deliver greater access to our holdings is a key development. In particular, in the digital arena, we are pointing the way for the future of moving images in research and education. More than 30 hours of moving image material in high quality (MPEG) digital form are now available via online terminals, together with hundreds of still photographs, script extracts, personal papers and recorded interviews from the *bfi* collections. The new-look *bfi* Online is sited at three locations: the *bfi* National Library, the NFT on London's South Bank and the Broadway Media Centre in Nottingham. We are also planning to pilot this facility at a number of specialist schools and media arts colleges. I am particularly pleased to report that our work to date in this area will be significantly enhanced by a £1.2m award from the New Opportunities Fund to deliver an educational resource that offers hundreds of hours of digitised moving images to all UK schools and public libraries.

More information about all of these plans, as well as regularly updated news about our ongoing activities is available on our website at **www.bfi.org.uk** I hope that you will continue to make good use of that facility and all of our many and diverse activities over the coming year.

Welcome to *bfi* Online

bfi Online is the British Film Institute's pilot resource for education and research in film and television. The service contains collections devoted to Alfred Hitchcock, Powell and Pressburger and Alexander Korda, as well as a fascinating selection of silent British comedies and a look at forty years of television drama. Other collections examine the shortlived but influential Free Cinema movement, and the representation of race on television.

bfi Online features more than forty hours of high quality video alongside hundreds of still photographs, scripts, posters, recorded audio interviews and more from the *bfi*'s massive collections.

bfi Online is currently available at three sites in London and Nottingham. It is not presently available via the internet.

Continue >

More about *bfi* Online >

Television Drama

Early TV drama consisted largely of live televised stage plays, while adapted plays and novels remained the main diet of TV drama well into the 1950s. From the early '50s however, writers, directors and producers were struggling to free the form from its theatrical origins, and to develop a style more suited to television. Nigel Kneale's Orwell adaptation *Nineteen Eighty-Four* (1954) for BBC integrated a number of filmed location sequences between the live studio performances. The abandonment of live performance was an early goal for many as they sought to make use of the greater creative freedom offered by recording and editing.

By the early '60s, writers and directors like Troy Kennedy Martin (*Z Cars*) and Ken Loach were calling for the development of a new form of realist drama written specially for television, relying on editing and techniques borrowed from other forms such as documentary. Loach's powerful *Cathy Come Home* (1966), written by Jeremy Sandford for the BBC's *The Wednesday Play*, and Peter Watkins' *The War Game* (1966) largely escaped the studio and made full use of the new techniques to create a passionate and energetic dramatic style that was uniquely televisual.

By the '80s, single drama was in decline (see *The South Bank Show* for a discussion), replaced by films made for cinema, and many drama series were genre based, with crime series such as *The Professionals* proving particularly popular. At the same time, soap opera, a mainstay in the schedules since the early 1960s, began to assume a new importance, with newer soaps like *EastEnders* challenging the position of the long-running *Coronation Street*.

Nineteen Eighty-Four
Quatermass & the Pit
Dixon of Dock Green
Cathy Come Home
Z Cars
The War Game
Upstairs, Downstairs
Cream in My Coffee
The South Bank Show
The Professionals
EastEnders

See also:

Timeline of British Television

British Silent Comedy

Early British film comedies have received little attention by comparison with their better known American counterparts, partly because most of the great silent screen comedians (many of them, like Charlie Chaplin, British) were working in Hollywood with higher production values, but also because British humour was regarded as quirky, wordy, anarchic and parochial.

Early films such as *Mary Jane's Mishap* (1903) or *Our New Errand Boy* (1905) reflect the trends of those early days in both American and European film, using devices such as facials, physical gags, the chase, and titillation. By the teens Fred Evans, aka *Pimple*, was making very popular parodies of contemporary plays and films, targeted narrowly at the British market in much the same way as today's television topical sketch shows. In the 1920s Adrian Brunel produced educated spoofs ridiculing film form itself, just as *Monty Python* was to do so successfully in the 1960s. The common factor here was cheapness, and British filmmakers excelled at making a virtue of low production values.

A little attention to the films themselves, rather than their reputation, pays dividends. Many remain genuinely funny, but more importantly they reveal the origins of a specifically British humour, notably absurdism, parody and the music hall tradition. These films anticipate the indigenous humour of the 1950s Ealing comedies, *Monty Python* or *Benny Hill* for which Britain is justly famous.

- Bryony Dixon, *bfi* Collections

Mary Jane's Mishap
Our New Errand Boy
The Man to Beat
Jack Johnson
Tilly, the Tomboy
Love and the Varsity
Daisy Doodad's Dial
Pimple in the Whip
Two-Chinned Chow
Bonzolino
Would You Believe It?

See also:

Powell & Pressburger
British Hitchcock
Timeline of British Cinema

bfi Online contains over 30 hours of moving image material

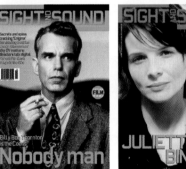

UK FILM, TELEVISION AND VIDEO: OVERVIEW

by Eddie Dyja

Depending on your point of view, it is easy to give two interpretations on the current state of film, television and interactive multi-media in Britain. The optimists are thrilled by the boom in the British film industry and look forward to integrated digital TV/DVD players which offer broadband access to the internet. The pessimists meanwhile, shake their heads and claim that the majority of British films are dire, that the internet as an entertainment source is unwieldy, and that it'll be at least a decade before the TV analogue signal is turned off. Somewhere in between these views is a narrow tightrope where an uneasy balance can be made.

Election
The result of the General Election was predictable with Labour easing themselves back into office but the subsequent reshuffle of the Department for Culture, Media and Sport was harder to call. Culture Secretary Chris Smith, who oversaw radical reform in the Communications White Paper, not to mention the setting up of the Film Council, was lambasted in the press for the Dome, the Lottery and Wembley Stadium. He was replaced by Tessa Jowell, while Kim Howells became the new minister for tourism, film and broadcasting replacing Janet Anderson.

The Communications White Paper
Outlines of a new single regulatory body for the media and telecommunications industry, Ofcom, were top of the reforms proposed in the Government's White Paper. Ofcom will replace the existing regulators which include the Independent Television Commission (ITC); the Broadcasting Standards Commission (BSC); the Radio Authority and Oftel. The BBC will be allowed to maintain its own self-regulation, although Ofcom will act as an ombudsman for BBC viewers whose complaints have not been fairly treated. The proposed Ofcom will have oversight of films shown on television and the

Bridget Jones's Diary – British film v.g.

internet, while the British Board of Film Classification (BBFC) will continue to review the same material for cinema, video and DVD.

The door was opened for the formation of a single company owning the ITV network. The rule limiting audience share of 15 per cent will go. Also scrapped was the rule barring one company from owning both the London weekday and weekend franchises. This was welcomed by television's current two giants Granada and Carlton who may yet merge at some point in the future. The panoply of control that has characterised the ITV since its creation in the mid-1950s looks like it might be coming to an end.

Cross-media ownership rules, which prevent national newspaper groups with more than 20 per cent of the market from owning terrestrial TV stations, stayed the same, although the Government invited comments for consultation.

The Film Council

The burden of responsibility for taking flak for Lottery-funded films passed over from the Arts Council of England to the sapling Film Council. Within a year the knives were out and slashing away.

The first cause for consternation in the media was the review of the licences for the three Lottery-funded franchises. The Film Consortium, which had pledged to make 39 films in return for a £30.25m handout had, at the time of writing, produced around a quarter of that total. In April 2001, the beleaguered franchise was taken over by Civilian Content, a UK-based media company, which looked to restructure the franchise with a new business plan. Similarly, Pathé Productions, who have maintained a steady if unspectacular output, and DNA Films who finally released its first film, *Beautiful Creatures* in April 2001, all passed their reviews.

There was also some concern at the Film Council's seemingly populist stance and desire to secure box office success. The debate centred on whether Robert Altman's *Gosford Park,* with its impressive cast and UK setting, was the type of film the Film Council should be backing. The same critics berated the Arts Council for subsidising films that flopped at the box office. The grumblers tended to focus on awards to the Premiere Fund – which was set up for the production of popular mainstream films. The Film Council was at pains to point out that it also had two funds aimed at less mainstream films and developing new talent – the New Cinema Fund and the Development Fund. All this was to no avail. Lottery-funded films look likely to be slated irrespective of whether they are good, bad or ugly.

Meanwhile, the Film Council's overhaul of English regional funding through its £6m Regional Investment Fund for England, aimed at encouraging regional film development, was introduced without the same level of brouhaha.

By August 2001 the Film Council had yet to deliver its promised strategy on distribution and exhibition, (although it had started a consultation process for these two sectors). For better or for worse, film production in the UK has been on the increase over the past few years, the problem in the industry comes from a tranche of small independent distributors trying to place small British films into a competitive marketplace. Exhibitors, at present are unlikely to choose cool, worthy British films ahead of blockbusters like *Planet of the Apes.* The exhibition sector is dominated by American and French-owned companies. Nevertheless, with doom and gloom merchants claiming that multiplexes have finally reached saturation point in the UK, there is certainly screen space available to accommodate a wider range of films. However, whether the will or the incentives are there is another matter. Whether the answer lies in imposing quotas – such as dictating that a percentage of screens must show a British film while offering initial subsidies for cinemas (to offset any initial losses) also remains to be seen. It is a conundrum worth solving if the Film Council is ever to come close to achieving its aim of a sustainable British film industry.

The Best of British

In many ways the British film industry is booming. Section 48 tax incentives were extended for a further three years in the March 2001 budget. These measures which allow producers to write off against tax all production or acquisition costs of films with budgets under £15m, have eased the pressure on UK film-makers. There remains a perception that Britain provides excellent acting, directing and movie-making talent, and British production facilities tend to be universally praised. In other words the British have the tools to make excellent films. How or where these tools are utilised isn't really so important. A good film is still a good film whether it is shot in the West Country or the West Coast of America.

In the early part of 2001 box office successes have already been scored by *Bridget Jones's Diary, Captain Corelli's Mandolin* and *Lara Croft Tomb Raider.* Add to this three box office hits from 2000, *Chicken Run, Billy Elliot* and *Snatch* and this constitutes the best run of British success for years. *Bridget Jones's Diary* not only became the

Gosford Park gave a clue to the Film Council's intentions

Harry Potter and the Sorcerer's Stone – you've read the book

second most successful UK film of all time (just behind the *Full Monty*) but also had the highest ever opening weekend for a British film of £5.72m. The film provided Hugh Grant with an enviable hat-trick of crowd-pleasing hits following on from *Notting Hill* and *Four Weddings and a Funeral*. These films have all helped to stimulate the industry, create jobs and a buzz that there is real export value in British titles. Films such as *Harry Potter and the Sorcerer's Stone* have boosted UK film production and kept UK film studios busy.

When looking for the best in British films the name Working Title bestrides the industry like a giant. At the risk of sounding repetitious their successes have included *Bridget Jones's Diary, Notting Hill, Four Weddings and a Funeral, Bean, Fargo, Billy Elliot, O Brother, Where Art Thou?, High Fidelity* and *Captain Corelli's Mandolin*. Success has been helped by securing a distribution deal with Universal and not surprisingly the company has an excellent track record globally.

Film-going remains popular in Britain, with attendances at their highest level for 26 years. Figures for 2000 showed a rise in audiences of three per cent. This came in a year with surprisingly few blockbusters, suggesting that British audiences aren't obsessed with American blockbusters as we are often led to believe. Also audiences in the UK are getting older with the baby-boomers of the 1960s perhaps looking for something a bit more challenging than the usually undemanding 18-24 demographically-challenged films.

The Worst of British

Last year's Handbook commented on how the likely success in America of Mike Hodges' *Croupier* would have

repercussions in Britain. Sure enough the film was re-released in the UK only for reviewers to assert that they always thought the film was great in the first place. *Croupier* was so highly regarded in the UK first time round that no distributor would touch it except for the *bfi* who managed two prints of the film. With that kind of backing the film, like so many other British films, sank without a trace.

It was only when the film resurfaced and took off in the States that a collective "Doh" could be heard in the pubs and clubs of Soho. Suddenly with revisionist zeal, the film was revived in the UK. That a half-decent UK film was treated with such scant regard in the first place speaks volumes at the present state of both distribution and exhibition in the UK which is dominated, and dictated to, by American products.

However, the blame cannot be entirely shouldered by distributors and exhibitors. The boom in film production in the UK has led to too many half-baked films going into production rather than being developed. As a result distributors and exhibitors are having to sift through a proportionately larger amount of poor quality films. The biggest blight in British films today is the lack of decent scripts, or decent script editing. No amount of expert editing can salvage a film, even if it contains a recognisable star. Too many British films appear flat because the script is poor and characters all seem one dimensional. The successful films released in the UK generally have tight scripts which have been through various stages of revision.

In 2000, a whole series of interesting non-mainstream American films were released such as *Being John Malkovich, Timecode, Fight Club, Memento* and *Magnolia*. Sadly, a comparable British list of films covering the same period cannot be drawn up. Indeed, the 2001 Cannes Film Festival took part with no British films in competition, much to the dismay of the British journalists covering the event.

Shorts

Despite the surprise decision by the BBC to scrap the British Short Film Festival, short films look like making a significant contribution to an artistic revival of British films. There are a growing number of websites dedicated to the burgeoning talents of British film-makers. For instance, www.in-movies.co.uk offers a jamboree bag of over 150 shorts, mini-shorts and micro-shorts featuring works by new directors, as well as more established names such as Peter Greenaway, Simon Beaufoy and

Being John Malkovich – no British equivalent

Shane Meadows. It can be argued that first time directors keen to impress with their potential, put more effort into the script and visuals of their work. They tend to be more eager to make an impression as a result. Also putting a short on the internet provides instant access to audiences worldwide.

Surveys have suggested that audiences would not mind seeing short films before their main feature. After all, at present audiences settle for expensive and arty commercials, advertising gin or Guinness. Audiences also get in-yer-face trailers for films which generally highlight every major scene in the film (although not in chronological order) – not so much an aperitif but rather the dessert. Well-programmed shorts might be a welcome relief not only in cinemas but also on the television.

Television
British television is often said to be the best in the world (usually by those working in it). It can be said that the British television industry does not suffer the same neurosis and inferiority complex that the British film industry does. Programmes are sold on a global scale and innovative gameshows such as *Who Wants to Be a Millionaire* and *The Weakest Link* are bought up by American companies. In that respect the TV industry can remain justifiably bullish. However, recent criticisms of the sharp decline in quality of current affairs programmes, dramas and sitcoms have led the pessimists to believe that the golden age of television has long passed us by.

It was an eventful year for terrestrial television where ratings and shifts in scheduling were intense. Parallel to the jostling for audience figures came the establishment of a plethora of digital TV channels.

ITV advertising revenue suffered a dramatic 8.9 per cent fall in 2001. This represented the worst advertising depression since commercial TV went on air. The pressure built up to create one single ITV company while the issue of cross-media ownership was not fully resolved. What was resolved was ITV's rebranding which meant amending its name to ITV1 thereby complementing its digital channel ITV2.

ITV launched its football highlights show *The Premiership* at 7.00pm on Saturday 18 August 2001, fronted by Des Lynham. The significance of the timing for the show was great. Saturday evening schedules for television have rarely, if ever, strayed from the inane light entertainment shows – ranging from circus style shows and holiday camp programmes in the fifties and sixties to shows like *The Generation Game, Blind Date, Big Break* and *Friends Like These* Whether or not the early-evening football slot will survive is debatable, but what it has done is forced the BBC to rethink its own scheduling to compete with the perceived audience-winner. Ironically, the BBC's coverage of England's 5-1 victory in Munich, on 1st September 2001, against Germany, during that early-evening Saturday slot surpassed any audience figure that *The Premiership* is ever likely to achieve.

The head-to-head ratings battles or ratings-charged episodes of soaps seemed to be a feature of the year. *News at Ten* appeared back in its slot on ITV while the BBC controversially moved the *Nine O'clock News* to ten

You are the The Weakest Link – goodbye

Channel 4's Black Books won a BAFTA for Best Sitcom

o'clock. This created the rather bizarre spectacle of a news ratings battle. Another notable battle took place when the last episode of *One Foot in the Grave* was pitted against *Who Wants to Be a Millionaire* (when Judith Keppel won the £1m). Soap operas came loaded with rape, murder and adulterous mayhem culminating in various storylines based on the theme of whodunit. The choice of suspects was offered in various guises by *EastEnders, Coronation Street, Emmerdale* and *Brookside*. The extreme nature of these soaps often stretched credibility to its limits. Nevertheless, the BBC thought it worth the effort to put *EastEnders* on for five nights a week. In the meantime, *Crossroads* returned to soap opera land. Fans of soaps certainly cannot complain about the lack of suds on the screen.

Both ITV and BBC were criticised by the ITC for providing too narrow a range of programmes. It claimed that viewers were being fed an unbalanced diet of programmes based around soaps, quizzes and leisure shows. The ITC particularly recommended that the ITV improved its factual programmes.

Others criticised the BBC for becoming too commercial and losing sight of its public service remit. A Government-commissioned report cleared the BBC of breaching its fair-trading rules and commercial policies. At the same time the corporation was generating extra income in sales of programmes such as *The Weakest Link* and the merchandising of popular programmes. There were also complaints about its digital service. During its coverage of Wimbledon for instance, the BBC gave digital viewers the chance to view any one of the matches played that day. However, analogue viewers had to be content with the usual coverage. It seemed that the

licence payers money was not benefiting all licence fee payers.

Channel 4 had a good year. The success of *Big Brother 2* was an obvious boost. However, the channel was by no means a one-hit wonder. The haul of 11 TV BAFTA awards including a range of categories such as Best News and Current Affairs Journalism *Out of Africa*; Best Documentary *True Stories – 100% White*; Best Sitcom *Black Books*; Best Drama Serial *Longitude;* Best Comedy Programme or Series *Da Ali G Show* and Best Entertainment Programme or Series *So Graham Norton* testified to that. This left outgoing Chief Executive Michael Jackson with reasons to be cheerful. Yet, Channel 4 didn't escape controversy when it screened and then repeated its *Brass Eye* special on paedophilia. The spoof documentary caused an almighty storm in the press and in Parliament, with complaints that the programme was in bad taste. This reaction seemed to mirror the kind of media hysteria that the programme-makers were aiming to satirise. It also highlighted the limited powers the ITC has as a watchdog and as a result might have added more power to the elbow of the new communications regulator Ofcom.

In the meantime Channel 5 continued to increase its audience-share and responded to an ITC request to reduce the number of adult-orientated programmes. The challenge for chief executive Dawn Airey, who succeeded David Elstein at the end of 2000, was to build on its steady audience figures.

Reality TV

The next big thing in convergence-style interactive TV to dominate our multi-media environments was Reality TV. It is hard to define Reality TV other than to say that it has nothing to do with reality and everything to do with TV. It involves an elimination element whereby either the audience at home or the contestants themselves get to vote each other off. It might have just as easily been labelled Addictive TV or Turn Off TV (depending on your point of view).

Channel 4 led the charge with the phenomenally successful *Big Brother 2* not to mention the charity version *Celebrity Big Brother*. This time to spice up the ratings ITV introduced *Survivor*. The two shows dominated the summer schedules. Ironically, part of the appeal of these goldfish bowl type shows is their soap-opera quality. They show ordinary (young) people interacting with each other in mundane and ordinary ways.

Hey, hey we're Hear'Say

The Weakest Link issued the year's most notable catchphrase: "You are the weakest link – goodbye," from its mean-spirited presenter Anne Robinson. There followed a bewildering array of *Weakest Link* specials (including a Reality TV Special). Anne Robinson also hosted the US version of the show.

Popstars produced the ever smiling, chart-topping, teen-group, Hear'Say, and no doubt there will be a slew of follow-up programmes based on similar formats – *Soapstars* currently proving that point.

Excess exposure of "celebrities" was exercised to its full by the tabloids who courted, signed up and generally pampered Reality TV contestants. No doubt Reality TV shows are hear to stay, and with the promise of saucier programmes, and variations on the same theme, this is excellent news... for the tabloids.

Digital Television
While TV, satellite and cable companies have been gearing themselves up for digital television by rigorous reorganisation, the fishing trip for new customers has proved less easy. The Government has even waded into the waters by suggesting that free digital set-tops might be dangled as an incentive for the nation's armchair army.

At present 30 per cent of the UK population receive digital television, but many of these homes also retain analogue televisions in other parts of their home. The headache for the Government and the digital TV players is to persuade the population to switch from analogue to digital TV. There have been mutterings that the projected switch-off timetable (between 2006 and 2010) is not realistic. It is ironic that the message "analogue TV will cease to exist, so switch to digital TV" is proving so difficult to put across, particularly through a medium which reaches so many households. Increasingly, cross-promotional advertising is appearing on all analogue channels. No doubt this will increase over the next few years as more and more popular programmes are moved across to digital channels.

ITV announced that it had exclusive rights to broadcast the first interactive television version of *Who Wants to Be a Millionaire* which is likely to be broadcast on ITV2.

Channel 4 raised eyebrows by creating its own pay-TV entertainment channel, E4 and frustrating its terrestrial viewers by packing off first runs of its popular imports such as the *West Wing* and *the Sopranos*.

Of the two main players BSkyB, who achieved modest consolidation, had an easier year than OnDigital. OnDigital struggled through the early part of 2001 before finding some stability by rebranding itself ITV Digital.

Video/DVD
Surprisingly, both video and DVD continued to flourish. DVD player sales continued to rise but, with integrated Digital TV/internet/DVD systems being refined sales in players may slow down. The public's appetite for DVD and home entertainment was reflected in a boom-time for DVD sales. As sales of widescreen systems, home cinema systems, back projection units and plasma

Swapping analogue TV for Digital TV proved to be problematic

Broadband streaming to a screen near you soon

televisions continue to rise, multiplexes and small independent cinemas may start to consider their own future strategies.

If one thing is certain it is the ability of video/DVD to withstand serious challenges from other media. The biggest threat now comes from broadband access to the internet and the development of TiVo which enables users to store and programme their recorded material more efficiently.

A development in video rentals came with the Blockbuster rental chains decision to fill their shelves with the same copy of its latest video release – *What Lies Beneath* being the film dominating the shelves at the time of writing. This policy came with the dubious claim that those renting videos would have more choice than ever before. Mind you, a chain called Blockbusters is hardly going to fill the shelves with arthouse and straight-to-video British films. Nevertheless, it is an interesting marketing exercise.

A report commissioned by the Video Standards Council returned an inconclusive verdict to prove or disprove a link with screen violence to actual violence. The report stated that the media tends to make the association irrespective of the evidence. It was interesting therefore that the BBFC vowed to tighten up some aspects of its policy on violence, particularly the depiction of knives in films, while relaxing its attitude to sex.

Broadband

To paraphrase from the film *The Graduate* "I just want to say just one word to you – broadband". At the time of writing NTL and Telewest joined forces in a joint marketing campaign to promote high-speed internet access. Under the hustings style slogan 'Building Broadband Britain' - the cable companies offer of broadband internet access of £24.99 per month was cheaper than the £40 per month offered by BT. The broadband connection was 10 times faster than standard dial-up connections over conventional telephone lines. It is not clear whether NTL and Telewest may yet merge to form one big company, but it seems likely that the two cable players will form an increasingly close relationship.

Broadband is important because it opens up the potential of the internet as an entertainment source. At present the internet is a pretty useful information tool (although pessimists claim that they can never find what they want), however, it falls a long way behind film, television, video/DVD, radio, CDs and computer games for pure entertainment value. The failure of Pop.com, the entertainment internet company backed by Steven Spielberg and Ron Howard, was proof that the internet as a showcase for films and programmes is still in its infancy. It will be interesting to note the uptake of broadband and to see how quickly it catches the public's imagination.

Perhaps by this time next year the merger of TV and the internet will have become more apparent and its advantages including personalisation and video on demand more obvious. Personal TV Services will mean that people wouldn't have to bother with the internet on their personal computers and this could spell the end for Internet Service Providers. However, the biggest losers may be the advertisers since viewers using systems like TiVo will be able to programme their viewing to avoid showing any adverts.

BFI Film and Television Handbook

Finally, evidence of how 21st century technology is affecting our lives has reached this edition of the Handbook, which now has its own website (**www.bfi.org.uk/handbook**). You now have the choice of reading this commentary online or reading it from the book. If you are reading in book form (which is obviously the best way) then this sentence is for you.

① Number and Value of UK Films* 1981-2000

Year	Titles produced	Current prices (£m)	Production cost (£m) (2001 prices**)
1981	24	61.2	139.8
1982	40	141.1	297.1
1983	51	251.1	505.9
1984	53	270.4	483.6
1985	54	269.4	487.6
1986	41	165.8	290.3
1987	55	195.3	327.7
1988	48	175.2	283.0
1989	30	104.7	155.8
1990	60	217.4	292.0
1991	59	243.2	306.6
1992	47	184.9	224.4
1993	67	224.1	271.9
1994	84	455.2	540.9
1995	78	402.4	474.5
1996	128	741.4	845.0
1997	116	562.8	626.5
1998	88	509.3	548.6
1999	100	549.2	574.1
2000	98	804.3	828.4

*UK films are defined here as films produced in the UK or with a UK financial involvement, they include majority and minority co-productions
** based on calendar year inflation figure of 3 per cent

Source: Screen Finance/x25 Partnership/*bfi*

The Martins – a fully funded British film

Film Production

While the 98 titles produced in the UK in 2000 was two short of the 1999 figures (Table 1) the investment of £804.3m shows an enormous increase of around 70 per cent. It would be easy to get too carried away with this figure, particularly if the average budget of £8.2m for UK films were also taken into consideration. This total average surpasses the record-breaking year of 1996 when 30 more films were produced. As a snapshot of the current state of the British film industry it would be fair to say that film production in the UK was booming. However, it is always worth looking in closer detail at the way the Handbook chooses to construct its film production statistics.

The job of putting together a definitive list of 'British' films produced every year is complex. Over the last eight years the Handbook has devised a system, which while not perfect, gives a pretty good indication of the state of UK film production. The definition of 'British' in what is now very much a film industry that supersedes national boundaries is open to endless interpretation.

The legal framework of what constitutes a British film is notoriously loose. Essentially, it is based on the 1985 Films Act that sets parameters based on a percentage of labour costs and registration of producing companies within the UK and the European Economic Area as a whole. In 1997 this was broadened still further to allow films to qualify as British if they used foreign post-production studios, as was the case with titles such as Mark Herman's *Little Voice*.

There is still no official comprehensive registration system for British films that would make the task easier; although it has been on the Government's agenda for some time. Since 1997 there is a system (Section 48 Finance (No. 2) Act) whereby moving image works can be registered as British for tax write-off purposes, but this is voluntary. The scheme was extended in 2001 to 2005.

It is not especially illuminating, however, to just have a raw list of titles in front of you. These might vary from a fully-funded British film about contemporary Hatfield, Herts (*The Martins*) to a film involving a British producer that details the problems of Czech war heroes under communism (*Dark Blue World*). Both should be listed but we need some way to differentiate between them. To this end we organise the films into five different categories. The idea of this is to give you some idea of how culturally British we consider them to be. It is this

UK Film Production 2000 - Category A

Feature films where the cultural and financial impetus is from the UK and where the majority of personnel are British.

Title	Production company(ies)	Production cost (£m)
Al's Lads	Alchemy Pictures/Evolution Films	3.50
Alone	CF1/Evolution Films	6.00
Beautiful Mistake	Boda Films/S4C/Arts Council of Wales	0.50
Born Romantic	Kismet Films/BBC/Harvest Pictures/Redbus	3.20
The Bunker	Millennium Pictures	1.92
Chunky Monkey	Open Roads Films	0.15
Club le Monde	Screen Associates	0.63
Crush	Pipedream Pictures/Lee Thomas Productions/Film Four/Film Council	4.30
Daddy	Imaginary Films	1.50
Dead Creatures	Long Pig Productions	0.10
Dead in the Water	Spice Factory/Redbarn/Enterprise Films	2.40
Dog Eat Dog	Tiger Aspect/FilmFour/Shona Prods	1.60
The Emperor's New Clothes	Redwave/FilmFour	6.00
End Game	Various Films	3.50
The Filth and the Fury	Film Four/Sex Pistols/Jersey Shore/Nitrate Film	0.60
The Final Curtain	Young Crossbow/DNA	4.00
Gabriel and Me	Samuelson Prods/Film Consortium/British Screen/Isle of Man Film Commission	3.75
Gypsy Woman	Sky Pictures/Starfield Productions/Imagico/Wave Pictures/Isle of Man Film Commission	2.90
Happy Now	Ruby Films/BBC/Distant Horizon/Arts Council of Wales	3.11
The Hole	Cowboy Films/Granada/Impact/Pathe	4.16
The Honeytrap	Honeytrap Prods	0.83
Hot Gold	Little Wing Films/SDA Prods	14.50
Injustice	Migrant Media	0.25
Is Harry on the Boat?	Sky/Ruby Films/Rapido	1.00
Jesus the Curry King	Aylesbury Films	0.01
Kiss Kiss Bang Bang	Pagoda Films/Sky/Television Production Company	4.30
Large	Picture Palace North/Film Four/Film Consortium/Yorkshire Media Production Agency	1.40
Last Resort	BBC Films	0.75
Late Night Shopping	Ideal World/Film Four/Glasgow Film Office/Scottish Screen	1.60
Liam	BBC Films/MIDA	1.60
Lawless Heart	Martin Pope Productions/ Isle of Man Film Commission/British Screen/Film Council/October Films	1.50
Mad Dogs	Roaring Mice Films	0.50
The Martins	Tiger Aspect/Isle of Man Film Commission	3.00
The Meeksville Ghost	Peakviewing Prods	2.34
Mrs. Caldicot's Cabbage War	Cabbage Films	3.00
My Kingdom	Close Grip Films/Primary Pictures/Sky	5.00
Pasty Faces	Noel Gay Motion Picture Co/Victor Film Co/Metrodome/Lone Wolf	0.50
Plato's Breaking Point	Robark Pictures/Shawthing Media	0.75
Randall's Flat	Stage to Screen	1.50
Revelation	Romulus Films	4.13
Shiner	Wisecroft Productions/IAC/Geoffrey Reeve Film and TV	7.00
South West Nine	Fruit Salad Films/Irish Screen	2.00
The Sorceror's Apprentice	Peakviewing Transatlantic	2.35
Tabloid TV	Ultimate Pictures	5.00
This Filthy Earth	Film Four/Tall Stories/Sky/Yorkshire Media Production Agency/East London Film Fund	1.10

TOTAL NUMBER OF FILMS   45
TOTAL COST   £119.73m
AVERAGE COST   £2.66m

Source: Screen Finance/*bfi*

UK Film Production 2000 - Category B

Majority UK Co-Productions. Films in which, although there are foreign partners, there is a UK cultural content and a significant amount of British finance and personnel.

Title	Production companies/participating countries	Production cost (£m)
The Abduction Club	Pathe/Gruber and Samson Films/KC Meridien (**Republic of Ireland/Germany**)	6.00
The 51st State	Momentum Pictures/ Focus Films/Alliance Atlantis/Film Consortium/ Artists Production Group (**Canada**)	19.38
The Fourth Angel	Rafford Films/Norstar Filmed Entertainment/Sky (**Canada**)	9.69
Last Orders	Scala prods/MBP/Metrodome (**Germany**)	8.30
Lucky Break	Fragile Films/FilmFour/Senator Films (**Germany**)	4.00
Me Without You	Dakota Films/Isle of Man Film Commission/British Screen/Banque Luxembourg/Matrix Film/Britannia (**Luxembourg**)	3.70
Mumbo Jumbo	Mumbo Jumbo Prods/Firelight/Apollo Media (**Germany**)	2.84
My Brother	Trijbits Productions/ Film Council/Film Four/British Screen/Media II/ Filimboard Berlin-Brandenburg (**Germany**)	1.00
The Navigators	Parallax Pictures/Road Movies/Tornasol/Alta/Film Four/ Film Consortium (**Spain/Germany**)	1.70
One of the Hollywood Ten	Alibi Films/Arts Council of Wales/BBC/Canal + Spain/Morena/Bloom Street/ Saltire Entertainment/TVE (**Spain**)	4.00
Puckoon	Insight Ventures//Northern Ireland Film Commission/Arts Council of Northern Ireland/Irish Govt Section 481 Tax Incentives/MBP (**Republic of Ireland/Germany**)	3.50
The Reckoning	Renaissance Films/KanZaman/MDA Films (**Spain**)	9.62
Quicksand	Geoffrey Reeve Film/Cinesand/Visionview/Cinerenta (**Germany**)	6.33

TOTAL NUMBER OF FILMS	13
TOTAL COST	**£80.06m**
AVERAGE COST	**£6.16m**

Source: Screen Finance/*bfi*

cultural dimension that marks out the tables in the Handbook from others of its type.

It would be wrong to suggest that all this did not involve the exercising of personal judgement in deciding what we considered to be British, or in deciding how British we felt it to be and which films fitted into the different categories. This is inevitable. If it sparks debate on our choices or about what British cinema really means then that is all to the good. For instance, *Pearl Harbour* was not included in the list of productions, although a couple of scenes were shot in England. This is because we felt that the vast total budget of the film would skew the figures for investment in such a way as to make proper comparisons too difficult. However, money spent on just a couple of scenes of such an expensive picture is likely to have amounted to at least £1m more invested in the UK film industry.

As well as the well-worn paths from Hollywood to use British locations and facilities, there was a big upsurge in interest in filming scenes in the UK by the Indian 'Bollywood' industry. The British Film Commission (BFC)

Lucky Break was released in 2001

4

UK Film Production 2000 - Category C

Minority UK Co-productions. Foreign (non US) films in which there is a small UK involvement in finance or personnel.

Title	Production company(ies)/participating countries	Production cost (£m)
The Biographer	First Biographer Films/Pipeline (**Germany**)	4.66
The Cat's Meow	Dan Films/ Cat's Meow/KC Medien (**Germany**)	4.30
Dark Blue World	Helkon Media/Portobello/Czech Film Fund/Phoenix Investments/Fandango/ Eurimages (**Germany/Czech Rep.**)	4.00
Disco Pigs	Temple Films/Renaissance Films/Irish Film Board/Irish Govt section 481 tax incentives (**Republic of Ireland**)	3.08
Dream	Final Cut/Scandinavian Entertainment (**Sweden**)	1.43
Dust	History dreams/Film Consortium/Ena Films/Fandango Prods/Sky/ European Co-Prod Fund/Filmstiftung/Shadow Doel (**Germany/Italy/Macedonia**)	11.00
Intimacy	Greenpoint/Telema/CNC/Canal + (**France**)	4.00
Invincible	Werner Herzog FilmProduktion/Tatfilm/Little Bird/Film Four/ Arte WDR/BR (**Germany**)	4.50
Off Key	Lola Films (**Spain**)	6.37
Princesca	Parallax Pictures/BIM/Road Movies (**Italy/Germany**)	0.97
Semana	SantaSchlemmer/Wandering St/Woodline/Movie Masters/De Lux Productions (**Netherlands/Luxembourg**)	4.50
Superstition	Woodline/Movie Masters/De Lux Productions (**Netherlands/Luxembourg**)	4.50
The Triumph of Love	Recorded Picture Company/Fiction (**Italy**)	3.50
Villa des Roses	Dan Films/Favourite Films/Isabella Films/Samsa Films (**Belgium/Netherlands/Luxembourg**)	2.40
The War Bride	Random Harvest/DB Entertainment/Vanguard Entertainment (**Canada**)	3.70

TOTAL NUMBER OF FILMS   15
TOTAL COST   **£63.18m**
AVERAGE COST   **£4.25m**

Source: Screen Finance/*bfi*

Lara Croft raided the UK Box Office in 2001

UK Film Production 2000 - Category D

American financed or part-financed films made in the UK. Most titles have a British cultural content.

Title	Production company(ies)	Production cost (£m)
Blow Dry	Intermedia/Miramax/West 11 Films/Mirage Enterprises/ Internationale Medien (Ger)	n/a
Bridget Jones' Diary	Working Title/Universal/Miramax	14.00
Buffalo Soldiers	Film Four/Good Machine/Gorilla Entertainment/Odeon Pictures/ Grosvenor Park	10.34
Captain Corelli's Mandolin	Working Title/Universal/Canal+	13.00
Chocolat	David Brown Prods/Miramax	18.00
A Christmas Carol: The Movie	Scala/Illuminated Film Company/Film Consortium/C4/Winchester/ UIP/Medien Beteiligungs	10.00
The Claim	Pathe/Revolution Films/United Artists/BBC/Canal +	12.50
Enigma	Intermedia/Broadway Pictures/Jagged Films/Mees Pierson	18.90
An Everlasting Piece	Dreamworks/Columbia/Bayakite/Baltimore/Everlasting Prods	n/a
The Four Feathers	Belhaven Prods/ High Command Prods/Paramount/Miramax	26.00
Global Heresy	GFT Entertainment/Ultimate Pictures	5.13
Harry Potter and the Sorcerer's Stone	Warner Brothers	90.00
High Heels and Low Lifes	Fragile Films/Buena Vista	6.50
Killing me Softly	Montecito Pictures/MGM	16.50
Lara Croft Tomb Raider	Paramount	60.00
Long Time Dead	WT2/Universal/Lola Productions	3.20
The Mummy Returns	Universal/Alphaville Prods	72.00
The Parole Officer	DNA/Figment Films/Toledo/Universal	5.99
Possession	Baltimore Spring Creek/Warner/USA Films	20.39
Proof of Life	Castle Rock/Warner/Bel Air Entertainment/Anvil Films	47.00
The Safety of Objects	Renaissance Films/Infilm/Killer Films/Clear Blue Sky Prods	4.86
The Search for John Gissing	Sunlight Prods	6.00
The Sleeping Dictionary	Fine Line	6.00
Spy Game	Universal/Beacon Pictures	55.00
Unconditional Love	Avery Pix/New Line/Zucca Bros	20.00

TOTAL NUMBER OF FILMS   25
TOTAL COST   £541.31m
AVERAGE COST   £21.65m

Source: Screen Finance/*bfi*

UK Film Production 2000 - Category E

'Bollywood' movies which shot sequences in the UK in 2000. Note these films are not included in the overall Film Production total

Title	Production company(ies)
A Couple of Words of Love	Inderjit
Kasam Se	Sai Tinetra Arts India
Khattee Methee	Bharat Productions
Love, Love, Love	Ashwammi Chopra Film
Mohabbetein	Yash Raj Films
Pyar Kiya Nahin Jata	Sutyashwami Production
Telegu Feature Film	Suresh Productions
Untitled	AK International
Untitled	Vigay Anthi Productions
Yaadein	Mukts Arts

TOTAL NUMBER OF FILMS   10

Source: Screen Finance/British Film Commission

7   Types of Release for UK films 2000

Proportion of films with a UK involvement which achieved;

a) Wide release. Opening or playing on 30 or more screens around the country within a year of production prior to 1 January 2000

b) Limited release, mainly in arthouse cinemas or a short West End run, prior to 1 January 2000.

c) Released or planned to be released during 2000

d) Unreleased with no plans to do so during 2000

Year	(a)%	(b)%	(c)%	(d)%
1997	15.5	19.0	22.4	43.1
1998	22.7	21.6	21.6	34.1
1999	30.0	10.0	22.0	38.0

Source: AC Nielsen EDI/*bfi*

Types of Release for UK films 1984-2000

Proportion of films with a UK involvement which achieved;

a) Wide release. Opening or playing on 30 or more screens around the country within a year of production

b) Limited release, mainly in art house cinemas or a short West End run

c) Unreleased a year after production

Year	(a)%	(b)%	(c)%
1984	50.00	44.00	6.00
1985	52.80	35.90	11.30
1986	55.80	41.90	2.30
1987	36.00	60.00	4.00
1988	29.50	61.20	9.30
1989	33.30	38.90	27.80
1990	29.40	47.10	23.50
1991	32.20	37.30	30.50
1992	38.30	29.80	31.90
1993	25.40	22.40	52.20
1994	31.00	22.60	46.40
1995	23.10	34.60	42.30
1996	19.00	14.00	67.00
1997	15.50	19.00	65.50
1998	22.70	21.60	55.70
1999	30.00	10.00	60.00

Source: Screen Finance/AC Nielsen EDI/*bfi*

helped to set up a number of shoots by Bollywood producers, often using dramatic Scottish scenery as the backdrop for spectacular dance sequences. Altogether the BFC believes this Indian investment was worth around £2m.

This year we have made a conscious effort to include some feature documentaries. In previous years films like these, such as *One Day in September* or *Kurt and Courtney*, have often slipped through our net, largely because their productions tend to span more than one year. There has been a renewed interest in exhibiting longer documentaries in cinemas and audiences have responded to this. You will, therefore, find Migrant Media's controversial *Injustice* and Julien Temple's Sex Pistols chronicle, *The Filth and the Fury*, in our list, with hopefully more to come in future Handbooks.

In nearly all cases you will find budget figures by productions. In most cases these are supplied from the estimable *Screen Finance*, with a few kindly supplied by the filmmakers. Film producers tend to be coy on financial matters however, and some decline to give this information (hence the two gaps in Table 5 this year). Budgets quoted are for negative costs (ie the cost of making the film) and do not cover the figures for prints, advertising and marketing which are incurred further down the line.

If there is an interest in real home-grown talent then Table 2 is a better indication of the fortunes of the British film industry. Only six out of 45 titles were made from budgets of £5m or greater and the average cost for all the films was £2.66m. What is surprising is that almost a third of the wholly-UK produced films are made on budgets of £1m or less. With the exception of two co-productions no other films are made for as little. As we have seen in previous years, very few of these films ever make it to the Top 20 Box Office tables.

The budgets for majority UK co-productions (Table 3) are up by around 16 per cent. Again this table is slightly distorted by *The 51st State* with a budget of £19.38m which makes it twice as expensive as the combined totals for *The Fourth Angel* (£9.69m) and *The Reckoning* (£9.62m). The pattern of rising budgets continued in minority UK co-productions (Table 4) with production costs averaging out at around £4.25m. The top film in this group was *Dust* with a budget of £11m.

As usual the big money came in American financed or part-financed films in the UK (Table 5). Last year's big budget production *Gladiator* was matched this year by

8   **What Happened to 1999 UK Films?**

Distribution of 1999 UK productions and foreign films made in the UK up to 1 July 2001

Released theatrically in 1999/2000	Released theatrically in 2001	No distribution deal
The Beach	All About Adam	Between Two Women
Billy Elliot	Another Life	Blood
Circus	Christie Malry's Own Double Entry	Cold Fish
Complicity *	The Criminal	The Company Man
Creatures (Beautiful Creatures)	Dead Bolt Dead	County Kilburn
The End of the Affair	Glory, Glory (Hooded Angels)	The Cup (A Shot at Glory)
Essex Boys	Inbetweeners	Daybreak
Gangster No.1	Kin	Deception
Gladiator	Lava	Emotional Backgammon
Going Off Big Time	The Low Down	Fed Rotten
The Golden Bowl	The Nine Lives of Tomas Katz	Five Seconds to Spare
Guest House Paradiso	Pandemonium	Hard News Soft Money
Honest	Quills	In the Light of the Moon
House!	Room to Rent	The Intruder
House of Mirth	Sexy Beast	Inside Outside Lydia's Head
Hotel Splendide	Strong Boys (Goodbye Charlie Bright)	The Last Minute
It was an Accident	Suspicious River	Londinium
Kevin and Perry go Large	The Truth Game	London Blues
The Little Vampire	Very Annie Mary	Love the One You're With
Love, Honour and Obey	Wild About Harry	New Year's Day
Love's Labours Lost	When Brendan Met Trudy	Offending Angels
The Luzhin Defence	Women Talking Dirty	One Life Stand
The Man Who Cried		Paradise Grove
Maybe Baby	**Distribution deal but no release date**	Secret Society
Miss Julie		Soul's Ark
Nasty Neighbours	Aberdeen	The Testimony of Teliesyn Jones
102 Dalmatians	Birthday Girl	Warrior Sisters
Purely Belter	Greenfingers	
Rat**	Shooters	* Scotland only
Relative Values	Strictly Sinatra	** Ireland only
Saltwater	That Girl From Rio	titles in parentheses ( ) indicate new title
Saving Grace		for release.
Second Generation	**Straight to TV or Video/DVD**	
Snatch		
Some Voices	Breathtaking	
Sorted	The Ghost of Greville Lodge	**Source: Screen Finance/**
There's Only One Jimmy Grimble	Paranoid	**ACNielsen EDI/bfi**
Thomas and the Magic Railway	Pilgrim	
Whatever Happened to Harold Smith?	Sabotage	
The World is Not Enough	Shaheed Udham Singh	

Harry Potter and the Sorcerer's Stone with a massive investment of £90m. This budget alone puts the previous four tables into some perspective. Imagine what the Harry Potter film would have been like if it had been made without American money.

At the time of writing many of the films in Table 5 have been released with *Bridget Jones's Diary, Captain Corelli's Mandolin, Chocolat* and *Lara Croft Tomb Raider* all enjoying box office success. We tend to refer to these mainly American financed films as British which is both confusing and misleading. Culturally it is easy to define films such *Bridget Jones's Diary* as British. However, it is when you follow the money that the Britishness of these films begins to lose its significance.

Looking across to some other countries in Europe, the UK lags some way behind the largest producer France, who made 171 films in 2000. Also for the first time in years the UK was overtaken by Spain who made 104 features and Italy who produced one less, 103.

There was good news and bad news concerning the extent to which films with UK involvement managed to get into cinemas. The good news is that the gradual trend for UK films to receive a wide release (defined here as opening or playing on 30 screens or more) (Table 7) rose by around eight per cent. This means that roughly a third of the films produced in 1999 reached a reasonable cinema audience. The bad news is that 70 per cent of UK films received a limited release or no release at all. Breaking down these figures shows that 10 per cent of films were released, while a considerable 22 per cent were awaiting release. The most worrying statistic, however, must be that 38 per cent of UK films remain unreleased after a year of production. This represents an unwelcome rise of around four per cent.

It is worth looking at Table 8 which gives a pretty good idea of the good and the not so good films produced in the UK. Closer examination reveals that of the 27 films listed without a distribution deal, 17 were wholly-UK productions. Breaking down this figure even further shows that 12 of the films were made for budgets of £1m or under. It is impossible to make an artistic or critical judgement on any of these films without actually seeing them, neither is it right to always equate low budgets with low quality. However, the facts remain that micro-budget films struggle to find a distributor let alone make it onto the smaller screen. If there ever was a celluloid cull of UK films to satisfy those concerned that the UK makes too many poor films then these micro-budget would surely be the first to go.

Additional material by Phil Wickham

The Reckoning – a British thriller set in the Middle Ages

9	**Number of UK Feature Films Produced 1912-2000**		
1912	2	1960	122
1913	18	1961	117
1914	15	1962	114
1915	73	1963	113
1916	107	1964	95
1917	66	1965	93
1918	76	1966	82
1919	122	1967	83
		1968	88
1920	155	1969	92
1921	137		
1922	110	1970	97
1923	68	1971	96
1924	49	1972	104
1925	33	1973	99
1926	33	1974	88
1927	48	1975	81
1928	80	1976	80
1929	81	1977	50
		1978	54
1930	75	1979	61
1931	93		
1932	110	1980	31
1933	115	1981	24
1934	145	1982	40
1935	165	1983	51
1936	192	1984	53
1937	176	1985	54
1938	134	1986	41
1939	84	1987	55
		1988	48
1940	50	1989	30
1941	46		
1942	39	1990	60
1943	47	1991	59
1944	35	1992	47
1945	39	1993	67
1946	41	1994	84
1947	58	1995	78
1948	74	1996	128
1949	101	1997	116
		1998	88
1950	125	1999	100
1951	114	2000	98
1952	117		
1953	138	**Source: Screen Digest/Screen Finance/bfi**	
1954	150		
1955	110		
1956	108		
1957	138		
1958	121		
1959	122		

National Lottery

Away from the accolades about the recent success that some British films have enjoyed over the past few years, the disbursement of National Lottery funds for UK film production provides an idea of the fragmented way the industry is run. This is the fifth year that we have included a table detailing National Lottery awards, and it is fair to say that each year assembling data has become more complicated.

Originally, the task of awarding some money towards the prospective budgets of films (both features and shorts) about to shoot were handled by the Arts Councils of the individual home nations. So far, so good.

In 1997 the Department for Culture, Media and Sport decreed that the job of selecting which feature film projects were commercially viable or artistically worthwhile was in most cases best decided by three film franchises. The three were allocated Lottery funds as follows: The Film Consortium (£30.25m), Pathé Pictures (£33m) and DNA Films (£29m). The hope was that they would have the creative and financial muscle to use the funding to produce a slate of films through development to release. At the same time, the Arts Councils of England, Scotland, Wales and Northern Ireland would also continue to award Lottery grants. The task of following the progress of National Lottery money was made slightly more complex.

2000 saw yet further changes in the way film Lottery awards were administered. All film matters were removed from the Arts Council of England and taken under the wing of the Film Council in March 2001. This included Lottery funding for shorts, features and, increasingly, script development, as well as ultimate responsibility for the franchises. The Film Council immediately set its stall out by restructuring Lottery funds further by organising different funds for different types of projects. The Premiere Fund – designed to look to finance big commercial pictures; the New Cinema Fund – aimed to nurture edgier or smaller scale material; the Development Fund – aimed at supporting innovative and commercially attractive screenplays; The Training Fund – supporting training initiatives for scriptwriters, film development executives, business executives, producers and distributors; First Movies – a pilot fund aimed at young filmmakers, and additionally, there was a Film Council pledge of 20 per cent of the budget of each fund for European co-productions.

Billy Elliot has proved to be the most successful Lottery-funded film to date – a late swansong for the Arts Council of England

The national picture remained devolved, but even there changes have occurred. In Scotland control passed from the Arts Council of Scotland to Scottish Screen. Only the Arts Councils of Wales and Northern Ireland have remained the same.

All these different bodies and different types of award have made collating information trickier. Total budgets are harder to gauge when projects are still at the drawing board stage. However, Lottery awards for film projects remain, and probably always will remain, a source of public controversy and it is important to at least attempt to track what is happening. One of the most potent cultural debates of the last few years in the UK is how public money (or money given by the public as National Lottery funds are) should be spent. Should they go on artistically valid projects that would otherwise not get made, or on popular titles that would bring pleasure to all those people who invested in Lottery tickets? Or indeed, as some claim, is neither defensible and public money should not be thrown away so carelessly.

To add fuel to the fire we have included a table this year listing the Top 20 most successful Lottery films by UK box office revenue since the inception of the scheme in 1995 up to 16 August 2001.

It would be an understatement to say that in terms of box office successes National Lottery funded films have been exceptionally disappointing. *Billy Elliot* is the most successful Lottery-funded film of all time – at least the Arts Council of England can claim that it went out with a bang rather than a whimper. *Shooting Fish* and *This Year's Love* were the only other two films to bring in more at the box office than they cost to make. As for recouping Lottery funds via box office receipts only three other films *An Ideal Husband*, *Plunkett and MacLeane* and *Land Girls* managed this feat. Bearing in mind that this table represents the most successful Lottery funded films, surely only stoke the fires of passion of those anti-lottery campaigners. Six out of 20 is bad enough – six out of approximately 250 Lottery funded films is abysmal.

10   Top 20 All-time Lottery Funded List by UK Box Office

	Title	Award (£m)	Budget (£m)	Box Office (£)
1	Billy Elliot	850,000	2.83	18,230,000
2	Shooting Fish	980,000	2.90	4,020,000
3	This Year's Love	750,000	2.75	3,600,000
4	An Ideal Husband	1,000,000	6.50	2,890,000
5	Plunkett and MacLeane	950,000	9.30	2,780,000
6	Land Girls	1,500,000	5.50	1,570,000
7	Topsy-Turvy	2,000,000	13.50	1,150,000
8	Hilary and Jackie	950,000	4.90	1,040,000
9	My Name is Joe	500,000	2.50	949,228
10	Still Crazy	1,890,000	7.00	933,574
11	Hideous Kinky	1,000,000	2.00	793,538
12	Mansfield Park	1,000,000	6.46	566,450
13	Love's Labours Lost	1,060,000	8.50	527,681
14	Divorcing Jack	1,000,000	2.70	469,961
15	Ratcatcher	615,000	2.00	429,980
16	Love and Death on Long Island	750,000	2.50	394,372
17	There's Only One Jimmy Grimble	1,600,000	3.31	352,173
18	Love is the Devil	364,551	1.00	277,366
19	Whatever Happened to Harold Smith?	500,000	5.64	253,530
20	The Winter Guest	500,000	4.50	250,689

Box office figures as of 16 August 2001

Source: ACNielsenEDI/Screen Finance/*bfi*

In order to add some balance to this pitiful table it is worth taking into consideration overseas sales or indeed international box office receipts. Since the Handbook is primarily interested in the UK market we have not attempted to produce a comparable international box office table. Had we done so we would have shown that a larger percentage of films such as *Topsy Turvy, Hilary and Jackie*, and *Love's Labours Lost* will have actually recouped their Lottery grants. What is startling perhaps is that the Arts Councils seemed reluctant to promote their successes. A yearly report ticking off those films that had finally paid off their Lottery grants would have been an astute strategy to quell those baying for blood. Perhaps the Film Council might oblige in the future.

Bemoaning the fate of Lottery-funded films is ultimately an unrewarding experience because in many ways the damage has already been done and the Film Council have introduced some new (if somewhat cumbersome) steps aimed at redressing the balance. It is too easy to be sidetracked by National Lottery funding issues. What the bigger picture shows is that the most successful British films of recent years – *The Full Monty, Bridget Jones's Diary, Notting Hill, Chicken Run, Lock Stock and Two Smoking Barrels, East is East* – have not relied on Lottery money. In all this naval gazing we should also bear in mind that Lottery money has been dished out to other cultural sectors. The amount of money allocated to film is rather modest compared with Heritage, Dance, Drama and Mime and Music (Table 11).

The complicated nature of the changes in allocation of funds means that most of the Lottery money shown in Table 12 was granted during the period when the Arts Council of England was handing over to the Film Council. *Long Time Dead* received the highest award of £1m during this period. The much maligned Lottery franchises continued to add films to their slates. DNA films continued to proceed with the utmost caution, investing £2m in the Steve Coogan vehicle *The Parole Officer*. The Film Consortium, which was bailed out during 2001 by Civilian Content, used Lottery money to either finance or develop a total of 19 films. *24 Hour Party People* and *The 51st State* were awarded £2m, while *Dust* received just under £2m on top of £50,000 for post-production purposes. Pathé spread its money out modestly among 13 films. It also invested money in film development. Its biggest feature, however, was *The Hole* which was given £1.5m. It was also the first Film Council sponsored film to get a release in April 2001. The good news for the Film Council is that, at the time of writing, box office figures for *The Hole* of just over £2m indicate that it paid off its Lottery allocation, but was still short of its total budget of just over £4m.

In Scotland, Wales and Northern Ireland the awards are usually on a smaller scale. In total five Scottish films received awards of £500,000. The total awards for Welsh feature films was £2.25m – four films receiving £250,000 each, while in Northern Ireland, *Puckoon* received the largest award of £120,000.

In the meantime the Film Council unveiled its first films to gain money from its Premiere Fund. Robert Altman's *Gosford Park*, headed an eclectic list which also included the mockumentary *Mike Bassett: England Manager* and FilmFour's romantic comedy *Miranda*. These films are of particular interest since the Film Council has placed its cards on the table by saying that the Premiere fund is aimed at commercially successful films. It will be interesting to see how these films fare against films funded through the New Cinema Fund. One thing is for certain, the debate about Lottery funded films is likely to run and run.

Additional material by Phil Wickham

11	**Total Lottery Grants to the Cultural Sector (£m)**					
Arts	**1994/95**	**95/96**	**96/97**	**97/98**	**98/99**	**TOTAL**
Combined Arts	n.a	66.45	72.02	71.96	25.88	236.31
Dance	n.a	30.82	32.02	48.5	9.48	120.82
Drama and mime	n.a	135.76	129.86	84.17	24.92	374.71
Film, Video and broadcasting	n.a	12.49	42.17	21.41	9.75	85.82
Literature	n.a	1.24	1.95	3.37	4.11	10.67
Music	n.a	45.84	61.91	58.02	39.28	205.05
Opera/music theatre	n.a	61.45	0.71	3.38	1.39	66.93
Visual arts	n.a	26.21	62.07	74.71	25.69	188.68
Other	n.a	1.75	1.76	7.67	9.93	21.11
Heritage	14.32	280.65	408.74	270.66	216.60	1190.97
TOTAL	**14.32**	**663.38**	**814.47**	**645.82**	**369.12**	**2507.11**

Source: PSI

Funding of Film Productions by National Lottery Awards 2000

Title	Amount of Award (£)	Total Budget (£)

ARTS COUNCIL OF ENGLAND/FILM COUNCIL – Features

	Title	Amount of Award (£)	Total Budget (£)
1	Crush	875,000	3,900,000
2	Long Time Dead	1,000,000	3,075,000
3	Morvern Callar	500,000	2,997,000
4	My Brother Rob	359,989	999,000
5	Pandaemonium	63,152 (Post Production)	
6	The Lawless Heart	200,000	1,205,000
7	Very Annie Mary	50,000 (Post Production)	
8	Simon Magus	21,730 (Post Production)	

ARTS COUNCIL OF ENGLAND/FILM COUNCIL – Short Films

	Title	Amount of Award (£)	Total Budget (£)
1	Delilah	21,325	45,469
2	Dish	30,000	60,000
3	Ho Ho Ho!	26,000	52,000
4	Home Ground	30,000	60,645
5	Intolerance	15,000	30,000
6	Just Like My Dad	26,870	53,740
7	Kings Ransom	27,025	54,050
8	Lambeth Marsh	40,000	80,000
9	Landmark	20,000	40,000
10	Maises Catch	41,226	86,226
11	Mapping Perception	32,400	62,526
12	Once Seen	28,157	59,546
13	The Elevator	13,350	26,700
14	Taxi!	11,825	36,970
15	The Tyre	45,258	90,516
16	To Have and to Hold	30,000	74,000
17	Trick of the Light	30,000	60,000
18	Vivid	26,000	96,500

DNA FILMS

	Title	Amount of Award (£)	Total Budget (£)
1	The Parole Officer	2,000,000	5,994,000

THE FILM CONSORTIUM

	Title	Amount of Award (£)	Total Budget (£)
1	24 Hour Party People	2,000,000	4,200,000
2	Blindfold	15,000 (Development)	
3	Brian Jones Project	19,000 (Development)	
4	Child of Air	11,500 (Development)	
5	Dust	1,950,000	5,236,000
6	Dust	50,000 (Post Production)	
7	Fattypuffs and Thinifers	20,000 (Development)	
8	Gabriel & Me	1,200,000	3,720,000
9	Haroun and the Sea of Stories	60,000 (Development)	
10	Innocence	19,750 (Development)	
11	Janice Beard	85,000 (Prints and Advertising)	
12	Large	75,000 (Post Production)	
13	Quiz Night	13,600 (Development)	
14	Room to Rent	20,000 (Post Production)	
15	Seven Against the West	34,000 (Development)	
16	Streets Above Us	10,000 (Development)	
17	The 51st State	2,000,000	16,340,000
19	Transgressions	15,000 (Development)	

Title	Amount of Award (£)	Total Budget (£)

PATHÉ PICTURES

	Title	Amount of Award (£)	Total Budget (£)
1	A Romantic Comedy About Divorce	38,750 (Development)	
2	Agent X	37,500 (Development)	
3	Dead Sexy	45,000 (Development)	
4	Feet Up	41,750 (Development)	
5	It Was An Accident	99,850 (Post Production)	
6	Minister of Fun	47,950 (Development)	
7	Ode to Pandora	34,750 (Development)	
8	The Abduction Club	1,200,000	4,297,000
9	The Alchemist	41,750 (Development)	
10	The Hole	1,500,000	4,158,000
11	The Wedding Gift	41,750 (Development)	
12	There's Only One Jimmy Grimble	60,000 (Post Production)	
13	Waterloo Sunset	50,000 (Development)	

NOTES

1 The above list includes hard awards only
2 Film Council Awards are given under the interim award process between the Arts Council of England and the Film Council
3 The Budget as provided at the time of the Award

SCOTTISH ARTS COUNCIL

Title	Amount (£)	Budget (£)
Features		
Child of Air	500,000	250,000
The Last Great Wilderness	375,000	500,000
Daybreak		
(supplementary funding)	26,500	63,536
Shorts		
Pastures New	11,080	36,503
Documentaries		
The Maggie Centre	38,000	70,215
Who Owns Jack Kerouac?	123,587	246,771
Louder than Bombs	25,000	48,911
Exploitation Fund		
A Small Piece of Paradise	17,500	24,316
Frog	10,000	13,400
Project Preparation Awards Scheme		
The Flying Scotsman	50,000	109,700
TOTAL		**1,176,667**

SCOTTISH SCREEN

Title	Amount (£)	Budget (£)
Features		
Late Night Shopping	100,000	1,600,000
Morvern Callar	500,000	3,000,000
Fly Me to Dunoon	500,000	
The Flying Scotsman	500,000	
Gas Attack	300,000	
Shorts		
The Hidden	17,000	
Over Land and Sea	13,697	
Annotations	12,000	
The Gift	21,146	
Reel in the Flickering	12,500	
Divine	25,000	
Looking for Karma	12,000	
Documentary		
The Millenium Clock	24,500	
The Sun Worshippers	95,401	
Company Development Awards		
4 Way Pictures	3,000	
Gabriel Films	61,750	
Saltire Productions	42,150	
Holdings Ecosse	3,000	
Moco Films	2,000	
Monogram Wark Clements	42,150	
Bronco Films	61,750	
January Films	3,000	
Umbrella Productions	3,000	
Ecosse Films	42,150	
TOTAL	**2,397,194**	

ARTS COUNCIL OF WALES

Title	Amount (£)	Budget (£)
Features		
Happy Now	250,000	3,110,000
The Tulse Luper Suitcase	250,000	
'360'	250,000	
The Amateur Photographer	250,000	
Very Annie Mary	25,000	3,090,000
Shorts		
Screen Gems		
(10x3 short films)	90,000	
Overland	74,114	
A Day Out	45,982	
Blue Kenny	31,228	
One Dau Trois	31,662	
Dance Floor	5,000	
Script Development		
Lavender	15,000	
Acting Up	14,445	
Caitlin	11,000	
Places of Greater Safety	10,000	
The Boy from Nowhere	9,825	
To Comfort the Brave	6,930	
TOTAL	**1,370,186**	

ARTS COUNCIL OF NORTHERN IRELAND

Title	Amount (£)	Budget (£)
Features		
Puckoon	120,000	2,784,648
Shorts		
The Devil You Know	32,967	65,967
Ireland	10,000	10,000
Mojo Mickybo	18,525	27,000
Teenage Kicks	35,000	105,000
English as a Foreign Language	12,000	49,925
Elsewhere	1,177	1,570
The Centre	6,000	45,250
A Multitude of Sins	35,000	110,000
The Last Storyteller/		
An Scealai Deanacn	50,000	170,758
TOTAL	**320,669**	

TOTAL AWARD   21,711,123

Source: Film Council/Screen Finance/Scottish Arts
Council/Arts Council of Wales/Arts Council of Northern
Ireland

Something to cheer about? Mike Bassett England Manager – one of the first films from the Film Council's Premiere Fund

13	Cinema Admissions 1933-2000 (millions)		
1933	903.00	1970	193.00
1934	950.00	1971	176.00
1935	912.33	1972	156.60
1936	917.00	1973	134.20
1937	946.00	1974	138.50
1938	987.00	1975	116.30
1939	990.00	1976	103.90
		1977	103.50
1940	1,027.00	1978	126.10
1941	1,309.00	1979	111.90
1942	1,494.00		
1943	1,541.00	1980	101.00
1944	1,575.00	1981	86.00
1945	1,585.00	1982	64.00
1946	1,635.00	1983	65.70
1947	1,462.00	1984	54.00
1948	1,514.00	1985	72.00
1949	1,430.00	1986	75.50
		1987	78.50
1950	1,395.80	1988	84.00
1951	1,365.00	1989	94.50
1952	1,312.10		
1953	1,284.50	1990	97.37
1954	1,275.80	1991	100.29
1955	1,181.80	1992	103.64
1956	1,100.80	1993	114.36
1957	915.20	1994	123.53
1958	754.70	1995	114.56
1959	581.00	1996	123.80
		1997	139.30
1960	500.80	1998	135.50
1961	449.10	1999	139.75
1962	395.00	2000	142.50
1963	357.20		
1964	342.80	**Source: Screen Digest/CAA/ AC Nielsen EDI**	
1965	326.60		
1966	288.80		
1967	264.80		
1968	237.30		
1969	214.90		

14	UK Box Office 2000
Admissions	142.50m
Total Cinema Sites	686
Total Cinema Screens	2,954
Total Multiplex Sites	209
Total Multiplex Screens	2,003
Box Office Gross	£577,280,342
Average Ticket Price	£4.00

Source: Screen Finance/Dodona Research/ CAA/AC Nielsen EDI

Cinemas

You would have to go back to 1972 to find a better year for cinema admissions in the UK, which totalled 142.50 million in 2000 (Table 13). In fact 2000 was the year that the box office in Britain was booming. The weekend of 11-13 February saw the biggest three-day figure ever recorded at the UK box office, with cinema tills ringing to the tune of £14.3m. The average number of people going to the cinema each week increased from 2.67 million in 1999 to 2.73 million in 2000. Interestingly, the gloom merchants looked to America to see admissions falling by three per cent over the same period and immediately predicted that the UK would inevitably follow suit.

The general upward trend seems a long way since the lowest point in UK cinema history which came in 1984. Since then cinemas, multiplexes and megaplexes have ensured that the UK cinema-going public are well catered for. Although the total of cinema sites dropped by six from 692 in 1999 to 686 in 2000 (Tables 14 and 15) the number of cinema screens actually increased. Multiplex sites broke through the 200 barrier, while multiplex screens nudged over 2,000. The number of new multiplex sites that opened in 2000 increased by 12.5 per cent – suggesting that the saturation point that many commentators predicted had not happened. Indeed, by the end of 2001 it was likely that there would be still more new sites opening.

Box office gross was up by around £7m and you may wish to compare the average price of a ticket of £4.00 to what you have to pay at your local cinema.

Toy Story 2 was the top box office film in the UK in 2000

**15   UK Sites and Screens
1984-2000**

Year	Total Sites	Total Screens
1984	660	1,271
1985	663	1,251
1986	660	1,249
1987	648	1,215
1988	699	1,416
1989	719	1,559
1990	737	1,685
1991	724	1,789
1992	735	1,845
1993	723	1,890
1994	734	1,969
1995	743	2,019
1996	742	2,166
1997	747	2,383
1998	759	2,564
1999	692	2,758
2000	686	2,954

Source: Screen Finance/X25 Partnership/Dodona Research

Saving Grace – drew in crowds in joints over the UK

In recent years the demographic breakdown of cinema-going has revealed the following paradox: the largest audience for films are those in the over 35 years age group (Table 16); the smallest group are those aged between 15-24. Yet, the smallest group goes to the cinema more often than the largest group. It would make sense if more films were made for the 35 plus audience instead of the steady stream of output for this small but regular audience. There were signs that the older audience was increasing, albeit marginally. Whether films will always be aimed at a younger audience is debatable. Age statistics on the other hand have thrown up some interesting nuggets of information. For instance, the 40 plus audience grew tenfold in the UK in the 1990s, a rate not matched by the 15-24 year-olds and when it comes to popular UK films the average audience often moves up from the 15-24 group – the average age of ticket buyers for *Notting Hill* was 39. It is also interesting to note that BBC Radio 2, which has recently focused on the thirty- and forty-something audience, is currently one of the most popular radio stations in Britain. Television continues to pander to the nostalgia trip with shows depicting eras which we were all supposed to have loved. But it is likely that the dawning of an older generation of cinema-goer may have to wait a little while longer.

What is surprising is the panic in multiplex land during a year where Hollywood did not churn out the prerequisite amount of blockbusters. Perhaps 2000 proved to be the year when the UK didn't need the blockbuster to keep its audiences happy. Indeed, the biggest threat to multiplex operators might be that they fail to recognise the need for diversity – after all the bogeyman of Home Cinema is only just around the corner.

16   Frequency of Cinema-going 2000

Age Group	4-14	15-24	25-34	35+	ABC1	C2DE	Male	Female
No.of People (m)	8.23	6.91	8.76	31.12	27.48	27.54	27.09	27.93
Once a month or more	26%	54%	31%	14%	27%	20%	25%	22%
Less than once a month	54%	33%	47%	31%	42%	32%	35%	39%
Once a year or less	13%	10%	17%	34%	21%	28%	25%	25%
Total who ever go to the cinema	93%	97%	95%	79%	90%	80%	85%	86%

Source: CAVIAR/Screen Finance

17 Top 20 Films at the UK Box Office 2000

	Film	Distributor	Country of Origin	Box Office Gross (£m)
1	Toy Story 2	Buena Vista	US	43,491,021
2	Gladiator	UIP	US	30,907,687
3	Chicken Run	Pathé	UK/US	29,428,037
4	American Beauty	UIP	US	21,340,511
5	Stuart Little	Columbia Tristar	US	17,828,403
6	Mission Impossible II	UIP	US/GER	17,291,606
7	Billy Elliot	UIP	UK	16,661,492
8	X-Men	20thC Fox	US	14,976,383
9	The Beach	20thC Fox	UK/US/TH	13,332,236
10	Dinosaur	Buena Vista	US	13,219,265
11	What Lies Beneath	20thC Fox	US	13,083,584
12	Snatch	Columbia Tristar	UK/US	12,326,923
13	The Grinch	UIP	US	11,393,599
14	Charlie's Angels	Columbia Tristar	US	11,143,821
15	Pokemon	Warner	US/JP	10,976,174
16	Erin Brockovich	Columbia Tristar	US	10,550,144
17	Final Destination	Entertainment	US	10,386,318
18	Kevin & Perry Go Large	Icon	UK/US	10,247,636
19	Scary Movie	Buena Vista	US	10,086,721
20	Sleepy Hollow	Pathé	US/GER	10,046,249

NB: Box office totals are for UK and Republic of Ireland for releases from 1 January 2000 – 5 January 2001

Source: AC Nielsen/EDI/Screen Finance/*bfi*

18 Top 20 UK Films at the UK Box Office 2000

	Film	Distributor	Country of Origin	Box Office Gross (£m)
1	Chicken Run	Pathé	UK/US	29,428,037
2	Billy Elliot	UIP	UK	16,661,492
3	The Beach	20thC Fox	UK/US/TH	13,332,236
4	Snatch	Columbia Tristar	UK/US	12,326,923
5	Kevin & Perry Go Large	Icon	UK/US	10,247,636
6	Angela's Ashes	UIP	UK/US	7,753,488
7	High Fidelity	Buena Vista	UK/US	4,871,947
8	The Little Vampire	Icon	UK/US/GER/NL	4,093,714
9	Maybe Baby	Redbus	UK/FR	3,474,530
10	Thomas & The Magic Railroad	Icon	UK/US	2,056,007
11	Saving Grace	20thC Fox	UK	1,919,572
12	A Clockwork Orange (re)	Warner	UK	1,905,983
13	Love Honour & Obey	UIP	UK	1,202,053
14	Topsy Turvy	Pathé	UK/US	1,081,918
15	The Miracle Maker	Icon	UK/RU	1,043,007
16	Wonder Boys	UIP	UK/US/GER/JP	994,139
17	Purely Belter	FilmFour	UK	765,509
18	The House Of Mirth	FilmFour	UK/US	636,835
19	Essex Boys	Pathé	UK	529,891
20	Mansfield Park	Buena Vista	UK/US	491,054

NB: Box office totals are for UK and Republic of Ireland for releases from 1 January 2000 – 5 January 2001

Source: ACNielsen EDI/Screen Finance/*bfi*

19   UK Box Office for UK Feature Films released in 2000 - UK Films

	Title	Distributor	Country of Origin	Box Office Gross (£m)
1	Billy Elliot	UIP	UK	16,661,492
2	Saving Grace	20thC Fox	UK	1,919,572
3	A Clockwork Orange (re)	Warner	UK	1,905,983
4	Love Honour & Obey	UIP	UK	1,202,053
5	Purely Belter	Film Four	UK	765,509
6	Essex Boys	Pathé	UK	529,891
7	Wonderland	UIP	UK	395,498
8	Rancid Aluminium	Entertainment	UK	325,106
9	Whatever Happened To Harold Smith	UIP	UK	253,530
10	Relative Values	Alliance Releasing	UK	244,415
11	The Filth And The Fury	Film Four	UK	117,282
12	House!	Pathé	UK	104,475
13	Complicity	Entertainment	UK	93,506
14	Going Off Big Time	Entertainment	UK	92,786
15	Sorted	Metrodome	UK	90,903
16	The Wedding Tackle	Viking	UK	41,078
17	One More Kiss	Metrodome	UK	40,751
18	The Long Good Friday (re)	Metrodome	UK	34,466
19	Some Voices	Film Four	UK	30,497
20	A Matter Of Life And Death (re)	BFI	UK	29,342
21	Brothers	Paradise	UK	25,890
22	Merlin: The Return	Peakviewing	UK	20,868
23	Manchester United: Beyond...	Icon	UK	15,109
24	Janice Beard: 45 wpm	UIP	UK	8,192
25	Nasty Neighbours	Redbus	UK	7,518
26	24 Hours In London	Blue Dolphin	UK	4,477
27	Small Time Obsession	Guerilla	UK	4,289
28	Bodywork	Guerilla	UK	3,161
29	Fast Food	Optimum	UK	2,617
30	Second Generation	Second Generation	UK	1,659
31	The Jolly Boys Last Stand	NFT	UK	1,408
32	Strong Language	NFT	UK	878
33	Sacred Flesh	Salvation Films	UK	823
				21,689,100

UK Box Office for UK Feature Films released in 2000 - Other UK Co-productions

	Title	Distributor	Country of Origin	Box Office Gross (£m)
1	The Beach	20thC Fox	UK/US/TH	13,332,236
2	The Little Vampire	Icon	UK/US/GER/NL	4,093,714
3	Maybe Baby	Redbus	UK/FR	3,474,530
4	The Miracle Maker	Icon	UK/RU	1,043,007
5	Wonder Boys	UIP	UK/US/GER/JP	994,139
6	The Golden Bowl	Buena Vista	UK/US/FR	474,768
7	Love's Labours Lost	Pathé	UK/FR/US	447,151
8	A Monkey's Tale	Miracom	UK/FR/GER/HU	382,802
9	Ordinary Decent Criminal	Clarence/Icon	UK/US/IE/GER	371,775
10	There's Only One Jimmy Grimble	Pathé	UK/FR	346,412
11	Gangster No1	Film Four	UK/GER/IE	328,682
12	The Closer You Get	20thC Fox	UK/US/IE	256,273
13	Eye Of The Beholder	Metrodome	UK/US/AU/CA	193,751
14	Honest	Pathé	UK/FR	189,567
15	Sunshine	Alliance Releasing	UK/HU/GER/CA/AT	175,77

Title	Distributor	Country of Origin	Box Office Gross (£m)
16 The Luzhin Defence	Entertainment	UK/US/FR/IT/HU	172,109
17 Nora	Alliance Releasing	UK/IE/GER/IT	170,917
18 Himalaya	Momentum	UK/FR/CH/NP	131,525
19 Grey Owl	20thC Fox	UK/CA	93,092
20 A Room For Romeo Brass	Alliance Releasing	UK/CA	86,463
21 Borstal Boy	Clarence	UK/IE	85,288
22 The Last September	Metro	UK/FR/IE	85,212
23 Saltwater	Buena Vista	UK/ES/IE	78,065
24 Where The Money Is	Warner	UK/US/GER	72,663
25 Tom's Midnight Garden	Downtown	UK/JP/US	67,054
26 The Man Who Cried	UIP	UK/FR	54,333
27 The Escort	Pathé	UK/FR	44,937
28 It Was An Accident	Pathé	UK/FR	30,462
29 Resources Humaines	NFT	UK/FR	14,725
30 Simon Magus	Film Four	UK/GER/FR/IT	13,161
31 Isn't She Great	UIP	UK/US/GER/JP	10,956
32 To Walk With Lions	Optimum	UK/CA/KE	10,502
33 Darkest Light	Pathé	UK/FR	10,500
34 Best	Optimum	UK/IE	9,801
35 I Could Read The Sky	Artificial Eye	UK/IE/FR	7,040
36 Hotel Splendide	Film Four	UK/FR	3,840
37 The King Of Paris	Gala	UK/FR	984
38 Siam Sunset	Blue Dolphin	UK/AU	957
			27,359,167

UK Box Office for UK Feature Films released in 2000 - US/UK Co-productions

Title	Distributor	Country of Origin	Box Office Gross (£m)
1 Chicken Run	Pathé	UK/US	29,428,037
2 Snatch	Columbia Tristar	UK/US	12,326,923
3 Kevin & Perry Go Large	Icon	UK/US	10,247,636
4 Angela's Ashes	UIP	UK/US	7,753,488
5 High Fidelity	Buena Vista	UK/US	4,871,947
6 Thomas & The Magic Railroad	Icon	UK/US	2,056,007
7 Topsy Turvy	Pathé	UK/US	1,081,918
8 The House Of Mirth	Film Four	UK/US	636,835
9 Mansfield Park	Buena Vista	UK/US	491,054
10 Circus	Columbia Tristar	UK/US	332,142
11 Titus	Buena Vista	UK/US	223,821
12 One Day In September	Redbus	UK/US	112,464
13 Up At The Villa	UIP	UK/US	107,451
14 Rat	UIP	UK/US	34,788
15 Miss Julie	Optimum	UK/US	28,384
16 Elephant Juice	Metrodome	UK/US	18,280
17 My Life So Far	Buena Vista	UK/US	16,702
18 The Loss Of Sexual Innocence	Columbia Tristar	UK/US	12,360
19 Wisconsin Death Trip	NFT	UK/US	6,752
			69,786,989

TOTAL   90 Titles   **122,121,180**

NB: Box office totals are for UK and Republic of Ireland for releases from 1 January 2000 – 5 January 2001

Source: AC Nielsen/EDI/Screen Finance/bfi

As reported in previous Handbooks some cinema chains are rising to the challenge of finding new audiences better than others. Following its trial run with Odeon cinemas, the *bfi* continued its bold experiment of programming non-mainstream films by linking up with UCI Cinemas This time the partnership covered 35 of UCI's multiplexes. 'Bollywood' movies continue to be booked in areas with large Asian communities, and some cinemas are also catering for older people with half-price afternoon matinees.

In recent years, due to technological advances and increasingly accurate sources, more information is available to us, giving a more realistic account of the distribution market. The primary source for box office figures is the AC Nielsen EDI tracking service. It is vital for our work that distributors log films with this service.

We collect the box office information on a monthly basis; note the distributor and the country of origin so that by the end of the year we should have information on every film released. The process of compiling the individual tables can then begin.

Looking at the top 20 films at the UK box office (Table 17) it is puzzling to comprehend how some commentators viewed 2000 as a poor year for the cinema. In fact the figures reflect UK audiences appetite for films. In 1999 *Wild Wild West* occupied 20th position in the chart with £6,845,175. It is worth comparing that figure with *Sleepy Hollow* which brought in £10,046,249.

Generally blockbusters and children's films proved the most lucrative with *Gladiator*, *Chicken Run*, *Stuart Little* and *Mission Impossible II* all in the top ten. There are

Chicken Run generally ruled the roost in UK cinemas in 2000

Top 20 EU Films at the UK Box Office 2000

	Film	Distributor	Country of Origin	Box Office Gross (£m)
1	Mission Impossible II	UIP	US/GER	17,291,606
2	Sleepy Hollow	Pathé	US/GER	10,046,249
3	Hollow Man	Columbia Tristar	US/GER	6,101,225
4	Double Jeopardy	UIP	US/GER	4,618,857
5	The Patriot	Columbia Tristar	US/GER	4,058,582
6	The End Of The Affair	Columbia Tristar	US/GER	3,471,852
7	Bedazzled	20thC Fox	US/GER	3,265,754
8	O Brother Where Art Thou?	Momentum	US/FR	3,114,223
9	Shaft	UIP	US/GER	2,969,360
10	The Cell	Entertainment	US/GER	1,950,977
11	Rules of Engagement	UIP	US/GER	1,109,480
12	Urban Legends	Columbia Tristar	US/FR	715,543
13	Elmo In Grouchland	Columbia Tristar	US/GER	532,351
14	Snow Day	UIP	US/GER	510,075
15	In The Mood For Love	Metro	FR/HK	460,982
16	Dancer In The Dark	Film Four	FR/DK/SE/IT/GER	417,111
17	Ghost Dog: Way Of The Samurai	Film Four	US/JP/FR/GER	394,976
18	Time Regained	Artificial Eye	FR/IT/PT	394,119
19	The Ninth Gate	UIP	US/FR/ES	281,463
20	Beau Travail	Artificial Eye	FR	276,544

NB: Box office totals are for UK and Republic of Ireland for releases from 1 January 2000 – 5 January 2001

Source: ACNielsen EDI/ Screen Finance/*bfi*

Top 20 Foreign Language Films Released in the UK 2000

	Title	Distributor	Country	Box Office (£)
1	Mohabbatein	Yash Raj	IN	967,803
2	Kaho Naa Pyaar Hai	Yash Raj	IN	474,751
3	In The Mood For Love	Metro	FR/HK	460,982
4	Dancer In The Dark	Film Four	FR/DK/SE/IT/GER	417,111
5	Dulhan Hum Le Jayenge	Yash Raj	IN	394,269
6	Time Regained	Artificial Eye	FR/IT/PT	394,119
7	Har Dil Jo Pyar Karega	Eros	IN	390,227
8	Fiza	Spark	IN	373,109
9	Phir Bhi Dil Hain Hindustani	Eros	IN	320,690
10	Hamara Dil Aapke Paas Hai	Eros	IN	310,422
11	Beau Travail	Artificial Eye	FR	276,544
12	Joan Of Arc	Columbia Tristar	FR	275,141
13	Mission Kashmir	Set Singa	IN	272,875
14	Asterix & Obelix V Caesar	Pathé	FR/GER/IT	260,627
15	The Girl On The Bridge	Pathé	FR	252,148
16	Harry He's Here To Help	Artificial Eye	FR	247,833
17	Dhadkan	Eros	IN	211,850
18	Chal Mere Bhai	Eros	IN	174,629
19	A Bout de Souffle (re)	Optimum	FR	170,864
20	Pukar	Eros	IN	163,320

NB: Box office totals are for UK and Republic of Ireland for releases from 1 January 2000 – 5 January 2001

Source: ACNielsen EDI/Screen Finance/*bfi*

22   Breakdown of UK Box Office by Country of Origin 2000

Territories	No of Titles	Box Office	%
US	140	353,085,344	61.16
Other US Co productions	34	91,156,601	15.79
UK	33	24,975,024	4.33
UK US	19	69,786,989	12.09
Other UK Co-productions	39	27,359,167	4.74
EU inc. other co-productions	63	4,932,787	0.85
Rest of world foreign language	49	5,711,917	0.99
Rest of world English language	5	272,513	0.01
Total	**382**	**577,280,342**	

NB: Box office totals are for UK and Republic of Ireland for releases from 1 January 2000 – 5 January 2001

Source: AC Nielsen EDI/*bfi*/Screen Finance

23   Top 10 US Box Office Revenue of UK Films Released in 2000

	Title	Distributor (US)	Country	Box Office ($m)
1	Chicken Run	Buena Vista	UK/US	106,834,564
2	The Beach	Fox	UK/US	39,785,027
3	Snatch	Sony	UK/US	30,328,156
4	Billy Elliot	Universal Focus	UK/US	21,995,263
5	Thomas and the Magic Railroad	Destination Films	UK/US	15,933,500
6	Saving Grace	Fine Line	UK	12,178,602
7	The End of the Affair*	Sony	UK/US	10,827,816
8	Croupier	Shooting Gallery	UK	6,201,143
9	Topsy-Turvy	USA Films	UK	6,208,548
10	East is East	Miramax	UK	4,177,818
Total				**232,475,174**

* Was released in December 1999 but not in last year's table

Source: AC Nielsen/EDI

The Beach proved popular with audiences in 2000

East is East was the tenth most popular UK film in the US

24   Top 20 of Admissions of Films Distributed in Europe in 2000

Based on data from 12 European Union Countries (78% of admissions)

	Title	Country	Admissions
1	Gladiator	US	24,649,032
2	Toy Story 2	US	23,751,342
3	American Beauty	US	21,416,993
4	Mission Impossible II	US	20,379,836
5	The Sixth Sense*	US	18,939,737
6	Scary Movie	US	14,123,441
7	Dinosaur	US	13,748,718
8	Erin Brockovich	US	12,474,099
9	Stuart Little	US	12,377,768
10	Chicken Run	UK/US	12,095,424
11	Pokemon:The First Movie	JP/US	11,555,667
12	Taxi 2	FR	11,317,034
13	X-Men	US	11,222,095
14	What Lies Beneath	US	11,052,359
15	Gone in Sixty Seconds	US	10,160,378
16	Sleepy Hollow	US	9,626,335
17	Hollow Man	US	9,570,561
18	Charlie's Angels	US	9,408,066
19	The Beach	US	9,284,789
20	American Pie*	US	9,066,508

*First Released in 1999
Source: European Audiovisual Observatory

25   Top 20 of Admissions of European Films Distributed in the European Union in 2000

Based on data from 12 European Union Countries (78% of admissions)

	Title	Country	Admissions
1	Chicken Run	UK/US	12,095,424
2	Taxi 2	FR	11,317,034
3	The World is Not Enough*	UK/US	6,395,673
4	Billy Elliot	UK	4,956,703
5	Les Rivieres Pourpres	FR	4,490,341
6	Le Gout des Autres	FR	4,100,165
7	Snatch	UK/US	4,002,905
8	Chiedimi se Sono Felice	IT	3,089,467
9	Angela's Ashes	IE/US	2,638,784
10	Dancer in the Dark	DEN/SWE/FR/GER	2,513,984
11	Kevin & Perry Go Large	UK	2,484,179
12	Anatomie	GER	2,289,536
13	High Fidelity	UK/US	2,279,508
14	Himalaya –L'Enfance d'un Chef	FR/CH/UK/NP	2.235,014
15	Harry, Un Ami Qui Vous Veut Du Bien	FR	2,061,253
16	Jet Set	FR	1,995,702
17	Harte Jungs	GER	1,666,031
18	Crazy	GER	1,467,029
19	Saving Grace (15)	UK	1,422,787
20	Ano Mariano	ES	1,357,867

* First Released in 1999
Country of origin defined here by the Observatory

Source: European Audiovisual Observatory

Kevin & Perry Go Large was largely a hit at the cinema

exceptions, *American Beauty* (number 4) and *Billy Elliot* (number 7) hardly fit into either genre but proved immensely popular, perhaps with older audiences.

Table 18 shows that the top five UK films in 2000 all managed to pass the £10m mark. The big successes of *Notting Hill*, *The World is Not Enough* and *Shakespeare in Love* in 1999 and successes of films like *Bridget Jones's Diary* in 2001 show that there is a small but potent market for UK products. However, it needs to be emphasised again and again that the cream of the UK crop comes courtesy of funding from the United States. Without that funding the UK really would be a nation producing one hit wonders.

Only four out of the 33 UK films managed to register box office receipts over the £1m mark (Table 19) and one of those films was the re-release of Kubrick's controversial film, *A Clockwork Orange*. As usual the majority of UK films were distributed by independents. However, pirouetting its way to the top of the list was the UK's genuine big hit *Billy Elliot* which took over £16m.

The film was one of those distributed by UIP and may give an insight into why the company appears willing to

take chances on low budget British fare which other distributors take on only in ones and twos. Of the five films in this category released by UIP it is the only one likely to have made a profit but it has made a considerable amount of money for a film with a budget of under £3 million. It may have made more had it not controversially been given a 15 certificate. *Billy Elliot* also provides an interesting example of the power of the press in the success or failure of a film. The film was covered in the dailies on an almost continual basis from its screening at the Cannes Film Festival and received uniformly excellent reviews on its release in UK cinemas, making it the must-see British film of the year.

The other categories in Table 19 show a downturn in box office while the actual numbers of films released remains the same. In 2000, there was no *Phantom Menace* or Bond movie to push up the returns. Ruling the roost was the claymation epic *Chicken Run* (£29,428,037), which was financed by US studio DreamWorks but made in Bristol by Aardman Animations. The huge hit had a box office total that surpassed the total for UK films (£21,689,100) and the total for other UK co-productions (£29,428,037).

26 Breakdown of UK Box Office by Distributor in 2000*

Distributor	Titles	Box office
UIP	43	160,153,643
Buena Vista	31	123,583,375
Columbia Tristar	30	76,507,851
Warner	23	36,396,845
20thC Fox	16	62,283,841
Total US Majors	**143**	**458,925,555**
Pathé	22	45,109,029
Entertainment	21	27,997,539
Icon	8	17,870,332
Momentum	6	6,306,136
Film Four	16	4,989,128
Redbus	7	3,705,679
Eros	16	2,185,131
Yash Raj	4	1,887,612
Artificial Eye	17	1,382,819
Metrodome	14	1,001,988
Alliance	8	973,898
Downtown	7	923,690
Metro	8	835,043
Optimum	10	603,953
Spark	3	434,396
Miracom	1	382,802
Clarence	4	322,312
Set Singa	1	272,875
ICA	8	177,733
BFI	8	160,533
Ink Pen	1	148,814
GVI	1	135,901
IFD	2	83,843
Bollywood	5	73,963
Tips	1	66,975
Blue Star	2	49,991
Gala	3	41,252
Viking	1	41,078
Paradise	1	25,890
Winchester	1	25,663
NFT	4	23,763
Peakviewing	1	20,868
Venus	1	16,729
Millivres	5	13,586
Celluloid	2	10,752
Peccadillo	1	10,095
Blue Dolphin	3	8,532
Guerilla	2	7,450
Barbican	3	5,087
Melanda	1	4,766
Bluelight	1	3,696
Winstone	1	3,666
Feature Film	1	3,094
Kino Kino	2	2,492
MFD	1	1,785
2nd Generation	1	1,659
Weinerworld	1	482
Sun Character	1	287
Total (independents)	**239**	**118,354,787**
Total	**382**	**577,280,342**

* only films released between January – December 2000 are included

Source: ACNielsen EDI/bfi/Screen Finance/X25

Mission Impossible II – top EU Film

Snatch was the next film in this category but it took just over £12 million, most of which presumably ended up with its financier and distributor Columbia Tristar. The real surprise of the table is TV spin-off *Kevin & Perry Go Large*. Partially financed, and distributed, by Icon. The film managed to bring in over £10 million and come 18th in the year overall.

The Beach has been included in the third category (other co-productions) as it was shot entirely in Thailand. Again the main finance for the film is from a US major, in this case 20th Century Fox, which also distribute the film in the UK. The inclusion of the film in this category has bumped up the box office total somewhat as it took over £13 million, but there are exactly the same number of releases in this category as the previous year, with more or less the same returns. Depressingly, the table overall is down by nine releases and about £70m on the previous year.

The global impact of US co-produced products are seen when we look at the fortunes of EU films at the UK box office (Table 20). Sixteen out of the 20 so-called EU films are US co-productions. The majority are produced with Germany. *Mission Impossible II* comes top as an EU film and only *In the Mood For Love*, *Time Regained* and *Beau Travail* are in foreign language. Europe is an important territory for the US. Films that don't necessarily take America by storm can usually offer decent or even better returns across Europe. Hence there are US films and then there are US films aimed at a global audience. Globalisation has meant that even some of the top films of all time have made more abroad than in the US.

Competition on the world stage from US domination comes from Asia. However, despite its size as a film producer, 'Bollywood' films have a modest impact on the UK box office. Thanks to multiplexes targeting ethnic minority audiences Hindi films dominate the top 20 foreign language films (Table 21). *Mohabbatein* was by far the most popular foreign language film. More people in the UK saw that film than the following top UK films – *Purely Belter, The House of Mirth, Essex Boys* and *Mansfield Park*. Encouraged by the successes of Indian films, producers have come to the UK to make films, and some films such as *Lagaan* are using British actors. The number of foreign language films released in the UK is increasing annually but, at least in 2000, none managed to break the £1m mark.

There was a time, not so long ago, when top foreign language films generally came from France, Germany, Spain and Italy. Now less than half of the foreign language films table is made up of European films. With the top film being *In the Mood For Love*.

It is a sad reflection of our times that UK audiences shy away from subtitled films unless they are encouraged to go by US backing or Oscar nominations. This point was emphasised in 2001 when Ang Lee's *Crouching Tiger*

Hidden Dragon broke all records for an opening weekend for a foreign language film.

In the UK this can be seen by the breakdown of box office by country of origin (Table 22). This table rather under cooks the US dominance of the UK market. If we treated US films (including co-productions) in the same way we regard UK films, it would be fairer to say that US films represent around 94 per cent of the box office total in the UK.

Interestingly, the top UK films at the US box office (Table 23) contain a few anomalies. The biggest difference being *Croupier* which out-performed *Topsy-Turvy* and *East is East.*

European audiences also love US movies. With the exception of *Taxi 2* the top films in Europe were from the States (Table 24). Evidence of the UK film industry's revival was hard to trace in the top 20 admissions table, *Chicken Run* and *The Beach*, were the UK's only two representatives.

Jumping to the wild conclusion that European audiences are not over keen on their own products would be easy to do – particularly when comparing the form of European films across Europe. *Chicken Run* was the most successful

Mohabbatein was the most popular foreign language film in the UK in 2000

27

UK Cinema Circuits 1984-2000
s (sites) scr (screens)

Year	ABC		UGC *(ex-Virgin)		Cine UK		Odeon**		Showcase		UCI		Warner Village		Small Chains		Independents	
	s	scr	s	scr	s	scr	s	scr	s	scr	s	scr	s	scr	s	scr	s	scr
1985	-	-	158	403*	-	-	76	194	-	-	3	17	1	5	-	-	-	-
1986	-	-	173	443*	-	-	74	190	-	-	3	17	1	5	-	-	-	-
1987	-	-	154	408*	-	-	75	203	-	-	5	33	1	5	-	-	-	-
1988	-	-	140	379*	-	-	73	214	7	85	12	99	1	5	-	-	-	-
1989	-	-	142	388*	-	-	75	241	7	85	18	156	3	26	-	-	-	-
1990	-	-	142	411*	-	-	75	266	7	85	21	189	5	48	-	-	-	-
1991	-	-	136	435*	-	-	75	296	8	97	23	208	6	57	-	-	-	-
1992	-	-	131	422*	-	-	75	313	9	109	25	219	7	64	-	-	-	-
1993	-	-	125	408*	-	-	75	322	10	127	25	219	9	84	-	-	-	-
1994	-	-	119	402*	-	-	76	327	11	141	26	232	10	93	-	-	437	631
1995	-	-	116	406*	-	-	71	320	11	143	26	232	12	110	-	-	469	716
1996	92	244	24	162*	2	24	73	362	14	181	26	232	16	143	58	139	437	679
1997	80	225	29	213*	5	66	73	362	15	197	26	263	17	152	68	166	434	739
1998	81	234	34	290*	10	116	79	415	15	199	29	287	22	200	73	100	416	633
1999	58	180	36	312	13	146	79	415	16	221	31	320	28	200	55	170	376	794
2000			41	363	20	219	118	634	19	244	35	345	33	331	54	159	366	659

Source: Screen Finance

* figures from 1985 to 1998 indicate Virgin Cinemas
** Odeon bought up the ABC chain in 2000

28

UK Cinema Advertising Revenue 1985-2000

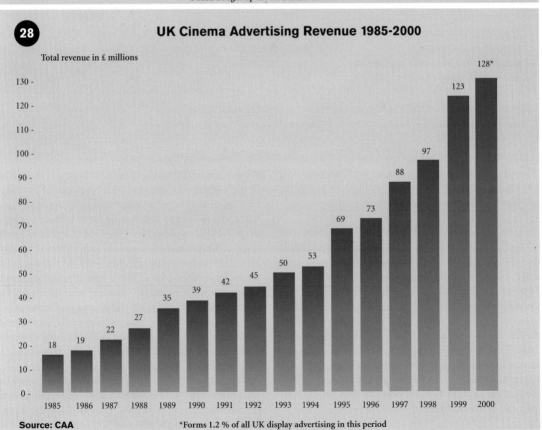

Total revenue in £ millions

| 1985 | 1986 | 1987 | 1988 | 1989 | 1990 | 1991 | 1992 | 1993 | 1994 | 1995 | 1996 | 1997 | 1998 | 1999 | 2000 |
| 18 | 19 | 22 | 27 | 35 | 39 | 42 | 45 | 50 | 53 | 69 | 73 | 88 | 97 | 123 | 128* |

Source: CAA   *Forms 1.2 % of all UK display advertising in this period

29   **All-time Top 20 UK Films at the UK Box Office**

	Title	Year of Release	Box Office Gross (£)
1	The Full Monty	1997	52,232,058
2	Bridget Jones' s Diary	2001	41,411,811
3	Notting Hill	1999	31,006,109
4	Chicken Run	2000	29,478,090
5	The World is Not Enough	1999	28,576,504
6	Four Weddings and a Funeral	1994	27,762,648
7	Shakespeare in Love	1999	20,814,996
8	Tomorrow Never Dies	1997	19,884,412
9	GoldenEye	1995	18,245,572
10	Billy Elliot	2000	18,232,327
11	Bean	1997	17,972,562
12	Sliding Doors	1998	12,457,984
13	Trainspotting	1996	12,443,450
14	Snatch	2000	12,337,505
15	A Fish Called Wanda	1988	12,034,286
16	Lock, Stock and Two Smoking Barrels	1998	11,784,141
17	Shirley Valentine	1990	11,548,196
18	Moonraker	1979	10,659,000
19	East is East	1999	10,373,945
20	Kevin & Perry Go Large	2000	10,256,520

Box office figures as of 16 August 2001
Source: ACNielsen EDI/bfi

N.B. Star Wars Episode 1 The Phantom Menace (1999) has grossed £51,031,269 in the UK.
It was partially produced in Britain, but for these purposes has been treated as a US film

'European' film. It is also worth noticing how many titles from Table 25 didn't seem to see the light of day in UK cinemas – and these are the best films in Europe.

As in 1999 the top two distributors in the UK in 2000 were UIP and Buena Vista (Table 26). Both experienced rises in their box office profits. UIP's biggest hit was the Oscar-laden *Gladiator* – although *American Beauty*, *Mission Impossible II* and *Billy Elliot* were leading players in its portfolio. Buena Vista's top two titles were the family-orientated hits – *Toy Story 2* and *Dinosaur*. Columbia TriStar leapt into third position with titles such as *Stuart Little*, *Snatch*, *Charlie's Angels* and award winning *Erin Brokovich*. Warners stayed in fourth position with only *Pokemon* making it into the top 20 films at the UK box office. 20th Century Fox slid down to fifth slot with *X-Men* and *The Beach* being its two leading titles.

What lies beneath the US major distributors is the bones of the UK distribution sector. The combined box office total of the 239 titles released by the independents (£118,354,787) were bettered by both UIP and Buena Vista. Pathé swapped places with Entertainment to reach top spot. Pathé's box office returns have increased steadily over the last few years and they were by far the most successful independent of 2000, with 22 titles and over £45m in box office receipts. This was achieved largely by doubling their output from the success of *Chicken Run*. Entertainment's biggest success was *Final Destination* while Icon had a good year largely off the back of *Kevin & Perry Go Large* and *Thomas and the Magic Railroad*.

By and large the remainder of the distribution network in the UK remains fragmented with most only releasing one or two titles a year. It is these companies in the main, which keep the supply of foreign language, art-house and re-released films available to UK audiences. Of note is the number of Asian distributors who have made modest inroads at the box office; Yash Raj, Set Singha, Eros and Bollywood among them. In Table 21 (Foreign Language Films) the films released by these companies make up over half the top 20, with three films from Yash Raj; *Mohabbatein, Kaho Naa Pyaar Hai* and *Dulhan Hum Le Jayenge* in the top five.

The top 10 independents managed box office receipts of £1m or more. However, it would be wrong to judge the output of this sector purely on box office receipts. What the independents give to the UK film industry is a smorgasbord of diversity. If the smaller independents were allotted more screen opportunities by the exhibition sector then their box office receipts would no doubt increase. But which exhibitor would be prepared to take such risks?

In 2000, Odeon bought up the ABC chain of cinemas and closures and re-openings of former ABC's will likely reach completion by 2002. This move has left Odeon cinemas with the most sites and screens in the UK (Table 27). There was much speculation about the fate of other smaller operators, such as Ster Century whether they would stay in the UK or sell up and go. Early in 2001 Showcase Cinemas took over Hoyts' massive Bluewater site and in March 2001 Zoo Cinema Exhibition was formed bringing together Oasis cinemas and Film Network.

With the UK experiencing a boom year in cinema attendances in 2000, it will be interesting to how the cinema circuits will respond to the market. Perhaps talk about saturation levels in the industry may have been slightly premature. However, half-way through 2001 indications are that admissions are down by about three per cent. While there is no reason to press the panic button just yet, the fear is that if audiences drop dramatically, a boom and bust effect may be felt through the exhibition sector creating a domino effect of closures.

This year we have included a top 20 UK films at the UK box office of all time (Table 29). Comprehensive box office figures for the UK prior to the mid-1980s are not readily available and the figures we have used have not been adjusted for inflation. The table throws up some 'cultural' anomalies, not least the fate of *Star Wars Episode 1 The Phantom Menace* which was partially produced in the UK, but has been treated as a US film.

The Full Monty still stands bold and proud at the top of the pile but is facing stiff opposition from *Bridget Jones's Diary* which was still on release at the time the table was completed. The films that work best are quirky British comedies (usually featuring an American actress) and Bond movies. *Shakespeare in Love* is the only costume drama to make it into the top 20 which is a bit of a surprise considering that costume dramas are perceived to be one of the strengths of British cinema.

We also have included a top 10 Indian movies in the UK to reflect the impact these films are having on the UK market (Table 30). The top film in this list being *Kuch, Kuch Hota Hai* which was the first Indian film ever to be screened at the Empire cinema in London's West End.

Additional material by Erinna Mettler

---

30   **Top 10 Indian Movies in the UK**

Title	Distributor	Opening Date	Total Box Office (£)
1 Kuch Kuch Hota Hai	Yash Raj	15-Oct-98	1,750,000
2 Mohabbatein	Yash Raj	27-Oct-00	1,100,000
3 Dil To Pagal Hai	Yash Raj	31-Oct-97	990,000
4 Hum Saath-Saath Hain	Eros	5-Nov-99	651,797
5 Taal	Eros	13-Aug-99	604,800
6 Kaho Naa Pyaar Hai	Yash Raj	14-Jan-00	495,531
7 Dil Se	Eros	21-Aug-98	467,271
8 Hum Aapke Dil Mein Rahte Hain	Eros	15-Jan-99	455,257
9 Dulhan Hum Le Jayenge	Yash Raj	24-Mar-00	394,269
10 Har Dil Jo Pyar Karega	Eros	4-Aug-00	390,227

Source: AC Nielsen EDI/Screen International

31   **BBFC Censorship of Videos 2000**

Certificate	Number of Films passed after cuts
U	6
PG	13
12	7
15	9
18	110
R18	28

Source: BBFC

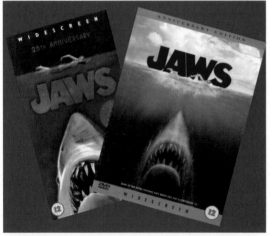

VHS and DVD formats performed surprisingly well in 2000

DVD/Video

It would have been logical to assume that the rise of DVD would signal the fall and eventual demise of VHS in the UK. The remarkable and unexpected news is that in 2000 both formats grew.

VHS retail transactions totalled 114 million which generated record sales of £1,104m (Table 32). The reason for this is that 90 per cent of the UK population have VHS players and there are plenty of VHS bargains to be had. What is interesting about this is that it implies that there are plenty of video collectors out there, still making additions to their video collections.

While the solid performance of VHS was not easy to forecast, the rise and rise of DVD was easier to call. But even then, the 300 per cent growth rate in DVD players was quite impressive. Disc sales rose massively to 16.6 million generating £264m. No doubt this figure will continue to grow, particularly when even more titles become available. It is interesting to compare the transactions totals and note that the current rate of DVD retail sales roughly corresponds to the levels VHS achieved in 1988. By this time next year DVDs may yet have surpassed the 1989 transactions total of 38 million units.

Video rentals were at the highest since 1992 with 186 million transactions also topping the previous year's total

32   **The UK Video/DVD Market 1986-2000**

Year	Retail Transactions (millions)		Value (£m)		Rental Transactions (millions)	Value (£m)
1986	6		55		233	284
1987	12		110		251	326
1988	20		184		271	371
1989	38		345		289	416
1990	40		374		277	418
1991	45		440		253	407
1992	48		506		222	389
1993	60		643		184	350
1994	66		698		167	339
1995	73		789		167	351
1996	79		803		175	382
1997	87		858		161	369
1998	100		940		186	437
1999	96	(4)	882	(68)	174	408
2000	114	(16.6)	1104	(264)	186	444

DVD retail transactions in parentheses

Source: BVA

33 Top 20 Rental Videos in the UK 2000

	Title	Distributor	Country
1	The Sixth Sense (15)	Buena Vista	US
2	Gladiator (15)	Universal	US
3	The Green Mile (18)	Universal	US
4	East is East (15)	FilmFour	UK
5	The Deep Blue Sea (15)	Warner	US
6	American Pie (15)	Universal	US
7	American Beauty (18)	Universal	US
8	Fight Club (15)	Fox Pathé	US
9	The Mummy (12)	Universal	US
10	End of Days (18)	Buena Vista	US
11	The World is Not Enough (12)	MGM	UK/US
12	Big Daddy (12)	Columbia TriStar	US
13	Three Kings (15)	Warner	US
14	The Bone Collector (18)	Columbia TriStar	US
15	Erin Brockovich (15)	Columbia Tristar	US
16	Sleepy Hollow (15)	Fox Pathé	US/GER
17	The Runaway Bride (PG)	Buena Vista	US
18	The Beach (15)	Fox Pathé	US/UK/TH
19	Blue Streak (12)	Columbia Tristar	US/GER
20	Stigmata (18)	MGM	US

Source: Rental Monitor

The Sixth Sense ghosted itself to the top of the rental chart

34 Distributors Share of UK Rental Transactions 2000 (%)

	Distributor	% share
1	Universal	20.2
2	Fox Pathé	17.5
3	Buena Vista	15.6
4	Warner	14.7
5	Columbia TriStar	12.6
6	EV	6.0
7	Film Four	5.2
8	Paramount	4.7
9	Metrodome	1.2
10	High Fliers/Alliance	1.1

Source: Rental Monitor/BVA

by a solid seven per cent. The value of these transactions soared to an all time high of £444m, evidence that home entertainment is as vibrant as cinema-going in the UK. Accurate figures for monitoring DVD rentals are not available, however the British Video Association (BVA) reckon that DVD rental transactions accounted for around four per cent of the overall total and is thought to have generated around £22m of the total spend.

Overall the most popular genre for rentals is comedy although this is not represented in the top 20 rentals (Table 33) which lean more towards thrills than laughs. *The Sixth Sense*, a suspense thriller, was the most rented title in 2000 having been rented over four million times. However, *Gladiator*, the Oscar winning, action, epic, was available to rent in mid October 2000 and accounted for over three million transactions. More suspense was offered from *The Green Mile* which also passed the three million transactions mark. FilmFour's *East is East* was the top UK rental title.

Universal leapt to the top of both the distributors rental and retail charts (Tables 34 & 37) wading in with a sizeable 20.2 per cent of the rental market and 19.4 per cent of the retail market. In rental terms they had five films in the top 10, with *Gladiator* the cream of the Universal crop. Pathé was in second place offering three films in the top 20 with the psychological action thriller, *Fight Club* punching itself into eighth spot. In third spot, Buena Vista could bask in the reflected glory of *the Sixth Sense*.

Just when it seemed that the retail market had begun a slide in 1999, figures went through the roof again in 2000 with 114 million sales netting £1,104m. VHS sales were undoubtedly boosted by the crop of crowd-pleasing family-orientated entertainment finding its way into homes. Hence, the top five retail films contained the likes of *Toy Story 2*, *Chicken Run* and *Stuart Little*. However, the top VHS retail film was *Star Wars Episode 1 - The Phantom Menace*. The UK's top representative was *Chicken Run*. Meanwhile, Ali G continued his popularity with the only non-film entry in the 2000 chart.

Last year the Handbook mused over the retail demographics between VHS and DVD. The DVD chart again contains fewer U certificate films than its older format. *Toy Story 2* and *Chicken Run* are the two token family-orientated films. A cursory look at the top titles leads to the highly contentious conclusion that the first batch of DVD owners were likely to be young thrill seeking men. Indeed, while Disney films remain

35   Top 20 Retail Videos in the UK 2000

	Title	Distributor	Country
1	Star Wars Episode 1 (U)	Fox	US
2	Toy Story 2 (U)	Buena Vista	US
3	Gladiator (15)	Universal	US
4	Chicken Run (U)	Fox	US/UK
5	Stuart Little (U)	Columbia Tristar	US
6	Tarzan (U)	Buena Vista	US
7	The Tigger Movie (U)	Buena Vista	US
8	Pokemon – the First Movie (PG)	Warner	US/JP
9	The World is Not Enough (12)	MGM	UK/US
10	American Pie (15)	Universal	US
11	Ali G-Aiii	VCI	UK
12	The Mummy (12)	Universal	US
13	Blade (18)	EV	US
14	Austin Powers – The Spy who Shagged Me (12)	EV	US
15	South Park – Bigger, Longer and Uncut (12)	Warner	US
16	Kevin and Perry Go Large (15)	Icon	UK/US
17	The Jungle Book (U)	Buena Vista	US
18	The Matrix (15)	Warner	US/AUS
19	Saving Private Ryan (15)	Paramount	US
20	The Sixth Sense (15)	Buena Vista	US

Source: BVA/CIN

36   Top 20 Retail DVDs in the UK 2000

	Title	Distributor	Country
1	Gladiator (15)	Columbia Tristar	US
2	The Matrix (15)	Warner	US
3	The Sixth Sense (15)	Buena Vista	US
4	Mission Impossible II (15)	Paramount	US
5	The Mummy (12)	Columbia TriStar	US
6	The World is Not Enough (12)	MGM	UK/US
7	Toy Story 2 (U)	Buena Vista	US
8	The Deep Blue Sea (15)	Warner	US
9	Chicken Run (U)	Fox	US/UK
10	The Perfect Storm (12)	Warner	US
11	The Green Mile (18)	VVL	US
12	Austin Powers – The Spy who Shagged Me (12)	EV	US
13	Three Kings (15)	Warner	US
14	Blade (18)	EV	US
15	American Pie (15)	Columbia Tristar	US
16	Lock, Stock and Two Smoking Barrels (18)	Universal	UK
17	End of Days (18)	Buena Vista	US
18	Men in Black (PG)	Columbia TriStar	US
19	Sleepy Hollow (15)	Pathé	US/GER
20	American Beauty (18)	Universal	US

Source: BVA/CIN

37   Video Retail Company Market Share by Volume (%) 2000

Distributor	% share
Universal	19.4
Warner	18.8
Columbia Tristar	16.1
Fox	10.0
Buena Vista	8.4
Paramount	7.5
EV	6.4
MGM	5.9
VCI	3.3
Icon	1.3

Includes VHS and DVD

Source: BVA/CIN

38   UK Video Games Market 2000 Computer Software Sales

Value	£934.4 million
Units	39.6 million

Source: Chartrack/Screen Digest/ELSPA

Star Wars Episode 1 was top of the video retail chart

prevalent in the top 20 videos of all time, the top 20 DVDs only contains the two Pixar Animation hits, *Toy Story 2* and *A Bug's Life*. It will be interesting to see if that trend continues as DVD players become even more part of people's home-viewing systems. *Gladiator* beat off all other challenges to reign supreme at the top of the DVD chart. The DVD retail chart is also made up exclusively of film titles. Whether television tie-in programmes such as *Big Brother*, fan-orientated sports programmes, or pop DVDs make a significant impact on the top 20 remains to be seen.

The proportion of videos cut by the British Board of Film Classification fell to 2.7 per cent. In July 2000, following a High Court ruling, the BBFC issued new guidelines for the adult R18 category which allowed more explicit videos to be permitted to enter licensed sex shops. Unsurprisingly, the Board reported that they received a greater increase in R18 submissions for consideration. Sex was also an issue which caused great excitement in the press as the Board passed more and more films such as *Intimacy* which contained sexually explicit material.

One of the consequences of the policy is the issuing of certificates to old titles which have courted controversy. As a result 2000 was notable for the release on video of the following titles to the delight of cineastes – *A Clockwork Orange*, *The Story of O*, *In the Realm of the Senses* and *Salò*.

Other issues that came to attention were bad language particularly in films aimed at younger audiences, (*Billy Elliot* received a 15 certificate for this reason) the portrayal of drug taking and the use of weapons, particularly knives, in films.

The video industry has adapted well to new challenges issued to it – notably from the Internet. It has worked with rather than against e-businesses who sell videos online. The industry's next challenge will be to see how it reacts to the growth of broadband services since downloading videos on demand will increasingly become an attractive proposition once broadband kicks into the consumer's consciousness.

Gladiator fought off all challenges to top the DVD retail chart

A Clockwork Orange was finally released on video in 2000

39   Trends in Television Viewing 2000

Average Daily Hours Viewing	3.68
Number of TV Households	24.2 million

Source: Taris-Taylor Nelson Sofres

40   Average TV Audience Share (%) of TV Channels 2000

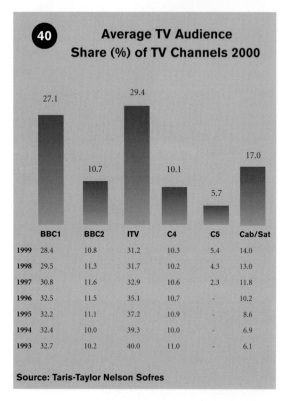

	BBC1	BBC2	ITV	C4	C5	Cab/Sat
	27.1	10.7	29.4	10.1	5.7	17.0
1999	28.4	10.8	31.2	10.3	5.4	14.0
1998	29.5	11.3	31.7	10.2	4.3	13.0
1997	30.8	11.6	32.9	10.6	2.3	11.8
1996	32.5	11.5	35.1	10.7	-	10.2
1995	32.2	11.1	37.2	10.9	-	8.6
1994	32.4	10.0	39.3	10.0	-	6.9
1993	32.7	10.2	40.0	11.0	-	6.1

Source: Taris-Taylor Nelson Sofres

41   Multichannel Subscriber Numbers 2000

Aggregate subscribers (millions)

Operator	Analogue	Digital	Total
Sky	0.5	4.6	5.1
Cable	2.6	0.9	3.5
OnDigital	-	1	1
Total	3.1	6.5	9.6

Source: ITC/Merrill Lynch/ITVDigital

Television

It has become clear that the familiar British television culture of the last 50 or so years is beginning to look very different. While television remains as popular as ever, analogue TV is slowly but surely reaching its retirement age and will eventually give way to the sharp gleaming signal of digital TV. Over the past few years the number of people using multichannel services has been steadily rising and this has been accelerated by the move to digital TV formats.

Regular readers will note that we have replaced our former table on cable and satellite penetration with one from the ITC on multichannel homes. This seemed more relevant in the new environment as the debate has moved on from the mechanics of access (and whether you put a dish on your house or had your street dug up) to the types of service people are choosing, whether it be analogue or digital; terrestrial or multichannel.

Digital services have been the Holy Grail for some in the industry but the public seem less than convinced about the desirability of trading in their old sets. There are fears that the percentage take up demanded by the Government before the analogue signal is turned off will be a long way off. Some believe that culturally the consequences of the shift when it happens will be immense. Early indications suggest that those already buying into the multichannel environment tend to be modest in the range of programmes they choose to watch. Generally, people still plump for popular programmes keeping their viewing to quite a narrow range. The difference in TV culture is also apparent in interactive TV, which has made its way on to terrestrial TV with a host of Reality TV shows. Where signs of viewer choice have become evident are in sporting events

Big Brother, where art thou?

42	ITV Companies Programme Supply to the Network 2000	
Company	**Hours of new programmes**	
Anglia	300	
Border	-	
Carlton	156	
Central	103	
Channel	-	
Grampian	-	
Granada	783	
HTV	29	
LWT	281	
Meridian	49	
STV	168	
Tyne Tees	15	
UTV	1	
West Country	6	
Yorkshire	70	

Source: ITC

Coronation Street was the top TV programme again

when the choice to watch different players playing football, golf or tennis has proved popular.

On the one hand multichannel life gives the choice to watch the types of programmes the viewer most enjoys, but on the other hand it runs the risk of reducing choice in other ways. Advertising revenues suffered badly during 2001 and the revenues that come from mass audiences might not be there to invest in new and challenging work (although this argument could apply as much to today's ratings-orientated programmes). Nevertheless, some argue that viewers may eventually be deprived of the choice to be part of a shared experience. The challenge to TV programme-makers is to provide a promotional mix heavily reliant on convergence to sell their wares. Programmes are no longer there to be watched – they are there to be absorbed. Hence, seen-the-film-read-the-book-bought-the-t-shirt culture has been injected to most TV programmes with the phrase – "you can learn more about this programme by clicking online to...."

British TV is experiencing a rate of change that shows no sign of abating. Paradoxically, TV archives are being constantly plundered to provide nostalgic themed shows, outtake shows, 100 best moment shows or just a steady stream of repeats harking back to simpler days when the viewer's choice of programmes was limited. The BBC's status and funding means that it will always be a political hot potato and commercial ITV seems to be moving inexorably towards being two or even one big monopoly after a year of frantic mergers, buy-outs and speculation.

Evidence of the digital TV future making an impact on broadcasting can be seen by the steady decline in audience share (Table 40). Both BBC channels and ITV saw their shares diminish slightly. ITV still commands the greater share of the market. Despite the success of *Big Brother* Channel 4's audience share did not increase. Meanwhile, the rise and rise of Channel 5 has continued to confound its critics. Perhaps a significant TV audience is not turned on by the TV ratings battles which TV executives and tabloid journalists seem eager to perpetuate.

The significant growth has been for Cable/Satellite audiences. The audience share rose by three per cent. The table to watch, however, will be the expected rise in multichannel subscribers (Table 41). The table confirms Sky as the leading digital provider and also shows, unsurprisingly, that the uptake in digital services is over double that of analogue services. However, as we have observed the road to digital domination is not an easy one. OnDigital reached 1 million subscribers in 2000 but needed help in 2001 when it was relaunched as ITV Digital.

Once again ITV dominated the top 20 programmes list (Table 43) with *Coronation Street* firmly installed as the most popular TV programme in the UK. The BBC's

Top 20 Programmes for all Terrestrial Channels 2000

Only top rated episodes of each series are included

	Title	Channel	TX date	Audience (m)
1	Coronation Street	ITV	1-Mar	19.0
2	Eastenders	BBC1	1-Mar	18.4
3	Who Wants to be a Millionaire?	ITV	19-Jan	15.9
4	Heartbeat	ITV	23-Jan	15.2
5	Euro 200: England V Portugal	ITV	12-Jun	14.9
6	Euro 200: England V Romania	BBC1	20-Jun	14.6
7	Inspector Morse	ITV	15-Nov	13.7
8	Emmerdale	ITV	22-Mar	13.3
9	One Foot in the Grave	BBC1	20-Nov	12.8
10	The Vicar of Dibley	BBC1	1-Jan	12.5
11	Casualty	BBC1	2-Dec	12.3
12	Seeing Red	ITV	19-Mar	12.3
13	Stars in their Eyes	ITV	12-Feb	12.1
14	The National TV Awards	ITV	10-Oct	12.0
15	A Touch of Frost	ITV	1-Jan	11.9
16	Garages from Hell	ITV	1-May	11.5
17	The Bill	ITV	4-Feb	11.5
18	Hero of the Hour	ITV	3-Dec	11.2
19	I Don't Believe It	BBC1	20-Nov	11.2
20	The Full Monty	ITV	29-Nov	11.1

Source: Taris-Taylor Nelson Sofres/BARB

Top 20 Original Drama Productions 2000

Including soap operas, series, serials and UKTV Movies.
Audience figures are for highest rated episodes of each production

	Title	Producer/Sponsor	Tx Date	Audience (m)
1	Coronation Street	Granada	1-Mar	19.0
2	EastEnders	BBC	1-Mar	18.4
3	Heartbeat	Yorkshire	23-Jan	15.2
4	Inspector Morse	Zenith/Carlton	15-Nov	13.7
5	Emmerdale	Yorkshire	22-Mar	13.3
6	Casualty	BBC	12-Dec	12.3
7	Seeing Red	Granada	19-Mar	12.3
8	A Touch of Frost	Yorkshire	1-Jan	11.9
9	The Bill	Pearson/Carlton	4-Feb	11.5
10	Hero of the Hour	LWT	3-Dec	11.2
11	London's Burning	LWT	16-Jan	10.7
12	Randall and Hopkirk (Deceased)	Working Title/BBC	18-Mar	10.6
13	Jonathan Creek	BBC	1-Feb	10.7
14	Monsignor Renard	Carlton	27-Mar	10.6
15	Where the Heart Is	United/Anglia	6-Apr	10.4
16	Fat Friends	Rollem/Tiger Aspect/Yorkshire	0-Dec	10.4
17	Holby City	BBC	13-Jan	10.1
18	Peak Practice	Central/Carlton	28-Mar	9.9
19	Cold Feet	Granada	19-Nov	9.9
20	My Fragile Heart	Tiger Aspect/LWT	17-Sep	9.8

Source: Taris-Taylor Nelson Sofres/BARB

45   **Television Advertising 2000**

	£m
Net TV Advertising Revenue	3,300
ITV	1,912
C4	652
C5	207
S4C & GMTV	67
Programme Sponsorship	67
Non-Terrestrial TV Revenue	462

Includes Advertising Revenue, Sponsorship and Subscriptions.

Source : ITC/C4

Seeing Red was the top single drama

flagship programme *EastEnders* improved its status in 2000 with a top audience figure of 18.4 million (and made even more strides in 2001 to consolidate its position by appearing four days a week with an omnibus edition on Sunday). The BBC notched up a disappointing six out of the 20 top shows. The surprise absence from the chart is *Big Brother*. Despite the ballyhoo surrounding Channel 4's ground-breaking show it remained elusively just outside the top 20. By 2001 *The Weakest Link* had been brought in to compete with *Who Wants to be a Millionaire* but in terms of popular TV, the ITV network was easily the leader.

46   **UK TV Films Premiered 2000**

Title	Tx date	BARB Rating(m)
BBC1		
The Great Gatsby	29-Mar	3.2
McCready and Daughter	15-Jun	7.6
Last of the Blonde Bombshells	9-Mar	7.7
Care	10-Aug	4.4
Thin Ice	12-Apr	5.7
BBC2		
Summer in the Suburbs	1-Oct	3.4
Storm Damage	23-Jan	1.4
Mojo*	20-Feb	1.0
Mrs Dalloway*	23-Feb	1.9
The James Gang*	27-Feb	1.2
Justice in Wonderland	3-May	1.9
Speak Like a Child	3-May	0.5
Metroland*	3-Dec	0.9
Love is the Devil*	26-Mar	0.7
A Love Divided	26-Mar	1.3
Nice Girl	5-Nov	2.6
TwentyFourSeven*	9-Oct	0.8
Divorcing Jack*	16-Dec	1.0
Wilde*	29-Dec	1.9
Gods and Monsters*	31-Dec	0.7

Source: BARB/*bfi*

Title	Tx date	BARB Rating(m)
ITV		
Forgive and Forget	1-Mar	5.9
Hero of the Hour	3-Dec	11.2
Seeing Red	19-Mar	12.3
The Last Musketeer	26-Mar	8.6
The Railway Children	23-Apr	9.6
Cor Blimey!	24-Apr	6.2
Inspector Wexford:Harm Done	10-Nov	9.8
Little Bird	11-Jan	6.0
Inspector Morse: The Remorseful Day	15-Nov	13.7
Channel 4		
Killing Time	1-Jan	0.5
Alice in Wonderland	23-Apr	4.0
The Land Girls*	19-Jun	3.9
Elizabeth*	9-Mar	3.8
Dancing at Lughnasa*	9-Oct	2.6
My Name is Joe*	17-Sep	1.0
Prometheus*	17-Sep	0.1
Under the Skin*	12-Dec	0.5
Hilary and Jackie*	5-Dec	0.7
Career Girls*	28-Dec	0.4

* denotes previous release in UK cinemas

47　　Top 20 Feature Films Shown on Terrestrial TV 2000

	Title	Country	Year	Channel	Audience (m)
1	The Full Monty	US/UK	1997	ITV	11.1
2	Liar Liar	US	1997	ITV	10.9
3	Men in Black	US	1997	BBC1	10.7
4	Dante's Peak	US	1997	ITV1	10.7
5	101 Dalmations	US	1996	BBC1	10.1
6	Titanic	US	1997	BBC1	10.0
7	Independence Day	US	1996	BBC1	9.9
8	Volcano	US	1997	ITV	9.7
9	Mrs Brown	UK/US/IE	1997	BBC1	9.3
10	Tomorrow Never Dies	UK/US	1997	ITV	9.3
11	The Lost World:Jurassic Park 2	US	1997	ITV	9.0
12	GoldenEye	UK/US	1995	ITV	8.9
13	Daylight	US	1996	ITV	8.3
14	One Fine Day	US	1996	ITV	8.2
15	Robin Hood:Prince of Thieves	US	1991	BBC1	8.1
16	Apollo 13	US	1995	BBC1	7.9
17	Sleepless in Seattle	US	1993	ITV	7.8
18	The Specialist	US	1994	ITV	7.8
19	Forrest Gump	US	1994	BBC1	7.8
20	Face/Off	US	1997	BBC1	7.7

Source: Taris-Taylor Nelson Sofres/BARB

Although the BBC lost out on the top football audience for Euro 2000 (with England's opening match against Portugal on ITV drawing a slightly bigger audience than England's final match against Romania) they gained comfort from viewing figures for the Euro 2000 clash with Germany. The match was shown on both channels (hence no top 20 appearance) with BBC coverage gaining 10.9 million viewers – some 4 million more than ITV.

ITV however, continued to score well in the table of original dramas (Table 44). Admittedly, this table is somewhat skewed by the reliance on soap operas and series. Nevertheless, the top series was *Heartbeat* which secured a top audience of 15.2 million compared with *Casualty,* which was the BBC's top series, watched by 12.3 million. ITV's series all proved popular whereas the BBC have really struggled in recent years to produce anything as durable as say, *Inspector Morse, A Touch of Frost,* or *London's Burning.* All three of these shows were more popular than the BBC's interesting attempt at reviving *Randall and Hopkirk (Deceased)* with Vic Reeves and Bob Mortimer. However, the thing that the ITV shows have had in common is the opportunity to establish themselves as the nation's favourite shows. In the last couple of years TV executives have been quick to press the panic button with shows that don't achieve instant

The Full Monty exposed itself as the top film on TV

48　　UK General Statistics 2000

Population	59.6 million
Number of Households	24.94 million
Inflation	3 per cent
Gross Domestic Product (Current Prices)	£934,924 million
Total TV Licences in Force	23 million
Licence Fee Income	£2,285,500

Source: ONS/BBC

success. It is a tall order and one that puts unnecessary pressure on the programme-makers. This applies to drama and sitcoms where in the past hit shows like *Dad's Army*, *Only Fools and Horses* and *Men Behaving Badly* took a while to establish themselves, and for the characters to grow on the audiences. Much of the problem with today's new drama programmes is that the eager-to-please element seems to destroy character development. Instead, the audience is subjected to parade of similar looking shows featuring twentysomethings or thirtysomethings, struggling to come to terms with life, and having relationships with their best friends – ie *This Life, Hearts and Bones.*

In fact, the top single TV drama in 2000 was Granada's *Seeing Red* starring Sarah Lancashire and based on the life of actress Coral Atkins which attracted 12.3 million. The most popular BBC1 single drama was *Last of the Blonde Bombshells* which drew an audience of 7.7 million. It is unlikely that either programmes would have drawn the same kind of audience had they been released in UK cinemas. It is a wonder why more single TV dramas are not made. Perhaps the perceived boom in the British film industry is partly responsible. It has been common to report in recent years about the casualty of micro-budget films that lie unwatched. A vast proportion of these films would have probably benefitted from TV values – not least with some tightening up of scripts. It could be argued that the majority of UK films shown on TV in 2000 (Table 46) should have been made for TV in the first place.

Meanwhile, the debate about the standard of British sitcoms rages. You're either in the "they don't make them like they used to" camp or "there's nothing wrong with British sitcoms" camp. The top sitcom show in 2000 was *One Foot in the Grave*, followed by the *Vicar of Dibley*. Neither of these two hit BBC shows were new – indeed *One Foot in the Grave* had been running for 10 years and its final episode was transmitted in November 2000. But as far as hit sitcoms go ITV has long been in the shadow of the BBC. Channel 4 on the other hand can point to the BAFTA success of *Black Books* as a measure of its own modest success in the sitcom area.

It is interesting to draw parallels again with the success of comedies in the UK film industry. *Bridget Jones's Diary* springs to mind since the film of the book would seem ideal material for TV comedy. In fact successful Bridget Jones type shows are currently screened on British TV, however, they are all American – *Friends, Ally McBeal* and *Frazier*. British attempts at the same genre have, to date, proved unmemorable.

There was a time when movies on terrestrial TV were big events. Now most movies shown on terrestrial TV have been round the block a few times having been released on Video/DVD and premiered on Cable/Satellite channels before making the last leg of their journeys on terrestrial TV. So, in 2000 half the big films in the top 20 came from 1997 (Table 47). The films were headed by *The Full Monty* which was watched by 11.1 million. The surprise is that *Titanic*, the biggest film of all time, was as low as number six in the TV chart.

Generally speaking, the terrestrial TV statistics for 2000 give no indication that a broadcasting revolution is taking place. The assumption is that we all will want to buy in to the multi-channel environment. TV programme makers will have to work harder to convince a nation of potential couch potatoes to tune in to whatever their services are. Along with the quantity of programmes it is reasonable for audiences to expect quality as well, otherwise, to paraphrase from a BBC campaign: "going out will be the new staying in".

Additional material by Phil Wickham

Further Reading

Statistics sources

AC Nielsen/EDI Database Reports
London: AC Nielsen/EDI, 2001
Key source for UK and US Box Office

British Films Catalogue 2001
British Council, 2001
*Annual listing of features,
documentary, short, and animation
films made in the UK.* (Available at
www.britfilms.com)

BVA Yearbook 2001
London: British Video Association,
2001
Key source for UK video/DVD data

**CAVIAR Report 1995 (+ Summary
findings 1996-99)**
CAVIAR Consortium/CAA.
*Three volume report on cinema
attendance and video watching. (Only
summary findings available in bfi
National Library from 1996)*

**Cinema exhibition and distribution
in Europe: market assessment and
forecast**
Screen Digest, 2001
*Likely to be an invaluable but
expensive resource*

Cinemagoing 9
Leicester: Dodona Research, 2001
*Key report on cinema attendance and
the state of the exhibition sector*

European Cinema Yearbook 2000
Media Salles, 2000
*Annual packed with tables on
European cinema admissions, market
shares, Top 10 domestic/European
films, admissions by large town, etc*

European Video Yearbook 2000/2001
Screen Digest: 2001
*Contains brief national market
summaries with accompanying tables
for VHS/DVD*

GB Cinema exhibitors
Office for National Statistics, 2000

**Overseas Transactions of the Film &
Television Industry**
Office for National Statistics, 1999.

**Statistical Yearbook: cinema,
television and new media in Europe
2001**
European Audiovisual Observatory,
2001
*Key source for European audiovisual
industry with summaries and tables on
the film production, distribution,
admissions, television, multimedia,
home video, and advertising*

**TaRIS UK Television & Video
Yearbook**
*Key source on audience share,
children's viewing, TV ratings, hours of
viewing, top 500 programmes and UK
video market*

*World Film & Television Market
(IDATE Report)*
Montpellier: IDATE, 2001
*Two-volume report covering
"industries & markets" and "the
players" from ARD to Walt Disney*

Suggested further reading and other useful sources

**Annuals Guide 2001
by Christophe Dupin and Andrea
King**
*Excellent guide to frequently used
sources held in the bfi National Library*
(Available to download at
www.bfi.org.uk/library/collections)

**British Cinema of the 90s,
ed by Robert Murphy**
*bfi , 1999.
Only up to date work on this subject*

**The British Cinema Book (2nd ed),
ed by Robert Murphy**
*bfi, 2001
Expanded survey with a new section
on contemporary British cinema*

Cable & Satellite Yearbook
Informa Media, 2001
A standard directory for the sector

**Childwise – the Monitor Report
Winter 2000-2001**
Norwich: Childwise, 2000
*Analysis and tables of children and
young persons' media consumption
from TV viewing to favourite pop star*

**Encore Hollywood: remaking French
cinema, by Lucy Mazdon**
bfi, 2000

The Film Industry Market Report
(Keynote Report)
Keynote, 2000.

**Film in England: a development
strategy for film and the moving
image in the English regions**
Film Council, 2000

Focus World Film Market
EAO, 2001
*Handy little pamphlet prepared for
Cannes extracted from Statistical
Yearbook above but with extra
international stats (US, Canada, Latin
America, Australia)*

**Global Film: Exhibition &
Distribution (4th ed), by Andy
Thomas & Stuart O'Brien**
Informa Media Group, 2001.
*Analysis and tables on exhibition,
admissions, box office & distribution*

**Global Hollywood,
by Toby Miller et al.**
bfi, 2001
Examination of Hollywood's cultural
and economic domination of cinema

**The Global Media Atlas,
by Mark Balnaves et al.**
bfi, 2001.
*Illustrated examination of the
dynamics of the media &
communications industries using
colour maps, charts and tables*

**International Film & Television
Rights 2000**
London: Market Tracking
International, 2000
*Well received analysis of the economics
of the film & TV industry*

**Media and meaning: an
introduction, by Colin Stewart**
bfi, 2001

*Aimed at students, this is sound
introduction which also examines
computer based media*

A New Future For Communications
HMSO, 2001.
*White paper from the DTI and DCMS
setting out the government's goals
regarding communications and how
the new regulator OFCOM will
operate*

TBI Yearbook
Informa Media, 2001.
*Long established reference source for
international TV with market
summaries and company listings.*

**Towards a Sustainable UK Film
Industry**
Film Council, 2000.
*First public document from the Film
Council outlining its plans and
initiatives*

Selected annual
reports

Arts Council of England annual
report 2000

BBC annual report & accounts
2000/2001

British Board of Film Classification
annual report 2000

BFI annual review 1999/2000

Broadcasting Standards
Commission annual report 2001

Independent Television Commission
annual report & accounts 2000

Periodicals

Broadcast (UK, weekly)
Screen Digest (UK, monthly)
Screen Finance (UK, fortnightly)
Screen International (UK, weekly)
Sight and Sound (UK, monthly)
Variety (US, weekly)

Compiled by Sean Delaney

AGENTS AND MANAGERS

Below is a selection of some film and television agents and managers. Compiled by Peter Todd

The Agency
24 Pottery Lane
London W11 4LZ
Tel: 020 7727 1346
Fax: 020 7727 1346

Artists Independent Network
32 Tavistock Street
London WC2E 7PB
Tel: 020 7257 8787
Fax: 020 7240 9029

Artists Management Group
9465 Wilshire Blvd
Beverly Hills
Ca 90212
USA
Tel: 001 310 860 8000
Fax: 001 310 860 8100

Artmedia
20 avenue Rapp
75007Paris
France
Tel: 33 01 43 17 33 00
Fax: 33 01 44 18 34 60
email: info@artmedia.fr
Website: www.artmedia.fr

Casarotto Ramsey & Associates
National House
60-66 Wardour Street
London W1V 4ND
Tel:. 020 7287 4450
Fax: 020 7287 5644
email: agents@casarotto.uk.com

Chatto & Linnit
123A Kings Road
London SW3 4PL
Tel: 020 7352 7722
Fax: 020 73523450
email: chattolinnnit@
kingsrdsw3.demon.co.uk

Conway Van Gelder
18-21 Jermyn Street
London SW1Y 6HP
Tel: 020 7287 0077
Fax: 020 7287 1940

Creative Artists Agency
9830 Wilshire Blvd.
Beverly Hills, CA 90212
USA
Tel: 001 310 288 4545
Fax: 001 310 288 4800

Curtis Brown
Haymarket House
28-29 Haymarket
London SW1Y 4SP
Tel: 020 7396 6600
Fax: 020 7396 0110

ICM (Internationl Creative Management)
Oxford House
76 Oxford Street
London W1N 0AX
Tel: 020 7636 6565
Fax: 020 7323 0101
8942 Wilshire Blvd
Beverly Hills, CA 90211
USA
Tel: 001 310 550 4000
Fax: 001 310 550 4100

Jonathan Altaras Associates
13 Short's Gardens
London WC2H 9AT
Tel: 020 7836 6565
Fax: 020 7836 6066

Judy Daish Associates
2 St. Charles Place
London W10 6EG
Tel: 020 8964 8811
Fax: 020 8964 8966

Julian Belfrage Associates
46 Albermarle Street
London W1X 3DH
Tel: 020 7491 4400
Fax: 020 7493 5460

Ken McReddie
91 Regent Street
London W1R 7TB
Tel: 020 7439 1456
Fax: 020 7734 6530

London Management
2-4 Noel Street
London W1V 3RB
Tel: 020 7287 9000
Fax: 020 7287 3036

Markham & Froggatt
4 Windmill Street
London W1P 1HF
Tel: 020 7636 4412
Fax: 020 7637 5233
email: markham@online.rednet.co.uk

Peters Fraser & Dunlop
Drury House
34-43 Russell Street
London WC2 5HA
Tel: 020 7344 10000
Fax: 020 7836 0444
email: postmaster@pfd.co.uk
Website: www.pfd.co.uk

Richard Stone Partnership
2 Henrietta Street
London WC2E 8PS
Tel: 020 7497 0849
Fax: 020 7497 0869

William Morris Agency
52-53 Poland Street
London W1F 7LX
Tel: 020 7534 6800
Fax: 020 7534 6900
One William Morris Place
Beverly Hills
CA 90212
USA
Tel: 001 310 859 4000
Fax: 001 310 859 4462

ARCHIVES AND FILM LIBRARIES

International Organisations

FIAF (International Federation of Film Archives)
1 Rue Defacqz
B-1000 Brussels
Belgium
Tel: 32 2 538 3065
Fax: 32 2 534 4774
email: info@fiafnet.org
Website: www.fiafnet.org
Christian Dimitriu
Founded in 1938, FIAF is a collaborative association of the world's leading film archives whose purpose is to ensure the proper preservation and showing of motion pictures. More than 120 archives in over 60 countries collect, restore, and exhibit films and cinema documentation spanning the entire history of film. It also publishes handbooks on film archiving practice which can be obtained from the above address

FIAT/IFTA (International Federation of Television Archives)
NRK Norwegian Broadcasting Corp.
DAFA
N-0340 OSLO
Norway
Tel: (+47) 2304 9135
Fax: (+47) 2304 9320
email: Office@fiatifta.org
Website: www.fiatifta.org
Liv Sonstebo, Administrative Coordinator
Peter Dusek (President)
Tedd Johansen (General Secretary)
FIAT membership is mainly made up of the archive services of broadcasting organisations. However, it also encompasses national archives and other television-related bodies. It meets annually and publishes its proceedings and other recommendations concerning television archiving

European Archives

Below are some European Film Archives of countries in the European Union. For more specialised information consult *Film and Television Collections in Europe – The MAP-TV Guide* published by Blueprint

Austria

Österreichishes Filmarchiv (Austrian Film Library)
Schaumburgergasse 11
1040 Wien
Tel: 0043 1 505 53 37 0
Fax: 0043 1 505 53 07
email: info@filmarchiv.org
Website: www.filmarchiv.org
Alexander V.Kammel

Belgium

Cinémathèque Royale/Koninklijk Filmarchief (Royal Film Archives)
Palais des Beaux Arts
Rue Ravenstein 23
1000 Bruxelles
Tel: 32 2 507 83 70
Fax: 32 2 513 12 72
email: filmarchive@ledoux.be
Gabrielle Claes
Film preservation. The collection can be consulted on the Archive's premises for research purposes

Denmark

Danish Film Institute
Archive and Cineatheque
Gothersgade 55
DK - 1123 Copenhagen K
Tel: 45 33 74 34 00
Fax: 45 33 74 35 99
email: museum@dfi.dk
Website: www.dfi.dk
Contact: Dan Nissen, Director

Finland

Suomen Elokuva-Arkisto (Finnish Film Archive)
PO Box 177
Fin 00151 Helsinki
Tel: 35 8 9 615 400
Fax: 35 8 9 615 40 242
email: sea@sea.fi
Website: www.sea.fi
Matti Lukkarila

France

Les Archives du Film du Centre National de la Cinématographie
7 bis rue Alexandre Turpault
78390 Bois D'Arcy Cedex
Tel: 33 1 30 14 80 00
Fax: 33 1 34 60 52 25
Website: www.cnc.fr
Michelle Aubert

Germany

Deutsches Rundfunkarchiv (DRA)/German Broadcast Archive
Marlene-Dietrich-Allee 20
D-14482 Potsdam-Babelsberg
Tel.: 49 331 58 12 0
Fax: 49 331 58 12 - 199
email: sekretariat@dra.de
Website: www.dra.de/Babelsberg
Director: Joachim-Felix Leonhard
Bertramstraße 8
D-60320 Frankfurt/M
Tel.: 49 69 15 687 - 0
Fax: 49 69 15 687 - 100
email: dra@hr-online.de
Website: dr@hr-online.de

Greece

Teniothiki Tis Elladas (Greek Film Archives)
1 Canari Street
Athens 10761
Tel: 30 1 361 2046
Fax: 30 1 362 8468
email: tain@otenet.gr
Website: www.tte.gr
Theodoros Adamopoulos, Director

Ireland

Irish Film Archive
Film Institute of Ireland
6 Eustace Street
Dublin 2
Tel: 353 1 679 5744
Fax: 353 1 677 8755
email: archive@ifc.ie
Website: www.fii.ie
Kasandra O'Connell, Head of Archive
Sunniva O'Flynn, Archive Curator
Eugene Finn, Film Archivist
Emma Keogh, Librarian/Paper
Archivist

Italy

Cineteca Nazionale (National Film Archive)
Centro Sperimentale di
Cinematografia
Via Tuscolana 1524
I-00173 Roma
Tel: 39 06 722 941
Fax: 39 06 722 3131
Website: snc.it
Angelo Libertini, General Director

Luxembourg

Cinémathèque Municipale de Luxembourg/Ville de Luxembourg (Luxembourg National Film Archive/City of Luxembourg
10 rue Eugène Ruppert
2453 Luxembourg
Tel: (352) 4796 2644
Fax: (352) 4075 19
Claude Bertemes

The Netherlands

Nederlands Filmmuseum, Stichting (Nederlands Film Museum)
Vondelpark 3
1071 AA Amsterdam
Tel: 31 20 589 1400
Fax: 31 20 683 3401
Peter Westervoorde, Head of
Cataloguing Department

Portugal

Cinemateca Portuguesa - Museu do Cinema (Portuguese Film Archive - Museum of Cinema)
Rua Barata Salgueiro, No 39
1200-059 Lisboa

Tel: 351 21 359 62 00
Fax: 351 21 352 31 80
email: cinemateca@cpmc.pt
João Bérnard da Costa, President
José Manuel Costa, Vice President
Rui Santana Brito, Vice President

Spain

Filmoteca Española (Spanish National Film Archive)
Caalle Magdalena 10
28012
Madrid
Tel: 34 91 369 21 18
Fax: 34 91 3699 12 50
Website: www.mcu.es

Sweden

Svenska Filminstitutet (Swedish Film Institute)
PO Box 27 126
Borgvägen 1-5
S-102 52 Stockholm
Tel: 46 8 665 11 00
Fax: 46 8 661 18 20
Website: www.sfise
Rolf Lindfors, Head of Archive

National Archives

bfi collections
(Incorporating The National
Film and Television Archive)
21 Stephen Street
London W1T 1LN
Tel: 020 7255 1444
Fax: 020 7580 7503
Website: www.bfi.org.uk/collections
Caroline Ellis, Heather Stewart
BFI collections contain more than
275,000 films and 200,000 TV
programmes, dating from 1895 to the
present. Related collections of stills,
posters, designs, scrips and printed
ephemera such as marketing
materials, technology, props and
costumes have been assembled
alongside the software to give added
context and meaning

Imperial War Museum Film and Video Archive
Lambeth Road
London SE1 6HZ
Tel: 020 7416 5000
Fax: 020 7416 5379
email: film@iwm.org.uk
Website: www.iwm.org.uk
Paul Sargent/Jane Fish
The national museum of modern
conflict, illustrating and recording
all aspects of modern war. The
Archive reflects these terms of
reference with an extensive
collection of film and video material,
which is widely used by historians
and by film and television
companies

Scottish Screen
1 Bowmont Gardens
Glasgow G2 9LR
Tel: 0141 337 7400
Fax: 0141 337 7413
email: archive@scottishscreen.com
Website: www.scottishscreen.com
Janet McBain: Curator
Annie Docherty:
Enquiries Tel: 0141 337 7402
Almost exclusively non-fiction film,
the collection dates from 1896 to the
present day and concerns aspects of
Scottish social, cultural and
industrial history. Available to
broadcasters, programme makers,
educational users and researchers.
Access charges and conditions
available on request

Wales Film and Television Archive
Unit 1
Parc Gwyddoniaeth
Cefn Llan, Aberystwyth
Ceredigion SY23 3AH
Tel: 01970 626007
Fax: 01970 626008
email: wftva@sgrin.co.uk
Website: www.sgrin.co.uk
Administrator: Jane Davies
c/o Sgrin
The Bank
10 Mount Stuart Square
Cardiff
CF10 5EE
Director: Iola Baines
The Archive locates, preserves and catalogues film and video material relating to Wales. The collection is made accessible where possible for research and viewing. The Archive is part of Sgrín, Media Agency for Wales

Regional Collections

East Anglian Film Archive
University of East Anglia
Norwich NR4 7TJ
Tel: 01603 592664
Fax: 01603 458553
email: eafa@uea.ac.uk
Website: www.uea.ac.uk/eafa/
David Cleveland, Director
Jane Alvey, Deputy Director
Preserving non-fiction films and videos, both amateur and professionally made, showing life and work in Bedfordshire, Cambridgeshire, Essex, Hertfordshire, Norfolk and Suffolk

North West Film Archive
Manchester Metropolitan University
Minshull House
47-49 Chorlton Street
Manchester M1 3EU
Tel: 0161 247 3097
Fax: 0161 247 3098
email: n.w.filmarchive@mmu.ac.uk
Website: www.nwfa.mmu.ac.uk
Maryann Gomes: Director
Enquiries: Lisa Ridehalgh
Preserves moving images showing life in the North West and operates as a public regional archive. Urban and industrial themes are particularly well illustrated. Online film and video catalogue at the Archive's website

Northern Region Film and Television Archive
Blanford House
Blanford Square
Newcastle upon Tyne NE1 4JA
Tel: 0191 232 6789
Fax: 0191 230 2614
email: lisa.bond@dial.pipex.com
Lisa Bond, Film Archive Access Officer Tyne & Wear
Director: Leo Enticknap
Middlesbrough Site:
School of Law
Arts and Humanities
University of Teesside
Room M616
Middlesbrough Tower
Middlesbrough, TS1 3BA
Tel. 01642 384022
Fax. 01642 384099,
email L.Enticknap@tees.ac.uk
Dr. Leo Enticknap
The NRFTVA was founded in 1998 in order to collect, preserve and provide access to moving images of historical, social and cultural relevance to an area covering Tyneside, Teesside, Cumbria, Northumberland and County Durham. The bulk of its current holdings (almost entirely non-fiction) consist of BBC North-East news footage from 1958-72, the news and documentary output of Tyne-Tees and Border Television and the productions of Trade Films, a Newcastle-based unit whose output is concerned with industry, in particular coal mining and its community. The Archive is in the process of building a purpose-designed storage and conservation centre at the University of Teesside which is expected to open in September 2002. In the meantime, enquiries concerning the BBC North East and Tyne-Tees collection should be directed to Teesside, whilst all other access enquiries should be made to Newcastle.

South East Film & Video Archive
University of Brighton
Grand Parade
Brighton BN2 2JY
Tel: 01273 643213
Fax: 01273 643214
email: sefva@brighton.ac.uk
Jane Pumford, Administrator
Established in 1992 the function of this regional film and video archive is to locate, collect, preserve and promote films and video tapes made in the four counties of Surrey, Kent, East Sussex and West Sussex and the unitary authorities of Brighton & Hove and Medway

South West Film and Television Archive The
New Cooperage
Royal William Yard
Stonehouse
Plymouth
Devon PL1 3RP
Tel: 01752 202650
Fax: 01752 205025
email: enquiries@tswfta.co.uk
Website: www.tswfta.co.uk
Elayne Hoskin
The official film archive for the South West of England. Holds south western film material and includes three television collections covering the period 1961 to 1992 - Westward Television, Television South West and BBC South West

Wessex Film and Sound Archive

Hampshire Record Office
Sussex Street
Winchester SO23 8TH
Tel: 01962 847742
Fax: 01962 878681
email: sadedm@hants.gov.uk
Website: www.hants.gov.uk/record-office/film.html
David Lee
Preserves and makes publicly accessible for research, films, video and sound recordings of local interest to central southern England

Yorkshire Film Archive

College of Ripon and York St John
College Road
Ripon HG4 2QX
Tel: 01765 602691
Fax: 01765 606267
email: s.howard@ucrysj.ac.uk
Website: www.yorkshire-media.co.uk
Sue Howard
The Yorkshire Film Archive exists to locate, preserve and show film about the Yorkshire region. Material dates from 1897 and includes newsreels, documentaries, advertising and amateur films

Newsreel, Production and Stock Shot Libraries

Adventure & Wildlife Stock Shot Library

Church House,
18 Park Mount, Leeds
Yorkshire LS5 3HE
Tel: 0113 230 7150
Fax: 0113 274 5387
Chris Lister
A wide range of adventure sports and wildlife footage, most shot on 16mm or Super 16mm and available on Beta SP or film

Archive Film Agency

21 Lidgett Park Avenue
Roundhay
Leeds LS8 1EU
Tel: 0113 2662454/0113 2684782
Fax: 0113 2662454
email: iacrchivefilmagency@email.com
Website: www.archivefilmagency.com
Agnèse Geoghegan
Film from 1898 to present day, including a current worldwide stock shot library. Specialists in early fiction, newsreel, documentary, Music Hall, Midlands, Yorkshire, British 1930s stills. Cassette services

Associated Press Television News (APTN)

The Interchange
Oval Road
Camden Lock
London NW1 7DZ
Tel: 020 7482 7482
Fax: 020 7413 8327
email: info@aptnlibrary.com
Website: www.aptnlibrary.com
David Simmons
Newsfilm and video from 1900 - and adding every day up to 100 new items from around the world. Hard news, stock footage, features, personalities, annual compilations, background packages etc. Story details and shotlists are stored on full-text easy-to-search database. Database also available on CD-Rom and online (see website address above)

BBC Information & Archives - Television Archive

Wood Lane
London W12 7RJ
Tel: 020 8225 9767
Fax: 020 8740 8755
The largest collection of broadcast programmes in the world reflecting the whole range of BBC output

 *bfi* Archival Footage Sales

21 Stephen Street
London W1P 2LN
Tel: 020 7957 8934
Fax: 020 7580 5830
email: footage.films@bfi.org.uk
Website: www.bfi.org.uk
Jan Faull or Simon Brown
Material from the largest collection of film footage in Britain - the National Film and Television Archive. Television, films, documentaries, newsreels and animation are all covered with over 350,000 titles to choose from, including material dating back to 1895. First stop for serious research on subjects that have shaped the 20th century. Research facilities available.

Boulton-Hawker Films

Hadleigh
near Ipswich
Suffolk IP7 5BG
Tel: 01473 822235
Fax: 01473 824519
Peter Boulton
Educational films and videos: health education, social welfare, home economics, P.S.E., P.E., Maths, biology, physics, chemistry, geography

The British Defence Film Library

SSVC, Chalfont Grove
Narcot Lane
Chalfont St. Peter
Gerrards Cross
Bucks SL9 8TN
Tel: 01494 878278/878252
Fax: 01494 878007
email: robertd@ssvc.com
Robert Dungate: BDFL Librarian
SSVC has many years experience in providing both entertainment and support for the military. The British Defence Library (BDFL) is an independent department within SSVC which holds and distributes audio visual training materials for use by the armed forces which have been specifically commissioned by the Ministry of Defence. The Library also supplies this footage to the film and television industry offering a unique collection of British military material

British Movietonews

North Orbital Road
Denham
Middx UB9 5HQ

Tel: 01895 833071
Fax: 01895 834893
email: library@mtone.co.uk
Website: www.movietone.com
Barbara Heavens
One of the world's major film archives featuring high quality cinema newsreels from the turn of the century, with an emphasis on 1929-1979. the library now represents on an exclusive basis the TV-AM News Library with over 1,100 hours of British and World news covering the period 1983-1991. This material is available on re-mastered digital tape

British Pathé Plc
New Pathé House
57 Jameston Road
London NW1 7DB
Tel: 020 7424 3650/020 7424 3636
Fax: 020 7485 3606
email:
larry.mckinna@britishpathe.com
Website: www.britishpathe.com
Larry McKinna: Chief Librarian
50 million feet of newsreel and social documentary from 1896 to 1970. Rapid research and sourcing through computerised catalogue

Canal + Image UK Ltd
Pinewood Studios
Pinewood Road, Iver
Bucks SL0 0NH
Tel: 01753 631111
Fax: 01753 655813
John Herron
Feature films, TV series, stock shots and stills, b/w and colour, 35mm, 1925 to present day

Central Office of Information Footage File
4th Floor
184-192 Drummond Street
London NW1 3HP
Tel: 020 7383 2292
Fax: 020 7383 2333
email: research@film-images.com.
Website: www.film-images.com
Tony Dykes
40,000 Crown Copyright titles from the Government's News and Information archives spanning over 75 years of British social and business history. Most of the collection has been thoroughly shot listed and is available on VHS viewing cassettes

Chain Production Ltd
2 Clanricarde Gardens
London W2 4NA
Tel: 020 7229 4277
Fax: 020 7229 0861

email: films@chain.production.co.uk
Website: www.chain.production.co.uk
Specialist in European films and world cinema, cult classics, handling European Film Libraries with all rights to over 1,000 films - also clip rights and clip search

Channel Four Clip Library
124 Horseferry Road
London SW1P 2TX
Tel: 020 7306 8490/8155
Fax: 020 7306 8362
email: ekelly@channel4.co.uk
Website: www.channel4.com
Eva Kelly
An ever growing portfolio of programmes and a diverse collection of library material. Also access to feature films when the copyright has been cleared with original copyright holders

The Cinema Museum
see The Ronald Grant Archive

Clips & Footage
2nd Floor
80a Dean Street
London W1D 3SN
Tel: 020 7287 7287
Fax: 020 7287 0984
email: clipsetc@easynet.co.uk
Website: www.clipsfootage.uk.com
Alison Mercer
Supplies historical and modern colour footage to broadcast, corporate and commercial producers. Special collections include B movies, feature film trailers, destinations, timelapse and lifestyle

Consignia
(formally Post Office Film and Video Library)
PO Box 145
Sittingbourne
Kent ME10 1NH
Tel: 01795 426465
Fax: 01795 474871
email: info@edist.co.uk
Barry Wiles, Linda Gates
Holds a representative selection of documentary programmes made under the GPO Film Unit, including the classic Night Mail, together with programmes produced from 1970s onwards

Contemporary Films
24 Southwood Lawn Road
Highgate
London N6 5SF
Tel: 020 8340 5715
Fax: 020 8348 1238

email: inquiries@
contemporaryfilms.com
Website: www.contemporaryfilms.
com
Documentaries on China, USSR, Cuba, Nazi Germany, South Africa. The library also covers areas like the McCarthy witch hunts in the '50s, the civil rights movements of the '60s, hippie culture, feminism

Editions Audiovisuel Beulah
18-20 St Dunstans Road
London SE25
Tel: 01892 652413
Fax: 01892 652413
email: beulah@enterprise.net
Website: www.eavb.co.uk/library
Beulah publish the following videos Vintage Music, Royal Navy, Military Transport, Yesterday's Britain. and operate a stock shot and sound affects library

Educational and Television Films (ETV)
247a Upper Street
London N1 1RU
Tel: 020 7226 2298
Fax: 020 7226 8016
email: zoe@etvlted.demon.co.uk
Website: www.etvltd.demon.co.u
Zoe Moore, Jack Amos
Established in 1950, ETV has amassed a wide and varied range of documentary archive material from the ex-Socialist world, with particular emphasis on the ex-Soviet Union, the former eastern Block countries and China. Material is also held from Vietnam, Cuba, Chile, Afghanistan and the other Arab Nations. ETV also houses material from the British Labour Movement and the Spanish Civil War

Environmental Investigation Agency
62/63 Upper Street
London N1 0NY
Tel: 020 7354 7960
Fax: 020 7354 7961
email: info@eia-internationl.org
Website: www.eia-international.org
Extensive and exclusive library of video and stills showing the exploitation of wildlife and the environment worldwide. Subjects include dolphin and whale slaughter, the bird trade, bear farms, animal products illegally on sale in shops and to undercover investigators, and other aspects of endangered species trade. All film sales help to fund future investigations and campaigns

Film and Video Umbrella

52 Bermondsey Street
London SE1 3UD
Tel: 020 7407 7755
Fax: 020 7407 7766
email: fvu@fvu.co.uk
Website: www.fvumbrella.com
Steve Bode
Film and Video Umbrella curates and produces film, video and new media projects by artists which are commissioned and presented in collaboration with galleries and venues across England

Film Images

2 The Quadrant
135 Salusbury Road
Tel: 020 7624 3388
Fax: 020 7624 3377
email: research@film-images.com
Website: www.film-images.com
Angela Saward
Thousands of hours of classic and contemporary film images from hundreds of different sources around the world. All fully catalogued and immediately available for viewing on VHS or U-Matic. Suppliers include Central Office of Information and Overseas Film and Television

Film Research & Production Services Ltd

Mitre House
177-183 Regent Street
London W1R 7SB
Tel: 020 7734 1525
Fax: 020 7734 8017
Amanda Dunne, James Webb
Film research and copyright clearance facilities, also third party clearance. Film holding of space footage

Fred Goodland Film, Video & Record Collections

81 Farmilo Road
Leyton
London E17 8JN
Tel: 020 8539 4412
Fax: 020 8539 4412
Fred Goodland MBKS
Factual and Fictional subjects held on 16mm film prints and brodcast video. Collections include examples of early sound films and a wide range of musical material (1920s-1960s). 1970s imported prints of superior quality include public domain shorts featuring popular American entertainers. Other subjects include vintage fashion, animation, amateur films, adverts, trailers and personalities. VHS previews with

BITC available to researchers. Copyright assistance given. Immediate access to all materials on sight of copyright owners authorisation where relevant.

Freemantle Media

1 Stephen Street
London W1P 1PJ
Tel: 020 7691 6732/6733
Fax: 020 7691 6080
email: archive@pearsontv.com
Website: www.pearsontvarchive.com
Len Whitcher
Over 15,000 hours of a wide range of TV programmes including all Thames, Grundy, Alomo, ACI and all American programming

GB Associates

7 Marion Grove
Woodford Green
Essex 9TA
Tel: 020 8505 1850
Fax: 020 8505 1850
email: filmview@dial.pipex.com
Malcolm Billingsley
An extensive collection, mainly on 35mm, of fact and fiction film from the turn of the century. The collection is particularly strong in vintage trailers, the early sound era, early colour systems and adverts

Granada Media Clip Sales - London Weekend TV

48 Leicester Square
London WC2H 7FB
Tel: 020 7389 8545
Fax: 020 7930 8498
email: clips.london@granadamedia.com
Julie Lewis
Clips and stockshots available from London Weekend Television's vast programme library, dating from 1968. Drama, entertainment, music, arts and international current affairs. Plus London's news, housing, transport, politics, history, wildlife etc

Huntley Film Archives

78 Mildmay Park
Newington Green
London N1 4PR
Tel: 020 7923 0990
Fax: 020 7241 4929
email: films@huntleyarchives.com
Website: www.huntleyarchives.com
Amanda Huntley, John Huntley, Sarah King
Archive film library for broadcast, corporate and educational purposes, specialising in documentary footage 1900-1980. Phone to make an

appointment or write for brochure detailing holdings. Now also 50,000 stills from films and film history, online film catalogue now available for research via website

Index Stock Shots

12 Charlotte Mews
London W1P 1LN
Tel: 020 7631 0134/7637 8741
Fax: 020 7436 8737
email: info@index-stockshots.com
Website: www.index-stockshots.com
Philip Hinds, Gerry Weinbren
Unique stock footage on 35mm film and tape. Including time-lapse and aerial photography, cities, landmarks, aviation, wildlife

ITN Archive

200 Gray's Inn Road
London WC1X 8XZ
Tel: 020 7430 4480
Fax: 020 7430 4453
email: archive.sales@itn.co.uk
Website: www.itnarchive.com
Karena Smith, Development Manager, Alwyn Lindsey
ITN Archive is one of the largest commercial archives in the world, providing access to over 250 000 hours of high quality news and feature material and dating back to 1986. The holdings comprise of all ITN's output, including award-winning reports and selected rushes since 1955. ITN Archive has exclusive world rights to the entire Reuters Television Archive which includes historical newsreel such as British Paramount News, Empire News Bulletin, Gaumont Graphic and Gaumont British.The entire full integrated database is available free on-line and much of the material is grouped into themed collections to aid research. ITN Archive also represents French Pathé in the UK

London Film Archive

c/o 78 Mildmay Park
Newington Green
London N1 4PR
Tel: 020 7923 4074
Fax: 020 7241 4929
email: info@londonfilmarchive.org
Website: www.londonfilmarchive.org
Robert Dewar
Dedicated to the acquisition and preservation of film relating to the Greater London region. The collection consists of material from 1895 to the present day and represents professional and amateur produced features and documentary films

The London Jewish Cultural Centre

The Old House
c/o King's College London
Kidderpore Avenue
London NW3 7SZ
Tel: 020 7431 0345
Fax: 020 7431 0361
email: admin@ljcc.org.uk
Website: www.ljcc.org.uk
The LJCC is an educational
organisation with an extensive library
of feature, documentary and Israeli
film containing rare and previously
unseen documentary footage,
educational compilation tapes, and a
vast archive of material on the
Holocaust. It offers some consultancy
services to researchers and producers
working in this field and organises
regular showings of films from the
collection. The Centre also uses
documentary and feature film widely
in all its academic programmes and
teaches a variety of film courses

The Lux Centre

2-4 Hoxton Square
London N1 6NU
Tel: 020 7684 0200
Fax: 020 7684 1111
email: dist@lux.org.uk
Website: www.lux.org.uk
Contact: Distribution
The Lux is Europe's largest
distributor of artists' film and video

Medi Scene

32-38 Osnaburgh Street
London NW1 3ND
Tel: 020 7387 3606
Fax: 020 7387 9693
email: info-uk@medi-cine.com
Website: medi-cine.com
Kevin Heath
Wide range of accurately catalogued
medical and scientific shots available
on film and video. Part of the Medi
Cine Group

Moving Image Communications

61 Great Titchfield Street
London W1W 7PP
Tel: 020 7580 3300
Fax: 020 7580 2242
email: mail@milibrary.com
Website: www.milibrary.com
Contact: Michael Maloney
Comprehensive footage resource
which covers an ever increasing range
of subjects both archival and
contemporary with material
originating from film and video.
Footage ranges from early silent
movies to celebrity chat shows; from
newsreels to travelogues. Collections
include: RSPB, Wild Islands, Flying
Pictures, TVAM, Channel X, British
Tourist Authority, Drummer Films,
Buff Films, Lonely Planet, Freud
Home movies, Cuban archives and
more. All collections are logged shot
by shot on a research database for
immediate access. In house
researchers service all enquires.
Compilation preview cassettes are
tailored to the footage brief.
Alternatively, clients can view on
premises.Internet online research
database of the Moving Image
Library is available on the web site.
Alternatively, a CD Rom is provided
to professional researchers at no cost.

Nova Film and Video Library

11a Winholme
Armthorpe
Doncaster DN3 3AF
Tel: 01302 833422
Fax: 08701 257917
email: library@novaonline.co.uk
Website: www.novaonline.co.uk
An extensive collection of unique
archive material of Britain and the
world. The Library holds a huge
selection of amateur cine film
documenting the changing social life
of Britain dating back to 1944 and
has a dedicated collection of
transport footage from 1949 to the
present day. The library also holds a
wide selection of specially shot
modern footage and interviews. A
catalogue and showreel is available,
and a selection of video clips are
available from the website

The Olympic Television Archive Bureau

4th Floor Axis Centre
Burlington Lane
Chiswick
London W4 2TH
Tel: 020 8233 5353
Fax: 020 8233 5354
email: jsieck@otab.com
Website: www.otab.com
The International Olympic
Committee owns a unique collection
of film and television material
covering the entire history of the
Olympic Games from 1896 to 1994.
Now it can be accessed via the
Olympic Television Archive Bureau,
which is administered by Trans World
International

Oxford Scientific Films

Lower Road
Long Hanborough
Oxford OX29 8LL
Tel: 01993 881881
Fax: 01993 883969 or 01993 882808
email: film.library@osf.uk.com
Website: www.osf.uk.com
Sandra Berry, Francesca Waldron,
Rachel Wakefield, Jane Mullenoux
Stock footage on 16mm, 35mm film
and video. Wide range of wildlife,
special fx, timelapse, slow motion,
scenics, world locations, macro, micro
etc. Catalogue and showreel available.
Extensive stills library

Pearson Television

see Freemantle Media

Reuters Television Library

(Managed and Distributed by ITN
Archive)
200 Grays Inn Road
London WC1X 8XE
Tel: 020 7430 4480
Fax: 020 7430 4453
email: archive.sales@itn.co.uk
Website: www.itnarchive.com
Alwyn Lindsey, Sales Director
Original newsreel, television news
and feature footage from 1896 to
present day. Special Collections.
Online database (free access) and
expert researchers

Ronald Grant Archive

The Cinema Museum
The Master's House
The Old Lambeth Workhouse
2 Dugard Way (off Renfrew
Road,Kennington)
London SE11 4TH
Tel: 020 7840 2200
Fax: 020 7840 2299
email: martin@
cinemamuseum.org.uk
Martin Humphries
15 million feet of fact and fiction film,
mainly 35mm, from 1896 on. Also 1
million film stills, posters,
programmes, scripts and information.
The museum is a FIAF subscriber

RSPB Film Unit

The Lodge
Sandy
Bedfordshire SG19 2DL
Tel: 01767 680 551
Fax: 01767 683 262
email: mark.percival@rspb.org.uk
Website: www.rspb.org.uk
Mark Percival: Producer and Unit
Manager
Natural history film-makers

specialising in UK birds and other plant and animal wildlife. Established in 1953, the RSPB Film Unit has produced over 120 wildlife films (filmed mostly in the '80s and '90s) generating a film archive of over 750 hours for commercial library sales. The RSPB Film Unit currently produces about one new wildlife film per year and a range of corporate programming

Sky News Library Sales
British Sky Broadcasting Ltd
6 Centaurs Business Park
Grant Way
Isleworth
Middlesex TW7 5QD
Tel: 020 7705 3132
Fax: 020 7705 3201
email: libsales@bskyb.com
Ben White, Pauliina Paorkka and Susannah Fritz
Extensive round the clock news and current affairs coverage since 1989. Entire library held on Beta SP on site. Library operates 24 hours a day

TWI Archive
Trans World International
McCormack House
Burlington Lane
Chiswick
London W4 2TH
Tel: 020 833 5500/5300
Fax: 020 8233 6476
Togo Keynes
email: twiarchive@imgworld.com
Website: www.twiarchive.com
Includes golf, tennis, World Cup rugby, America's Cup, Test cricket, skating, snooker, gymnastics, yachting, motorsport, adventure sport, many minor and ethnic sports plus expanding catalogue of worldwide stockshots

Undercurrents Archive
16b Cherwell Street
Oxford OX4 1BG
Tel: 01865 203661/662
Fax: 08701 316103
email: underc@gn.apc.org
Website: www.undercurrents.org
Paul O'Connor
Undercurrents is an archive of grassroots environmental and social protest and dissent and community issues from 1990 to present day. Over 2,000 hours archived and supplied on Betacam SP

World Backgrounds Film Production Library
Millenium Studios

Elstree Way
Borehamwood, Herts WD6 1SF
Tel: 020 8207 4747
Fax: 020 8207 4276
email: films@world-backgrounds
Website: www.world-backgrounds.com
Ralph Rogers
Locations around the world. Fully computerised. All 35mm including 3,000 back projection process plates. Numerous video masters held. Suppliers to TV commercials, features, pop promos, TV series, corporate videos etc

Photographic Libraries

BBC Photograph Library
B116 Television Centre
Wood Lane
London W12 7RJ
Tel: 020 8225 7193
Fax: 020 8746 0353
The BBC's unique archive of radio and television programme stills, equipment, premises, news and personalities dating from 1922. B/w and colour. Visits by appointment

bfi Stills, Posters and Designs
21 Stephen Street
London W1T 1LN
Tel: 020 7255 1444
Fax: 020 7323 9260
Website: www.bfi.org.uk/collection/about
A visual resource of around seven million images, illustrating every aspect of the development of world cinema and television. The collection also holds approximately 15,000 film posters and 2,000 production and costume designs. Other material includes animation cells, storyboards, sketches and plans

The Bridgeman Art Library
17-19 Garway Road
London W2 4PH
Tel: 020 7727 4065
Fax: 020 7792 8509
email: info@bridgeman.co.uk
Website: www.bridgeman.co.uk
Peticia Watson
The Bridgeman Art Library is the world's leading source of fine art images for reproduction. From Renaissance classics to Pop Art and beyond, all styles and periods are covered. Images can be viewed and ordered online and a free printed catalogue is available

Corbis
12 Regents Wharf
All Saints Street
London N1 9RL
Tel: 020 7843 4444
Fax: 020 7278 1408
email: info@corbisimages.com
Website: www.corbis.com
Photographic stills agency/library

Freemantle Media Television Stills Library
Teddington Studios

Broom Road
Teddington TW11 9NT
Tel: 020 8781 2789
Fax: 020 8614 2250
email: stills.library@pearsontv.com
Website: www.pearsontv.com
Colleen Kay
The Pearson Television Stills Library
contains over a million different
images from programmes such as
Neighbours, the Sweeney,
Morecombe and Wise, and many
others produced by Thames TV,
Alomo, Grudy and Talkback.

Hulton Archive
Unique House
21-31 Woodfield Road
London W9 2BA
Tel: 020 7266 2662
Fax: 020 7266 3154
email: hultonresearch@getty-
images.com
Website: www.hultonarchive.com
One of the world's largest stills
archives with over 15 million
photographs, prints and engravings
covering the entire history of
photojournalism

The Image Bank
17 Conway Street
London W1 6EE
Tel: 020 7554 2607
Fax: 020 7391 9123
email: bryn.downing@
gettyimages.com
Website: www.imagebank.co.uk
Bryn Downing, Business
Development Team Lead
Chris Blakeston, Customer sales and
service team
Includes the Energy Film Collection
and the Archive Films Collection

Image Diggers Picture and Tape Library
618b Finchley Road
London NW11 7RR
Tel: 020 8455 4564
Fax: 020 8455 4564
email: ziph@appleonline.net
Neil Hornick
35mm slides, stills, postcards, sheet
music, magazine and book material
for hire. Cinema, theatre and
literature clippings archive.
Audio/visual tape resources in
performing arts and other areas, plus
theme research

image.net
18 Vine Hill
London EC1
Tel: 08701 522 333

Fax: 020 7216 9014
email: solutions@imagenet.co.uk
Website: www.imagenet.co.uk
Simon Townsley

Imperial War Museum
Photograph Archive
All Saints Annexe
Austral Street
London SE11 4SL
Tel: 020 7416 5333/8
Fax: 020 7416 5355
email: photos@iwm.org.uk
Website: www.iwm.org.uk
Bridget Kinally
A collection of some 6 million images
illustrating all aspects of 20th century
warfare. Film stills can also be made
from material held by the IWM's Film
& Video Archive, by prior arrangement

Institute of Contemporary History & Wiener Library
4 Devonshire Street
London W1W 5BH
Tel: 020 7636 7247
Fax: 020 7436 6428
email: lib@wl.u-net.com
Website: www.wienerlibrary.co.uk
Rosemarie Nief: Head Librarian
Ben Barkow: Photo Archive, Christine
Patel: Video Collection
The Wiener Library is a private
research library and institute
specialising in contemporary
European and Jewish history,
especially the rise and fall of the
Third Reich, Nazism and fascist
movements, anit-Semitism, racism,
the Middle East and post-war
Germany. It holds Britain's largest
collection of documents, testimonies,
books and videos on the Holocaust.
The photographic archive contains
stills, postcards, posters and portraits,
illustrated books, approx. 2,000
videos and recordings

Kobal Collection
4th Floor
184 Drummond Street
London NW1 3HP
Tel: 020 7383 0011
Fax: 020 7383 0044
Website: www.kobal-collection.com
David Kent
One of the world's leading film photo
archives in private ownership. Film
stills and portraits, lobby cards and
posters, from the earliest days of the
cinema to modern times

Mckenzie Heritage Picture Archive
Studio 226

Station House
Greenwich Commercial Centre
49 Greenwich High Road
London SE10 8JL
Tel: 020 8469 2000
Fax: 020 8469 2000
email: info@mckenziehpa.com
Website: www.mckenziehpa.com
Jeni Mckenzie
Mckenzie Heritage picture archive
specialises in pictures of black
communities from Britain and
abroad. The images span the 19th and
20th centuries.

The Moviestore Collection Ltd
3 Jonathan Street
London SE11 5NH
Tel: 020 7820 3820
Fax: 020 7820 8420

Pearson Television Stills Library
see Freemantle Media Television
Stills Library

Retrograph Nostalgia Archive
164 Kensington Park Road
London W11 2ER
Tel: 020 7727 9378
Fax: 020 7229 3395
email: retropix1@aol.com
Jilliana Ranicar-Breese, Martin Breese
Vintage worldwide advertising labels,
packaging, magazine advertisements,
posters and prints. Commercial art
and fine art from 1860-1960. Supplier
to film and TV companies. Visual
research and photography service.
Transparencies or high resolution
colour laser prints supplied. Travel,
food and drink a speciality. Free
colour brochure on request

Museums

Bill Douglas Centre for the History of Cinema and Popular Culture, The
University of Exeter
Queen's Building
Queen's Drive
Exeter EX4 4QH
Tel: 01392 264263
Fax: 01392 264361
email: h.k.higton@exeter.ac.uk
Website: www.ex.ac.uk/bill.douglas/
Dr Hester Higton
The core of the Centre's collection was assembled over many years by film-maker Bill Douglas and his friend Peter Jewell. Since the original donation, important additions have come from film-makers Roy Fowler and Don Boyd, and from cinematographer Ossie Morris. The collection comprise a very extensive range of books, periodicals, programmes, posters, sheet music, cards, toys and games related to the cinema, in addition to 19th century pre-cinema artefacts such as zoetropes, magic lanterns, panoramas, peepshows and other optical toys and devices

The Cinema Museum
Ronald Grant Archive
The Master's House
The Old Lambeth Workhouse
2 Dugard Way (off Renfrew Road,Kennington)
London SE11 4TH
Tel: 020 7840 2200
Fax: 020 7840 2299
email: martin@ cinemamuseum.org.uk
Martin Humphries
The museum is a FIAF subscriber

Imperial War Museum Film and Video Archive
Lambeth Road
London SE1 6HZ
Tel: 020 7416 5291/5292
Fax: 020 7416 5299
email: film@iwm.org.uk
Website: www.iwm.org.uk
Paul Sargent/Jane Fish
The national museum of modern conflict, illustrating and recording all aspects of modern war. The Archive reflects these terms of reference with an extensive collection of film and video material, which is widely used by historians and by film and television companies

Laurel and Hardy Museum
4C Upper Brook Street
Ulverston
Cumbria LA12 7BH
Tel: 01229 582292
The is in Ulverston, Cumbria, Stan Laurel's birthplace. Open all year 7 days a week for talks about Laurel and Hardy. It contains photos, letters, and memorabilia

National Museum of Photography Film & Television
Bradford BD1 1NQ
Tel: 01274 202030
Fax: 01274 723155
Website: www.nmpft.org.uk
Bill Lawrence, Head of Film
The world's only museum devoted to still and moving pictures, their technology and history. Features Britain's first giant IMAX film system; the world's only public Cinerama; interactive galleries and 'TV Heaven', reference library of programmes and commercials

FILM

AT THE NATIONAL MUSEUM
OF PHOTOGRAPHY, FILM & TELEVISION

 8th Bradford Film Festival 8 - 23 March 2002

 BAF! Bradford Animation Festival Autumn 2002

 Bite the Mango September 2002
Europe's premier Black & Asian Film Festival

- Film and television galleries
- Cubby Broccoli and Pictureville Cinemas
- 2D and 3D IMAX® Cinema
- Double band 35mm & 16mm preview facilities

National Museum of Photography,
Film & Television, Bradford, BD1 1NQ
Tel (01274) 202030   Fax (01274) 394540
www.nmpft.org.uk   talk.nmpft@nmsi.ac.uk

AWARDS

This section features some of the principal festival prizes and awards from 1 January 2000 to 31 December 2000. Compiled by Linda Wood

Awards 2000

BAFTA FILM AWARDS

Awarded 9th April 2000, London
195 Piccadilly
London W1V OLN
Tel: 020 7734 0022
Fax: 020 7734 1792
Website: www.bafta.org

The Academy Fellowships: Michael Caine & Stanley Kubrick
The Michael Balcon Award for Outstanding British Contribution to Cinema: Joyce Herlihy
The Alexander Korda Award for Outstanding British Film of the Year: EAST IS EAST (UK) Dir Damien O'Donnell
Best Film: AMERICAN BEAUTY (US) Dir Sam Mendes
The David Lean Award for Best Achievement in Direction: Pedro Almodòvar for TODO SOBRE MI MADRE (Spain/France)
Best Original Screenplay: Charlie Kaufman for BEING JOHN MALKOVICH (US) Dir Spike Jonze
Best Adapted Screenplay: Neil Jordan for The END OF THE AFFAIR (US/Germany) Dir Neil Jordan
Best Actress: Annette Bening for AMERICAN BEAUTY (US) Dir Sam Mendes
Best Actor: Kevin Spacey for AMERICAN BEAUTY (US) Dir Sam Mendes
Best Supporting Actress: Maggie Smith for Un Té CON IL DUCE (Italy/UK) Dir Franco Zeffirelli
Best Supporting Actor: Jude Law for The TALENTED MR RIPLEY (US) Dir Anthony Minghella
Best Film not in the English Language: TODO SOBRE MI MADRE (Spain/France) Dir Pedro Almodòvar
The Anthony Asquith Award for Achievement in Film Music: Thomas Newman for AMERICAN BEAUTY (US) Dir Sam Mendes
The Carl Foreman Award for Newcomer in British Film: Lynne Ramsay for RATCATCHER (UK) Dir Lynne Ramsay
Best Cinematography: Conrad L. Hall for AMERICAN BEAUTY (US) Dir Sam Mendes
Best Production Design: Rick Heinrichs for SLEEPY HOLLOW (US/Germany) Dir Tim Burton
Best Costume Design: Colleen Atwood for SLEEPY HOLLOW (US/Germany) Dir Tim Burton
Best Editing: Tariq Anwar and Christopher Greenbury for AMERICAN BEAUTY (US) Dir Sam Mendes
Best Sound: David Lee, John Reitz, Gregg Rudloff, David Campbell and Dane A. Davis for The MATRIX (US/Australia) Dir Andy Wachowski
Best Achievement in Special Visual Effects: John Gaeta, Steve Courtley, Janek Sirrs and Jon Thum for The MATRIX (US/Australia) Dir Andy Wachowski

Best Makeup/Hair: Christine Blundell for TOPSY TURVY (UK/US) Dir Mike Leigh
Best Short Film: WHO'S MY FAVOURITE GIRL (Scotland) Dir Adrian McDowall
Best Short Animation: The MAN WITH BEAUTIFUL EYES (UK) Dir Jonathan Hodgson
The Orange Audience Award: NOTTING HILL (US/UK) Dir Roger Michell

BAFTA TELEVISION AWARDS

Awarded 13th May 2001,

Best Actress: Thora Hird for LOST FOR WORDS (Yorkshire Television in association with Bard Entertainment for ITV)
Best Actor: Michael Gambon for WIVES & DAUGHTERS (WGBH (Boston)/BBC for BBC1)
Best Entertainment Performance: Graham Norton for SO GRAHAM NORTON (United Film & Television Production for C4)
Best Comedy Performance: Caroline Aherne for The ROYLE FAMILY (Granada Television for BBC Manchester, BBC1)
The Richard Dimbleby Award for Best Presenter (Factual, Features and News): Jeremy Paxman for NEWSNIGHT (BBC2)
Best Single Drama: Mark Redhead and Paul Greengrass for The MURDER OF STEPHEN LAWRENCE (Granada Television in association with Vanson Productions for ITV)
Best Drama Series: The COPS (World Productions for BBC2)
The Lew Grade Award (voted by readers of the Radio Times): A TOUCH OF FROST (Yorkshire TV for ITV)
Best Soap: Matthew Robinson for EASTENDERS (BBC1)
Best Drama Serial: Nigel Stafford-Clark, Peter Kosminsky and Leigh Jackson for WARRIORS (BBC Films in association with Deep Indigo Productions for BBC1)
Best Factual Series: Adam Curtis for The MAYFAIR SET (BBC2)
Best Entertainment (Programme or Series): ROBBIE THE REINDEER: HOOVES OF FIRE (BBC Animation Unit for BBC1)
Best Comedy (Programme or Series): The LEAGUE OF GENTLEMEN (BBC2)
Best Situation Comedy Award: Kenton Allen, Caroline Aherne and Craig Cash for The ROYLE FAMILY (Granada Television for BBC Manchester, BBC1)
Best Features: Robert Thirkell and Nick Mirsky for BLOOD ON THE CARPET (BBC2)
The Huw Wheldon Award for the Best Arts Programme or Series: Ian MacMillan and Matt Collings for THIS IS MODERN ART (Oxford Television Company for C4)
Best Sports Programme: Jeff Foulser and Gary Franses for TEST CRICKET (Sunset and Vine Productions for C4)
News and Current Affairs Journalism: John Simpson and the BBC News team for their coverage of the Kosovo conflict (BBC1)
Innovation: John Lynch, Tim Haines and Mike Milne for WALKING WITH DINOSAURS (BBC/Discovery

Channel/TV Asahi in association with ProSieben and France 3 for BBC1)
The Flaherty Documentary Award: Kim Longinotto and Ziba Mir-Hosseini for TRUE STORIES - DIVORCE IRANIAN STYLE (20th Century Vixen Productions for C4)
The Academy Fellowship: Peter Bazalgette
The Dennis Potter Award: Tony Marchant
The Special Award: Honor Blackman, Joanna Lumley, Diana Rigg and Linda Thorson for The AVENGERS series (ABC Television)

BAFTA TELEVISION CRAFT AWARDS
(1st presentation)
Awarded in London 30th April 2000

Best Costume Design: Odile Dicks-Mireaux for GREAT EXPECTATIONS (WGBH (Boston)/BBC for BBC2)
Best Design: Gerry Scott for WIVES & DAUGHTERS (WGBH (Boston)/BBC for BBC1)
Best Editing (Factual): Malcolm Daniel for INSIDE STORY - CHILD OF THE DEATH CAMPS (BBC1)
Best Editing (Fiction/Entertainment): Tony Cranstoun for The ROYLE FAMILY (Granada Television for BBC Manchester, BBC1)
Best Graphic Design: Philip Dupee for The VICE (Carlton UK Television for ITV)
Best Hair & Makeup: Lisa Westcott for WIVES & DAUGHTERS (WGBH (Boston)/BBC for BBC1)
Best Original Television Music: Ben Bartlett for WALKING WITH DINOSAURS (BBC/Discovery Channel/TV Asahi in association with ProSieben and France 3 for BBC1)
Best Photography (Factual): Chip Houseman and Hugh Miles for WILDLIFE SPECIAL - TIGER (BBC Bristol/Mike Birkhead Associates for BBC1)
Best Photography & Lighting (Fiction/Entertainment): Fred Tammes for WIVES & DAUGHTERS (WGBH (Boston)/BBC for BBC1)
Best Sound (Factual): John Pritchard and Bob Jackson for MICHAEL PALIN'S HEMINGWAY ADVENTURE (Prominent Television for BBC1)
Best Sound (Fiction/Entertainment): David Old, Graham Headicar, Maurice Hillier, Danny Longhurst for WARRIORS (BBC Films in association with Deep Indigo Productions)

5TH BAFTA CHILDREN'S FILM AND TELEVISION AWARDS
(in association with the Lego Company)
Awarded in London 12th November 2000 at the London Hilton, Park Lane

Animation: Jon Doyle, John Offord for FOXBUSTERS (CiTV/Cosgrove Hall Films)
Drama: Diana Kyle, Kate Cheeseman, Malorie Blackman for PIG HEART BOY (BBC1/BBC)
Entertainment: Conor McAnally, David Staite, John FD Northover for SMTV:LIVE (CiTV/Blaze Television)
Factual: Ian Prince, Roy Milani for NEWSROUND EXTRA - RUSSIAN ORPHANAGES (BBC1/BBC)
Feature Film: Allison Abbate, Des McAnuff, Brad Bird, Tim McCanlies for THE IRON GIANT (Warner Bros Distributors Ltd/Warner Bros Animation)
International: The Production Team for PABLO - THE LITTLE RED FOX (BBC1/RedFoxProductions/Millimages)
Pre-school animation: Clive Juster, Leo Nielsen for MAISY (CiTV/King Rollo Films)
Pre-School Live Action: Iain Lauchlan, Will Brenton

TWEENIES (BBC1/Tell-Tale Productions)
Schools Drama: Hilary Durman, Cilla Ware, Ray Harrison Graham for DREAM ON (Channel 4/The Resource Base)
Schools Factual Primary: Sarah Miller, Dan Zeff for ENGLISH EXPRESS: TEXTS - FOOTBALL (BBC2/BBC)
Schools Factual Secondary: Sara Feilden for LIFESCHOOL SEX - SAYING IT FOR THE GIRLS (BBC2/BBC)
The Special Award: Anne Wood (Ragdoll Productions)
The Presenter's Award: Katy Hill
The Writer's Award: Richard Carpenter, Helen Cresswell

50TH BERLIN INTERNATIONAL FILM FESTIVAL
Held 9th-20th February 2000, Berlin
Internationale Filmfestspiele Berlin
Potsdamer Strafle 5
D-10785 Berlin
Tel: (49) 030 25 920
Fax: (49) 030 25 920 299
Email: info@berlinale.de
Website: www.berlinale.de

INTERNATIONAL JURY
Golden Bear: MAGNOLIA (US) Dir Paul Thomas Anderson
Silver Bear (Grand Jury Prize): WO DE FU QIN MU QIN (China) Dir Zhang Yimou
Silver Bear - Best Actress: Bibiana Beglau and Nadja Uhl for Die STILLE NACH DEM SCHUSS (Germany) Dir Volker Schloendorff
Silver Bear - Best Actor: Denzel Washington for The HURRICANE (US) Dir Norman Jewison
Silver Bear - Best Director: Milos Forman for MAN ON THE MOON (US)
Silver Bear (Jury Prize): The MILLION DOLLAR HOTEL (Germany/US) Dir Wim Wenders
Silver Bear - Oustanding Artistic Achievement: to the entire cast of PARADISO - SIEBEN TAGE MIT SIEBEN FRAUEN (Germany) Dir Rudolf Thome
Golden Bear - Best Short Film: HOMMAGE ¿ ALFRED LEPETIT (France) Dir Jean Rousselot
Silver Bear - Best Short Film: MEDIA (Czech Republic) Dir Pavel Koutsky
Blue Angel (AGICOA Copyright) Prize for Best European Film: Die STILLE NACH DEM SCHUSS (Germany) Dir Volker Schloendorff
Alfred Bauer Prize for Debut Film: DOKURITSU SHONEN GASSHOUDAN (Japan) Dir Akira Ogata
OTHER AWARDS
FIPRESCI (International Critics) Prizes: Competition - La CHAMBRE DES MAGICIENNES (France) Dir Claude Miller
Forum - MONDAY (Japan) Dir Sabu
Panorama - PARAGRAPH 175 (US) Dir Rob Epstein and Jeffrey Friedman
Ecumenical Jury Prizes: Competition - WO DE FU QIN MU QIN (China) Dir Zhang Yimou
Short Film: - MEDIA (Czech Republic) Dir Pavel Koutsky
Panorama - BOTIN DE GUERRA (Argentina/Spain) Dir David Blaustein
Special Prize, Short Film - ECHO (Belgium) Dir Frédéric Roullier-Gall
Forum - De GROTE VAKANTIE (Netherlands) Dir Jan van der Keuken
Special Prize - CINÉ.MA VÉRITÉ: DEFINING THE MOMENT (Canada) Dir Peter Wintonick
Peace Film Prize: LONG DAY'S JOURNEY INTO DAY -

SOUTH AFRICA'S SEARCH FOR TRUTH AND RECONCILIATION (US) Dir Deborah Hoffmann and Frances Reid
Wolfgang Staudte Prize: Forum - MARSAL (Croatia) Dir Vinco Bresan
Special Mention - TRUTHS: A STREAM (Japan) Dir Masahiro Tsuchi
Don Quixote Prize: Forum - I EARINI SYNAXIS TON AGROFYLAKON (Greece) Dir Dimos Avdeliodis
Special Mention - MONDAY (Japan) Dir Sabu
Special Mention - RUANG TALOK 69 (Thailand) Dir Pen-ek Ratanaruang
CICAE Prizes: Panorama - SALTWATER (Ireland) Dir Conor McPherson
Forum - I EARINI SYNAXIS TON AGROFYLAKON (Greece) Dir Dimos Avdeliodis
Guild of German Art House Cinemas Prize: The HURRICANE (US) Dir Norman Jewison
Caligari Prize: I EARINI SYNAXIS TON AGROFYLAKON (Greece) Dir Dimos Avdeliodis
Special Mention - MONDAY (Japan) Dir Sabu
NETPAC PRIZE: Forum - BARIWALI (India) Dir Rituparno Ghosh and NABBIE NO KOI (Japan) Dir Yuji Nakae
Special Mention - GOCHOO MALIGEE (Korea) Dir Jan Hee-Sun
International Jury, Children's Film Festival: MAN VAN STAAL (Belgium) Dir Vincent Bal and TSATSIKI, MORSAN OCH POLISEN (Sweden/Norway/Denmark) Dir Ella Lemhagen
Special Mention - MANOLITO GAFOTAS (Spain) Dir Miguel Albaladejo
Special Mention - DOKHTARI BA KAFSH-HAYE-KATANI (Iran) Dir Rassul Sadr Ameli
Best Short Film - KONGEN SOM VILLE HA MER EN KRONE (Norway) Dir Randall Meyers and Anita Killi and PUGALO (Russia) Dir Alexander Kott
Crystal Bear, Young People's Jury, Children's Film Festival: TSATSIKI, MORSAN OCH POLISEN (Sweden/Norway/Denmark) Dir Ella Lemhagen
Special Mention - MR. RICE'S SECRET (Canada) Dir Nicholas Kendall
Crystal Bear Best Short Film - En DJEVEL I SKAPET (Norway) Dir Lars Berg
Reader's Prize of the 'Berliner Morgenpost': MAGNOLIA (US) Dir Paul Thomas Anderson
Manfred Satzgeber Prize: El MAR (Spain) Dir Augusti Villaronga
Panorama Short Film Prize of the New York Film Academy: HARTES BROT (Germany) Dir Nathalie Percillier and HOP, SKIP & JUMP (Slovenia/Bosnia) Dir Srdjan Vuletic
Special Mention - SPARKLEHORSE (Canada) Dir Gariné Torossian
Special Mention - 2~3 (US) Dir Richard Press
New York Film Academy Scholarship: Gianluca Vallero for FINIMONDO (Germany)
Panorama Audience Prize: NATIONALE 7 (France) Dir Jean-Pierre Sinapi
Gay Teddy Bear for Best Feature: GOUTTES D'EAU SUR PIERRES BRÛLANTES Dir Franáois Ozon
Gay Teddy Bear for Best Documentary: PARAGRAPH 175 (US) Dir Rob Epstein and Jeffrey Friedman
Gay Teddy Bear for Best Short: HARTES BROT (Germany) Dir Nathalie Percillier
Gay Teddy Bear Jury Award: DR'LE DE FELIX (France) Dir Olivier Ducastel and Jacques Martineau and CHRISSY (Australia) Dir Jacqui North

Reader's Prize of the 'Siegessäule' [Berlin's gay/lesbian magazine]: DRÔLE DE FELIX (France) Dir Olivier Ducastel and Jacques Martineau
Reader's Prize of the 'Berliner Zeitung': LONG NIGHT'S JOURNEY INTO DAY - SOUTH AFRICA'S SEARCH FOR TRUTH AND RECONCILIATION (US) Dir Deborah Hoffman and Frances Reid
Special Mention - I EARINI SYNAXIS TON AGROFYLAKON (Greece) Dir Dimos Avdeliodis
Special Mention - BEAU TRAVAIL (France) Dir Claire Denis

BFI FELLOWSHIPS
London
British Film Institute
21 Stephen Street
London W1P
Tel: (44) 020 7255 1444
Fax: (44) 020 7436 0439
Web site: www.bfi.org.uk
Awarded 24th May 2000 to Dame Elizabeth Taylor

BROADCASTING PRESS GUILD AWARDS 1999
Held mid-April 2000, London
c/o Richard Last
Tiverton, The Ridge
Woking
Surrey GU22 7EQ
Tel: 01483 764895

Writer's Award: Stephen Poliakoff for SHOOTING THE PAST (Talkback for BBC Television, BBC2)
Harvey Lee Award: Cilla Black
Best Actress: Justine Waddell for WIVES AND DAUGHTERS (BBCTV in association with WGBH (Boston) for BBC1)
Best Actor: Tony Doyle for BALLYKISSANGEL (World Productions/BBC Northern Ireland for BBC1) and FOUR FATHERS (Sally Head Productions for ITV)
Best Drama Serial: WIVES AND DAUGHTERS (BBC TV in association with WGBH (Boston) for BBC1)
Best Entertainment: BREMNER, BIRD AND FORTUNE (Vera Productions for C4)
Best Performer: Chris Tarrant for WHO WANTS TO BE A MILLIONAIRE? (Celador Productions for ITV)
Best Single Drama: WARRIORS (BBC TV in association with Deep Indigo Productions)

3rd BRITISH INDEPENDENT FILM AWARDS
Held on 25 October 2000 at the Cafe Royal London
81 Berwick Street
London W1F 3TW
Tel: 020 7287 3833
Fax; 020 7439 2243
email: info@bifa.org.uk
Website: www.bifa.org.uk

Douglas Hickox Award For a British Director On Their Debut Feature: Kevin Macdonald for ONE DAY IN SEPTEMBER (UK) Dir Kevin Macdonald
Producer of the Year: Andrew Eaton
Best Foreign Independent Film - Foreign Language: KADOSH (Israel, France, Italy) Dir Amos Gitai
Best Foreign Independent Film – English Language: THE STRAIGHT STORY (US, France,UK) Dir David Lynch

Best Achievement In Production: ONE LIFE STAND (UK) Dir May Miles Thomas
Best Actor: Daniel Craig for SOME VOICES (UK) Dir Simon Cellan Jones
Best Screenplay: Lee Hall for BILLY ELLIOT (UK) Dir Stephen Daldry
The Film Four Special Jury Prize: Mike Figgis
Best Newcomer (Off Screen): Justine Wright (Editor) for ONE DAY IN SEPTEMBER (UK) Dir Kevin Macdonald
Best Newcomer (On Screen): Jamie Bell for BILLY ELLIOT (UK) Dir Stephen Daldry
Best Actress: Gillian Anderson for THE HOUSE OF MIRTH (UK/US) Dir Terence Davis
Lifetime Achievement Award: Colin Young
Best Director: Stephen Daldry for BILLY ELLIOT (UK)
Best Film: BILLY ELLIOT (UK) Dir Stephen Daldry

53rd CANNES FESTIVAL

10th-21st May 2000, Cannes
99 Boulevard Malesherbes
75008 Paris
Tel: (33) 1 45 61 66 00
Fax: (33) 1 45 61 45 88
Email: RDF@festival-cannes.fr
Website: www.festival-cannes.org
Feature Film Palme d'Or: DANCER IN THE DARK (Denmark/Sweden/France/Germany) Dir Lars von Trier
Grand Jury Prize: GUIZI LAI LE (China) Dir Jiang Wen
Best Actress: Björk for DANCER IN THE DARK (Denmark/Sweden/France/Germany) Dir Lars von Trier
Best Actor: Tony Leung Chiu-Wai for IN THE MOOD FOR LOVE (Hong Kong/France) Dir Wong Kar-Wai
Best Director: Edward Yang for YI YI (Taiwan/Japan)
Best Screenplay: Neil LaBute for NURSE BETTY (US) Dir Neil LaBute
Jury Prize: (co-winners) SÅNGER FRÅN ANDRA VÅNINGEN (Sweden/Denmark/Norway/France/Germany) Dir Roy Andersson and TAKHTÉ SIAH (Iran/Italy/Japan) Dir Samira Makhmalbaf
Camera d'Or: (co-winners) DJOMEH (Iran/France) Dir Hassan Yektapanah and ZAMANI BARAYE MASTI ASBHA (Iran) Dir Bahman Ghobadi
Grand Prix Technique de la Commission Supèrieure
Technique de L'image et du Son: Christopher Doyle, Mark Li Ping Bing and William Chang Suk-Ping for IN THE MOOD FOR LOVE (Hong Kong/France) Dir Wong Kar-Wai
Short Films
Palme d'Or: ANINO (Philippines) Dir Raymond Red
CineFondation
First Prize: FIVE FEET HIGH AND RISING (US) Dir Peter Sollett
Second Prize: (co-winners) KISS IT UP TO GOD (US) Dir Caran Hartsfield and KINU'ACH (Israel) Dir Amit Sakomski
Third Prize: (co-winners) INDIEN (Denmark) Dir Pernille Fisher Christensen and CUOC XE DEM (Vietnam/France) Dir Bui Thac Chuyên

25th CÉSARS

Awarded in Paris 19th February 2000
Césars du Cinéma Français
19 av.du Pdt Wilson
75116 Paris
Tel.01 47 23 72 33
Fax.01 40 70 02 91
Web site: www.césars.com
Best Film: VÉNUS BEAUTÉ (INSTITUT) (France) Dir Tonie Marshall

Best Actress: Karin Viard in HAUT LES COEURS! (France/Belgium) Dir Solveig Anspach
Best Actor: Daniel Auteuil in La FILLE SUR LE PONT (France) Dir Patrice Leconte
Best Supporting Actress: Charlotte Gainsbourg in La BÛCHE (France) Dir Danièle Thompson
Best Supporting Actor: François Berléand in MA PETITE ENTREPRISE (France) Dir Pierre Jolivet
Best Female Newcomer: Audrey Tautou in VÉNUS BEAUTÉ (INSTITUT) (France) Dir Tonie Marshall
Best Male Newcomer: Eric Caravaca in C'EST QUOI LA VIE? (France) Dir FranÁois Dupeyron
Best Director: Tonie Marshall for VÉNUS BEAUTÉ (INSTITUT) (France)
Best Original Screenplay: Tonie Marshall for VÉNUS BEAUTÉ (INSTITUT) Dir Tonie Marshall
Best Foreign Film: TODO SOBRE MI MADRE (Spain/France) Dir Pedro Almodòvar
Best Music: Bruno Coulais for HIMALAYA, L'ENFANCE D'UN CHEF (France/China/UK/Nepal) Dir Eric Valli
Best Photography: Eric Guichard for HIMALAYA, L'ENFANCE D'UN CHEF (France/China/UK/Nepal)
Best First Film: VOYAGES (France/Poland/Belgium) Dir Emmanuel Finkiel
Best Editing: Emmanuelle Castro for VOYAGES (France/Poland/Belgium) Dir Emmanuel Finkiel
Best Sound: Vincent Tulli, FranÁois Grouli, Bruno Tarrière for JEANNE D'ARC (France) Dir Luc Besson
Best Costume Design: Catherine Leterrier for JEANNE D'ARC (France) Dir Luc Besson
Best Set Design: Philippe Chiffre for REMBRANDT (France) Dir Charles Matton
Best Short Film: SALE BATTARS (France) Dir Delphine Gleize
Césars d'Honneur: Jean-Pierre Léaud, Josiane Balasko, and Georges Cravenne

54th EDINBURGH INTERNATIONAL FILM FESTIVAL

Held 13th-27th August 2000, Edinburgh
88 Lothian Road
Edinburgh EH3 9BZ
Tel: (44) 131 229 2550
Fax: (44) 131 229 5501
Website: www.edfilmfest.org.uk/

Best New British Feature: THE LAST RESORT (UK) Dir Paul Pawlikowski
Pathé Best British Performance Award: Aidan Gillen for THE LOW DOWN (UK) Dir Jamie Thraves
New Director's Award: AMORES PERROS (Mexico) Dir Alejandro González Iñárritu
Standard Life Audience Award: BILLY ELLIOT (UK) Dir Stephen Daldry
Best British Shorts: A GOOD MAN IS HARD TO FIND (UK) Dir Martin Radich; JOMEO AND RULIET (UK) Dir Alnoor Dewshi
Best British Animation: ROBOTS – THE ANIMATED DOCU-SOAP (UK) Dir John Williams

EMMY AWARDS - 28TH INTERNATIONAL EMMY AWARDS GALA

Awarded on November 20, at the Sheraton New York Hotel, New York City
International Council for the National Academy of TV Arts & Sciences
142 West 57th Street
New York

NY 10019
Tel: (212) 489 6969
Fax: (212) 489 6557
Website: www.intlemmyawards.com/

Drama: ALL STARS (The Netherlands) NOS/VARA
Broadcasting Organizations
Documentary: KAPO (Israel) Set Productions
Arts Documentary: THE JAZZMAN FROM THE
GULAG (France) France 3
Performing Arts: GLORIANA (UK) BBC
Popular Arts: SMACK THE PONY SERIES II,
PROGRAM 1 (UK) Channel 4
Children & Young People: THE MAGICIAN'S HOUSE
EPISODES 1, 3 & 6 (UK)
News:
ITN NEWS ON ITV: THE MOZAMBIQUE FLOOD (UK)
ITN

52nd ANNUAL PRIME TIME EMMY AWARDS

(for nighttime programming USA)
Awards in 52 categories presented in Pasadena
(selection)

**Outstanding Achievement in Non-Fiction Programming
– Cinematography:** Didier Portal, Robert Pauly for
RAISING THE MAMMOTH (DSC)
**Outstanding Achievement in Non-Fiction Programming
- Picture Editing:** Nina Schulman, Li Yu for NEW YORK
(THE AMERICAN EXPERIENCE) (PBS)
**Outstanding Achievement in Non-Fiction Programming
- Sound Editing:** Andrew Sherriff, Simon Gotel,
WALKING WITH DINOSAURS (DSC)
**Outstanding Animated Program (For Programming
More Than One Hour):** WALKING WITH DINOSAURS
(DSC)
**Outstanding Animated Program (For Programming One
Hour or Less):** THE SIMPSONS (FOX)
**Outstanding Art Direction For A Miniseries Movie or a
Special:** Leslie Thomas Art Director, Robert Greenfield Set
Decorator, James Spencer Production Designer for
INTRODUCING DOROTHY DANDRIDGE (HBO)
Outstanding Art Direction For a Multi-Camera Series:
Rusty Lipscomb Set Decorator, Dahl Delu, Production
Designer for LOVE & MONEY (CBS)
Outstanding Art Direction For a Single-Camera Series:
Ellen Totleben Set Decorator, Jon Hutman, Production
Designer, Tony Fanning Art Director for THE WEST
WING (NBC)
**Outstanding Art Direction For a Variety or Music
Program:** Bob Keene Production Designer, Brian
Stonestreet Art Director THE 42ND ANNUAL GRAMMY
AWARDS (CBS)
Outstanding Casting For a Comedy Series: Allison Jones
Casting Executive, Jill Sands Casting Executive (Location),
Coreen Mayrs C.S.A. Casting Executive (Location) for
FREAKS AND GEEKS (NBC)
Outstanding Casting For a Drama Series: Kevin Scott
C.S.A. Casting Executive, John Levey C.S.A. Casting
Executive, Barbara Miller C.S.A. Casting Executive for THE
WEST WING (NBC)
Outstanding Casting For a Miniseries Movie or a Special:
Lora Kennedy C.S.A. Casting Executive, Joyce Nettles
Casting Executive (Location) for RKO 281 (HBO)
Outstanding Children's Program: GOODNIGHT MOON
AND OTHER SLEEPYTIME TALES (HBO) and
THE COLOR OF FRIENDSHIP (DIS)

Outstanding Choreography: Rob Marshall for ANNIE
(ABC)
**Outstanding Cinematography For a Mulit-Camera
Series:** Dick Quinlan for SPIN CITY (ABC) and
Peter Smokler for SPORTS NIGHT (ABC)
**Outstanding Cinematography For a Single-Camera
Series:** Thomas Del Ruth A.S.C. for THE WEST WING
(NBC)
Outstanding Classical Music Dance Program: DANCE IN
AMERICA: AMERICAN BALLET THEATRE IN LE
CORSAIRE (PBS)
Outstanding Comedy Series: WILL & GRACE (NBC)
Outstanding Commercial: THE MORNING AFTER
Propaganda/Satellite Production Co. Wieden & Kennedy
Ad Agency
**Outstanding Costumes For a Miniseries, Movie or a
Special:** Lucinda Campbell Costume Supervisor, Shelley
Komarov Costume Designer for INTRODUCING
DOROTHY DANDRIDGE (HBO)
Outstanding Costumes For a Series: Giovanna Melton
Costume Designer, Sandy Kenyon Costume Supervisor for
PROVIDENCE (NBC)
Outstanding Costumes For a Variety and Music Program:
David Cardona Dancer's Costume Designer, Bob Mackie
Cher's Costume Designer, Helen Hiatt Costume Supervisor
CHER: LIVE IN CONCERT - FROM THE MGM GRAND
IN LAS VEGAS (HBO)
Outstanding Directing For a Comedy Series: Todd
Holland for MALCOLM IN THE MIDDLE (FOX)
Outstanding Directing For a Drama Series: Thomas
Schlamme for THE WEST WING (NBC)
**Outstanding Directing For a Miniseries, Movie or a
Special:** Charles Dutton for THE CORNER (HBO)
Outstanding Directing For a Variety or Music Program:
Louis Horvitz for 72ND ANNUAL ACADEMY AWARDS
(ABC)
Outstanding Drama Series: THE WEST WING (NBC)
Outstanding Guest Actor in a Comedy Series: Bruce Willis
in FRIENDS (NBC)
Outstanding Guest Actor in a Drama Series: James
Whitmore in THE PRACTICE (ABC)
Outstanding Guest Actress in a Comedy Series: Jean
Smart in FRASIER (NBC)
Outstanding Guest Actress in a Drama Series: Beah
Richards in THE PRACTICE (ABC)
**Outstanding Hairstyling For a Miniseries, Movie or a
Special:** Kathrine Gordon Key, Katherine Rees, Virginia
Kearns, Jennifer Bell, Hazel Catmull for INTRODUCING
DOROTHY DANDRIDGE (HBO)
Outstanding Hairstyling For a Series: Bobby Grayson for
SATURDAY NIGHT LIVE (NBC)
**Outstanding Individual Performance in a Variety or
Music Program:** Eddie Izzard in EDDIE IZZARD: DRESS
TO KILL (HBO)
Outstanding Lead Actor in a Comedy Series: Michael J
Fox in SPIN CITY (ABC)
Outstanding Lead Actor in a Drama Series: James
Gandolfini in THE SOPRANOS (HBO)
Outstanding Lead Actor in a Miniseries or Movie: Jack
Lemmon in OPRAH WINFREY PRESENTS: TUESDAYS
WITH MORRIE (ABC)
Outstanding Lead Actress in a Comedy Series: Patricia
Heaton in EVERYBODY LOVES RAYMOND (CBS)
Outstanding Lead Actress in a Drama Series: Sela Ward in
ONCE AND AGAIN (ABC)
Outstanding Lead Actress in a Miniseries or a Movie:
Halle Berry in INTRODUCING DOROTHY
DANDRIDGE (HBO)

Outstanding Lighting Direction (Electronic): Kim Killingsworth Lighting Designer, John Alonzo, Director of Photography for FAIL SAFE (CBS)

Outstanding Made For Television Movie: OPRAH WINFREY PRESENTS: TUESDAYS WITH MORRIE (ABC)

Outstanding Main Title Design: Tim Webber for THE 10TH KINGDOM (NBC)

Outstanding Main Title Theme: W.G. Walden for THE WEST WING (NBC)

Outstanding Makeup For a Miniseries, Movie or a Special: Annie Spiers Head Makeup Artist, Mark Coulier Prosthetic Makeup Artist, Diane Chenery-Wickens Makeup Artist, Darren Phillips Makeup Artist, Duncan Jarman Prosthetic Makeup Artist for ARABIAN NIGHTS (ABC)

Outstanding Makeup For a Series: Cheri Medcalf, Head Makeup Artist, Kevin Westmore, Makeup Artist, LaVerne Basham, Makeup Artist, Gregory Funk Makeup Artist, Cindy Williams, Makeup Artist for THE X-FILES (FOX)

Outstanding Miniseries: THE CORNER (HBO)

Outstanding Multi-Camera Picture Editing For a Miniseries, Movie or a Special: Bill DeRonde for A SUPERNATURAL EVENING WITH SANTANA (FOX)

Outstanding Multi-Camera Picture Editing For a Series: Ron Volk, Scott Maisano for FRASIER (NBC)

Outstanding Music and Lyrics: John Kimbrough for NICKELLENNIUM (NIK)

Outstanding Music Composition For a Miniseries, Movie or a Special: John Altman for RKO 281 (HBO)

Outstanding Music Composition For a Series (Dramatic Underscore): Joseph LoDuca for XENA: WARRIOR PRINCESS (SYN)

Outstanding Music Direction: Paul Bogaev for ANNIE (ABC)

Outstanding Non-Fiction Series: AMERICAN MASTERS (PBS)

Outstanding Non-Fiction Special: CHILDREN IN WAR (HBO)

Outstanding Single-Camera Picture Editing For a Miniseries, Movie or a Special: Carol Littleton A.C.E. for OPRAH WINFREY PRESENTS: TUESDAYS WITH MORRIE (ABC)

Outstanding Single-Camera Picture Editing For a Series: Kevin Casey for ER (NBC)

Outstanding Sound Editing For a Miniseries, Movie or a Special: Suzanne Angel ADR Supervisor, Bob Costanza Sound Editor, Bill Bell Sound Editor, Anton Holden Sound Editor, Mike Dickeson Sound Editor, Rick Crampton Sound Editor, Rick Steele Sound Editor, Rusty Tinsley Sound Editor, Rob Webber Sound Editor, Gary Macheel Sound Editor, Tim Terusa Sound Editor, Lou Thomas Sound Editor, Mike Lyle Sound Editor, Tim Chilton Foley Artist, Jill Schachne Foley Artist, Michael Graham M.P.S.E. Supervising Sound Editor, David Bondelevitch Music Editor for THE HUNLEY (TNT)

Outstanding Sound Editing For a Series: Walter Newman Supervising Sound Editor, Darren Wright Sound Editor, Rick Hromadka Sound Editor, Rick Camara Sound Editor, Darleen Kageyama Dialogue Editor, Thomas Harris ADR Editor, Kenneth Young Sound Editor, Casey Crabtree Foley Artist, Mike Crabtree Foley Artist, Clay Collins Dialogue Editor, Allan Rosen Music Editor, Karyn Foster Dialogue Editor for THIRD WATCH (NBC)

Outstanding Sound Mixing For a Comedy Series or a Special: Nello Torri Re-Recording Mixer, Peter Kelsey, Re-Recording Mixer, Paul Lewis Production Mixer for ALLY MCBEAL (Fox)

Outstanding Sound Mixing For a Drama Series: Harry Andronis Re-Recording Mixer, David West, Re-Recording Mixer, Ray O'Reilly Re-Recording Mixer, Steve Cantamessa Production Mixer for THE X-FILES (FOX)

Outstanding Sound Mixing For a Miniseries, Movie or a Special: Clive Derbyshire Production Mixer, Mike Dowson, Re-Recording Mixer, Mark Taylor, Re-Recording Mixer for RKO 281 (HBO)

Outstanding Special Visual Effects For a Miniseries, Movie or a Special: Tim Greenwood Visual Effects Supervisor, Jez Harris Lead Special Effects Supervisor, Mike Milne CGI Supervisor, Virgil Manning Lead CGI Artist/Animator, David Marsh Lead CGI Artist/Animator, Daren Horley Lead CGI Artist/Animator, Alec Knox Lead CGI Artist/Animator, Carlos Rosas, Lead CGI Artist/animator, Mike McGee, Visual Effects Supervisor for WALKING WITH DINOSAURS (DSC)

Outstanding Special Visual Effects For a Series: Bill Millar Visual Effects Producer, Deena Burkett, Visual Effects Supervisor, Monique Klauer, Visual Effects Coordinator, Don Greenberg Visual Effects Compositor, Cory Strassburger Visual Effects Animator, Steve Scott Visual Effects Compositor, Jeff Zaman, Visual Effects Compositor, Steve Strassburger, Visual Effects Compositor for THE X-FILES (FOX)

Outstanding Supporting Actor in a Comedy: Sean Hayes in WILL & GRACE (NBC)

Outstanding Supporting Actor in a Drama: Richard Schiff in THE WEST WING (NBC)

Outstanding Supporting Actor in a Miniseries or a Movie: Hank Azaria in OPRAH WINFREY PRESENTS: TUESDAYS WITH MORRIE (ABC)

Outstanding Supporting Actress in a Comedy Series: Megan Mullally in WILL & GRACE (NBC)

Outstanding Supporting Actress in a Drama Series: Allison Janney in THE WEST WING (NBC)

Outstanding Supporting Actress in a Miniseries or Movie: Vanessa Redgrave in IF THESE WALLS COULD TALK 2 (HBO)

Outstanding Technical Direction, Camerawork, Video For a Miniseries, Movie or a Special: Gene Crowe Technical Director, Ted Ashton Camera, Dave Chameides Camera, Rocky Danielson Camera, Sam Drummy Camera, David Eastwood Camera, Tom Geren, Camera, Hank Geving Camera, Larry Hieder Camera, Easter Xua Camera, David Irite Camera, Dave Levisohn Camera, Wayne Orr Camera, Bill Philbin Camera, Hector Ramirez Camera, Dennis Turner Camera, John O'Brien Video, Chuck Reilly , Video for FAIL SAFE (CBS)

Outstanding Technical Direction, Camerawork, Video For a Series: Paul Johnson Camera, Jim Velarde Camera, Richard Davis Camera, Thomas Luth Camera, Michael Schwartz Camera, Rick Labgold Video, Terry Clark Camera, Donna Stock Technical Director for POLITICALLY INCORRECT WITH BILL MAHER (ABC) and Steven Cimino Technical Director, Jan Kasoff Camera, Michael Bennett, Camera, Richard Fox Camera, Carl Eckett Camera, John Pinto, Camera, Susan Noll. Video, Frank Grisanti, Video for SATURDAY NIGHT LIVE (NBC)

Outstanding Variety, Music or Comedy Series: LATE SHOW WITH DAVID LETTERMAN (CBS)

Outstanding Variety, Music or Comedy Special: SATURDAY NIGHT LIVE: THE 25TH ANNIVERSARY SPECIAL (NBC)

Outstanding Writing For a Comedy Series: Linwood Boomer for MALCOLM IN THE MIDDLE (FOX)

Outstanding Writing For a Drama Series: Aaron Sorkin, Rick Cleveland for THE WEST WING (NBC)

Outstanding Writing For a Miniseries or a Movie: David Simon, David Mills for THE CORNER (HBO)
Outstanding Writing For a Variety, Music or Comedy Program: Eddie Izzard for EDDIE IZZARD: DRESS TO KILL (HBO)

13th EUROPEAN FILM AWARDS
2nd December 2000, Théatre National de Chaillot in Paris
European Film AcademyKurfürstendamm 225
10719 Berlin
Tel: 49 (30) 887 167 0
Fax: 49 (30) 887 167 77
Website: www.europeanfilmacademy.org

Best European Film: DANCER IN THE DARK, (Denmark/Sweden/France) Dir Lars von Trier
Best European Actor: Sergi Lopez in HARRY, UN AMI QUI VOUS VEUT DU BIEN (France) Dir Dominik Moll
Best European Actress: Björk in DANCER IN THE DARK, (Denmark/Sweden/France) Dir Lars von Trier
Best European Screenwriter: Agnès Jaoui and Jean-Pierre Bacri for LE GOÛT DES AUTRES (France) Dir Agnès Jaoui
Best European Cinematographer: Vittorio Storaro for GOYA EN BURDEOS (Spain) Dir Carlos Saura
European Achievement in World Cinema: Jean Reno, Roberto Benigni
Screen International European Film Award: IN THE MOOD FOR LOVE (France/Hong Kong) Dir Wong Kar-Wai
THE PEOPLE'S CHOICE AWARDS:
Best European Director: LARS VON TRIER, Dancer In The Dark
Best European Actor: Ingvar E. Sigurdsson for ENGLAR ALHEIMSINS (Iceland, Norway, Demark, Sweden, Germany)Dir Fridrik Thór Fridriksson
Best European Actress: Björk for DANCER IN THE DARK (Denmark/Sweden/France) Dir Lars von Trier
European Discovery 2000 - Fassbinder Award: RESSOURCES HUMAINES (France/UK) Dir Laurent Cantet
European Documentary Award 2000 - Prix Arte: LES GLANEURS ET LA GLANEUSE (France) Dir Agnès Varda,
Special Mention: HEIMSPIEL Germany, Dir Pepe Danquart
European Short Film 2000 - Prix UIP: A MI GÓLYÁNK (Hungary) Dir Livia Gyarmathy
European Critics' Award 2000 - Prix Fipresci: MAYIS SIKINTISI (Turkey) Dir Nuri Bilge Ceylan
European Film Academy Lifetime Achivement Award 2000: Richard Harris

EVENING STANDARD BRITISH FILM AWARDS
Awarded 6th February 2000, Savoy Hotel, London

Best Film: EAST IS EAST (UK) Dir Damien O'Donnell
Best Actor: Jeremy Northam in IDEAL HUSBAND (UK/US) Dir Oliver Parker and also in WINSLOW BOY (US) Dir David Mamet
Best Actress: Samantha Morton in DREAMING OF JOSEPH LEES (US/UK) Dir Eric Styles
Best Screenplay: Tom Stoppard for SHAKESPEARE IN LOVE (US) Dir John Madden
Most Promising Newcomer: Peter Mullan for ORPHANS (UK)
Best Technical/Artistic Achievement: John de Borman for HIDEOUS KINKY (UK/France) Dir Gillies MacKinnon

Peter Sellers Award for Comedy: NOTTING HILL (US/UK) Dir Roger Michell
Special Award (Lifetime Achievement): Freddie Francis

57th GOLDEN GLOBE AWARDS
Awarded 23rd January 2000, Los Angeles
Hollywood Foreign Press Association
646 North Robertson Boulevard
West Hollywood
California 90069
Tel.(310) 657 1731
Fax.(310) 657 5576
Email: hfpa95@aol.com
Web site: www.hfpa.com

FILM
Best Motion Picture (Drama): AMERICAN BEAUTY (US) Dir Sam Mendes
Best Motion Picture (Comedy/Musical): TOY STORY 2 (US) Dir John Lasseter
Best Actor (Drama): Denzel Washington in The HURRICANE (US) Dir Norman Jewison
Best Actor (Comedy/Musical): Jim Carrey in MAN ON THE MOON (US) Dir Milos Forman
Best Actress (Drama): Hilary Swank in BOYS DON'T CRY (US) Dir Kimberly Peirce
Best Actress (Comedy/Musical): Janet McTeer in TUMBLEWEEDS (US) Dir Gavin O'Connor
Best Supporting Actor: Tom Cruise in MAGNOLIA (US) Dir Paul Thomas Anderson
Best Supporting Actress: Angelina Jolie in GIRL, INTERRUPTED (US) Dir James Mangold
Best Director: Sam Mendes for AMERICAN BEAUTY (US)
Best Screenplay: Alan Ball for AMERICAN BEAUTY (US) Dir Sam Mendes
Best Original Song: Phil Collins for "You'll Be In My Heart" for TARZAN (US) Dir Kevin Lima
Best Original Score: Ennio Morricone for La LEGGENDA DEL PIANISTA SULL'OCEANO (Italy/US) Dir Giuseppe Tornature
Best Foreign Language Film: TODO SOBRE MI MADRE (Spain/France) Dir Pedro Almodòvar

TELEVISION
Best Actor in a TV-Series (Drama): James Gandolfini in The SOPRANOS (HBO Productions/Brillstein-Grey Entertainment)
Best Actor in a TV-Series (Comedy/Musical): Michael J. Fox in SPIN CITY (ABC TV)
Best Actor in a Mini-Series or Motion Picture Made for TV: Jack Lemmon in INHERIT THE WIND (Showtime)
Best Actress in a TV-Series (Drama): Edie Falco in The SOPRANOS (HBO Productions/Brillstein-Grey Entertainment)
Best Actress in a TV-Series (Comedy/Musical): Sarah Jessica Parker in SEX AND THE CITY (HBO)
Best Actress in a Mini-Series or Motion Picture Made for TV: Halle Berry in INTRODUCING DOROTHY DANDRIDGE (HBO) Dir Martha Coolidge
Best Supporting Actor in a Series, Mini-Series or Motion Picture Made for TV: Peter Fonda in The PASSION OF AYN RAND (Showtime) Dir Chris Menaul
Best Supporting Actress in a Series, Mini-Series or Motion Picture Made for TV: Nancy Marchand in The SOPRANOS (HBO Productions/Brillstein-Grey Entertainment)
Best TV Series (Comedy/Musical): SEX AND THE CITY (HBO)

Best TV Series (Drama): The SOPRANOS (HBO Productions/Brillstein-Grey Entertainment)
Best Mini-Series or Motion Picture Made for TV: RKO 281 (HBO Pictures) Dir Benjamin Ross
Cecil B. DeMille Award: Barbra Streisand

40th GOLDEN ROSE OF MONTREUX

Held 4th-9th May 2000, Montreux
Télévision Suisse Romande
Quai E. Anserment 20
P.O. Box 234
CH-1211 Geneva 8
Tel: (41) 22 708 89 98
Fax: (41) 22 781 52 49
Email: Sarah.Fanchini@tsr.ch
Website: www.rosedor.ch

Rose D'Or: The MOLE (VRT/Vlaamse Radio- en Televisieomroep) (Belgium)
Silver Rose (Sitcoms): ALL STARS (Vara Television) (Netherlands)
Bronze Rose (Sitcoms): WILL & GRACE (NBC Enterprises/Everything Entertainment) (US)
Silver Rose (Music): JOSEPH AND THE AMAZING TECHNICOLOR DREAMCOAT (Really Useful Picture Company) (UK)
Bronze Rose (Music): ROBBIE WILLIAMS LIVE AT SLANE CASTLE (Done & Dusted for Robert Williams Productions) (UK)
Silver Rose (Variety): FRANCAMENTE...ME NE INFISCHIO (Rai UNO) (Italy)
Bronze Rose (Variety): MICHAEL MOORE: THE AWFUL TRUTH (Dog Eat Dog Films) (US/UK)
Silver Rose (Comedy): PEOPLE LIKE US (Talkback Productions for BBC2) (UK)
Bronze Rose (Comedy): TRIGGER HAPPY TV (Absolutely Productions for C4) (UK)
Silver Rose (Gameshows): The BIG CLASS REUNION (Wegelius Television APS) (Denmark)
Bronze Rose (Gameshows): FRIENDS LIKE THESE (BBC1) (UK)
Special Prize of the City of Montreux Egg: The ARTS SHOW #101 (Thirteen/WNET) (US)
Press Prize: ALL STARS (Vara Television) (Netherlands)
UNDA Prize: The REST (Langteaux/A.D.D. Prod./TLN Television (US)

GRIERSON AWARD 1999

Awarded 23rd March 2000, Savoy Hotel, London
The Grierson Memorial Trust
37 Gower Street
London WC1E 6HH
Tel: 020 7580 1502
Fax: 020 7580 1504
Email: john.chittock@which.net
Website: www.editor.net/griersontrust
Best Documentary: GULAG (ENEMY OF THE PEOPLE) Dir Angus Macqueen (BBC2 Television)
Commended: TRUE STORIES: KOSOVO THE VALLEY Dir Dan Reed (Mentorn Barraclough Carey/Suspect Device for C4)
Commended: TRUE STORIES: DIVORCE IRANIAN STYLE Dir Kim Longinotto and Ziba Mir-Hosseini (Twentieth Century Vixen for C4)
Special Mention: TIMEWATCH: TALES OF THE EIFFEL TOWER Dir Jonathan Gill (BBC2)
Trustees' Tribute: David Munro and Philip Donnellan

INTERNATIONAL INDIAN FILM AWARDS

Awarded 24th June 2000 at the Millennium Dome, London

Best Film: HUM DIL DE CHUKE SANAM (India) Dir Sanjay Leela Bhansali
Best Director: Sanjay Leela Bhansali for HUM DIL DE CHUKE SANAM (India)
Best Story: Sanjay Leela Bhansali and Pratap Karvat for HUM DIL DE CHUKE SANAM (India) Dir Sanjay Leela Bhansali
Best Actress in a Leading Role: Aishwarya Rai for HUM DIL DE CHUKE SANAM (India) Dir Sanjay Leela Bhansali
Best Actor in a Leading Role: Sanjay Dutt for VAASTAV (India) Dir Mahesh Manjrekar
Lifetime Achievement Award: Jackie Chan
Special Prize: EAST IS EAST (UK) Dir Damien O'Donnell
Special Prize: ELIZABETH (UK) Dir Shekhar Kapur
Best Lyrics: Anand Bakshi for the song "Ishq Bina" from TAAL (India) Dir Subhash Gai
Best Music Direction: AR Rehman for TAAL (India) Dir Subhash Gai
Best Female Playback Singer: Alka Yagnik for the song "Taal Se Taal" from TAAL (India) Dir Subhash Gai
Best Male Playback Singer: Udit Narayan for "Chand Chupa" from HUM DIL DE CHUKE SANAM (India) Dir Sanjay Leela Bhansali
Best Performance in a Negative Role: Naseeruddin Shah for SARFAROSH (India) Dir John Mathew Matthan
Best Actor in a Supporting Role: Anil Kapoor for TAAL (India) Dir Subhash Gai
Best Actress in a Supporting Role: Sushmita Sen for BIWI NO.1 (India) Dir David Dhawan
Best Performance in a Comic Role: Anil Kapoor for BIWI NO.1 (India) Dir David Dhawan

35th KARLOVY VARY INTERNATIONAL FILM FESTIVAL

Held 5th-15th July 2000, Karlovy Vary
Panska 1
110 00 Prague 1
Czech Republic
Tel: (420) 224 23 54 13
Fax: (420) 224 23 34 08
Email: Foundation@iffkv.cz
Web site: www.iffkv.cz/

Crystal Globe: EU TU ELES (Brazil) Dir Andrucha Waddington
Special Jury Prize: DUZE ZWIERZE (Poland) Dir Jerzy Stuhr and
BAKHA SATANG (Korea), Dir Lee Chang-Dong
Best Director Award: Vinko Bresan for MARSAL (Croatia)
Best Actress Award: Regina Casé for EU TU ELES (Brazil)
Best Actor Award: Ian Hart for ABERDEEN (Norway/UK) Dir Hans Petter Moland and
Hamid Farokhnezad for AROUS-E ATASH (Iran) Dir Khosro Sinai
Special Jury Mention: UNE AFFAIRE DE GOÛT (France) Dir Bernard Rapp and
ENGLAR ALHEIMSINS (Iceland, Norway, Sweden, Germany, Denmark) Dir Fridrik Thór Fridriksson
Prize For Outstanding Contribution to World Cinema: Vera Chytilová, (Czech Republic); Carlos Saura (Spain)
Prize of the City of Karlovy Vary: Károly Makk (Hungary)
Mladá Fronta Dnew Audience Prize: ANGELA'S ASHES (US/UK) Dir Alan Parker

Best Documentary Film Lasting 30 Minutes or Less: DEL AV DEN VÄRLD SOM TILLHÖR DIG (Sweden) Dir Karin Wegsjö

Best Documentary Film More Than 30 Minutes in Length:
MIN MAMMA HADE FJORTON BARN (Sweden) Dir Lars-Lennart Forsberg

Special Mention: PRISADATA-OBVINENIENTO (Bulgaria) Dir Anna Petkova and
THE FIGHTER (US/Czech Republic) Dir Amir Bar-Lev

Philip Morris Freedom Award: SARI GYALIN (Azerbaijan) Dir Yaver Rzayez

FIPRESCI Award: ENGLAR ALHEIMSINS (Iceland) Dir Fridrik Thor Fridriksson

Special Mention: ENE BENE (Czech Republic) Dir Alice Nellis

53rd LOCARNO INTERNATIONAL FILM FESTIVAL

Held 2nd-12th August 2000, Locarno
Via Luini 3a
CH-6601 Locarno
Switzerland
Tel: (41) 91 756 2121
Fax: (41) 91 756 2149
Email: info@pardo.ch
Website: www.pardo.ch

Golden Leopard: BABA (China) Dir Wang Shuo

Silver Leopard (New Cinema): SAI LO CHEUNG (Hong Kong/Japan) Dir Kuo, Fruit Chan

Silver Leopard (Young Cinema): MANILA (Germany) Dir Romuald Karmakar

Bronze Leopard (Actress): Sabine Timoteo for L'AMOUR L'ARGENT L'AMOUR (Germany, Switzerland, France) Dir Philip Gröning

Bronze Leopard (Actor): Roland Düringer, Joachim Bissmeier, Josef Hader for DER ÜBERFALL (Austria) Dir Florian Flicker

Special Jury Prize (Crossair): GOSTANZA DA LIBIANNO (Italy) Dir Paolo Benvenuti

Leopard of Honour: Paul Verhoeven

Public Choice Award: HOLLOW MAN (US) Dir Paul Verhoeven

LONDON CRITICS' CIRCLE FILM AWARDS

Awarded 2nd March 2000, London

Best Actor: Kevin Spacey in AMERICAN BEAUTY (US) Dir Sam Mendes

Best Actress: Annette Bening in AMERICAN BEAUTY (US) Dir Sam Mendes

Best British Film: EAST IS EAST (UK) Dir Damien O'Donnell

Best British Producer: Leslee Udwin for EAST IS EAST (UK) Dir Damien O'Donnell

Best British Screenwriter: Ayub Khan-Din for EAST IS EAST (UK) Dir Damien O'Donnell

Best Director: Sam Mendes for AMERICAN BEAUTY (US)

Best English Language Film: AMERICAN BEAUTY (US) Dir Sam Mendes

Best Foreign Language Film: TODO SOBRE MI MADRE (Spain/France) Dir Pedro Almodòvar

Best Screenplay: Alan Ball for AMERICAN BEAUTY (US) Dir Sam Mendes

Best British Supporting Actor: Michael Caine in LITTLE VOICE (UK/US) Dir Mark Herman

Special Award: Mike Leigh

40th MONTE CARLO TELEVISION FESTIVAL

Held 17th-23rd February 2000, Monte Carlo
4 Boulevard de Jardin Exotique
98000 Monte Carlo
Monaco
Tel: (37) 793 10 40 60
Fax: (37) 793 50 70 14
Email: info@tvfestival.com
Website: www.tvfestival.com/

TELEVISION FILMS
Gold Nymphs:

Best Film: BONHOEFFER DIE LEZTE STUFE (Germany/Canada) Dir Eric Till (Norflicks/NFP/Teleart GmbH & Co.)

Best Script: Theo Hakola for The FAVOURITE DAUGHTER (France) (M6 Droits Audivisuels)

Best Direction: Daniel Alfredson for D÷DSKLOCKAN (Sweden) (Sveriges Television)

Best Actor: Lino Banfi in VOLA SCIUSCIU, THE SAVIOR OF SAN NICOLA (Italy) (Lux Vide)

Best Actress: Orla Brady in A LOVE DIVIDED (Ireland) (Parallel Films Productions)

MINI-SERIES
Gold Nymphs:

Best Mini-Series: WARRIORS (UK) Dir Peter Kosminsky (BBC Films in association with Deep Indigo Productions)

Best Script: Tony Marchant for KID IN THE CORNER (UK) (Tiger Aspect Production for C4)

Best Direction: Billie Eltringham for KID IN THE CORNER (UK) (Tiger Aspect Production for C4)

Best Actor: Douglas Henshall in KID IN THE CORNER (UK) (Tiger Aspect Production for C4)

Best Actress: Virna Lisi in BALZAC (France) (TF1)

NEWS PROGRAMMES
Gold Nymph (Best News Programme): ITN News compilation of reports on the Kosovo conflict (UK) (ITN)

Silver Nymph (News Programme): NEWSNIGHT: SOUTH AFRICA POLICE (UK) (BBC News)

Gold Nymph (Best Current Affairs Programme): KOSOVO THE VALLEY (UK) (C4)

Silver Nymph (Current Affairs Programme): RINJINTACHI NO SENSO KOSOVO: HAJDAR DUSHI DORI NO HITOBITO (Japan) (NHK Japan Broadcasting Corporation)

Special Mention: FMI - RUSSIE: L'ENJEU (France) (La Sept Arte)

SPECIAL PRIZES
Special Prize of H.S.H. Prince Rainier III: L'OR VERT (ENVOYE SPECIAL) (France) (France 2)

Prize of the Monaco Red Cross: BEHIND THE MASK (US) (Pearson Television International)

AMADE & UNESCO Prize: DESSINE MOI UN JOUET (France) (France 3)

Prix UNDA: NEWS: MAS ENLLA DEL DOLOR (Spain) (TV3/Televisio de Catalunya S.A.)

European Producer Award: Zentropa Productions (Denmark) for its fiction productions over the last two years

72ND OSCARS - ACADEMY OF MOTION PICTURE ARTS AND SCIENCES

Awarded 26th March 2000, Los Angeles
8949 Wilshire Boulevard
Beverly Hills
California 90211
Tel: (310) 247 3000
Fax: (310) 859 6919
Website: www.oscar.com and www.oscars.org

Best Film: AMERICAN BEAUTY (US) Dir Sam Mendes
Best Director: Sam Mendes for AMERICAN BEAUTY (US)
Best Actor: Kevin Spacey in AMERICAN BEAUTY (US) Dir Sam Mendes
Best Actress: Hilary Swank in BOYS DON'T CRY (US) Dir Kimberly Peirce
Best Supporting Actor: Michael Caine in The CIDER HOUSE RULES (US) Dir Lasse Hallstr´m
Best Supporting Actress: Angelina Jolie in GIRL, INTERRUPTED (US) Dir James Mangold
Best Screenplay: Alan Ball for AMERICAN BEAUTY (US) Dir Sam Mendes
Best Adapted Screenplay: John Irving for The CIDER HOUSE RULES (US) Dir Lasse Hallstr´m
Best Cinematography: Conrad L. Hall for AMERICAN BEAUTY (US) Dir Sam Mendes
Best Editing: Zach Staenberg for The MATRIX (US/Australia) Dir Andy Wachowski
Best Music (Original Score): John Corigliano for The RED VIOLIN (Canada/Italy/US/UK) Dir FranÁois Girard
Best Music (Original Song): Phil Collins for "You'll Be In My Heart" from TARZAN (US) Dir Kevin Lima
Best Art Direction: Rick Heinrichs for SLEEPY HOLLOW (US/Germany) Dir Tim Burton
Best Costume Design: Lindy Hemming for TOPSY-TURVY (UK/US) Dir Mike Leigh
Best Sound: John Reitz, Gregg Rudloff, David Campbell and David Lee for The MATRIX (US/Australia) Dir Andy Wachowski
Best Sound Effects Editing: Dane A. Davis for The MATRIX (US/Australia) Dir Andy Wachowski
Best Visual Effects: John Gaeta, Janek Sirrs, Steve Courtley and Jon Thum for The MATRIX (US/Australia) Dir Andy Wachowski
Best Foreign Language Film: TODO SOBRE MI MADRE (Spain/France) Dir Pedro Almodòvar
Best Make-up: Christine Blundell and Trefor Proud for TOPSY-TURVY (UK/US) Dir Mike Leigh
Best Documentary Feature: ONE DAY IN SEPTEMBER (UK) Dir Kevin MacDonald
Best Documentary Short Subject: KING GIMP (US) Dir Susan Hannah Hadary and William A. Whiteford
Best Animated Short Film: The OLD MAN AND THE SEA (Quebec/Japan/Russia) Dir Alexander Petrov
Best Live Action Short Film: MY MOTHER DREAMS THE SATAN'S DISCIPLES IN NEW YORK (US) Dir Barbara Schock

ROYAL TELEVISION SOCIETY AWARDS

Awarded in London March 2000
100 Gray's Inn Road
London WC1X 8AL
Tel: 020 7430 1000
Fax: 020 7430 0924
Email: info@rts.org.uk
Website: www.rts.org.uk/

RTS PROGRAMME AWARDS
Situation Comedy/Comedy Drama: PEOPLE LIKE US (BBC Production for BBC2)
Entertainment: The LEAGUE OF GENTLEMEN (BBC Production for BBC2)
Single Documentary: MALCOLM AND BARBARA: A LOVE STORY (Granada Television)
Documentary Series: The DECISION (A Windfall Film Production for C4)
Documentary Strand: HORIZON (BBC Production for BBC2)
Regional Documentary: SPINNERS AND LOSERS (Scottish Television)
Regional Programme: NUTS AND BOLTS (HTV)
Regional Presenter: Roy Noble for COMMON GROUND: THE SHED (Presentable Productions for BBC Wales)
Features - Daytime: SHOW ME THE MONEY (Princess Productions for C4)
Features - Primetime: 1900 HOUSE (Wall To Wall Television for C4)
Children's Drama: SEE HOW THEY RUN (BBC Production in association with ABC Australia for BBC1)
Children's Entertainment: SM:TV LIVE (Blaze Television for ITV)
Children's Factual: NICK NEWS (Wised Up Productions for Nickelodeon UK)
Presenter: Johnny Vaughan for The BIG BREAKFAST (Planet 24 for C4)
Arts: THIS IS MODERN ART (Oxford TV Productions for C4)
Network Newcomer - On Screen: Jamie Oliver for The NAKED CHEF (Optomen Television for BBC2)
Network Newcomer - Behind the Screen: David Wolstencroft for PSYCHOS (A Kudos Production for C4)
Television Performance: Rory Bremner for BREMNER, BIRD & FORTUNE (Vera for C4)
Single Drama: WARRIORS (BBC Films in association with Deep Indigo Productions for BBC1)
Drama Serial: SHOOTING THE PAST (Talkback Productions for BBC2)
Drama Series: The COPS (World Productions for BBC2)
Actor - Female: Thora Hird for LOST FOR WORDS (Yorkshire Television in association with Bard Entertainments for ITV)
Actor - Male: Michael Gambon for WIVES & DAUGHTERS (BBC Production for BBC1)
Writer: Caroline Aherne & Craig Cash for The ROYLE FAMILY (Granada Television for BBC1)
Team: WALKING WITH DINOSAURS (BBC Production for BBC1)
Cyril Bennett Award/Judges Award: Peter Symes
Gold Medal: BSkyB

RTS EDUCATIONAL AWARDS
SCHOOLS TELEVISION
Pre-School & Infants: TWEENIES (Blow Tell-Tale Productions for BBC Education)
Primary Numeracy & Literacy: NUMBER CREW (Sports Day Open Mind for C4)
Primary Arts & Humanities: ZIG ZAG: A WALK THROUGH TIME - WORK (BBC Education)
Primary & Secondary Science & Maths: SCIENTIFIC EYE: MATERIALS AND THEIR PROPERTIES - CHANGING STATE (Yorkshire Television for C4)
Primary & Secondary Multimedia & Interactive: RAINFOREST DEVELOPMENT: The AMAZONIA EXPERIENCE (Channel 4 Learning with InSignificant Productions for C4)

Secondary Arts & Language: ENGLISH FILE: ROOTS & WATER (BBC Education)
Secondary Humanities: PLACE & PEOPLE: LAND FORMS (Ice Flying Pictures for C4)
ADULT EDUCATIONAL TELEVISION
Campaigns & Seasons - RTS/NIACE Award: BROOKIE BASICS (C4)
Vocational Training: STUDENT CHOICE í99 (Wobbly Picture Productions for BBC Education)
Single Programme: EMBARASSING ILLNESSES: TESTICULAR CANCER (A Maverick Production for C4)
Educational Impact In The Prime Time Schedule: The SECOND WORLD WAR IN COLOUR
(A TWI/Carlton Co-Production for ITV)
Judges Award: BBC Education Online

RTS TELEVISION SPORTS AWARDS
Live Outside Broadcast Coverage Of The Year: TEST CRICKET (A Sunset & Vine Production for C4)
Sports News: OLYMPIC CORRUPTION - CHANNEL 4 NEWS (ITN/Atlantic Television for Channel 4 News)
Sports Documentary: CLASH OF THE TITANS: BENN V EUBANK (BBC Television)
Regional Sports News: DOUGIE WALKER - REPORTING SCOTLAND (BBC Scotland Sport)
Regional Sports Documentary: WORKING CLASS HERO - NEIL JENKINS (BBC Wales)
Regional Sports Programme Of The Year -
Entertainment:
OFFSIDE (BBC Scotland Sport)
Regional Sports Programme Of The Year - Actuality:
FRIDAY SPORTSCENE (BBC Scotland Sport
Regional Sports Presenter Or Commentator: Jonathan Wills (London News Network)
Sports Presenter: Jim Rosenthal (ISN/Carlton/MACh 1 for ITV)
Sports Commentator: Peter Alliss (BBC Sport)
Sports Pundit: Martin Brundle (Chrysalis Sport/United Productions for ITV)
Sports Innovation: SKY SPORTS ACTIVE/INTERACTIVE FOOTBALL (Sky Sports)
Television Image Of The Year: F1: BRITISH GRAND PRIX LIVE - MICHAEL SCHUMACHER CRASH (Chrysalis Sport/United Productions for ITV)
Sports Programme Of The Year - Entertainment:
SPORTS PERSONALITY OF THE CENTURY (BBC Sport)
Sports Programme Of The Year - Actuality: SCOTLAND V ENGLAND (Sky Sports)
Television Sports Award Of The Year: TEST CRICKET (A Sunset & Vine Production for C4)
Judges' Award: Bill McLaren

RTS TELEVISION JOURNALISM AWARDS
News Award - International: NINE OíCLOCK NEWS - DILI INDONESIA (BBC News)
News Award - Home: CHANNEL 4 NEWS - The PADDINGTON CRASH & ITS CAUSES (ITN for C4)
Regional Daily News Magazine: LOOK NORTH (BBC North East and Cumbria)
News Event Award: SKY NEWS - KOSOVO LIBERATION DAY (Sky News)
Television Technician Of The Year: Miguel Gil (APTN)
Interviewer Of The Year: Tim Sebastian for BBC News
Regional Current Affairs: LONDON TONIGHT SPECIAL - SOHO BOMBING (London News Network)
Current Affairs - International: DISPATCHES - PRIME SUSPECTS (Hardcash for C4)
Current Affairs - Home: BLACK BRITAIN SPECIAL -

WHY STEPHEN? (BBC News)
Production Award: CHANNEL 4 NEWS (ITN for C4)
Television Journalist Of The Year: John Simpson for BBC News
Young Journalist Of The Year: Matthew Price for BBC Newsround
Specialist Journalism: Susan Watts for BBC News
Programme Of The Year: TONIGHT WITH TREVOR McDONALD (Granada Television)
Judges Award: Michael Brunson

RTS CRAFT & DESIGN AWARDS
(Awarded in London 25 November 1999)

Production Design - Drama: Alice Normington for GREAT EXPECTATIONS (A BBC/WGBH Boston Co-Production for BBC2)
Production Design - Entertainment & Non-Drama: Simon Jago for CHANNEL 4 NEWS (Jago Design for C4)
Costume Design - Drama: Susannah Buxton for SHOOTING THE PAST (A Talkback Production for BBC2)
Make-Up - Drama: Ann Humphreys for GIRLS NIGHT (Granada Film)
Make-Up: Non-Drama: Helen Barrett for The GREATEST RORY EVER TOLD (Made By Vera for C4)
Graphic Design - Channel Idents: Jane Wyatt & Sean De Sparengo for CHRISTMAS ON BBC TWO (BBC2)
Graphic Design - Titles: Paul Baguley MAD FOR IT (Carlton Television)
Graphic Design - Programme Content Sequences: Sarah Grigg, Howard Jones & Marlon Griffin for SUPERNATURAL
(John Downer Productions for BBC1)
Lighting, Photography & Camera - Photography Drama: David Odd for GREAT EXPECTATIONS (BBC/WGBH (Boston) for BBC2)
Lighting, Photography & Camera - Photography Documentary & Factual & Non-Drama Production: Jacek Petrycki for KOSOVO - The VALLEY (Mentorn Barraclough Carey for C4)
Lighting, Photography & Camera - Lighting For Multicamera: Bernie Davis for MASTERWORKS - VAUGHAN WILLIAMS (BBC2)
Lighting, Photography & Camera - Multicamera Work: GLADIATORS Camera Team (London Weekend Television)
Tape & Film Editing - Drama: Beverley Mills Dalziel and Pascoe for BONES AND SILENCE (BBC1)
Tape & Film Editing - Documentary & Factual: Kim Horton Malcolm and Barbara for A LOVE STORY (Granada Television)
Tape & Film Editing - Entertainment & Situation Comedy:
Tony Cranstoun for The ROYLE FAMILY (Granada Television for BBC2)
Sound - Drama: Richard Manton for GREAT EXPECTATIONS (BBC/WGBH (Boston) for BBC2)
Sound - Entertainment & Non-Drama: Patrick Boland for KOSOVO - The VALLEY (Mentorn Barraclough Carey for C4)
Music - Original Title Music: Hal Lindes for RECKLESS - The MOVIE (Granada Television)
Music - Original Score: Murray Gold for QUEER AS FOLK (Red Productions for C4)
Team Award: MASTERWORKS - SIX PIECES OF BRITAIN (BBC2)
Craft & Design Innovation: John Downer, Mark Brownlow, Rod Clarke, Steve Downer, Sarah Grigg, James

Honeyborne, Howard Jones, Susan Macmillan & Tim
Macmillan for SUPERNATURAL (BBC1)
Judges' Award: Cosgrove Hall Films

RTS TECHNOLOGY AWARDS

Innovative Applications: "Specter" Virtual DataCine -
Philips Digital Video Systems
Research & Development: The Commute-Interactive
Project
ITC/ComTel/Convergence/DTI(RA)/Eurobell/GEC-
Marconi/
Sony/Thomson
Special Award: The Digital Television Group
Judges' Award: Digital Services - British Sky Broadcasting

RTS STUDENT TELEVISION AWARDS

Animation: Anwyn Beier for NIGHTLIFE (Edinburgh
College of Art)
Factual: Talya Exrahi & Lewie Kerr for The JAHALIN
(London College of Printing)
Non Factual: Adrian J McDowall, Kara Johnston, Joern
Utkilen, Martin Radich & Monica Heilpern for WHO'S
MY FAVOURITE GIRL? (Edinburgh College of Art)

57th VENICE FILM FESTIVAL

Held 30th August – 9th September 2000 Venice
San Marco, 1364/a Ca'Giustinian
30124 Venice
Tel: 0039 41 5218711
Fax: 0039 41 5227539
Email: das@labiennale.com
Website: 194.185.28.38/
Golden Lion For Best Film: DAYEREH (Iran/Italy) Dir
Jafar Panahi
Jury Grand Prix: BEFORE NIGHT FALLS (US) Dir Julian
Schnabel
Special Director's Award: UTTARA (India) Dir
Buddhadeb Dasgupta
Award For Best Screenplay: Claudio Fava, Monica
Zappelli, Marco Tullio Giordana for I CENTO PASSI
(Italy) Dir Marco Tullio Giordana
Coppa Volpi For Best Actor: Javier Bardem for BEFORE
NIGHT FALLS (US) Dir Julian Schnabel
Coppa Volpi For Best Actress: Rose Byrne for THE
GODDESS OF 1967 (Australia/Hong Kong) Dir Clara Law
Marcello Mastroianni Award: Megan Burns for LIAM
(UK/Germany/Italy) Dir Stephen Frears
Golden Medal of the Italian Senate: LA VIERGE DES
TUEURS (France/Columbia) Dir Barbet Schroeder
Premio Venezia Opera Prima - "Luigi De Laurentiis"
The Jury of Premio Venezia Opera Prima: LA FAUTE À
VOLTAIRE (France) Dir Abdel Kechiche
Golden Lion for Lifetime Achievement: Clint Eastwood
Corto-Cortissimo
The jury of Corto-Cortissimo assigned the following
awards:
The Silver Lion For the Best Short Film: A TELEPHONE
CALL FOR GENEVIEVE SNOW (Australia) by Peter Long
Special Mention: TRAJETS (France/Malasia) by Faouzi
Bensaïdi
Special Mention: SEM MOVIMENTO (Portugal) by
Sandro Aguilar
FIPRESCI Award:
Best Feature - DAYEREH (Iran/Italy) Dir Jafar Panahi
Best First Feature - THOMAS EST AMOREUX
(Belgium/France) Dir Pierre-Paul Renders

This section features some of the principal festival prizes and awards from 1 January 2001 to 30 June 2001. Compiled by Linda Wood

Awards 2001

BAFTA FILM AWARDS

Awarded on 25th February 2001 at The Odeon Leicester Square, London
195 Piccadilly
London W1V OLN
Tel: 020 7734 0022
Fax: 020 7734 1792
Website: www.bafta.org

Academy Fellowship: Albert Finney
Michael Balcon Award For Outstanding British Contribution to Cinema: Mary Selway
Alexander Korda Award For Outstanding British Film of the Year: BILLY ELLIOT (UK) Dir Stephen Daldry
Best Film: GLADIATOR (US) Dir Ridley Scott
David Lean Award For Achievement in Direction: Ang Lee for CROUCHING TIGER, HIDDEN DRAGON (Taiwan/China/US)
Best Screenplay (Original): Cameron Crowe for ALMOST FAMOUS (US) Dir Cameron Crowe
Best Screenplay (Adapted): Stephen Gaghan for TRAFFIC (US) Dir Steven Soderbergh
Performance by an Actress in a Leading Role: Julia Roberts in ERIN BROCKOVICH (US) Dir Steven Soderbergh
Performance by an Actor in a Leading Role: Jamie Bell in BILLY ELLIOT (UK) Dir Stephen Daldry
Performance by an Actress in a Supporting Role: Julie Walters in BILLY ELLIOT (UK) Dir Stephen Daldry
Performance by an Actor in a Supporting Role: Benicio Del Toro in TRAFFIC (US) Dir Steven Soderbergh
Film Not in the English Language: CROUCHING TIGER, HIDDEN DRAGON (Taiwan/China/US) Dir Ang Lee
Anthony Asquith Award For Achievement in Film Music: Tan Dun for CROUCHING TIGER, HIDDEN DRAGON (Taiwan/China/US) Dir Ang Lee
Carl Foreman Award For Most Promising Newcomer to British Film: Pawel Pawlikowski
Best Cinematography: John Mathieson for GLADIATOR (US) Dir Ridley Scott
Best Production Design: Arthur Max for GLADIATOR (US) Dir Ridley Scott
Best Costume Design: Tim Yip for CROUCHING TIGER, HIDDEN DRAGON (Taiwan/China/US) Dir Ang Lee
Best Editing: Pietro Scalia for GLADIATOR (US) Dir Ridley Scott
Best Sound: Jeff Wexler, D.M. Hemphill, Rick Kline, Paul Massey, Mike Wilhoit for ALMOST FAMOUS (US) Dir Cameron Crowe
Achievement in Special Visual Effects: Stefen Fangmeier, John Frazier, Walt Conti, Habib Zargarpour, Tim Alexander for THE PERFECT STORM (US) Dir Wolfgang Peterson
Best Make Up/Hair: Rick Baker, Kazuhiro Tsuji, Toni G. Gail Ryan, Sylvia Nava for THE GRINCH (US/Germany) Dir Ron Howard
Best Short Film: SHADOWSCAN (UK) Dir Tinge Krishnan
Best Short Animation: FATHER AND DAUGHTER

(UK/Netherlands) Dir Michael Dudok de Wit
Orange Audience Award: GLADIATOR (US) Dir Ridley Scott

BAFTA TELEVISION CRAFT AWARDS

Awarded in London on 22nd April 2001

Best Costume Design: Yves Barre for THE LEAGUE OF GENTLEMAN (BBC for BBC2)
Best Editing (Factual): Andrew Fegen for DUDLEY MOORE - AFTER THE LAUGHTER (OMNIBUS) (BBC1)
Best Editing (Fiction/Entertainment): Jon Costello for NORTH SQUARE (Channel 4)
Best Make Up & Hair Design: Joan Hills & Christine Greenwood for GORMENGHAST (BBC2)
New Director Factual: Sarah MacDonald for NEWSNIGHT SPECIAL: A FAMILY AFFAIR (BBC2)
New Director Fiction: Dominic Savage for NICE GIRL (BBC2)
New Writer: Ed McCardie for TINSEL TOWN (BBC2)
Original Television Music: Geoffrey Burgon for LONGITUDE (Granada Film, Channel 4)
Photography Factual: Eigil Bryld for WISCONSIN DEATH TRIP (ARENA)(BBC2)
Photography & Lighting Fiction/Entertainment: Peter Hannan for LONGITUDE (Granada Film, Channel 4)
Production Desgin: Eileen Diss and Chris Lowe for LONGITUDE (Granada Film, Channel 4)
Sound Factual: Paul Vigars and Alex Thomson for SOUTH BANK SHOW: SIMON RATTLE ON JUDITH WEIR (ITV)
Sound Fiction/Entertainment: ANNA KARENINA (Channel 4) (Team)
Visual Effects & Graphic Design: GORMENGHAST (BBC2) (Team)
World Productions: Brian Tufano

BAFTA TELEVISION AWARDS

Awarded in London 13th May 2001

Best Actress: Judi Dench for LAST OF THE BLONDE BOMBSHELLS (Working Title Television, HBO Films, BBC1)
Best Actor: Michael Gambon for LONGITUDE (Granada Film, Channel 4)
Best Entertainment Performance: Graham Norton for SO GRAHAM NORTON (So TV, Channel 4)
Comedy Performance: Sacha Baron Cohen for DA ALI G SHOW (Talkback, Channel 4)
The Richard Dimbleby Award For The Best Presenter (Factual, Features and News): Louis Theroux for LOUIS THEROUX'S WEIRD WEEKENDS (BBC2)
Best Single Drama: CARE (BBC Drama, BBC Wales, BBC1)
Best Drama Series: CLOCKING OFF (Red Productins, BBC 1)
Lew Grade Award as voted by readers of the Radio Times: THE REMORSEFUL DAY - INSPECTOR MORSE (Central Independent Television, ITV)
Best Soap: EMMERDALE (Yorkshire Television, ITV)
Best Drama Serial: LONGITUDE (Granada Film, Channel 4)
Best Factual Series or Strand: BRITAIN AT WAR IN COLOUR (Transworld International, Carlton Television, ITV))
Best Entertainment (Programme or Series): SO GRAHAM NORTON (So TV, Channel 4)

Best Comedy (Programme or Series): DA ALI G SHOW (Talkback, Channel 4)
Best Situation Comedy: BLACK BOOKS (Assembly Film and Televison, Channel 4)
Best Features: THE NAKED CHEF (Optomen Television, BBC2)
The Huw Wheldon Award for Specialised Programme or Series (Arts, History, Religion and Science): HOWARD GOODALL'S BIG BANGS (Tiger Aspect, Channel 4)
Best Sport Coverage: SYDNEY OLYMPICS 2000 (BBC Sport)
Best News and Current Affairs Programme: OUT OF AFRICA (Insight News Television, Channel 4)
Best Innovation: BIG BROTHER (Bazal Productions, Channel 4)
The Flaherty Documentary Award: Leo Regan for 100% WHITE (Diverse Production, Channel 4)
The Academy Fellowship: John Thaw
The Alan Clarke Award for Creative Contribution to Television: Ruth Caleb
The Dennis Potter Award: Lynda La Plante
Special BAFTA Awards: Patrick Moore and CORONATION STREET

51TH BERLIN INTERNATIONAL FILM FESTIVAL
Held 7th-18th February 2001, Berlin
Internationale Filmfestspiele Berlin
Potsdamer Straße 5
D-10785 Berlin
Tel: (49) 030 25 920
Fax: (49) 030 25 920 299
Email: info@berlinale.de
Website: www.berlinale.de

INTERNATIONAL JURY
Golden Bear: INTIMACY (France) Dir Patrice Chéreau
Silver Bear (Grand Jury Prize): BEIJING BICYCLE (China/France) Dir Wang Xiaoshuai
Silver Bear - Best Actress: Kerry Fox for INTIMACY (France) Dir Patrice Chéreau
Silver Bear - Best Actor: Benicio Del Toro for TRAFFIC (US) Dir Steven Soderbergh
Silver Bear - Best Director: Lin Cheng-Sheng for BETELNUT BEAUTY (Taiwan/China/France)
Silver Bear (Jury Prize): ITALIAN FOR BEGINNERS (Denmark) Dir Lone Scherfig
Silver Bear - Oustanding Artistic Achievement: Raúl Pérez Cubero for YOU'RE THE ONE (A TALE FROM THEN) (Spain) Dir José Luis Garcia
Golden Bear - Best Short Film: BLACK SOUL (Canada) Dir Martine Chartrand
Silver Bear - Best Short Film: JUNGLE JAZZ: PUBLIC ENEMY #1 (US) Dir Frank Fitzpatrick
Blue Angel (AGICOA Copyright) Prize for Best European Film: INTIMACY (France) Dir Patrice Chéreau
Alfred Bauer Prize for Debut Film: THE SWAMP (Argentina/Spain) Dir Lucrecia Martel
The Piper Heidsieck New Talent Award for Best Young Actress: Angelica Lee Sinje for BETELNUT BEAUTY (Taiwan/China/France) Dir Lin Cheng-sheng
The Piper Heidsieck New Talent Award for Best Young Actor: Cui Lin and Li Bin for BEIJING BICYCLE (China/France) Dir Wang Xiaoshuai
Honorary Golden Bear: Kirk Douglas

OTHER AWARDS
FIPRESCI (International Critics) Prizes:
Competition - ITALIAN FOR BEGINNERS (Denmark) Dir Lone Scherfig
Forum - DANACH HÄTTE ES SCHÖN SEIN MÜSSEN (Germany) Dir Karin Jurschick
Panorama - MAELSTRÖM (Canada) Dir Denis Villeneuve
Ecumenical Jury Prizes:
Competition - ITALIAN FOR BEGINNERS (Denmark) Dir Lone Scherfig
Forum - DET NYA LANDET (Sweden) Dir Geir Hansteen Jörgensen
Panorama - BLUE END (Switzerland) Dir Kaspar Kasics
Special Prize - WIT (US) Dir Mike Nichols
Peace Film Prize: VIVRE APRÈS - PAROLES DE FEMMES (France) Dir Laurent Bécue-Renard
Wolfgang Staudte Prize: Forum - LOVE/JUICE (Japan) Dir Kaze Shindo
Don Quixote Prize: Forum - KARUNAM (India) Dir Jayaraaj Raja Sekharan Nair
Special Mention - TREMBLING BEFORE G-D (US) Dir Sandi Simcha Dubowski
Special Mention - XIARI NUANYANGYANG (China) Dir Ning Ying
CICAE Prizes: Panorama - LATE NIGHT SHOPPING (UK) Dir Saul Metzstein
Forum - LOVE/JUICE (Japan) Dir Kaze Shindo
Guild of German Art House Cinemas Prize: FINDING FORRESTER (US) Dir Gus Van Sant
Caligari Prize: CRÓNICA DE UN DESAYUNO () Dir Benjamín Cann, E Carranza (Mexico)
NETPAC Prize: Forum - BOOYE KAFOOR, ATRE YAS (Iran) Dir Bahman Farmanara
Special Mention - BEN KHONG CHONG (Vietnam) - Dir Trong Ninh Luu
UIP Berlin Award (European Short Film): Å SE EN BÂT MED SEIL (Norway) Dir Anja Breien
International Jury, Children's Film Festival:
Best Feature Film - NAGISA (Japan) Dir Masaru Konuma
Best Short Film - HOOVES OF FIRE (UK) Dir Richard Goleszowski
Special Mention Feature - IL CIELO CADE (Italy) Dir Andrea Frazzi, Antonio Frazzi
Special Mention Short - LA NOTA FINAL (Spain/Cuba) Dir Malte Rivera Carbone
Crystal Bear, Young People's Jury, Children's Film Festival:
Crystal Bear Best Feature - THERE'S ONLY ONE JIMMY GRIMBLE (UK) Dir John Hay
Special Mention - O BRANCO (Brazil) Dir Ángela Pires, Liliana Sulzbach and THE TESTIMONY OF TALIESIN JONES (UK) Dir Martin Duffy
Crystal Bear Best Short Film - HOOVES OF FIRE (UK) Dir Richard Goleszowski
Reader's Prize of the 'Berliner Morgenpost': ITALIAN FOR BEGINNERS (Denmark) Dir Lone Scherfig
Manfred Satzgeber Prize: À MA SOEUR! (France) Dir Catherine Breillat
Panorama Short Film Prize of the New York Film Academy: TYR (Ukraine) Dir Taras Tomenko
Special Mention - JE T'AIME JOHN WAYNE (UK) Dir Toby MacDonald
Special Mention - VETA (Macedonia) Dir Teona Strugar Mitevska
Panorama Audience Prize: BERLIN IS IN GERMANY (Germany) Dir Hannes Stöhr
Gay Teddy Bear for Best Feature: HEDWIG AND THE

ANGRY INCH (US) Dir John Cameron Mitchell
Gay Teddy Bear for Best Documentary: TREMBLING BEFORE G-D (US) Dir Sandi Simcha Dubowski
Gay Teddy Bear for Best Short: ERÈ MÈLA MÈLA () Dir Daniel Wiroth
Gay Teddy Bear Jury Award: FORBIDDEN FRUIT (Zimbabwe/Germany) Dir Sue Maluwa-Bruce
Special Teddy: Moritz de Hadeln
Reader's Prize of the 'Siegessäule' [Berlin's gay/lesbian magazine]: SA TREE LEX (Thailand) Dir Yongyooth Thongkonthun
Reader's Prize of the 'Berliner Zeitung': WERCKMEISTER HARMÓNIÁK (Hungary/Germany) Dir Béla Tarr

BROADCASTING PRESS GUILD TELEVISION AND RADIO AWARDS 2000
Awarded in London 29th March 2001

c/o Richard Last
Tiverton, The Ridge
Woking
Surrey GU22 7EQ
Tel: 01483 764895

Best Single Drama: LONGITUDE (Granada Film, Channel 4)
Best Drama Series: NORTH SQUARE (Company Pictures, Channel 4)
Best Documentary Series: A HISTORY OF BRITAIN (BBC2)
Best Single Documentary: WHO BOMBED OMAGH? (Panorama for BBC1)
Best Entertainment: MARION AND GEOFF (BBC2)
Best Actor: Phil Davies for NORTH SQUARE (Company Pictures, Channel 4)
Best Actress: Helen McCrory for NORTH SQUARE (Company Pictures, Channel 4)
Best Performer: Graham Norton for SO GRAHAM NORTON (So TV, Channel 4)
Writer's Award: Peter Moffat for NORTH SQUARE (Company Pictures, Channel 4) and Simon Schama A HISTORY OF BRITAIN (BBC2)
Radio Programme of the Year: DEAD RINGERS (BBC Radio 4)
Radio Broadcaster of the Year: Nick Clarke for THE WORLD AT ONE (BBC Radio 4)
Multichannel Award: BALACLAVA (Cromwell Productions for the History Channel)
Harvey Lee Award for Outstanding Contribution to Broadcasting: Ted Childs.

54th CANNES FESTIVAL
Held in Cannes 9th to 20th May 2001

Feature Film Palme D'Or: THE SON'S ROOM (Italy) Dir Nanni Moretti
Grand Prix of the Jury: THE PIANO PLAYER (France/Austria) Dir Michael Haneke
Best Actress: Isabelle Huppert for THE PIANO PLAYER (France/Austria) Dir Michael Haneke
Best Actor: Benoît Magimel for THE PIANO PLAYER (France/Austria) Dir Michael Haneke
Best Director: Joel Coen for THE MAN WHO WASN'T THERE (US) and David Lynch for MULHOLLAND DRIVE (US)
Best Screenplay: NO MAN'S LAND (France/Belgium/Italy/Slovenia) from Danis Tanovic
Technical Prize: Tuu Duu-Chih for MILLENNIUM

MAMBO (Taiwan) Dir Hou Hsiao-Hsien and NI NEI PIEN CHI TIEN (Taiwan) Dir Tsai Ming-Liang
Caméra d'or Winner: ATANARJUAT, THE FAST RUNNER (Canada) Dir Zacharias Kunuk
Short Film Palme D'Or: BEAN CAKE (Japan) Dir David Greenspan
Jury Prize: PIZZA PASSIONATA (Finland)Dir Kari Juusonen
Special Jury Prize: DADDY'S GIRL (UK)Dir Irvine Allan

26th CÉSARS
Awarded in Paris 24th February 2001

Best French Film: LE GOÛT DES AUTRES (France) Dir Agnès Jaoui
Best Actor: Sergi Lopez for HARRY, UN AMI QUI VOUS VEUT DU BIEN (France) Dir Dominik Moll
Best Actress: Dominique Blanc for STAND-BY (France) Dir Roch Stéphanik
Best Supporting Actor: Gérard Lanvin for LE GOÛT DES AUTRES (France) Dir Agnès Jaoui
Best Supporting Actress: Anne Alvaro for LE GOÛT DES AUTRES (France) Dir Agnès Jaoui
Best Director: Dominik Moll for HARRY, UN AMI QUI VOUS VEUT DU BIEN (France)
Best Foreign Film: IN THE MOOD FOR LOVE (Hong Kong/France) Dir Wong Kar-wai
Best First Feature Film: RESSOURCES HUMAINES (France/UK) Dir Laurent Cantet
Best Short Film: SALAM (France) Dir Souad El Bouhati and UN PETIT AIR DE FÊTE (France) Dir Eric Guirado
Best Original or Adapted Screenplay: Agnès Jaoui and Jean-Pierre Bacri for LE GOÛT DES AUTRES (France) Dir Agnès Jaoui
Best Art Direction: Jean Rabasse for VATEL (France/US) Dir Roland Joffé
Best Cinematography: Agnès Godard for BEAU TRAVAIL (France) Dir Claire Dennis
Best Costume Design: Edith Vesperini and Jean-Daniel Vuillermoz for SAINT-CYR (France/Germany/Belgium) Dir Patricia Mazury
Best Editing: Yannick Kergoat for HARRY, UN AMI QUI VOUS VEUT DU BIEN (France) Dir Dominik Moll
Best Music: Tomatito, Sheikh Ahmad Al Tuni, La Caita, and Tony Gatlif for VENGO (France) Dir Tony Gatlif
Best Sound: François Maurel, Gérard Lamps and Gérard Hardy for HARRY, UN AMI QUI VOUS VEUT DU BIEN (France) Dir Dominik Moll
Best Newcomer, Actor: Jalil Lespert for RESSOURCES HUMAINES (France/UK) Dir Laurent Cantet
Best Newcomer, Actress: Sylvie Testud, LES BLESSURES ASSASSINES (France) Dir Jean-Pierre Denis
Honorary Cesars:
Darry Cowl
Charlotte Rampling
Agnès Varda

EVENING STANDARD BRITISH FILM AWARDS

Awarded in London 4th February 2001
Best Film: Topsy-Turvy (UK/US) Dir Mike Leigh
Best Actor: Jim Broadbent for Topsy-Turvy (UK/US) Dir Mike Leigh
p Actress: Julie Walters for Billy Elliot (UK) Dir Stephen Daldry
Peter Sellers Award for Comedy: Peter Lord and Nick Park for Chicken Run (US/UK)

Best Screenplay: Neil Jordan for The End Of The Affair (US/Germany) Dir Neil Jordan
Most Promising Newcomer: Jamie Bell in BILLY ELLIOT (UK) Dir Stephen Daldry
Technical Achievement: Andrew Saunders for THE GOLDEN BOWL (UK/France/US) Dir James Ivory
Best Documentary: INTO THE ARMS OF STRANGERS: STORIES OF THE KINDERTRANSPORT (US) Dir Mark Jonathan Harris
Special Award: Peter Yates

58th GOLDEN GLOBE AWARDS
Awarded 21st January 2001, Los Angeles
Hollywood Foreign Press Association
646 North Robertson Boulevard
West Hollywood
California 90069
Tel.(310) 657 1731
Fax.(310) 657 5576
Email: hfpa95@aol.com
Web site: www.hfpa.com

FILM
Best Motion Picture - Drama: GLADIATOR (US) Dir Ridley Scott
Best Motion Picture - Musical or Comedy: ALMOST FAMOUS (US) Dir Cameron Crowe
Best Director: Ang Lee for CROUCHING TIGER, HIDDERN DRAGON (China/Taiwan/US)
Best Foreign Language Film: CROUCHING TIGER, HIDDERN DRAGON (China/Taiwan/US) Dir Ang Lee
Best Performance by an Actor in a Motion Picture - Drama: Tom Hanks in CAST AWAY (US) Dir Robert Zemeckis
Best Performance by an Actor in a Motion Picture Comedy or Musical: George Clooney in O BROTHER, WHERE ART THOU? (US/France/UK) Dir Joel Coen
Best Performance by an Actor in a Supporting Role in a Motion Picture: Benecio Del Toro in TRAFFIC (US) Dir Steven Soderbergh
Best Performance by an Actress in a Motion Picture - Comedy or Musical: Renee Zellweger in NURSE BETTY (US) Dir Neil LaBute
Best Performance by an Actress in a Motion Picture - Drama: Julia Roberts in ERIN BROCKOVICH (US) Dir Steven Soderbergh
Best Performance by an Actress in a Supporting Role in a Motion Picture: Kate Hudson in ALMOST FAMOUS (US) Dir Cameron Crowe
Best Screenplay - Motion Picture: Stephen Gaghan in TRAFFIC (US) Dir Steven Soderbergh
Best Original Score - Motion Picture: Hans Zimmer, Lisa Gerrard for GLADIATOR (US) Dir Ridley Scott
Best Original Song - Motion Picture: Bob Dylan for Things Have Changed from WONDER BOYS (US/Germany/UK/Japan) Dir Curtis Hanson

TELEVISION
Best Mini-Series or Motion Picture Made for Television: DIRTY PICTURES (Manheim Company, MGM Television Entertainment, Showtime)
Best Performance by an Actor in a Mini-Series or a Motion Picture made for Television: Brian Dennehy in DEATH OF A SALESMAN (Showtime)
Best Performance by an Actor in a Supporting Role in a Series, Mini-Series or Motion Picture Made for Televison: Robert Downey Jr. in ALLY MCBEAL (Twentieth Century-Fox Television, David E Kelley)

Best Performance by an Actor in a Television Series - Drama: Martin Sheen THE WEST WING (Warner Bros. Television, John Wells Productions)
Best Performance by an Actor in a Television Series - Musical or Comedy: Kelsey Grammer in FRASIER (Paramount Television, Grub Street)
Best Performance by an Actress in a Mini-Series or a Motion Picture made for Television: Judi Dench in THE LAST OF THE BLONDE BOMBSHELLS (Working Title Television for BBC)
Best Performance by an Actress in a Supporting Role in a Series, Mini-Series or Motion Picture Made for Televison: Vanessa Redgrave in IF THESE WALLS COULD TALK II (Moving Pictures)
Best Performance by an Actress in a Television Series - Drama Sela Ward in ONCE AND AGAIN (Bedford Falls Productions, Touchstone Television)
Best Performance by an Actress in a Television Series - Musical or Comedy: Sarah Jessica Parker in SEX AND THE CITY (Darren Star Productions, HBO)
Best Television Series - Drama: THE WEST WING (NBC, John Wells Productions, Warner Bros. TV)
Best Television Series - Musical or Comedy: SEX AND THE CITY (Darren Star Productions, HBO)

41st GOLDEN ROSE OF MONTREUX
Held 26th April – 1st May 2001, Montreux
Télévision Suisse Romande
Quai E. Anserment 20
P.O. Box 234
CH-1211 Geneva 8
Tel: (41) 22 708 89 98
Fax: (41) 22 781 52 49
Email: Sarah.Fanchini@tsr.ch
Website: www.rosedor.ch

Rose d'or: LENNY HENRY IN PIECES (UK) Tiger Aspect Productions, BBC
Honorary Rose: Rudi Carrell
COMEDY
Silver Rose: MIRCOMANIA (Germany) Zeitsprung Film TV Produktions & Brainpool TV
Bronze Rose: ALI G (UK) Talkback, Channel 4
MUSIC
Silver Rose: DON GIOVANNI UNMASKED Rhombus Media
Bronze Rose: BADEN POWELL – VELHO AMIGO (France) G2 Films
SITCOM
Silver Rose: COUPLING (UK) Hartswood Films
Bronze Rose: BLACK BOOKS (UK) Assembley Film and Television, Channel 4
GAMES SHOW
Silver Rose: THE WEAKEST LINK (UK)BBC2
Bronze Rose: THE VAULT (Israel) Keshet Broadcasting & Menta Productions
VARIETY:
Silver Rose: POPSTARS (UK) LWT – London Weekend Television
Bronze Rose: THE BEST OF TV TOTAL (Germany) Raab TV Produktion
ARTS & SPECIAL
Special Prize of the City of Montreux : THE JOEL FILES (Austria) DoRo Productions Vienna
Press Prize: FREDDIE MERCURY – THE UNTOLD STORY (Austria) DoRo Productions Vienna
UNDA Prize: THE THING ABOUT VINCE (UK) Carlton Television

INDIAN INTERNATIONAL FILM ACADEMY AWARDS

The Kelvinator IIFA Awards
Held in Johannesberg, South Africa on 17 May 2001
Website: www.iifa.com

POPULAR AWARD CATERGORY

Best Director: Rakesh Roshan for KAHO NAA… PYAAR HAI
Best Picture: KAHO NAA… PYAAR HAI
Lyrics: Javed Akhtar for REFUGEE: Panchhi Nadiyan Pawan Ke
Performance In A Negative Role: Sushant Singh in JUNGLE
Performance In A Comic Role: Paresh Rawal in HERA PHERI
Actress In A Supporting Role: Jaya Bachchan in FIZA
Actor In A Supporting Role: Amitabh Bachchan in MOHABBATEIN
Music Direction: Rajesh Roshan for KAHO NAA… PYAAR HAI
Male Playback Singer: Lucky Ali for KAHO NAA… PYAAR HAI: Ek Pal Ka Jeena
Female Playback Singer: Alka Yagnik for KAHO NAA… PYAAR HAI: Kaho Naa… Pyaar Hai
Best Story: Aditya Chopra for MOHABBATEIN
Actress In A Leading Role: Karisma Kapoor in FIZA
Actor In A Leading Role: Hrithik Roshan in KAHO NAA… PYAAR HAI

TECHNICAL AWARD CATEGORY

Sound Recording: Sona Chaudhary for JUNGLE
Costume Designer: Manish Malhotra /Karan Johar for MOHABBATEIN
Song Recording: Satish Gupta for KAHO NAA… PYAAR HAI
Art Direction: Nitin Desai for JOSH
Dialogue: O.P.Dutta for REFUGEE
Choreography: Farah Khan for KAHO NAA.. PYAAR HAI: Ek Pal Ka Jeena
Cinematography: Binod Pradhan for MISSION KASHMIR **Background Score:** Aadesh Shrivastava for REFUGEE **Editing:** Sanjay Verma for KAHO NAA… PYAAR HAI **Screenplay:** Honey Irani for Kya Kehna
Sound Re-recording: Hitendra Ghosh for Jungle
Special Effects (Visual): Rajtaru Videosonic Limited for PHIR BHI DIL HAI HINDUSTANI

SPECIAL AWARD

Invaluable Contribution to Indian Cinema: Waheeda Rehman
Invaluable Contribution to Indian Cinema: Shammi Kapoor

41st MONTE CARLO TELEVISION FESTIVAL

Held 16-21st February Monte Carlo

TELEVISION FILMS

Gold Nymphs:
Best Film: DIRTY PICTURES (US) Showtime, MGM
Best Script: Max Färberböck for JENSEITS (Germany) ZDF -Allemagne
Best Direction: Max Färberböck for JENSEITS (Germany) ZDF -Allemagne
Best Actor: Nikolai Volkov in THAT ORCHARD FULL OF MOON (Russia) Pelican Film Studio Russie
Best Actress: Zinaida Sharko in THAT ORCHARD FULL OF MOON (Russia) Pelican Film Studio Russie
Special mention: Tatiana Vilhemova in SPOLECNICE (Czech Republic) Télévision Tchèque /Czech Television.

MINI-SERIES

Best Mini-Series: UN PIC NIC CHEZ OSIRIS (France) Mag Bodard, SFP, France 2
Best Script: Guy Hibbert for THE RUSSIAN BRIDE (UK) ITV
Best Direction: John Strickland for REBEL HEART (UK) BBC Northern Ireland
Best Actor: Ino Manfredi in UNA STORIA QUALUNQUE (Italy)RAI Uno
Best Actress: Marina Hands for UN PIC NIC CHEZ OSIRIS (France) Mag Bodard, SFP, France 2
Special mention: THE NEW COUNTRY (Sweden) Göta

NEWS PROGRAMMES

Best News Programme: THE MOZANBIQUE FLOODS (UK)
Silver Nymph: PALESTINIAN UPRISING -
Best Current Affairs Programme: KURSK - TRAGEDY IN THE BARENTS SEA (Norway) - TV2 Norvege/ Norway
Silver Nymph: CONVOY TO MOLDOVA - CORRESPONDENT (UK) BBC World
Special Mention: BLACK SEPTEMBER IN EAST TIMOR (Japan) NHK

SPECIAL PRIZES

The Special Prize of H.S.H. Prince Rainier III: KAMPEN OM KLIMAET (Denmark) Lars Mortensen TV Production
Prize of The Monaco Red Cross: CONVOY TO MOLDOVA - CORRESPONDENT (UK) BBC World
UNESCO Prize Fiction: L'ENFANT DE LA NUIT, COLLECTION "COMBATS DE FEMMES" (France) Capa Drama
UNESCO Prize Facts: THE DIAMOND TRAGEDY (Czech Republic) République Tchèque, Czech Republic
UNDA Prize Fiction: UN DONO SEMPLICE (Italy) RAI Due
UNDA Prize News: CONVOY TO MOLDOVA CORRESPONDENT (UK) BBC World
European Producer Award: GTV (France) for its fiction production over the last two years

73rd OSCARS -ACADEMY OF MOTION PICTURE ARTS AND SCIENCES

Awarded 25 March 2001, Los Angeles

Best Film: GLADIATOR (US) Dir Ridley Scott
Best Director: Steven Soderbergh for TRAFFIC (US)
Best Actor: Russell Crowe GLADIATOR (US) Dir Ridley Scott
Best Supporting Actor: Benicio Del Toro for TRAFFIC (US) Dir Steven Soderbergh
Best Actress: Julia Roberts for ERIN BROCKOVICH (US) Dir Steven Soderbergh
Best Supporting Actress: Marcia Gay Harden for POLLOCK (US)
Best Art Direction: Tim Yip for CROUCHING TIGER, HIDDEN DRAGON (Taiwan/China/US) Dir Ang Lee
Best Cinematography: Peter Pau CROUCHING TIGER, HIDDEN DRAGON (Taiwan/China/US) Dir Ang Lee
Best Costume Design: Janty Yates for GLADIATOR (US) Dir Ridley Scott
Best Documentary Short: BIG MAMA (US) Dir Tracy Seretean
Best Documentary Feature: INTO THE ARMS OF STRANGERS: STORIES OF THE KINDERTRANSPORT (US) Dir Mark Jonathan Harris
Best Film Editing: Stephen Mirrione for TRAFFIC (US) Dir Steven Soderbergh
Best Foreign Language Film:
CROUCHING TIGER, HIDDEN DRAGON (Taiwan, China, US) Dir Ang Lee

Best Make Up: Rick Baker, Gail Ryan for DR. SEUSS' HOW THE GRINCH STOLE CHRISTMAS (US) Dir Ron Howard
Best Music (Score): CROUCHING TIGER, HIDDEN DRAGON (Taiwan/China/US) Dir Ang Lee
Best Music (Song): Bob Dylan for "Things Have Changed" from WONDER BOYS (US/Germany/UK/Japan) Dir Curtis Hanson
Best Short - Live Action: QUIERO SER (Germany) Dir Florian Gallenberger
Best Short Animated: FATHER AND DAUGHTER (UK/Holland) Dir Michael Dudok de Wit
Best Sound: Scott Millan, Bob Beemer, Ken Weston for GLADIATOR (US) Dir Ridley Scott
Best Sound Editing: Jon Johnson for U-571 (US) Dir Jonathan Mostow
Best Visual Effects: John Nelson, Neil Corbould, Tim Burke, Rob Harvey for GLADIATOR (US) Dir Ridley Scott
Best Screenplay (Adapted): Stephen Gaghan for TRAFFIC (US) Dir Steven Soderbergh
Best Screenplay (Original): Cameron Crowe for ALMOST FAMOUS (Dir Cameron Crowe)
Honorary Oscars: Jack Cardiff, Ernest Lehman

ROYAL TELEVISION SOCIETY AWARDS
RTS PROGRAMME AWARDS
Awarded in London

RTS PROGRAMME AWARDS
Situation Comedy/Comedy Drama: THE ROYLE FAMILY (A Granada Production for BBC 1)
Entertainment: DA ALI G SHOW (A TalkBack Production for Channel 4)
Single Documentary: 100% WHITE - TRUE STORIES (A Diverse Production for Channel 4)
Documentary Series: 15 (A Windfall Film Production for Channel 4)
Documentary Strand: CORRESPONDENT (BBC News for BBC 2)
Regional Documentay: SPOTLIGHT: CAPITOL HILL (BBC Northern Ireland)
Regional Programme: NEW FOUND LAND: I SAW YOU (Umbrella Productions/Scottish Screen/Scottish Television for Grampian Television)
Regional Presenter: Stephen Jardine, Scottish Television
Features - Daytime: WATERCOLOUR CHALLENGE A (Planet 24 Production for Channel 4)
Features - Primetime: BIG BROTHER (Bazal (part of Endemol UK Entertainment) for Channel 4)
Children's Drama: MY PARENTS ARE ALIENS (Granada Media Children's for ITV)
Children's Entertainment: SM:TV LIVE (Blaze Television for ITV)
Children's Factual: BLUE PETER (BBC Children's for BBC 1)
Presenter: Graham Norton SO GRAHAM NORTON (A So Television Production for Channel 4)
Arts: ARENA: WISCONSIN DEATH TRIP (BBC Specialist Factual for BBC 2)
Network Newcomer - On Screen: Rob Brydon in MARION AND GEOFF (BBC Entertainment for BBC 2)
Network Newcomer - Behind the Screen: Liza Marshall for THE SINS (BBC1)
Television Performance: Julia Davis for HUMAN REMAINS (A Baby Cow Production for BBC 2)
Single Drama: STORM DAMAGE (BBC Drama for BBC 2)
Drama Serial: NATURE BOY (BBC Drama for BBC 2)
Drama Series: CLOCKING OFF (Red Production Company for BBC 1)

Actor - Female: Katy Murphy for DONOVAN QUICK (Making Waves Film & Television for BBC Scotland)
Actor - Male: Steven Mackintosh for CARE (BBC Drama for BBC 1)
Writer: Paul Abbott for CLOCKING OFF (Red Production Company for BBC 1)
Team: BIG BROTHER (Bazal (part of Endemol UK Entertainment) for Channel 4)
Cyril Bennett Judges' Award: John Willis

RTS TELEVISION JOURNALISM AWARDS
News Award - International: ZIMBABWE FARM - BBC NEWS AT NINE O'CLOCK (BBC News for BBC 1)
News Award Home: WHAT CAUSED HATFIELD? Channel 4 News (ITN for Channel 4)
Regional Daily News Magazine: SCOTLAND TODAY (Scottish Television)
News Event: BELGRADE REVOLUTION BBC News 24 BBC
Television Technician of the Year: Andy Rex ITV News (ITN for ITV)
Interviewer of the Year: Tim Sebastian (BBC)
Regional Current Affairs: LIFE AND DEATH OF AN IRA QUARTERMASTER: SPOTLIGHT (BBC Northern Ireland)
Current Affairs - International: LICENCE TO KILL – CORRESPONDENT (BBC 2)
Current Affairs Home: WHO BOMBED OMAGH? – PANORAMA (BBC 1)
Production Award: Photo Journalism – Channel 4 News (ITN for Channel 4)
Television Journalist of the Year: John Ware (BBC)
Young Journalist of the Year: Nicola Pearson (BBC)
Specialist Journalism: Nicholas Glass (ITN for Channel 4)
Programme of the Year: WHO BOMBED OMAGH? Panorama (BBC 1)
Judges Award: Peter Taylor

RTS STUDENT TELEVISION AWARDS
Animation: HOURGLASS Matthew Hood, Douglas Ray, Kieron Connolly, Alastair Reid, Simon Chase & Ruben Kenig (National Film & Television School)
Factual: HAMMAM MEMORIES Peggy Vassiliou (Goldsmiths' College)
Non-Factual: LOSING TOUCH Sarah Gavron, Jonny Persey, Antonia Baldo, David Katznelson, Jane Harwood, Riaz Meer, Maj-Linn Preiss & Tara Creme (National Film & Television School)

RTS CRAFT & DESIGN AWARDS
Production Design - Drama: Christopher Hobbs for GORMENGHAST (BBC Drama for BBC 2)
Production Design - Entertainment & Non-Drama: Grenville Horner for THE LEAGUE OF GENTLEMEN (BBC Entertainment for BBC 2)
Visual Effects: Framestore for ALICE IN WONDERLAND (Hallmark Entertainment in Association with NBC for Channel 4)
Costume Design - Drama: James Keast for WARRIORS (BBC Films in Association with Deep IndigoProductions for BBC 1)
Costume Design - Entertainment & On-Drama: Yves Barre for THE LEAGUE OF GENTLEMEN (BBC Entertainment for BBC 2)
Make-up Design - Drama: Lisa Westcott for WIVES & DAUGHTERS (BBC Drama for BBC 1)
Make-up Design - Entertainment & Non-Drama: Heather Squire for ALISTAIR MCGOWAN'S BIG IMPRESSION (Vera for BBC 1)

Graphic Design - Trails & Packaging: Simon Pullinger for DON'T MENTION THE SCORE (Television Department for ONdigital)

Graphic Design - Titles: Garth Jennings and Dan Mazer for ALI G (Hammer & Tongs/Talkback Productions for Channel 4)

Graphic Design: Programme Contents Sequences: Rob Hifle, Alan Short and Stefan Narjoram for PREDATORS BBC (Natural History Unit/Burrell Durrant Hifle for BBC 1)

Lighting, Photography & Camera - Photography Drama: Gavin Finney for GORMENGHAST (BBC Drama for BBC 2)

Lighting, Photography & Camera: Photography Documentary & Factual and Non-Drama Productions: Sorious Samura for OUT OF AFRICA (An Insight News Production for Channel 4)

Lighting, Photography & Camera: Lighting For Multicamera: Tom Kinane and Alan Fawcus for SM:TV LIVE/CD:UK (Blaze TV for ITV)

Lighting, Photography & Camera: Multicamera Work: Michael Lingard and Simon Stafforth for BIG BROTHER (Bazal Productions for Channel 4)

Tape & Film Editing - Drama: Philip Kloss for DAVID COPPERFIELD (BBC Drama for BBC 1)

Tape & Film Editing - Documentary & Factual: Dave King for A WEDDING IN THE FAMILY (United Productions for Channel 4)

Tape & Film Editing - Entertainment & Situation Comedy: Perry Widdowson, Paul Richmond, Steve Murray and Peter Spink for WHO WANTS TO BE A MILLIONAIRE? (Celador for ITV)

Sound - Drama: Maurice Hillier, Danny Longhurst, Graham Headicar and David Old for WARRIORS (BBC Films in Association with Deep Indigo Productions for BBC 1)

Sound - Entertainment & Non-Drama: Tim Summerhayes and John Middleton for FIGARO LIVE (Fleetwood for BBC Classical Music for BBC 2)

Music - Original Title Music: Joby Talbot for THE LEAGUE OF GENTLEMEN (BBC Entertainment for BBC 2)

Music - Original Score: Debbie Wiseman for WARRIORS (BBC Films in Association with Deep Indigo Productions for BBC 1)

Team Award: Richard Hopkins, Ruth Wrigley & Conrad Green for BIG BROTHER (Bazal Productions for Channel 4)

Design & Craft Innovation: Mike Milne and Jez Harris for WALKING WITH DINOSAURS (BBC Science for BBC 1)

Picture Manipulation: Phil Moss, Gerry Gedge, Steve Moore and Maggie Choyce for THE SECOND WORLD WAR IN COLOUR (A TWI/Carlton Co-Production for ITV)

Lifetime Achievement Award: Edward Roberts

Judges' Award: Framestore

RTS TELEVISION SPORTS AWARDS

Held at London Hilton, Park Laneon Thursday 24 May 2001

Live Outside Broadcast Coverage of the Year: SYDNEY OLYMPIC GAMES: MEN'S COXLESS FOURS 'REDGRAVE DAY' (BBC Sport)

Sports News: FOOTBALL VIOLENCE - ITV EVENING NEWS (ITN for ITV)

Sports Documentary: FOOTBALL STORIES: MAN IN BLACK (A Scottish Television Production for Channel 4)

Regional Sports Documentary: CHESTER CITY - AN AMERICAN DREAM (Granada Television)

Regional Sports Programme of the Year - Entertainment: RUGBY LEAGUE RAW (Yorkshire Television)

Regional Sports Programme of the Year - Actuality: SLAM XXL (Yorkshire-Tyne Tees Television)

Regional Sports Presenter or Commentator: Alistair Mann (Granada Television)

Sports Presenter: Mark Nicholas (Sunset & Vine for Channel 4)

Sports Commentator: Clive Tyldesley (ISN/Carlton for ITV Sport)

Sports Pundit: Alan Hansen (BBC Sport)

Sports Programme of the Year - Entertainment: A QUESTION OF SPORT (BBC Manchester for BBC 1)

Sports Programme of the Year - Actuality: SYDNEY OLYMPIC GAMES: FREEMAN/EDWARDS NIGHT (BBC Sport)

Creative Sports Sequence: SPORTS PERSONALITY OF THE YEAR: REVIEW OF THE DOMESTIC FOOTBALL SEASON (BBC Sport)

Judges' Award: BBC Coverage: SYDNEY OLYMPIC GAMES 2000

Lifetime Achievement Award: Murray Walker OBE

Gold Medal: John Bromley OBE

RTS EDUCATIONAL AWARDS 2000

SCHOOLS TELEVISION

Pre-School & Infants: TELETUBBIES - SCRAPBOOK (Ragdoll for BBC Education/ Children's BBC)

Primary Literacy & Numeracy: PUZZLE MATHS 2: MULTIPLICATION AND DIVISION Double Exposure for (Channel 4)

Primary Arts & Humanities: DREAM ON (The Resource Base for Channel 4)

Primary & Secondary Science & Maths: STAGE ONE - GROWING PLANTS: HOW DO PLANTS GROW AND CHANGE? (Television Junction for Channel 4)

Secondary Arts & Language: THE ENGLISH PROGRAMME: FILM FOCUS – THE FILMS OF BAZ LUHRMANN: ROMEO AND JULIET (Double Exposure and Film Education for Channel 4)

Secondary Humanities: HISTORY FILE: THE COLD WAR - U-2 AND THE ARMS RACE (Lodestar Productions for BBC Education)

Primary & Secondary Multimedia & Interactive: TVM - PUZZLE MATHS (Double Exposure and Cimex Media for Channel 4)

ADULT EDUCATIONAL TELEVISION

Vocational Training: STUDENT ESSENTIALS (A Wobbly Picture Production for BBC Education)

Single Programme: WHEN I GET OLDER.... (BBC for BBC Adult Learning)

Campaigns & Seasons – Rts/Niace Award: ADOPTION ON TRIAL (Channel 4)

Educational Impact In The Prime Time Schedule: NEANDERTHAL (A Wall to Wall Production for Channel 4)

Judges' Award: Andrew Bethell, Director Double Exposure

RTS TECHNOLOGICAL INNOVATION AWARDS

Innovative Applications: Assisted Subtitling, BBC, 20/20 Speech and Softel

Research And Development: Standard Media Exchange Framework, BBC Distribution & Technology

Judges' Award: The BBC DTT Technical Team

British Successes in the Academy Awards 1927–2000

The following list chronicles British successes in the Academy Awards. It includes individuals who were either born, and lived and worked, in Britain into their adult lives, or those who were not born here but took on citizenship.
Compiled by Erinna Mettler

(1st) 1927/28 held in 1930

Charles Chaplin
- **Special Award (acting, producing, directing and writing):** THE CIRCUS

(2nd) 1928/29 held in 1930

Frank Lloyd
- **Best Direction:** THE DIVINE LADY

(3rd) 1929/30 held in 1930

George Arliss
- **Best Actor:** THE GREEN GODDESS

(6th) 1932/33 held in 1934

William S. Darling
- **Best Art Direction:** CAVALCADE
Charles Laughton
- **Best Actor:** THE PRIVATE LIFE OF HENRY VIII
Frank Lloyd
- **Best Direction:** CAVALCADE

(8th) 1935 held in 1936

Gaumont British Studios
- **Best Short Subject:** WINGS OVER MT. EVEREST
Victor Mclaglen
- **Best Actor:** THE INFORMER

(11th) 1938 held in 1939

Ian Dalrymple, Cecil Lewis & W.P. Lipscomb
- **Best Screenplay:** PYGMALION

(12th) 1939 held in 1940

Robert Donat
- **Best Actor:** GOODBYE MR. CHIPS

Vivien Leigh
- **Best Actress:** GONE WITH THE WIND

(13th) 1940 held in 1941

Lawrence Butler & Jack Whitney
- **Special Visual Effects:** THE THIEF OF BAGDAD
Vincent Korda
- **Best Colour Set Design:** THE THIEF OF BAGDAD

(14th) 1941 held in 1942

British Ministry of Information
- **Honorary Award:** TARGET FOR TONIGHT
Donald Crisp
- **Best Supporting Actor:** HOW GREEN WAS MY VALLEY
Joan Fontaine
- **Best Actress:** SUSPICION
Jack Whitney & The General Studios Sound Department
- **Best Sound:** THAT HAMILTON WOMAN

(15th) 1942 held in 1943

Noel Coward
- **Special Award:** IN WHICH WE SERVE
Greer Garson
- **Best Actress:** MRS. MINIVER

(16th) 1943 held in 1944

British Ministry of Information
- **Best Documentary:** DESERT VICTORY
William S. Darling
- **Best Art Direction:** THE SONG OF BERNADETTE

(18th) 1945 held in 1946

The Governments of the United States & Great Britain
- **Best Documentary:** THE TRUE GLORY
Ray Milland
- **Best Actor:** THE LOST WEEKEND
Harry Stradling
- **Best Cinematography (b/w):** THE PICTURE OF DORIAN GRAY

(19th) 1946 held in 1947

Muriel & Sydney Box
- **Best Original Screenplay:** THE SEVENTH VEIL

Clemence Dane
- **Best Original Story:** VACATION FROM MARRIAGE

Olivia de Havilland
- **Best Actress:** TO EACH HIS OWN

Laurence Olivier
- **Special Award:** HENRY V

Thomas Howard
- **Best Special Effects:** BLITHE SPIRIT

William S. Darling
- **Best Art Direction (b/w):** ANNA AND THE KING OF SIAM

(20th) 1947 held in 1948

John Bryan
- **Best Art Direction:** GREAT EXPECTATIONS

Jack Cardiff
- **Best Cinematography (col):** BLACK NARCISSUS

Ronald Colman
- **Best Actor:** A DOUBLE LIFE

Guy Green
- **Best Cinematography (b/w):** GREAT EXPECTATIONS

Edmund Gwen
- **Best Supporting Actor:** MIRACLE ON 34TH STREET

(21st) 1948 held in 1949

Carmen Dillon & Roger Furse
- **Best Art Direction (b/w):** HAMLET

Brian Easdale
- **Best Score:** THE RED SHOES

Roger Furse
- **Best Costume Design:** HAMLET

Laurence Olivier
- **Best Picture:** HAMLET

Laurence Olivier
- **Best Actor:** HAMLET

(22nd) 1949 held in 1950

British Information Services
- **Best Documentary:** DAYBREAK IN UDI

Olivia de Havilland
- **Best Actress:** THE HEIRESS

(23rd) 1950 held in 1951

George Sanders
- **Best Supporting Actor:** ALL ABOUT EVE

(24th) 1951 held in 1952

James Bernard & Paul Dehn
- **Best Motion Picture Story:** SEVEN DAYS TO NOON

Vivien Leigh
- **Best Actress:** A STREETCAR NAMED DESIRE

(25th) 1952 held in 1953

T.E.B. Clarke
- **Best Story & Screenplay:** THE LAVENDER HILL MOB

London Films Sound Dept.
- **Best Sound:** THE SOUND BARRIER

(26th) 1954 held in 1955

British Information Services
- **Best Documentary Short Subject:** THURSDAY'S CHILDREN

S. Tyne Jule
- **Best Song:** THREE COINS IN THE FOUNTAIN

Jon Whitely & Vincent Winter
- **Special Award (Best Juvenile Performances):** THE KIDNAPPERS

(29th) 1956 held in 1957

George K. Arthur
- **Best Short Subject:** THE BESPOKE OVERCOAT

(30th) 1957 held in 1958

Malcolm Arnold
- **Best Musical Score:** THE BRIDGE ON THE RIVER KWAI

Alec Guinness
- **Best Actor:** THE BRIDGE ON THE RIVER KWAI

Jack Hildyard
- **Best Cinematography:** THE BRIDGE ON THE RIVER KWAI

David Lean
- **Best Director:** THE BRIDGE ON THE RIVER KWAI

Pete Taylor
- **Best Editing:** THE BRIDGE ON THE RIVER KWAI

(31st) 1958 held in 1959

Cecil Beaton
- **Best Costumes:** GIGI

Wendy Hiller
- **Best Supporting Actress:** SEPARATE TABLES

Thomas Howard
- **Special Visual Effects:** TOM THUMB

David Niven
- **Best Actor:** SEPARATE TABLES

(32nd) 1959 held in 1960

Hugh Griffith
- **Best Supporting Actor:** BEN HUR

Elizabeth Haffenden
- **Best Costume Design (col.):** BEN HUR

(33rd) 1960 held in 1961

Freddie Francis
- **Best Cinematography (b/w):** SONS & LOVERS

James Hill
- **Best Documentary:** GIUSEPPINA

Hayley Mills
- **Special Award (Best Juvenile Performance):** POLLYANNA

Peter Ustinov
- **Best Supporting Actor:** SPARTACUS

(34th) 1961 held in 1962

Vivian C. Greenham
- **Best Visual Effects:** THE GUNS OF NAVARONE

(35th) 1962 held in 1963

John Box & John Stoll
- **Best Art Direction:** LAWRENCE OF ARABIA

Anne V. Coates
- **Best Editing:** LAWRENCE OF ARABIA

Jack Howells (Janus Films)
- **Best Documentary:** DYLAN THOMAS

David Lean
- **Best Director:** LAWRENCE OF ARABIA

Shepperton Studios Sound Dept. (John Cox Sound Director)
- **Best Sound:** LAWRENCE OF ARABIA

Freddie Young
- **Best Cinematography:** LAWRENCE OF ARABIA

(36th) 1963 held in 1964

John Addison
- **Best Score:** TOM JONES

John Osborne
- **Best Adapted Screenplay:** TOM JONES

Tony Richardson
- **Best Director:** TOM JONES

Tony Richardson (Woodfall Films)
- **Best Picture:** TOM JONES

Margaret Rutherford
- **Best Supporting Actress:** THE V.I.P.S

(37th) 1964 held in 1965

Julie Andrews
- **Best Actress:** MARY POPPINS

Cecil Beaton
- **Best Art Direction (col):** MY FAIR LADY

Cecil Beaton
- **Best Costume Design (col):** MY FAIR LADY

Rex Harrison
- **Best Actor:** MY FAIR LADY

Walter Lassally
- **Best Cinematography (b/w):** ZORBA THE GREEK

Harry Stradling
- **Best Cinematography (col):** MY FAIR LADY

Peter Ustinov
- **Best Supporting Actor:** TOPKAPI

Norman Wanstall
- **Best Sound Effects:** GOLDFINGER

(38th) 1965 held in 1966

Julie Christie
- **Best Actress:** DARLING

Robert Bolt
- **Adapted Screenplay:** DOCTOR ZHIVAGO

Frederic Raphael
- **Original Screenplay:** DARLING

Freddie Young
- **Colour Cinematography:** DOCTOR ZHIVAGO

John Box, Terence Marsh
- **Best Art Direction (colour):** DOCTOR ZHIVAGO

Julie Harris
- **Costume (b/w):** DARLING

Phyllis Dalton
- **Costume (col):** DOCTOR ZHIVAGO

John Stears
- **Special Visual Effects:** THUNDERBALL

(39th) 1966 held in 1967

John Barry
- **Best Original Score:** BORN FREE

John Barry & Don Black
- **Best Song:** BORN FREE

Robert Bolt
- **Best Adapted Screenplay:** A MAN FOR ALL SEASONS

Joan Bridge & Elizabeth Haffenden
- **Best Costume (col):** A MAN FOR ALL SEASONS

Gordon Daniel
- **Best Sound:** GRAND PRIX

Ted Moore
- **Best Cinematography (col):** A MAN FOR ALL SEASONS

Ken Thorne
- **Best Adapted Score:** A FUNNY THING HAPPENED ON THE WAY TO THE FORUM

Peter Watkins
- **Best Documentary Feature:** THE WAR GAME

(40th) 1967 held in 1968

Leslie Bricusse
- **Best Song:** DOCTOR DOLITTLE (TALK TO THE ANIMALS)

Alfred Hitchcock
- **Irving Thalberg Memorial Award**

John Poyner
- **Best Sound Effects:** THE DIRTY DOZEN

(41st) 1968 held in 1969

John Barry
- **Best Original Score:** THE LION IN WINTER

Vernon Dixon & Ken Muggleston
- **Best Art Direction:** OLIVER!

Carol Reed
- **Best Director:** OLIVER!

Shepperton Sound Studio
- **Best Sound:** OLIVER!

Charles D. Staffell
- **Scientific, Class I Statuett -**
for the development of a successful embodiement of the reflex background projection system for composite cinematography

John Woolf
- **Best Picture:** OLIVER!

(42nd) 1969 held in 1970

Margaret Furfe
- **Best Costume:** ANNE OF THE THOUSAND DAYS

Cary Grant
- **Honorary Award**

John Schlesinger
- **Best Director:** MIDNIGHT COWBOY

Maggie Smith
- **Best Actress:** THE PRIME OF MISS JEAN BRODIE

(43rd) 1970 held in 1971

The Beatles
- **Best Original Score:** LET IT BE

Glenda Jackson
- **Best Actress:** WOMEN IN LOVE

John Mills
- **Best Supporting Actor:** RYAN'S DAUGHTER

Freddie Young
- **Best Cinematography:** RYAN'S DAUGHTER

(44th) 1971 held in 1972

Robert Amram
- **Best Short:** SENTINELS OF SILENCE

Ernest Archer, John Box, Vernon Dixon & Jack Maxsted
- **Best Art Direction:** NICHOLAS & ALEXANDRA

Charles Chaplin
- **Honorary Award**

David Hildyard & Gordon K. McCallum
- **Best Sound:** FIDDLER ON THE ROOF

Oswald Morris
- **Best Cinematography:** FIDDLER ON THE ROOF

(45th) 1972 held in 1973

Charles Chaplin
- **Best Original Score:** LIMELIGHT

David Hildyard
- **Best Sound:** CABARET

Anthony Powell
- **Best Costume Design:** TRAVELS WITH MY AUNT

Geoffrey Unsworth
- **Best Cinematography:** CABARET

(46th) 1973 held in 1974

Glenda Jackson
- **Best Actress:** A TOUCH OF CLASS

(47th) 1974 held in 1975

Albert Whitlock
- **Special Achievement In Visual Effects:** EARTHQUAKE

(48th) 1975 held in 1976

Ben Adam, Vernon Dixon & Roy Walker
- **Best Art Direction:** BARRY LYNDON

John Alcott
- **Best Cinematography:** BARRY LYNDON

Bob Godfrey
- **Best Animated Short:** GREAT

Albert Whitlock
- **Special Achievement In Visual Effects:** THE HINDENBERG

(49th) 1976 held in 1977

Peter Finch
- **Best Actor:** NETWORK

(50th) 1977 held in 1978

John Barry, Roger Christians & Leslie Dilley
- **Best Art Direction:** STAR WARS

John Mollo
- **Best Costume Design:** STAR WARS

Vanessa Redgrave
- **Best Supporting Actress:** JULIA

John Stears
- **Best Visual Effects:** STAR WARS

(51st) 1978 held in 1979

Les Bowie, Colin Chilvers, Denys Coop, Roy Field & Derek Meddings
- **Special Achievement In Visual Effects:** SUPERMAN

Michael Deeley, John Peverall & Barry Spikings
- **Best Picture:** THE DEER HUNTER

Laurence Oilvier
- **Lifetime Achievement Award**

Anthony Powell
- **Best Costume Design:** DEATH ON THE NILE

Maggie Smith
- **Best Supporting Actress:** CALIFORNIA SUITE

(52nd) 1979 held in 1980

Nick Allder, Denis Ayling & Brian Johnson
- **Special Achievement In Visual Effects:** ALIEN

Alec Guinness
- **Honorary Award**

Tony Walton
- **Best Art Direction:** ALL THAT JAZZ

(53rd) 1980 held in 1981

Brian Johnson
- **Special Achievement In Visual Effects:** THE EMPIRE STRIKES BACK

Lloyd Phillips
- **Best Live Action Short:** THE DOLLAR BOTTOM

Anthony Powell
- **Best Costume Design:** TESS

David W. Samuelson
- **Scientific and Engineering Award -**
for the engineering and development of the Louma Camera Crane and remote control system for motion picture production

Jack Stevens
- **Best Art Direction:** TESS

Geoffrey Unsworth
- **Best Cinematography:** TESS

(54th) 1981 held in 1982

Leslie Dilley & Michael Ford
- **Best Art Direction:** RAIDERS OF THE LOST ARK

John Gielgud
- **Best Supporting Actor:** ARTHUR

Nigel Nobel
- **Best Documentary Short:** CLOSE HARMONY

David Puttnam
- **Best Picture:** CHARIOTS OF FIRE

Arnold Schwartzman
- **Best Documentary Feature:** CLOSE HARMONY

Colin Welland
- **Best Original Screenplay:** CHARIOTS OF FIRE

Kit West
- **Special Achievement In Visual Effects:** RAIDERS OF THE LOST ARK

(55th) 1982 held in 1983

Richard Attenborough
- **Best Picture:** GANDHI

Richard Attenborough
- **Best Director:** GANDHI

John Briley
- **Best Original Screenplay:** GANDHI

Stuart Craig, Bob Laing & Michael Seirton
- **Best Art Direction:** GANDHI

Ben Kingsley
- **Best Actor:** GANDHI

John Mollo
- **Best Costume Design:** GANDHI

Sarah Monzani
- **Best Achievement In Make Up:** QUEST FOR FIRE

Colin Mossman & Rank Laboratories
- **Scientific and Engineering Award -**
for the engineering and implementation of a 4,000 meter printing system for motion picture laboratories

Christine Oestreicher
- **Best Live Action Short:** A SHOCKING ACCIDENT

Ronnie Taylor & Billy Williams
- **Best Cinematography:** GANDHI

(56th) 1983 held in 1984

Gerald L. Turpin (Lightflex International)
- **Scientific And Engineering Award**
- for the design, engineering and development of an on-camera device providing contrast control, sourceless fill light and special effects for motion picture photography

(57th) 1984 held in 1985

Peggy Ashcroft
- **Best Supporting Actress:** A PASSAGE TO INDIA

Jim Clark
- **Best Editing:** THE KILLING FIELDS

George Gibbs
- **Special Achievement In Visual Effects:** INDIANA JONES AND THE TEMPLE OF DOOM

Chris Menges
- **Best Cinematography:** THE KILLING FIELDS

Peter Shaffer
- **Best Adapted Screenplay:** AMADEUS

(58th) 1985 held in 1986

John Barry
- **Best Original Score:** OUT OF AFRICA

Stephen Grimes
- **Best Art Direction:** OUT OF AFRICA

David Watkin
- **Best Cinematography:** OUT OF AFRICA

(59th) 1986 held in 1987

Brian Ackland-Snow & Brian Saregar
- **Best Art Direction:** A ROOM WITH A VIEW

Jenny Beavan & John Bright
- **Best Costume Design:** A ROOM WITH A VIEW

Michael Caine
- **Best Supporting Actor:** HANNAH & HER SISTERS

Simon Kaye
- **Best Sound:** PLATOON

Lee Electric Lighting Ltd.
- **Technical Achievement Award**

Chris Menges
- **Best Cinematography:** THE MISSION

Peter D. Parks
- **Technical Achievement Award**
William B. Pollard & David W. Samuelson - Technical Achievement Award

John Richardson
- **Special Achievement In Visual Effects:** ALIENS

Claire Simpson
- **Best Editing:** PLATOON

Don Sharpe
- **Best Sound Effects Editing:** ALIENS

Vivienne Verdon-Roe
- **Best Documentary Short:** WOMEN - FOR AMERICA, FOR THE WORLD

(60th) 1987 held in 1988

James Acheson
- **Best Costume Design:** THE LAST EMPEROR

Sean Connery
- **Best Supporting Actor:** THE UNTOUCHABLES

Mark Peploe
- **Best Adapted Screenplay:** THE LAST EMPEROR

Ivan Sharrock
- **Best Sound:** THE LAST EMPEROR

Jeremy Thomas
- **Best Picture:** THE LAST EMPEROR

(61st) 1988 held in 1989

James Acheson
- **Best Costume Design:** DANGEROUS LIAISONS

George Gibbs
- **Special Achievement In Visual Effects:** WHO FRAMED ROGER RABBIT

Christopher Hampton
- **Best Adapted Screenplay:** DANGEROUS LIAISONS

(62nd) 1989 held in 1990

Phyllis Dalton
- **Best Costume:** HENRY V

Daniel Day-Lewis
- **Best Actor:** MY LEFT FOOT

Freddie Francis
- **Best Cinematography:** GLORY

Brenda Fricker
- **Best Supporting Actress:** MY LEFT FOOT

Anton Furst

- **Best Art Direction:** BATMAN

Richard Hymns
- **Best Sound Effects Editing:** INDIANA JONES AND THE LAST CRUSADE

Jessica Tandy
- **Best Actress:** DRIVING MISS DAISY

James Hendrie
- **Best Live Action Short:** WORK EXPERIENCE

(63rd) 1990 held in 1991

John Barry
- **Best Original Score:** DANCES WITH WOLVES

Jeremy Irons
- **Best Actor:** REVERSAL OF FORTUNE

Nick Park
- **Best Animated Short:** CREATURE COMFORTS

(64th) 1991 held in 1992

Daniel Greaves
- **Best Animated Short:** MANIPULATION

Anthony Hopkins
- **Best Actor:** SILENCE OF THE LAMBS

(65th) 1992 held in 1993

Simon Kaye
- **Best Sound:** THE LAST OF THE MOHICANS

Tim Rice
- **Best Original Song:** ALADDIN (A WHOLE NEW WORLD)

Emma Thompson
- **Best Actress:** HOWARDS END

Ian Whittaker
- **Best Art Direction:** HOWARDS END

(66th) 1993 held in 1994

Richard Hymns
- **Best Sound Effects Editing:** JURASSIC PARK

Nick Park
- **Best Animated Short:** THE WRONG TROUSERS

Deborah Kerr
- **Career Achievement Honorary Award**

(67th) 1994 held in 1995

Ken Adam & Carolyn Scott
- **Best Art Direction:** THE MADNESS OF KING GEORGE

Peter Capaldi & Ruth Kenley-Letts
- **Best Live Action Short:** FRANZ KAFKA'S IT'S A WONDERFUL LIFE

Elton John & Tim Rice
- **Best Song:** THE LION KING (CAN YOU FEEL THE LOVE TONIGHT)

Alison Snowden & David Fine
- **Best Animated Short:** BOB'S BIRTHDAY

(68th) 1995 held in 1996

James Acheson
- **Best Costume Design:** RESTORATION

Jon Blair
- **Best Documentary Feature:** ANNE FRANK REMEMBERED

Lois Burwell & Peter Frampton
- **Special Achievement In Make Up:** BRAVEHEART

Emma Thompson
- **Best Adapted Screenplay:** SENSE & SENSIBILITY

Nick Park
- **Best Animated Short:** A CLOSE SHAVE

(69th) 1996 held in 1997

Anthony Minghella
- **Best Director:** THE ENGLISH PATIENT

Rachel Portman
- **Best Original Score Musical or Comedy:** EMMA

Tim Rice & Andrew Lloyd Webber
- **Best Original song:** EVITA (YOU MUST LOVE ME)

Stuart Craig & Stephanie McMillan
- **Best Art Direction:** THE ENGLISH PATIENT

(70th) 1997 held in 1998

Peter Lamont and Michael Ford
- **Best Achievement In Art Direction:** TITANIC

Anne Dudley
- **Best Original Score Musical or Comedy:** THE FULL MONTY

Jan Pinkava
- **Best Animated Short:** GERI'S GAME

(71st) 1998 held in 1999

David Parfitt
- **Best Film:** SHAKESPEARE IN LOVE

Judi Dench
- **Best Actress in a Supporting Role:** SHAKESPEARE IN LOVE

Tom Stoppard
- **Best Original Screenplay:** SHAKESPEARE IN LOVE

Martin Childs and Jill Quertier
- **Best Art Direction:** SHAKESPEARE IN LOVE

Sandy Powell
- **Best Costume Design:** SHAKESPEARE IN LOVE

Jenny Shircore
- **Best Make-up:** ELIZABETH

Stephen Warbeck
- **Best Original Score Musical or Comedy:** SHAKESPEARE IN LOVE

Andy Nelson
- **Best Sound:** SAVING PRIVATE RYAN

(72nd) 1999 held in 2000

Michael Caine
- **Actor in a Supporting Role:** CIDER HOUSE RULES

Peter Young
- **Art Direction:** SLEEPY HOLLOW

Lindy Hemming
- **Costume Design:** TOPSY-TURVY

Sam Mendes
- **Directing:** AMERICAN BEAUTY

Kevin MacDonald, John Battsek,
- **Documentary Feature:** ONE DAY IN SEPTEMBER

Christine Blundell, Trefor Proud
- **Make up:** TOPSY-TURVY

Phil Collins
- **Original Song:** TARZAN "You'll Be In My Heart"

(73rd) 2000 held in 2001

Janty Yates
- **Costume Design:** GLADIATOR

Claire Jennings
- **Best Animated Short:** FATHER AND DAUGHTER

Ken Weston
- **Best Sound:** GLADIATOR

Tim Burke
- **Best Visual Effects:** GLADIATOR

SPECIAL AWARDS

Jack Cardiff
- **Honorary Oscar**

Vic Armstrong
- **Scientific and Technical Award**

BOOKS

Below is a selective list of books, in the English language, published in 2000 on the subject of film and television, all of which can be found at the *bfi* National Library. An ISBN has been provided where known. Compiled by Louise Johnston

Broadcasting

The daily globe: environmental change, the public and the media
SMITH, Joe.
Earthscan, vii-xii, 263p. bibliog. index.
ISBN 1853836648

De-westernizing media studies
CURRAN, James and PARK, Myung-Jin (eds.)
Routledge, vi-ix, 342p. index.
ISBN 0415193958

Degraded capability: the media and the Kosovo crisis
HAMMOND, Philip and HERMAN, Edward S (eds.)
Pluto Press, vii-x, 222p. bibliog. index.
ISBN 074531631X

Democracy and the Philippine media, 1983-1993
SMITH, Desmond.
Edwin Mellen Press, ix-xix, 382p. bibliog. index.
ISBN 0773478167

The economy, media and public knowledge
GAVIN, Neil T.
Leicester University Press, x, 198p. illus. index.
ISBN 0718502418

Emancipation, the media, and modernity: arguments about the media and social theory
GARNHAM, Nicholas.
Oxford University Press. vii, 206p. refs. index.
ISBN 019874224X

Environmental risks and the media
ALLAN, Stuart and CARTER, Cynthia.
Routledge, vi-xiv, 278p. illus. bibliog. index.
ISBN 0415214475

Ethics and media culture: practices and representations
BERRY, David.
Focal Press, v-xix, 350p. bibliogs. index.
ISBN 0240516036

Ethnic minorities and the media: changing cultural boundaries
COTTLE, Simon.
Open University Press, vi-xii, 251p. refs. index.
ISBN 0335202705

From Callaghan to Kosovo: changing trends in British television news 1975-1999
BARNETT, Steven and SEYMOUR, Emily and GABER, Ivor.
University of Westminster, 18p. illus. tables. appendices

Haunted media: electronic presence from telegraphy to television
SCONCE, Jeffrey.
Duke University Press, x, 257p. illus. notes. bibliog. index.
ISBN 0822325721

Holding the media accountable: citizens, ethics, and the law
PRITCHARD, David.
Indiana University Press, vi-viii, 203p. index.
ISBN 0253213576

In the company of media: cultural constructions of communication, 1920s-1930s
HARDT, Hanno.
Westview, vii-xii, 186p. illus. bibliog. index.
ISBN 0813314224

International communication: continuity and change
THUSSU, Daya Kishan.
Arnold, viii-ix, 342p. tables. figs. gloss. appendices. bibliog. index.
ISBN 0340741317

bfi Interpreting Diana: television audiences and the death of a princess
TURNOCK, Robert.
British Film Institute, iv-v, 138p. bibliog. index.
ISBN 0851707890

The making of citizens: young people, news and politics
BUCKINGHAM, David.
Routledge, vii-x, 235p. bibliog. index.
ISBN 0415214610

Mass media and society: 3rd ed
CURRAN, James and GUREVITCH, Michael (eds.)
Arnold, vi, 408p. index.
ISBN 0340732016

The media and international security
BADSEY, Stephen.
Frank Cass, viii-xxxii, 264p. index.
ISBN 0714644064

The media at war: communication and conflict in the twentieth century
CARRUTHERS, Susan L.
St. Martin's Press, vii-xii, 321p. bibliog. index.
ISBN 0312228015

Media organisations in society
CURRAN, James.
Arnold, vii, 292p. figs. index, tables.
ISBN 0340720158

Media power, professionals and policies
TUMBER, Howard (ed.)
Routledge, vii-xii, 342p. index.
ISBN 0415196698

Media studies: an introduction
DUTTON, Brian.
3rd. Longman, 157p. illus. index.
ISBN 0582411181

Media, communication, culture: a global approach: 2nd ed
LULL, James.
Polity Press, vi-x, 308p. notes. gloss. refs. index.
ISBN 0745621910

The media, journalism and democracy
SCAMMELL, Margaret and SEMETKO, Holli.
Dartmouth Publishing Company Limited, xlix, 432p. illus. index.
ISBN 1855215411

Monitoring community attitudes in changing mediascapes
DICKINSON, Garry and HILL, Michael and ZWAGA, Wiebe.
Dunmore Press, 131p. tables. figs. appendices.
ISBN 0864693656

The new communications landscape: demystifying media globalization
WANG, Georgette and SERVAES, Jan and GOONASEKERA, Anura (eds.)
Routledge, v-xvi, 336p. figs. tables. bibliog. index.
ISBN 0415223253

A new future for communications: Presented to Parliament by the Secretary of State for Trade and Industry and the Secretary of State for Culture, Media and Sport
Great Britain Department of Trade and Industry and Great Britain Department for Culture, Media and Sport.
The Stationery Office, illus. appendices. glossary.
ISBN 0101501021

The place of media power: pilgrims and witnesses of the media age
COULDRY, Nick.
Routledge, x-xii, 238p. appendix. bibliog. index.
ISBN 0415213150

Postmodern media culture
BIGNELL, Jonathan.
Edinburgh University Press, vii-viii, 240p. bibliog. index.
ISBN 0748609881

Power play: sport, the media popular culture

BOYLE, Raymond and HAYNES, Richard.
Longman, vi-xii, 244p. bibliog. index.
ISBN 0582369398

Race, media and the crisis of civil society: from Watts to Rodney King
JACOBS, Ronald
Cambridge University Press, xii. 189p. notes. bibliog. index.
ISBN 0521625785

Radio in the global age
HENDY, David.
Polity Press, vi-xiii, 260p. bibliog. index.
ISBN 0745620698

Radio live! Television live!: those golden days when horses were coconuts
MOTT Robert L.
McFarland, v-vi, 234p. illus. appendix. bibliog. index.
ISBN 0786408162

Raised on radio: in quest of...
NACHMAN, Gerald.
University of California Press, vi-ix, 535p. bibliog. index.
ISBN 0520223039

The reality of the mass media
LUHMAN, Niklas and CROSS, Kathleen.
Polity Press, vi, 154p. index.
ISBN 0745621325

Simulacrum America: the USA and the popular media
KRAUS, Elisabeth and AUER, Carolin (eds.)
Camden House, xi, 259p. index.
ISBN 1571131876

Studying radio
BARNARD, Stephen and CARNEY, Raymond.
Arnold, vi, 282p. figs. bibliog. index.
ISBN 0340719664

Turning the century: essays in media and cultural studies
STABILE, Carol A. Boulder.
Westview, 256p. illus. index.
ISBN 0813368200

Windows on the sixties: exploring key texts of media and culture

ALDGATE, Anthony and CHAPMAN, James and MARWICK, Arthur (eds.)
I.B.Tauris, 194p. index.
ISBN 1860643833

Careers

Agents on actors: over sixty professionals share their secrets on finding work on the stage and screen
HURTES, Hetty Lynne.
Back Stage Books, 173p.
ISBN 0823088030

Broadcast announcing worktext: performing for radio, television and cable
REESE, David A and BEADLE, Mary E and STEPHENSON, Alan R.
Focal Press, vii-xv, 173p. illus. appendix. gloss. index.
ISBN 0240803566

Broadcasting: breaking down the barriers
BAKER, Nick.
University of Luton Press, iv-viii, 232p.
ISBN 1860205720

A career handbook for TV, radio, video and interactive media
LLEWELLYN, Shiona.
A C Black, iii-xv, 288p. index.
ISBN 0713656980

The continuity supervisor: 4th ed
ROWLANDS, Avril.
Focal Press, v-x, 193p.
ISBN 0240516133

Guerrilla TV: low budget programme making
LEWIS, Ian.
Focal Press, 247p. figs. appendix. index.
ISBN 024051601X

How to be a working actor: the insider's guide to finding jobs in theater, film and television: 4th ed
HENRY, Mari Lyn and ROGERS, Lynne.
Back Stage Books, 367p. bibliog. appendices. index.
ISBN 0823088944

Multiskilling for television production
WARD, Peter and BERMINGHAM, Alan and WHERRY, Chris.
Focal Press, xii, 404p. illus. bibliog. glossary. index.
ISBN 0240515579

Practical cinematography
WHEELER, Paul.
Focal Press, viii, 178p. illus. index.
ISBN 0240515552

The producer's business handbook
LEE, John J.
Focal Press, v-xv, 173p. figs. index.
Includes CD-ROM.
ISBN 0240803965

Collected Films

1001: a video Odyssey: movies to watch for your every mood
TATHAM, Steve.
Lone Eagle, vi-xi, 288p. index.
ISBN 1580650236

American films of the 70s: conflicting visions
LEV, Peter.
University of Texas Press, viii-xxii, 238p. appendix. filmog. bibliog. index.
ISBN 0292747160

The Cambridge companion to Shakespeare on film
JACKSON, Russell.
Cambridge University Press, xiv, 342p. filmog. Index.
ISBN 0521639751

A century of films: Derek Malcolm's personal best
MALCOLM, Derek.
I.B.Tauris, 184p. illus. index.
ISBN 186064645X

Christmas at the movies: images of Christmas in American, British and European cinema
CONNELLY, Mark.
I.B.Tauris, [xiv], 242p. illus. filmog. Indices.
ISBN 1860643973

A Christmas Carol and its adaptations: a critical examination of Dickens's story and its productions

on screen and television
GUIDA, Fred.
McFarland, vii-xii, 264p. illus. filmog. notes. bibliog. index.
ISBN 0786407387

Reel spirit: a guide to movies that inspire, explore and empower
TEAGUE, Raymond.
Unity House, 438p. index.
ISBN 0871592487

Cultural Studies

American cultural studies: a reader
HARTLEY, John and PEARSON, Roberta E (eds.)
Oxford University Press, vi-xiii, 439p. illus. index.
ISBN 0198742541

Arts - what's in a word? Ethnic minorities and the arts
JERMYN, Helen and DESAI, Philly.
The Arts Council of England, 96p. tables. bibliog.
ISBN 0728708078

Artstat: digest of arts, statistics and trends in the UK, 1986/87-1997/98
Arts Council of England, ii-xv, 119p. tables. appendix. bibliog.
ISBN 0728708000

Brit cult: an A-Z of British pop culture
CALCUTT, Andrew.
Prion, 448p. illus.
ISBN 1853753211

British television advertising: cultural identity and communication
DICKASON, Renée.
University of Luton Press, v-vii, 188p. bibliog. index.
ISBN 1860205712

The children are watching: how the media teach about diversity
CORTES, Carlos E.
Teachers College Press, vi-xxi, 201p. bibliog. index.
ISBN 0807739375

Cultural encounters: representing 'otherness'
HALLAM, Elizabeth and STREET, Brian. V. (eds.)
Routledge, vi-xi, 292p. illus. refs.

index.
ISBN 0415202809

Cultural industries key data: cultural industries in Yorkshire and the Humber
ROODHOUSE, Simon.
Bretton Hall, 36p. figs. appendix.

The daily planet: a critic on the capitalist culture beat
AUFDERHEIDE, Patricia.
University of Minnesota Press, ix-xv, 347p.
ISBN 0816633428

Delete expletives?
MILLWOOD-HARGRAVE, Andrea.
Advertising Standards Authority, 60p. tables,appendices.
ISBN 1872521428

E-Britannia: the communications revolution
Barnett, Steven et al.
University of Luton Press, 165p.
ISBN 1860205763

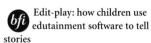 **Edit-play: how children use edutainment software to tell stories**
SEFTON-GREEN, Julian and PARKER, David.
British Film Institute, 64p. illus. bibliog. (BFI Education research report)

"Here, there and everywhere": the foreign politics of American popular culture
WAGNLEITNER, Reinhold and MAY, Elaine Tyler.
University Press of New England, vii-xi, 356p. index.
ISBN 1584650354

The hidden meaning of mass communications: cinema, books, and television in the age of computers
HOVEYDA, Fereydoun.
Praeger, vii-xii, 170p. bibliog. index.
ISBN 0275969967

The idea of culture
EAGLETON, Terry.
Blackwell, 156p. index.
ISBN 0631219668

Illusions of immortality: a psychology of fame and celebrity

GILES, David.
Macmillan, v-viii, 187p. refs. bibliog.
index.
ISBN 033375450

Information society studies
DUFF, Alistair S.
Routledge, vi-x, 204p. tables. figs.
appendices. bibliog. index.
ISBN 041521551X

An introduction to studying popular culture
STRINATI, Dominic. Routledge, viii-xvi, 288p. bibliog. index.
ISBN 0415157676

Mass mediations: new approaches to popular culture in the Middle East and Beyond
ARMBRUST, Walter.
University of California Press, vi-xi, 378p. illus. bibliog. index.
ISBN 0520219252

Mind abuse: media violence in an information age
DYSON, Rose A.
Black Rose Books, vi-xii, 225p.
bibliog. index.
ISBN 1551641526

Nobrow: the culture of marketing, the marketing of culture
SEABROOK, John.
Alfred A. Knopf, 215p.
ISBN 0375405046

Overloaded: popular culture and the future of feminism
WHELEHAN, Imelda.
The Women's Press, ix-x, 202p.
bibliog. index.
ISBN 0704346176

Placing art in new contexts: summary of a report to the Arts Council of England
JERMYN, Helen and BMRB.
Arts Council of England, 51p.

Regulation on advertising aimed at children in EU-Member states and some neighbouring states: the legal framework
EUROPEAN AUDIOVISUAL OBSERVATORY.
European Audiovisual

Report on the UK music video industry in 1998 and 1999
The Video Group
The Video Group. 6p.

Research in media promotion
EASTMAN, Susan Tyler.
Lawrence Erlbaum, xiii, 365p. tables.
charts. index.
ISBN 080583382X

Science fiction, children's literature, and popular culture: coming of age in Fantasyland
WESTFAHL, Gary
Greenwood Press, viii, 157p. bibliog.
index.
ISBN 0313308470

Setting the standards: the regulation of home video and video games in the United Kingdom
Video Standards Council.
Video Standards Council, 8p. illus.

Thirty frames per second: the visionary art of the music video
REISS, Steve and FEINEMAN, Neil.
Harry N. Abrams, 272p. cred. index.
biogs.
ISBN 0810943573

Video violence: villain or victim? A review of the research evidence concerning screen violence (video and computer games) and violence in the real world
CUMBERBATCH, Guy and Video Standards Council.
Video Standards Council, 27p.
bibliog.

Visual communication: images with messages: 2nd ed.
LESTER, Paul Martin.
Wadsworth, v-xiv, 402p. illus. [8] col.
plates. figs. gloss. bibliog. index.
ISBN 053456142X

When law goes pop: the vanishing line between law and popular culture
SHERWIN, Richard K.
University of Chicago Press, 325p.
index.
ISBN 0226752917

Dictionaries/ Encyclopedias

"A" western filmmakers: a biographical dictionary of writers, directors, cinematographers, composers, actors and actresses
HOFFMANN, Henryk.
McFarland, vii-viii. 647p. illus.
appendices. bibliog. index.
ISBN 078640968

The animated film encyclopedia: a complete guide to American shorts, features, and sequences, 1900-1979
WEBB, Graham.
McFarland, v-vi, 634p. appendix.
index.
ISBN 0786407288

A dictionary of media and communication studies: 5th ed
WATSON, James and HILL, Anne.
Arnold, vi-xiii, 364p. diags. Appendix.

The encyclopedia of fantastic film: Ali Baba to Zombies
YOUNG, R.G.
Applause, 1018p. illus. Appendices.
chronolog. indices.
ISBN 1557832692

Encyclopedia of film themes, settings and series
ARMSTRONG, Richard and ARMSTRONG, Mary Willems.
McFarland, vii-xii, 225p.
ISBN 0786408936

Encyclopedia of movie special effects
NETZLEY, Patricia D.
Oryx Press, iii-xi, 291p. illus.
appendices. bibliog. index.
ISBN 1573561673

Encyclopedia of TV science fiction: 4thed
FULTON, Roger.
Boxtree, 836p. illus. chronolog.
ISBN 0752271679

Filmmaker's dictionary: 2nd ed
SINGLETON, Ralph S and CONRAD, James A. and HEALY, Janna Wong.
Lone Eagle, 356p.
ISBN 1580650228

International dictionary of
broadcasting and film: 2nd ed
BOGNAR, Desi K.
Focal Press, iv-xi, 316p.
ISBN 0240803760

Film Studies, Theory and Criticism

Art and politics of film
ORR, John.
Edinburgh University Press, ix, 198p.
illus. notes. bibliog. index.
ISBN 0748611991

The art of watching films: 5th ed
BOGGS, Joseph M and PETRIE,
Dennis W.
Mayfield, vii-xxii, 570p. illus.
appendices. gloss. bibliog. index.
ISBN 0767405323

The brain is the screen: Deleuze and
the philosophy of cinema
FLAXMAN, Gregory.
University of Minnesota Press, ix-x,
395p. index.
ISBN 0816634475

bfi Cahiers du cinéma, volume
four, 1973-1978: history,
ideology, cultural struggles: an
anthology from Cahiers du cinéma
nos 248-292, September 1973-
September 1978, 1969-1972: the
politics of representation
WILSON ,David.
Routledge in association with British
Film Institute, i-xi, 323p. index.
ISBN 0415029880

Cinema and cultural modernity
BRANSTON, Gill.
Open University Press, x, 207p. gloss.
bibliog. index.
ISBN 0335200761

Cinema studies: the key concepts:
2nd ed
HAYWARD, Susan.
Routledge, vii-xx, 528p. bibliog.
index.
ISBN 0415227402

The cognitive semiotics of film
BUCKLAND, Warren.
Cambridge University Press, vii-xi,
174p. notes. bibliog. index.

ISBN 0521780055
Disclosure of the everyday:
undramatic achievement in narrative
film
KLEVAN, Andrew.
Flicks Books, vi-vii, 230p. filmog.
bibliog. index.
ISBN 1862360049

Feminism and film
KAPLAN, Ann E.
Oxford University Press, v-xiv, 566p.
illus. bibliog. index.
ISBN 0198782349

Film and theory: an anthology
MILLER, Toby and STAM, Robert
(eds.)
Blackwell, vi-xviii, 862p. bibliog.
index.
ISBN 0631206264

The film studies reader
HOLLOWS, Joanne and
HUTCHINGS, Peter and
JANCOVICH, Mark (eds.)
Arnold, xii, 368p. index.
ISBN 0340692790

Film studies: critical approaches
HILL, John and GIBSON, Pamela
Church (eds.)
Oxford University Press, vii-xv, 229p.
illus. index.
ISBN 0198742800

Film theory: an introduction
STAM, Robert.
Blackwell, vi-x, 381p. bibliog. index.
ISBN 063120654X

How to read a film: the world of
movies, media and multimedia:
language, history, theory: 3rd ed
MONACO, James.
Oxford University Press, 672p. illus.
bibliog. chronolog. indices.
ISBN 019503869X

Imagining selves: the politics of
representation, film narratives, and
adult education
GAZETAS, Aristides.
Peter Lang, ix-xi, 219p. bibliog.
filmog. index.
ISBN 0820445665

Literature and film as modern
mythology

FERRELL, William K.
Praeger, vi, 216p. appendices. bibliog.
index.
ISBN 0275968138

Moving images, culture and the mind
BONDEBJERG, Ib (ed.)
University of Luton Press, v-x, 255p.
illus. figs. bibliogs.
ISBN 1860205739

Narrative in fiction and film: an
introduction
LOTHE, Jakob.
Oxford University Press, xii, 253p.
refs. filmog. index.
ISBN 0198752326

New developments in film theory
FUERY, Patrick.
Macmillan, vii-x, 211p. gloss. filmog.
bibliog.
ISBN 0333744918

Overhearing film dialogue
KOZLOFF, Sarah.
University of California Press, ix,
323p. illus. filmog. bibliog.
index.
ISBN 0520221389

Perverse spectators: the practices of
film reception
STAIGER, Janet.
New York University Press, v-vi, 242p.
notes. index.
ISBN 0814781381

Reading Cavell's The World Viewed:
a philosophical perspective on film
ROTHMAN, William and KEANE,
Marian.
Wayne State University Press, 294p.
illus. appendix. notes. index.
ISBN 0814328962

Reinventing film studies
GLEDHILL, Christine and
WILLIAMS, Linda (eds.)
Arnold, viii-xvi, 464p. illus. index.
ISBN 0340677236

The Routledge reader in politics and
performance
GOODMAN, Lizbeth and de GAY,
Jane.
Routledge, xxvii, 322p. illus. bibliog.
index.
ISBN 0415174732

Savage theory: cinema as modern magic
MOORE, Rachel O.
Duke University Press, 199p. illus. bibliog. index.
ISBN 0822323885

Semiotics and the analysis of film
MITRY, Jean and KING,Christopher (transl)
Athlone Press, vi-xi, 277p. illus. bibliog. index.
ISBN 0485121514

Siegfried Kracauer: an introduction
KOCH, Gertrud and GAINES, Jeremy (transl)
Princeton University Press, vii-xii, 137p. bibliog. index.
ISBN 0691049920

The skin of the film: intercultural cinema, embodiment and the senses
MARKS, Laura U.
Duke University Press, vii-xvii, 298p. illus. bibliog. filmog. index. ISBN 0822323915

Theories of the new media: a historical perspective
CALDWELL, John Thornton.
Athlone Press, vii-viii, 331p. bibliog. index.
ISBN 0485300915

 Understanding film texts: meaning and experience
PHILLIPS, Patrick.
British Film Institute, xiii, 158p. illus. index.
ISBN 085170798X

Film-General

All about the movies: a handbook for the movie-loving layman
RAPF, Maurice.
The Scarecrow Press, v-xi, 116p. illus. bibliog. index.
ISBN 0810837919

Architecture and film
LAMSTER, Mark (ed.)
Princeton Architectural Press, 254p. illus.
ISBN 1568982070

Between cinema and a hard place
Tate Modern.

Tate Modern, 22p. illus

BVA: the first 20 years
British Video Association.
Square One, 77p. illus

Cinema and nation
HJORT, Mette and MacKENZIE, Scott.
Routledge, vii-xvi, 331p. illus. index.
ISBN 0415208637

Film adaptation
NAREMORE, James (ed.)
Rutgers University Press, vii-x, 258p. illus. bibliog. index.
ISBN 0813528143

Film music
RUSSELL, Mark and YOUNG, James.
RotoVision, 192p. col. illus. gloss. index.
ISBN 2880464412

Film posters of the 50s: the essential movies of the decade, from the reel poster gallery collection
NOURMAND, Tony and MARSH, Graham (eds.)
Aurum, 128p. col. illus. index.
ISBN 1854107194

The FilmFour book of film quotes
FilmFour, 60p. col. illus.
ISBN 0752271571

 A Guide to the British Film Institute
British Film Institute.
British Film Institute, 20p

Icons of film: the 20th century
ENGELMEIER, Peter W.
Prestel, 191p. illus. index.
ISBN 3791323946

Movie locations: a guide to Britain and Ireland
ADAMS, Mark.
Boxtree, 256p. illus. index.
ISBN 0752271695

The movie traveller: a film fan's travel guide to the UK and Ireland
FOSTER, Allan.
Polygon, v-ix, 300p. illus. appendix. index.
ISBN 0748662499

Movie worlds: production design in film. Das Szenenbild im Film
LÜDI, Heidi and LÜDI, Toni.
Axel Menges, 127p. col. illus. filmog. notes.
ISBN 3932565134

The movies as history: visions of the twentieth century
ELLWOOD, David W.
Sutton, vi-x, 214p. illus. bibliog. Index.
ISBN 0750923318

 Moving images in the classroom: a secondary teachers' guide to using film and television
British Film Institute and English and Media Centre and Film Education.
British Film Institute, 64p. illus.
ISBN 0851708315

Poster artist Chen Zi Fu
CHINESE TAIPEI FILM ARCHIVE.
Chinese Taipei Film Archive, 176p. col. illus.
ISBN 9570259310

Screen style: fashion and femininity in 1930s Hollywood
BERRY, Sarah.
Minnesota University Press, ix-xxiv, 234p. illus. filmog. index.
ISBN 0816633126

Sound
KRUTH, Patricia and STOBART, Henry.
Cambridge University Press, v, 235p. illus. index.
ISBN 0521572096

Sound and vision: sixty years of motion picture soundtracks
BURLINGAME, Jon.
Billboard Books, vii-xi, 244p. illus. bibliog. indices.
ISBN 0823084272

Sound technology and the American cinema: perception, representation, modernity
LASTRA, James.
Columbia University Press, ix-x, 270p. illus. Index.
ISBN 0231115172

Sundancing: hanging out and listening in at America's most

important film festival
ANDERSON, John.
Spike, v-xiii, 268p. illus. appendix.
index.
ISBN 0380804808

Film-Genre

 Action/spectacle cinema: a Sight and Sound reader
ARROYO, José.
British Film Institute, 272p. illus.
index.
ISBN 0851707572

 Animation: 16+ Guide
KERAMEOS, Anastasia and RASMUSSEN, Heidi.
BFI National Library, 50p.
ISBN 0851708250

Arthurian legends on film and television
OLTON, Bert.
McFarland, vii-ix, 341p. illus.
appendices. bibliog. index.
ISBN 0786407182

Artistry in noir: the use and representation of jazz in film noir
BUTLER, David.
271p. bibliog.

Brassey's guide to war films
EVANS, Alun.
Brassey's, 256p. illus. bibliog. indices.
ISBN 1574882635

Children's film: history, ideology, pedagogy, theory
WOJCIK-ANDREWS, Ian.
Garland, vii-xiii, 257p. filmog.
bibliog. index.
ISBN 0815337949

A chorus of raspberries: British film comedy 1929-1939
SUTTON, David.
University of Exeter Press, ix, 294p.
illus. notes. filmog. bibliog. index.
ISBN 085989603X

The classic novel from page to screen
GIDDINGS, Robert and SHEEN, Erica.
Manchester University Press, v-viii, 243p. illus. index.
ISBN 0719052319

Classics in film and fiction
CARTMELL, Deborah and HUNTER, I.Q and KAYE, Heidi and WHELEHAN, Imelda (eds.)
Pluto Press, vii-x, 240p. index.
ISBN 0745315933

Creatures of darkness: Raymond Chandler, detective fiction, and film noir
PHILLIPS, Gene D.
The University Press of Kentucky, xxiv, 311p. notes. bibliog. filmog.
index.
ISBN 0813121744

Cutting edge: art-horror and the horrific avant-garde
HAWKINS, Joan.
University of Minnesota Press, ix-xiii, 326p. illus. bibliog. filmog. index.
ISBN 0816634130

The dead walk
BLACK, Andy.
Noir Publishing, 160p. illus. filmog.
index.
ISBN 095365642X

Death on the cheap: the lost B movies of film noir
LYONS, Arthur.
Da Capo, x, 212p. illus. bibliog.
filmog. index.
ISBN 0306809966

English gothic: a century of horror cinema
RIGBY, Jonathan.
Reynolds Hearn Ltd, 256p. illus.
index.
ISBN 1903111013

The essential Bond: the authorized guide to the world of 007
PFEIFFER, Lee and WORRALL, Dave.
213p. col. illus.
ISBN 0752217585

Film genre 2000: new critical essays
DIXON, Wheeler Winston (ed.)
State University of New York Press, v-vii, 266p. illus. index.
ISBN 0791445143

 Film parody
HARRIES, Dan.
British Film Institute, 153p. illus.

bibliog. filmog. index.
ISBN 085170803X

Genre and Hollywood
NEALE, Steve.
Routledge, vii-viii, 336p. appendix.
bibliog. index.
ISBN 0415026067

The horror reader
GELDER, Ken.
Routledge, vi-xiii, 414p. illus. bibliog.
index.
ISBN 0415213568

Insideaard
OLIVER, James.
Aardman Animations. ScreenPress, 64p. [16] col. plates. filmog.
ISBN 1901680525

 James Bond: 16+ guide
CLARKE, Nicola and DELANEY, Sean and KHAN, Ayesha and SMART, Emma.
BFI National Library, 42p. illus.
ISBN 0851708269

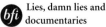 Lies, damn lies and documentaries
WINSTON, Brian.
British Film Institute, iv-v, 186p.
bibliog. index.
ISBN 0851707963

Monsters from the id: horror in fiction and film
JONES, E. Michael.
Spence, ix-xii, 298p. index.
ISBN 1890626066

Musicals: Hollywood and beyond
MARSHALL, Bill and STILWELL, Robynn (eds.)
Intellect Books, iv, 188p. illus. index.
ISBN 1841500038

The naked and the undead: evil and the appeal of horror
FREELAND, Cynthia A.
Westview, vii-xv, 320p. illus. filmog.
bibliog. index.
ISBN 0813367026

New documentary: a critical introduction
BRUZZI, Stella.
Routledge, 199p. illus. bibliog. index.
ISBN 0415182964

Opera on film
FAWKES, Richard.
Duckworth, 262p. [16] plates. bibliog.
index.
ISBN 0715629433

Opera on screen
CITRON, Marcia J.
Yale University Press, 295p. illus.
index.
ISBN 0300081588

Picturing culture: explorations of film and anthropology
RUBY, Jay.
University of Chicago Press, ix-xiii,
339p. bibliog. index.
ISBN 0226730999

Pimple, pranks pratfalls: British film comedy before 1930
BURTON, Alan and PORTER,
Laraine.
Flicks Books, 122p. [16] plates, index.
ISBN 1862360103

The pocket essential slasher movies
WHITEHEAD, Mark.
Pocket Essentials, 96p. filmog. bibliog.
ISBN 1903047277

Psycho paths: tracking the serial killer through contemporary American film and fiction
Simpson, Philip L.
Southern Illinois University Press,
xvi, 244p. bibliog. index.
ISBN 080932329X

Realism and popular cinema
HALLAM, Julia and MARSHMENT,
Margaret.
Manchester University Press, xvi,
280p. illus. bibliog. index.
ISBN 0719052513

Science fiction cinema: from outerspace to cyberspace
KING, Geoff and KRZYWINSKA,
Tanya.
Wallflower, 128p. illus. bibliog.
filmog. glossary.
ISBN 1903364035

Screen sirens scream! Interviews with 20 actresses from science fiction, horror, film noir and mystery movies, 1930s to 1960s
PARLA, Paul and MITCHELL,

Charles P.
McFarland, v-viii, 248p. illus. index.
ISBN 0786407018

Shots in the mirror: crime films and society
RAFTER, Nicole.
Oxford University Press, ix, 201p.
illus. bibliog. filmog. index.
ISBN 0195129830

A skin for dancing in: possession, witchcraft and voodoo in film
KRZYWINSKA, Tanya.
Flicks Books, x, 214p. illus. [2] leaves
of plates, bibliog. index.
ISBN 186236009X

States of emergency: documentaries, wars, democracies
ZIMMERMANN, Patricia R.
University of Minnesota Press, ix-
xxiii, 229p. illus. index.
ISBN 0816628238

Uneasy dreams: the golden age of British horror films, 1956-1976
SMITH, Gary A.
McFarland, vii-ix, 267p. illus. bibliog.
index.
ISBN 0786406046

Universal-International westerns, 1947-1963: the complete filmography
BLOTTNER, Gene.
McFarland, v-vi, 362p. illus. bibliog.
filmog. index.
ISBN 0786407913

 The western: a teacher's guide
Film Education and British
Film Institute.
Film Education, 18p. illus.

Wildlife films
BOUSÉ, Derek.
University of Pennsylvania Press, xii-
xv, 280p. illus. chronol. bibliog. index.
ISBN 0812217284

Filmographies

Guide to Jewish films on video
ANKLEWICZ, Larry.
KTAV, v-xxiv, 378p.
ISBN 0881256056

The Hong Kong filmography, 1977-1997: a complete reference to 1,100 films produced by British Hong

Kong studios
CHARLES, John.
McFarland, viii, 387p. gloss. bibliog.
index.
ISBN 0786408421

Lesbian film guide
DARREN, Alison.
Cassell, vii-ix, 246p. illus. indices.
ISBN 030433376X

Missing reels: lost films of American and European cinema
WALDMAN, Harry.
McFarland, 313p. illus. bibliog. index.
ISBN 0786407247

Radio Times guide to films
FANE-SAUNDERS, Kilmeny.
BBC Worldwide Ltd, 1924p.
appendices. indices.
ISBN 0563537108

Video movie guide
MARTIN, Mick and PORTER,
Marsha.
Ballantine, vi-xi, 1582p. indices.
ISBN 0345420942

Video versions: film adaptations of plays on video
ERSKINE, Thomas L and
WELSH,James M and TIBBETTS,
John C and WILLIAMS, Tony.
Greenwood Press, vii-xix, 418p.
index.
ISBN 0313301859

Films-Social Aspects

The AIDS movie: representing a pandemic in film and television
HART, Kylo-Patrick R.
Haworth Press, ix-xiii, 120p.
appendices. bibliog. index.
ISBN 0789011085

 Black British film TV: 16+ guide
CLARKE, Nicola and KING, Andrea
and KER, Matt.
BFI National Library, 36p.
ISBN 0851708277

Black film as a signifying practice: cinema, narration and the African-American aesthetic tradition
YEARWOOD, Gladstone L.
Africa World Press, vii-ix, 263p.

bibliog. index.
ISBN 0865437157

The black image in the white mind: media and race in America
ENTMAN, Robert M and ROJECKI, Andrew.
University of Chicago Press, vii-xix, 305p. tables. refs. index.
ISBN 0226210758

 The British Film Institute: black and Asian film research
Surrey Social and Market Research Ltd. 152p. tables

Complicated women: sex and power in pre-code Hollywood
LASALLE, Mick.
A Thomas Dunne Book/St. Martin's Press, 293p. [32] plates. bibliog. index.
ISBN 0312252072

Countervisions: Asian American film criticism
LIU, Sandra and HAMAMOTO, Darrell Y (eds.)
Temple University Press, viii-xiv, 317p. illus. bibliogs.
ISBN 156639776

Flaming classics: queering the film canon
DOTY, Alexander.
Routledge, 194p. illus. index.
ISBN 041592345X

For entertainment purposes only? An analysis of the struggle to control filmic representations
CHAISSON, Reba.
Lexington Books, 101p. bibliog. index.
ISBN 0739101560

Framed: lesbians, feminists, and media culture
MAYNE, Judith.
University of Minnesota Press, ix-xxiii, 224p. illus. index.
ISBN 0816634572

The fruit machine: twenty years of writings on queer cinema
WAUGH, Thomas.
Duke University Press, xii, 312p. illus. bibliog. index.
ISBN 0822324687

God in the movies
BERGESEN, Albert J and GREELEY, Andrew M.
Transaction, vii-ix, 186p. index.
ISBN 0765800209

Green screen: environmentalism and Hollywood cinema
INGRAM ,David.
University of Exeter Press, x, 230p. notes. filmog. bibliog. index.
ISBN 0859896080

Hollywood v. hard core: how the struggle over censorship saved the modern film industry
LEWIS, Jon.
New York University Press, vii-xi,377p. illus. appendix, index.
ISBN 0814751423

Hollywood's frontier captives: cultural anxiety and the captivity plot in American film
NADELHAFT, Jerome.
Garland, v, 184p. filmog. bibliog. Index
ISBN 0815331169

Is that a gun in your pocket? Women's experience of power in Hollywood
ABRAMOWITZ, Rachel.
Random House, xv, 494p. illus. index.
ISBN 0679437541

Media messages: what film, television, and popular music teach us about race, class, gender and sexual orientation
HOLTZMAN, Linda.
M.E. Sharpe, xiv. 346p. illus. bibliogs. index.
ISBN 0765603373

More than a movie: ethics in entertainment
VALENTI, Miguel.
Westview, v-xxxi, 272p. filmog. index.
ISBN 0813390753

Movie wars: how Hollywood and the media conspire to limit what films we can see
ROSENBAUM, Jonathan.
A Capella Books, 234p. index.
ISBN 1556524064

The new avengers: feminism, femininity and the rape-revenge cycle
READ, Jacinda. Manchester University Press, vi-viii, 290p. illus. filmog. bibliog. index.
ISBN 0719059054

On location: cinema and film in the Anglophone Caribbean
WARNER, Keith Q.
Macmillan Education, iii-xii, 194p. appendices. index.
ISBN 033379211

Ratings analysis: the theory and practice of audience research: 2nd ed
WEBSTER, James G and PHALEN, Patricia F. and LICHTY, Lawrence W.
Lawrence Erlbaum, vii-x, 282p. tables. figs. gloss. bibliog. index. ISBN 0805830987

Reel spirituality: theology and film in dialogue
JOHNSTON, Robert K.
Baker Academic, 236p. illus. notes. bibliog. index.
ISBN 080102241X

Screening violence
PRINCE, Stephen.
Rutgers University Press, viii, 275p. illus. index.
ISBN 0813528178

Signifying female adolescence: film representations and fans, 1920-1950
SCHEINER, Georganne.
Praeger, ix-x, 171p. filmog. bibliog. index.
ISBN 0275968952

Slaves on screen: film and historical vision
DAVIS, Natalie Zemon.
Vintage Canada, ix-xi, 164p. illus.
ISBN 0679310231

Spectacular passions: cinema, fantasy, gay male spectatorships
FARMER, Brett.
Duke University Press, x, 305p. illus. notes. filmog. bibliog. index.
ISBN 0822325896

Vishnu in Hollywood: the changing image of the American male
GROSSVOGEL, David I.
The Scarecrow Press, iii-xx, 225p. illus. bibliog. index.
ISBN 0810837676

Histories-Africa, Asia, Australasia

African cinemas: decolonizing the gaze
BARLET, Olivier and TURNER, Chris.
Zed Books, viii-xii, 315p. illus. bibliog. appendix. index.
ISBN 1856497437

All you want is money, all you need is love: sexuality and romance in modern India
DWYER, Rachel.
Cassell, vii-viii 248p. [8] plates. bibliog. index.
Includes filmography of Yash Chopra.
ISBN 0304703214

The cinema of Hong Kong: history, arts, identity
FU, Poshek and DESSER, David (ed.)
Cambridge University Press, v-xi, 333p. illus. index.
ISBN 0521772354

Colonial India and the making of empire cinema: image, ideology and identity
CHOWDHRY, Prem.
Manchester University Press, vi-viii, 294p. illus. bibliog. index.
ISBN 0719057922

Contemporary Australian cinema: an introduction
RAYNER, Jonathan.
Manchester University Press, xiii, 203p. illus. bibliog. filmog. index.
ISBN 0719053277

The essential mystery: the major filmmakers of Indian art cinema
HOOD, John W.
Sangam Books, 474p. filmog. index.
ISBN 0863118526

From book to screen: modern Japanese literature in film
MCDONALD, Keiko I.
M.E. Sharpe, vii-xv, 326p. illus. bibliog. index.
ISBN 076560387X

Hollywood east: Hong Kong movies and the people who make them
HAMMOND, Stefan.

Contemporary Books, 274p. illus. [16]col. plates. glossary. index.
ISBN 0809225816

Making meaning in Indian cinema
VASUDEVAN, Ravi S.
Oxford University Press, viii-x, 317p. bibliogs.
ISBN 0195645456

Movies, masculinity and modernity: an ethnography of men's filmgoing in India
DERNÉ, Steve.
Greenwood Press, vii-viii, 211p. appendix. bibliog. Index.
ISBN 0313312877

New Zealand - a pastoral paradise?
CONRICH, Ian and WOODS, David (eds.)
Kakapo Books, 128p. index.
ISBN 0953917753

Planet Hong Kong: popular cinema and the art of entertainment
BORDWELL, David.
Harvard University Press, ix-xii, 329p. illus. bibliog. index.
ISBN 0674002148

Profiling Sri Lankan cinema
DISSANAYAKE, Wimal and RATNAVIBHUSHANA, Ashley.
Asian Film Centre, 152p. illus. bibliog. indices.
ISBN 9558008001

Public secrets, public spaces: cinema and civility in China
DONALD, Stephanie.
Rowman and Littlefield, v-xii, 201p. illus. bibliog. filmog. gloss. index.
ISBN 0847698777

Sequel of 80 glorious years of Indian cinema: complete filmography of all released Hindi films from 1994-1999
OJHA, Rajendra.
Screen World Publication, 72p.

Sisters of the screen: women of Africa on film, video and television
ELLERSON, Beti.
Africa World Press, 395p. filmog. bibliog.
ISBN 0865437130

Sisters on screen: siblings in contemporary cinema
RUESCHMANN, Eva.
Temple University Press, vii-x, 221p. illus. filmog. index.
ISBN 1566397472

 Symbolic narratives/African cinema: audiences, theory and the moving image
GIVANNI, June.
British Film Institute, xvi, 256p. index.
ISBN 0851707378

Histories-Europe

 The BFI companion to Eastern European and Russian cinema
TAYLOR, Richard and WOOD, Nancy and GRAFFY, Julian and IORDANOVA, Dina (eds.)
British Film Institute, 288p. bibliog.
ISBN 085170753X

Cultural history through a National Socialist lens: essays on the cinema of the Third Reich
REIMER, Robert C.
Camden House, vii-xvi, 301p. illus. bibliog. index.
ISBN 1571131647

The film minister: Goebbels and the cinema in the "Third Reich"
MOELLER, Felix and ROBINSON, Michael (trans.)
Axel Menges, 216p. illus. bibliog. index.
ISBN 393256510X

Filming women in the Third Reich
FOX, Jo.
Berg, v-xi, 268p. illus. filmog. bibliog. index.
ISBN 1859733913

Filmmuseum Berlin
JACOBSEN, Wolfgang and PRINZLER, Hans Helmut and SUDENDORF, Werner.
Berlin Nicolai, 351p. col. and bw plates. notes. index.
ISBN 3875849078

French films: texts and contexts: 2nd ed
HAYWARD, Susan and

VINCENDEAU, Ginette (eds.)
Routledge, 309p. illus. bibliogs.
filmogs. index.
ISBN 0415161185

French science fiction, fantasy,
horror and pulp fiction: a guide to
cinema, television, radio, animation,
comic books and literature from the
Middle Ages to the present
LOFFICIER, Jean-Marc and
LOFFICIER, Randy.
McFarland, vii-x1, 787p. illus. bibliog.
index.
ISBN 0786405961

Guide to the cinema of Sweden and
Finland
QVIST, Per Olov and BAGH, Peter
von.
Greenwood Press, vi-vii, 308p.
filmogs. bibliogs. index.
ISBN 0313303770

Heroines without heroes:
reconstructing female and national
identities in European cinema 1945-51
SIEGLOHR, Ulrike.
Cassell, xi, 212p. illus. bibliog. filmog.
index.
ISBN 0304702501

Italian film
LANDY, Marcia.
Cambridge University Press, vii-xxiii,
434p. illus. bibliog. filmog. index.
ISBN 0521640091

The queer German cinema
KUZNIAR, Alice A.
Stanford University Press, vi-x, 314p.
illus. bibliog. index.
ISBN 0804739951

Real images: Soviet cinema and the
thaw
WOLL, Josephine.
I.B.Tauris, vii-xvi, 267p. illus. filmog.
bibliog. index
ISBN 1860643698

Revolt of the filmmakers: the
struggle for artistic autonomy and
the fall of the Soviet film industry
FARADAY, George.
Pennsylvania State University Press,
252p. illus. bibliog. index.
ISBN 0271019832
"Some big bourgeois brothel":

contexts for France's culture wars
with Hollywood
GRANTHAM, Bill.
University of Luton Press, 184p.
tables. bibliog. filmog.
ISBN 1860205356

Spaces in European cinema
KONSTANTARAKOS, Myrto (ed.)
Intellect Books, 188p. illus.
ISBN 1841500046

Stars and stardom in French cinema
VINCENDEAU, Ginette
Continuum, xii, 275p. illus. bibliog.
index.
ISBN 0826447317

Weimar cinema and after: Germany's
historical imaginary
ELSAESSER, Thomas.
Routledge, v-viii, 472p. illus. bibliog.
index.
ISBN 141501235X

Histories-General

The great art of light and shadow:
archaeology of the cinema
MANNONI, Laurent and Crangle,
Richard (ed and transl.)
University of Exeter Press, xxx, 546p.
bibliog. notes. index. appendices.
ISBN 085989665X

A history of pre-cinema
HERBERT, Stephen.
Routledge, iv-xxviii, 329, iv-xi, 525,
iv-vi, 142p. illus. index.
ISBN 0415211476

The international movie industry
KINDEM, Gorham.
Southern Illinois University Press, v-
vi, 417p. bibliog. index.
ISBN 0809322994

An introduction to world cinema
GAZETAS, Aristides.
McFarland, vii-viii, 340p. illus. index.
ISBN 078640809X

Moving images: from Edison to the
webcam
FULLERTON, John and
SODERBERGH WIDDING, Astrid
(ed.)
John Libbey, 201p. illus. index.
ISBN 1864620544

A short history of the movies: 7th ed
MAST, Gerald and KAWIN ,Bruce F.
Allyn Bacon, iii-x, 702p. [16] col.
plates. bibliog. gloss. index.
ISBN 0205296858

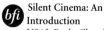 Silent Cinema: An
Introduction
USAI, Paolo Cherchi
British Film Institute, xi, 212p. illus.
tables. bibliog. index.
ISBN 851707 467

World cinema: critical approaches
HILL, John and GIBSON, Pamela
Church.
Oxford University Press, vii-xv, 234p.
illus. bibliogs. index.
ISBN 0198742827

Histories-Great Britain

British cinema and the Second World
War
MURPHY, Robert.
Continuum, viii, 340p. illus. bibliog.
filmog. indices.
ISBN 082645139X

British cinema in documents
STREET, Sarah.
Routledge, x, 194p. illus. appendices.
bibliog. index.
ISBN 0415168015

British cinema in the fifties: gender,
genre and the 'new look'
GERAGHTY, Christine.
Routledge, xv, 221p. illus. bibliog.
filmog. index.
ISBN 041517158X

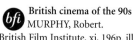 British cinema of the 90s
MURPHY, Robert.
British Film Institute, xi, 196p. illus.
tables. bibliog. index.
ISBN 0851707629

British cinema, past and present
ASHBY, Justine and HIGSON,
Andrew (eds.)
Routledge, vii-xx, 385p. illus. bibliog.
index.
ISBN 0415220629

Cinecenta cinemas: an outline
history
TURNER, Philip.

Brantwood Books,(ii) 30p. illus.
ISBN 0953102173

Edinburgh theatres, cinemas and circuses, 1820-1963
BAIRD, George.
George Baird, ii-xii, 526p. index

Film, television and the Left in Britain 1950 to 1970
HOGENKAMP, Bert.
Lawrence Wishart, vii-xiv, 178p. illus.
filmog. bibliog. index.
ISBN 085315905X

Going to the pictures: Scottish memories of cinema
MARTIN, Andrew.
NMS Publishing, 159p. illus. filmog.
bibliog.
ISBN 1901663442

 Irish film: the emergence of a contemporary cinema
MCLOONE, Martin.
British Film Institute, vi, 234p. illus.
bibliog. index.
ISBN 0851707920

Moving performance: British stage and screen, 1890s-1920s
FITZSIMMONS, Linda and STREET, Sarah.
Flicks Books, 178p. [4] plates. index.
ISBN 0948911549

The Pinewood story: the authorised history of the world's most famous film studio
OWEN, Gareth and BURFORD, Brian.
Reynolds Hearn Ltd, 208p. illus.
bibliog. filmog. index.
ISBN 1903111099

Popular filmgoing in 1930s Britain: a choice of pleasures
SEDGWICK, John.
University of Exeter Press, v-x, 316p.
bibliog. figs. index. tables.
ISBN 0859896609

Screening Ireland: film and television representation
PETTITT, Lance.
Manchester University Press, 320p.
illus. appendices. bibliog. index.
ISBN 071905270X

 Screening Scotland
PETRIE, Duncan.
British Film Institute, 250p. illus.
appendices. bibliog. index.
ISBN 0851707858

Searching for stars: stardom and screen acting in British cinema
MACNAB, Geoffrey.
Cassell, vi-vii, 216p. [8] plates.
bibliog. index.
ISBN 0304333514

 Sixties British cinema: 16+ guide
DUPIN, Christophe and NEWMAN, Sara and ORMSBY, Andrew and O'SULLIVAN, Ian.
BFI National Library, 42p.
ISBN 0851708285

Structures of desire: British cinema, 1939-1955
WILLIAMS, Tony.
State University of New York Press, v-xi, 213p. illus. bibliog. index.
ISBN 0791446441

Towards a sustainable UK film industry
Film Council
Film Council, 36p. illus.

 Towards visibility: a three-year cultural diversity strategy (phase 1): consultation draft
British Film Institute.
British Film Institute, 92p.

Women in British cinema: mad, bad and dangerous to know
HARPER, Sue.
Continuum, vii, 261p. plates. bibliog.
indices.
ISBN 0826447333

Histories-USA and America

100 years of American film
BEAVER, Frank Eugene (ed.)
Macmillan Library Reference, v-xxiv, 840p. illus. gloss.
bibliog. index.
ISBN 0028653807

American cinema and Hollywood: critical approaches
HILL, John and GIBSON, Pamela

Church.
Oxford University Press, vi-xiii, 160p.
illus. bibliogs. index.
ISBN 019874281

American politics in Hollywood film
SCOTT, Ian. Edinburgh University Press, vii-viii, 184p. illus. index.
ISBN 0748612467

The big picture: who killed Hollywood? and other essays
GOLDMAN, William and LOUVISH, Simon.
Applause, 283p.
ISBN 1557834067

The big tomorrow: Hollywood and the politics of the American way
MAY, Lary.
University of Chicago Press, vii-xv, 348p. illus. appendices. index.
ISBN 0226511626

Canada's film century: traditions transitions transcendence Special theme
Lonergan University College.
Lonergan University College, i-ix.
237p. illus.
ISBN 0969630956

Celluloid mavericks: a history of American independent film
MERRITT, Greg.
Thunder's Mouth Press, ix-xv, 463p.
illus. chronol. appendices. bibliog.
index.
ISBN 1560252324

Cinema southwest: an illustrated guide to the movies and their locations
MURRAY, John A.
Northland, ix-xi, 161p. illus.
appendix. bibliog. index.
ISBN 0873587472

Destination Hollywood: the influence of Europeans on American filmmaking
LANGMAN, Larry.
McFarland, vii, 278p. illus. bibliog.
index.
ISBN 078640681X

The Emmys: the ultimate, unofficial guide to the battle of TV's best shows and greatest stars: 3rd ed

O'NEIL, Thomas.
Perigee, vi-ix, 691p. index.
ISBN 0399526110

 Encore Hollywood: remaking French cinema
MAZDON, Lucy.
British Film Institute, vi, 169p.
bibliog. index.
ISBN 0851708013

Feminist Hollywood: from Born in flames to Point break
LANE, Christina.
Wayne State University Press, 261p.
illus. bibliog. index.
ISBN 0814327990

Film composers in America: a filmography, 1911-1970: 2nd ed
MCCARTY, Clifford.
Oxford University Press, viii, 534p.
index.
ISBN 0195114736

The girls: Sappho goes to Hollywood
MCLELLAN, Diana.
St. Martin's Press, vii-xxiii, 440p. [16] plates. index.
ISBN 0312246471

Heroes, monsters, and messiahs: movies and television shows as the mythology of American culture
HIRSCHMANN, Elizabeth.
Andrews McMeel, 353p. illus. bibliog.
ISBN 0740704850

Hollywood candid: a photographer remembers
GARRETT, Murray.
Harry N. Abrams, 167p. illus. index.
ISBN 0810934418

Hollywood death and scandal sites: sixteen driving tours with directions and the full story, from Tallulah Bankhead to River Phoenix
FLEMING, E. J.
McFarland, v, 281p. illus. bibliog.
index.
ISBN 0786401605

Hollywood fictions: the dream factory in American popular literature
SPRINGER, John Parris.
University of Oklahoma Press, ix-xvi, 319p. bibliog. index.
ISBN 0806132035

Hollywood goes shopping
DESSER, David and JOWETT, Garth S (eds.)
University of Minnesota Press, ix-xxi, 363p. illus. index.
ISBN 0816635137

Inside "Variety": the story of the bible of showbusiness (1905-1987) (unauthorized)
BESAS, Peter.
Ars Millenii, x-xxi, 563p. illus. chronol. bibliog. index.
ISBN 8493021156

Lost illusions: American cinema in the shadow of Watergate and Vietnam, 1970-1979
COOK, David A.
Charles Scribner's Sons, xi-xxii, 695p. illus. filmog. appendices. bibliog. indices.
ISBN 0684804638

Magic moments: first 20 years of moving pictures in Toronto (1894-1914)
GUTTERIDGE, Robert W.
Gutteridge-Pratley, ii-x, 258p. illus. appendices. indices.
ISBN 0968612504

Magical reels: a history of cinema in Latin America: 2nd ed
KING, John.
Verso, vi. 314p. notes. index.
ISBN 185984233X

The making of American audiences: from stage to television, 1750-1990
BUTSCH, Richard.
Cambridge University Press, v-x, 438p. [16] plates. bibliog. index.
ISBN 0521664837

Movies and television locations: 113 famous filming sites in Los Angeles and San Diego
SMITH, Leon.
McFarland, vii-x, 285p. illus. index.
ISBN 0786406054

Movie-struck girls: women and motion picture culture after the Nickelodeon
STAMP, Shelley.
Princeton University Press, x, 274p.
28 illus. bibliog. index.
ISBN 0691044570

A new pot of gold: Hollywood under the electronic rainbow, 1980-1989
PRINCE, Stephen.
Charles Scribner's Sons, x-xxi, 564p.
illus. appendices. bibliog. indices.
ISBN 068480493X

Radicalism in American silent films, 1909-1929: a filmography and history
SHULL, Michael S.
McFarland, vii-x, 345p. illus. bibliog. index.
ISBN 0786406925

Shot in America: television, the state, and the rise of Chicano cinema
NORIEGA, Chon A.
Minnesota University Press, xi-xxxiii, 305p. filmog. bibliog. index. ISBN 0816629315

Silent screens: the decline and transformation of the American movie theatre
PUTNAM, Michael.
Johns Hopkins University Press, xi-xv, 102p. illus.
ISBN 0801863295

Spectacular narratives: Hollywood in the age of the blockbuster
KING, Geoff.
I.B.Tauris, 213p. illus. bibliog. index.
ISBN 1860645720

Tinker belles and evil queens: the Walt Disney Company from the inside out
GRFFIN, Sean
New York University
Press, v-xxiii, 292p. [4] plates. bibliog. index.
ISBN 0814731236

Visible nations: Latin American cinema and video
NORIEGA, Chon A.
University of Minnesota Press, xxv, 305p. illus.
ISBN 0816633487

Individual Films

Alfred Hitchcock's Rear window
BELTON, John.
Cambridge University Press, ix-xiv, 177p. illus. filmog. bibliog. index.
ISBN 0521564530

Alien: the complete illustrated screenplay
O'BANNON, Dan. SAMMON, Paul M. London: Orion, 2000. 191p. illus.
ISBN 0752831917

All about "All About Eve": the complete behind-the-scenes story of the bitchiest film ever made
STAGGS, Sam.
St. Martin's Press, xi, 388p. illus. index
ISBN 0312252684

Almost famous
CROWE, Cameron.
Faber and Faber, vii-xxiv, 188p. illus.
ISBN 0571205690

 L'année derniere a Marienbad (Last year in Marienbad)*
LEUTRAT, Jean-Louis and HAMMOND, Paul (transl.)
British Film Institute, 72p. illus.
bibliog.
ISBN 0851708218

The Apocalypse Now book
COWIE, Peter.
Faber and Faber, x, 212p. illus,
bibliog, index.
ISBN 0571203698

Arthur Penn's Bonnie and Clyde
FRIEDMAN, Lester D.
Cambridge University Press, xvii, 211p. illus. filmog. index.
ISBN 0521596971

Asthenic syndrome = Asteniceskij sindrom
TAUBMAN, Jane A.
Flicks Books, 54p. illus. index.
ISBN 0948911336

The Battleship Potemkin: the film companion
TAYLOR, Richard.
I.B.Tauris, xiv, 129p. illus.
ISBN 1860643930

The beach
HODGE, John.
Faber and Faber, 153p. illus.
ISBN 0571204864

Being John Malkovich
KAUFMAN, Charlie.
Faber and Faber, vii-xi, 129p. illus. credits.
ISBN 0571205860

 Belle de jour
WOOD, Michael.
British Film Institute, 79p. illus.
bibliog.
ISBN 0851708234

Billy Elliot
HALL, Lee.
Faber and Faber, vii-xi, 97p. illus.
credits.
ISBN 0571207030

Blade Runner: the inside story
SHAY, Don.
Titan, 72p. col. illus.
ISBN 1840232102

 Bonnie and Clyde
FRIEDMAN, Lester D.
British Film Institute, 78p. illus.
ISBN 0851705707

Bringing out the dead
SCHRADER, Paul.
Faber and Faber, 116p. illus.
ISBN 0571204899

Buena Vista Social Club: the book of the film
WENDERS, Wim and WENDERS, Donata.
Thames and Hudson, 131p. col. plates.
ISBN 050028220X

Burnt by the sun
BEUMERS, Birgit.
I.B.Tauris, xii, 134p. illus. bibliog.
ISBN 1860643965

Chicken Run: hatching the movie
SIBLEY, Brian.
Harry N. Abrams, 191p. illus. credits.
ISBN 0810941244

Cradle will rock: the movie and the moment
ROBBINS, Tim.
Newmarket Press, 150p. illus. index.
ISBN 155704399X

Dancer in the dark
TRIER, Lars von.
FilmFour, v-xv, 153p. [8] plates.
ISBN 0752219308

 Dead Man
ROSENBAUM, Jonathan.
British Film Institute, 93p. illus.
appendix. bibliog.
ISBN 0851708064

Diner
LEVINSON, Barry.
Faber and Faber, 110p.
ISBN 0571202349

Dinosaur: the evolution of an animated movie
KURTTI, Jeff.
Disney Editions, 128p. col. illus.
ISBN 0786851058

Double indemnity: screenplay
WILDER, Billy and CHANDLER, Raymond.
University of California Press, vii-xvi, 123p.
ISBN 0520218485

Erin Brockovich
GRANT, Susannah.
Nick Hern Books, iv-vi, 135p. illus.
credits.
ISBN 1854596330

The Evil Dead companion
WARREN, Bill and RAIMI, Sam.
Titan, 271p. illus. gloss. filmog. index.
bibliog.
ISBN 1840231874

Forever Liesl: my Sound Of Music story
CARR, Charmian and STRAUSS, Jean A.S.
Sidgwick & Jackson, viii-x, 254p. [8] plates. index.
ISBN 0283072962

Fritz Lang's Metropolis: cinematic visions of technology and fear
MINDEN, Michael and BACHMANN, Holger.
Camden House, xi, 326p. illus.
bibliog. index.
ISBN 1571131221

High Fidelity
CUSACK, John and DeVINCENTIS, D.V. and PINK, Steve and ROSENBERG, Scott.
FilmFour, ix-xiii, 170p. [8] plates.
ISBN 0752219197

Ingmar Bergman's Persona
MICHAELS, Lloyd and BERGMAN, Ingmar.
Cambridge University Press, ix-xiv, 191p. illus. bibliog. index.
ISBN 0521656982

Inside The Wicker man: the morbid ingenuities
BROWN, Allan.
Sidgwick Jackson, x-xxvi, 241p. [24] plates. appendices. bibliog. index.
ISBN 0283063556

Into the woods: the definitive story of The Blair witch project
POTTON, Ed and COWAN, Amber.
ScreenPress, xiii, 64p. illus

Jane Campion's The Piano
MARGOLIS, Harriet E (ed.)
Cambridge University Press, vii-xiv, 204p. filmog. bibliog. index.
ISBN 0521592585

Jean-Luc Godard's Pierrot le fou
WILLS, David.
Cambridge University Press, vii-xiv, 191p. bibliog. index.
ISBN 0521573750

The lost "Carry Ons": scenes that never made it to the screen
BRIGHT, Morris and ROSS, Robert.
Virgin, 160p. illus.
ISBN 1852279907

The lost weekend: screenplay
WILDER, Billy and BRACKETT, Charles.
University of California Press, vii-xiv, 110p.
ISBN 0520218566

M
KAES, Anton.
British Film Institute, 87p, illus.
ISBN 0851703704

Magnolia: the shooting script
ANDERSON, Paul Thomas.
Newmarket Press, vii-ix, 212p. illus. [16] plates.
ISBN 1557044066

The making of 2001: a space Odyssey
SCHWAM, Stephanie (compiler)
Modern Library, viii-xviii, 326p. filmog.
ISBN 0375755284

The making of The Crow
BAISS, Bridget.
Making of The Crow Inc. 272p. illus. appendices.
ISBN 1870048547

The man who cried
POTTER, Sally.
Faber and Faber, vii-xlii, 102p. illus. credits.
ISBN 0571207480

The man with the movie camera
ROBERTS, Graham.
I.B.Tauris, xv,108p. illus.
ISBN 1860643949

Manhattan: scenario bilangue
ALLEN, Woody and BRICKMAN, Marshall and DUTTER, Georges (transl.)
Cahiers du Cinéma, 191p.
ISBN 286642204X

A matter of life and death
CHRISTIE, Ian.
British Film Institute, 87p, illus.
ISBN 0851704794

Max Steiner's Now, Voyager: a film score guide
DAUBNEY, Kate
Greenwood Press, ix-xviii, 112p. figs. appendix. bibliog. index.
ISBN 0313312532

Memories of Hollywood 1944: Uncertain Glory: a reappraisal of the Warner Bros
First National Picture
LAZAROU, George A.
George A. Lazarou (10 Lamias Street) ii-vi, 22p. illus. bibliog.

Metropolis
ELSAESSER, Thomas.
British Film Institute, 87p. illus. appendix. bibliog.
ISBN 0851707777

Mourir a tue-tete / A scream from silence
LOISELLE, Andre.
Flicks Books, 71p. notes. index.
ISBN 0948911328

The Navigator: a mediaeval odyssey
DOWNIE, John.
Flicks Books, 58p.
ISBN 0948911654

The night of the hunter
CALLOW, Simon.
British Film Institute, 79p. illus.
ISBN 0851708226

O brother, where art thou?
COEN, Ethan and COEN, Joel.
Faber and Faber, vii-viii, 111p. illus.
ISBN 0571205186

The Odd Couple I and II: the original screenplays
SIMON, Neil.
Touchstone, 318p.
ISBN 0684859254

Oz before the rainbow: L. Frank Baum's The Wonderful Wizard of Oz on stage and screen to 1930
SWARTZ, Mark Evan.
Johns Hopkins University Press, xii, 291p. illus. bibliog. index.
ISBN 0801864771

The patriot: the official companion
FRITZ, Suzanne and ABERLY, Rachel.
Carlton Books, 96p. col. illus.
ISBN 1842220764

Pulp Fiction
POLAN, Dana.
British Film Institute, 95p. illus. bibliog.
ISBN 0851708080

Purely belter
HERMAN, Mark.
FilmFour, v-x, 182p. [8]plates.
ISBN 0752219049

Red River
LIANDRAT-GUIGUES, Suzanne and COATES, Nick (transl.)
British Film Institute, 72p. illus.
ISBN 0851708196

Requiem for a dream
ARONOFSKY, Darren and SELBY, Jr, Hubert.
Faber and Faber, vii-xv, 127p. illus.
ISBN 057120631X

Rome open city (Roma citta aperta)
FORGACS, David.
British Film Institute, 79p. illus. bibliog.
ISBN 0851708048

A room for Romeo Brass: the original shooting script
FRASER, Paul and MEADOWS, Shane.
ScreenPress, 120p. illus.
ISBN 1901680452

Salò or the 120 days of Sodom
(Salo o le 120 giornate di
Sodoma)
INDIANA, Gary.
British Film Institute, 95p. illus.
bibliog.
ISBN 0851708072

 Sansho dayu
ANDREW, Dudley and
CAVANAUGH, Carole.
British Film Institute, 79p. illus.
bibliog.
ISBN 0851708153

 The Searchers
BUSCOMBE, Edward.
British Film Institute, 80p. illus.
bibliog.
ISBN 085170820X

Snatch: the screenplay
RITCHIE, Guy.
Orion, 224p. illus.
ISBN 0752837729

Snow falling on cedars: [a]
screenplay
BASS, Ron and HICKS, Scott.
Bloomsbury, vi-vii, 166p. illus.
ISBN 0747544778

Stuart Little: the art, the artists, and
the story behind the amazing movie
SUNSHINE, Linda (ed) and
SHYAMALAN, M. Night and
BROOKER, Greg.
Newmarket Press, 160p. col. illus.
ISBN 1557044074

The talented Mr. Ripley: screenplay
MINGHELLA, Anthony.
Methuen, vii-xvi, 157p. [8] plates.
ISBN 0413742008

 Taxi driver
TAUBIN, Amy.
British Film Institute, 79p. col. illus.
ISBN 0851703933

 Thelma and Louise
STURKEN, Marita.
British Film Institute, 94p. illus.
ISBN 0851708099

Traffic
GAGHAN, Stephen.
Faber and Faber, 158p. illus.
ISBN 0571212700

Individual Television Programmes

The art of Gormenghast: the making
of a television fantasy
DANIEL, Estelle and PEAKE,
Mervyn.
HarperCollins, 160p. col. illus.
ISBN 0002571560

Backstage at the Dean Martin Show
HALE, Lee and NEELY, Richard.
Taylor Publishing Company, ix-xv,
254p. illus. [16] col. plates. index.
ISBN 0878331700

Big brother: the official unseen story
RITCHIE, Jean.
Channel 4 Books, 250p. [16] plates.
ISBN 075221912X

Dreaming of Jeannie: tv's prime time
in a bottle
COX, Stephen.
St. Martin's Griffin, ix-xi, 285p. illus.
[16] col. plates.
ISBN 0312204175

Eliot Ness and the Untouchables: the
historical reality and the film and
television depictions
TUCKER, Kenneth.
McFarland, v, 202p. illus. bibliog.
index.
ISBN 0786407727

Father Ted: the complete scripts
LINEHAN, Graham and MATHEWS,
Arthur
Boxtree, iv-vii, 368p. illus.
ISBN 0752272357

"From beautiful downtown
Burbank": a critical history of Rowan
and Martin's laugh-in, 1968-1973
ERICKSON, Hal.
McFarland, vii-viii. 333p. appendix.
bibliog. index.
ISBN 0786407662

A history and critical analysis of
Blake's 7, the 1978-1981 British
television space adventure
MUIR, John Kenneth.
McFarland, v-vi, 217p. illus.
appendix. videog. bibliog. index.
ISBN 078640600

The pocket essential Doctor Who
CAMPBELL, Mark.
Pocket Essentials, 95p. bibliog.
ISBN 1903047196

Poplit, popcult and The X-Files: a
critical exploration
DELASARA, Jan.
McFarland, v, 247p notes. bibliog.
index.
ISBN 0786407891

Star Trek: parallel narratives
GREGORY, Chris.
Macmillan, viii, 225p. app. bibliog.
ISBN 0333744896

Who's who in Eastenders
LOCK, Kate.
BBC Worldwide, 128p. col. Illus
ISBN 056355178X

New Technologies

After the death of childhood:
growing up in the age of electronic
media
BUCKINGHAM, David.
Polity Press and Basil Blackwell, vii,
245p. refs. index.
ISBN 0745619339

The art of digital video: 3rd ed
WATKINSON, John.
Focal Press, 774p. figs. index.
ISBN 0240515862

Broadcasting, cable, the internet, and
beyond: an introduction to modern
electronic media: 4th ed
DOMINICK, Joseph R and
SHERMAN, Barry L and MESSERE,
Fritz.
McGraw-Hill, v-xvii. 330p. illus. figs.
gloss. index.
ISBN 0070179883

The business of digital television
FORRESTER, Chris.
Focal Press, viii-xii, 275p. charts.
index.
ISBN 0240516060

The digital dialectic: new essays on
new media
LUNENFELD, Peter.
MIT Press, x-xxi, 298p. bibliog. index.
ISBN 0262122138

Electronic cinema: the big screen goes digital
SYCHOWSKI, Patrick von.
Screen Digest, 244p. tables. figs. gloss. appendices.

The internet and society
SLEVIN, James.
Polity Press, xi, 266p. figures. index.
ISBN 0745620876

Is regulation still an option in a digital universe? Papers from the 30th University of Manchester International broadcasting Symposium LEES, Tim and RALPH, Sue and BROWN, Jo Langham.
University of Luton Press, iv-xii, 326p. figs.

Journalism in the digital age: theory and practice for broadcast, print and on-line media
HERBERT, John.
Focal Press, v-xiv, 349p. appendix. gloss. bibliog. index.
ISBN 0240515897

Multimedia: a critical introduction
WISE, Richard.
Routledge, 228p. bibliog. index.
ISBN 0415121515

Old media, new media: mass comunications in the information age: 3rd ed
DIZARD, Wilson Jnr.
Longman, vii-xv, 233p. tables. appendix. gloss. bibliog.
ISBN 080133277X

Trigger happy: the inner life of videogames
POOLE, Steven.
Fourth Estate, 254p. illus. bibliog. index.
ISBN 1841151203

Web.Studies: rewiring media studies for the digital age
GAUNTLETT, David.
Arnold, ix. 250p. illus. gloss. ref. index.
ISBN 0340760494

Personalities: Collected Studies

After image: the indelible Catholic imagination of six American filmmakers
BLAKE, Richard.
Loyola Press, ix-xxi, 274p. filmog. bibliog. notes. index.
ISBN 0829415505

America noir: underground writers and filmmakers of the postwar era
COCHRAN, David.
Smithsonian Institution, viii-xiii, 280p. notes. bibliog. index.
ISBN 1560988134

Brat pack: confidential
PULVER, Andrew and DAVIES, Steven Paul.
B.T. Batsford, 158p. illus. index.
ISBN 0713486856

Brotherhood in rhythm: the jazz tap dancing of the Nicholas brothers
HILL, Constance Valis.
Oxford University Press, ix-xvi, 320p. illus. gloss. bibliog. index.
ISBN 0195131665

A cinema of loneliness: Penn, Stone, Kubrick, Scorsese, Spielberg, Altman: 3rd ed
KOLKER, Robert
Oxford University Press, ix-xvii, 484p. illus. filmog. index.
ISBN 0195123506

The Coen brothers
BERGAN, Ronald.
Orion, 242p. illus. bibliog. filmog. index.
ISBN 0752818147

The directors - take two: in their own words
EMERY, Robert J.
TV Books, 381p. illus. filmogs. index.
ISBN 1575001292

Directors close-up: interviews with directors nominated for outstanding directorial achievement in a feature film by the Directors Guild of America
KAGAN, Jeremy (ed.)
Focal Press, v-ix, 253p. [16] plates.
appendix.
ISBN 0240804066

Double vision: Stan Douglas and Douglas Gordon
COOKE, Lynne and KELLY, Karen.
Dia Center for the Arts, 51p. col. plates. bibliog.
ISBN 0944521371

The family way : the Boulting brothers and postwar British film culture
BURTON, Alan and O'SULLIVAN, Tim and WELLS, Paul (eds.)
Flicks Books, vi, 298p. [8] plates. filmog. bibliog. index.
ISBN 094891159X

Film crazy: interviews with Hollywood legends
MCGILLIGAN, Patrick.
St. Martin's Press, viii, 279p. [8] plates. index.
ISBN 0312261314

The horror spoofs of Abbott and Costello: a critical assessment of the comedy team's monster films
MILLER, Jeffrey S.
McFarland, vii-ix, 241p. bibliog. index.

The Hustons: the life and times of a Hollywood dynasty
GROBEL, Lawrence.
Cooper Square Press, viii-xx, 830p. [16] plates. theatrog. filmog. index.
ISBN 0815410263

Joel and Ethan Coen: blood siblings
WOODS, Paul A (ed.)
Plexus, 180p. illus.
ISBN 0859652858

Last of the cowboy heroes: the westerns of Randolph Scott, Joel McCrea, and Audie Murphy
NOTT, Robert.
McFarland, ix, 195p. illus. bibliog. filmog. index.
ISBN 078640762X

More contemporary cinematographers on their art
ROGERS, Pauline B
Focal Press, v-xii, 199p.
ISBN 024080368X

My first movie
LOWENSTEIN, Stephen.
Faber and Faber, xiv, 360p.
ISBN 0571196691

Personal visions: conversations with
contemporary film directors
FALSETTO, Mario.
Silman-James Press, ix-xviii, 529p.
ISBN 1879505517

Projections 11: New York film-
makers on film-making
LIPPY, Todd and BOORMAN, John
and DONOHUE, Walter (eds.)
Faber and Faber, vii-ix, 332p. illus.
ISBN 0571205917

Ready when you are, Mr. Coppola,
Mr. Spielberg, Mr. Crowe
ZIESMER, Jerry.
The Scarecrow Press, xi-xviii, 436p.
[16] plates. index.
ISBN 0810836572

Reel cowboys: western movie stars
who thrilled young fans and helped
them grow up decent and strong
O'NEAL, Bill.
Eakin Press, vi, 90p. illus. index.
ISBN 1571683300

Rudyard Kipling and Sir Henry Rider
Haggard on screen, stage, radio and
Television
LEIBFRIED, Philip. McFarland, vii-ix,
214p. illus. bibliog. index.
ISBN 0786407077

Salaam cinema! Films of
Makhmalbaf family
Pusan International Film Festival.
Pusan International Film Festival,
120p. illus. filmog

Science fiction film directors, 1895-
1998
FISCHER, Dennis.
McFarland, vi-viii, 759p. illus.
appendices. bibliog. index.
ISBN 0786407409

Stars in my eyes
BACHARDY, Don.
University of Wisconsin Press, vii-ix,
262p. illus.
ISBN 0299167305

Voices from the set: the Film
Heritage interviews

MACKLIN, Tony and PICI, Nick.
The Scarecrow Press, vii-xiii, 335p.
[8] plates. index.
ISBN 0810837951

You should have been here yesterday:
a life in television news
UTLEY, Garrick.
Public Affairs Press, ix-xvi, 285p. illus.
index. Includes cd-rom.
ISBN 1891620940

Personalities –
Individual Studies

Alex Cox: film anarchist
DAVIES, Steven Paul.
Batsford, 191p. illus. filmog.
ISBN 0713486708

An unspeakable betrayal: selected
writings of Luis Buñuel
BUÑUEL, Luis and WHITE, Garrett
(trans.)
University of California Press. 235p.
Poetry, short stories, and an essay.
ISBN:0520208404

An Argentine passion: María Luisa
Bemberg and her films
KING, John and WHITAKER, Sheila
and BOSCH, Rosa (eds.)
Verso, vi-xiii, 234p. illus. Filmog.
index.
ISBN 1859843085

The art of Charlie Chaplin
KIMBER, John.
Sheffield Academic Press, 291p. illus.
filmog. bibliog.
ISBN 1841270776

Arthur Godfrey: the adventures of an
American broadcaster
SINGER, Arthur J.
McFarland, vii-x, 246p. illus. bibliog.
index.
ISBN 0786407042

Bernardo Bertolucci: interviews
GERARD, Fabien S and KLINE, T
Jefferson and SKLAREW, Bruce H
(eds.)
University Press of Mississippi, xvi,
276p. filmog. [8] plates index.
ISBN 1578062055

Bertrand Tavernier: the film-maker
of Lyon
HAY, Stephen.
I.B.Tauris, vii-xviii, 244p. illus.
filmog. bibliog. index.
ISBN 1860644627

Billy Wilder: American film realist
ARMSTRONG, Richard.
McFarland, v-vii, 164p. illus. filmog.
bibliog. index.
ISBN 0786408219

Bunuel 100 years
CAMACHO, Enrique and BAZO,
Javier Pérez and BLANCO, Manuel
Rodriguez and BRANGER, Alejandro
(eds.)
Museum of Modern Art/Instituto
Cervantes, 339p. illus.
ISBN 0870700154

Burt Lancaster: a filmography and
biography
ANDREYCHUK, Ed.
McFarland, vi-vii, 248p. illus. bibliog.
filmog. index.
ISBN 0786404361

Burt Lancaster: an American life
BUFORD, Kate.
Alfred A. Knopf, ix, 447p. illus.
bibliog. fimog. index.
ISBN 0679446036

Burton on Burton
SALISBURY, Mark.
Faber and Faber, vii-xviii, 205p, illus.
filmog. index.
ISBN 0571205070

Carol Reed
Festival Internacional de Cine de San
Sebastian.
Festival Internacional de Cine de San
Sebastian/Filmoteca Espanola, 459p.
illus. filmog. bibliog. index.
ISBN 8486877261

The Charlie Chan film encyclopedia
BERLIN, Howard M.
McFarland, vii, 375p. illus. index.
ISBN 0786407093

The cinema alone: essays on the work
of Jean-Luc Godard 1985-2000
TEMPLE, Michael and WILLIAMS,
James S (eds.)
Amsterdam University Press, 269p.

bibliog. filmog. index.
ISBN 9053564551

The cinema of Satyajit Ray: between tradition and modernity
COOPER, Darius.
Cambridge University Press, xii, 260p.
filmog. bibliog. index.
ISBN 0521629802

Claire Danes
AMBROSE, Jennifer.
ECW Press, 156p. illus. bibliog.
ISBN 1550224026

The complete Kubrick
HUGHES, David.
Virgin, 303p. [16] col. plates. filmog.
bibliog. indices.
ISBN 0753504529

The court of king Rolf: a tribute to Rolf Harris
WALKER, Mark.
Partridge, 201p. [16] plates. illus.
ISBN 1852252863

Cyberpunk and cyberculture: science fiction and the work of William Gibson
CAVALLARO, Dani.
Athlone Press, viii-xvi, 258p. refs.
bibliog. index.
ISBN 0485006073

Cybil disobedience
SHEPHERD, Cybill and BALL, Aimee Lee.
HarperCollins, 294p. [24] plates.
ISBN 0060193506

David Geffen: a biography of new Hollywood
KING, Tom.
Hutchinson, ix-xiv, 670p. illus. index.
ISBN 0091802342

Desire unlimited: the cinema of Pedro Almódovar: 2nd ed
SMITH, Paul Julian.
Verso, vii-xvii, 217p. illus. bibliog.
filmog. index.
ISBN 1859843042

Directing film: from pitch to premiere
RUSSELL, Ken.
B.T. Batsford, 127p. illus. filmog.
index.
ISBN 071348554X

The director's cut: a memoir of 60 years in film and television
BAKER, Roy Ward.
Reynolds Hearn Ltd, 185p. [16] plates. filmog. index.
ISBN 1903111021

Dreams within a dream: the films of Peter Weir
BLISS, Michael.
Southern Illinois University Press, x, 243p. illus. bibliog. filmog. index.
ISBN 0809322846

The drunken journalist: the biography of a film stereotype
GOOD, Howard.
The Scarecrow Press, v-vii, 200p, illus.
bibliog. filmog.
ISBN 081083717X

Elia Kazan: interviews
BAER, William.
University Press of Mississippi, vii-xxxiii, 250p. [8] plates. index. ISBN 1578062241

Emile de Antonio: a reader
KELLNER, Douglas and STREIBLE, Dan (eds.)
University of Minnesota Press, xi-xiii, 434p. illus. filmog. bibliog. index.
ISBN 0816633649

The enemy within: the films of Mrinal Sen
CHAKRAVARTY, Sumita S.
Flicks Books, vi, 201p. filmog. bibliog.
index.
ISBN 094891145X

Evergreen: Victor Saville in his own words
MOSELEY, Roy.
Southern Illinois University Press, xi-xxiv, 227p. [16] plates. filmog.
ISBN 080932315X

Face to face: Liv Ullmann and film: filmography
HADDAL, Per.
Norwegian Film Institute, 104p. illus.
filmog.
ISBN 8290463960

The films of Fritz Lang: allegories of vision and modernity
GUNNING, Tom.
British Film Institute, vi-xiii, 528p.

illus. bibliog. index.
ISBN: 0851707432

Films of John Carpenter
MUIR, John Kenneth.
McFarland, vii-x, 265p. illus. filmog.
appendices. bibliog. index.
ISBN 0786407255

The films of Leni Riefenstahl : 3rd ed
HINTON, David B.
The Scarecrow Press, v-ix, 145p [16] plates, appendices, bibliog. filmog.
index.
ISBN 0578860091

The films of Martin Ritt: fanfare for the common man
MILLER, Gabriel.
University Press of Mississippi, xvi.
240p, filmog. index.
ISBN 1578062772

The films of Martin Scorsese, 1963-77: authorship and context
GRIST, Leighton.
Macmillan, vii-ix, 250p. [8] plates.
bibliog. filmog. index.
ISBN 0312229917

The films of Mike Leigh: embracing the world
CARNEY, Ray.
Cambridge University Press, ix-xii, 292p. illus. filmog. bibliog. index.
ISBN 0521485185

Framing Shakespeare on film
HOWLETT, Kathy M.
Ohio University Press, xvii, 255p.
illus. bibliog. filmog. index.
ISBN 0821412477

The gaze and the labyrinth: the cinema of Liliana Cavani
MARRONE, Gaetana.
Princeton University Press, ix-xviii, 308p. illus. bibliog. index.
ISBN 0691008736

George Lucas
WOOG, Adam.
Lucent Books, 112p. illus. bibliog.
index.
ISBN 156006434X

George Lucas: biography
WHITE, Dana.
Lerner, 127p. illus. bibliog. filmog.

index.
ISBN 0822596849

George Méliès: the birth of the auteur
EZRA, Elizabeth.
Manchester University Press, vi-viii, 166p. illus. filmog. bibliog. index.
ISBN 07190539X

Get happy: the life of Judy Garland
CLARKE, Gerald.
Little, Brown, 510p. illus. bibliog. index.
ISBN 0316855952

Girl reel: memoir: a lesbian remembers growing up at the movies
MORRIS, Bonnie J
Coffee House Press, 166p.
ISBN 156890942

Gold digger: the outrageous life and times of Peggy Hopkins Joyce
ROSENBLUM, Constance.
Henry Holt, 293p. illus. bibliog. index.
ISBN 0805050892

Gore Vidal
KAPLAN, Fred.
Bloomsbury, x-xi, 850p. [16] plates. index.
ISBN 0747548188

Greg Williams on set
WILLIAMS, Greg.
Vision On Publishing, 221p. col and bw plates.
ISBN 1903399017

 The Griffith Project volume 4: films produced in 1910*
USAI, Paolo Cherchi.
British Film Institute, ix, 286p. bibliog. index.
ISBN 0851708056

Gwyneth Paltrow
MILANO, Valerie.
ECW Press, 207p. illus. bibliog. filmog.
ISBN 1550224077

Henry James on stage and screen
BRADLEY, John R.
Palgrave, vii-xi, 264p. index.
ISBN 0333792149

Herschell Gordon Lewis, godfather of gore: the films
PALMER, Randy.
McFarland, vii-ix, 193p. illus. filmog. index.
ISBN 078640808

High spirits
SIMS, Joan.
Partridge, vii-ix, 212p. [16] plates.
ISBN 1852252804

 Hitchcock: a teacher's guide
Film Education and British Film Institute.
Film Education, 12p. illus. bibliog.

 Hitchcock: suspense, humour and tone
SMITH, Susan.
British Film Institute, vi-xiii, 162p. illus. filmog. bibliog.
ISBN 0851707793

Interpreting Shakespeare on the screen
CARTMELL, Deborah.
Macmillan, vii-xiii, 170p. appendices. bibliog. filmog. index.
ISBN 0333652126

Inventing Jerry Lewis
KRUTNIK, Frank.
Smithsonian Institution Press, viii, 317p. bibliog. filmog. index.
ISBN 1560983698

The invention of Dolores del Río
HERSHFIELD, Joanne.
University of Minnesota Press, xvi, 165p. illus. bibliog. index.
ISBN 0816634092

J. Lee Thompson
CHIBNALL, Steve.
Manchester University Press, xii, 380p. illus. bibliog. filmog. index.
ISBN 0719060125

Jack Clayton
SINYARD, Neil.
Manchester University Press, xiv. 289p. illus. filmog. bibliog. index.
ISBN 0719055059

James Cameron: an unauthorized biography
SHAPIRO, Marc.
Renaissance Books, 350p. illus. filmog. bibliog. index.
ISBN 158063124X

Jean Renoir
O'SHAUGHNESSY, Martin.
Manchester University Press, viii, 251p. illus. bibliog. filmog. index.
ISBN 0719050634

Jerusalem, take one!: memoirs of a Jewish filmmaker
ROSENTHAL, Alan.
Southern Illinois University Press, ix-xii, 287p. illus. filmog. index.
ISBN 0809323125

John Grierson: life, contributions, influence
ELLIS, Jack C.
Southern Illinois University Press, vii-xiv, 441p. bibliog. index.
ISBN 0809322420

John Sayles: an unauthorized biography of the pioneering indie filmmaker
MOLYNEAUX, Gerard.
Renaissance Books, ix, 317p. illus. filmog. videog. bibliog. index.
ISBN 1580631258

The keys to the kingdom: how Michael Eisner lost his grip
MASTERS, Kim.
William Morrow, 469p. [16] plates. index.
ISBN 0688174493

Kubrick
HERR, Michael.
Grove Press, 96p. illus.
ISBN 0802116701

Kubrick's 2001: a triple allegory
WHEAT, Leonard F.
The Scarecrow Press, v-vi, 181p. bibliog. index.
ISBN 081083796X

Kubrick: inside a film artist's maze: new ed
NELSON, Thomas Allen.
Indiana University Press, ix, 333p. illus. bibliog. filmog. index.
ISBN 0253213908

Kurosawa: film studies and Japanese cinema
YOSHIMOTO, Mitsuhiro.
Duke University Press, vii-x, 485p. illus. filmog. bibliog. index.
ISBN 0822325195

Lee Marvin: his films and career
LENTZ, Robert J.
McFarland, ix, 228p. illus. bibliog.
index.
ISBN 0786407239

Liberace: an American boy
PYRON, Darden Asbury.
University of Chicago Press, vii-xvi,
494p. [36] plates. index.
ISBN 0226686671

The life and humour of Robin
Williams: a biography
DAVID, Jay.
Robert Hale, 192p. illus. appendices,
index.
ISBN 0709067356

Like a bullet of light: the films of Bob
Dylan
LEE, C. P.
Helter Skelter Publishing, 219p. illus.
8 plates. bibliog.
ISBN 1900924064

Lillian Gish: a life on stage and
screen
ODERMAN, Stuart.
McFarland, vii-viii, 400p. illus.
bibliog. index.
ISBN 0786406445

Living dangerously: a biography of
Joris Ivens
SCHOOTS, Hans.
Amsterdam University Press, 443p.
bibliog. filmog. index.
ISBN 9053563881

Looking for Robbie: a biography of
Robbie Coltrane
NORMAN, Neil.
Orion, 277p. [16] plates. filmog.
index.
ISBN 0752837567

Lost in the funhouse: the life and
mind of Andy Kaufman
ZEHME, Bill.
Fourth Estate, 368p. [16] plates.
ISBN 1841152307

Lulu in Hollywood
BROOKS, Louise Randolph.
University of Minnesota Press, xlvi,
115p.
ISBN 0816637318

Mainly about Lindsay Anderson
LAMBERT, Gavin.
Alfred A. Knopf, 369p. illus. index.
ISBN 0679445986

Making music with Charlie Chaplin:
an autobiography by Eric James
JAMES, Eric.
The Scarecrow Press, xvii, 122p. illus.
index.
ISBN 0810837412

Manuel Puig and the spider woman:
his life and fictions
LEVINE, Suzanne Jill.
Faber and Faber, vi-xvi, 448p. [8]
plates.
index.
ISBN 0571176666

Margaret O'Brien: a career chronicle
and biography
ELLENBERGER ,Allan R.
McFarland, xiii. 239p. illus. filmog.
bibliog. index.
ISBN 0786408855

The measure of a man: a memoir
POITIER, Sidney.
Simon Schuster, xiii, 255p. index.
ISBN 0743208684

Mike Leigh: interviews
MOVSHOVITZ, Howie.
University Press of Mississippi, vi-
xxii, 138p. [8] plates. index.
ISBN 1578060680

Mitchum in his own words
ROBERTS, Jerry.
Limelight Editions, 256p. illus. [8
leaves of plates], filmog. index.
ISBN 0879102926

The modern fantastic: the films of
David Cronenberg
GRANT, Michael.
Flicks Books, 218p. bibliog. filmog.
index.
ISBN 1862360006

Moonraker, Strangelove and other
celluloid dreams: the visionary art of
Ken Adam
SYLVESTER, David.
Serpentine Gallery, 143p. illus. filmog.
bibliog.
ISBN 1870814274

My time with Antonioni: the diary of
an extraordinary experience
WENDERS, Wim.
Faber and Faber, xviii, 183p. illus.
ISBN 0571200761

My only great passion: the life and
films of Carl Th. Dreyer
DRUM, Jean and DRUM, Dale D.
The Scarecrow Press, xx, 329p. illus.
bibliog. filmog. index.
ISBN 0810836793

My week with Marilyn
CLARK, Colin.
HarperCollins, 159p. [8] plates.
index.
ISBN 0002571277

Oliver Stone's USA: film, history, and
controversy
TOPLIN, Robert Brent.
University Press of Kansas, 335p. [16]
plates. bibliog. index.
ISBN 0700610359

An open window: the cinema of
Víctor Erice
EHRLICH, Linda C.
The Scarecrow Press, 304p. filmog.
bibliog. index.
ISBN 0810837668

Order in the universe: the films of
John Carpenter: 2nd ed
CUMBOW, Robert C.
The Scarecrow Press, xi. 295p. illus.
filmog. index.
ISBN 0810837196

The passion of Dennis Potter:
international collected essays
GRAS, Vernon and W.COOK, John R
(eds.)
St. Martin's Press, vi-xvi, 279p.
ISBN 0312218036

The Peter Cushing companion
MILLER, David.
Reynolds Hearn Ltd, 192p. chronol.
bibliog. index.
ISBN 190311103X

Peter Greenaway interviews
GRAS, Vernon and GRAS, Marguerite
(eds.)
University Press of Mississippi, vi-
xxviii, 200p. 8 plates. index.
ISBN 1578062551

The pocket essential David Lynch
LE BLANC, Michelle and ODELL, Colin.
Pocket Essentials, 96p. bibliog
ISBN 1903047064

The pocket essential Orson Welles
FITZGERALD, Martin.
Pocket Essentials, 95p. bibliog.
ISBN 1903047048

The pocket essential Sam Peckinpah
LUCK, Richard.
Pocket Essentials, 96p. filmog. Bibliog.
ISBN 190304720X

The pocket essential Steve McQueen
LUCK, Richard.
Pocket Essentials, 95p. filmog. bibliog.
ISBN 1903047234

Quentin Tarantino: the film geek files
WOODS, Paul A.
Plexus, 183p. illus. filmog.
ISBN 085965284X

Reminder
WATERMAN, Dennis and ARLON, Jill.
Hutchinson, viii, 304p. [16] plates. index.
ISBN 0091801087

Robert Altman interviews
STERRITT, David.
University Press of Mississippi, xxxv, 225p. filmog. [8] plates. index.
ISBN 1578061865

Robert Bresson
READER, Keith.
Manchester University Press, vi-viii, 166p. illus. filmog. bibliog. index.
ISBN 0719053668

 Roberto Rossellini: magician of the real
FORGACS, David and LUTTON, Sarah and NOWELL-SMITH, Geoffrey (eds.)
British Film Institute, xxii. 208p. illus. filmog. bibliog. index.
ISBN 0851707947

Satyajit Ray: in search of the modern
GANGULY, Suranjan.
The Scarecrow Press, 175p. [8] plates. chronol. filmog. bibliog.
ISBN 0810837692

Science is fiction: the films of Jean Painlevé
BERG, Brigitte and BELLOWS, Andy Masaki and McDOUGALL, Marina (eds.)
Brico Press, xv-xviii, 213p. illus. index. filmog. bibliog.
ISBN 0262024721

Sean Bean: the biography
JACKSON, Laura.
Piatkus, vi-vii, 231p. [8] col. plates. filmog. index.
ISBN 0749921501

Seeing things: an autobiography
POSTGATE, Oliver.
Sidgwick Jackson, 422p. illus. [16] plates.
ISBN 0283063637

Sergio Leone: something to do with death
FRAYLING, Christopher.
Faber and Faber, ix-xvi, 570p. [16] plates. bibliog. filmog. index.
ISBN 0571164382

Shakespeare in Hollywood, 1929-1956
WILLSON, Robert F.Jr.
Associated University Presses, 190p. filmog. bibliog. index.
ISBN 0838638325

Shakespeare in the movies: from the silent era to Shakespeare in Love
BRODE, Douglas.
Oxford University Press, ix, 257p. illus. index.
ISBN 0195139585

Shakespeare on love & lust
CHARNEY, Maurice.
Columbia University Press, 234p. index.
ISBN 0231104286

Shakespeare, film, fin de siècle
BURNETT, Mark Thornton and WRAY, Ramona.
Macmillan, vii-xiv, 244p. index.
ISBN 033377664X

Shakespeare: a hundred years on film
SAMMONS, Eddie.
Shepheard Walwyn, iii-viii, 249, 16p. [16] plates. appendix.
ISBN 0856831883

Silent echoes: discovering early Hollywood through the films of Buster Keaton
BENGTSON, John.
Santa Monica Press, 231p. illus.
ISBN 189166106X

Smiling in slow motion
JARMAN, Derek.
Century, 388p. [24] plates.
ISBN 0712680047

Steven Spielberg: interviews
FRIEDMAN, Lester D.
University of Mississippi, vi-xxxii, 250p. [8] plates. index.

Still memories
MILLS, John.
Hutchinson, 208p. illus (some col.)
ISBN 0091793912

Straight lick: the cinema of Oscar Micheaux
GREEN, J. Ronald.
Indiana University Press, xvi, 295p. illus.,appendices, bibliog. filmog. index.
ISBN 0253337534

Stroheim
LENNIG, Arthur.
University Press of Kentucky, xv, 514p. illus. bibliog. filmog. index.
ISBN 0813121388

Tacita Dean
DEAN, Tacita.
Museu d'art contemporani de Barcelona, 122p. filmog. biog. bibliog.
ISBN 8495273713

The tao of Bruce Lee
MILLER, Davis.
Vintage, xi-xiii, 177p.
ISBN 0002571277

Travels in Greeneland: the complete guide to the cinema of Graham Greene: 3rd ed.
FALK, Quentin.
Reynolds Hearn Ltd, 158p. illus. bibliog. filmog. index.
ISBN 1903111137

 The ultimate Hitchcock
British Film Institute.
British Film Institute.

Under no illusion
DANIELS, Paul and GIDNEY, Chris.

Blake Publishing, 313p.
ISBN 1857823141

The unruly life of Woody Allen: a biography
MEADE, Marion.
Scribner, 384p. [16] plates. filmog. index.
ISBN 0684833743

Vsevolod Pudovkin: classic films of the Soviet avant-garde
SARGEANT, Amy.
I.B.Tauris, vii-xxxvii, 207p. illus. bibliog. index.
ISBN 1860644554

Which lie did I tell? More adventures in the screen trade
GOLDMAN, William.
Pantheon, ix-x, 485p. index.
ISBN 0375403493

Woody, from Antz to Zelig: a reference guide to Woody Allen's creative work, 1964-1998
SCHWARTZ, Richard A.
Greenwood Press, xi-xvi, 314p. illus. filmog. bibliog. index.
ISBN 0313311331

Writing himself into history: Oscar Micheaux, his silent films, and his audiences
BOWSER, Pearl and SPENCE, Louise.
Rutgers University Press, ix-xxv, 288p. illus. bibliog. filmog. index.
ISBN 0813528038

Scriptwriting

Crafting short screenplays that connect
JOHNSON, Claudia Hunter.
Focal Press, xiv, 273p. appendices, index.
ISBN 0240803787

Developing story ideas
RABIGER, Michael.
Focal Press, vii-viii, 214p. appendix. index.
ISBN 0240803981

Laughing out loud: writing the comedy-centered screenplay
HORTON, Andrew.
University of California Press, xii, 218p. apps. bibliog. index.
ISBN 0520220153

Screenwriting from the heart: the technique of the character-driven screenplay
RYAN, James. Billboard Books, 186p. bibliog. index.

Screenwriting: a manual
DAWSON, Jonathan.
Oxford University Press, ix,230p. illus. appendices, glossary, index, refs.
ISBN 0195508327

Script magic: subconscious techniques to conquer writer's block
D'VARI, Marisa.
Wiese Film Productions, ix-x, 191p bibliog.
ISBN 0941188744

Writing the short film: 2nd ed
COOPER, Pat and DANCYGER, Ken.
Focal Press, ix, 308p. appendix, index
ISBN 0240803698

Television and Society

British television drama: past, present and future
BIGNELL, Jonathan and LACEY, Stephen and MACMURRAUGH-KAVANAGH, Madeleine (eds.)
Palgrave, xi, 200p. bibliog. index.
ISBN 0333774965

British television: a reader
BUSCOMBE, Edward (ed.)
Clarendon Press, viii-xiii, 348p. bibliog. index.
ISBN 0198742657

British television: an insider's history
SCOTT, Peter Graham.
McFarland, vii-ix, 323p. illus, plates, bibliog, index.

Broadcasting Committee, first report: the development of Parliamentary broadcasting: report, together with appendices, proceedings of the Committee and minutes of evidence
GREAT BRITAIN HOUSE OF COMMONS BROADCASTING COMMITTEE.
The Stationery Office, 67p. (House of Commons papers, session 1999-2000)
ISBN 0102442002

A concise history of British television, 1930-2000
CURRIE, Tony.
Kelly Publications, 112p. illus.
ISBN 1903053072

Cracking Morse code: semiotics and television drama
PAGE, Adrian.
University of Luton Press, iv-vi, 194p. refs.
ISBN: 1860205704

Frames and fictions on television: the politics of identity within drama
CARSON, Bruce and LLEWELLYN-JONES, Margaret.
Intellect Books, iv, 156p. bibliog. index.
ISBN 184150009

The intimate screen: early British television drama
JACOBS, Jason.
Clarendon Press, xiii, 175p. tables. bibliog. index.
ISBN 0198742339

Seeing things: television in the age of uncertainty
ELLIS, John.
I.B.Tauris, 193p. bibliog. index.
ISBN 1860641253

Talking television: an introduction to the study of television
BURTON, Graeme.
Arnold, xii, 319p. illus. bibliog. figures. indices.
ISBN 0340589647

Television
DINSDALE, Alfred.
Kelly Publications, 62p. illus. [6] plates.
ISBN 1903053056

The television handbook: 2nd ed
HOLLAND, Patricia.
Routledge, vi-ix, 303p. illus. figs. gloss. bibliog. index.
ISBN 0415212820

Television: the critical view: 6th ed
NEWCOMB, Horace.
Oxford University Press, 721p.
ISBN 0195119274

Thinking through television
LEMBO, Ron.

Cambridge University Press, xiii. 254p. index.
ISBN 0521585775

Watching television audiences: cultural theories and methods
TULLOCH, John.
Arnold, 264p. bibliog. index.
ISBN 0340741422

Television-National and International

Broadcasting politics in Japan: NHK and television news
KRAUSS, Ellis S.
Cornell University Press, ix-xiv, 278p, illus, index.
ISBN 0801437482

Closing the shop: information cartels and Japan's mass media
FREEMAN, Laurie Anne.
Princeton University Press, xi-xix, 255p. appendices. bibliog. index.
ISBN 0691059543

Continuity and change: television fiction in Europe: Eurofiction third report
BUONANNO, Milly.
University of Luton Press, iv-xv, 214p. illus, figs, tables, appendix.
ISBN 1860205755

Culture, Media and Sport Committee, ninth report: report and accounts of the BBC for 1999-2000: report, together with proceedings of the committee and minutes of evidence
Great Britain House of Commons Culture and Media and Sport Committee KAUFMAN, Gerald (chair.)
The Stationery Office, ii-xx, 24p. (House of Commons papers, session 1999-2000)
ISBN 0102561001

The funding of the BBC: government response to the third report from the Culture, Media and Sport Committee, session 1999-2000
Great Britain Department for Culture, Media and Sport.
The Stationery Office, 13p.
ISBN 0101467427

Inside the BBC and CNN: managing media organisations
KÜNG-SHANKLEMAN, Lucy.
Routledge, vi-viii, 245p. figs. bibliog. index.
ISBN 0415213223

Media, culture and politics in Indonesia
SEN, Krishna and HILL, David T.
Oxford University Press, v-x, 245p. bibliog, index.
ISBN 0195537033

Select Committee on delegated powers and deregulation: Royal Parks (trading) Bill; Television Licences (Disclosure of Information) Bill; Wireless Telegraphy (Television Licence Fees) Bill...
Great Britain House of Lords Select Committee on Delegated Powers and Deregulation.
The Stationery Office, 10p. (House of Lords papers, session 1999-2000)
ISBN 0104810009

Something completely different: British television and American culture
MILLER, Jeffrey S.
University of Minnesota Press, ix-xvii, 250p. illus. index.
ISBN 0816632413

Spy TV
BURKE, David.
Slab-O-Concrete Publications, 159p. appen. bibliog.
ISBN 1899866256

Tabloid culture: trash taste, popular power, and the transformation of American Television
GLYNN, Kevin.
Duke University Press, x. 324p. illus. notes. bibliog. index.
ISBN 0822325691

Technological and organisational changes in the European audiovisual industries: an exploratory analysis of the consequences for employment
EUROPEAN AUDIOVISUAL OBSERVATORY.
European Audiovisual Observatory, 13p.

Televised election debates: international perspectives
COLEMAN, Stephen.
Macmillan, x, 211p. index.
ISBN 0333732634

Television news: 4th ed
YORKE, Ivor and revised by ALEXANDER, Ray.
Focal Press, vi-xi, 233p. figs.
ISBN 024051615X

Terrestrial TV news in Britain: the culture of production
HARRISON, Jackie.
Manchester University Press, vii-xiii, 256p. tables. appendices. bibliog. index.
ISBN 0719055903

Vivendi SA and British Sky Broadcasting Group plc: a report on the merger situation
Great Britain Competition Commission
The Stationery Office, 209p. appendices. gloss.
ISBN 0101469128

The work of BBC Scotland and the Broadcasting Council for Scotland, minutes of evidence, Wednesday 19 January 2000
Great Britain House of Commons Scottish Affairs Committee.
The Stationery Office, 27p. (House of Commons papers, session 1999-2000)
ISBN 0102154007

BOOKSELLERS

Stock

A   Books

B   Magazines

C   Posters

D   Memorabilia eg Stills

E   Cassettes, CDs, Records Videos and DVDs

F   Postcards and Greetings Cards

Arnolfini Bookshop
16 Narrow Quay
Bristol BS1 4QA
Tel: 0117 9299191
Fax: 0117 9253876
email: bookshop@arnolfini.demon.co.uk
Website: www.arnolfini.demon.co.uk
Peter Begen, Bookshop Manager
Open: 10.00-7.00 Mon-Sat, Thurs 10.00-9.00pm
12.00-7.00pm Sun
Stock: A, B, F
Based in the Arnolfini Gallery, concentrating on the visual arts. No catalogues issued. Send requests for specific material with SAE

At the Movies
9 Cecil Court
London WC2N 4EZ
Tel: 020 7240 7221
Stock includes books, stills and memorabilia. No catalogue
Open: 11.00-6.00 Mon-Fri
11.30-6.00 Sat

Blackwell's
48-51 Broad Street
Oxford OX1 3BQ
Tel: 01865 792792
Fax: 01865 794143
email: blackwells.extra@
blackwell.co.uk
Website: www.bookshop.
blackwell.co.uk
Open: 9.00-6.00 Mon, Wed-Sat, 9.30-6.00 Tue, 11.00-5.00 Sun
Stock: A
Literature department has sections on cinemas and performing arts, sociology department has a Media Studies section `and performing arts. International charge and send service available

Blackwell's Art & Poster Shop
27 Broad Street
Oxford OX1 2AS
Tel: 01865 792792
Open: 9.00-6.00 Mon, Wed-Sat, 9.30-6.00 Tues, 11.00-5.00 Sun
Stock: A, B, C, F
A wide selection of books, posters, cards, calendars and gift items, all available by mail order

Brockwell Books
5 Old School House Court
High Street
Honiton
Devon EX14 8NZ
Tel: 01404 42826
Stock: A, B, C, D
Film books offered by mail order only. Mainly deal in out of print books but also some new titles. Catalogue 'Serious about Cinema' produced three times a year

Cinegrafix Gallery
4 Copper Row
Shad Thames
Tower Bridge Piazza
London SE1 2LH
Tel: 020 7234 0566
Fax: 020 7234 0577
Gallery open Tues-Sat 11.00-7.00
Stock: A, B, C, D, F
Specialist in rare film posters. Poster catalogues available at £5. Fully illustrated Portrait catalogue available at £4

The Cinema Bookshop
13-14 Great Russell Street
London WC1B 3NH
Tel: 020 7637 0206
Fax: 020 7436 9979
Open: 10.30-5.30 Mon-Sat
Stock: A, B, C, D
Comprehensive stock of new, out-of-print and rare books. Posters, Pressbooks and stills etc. No catalogues are issued. Send requests for specific material with SAE

The Cinema Store
Unit 4B, Orion House
Upper Saint Martin's Lane
London WC2H 9EJ
Tel: 020 7379 7838 (general enquiries)
Fax: 020 7240 7689
email: cinemastor@aol.com
Website: www. thecinemastore.com
Tel: 0171 379 7865 (DVD mail order books, cd's)
Tel: 0171 379 7895 (trading cards, VHS)
Open: 10.00-6.00 Mon-Wed, Sat, 10.00-7.00 Thu-Fri
12-6 Sun
Stock: A, B, C, D, E, F
Mail order available worldwide. Latest

and vintage posters/stills, magazines, models and DVD, new/rare VHS, soundtracks and trading cards

Cornerhouse Books

70 Oxford Street
Manchester M1 5NH
Tel: 0161 228 7621
Fax: 0161 200 1506
Stock: A, B, F
Open: 12.00-8.30 daily
No catalogues issued. Send requests for specific material with SAE

Culture Vultures Books

329 St Leonard's Road
Windsor SL4 3DS
Tel: 01753 851 693
Fax: 01923 224714
Stock: A
Mail order only. Periodic catalogues issued (separate catalogues for cinema, theatre, music). SAE appreciated. Comprehensive stock of out-of-print titles

Dasilva Puppet Books Ray

63 Kennedy Road
Bicester
Oxfordshire OX6 8BE
Tel: 01869 245793
email: dasilva@puppetbooks.co.uk
Website: www.puppetbooks.com
Mail order (visitors by appointment). New and second hand books on puppetry and animation including film and television. Catalogue available

David Drummond at Pleasures of Past Times

11 Cecil Court
Charing Cross Road
London WC2N 4EZ
Tel: 020 7836 1142
Fax: 020 7836 1142
email: drummond@popt.fsnet.co.uk
David Drummond
Open: 11.00-2.30, 3.30-5.45 Mon-Fri.
First Sat in month 11.00-2.30
Stock: A, D, F
Extended hours and other times by arrangement. No catalogue

Decorum Books

24 Cloudsley Square
London N1 0HN
Tel: 020 7278 1838
Fax: 020 7837 6424
email: decorumbooks@lineone.net
Website: www.decorumbooks.co.uk
Mail order only. Secondhand books on film and theatre; music and art. Also secondhand scores and sheet music

Dress Circle

57-59 Monmouth Street
Upper St Martin's Lane
London WC2H 9DG
Tel: 020 7240 2227
Fax: 020 7379 8540
Website: www.dresscircle .co.uk
Open: 10.00-7.00 Mon-Sat
Stock: A, B, C, D, E, F
Specialists in stage music and musicals. Catalogue of the entire stock issued annually with updates twice yearly. Send SAE for details

Everyman Cinema Club

5 Holly Bush Vale
Hampstead
London NW3 6TX
Tel: 020 7431 1818
Fax: 020 7435 2292
email: mail@everymancinema.com
Website: www.everymancinema.com
Angela Cunningham
Stock: A, B, C, D, E, F
The Everyman Film Books Store offers wide range of materials for scholars and enthusiasts alike

Anne FitzSimons

62 Scotby Road
Scotby
Carlisle CA4 8BD
Tel: 01228 513815
Stock: A, B, C, D, F
Mail order only. Antiquarian and out-of-print titles on cinema, broadcasting and performing arts. A catalogue is issued twice a year. Send three first-class postage stamps for current issue

Flashbacks

6 Silver Place
Beak Street
London W1F 0JS
Tel: 020 7437 8562
Fax: 020 7437 8562
email: shop@flashbacks.freeserve.co.uk
Website: www.dacre.org
Richard Dacre, Chris Voisey
Stock: C, D
Stockist of vintage and modern movie posters and stills. Shop and mail order service. Send SAE and 'wanted' list for stock details

Forbidden Planet

71-75 New Oxford Street
London WC1A 1DG
Tel: 020 7836 4179
Fax: 020 7240 7118
Open: 10.00-6.00 Mon-Wed, Sat, 10.00-7.00 Thur, Fri
Stock: A, B, C, D, E, F

Science fiction, horror, fantasy and comics specialists. Mail order service available on 0171 497 2150

Grant and Cutler

Language Booksellers
55-57 Great Marlborough Street
London W1V 2AY
Tel: 020 7734 2012
Fax: 020 7734 9272
email: postmaster@grant-c.demon.co.uk
Website: www.grant-c.demon.co.uk
Stock A,E
Foreign language book specialist. World cinema books and screenplays
Open 9:00 to 17:30 Monday to Saturday.
Thursdays, 9:00 to 19:00

Hay Cinema Bookshop

(including Francis Edwards)
The Old Cinema
Castle Street
Hay-on-Wye
via Hereford HR3 5DF
Tel: 01497 820071
email: sales@haycinemabookshop.co.uk
(sales@francisedwards.co.uk)
Website: www.haycinemabookshop.co.uk
(www.francisedwards.co.uk)
Large second hand stock. Open 9.00-7.00 Mon-Sat, 11.30-5.30 Sun
Includes an antiquaria bookshop within the Hay Cinema Bookshop (Francis Edwards).

Heffers Booksellers

20 Trinity Street
Cambridge CB2 1TY
Tel: 01223 568568
Fax: 01223 568591
email: heffers@heffers.co.uk
Website: www.heffers.co.uk
Open: 9.00-5.30 Mon-Sat
Tuesdays from 9.30 am
11.00-5.00 Sun
Stock: A, E
Catalogues of videocassettes and spoken word recordings issued. Copies are available on request

Hoxton Book Depository

97 Hoxton Street
Shoreditch
London N1 6QL
Tel: 020 7613 4841
Website: www.hoxtonbooks.com
Stock: A, B, E
Used, new and remainder books including film theory, biographies, filmographies, film and television tie-

ins. Also stock videos, vintage magazines and vinyl soundtracks

David Henry
PO Box 9146
London W3 8WZ
Tel: 020 8993 2859
email: Filmbooks@Compuserve.com
Stock: A, B
Mail order only. A catalogue of out-of-print and second-hand books is issued two or three times a year and available on request. Search service for titles not in stock. New books can be obtained to order, including those published in USA

LV Kelly Books
6 Redlands
Blundell's Road
Tiverton
Devon EX16 4DH
Tel: 01884 256170
Fax: 01884 251063
email: lenkelly@topservice.com
Website:www.lvkellybooks.
webjump.com
Stock: A, B, E
Principally mail order but visitors welcome by appointment. Catalogue issued regularly on broadcasting and mass communications. Occasional lists on cinema, music, journalism

Ed Mason
Room 301
Third Floor
River Bank House Business Centre
1, Putney Bridge Approach
London SW6 3JD
Tel: 020 7736 8511
Stock: A, B, C, D
Specialist in original film memorabilia from the earliest onwards. Also organises the Collectors' Film Convention six times a year
Office only - all memorabilia stock is re-located to Rare Discs (see entry)

National Museum of Photography, Film & Television
Bradford BD1 1NQ
Tel: 01274 202030
Fax: 01274 723155
Website: www.nmpft.org.uk
Bookshop run by A Zwemmer
Open: 10.00-6.00 Tue-Sun
Closed Mondays (except Bank Holidays and School Holidays)
Stock: A, C, D, F
Mail order available. Send SAE with requests for information

Offstage Theatre & Film Bookshop
37 Chalk Farm Road
London NW1 8AJ
Tel: 020 7485 4996
Fax: 020 7916 8046
email: offstage@btinternet.com
Brian Schwartz
Free cinema and media catalogues available. Send SAE. Open 7 days a week

C D Paramor
25 St Mary's Square
Newmarket
Suffolk CB8 0HZ
Tel: 01638 664416
Fax: 01638 664416
C.D. Paramor
Stock: A, B, C, F, E
Mail order only. Visitors welcome strictly by appointment. Catalogues on most of the performing arts issued regularly free of charge

Rare Discs
18 Bloomsbury Street
London WC1B3 QA
Tel: 020 7580 3516
Open: 10.00-6.30 Mon-Sat
Stock: E
Retail shop with recorded mail order service. Over 7,000 titles including soundtracks, original cast shows, musicals and nostalgia. Telephone for information

Screenwriter's Store
10-11 Moor Street
London W1D 5NE
Tel: 020 7287 9009
Fax: 020 7287 6009
email: info@thescreenwritersstore.co.uk
Website: www.screenwriters.co.uk
Rinaldo Quacquarini
Sells screenwriting and production software and resources

Spread Eagle Bookshop
(Incorporates Greenwich Gallery)
9 Nevada Street
London SE10 9JL
Tel: 020 8305 0447
Fax: 020 8305 1666
email: antiques@spreadeagle.ogr.uk
Open: 10.00-5.30 daily
Stock: A, B, C, D
All second-hand stock. Memorabilia, ephemera. Large stock of books on cinema, theatre, posters and photos

Stable Books
Holm Farm
Coldridge

Crediton
Devon EX17 6BR
Tel: 01363 83227
Mail order (visitors by appointment only). Second hand stock concerning theatre, cinema and puppetry

Stage and Screen
34 Notting Hill Gate
London W11
Tel: 020 7221 3646

Stage Door Prints
9 Cecil Court
London WC2N 4EZ
Tel: 020 7240 1683
General stock of performing arts titles including antiquarian prints, ephemera and movie memorobilia.
Open 11.00-6.00 Mon-Fri, 11.30-6.00 Sat

Tate Modern Shop - Cinema Section
25 Summer Street
London SE1 9JX
Tel: 020 7401 5156
Fax: 020 7401 5152
Open: Mon-Thurs 10.00-6.00pm Fri-Sat 10.00am-10.00pm, Sun 10.00-6.00pm
Stock: A, B, E, F
Tate Modern Shop Cinema Section is situate within Tate Modern gallery main book shop on level 1. Selection includes books about film history, theory and practice as well as vidos and DVDs of classic, art house and arts related films and documentaries. Shop offers mail-order service

Terence H Kaye
Rare and Collectable Books
Specialist in Books About Theatre Cinema & Performing Arts
52 Neeld Crescent
London NW4 3RR
Tel: 020 8202 8188
Fax: 020 8202 8188

Treasure Chest
61 Cobbold Road
Felixstowe
Suffolk 1P11 7BH
Tel: 01394 270717
Second hand stock specialising in cinema and literature. Open 9.30-5.30 Mon-Sat

Vinmagco limited
39-43 Brewer Street
London W1R 9UD
Tel: 020 7439 8525
Fax: 0204 398 527
email: vintage.soho@ndirect.co.uk

Website: www.vinmag.com
Open: 10.00-8.00 Mon-Sat,
12.00-7.00 Sun
Stock: B, C, D, F
Other Branch;
247 Camden High Street, London
NW1
Tel: 0171 482 0587
Open: 10.00-6.00
Mon-Fri, 10.00-7.00 Sat, Sun
Stock: B,C,D,F
Other branch;
55 Charing Cross Road, London
WC2H ONE
OPEN: 10.00 - 10.00
TEL: 02307 494 4064

Peter Wood
20 Stonehill Road
Great Shelford
Cambridge CB2 5JL
Tel: 01223 842419
Stock: A, D, F
Mail order. Visitors are welcome by
appointment. A free catalogue is
available of all books in stock

A Zwemmer
80 Charing Cross Road
London WC2H 0BB
Tel: 020 7240 4157
Fax: 020 7240 4186
email: enquiries@zwemmer.co.uk
Website: www.zwemmer.co.uk
Claire de Rouen
Open: 9.30-6.00 Mon-Fri,
10.00-6.00 Sat
Stock: A, B
A catalogue of new and in-print titles
on every aspect of cinema is available
on request. Mail order service for all
books available through Mail Order
Department

CABLE, SATELLITE AND DIGITAL

Information in this section is provided by Linda Wood whose continuing support we gratefully acknowledge

As the number of channels and digital services expands, the number of companies involved in delivering multichannel television to UK homes is rapidly diminishing. In the satellite orbit there has been one dominant operator—British Sky Broadcasting (BSkyB)—for some years. The cable business is moving towards a comparable position now that the third largest operator, NTL, has taken over the domestic cable television operations of the biggest, Cable & Wireless Communications, leaving only two major multiple system operators (MSOs). The second largest MSO, Telewest, is widely expected to become part of one major cable company in due course through a merger with NTL. The cost to NTL of the CWC acquisition is £8.2 billion, whilst Cable & Wireless is paying £6.5 billion to take full ownership of CWC's business operations. These figures indicate the massive financial scale of cable investment and costs.

This process of merger and takeover has radically altered the structure of the UK's broadband cable industry as envisaged when the first franchises were awarded in November 1983. With 12.5m homes already passed by cable systems that are continuing to build—and only 4m homes outside franchise areas—a new phase is beginning as the exclusivity that operators enjoyed as part of their franchises is abandoned. Competition between cable companies is thus possible, although the prospect of operators spending huge sums of money on building competitive cable networks in the foreseeable future is remote. While cable has up to now tended to be the Cinderella partner, its ability to provide broadband facilities has resulted in a range of new - and potentially extremely lucrative - services being added to the cable portfolio.

MULTIPLE SYSTEM OPERATORS

Almost all franchises are held as part of groups of holdings. Such groups are called multiple system operators (MSOs). Extensive consolidation has taken place since 1995 and especially during the first half of 1998, which resulted in the emergence of two dominant groups: NTL and Telewest.

AT&T
US telecom operator, which acquired Tele-Communications Inc (TCI), the largest US cable operator, holder of 50% share in TW Holdings, which owns 53% of Telewest [qv]

Atlantic Telecom Group
Holborn House
475-485 Union St
Aberdeen AB11 6DB
Tel: 01224 454 000
Fax: 01224 454 0111
Website: www.atlantic-telecom.co.uk
Areas: Aberdeen

British Telecommunications (BT)
87-89 Baker Street
London W1M 2LP
Tel: 020 7487 1254
Fax: 020 7487 1259
Areas: as BT New Towns Cable TV Services: Milton Keynes
as Westminster Cable Company: Westminster LB.
Also upgrade systems at Barbican (London), Brackla, Martlesham, Walderslade, Washington
Note: From 1 January 2001 BT will be allowed to compete in delivery of television-related services with existing cable networks.

Cable & Wireless Communications
Cable franchises now owned by NTL

Cox Communications
US cable operator
10% stake in Telewest (23% of preference shares) [qv]

Eurobell (Holdings)
Multi-Media House
Lloyds Court, Manor Royal
Crawley, West Sussex RH10 2PT
Tel: 01293 400444
Fax: 01293 400440
Ownership: Detecon (Deutsche Telepost Consulting)
Areas: Crawley/Horley/Gatwick, Devon South, Kent West

NTL
Bristol House
1 Lakeside Road
Farnborough
Hampshire GU14 6XP
Tel 01252 402662
Fax 01252 402665
Website: www.cabletel.co.uk
HQ: **110 East 59th Street, New York, NY 10022 USA**
Tel +1/212 906 8440
Fax +1/212 752 1157
Formerly: International CableTel
Ownership: Rockefeller family, Capital Cities Broadcasting Company (subsidiary of Walt Disney Company), Microsoft, France Télécom (eventually will be largest shareholder with 25%)
NTL has acquired Cable & Wireless Communications cable franchises and is replacing that brand with its own.
Areas: former CableTel franchises
as CableTel Bedfordshire: Bedford
as CableTel Glasgow: Bearsden/Milngavie, Glasgow Greater, Glasgow North West/Clydebank, Invercylde, Paisley/Renfrew
as CableTel Herts & Bedfordshire: Luton/South Bedfordshire
as CableTel Hertfordshire: Hertfordshire Central, Hertfordshire East,
as CableTel Kirklees: Huddersfield/Dewsbury
as CableTel Northern Ireland: Northern Ireland
as CableTel South Wales: Cardiff/Penarth, Glamorgan West, Glamorgan/Gwent, Newport/Cwmbran/Pontypool
as CableTel Surrey: Guildford/West Surrey
former Comcast UK franchises:

as Anglia Cable: Harlow/Bishops Stortford/Stansted Airport
as Cambridge Cable: Cambridge/Ely/Newmarket,
as Comcast Teesside: Darlington, Teeside
as East Coast Cable: Colchester/Ipswich/etc,
as Southern East Anglia Cable: East Anglia South,
Sold its 50% stake in Cable London to Telewest (qv) August 1999.
former ComTel franchises:
Andover/Salisbury/Romsey, Daventry, Corby/Kettering/Wellingborough, Hertfordshire West, Litchfield/Burntwood/Rugeley, Northampton, Nuneaton/Bedworth/Rugby, Oxford/Abingdon, Stafford/Stone, Swindon, Tamworth/North Warwickshire/Meriden, Thames Valley, Warwick/Stratford-upon-Avon/Kenilworth/Leamington Spa
former Diamond Cable franchises: Bassetlaw, Burton-on-Trent, Coventry, East Derbyshire, Grantham, Grimsby/Immingham /Cleethorpes, Hinckley/Bosworth, Huddersfield/Dewsbury, Leicester, Lincoln, Lincolnshire/South Humberside, Loughborough/ Shepshed, Mansfield/Sutton/Kirkby-in-Ashfield, Melton Mowbray, Newark-on-Trent, Northern Ireland, Nottingham, Ravenshead, Vale of Belvoir
fomerly Cable & Wireless Communications franchises
Areas: Aylesbury/Amersham/ Chesham, Bolton, Bournemouth/Poole/Christchurch, Brighton/Hove/Worthing, Bromley, Bury/Rochdale, Cheshire North, Chichester/Bognor, Dartford/Swanley, Derby/Spondon, Durham South /North Yorkshire, Ealing, Eastbourne/Hastings, Epping Forest/Chigwell/Loughton/O ngar, Fenland, Great Yarmouth/Lowestoft/ Caister, Greater London East, Greenwich/Lewisham, Harrogate/Knaresborough, Harrow, Havering, Hertfordshire South, Kensington/Chelsea, Kent South East, Lambeth/Southwark, Lancashire East, Leeds, London North West, Macclesfield/Wilmslow, Manchester/Salford, Newham/Tower Hamlets, Norwich, Oldham/Tameside, Peterborough, Portsmouth/Fareham/Gosport/Havan t, Southampton/Eastleigh, Stockport, Stoke-on-Trent/Newcastle, Surrey North, Surrey North East,

Thamesmead, Totton/Hythe, Waltham Forest, Wandsworth, Wearside, Whittlesey/March/Wisbech, Winchester, The Wirral, York

SBC International
Ownership: Southwestern Bell Telecom [US telecom operator] 10% stake in Telewest (23% of preference shares) [qv]

Telewest Communications
Unit 1, Genesis Business Park
Albert Drive
Woking, Surrey GU21 5RW
Tel: 01483 750900
Fax 01483 750901
Website: www.telewest.co.uk
Ownership: TW Holdings (= Tele-Communications International (TINTA) 50% and US West International 50%) 53%, Microsoft 29.9%, Liberty Media (=AT&T), Cox Communications 10%, SBC International (= Southwestern Bell Telecom) 10%
Acquired NTL's (formerly Comcast UK's) half-share in Cable London in August 1999.
Areas:
as Birmingham Cable: Birmingham/Solihull, Wythall
as Cable Corporation: Hillingdon/Hounslow, Windsor
as Cable London: Camden, Enfield, Hackney & Islington, Haringey
as Telewest London & the South East): Croydon, Kingston/Richmond, Merton/Sutton, Thames Estuary North, Thames Estuary South
as Telewest Midlands & the South West: Avon, Black Country, Cheltenham/Gloucester, Taunton/Bridgewater, Telford, Worcester
as Telewest North West):
Blackpool/Fylde, Lancashire Central, Liverpool North/Bootle/Crosby, Liverpool South, St Helens/Knowsley, Southport, Wigan
as Telewest Scotland & North East: Cumbernauld, Dumbarton, Dundee, Edinburgh, Falkirk/West Lothian, Fife, Glenrothes/Kirkaldy/Leven, Motherwell/East Kilbride/Hamilton/Wishaw/Lanark, Perth/Scone, Tyneside
as Yorkshire Cable Communications: Barnsley, Bradford, Calderdale, Doncaster/Rotherham, Sheffield, Wakefield/Pontefract/Castleford

US West International
50% share in TW Holdings, which owns 53% of Telewest [qv]

CABLE FRANCHISES

All broadband cable franchises to date were granted by the Cable Authority (apart from 11 previously granted by the Department of Trade and Industry), the role of which was taken over by the Independent Television Commission (ITC) in January 1991, under the Broadcasting Act 1990.

The Act empowered the ITC to grant fifteen-year 'local delivery licences', which can include use of microwave distribution. Licences must be awarded to the highest bidder on the basis of an annual cash bid in addition to forecasts of the sums that will be paid to the Exchequer as a percentage of revenue earned in the second and third five-year periods of the licence.

The biggest change since the last edition of the Handbook is that the major operators, by agreement with the ITC, have each opted for a single non-exclusive local delivery service licence, thus allowing the possibility of competitive marketing and delivery on a potentially national basis. The individual franchise exclusive licences held by NTL were consequently revoked by the ITC on 31 December 1999 and those of Telewest on 31 May 2000.

In some towns an older cable system still exists. These are not franchised but are licensed by the ITC to provide limited services. They are gradually being superseded by new broadband networks

Details of who holds the franchise for a particular town/area can be obtained from the ITC.

SATELLITE AND CABLE TELEVISION CHANNELS

All channels transmitting via cable or satellite within or to the UK, wholly or partly in the English language or intended for viewing by other linguistic groups within the UK. Services are licensed and monitored by the Independent Television Commission (ITC). Channels not intended for reception in the UK are excluded, as are those that are licensed but not actively broadcasting (many licensed channels never materialise).

The television standard and encrypting system used are indicated after the name of the satellite. Services for which a separate charge is made are marked 'premium' after the programming type.

The advent of digital television from late 1998 has already created many new channels. Although initially most digital channels are conversions of services already available in analogue form, by 2000 this was no longer the case.

MULTIPLE SERVICE PROVIDERS (MSP)

BBC Worldwide
Woodlands
80 Wood Lane
London W12 0TT
Tel: 020 8433 2000
Fax: 020 8749 0538
Services: Animal Planet 50%, BBC News 24%, UK Gold 50%, UK Horizons 50%, UK Style 50%, PLAY UK 50%

British Sky Broadcasting (BSkyB)
6 Centaurs Business Park
Grant Way, Syon Lane
Isleworth
Middlesex TW7 5QD
Tel: 0870 240 3000
Fax: 020 7705 3030
Website: www.sky.co.uk
Ownership: News International Television 39.88 %, BSB Holdings (= Pathé 30.27%, Granada 36.22%, Pearson 4.29%) 12.82 %, Pathé 12.71 %, Granada Group 6.48 %
Services: The Computer Channel, The History Channel 50%, National Geographic Channel 50%, Nickelodeon 50%, QVC 20%, Sky Box Office, Sky Cinema, Sky MovieMax, Sky News, Sky One, Sky Premier, Sky Soap, Sky Sports1 , Sky Sports 2, Sky Sports 3, Sky Sports Extra, Sky Travel. 40% stake in Granada Sky Broadcasting

Carlton Communications
25 Knightsbridge
London SW1X 7RZ
Tel: 020 7663 6363
Website: www.carlton.com
Services: Taste, Carlton Cinema, ITVDigital (50%)

Discovery Communications
160 Great Portland Street
London W1N 5TB
Tel: 020 7462 3600
Fax: 020 7462 3700
Services: Animal Planet, Discovery Channel Europe, TLC Europe

Flextech Television
160 Great Portland Street
London W1N 5TB
Tel: 020 7299 5000
Fax: 020 7299 5400
Ownership: Telewest (see MSOs)
Services: Bravo, Challenge TV, Living, Trouble, bid-up TV, Screenshop, UK Gold 50%, UK Gold 2 50%, UK Horizons 50%, UK Style 50%, UK Drama, Play UK 50%, TV Travel Shop 37%, Sit-Up TV 38%
Service management: Discovery, Discovery Home & Leisure, Playboy TV, Screenshop

Granada Sky Broadcasting
Franciscan Court
16 Hatfields
London SE1 8DJ
Tel: 020 7578 4040
Fax: 020 7578 4176
email: malcolm.packer@gsb.co.uk
Website:gsb.co.uk
Ownership: Granada Group 60%, British Sky Broadcasting 40%
Services: Granada Breeze, Granada Plus, Granada Men & Motors

Home Video Channel
Aquis House
Station Road
Hayes
Middlesex UB3 4DX
Tel: 020 8581 7000
Fax: 020 8581 7007
Ownership: Spice Entertainment Companies
Services: The Adult Channel, HVC

Landmark Communications
64-66 Newman Street
London W1P 3PG
Tel: 020 7665 0600
Fax: 020 7665 0601
Ownership: Landmark Communications Inc
Services: Travel Channel

Portland Enterprises
Portland House
Portland Place
London E14 9TT
Tel: 020 7308 5090
Services: Gay TV, Television X The Fantasy Channel

Turner Broadcasting System (TBS)
CNN House
19-22 Rathbone Place
London W1P 1DF
Tel: 0171 637 6700
Fax: 0171 637 6768
Ownership: Time Warner
Services: Cartoon Network, CNN International, Turner Network Television

UK Channel Management
160 Great Portland Street
London W1N 5TB
Tel: 020 7765 1959
Ownership: BBC Worldwide, Flextech [qqv]

CHANNELS

The Adult Channel
Aquis House
Station Rd
Hayes
Tel: 020 8581 7000
Fax: 020 8581 7007
email: adultch@spicetv.com
Website: www.spicetv.com
Ownership: Home Video Channel
[see MSP above]
Service start: Feb 1992
Satellite: Astra 1B (PAL/Videocrypt)
Programming: 'adult' entertainment
(premium)

Adventure One
NGC-UK Partnership
Grant Way
Isleworth
Middlesex TW7 5QD
Tel: 020 7705 3000
Fax: 020 7805 2296
Programming: documentaries on
exploration and adventure

The Afro-Caribbean Channel
Takerak Ltd
81 Seaford Road
London N15 5DX
Tel: 020 8802 4576
Fax: 020 8211 7499
email: vernonking@btinternet.com
Programming: Afro-Caribbean
material

Animal Planet
160 Great Portland St
London W1W 5TB
Tel: 020 7462 3600
Website: www.animal.discovery.com
Ownership: BBC Worldwide,
Discovery Communications [see MSP
above]
Service start: Sep 98
Satellite: Astra 1E, Hot Bird 1
(PAL/encrypted)
Programming: natural history
documentaries

Apna TV
60 Aubert Park
London N5 1TS
Tel: 020 7831 2525
Fax: 020 7242 2860
Website: www.apnatv.com
Programming: entertainment, arts,
music programmes from/about India,
Pakistan and Bangladesh

Arsenal
Arsenal Football Club
Highbury
London N5 1BU
Tel: 020 7704 4000
Website: www.arsenal.co.uk
Programming: football

Arts World
Artsworld Channels Ltd.
80 Silverthorne Road
London
SW8 3XA
Tel 020 7819 1160
Fax 020 7819 1161
email: tv@artsworld.com
Website: www.artsworld.com
Ownership: BSkyB, Caledonia
Investments, Guardian Media Group,
and private investors
Programming: arts

Asian Music Channel
Vis Television Media International
Fountain House,
140 Dudley Port
Tipton,
West Midlands. DY4 7RE.
Tel: 08700 110020
Fax: 08700 110030
email: info@vismediaint.com
Website: vismediaint.com
Programming: Material for Asian,
African and UK broadcasters

Asianet
PO Box 38
Greenford
Middlesex UB6 7SB
Tel: 020 8566 9000
Fax: 020 8810 5555
Website: www.asianet-tv.com
Cable only from videotape
Programming: movies and
entertainment in Hindi, Punjabi and
other languages

Asset Television
Management Plus
548 Ley Street
Newbury Park
Ilford
Essex 1G2 7DB
Tel: 020 8554 7766
Fax: 020 8554 8881
Programming: family entertainment
with some sport for a multi-cultural
audience

BBC Choice
Woodlands
80 Wood Lane
London W12 0TT
Tel: 020 8433 2000
Fax: 020 8749 0538
Website: www.bbc.co.uk/choice
Ownership: BBC Worldwide [See
MSP above]
Programming: general entertainment
Digital

BBC Knowledge
Woodlands
80 Wood Lane
London W12 0TT
Tel: 020 8433 2000
Fax: 020 8749 0538
Website: www.bbc.co.uk/knowledge
Ownership: BBC Digital Programme
Services [See MSP above]
Programming: educational
Digital

BBC News 24
Woodlands
80 Wood Lane
London W12 0TT
Tel: 020 8433 2000
Fax: 020 8749 0538
Website: www.bbc.co.uk
Ownership: BBC Worldwide [See
MSP above]
Programming: news

BBC Parliamentary Channel
BBC Westminster
4 Millbank
London SW1P 3JA
Tel: 020 973 6048
Fax: 020 0793 6049
Ownership: BBC
Programming: daily coverage of
Parliamentary proceedings

Bet International
Kershaw House
Great West Rd
Hounslow
Middlesex TW5 0BU
Tel: 020 8814 2357
Fax: 020 8814 2358
Website: www.betint.com
Ownership: Viacom
Service start: August 1993
Programming: Jazz

B4U
Bollywood Eros Network
Unit 23, Sovereign Park
Coronation Road
London NW10
Tel: 020 8963 8400
email:b4utv@b4utv.com
Website: www.b4utv.com
Programming: Hindi feature films

Bid-up TV
160 Great Portland Street
London W1N 5TB
Tel: 020 7299 5000
Fax: 020 7299 5400
Website: www.bid-up.tv
Ownership: Flextech [see MSP]
Programming: on-screen auctions

The Biography Channel
Grant Way, Syon Lane
Isleworth
Middlesex TW7 5QD
Tel: 0870 240 3000
Service start: 2000
Programming: biographical material

Bloomberg Television
City Gate House
39-45 Finsbury Square
London EC2A 1PQ
Tel: 020 7330 7500
Fax: 020 7661 5748
email: ukfeedback@bloomberg.net
Website: www.bloomberg.co.uk
Service start: 1 Nov 1995
Satellite: Astra 1E, Eutelsat II-F1
Programming: business and finance

The Box
Imperial House
11-13 Young Street
London W8 5EH
Tel: 020 7376 2000
Fax: 020 7376 1313
Website: www.thebox.com
Ownership: Emap
Service start: 2 Mar 1992
Satellite: Astra 1A (PAL/Videocrypt;
cable only)
Programming: interactive pop music

Boomerang
Turner House
16 Great Marlborough St
London W1F 7HS
Tel: 020 7693 1000
Fax: 020 7693 1001
Website: www.cartoonnetwork.co.uk
Ownership: Turner Broadcasting [see
MSP above]
Service start: 27 May 2000
Programming: classic cartoons

Bravo
160 Great Portland St
London W1W 5QA
Tel: 020 7299 5000
Fax: 020 7299 6000
email: enquiries@bravo.co.uk
Website: www.bravo.co.uk
Ownership: Flextech Television [see
MSP above]
Service start: Sept 1985
Satellite: Astra 1C (PAL/Videocrypt)
Programming: old movies and
television programmes

British Eurosport see
Eurosport

British Interactive Video
34-35 Faringdon St
London EC4A 4HL

Tel: 020 7332 7000
Fax: 020 7332 7100
email: name@open-here.co.uk
Website: www.open-here.co.uk
Programming: interactive television

Carlton Cinema
Website: www.carltoncinema.co.uk
Ownership: Carlton Communications
[see MSP above]
Service start: 2 Sep 1996
Also digital

Carlton Kids
Ownership: Carlton Entertainment
[see MSP above]
Programming: children's
Digital, included in ITV Digital

Carlton World
Ownership: Carlton Entertainment
[see MSP above]
Programming: documentary
Digital, included in ITV Digital

Cartoon Network
Turner House
16 Great Marlborough St
London W1F 7HS
Tel: 020 7693 1000
Fax: 020 7693 1001
email: toon.pressoffice@turner.com
Website: www.cartoonnetwork.co.uk
Ownership: Turner Broadcasting [see
MSP above]
Service start: 17 Sept 93
Satellite: Astra 1C, Astra 1F
(PAL/clear)
Programming: children's animation
Also digital

Challenge TV
160 Great Portland St
London W1W 5QA
Tel: 020 7299 5000
Fax: 020 7299 6000
Website: www.challengetv.co.uk
Ownership: Flextech [see MSP above]
Service start: 3 Feb 1997
Satellite: Astra 1C (PAL/Videocrypt)
Programming: general entertainment,
game shows

The Channel Guide
1 Yeoman's Court
Ware Road
Ware, Herts SG13 7HJ
Tel: 01920 469238
Fax: 01920 468372
Ownership: Picture Applications
Service start: May 1990
Cable only (text)
Programming: programme listings

Channel One
PO Box 336

Old Hall Street
Liverpool L69 3TE
Tel: 0151 472 2700
Fax: 0151 472 2702
email: Ch1.lpl@cybase.co.uk
Service start: November 1994
Programming: local news and
features

The Chinese Channel
Teddington Studios
Broom Road
Teddington
Middlesex TW11 9NT
Tel: 020 8614 8300
Fax: 020 8943 0982
email: tvbseurope@chinese-
channel.co.uk
Website: www.chinese-channel.co.uk
Ownership: TVBI 64%, Pacific Media
36%
Service start: 31 March 1997
Programming: Entertainment, films
and new in Mandarin and Cantonese

Chinese News and
Entertainment see Phoenix
Chinese News and
Entertainment

Christian Channel Europe
Christian Channel Studios
Stonehills, Shields Road
Gateshead NE10 0HW
Tel: 0191 4952244
email: info@godnetwork.com
Website:
www.indigo.ie/spugradio/cce.html
Service start: 1 Oct 1995
Satellite: Astra 1B
Programming: Christian

CNBC Europe
10 Fleet Place
London EC4M 7QS
Tel: 0181 653 9300
email: talkback@nbc.com
Website: www.cnbceurope.com
Ownership: International General
Electrics
Service start: 11 Mar 1996
Satellite: Astra 1E
Programming: business news

CNN International
CNN House
19-22 Rathbone Place
London W1P 1DF
Tel: 020 7637 6921
Fax: 020 7637 6868
email: cnni@turner.com
Website: www.europe.cnn.com
Ownership: Time Warner Inc
Service start: Oct 1985
Satellite: Astra 1B, Intelsat 605

(PAL/clear)
Programming: news

The Computer Channel
6 Centaurs Business Park
Grant Way, Syon Lane
Isleworth
Middlesex TW7 5QD
Tel: 0870 240 3000
Fax: 020 7705 3030
Website: www.sky.co.uk
Ownership: British Sky Broadcasting
(see MSP)
Satellite: Astra 1D
Programming: computer topics and
programs

The Discovery Channel
160 Great Portland Street
London W1N 5TB
Tel: 020 7462 3600
Fax: 020 7462 3700
Website: www.discovery.com
Ownership: Discovery
Communications [see MSP above]
Service start: Apr 89
Satellite: Astra 1C, Hot Bird 1
(PAL/encrypted)
Programming: documentaries

Discovery Civilization
see above
Programming: ancient history

Discovery Health
see above
Programming: health

Discovery Home & Leisure
See above
Programming: lifestyle

Discovery Kids
see above
Programming: childrens

Discovery Sci-Trek
see above
Programming: science

Discovery Travel & Adventure
see above
Programming: travel

Discovery Wellbeing
see above
Programming: healthy living

Discovery Wings
see above
Programming: flight

The Disney Channel UK
3 Queen Caroline St
Hammersmith
London W6 9PE
Tel: 020 8222 1000
Fax: 020 8222 2795
Website: www.disneychannel.co.uk
Ownership: Walt Disney Company
Satellite: Astra 1B (PAL/Videocrypt)
Programming: children's (supplied as
bonus with Sky Premier and
Moviemax)

EBN: European Business News
10 Fleet Place
London EC4M 7RB
Tel: 020 7653 9300
Fax: 020 7653 9333
Website: www.ebn.co.uk
Ownership: Dow Jones & Co 70%,
Flextech 30%
Service start: 27 Feb 95
Satellite: Eutelsat II F6 (PAL/clear)
Programming: financial and business
news

EDTV (Emirates Dubai TV)
c/o Teleview Productions
7a Grafton Street
London W1X 3LA
Tel: 020 7493 2496
Fax: 020 7629 6207
Ownership: Dubai government
Service start: Dec 93
Satellite: Arabsat 2A, Intelsat K
Programming: news (from ITN),
entertainment, film, sports, children's
in Arabic and English
Website: www.edtv.com

EFour
124 Horseferry Road
London SW1P 2TX
Tel: 020 7396 4444
Website: www.efour.com
Ownership: Channel Four Television
Programming: entertainment
[premium]
Digital

EuroNews
60 Chemin des Mouilles
69131 Lyon Ecully
France
Tel: (33) 4 72 18 80 00
Fax: (33) 4 72 18 93 71
email: info@euronew.net
Website: www.euronews.net
Ownership: 18 European
Broadcasting Union members 51%,
Générale Occidentale 49%
Service start: 1 Jan 1993
Satellite: Hot Bird 3, Eutelsat II-F1
(PAL/clear)
Programming: news in English,
French, Spanish, German and Italian

Eurosport
84 Theobalds Rd
London WC1X 8RW
Tel: 020 7468 7777
Fax: 020 7468 0024
Website: www.eurosport-tv.com
Ownership: ESO Ltd = TF1 34%,
Canal Plus 33%, ESPN 33%
Service start: Feb 89
Satellite: Astra 1A, Hot Bird 1
(PAL/clear)
Programming: sport
Also digital

FilmFour
124 Horseferry Road
London SW1P 2TX
Tel: 020 7396 4444
Website: www.filmfour.com
Ownership: Channel Four Television
Programming: feature and short films
[premium]
Digital

Fox Kids UK
338 Euston Road
London NW1 3AZ
Tel: 020 7554 9000
Fax: 020 7554 9005
Website: www.foxkids.co.uk
Ownership: Fox Television 50%,
Saban 50%
Satellite: Astra 1A (PAL/Videocrypt)
Programming: children's

Front Row
Front Row Television
64 Newman Street
London W1P 3PG
Tel: 020 7551 5956
Ownership: NTL, Telewest
Programming: movies [pay-per-view]

Gay TV
Portland House
Portland Place
London E14 9TT
Tel: 020 7308 5090
Ownership: Portland Enterprises [see
MSP above]
Satellite: Astra 1C (PAL/encrypted)
Programming: erotic

GMTV2
The London Television Centre
Upper Ground
London SE1 9TT
Tel: 020 7928 5884
Fax: 020 7633 0919
Emai: laura.lewis@gmtv.co.uk
Website: gmtv.co.uk
Programming: morning general
interest
Digital

Granada Breeze

Franciscan Court
16 Hatfields
London SE1 8DJ
Tel: 020 7578 4040
Fax: 020 7578 4176
Website: www.gbreeze.co.uk
Ownership: Granada Sky
Broadcasting
Satellite: Astra 1E (PAL/encrypted)
Programming: lifestyle
Also digital

Granada Men & Motors

Franciscan Court
16 Hatfields
London SE1 8DJ
Tel: 020 7578 4040
Fax: 020 7578 4176
Website: www.menandmotors.co.uk
Ownership: Granada Sky
Broadcasting
Satellite: Astra 1A (PAL/Videocrypt)
Programming: male-oriented,
motoring
Also digital

Granada Plus

Franciscan Court
16 Hatfields
London SE1 8DJ
Tel: 020 7578 4040
Fax: 020 7578 4176
Website:: www.gplus.co.uk
Ownership: Granada Sky
Broadcasting
Satellite: Astra 1A (PAL/Videocrypt)
Programming: classic TV
programmes
Also digital

The Hallmark Channel

234a King's Road
London SW3 5UA
Tel: 020 7368 9100
Fax: 020 7368 9101
Website: hallmarkchannelint.com
Programming: drama

Hellenic Television

50 Clarendon Road
London N8 0DG
Tel: 020 8292 7037
Fax: 020 8292 7042
email: hellenictv@btinternet.com
Programming: Greek language
material

The History Channel

6 Centaurs Business Park
Grant Way, Syon Lane
Isleworth
Middlesex TW7 5QD
Tel: 0870 240 3000
Fax: 020 7705 3030

Website: www.sky.co.uk
Ownership: BSkyB 50%, A&E
Television Networks 50%
Service start: 1 Nov 1995
Satellite: Astra 1B (PAL/Videocrypt)
Programming: history
Website: www.thehistorychannel.
co.uk
Also digital

The Home Shopping Channel

Sir John Moores Building
100 Old Hall Street
Liverpool
Merseyside L70 1AB
Tel: 0800 775533
Ownership: The Home Shopping
Channel Ltd
Digital

HVC: Home Video Channel

Aquis House
Station Rd
Hayes
Tel: 020 8581 7000
Fax: 020 8581 7007
Website: www.theadultchannel.co.uk
Ownership: Home Video Channel
[see MSP above]
Service start: Sept 1985
Satellite: Astra 1D (cable exclusive)
Programming: movies (premium)

ITN News Channel

200 Gray's Inn Road
London WC1X 8XZ
Tel: 020 7833 3000
Fax: 020 7430 4700
Website: www.itv.co.uk
Programming: news

ITV Select

346 Queenstown Road
London SW8 4NE
Tel: 020 7819 8000
Fax: 020 819 8100
Website: www.itv-digital.co.uk
Programming: entertainment,
movies, sport

ITV Sports Channel

346 Queenstown Road
London SW8 4NE
Tel: 020 7819 8000
Fax: 020 819 8100
Website: www.itv-digital.co.uk
Programming: sport

ITV2

200 Gray's Inn Road
London WC1X 8HF
Tel: 020 7843 8000
Fax: 020 7843 8443
Website: www.itv.co.uk
Ownership: ITV companies
Digital; also on analogue cable

Japan Satellite TV (JSTV)

Quick House
65 Clifton Street
London EC2A 4JE
Tel: 020 7426 7330
Fax: 020 7426 7333
Website: www.jstv.co.uk
Ownership: NHK, private Japanese
investors
Satellite: Astra 1E (PAL/Videocrypt)
Programming: Japanese news, drama,
documentary, entertainment, sport

Kiss TV

80 Holloway Road
London N7
Tel: 020 7700 6100
Website: www.kissonline.co.uk
Programming: music

The Landscape Channel Europe

Landscape Studios
Hye House
Crowhurst, East Sussex TN33 9BX
Tel: 01424 830900
Fax: 01424 83680
email: info@landscapetv.com
Website: www.landscapetv.com
Service start: Nov 1988 (on
videotape); Apr 1993 (on satellite)
Satellite: Orion, Hispasat (PAL/clear)
Programming: music and visual
wallpaper

Live TV

24th floor
1 Canada Square
Canary Wharf
London E14 5AP
Tel: 0171 293 3900
Fax: 0171 293 3820
email: cable@livetv.co.uk
Ownership: Mirror Group
Newspapers
Service start: 12 June 95
Programming: general entertainment
Website: www.livetv.co.uk

Living

160 Great Portland St
London W1W 5QA
Tel: 020 7299 5000
Fax: 020 7299 6000
Website: www.livingtv.co.uk
Ownership: Flextech [see MSP above]
Service start: Sept 93
Satellite: Astra 1C (PAL/Videocrypt)
Programming: daytime lifestyle,
evening general entertainment,
particularly aimed at women

Magazine Showcase

Millenium 7 Television
Knightrider House

Knightrider Street
Maidstone ME15 6LU
Tel: 01622 776776
Fax: 01622 678080
email: info@m7tv.co.uk
Website: www.m7tv.co.uk
Programming: general entertainment

MBC: Middle East Broadcasting Centre
80 Silverthorne Road
Battersea
London SW8 3XA
Tel: 020 7501 1111
Fax: 020 7501 1110
Website: www.mbctvsat.com
Service start: Sept 91
Programming: general entertainment
and news in Arabic

Med TV
The Linen Hall
162-168 Regent Street
London W1R 5AT
Tel: 020 7494 2523
Fax: 020 7494 2528
Website: www.ib.be/med
Service start: March 1995
Programming: general entertainment
for Kurdish Turkish communities

Men & Motors see Granada Men & Motors

The Money Channel
Princes Court
Wappiing Lane
London E1W 2DA
Tel: 020 7942 7942
Fax: 020 7942 7943
email: reception@themoneychannel.
co.uk
Website: www.themoneychannel.
co.uk
Programming: financial news

MTV UK
180 Oxford Street
London W1N 0DS
Tel: 020 7478 6000
Website: www.mtv.co.uk
Ownership: Viacom
Service start: Aug 87
Satellite: Astra 1A (PAL/Videocrypt)
Programming: pop music
Also digital

Music Box Channel
Zone Broadcasting
Queen's Studios
117-121 Salisbury Road
London NW6 6RG
Tel: 020 7328 8808
Fax: 020 7328 8858
email: pobox@zonevision.com

Website: www.zonevision.com
Programming: interactive TV juke
box

Music Choice
Turner House
16 Great Marlborough St
London W1F 7AW
Tel: 020 7534 4700
Programming: music

Muslim TV Ahmadiyyah
16 Gressenhall Road
London SW18 5QL
Tel: 020 8870 0922
Fax: 020 8870 0684
Website: www.alislam.org
Ownership: Al-Shirkatul Islamiyyah
Service start: Jan 94
Satellite: Intelsat 601
Programming: spiritual, educational,
training

MUTV
Manchester United Television
274 Deansgate
Manchester M3 4SB
Tel: 0161 834 1111
Website: www.manutd.com
Ownership: Manchester United FC,
BSkyB, Granada
Programming: Manchester United FC

Namaste Television
7 Trafalgar Business Centre
77-87 River Road
Barking
Essex IG11 0EZ
Tel: 0181 507 8292
Fax: 0181 507 8292
Website: www.namastev.co.uk
Service start: Sept 92
Satellite: Intelsat 601
Programming: Asian entertainment

National Geographic Channel
Grant Way, Syon Lane
Isleworth
Middlesex TW7 5QD
Tel: 0870 240 3000
Fax: 020 7705 3030
Ownership: British Sky Broadcasting
(see MSP), National Geographic
Website: www.nationalgeographic.
com
Service start: 1997
Satellite: Astra 1A (PAL/Videocrypt)
Programming: natural history
documentaries

Nickelodeon
15-18 Rathbone Place
London W1P 1DF
Tel: 0171 462 1000

Fax: 0171 462 1030
Website: www.nicktv.co.uk
Ownership: British Sky Broadcasting
50% [see MSP above], MTV
Networks 50%
Service start: 1 Sept 93
Satellite: Astra 1C (PAL/Videocrypt)
Programming: children's

Nick Jr
15-18 Rathbone Place
London W1P 1DF
Tel: 0171 462 1000
Fax: 0171 462 1030
Website: www.nicktv.co.uk
Ownership: British Sky Broadcasting
50% [see MSP above], MTV
Networks 50%
Service start: 1 Sept 99
Programming: young children

OpenTV UK
90 Long Acre
Covent Garden
London WC2E 9RZ
Tel: 020 7849 3004
Fax: 020 7849 3140
Website: opentv.com
Programming: interactive television

The Paramount Comedy Channel
3-5 Rathbone Place
London W1P 1DA
Tel: 020 7399 7700
Website: www.paramountcomedy.
com
Ownership: British Sky Broadcasting
[see MSP above], Viacom
Service start: 1 Nov 1995
Satellite: Astra 1C (PAL/Videocrypt)
Programming: comedy

Performance: The Arts Channel
New Pathe House
57 Jamestown Rd
London NW1P TBD
Tel: 020 7424 3688
Fax: 020 7424 3689
Website: www.performance-
channel.com
Ownership: Arts & Entertainment
Service start: Oct 92
Cable only from videotape
Programming: opera, jazz and
classical concerts, drama

Playboy TV
Aquis House
Station Rd
Hayes
Tel: 020 8581 7000
Fax: 020 8581 7007
Website: www.playboytv.co.uk

Ownership: Flextech 51% [see MSP above], BSkyB, Playboy
Service start: 1 Nov 1995
Satellite: Astra 1B (PAL/Videocrypt)
Programming: erotic (premium)

Phoenix Chinese News and Entertainment (CNE)
Marvic House
Bishops Road, Fulham
London SW6 7AD
Tel: 020 7610 3880
Fax: 020 7610 3118
email: chinesemarkets@
cnetv.demon.co.uk
Website: phoenixtv.com
Ownership: The CNT Group
Service start: Nov 92
Satellite: Astra 1C (PAL/Clear)
Programming: news, current affairs, films, dramas, lifestyle

PLAY UK
160 Great Portland Street
London W1N 5TB
Tel: 020 7299 5000
Fax: 020 7299 6000
Website: www.telewest.co.uk/flextech
Ownership: UKTV = BBC
Worldwide, Flextech [see MSP above]
Programming: popular music, comedy
Digital

QVC: The Shopping Channel
Marco Polo House, Chelsea Bridge
Queenstown Road
London SW8 4NQ
Tel: 020 7705 5600
Fax: 020 7705 5602
Website: www.qvc.com
Ownership: QVC (= Comcast, TCI) 80%, BSkyB 20%
Satellite: Astra 1C (soft scrambled)
Service start: Oct 93
Programming: home shopping

The Racing Channel
17 Corsham Street
London N1 6DR
Tel: 020 7253 2232
Fax: 020 7490 0017
email: info@satelliteinfo.co.uk
Service start: Nov 1995
Satellite: Astra 1D
Programming: horse racing

Reality Television
Zone Broadcasting
Queen's Studios
117-121 Salisbury Road
London NW6 6RG
Tel: 020 7328 8808
Fax: 020 7328 8858
email: pobox@zonevision.com

Website: www.zonevision.com
Programming: documentaries/fly-on-the-wall programmes

The Sci-Fi Channel Europe
5-7 Mandeville Street
London W1U 3AR
Tel: 020 7535 3300
Website: www.scifi.com
Service start: 1 Nov 1995
Satellites: Astra 1B, Hot Bird 1 (PAL/encrypted)
Programming: science fiction

Screenshop
160 Great Portland Street
London W1N 5TB
Tel: 020 7299 5000
Fax: 020 7299 5400
Website: screenshop.co.uk
Ownership: Flextech
Programming: shopping

Setanta
52 The Haymarket
London SW1Y 4RP
Tel: 020 7930 8926
Fax: 020 7930 2509
email: setanta.uk@setanta.com
Website: www.setanta.com
Programming: Gaelic sports for pubs

S4C2
Sianel Pedwar Cymru
Parc Ty-Glas
Llanisien
Cardiff CF4 5DU
Wales
Tel: 029 2074 7444
Fax: 020 2075 4444
Website: www.s4c..co.uk
Programming: coverage of the Welsh Assembly in session initially, news and general entertainment in Welsh and English
Digital

Showtime (The Movie Channel)
Gulf DTH Productions
180 Oxford Street
London W1N 0DS
Tel: 020 7487 6900
Fax: 020 7478 6945
Programming: feature films

Simply Shopping
103a Oxford St
London W1D 2HG
Tel: 020 7758 3000
Fax: 020 7758 3101
Website: www.simplyshoppingtv.com
Programming: home shopping

Sky Box Office
6 Centaurs Business Park

Grant Way
Syon Lane
Isleworth
Middlesex TW7 5QD
Tel: 0870 240 3000
Fax: 020 7705 3030
Ownership: British Sky Broadcasting [see MSP above]
Service start: 1 Dec 97
Satellite: Astra 1E (PAL/Videocrypt)
Programming: movies, concerts, events (pay-per-view)
Also digital

Sky Cinema
Ownership: British Sky Broadcasting [see MSP above]
Service start: Oct 92
Satellite: Astra 1C (PAL/Videocrypt)
Programming: movies (premium)

Sky MovieMax
Ownership: British Sky Broadcasting [see MSP above]
Service start: Feb 89
Satellite: Astra 1A (PAL/Videocrypt)
Programming: movies (premium)
Also digital

Sky News
Ownership: British Sky Broadcasting [see MSP above]
Service start: Feb 89
Satellite: Astra 1A (PAL/Videocrypt)
Programming: news

Sky One
Ownership: British Sky Broadcasting [see MSP above]
Service start: Feb 89
Satellite: Astra 1A (PAL/Videocrypt)
Programming: entertainment
Also digital

Sky Premier
Ownership: British Sky Broadcasting [see MSP above]
Service start: Apr 91
Satellite: Astra 1B (PAL/Videocrypt)
Programming: movies (premium)
Also digital

Sky Scottish
Ownership: British Sky Broadcasting [see MSP above]
Programming: Scottish programmes
Satellite: Astra 1A (PAL/Videocrypt)

Sky Soap
Ownership: British Sky Broadcasting [see MSP above]
Satellite: Astra 1B (PAL/Videocrypt)
Programming: entertainment

Sky Sports 1
Ownership: British Sky Broadcasting [see MSP above]

Service start: Apr 91
Satellite: Astra 1B (PAL/Videocrypt)
Programming: sport (premium)
Also digital

Sky Sports 2
Ownership: British Sky Broadcasting
[see MSP above]
Service start: Aug 94
Satellite: Astra 1C (PAL/Videocrypt)
Programming: sport (premium)
Also digital

Sky Sports 3
Ownership: British Sky Broadcasting
[see MSP above]
Service start: Aug 94
Satellite: Astra 1B (PAL/Videocrypt)
Programming: sport (premium)
Also digital

Sky Sports Extra
Ownership: British Sky Broadcasting
[see MSP above]
Service start: Aug 99
Satellite: Astra 1B (PAL/Videocrypt)
Programming: sport (bonus with
premium channels)
Digital

Sky Travel
Ownership: British Sky Broadcasting
[see MSP above]
Satellite: Astra 1C (PAL/Videocrypt)
Programming: travel documentaries

STEP-UP
University of Plymouth
Notte Street
Plymouth PL1 2AR
Tel: 01752 233635
Programming: educational and
business

The Studio
5-7 Mandeville Street
London W1U 3AR
Tel: 020 7535 3300
Website: www.thestudio.com
Programming: Classic Hollywood
films

Tara Television
60 Charlotte St
London W1T 4DA
Tel: 020 7612 0180
Fax: 020 7612 0181
Website::www.tara-tv.co.uk
Service start: 15 Nov 1996
Satellite: Intelsat 601 (MPEG-2
encrypted)
Programming: Irish entertainment

Taste (formerly Carlton Food Network)
Website: www.cfn,co.uk

Ownership: Carlton Communications
[see MSP above]
Service start: 2 Sep 1996
Satellite: Intelsat 601 (MPEG2 encrypted)
Programming: food
Also digital

TCM Turner Classic Movies
Turner House
160 Great Marlborough St
London W1F 7HS
Tel: 020 7693 1000
Fax: 020 7693 1001
email: tcmeurope@turner.com
Website: www.tcmonline.co.uk
Ownership: Turner Broadcasting [see
MSP above]
Service start: Sept 93
Satellite: Astra 1C, Astra 1F
(PAL/clear)
Programming: movies

Television X: The Fantasy Channel
Northern Shell Building
4 Salesdon Way
City Harbour
London E14 9GL
Tel: 020 7308 5090
Fax: 020 7308 6001
Website: www.televisionx.co.uk
Service start: 2 Jun 1995
Satellite: Astra 1C (PAL/Videocrypt)
Programming: erotic

TLC Life Unscripted
160 Great Portland Street
London W1N 5TB
Tel: 020 7462 3600
Fax: 020 7462 3700
Website: tlc.discovery.com
Ownership: Discovery
Communications
Service start: 1992
Programming: educational/
instructional

The Travel Channel
66 Newman Street
London W1P 3LA
Tel: 020 7636 5401
Fax: 020 7636 6424
Website: www.travelchannel.co.uk
Ownership: Landmark
Communications [see MSP above]
Service start: 1 Feb 94
Satellite: Astra 1E
Programming: travel

Trouble
160 Great Portland Street
London W1N 5TB
Tel: 020 7299 5000
Fax: 020 7299 6000
Website: www.trouble.co.uk

Ownership: Flextech Television [see
MSP above]
Service start: February 1997
Satellite: Astra 1C (PAL/Videocrypt)
Programming: teenagers
email: webmaster@trouble.co.uk

[.tv]
96-97 Wilton Road
London SW1V 1DW
Tel: 020 7691 6112
Website: www.tvchannel.co. uk
Satellite: Astra 1E
Programming: computer-related topics
Website: www.tvchannel.co.
uk/dottv/

TVBS Europe
30-31 Newman Street
London W1P 3PE
Tel: 020 7636 8888
Website: www.chinese-channel.co.uk
Satellite: Astra 1E (digital)
Programming: Chinese-language

TV Travel Shop
1st Floor
1 Stephen St
London W1P 1AL
Tel: 020 7691 6112
Website: www.tvtravelshop.co.uk
Service start: 4 April 1998
Satellite: Astra 1C
Also digital

UK Drama
160 Great Portland Street
London W1N 5TB
Tel: 020 7299 5000
Fax: 020 7299 6000
Website: www.telewest.co.uk/flextech
Ownership: UKTV = BBC
Worldwide, Flextech [see MSP above]
Service start: 31 March 2000
Programming: drama
Also digital

UK Gold/UK Gold 2
160 Great Portland Street
London W1N 5TB
Tel: 020 7299 5000
Fax: 020 7299 6000
Website: www.telewest.co.uk/flextech
Ownership: UKTV = BBC
Worldwide, Flextech [see MSP above]
Service start: Nov 92
Satellite: Astra 1B (PAL/Videocrypt)
Programming: entertainment
Also digital

UK Horizons
160 Great Portland Street
London W1N 5TB
Tel: 020 7299 5000
Fax: 020 7299 6000
Website: www.telewest.co.uk/flextech

Ownership: UKTV = BBC
Worldwide, Flextech [see MSP above]
Satellite: Astra 1E
Programming: documentaries
Also digital

UK Style
160 Great Portland Street
London W1N 5TB
Tel: 020 7299 5000
Fax: 020 7299 6000
Website: www.telewest.co.uk/flextech
Ownership: UKTV = BBC
Worldwide, Flextech [see MSP above]
Satellite: Astra 1E
Programming: lifestyle

VH-1
180 Oxford Street
London W1N 0DS
Tel: 020 7284 7777
Fax: 020 7284 7788
Website: www.vh1online.co.uk
Ownership: MTV Networks =
Viacom (100%)
Satellite: Astra 1B (PAL/encrypted)
Programming: pop music

Wellbeing see Discovery Wellbeing

Zee TV Europe
Unit 5-9
Belvue Business Centre
Belvue Road
Northolt
Middlesex UB5 5QQ
Tel: 020 8839 4000
Fax: 020 8842 3223
email: info@zeetv.co.uk
Website: www.zeetelevision.com
Ownership: Asia TV Ltd
Service start: March 1995
Satellite: Astra 1E (PAL/Videocrypt)
Programming: films, discussions,
news, game shows in Hindi, Punjabi,
Urdu, Bengali, Tamil, English, etc

DIGITAL TELEVISION

BBC Digital Services
TV Centre
Wood Lane
London W12 7RJ
Tel: 020 8743 8000
All the BBC's digital services are
funded by the licence fee and are
therefore non-subscription.

ITVdigital
346 Queenstown Road
London SW8 4NE
Tel: 020 7819 8000
Fax: 020 819 8100
Website: www.itv-digital.co.uk

Sky Digital
6 Centaurs Business Park
Grant Way
Syon Lane
Isleworth
Middlesex TW7 5QD
Tel: 0870 240 3000
Fax: 020 7705 3030
Website: www.skydigital.co.uk

CAREERS AND TRAINING

Careers

No one organisation gives individually-tailored advice about careers in the media industries, but it is an area much written about, and we have included in this section details of some books and other sources or contacts that may help. Compiled by David Sharp.

There is no doubt that the media industries are perceived as being "glamourous" and young people are attracted to them. Opportunities in television appear to be increasing as the number of companies and organisations continues to grow, boosted by the growth of digital delivery and the new technologies. The film sector too, continues to appear reasonably healthy.
Anyone wanting to work in these industries should expect to be open to the idea of working with new technologies and should anticipate the need to update their skills regularly. Offering a range of skills, rather than just one can be to an applicant's benefit.

Finally, it is important to recognise that this area of training and learning, like many others, has been undergoing shifts of emphasis that provide vocational alternatives to more traditional ways of obtaining qualifications and experience.
Health warning! it is still the case that formal qualifications are only part of the picture. If you do get a foot in the door and show initiative and skill you can still get on.

For these reasons it is important that anyone considering a career in the industry takes care to investigate what courses are available that will help prepare the way, and if possible, although this is rarely easy, talks to someone already doing a job similar to the one they are interested in.

WEBSITE
A very useful site is skillsformedia, jointly developed by Skillset and BECTU. Although partly aimed at people already in the industry, this excellent site provides a lot of useful information for industry hopefuls.
www.skillsformedia.com

The Jobs

The media industry contains a wide range of jobs, some of which, usually of a support or administrative nature (eg librarian; accountant) have equivalents in many other areas, and some of which are quite specialised and have unique, though possibly misleading titles (eg best boy; gaffer).

The bibliography, below, will help guide you.

Bibliography
Below is a selected list, based on holdings at the BFI National Library. These will give you some guidance as to the range of jobs available, the structure of the industry, and they will offer some general guidance on preparing a CV. There are publications (and short courses) devoted to creating and presenting CVs, and you should check with your nearest library about these.

A CAREERS HANDBOOK FOR TV, RADIO, FILM, VIDEO & INTERACTIVE MEDIA
Llewellyn, Shona
A&C Black, 2000
ISBN 0713656981

GETTING INTO FILMS & TELEVISION
Angell, Robert
How To Books, 6th ed., 1999
ISBN 1-85703-5453

HOW TO GET INTO THE FILM & TV BUSINESS
Gates, Tudor
Alma House, 1995
ISBN 0-415-15112-0

INSIDE BROADCASTING
Newby, Julian

Routledge, 1997
ISBN 0-415-15112-0

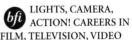 LIGHTS, CAMERA, ACTION! CAREERS IN FILM, TELEVISION, VIDEO
Langham, Josephine
BFI, 2nd ed., 1997
ISBN 0-85170-573-1

MAKING ACTING WORK
Salt, Chrys
Bloomsbury, 1997
ISBN 0-74753-595-7

WORKING IN TELEVISION, FILM & RADIO
Foster, Val et al
DCMS/Design Council/ACE, 1999

YOUR CREATIVE FUTURE
Burnside, Amanda
DfEE, 1997
ISBN 0-86111-0696-2

Courses

The following titles are recommended for information on courses. You will need to consider what balance between theory, practice and academic study you wish to undertake, and plan accordingly. Decide what qualifications and skills you want to acquire, check who validates the course, and for practical courses, what equipment is available to learn with.

 MEDIA COURSES UK
Orton, Lavinia
BFI, Annual.

 MEDIA AND MULTIMEDIA SHORT COURSES
Orton, Lavinia
BFI/Skillset (3 issues per year)
This is also available on the BFI website; and at some Regional Arts Boards. You can find a fully searchable version of this list on the BFI's website at
www.bfi.org.uk/mediacourses

FLOODLIGHT
(covers the Greater London region)

and other local guides to courses may be worth checking at your local library

Courses Abroad

COMPLETE GUIDE TO AMERICAN FILM SCHOOLS AND CINEMA AND TELEVISION COURSES
Pintoff, Ernest
Penguin, 1994
ISBN 0-1401-7226-2

COMPLETE GUIDE TO ANIMATION AND COMPUTER GRAPHICS SCHOOLS
Pintoff, Ernest
Watson-Guptill, 1995
ISBN 0-8230-2177-7
Restricted to American courses only

VARIETY INTERNATIONAL FILM GUIDE
Cowie, Peter, ed.
This annual guide includes an international film schools section.

WHERE TO GET MULTIMEDIA TRAINING IN EUROPE
Institut National de L' Audiovisuel
4th edition CIDJ 1999
ISBN 2-86938-136-0

Bi-lingual guide online version on http//: www.inafr/guide

For courses abroad:

CILECT (Centre International de Liaison Ecoles de Cinema et de Télévision)
8 rue Theresienne
1000 Bruxelles
Belgique
Tel: 00 32 2 511 98 39
Fax: 00 32 2 511 00 35
Contact: Executive Secretary, Henry Verhasselt.
email: hverh.cilect@skynet.be

Training Organisations

Cyfle
Gronant, Penrallt Isaf
Caernarfon, Gwynedd
LL55 1NS
Tel: 01286 671000
Fax: 01286 678831
email: cyfle@cyfle.co.uk
Website: www.cyfle.cyfle.co.uk
This organisation supports the training needs of the Welsh film and television industry
Cyfle
Crichton House
11-12 Mount Stuart Square
Cardiff CF10 5EE

Eastern Media Training Consortium
Anglia House
Norwich
NR1 3JG
Tel: 01603 756839

Film Education
Film Education
Alhamba House
27-31 Charing Cross Road
London WC2H OAU
Tel: 020 7976 2291
Fax: 020 7839 5052
email: postbox@filmeducation.org
Website: www.filmeducation.org
Useful general background on how films are put together, generally as part of their study packs on particular titles

FT2 - Film & Television Freelance Training
4th Floor
Warwick House
9 Warwick Street
London W1R 5LY
Tel: 020 7734 5141
Fax: 020 787 9899
email: ft2@ft2.org.uk
Website: www.ft2.org.uk
Sharon Goode
FT2 is the only UK-wide provider of new entrant training for young people wishing to enter the freelance sector of the industry in the junior construction, production and technical grades. Funded by Skillset Investment Fund, European Social Fund, the AFVPA and Channel 4, FT2 is the largest industry managed training provider in its field and has a 100 per cent record of people

graduating from the scheme and entering the industry. FT2 is also an approved Assessment Centre and offers assessment to industry practitioners for the Skillset Professional Qualifications

4FIT
C/o ft2
4th Floor
Warwick House
9 Warwick Street
London W1R 5RA
Tel: 020 7734 5141
Fax: 020 7287 9899
Sharon Good
Managed by ft2, this is Channel 4's training programme for people from ethnic minority backgrounds wishing to train as new entrants in junior production grades

Gaelic Television Training Trust
Sabhal Mor Ostaig
An Teanga
Isle of Skye, IV44 8RQ
Tel: 01471 888 000
Fax: 01471 888 001
Website: www.smo.uhi.ac.uk
Catriona NicIain

Intermedia Film and Video
19 Heathcote Street
Nottingham NG1 3AF
Tel: 0115 955 6909
Fax: 0115 955 9956
email: info@intermedianotts.co.uk
Website: intermedianotts.co.uk
Ken Hay, Director
Offers a series of training courses, seminars and workshops each year - targeting everyone from new entrants to established producers

Media Skills Wales
Ty Crichton
3rd Floor
11-12 Sgwar Mount Stuart Square
Caerdydd CF10 5EE
Tel: 029 465533
Fax: 029 463344
email: info@mediaskillswales.com
Website: www.mediaskillswales.com
Nadine Griffiths
The regional/national training consortium for Wales

Midlands Media Training Consortium (MMTC - East)
Broadway
Broad St House
14-18 Broad Street
Nottingham NG1 3AL
Tel: 0115 993 0151

Fax: 0115 993 0151
email: training@mmtc.co.uk
Website: www.mmtc.co.uk
Jo Welch, Training Manager
Midlands Training Consortium
provides substantial funding to
Midlands professional freelancers and
broadcast staff to help them keep up
with new technology, new working
practices and new markets

Midlands Media Training Consortium (MMTC - West)
3rd Floor
212 Broad Street
Birmingham B15 1AY
Tel: 0121 643 5504
Fax: 0121 643 5504
email: training@mmtc.co.uk
Website: www.mmtc.co.uk
Bryan Horne
Midlands Training Consortium
provides substantial funding to
Midlands professional freelancers and
broadcast staff to help them keep up
with new technology, new working
practices and new markets

National Film & Television School
National Short Course Training
Programme
Beaconsfield Film Studios
Station Road,
Beaconsfield,
Bucks, HP9 1LG
Tel: 01494 677903
Fax: 01494 678708
email: info@nfts-scu.org.uk
Website: www.nftsfilm-tv.ac.uk
Deanne Edwards
Short course training for people
already working in the industry

North West Media Training Consortium
c/o Mersey Television
Campus Manor
Childwall Abbey Road
Liverpool L16 0JP
Tel: 0151 722 9122
Fax: 0151 722 6839
Regional training body with a brief to
develop a training strategy for those
who already have industry experience

Northern Ireland Film Commission
21 Ormeau Avenue
Belfast BT2 8HD
Tel: 01232 232444
Fax: 01232 239918
email: info@nifc.co.uk
Website: www.nifc.co.uk

Scottish Screen Training
Second Floor
249 West George Street
Glasgow G2 4QE
Tel: 0141 302 1700
Fax: 0141 302 1711
email: info@scottishscreen.com
Website: www.scottishscreen.com

Skillnet South West
The Regional Training Consortium
for the South West
59 Prince Street
Bristol BS1 4QH
Tel: 0117 925 4011
Fax: 0117 925 3511
email: info@skilnetsouthwest.com
Website: www.skillnetsouthwest.com
Jules Channer, Amanda Doughty
Additionally all the Regional Arts
Boards and Media Development
Agencies are involved with or have
information on training. These are
listed in the separate section of this
handbook under Funding.

Skillset
103 Dean Street
London W1V 5RA
Tel: 020 7534 5300
Fax: 020 7534 5333
email: info@skillset.org
Website: www.skillset.org
Skillset is the industry training
organisation for broadcast film and
video. It takes an overview and does
not carry out training itself. It
produces a free (and copyright free)
careers pack for people interested in
entering the industry, but please send
SAE with £1 stamp

Skillstrain South East
c/o Skillset (see above)
Contact: Tricia Boland

Yorkshire Media Training Consortium
30-38 Dock Street
Leeds LS10 1JF
Tel: 0113 294 4410
Fax: 0113 294 4989
email: info@ymtc.co.uk
A regional agency, YMTC is
concerned to develop a strategy to
identify, develop and provide training
for those who are already working
within the industry in the region

Paying Your Way

It is important to be clear on the cost
of any course you embark on and
sources of grants or other funding.
Generally speaking short courses do
not attract grants, but your local
authority or local careers office may
be able to advise on this. Check
directories of sources for grants at
your local library. Learn Direct may
also be able to advise. They are on
0800 100 900 with a (multilingual)
website at **www.learndirect.co.uk**.
(Learn Direct, PO Box 900,
Manchester M60 3LE)
UK residents over 19, not receiving
other government funding for
education may be eligible for an
Individual Learning Account (ILA)
towards costs if their course leads to a
recognised qualification such as an
NVQ. Contact them on 0800-072 -
5678, ILA Centre, PO Box 122,
Newmarket CB8 7YA
Website: www.my-ila.com

CINEMAS

Listed below are the companies who control the major cinema chains and multiplexes in the UK, followed by the cinemas themselves listed by county and town, and including seating capacities. The listing also includes disabled access information, where available. Compiled by Allen Eyles

KEY TO SYMBOLS

 bfi supported - either financial and/or programming assistance

P/T   Part-time screenings
S/O   Seasonal openings

DISABILITY CODES

West End/Outer London

E   Hearing aid system installed. Always check with venue whether in operation
W   Venue with unstepped access (via main or side door), wheelchair space and adapted lavatory
X   Venue with flat or one step access to auditorium
A   Venue with 2-5 steps to auditorium
G   Provision for Guide Dogs

England/Channel Islands/Scotland/Wales/Northern Ireland

X   Accessible to people with disabilities (advance arrangements sometimes necessary - please phone cinemas to check)
E   Hearing aid system installed. Always check with venue whether in operation

The help of Artsline, London's Information and Advice Service for Disabled People on Arts & Entertainment, in producing this section, including the use of their coding system for venues in the Greater London area, is gratefully acknowledged. Any further information on disability access would be welcome.

CINEMA CIRCUITS

Apollo Leisure Group
7 Palatine Suite
Coppull Enterprises Centre
Mill Lane, Coppull
Lancs PR7 5AN
Tel: 01257 471012
Fax: 01257 794109
14 cinemas with 64 screens in the North West of England, Wales, Yorkshire and the Midlands, and a 9 screen multiplex at Paignton, Devon

Artificial Eye Film Company
14 King Street
London WC2E 8HN
Tel: 020 7240 5353
Fax: 020 7240 5242
Film distributors operating the Chelsea Cinema and Renoir in London's West End

Cine-UK Ltd
Chapter House
22 Chapter Street
London SW1P 4NP
Tel: 020 7932 2200
Fax: 020 7932 2222
Website: www.cineworld.co.uk
23 multiplexes (245 screens) in August 2001 with others under construction or planned for 15 further locations

Circle Cinemas
Pantbach Road, Rhiwbina
Cardiff
Tel: 029 20693426
Operate the Monico, Cardiff, Theatre Royal, Barry and Studio, Coleford

City Screen
86 Dean Street
London W1V 5AA
Tel: 020 7734 4342
Fax: 020 7734 4027
Website: www.picturehouse-cinemas.co.uk
Picture House cinemas in Clapham, Brighton (Duke of York's), Oxford (Phoenix), Exeter, Stratford upon Avon, Stratford East (London), East Grinstead, Southampton (Harbour Lights) York and Cambridge (Arts). The company also operates cinemas at Aberdeen and elsewhere and programmes or manages the Curzon

group of cinemas in London's West End, Metro and others

Film Network
23 West Smithfield
London EC1A 9HY
Tel: 020 7489 0531
Fax: 020 7248 5781
Nine screens on two sites at Greenwich and Peckham in South East London

Graves (Cumberland) Ltd
8 Falcon Place
Workington
Cumbria CA14 2EX
Tel: 01900 64791
Fax: 01900 601625
Established 1910. Four sites in Cumbria including a new multiplex at Workington

Hollywood Screen Entertainment
41 London Road South
Lowestoft
Suffolk NR33 0AS
Tel: 01502 564567
Operate the cinemas in Lowestoft, Dereham, Fakenham, Great Yarmouth and Norwich

Mainline Pictures
37 Museum Street
London WC1A 1LP
Tel: 020 7242 5523
Fax: 020 7430 0170
Website: www.screencinemas.co.uk
Screen cinemas at Baker Street, Haverstock Hill, Islington Green, Reigate, Walton-on-Thames and Winchester with a total of 10 screens

National Amusements (UK)
Showcase Cinema
Redfield Way
Lenton
Nottingham NG27 2UW
Tel: 0115 986 2508
Website: www.showcasecinemas.co.uk
16 Showcase cinemas with 211 screens in August 2001 with two further multiplexes opening imminently

Oasis Cinemas
20 Rushcroft Road
Brixton
London SW2 1LA

Tel: 020 7733 8989
Fax: 020 7733 8790
Gate Notting Hill, Cameo Edinburgh, and Ritzy Brixton

Odeon Cinemas
54 Whitcomb Street
London WC2H 7DN
Tel: 0207 321 0404
Fax: 0207 321 0357
Website: www.odeon.co.uk
115 sites with 617 screens in June 2001, including ABC cinemas

Reeltime Cinemas Limited
Carlton
Westgate-on-Sea Kent
St Mildreds Road CT8 8RE
Tel: 01843 834290
Based at the Carlton Westgate Reeltime operates Herne Bay Kavanagh, Margate Dreamland, Dorchester Plaza, Cannock Picture House, Bristol Orpheus, Sittingbourne New Century and Ryde Commodore

Scott Cinemas
Alexandra
Newton Abbot
Devon
Tel: 01626 65368
West Country circuit with cinemas at Barnstaple, Bridgwater, Exmouth, Lyme Regis, Newton Abbot and Sidmouth

Ster Century Europe
3rd floor, St. George's House
Knoll Road, Camberley
Surrey GU15 3SY
Tel: 01276 605 605
Fax: 01276 605 600
Website: www.stercentury.net
Multiplexes at Norwich and Romford with four others scheduled to open in UK

UCI Cinemas
7th Floor, Lee House
90 Great Bridgewater Street
Manchester M1 5JW
Tel: 0161 455 4000
Fax: 0161 455 4076
Website: www.uci-cinemas.co.uk
34 purpose-built multiplexes plus the Empire and Plaza in London's West End with 369 screens in the UK and no additional multiplexes imminent

UGC Cinemas
6th Floor, Adelaide House
626 High Road, Chiswick
London W4 5RY
Tel: 020 8987 5000
Fax: 020 8742 7984
35 multiplexes and 4 subdivided traditional cinemas in UK in August 2001 with total of 352 screens

Ward-Anderson Cinema Group
Film House
35 Upper Abbey Street, Dublin 1
Ireland
Tel: (353) 1 872 3422/3922
Fax: (353) 1 872 3687
Leading cinema operator in Northern and Southern Ireland. Sites include Ballymena, Belfast, Londonderry, Lisburn and Newry

Warner Village Cinemas
Warner House
98 Theobald's Road
London WC1X 8WB
Tel: 020 7984 6600
Website: www.warnervillage.co.uk
34 multiplex cinemas in the UK with 292 screens in August 2001, including the 9-screen Warner Village West End in London's Leicester Square and the 30-screen Birmingham StarCity site. Many further sites are under construction

West Coast Cinemas
Studio, John Street
Dunoon
Strathclyde
Scotland
Tel: 01369 704545
Operate cinemas in Dunoon, Greenock and Fort William

WTW Cinemas
Regal, The Platt
Wadebridge
Cornwall PL27 7AD
Tel: 01208 812791
Operate Wadebridge Regal, St Austell Film Centre, Truro Plaza and Padstow Cinedrome

Zoo Cinema Exhibition Ltd
20 Rushcroft Road
SW2 1LA
Tel: 020 7733 8989
Fax: 020 7733 8790
email: info@zoocinemas.co.uk
Clare Binns
New British cinema company launched in 2001. Zoo manages the Oasis group of cinemas (the Ritzy Brixton, Gate Notting Hill and Cameo Edinburgh) and programme the Everyman Hampstead, Phoenix East Finchley, The David Lean Cinema in Croydon and the Broadway, Letchworth. The company has also taken on the programming contract for the Film Network group, which includes the 3-screen Greenwich Cinema, the 6-screen Premier in Peckham and the Richmond Filmhouse

LONDON WEST END - PREMIERE RUN

BAKER STREET
Screen on Baker Street
Baker Street, NW1
Tel: 020 7935 2772
Seats: 1:95, 2:100

Bayswater
UCI Whiteleys
Queensway, W2
WG
Tel: 08700 102030
Seats: 1:333, 2:281, 3:196, 4:178, 5:154, 6:138, 7:147, 8:125

Bloomsbury
Renoir
Brunswick Square, WC1
Tel: 020 7837 8402
Seats: 1:251, 2:251

Chelsea
Chelsea Cinema
Kings Road, SW3
Tel: 020 7351 3742
Seats: 713

UGC Cinemas,
Kings Road, SW3
Tel: 0870 907 0710
Seats: 1:220, 2:238, 3:122, 4:111

City of London
Barbican Centre,
Silk Street, EC2
WE
Tel: 020 7382 7000
Seats: 1:288, 2:255

Fulham Road
UGC Cinemas
Fulham Road, SW10
Tel: 0870 907 0711
Seats: 1:348 X, 2:329 X, 3:173 X, 4:203 X, 5:218, 6:154

Haverstock Hill
Screen on the Hill
Haverstock Hill, NW3
A
Tel: 020 7435 3366/9787
Seats: 339

Haymarket
UGC Cinemas
Haymarket, SW1
Tel: 0870 907 0712
Seats: 1:448, 2:200, 3:201

Odeon,
Haymarket, SW1
A
Tel: 0870 50 50 007

Seats: 600
(temporarily closed in August 2001)

Hoxton
The Lux Cinema,
2-4 Hoxton Square, N1
Tel: 020 7684 0200/0201
Seats: 120

Islington
Screen on the Green,
Upper Street, Islington, N1
A
Tel: 020 7226 3520
Seats: 280

Kensington
Odeon,
Kensington High Street, W8
Tel: 0870 50 50 007
Seats: 1:645, 2:73, 3:110, 4:297 X,
5:190 X, 6:234 X

Leicester Square
Odeon,
Panton Street, SW1
Tel: 0870 50 50 007
Seats: 1:127 X, 2:144 X, 3:138, 4:136

Odeon Wardour Street,
Swiss Centre, W1
Tel: 0870 50 50 007
Seats: 1:97, 2:101, 3:93, 4:108

Empire,
Leicester Square, WC2
Tel: 028700 102030
Seats: 1:1,330 X, 2:353, 3:77

Odeon,
Leicester Square, WC2
Tel: 0870 50 50 007
Seats: 1,943 EX; Mezzanine: 1:60 W,
2:50, 3:60, 4:60, 5:60

Odeon West End,
Leicester Square, WC2
E
Tel: 0870 50 50 007
Seats: 1:503, 2:838

Prince Charles,
Leicester Place, WC2
X
Tel: 020 7437 8181
Seats: 488

Warner Village West End,
Cranbourne Street, WC2
Tel: 020 7437 4347/3484
Seats: 1:187, 2:126, 3:300, 4:298,
5:414, 6:264, 7:410, 8:180, 9:303

The Mall
ICA Cinema,

The Mall, SW1
AG
Tel: 020 7930 3647
Seats: 185, C'th_que: 45

Marble Arch
Odeon,
Edgware Road, W1
E
Tel: 0870 50 50 007
Seats: 1:254, 2:126, 3:174, 4:229, 5:239

Mayfair
Curzon Mayfair,
Curzon Street, W1
Tel: 020 7369 1720/7465 8865
Seats: 542

Notting Hill
Coronet,
Notting Hill Gate, W11
A
Tel: 020 7727 6705
Seats: 1:388, 2:147

Electric,
Portobello Road, W11
X
Tel: 020 7727 9958
Seats: 220 plus sofas

Gate,
Notting Hill Gate, W11
Tel: 020 7727 4043
Seats: 240

Piccadilly Circus
Metro,
Rupert Street, W1
W
Tel: 020 7437 0757
Seats: 1:195, 2:84

Plaza,
Lower Regent Street, W1
Tel: 0990 888990
Seats: 1:752, 2:370 X, 3:161, 4:187

UGC Cinemas,
Trocadero Centre, Piccadilly Circus, W1
XE
Tel: 0870 907 0716
Seats: 1:548, 2:240, 3:146, 4:154,
5:122, 6:94, 7:89

Shaftesbury Avenue
Odeon Covent Garden, Shaftesbury
Avenue, WC2
Tel: 0870 50 50 007
Seats: 1:146, 2:268, 3:167, 4:156

Curzon Soho,
Shaftesbury Avenue, W1
Tel: 020 7734 2255
Seats: 1:249, 2:110, 3:130

South Kensington
Ciné Lumiére,
French Institute, Queensberry Place,
SW7
(P/T)
Tel: 020 7838 2144/2146
Seats: 350

Goethe Institute,
50 Princes Gate,
Exhibition Rd, SW7 (P/T)
Tel: 020 7596 4000
Seats: 170

IMAX, Science Museum
Tel: 0870 870 4868
Seats: 450

Tottenham Court Road
Odeon,
Tottenham Court Road, W1
Tel: 0870 50 50 007
Seats: 1:328, 2:145, 3:137

Waterloo
 bfi London IMAX, Charlie
Chaplin Walk, SE1
Tel: 020 7902 1234
Seats: 482

 National Film Theatre, South
Bank, Waterloo, SE1
WE
Tel: 020 7928 3232
Seats: 1:450, 2:160, 3:135

Queen Elizabeth Hall, South Bank,
Waterloo, SE1 (P/T)
X
Tel: 020 7928 3002
Seats: 906

Royal Festival Hall, South Bank,
Waterloo, SE1 (P/T)
X
Tel: 020 7928 3002
Seats: 2,419

OUTER LONDON

Acton
Warner Village Cinemas, Royale
Leisure Park, Park Royal
Tel: 020 8896 0099
Seats: 1:425, 2:159, 3:205, 4:274,
5:314, 6:274, 7:205, 8:159, 9:425

Barnet
Odeon, Great North Road
Tel: 0870 50 50 007
Seats: 1:528 E, 2:140, 3:150, 4:193 W,
5:158

Beckenham
Odeon, High Street
Tel: 0870 50 50 007
Seats: six screens

Studio, Beckenham Road
Tel: 020 8663 0103
Seats: 84

Bexleyheath
Cineworld, The Broadway
Tel: 020 8303 0015
Seats: 1:157, 2:128, 3:280, 4:244, 5:88,
6:84, 7:111, 8:168, 9:221

Brentford
Watermans Arts Centre,
High Street
WEG
Tel: 020 8568 1176
Seats: 240

Brixton
Ritzy, Brixton Oval, Coldharbour
Lane, SW2
Tel: 020 7737 2121/7733 2229
Seats: 1:353, 2:179, 3:125, 4:108, 5:84

Bromley
Odeon, High Street
Tel: 0870 50 50 007
Seats: 1:392, 2:129 X, 3:105 X, 4:273

Camden Town
Odeon, Parkway
Tel: 0870 50 50 007
Seats: 1:403, 2:92, 3:238, 4:90, 5:103

Catford
ABC, Central Parade, SE6 2TF
Tel: 020 8698 3306/697 6579
Seats: 1:519 X, 2:259

Clapham
Picture House
Venn Street, SW4
Tel: 020 7498 3323
Seats: 1:202, 2:153 X, 3:134 X, 4:115

Croydon
Safari, London Road

Tel: 020 8688 3422
Seats: 1:650, 2:399 X, 3:187 X

David Lean Cinema, Clock Tower,
Katherine St
X
Tel: 020 8253 1030
Seats: 68

Fairfield Halls/Ashcroft Theatre,
Park Lane (P/T)
Tel: 020 8688 9291
Seats: Fairfield: 1,552 WEG, Ashcroft:
750

Warner Village Cinemas, Grant's site
Seats: 1,900 (10 screens)
(scheduled to open February 2002)

Dagenham
Warner Village Cinemas, Dagenham
Leisure Park, Cook Road
Tel: 020 8592 2211
Seats: 1:404, 2:146, 3:189, 4:252,
5:305, 6:252, 7:189, 8:146, 9:404

Dalston
Rio, Kingsland High Street, E8
WEG
Tel: 020 7241 9410
Seats: 405

Ealing
UGC Cinemas, Uxbridge Road, W5
Tel: 0870 907 0719
Seats: 1:576, 2:371, 3:193

East Finchley
Phoenix, High Road, N2
XG
Tel: 020 8444 6789
Seats: 308

East Ham
Boleyn, Barking Road
Tel: 020 8471 4884
Seats: 1:800, 2:250, 3:250

Edgware
Cinemax, Station Road
Tel: 020 8381 2556
Seats: 1:700, 2:200, 3:158

Enfield
UGC Cinemas, Southbury Leisure
Park, Southbury Road
Tel: 0870 90 70 745
Seats: 1:156, 2: 270, 3:236, 4:186,
5:156, 6:192, 7:277, 8:522, 9:273,
10:203, 11:156, 12:270, 13:236,
14:186, 15:98

Feltham
Cineworld, Leisure West, Browells
Lane
Tel: 020 8867 0888

Seats: 1:104, 2:116, 3:132, 4:205,
5:253, 6:351, 7:302, 8:350, 9:265,
10:90, 11:112, 12: 137, 13:124, 14:99

Finchley Road
Warner Village Cinemas, 02 Centre
Tel: 020 7604 3066
Seats: 1:359, 2:324, 3:159, 4:261,
5:376, 6:258, 7:134, 8:86

Greenwich
The FilmWorks, Bugsby's Way
Tel: 08700 10 20 30
Seats: 1:115, 2:138, 3:157, 4:178,
5:178, 6:157, 7:138, 8:115, 9:279,
10:338, 11:372, 12:261, 13:44, 14:44

Greenwich Cinema,
High Road, SE10
WEG
Tel: 01426 919 020
Seats: 1:350, 2:288, 3:144

Hammersmith
UGC Cinemas, King Street, W6
Tel: 0870 907 0718
Seats: 1:322, 2:322, 3:268 A, 4:268 A

Riverside Studios,
Crisp Road, W6
E
Tel: 020 8237 1111
Seats: 200

Hampstead
Everyman, Holly Bush Vale, NW3
X
Tel: 020 7431 1777
Seats: 184

Harringey
New Curzon, Frobisher Road
Tel: 020 8347 6664
Seats: 498

Harrow
Safari, Station Road
Tel: 020 8426 0606
Seats: 1:612, 2:133

Warner Village Cinemas, St George's
Centre, St. Anne's Road
Tel: 020 8427 9900/9944
Seats: 1:347, 2:288, 3:424, 4:296,
5:121, 6:109, 7:110, 8:87, 9:96

Hayes
Beck Theatre, Grange Road (P/T)
XE
Tel: 020 8561 8371
Seats: 518

Holloway
Odeon, Holloway Road, N7
Tel: 0870 50 50 007
Seats: 1:330, 2:315, 3:72, 4:239, 5:187,
6:252, 7:94, 8:105

Ilford
Cinemas
High Road
Tel: 020 8514 4400
Seats: 650

Cineworld, Clements Road
Seats: 2200 (11 screens)
(Scheduled to open Spring 2002)

Odeon, Gants Hill
Tel: 0870 50 50 007
Seats: 1:768, 2:255 X, 3:290 X, 4:190,
5:62

Kilburn
Tricycle Cinema, High Road
Tel: 020 7328 1000
Seats: 280

Kingston
ABC Options, Richmond Road
Tel: 020 8546 0404/547 2860
Seats: 1:303 X, 2:287 X, 3:208

Odeon
Seats: (14 screens)
(Scheduled to open October 2002)

Lambeth
Imperial War Museum, Lambeth
Road, SE1 (P/T)
X
Tel: 020 7735 8922
Seats: 216

Lee Valley
UCI Cinemas, Picketts Lock Lane,
Meridian Way, Edmonton
X
Tel: 08 700 10 20 30
Seats: 164 (6 screens), 206 (4 screens),
426 (2 screens)

Mile End
Genesis, Mile End Road
Tel: 020 7780 2000
Seats: 1:575, 2:159, 3:159, 4:101, 5:95

Muswell Hill
Odeon, Fortis Green Road, N10
Tel: 0870 50 50 007
Seats: 1:610, 2:134 X, 3:130 X

Newham
Showcase Cinemas,
Jenkins Lane, off A13
X
Tel: 020 8477 4500
Seats: 3,664 (14 screens)

North Finchley
Warner Village Cinemas, Great North
Leisure Park, Chaplin Square, N12
Tel: 020 8446 9977/9933
Seats: 1:377, 2:164, 3:219, 4:333,
5:333, 6:219, 7:164, 8:377

Peckham
Premier, Rye Lane
X
Tel: 020 7732 1010
Seats: 1:397, 2:255, 3:275, 4:197,
5:218, 6:112

Purley Way
Warner Village Cinemas, Valley Park
Leisure Complex, Croydon
Tel: 020 8680 1968/6881
Seats: 1:253, 2:205, 3:178, 4:396,
5:396, 6:178, 7:205, 8:253

Putney
Odeon, High Street, SW15
AWG
Tel: 0870 50 50 007
Seats: 1:434, 2:312, 3:147

Richmond
Filmhouse, Water Lane
WG
Tel: 020 8332 0030
Seats: 150

Odeon, Hill Street
Tel: 0870 50 50 007
Seats: 1:478, 2:201 X, 3:201 X

Odeon Studio, Red Lion Street
Tel: 0870 50 50 007
Seats: 1:81, 2:78, 3:78, 4:92

Romford
Ster Century, The Brewery,
Waterloo Road
Tel: 01708 759100
Seats: 3,800 (16 screens)

Shepherds Bush
Warner Village Cinemas
Seats: 2,487 (12 screens)
(Scheduled to open December 2001)

Staples Corner
UGC Cinemas, Geron Way
WE
Tel: 0870 907 0717
Seats: 1:455, 2:362, 3:214, 4:210,
5:166, 6:166

Stratford
Picture House, Gerry Raffles Square,
Salway Road, E15
Tel: 020 8555 3311/66
Seats: 1:260, 2:242, 3:215, 4:151

Streatham
Odeon, High Road, SW16
Tel: 0870 505 000
Seats: 1:451, 2:110, 3:110, 4:103,
5:237, 6:209, 7:93, 8:172

Surrey Quays
UCI Cinemas, Redriff Road, SE16

Tel: 0870 102030
Seats: 1:411, 2:401, 3:328, 4:200,
5:198, 6:198, 7:164, 8:164, 9:164

Sutton
Secombe Centre, Cheam Road
XE
Tel: 020 8661 0416
Seats: 330

UCI Cinemas, St Nicholas Centre, St
Nicholas Way
X
Tel: 0870 010 2030
Seats: 1:305, 2:297, 3:234, 4:327,
5:261, 6:327

Swiss Cottage
Odeon, Finchley Road, NW3
Tel: 0870 50 50 007
Seats: 1:658, 2:112, 3:267, 4:118,
5:150, 6:150

Walthamstow
EMD, Hoe Street, London E17
Tel: 020 8520 7092
Seats: 1:592, 2:183 A, 3:174 A

West India Quay
UGC Cinemas, Hertsmere Road
Tel: 0207 517 7860
Seats: 1:111, 2:168, 3:216, 4: 275,
5:360, 6: 104, 7:164, 8: 216, 9:275,
10:359

Willesden
Belle Vue, Willesden Green Library
Centre, NW10
Tel: 020 8830 0822
Seats: 204

Wimbledon
Odeon, The Broadway, SW19
Tel: 0870 50 50 007
Seats: 1:702, 2:90, 3:190 X, 4:175,
5:218 X

Woodford
Odeon, High Road, E18
Tel: 0870 50 50 007
Seats: (seven screens)

Wood Green
Cineworld, Shopping City, High
Road
Tel: 020 8829 1400
Seats: 1:267, 2:315, 3:106, 4:152,
5:185, 6:111, 7:180, 8:137, 9:172,
10:140, 11:162, 12:105

Showcase
Seats: 1,600 (6 screens)
(Scheduled to open Autumn 2001)

ENGLAND

Accrington – Lancashire
Metro
Seats: 950 (4 screens)
(Scheduled to open June 2002)

Aldeburgh - Suffolk
Aldeburgh Cinema, High Street
X
Tel: 01728 452996
Seats: 284

Aldershot - Hants
ABC, High Street
Tel: 01252 317223/320355
Seats: 1:313, 2:187, 3:150

West End Centre, Queens Road
(P/T)
X
Tel: 01252 330040
Seats: 98

Alnwick - Northumberland
Playhouse, Bondgate Without (P/T)
Tel: 01665 510785
Seats: 272

Alton - Hants
Palace, Normandy Street
Tel: 01420 82303
Seats: 111

Ambleside - Cumbria
Zeffirelli's, Compston Road
X
Tel: 01539 431771
Seats: 1:205, 2:63

Ardwick - Greater Manchester
Apollo, Ardwick Green (P/T)
X
Tel: 0161 273 6921
Seats: 2,641

Ashford - Kent
Cineworld, Eureka Leisure Park, Trinity Road
Tel: 01233 620568/622226
Seats: 1:344, 2:75, 3:63, 4:89, 5:156, 6:254, 7:254, 8:156, 9:89, 10:63, 11:215, 12:345

Ashton-under-Lyne - Greater Manchester
Metro, Old Street
Tel: 0161 330 1993
Seats: 987

Aylesbury - Buckinghamshire
Odeon, The Exchange
Tel: 0870 50 50 007
Seats: 1: 399, 2:283, 3:266, 4:230, 5:205, 6:194

Banbury - Oxfordshire
ABC, Horsefair
Tel: 01295 262071
Seats: 1:430, 2:225

Barnsley - South Yorkshire
Odeon, Eldon Street
Tel: 0870 50 50 007
Seats: 1:419, 2:636X

Barnstaple - Devon
Central, Boutport Street
Tel: 01271 342550
Seats: 1:360, 2:80, 3:80, 4:130

Barrow - Cumbria
Apollo, Hollywood Park, Hindpool Road
Tel: 01229 825354
Seats: 1:118, 2:103, 3:258, 4:258, 5:118, 6:118

Basildon - Essex
UCI, Festival Leisure Park, Pipps Hill
Tel: 0870 010 2030
Seats: 2,909 (12 screens)

Basingstoke - Hants
Anvil, Churchill Way (P/T)
X
Tel: 01256 844244
Seats: 70

Ster Century, Festival Place
Seats: 2,116 (10 screens)
(Scheduled to open in 2002)

Warner Village Cinemas, Basingstoke Leisure Park, Churchill Way West, West Ham
XE
Tel: 01256 818739/818517
Seats: 1:427, 2:238, 3:223, 4:154, 5:157, 6:157, 7:154, 8:223, 9:238, 10:427

Bath - Avon
ABC, Westgate Street X
Tel: 01225 461730/462959
Seats: 652

Little Theatre, St Michael's Place
Tel: 01225 466822
Seats: 1:192, 2:74

Robins, St John's Place
Tel: 01225 461506
Seats: 1:151, 2:126 X, 3:49

Bedford - Bedfordshire
Civic Theatre, Horne Lane (P/T)
Tel: 01234 44813
Seats: 266

UGC Cinemas, Aspect Leisure Park, Newnham Avenue   XE
Tel: 0541 555 130
Seats: 1:334, 2:292, 3:291, 4:289, 5:187, 6:187

Berwick - Northumberland
Maltings Art Centre, Eastern Lane (P/T)
Tel: 01289 330999/330661
Seats: 100

Playhouse, Sandgate
Tel: 01289 307769
Seats: 650

Beverley - East Yorkshire
Picture Playhouse, Market Place
Tel: 01482 881315
Seats: 310

Bexhill - East Sussex
Curzon Picture Playhouse, Western Road
Tel: 01424 210078
Seats: 175

Bideford - Devon
College Theatre (P/T)
Tel: 01237 428110
Seats: 181

Billingham - Cleveland
Forum Theatre, Town Centre (P/T)
Tel: 01642 552663
Seats: 494

Birkenhead - Merseyside
Warner Village Cinemas, Europa Boulevard, Conway Park
Tel: 0151 649 8822
Seats: 1:298, 2:359, 3:164, 4:206, 5:433, 6:206, 7:164

Birmingham - West Midlands
Electric, Station Street
X
Tel: 0121 643 7277
Seats: 1:200, 2:100

MAC
Cannon Hill Park, Edgbaston
Tel: 0121 440 3838
Seats: 1:202, 2:144

Odeon, New Street
Tel: 0870 50 50 007
Seats: 1:238, 2:387, 3:308, 4:239, 5:204, 6:190, 7:126, 8:80

Piccadilly, Stratford Road, Sparkhill
Tel: 0121 773 1658

Showcase Cinemas, Kingsbury Road

Erdington
Tel: 0121 382 9779
Seats: 3,599 (12 screens)

UGC Cinemas, Arcadian Centre,
Hurst Street
XE
Tel: 0121 155 5177
Seats: 1:419, 2:299, 3:275, 4:240,
5:192, 6:222, 7:210, 8:196, 9:168

UGC Cinemas, Five Ways Leisure,
Broad Street
Tel: 0870 907 0723
Seats: 1:371, 2:330, 3:269, 4:181.
5:287, 6:434, 7:341, 8:185, 9:269, 10:
240, 11:263, 12:167

Warner Village Cinemas
StarCity, Watson Road, Nechells
Tel: 0121 326 0246
Seats: 1:432, 2:126, 3:112, 4:175,
5:245, 6:245, 7:179, 8:142, 9:142,
10:142, 11:142, 12:534, 13:135,
14:192, 15:201, 16:135, 17:192,
18:201, 19:534, 20:128, 21:128,
22:120, 23:115, 24:146, 25:143,
26:181, 27:245, 28:245, 29:159, 30:318

Bishop's Stortford - Herts
Cineworld, Anchor Street
Tel: 01279 710 000
Seats: 1:299, 2:104, 3:160, 4:259,
5:230, 6:185

Blackburn - Lancashire
Apollo Five, King William Street
Tel: 01254 695979
Seats: 1:295, 2:205, 3:115, 4:100, 5:95

Blackpool - Lancashire
Odeon, Rigby Road
Tel: 0870 50 50 007
Seats: 1:416, 2:137, 3:347, 4:155,
5:202, 6:391, 7:158, 8:344, 9:371,
10:203

Bluewater - Kent
Showcase
Tel: 0870 242 7070
Seats: 1:129, 2:197, 3:361, 4:464,
5:245, 6:176, 7:80, 8:139, 9:298,
10:379, 11:193, 12:132, Studio:86

Blyth - Northumberland
Wallaw, Union Street
Tel: 01670 352504
Seats: 1:850, 2:150, 3:80

Bognor Regis - West Sussex
Picturedrome, Canada Grove
Tel: 01243 841015
Seats: 1:399, 2:100

Odeon, Butlin's Southcoast World
Tel: 0870 841916
Seats: 1:240, 2:240

Boldon - Tyne and Wear
UGC Cinemas, Boldon Leisure Park,
Boldon Colliery
Tel: 0541 550512
Seats: 1:284, 2:197, 3:80, 4:119, 5:263,
6:529, 7:263, 8:136, 9:119, 10:197,
11:284

Bolton - Greater Manchester
Warner Village Cinemas,
Middlebrook Leisure Park, Horwich
Tel: 01204 669668
Seats: 1:375, 2:124, 3:124, 4:166,
5:244, 6:269, 7:269, 8:244, 9:166,
10:124, 11:124, 12:368

UGC Cinemas, Eagley Brook Way
Tel: 01204 366200
Seats: 1: 143, 2:144, 3:118, 4:155,
5:230, 6:467, 7:635, 8:522, 9:233,
10:156, 11:156, 12:193, 13:193, 14:72,
15:72

Boston - Lincolnshire
Blackfriars Arts Centre, Spain Lane
(P/T)
Tel: 01205 363108
Seats: 237

Bournemouth - Dorset
ABC, Westover Road
Tel: 01202 558433
Seats: 1:650, 2:583, 3:221

Odeon, Westover Road
Tel: 0870 50 50 007
Seats: 1:757, 2:359, 3:267, 4:119,
5:121, 6:140

Bowness-on-Windermere - Cumbria
Royalty, Lake Road
X
Tel: 01539 443364
Seats: 1:400, 2:100, 3:65

Bracknell - Berkshire
South Hill Park Arts Centre
X
Tel: 01344 427272/484123
Seats: 1:60, 2:200 m

UCI Cinemas, The Point,
Skimpedhill Lane
X
Tel: 0870 010 2030
Seats: 1:177, 2:205, 3:205, 4:177,
5:316, 6:316, 7:177, 8:205, 9:205,
10:177

Bradford - West Yorkshire
Cineworld, Vicar Lane
Seats: 3,300 (16 screens)
(Scheduled to open December 2001)

National Museum of Photography,
Film and Television,
Prince's View (P/T)
Tel: 01274 202030
Seats: (IMAX) 340,(Pictureville) 306

Odeon, Gallagher Leisure Park,
Thornbury
X
Tel: 0870 50 50 007
Seats: 1:128, 2:217, 3:155, 4:231,
5:300, 6:443, 7:438, 8:215, 9:154,
10:159, 11:148, 12:142, 13:147

Pictureville Cinema,
Priestley Centre for the Arts, Chapel
Street, Little Germany BD1 5DL
(P/T)
XE
Tel: 01274 820666
Seats: 290

Bridgnorth - Shropshire
Majestic, Whitburn Street
Tel: 01746 761815/761866
Seats: 1:500, 2:86, 3:86

Bridgwater - Somerset
Film Centre, Penel Orlieu
Tel: 01278 422383
Seats: 1:223, 2:232

Bridlington - Humberside
Forum, The Promenade
Tel: 01262 676767
Seats: 1:202, 2:103, 3:57

Bridport - Dorset
Palace, South Street
(temporarily closed)
Seats: 420

Brierley Hill - Staffordshire
UCI Cinemas, Merry Hill Shopping
Centre
X
Tel: 0870 0102030
Seats: 1:350, 2:350, 3:274, 4:274,
5:224, 6:224, 7:254, 8:254, 9:178,
10:178

Brighton - East Sussex
Cinematheque, Media Centre,
Middle Street
Tel: 01273 739970

Duke of York's Premier Picture
House, Preston Circus
Tel: 01273 626 261
Seats: 327

Gardner Arts Centre, University of Sussex, Falmer (P/T)
Tel: 01273 685861
Seats: 354

Odeon Cinemas, Kingswest, West Street
Tel: 0870 50 50 007
Seats: 1:388, 2:883, 3:504, 4:275, 5:242, 6:103

UGC Cinemas, Brighton Marina
Tel: 0541 555 145
Seats: 1:351, 2:351, 3:251, 4:251, 5:223, 6:223, 7:202, 8:203

Bristol - Avon
ABC, Whiteladies Road, Clifton
Tel: 0117 973 0679/973 3640
Seats: 1:372, 2:253 X, 3:135 X

Arnolfini, Narrow Quay
XE
Tel: 0117 929 9191
Seats: 176

Cineworld, Hengrove Leisure Park, Hengrove Way
Tel: 01275 831099
Seats: 1:97, 2:123, 3:133, 4:211, 5:264, 6:343, 7:312, 8:344, 9:262, 10:88, 11:113, 12:152, 13:123, 14:98

The Cube, King Square
X
Tel: 0117 907 4190/4191
Seats: 124

IMAX, Canon's Marsh
Tel: 0117 915 5000
X
Seats: 250

Odeon, Union Street
Tel: 0870 50 50 007
Seats: 1:399, 2:224, 3:215

Orpheus, Northumbria Drive, Henleaze
Tel: 0117 962 1644
Seats: 1:186, 2:129, 3:125

Showcase Cinemas, Avon Meads off Albert Road, St Phillips Causeway
Tel: 0117 972 3800
Seats: 3,408 (14 screens)

Warner Village Cinemas
The Venue, Cribbs Causeway Leisure Complex, Merlin Road
Tel: 0117 950 0222
Seats: 1:385, 2:124, 3:124, 4:166, 5:239, 6:273, 7:273, 8:239, 9:166, 10:124, 11:124, 12:385

Warner Village Cinemas, Aspects Leisure Park, Longwell Green
Tel: 0117 960 0021
Seats: 1:382, 2:165, 3:122, 4:122, 5:165, 6:290, 7:342, 8:290, 9:165, 10:122, 11:122, 12:165, 13:382

 Watershed, 1 Canon's Road, BS1 5TX
XE
Tel: 0117 927 6444/925 3845
Seats: 1:200, 2:50

Broadstairs - Kent
Windsor, Harbour Street
Tel: 01843 865726
Seats: 120

Bromborough - Merseyside
Odeon, Wirral Leisure Retail Park, Welton Road
X
Tel: 0870 50 50 007
Seats: 1:465, 2:356, 3:248, 4:203, 5:338, 6:168, 7:168, 8:86, 9:135, 10:71, 11:121

Bude - Cornwall
Rebel, off A39, Rainbow Trefknic Cross
Tel: 01288 361442
Seats: 120

Burgess Hill - West Sussex
Orion, Cyprus Road
Tel: 01444 232137/243300
Seats: 1:150, 2:121

Burnham-on-Crouch - Essex
Rio, Station Road
Tel: 01621 782027
Seats: 1:220, 2:60

Burnham-on-Sea - Somerset
Ritz, Victoria Street
Tel: 01278 782871
Seats: 204

Burnley - Lancashire
Apollo, Hollywood Park, Centenary Way, Manchester Road
Tel: 01282 456222/456333
Seats: 1:61, 2:238, 3:93, 4:339, 5:93, 6:339, 7:93, 8:238, 9:93

Burton-on-Trent - Staffordshire
Cineworld, Middleway Leisure Park, Guild Street
Tel: 01283 511561
Seats: 1:225, 2:98, 3:136, 4:107, 5:316, 6:289, 7:203, 8:132, 9:98

Bury - Greater Manchester
Warner Village Cinemas, Park 66, Pilsworth Road   X
Tel: 0161 766 2440/1787
Seats: 1:559, 2:322, 3:278, 4:434, 5:208, 6:166, 7:166, 8:208, 9:434, 10:278, 11:322, 12:573

Bury St Edmunds - Suffolk
ABC, Hatter Street
Tel: 01284 754477
Seats: 1:196, 2:117

Camberley - Surrey
ArtsLink, Knoll Road (P/T)
Tel: 01276 707600
Seats: 338

Globe, Hawley (P/T)
Tel: 01252 876769
Seats: 200

Robins, London Road
Tel: 01276 63909/26768
Seats: 1:420, 2:114, 3:94

Cambridge - Cambridgeshire
Arts Picture House, St Andrews Street
Tel: 01223 504444/578939
Seats: 1: 250, 2:150, 3:98

Warner Village Cinemas, Grafton Centre, East Road
XE
Tel: 01223 460442/460225
Seats: 1:162, 2:168, 3:182, 4:205, 5:166, 6:175, 7:321, 8:442

Cannock - Staffordshire
Picture House, Walsall Road
Tel: 01543 502226
Seats: 1:368, 2:185

Canterbury - Kent
ABC, St Georges Place
Tel: 0870 155 5133
Seats: 1:536, 2:404

Cinema 3, Cornwallis South, University of Kent, CT2 7NX
Tel: 01227 769075/764000 x4017
Seats: 300

Canvey Island - Essex
Movie Starr Cineplex, Eastern Esplandade
Tel: 01268 699799
Seats: 1:134, 2:122, 3:104, 4:73

Carlisle - Cumbria
Lonsdale, Warwick Road
Tel: 01228 514654
Seats: 1:375, 2:216, 3:54

City Cinemas 4 & 5, Mary Street

X
Tel: 01228 514654
Seats: 4:122, 5:112

Warner Village Cinemas, Botchergate
X
Tel: 01228 819 104
Seats: 1:145, 2:242, 3:242, 4:145, 5:295, 6:295, 7:334

Chatham - Kent
ABC, High Street
Tel: 01634 846756/842522
Seats: 1:520, 2:360, 3:169

Chelmsford - Essex
Cramphorn Theatre, High Street (P/T)
Tel: 01245 606 505
Seats: 140

Odeon, Kings Head Walk
EX
Tel: 0870 50 50 007
Seats: 1:338, 2:110, 3:160, 4:236, 5:174, 6:152, 7:131, 8:140

Cheltenham - Gloucestershire
Odeon, Winchcombe Street
Tel: 0870 50 50 007
Seats: 1:252, 2:184, 3:184, 4:90, 5:129, 6:104, 7:177

Chesham - Buckinghamshire
New Elgiva Theatre, Elgiva Lane (P/T)
XE
Tel: 01494 582900
Seats: 328

Cheshire Oaks - Cheshire
Warner Village Cinemas, The Coliseum, Stannley Lane, Ellesmere Port
Tel: 0151 356 2261
Seats: 1:345, 2:166, 3:124, 4:166, 5:239, 6:252, 7:345, 8:252, 9:239, 10:166, 11:124, 12:124, 13:166, 14:345, Iwerks:312

Chester - Cheshire
Odeon, Northgate Street
Tel: 0870 50 50 007
Seats: 1:408, 2:148, 3:148, 4:123, 5:123

UGC Cinemas, Chaser Court, Greyhound Park, Sealand Road
XE
Tel: 01244 380459/380301/380155
Seats: 1:366, 2:366, 3:265, 4:232, 5:211, 6:211

Chesterfield - Derbyshire
Cineworld, Derby Road, Alma Leisure Park

Tel: 0246 229172/278000
Seats: 1:245, 2:128, 3:107, 4:150, 5:291, 6:291, 7:150, 8:107, 9:128, 10:237

Chichester - West Sussex
Minerva Movies, Chichester Festival Theatre, Oaklands Park (S/O)
X
Tel: 01243 781312
Seats: 214

New Park Film Centre, New Park Road
X
Tel: 01243 786650
Seats: 120

Chippenham - Wiltshire
Astoria, Marshfield Road
Tel: 01249 652498
Seats: 1:215, 2:215

Chipping Norton - Oxfordshire
The Theatre, Spring Street (P/T)
Tel: 01608 642349/642350
Seats: 195

Christchurch - Dorset
Regent Centre, High Street (P/T)
Tel: 01202 479819/499148
Seats: 485

Cinderford – Gloucestershire
Palace, Bellevue Road
Tel: 01594 822555

Cirencester - Gloucestershire
Regal, Lewis Lane
Tel: 01285 658755
Seats: 1:100, 2:100

Clacton - Essex
Flicks, Pier Avenue
Tel: 01255 429627/421188
Seats: 1:625, 2:135

Clevedon - Avon
Curzon, Old Church Road
Tel: 01275 871000
Seats: 392

Clitheroe - Lancashire
Grand, York Street
Tel: 01200 423278
Seats: 400

Colchester - Essex
Odeon, Crouch Street
Tel: 0870 50 50 007
Seats: 1:480, 2:235, 3:118, 4:133, 5:126, 6:177

Odeon
Seats: (8 screens)
(Scheduled to replace existing Odeon in Spring 2002)

Coleford - Gloucestershire
Studio, High Street
Tel: 01594 833331
Seats: 1:200, 2:80

Consett - Co Durham
Empire, Front Street   XE
Tel: 01207 506751
Seats: 535

Cosham - Hants
ABC, High Street
Tel: 023 92376635
Seats: 1:441, 2:118, 3:107

Coventry - West Midlands
Odeon, Sky Dome, Croft Road
X
Tel: 0870 50 50 007
1: 231, 2:419, 3:182, 4:363, 5:176, 6:139, 7:117, 8:165, 9:174

Showcase Cinemas, Gielgud Way, Walsgrave
Tel: 0247 660 2111
Seats: 4,413 (14 screens)

Warwick Arts Centre, University of Warwick, CV4 7AL
X
Tel: 0247 652 4524/3060
Seats: 240

Cranleigh - Surrey
Regal, High Street
Tel: 01483 272373
Seats: 268

Crawley - West Sussex
UGC Cinemas, Crawley Leisure Park, London Road
Tel: 0870 902 0411
Seats: 1:236, 2:421, 3:186, 4:551, 5:186, 6:129, 7:129, 8:318, 9:173, 10:231, 11:184, 12:156, 13:173, 14:173, 15:70

Crewe - Cheshire
Apollo, High Street
Tel: 0870 444 3149
Seats: 1:107, 2:110, 3:91

Lyceum Theatre, Heath Street (P/T)
Tel: 01270 215523
Seats: 750

Cromer - Norfolk
Regal, Hans Place
Tel: 01263 513311
Seats: 1:129, 2:136, 3:66, 4:55

Crookham - Hants
Globe, Queen Elizabeth Barracks
Tel: 01252 876769
Seats: 340

Crosby - Merseyside
Plaza, Crosby Road North, Waterloo
Tel: 0151 474 4076
Seats: 1:600, 2:92, 3:74

Dartford - Kent
Orchard Theatre, Home Gardens
(P/T)
XE
Tel: 01322 343333
Seats: 930

Darlington - Co Durham
Arts Centre, Vane Terrace (P/T)
XETel: 01325 483168/483271
Seats: 100

Odeon, Northgate
Tel: 0870 50 50 007
Seats: 1:590, 2:218, 3:148

Dartington - Devon
 Barn Theatre, Arts Society,
The Gallery, TQ9 6DE (P/T)
X
Tel: 01803 865864/863073
Seats: 208

Deal - Kent
Flicks, Queen Street
Tel: 01304 361165
Seats: 1:162, 2:99

Derby - Derbyshire
 Metro Cinema, Green Lane,
DE1 1SA
XE
Tel: 01332 340170/347765
Seats: 128

Showcase Cinemas,
Foresters Park, Osmaston Park Road
at Sinfin Lane
X
Tel: 01332 270300
Seats: 2,557 (11 screens)

UCI Cinemas, Meteor Centre 10,
Mansfield Road
X
Tel: 0870 0102030
Seats: 1:191, 2:188, 3:188, 4:191,
5:276, 6:276, 7:191, 8:188, 9:188,
10:191

Dereham - Norfolk
Hollywood, Dereham Entertainment
Centre, Market Place
Tel: 01362 691133
Seats: 1:147, 2:95, 3:57

Devizes - Wiltshire
Palace, Market Place
Tel: 01380 722971
Seats: 253

Didsbury – Greater Manchester
UGC Cinemas, Parrs Wood
Entertainment Centre, East Didsbury
Tel: 0161 434 0909
Seats: 1:592, 2:261, 3:181, 4:214,
5:235, 6:214, 7:186, 8:350, 9:193,
10:277, 11:145

Doncaster - South Yorkshire
Civic Theatre, Waterdale (P/T)
Tel: 01302 62349
Seats: 547

Odeon, Hallgate
X
Tel: 0870 50 50 007
Seats: 1:1,003, 2:155, 3:155

Warner Village Cinemas, Doncaster
Leisure Park, Bawtry Road
Tel: 01302 371313/371020
Seats: 1:224, 2:212, 3:252, 4:386,
5:252, 6:212, 7:224

Dorchester - Dorset
Plaza, Trinity Street
Tel: 01305 262488
Seats: 1:100, 2:320

Dorking - Surrey
Dorking Halls
Tel: 01306 881717
Seats: 198

Douglas - Isle of Man
Palace Cinema
Tel: 01624 76814
Seats: 1:319, 2:120

Summerland Cinema
Tel: 01624 25511
Seats: 200

Dover - Kent
Silver Screen, White Cliffs
Experience, Gaol Lane
Tel: 01304 228000
Seats: 110

Dudley - West Midlands
Limelight Cinema, Black Country
Living Museum
Tel: 0121 557 9643
Seats: 100

Showcase Cinemas
Seats: 2,850 (14 screens)
(Scheduled to open Autumn 2001)

Durham - Co Durham
Robins, North Road
Tel: 0191 384 3434
Seats: 1:312 X, 2:98, 3:96, 4:74

Eastbourne - East Sussex
Curzon, Langney Road
Tel: 01323 731441
Seats: 1:530, 2:236, 3:236

UGC Cinemas, Sovereign Harbour
Retail Park, Pevensey Bay Road
XE
Tel: 0541 555159
Seats: 1:322, 2:312, 3:271, 4:254,
5:221, 6:221

East Grinstead - West Sussex
King Street Picture House
Atrium Building, King Street
Tel: 01342 321666/321216
Seats: 1:240, 2:240

Eastleigh - Hants
Point Dance and Arts Centre
Town Hall Centre, Leigh Road (P/T)
Tel: 023 8065 2333
Seats: 264

Elland - North Yorkshire
Rex, Coronation Street
X
Tel: 01422 372140
Seats: 294

Ellesmere Port - Cheshire
Epic Cinema, Epic Leisure Centre
(P/T)   X
Tel: 0151 355 3665
Seats: 163

Ely - Cambridgeshire
The Maltings, Ship Lane (P/T)
Tel: 01353 666388
Seats: 200

Epsom - Surrey
Odeon, Upper High Street
Tel: 0870 50 50 007
Seats: 1:325, 2:213, 3:274, 4:249,
5:174, 6:301, 7:245, 8:396

Playhouse, Ashley Avenue (P/T)
XE
Tel: 01372 742555/6
Seats: 300

Esher - Surrey
Odeon, High Street
Tel: 0870 50 50 007
Seats: 1:520, 2:113, 3:114, 4:114

Evesham - Hereford & Worcs
Regal, Port Street

Tel: 01386 446002
Seats: 540

Exeter - Devon
Northcott Theatre,
Stocker Road (P/T)
Tel: 01392 54853
Seats: 433

Odeon, Sidwell Street
Tel: 0870 50 50 007
Seats: 1:744, 2:119, 3:105, 4:344

Picture House
51 Bartholomew Street West
Tel: 01392 251341/435522
Seats: 1:220, 2:156

Exmouth - Devon
Savoy, Rolle Street
Tel: 01395 268220
Seats: 1:204, 2:100, 3:70

Fakenham - Norfolk
Hollywood Cinema, The Market
Place
Tel: 01328 856 466
Seats: 1:120, 2:60

Falmouth - Cornwall
Arts, Church Street (P/T)
Tel: 01326 212300
Seats: 199

Farnham - Surrey
Redgrave Theatre, Brightwells
(P/T)
X
Tel: 01252 727 720
Seats: 362

Faversham - Kent
New Royal, Market Place
Tel: 01795 591211
Seats: 448

Felixstowe - Suffolk
Palace, Crescent Road
Tel: 01394 282787
Seats: 1:150, 2:90

Folkestone - Kent
Silver Screen, Guildhall Street
Tel: 01303 221230
Seats: 1:435, 2:106

Forest, Guernsey - Channel Islands
Mallard Cinema, Mallard Hotel, La
Villiaze
Tel: 01481 64164
Seats: 1:154, 2:54, 3:75, 4:75

Frome - Somerset
Westway, Cork Street
Tel: 01373 465685
Seats: 304

Gainsborough - Lincolnshire
Trinity Arts Centre, Trinity Street
(P/T)
X
Tel: 01427 810710
Seats: 210

Gateshead - Tyne and Wear
UCI Cinemas, Metro Centre
Tel: 0191 493 2022/3
Seats: 1:200, 2:200, 3:228, 4:256,
5: 370, 6:370, 7:256, 8:228, 9:200,
10:200, 11:520

Gerrards Cross - Buckinghamshire
Odeon, Ethorpe Crescent
Tel: 0870 50 50 007
Seats: 1:350, 2:212

Gloucester - Gloucestershire
Guildhall Arts Centre,
Eastgate Street
X
Tel: 01452 505086/9
Seats: 1:120, 2:150(P/T)

New Olympus Theatre, Barton Street
(P/T)
Tel: 01452 505089
Seats: 375

UGC Cinemas, Peel Centre, St. Ann
Way, Bristol Road
XE
Tel: 0541 555 174
Seats: 1:354, 2:354, 3:238, 4:238,
5:219, 6:219

Godalming - Surrey
Borough Hall (P/T)
Tel: 01483 861111
Seats: 250

Goole - Humberside
The Gate, Dunhill Road (P/T)
Tel: 01405 720219
Seats: 90

Grantham - Lincolnshire
Paragon, St Catherine's Road
X
Tel: 01476 570046
Seats: 1:270, 2:160

Gravesend - Kent
EMD, King Street
Tel: 01474 356947/352470
Seats: 1:571, 2:296, 3:109

Grays - Essex
Thameside, Orsett Road (P/T)
Tel: 01375 382555
Seats: 303

Great Yarmouth - Norfolk
Hollywood, Marine Parade
Tel: 01493 842043
Seats: 1:500, 2:296, 3:250, 4:250

Grimsby - Lincolnshire
ABC, Freeman Street
Tel: 01472 342878/349368
Seats: 1:419, 2:251, 3:130

Screen, Crosland Road, Willows
DN37 9EH (P/T)
X
Tel: 01472 240410
Seats: 206

Guildford - Surrey
Odeon, Bedford Road
Tel: 0870 50 50 007
Seats: 1:426, 2:357, 3:271, 4:271,
5:295, 6:146, 7:110, 8:128, 9:128

Hailsham - East Sussex
Pavilion, George Street (P/T)
Tel: 01323 841414
Seats: 203

Halifax - West Yorkshire
ABC, Ward's End
Tel: 01422 352000/346429
Seats: 1:670, 2:199, 3:172

Halstead - Essex
Empire, Butler Road
Tel: 01787 477001
Seats: 320

Halton - Buckinghamshire
Astra, RAF Halton (P/T)
Tel: 01296 623535
Seats: 570

Forum Theatre,
Stoke-on-Trent City Museum,
Bethesda Street (P/T)
Tel: 01782 232799
Seats: 300

Harlow - Essex
Odeon, The High
Tel: 0870 50 50 007
Seats: 1:450, 2:243, 3:201

Playhouse, The High (P/T)
XE
Tel: 01279 431945
Seats: 330

UGC Cinemas, Queensgate Centre,
Edinburgh Way
XE
Tel: 0870 907 0713
Seats: 1:356, 2:260, 3:240, 4:234,
5:233, 6:230

Harrogate - North Yorkshire
Odeon, East Parade
Tel: 0870 50 50 007
Seats: 1:532, 2:108 X, 3:75 X, 4:259

Hartlepool - Cleveland
Warner Village Cinemas
The Lanyard, Marina Way
Tel: 01429 261 177/263 263
Seats: 1:295, 2:336, 3:160, 4:204,
5:430, 6:204, 7:160

Harwich - Essex
Electric Palace, King's Quay Street
(P/T)
Tel: 01255 553333
Seats: 204

Haslemere - Surrey
Haslemere Hall, Bridge Road (P/T)
Tel: 01428 661793
Seats: 350

Hastings - East Sussex
Odeon, Queens Road
Tel: 0870 50 50 007
Seats: 1:376, 2:176, 3:128

St Mary-in-the-Castle Arts Centre,
Pelham Crescent (P/T)
Tel: 01424 781624
Seats: 590

Hatfield - Herts
UCI Cinemas, The Galleria, Comet
Way
Tel: 0870 010 2030
Seats: 1:172, 2:235, 3:263, 4:167,
5:183, 6:183, 7:260, 8:378, 9:172

Havant - Hants
Arts Centre, East Street (P/T)
X
Tel: 023 92472700
Seats: 130

Haverhill - Suffolk
Arts Centre, Town Hall, High Street
(P/T)
Tel: 01440 714140
Seats: 210

Hayling Island - Hants
Hiads Theatre, Station Road (P/T)
Tel: 02392 466363
Seats: 150

Haywards Heath - West Sussex
Clair Hall, Perrymount Road (P/T)
Tel: 01444 455440/454394
Seats: 350

Heaton Moor - Greater Manchester
Savoy, Heaton Moor Road
Tel: 0161 432 2114
Seats: 476

Hebden Bridge - West Yorkshire
Picture House, New Road
XE
Tel: 01422 842807
Seats: 498

Helston – Cornwall
Flora, Wendron Street
Tel: 01326 573377
Seats: 80

Hemel Hempstead - Herts
Odeon, Leisure World,
Jarmans Park
XE
Tel: 0870 50 50 007
Seats: 1:120, 2:170, 3:170, 4:276,
5:210, 6:401, 7:152, 8:152

Henley-on-Thames - Oxfordshire
Kenton Theatre, New Street (P/T)
X
Tel: 01491 575698
Seats: 240

Regal, Broma Way, off Bell Street
Tel: 01491 414160
Seats: 1:152, 2:101, 3:85

Hereford - Hereford & Worcs
ABC, Commercial Road
Tel: 01432 272554
Seats: 378

The Courtyard Theatre and Arts
Centre, Edgar Street (P/T)
X
Tel: 01432 359252
Seats: 1:364, (Studio:)124

Herne Bay - Kent
Kavanagh, William Street
X
Tel: 01227 362228
Seats: 1:137, 2:95

Hexham - Northumberland
Forum, Market Place
Tel: 01434 601144
Seats: 207

High Wycombe - Buckinghamshire
UCI Cinemas, Crest Road,
Cressex
X
Tel: 0870 010 2030
Seats: 1:388, 2:388, 3:284, 4:284,
5:202, 6:202

Hoddesdon - Herts
Broxbourne Civic Hall, High Street
(P/T)
Tel: 01992 441946/31
Seats: 564

Hollinwood - Greater Manchester
Roxy, Hollins Road
Tel: 0161 681 1441
Seats: 1:470, 2:130, 3:260, 4:260,
5:320, 6:96, 7:140

Horsham - West Sussex
Arts Centre (Ritz Cinema and
Capitol Theatre), North Street
Tel: 01403 274325
Seats: 1:126, 2:450 (P/T)

Horwich - Lancashire
Leisure Centre, Victoria Road (P/T)
Tel: 01204 692211
Seats: 400

Hucknall - Notts
Byron, High Street
Tel: 0115 963 6377
Seats: 430

Huddersfield – West Yorkshire
UCI Cinemas, McAlpine Stadium,
Bradley Mills Road
Tel: 0870 0102030
Seats: 1:375, 2:296, 3:296, 4:268,
5:268, 6:176, 7:176, 8:148, 9:148

Hull - Humberside
Odeon, Kingston Street
X
Tel: 0870 50 50 007
Seats: 1:172, 2:172, 3:152, 4:174,
5:468, 6:275, 7:134, 8:152, 9:110,
10:89

 Screen, Central Library,
Albion Street HU1 3TF
XE
Tel: 01482 226655
Seats: 247

UCI Cinemas, St Andrew's Quay,
Clive Sullivan Way
X
Tel: 0870 0102030
Seats: 1:166, 2:152, 3:236, 4:292,
5:292, 6:236, 7:152, 8:166

UGC Cinemas, Kingswood Leisure
Park, Ennerdale Link Road
Tel: 01482 835035
Seats: 1:165, 2:211, 3:253, 4:498,
5:253, 6:211, 7:165, 8:165, 9:98

Hunstanton - Norfolk
Princess Theatre, The Green (P/T)
Tel: 01485 532252
Seats: 467

Huntingdon - Cambridgeshire
Cromwell Centre, Princes Street
Tel: 01480 433499
Seats: 264

Cineworld, Towerfields, Abbot's
Ripton Road
Tel: 01480 412255
Seats: 1:224, 2:126, 3:90, 4:125, 5:110,
6:317, 7:284, 8:208, 9:208, 10:101

Ilfracombe - Devon
The Landmark Theatre, Wilder Road
(P/T)
Tel: 01271 324242
Seats: 175

Pendle Stairway, High Street
X
Tel: 01271 863260
Seats: 460

Ilkeston - Derbyshire
Scala, Market Place
Tel: 0115 932 4612
Seats: 500

Ipswich - Suffolk
 Film Theatre, Corn Exchange,
King Street, IP1 1DH
XE
Tel: 01473 433100
Seats: 1:220, 2:40

Odeon, St Margaret's Street
Tel: 0870 50 50 007
Seats: 1:506, 2:318, 3:290, 4:218, 5:218

UGC Cinemas, Cardinal Park,
Greyfriars Road
Tel: 0870 907 0748
Seats: 1:168, 2:186, 3:168, 4:270,
5:179, 6:510, 7:238, 8:398, 9:186,
10:168, 11:83

Keighley - West Yorkshire
Picture House
Tel: 01535 602561
Seats: 1:364, 2:95

Kendal - Cumbria
Brewery Arts Centre, Highgate, LA9
4HE (S/O)
XE
Tel: 01539 725133
Seats: 1:192, 2:115, Theatre (P/T) 250

Keswick - Cumbria
Alhambra, St John Street

X
Tel: 017687 72195
Seats: 270

Kettering - Northants
Odeon, Pegasus Court,
Wellingborough Road
Tel: 0870 50 50 007
Seats: 1:175, 2:125, 3:232, 4:349,
5:105, 6:83, 7:105, 8:310

Kingsbridge - Devon
The Reel Cinema, Fore Street
Tel: 01548 856636
Seats: 190

King's Lynn - Norfolk
Arts Centre, King Street
Tel: 01553 774725/773578
Seats: 359

Majestic, Tower Street
Tel: 01553 772603
Seats: 1:450, 2:123, 3:400

Knutsford - Cheshire
Studio, Toft Road
X
Tel: 01565 633005
Seats: 400

Lancaster - Lancashire
ABC, King Street
Tel: 01524 64141/841149
Seats: 1:250, 2:244

The Dukes Playhouse, Moor Lane,
LA1 1QE (P/T)
XE
Tel: 01524 66645/67461
Seats: 307

Warner Village Cinemas, Church
Road
Seats: (6 screens)
(Under development)

Leamington Spa - Warwicks
Apollo, Portland Place
Tel: 0906 294 3456/0870 444 3148
Seats: 1:309 X, 2:199 X, 3:138, 4: 112
X

Royal, Spa Centre,
Newbold Terrace
Tel: 01926 887726/888997
Seats: 208

Leeds - West Yorkshire
Cottage Road Cinema, Headingley
Tel: 0113 230 2562
Seats: 468

Hyde Park Cinema, Brudenell Road
Tel: 0113 275 2045
Seats: 360

Lounge, North Lane, Headingley
Tel: 0113 275 1061/258932
Seats: 691

Odeon, The Headrow
Tel: 0870 50 50 007
Seats: 1:982, 2:441 X, 3:200 X, 4:174,
5:126

Showcase Cinemas, Gelderd Road,
Birstall
X
Tel: 01924 420622
Seats: 4,250 (16 screens)

Ster Century, The Light, Headrow
Seats: 2,789 (13 screens)
(Scheduled to open early 2002)

Warner Village Cinemas, Cardigan
Fields, Kirkstall Road
Tel: 0113 279 9855
Seats: 1: 345, 2: 124, 3:166, 4: 245, 5:
252, 6: 245, 7:166, 8:124, 9:345
Leicester - Leicestershire
Bollywood, Melton Road
Tel: 0116 268 1422
Seats: (3 screens)

Odeon, Aylestone Road, Freemans Park
XE
Tel: 0870 50 50 007
Seats: 1:129, 2:165, 3:154, 4:239,
5:230, 6:362, 7:332, 8:230, 9:329,
10:154, 11:165, 12:127

 Phoenix Arts
21 Upper Brown Street
LE1 5TE (P/T)
XE
Tel: 0116 255 4854/255 5627
Seats: 274

Piccadilly, Abbey Street
Tel: 0116 262 0005
Seats: 1:250, 2:180

Piccadilly, Green Lane Road
Tel: 0116 251 8880
Seats: (2 screens)

Warner Village Cinemas, Meridian
Leisure Park, Lubbesthorpe Way,
Braunstone
Tel: 0116 282 7733/289 4001
Seats: 1:423, 2:158, 3:189, 4:266,
5:306, 6:266, 7:202, 8:158, 9:423

Leighton Buzzard - Bedfordshire
Theatre, Lake Street (P/T)
Tel: 01525 378310
Seats: 170

Leiston - Suffolk
Film Theatre, High Street
Tel: 01728 830549
Seats: 288

Letchworth - Herts
Broadway, Eastcheap
Tel: 01462 681 223
Seats: 1:488, 2:176 X, 3:174 X

Leyburn - North Yorkshire
Elite, Railway Street (P/T)
Tel: 01969 624488
Seats: 173

Lincoln - Lincolnshire
Odeon,
Tritton Trading Estate
Valentine Road
Tel: 0870 50 50 007
Seats: 1:276, 2:162, 3:179, 4:136,
5:132, 6:136
(Scheduled for replacement by 9-
screen Odeon in November 2001)

Littlehampton - West Sussex
Windmill Theatre, Church Street
(P/T)
Tel: 01903 722224
Seats: 252

Liverpool - Merseyside
ABC, Allerton Road
Tel: 0151 724 3550/5095
Seats: 493

Odeon, London Road
Tel: 0870 50 50 007
Seats: 1:482, 2:154, 3:155, 4:149,
5:217, 6:134, 7:134, 8:125, 9:194,
10:137

Philharmonic Hall, Hope Street
(P/T)
X
Tel: 0151 709 2895/3789
Seats: 1,627

Showcase Cinemas, East Lancashire
Road, Norris Green   X
Tel: 0151 549 2021
Seats: 3,415 (12 screens)

UGC Cinemas, Edge Lane Retail
Park, Binns Road
XE
Tel: 0151 252 0544
Seats: 1:356, 2:354, 3:264, 4:264,
5:220, 6:220, 7:198, 8:200
Woolton, Mason Street
X
Tel: 0151 428 1919
Seats: 256

Longridge - Lancashire
Palace, Market Place
Tel: 01772 785600
Seats: 200

Loughborough - Leicestershire
Curzon, Cattle Market
Tel: 01509 212261
Seats: 1:420, 2:303, 3:199, 4:186,
5:140, 6:80

Stanford Hall Cinema at the Co-
operative College (P/T)
Tel: 01509 852333
Seats: 352

Louth - Lincolnshire
Playhouse, Cannon Street
Tel: 01507 603333
Seats: 1:215, 2:158 X, 3:78 X

Lowestoft - Suffolk
Hollywood Cinemas, London Road
South
Tel: 01502 564567
Seats: 1:200, 2:175, 3:65, 4:40

Marina Theatre, The Marina (P/T)
Tel: 01502 573318
Seats: 751

Ludlow - Shropshire
Assembly Rooms, Mill Street (P/T)
X
Tel: 01584 878141
Seats: 320

Luton - Bedfordshire
Artezium, Arts and Media Centre
Tel: 01582 707100
Seats: 96

Cineworld, The Galaxy, Bridge Street
Tel: 01582 401092/400705
Seats: 1:114, 2:75, 3:112, 4:284, 5:419,
6:212, 7:123, 8:217, 9:137, 10:213,
11:240

St George's Theatre
Central Library (P/T)
Tel: 01582 547440
Seats: 238

Lyme Regis - Dorset
Regent, Broad Street
X
Tel: 01297 442053
Seats: 400

Lymington - Hants
Community Centre, New Street
(P/T)
Tel: 015907 2337
Seats: 110

Lytham St. Annes - Lancashire
Pleasure Island Cinemas, South
Promenade
Tel: 01253 780085
Seats: 1:170, 2:92, 3:117, 4:105

Lynton – Devon
Cinema
Tel: 01598 752 275
Seats: 100

Mablethorpe - Lincolnshire
Loewen, Quebec Road
Tel: 0150 747 7040
Seats: 1:203, 2:80

Maidenhead - Berkshire
UCI Cinemas, Grenfell Island
Tel: 0870 0102030
Seats: 1:319, 2:246, 3:139, 4:113,
5:201, 6:179, 7:87, 8:146

Maidstone - Kent
Odeon, Lockmeadow
Tel: 0870 50 50 007
Seats: 1:86, 2:89, 3:127, 4:111, 5:240,
6:240, 7:398, 8:347

Malvern - Hereford & Worcs
Festival Cinema, Winter Gardens
Complex, Grange Road
Tel: 01684 892277/892710
Seats: 407

Manchester - Greater Manchester
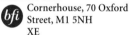 Cornerhouse, 70 Oxford
Street, M1 5NH
XE
Tel: 0161 228 2467/7621
Seats: 1:300, 2:170, 3:60

Odeon, Oxford Street
Tel: 0870 50 50 007
Seats: 1:629 E, 2:326 E, 3:145 X, 4:97,
5:203 E, 6:142 X, 7:97

Showcase Cinemas, Hyde Road, Belle
Vue
Tel: 0161 220 8765
Seats: 3,191 (14 screens)

UCI Cinemas, Trafford Centre, The
Dome, Dumplington
X
Tel: 0870 0102030
Seats: 1:427, 2:427, 3:371, 4:301,
5:243, 6:243, 7:181, 8:181, 9:181,
10:181, 11:181, 12:181, 13:152,
14:152, 15:140, 16:140, 17:112,
18:112, 19:112, 20:112
UCI The PrintWorks
X
Tel: 0870 0102030

Seats: 1 (IMAX) 368, 2: 217, 3:122,
4:140, 5:140, 6:140, 7:122, 8:214,
9:120, 10:138, 11:228, 12:371, 13:422,
14:164, 15:140, 16:140, 17:322,
18:564, 19:122, 20:122

Mansfield - Notts
Odeon, Mansfield Leisure Park, Park
Lane
Tel: 0870 50 50 007
Seats: 1:393, 2:393, 3:246, 4:246,
5:221, 6:221, 7:193, 8:193

March – Cambridgeshire
Hippodrome, Dartford Road
Tel: 01354 653178
Seats: 96

Margate - Kent
Dreamland, Marine Parade
Tel: 01843 227822
Seats: 1:378, 2:376

Marple - Greater Manchester
Regent, Stockport Road
X
Tel: 0161 427 5951
Seats: 285

Market Drayton - Shropshire
Royal Festival Centre (P/T)
Seats: 165

Melton Mowbray - Leicestershire
Regal, King Street
Tel: 01664 562251
Seats: 226

Middlesbrough - Cleveland
UGC Cinemas, Leisure Park, Marton
Road
Tel: 01642 247766
Seats: 1:204, 2:151, 3:141, 4:271,
5:401, 6:204, 7:125, 8:141, 9:230,
10:271, 11:402

Milton Keynes - Buckinghamshire
Cineworld, Xscape, Marlborough
Gate
Tel: 01908 230 088
Seats: 1:137, 2:234, 3:205, 4:170,
5:214, 6:281, 7:304, 8:158, 9:158,
10:316, 11:281, 12: 214, 13:170, 14:
205, 15: 234, 16:135

UCI Cinemas, The Point,
Midsummer Boulevard
Tel: 0870 010 2030
Seats: 1:156, 2:169, 3:250, 4:222,
5:222, 6:222, 7:222, 8:250, 9:169,
10:156

Minehead - Somerset
Odeon, Butlin's Summerwest World
X
Tel: 0870 50 50 007
Seats: 218

Morecambe - Lancashire
Apollo, Central Drive
Tel: 01524 426642
Seats: 1:207, 2:207, 3:106, 4:106

Nailsea - Avon
Cinema, Scotch Horn Leisure Centre,
Brockway (P/T)
Tel: 01275 856965
Seats: 250

Nantwich - Cheshire
Civic Hall, Market Street (P/T)
Tel: 01270 628633
Seats: 300

Newark - Notts
Palace Theatre, Appleton Gate (P/T)
Tel: 01636 671156
Seats: 351

Newbury - Berkshire
Corn Exchange, Market Place (P/T)
X
Tel: 01635 522733
Seats: 370

Newcastle-under-Lyme - Staffordshire
Warner Village Cinemas, The Square,
High Street
Tel: 01782 711666
Seats: 2,000 (8 screens)

Newcastle-upon-Tyne - Tyne and Wear
Odeon, Pilgrim Street
Tel: 0870 50 50 007
Seats: 1:1,171, 2:155, 3:250, 4:361

 Tyneside, 10-12 Pilgrim
Street, NE1 6QG
XE
Tel: 0191 232 8289
Seats: 1:296, 2:122

Warner Village Cinemas, New Bridge
Street
Tel: 0191 221 0202/0222
Seats: 1:404, 2:398, 3:236, 4:244,
5:290, 6:657, 7:509, 8:398, 9:248

Newport - Isle of Wight
Cineworld, Coppins Bridge
Tel: 01983 550800
1:300, 2:96, 3:202, 4:178, 5:152, 6:101,
7:84, 8:132, 9:169, 10:195, 11:263
Medina Movie Theatre, Mountbatten
Centre, Fairlee Road (P/T)
XE

Tel: 01983 527 020
Seats: 419

Newton Abbot - Devon
Alexandra, Market Street
X
Tel: 01626 365368
Seats: 1:206, 2:127

Northampton - Northants
UGC Cinemas, Sixfields Leisure,
Weeden Road, Upton
Tel: 0541 560564
Seats: 1:452, 2:287, 3:287, 4:207,
5:207, 6:147, 7:147, 8:147, 9:147

 Forum Cinema, Lings Forum,
Weston Favell Centre, NN3
4JR (P/T)
Tel: 01604 401006/ 402 833
Seats: 270

North Shields - Tyne and Wear
UCI Cinemas, Silverlink
Tel: 0870 0102030
Seats: 1:326, 2:156, 3:185, 4:198,
5:410, 6:198, 7:185, 8:156, 9:326

Northwich - Cheshire
Regal, London Road
Tel: 01606 43130
Seats: 1:797, 2:200

Norwich - Norfolk
Cinema City, St Andrew's Street,
NR2 4AD
X
Tel: 01603 625145/622047
Seats: 230

Hollywood Cinemas, Anglia Square
E
Tel: 01603 621903
Seats: 1:442, 2:197, 3:195 X

Ster Century, Castle Mall
Tel: 01603 221 900
Seats: 1:170, 2:143, 3:216, 4:324,
5:313, 6:294, 7:331, 8:126

UCI Cinemas, Riverside
Tel: 0870 010 2030
Seats: 1:168, 2:349, 3:123, 4:138,
5:157, 6:269, 7:464, 8:247, 9:157,
10:138, 11:138, 12:156, 13:247, 14:212

Nottingham - Notts
 Broadway, Nottingham Media
Centre, 14 Broad Street, NG1
3AL
Tel: 0115 952 6600/952 6611
Seats: 1:379 E, 2:155 XE

Royal Centre, Theatre Square (P/T)
Tel: 0115 989 5555
Seats: 1,000

Savoy, Derby Road
Tel: 0115 947 2580/941 9123
Seats: 1:386, 2:128, 3:168

Showcase Cinemas,
Redfield Way, Lenton
Tel: 0115 986 6766
Seats: 3,307 (12 screens)

Warner Village Cinemas, The
Cornerhouse, Forman Street
Tel: 0115 950 0163/5
Seats: 1:398, 2:108, 3:146, 4:130,
5:237, 6:139, 7:593, 8:108, 9:146,
10:146, 11:146, 12:130

Nuneaton - Warwicks
Odeon, St. David's Way, Bermuda
Park
Tel: 0870 50 50 007
Seats: 1:475, 2:390, 3:318, 4:318,
5:257, 6:257, 7:212, 8:212

Okehampton - Devon
Carlton, St James Street
Tel: 01837 52167
Seats: 380

Oldham - Lancashire
Roxy, Hollins Road
Tel: 0161 683 4759
Seats: 1:400, 2:300, 3:130

Oxford - Oxfordshire
Odeon, George Street
Tel: 0870 50 50 007
Seats: (six screens)

Odeon, Magdalen Street
Tel: 0870 50 50 007
Seats: 1:600, 2:61

Phoenix Picture House,
57 Walton Street
X
Tel: 01865 554909
Seats: 1:220, 2:105

Ultimate Picture Palace, Jeune Street
X
Tel: 01865 245288
Seats: 185

Oxted - Surrey
Plaza, Station Road West
X
Tel: 01883 712567
Seats: 442

Padstow - Cornwall
Cinedrome, Lanadwell Street
Tel: 01841 532344
Seats: 183

Paignton - Devon
Apollo Cinemas, Esplanade

Tel: 0870 444 3140
Seats: 1:360, 2:184, 3: 184, 4:219,
5:360, 6:77, 7:86, 8:33, 9:97

Penistone - South Yorkshire
Paramount, Town Hall
Tel: 01226 762004
Seats: 348

Penrith - Cheshire
Rhegel Discovery Centre
Tel: 01768 868000
Seats: 258 (large screen format)

Penrith - Cumbria
Alhambra, Middlegate
Tel: 01768 862400
Seats: 1:167, 2:90

Penzance - Cornwall
Savoy, Causeway Head
Tel: 01736 363330
Seats: 1:200, 2:50, 3:50

Peterborough – Cambridgeshire
Broadway, 46 Broadway (P/T)
Tel: 01733 316100
Seats: 1,200

Showcase Cinemas, Mallory Road,
Boon Gate
X
Tel: 01733 555636
Seats: 3,365 (13 screens)

Pickering - North Yorkshire
Castle, Burgate
Tel: 01751 472622
Seats: 250

Plymouth - Devon
ABC, Derry's Cross
Tel: 01752 663300/225553
Seats: 1:583, 2:340, 3:115

Arts Centre, Looe Street
X
Tel: 01752 660060
Seats: 73

Warner Village Cinemas, Barbican
Leisure Park, Shapters Road, Coxside
Tel: 01752 223435
Seats: 1:175, 2:189, 3:153, 4:196,
5:188, 6:133, 7:292, 8:454, 9:498,
10:257, 11:215, 12:133, 13:127,
14:190, 15:187

Poole - Dorset
Arts Centre, Kingland Road (P/T)
X
Tel: 01202 685222
Seats: 143

UCI Cinemas, Tower Park, Mannings
Heath
Tel: 0870 010 2030
Seats: 1:194, 2:188, 3:188, 4:194,
5:276, 6:276, 7:194, 8:188, 9:188,
10:194

Portsmouth - Hants
Odeon, London Road, North End
Tel:0870 50 50 007
Seats: 1:524, 2:225, 3:173, 4:259

Rendezvous
Lion Gate Building
University of Portsmouth (S/O)
Tel: 023 92833854
Seats: 90

UCI Cinemas, Port Way, Port Solent
X
Tel: 0870 010 2030
Seats: 1:214, 2:264, 3:318, 4:264,
5:257, 6:190

Warner Village Cinemas, Gunwharf
Quays
Tel: 02392 827600/827644
1:228, 2:332, 3:427, 4:332, 5:228,
6:244, 7:181, 8:190, 9:374, 10:164,
11:153

Potters Bar - Herts
Wyllyotts Centre,
Darkes Lane (P/T)
X
Tel: 01707 645005
Seats: 345

Preston - Lancashire
Guild Hall, Lancaster Road (P/T)
X
Tel: 01772 258858

UCI Cinemas, Riversway
Ashton-on-Ribble
X
Tel: 0870 0102030
Seats: 1:194, 2:188, 3:188, 4:194,
5:276, 6:276, 7:194, 8:188, 9:188,
10:194

Warner, The Capitol Centre, London
Way, Walton-le-Dale
X
Tel: 01772 881100/882525
Seats: 1:180, 2:180, 3:412, 4:236,
5:236, 6:412, 7:192

Quinton - West Midlands
ABC, Hagley Road West
Tel: 0121 422 2562/2252
Seats: 1:300, 2:236, 3:232, 4:121

Ramsey - Cambridgeshire
Grand, Great Whyte (P/T)

Tel: 01487 710221
Seats: 173

Ramsgate - Kent
Granville Premier, Victoria Parade
(P/T)
Tel: 01843 591750
Seats: 1:210, 2:230

Reading - Berkshire
Film Theatre, Whiteknights (P/T)
Tel: 0118 986 8497
Seats: 409

The Hexagon, South Street (P/T)
Tel: 0118 960 6060
Seats: 450

Warner Village Cinemas, Oracle
Centre
Tel: 0118 956 0047
Seats: 1:134, 2:146, 3:264, 4:384,
5:212, 6:212, 7:246, 8:158, 9:113,
10:84

Redcar - Cleveland
Regent, Newcomen Terrace
Tel: 01642 482094
Seats: 350

Redhill - Surrey
The Harlequin, Warwick Quadrant
(P/T)
X
Tel: 01737 765547
Seats: 494

Redruth - Cornwall
Regal Film Centre, Fore Street
Tel: 01209 216278
Seats: 1:171, 2:121, 3:600, 4:95

Reigate - Surrey
Screen, Bancroft Road
Tel: 01737 223200
Seats: 1:139, 2:142

Rickmansworth - Herts
Watersmeet Theatre, High Street
(P/T)
Tel: 01923 771542
Seats: 390

**Rochdale - Greater
Manchester**
Odeon, Sandbrook Way, Sandbrook
Park
Tel: 0870 50 50 007
Seats: 1:469, 2:306, 3:306, 4:231,
5:231, 6:206, 7:206, 8:167, 9:167

Rochester - Kent
UGC Cinemas, Valley Park, Chariot
Way, Strood
Tel: 0541 560 568
Seats: 1:485, 2:310, 3:310, 4:217,

5:220, 6:199, 7:199, 8:92, 9:142

Royston - Herts
Priory, Priory Lane
Seats: 305
(Temporarily closed in August 2001)

Rubery - West Midlands
UGC Cinemas, Great Park
Tel: 0870 907 0726
Seats: 1:165, 2:187, 3:165, 4:149,
5:288, 6:194, 7:523, 8:247, 9:400
10:149 11:187 12:165, 13:82

Rugby - Warwicks
Cineworld, Junction One Retail &
Leisure Park, Junction One, Leicester
Road
Tel: 01788 551110
Seats: 1:222, 2:95, 3:131, 4:120, 5:311,
6:290, 7:202, 8:131, 9:96

Runcorn - Cheshire
Cineworld, Trident Park, Halton Lea
Tel: 01928 759811
Seats: 1:127, 2:121, 3:94, 4:87, 5:317,
6:283, 7:164, 8:184, 9:214

Ryde - Isle of Wight
Commodore, Star Street
Tel: 01983 564064
Seats: 1:186, 2:184, 3:180

St Albans - Herts
Alban Arena, Civic Centre (P/T) XE
Tel: 01727 844488
Seats: 800

St Austell - Cornwall
Film Centre, Chandos Place
Tel: 01726 73750
Seats: 1:274, 2:134, 3:133, 4:70, 5:70

St Helens - Merseyside
Cineworld, Chalon Way West
Tel: 01744 616576
Seats: 1:180, 2:139, 3:210, 4:180,
5:115, 6:103, 7:129, 8:94, 9:283,
10:302, 11:269

**St Helier Jersey - Channel
Islands**
Odeon, Bath Street
Tel: 0870 50 50 007
Seats: 1:412, 2:247, 3:184X, 4:162X

St Ives - Cornwall
Royal, Royal Square
Tel: 01736 796843
Seats: 1:409, 2:244, 3:213, 4:171

**St Peter Port Guernsey -
Channel Islands**
Beau Sejour Centre
Tel: 01481 26964
Seats: 250

**St Saviour Jersey - Channel
Islands**
Cine Centre, St Saviour's Road
Tel: 01534 871611
Seats: 1:400, 2:291, 3:85

**Salford – Greater
Manchester**
Warner Village Cinemas, Lowry
Centre
Seats: 2,500 seats (9 screens)
(Scheduled to open late 2001)

Salisbury - Wiltshire
Odeon, New Canal
Tel: 0870 50 50 007
Seats: 1:471, 2:278 X, 3:120 X, 4:120
X, 5:70

Sandwich - Kent
Empire, Delf Street
Tel: 01304 620480
Seats: 136

**Scarborough - North
Yorkshire**
Futurist, Forshaw Road (P/T)
X
Tel: 01723 370742
Seats: 2,155

Hollywood Plaza
North Marine Road
Tel: 01723 365119
Seats: 275

Stephen Joseph Theatre,
Westborough (P/T)
XE
Tel: 01723 370541
Seats: 165 (McCarthy Auditorium)

YMCA Theatre, St Thomas Street
(P/T)
Tel: 01723 506750
Seats: 290

Scunthorpe - Herts
Majestic, Oswald Road
Tel: 01724 842352
Seats: 1:176, 2:155 X, 3:76 X, 4:55 X,
5:38

Screen, Central Library, Carlton
Street, DN15 6TX (P/T)
X
Tel: 01724 860190/860161
Seats: 253

Sevenoaks - Kent
Stag Cinemas 1 & 2, London Road
Tel: 01732 450175/451548
Seats: 1:126, 2:108

Shaftesbury - Dorset
Arts Centre, Bell Street (P/T)
Tel: 01747 854321
Seats: 160

Sheffield - South Yorkshire
 The Showroom, Media and
Exhibition Centre,
Paternoster Row, S1 2BX
X
Tel: 0114 275 7727
Seats: 1:83, 2:110, 3:178, 4:282

Odeon, Arundel Gate
Tel: 0870 50 50 007
Seats: 1:253 XE, 2:231 XE,
3:259 XE, 4:117 XE, 5:115 XE, 6:135
XE, 7:177XE, 8:160XE, 9:161XE,
10:123XE

UCI Cinemas, Crystal Peaks,
Eckington Way, Sothall
XE
Tel: 0870 0102030
Seats: 1:202: 2:202, 3:230, 4:226, 5:316,
6:316, 7:226, 8:230, 9:202, 10:202

UGC Cinemas, Broughton Lane
Tel: 0114 242 1237
Seats: 1:143, 2:141, 3:164, 4:262,
5:262, 6:551, 7:691, 8:551, 9:262,
9:262, 10:262, 11:173, 12:193, 13:115,
14:197, 15:197, 16:197, 17:197, 18:93,
19:82, 20:82

Warner Village Cinemas, Meadowhall
Centre
X
Tel: 0114 256 9825
Seats: 1:200, 2:200, 3:97, 4:238, 5:200,
6:365, 7:195, 8:195, 9:73, 10:195,
11:323

Shepton Mallet - Somerset
Amusement Centre, Market Place
(P/T)
Tel: 01749 3444688
Seats: 270

Sheringham - Norfolk
Little Theatre, Station Road (S/O)
Tel: 01263 822347
Seats: 198

Shrewsbury - Shropshire
Cineworld, Old Potts Way
Tel: 01743 340726/240350
Seats: 1:224, 2:157, 3:226, 4:280,
5:135, 6:100, 7:81, 8:222

The Music Hall Film Theatre,
The Square, SY1 1LH
Tel: 01743 281281
Seats: 100

Sidmouth - Devon
Radway, Radway Place X
Tel: 01395 513085
Seats: 272

Sittingbourne - Kent
New Century, High Street
Tel: 01795 423984/426018
Seats: 1:300, 2:110

Skegness - Lincolnshire
Odeon, Butlins Family
Entertainment Resort, Roman Bank
Tel: 0870 50 50 007
Seats: 1:120, 2:120

Tower, Lumley Road
Tel: 01754 3938
Seats: 401

Skipton - North Yorkshire
Plaza, Sackville Street
X
Tel: 01756 793417
Seats: 320

Slough - Berkshire
UGC Cinemas, Queensmere Centre
Tel: 0870 907 0715
Seats: 2,113 (10 screens)

Solihull - West Midlands
Cineworld, Mill Lane Arcade,
Touchwood, Solihull
Seats: 1,700 (9 screens)
(Scheduled to open September 2001)

UCI Cinemas, Highland Road,
Shirley
X
Tel: 0870 010 2030
Seats: 286 (2 screens), 250 (2 screens),
214 (2 screens), 178 (2 screens)

South Shields - Tyne and Wear
Customs House, Mill Dam
Tel: 0191 455 6655
Seats: 1:400, 2:160

South Woodham Ferrers - Essex
Flix, Market Street
Tel: 01245 329777
Seats: 1:249, 2:101

Southend - Essex
Odeon, Victoria Circus
XE
Tel: 0870 50 50 007
Seats: 1:198, 2:262, 3:146, 4:222,
5:390, 6:261, 7:261, 8:200

Southampton - Hants
 The Gantry, Off Blechynden
Terrace, SO15 1GW
X
Tel: 023 8022 9319
Seats: 198

Harbour Lights Picture House
Ocean Village SO14 3TL
Tel: 023 8033 5533/8063 5335
Seats: 1:325, 2:144

Mountbatten Theatre
East Park Terrace (P/T)
Tel: 023 80221991
Seats: 515

Northguild Lecture Theatre
Guildhall (P/T)
XE
Tel: 023 80632601
Seats: 118

Odeon, Leisure World, West Quay
Road
Tel: 0870 50 50 007
Seats: 1:540, 2:495, 3:169, 4:111,
5:112, 6:139, 7:270, 8:318, 9:331,
10:288, 11:102, 12:102, 13:138

UGC Cinemas, Ocean Way, Ocean
Village
Tel: 0541 555132
Seats: 1:421, 2:346, 3:346, 4:258, 5:258

Southport - Merseyside
Arts Centre, Lord Street (P/T)
X
Tel: 01704 540004/540011
Seats: 400

ABC, Lord Street
X
Tel: 01704 530627
Seats: 1:494, 2:385

Spilsby - Lincolnshire
Phoenix, Reynard Street
Tel: 01790 753 675
Seats: 264

Stafford - Staffordshire
Apollo, Newport Road
Tel: 0870 444 3150
Seats: 1:305, 2:170, 3:164

Staines - Middlesex
Warner Village Cinemas, Tilly's Lane
Seats: 2,500 (10 screens)
(Scheduled to open February 2002)

Stalybridge - Greater Manchester
Palace, Market Street
Tel: 0161 330 1993
Seats: 414

Stanley - Co Durham
Civic Hall (P/T)

Tel: 01207 32164
Seats: 632

Stamford - Lincolnshire
Arts Centre, St. Mary's Street
Tel: 01780 763203
Seats: 166

Stevenage - Herts
Cineworld, Stevenage Leisure Park,
Six Hills Way
Tel: 01438 740944/740310
Seats: 1:357, 2:289, 3:175, 4:148, 5:88,
6:99, 7:137, 8:112, 9:168, 10:135,
11:173, 12:286

Gordon Craig Theatre, Lytton Way
(P/T)
Tel: 01438 766 866
Seats: 507

Stockport - Greater Manchester
Plaza Super Cinema, Mersey Square
(P/T)
Tel: 0161 477 7779
Seats: 1,200

UGC Cinemas, Grand Central
Square, Wellington Road South
XE
Tel: 08701 555 157
Seats: 1:303, 2:255, 3:243, 4:243,
5:122, 6:116, 7:96, 8:120, 9:84, 10:90

Stockton - Cleveland
The Arc, Dovecot Street
Tel: 01642 666600/666606/666669
Seats: 130

Showcase Cinemas, Aintree Oval
Teeside Leisure Park
Tel: 01642 633111
Seats: 3,400 (14 screens)

Stoke-on-Trent - Staffordshire
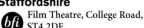 Film Theatre, College Road,
ST4 2DE
Tel: 01782 411188/413622
Seats: 212

Odeon, Festival Park,
Etruria Road
X
Tel: 0870 50 50 007
Seats: 1:177, 2:177, 3:309, 4:150,
5:160, 6:160, 7:521, 8:150, 9:80, 10:80

Stourport - Hereford & Worcs
Civic Centre, Civic Hall,
New Street
Tel: 01562 820 505
Seats: 399

Stowmarket - Suffolk
Regal, Ipswich Street (P/T)
Tel: 01449 612825
Seats: 234

Stratford-on-Avon - Warwicks
Picture House, Windsor Street
X
Tel: 01789 415511
Seats: 1:208, 2:104

Street - Somerset
 Strode Theatre, Strode
College, Church Road, BA16
0AB (P/T)
XE
Tel: 01458 442846/46529
Seats: 400

Sudbury - Suffolk
Quay Theatre, Quay Lane
Tel: 01787 374745
Seats: 129

Sunninghill - Berkshire
Novello Theatre, High Street (P/T)
Tel: 01990 20881
Seats: 160

Sutton Coldfield - West Midlands
Odeon, Birmingham Road
Tel: 0870 50 50 007
Seats: 1:598, 2:132 X, 3:118 X, 4:307 X

Swanage - Dorset
Mowlem, Shore Road (P/T)
Tel: 01929 422239
Seats: 411

Swindon - Wiltshire
Arts Centre, Devizes Road, Old Town
(P/T)
E
Tel: 01793 614 837
Seats: 228

Cineworld, Greenbridge Retail & Leisure Park, Drakes Way
Tel: 01793 484322/420710
Seats: 1:327, 2:282, 3:170, 4:154, 5:94,
6:102, 7:134, 8:105, 9:139, 10:129,
11:137, 12:263

UGC Cinemas, Shaw Ridge Leisure Park, Whitehill Way
XE
Tel: 0541 555134
Seats: 1:349, 2:349, 3:297, 4:297,
5:272, 6:166, 7:144

Wyvern, Theatre Square (P/T)
Tel: 01793 524481

Seats: 617

Switch Island - Merseyside
Odeon, Dunnings Bridge Road,
Netherton
Tel: 0870 50 50 007
Seats: 1:373, 2: 230, 3:132, 4:181,
5:245, 6:158, 7:342, 8:230, 9:132,
10:151, 11:245, 12:158

Tadley - Hants
Cinema Royal, Boundary Road
(P/T)
Tel: 01734 814617

Tamworth - Staffordshire
Palace, Lower Gungate (P/T)
Tel: 01827 57100
Seats: 325

UCI Cinemas, Bolebridge Street
X
Tel: 0870 010 2030
Seats: 203 (8 screens), 327 (2 screens)

Taunton - Somerset
Odeon, Heron Gate, Riverside
X
Tel: 0870 50 50 007
Seats: 1:106, 2:316, 3:218, 4:252, 5:106

Tavistock - Devon
The Wharf, Canal Street (P/T)
Tel: 01822 611166
Seats: 212

Telford - Shropshire
UCI Cinemas, Telford Centre,
Forgegate
X
Tel: 0870 010 2030
Seats: 1:194, 2:188, 3:188, 4:194,
5:276, 6:276, 7:194, 8:188, 9:188,
10:194

Tenbury Wells - Hereford & Worcs
Regal, Teme Street (P/T)
Tel: 01584 810971
Seats: 260

Tewkesbury - Gloucestershire
Roses Theatre, Sun Street (P/T)
Tel: 01684 295074
Seats: 375

Thirsk - North Yorkshire
Ritz
Tel: 01845 523484
Seats: 238

Tiverton - Devon
Tivoli, Fore Street
Tel: 01884 252157
Seats: 364

Tonbridge - Kent
Angel Centre, Angel Lane (P/T)
Tel: 01732 359588
Seats: 306

Torquay - Devon
Central, Abbey Road
Tel: 01803 380001
Seats: 1:308, 2:122, 3:78, 4:42

Torrington - Devon
Plough Arts Centre, Fore Street
Tel: 01805 622552/3
Seats: 108

Totnes - Devon
Dartington Arts Centre, Dartington Hall (P/T)
Tel: 01803 863073
Seats: 185

Truro - Cornwall
Plaza, Lemon Street
Tel: 01872 272 894
Seats: 1:300, 2:198, 3:135, 4:70

Tunbridge Wells - Kent
Odeon, Knights Way, Pembury
Tel: 0870 50 50 007
Seats: 1:445, 2:275, 3:261, 4:224, 5:142, 6:275, 7:261, 8:224, 9:142

Uckfield - East Sussex
Picture House, High Street
Tel: 01825 763822/764909
Seats: 1:150, 2:100, 3:100

Ulverston - Cumbria
Laurel & Hardy Museum
Upper Brook Street (P/T) (S/O)
Tel: 01229 52292/86614
Seats: 50

Roxy, Brogden Street
Tel: 01229 53797/56211
Seats: 310

Urmston - Greater Manchester
Curzon, Princess Road
Tel: 0161 748 2929
Seats: 1:400, 2:134

Uxbridge - Middlesex
Odeon, The Chimes
Tel: 0870 50 50 007
Seats: 2,500 (9 screens)

Wadebridge - Cornwall
Regal, The Platt
Tel: 01208 812791
Seats: 1:224, 2:98

Wakefield - West Yorkshire
Cineworld, Westgate Leisure Centre
X
Tel: 01924 332114

Seats: 1:323, 2:215, 3:84, 4:114, 5:183, 6:255, 7:255, 8:183, 9:114, 10:84, 11:215, 12:323

Wallingford - Oxfordshire
Corn Exchange (P/T)
Tel: 01491 825000
Seats: 187

Walsall - West Midlands
Showcase Cinemas, Bentley Mill Way, Junction 10, M6
X
Tel: 01922 22123
Seats: 2,870 (12 screens)

Walton on Thames - Surrey
The Screen at Walton, High Street
Tel: 01932 252825
Seats: 1:200, 2:140

Wantage - Oxfordshire
Regent, Newbury Street
Tel: 01235 771 155
Seats: 1:110, 2:87

Wareham - Dorset
Rex, West Street
Tel: 01929 552778
Seats: 151

Warrington - Cheshire
UCI Cinemas, Westbrook Centre, Cromwell Avenue
X
Tel: 08700 102030
Seats: 1:186, 2:180, 3:180, 4:186, 5:276, 6:276, 7:186, 8:180, 9:180, 10:186

Watford - Herts
Warner Village Cinemas, Woodside Leisure Park, Garston
Tel: 01923 682886/682244
Seats: 1:249, 2:233, 3:264, 4:330, 5:221, 6:208, 7:215, 8:306

Wellingborough - Northants
Castle, Castle Way, Off Commercial Way (P/T)
Tel: 01933 270007
Seats: 500

Wellington - Somerset
Wellesley, Mantle Street
Tel: 01823 666668/666880
Seats: 432

Wells - Somerset
Film Centre, Princes Road
Tel: 01749 672036/673195
Seats: 1:116, 2:113, 3:82

Welwyn Garden City - Herts
Campus West,
The Campus, AL8 6BX (P/T)

Tel: 01707 357117/357165
Seats: 300

West Bromwich - West Midlands
Kings, Paradise Street
X
Tel: 0121 553 0192
Seats: 1:450, 2:260

Westgate-on-Sea - Kent
Carlton, St Mildreds Road
Tel: 01843 832019
Seats: Premiere: 297, Century: 56, Bijou: 32

Weston-Super-Mare - Avon
Odeon, The Centre
Tel: 0870 50 50 007
Seats: 1:590, 2:109, 3:130, 4:264

Playhouse, High Street (P/T)
Tel: 01934 23521/31701
Seats: 658

West Thurrock - Essex
UCI Cinemas,
Lakeside Retail Park
X
Tel: 0870 010 2030
Seats: 276 (2 screens), 194 (4 screens), 188 (4 screens)

Warner, Village Cinemas, Lakeside Shopping Centre
X
Tel: 01708 860 393
Seats: 1:382, 2:184, 3:177, 4:237, 5:498, 6:338, 7:208

Wetherby - West Yorkshire
Film Theater, Crossley Street
Tel: 01937 580544
Seats: 156

Weymouth - Dorset
Cineworld, New Bond Street
Tel: 01305 768798
Seats: 1:299, 2:218, 3:265, 4:102, 5:136, 6:187, 7:139, 8:132, 9:148

Whitby – North Yorkshire
Coliseum, Victoria Place
Tel: 01947 825000
Seats: 99

Whitehaven - Cumbria
Gaiety, Tangier Street
Tel: 01946 693012
Seats: 264
Rosehill Theatre, Moresby (P/T)
X
Tel: 01946 694039/692422
Seats: 208

Whitley Bay - Tyne and Wear
Playhouse, Marine Avenue (P/T)
Tel: 0191 252 3505
Seats: 746

Whitstable - Kent
Imperial Oyster, The Horsebridge, Horsebridge Road
Tel: 01227 770829
Seats: 144

Wigan - Greater Manchester
UGC Cinemas, Robin Park Road, Newtown
X
Tel: 08701 555 157
Seats: 1:554, 2:290, 3:290, 4:207, 5:207, 6:163, 7:163, 8:163, 9:163, 10:207, 11:129

Wilmslow - Cheshire
Rex, Alderley Road (P/T)
Tel: 01625 522266
Seats: 838

Wimborne - Dorset
Tivoli, West Borough (P/T)
Tel: 01202 848014
Seats: 500

Winchester - Hants
The Screen at Winchester, Southgate Street
X
Tel: 01962 856009
Seats: 1:214, 2:170

Windsor - Berkshire
Arts Centre, St Leonards Road (P/T)
Tel: 01753 8593336
Seats: 108

Witney - Oxfordshire
Corn Exchange, Market Square (P/T)
Tel: 01993 703646
Seats: 207

Woking - Surrey
Ambassador Cinemas, Peacock Centre off Victoria Way
X
Tel: 01483 761144
Seats: 1:434, 2:447, 3:190, 4:236, 5:268, 6:89

Wokingham - Berkshire
Showcase Cinemas, Loddon Bridge, Reading Road, Winnersh

X
Tel: 0118 974 7711
Seats: 2,980 (12 screens)

Wolverhampton - West Midlands
Cineworld, Bentley Bridge Leisure, Wednesfield Way, Wednesfield
Tel: 01902 306922/306911
Seats: 1:103, 2:113, 3:151, 4:205, 5:192, 6:343, 7:379, 8:343, 9:184, 10:89, 11:105, 12:162, 13:143, 14:98

Light House, Chubb Buildings, Fryer Street
XE
Tel: 01902 716055
Seats: 1:242, 2:80

Woodbridge - Suffolk
Riverside Theatre, Quay Street
Tel: 01394 382174/380571
Seats: 280

Woodhall Spa - Lincolnshire
Kinema in the Woods, Coronation Road
Tel: 01526 352166
Seats: 1:290, 2:90

Worcester - Hereford & Worcs
Odeon, Foregate Street
Tel: 0870 50 50 007
Seats: 1:260, 2:175, 3:175, 4:68, 5:130, 6:100, 7:205

Warner Village Cinemas, Friar Street
Tel: 01905 617806/617737
Seats: 1,351 (6 screens)

Workington - Cumbria
Plaza, Dunmail Park Shopping Centre, Maryport Road
X
Tel: 01900 870001
Seats: 1:307, 2:229, 3:174, 4:95, 5:95, 6:95

Worksop - Notts
Regal, Carlton Road
Tel: 01909 482896
Seats: 1:326 (P/T), 2:154

Worthing - West Sussex
Connaught Theatre, Union Place
Tel: 01903 231799/235333
Seats: 1:512 (P/T), 2(Ritz): 220

Dome, Marine Parade
Tel: 01903 200461
Seats: 425

Wotton Under Edge - Gloucestershire
Town Cinema
Tel: 01453 521666
Seats: 200

Yeovil - Somerset
ABC, Court Ash Terrace
Tel: 01935 413333/413413
Seats: 1:602, 2:248, 3:246

Cineworld
Seats: 1,900
(Scheduled to open Spring 2002)

York - North Yorkshire
Odeon, Blossom Street
Tel: 0870 50 50 007
Seats: 1:799, 2:111 X, 3:111 X

Picture House, Coney Street
Tel: 01904 541144/612940
Seats: 1:226, 2:142, 3:135

Warner Village Cinemas, Clifton Moor Centre, Stirling Road
X
Tel: 01904 691147/691094
Seats: 1:128, 2:212, 3:316, 4:441, 5:185, 6:251, 7:251, 8:185, 9:441, 10:316, 11:212, 12:128

SCOTLAND

A number of bfi-supported cinemas in Scotland also receive substantial central funding and programming/management support via Scottish Screen

Aberdeen - Grampian
The Belmont, Belmont Street
Tel: 01224 343536/343500
Seats 1:272, 2:146, 3:67

The Lighthouse, Shiprow
Tel: 084560 20266
Seats: 1:321, 2:221, 3:180, 4:236, 5:219, 6:165, 7:190

UGC Cinemas, Queens Link, Leisure Park, Links Road
Tel: 01224 572228
Seats: 1:160, 2:86, 3:208, 4:290, 5:560, 6:280, 7:208, 8:160, 9:160

Annan - Dumfries & Gall
Londsdale Cinemas, Lady Street Leisure Centre, Moat Street
Tel: 01461 202796
Seats: 1:107, 2:57

Aviemore - Highlands
Speyside, Aviemore Centre
X
Tel: 01479 810624/810627
Seats: 721

Ayr - Strathclyde
Odeon, Burns Statue Square
Tel: 0870 50 50 007
Seats: 1:388, 2:168, 3:135, 4:371

Brodick, Arran - Strathclyde
Brodick, Hall Cinema
Tel: 01770 302065/302375
Seats:250

Campbeltown - Strathclyde
Picture House, Hall Street (P/T)
Tel: 01586 553899
Seats: 265

Castle Douglas - Dumfries & Gall
Palace, St Andrews Street (S/O)
Tel: 01556 2141
Seats: 400

Clydebank - Strathclyde
UCI Cinemas, Clyde Regional Centre, Britannia Way
Tel: 0870 0102030
Seats: 1:202, 2:202, 3:230, 4:253, 5:390, 6:390, 7:253, 8:230, 9:202, 10:202

Coatbridge - Strathclyde
Showcase Cinemas, Langmuir Road, Bargeddie, Bailleston
X
Tel: 01236 434 434
Seats: 3,664 (14 screens)

Dumfries - Dumfries & Gall
ABC, Shakespeare Street
Tel: 01387 253578
Seats: 526

Robert Burns Centre Film Theatre, Mill Road (P/T)
Tel: 01387 264808
Seats: 67

Dundee - Tayside
Dundee Contemporary Arts, Nethergate
Tel: 01382 432000
Seats: 1:217, 2:77

Odeon, Eclipse Leisure Park
Tel: 0870 50 50 007
Seats: 1:411, 2:234, 3:317, 4:182, 5:102, 6:481, 7:256, 8:294, 9:161, 10:119

Steps Theatre
Central Library, The Wellgate, DD1 1DB
Tel: 01382 432082
Seats: 250

UGC Cinemas, Camperdown Park, Kingsway West
Tel: 01382 828793
Seats: 1:263, 2: 180, 3:109, 4:224, 5:512, 6:224, 7:130, 8:109, 9:79

Dunfermline - Fife
Odeon, Whimbrel Place, Fife Leisure Park
Tel: 0870 50 50 007
Seats: 1:268, 2:337, 3:268, 4:210, 5:139, 6:419, 7:268, 8:337, 9:210, 10:139

Robins, East Port
Tel: 01383 623535
Seats: 1:209, 2:156, 3:78

Dunoon - Strathclyde
Studio, John Street
Tel: 01369 704545
Seats: 1:188, 2:70

East Kilbride - Strathclyde
Arts Centre, Old Coach Road (P/T)
Tel: 01355 261000

UCI Cinemas, Olympia Shopping Centre
Rothesay Street, Town Centre

Tel: 0870 0102030
Seats: 1:319, 2:206, 3:219, 4:207, 5:207, 6:219, 7:206, 8:206, 9:219

Edinburgh - Lothian
Cameo, Home Street, Tollcross
X
Tel: 0131 228 4141/2800
Seats: 1:253, 2:75, 3:66

Dominion, Newbattle Terrace, Morningside
Tel: 0131 447 2660/4771
Seats: 1:586, 2:317, 322:47, 4:67

Filmhouse, 88 Lothian Road, EH3 9BZ
XE
Tel: 0131 228 2688/6382
Seats: 1:280, 2:97, 3:73

The Lumiére, Royal Museum Chambers Street,
Edinburgh EH1 1JF
Tel: 0131 247 4219
Seats: 280

Odeon, Clerk Street
Tel: 0870 50 50 007
Seats: 1:695, 2:293 X, 3:201 X, 4:259, 5:182

Odeon, Lothian Road
Seats: 800 (4 screens)
(Former ABC under redevelopment)

Odeon, Westside Plaza, Wester Hailes Road
Tel: 0870 50 50 007
Seats: 1:416, 2:332, 3:332, 4:244, 5:228, 6:213, 7:192, 8:171

Ster Century, Ocean Terminal
Seats: 2,730 (12 screens)
(Scheduled to open late 2001)

UCI Cinemas, Kinnaird Park, Newcraighall Road
Tel: 0870 0102030
Seats: 170 (6 screens), 208 (4 screens), 312 (2 screens)

UGC Cinemas, Fountain Park, Dundee Street
Tel: 0131 228 8788
Seats: 1:(Iwerks) 298, 2:339, 3:228, 4:208, 5:174, 6:159, 7:527, 8:248, 9:188, 10:194, 11:194, 12:177, 13:88

Elgin - Grampian
Moray Playhouse, High Street
Tel: 01343 542680
Seats: 1:300, 2:250

Falkirk – Central
Cineworld, Central Retail Park, Old
Bison Works, off Stewart
Road/Queen's Street
Tel: 01324 617860
Seats: 1:311, 2:218, 3:103, 4:128,
5:171, 6:253, 7:253, 8:171, 9:128,
10:103, 11:243, 12:232

FTH Arts Centre, Town Hall,
West Bridge Street
Tel: 01324 506850

Fort William - Highlands
Studios 1 and 2, Cameron Square
Tel: 01397 705095
Seats: 1:126, 2:76

Galashiels - Borders
Pavilion, Market Street
Tel: 01896 752767
Seats: 1:335, 2:172, 3:147, 4:56

Glasgow - Strathclyde
ABC, Clarkston Road, Muirend
X
Tel: 0141 637 2641
Seats: 1:482, 2:208, 3:90

Bombay Cinema, Lorne Road
Ibrox
Tel: 0141 419 0722

 Glasgow Film Theatre,
12 Rose Street, G3 6RB
XE
Tel: 0141 332 6535/8128
Seats: 1:404, 2:144

Grosvenor, Ashton Lane, Hillhead
Tel: 0141 339 4298
Seats: 1:274, 2:252

Odeon, Springfield Quay, Paisley
Road
Tel:0870 50 50 007
X
Seats: 1:428, 2:128, 3:89, 4:201, 5:200,
6:277, 7:321, 8:128, 9:89, 10:194,
11:242, 12:256

Odeon, Renfield Street
X
Tel: 0870 50 50 007
Seats: 1:555, 2:153, 3:113, 4:174,
5:189, 6:230, 7:238, 8:251, 9:222

UGC Cinemas, The Forge,
Parkhead
XE
Tel: 0141 556 4282
Seats: 1:434, 2:434, 3:322, 4:262,
5:208, 6:144, 7:132

UGC Cinemas, Nile Street

Seats: 4,100 (18 screens)
(Scheduled to open late 2001)

Glenrothes - Fife
Kingsway, Church Street
Tel: 01592 750980
Seats: 1:294, 2:223

Greenock - Strathclyde
Waterfront, off Container Way
Tel: 01475 732201
Seats: 1:258, 2:148, 3:106, 4:84

Inverness - Highlands
Eden Court Theatre, Bishops Road
Tel: 01463 234234
Seats: 84

Warner Village Cinemas
Inverness Business and Retail Park,
Eastfield Way
Tel: 01463 711 175/147
Seats: 1:314, 2:352, 3:160, 4:203,
5:430, 6:203, 7:160

Irvine - Stathclyde
Magnum, Harbour Street
X
Tel: 01294 278381
Seats: 323

Kelso - Borders
Roxy, Horse Market
Tel: 01573 224609
Seats: 260

Kilmarnock - Strathclyde
Odeon, Queens Drive
Tel: 0870 50 50 007
Seats: 1:308, 2:308, 3:145, 4:185,
5:437, 6:185, 7:145, 8:201

Kirkcaldy - Fife
 Adam Smith Theatre
Bennochy Road, KY1 1ET
(P/T) XE
Tel: 01592 412929
Seats: 475

Kirkwall - Orkney
New Phoenix, Pickaquoy Centre,
Muddisdale Road
Tel: 01856 879900
Seats: 244

Largs - Strathclyde
Vikingar Cinema, Greenock Road
Tel: 01475 689777
Seats: 470

Livingston – West Lothian
The Circuit, McArthur Glen
Designer Outlet, Almondvale North
Tel: 0845 60 20 266
Seats: 1:402, 2:178, 3:140, 4:211,
5:254, 6:140, 7:140, 8:195

Lockerbie - Dumfries & Gall
Rex, Bridge Street (S/O)
Tel: 01576 202547
Seats: 195

Millport - Strathclyde
The Cinema (Town Hall), Clifton
Street (S/O)
Tel: 01475 530741
Seats: 250

Motherwell - Lanarkshire
Civic Theatre, Civic Centre (P/T)
Tel: 01698 66166
Seats: 395

**Newton Stewart - Dumfries
& Gall**
Cinema, Victoria Street
Tel: 01671 403 333

Oban - Strathclyde
Highland Theatre, Highland
Discovery Centre, George Street
(P/T)
Tel: 01631 563794
Seats: 1:277, 2:25

Paisley - Strathclyde
Showcase Cinemas, Phoenix Business
Park, Linwood
Tel: 0141 887 0011
Seats: 3,784 (14 screens)

Perth - Tayside
Playhouse, Murray Street
Tel: 01738 623126
Seats: 1:606, 2:56, 3:156, 4:144, 5:131,
6:113, 7:110

Pitlochry - Tayside
Regal, Athal Road (S/O)
Tel: 01796 2560
Seats: 400

Portree - Highland
Aros Cinema, Viewfield Road
Tel: 01478 613750
Seats: 400

Rothesay - Isle of Bute
MBC Cinema, Winter Gardens,
Victoria Centre, Victoria Street
Tel: 01700 505462
Seats: 98

St Andrews - Fife
New Picture House, North Street
Tel: 01334 473509
Seats: 1:739, 2:94

Stirling - Central
Allanpark Cinema, Allanpark
Tel: 01786 474137
Seats: 1:399, 2:289

MacRobert Arts Centre,
University of Stirling,
FK9 4LA (P/T)
XE
Tel: 01786 461081
Seats: 495

Stornoway - Western Isles
Twilights, Seaforth Hotel
James Street (P/T)
Tel: 01851 702740
Seats: 60

Thurso – Highland
All Star Factory, Ormlie Road
Tel: 01847 890890
Seats: 1:88, 2:152

WALES

Aberaman - Mid Glamorgan
Grand Theatre, Cardiff Road (P/T)
Tel: 01685 872310
Seats: 950

Abercwmboi - Mid Glamorgan
Capitol Screen
Tel: 01443 475766
Seats: 280

Aberdare - Mid Glamorgan
Coliseum, Mount Pleasant Street
(P/T)
X
Tel: 01685 881188
Seats: 621

Aberystwyth - Dyfed
Arts Centre, Penglais, Campus,
University of Wales (P/T)
Tel: 01970 623232
Seats: 125

Commodore, Bath Street
Tel: 01970 612421
Seats: 410

Bala - Gwynedd
Neuadd Buddig (P/T)
Tel: 01678 520 800
Seats: 372

Bangor - Gwynedd
Plaza, High Street
X
Tel: 01248 371080
Seats: 1:310, 2:178

Theatr Gwynedd, Deiniol Road
(P/T)
X
Tel: 01248 351707/351708
Seats: 343

Barry - South Glamorgan
Theatre Royal, Broad Street
Tel: 01446 735019
Seats: 496

Bethesda - Gwynedd
Ogwen, High Street (P/T)
Tel: 01286 676335
Seats: 315

Blackwood - Gwent
Miners' Institute, High Street (P/T)
X
Tel: 01495 227206
Seats: 409

Blaenavon - Gwent
Workman's Hall, High Street (P/T)
Tel: 01495 792661
Seats: 80

Blaengarw - Mid Glamorgan
Workmen's Hall, Blaengarw Rd (P/T)
X
Tel: 01656 871911
Seats: 250

Brecon - Powys
Coliseum Film Centre
Wheat Street
Tel: 01874 622501
Seats: 1:164, 2:164

Bridgend - Mid Glamorgan
Odeon, McArthur Glen Designer
Outlet
Tel: 0870 50 50 007
Seats: 1:432, 2:326, 3:252, 4:245,
5:219, 6:176, 7:154, 8:162, 9:110

Brynamman - Dyfed
Public Hall, Station Road
Tel: 01269 823232
Seats: 838

Brynmawr - Gwent
Market Hall, Market Square
Tel: 01495 310576
Seats: 320

Builth Wells - Powys
Castle Cinema, Wyeside Arts Centre,
Castle Street
Tel: 01982 552555
Seats: 210

Cardiff - South Glamorgan
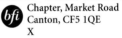 Chapter, Market Road
Canton, CF5 1QE
X
Tel: 029 20304 400
Seats: 1:194, 2:68

Galaxy, Albany Road
Tel: 02920 495065
Seats: 200

Monico, Pantbach Road, Rhiwbina
Tel: 029 20693426
Seats: 1:500, 2:156

St David's Hall, The Hayes (P/T)
Tel: 029 20371236/42611
Seats: 1,600

Ster Century, Millennium Plaza
Seats: 1:124, 2:132, 3:265, 4:358,
5:333, 6:257, 7:177, 8:124, 9:132,
10:265, 11:358, 12:333, 13:257, 14:177
(Scheduled to open late 2001)

UCI Cinemas, Hemingway Road
Atlantic Wharf, Cardiff Bay
Tel: 0870 010 2030
Seats: 1:520, 2:353, 3:351, 4:313,
5:267, 6:267, 7:200, 8:200, 9:153,
10:153, 11:147, 12:147

UGC Cinemas, Mary Ann Street
Tel: 02920 667718
Seats: 1:132, 2:195, 3:195, 4:126,
5:155, 6:206, 7:248, 8:375, 9:478,
10:125, 11:154, 12:206, 13:248,
14:183, 15:183

Cardigan - Dyfed
Theatr Mwldan, Bath House Road
(P/T)
X
Tel: 01239 621200
Seats: 210

Carmarthen - Dyfed
Lyric, King's Street (P/T)
Tel: 01267 232632
Seats: 740

Colwyn Bay – Clwyd
Theatr Colwyn, Abergele Road (P/T)
Tel: 01492 872000
Seats: 386

Cross Hands - Dyfed
Public Hall
Tel: 01269 844441
Seats: 300

Cwmaman - Mid Glamorgan
Public Hall, Alice Place (P/T)
Tel: 01685 876003
Seats: 344

Cwmbran - Gwent
Scene, The Mall
Tel: 016338 66621
Seats: 1:115, 2:78, 3:130

Ferndale - Mid Glamorgan
Cinema, Hall, High Street (P/T)
Seats: 190

Fishguard - Dyfed
Theatr Gwaun, West Street
Tel: 01348 873421/874051
Seats: 252

Harlech - Gwynedd
Theatr Ardudwy Coleg Harlech (P/T)
Tel: 01766 780667
Seats: 266

Haverfordwest - Dyfed
Palace, Upper Market Street
Tel: 01437 767675
Seats: 500

Holyhead - Gwynedd
Empire, Stanley Street
Tel: 01407 761458
Seats: 160

**Llandudno Junction -
Gwynedd**
Cineworld,
Junction Leisure Park
Off Junction Way
Tel: 01492 580503

Seats: 1:228, 2:100, 3:138, 4:107,
5:322, 6:292, 7:207, 8:138, 9:100

Llanelli - Dyfed
Entertainment Centre, Station Rd
Tel: 07000 001234
Seats: 1:516, 2:310, 3:122

**Llantwit Major - Mid
Glamorgan**
St Donat's Arts Centre
St Donat's Castle
Tel: 01446 799099
Seats: 220

Maesteg - Mid Glamorgan
Town Hall Cinema,
Talbot Street
Tel: 01656 733269
Seats: 170

**Merthyr Tydfil - Mid
Glamorgan**
Castle
Tel: 01685 386669
Seats: 1:98, 2:198

Milford Haven - Dyfed
Torch Theatre, St Peters Road
Tel: 01646 695267
Seats: 297

Mold - Clwyd
Theatr Clwyd, County Civic Centre,
CH7 1YA
X
Tel: 01352 756331/755114
Seats: 1:530, 2:129

Monmouth - Gwent
Savoy, Church Street
Tel: 01600 772467
Seats: 450

Nantgarw – Mid Glamorgan
Showcase Cinemas, Treforest
Tel: 01443 846 908
Seats: 2,604 (12 screens)

Newport – Gwent
Metro, Bridge Street
Tel: 01633 224040
Seats: 1:406, 2:170, 3:117

UGC Cinemas, Retail Park, Seven
Styles Avenue
Tel: 0541 550516
Seats: 1:199, 2:178, 3:123, 4:187,
5:267, 6:405, 7:458, 8:287, 9:180,
10:123, 11:211, 12:156, 13:77

Newtown - Powys
Regent, Broad Street
Tel: 01686 625917
Seats: 210

**Pontardawe - West
Glamorgan**
Arts Centre, Herbert Street

Tel: 01792 863722
Seats: 450

Pontypool - Gwent
Scala, Osborne Road
Tel: 0149 575 6038
Seats: 197

**Pontypridd - Mid
Glamorgan**
Muni Screen, Gelliwastad Rd (P/T)
XE
Tel: 01443 485934
Seats: 400

**Port Talbot - West
Glamorgan**
Apollo, Hollywood Park, Aberavon
Sea Front, Princess Margaret Way
Tel: 01639 895552
Seats: 1:118, 2:103, 3:258, 4:258,
5:118, 6:118

Porthcawl - Mid Glamorgan
Grand Pavilion (S/O) (P/T)
Tel: 01656 786996
Seats: 500

Portmadoc - Gwynedd
Coliseum, Avenue Road
Tel: 01766 512108
Seats: 582

Pwllheli - Gwynedd
Odeon, Butlin's Starcoast World
Tel: 0870 50 50 007
Seats: 200

Town Hall Cinema (P/T)
Tel: 01758 613371
Seats: 450

Rhyl - Clwyd
Apollo, Children's Village, West
Promenade
Tel: 01745 353856
Seats: 1:206, 2:206, 3:117, 4:107, 5:107

Swansea - West Glamorgan
Taliesin Arts Centre, University
College, Singleton Park, SA2 8PZ
XE
Tel: 01792 296883/295491
Seats: 328

UCI Cinemas, Quay Parade, Parc
Tawe
Tel: 01792 645005
Seats: 1:180, 2:188, 3:188, 4:194,
5:276, 6:276, 7:194, 8:188, 9:188,
10:180

Tenby - Dyfed
Royal Playhouse, White Lion Street
Tel: 01834 844809
Seats: 400

Treorchy - Mid Glamorgan
Parc and Dare Theatre, Station Road
Tel: 01443 773112
Seats: 794

Tywyn - Gwynedd
The Cinema, Corbett Square
X
Tel: 01654 710260
Seats: 368

Welshpool - Mid Glamorgan
Pola, Berriew Street
Tel: 01938 555715
Seats: 1:150, 2:40

Wrexham - Clwyd
Odeon Plas Coch Retail Park, Plas
Coch Road
Tel: 0870 50 50 007
Seats: 1:354, 2:191, 3:148, 4:254,
5:112, 6:112, 7:112

**Ystradgynlais - Mid
Glamorgan**
Miners' Welfare and Community
Hall, Brecon Road (P/T)
X
Tel: 01639 843163
Seats: 345

NORTHERN IRELAND

Antrim - Antrim
Cineplex, Fountain Hill
Tel: 028 94 461 111
Seats: 1:312, 2:232, 3:132, 4:112

Armagh - Armagh
City Film House
Tel: 028 37 511033
Four screens

Ballymena - Antrim
IMC, Larne Link Road
Tel: 028 25 631111
Seats: 1:342, 2:261, 3:160, 4:160,
5:109, 6:112, 7:109

Bangor - Down
Cineplex, Valentine's Road,
Castlepark
Tel: 028 91454729
Seats: 1:287, 2:196, 3:164, 4:112

Belfast - Antrim
Cineworld, Kennedy Centre, Falls
Road   E
Tel: 028 90 600988
Seats: 1:296, 2:190, 3:178, 4:178, 5:165

IMAX Queen's Quay
Seats: 380
(Scheduled to open late 2001)

Movie House, Yorkgate Shopping
Centre
X
Tel: 028 90 755000
Seats: 1:314, 2:264, 3:248, 4:181,
5:172, 6:97, 7:97, 8:332, 9:72, 10:67,
11:67, 12:83, 13:83, 14:475

Queen's Film Theatre, 25 College
Gardens, BT9 6BS
X
Tel: 028 90 244857/667687
Seats: 1:250, 2:150

The Strand, Hollywood Road
Tel: 028 90 673500
Seats: 1:250, 2:193, 3:84, 4:98

UGC Cinemas, Dublin Road
Tel: 028 90 245700
Seats: 1:436, 2:354, 3:262 X, 4:264 X,
5:252, 6:272, 7:187 X, 8:187 X, 9:169,
10:118 X

Warner Village Cinemas, The
Pavillion, Odyssey Centre 2, Queens
Quay
Tel: 028 90 739072/739134
1:402, 2:153, 3:153, 4:153, 5:473,
6:186, 7:186, 8:265, 9:292, 10:278,
11:242, 12:242

Carrickfergus - Antrim
Omniplex, Marina, Rogers Quay
Tel: 02893 351111
Seats: 1: 378, 2:232, 3:210, 4:153,
5:117, 6:128

Coleraine - Londonderry
Jet Centre, Riverside Park
Tel: 01265 58011
Seats: 1:273, 2:193, 3:152, 4:104

Cookstown - Tyrone
Ritz, Burn Road
Tel: 02886 765182
Five screens

Dungannon - Tyrone
Global Cinemas, Oaks Centre, Oaks
Road
Tel: 02887 727733
Seats: (6 screens)

Dungiven - Londonderry
St Canice's Hall, Main Street
Seats: 300

Enniskillen - Fermanagh
Ardhowen Theatre,
Dublin Road (P/T)
Tel: 028 66325440
Seats: 295

Omniplex, Factory Road
Tel: 02866 324777
Seats: 1:300, 2:126, 3:104, 4:154,
5:254, 6:165, 7:78

Glengormley - Antrim
Movie House, Glenville Road
Tel: 028 90 833424
Seats: 1:309, 2:243, 3:117, 4:110, 5:76,
6:51

Kilkeel - Down
Vogue, Newry Road
Tel: 016937 63092
Seats: 295

Larne - Antrim
Regal, Curran Road
Tel: 028 28 277711
Seats: 1:300, 2:220, 3:120, 4:120

Lisburn - Antrim
Omniplex, Governors Road
Tel: 028 92 663664
Seats: 1:489, 2:219, 3:161, 4:112,
5:176, 6:234, 7:142, 8:112, 9:84, 10:66,
11:66, 12:84, 13:97, 14:148

Londonderry - Londonderry
Orchard, Orchard Street
Tel: 028 71 267789
Seats: 132, 700 m

Strand, Quayside Centre, Strand
Road
Tel: 028 71 373939
Seats: 1:317, 2:256, 3:227, 4:227,
5:134, 6:124, 7:90

Lurgan - Armagh
Centre Point Cinemas, Portadown
Road
Tel: 01762 324667
Seats: 1:281, 2:182, 3:142, 4:90

Maghera - Londonderry
Movie House, St Lurach's Road
Tel: 028 796 43872/42936
Seats: 1:221, 2:117, 3:95

Newry - Down
Savoy 2, Merchant's Quay
Tel: 028 028 30260000
Seats: 1:197, 2:58

Omniplex, Quays Shopping Centre,
Albert Basin
Tel: 028 30256098
Seats: 1:470, 2:219, 3:168, 4:2003,
5:203, 6:168, 7:219, 8:333, 9:122

Newtownards - Down
Movieland, Ards Shopping Centre
Tel: 028 9182 2000/01247 821000
Seats: 1:278, 2:238, 3:155, 4:155,
5:119, 6:119

Omagh - Tyrone
Studios 1-6, Gillyhooley Road
Tel: 02882 242034
Six screens

Portrush - Antrim
Playhouse, Mainstreet
Tel: 01265 823917
Seats: 1:299, 2:65

COURSES

Listed here is a selection of educational establishments which offer courses in film, television and media studies. Some of the courses are Further Education course but the majority are Undergraduate or Postgraduate courses. (P) indicates where a course is mainly practical. Emphasis on the remaining courses is usually on theoretical study; some of these courses include minor practical components.

A wider range of courses and more detailed information can be found in two indispensable bfi publications, Media Courses UK 2002 and Media and Multimedia Short Courses both edited by Lavinia Orton.

It is worth checking individual college websites for up to date course details.

AFECT (Advancement of Film Education Charitable Trust)
52a Walham Grove
London SW6 1QR
Tel: 020 7609 2992
Contact:: Jeremy Ross
(P) Practical 16mm Film-Making Course
Part-time, 2 years for those seeking professional-level training.
(P) Practical 16mm Film-Making Course: Post-Course, Semi-Independent Third-Year Projects
Part-time, 1 year
Patron: Mike Leigh
Makes professional-level, practical film education available on a part-time basis to those who may have neither the means nor the time to attend a full-time film course

ARTTS International
Highfield Grange
Bubwith
North Yorks YO8 6DP
Tel: 01757 288088
Fax: 01757 288253
Website: www.artts.co.uk
email: admin@artts.co.uk
Contact: Duncan Lewis
(P) Acting Diploma
Full-time 40 weeks
(P) Directing Diploma
Full-time 40 weeks
(P) Production Operations Diploma
Full-time 40 weeks

AIU – London
Department of Media Production
110 Marylebone High Street
London W1U 4RY
Tel: 020 7467-5600
Fax: 020 7467 5641
email: admissions@aiulondon.ac.uk
Website: www.aiulondon.ac.uk
Contact: Emma Wood, Alison McCale
(P) Associate of Arts and BFA Media Production
The Associate of Arts is a two-year, full or part-time course; and the BFA is a four-year, full or part-time course.
The University operates on a modular basis, enabling students to tailor the programme to their individual needs. The year is divided into five terms, beginning in October. Included are courses in: scriptwriting; producing and directing; cinematography; electronic music; audio engineering; computer graphics; multimedia; streaming and web-based media; animation; editing; and all aspects of video and audio production.
Facilities include industry-standard video equipment for video and audio production and editing

Barking College
Dagenham Road
Romford RM7 0XU
Tel: 01708 770000
Fax: 01708 770007
(P) B/TEC National Diploma Media
This two year broad based media course covers video, radio and sound recording, print and journalism. Facilities include: television studio; portable video; video editing suites; sound recording studio and DTP equipment. There is a practical and vocational emphasis and students are prepared for either a career in the media industries, or for entry to higher education. The entry requirements are 4 GCSEs at C or above. Applications from mature students are welcome
(P) BTEC National Diploma in Multimedia
This two year full-time course includes digital imaging using Photoshop,Premier and Multimedia programs including Flash, Dreamweaver and Director.There is a practical and vocational emphasis and students are prepared for either a career in multimedia or for entry to Higher Education. Applications from mature students are welcome.The entry requirements are 4 GCSEs at C or above.
(P) GNVQ Intermediate in Media
This one year course provides an introduction to media work and has a 50% practical 'hands on' approach to video production and photography and provides an oportunity to improve general communications to progress on to either National Diploma courses in either Media, Photography or Multimedia.The entry requirements are 3 Ds at GCSE or above.
HND in Multimedia.
This full-time Higher Education course includes digital video editing, digital sound recording, web site design and 2D and 3D design and animation. Entry requirements are 2 A levels or National Diploma or GNVQ Advanced in relevant subjects

University of Bath
Department of European Studies and Modern Languages
Claverton Down
Bath BA2 7AY
Tel: 01225 826482
Fax: 01225 826099
email: w.everett@bath.ac.uk
Website: www.bath.ac.uk
Contact: Wendy E. Everett
BA (Hons) Modern Languages and European Studies
This is a four-year, full-time course which includes a year abroad. Film and Media Studies form an integral

part of the Modern Languages and European Studies degree scheme. In the first year, there is an introductory course in French film. The second and fourth years have options covering French, German, Italian and Russian film, plus French and German television. In the final year, an option in European film is offered

Birkbeck College University of London

Media Studies
Faculty of Continuing Education,
Birkbeck College
26 Russell Square
London WC1B 5DQ
Tel: 020 7631 6667/6663
Fax: 020 7631 6683
email: m.talukdar@bbk.ac.uk
Website: bbk.ac.uk
Certificate and Diploma in Media Studies
Part-time courses in film, television, journalism and in areas of media practice such as screenwriting, freelance journalism, video, radio, leading to the Certificate/Diploma in Media Studies or in Media Practice.
Contact: Manize Talukdar
BA in Film and Media
Four year part-time degree which offers a multi-disciplinary approach to the study of film and media

University of Birmingham

Department of Cultural Studies and Sociology
Edgbaston
Birmingham B15 2TT
Tel: 0121 414 6060
Website: www.bham.ac.uk
Ann Gray
BA Media, Culture and Society
Full degree or combined half degree, looking at a range of contemporary social and cultural issues, in a cross-disciplinary way. Representation through dominant and alternative media are explored throughout the degree strands on gender, race and ethnicity, etc. A compulsory dissertation may be interview or video-based

Bournemouth University

School of Media Arts and Communication, Poole House
Talbot Campus, Fern Barrow
Poole
Dorset BH12 5BB
Tel: 01202 595553
Fax: 01202 595314
email: tboucouv@bournemouth.ac.uk

Website: www.bournemouth.ac.uk
Contact: Anthony C. Boucouvalas
BSc in Multimedia Communications
The course aims to develop knowledge and skills in creating effective multimedia interfaces coupled with expertise in designing communication systems and network infrastructure to support distributed multimedia applications. The course content includes: multimedia development; communication systems software development; creative multimedia design; computer networks; databases; graphics; and human computer interfaces

The Arts Institute of Bournemouth School of Media

Wallisdown
Poole,
Dorset BH12 5HH
Tel: 01202 363281
Fax: 01202 537729
(P) B/TEC National Diploma in Moving Image (Media Production)
Contact: Jon Towlson
Tel: 01202 363289
Fax: 01202 537729
Two year vocational course centred around the disciplines of video and audio production. These practical studies are supported by elements of design studies, drama, music, scriptwriting, animation, Contextual Studies, Business and Professional Studies. The course is recognised by BKSTS
BA Hons Film and Animation Production
Contact: Nik Stratton
Tel: 01202 363269
Fax: 01202 537729
The course offers experience of film and video production for either live action or animation and within this, the opportunity to specialise in either camera editing, producing, directing etc. It also encourages engagement with the history of the moving image of the relationship between contemporary media theory and practice

University of Bradford

Department of Electronic Imaging and Media Communications
Richmond Road
Bradford BD7 1DP
Tel: 01274 235963
Fax: 01274 233727
email: P.E.Dale@bradford.ac.uk

Website: www.eimc.brad.ac.uk
Paula Dale, EIMC Admissions Office
(P) BSc Electronic Imaging and Media Communications
A three year, full-time course, developed by a group of staff with various specialities – electronics, art and design, digital music, sociology, photography and television. The breadth of the course is unusual and offers real advantages in preparing students for a career in the media. A Foundation Year is available
(P) BSc Media Technology and Production
In this course high calibre candidates will be able to develop full media products in realistic environments
(P)BSc Interactive Systems Video Games Design
(P) BSc Computer Animation and Special Effects
(P) BSc Internet Product Design
Three new courses offering Bradford's successful new media background alongside the opportunity to specialise in these areas

Brighton Film School

Admin Office
13 Tudor Close
Dean Court Road
Rottingdean, East Sussex BN2 7DF
Tel: 01273 302166
Fax: 01273 302163
email: brightonfilmschool@cwcom.net
Website: www.brightonfilmschool.org.uk
Franz von Habsburg MBKS, (BAFTA Member) Senior Lecturer
Admissions: Meryl von Habsburg
BSc MSc Cert Ed
Studio:
Phoenix Arts Centre, Wellesley House
10-14 Waterloo Place, Brighton BN2 2NB
Tel: 01273 602070
The Brighton Film School is a member of Centre International de Liaison des Ecoles de Cinéma et Télévision (www.cilect.org) via the National Association
for Higher Education in the Moving Image (NAHEMI) and fees (DofEE ILAs accepted) include one year's student membership of both The Moving Image Society (BKSTS) (www.bksts.demon.co.uk) and the Directors' Guild of Great Britain.
Director's Courses in Cinematography (Part-time)
Six one-term part-time courses plus a

full-time three week Summer School are offered each year: In Sept, Jan and April you can choose from one day a week (Weds) or two evenings a week (Tues and Thurs) to learn the cinematic skills which should be known by the competent director and include Camera, Film Stock, Lighting, Sound, Editing, Film Grammar, Screenwriting (we use Final Draft 5.13e, Screenwriter 2000 plus Storyboard Quick and Shotmaster for storyboarding), Production Management (Movie Magic Scheduling and Budgeting are taught) plus Stagecraft skills (incl Acting and Makeup). Tuition by a variety of lecturers in all disciplines followed by practical exercises (in small groups) is combined with film company and studio visits, including Pinewood and RADA, providing a route which may be available as an Access Course.

Director's Diploma Course in Cinematography
This is planned to start in Sept 2001 as a one-year part-time course, ie three academic terms for one day a week, the third being for practical assignments in small groups on 16mm.

Weekend Courses
We also hold Courses in TV Presenting and weekend residential courses in Screenwriting.
All our film courses are designed to meet industry needs and we work closely with the education committee of the BKSTS, to which all our students belong. Graduates may submit their CVs to the Guild of British Camera Technicians and are also issued with passes so that they may attend certain BAFTA events

University of Bristol
Department of Drama
Cantocks Close
Woodland Road
Bristol BS8 1UP
Tel: 0117 928 7833
Fax: 0117 928 7832
email: mark.sinfield@bristol.ac.uk
Website: www.bris.ac.uk
Mark Sinfield
BA Drama
Three year course with theatre, film and TV options. Alongside theatre-based Units, critical and theoretical approaches to film and TV are part of the core syllabus in year 1. Additional critical and practical options are offered in years 2 and 3. Practical

work is group-based, extends and enriches critical study in a range of forms in fiction and non-fiction, and results in the production of original work. Theoretical work may be developed through individual dissertations as well as a range of seminar courses

(P) MA in Film and Television Production
This one-year course was the first of its kind in a British university and has produced numerous distinguished practitioners working internationally. It offers a broad grounding in practical skills in film and television production, regular consultation with professional practitioners, and a collective forum for the development of critical thinking and creative practice. Based around a core of group-based practical work, the course offers modular options in a range of practical and critical disciplines, leading to group-based production for public festival entry and/or broadcast, and individual analysis. Production platforms include broadcast-standard video and 16mm film, as well as digital media. The course enjoys widespread support from film and television organisations and leading practitioners

University of the West of England, Bristol
Coldharbour Lane
Bristol BS16 1QY
email: Andrew2.Spicer@uwe.ac.uk
Website: www.uwe.ac.uk
Andrew Spicer
Film Studies and European Cinema
A wide–ranging study of film theory and history through four interlinked modules: 'Questions of Aesthetics, Representation and Identity', 'Theory, Criticism, Practice', 'British Cinema', 'Modernity and Identity'. Students choose a topic independently for their dissertation and receive individual supervision. In some cases this can be replaced by a project involving some aspect of filmmaking

Brunel University
Department of Human Sciences
Uxbridge
Middx UB8 3PH
Tel: 01895 274000
Fax: 01895 232806
Contact: Suzette Heald
BSc Communication and Media Studies

This four-year, full-time course is broad-based and multi-disciplinary. Students will receive a substantial grounding in sociology, psychology, anthropology and communication studies in their first year, and will then be able to specialise in communications as they progress through the other three years. Students are required to undertake project-work in both computing and video, and to undertake two periods of work experience of approximately five months each, during their first three years. This combination of academic and practical training should prove to be of substantial benefit on graduation.

BSc Sociology and Communications
This four-year, full-time course is unusual in bringing together a wide variety of social sciences in the study of communications. Students receive a multi-disciplinary grounding in social sciences in the first year, then specialise in both sociology and communications as they progress through the other three years. Students are required to undertake two six-month periods of work placement as an integral part of their degree

BA (Single and Joint Hons) Film and Television Studies
Film and Television Studies is offered as a single, major or minor programme of study within a Combined Studies degree. It offers students the opportunity to study film and television (and other related media) from various disciplinary perspectives. The course modules are designed to develop and promote theoretical and conceptual understanding of how these media produce and project meaning, as well as offering critical, creative and basic practical skills. Modules cover a range of cinemas and television, and are taught by research-active staff. This is not a training or heavily practical course. Practical work is principally perceived as a means of exploring theory

Canterbury Christ Church University College
Dept of Radio, Film and Television
North Holmes Road
Canterbury CT1 1QU
Tel: 01227 767700
Fax: 01227 782914
email: n.burton@cant.ac.uk

Website: www.cant.ac.uk
Nick Burton
(P) BA in Radio, Film and Television Single Honours
Contact: Nick Burton
RFTV single honours is an integrated theory and practice course in these three media, with students having the options to specialise in one or two of them on the practical courses in year two and three. The basic ratio between theory and practice is 50:50, but there is some flexibility to weight the programme in either direction. This well resourced programme introduces students to an understanding and appreciation of radio, film and television as media of communication and creative expression, stressing their relevance to the individual and society, as well as offering an opportunity to develop and practice production skills in 16mm film and digital video and sound. The programme also includes an option in animation. There are strong links with the industry, and the BBC has a studio in the department.
The BA/BSc Joint and Combined Honours offers the opportunity to study part of the above programme with fewer options and less practical work, but to combine it with Media and Cultural Studies, Art, American Studies, English, Music, Religious Studies, Science, Mathematics, Business Studies, Tourism, History or Geography.
(P) MA Media Production
Contact: Andy Birtwistle
A one year taught MA which concentrates on production in radio, film and television. Part I of the course introduces relevant production skills; in Part II members will fulfil a measurable major role in a production project. Course members with practical experience can update their skills and concentrate on one medium in Part I. All course members attend theory seminars through the course. Assessment will be based on the major piece of practical work and an extended essay.

The City College Manchester
Arden Centre
Manchester M23 0DD
Tel: 0161 957 1749
Fax: 0161 935 3854
email: smarland@ccm.ac.uk

Website: www.manchester-city-coll.ac.uk
Steve Marland
(P) B/TEC National Diploma Multimedia
Multi-disciplinary course bringing together video, photography, digital imaging and and design. Teaching practical production skills in analogue and new media, based on practical projects integrating theoretical studies

Coventry University
Coventry School of Art and Design
Priory Street
Coventry CV1 5FB
Tel: 024 7688 7478
Fax: 024 76887440
email: a.beck@coventry.ac.uk

(P) BA (Hons) Communication, Culture and Media
This three-year, full-time course, which includes specialisms in Cultural and Media Studies, and in Communication and Media Practice, is built around a core of studies in communication, culture and media, with a range of options for students to select from. European exchange and work placement programmes are included; and there are options in advertising, television, film, print and broadcast journalism, popular music, photography, video, and multimedia. Projects enable students to combine theoretical and practical work according to their particular interests

De Montfort University Bedford
Polhill Avenue
Bedford MK41 9EA
Tel: 01234 793117
Fax: 01234 217738
Contact: Carole Wood
BA (Hons) English
Screening the Text. A module in Part 2 which examines the transposition of a written text to the screen from a range of periods and genre from Shakespeare to the postmodern novel. Visual Fictions and Imagining the Contemporary. Two modules in Part 2 which explore film as a cultural product and address a range of issues including narrative and visual pleasure, gender and sexuality, and genre

De Montfort University Leicester
School of Arts
The Gateway
Leicester LE1 9BH

Tel: 0116 255 1551 or 0116 257 8391
Fax: 0116 257 7199
Dr A.Tolson/Tim O'Sullivan
(P) BA (Hons) Media Studies (Single, Joint or Combined Honours Degrees)
As a Single Honours degree, Media Studies offers a range of courses which focus specifically on Film, Television/Video, Photography and Media institutions. It offers courses in both theoretical and practical work which provide students with the opportunity to develop their skills and learning through detailed analysis of media texts, through understanding the social and political processes of media industries and institutions and through practical work in video, photography, radio and journalism. With Joint Honours, it is possible to take Media Studies in conjunction with one other arts discipline; for Combined Honours, with two other disciplines

University of Derby
Film and Video Department
Green Lane
Derby DE1 1RX
Tel: 01332 593065
Fax: 01332 622296
email: t.hill2@derby.ac.uk
Tony Hill
(P) BA (Hons) Film and Video
The programme is a visual arts course designed to help develop film-making and video-making skills by offering students the challenge to evolve their own vision through media production. The practical modules are structured to allow technical knowledge and skills to be learnt through their application to individual work. The programme does not attempt to prescribe content, technique, genre or approach, but offers a stimulating environment in which students are exposed to a wide range of contemporary film and video artworks. It prepares students to take advantage of the opportunities in the arts and industry

Dewsbury College
Batley School of Art & Design
Wheelwright Campus
Birkdale Road
Dewsbury, West Yorks WF13 4HQ
Tel: 01924 451649
Fax: 01924 469491
email: Sharman@dewsbury.ac.uk
BA (Hons) Moving Image Design

This course provides an opportunity to study one of the most rapidly developing areas of design. Using computer technology, the course combines live action video techniques with 3D animation to produce time-based imagery for the broadcast media, advertising and publicity. The course demands an imaginative approach with an understanding of both 2D and 3D design

University of East Anglia
School of English and American Studies,
Norwich NR4 7TJ
Tel: 01603 592283
Fax: 01603 593799
email: eas.admiss@uea.ac.uk
Website: www.uea.ac.uk
Yvonne Tasker
BA (Hons) Film and English Studies
A Joint Major programme which integrates Film and Television history and theory with work on English literature, history and cultural studies; the film work deals mainly with Hollywood, but also with British cinema. Course includes instruction in film and video production, and the option of submitting a practical project. All students submit an independent dissertation on a film or television topic.
BA (Hons) Film and American Studies
A four year Joint Major programme which integrates Film and Television history and theory with work on American literature, history, cultural studies and politics. Course includes instruction in film and video production, and the option of submitting a practical project. All students spend a year at a University in the USA, and submit an independent dissertation on a film or television topic.
BA (Hons) Modular System
Students admitted to the University to major in other subjects including Literature, Drama, American Studies etc have the option of taking one or more units in film and television study: together, these may comprise up to one third of the degree work. Limited practical element.
Contact: Undergraduate: Ros Montague 01603 592283
BA Film and Television Studies
this new programme allows the study of history, theory and politics of moving images and introduces critical approaches to film and

television. there is a strong emphasis on film and television history, from silent cinema to the contemporary scene. Work in cultural history provides a broader context in which to understand the development of cinema and television. Introductory and survey units are complemented by a broad range of specialist units on aspects of British and North American cinema and television. Some units focus on particular filmmakers or genres; other s deal with critical issues such as video activism, gender and film, or the cinema as industry. In your final year you research a dissertation topic of your own devising. You can also choose to engage in some practical work as part of your studies, with units including 16mm film, video, photography and television studio production
MA Film Studies
One year full-time taught programme. MA is awarded 50 per cent on coursework and 50 per cent on dissertation. Within the School's modular system, it is possible to replace one or two of the four film seminars with others chosen from a range of topics in literary theory, creative writing, American studies and cultural studies. The film seminars deal with early cinema, British film history, film and narrative theory, screen costume and theories of the image, and research resources and methodology. Dissertation topics are freely chosen and may deal with television as well as cinema.
MA Film Studies: Film Archive option
One year full-time taught programme, run in conjunction with the East Anglian Film Archive (located in the University). Students take two of the MA film seminars, plus two more that deal with the practical and administrative aspects of film archive work. Course includes visits to other archives, and a one-month placement at a chosen archive in Britain or overseas. Assessment is based on two essays, a video production, a placement report, and an independent dissertation (counting 50 per cent)
MPhil and PhD
Students are accepted for research degrees. Areas of special expertise include early cinema, British film history, television history, gender and

cinema, classical and contemporary Hollywood, and gender and authorship
Contact: Postgraduate: Lorraine Faith 01603 3262

University of East London
Department of Cultural Studies
Docklands Campus
4-6 University Way
Off Royal Albert Way
London E16 2RD
Tel: 020 8223 2743
Fax: 020 8223 2898
email: y.fitzgerald@uel.ac.uk
BA (Hons) Media and Gender
This degree, based in the new media centre in Docklands, takes a theory and practice approach to the politics of representation, combining an understanding of media theories with a focus on issues of gender and identity. In the first year, students acquire practical skills via media workshops (across the areas of sound, radio, video, photography, desktop publishing, and multimedia); and, in addition, they gain a theoretical grounding in media studies and gender theory. In the second and third years, they may explore their own perspectives on these issues via a range of more specialised theory units, and put the theory into practice in practical media project-work.

BA (Hons) Media Studies
Media Studies is offered as a single honours degree or as a major, minor or joint degree in combination with other subjects such as: Cultural Studies; History; Literature; and Information Technology.
All students are required to take a set of core history and theory units, particularly in their first year, and select from approved optional units in Media Studies and related subject areas. Single honours students are required to take production units (one-third of the course) in the areas of video, audio, photography, graphics and multimedia. They also take a working-in-the-media-industries unit which includes short placements and visiting lecturers from culture industries. Production units are optional.

(P) BSc (Hons) Multimedia Studies
Multimedia Studies is available as a single honours and a combined (minor, major or joint) honours pathway. It is not possible to combine Multimedia Studies with any other

pathway within Innovation Studies. This degree aims to develop theoretical and practical skills relevant to multimedia production, as well as sharing broad aims with other degrees in the department.

BSc (Hons) Media and Communication Technologies

This course is an innovative and challenging programme which combines specialist study of the media industries with a wider focus on changing developments in the field of information communications technologies. It aims to provide students with the expertise to analyse and evaluate the relationship between technical, social, economic, cultural and political change in the context of the media industries. Students also build skills in the key practical areas of information technology, computer graphics, electronic publishing and video production; and develop the ability to link the practical and theoretical aspects of their studies in creative tension.

BA (Hons) Film History

This course is structured in modular units, offering flexibility and choice. Introductory units, in Hollywood cinema and in the history and theory of film, television and video, are followed by more advanced work in the areas of: film theory; Soviet cinema; avant-garde; art cinema; new American cinema; British cinema; world cinema; horror and fantasy; film theory; screenwriting; and film animation. In addition to the main studies in Film History, students may select options from the Art and Design History courses. Alternatively, students may link Film History with other subjects within the university (such as Communication Studies or Media Studies) in a Combined Honours degree.

Edinburgh College of Art
School of Visual Communication
Lauriston Place
Edinburgh EH3 9DF
Tel: 0131 221 6138
Fax: 0131 221 6100

These courses are strongly based on practical production work and run for three years.

BA (Hons) Visual Communications (Film and Television)

The course runs for three years and most applicants have done either a foundation course in art and design,

or a further education course in video/audio-visual. Film/television students will generally combine individual projects with participation in group projects. All kinds of work can be tackled – drama, documentary and experimental. The course includes possibilities of cross-disciplinary projects with other departments in the school - animation, illustration, photography, and graphic design. All students are also encouraged to use the school's computer workshop

Masters Degree

A small number of postgraduates can be accepted, studying either for a diploma (three terms) or a masters degree (four terms). In both cases there is no formal taught course – the programme is tailored to the practical production proposals of the individual student. Postgraduates must already have appropriate skills and experience to use the resources available. The masters degree is awarded on the strength of the practical work produced

University of Exeter
School of Modern Languages
Department of French
Queen's Building,
The Queen's Drive
Exeter EX4 4QH
Tel: 01392 264263
Fax: 01392 264361
Website: www.ex.ac.uk

BA (Hons) Cinema Studies (Modular Degree)

A number of modules have been selected from the Schools of English and of Modern Languages to create a two-year modular degree in Film Studies. Candidates may either take modules to the full value of 240 credits to obtain a degree in Film Studies or choose individual modules to combine with other fields of study, for example, Information Technology. No foreign language ability is needed as all modules are taught in English. The areas covered are: Hollywood, British, French, Italian, and Post-Colonial Cinemas.
The course includes a video-making project as an option module.

BA (Hons) Film Studies

This is a three-year degree programme in Film Studies established across two schools, the School of Modern Languages and the School of English. Students take core

courses: Culture and Criticism, and Approaches to Film (in the first year); and Introduction to Film, Hollywood and Europe, French National Cinema, and World Cinema (in the second year). In the third year, all the courses are option-based including: to make a film; British Cinema Image and Identity; Auteur Theory; Italian Cinema; French Women Film-Makers; Francophone Cinema; The City as Film Narrative; video-making project; and dissertation.

Farnborough College of Technology
Media and Visual Arts
Boundary Road, Farnborough
Hants GU14 6SB
Tel: 01252 407270
Fax: 01252 407271
email: a.harding@farn-ct.ac.uk
Website: farn-ct.ac.uk
Alan Hardy

(P) HND Media Technology and Business

Two year full-time course to study media production techniques with business studies. Course includes television and video production, video and audio systems, radio, journalism and finance in the media

(P) HND Design Technology (Multimedia, Video Graphics & Animation)

Provides training in television and video production, animation and computerised video graphics. In the first and second years, all students undertake the following modules: visual studies, television and video production, animation and graphics, historical and contextual studies and business management. In the second year, students select three options from the following: video systems, documentary and drama production, advertising copywriting, photography, marketing and the media, journalism, desktop publishing and radio production

(P) BSc (Hons) Media (Production) Technology

This popular degree adopts a bi-media approach studying both Television and Radio. Students will be expected to develop and demonstrate technical skills, as well as an understanding of the appropriate theories and concepts. This will be achieved by practical units in television/video and radio, as well as theoretical ones such as audio-visual

systems, television and film, radio in society etc. Optional units enable the students to create a vocational or academic pathway of their choice
(P) Higher National Diploma in Media Technology (Broadcast Systems and Operations)
This new programme has been created at the specific request of the broadcast industries. As a result of he digital revolution there is a dramatic increase in the number of broadcasters of both television and radio. Through this programme of study students learn to become broadcast engineers using and maintaining a range of equipment necessary to provide television and radio broadcasts.

University of Glasgow
Department of French
Glasgow University
Glasgow G12 8QQ
Tel: 0141 339 8855
Fax: 0141 330 4234
MA (Hons) French: Option on French Cinema
A one-year, special subject for honours students of French. Two areas are treated. Firstly, cinema and society in 1930s France, with special emphasis on the Popular Front, including films by Renoir, Duvivier and Carné. Secondly, issues of narrative, *mise en scène* and politics, concentrating on French cinema from the 1960s to the present day. Directors studied include Truffaut, Beineix, Malle and Godard. Screenings and classes are weekly, and assessment is by examination or dissertation.

Department of Theatre,
Film and Television Studies
University of Glasgow
Glasgow G12 8QQ
Tel: 0141 330 5162
Fax: 0141 330 4142
email: tfts.office@arts.gla.ac.uk
Website: www.arts.gla.ac.uk/tfts/
Ian P. Craven
MA Joint Honours Film and Television Studies
Four year undergraduate course. Film/Television Studies represents 50 per cent of an Honours degree or 30 per cent of a non-Honours degree. Year 1 is concerned with Film and TV as 'languages', and with the institutional, industrial and technological contexts of cinema and television.Year 2 is structured under

two headings; Film and Television: Theories and Methods and Film and Television: National and Cultural Identities. Years 3 and 4 consist of a range of Honours optional courses, seven to be taken over two years in addition to a dissertation. There is also a compulsory practical course, involving either the production of a video, a contractual work placement or an applied research project
MPhil Screen Studies
One-year postgraduate course. Consisting of a core course on research methods, a range of specialist options and a supervised dissertation component, the M.Phil. in Screen Studies aims to offer an opportunity for advanced level study of cinema and television. It is geared towards the needs of well-qualified students contemplating a career in media research, criticism or administration, and also seeks to provide a preparation for applicants whose intention is to pursue research in Film and Television Studies at Doctoral level. Options within the course vary from year to year, according to the research priorities of academic staff. Please contact the department at the addresses above for further details

Glasgow Caledonian University
Division of Journalism & Media
Cowcaddens Road
Glasgow G4 0BA
Tel: 0141 331 3259
Fax: 0141 331 3264
email: hod@gcal.ac.uk
Website: www.gcal.ac.uk
Dr Hugh O'Donnell, Admissions Tutor
BA Communication and Mass Media
Four year course (unclassified and honours) examining the place of mass communication in contemporary society. Includes practical studies in television, advertising and public relations

Goldsmiths College
University of London
Lewisham Way
London SE14 6NW
Tel: 020 7919 7171
Fax: 020 7919 7509
email: admissions@gold.ac.uk
Website: www.goldsmiths.ac.uk
Colin Aggett
BA Media and Communications
This programme will give students a

broad understanding of media, communications and culture in Britain and globally through integrated studies in theory and practice. The theory courses incorporate a wide range of perspectives in the study of media, communications and culture and adopt approaches from cultural studies, semiotics, history, linguistics, psychology, sociology, antrhropology and economics. Practice courses provide an initial introduction to different media, after which students specialise and gain considerable expertise in their chosen medium
BA Anthropology and Communications
Half of this course constitutes Communication Studies.The course is mainly theoretical but does include two short practical courses of ten weeks in length in two of the practice areas. These include television, videographics and animation, radio, print journalism, photography, creative writing and script writing. The theory component is concerned with media history, sociology, psychology, textual and cultural studies
BA Communications and Cultural Studies
This theory-only degree offers an innovative programme. The course draws on a broad spectrum of critical approaches to the media, culture and communications, and encourages students to develop their own understanding of the mass media and contemporary culture. It enables students to study particular examples of media use and cultural practice in the context of broader theories of production, development and consumption, and to study global and national concentrations of media power and new forms of identity and consumption
MA in Feature Film
This one-year programme combines the exploration and understanding of the creative process with the acquisition of business acumen. It adopts a bilateral approach to the idea of cultural production through cinema. Firstly, by generating research and debates on the nature of the forms and genres in contemporary cinema and their impact on societies both nationally and globally. Secondly, to take a very practical approach to the way snew voices, producers, directors and writers can

gain an understanding of how the world of feature film-making works

MA Image and Communication (Photography or Electronic Graphics)

One year full-time course combines theory and practice, specialising in either photography or electronic graphics. Practical workshops cover medium and large format cameras, flash, colour printing, lighting, computer and video graphics, design, desktop publishing, animation, animatics, two and three dimensional computer animation. Assessment by coursework, practical production and viva voce

MA in Television Documentary

This course comprises a series of lectures, workshops, exercises and projects exploring the production of television documentary, culminating in the making of a 15-25 minute piece by each student as their final project. In the first term, there are also two theoretical courses: Representing Reality, a series of seminars on documentary; and Issues in Media and Culture, exploring wider critical and theoretical perspectives

MA in Television Drama

The core drama production component is taught throughout the three terms of the programme. A series of lecutres, workshops, exercises and projects explore the creation of drama narrative and the development of a wide range of writing production and direction skills, culminating in the production of a major piece of drama by each student in the latter half of the final year. The core course is supported by two subsidiary theoretical courses: Television Drama Narrative; and Issues in Media and Culture

MA in Television Journalism

The course is a practical introduction to journalism with the emphasis on television news and current affairs. There are three compulsory elements; TV Journalism Practice, Journalism and Professional Studies, and Media Law and Ethics. The course includes a one month placement and optional subsidiary courses in the history of documentary-making, issues in media and culture and the political economy of the mass media

MA Media and Communication Studies

This course offers an inter-disciplinary approach as well as the opportunity to specialise in media and communications. The course is based around a series of compulsory courses and options drawing on theoretical frameworks from cultural studies, political economy, sociology, anthropology, and psychology to develop a critical understanding of the role of the media and communications industries in contemporary culture. Assessment is by coursework, written examinations and dissertation

MA Journalism

The course is essentially a practical introduction to journalism as a multi-media skill with the emphasis on print journalism. In addition, you will take a subsidiary course dealing, in the first term, with the Law and ethical issues and in the second term, with the history and changing structure of the media industry.

MA Radio

This course provides an opportunity for postgraduates with some knowledge and experience of radio, to explore the medium in depth, both in theory and in practice. During the first half of the course, students study both Radio Drama and Features, and Radio Journalism and Documentary before specialising in either mode of radio production for their projects. A third element, Media Law and Ethics is taken by all students

MA in Transnational Communications and the Global Media

This programme builds on the department's strengths in the study of communications in a global and international context. It is particularly appropriate for those who have some experience of studying or working in the media and the innovations associated with the development of new modes of communications with an emphasis on the transnational context. Particular priority is given to the development of the sudents' interests and research which will be supported through specialist core courses. There are also opportunities to study relevant options offered by other departments including Anthropology, Sociology and the Centre for Cultural Studies

University of Hertfordshire

Watford Campus, Wall Hall, Aldenham
Watford
Herts WD2 8AT
Tel: 01707 285643
Fax: 01707 285616
email: s.tegel@herts.ac.uk
Susan Tegel

BA (Hons) Humanities

Full- or part-time degree. Within the History major/minor and single honours there is a second year option, Film and History, which examines the inter-war period through film and focuses on the historian's use of film, and the opportunity in the final year to undertake a dissertation using films as an historical source

University of Lincolnshire and Humberside

Hull School of Art and Design
Queens Gardens
Hull HU1 3DQ
Website: www.ulh.ac.uk
Tel: 01482 440550
Fax: 01482 462101

(P) BA (Hons) Animation

The course provides a contemporary environment in which the undergraduate animators may freely develop their creative signature as both an artist and animation designer. Staffed by practising animators and supported by visiting lecturers from all aspects of film and television production, the emphasis of the course is firmly rooted in effective communication with an audience through the creative development of mood, atmosphere, narrative and graphic depth. Students learn to use animation as an abstract, narrative or commercial media tool within the context of film and television

Kent Institute of Art and Design

Maidstone College
Oakwood Park
Maidstone
Kent ME16 8AG
Tel: 01622 757286
Fax: 01622 621100
email: cjohnson@kiad.ac.uk

BA (Hons) Video with Film

The course aim is to develop students' critical, aesthetic and cultural understanding, with special interests in new ideas within all aspects of production in any genre style. In the first two years, all practical projects, both group and individual, are encouraged to be exploratory and experimental.

Technical skills are learnt through introductory workshops and by hands-on experience across all areas of production (video, film, sound, performance, animation and paper, electronic, and model), and include live multi-camera shoots with dance groups. The final year is self-motivated and authorship is encouraged, either as individuals or through group collaboration.

MA in Visual Communication: New Media Practices

The course sets out to address new creative practices that have developed in the context of new media and technologies. Electronic technologies have transformed the way in which designers and artists relate to traditional media and processes. The interfaces between site-based, screen-based and time-based work have become the point of departure for contemporary forms of creative practice that address the symbiotic relationship between design and art, and the establishment of new parameters for visual communication. Students are encouraged to draw upon their previous experience in formulating a research project that can be explored and extended in the context of contemporary media technologies and production

University of Kent
Rutherford College
Canterbury
Kent CT2 7NX
Tel: 01227 764000
Fax: 01227 827846

BA (Hons) Film Studies
BA (Joint Hons) Film Studies and another subject

Film Studies may be taken as single or joint honours degree.

Year 1. Students must take An Introduction to Narrative Cinema. This involves predominantly the study of American Cinema 1910-1960. Years 2 and 3. All students take Film Theory which considers realism, montage and semiotics. Students taking four or more courses take the Unseen Film Analysis examination in the third year. Students taking five or more courses write an extended essay on a single film in the second year. Options are chosen from: Non-Narrative Cinema; British Cinema; Documentary; Reading the Image; French Film; Sexual Difference; Post-War American Cinema; Fantastic Cinema; Roberto Rossellini; Film Production; and Early Film Form

King Alfred's College Winchester (Affiliated to Southampton University)
School of Community and Performing Arts
Sparkford Road
Winchester SO22 4NR
Tel: 01962 827368
Fax: 01962 827458

BA (Hons) Media and Film Studies

All students study Media and Film with another subject in the first year. In the second and third year, students may either take Media and Film Studies as a Single Honours degree or as a Main, Joint or Minor with another subject on a Combined Honours degree. This course enables students to study media and film, initially as separate and later as integrated academic disciplines. Students may choose from a broad range of theoretical modules which cover: film; television; print media; popular music; and radio. Optional modules in video production and screenwriting are available for single honours and main students only.

BA (Hons) Drama, Theatre and Television

A three-year course that relates theories of contemporary television and drama to practical work in both media. The course looks at both the institutions and the practices of the two media from the perspectives of the psychology and critical ideologies (including women's studies) of the 20th century. The course includes three major television projects in documentary or drama documentary. Students interested in television may apportion two-thirds of their time to this medium. Staff members are active practitioners in the film and television industries. Modular units are available for suitably qualified mature and overseas students.

Kingston University
School of Art and Design History
Kingston-Upon-Thames
Surrey KT1 2QJ
Tel: 020 8547 7112
Website: www.kingston@ac.uk

BA/BA (Hons) Combined Studies: History of Art, Architecture and Design

Five to six year part-time or three year full-time. Optional film strand: three Film Studies modules, each representing one sixth of a full-time student's yearly programme, one third of a part-time student's. Foundation level: concepts of 'Art' cinema. Intermediate level: photographic issues. Advanced level; the study of a selected artist.

School of Three Dimensional Design, Knights Park
Kingston-Upon-Thames
Surrey KT1 2QJ
Tel: 020 8547 7165
Fax: Fax; 020 8547 7365
email: s.edwards@kingston.ac.uk
Website: www.kingston@ac.uk
Sarah Edwards

MA Production Design for Film and Television

One year MA Course in scenic design tailored to the needs of those who wish to enter the industry with the eventual aim of becoming production designers or art directors. The course is constructed as a series of design projects to cover different types of film and television production

School of Humanities
Kingston University, Penrhyn Road
Kingston-Upon-Thames
Surrey KT1 2EE
Tel: 020 8547 2000
Fax: 020 8547 7392

BA (Hons) French Major and Half-field, Full and Part-time

Introduction to French Cinema. Year two on French Cinema. Year four special subject on New Wave Cinema

University of Leicester
Centre for Mass Communication Research
104 Regent Road
Leicester LE1 7LT
Tel: 0116 252 3863
Fax: 0116 252 3874
email: cmcr@le.ac.uk
Website: le.ac.uk/cmcr/

BSc Communications and Society

A three-year social science based undergraduate course. The modules taught cover a wide range of areas including media institutions, research methods in mass communications, film and TV forms and television production. Students are assessed by a combination of continuous assessment and examination

MA Mass Communications

One year taught course studying the organisation and impact of the mass media both nationally and internationally and providing practical training in research methods

MA Mass Communications (by

Distance Learning)
Two year part-time course by distance learning. Organized in 10 modules plus dissertation. Course materials include 60 course units, readers, set books, AV materials. Contributions from a team of international experts. The course covers media theories, history, regulation, media in global context, methodology, media industries, professional practices, audiences, texts and issues of representation. Options include media education, film. Day and weekend schools are voluntary but highly recommended

University of Liverpool
School of Politics and
Communication Studies
Roxby Building
PO Box 147
Liverpool L69 3ZT
Tel: 0151 794 2890
Fax: 0151 794 3948
email: jhallam@liv.ac.uk
Website: www.live.ac.uk/polcomm
Julia Hallam
BA Combined Hons (Social and Environmental Studies)
Contact Julia Hallam,
email: jhallam@live.ac.uk
BA Joint Hons (English and Communication Studies)
Contact: John Corner, email: corner@liv.ac.uk
BA Joint Hons (Politics and Communication Studies)
Contact: Adrian Quinn,
 email: aquinn@liv.ac.uk
Combined Honours (Social and Environmental Studies)
Contact: Kay Richardson,
email: Kay100@liv.ac.uk
In all these programmes, students combine work in the Communication Studies Department with largely non media-related work in other Departments; Communication Studies forms 50 per cent of their programme and offers specialisms in public communication (press, broadcasting and political journalism) screen fictions (film, TV drama, contemporary production and policy issues) and sociolinguistics. No practical component
MA Mass Media and Politics
Contact: Piers Robinson,
email: piersgr@liv.ac.uk
This new and unique programme combines mainstream politics with mass media studies. The core

modules focus on political communication in modern democracies; media and the democratic idea, news management and censorship, political journalism, political campaigning, globalisation of media and electioneering, media and public policy in Britain, Europe and the USA and research methods and issues for media and politics

Liverpool John Moores University
School of Media, Critical and Creative Arts
Dean Walters Building
St James Road
Liverpool L1 7BR
Tel: 0151 231 5052
Website: www.livjm.ac.uk
BA (Hons) Media and Cultural Studies
This is a three-year, full-time or four-year, part-time modular course. In the first year, there are courses in media institutions, media texts, television, film, popular music, photography, journalism and cultural studies. In the second and third years, students may take modules in film studies, television studies, mass communications, photography, as well as courses in cultural studies (for example, popular culture and popular fiction) and ethnography of audiences. The course is not practical or vocational, however, students do have the opportunity of taking a work-experience module in local media and cultural organisations. The course may be taken as a joint honours programme with Screen Studies which does have practical work.
BA (Hons) Media Professional Studies
As an industry-linked degree, this course brings together theoretical and vocational approaches to the study of television and related media. It combines: production; business and management; enterprise; information technology; law; and media theory. The wide-ranging programme aims to meet the demands for multi-skilled graduates in the media production industries. The course is mounted in collaboration with local media companies, notably Mersey Television.
BA (Hons) Screen Studies
In the first year, Screen Studies must be taken with another subject such as Media and Cultural Studies, Theatre

Studies or Imaginative Writing. The course spans the separate but increasingly interwoven histories of film and television. It provides the opportunity to develop a critical understanding of the moving image alongside the acquisition of organisational and practical skills in film and video production. In the first year, there are courses in Film and Television Studies, and Production Practice. In the second and third years, available modules include: Production Practice; Hollywood Cinema; Film and Television Research; Aesthetics of the Moving Image; and Experimental Video. Opportunities also exist for work-based learning on an industrial placement.

London College of Printing & Distributive Trades
Media School
Backhill
Clerkenwell EC1R 5LQ
Tel: 020 7514 6500

(P) MA in Feature Film
Both practical and critical students will be recruited on to this degree. Students will not be able to make a feature film but will make a short and prepare for the development of a feature project. Critical research will be encouraged in terms of the practical criticism of great works of the past and current British cinema, and into strategic business issues, such as finance and distribution. The idea is to develop an intellectual hothouse which encourages the highest artistic standards and a sharp understanding of the politics of the global film industry.
(P) MA in Screenwriting
A two-year, part-time course providing students with the opportunity to create a portfolio of work ranging from short screenplays to feature length projects. The course has a comprehensive range of visiting lecturers including producers, agents and writers.
MA in Documentary Research
This is a two-year, part-time course, targeting industry employees and others who wish to develop documentary research skills.
The aim of this course is to develop research and marketing skills around project proposals in the area of documentary for television and film. Lectures and workshops support project-work in pre-production

research, feasibility testing and marketing of proposals for documentary

London Guildhall University
Sir John Cass Department of Art
133 Whitechapel High Street
London E1 7QA
Tel: 020 7320 1956
Fax: 020 7320 1938
(P) PgCert, PgDip and MA in Audio-Visual Production
The course is based on a commitment to high level film-making across a range of genres including documentary and drama. A core programme of creative research will be complemented by an agreed programme of hands-on independent study, focused on specific film projects and structured via individually negotiated learning agreements. Film-making is essentially a collaborative process and a strong commitment to teamwork will be an integral part of the course. At the same time students will be offered the opportunity to specialise in the key areas of production such as scriptwriting, producing, editing, camera and sound

London Film School
Department F17
24 Shelton Street
London WC2H 9UB
Tel: 020 7836 9642
Fax: 020 7497 3718
email: film.school@lifs.org.uk
Website: www.lifs.org.uk
Ben Gibson, Director
(P) Diploma in Film Making
A two year full-time practical course teaching skills to professional levels. All students work on one or more films each term and are encouraged to interchange unit roles termly to experience different skill areas. Approximately half each term is spent in film making, half in practical instruction, seminars, workshops, tutorials, and script writing. Established for over 40 years, the school is constituted as an independent, non profit-making, educational charity and is a member of NAHEFV and CILECT – respectively the national and international federations of film schools. Graduates include Bill Douglas, Danny Huston, John Irwin, Mike Leigh, Michael Mann and Franc Roddam. The course is accredited by

BECTU and widely recognised by local education authorities for grants. New courses commence each January, April and September

London School of Economics and Political Science
Department of Social Psychology
Media and Communications
Houghton Street
London WC2A 2AE
Tel: 020 7955 7710/7714
Fax: 020 7955 7565
MSc Media and Communications
One year MSc programme (two years part-time) provides an advanced understanding of the development and forms of media systems (eg text, audience, organisation, effects) in Britain and elsewhere. Students take two core courses, one inter-disciplinary theoretical approaches to media and communications, and one research methodology in media and communications. Additionally, students choose from a range of optional courses reflecting social science approaches to media and communications, and complete an original, supervised, research report on a subject of their choice

The Lux Centre

2-4 Hoxton Square
London N1 6NU
Tel: 020 7684 2783
Fax: 020 7684 2222
email: hemanth.rao@lux.org.uk
Website: www.lux.org.uk
Hemanth Rao
The training and education
programme at the Lux Centre aims to
broaden practical and theoretical
understanding of film, video and
emergent media. Lux training
combines artistic and technical
perspectives, taught by tutors
experienced in the arts and industry.
Continually reviewed and updated,
Lux short courses provide affordable
training in a relaxed environment
with maximum hands on experience.
Courses run on a rolling basis, all
year round. Dates and times are listed
on the website the training diary and
the Lux Programme. Alternatively
you can join our mailing list;
specifying which course you are
interested in
Introduction to Digital Video
Camera and Lighting
Super 8 Film-making
16mm Film Production
Directing Performers
Optical Printing
Desktop Video: Adobe Premier
Streaming Media Workshop
Introduction to Digital Video Editing
(AVID)
Final Cut Pro

University of Manchester

Department of Drama
Oxford Road, Manchester M13 9PL
Tel: 0161 275 3347
Fax: 0161 275 3349
MA in Screen Studies
The MA in Screen Studies is a taught
Masters course which capitalises on
expertise in Screen Studies
throughout the Faculty of Arts.
Participating schools include the
School of Music and Drama; the
Department of English and American
Studies (Hollywood Cinema, star
cultures), and the School of Modern
Languages (including French,
German, Italian and Latin American
cinema). Courses are available in all
these areas
MPhil and PhD in Drama (Screen
Studies)
Research by thesis for MPhil and
PhD. Subjects accepted depend on
staff supervision interests but usually
include: Aspects of Silent Film;

Italian, Scandinavian, British and
American Film; British and American
Television and Drama; Documentary
Film; European and American
Cinema History; Women and Film;
Critical Theory; and Representation
of Native Peoples on Film

Manchester Metropolitan University

Department of Communication
Media, Chatham Building
Cavendish Street
Manchester M15 6BR
Tel: 0161 247 1284
Fax: 0161 247 6393
Website: www.mmu.ac.uk
BA (Hons) Film and Media Studies
The course provides an opportunity
to study film, photography and
popular printed media such as
advertisements, posters, comics and
cartoons in social and political
contexts. Historical studies in film,
photography and graphic arts are
balanced by more vocational course
elements. One optional unit focuses
on the conservation of film and
photographic materials, and another
on the history of processes and
techniques in the media. Practical
studio-work in communication
media (including photography,
scriptwriting, and graphic design and
advertising) is a further option. All
students undertake an organised five-
week placement with an arts, media
or broadcasting organisation,
company, public institution or
museum. Where appropriate, course
units draw on firsthand experience of
museums and archives

Middlesex University

Faculty of Art, Design & Performing
Arts
Cat Hill, Barnet
Herts EN4 8HT
Tel: 020 8362 5000
Fax: 020 8362 6339
email: admissions@mdx.ac.uk
BA (Hons and Joint Hons) Film
Studies
Film Studies may be taken as a single
honours degree or as a joint honours
degree with Film Studies as a major
or minor. The course is based on
academic studies in film theory, film
history and film criticism. It is not a
practical course in film-making but
nevertheless provides a fine basis for
those who wish to pursue a career in
the industry. A wide range of
modules includes a core of key

concepts which may be combined
with option modules ranging from
screenwriting and film journalism to
technoculture and film music.
The course is offered on a campus
specialising in fine and applied arts
(such as fashion, jewellery design and
electronic media) and offering a
richly creative environment for visual
studies

Napier University

Department of Photography, Film
and Television
61 Marchmont Road
Edinburgh EH9 1HU
Tel: 0131 466 7321
(P) BA (Hons) Photography, Film
and Television
With option of specialising in Film
and Television production from the
start of the 3rd year. At the end of the
2nd year students take either the still
image stream or the moving image
stream in this four year course.
MPhil/PhD
A 2/3 year research programme with
tutorial support facilitating
opportunities for advanced study in
creative practice in the moving image,
including production of a major film
or multimedia project
Department of Print Media,
Publishing and Communication
Craighouse Road
Edinburgh EH10 5LG
MA in European Film and
Multimedia Development
Tel: 0131 455 5203
The first semester is online and the
second semester is by weekly
attendance. Students are offered a
range of specialised modules in
screenwriting and in project
development in film and the media

National Film and Television School

Beaconsfield Studios
Station Road
Beaconsfield
Bucks HP9 1LG
Tel: 01494 671234
Fax: 01494 674042
email: admin@nftsfilm-tv.ac.uk
Website: www.nftsfilm-tv.ac.uk
Full-time professional training
leading to an NFTS Associateship; it
is expected that the NFTS will offer
an MA in most Diploma Courses
from January 2001. The 2-year
Diploma Course develops creative
and technical skills in people with
some experience while the one-year,

project-based Advanced Programme is designed for those with substantial experience in the media or a related field. Both Diploma and Advanced students train in one of the following specialisations: producing, screenwriting, animation, documentary or fiction direction, screen design, cinematography, editing, sound, screen music and television. In most departments, shorlisted applicants take part in a short course prior to final selection. In addition, the National Short Course Training Programme runs a continuous programme of short course for freelancers, while the Finishing School, a joint venture between the NFTS and the Lux Centre, in Shoreditch, offers industry-accredited training in digital post-production. The NFTS is funded by a partnership of Government and the screen industries. Its graduates occupy leading roles in all aspects of film, television and new media

University of Newcastle upon Tyne

Centre for Research into Film
Newcastle upon Tyne NE1 7RU
Tel: 0191 222 7492
Fax: 0191 222 5442
email: p.p.powrie@ncl.ac.uk
Website: www.ncl.ac.uk/ncrif
Diploma/MA in Film Studies
One year full-time; two year part-time course. Obligatory research training and introduction to the study of film, followed by 4 from 19 day-time and evening options, although not all are taught in every year: Almodóvar, The Biblical Epic, British Cinema 1930s-1950s, British Cinema 1960s-1990s, Carmen Adaptations, Class & Sex in British Cinema, Gender in the Hollywood Action Film, Film Programming and Marketing, Les Films de Jean-Jacques Beineix, Financial Structures of the Industry, French Cinema 1980s-1990s, Hollywood Film Noir, the Hollywood Musical, Lubitsch, New Zealand Cinema, Spanish Cinema 1960s-1970s, Spanish Cinema 1980s-1990s, Television Comedy, Westerns: The Evolution of the Hero. Dissertation required for the MA
MLitt in Film Studies
Research-based course tailor-made for individual students. Three/four essays followed by a dissertation on negotiated topic in British, French, Hollywood, or Spanish cinemas.

PhD in Film Studies
Supervision offered in British, French, Hollywood, and Spanish cinemas. for current and suggested postgraduate projects
Department of French Studies
Newcastle upon Tyne NE1 7RU
Tel: 0191 222 7441
Fax: 0191 222 5442
Keith Reader
BA (Hons) French, French/Spanish, French/German
Optional modules in film studies. Stage 1: introduction to the study of film. Stage 2: introduction to film theory

University of North London

School of Literary and Media Studies
116-220 Holloway Road
London N7 8DB
Tel: 020 7753 5111

BA (Hons) Film Studies
BA (Hons) Humanities
A three or four-year, full-time course (four years with a language) or a part-time course, normally over six years.Film Studies may be taken as a single, major, joint or minor with one of thirteen other subjects within BA (Hons) Humanities. Preliminary-level units consist of: An Introduction to Film Studies, and to National Cinemas; Authorship; Readership; Melodrama; and Photographic Image.
Advanced level study includes: Questions of Visual Pleasure; Realism; The Film Industry; Questions of Third Cinema; Genre; Feminism and Sexuality; Male Objectification and Representation of AIDS, as these relate to film. Additionally, there is an option concerned with Television Drama, and another offering experience in small-group video production. The final-year project (double unit) may be submitted on video

Northern Media School

The Workstation
15 Paternoster Row
Sheffield S1 2BX
Tel: 0114 272 0994
Fax: 0114 275 6816
(P) PgDip Broadcast Journalism
Main focus is on practical work. Much of the teaching is conducted through workshops and practical exercises supplemented by seminars and lectures
(P) PgDip and MA in Screenwriting (Fiction)

Intensive practical course covering fiction scriptwriting for film and television

Northern School of Film and Television

Leeds Metropolitan University
2 Queen Square
Leeds LS2 8AF
Tel: 0113 283 1900
Fax: 0113 283 1901
email: nsftv@lmu.ac.uk
Website: www.lmu.ac.uk/
This is run by Leeds Metropolitan University, with the support of Yorkshire Television, providing postgraduate level professional training in practical film production
(P) MA/PgD Scriptwriting for Film and TV (Fiction)
An intensive practical course running from February, one year full-time, and one year part-time (off site). Staffed largely by working professional writers, it covers the various forms of fiction scriptwriting for film and television – short film, feature film, television drama, soap opera, series etc. The course has a strong emphasis on professional presentation, and aims to help graduates to set up a credible freelance practice. Work consists of a short film script, a 30 minute script, a 60 minute script proposal and a full length feature script or television equivalent.
(P) PgD Film Production (Fiction)
An intensive one year practical course running from October to October. Students are admitted into specialist areas: Direction (six students per year), Production (six), Camera (three), Art-Direction (six), Editing (three) and Sound (three). Students work in teams to produce six short films, in two batches of three. The resulting films may be broadcast on Yorkshire Television, which provide the base production funding and some facilities. Scripts are normally drawn from the product of the Scriptwriting Course and the emphasis is on team working and joint creativity under pressure. It is not a course for 'auteur' film makers. There is also a theoretical studies component
(P) MA Film Production (Fiction)
Part-time course. Normally taken up by students who have completed the Postgraduate Diploma (see above), the MA is available via several options: 1) a 10,000 word

dissertation; 2) 2 x 5,000 word extended essays; 3) exchange placement with one of NSFTV's exchange partners (Poland, Germany, Holland)

University of Northumbria at Newcastle
Faculty of Art & Design
Squires Building
Sandyford Road
Newcastle upon Tyne NE1 8ST
Tel: 0191 227 4935
Fax: 0191 227 3632
BA and BA (Hons) History of Modern Art, Design and Film
This course provides the opportunity to study film with an increasing degree of specialisation throughout the three years. Film topics include: Year 1. The Institution of Cinema; Classical Hollywood Narrative; The Film Industry; and Genre and Stars. Year 2. Melodrama; Wartime and Post-War British Cinema; Hitchcock and Authorship; and Realism and Anti-Realism. Year 3. Arts Cinema; The Horror Film; Gender and Film; and Film Programming and Marketing.
BA (Hons) English and Film
This is a modular course in which students spend approximately half their time studying film-related modules
BA (Hons) Media Production
Practical three year course with fully integrated theoretical and critical components in which students are offered the opportunity to specialise in individual programmes of work.
BA (Hons) History of Modern Art, Design and Film
Offered as a three year full-time course. Film Studies is given equal weighting with painting and design in the first year. In the second year up to 60 per cent of a student's time can be devoted to Film Studies, with this rising to nearly 100 per cent in the third year
MPhil
There are possibilities for research degrees in either film theory or practice

Nottingham Trent School of Art and Design
The Nottingham Trent University
Burton Street
Nottingham NG1 4BU
Tel: 0115 848 4850
Fax: 0115 848 4086
BA (Hons) Design for Television
This specialist programme concentrates on Production Design with an emphasis on Design for Television, involving a wide range of creative, communicative and intellectual skills. The industry-modelled projects develop professional skill sets and awareness of space, form, texture, colour and light as a means of communicating information and creating atmosphere. Students are challenged to produce professional output to assist them into the industrial workplace. The evolution and future of industrial practice is complemented by a comprehensive understanding of the media industry. The programme is practically based in a design studio environment.

Nova Camcorder School
11a Winholme
Armthorpe
Doncaster DN3 3AF
Tel: 01302 833422
Fax: 08701 257917
email: ncs@novaonline.co.uk
Website: www.novaonline.co.uk/ncs
Practical evening course for camcorder beginners
A 10 week course, one night a week

running throughout the year, for people who want to learn how to use their camcorders properly. The course explains all the features and functions of a camcorder before moving onto basic film-making techniques and home editing and titling. The course is specifically designed for beginners, and participants receive a worksheet every week which summarises the topics covered

Panico London Ltd

PO Box 19054
London N7 0ZB
Tel: 020 7485 3533
Fax: 020 7485 3533
email: panico@panicofilms.com
Website: www.panicofilms.com
Panico offers a range of weekend courses, which provide training and practical experience with tutors who are well known in the British Film Industry.
Panico courses include:
Foundation Course – Designed to give students an overall view and practical experience of the film-making process. It is spread over six days either six Saturdays or six Sundays. The aim of the course is to give students enough knowledge and practical experience to be able to undertake their own productions. The course also gives students an insight into the working conditions, practices and opportunities in the British Film Industry. Students gain experience working in both video and film formats, and get practical experience in drama and documentary film.
Panico also runs a number of advanced courses for individuals who already have some experience of film making

Plymouth College of Art and Design

School of Media and Photography
Tavistock Place
Plymouth
Devon PL4 8AT
Tel: 01752 203434
Fax: 01752 203444
B/TEC HND Media Production
(in partnership with the University of Plymouth). A two year modular course with pathways in film, video, animation and electronic imaging. All areas of film, video and television production are covered and the course is well supported by visiting

lecturers and workshops. Strong links with the industry have been developed and work based experience forms an important part of the course. The course has BKSTS accreditation. Opportunities exist through the ERASMUS programme to undertake a programme of exchange with European universities or polytechnics during the course. In addition suitably qualified students can progress to third level modules for the award of a BA (Hons) PhotoMedia
Advanced Diploma Photography, Film and Television leading to the BIPP Professional Qualifying Exam
A one year course post HND and postgraduate. The photography, film and television option allows students to plan their own line of study, including practical work, dissertation and an extended period of work based experience. Students from both courses have had considerable success in film and video scholarships and competitions. Students on both courses have the opportunity for three month work placements in the media industry in Europe
(P) NCFE Foundation in Lens Based Media
A one year full time foundation course for those wishing to progress to Higher Education in one of the many exciting areas of lens based media. This practical course covers: photography, video, electronic imaging, multi-imaging and contextual studies. The course aims to help the student develop a portfolio which shows how the student has integrated technical skills with creative concepts and critical analysis. (This course may also be studied part time over two academic years)
National Diploma Programmes
ND Photography; ND MultiMedia, ND Media Studies

University of Portsmouth

Department of Design
Lion Gate Building, Lion Terrace
Portsmouth PO1 3HF
Tel: 01705 843805
Fax: 01705 843808
email: lingardm@env2.enf.port.ac.uk
BA (Hons) Art, Design and Media
Three year unitised programme has six specialist pathways. All are structured around historical, cultural and theoretical analysis which form an important part of the degree.

Student placements in Europe and the UK and outside projects maintain the degree's links with industry and art practice.
Media Arts - Moving Image Strand
In the first and second years, students undertake briefs around personal and cultural identity, gender, media arts practice, documentary as intervention etc. Students work in video, sound, multimedia and photography. In the third year students work on self-directed projects
Media Arts - Photography Strand
Encourages collabarative work with moving image and sound artists
Communication Design
Design for television, video graphics and multimedia are central areas of concern
History and Cultural Theory
Aim to produce graduates with particular skills in research and communication
School of Social and Historical Studies, Milldam
Burnaby Road
Portsmouth PO1 3AS
Tel: 01705 876543
Fax: 01705 842174
BA (Hons) Cultural Studies
Year 3: options on British Cinema 1933-70, British television Drama, Avant-Garde Films and Feminism

Ravensbourne College of Design & Communication

Walden Road
Chislehurst
Kent BR7 5SN
Tel: 020 8289 4900
Fax: 020 8325 8320
email: info@rave.ac.uk
Website: www.rave.ac.uk
(P) HND Broadcast Post Production
BA (Hons) Content Creation for Broadcasting and New Media
Foundation Degree in Broadcasting and Digital Technology (or upon completion of extra year leading to)
BSc (Hons) Broadcast Technology or BA (Hons) Broadcast Production
The University Sector College, a National Centre of Broadcasting Excellence, is the preferred supplier of education and training to the independent television companies. The £6 million facility is amongst the best in Europe. Equipment ranges from Hitachi studio cameras, Beta SP and DV-cam VTRs. Post-production systems include Avid Symphony and Media Composer, Quantel Editbox, Lightworks and Discreet's Smoke,

Flame and Frost. Each year culminates in 'Ravensbourne On Air' where students turn broadcasting into a fully functional TV station. Work placements have included: The Bill, Big Brother, Wimbledon, BBC Drama and LWT and have helped result in over 90 per cent of students gaining employment in their first 3 months of graduation

University of Reading
Department of Film and Drama
Bulmershe Court
Woodlands Ave
Reading RG6 IHY
Tel: 0118 931 8878
Fax: 0118 931 8873
email: e.a.silvester@reading.ac.uk
Website: www.reg.ac.uk/FD
Jim Hillier, Head Film& Drama
(P) BA Film and Drama (Single Subject)
After the first two terms in which three subjects are studied (two being in film and drama), students work wholly in film and drama. The course is critical but with significant practical elements which are designed to extend critical understanding. It does not provide professional training
BA Film and Drama (Combined Subject) with English, German, Italian, History of Art
Students in general share the same teaching as Single Subject students but do not do any practical work
MA Film Studies, MA Theatre Studies, MA Film and Theatre Studies
One year taught courses specialising in Film or Theatre or combining study of the two, incorporating research methodologies and the possibility of practical work
MPhil and PhD
Research applications for MPhil and PhD degrees are invited in areas of cinema, television and theatre of the nineteenth century and after
Department of English
Whiteknights
Reading RG6 6AA
Tel: 0118 931 8361
Fax: 0118 931 6561
email: English@reading.ac.uk
Website: www.reading.ac.uk/english/
Dr M.K. Davies
BA (Hons) English
Second year optional course on film, television and literature. Third year optional course in TV Crime Drama
PhD

Research can be supervised on the history of the BBC and other mass media topics
Department of French Studies
Whiteknights
Reading RG6 6AA
Fax: 0118 931 8122
BA (Hons) French
Four-year French degree with courses in film.
Year 1 (one half-term). Introductory course with detailed study of one film.
Year 2 (one half-term module) The Individual and War in French Cinema
Year 2 (one half-term module) Quebec Cinema: Literature in Film
Year 4 (two-term option). French Cinema from the 1920s to the present, with special emphasis on the 30s, 40s and the New Wave. It includes introductory work on the principle of film study. The films are examined using a variety of critical disciplines: psychoanalysis, semiotics, sociology, etc. Also available to students combining French with certain other subjects.
Year 4 (two-term option). French-Canadian Cinema. The course introduces students to the diversity of French-Canadian cinema and its historical, socio-political and cultural underpinnings
Department of German Studies, University of Reading
Whiteknights
Reading RG6 6AA
Tel: 0118 931 8332
Fax: 0118 931 8333
email: j.e.sandford@reading.ac.uk
Website: www.rdg.ac.uk/german
Prof John. Sandford
BA (Hons) German
Two-term Finals option: The German Cinema. Course covers German cinema from the 1920s to the present, with special emphasis on the Weimar Republic, the Third Reich, the 'New German Cinema', and GDR cinema
Department of Italian Studies
Whiteknights
Reading RG6 2AA
Tel: (0118) 931 8402
Fax: (0118) 931 6797
email: c.g.wagstaff@reading.ac.uk
Website: www.reading.ac.uk
Chris Wagstaff
BA (Hons) Italian/French and Italian with Film Studies
First year introductory course: Post-War Italian Cinema (one half-term). Second year course: Italian Cinema (three terms). Final year course:

Italian Cinema in its European and American context (two terms). Dissertation on an aspect of Italian cinema. These courses available to students reading other subjects in the Faculty.
MA Italian Cinema
One year full-time or two year part-time course on Italian cinema: compulsory theory course, options on film and literature, Bertolucci, Italian industry and genre – the Spaghetti Western.
MPhil and PhD
Research can be supervised on Italian cinema for degree by thesis

College of Ripon and York St John
Faculty of Creative and Performing Arts
Lord Mayor's Walk
York 7EX
Tel: 01904 616672
Fax: 01904 616931
email: r.edgar@ucrysj.ac.uk
Website: www.ucrysj.ac.uk/academic/tftv/default.htm
Robert Edgar-Hunt
(P) BA (Hons) Theatre, Film and Television
This degree programme embraces theoretical and practical aspects of theatre, film and television. 'Core' theories and concepts are taught alongside practical, production modules and all activity is focussed on the development of both intellectual and practical skills. Emphasis is placed upon the interrelationship of the three areas alongside theories and skills specific to each. Workshops and specialist modules allow a focus of interests and skills, but students are expected to engage with all three areas of the degree. There are opportunities to study abroad in Europe or North America, and to undertake work placements and internships. There are excellent facilities for performance activity and video production

University of Surrey Roehampton
Faculty of Arts and Humanities
Digby Stuart College
Roehampton Lane
London SW15 5PU
Tel: 020 8392 3230
Fax: 020 8392 3289
email: j.ridgman@roehampton.ac.uk
BA Film and Television Studies
A three year modular degree

programme, which may be combined with a variety of other subjects. Several core courses are available (Genre and Gender, Issues of Authorship, Hollywood, British Television Drama, French National Cinema etc) to which may be added selected topic modules. The course includes up to 40 per cent practical work in television and video, moving from principles of single camera production in year one to sustained, independent project work in the final year

University of Salford
School of Media, Music and Performance
Adelphi, Peru Street
Salford, Manchester M3 6EQ
Tel: 0161 295 6026
Fax: 0161 295 6023
Website: www.salford.ac.uk

(P) HND in Media Performance
Full-time, 2 years
(P) HND in Media Production
Full-time, 2 years
(P) HND in Physical Theatre and Dance
Full-time, 2 years
HND in Audio and Video Systems
Full-time and Part-time, 2 years
(P) HND in Professional Sound and Video Technology
Full-time, 2 years

University of Sheffield
Department of English Literature
Shearwood Mount
Shearwood Road
Sheffield S10 2TD
Tel: 0114 222 8480
Fax: 0114 282 8481
BA (Hons) English Literature
Students may study several Special Subjects in Film in their second and third years, and may take a Hollywood course in the first year

Sheffield Hallam University
Communications Subject Group
School of Cultural Studies
36 Collegiate Crescent
Sheffield S10 2BP
Tel: 0114 255 5555
Fax: 0114 253 2344
(P) BA (Hons) Fine Art (Time-Based Art)
Within the Fine Art degree, students are able to undertake major study in the Time-Based Art programme which covers the new media that have made a significant impact on the world of fine art: film, photography, video, sound, performance art, and

digital imaging. Students on the programme are able to specialise in any one of the areas after initial work in each medium.
Film productions can range from short 8mm films, through 16mm documentaries to features; there are excellent professional facilities for shooting, processing, editing, recording and dubbing 16mm films, and good animation equipment. The video and sound section is primarily concerned with enabling students to express and develop their personal interests. There are well-equipped video studios, with studio and portable cameras using SVHS, MII and D3 formats. There are many off-line two and three-machine edit suites in the school, including SVHS, Premiere, Avids and a broadcast quality digital D3 edit suite. There is an increasing role for digital imaging via a suite of Apple Macs. The emphasis is not only on single screen work, but also on installation and the relationship to live and photographic work, within a Fine Art context.
School of Cultural Studies
Psalter Lane
Sheffield S11 8UZ
Tel: 0114 253 2601 /272 0911
Film and Media Studies Programme
BA (Hons) Film Studies
BA (Hons) Media Studies
The Film and Media Studies Programme consists of two degree routes. The courses provide opportunities for the study of film and a range of media (including television, radio and journalism) from a variety of perspectives including historical development, social, political and economic contexts, and the artistic and aesthetic dimensions of film and media. The courses also provide a grounding in basic media production skills with units in film, video etc and scriptwriting
BA (Hons) History of Art, Design and Film
Film studies is a major component of this course. Year 1: introduction to film analysis and history. Year 2: special study on Hollywood. Year 3: critical and theoretical studies in Art, Design and Film and Contemporary Film Theory and Practice.
MA Film Studies
Two year part-time course; two evenings per week, plus dissertation to be written over two terms in a third year. Main areas of study:

Problems of Method; The Classical Narrative Tradition; British Cinema 1927-45; Hollywood and Popular culture
BA (Hons) Fine Art (Combined and Media Arts)
After initial work with a range of media, students can specialise in film and/or video. Film productions range from short 8mm films to 16mm documentaries or widescreen features, to small 35mm productions

South Bank University
Education, Politics and Social Science
103 Borough Road
London SE1 1AA
Tel: 020 7928 8989
Fax: 020 7815 8273
email: registry@sbu.ac.uk
BSc (Hons) Media and Society
Three year full time course. Two thirds critical studies, one third practical work. This course combines units assessing the social and political significance of the mass media, together with units introducing practical production skills. Critically, the course grows from studies of the media in the Britain during year one, to studies of European and global media in years tow and three. Other units also address the understanding of media audiences, news forms and media law. Individual research leads to the completion of a disserattion thesis in year three. Practically, the course develops skills in audio, radio, video and multimedia production. These skills are then employed by students in the creation of their own final year projects
BSc (Combined Hons) Media Studies
The course will give students an understanding of how mass media industries create images and meanings in British, European and international contexts; and will introduce them to some of the key issues facing the media, such as the roles of the news, audiences, public policy and law. The course does not include the practical skills of media production. The course can be combined with a variety of other subjects including Languages, History and Music

South Kent College
Creative Arts
Maison Dieu Road
Dover CT16 1DH
Tel: 01304 244355
Fax: 01304 244301
email: admissions@southkent.ac.uk

Website: www.southkent.ac.uk
Freddie Gaffney
(P) B/TEC National Diploma Media Studies (Moving Image and Information Design)
Two year full-time course covering video, 16mm film, print/DTP, digital photography and radio. Students complete advertising, drama, news and documentary projects closely linked to community groups. The course is modular and work experience is offered

South Thames College
Department of Design and Media
Wandsworth High Street
London SW18 2PP
Tel: 020 8918 7043
(P) AVCE in Media: Communication and Production
Full-time, 2 years
16-18 year-olds, with proven interest in media industry or progression to university.
(P) GNVQ in Media: Communication and Production (Intermediate)
Full-time, 1 year
16-18 year-old. Beginners in a media career.
(P) HNC in Media Production (16mm Film Pathway)
Part-time, 36 weeks
(P) HNC in Media Production (Moving Image Pathway - Television and Video)
Part-time, 1 year
Those wanting a formal qualification in media production.

(P) HNC in Multimedia
Part-time, 36 weeks
(P) HNC in Writing and Journalism
Part-time, 1 year
(P) National Certificate in Media Production (Audio)
National Certificate in Media Production (Moving Image Pathway - Television and Video)
Full-time, 1 year
National Certificate in Media Production (Moving Image Pathway - 16mm Film)
Full-time, 1 year

University of Southampton
Research and Graduate School of Education
Faculty of Educational Studies
Southampton
Hants SO9 5NH
Tel: 01703 593387
Fax: 01703 593556

BA (Hons) English and Film Studies
The core units in the first year are followed by a wide choice of units in the second and third years including units in European Film. There are varied learning and assessment styles with an emphasis on essay-work. The course closely integrates English and Film with shared theoretical approaches. Specialisation is possible through double units and a dissertation.The emphasis of the course is on the theoretical study of film rather than the practical side of film-making.
BA (Hons) Film Studies and a Modern Language
Film may be combined with French, German or Spanish. The course includes: a study of Hollywood Cinema; a grounding in European Film History; a solid foundation in Film Theory and critical debates; an opportunity to focus, through the option units, on a students particular area of interest. Students will develop their practical language skills to a high level of proficiency, particularly in relation to text handling and oral communication; and will spend their third year in a country where French, German or Spanish is spoken, either working as a language assistant in a school, studying in a university, or on a placement in an approved workplace.
School of Research & Graduate Studies, Highfield
Southampton
Hants SO17 1BJ
Tel: 023 80 593406/592248
Fax: 023 80 593288/595437
email: srgs@soton.ac.uk
Website: www.soton.ac.uk/~srgs
Pam Cook, MA Coordinatior
MA Film Studies
The course aims to equip students with the capacity to engage intellectually with significant developments in film theory and history, together with the skills required to undertake contextual and textual analysis of films and critical writing. The weight given to European cinemas, including British cinema, and to transnational perspectives, is a unique feature, and Hollywood and American independent cinema represent core elements. Tutors include Tim Bergfelder, Caroline Blinder, Pam Cook, Deniz Göktürk, Sylvie Lindeperg, Bill Marshall, Lucy Mazdon, David Vilaseca and Linda Ruth Williams

Staffordshire University
School of Art & Design
College Road
Stoke on Trent ST4 2DE
Tel: 01782 294565
Fax: 01782 294873
email: j.holden@staffs.ac.uk
John Holden
(P) BA(Hons) Design (Media Production)
Media Production is a route within a broad-based modular design programme. The aim is for graduates to be confident, articulate communicators with minds flexible enough to meet the creative and technical challenges of a rapidly changing world. Students experience a range of media (video, animation and sound) and use these to explore, for example, storytelling, drama, documentary, and educational, persuasive and factual topics. Opportunities are available to work formally for real clients, and to explore a variety of personal directions. After graduation students should be equipped to enter the media labour-market directly or to proceed to postgraduate study. The aim is to produce students who can communicate effectively and creatively using sound and vision. Full-time , 3 year course with 80 per cent practical work

University of Stirling
Film and Media Studies
Stirling FK9 4LA
Tel: 01786 467520
Fax: 01786 466855
email: stirling.media@stir.ac.uk
Website: www.fms.stir.ac.uk
Dr Raymond Boyle
BA (Hons) Film and Media Studies (Single and Joint Hons)
Four year degree in the theory and analysis of all the principal media. All students take courses in the theories of mass communication and in cultural theories, as well as problems of textual analysis and then select from a range of options, including practical courses in the problems of news reporting in radio and television and in television documentary. As a joint honours degree Film and Media Studies can be combined with a variety of other subjects
BA General Degree
Students can build a component of their degree in film and media studies ranging from as much as eight units

(approximately 50 per cent of their degree) if they take a major in the subject, down to as little as three if they wish merely to complete a Part 1 major. For the most part students follow the same units as do Film and Media Studies Honours students

MSc/Diploma Media Management
One year full-time programme consisting of two taught terms (Sept-May) followed by a dissertation (May-Aug). Internationally oriented and comparative in approach, the course offers media practitioners a wider analytical perspective on the key issues affecting their work and offers graduates a rigorous foundation for a career in the media industry. Areas covered include media policy and regulation, media economics, management and marketing, analytical methods and case studies and advanced media theory

MLitt and PhD
The specialist fields of the Stirling Media Research Institute: Media and National/Cultural identity; political communication and the sociology of journalism; screen interpretation; media management and media policy; public relations. Further details of the Institute's work are obtainable on request

MSc/Diploma Public Relations
Available in full time (12 months) and online learning (30 months) formats. The degree develops the key analytical and practical skills for a career in Public Relations. Areas covered incllude; Public Relations; management and organisational studies; research and evaluation; media and communication studies; marketing and political communication

MSc/Diploma in Media Management by Online Learning (PT)
Studies entirely on the web, this course is designed for media practitioners who want a broader analytical understanding of the industry

MSc/Diploma in Creative and Cultural Industries by Online Learning (PT)
This new masters programme addresses the increasing academic and policy interest in the cultural industries. Taught via the Internet, the programme is designed to provide a theoretical and case-study based foundation in the political economy of the cultural industries

MSc/Diploma in Media, Sport and Promotional Industries by Online Learning
The programme addresses the growing interest in the media sport industries, covering issues of media rights, sports PR and the business of sport

MSc/Diploma in Media Research
A comprehensive postgraduate training and education in media research. On completion there is a possibility of registering for a PhD

University of Sunderland
School of Arts, Design and Media
Ashburne House
Backhouse Park
Ryhope Road
Sunderland SR2 7EF
Tel: 0191 515 2125
Fax: 0191 515 2132
Website: www.sunderland.ac.uk

(P) BA (Hons) Photography, Video and Digital Imaging
This is a new degree programme which amalgamates three important areas within a creative and fine art context. The programme is concerned with the individual creative and intellectual development of students in all three subject areas, producing multi-skilled and creative practitioners who can see the boundaries of the still, moving and interactive image. An extensive combination of modules is offered, providing students with a flexible package, which by the time they reach the third year can develop into specialisms in one or all three areas.

BA and BSc (Hons) Media Studies and another subject
Media Studies covers the study of social, historical and artistic aspects of the mass media and popular culture, and the development of optional practical skills in a range of media. Students study a theoretical core in media, cultural and film studies, with options in theoretical and practical areas of radio and video production, and journalism.

(P) BA (Hons) Electronic Media Design
This is a modular programme which combines conventional design skills and creativity with cutting-edge technology. Students produce digital design solutions for screen-based applications such as multimedia and web design, as well as conventional print and other forms of graphic publications.

BA (Hons) Film and Media Studies
This programme is structured around modules in film studies, media studies and cultural studies. This theoretical base is complemented by practical and studio-based modules across a range of media (photography, print, radio and video).

(P) BA (Hons) Media Production (Television and Radio)
Structured around core modules in media studies and media production, this programme allows students to study and practice radio and television production alongside theoretical subjects. Students may study both television and radio or they may choose to specialise after the first year.
School of Arts, Design and Media
Forster Building
Chester Road
Sunderland SR1 3SD
Tel: 0191 515 3347
Fax: 0191 515 2178

BA and BA (Hons) Communication, Cultural and Media Studies
The course is based on media and cultural studies, including the study of language. Core study may be supplemented by options in sociology and psychology, and media practice and production modules, including radio, television and print journalism.
Engineering and Technology
Information Centre
St Peter's Campus
St Peter's Way
Sunderland SR6 0DD
Tel: 0191 515 2758
Fax: 0191 515 2703

(P) BSc (Hons) Interactive Media
This programme is a diverse mix of art and technology. It will give students the graphic design skills to produce visually impressive images and the technological skills to complement this with sound, moving images, intelligence and interactivity

Surrey Institute of Art and Design
Faculty of Arts and Media
Falkner Road, The Hart
Farnham, Surrey GU9 7DS
Tel: 01252 722441
Fax: 01252 732213

(P) BA (Hons) Film and Video
The college offers two pathways through the programme: Film and Video Production; and Broadcast and New Media Practices. Both pathways

offer the same degree award and are delivered through the same structure. Film and Video Production focuses on traditional film and video-making, while Broadcast and New Media offers a more experimental approach to new media technologies. The course is designed to provide students with a thorough grounding in all aspects of film and video production, and the history and theory of the media. It aims to promote an engagement with social issues as well as experimentation through critical practice

University of Sussex

School of Cultural and Community Studies
Media Studies Co-Ordinator
Essex House, Falmer
Brighton BN1 9RQ
Tel: 01273 872574
Fax: 01273 678644
email: media@sussex.ac.uk
Website: www.sussex.ac.uk/units/media-studies/
BA Media Studies
The degree course in Media Studies enables students to develop a critical understanding of the press, cinema, radio, television, new information technologies and of the particular character of media communications. The Major in Media Studies is taught in two Schools of Studies – Cultural and Community Studies (CCS) and European Studies (EURO): different School Courses accompany it according to the School. The course in EURO also involves study of a modern European language and an additional year abroad in Europe
BA English and Media Studies
BA Music and Media Studies
A three year full-time degree course which includes analysis of television, film and other media, together with some opportunity to be involved in practical television, video and radio production
MA in Media Studies
The MA comprises a two-term core course in media theory and research which students study the conceptual, methodological and policy related issues emerging from the study of the media. In addition, students choose, in each of the first two terms, an optional course from: European Media in Transition; Media Technology and Everyday Life; Media Audiences; The Political Economy of the New Communications Media;

Promotional Culture; Queering Popular Culture; Sexual Difference; Theories of Representation; Memories of the Holocaust
MA in Digital Media
The course shares a core course, Media Theory and Research, with the MA in Media Studies. In addition, students take two dedicated courses: The Political Economy of the New Communications Media, and Theory and Practice of Interactive Multimedia. After two terms students either complete an academic dissertation, or undertake an industry placement and a multimedia project

Thames Valley University, London

London College of Music and Media
St Mary's Road
Ealing
London W5 5RF
Tel: 020 8231 2304
Fax: 020 8231 2656
email: enquiries@elgar.tvu.ac.uk
Website: www.elgar.tvu.ac.uk
Carla Willis-Smith
(P) BA (Combined Hons) Digital Arts with another subject
A Digital Arts major can be combined with a range of minor pathways including: Advertising, Multimedia Computing; Music; Photography; Sound and Music Recording and Video Production
BTEC Higher National Diploma and BSc in Media Technology
This course enables students to develop creative, technical, analytical and evaluative skills using a broad range of audio and visual media and their associated technology for application within the creative, cultural, leisure and business industries
MA in Film and the Moving Image
This three-year , full or part-time course comprises the study of: Film Theory; Cinemas of Places and Peoples (national and ethnic cinemas) Genres; and Exhibition and Audiences.
(P) MA in Digital Arts
This one-year, full-time or two-year, part-time programme is designed to extend the existing skills of those currently working within the creative and visual industries

Trinity and All Saints College

(A College of the University of Leeds)

Brownberrie Lane, Horsforth
Leeds LS18 5HD
Tel: 0113 283 7100
Fax: 0113 283 7200
email: M_hampton@tasc.ac.uk
Website: www.tasc.ac.uk
Margaret Hampton
Postgraduate Diploma/MA in Broadcast, Radio or Print Journalism
These full-time accredited courses are designed to provide trainees with the practical skills required for radio and television, radio or print journalism. The journalism programme runs from the end of January to the end of November and includes a minimum of four weeks attachment at a news organisation

University of Ulster at Belfast

School of Design & Communication
Faculty of Art and Design
York Street
Belfast BT15 1ED
Tel: 01232 328515
Fax: 01232 321048
(P) DipHE/BA (Hons) Visual Communication
Practical and theoretical film/video/media studies available to all students plus a specialist pathway, Screen Based Imaging (SBI) which includes Video production, Animation and Multimedia Design
DipHE/BA (Hons) Combined Studies
Students choose from modules across all courses and many specialise in a combination of Visual/Communication SBI and Fine Art Video plus media studies theory modules
School of Fine and Applied Arts
DIPHE/BA Hons Fine and Applied Arts
Students specialising in the Fine Art pathway may specialise in video from year two

University of Ulster at Coleraine

School of Media and Performing Arts, Coleraine
Co Londonderry
Northern Ireland BT52 1SA
Tel: 02870 324196
Fax: 02870 324964
Website: www.ulst.ac.uk
Dan Fleming
(P) BA (Hons) Media Studies
Three year course integrating theoretical, critical and practical approaches to film, television,

photography, radio, the press and the new technologies. Important practical component

MA Media Studies

A one-year full-time course designed to provide an opportunity to study the mass media (especially film, television, the press and the new technologies) in an international context. Students will also be provided with opportunities for undertaking media practice (in video, radio, photography and practical journalism). MA is awarded 40 per cent on coursework, 60 per cent on dissertation (which may incorporate a production element)

MPhil and PhD

Students are accepted for MPhil and PhD by thesis. Particular expertise is offered in the area of the media and Ireland, although supervision is provided in most areas of Media Studies

University of Wales College, Newport

University Information Centre
Caerleon Campus
PO Box 101
Newport NP6 1YH
Tel: 01633 432432
Fax: 01633 432850
email: uic@newport.ac.uk
Website: www.newport.ac.uk

BA (Hons) Film and Video

The course is intended for students wishing to explore the moving image in the broadest possible sense as an expressive and dynamic medium. It provides them with a programme of work designed to support and stimulate their personal development as creative and aware practitioners of film, regardless of their ultimate ambition. The practice of film is studied in a wider culture and intellectual context and students are encouraged to be analytical and critical. Their study acknowledges existing conventions in dominant cinema but seeks to extend them through experimentation and exploration

BA (Hons) Animation

Intended for students wishing to use animation as part of a wider personal practice, as well as becoming professional animators working in independent production, advertising and design. The course is designed to develop students imaginations and ideas to explore and extend their animation technique. Therefore it is

presented in a cultural context which promotes critical debate and rigorous analysis in terms of representation and expression. In Year 3 students develop their own programme for the production of major pieces of animation on high quality production equipment to broadcast standards

BA (Hons) Media and Visual Culture

At a time when our culture seems dominated as never before by the presence of media systems and images, this stimulating programme critically examines issues relating to media and visual culture. Specialist courses in the theory and history of film, photography design and contemporary art complement the central study of media culture. Practical options in subjects such as film, photography and new media can be selected, leading to major work involving practice in the final year.

MA Film

This practical MA programme will offer an opportunity to: complete a short broadcast standard film explore and challenge the notions of the cinematic subject and language explore developing forms and changing technologies
The course will include:

teaching through group and individual tutorials
close links with the film and television industry and media agencies in Wales
visiting masterclasses and facilities made available in professional production houses . The discursive and practical work on a short film wil be in one of the following areas; Fiction, Faction, Animation, Non-genre/experimental. Acceptance of the course will be based on interview including: the submission of a treatment of a proposed film to be made during the course, the screening of a previous film, some fees/production bursaries could be available.

Warrington Collegiate Institute

Faculty of Higher Education
(Affiliated to the University of Manchester)
Media and Performing Arts
Padgate Campus
Crab Lane WA2 0DB
Tel: 01925 494205
Fax: 01925 494289
email: Media@Warr.ac.uk
Website: www.warr.ac.uk

BA (Hons) Media and Cultural

Studies
This University of Manchester degree combines academic study in Media and Cultural Studies with extensive specialist production work chosen from television production, radio production, multimedia journalism or commercial music production. In addition to the core course in Media and Cultural Studies, the course offers students the opportunity to undertake academic specialisms in television, film, radio, the print media, popular music, and new communication technologies. The course also offers a range of more vocationally-related modules, such as Media Professional Studies, and Media Law, and includes an extensive period of work placement in a media industry.

BA (Hons) Media with a practical specialism
The new Modular Scheme allows students to combine academic study of media with specialist practical production work chosen from: Television Production; Radio Production; Commercial Music Production; Multimedia Journalism; and Multimedia Web Production. Students may choose to take either a Single Honours programme in Media or may combine Media as a major subject with a range of other minor subjects such as: Business; Information Technology and Management; Sports Studies; Performing Arts; Leisure; and Professional Studies in Social Work and Education, in a Joint Honours programme

University of Warwick
Department of Film and Television Studies
Faculty of Arts
Coventry CV4 7AL
Tel: 024 7652 3511
Fax: 024 7652 4757
Website: www.warwick.ac.uk/fac/arts/Film
BA Joint Degree Film and Literature
Four courses offered each year, two in film and two in literature. Mainly film studies but some television included.
BA in Film with Television Studies
Four courses offered each year, three of which on film and, from year two, television. Further options available in film and/or television in year three
BA French or Italian with Film Studies

This degree puts a particular emphasis on film within and alongside its studies of French or Italian language, literature and society.
MA Film and Television Studies
Taught courses on Textual Analysis, Methods in Film History, Modernity and Innovation, and Issues of Representation, Introduction to Film and Television Studies for Graduates
MA for Research in Film and Television Studies
Combination of taught course and tailor-made programme of viewing and reading for students with substantial knowledge of film and television studies at BA level. For students wishing to proceed to PhD research
MA, MPhil and PhD
Students are accepted for research degrees

University of Westminster
School of Communication and Creative Industries
Harrow Campus, Watford Road
Northwick Park HA1 3TP
Tel: 020 7911 5944
Fax: 020 7911 5943
email: cdm@wmin.ac.uk
Website: www.wmin.ac.uk/media
BA (Hons) Film and Television
A modular degree course for young and mature students interested in film-making (fiction, documentary and experimental), television drama and documentary, screenwriting and film and television theory and criticism. The course emphasises creative collaboration and encourages some specialisation. It aims to equip students with understanding and competence in relevant critical ideas and the ability to work confidently and professionally in film and allied media using traditional and new technologies
BA (Hons) Media Studies
This degree studies the social context in which the institutions of mass communications operate, including film and television, and teaches the practice of print and broadcasting journalism and video production. On levels 2 and 3 students choose one of the following pathways: radio, journalism or video production. The course gives equal emphasis to theory/criticism and practice. The video pathway is accredited by BECTU
MA PgD Film and Television Studies

Advanced level part-time course taught in Central London (evenings and study weekends) concerned with theoretical aspects of film and television. Modular credit and accumulation scheme, with exemption for work previously done. The MA is normally awarded after three years' study (120 credits). A Postgraduate Certificate can be awarded after one year (45 credits) or a Diploma after two years (75 credits)
BA (Hons) Contemporary Media Practice
A modular three year full-time course offering an integrated approach to photography, film, video and digital-imaging. Students are encouraged to use a range of photographic and electronic media and theoretical studies are considered crucial to the development of ideas. In Years 1 and 2, the taught programme covers basic and applied skills on a project basis; these are complemented by a range of options. In Year 3 students are given the opportunity to develop their own programme of study, resulting in the production of major projects in practice and dissertations

Weymouth College
Creative & Performing Arts
Cranford Avenue
Weymouth
Dorset DT4 7LQ
Tel: 01305 208856
Fax: 01305 208892
email: paul_kaspar@weymouth.ac.uk
Paul Kaspar
(P) BTEC National Diploma in Media Production.
This two year, full-time programme offers a broad foundation in media production skills, working practices and contextual knowledge. Two main streams are combined: Moving Image Production and Design Communication, both using digital media, reflecting convergence within New Media forms.
(P) HND Video Production (in partnership with Bournemouth University)
This two-year intensive production course, accredited by Bournemouth University, develops a multi-skilled approach to all aspects of television and video production. Students are continuously at work on a range of productions, including factual, experimental, narrative, and client-led programmes. Skill areas particularly developed through the

course are production management and post-production digital editing, whilst extended professional placements ensure realistic, vocational relevance. The programme is sponsored by Total Video, a community-based production company working in partnership with the college Media Centre. The HND provides progression opportunities onto Year Three B.A. programmes

Wimbledon School of Art
Merton Hall Road
London SW19 3QA
Tel: 020 8408 5072
Fax: 020 8408 5050
BA (Hons) Technical Arts: Design
This course offers a programme focusing on set design for theatre, film and television

University of Wolverhampton
School of Humanities and Social Sciences, Castle View, Dudley
West Midlands DY1 3HR
Tel: 01902 323400
Fax: 01902 323379
BA (Hons) Media and Cultural Studies
This is a modular programme which may be studied as a Specialist or Combined Award. Students follow a core programme covering key theoretical, historical and critical debates in both Media and Cultural Studies.
BA (Hons) Applied Communications
This modular programme may be studied as a Specialist or Combined Award and is concerned with issues and problems of human communication in their professional or industrial context. It draws upon media studies and planned communication, including marketing, journalism, public relations, corporate communication and interactive multimedia.
BA (Hons) Film Studies
This modular programme is available as a Joint degree, which can be studied in combination with another subject. Students take a general foundation in Media Studies and then follow modules which introduce approaches to the analysis of films, studies of different genres (musicals, melodrama, film noir), theories of authorship, and the Hollywood studio system. The study of national cinemas includes options on British, French and Spanish cinema and special study of contemporary America. Film modules are taught at Wolverhampton's award-winning Light House Media Centre, which offers two purpose-built and fully equipped cinemas, library and exhibition facilities. The majority of films studied are screened in full cinema format

DISTRIBUTORS (NON-THEATRICAL)

Companies here control UK rights for non–theatrical distribution (for domestic and group viewing in schools, hospitals, airlines and so on).

For an extensive list of titles available non–theatrically with relevant distributors' addresses, see the *British National Film & Video Catalogue*, available for reference from the *bfi* National Library and major public libraries. Other sources of film and video are listed under Archives and Film Libraries and Workshops

Amber Films
5-9 Side
Newcastle upon Tyne NE1 3JE
Tel: 0191 232 2000
Fax: 0191 230 3217
email: amberside@btinternet.com

Arts Council Film and Video Library
Concord Video and Film Council
22 Hines Road
Ipswich 1P3 9BG
Tel: 01473 726012
Fax: 01473 274531
email: concordvideo@btinternet.com
Website: www.btinternet.com/~concordvideo
Lydia Vulliamy

BBC for Business
Woodlands
80 Wood Lane
London W12 0TT
Tel: 020 8576 2088
Fax: 020 8433 2867

 bfi Films
21 Stephen Street
London W1T 1LN
Tel: 020 7957 89o9
Fax: 020 7580 5830
email: bookings@bfi.org.uk
Website: www.bfi.org.uk
Handles non-theatrical 16mm, 35mm and video. Subject catalogues available

Big Bear Records
PO Box 944
Birmingham B16 8UT
Tel: 0121 454 7020/8100
Fax: 0121 454 9996

email: bigbearmusic@compuserve.com
Website: bigbearmusic.com
Jim Simpson

Boulton-Hawker Films
Hadleigh
near Ipswich
Suffolk IP7 5BG
Tel: 01473 822235
Fax: 01473 824519
Educational films and videos: health education, social welfare, home economics, P.S.E., P.E., Maths, biology, physics, chemistry, geography

BUFVC (British Universities Film & Video Council)
77 Wells Street
London W1T 3QJ
Tel: 020 7393 1500
Fax: 020 7393 1555
email: ask@bufvc.ac.uk
Website: bufvc.ac.uk
Geoffrey O'Brien, Assistant Director
Videocassettes for sale direct from above address. Film hire via Concord Video and Film Council. The BUFVC maintains an Off-Air Recording Back-Up Service available to any educational institution in BUFVC membership holding an Educational Recording Agency license.

Bureau Films
c/o The Short Film Bureau
47 Poland Street
London W1F 7NB
Tel: 020 7734 8708
Fax: 020 7734 2406
email: info@shortfilmbureau.com
Website: www.shortfilmbureau.com
(see The Short Film Bureau)

Carlton UK Television
Video Resource Unit
Lenton Lane
Nottingham NG7 2NA
Tel: 0115 964 5477
Fax: 0115 964 5202
email: sarah.hoyle@carltontv.co.uk
Sarah Hoyle

CFL Vision Euroview Management Services Limted
PO Box 80
Wetherby

Yorks LS23 7EQ
Tel: 01937 541010
Fax: 01937 541083
email: euroview@compuserve.com
Website: www.euroview.co.uk

Chain Production Ltd
2 Clanricarde Gardens
London W2 4NA
Tel: 020 7229 4277
Fax: 020 7229 0861
email: films@chainproduction.co.uk
Website: www.chainproduction.co.uk
Specialist in European films and world cinema, cult classics, handling European Film Libraries with all rights to over 1,000 films - also clip rights and clip search

Cinenova: Promoting Films by Women
113 Roman Road
Bethnal Green
London E2 0QN
Tel: 020 8981 6828
Fax: 020 8983 4441
email: shona@cinenova.org.uk
Website: www.cinenova.org.uk
Shona Barrett, Distribution
Laura Hudson: Development
Cinenova acts as a champin for the equality of women behind the camera, taking the diversity of women's voices to a global audience. It is committed to the acquisition, promotion, distribution and exhibition of films and videos directed by women and to provide the context to support women's film

Concord Video and Film Council
22 Hines Road
Ipswich IP3 9BG
Tel: 01473 726012
Fax: 01473 274531
email: concordvideo@btinternet.com
Website: www.btinternet.com/~concordvideo
Lydia Vulliamy
Videos and films for hire/sale on domestic and international social issues - counselling, development, education, the arts, race and gender issues, disabilities, etc - for training and discussion. Also incorporates Graves Medical Audio Visual Library

CTVC Video
Hillside Studios
Merry Hill Road
Bushey
Watford WD2 1DR
Tel: 020 8950 4426
Fax: 020 8950 1437
email: ctvc@ctvc.co.uk
Website: www.ctvc.co.uk
Christian, moral and social
programmes

Derann Film Services
99 High Street
Dudley
West Mids DY1 1QP
Tel: 01384 233191/257077
Fax: 01384 456488
Website: www.derran.com
D Simmonds, S Simmonds
8mm package movie distributors;
video production; bulk video
duplication; laser disc stockist

Education Distribution Service
Education House
Castle Road
Sittingbourne
Kent ME10 3RL
Tel: 01795 427614
Fax: 01795 474871
email: eds@edist.co.uk
Distribution library for many clients
including film and video releases.
Extensive catalogue available

Educational and Television Films
247A Upper Street
London N1 1RU
Tel: 020 7226 2298
Fax: 020 7226 8016
email: zoe@etvltd.demon.co.uk
Website: www.etvltd.demon.co.uk
Zoe More, Jack Amos
Established in 1950, ETV has amassed
a wide and varied range of
documentary archive materia from
the ex-Socialist world, with particular
emphasis on the ex-Soviet Union, the
former eastern Block countries and
China. Material is also held from
Vietnam, Cuba, Chile, Afghanistan
and the other Arab Nations. ETV also
houses material from the British
Labour Movement and the Spanish
Civil War

Educational Media, Film & Video
235 Imperial Drive
Rayners Lane
Harrow HA2 7HE
Tel: 020 8868 1908/1915
Fax: 020 8868 1991
email: edmedia@dircon.co.uk
Website: www.emfv.com
Lynda Morrell
Distributors of British and overseas
educational, health, training/safety
video games as well as new CD-ROM
titles. Act as agent for the promotion
of British productions overseas. Free
catalogue

Film Quest Ltd
71 (b) Maple Road
Surbiton
Surrey KT6 4AG
Tel: 020 8390 3677
Fax: 020 8390 1281
Booking agents for university, school
and private film societies

Filmbank Distributors
Grayton House
98 Theobalds Road
London WC1X 8WB
Tel: 0207 984 5950
Fax: 0207 984 5951
Bookings Department
Filmbank represents all of the major
film studios for the non-theatrical
market (group screenings) and
distributes titles on either 16mm film
or video

Golds
The Independent Home
Entertainment Wholesaler
Gold House,
69 Flempton Street
Leyton
London E10 7NL
Tel: 020 8539 3600
Fax: 020 8539 2176
Contact: Garry Elwood, Sales &
Marketing Director
Gold product range ever increasing
multi-format selection including:
Audio cassettes, CD's, T-Shirts, DVD,
Spoken Word Cassettes and CDs,
Video, CD Rom, CDi, Video CD,
Laserdisc, computer games and
accessories to all formats. 42 years of
service and expertise 32 years spent in
home entertainment market

Granada Learning/SEMERC
Granada Television
Quay Street
Manchester M60 9EA
Tel: 0161 827 2927
Fax: 0161 827 2966
email: info@granada-learning.co
Paula Warwick
Granada Learning Ltd is the UK's
leading publisher of educational
software. Its extensive range of CD-
ROMs spans the syllabus of primary
and secondary schools to meet the
requirements of learners of all ages
and abilities, including those with
special educational needs. Granada
Learning recently acquired Letts
Educational, the UK's leading
provider of educational textbooks
and revision guides for the home
market, and BlackCat, the UK's
market-leading supplier of
educational tools and applications for
younger children

IAC (Institute of Amateur Cinematographers)
24c West Street, Epsom
Surrey KT18 7RJ
Tel: 01372 739672
Fax: 01372 739672
email: iacfilmvideo@compuserve.com
Website: www.theiac.org.uk
Janet Smith

Imperial War Museum
Film and Video Archive (Loans)
Lambeth Road
London SE1 6HZ
Tel: 020 7416 5293/4
Fax: 020 7416 5299
email: film@iwm.org.uk
Website: www.iwm.org.uk
Toby Haggith, Matthew Lee
Documentaries, newsreels and
propaganda films from the Museum's
film archive on 16mm, 35mm and
video

IUN Entertainment
Centre 500
500 Chiswick High Road
London W4 5RG
Tel: 020 8956 2340
Fax: 020 8956 2339
email: bobburgis@aol.com
Website: www.iun.com
Bob Burvis

Leeds Animation Workshop (A Women's Collective)
45 Bayswater Row
Leeds LS8 5LF
Tel: 0113 248 4997
Fax: 0113 248 4997
Milena Dragic
Producers and distributors of
animated films on social issues

The Lux Centre
2-4 Hoxton Square
London N1 6NU
Tel: 020 7684 2782
Fax: 020 7684 1111
email: dist@lux.org.uk

Website: www.lux.org.uk
The Lux Centre house the distribution collections of the former London Film Makers' Co-op and London Electronic Arts, with over 3,500 artists' films, videos and works in new media, ranging from 1920s animations by Len Lye through classic avant garde films by Maya Deren, Stan Brakhage and others, to the latest work by international artists such as Sadie Benning and John Maybury

Melrose Film Productions
Dumbarton House
68 Oxford Street
London WIN OLH
Tel: 020 7627 8404
Fax: 020 7622 0421

National Educational Video Library
Arfon House
Bontnewydd
Caernarfon
Bangor
Gwynedd LL57 7UD
Tel: 01286 676001
Fax: 01286 676001
email: nevl@madasafish.com
Website: www.madasafish.com/~neul
John Lovell
Supply of educational videotapes and loan of sponsored videotapes and film

National Film and Television School
Beaconsfield Studios
Station Road
Beaconsfield
Bucks HP9 1LG
Tel: 01494 671234
Fax: 01494 674042
email: rjenkins@nftsfilm-tv.ac.uk
Website: www.nftsfilm-tv.ac.uk
Richard Jenkins

Open University Worldwide
The Berrill Building
Walton Hall
Milton Keynes NK7 6AA
Tel: 01908 858785
Fax: 01908 858787
email: s.l.mccormack@open.ac.uk
Sarah McCormack

Post Office Video and Film Library
PO Box 145
Sittingbourne
Kent ME10 1NH
Tel: 01795 426465
Fax: 01795 474871
email: poful@edist.co.uk
Includes many video programmes

and supporting educational material including curriculum guidelines. Also a comprehensive range of extension and other curriculum linked material. TV rights available

Royal Danish Embassy
55 Sloane Street
London SW1X 9SR
Tel: 020 7333 0200
Fax: 020 7333 0270
email: alemei@um.dk
Website: www.denmark.org.uk
Alexander Meinertz, Cultural Attaché

RSPCA
Causeway
Horsham
West Sussex RH12 1HG
Tel: 01403 264181
Fax: 01403 241048
email: webmail@rspca.org.uk
Website: www.rspca.org.uk
Michela Miller

Sheila Graber Animation Limited
50 Meldon Avenue
South Shields
Tyne and Wear NE34 0EL
Tel: 0191 455 4985
Fax: 0191 455 3600
email: sheila@graber.demon.co.uk
Over 70 animated shorts available - 16mm, video and computer interactive featuring a range of 'fun' educational shorts on art, life, the universe and everything. Producers of interactive CD-Roms

The Short Film Bureau
47 Poland Street
London W1F 7NB
Tel: 020 7734 8708
Fax: 020 7734 2406
email: info@shortfilmbureau.com
Website: www.shortfilmbureau.com
Kim Leggatt
Specialising in the promotion and distribution of short films for theatrical and non-theatrical release world wide. The Bureau also runs a script consultancy service for short films which looks at helping the writer rework their projects to maximise commercial success

South West Arts
Bradninch Place
Gandy Street
Exeter EX4 3LS
Tel: 01392 218188
Fax: 01392 229229
email: info@swa.co.uk
Website: www.swa.co.uk

Clare Frank, Ruth Bint: Information Advisers
Sara Williams: Visual Arts and Media Administrator

Team Video Productions
Canalot
222 Kensal Road
London W10 5BN
Tel: 020 8960 5536
Fax: 020 8960 9784
Chris Thomas, Billy Ridgers
Producer and distributor of educational video resources

THE (Total Home Entertainment)
National Distribution Centre
Rosevale Business Park
Newcastle-under-Lyme
Staffs ST5 7QT
Tel: 01782 566566
Fax: 01782 568552
email: jed.taylor@the.co.uk
Website: www.the.co.uk
Jed Taylor
Exclusive distributors for Visual Corp, ILC, Quantum Leap, Mystique, Prime Time, IMS, Wardvision, Academy Media, Empire, RWP (over 6,000 titles) (see also Video Labels)

Training Services
Brooklands House
29 Hythegate
Werrington
Peterborough PE4 7ZP
Tel: 01733 327337
Fax: 01733 575537
email: tipton@training.services.demon.co.uk
Website: www. trainingservices.demon.co.uk/index.htim
C.Tipton
Distribute programmes from the following producers:
3E's Training
Aegis Healthcare
Angel Productions
Barclays Bank Film Library
John Burder Films
Career Strategies Ltd
CCD Product & Design
Easy-i Ltd
Flex Training
Flex Multi-Media Ltd
Grosvenor Career Services
Hebden Lindsay Ltd
Kirby Marketing Associates
McPherson Marketing
Promotions Sound & Vision
Schwops Productions
Touchline Training Group
Video Communicators Pty

TV Choice
22 Charing Cross Road
London WC2H 0HR
Tel: 020 7379 0873
Fax: 020 7379 0263

Vera Media
30-38 Dock Street
Leeds LS10 1JF
Tel: 0113 242 8646
Fax: 0113 242 8739
email: vera@vera-media.co.uk
Website: www.vera-media.co.uk
Al Garthwaite
Catherine Mitchell

Video Arts
Dumbarton House
68 Oxford Street
London W1N 0LH
Tel: 020 7637 7288
Fax: 020 7580 8103
Video Arts produces and exclusively
distributes the John Cleese training
films; Video Arts also distributes a
selection of meeting breaks from
Muppet Meeting Films TM as well as
Tom Peters programmes (produced
by Video Publishing House Inc) and
In Search of Excellence and other
films from the Nathan/Tyler Business
Video Library

Viewtech Film and Video
7-8 Falcons Gate
Northavon Business Centre
Dean Road Yate
Bristol BS37 5NH
Tel: 01454 858055
Fax: 01454 858056
email: info@viewtech.co.uk
Website: www.viewtech.co.uk
Safety films

Westbourne Film Distribution
1st Floor, 17 Westbourne Park Road
London W2 5PX
Tel: 020 7221 1998
Fax: 020 7221 1998
Agents for broadcasting/video sales
for independent animators from
outside the UK, particularly Central
Eastern Europe. Classic children's
film The Singing Ringing Tree

The University of Westminster
School of Communications and
Creative Industries
Harrow Campus, Watford Road
Northwick Park HA1 3TP
Tel: 020 7911 5944
Fax: 020 7911 5943
email: cdm@wmin.ac
Website: www.wmin.ac.uk/media
Professor Brian Winston

WFA
9 Lucy Street
Manchester M15 4BX
Tel: 0161 848 9782/5
Fax: 0161 848 9783
email:wfa@timewarp.com.uk
Website: www.wfamedia.co.uk
Fiona Johnson

DISTRIBUTORS (THEATRICAL)

Alibi Communications plc

35 Long Acre
London WC2E 9JT
Tel: 020 7845 0400
Fax: 020 7379 7035
email: info@alibifilms.co.uk
Website: www.alibifilms.co.uk
Roger Holmes
Alibi is active in the financing,
international sales and distirbution of
theatrical feature films and the
production of feature film, television
drama and children's programming.
Titles include: *One More Kiss* (1999),
One of the Hollywood Ten (2000)

Arrow Film Distributors

18 Watford Road
Radlett
Herts WD7 8LE
Tel: 01923 858306
Fax: 01923 859673
Email: Neil@.arrowfilms.co.uk
Website: www.arrowfilms.co.uk/
Neil Agran

Artificial Eye Film Company

14 King Street
London WC2E 8HN
Tel: 020 7240 5353
Fax: 020 7240 5242
Website: www.artificial-eye.com
Robert Beeson
Titles include: *Time Regained, Rosetta,
The Carriers Are Waiting, L'Ennui,
Mal, Beau Travail, Pola-X, Those Who
Love Me Can Take..., Whatever,
L'Humanite, Abendland, Water Drops
on Burning Rocks, I Could Read the
Sky, Harry, He's Here To Help, Suzhou
River, La Fidelite, Blackboards*

bfi Collections

21 Stephen Street
London W1T 1LN
Tel: 020 7957 8905
Fax: 020 7580 5830
email: bookings@bfi.org.uk
Website: www.bfi.org.uk
Heather Stewart
Titles include: *George Washington,
Deux ou trois choses que je sais d'elle
(2 or 3 things I know about her),
Bande À Part, As You Like It,
Alfie, Mildred Pierce, Kiss Me Kate,
Breakfast at Tiffany's, Don't Look Now*

Blue Dolphin Film & Video

40 Langham Street
London W1N 5RG
Tel: 020 7255 2494
Fax: 020 7580 7670
Joseph D'Morais

Blue Light

231 Portobello Road
London W11 1LT
Tel: 020 7792 9791
Fax: 020 7792 9871
email: kevan@bluelight.co.uk
Website: www.bluelight.co.uk
Kevan Wilkinson
Alain De La Mata
see Made in Hong Kong

Boudicca

75 East Road
London N1 6AH
Tel: 020 7490 1724
Fax: 020 7490 1764
email: sales@boudiccafilms.com
Website: www.boudiccafilms.com
Ray Brady
A new British independent Sales &
Distribution Company set up by the
Producer/Director Ray Brady
attempting to produce, promote, sell
and distribute its own and other
British feature films

Buena Vista International (UK)

3 Queen Caroline Street
Hammersmith
London W6 9PE
Tel: 020 8222 1000
Fax: 020 8222 2494
Website: www.thefilmfactory.co.uk
Daniel Battsek
Titles include: *Bringing Out the Dead,
Music of the Heart, Toy Story 2, The
Talented Mr Ripley, The Insider, The
Cider House Rules, The Hurricane,
Mansfield Park The Tigger Movie,
Mission to Mars, Cradle Will Rock,
Scream 3, My Life So Far, Deuce
Bigalow: Male Gigolo, Fantasia 2000,
Deception, The Next Best Thing, High
Fidelity, Gone in 60 Seconds, Me Myself
I, Shanghai Noon, Titus, Scary Movie,
Keeping the Faith, Saltwater, Dinosaur,
Cayote Ugly, The Golden Bowl, Disney's
The Kid, 102 Dalmatians, Unbreakable*

John Burder Films

7 Saltcoats Road
London W4 1AR
Tel: 020 8995 0547
Fax: 020 8995 3376
email: jburder@aol.com
Website: www.johnburder.co.uk

Chain Production Ltd

2 Clanricarde Gardens
London W2 4NA
Tel: 020 7229 4277
Fax: 020 7229 0861
email: films@chain.production.co.uk
Website:
www.chain.production.co.uk
Specialist in European films and
world cinema, cult classics, handling
European Film Libraries with all
rights to over 1,000 films - also clip
rights and clip search

Children's Film Unit

South Way
Leavesden
Herts WD2 7LZ
Tel: 01923 354656
Fax: 01923 354656
email: cfilmunit@aol.com
Website: www.btinternet.com/~cfu
Carol Rennie

Cinenova: Promoting Films by Women

113 Roman Road
Bethnal Green
London E2 0QN
Tel: 020 8981 6828
Fax: 020 8983 4441
email: shona@cinenova.org.uk
Website: www.cinenova.org.uk
Shona Barrett, Distribution
Cinenova acts as a champion for the
equality of women behind the
camera, taking the diversity of
women's voices to a global audience.
It is committed to the acquisition,
promotion, distribution, and
exhibition of films and videos
directed by women and to provide
the context to support women's film

City Screen

86 Dean Street
London W1D 3SR
Tel: 020 7734 4342
Fax: 020 7734 4027

email: enquiries@picturehouse-
cinemas.co.uk
Website: www.picturehouse-
cinemas.co.uk

Columbia TriStar Films (UK)
Europe House
25 Golden Square
London W1R 6LU
Tel: 020 7533 1111
Fax: 020 7533 1105
Website: www.spe.sonycom
A division of Sony Pictures
International, the company handles
releases from Columbia and TriStar,
Releases include: *The Loss of Sexual
Innocence, The Bone Collector,
Bicentenial Man, Limbo, The End of
the Affair, Joan of Arc, SLC Punk, Girl
Interrupted, Erin Brockovich, Circus,
Hanging Up, Elmo in Grouchland,
Sweet and Lowdown, 28 Days, Bats,
Not One Less, Stuart Little, American
Movie, The Patriot, The Emperor and
the Assassin, Fortress 2, Timecode,
Snatch, Hollow Man, The Road Home,
Loser, Black and White, Charlie's
Angels, Urgan Legends: Final Cut, The
6th Day*

Contemporary Films
24 Southwood Lawn Road
Highgate
London N6 5SF
Tel: 020 8340 5715
Fax: 020 8348 1238
email: contemporaryfilms@
compuserve.com
Website: www.contemporaryfilms.com
Eric Liknaitzky
*Strangers on a Train
Battleship Potemkin*

Distribution & Licensing Company (TDLC)
13 Berners Street
London W1P 3DE
Tel: 020 7580 0088
Fax: 020 7580 3468
email: dlamping@
tdlcentertainment.com
David Lamping

Documedia International Films Ltd
Programme Sales/Acquistitions
19 Widegate Street
London E1 7HP
Tel: 020 7625 6200
Disbributors of award winning drama
specials, drama shorts and feature
films for theatrical release, also video
sales/Internet and video on demand.
Drama specials - *Soulscapes;*

Telemovies/Features - *Deva's Forest,
Leaves and Thorns*
International short drama for
theatrical release, also
educational/film club and non
theatrical release - *Pile of Clothes,
JoyRidden, The Cage, Nazdrovia, Thin
Lines, Late Fred Morse, The
Extinguisher, The Summer Tree, Arch
Enemy, Tea and Bullets, Isabelle,
Peregrine, Beyond Reach, Trauma,
Edge of Night, Something Wonderful*

Double: Take
21 St Mary's Grove
London SW13 0JA
Tel: 020 8788 5743
Fax: 020 8785 3050
Maya Kemp
Distributors and producers of
children's TV
*Beachcomber Bay, Dappledown Farm,
Crystal Tipps and Alistair, Fred Basset,
Willo the Wisp, Bod, Puppydog Tales,
Doris*

Downtown Pictures Ltd
4th Floor, Suite 2
St Georges House
14-17 Wells Street
London W1P 3FP
Tel: 020 7323 6604
Fax: 020 7636 8090

Entertainment Film Distributors
Eagle House
108-110 Jermyn Street
London SW1Y 6HB
Tel: 020 7930 7744
Fax: 020 7930 9399
Titles Include: *Rancid Aluminium,
Complicity, Julian Po, The Bachelor,
Body Shots, Tumbleweeds, Next Friday,
Magnolia, American Psycho, Boiler
Room, Final Destination, U-571,
Frequency, Love and Basketball,
Cherry Falls, The Luzhin Defense, The
Cell, Going Off Big Tie, Bring It On,
The Family Man*

Feature Film Company
19 Heddon Street
London W1B 4BG
Tel: 020 7851 6560
Fax: 020 7851 6505
Website: featurefilm.co.uk
(the company is a wholly owned
subsidiary of Winchester
Entertainment plc). Titles include:
*Ulees Gold, My Son the Fanatic, The
Blackout, It's A Wonderful Life,
Quadrophenia, Das Boot; the
Director's Cut, Wild Man Blues, Gang
Related, Broken Vessels*

FilmFour Distributors
76-78 Charlotte Street
London W1P 1LX
Tel: 020 7868 7700
Fax: 020 7868 7767
Website: www.filmfour.com
The distribution arm of C4's stand-
alone film company FilmFour Ltd.
Handles the theatrical and video
distribution in the UK of all
FilmFour Productions and an
expanding slate of third party
acquisitions. Recent releases:
*East is East, Ghost Dog, The Filth and
the Fury, Down To You, Holy Smoke,
Simon Magus, Gangster No 1, La
Veuve de Saint-Paul, Some Voices,
Dancer in the Dark, Hotel Splendide,
Les Enfants du Siecle, The House of
Mirth, Purely Belter, The Yards, Small
Time Crooks, Hamlet*

Fine Line Features
CNN House
19-22 Rathbone Place
London W1T 1HY
Tel: 020 7307 6700
Fax: 020 7307 6264
Website: www.newline.com

Gala
26 Danbury Street
Islington
London N1 8JU
Tel: 020 7226 5085
Fax: 020 7226 5897
email: galafilms@hotmail.com

GVI Distributors
2 King Street
Southall
Middlesex UB2 4DA
Tel: 020 8813 8059
Fax: 020 8813 8062

Helkon SK
17-18 Henrietta Street
London WC2E 8QH
Tel: 020 7257 2000
Fax: 020 7257 2300
Website: www.films.helkon.co.uk
Simon Franks, CEO
Zygi Kamsa, COO, Christopher
Bailey, Managing Director
Titles include: *Strange Planet, Open
Your Eyes, One Day in September,
Maybe Baby, Play It to the Bone, Nasty
Neighbours, Gun Shy*

ICA Projects
12 Carlton House Terrace
London SW1Y 5AH
Tel: 020 7766 1416
Fax: 020 7930 9686
email: projects@ica.org.uk

Website: www.ica.org.uk/icaprojects
David Sin/Edward Fletcher
Titles include: *Videodrome, Ring/Ring 2, Songs From the Second Floor, A One and A Two - Yi Yi, The Season of Men, Iron Ladies*

Icon Film Distributors
The Quadrangle , 4th Floor
180 Wardour Street
London W1A 4YG
Tel: 020 7494 8100
Fax: 020 7494 8151
Titles include: *Ordinary Decent Criminal, The Miracle Maker, Kevin and Perry Go Large, The Million Dollar Hotel, Thomas and the Magic Railroad, The Little Vampire, Manchester United: Beyond..., Duets*

Indy UK
Independent Feature Film
Distributors
13 Mountview
Northwood
Middlesex HA6 3NZ
Tel: 07000 463985
Fax: 0870 161 7339
email: info@indyuk.co.uk
Stuart Aikman
The Scarlet Tunic, The Usual Children

Brian Jackson Films Ltd
39/41 Hanover Steps
St George's Fields
Albion Street
London W2 2YG
Tel: 020 7402 7543
Fax: 020 7262 5736
email: brianjfilm@aol.com
Brian Jackson

Kino Kino!
24c Alexandra Road
London N8 OPP
Tel: 020 8881 9463
Fax: 020 8881 9463
email: vitaly@kinokino.u-net.com
Website: Kinokino.u-net.com
Brother (Dir Alexei Balabanov),
Happy Days (Dir Alexei Balabanov)
Maria (Dir Artur Aristakisyan)

The David Lamping Company
13 Berners Street
London W1T 3LH
Tel: 020 7580 0088
Fax: 020 7580 3468
email: dlamping@
tdlcentertainment.com
David Lamping

Made in Hong Kong/Blue Light
231 Portobello Road

London W11 1LT
Tel: 020 7792 9791
Fax: 020 7792 9871
Website: www.madeinhongkong.co.uk
Kevan Wilkinson
Made in Hong Kong releases the finest in Hong Kong cinema
Bullet in the Head, Chinese Ghost Story, City on Fire, Days of Being Wild, Full Contact, Heroic Trio, The Killer, Saviour of the Soul
Blue Light distributes European and other titles

Mainline Pictures
37 Museum Street
London WC1A 1LQ
Tel: 020 7242 5523
Fax: 020 7430 0170
Website: www.screencinemas..co.uk
Romaine Hart

Mayfair Entertainment UK Ltd
20-22 Stukeley Street
London WC2B 5LF
Tel: 020 7304 7922
Fax: 020 7867 1121

Medusa Communications & Marketing Ltd
Regal Chambers, 51 Bancroft
Hitchin
Herts SG5 1LL
Tel: 01462 421818
Fax: 01462 420393
email: steve@medusacom.co.uk
Website: www.getplayboy.co.uk
Stephen Rivers
Medusa Pictures
Odyssey, Playboy, Adult Channel, Hong Kong Legends, Eastern Hero's Jerry Springer, Spawn Animation

Metro Tartan Distribution Ltd
Atlantic House
5 Wardour Street
London W1D 6PB
Tel: 020 7494 1400
Fax: 020 7439 1922
Laura De Casto
Lovers of the Arctic Circle, Of Freaks and Men, The Last September, Donald Cammell's Wild Side, Siberia, Julien Donkey-Boy, In the Mood for Love, Confessions of a Trick Baby

Metrodome Distribution
110 Park Street
London W1Y 3RJ
Tel: 020 7408 2121
Fax: 020 7409 1935
Website: www.metrodomegroup.com
Metrodome Distribution is part of

the Metrodome Group. The distribution arm was set up in order to distribute films that Metrodome Films produces, as well as to actively acquire and release another 8-10 films per year.
Titles include: *Buffalo 66, The Real Blonde, The Daytrippers, Human Traffic, The Bride of Chucky, Tango, Taxi, Eye of the Beholder, Sex - The Annabel Chong Story, Rage, Chuck & Buck, Elephant Juice*

Millivres Multimedia
Ground Floor
Worldwide House
116-134 Bayham St
London NW1 0BA
Tel: Tel. 020 7482 2576
Fax: 020 7482 2576
email: kim@millivres.co.uk
Website: www.millivres.co.uk
Kim Watson

Miracle Communications
38 Broadhurst Avenue
Edgware
Middx HA8 8TS
Tel: 020 8958 8512
Fax: 020 8958 5112
email: martin@
miracle63.freeserve.co.uk
Martin Myers
Handles all First Independent titles

Momentum Pictures
2nd Foor
184-192 Drummond Street
London NW1 3HP
Tel: 020 7388 1100
Fax: 020 7383 0404
email: sam.nichols@
momentumpictures.co.uk
Sam Nichos
Film distribution: *Lies, Simpatico, A Room for Romeo Brass, Show Me Love, Nora, Sunshine, Une Liaison Pornographique, Relative Values, Jesus' Son, Himalaya, O Brother, Where Art Thou?, Blair Witch 2: Book of Shadows, The Way of the Gun, Cecil B. Demented*

Oasis Cinemas and Film Distribution
20 Rushcroft Road
Brixton
London SW2 1LA
Tel: 020 7733 8989
Fax: 020 7733 8790
email: mail@oasiscinemas.co.uk
Mike Ewin
at Winstone for all except *Dancehall Queen, Laws of Gravity The Lunatic, The Secret Rapture, Gravesend*

Optimum Releasing
9 Rathbone Place
London W1T 1HW
Tel: 020 7637 5403
Fax: 020 7637 5408

Pathé Distribution
Kent House
14-17 Market Place
Great Titchfield Street
London W1N 8AR
Tel: 020 7323 51 51
Fax: 020 7631 3568
Website: www.pathe.co.uk
Majbritt Kirchner
Titles include: *Sleepy Hollow, The Darkest Light, Three Seasons, Topsy-Turvy, Love's Labours Lost, Asterix & Obelix Vs. Caesar, Earth, In All Innocence, House!, Virgin Suicides, The Girl on the Bridge, Honest, The Barber of Siberia, Chicken Run, Kikujiro, Essex Boys, There's only One Jimmy Grimble, Nurse Betty, Memento, It Was an Accident, The Escort, Les Destinees sentimentales*

PD&B Films
c/o The Short Film Bureau
47 Poland Street
London W1F 7NB
Tel: 020 7734 8708
Fax: 020 7734 2406
email: info@shortfilmbureau.com
Website: www.shortfilmbureau.com
(See The Short Film Bureau)

Poseidon Film Distributors
Hammer House
117 Wardour Street
London W1V 3TD
Tel: 020 7734 4441
Fax: 020 7437 0638
email: poseidon@posfilm.demon.co.uk
Website: www.poseidonfilms.com
Frixos Constantine
Autism, Dyslexia, Russian Composers - Writers, The Steal, Animation series *The Bears, "The Odyssey", The Night Witches*

Smoking Dogs Films
26 Shacklewell Lane
London E.8 2EZ
Tel: 020 7249 6644
Fax: 020 7249 6655
email: smart@smokingdogsfilms.com
John Akomfrah, Lina Gopaul, David Lawson
Independent films (see Production Companies)

Squirrel Films Distribution
119 Rotherhithe Street

London SE16 4NF
Tel: 020 7231 2209
Fax: 020 7231 2119
email: ostockman@sandsfilms.co.uk
Olivier Stockman
Slate of 6 feature films for children in preparation - current releases include the highly successful *The Children's Midsummer's Dream*

TKO Communications
PO Box 130
Hove, East Sussex BN3 6QU
Tel: 01273 550088
Fax: 01273 540969
email: jkruger02@aol.com
Gallavants (Animated)
3 Musketeers (Animated)
In Concert with Marvin Gaye
Jerry Lee Lewis - live in concert
Glen Campbell - live in concert
Catch Me a Spy (Kirk Douglas)
Sons of Captain Blood (Sean Flynn)
Diamond Mercenaries (Telly Savalis, Peter Fonda, O.J.Simpson)

Twentieth Century Fox Film Co
20th Century House
31-32 Soho Square
London W1V 6AP
Tel: 020 7437 7766
Fax: 020 7734 2170
Website: www.fox.co.uk
Titles include: *The Beach, Lake Placid, Boys Don't Cry, Saving Grace, Stir of Echoes, Drive Me Crazy, When the Sky Falls, Big Momma's House, Titan A.E., X-Men, The Closer You Get, My, Myself ad Irene, What Lies Beneath, Grey Owl, Bedazzled, Where the Heart Is*

UIP (United International Pictures (UK))
12 Golden Square
London W1A 2JL
Tel: 020 7534 5200
Fax: 020 7636 4118
Website: www.uip.com
Releases product from Paramount, Universal, MGM/UA and SKG DreamWorks
Titles include: *Angela's Ashes, Wonderland, Stigmata, American Beauty, Double Jeopardy, The Wood, Rear Window, The Green Mile, Whatever Happened to Harold, Being John Malkovich, Superstar, Love, Honour and Obey, Up at the Villa, Snow Day, Galaxy Quest, Janice Beard: 45 WPM, Man on the Moon, Gladiator, Snow Falling on Cedars, The Ninth Gate, Return to Me, For the Love of the Game, Supernova, Isn't She Great, The Best Man, Beyond the Mat,*

Mission: Impossible 2, Flintstones in Viva Rock Vegas, The Road to El Dorado, Rules of Engagement, Shaft, Billy Elliot, Nutty 2: The Klumps, Rat, Road Trip, Wonder Boys, Pitch Black, The Original Kings of Comedy, The Skulls, The Grinch, The Man Who Cried, Meet the Parents

United Artists Corporation, Ltd (MGM/United Artists)
5 Kew Road
Richmond
Surrey TW9 2PR
Tel: 020 8939 9300
Fax: 020 8939 9411
Anke Folchert
Tomorrow Never Dies, Man in the Iron Mask

Warner Bros. Pictures
International Distribution
98 Theobalds Road
London WC1X 8WB
Tel: 020 7984 5205
Fax: 020 7984 5211
Website: www.warnerbros.com
Nigel Sharrocks
Titles include: *House on Haunted Hill, Three Kings, A Clockwork Orange, Any Given Sunday, Pokemon: The First Movie, The Story of Us, The Whole Nine Yards, Battlefield Earth, Chill Factor, Three to Tango, Breakfast of Champions, The Perfect Storm, My Dog Skip, Gossip, Liberty Heights, Space Cowboys, Where the Money Is, Romeo Must Die, The Exorcist (Director's Cut), Into the Arms of Strangers, Ready to Rumble, Red Planet, The Art of War, Pokemon: The Movie 2000*

Winstone Film Distributors
18 Craignish Avenue
Norbury
London SW16 4RN
Tel: 020 8765 0240
Fax: 020 8765 0564
email: winstonefilmdist@aol.com
Mike.G.Ewin, Sara Ewin
Sub-distribution for Canal + Image UK Ltd)- Library only
Judy Berlin, Uneasy Riders, Inbetweeners, Two days nine lives

Yash Raj Films
3rd Floor Wembley Point
1 Harrow Road
Middlesex HA9 6DE
Tel: 0870 7397345
Fax: 0870 7397346
email:ukoffice@yashrajfilms.com
Website: www.yashrajfilms.com
Mohabbatein, Zubeidaa, Aashiq, Refugee

FACILITIES

Abbey Road Studios
3 Abbey Road
St John's Wood
London NW8 9AY
Tel: 020 7266 7000
Fax: 020 7266 7250
email: bookings@abbeyroad.co.uk
Website: www.abbeyroad.co.uk
Colette Barber
4 recording studios:
Studio 1: AMS Neve VRP 72 channel.
New improved facilities, capacity 100
orchestra, 120 piece choir, 444ft
screen, 35mm projection, 2xi
isolation rooms, large client lounge,
shower room, private office.
Studio 2: AMS Neve VRP 60 channel,
capacity 55 musicians
Studio 3: NEW SSL 9000 J series 96
channel mixing console (for stereo
and surround recording and mixing)
Penthouse: AMS Neve Capricorn
Digital (ideal for mixing/vocal
overdubs) 2 mobile location
recording units;
Audio post production: mastering, re-
mastering, editing, 5.1 audio
preparation and restoration, CD
preparation, copying; Interactive
design and digital video studio

AFM Lighting Ltd
Waxlow Road
London NW10 7NU
Tel: 020 8233 7000
Fax: 020 8233 7001
Gary Wallace
Lighting equipment and crew hire;
generator hire

After Image Facilities
32 Acre Lane
London SW2 5SG
Tel: 020 7737 7300
Website: www.after.arc.co.uk
Jane Thorburn, Mark Lucas
Full broadcast sound stage - Studio A
(1,680 sq ft, black, chromakey, blue,
white cyc) and insert studio (730 sq ft
hard cyc). Multiformat broadcast on-
line post production. Special effects -
Ultimatte/blue screen

Air Studios
Lyndhurst Hall, Lyndhurst Road
Hampstead
London NW3 5NG
Tel: 020 7794 0660
Fax: 020 7794 8518
Alison Burton
Lyndhurst Hall: capacity - 500 sq m
by 18m high with daylight; 100 plus
musicians; four separation booths.
Full motion picture scoring facilities.
Neve VRP Legend 72ch console,
flying fader automation. LCRS
monitoring. Studio 1: capacity - 60 sq
m with daylight. 40 plus musicians.
Neve/Focusrite 72ch console; GML
automation; LCRS monitoring.
Studio 2: Mixing Room; SSL8000G
plus series console with Ultimation;
ASM system. Film and TV dubbing
facilities; two suites equipped with
AMS Logic II consoles; 16 output;
AudioFile spectra plus; LCRS
monitoring. Exabyte back-up. One
suite equipped with an AMS Logic III
console. Every tape machine format
available

Alphabet Communications
Haig Road
Parkgate Estate
Knutsford
Cheshire WA16 8DX
Tel: 01565 755678
Fax: 01565 634164
email: info@alphabet.co.uk
Website: www.alphabet.co.uk
Simon Poyser
Digital Beta on line digital edit suites
Charisma DVE
Aston Motif caption generator
Sony 6000 vision switcher
Sony 9100 edit controller
Beta SP component edit suite
Avid 100 OXL Media Composer
online suite
Avid 800 offline 18Gbyte memory
2D Computer graphic Pixell Collage
3D Computer graphics Softimage 3D
Extreme Mental Ray render
Standards conversion
All tape formats available
Commentary recording and rostrum
camera
1800sq ft drive in studio
Digital Beta DVW700P 16: 9 & 4:3
camera
Beta SP
VHS Duplication
Authoring of Interactive DVD & CD

ROM packages
Website building

Angel Recording Studios
311 Upper Street
London N1 2TU
Tel: 020 7354 2525
Fax: 020 7226 9624
email: angel@angelstudios.co.uk
Gloria Luck
Two large orchestral studios with
Neve desks, and one small studio. All
with facilities for recording to picture

Anvil Post Production Ltd
Denham Studios
North Orbital Road, Denham
Uxbridge
Middx UB9 5HL
Tel: 01895 833522
Fax: 01895 835006
email: *@anvil.nildram.co.uk
Sound completion service; re-
recording, ADR, post-sync, Fx
recording, transfers, foreign version
dubbing; non-linear and film editing
rooms, neg cutting, off-line editing,
production offices

ARRI Lighting Rental
20a The Airlinks,
Spitfire Way,
Heston,
Middx TW5 9NR
Tel: 020 8561 6700
Fax: 020 8569 2539
Tim Ross
Lighting equipment hire

Jim Bambrick and Associates
William Blake House
8 Marshall Street
London W1V 2AJ
Tel: 020 7434 2351
Fax: 020 7734 6362
6 x Avid Editing Suite with versions
6.5 software, 35mm Steinbeck

Barcud
Cibyn
Caernarfon
Gwynedd LL55 2BD
Tel: 01286 671671
Fax: 01286 671679
Video formats: 1"C, Beta SP, D2 OB
Unit 1: up to 7 cameras 4VTR OB

Unit 2: up to 10 cameras 6VTR, DVE, Graphics Betacam units. Studio 1: 6,500 sq ft studio with audience seating and comprehensive lighting rig. Studio 2: 1,500 sq ft studio with vision/lighting control gallery and sound gallery. Three edit suites; two graphics suites, one with Harriet. DVE: three channels Charisma, two channels Cleo. Two Sound post-production suites with AudioFile and Screen Sound; BT lines. Wales' leading broadcast facility company can supply OB units, studios, Betamac Kits (all fully crewed if required) and full post production both on and off-line

Bell Digital Facilities
Lamb House
Church Street
Chiswick Mall
London W4 2PD
Tel: 020 8996 9960
Fax: 020 8996 9966
email: sales@bel-media.co
ProTools IV sound dubbing studio with non-linear picture. VocAlign & other ADR and outboard tools. Voice booth accessible from all suites. Extensive 3D animation & 2D graphics studio. Sound proofed, air-conditioned. 600 sq ft video studio available as 4-waller or with cameras. Avid off and on-line and After Effects

Blue Post Production
58 Old Compton Street
London W1V 5PA
Tel: 020 7437 2626
Fax: 020 7439 2477
Contact: Catherine Spruce, Director of Marketing
Digital Online Editing with Axial edit controllers, GVG 4000 digital vision mixers, Kaleidoscope DVEs, disc recorders, Abekas A72, digital audio an R-Dat
Quantel Edit Box 4000 with 2 hours non-compressed storage
Sound Studio with Avid Audio Vision, 32 input MTA fully automated desk
Offline Editing on Avid Media Composer 800
Telecine Ursa Diamond System, incorporating Pogle Platinium DCP with ESR & TWiGi

BUFVC
77 Wells Street
London W1T 3QJ
Tel: 020 7393 1500
Fax: 020 7393 1555
email: ask@bufvc.ac.uk

Website: www.bufvc.ac.uk
16mm video steenbeck plus 35mm and 16mm viewing facilities. Betacam 2 machine edit facility for low-cost assembly off-line work.

Canalot Production Studios
222 Kensal Road
London W10 5BN
Tel: 020 8960 8580
Fax: 020 8960 8907
Nieves Heathcote
Media business complex housing over 80 companies, involved in TV, film, video and music production, with boardroom to hire for meetings, conferences and costings

Capital FX
21A Kingly Court
London W1R 5LE
Tel: 020 7439 1982
Fax: 020 7734 0950
Graphic design and production, laser subtitling, opticals effects and editing

Capital Studios
Wandsworth Plain
London SW18 1ET
Tel: 020 8877 1234
Fax: 020 8877 0234
Central London: 3,000 and 2,000 sq ft fully equipped broadcast standard television studios. 16x9/4x3 switchable, two on-line edit suites (D3, D2, D5, Digital Betacam & Beta SP). Avid on/off line editing. Multi track and digital sound dubbing facilities with commentary booth. 'Harriet' graphics suite. BT lines. All support facilities. Car park. Expert team, comfortable surroundings, immaculate standards

Chromacolour International Ltd
Unit 5 Pilton Estate
Pitlake
Croydon
Suurrey CRO 33RA
Tel: 020 8688 1991
Fax: 020 8688 1441
email: sales@chromacolour.co.uk
Website: www.chromacolour.co.uk
Contact: Joanne Hogan
Animation supplies/equipment

Cinebuild
Studio House
Rita Road
Vauxhall
London SW8 1JU
Tel: 020 7582 8750
Fax: 020 7793 0467
Special effects: rain, snow, fog, mist,

smoke, fire, explosions; lighting and equipment hire. Studio: 200 sq m

Cinecontact
27 Newman Street
London W1T 1AR
Tel: 020 7323 0618
Fax: 020 7323 1215
Contact: Jacqui Timberlake
Documentary film-makers. Avid post production facilities

Cinesite (Europe) Ltd
9 Carlisle Street
London W1V 5RG
Tel: 020 7973 4000
Fax: 020 7973 4040
Website: www.cinesite.com
Utilising state-of-the art technology, Cinesite provides expertise in every area of resolution-free digital imaging and digital special effects for feature films. Our creative and production teams offer a full spectrum of services from the storyboard to the final composite, including digital effects, and shoot supervision. Credits include: *Devil's Advocate, Air Force One, Event Horizon, Tommorow Never Dies, Batman and Robin, Jerry Maguire, Space Jam, Smilla's Sense of Snow*

Colour Film Services
10 Wadsworth Road
Perivale
Middx UB6 7JX
Tel: 020 8998 2731
Fax: 020 8997 8738
email: ruthlawton@ colourfilmservices.co.uk
Website: www.colourfilmservices. co.uk
Ruth Lawton
CFS in soho
26 Berwick Street
London W1F 8RG
Tel: 020 7734 4543
Fax: 020 7734 6600
email: cfsinsoho@ colurfilmservices.co.uk
Website: www.colourfilmservices. co.uk
Contact: GrahamTolley

Communicopia Ltd
The Old Town Hall
Albion Street
Southwick
West Sussex BN42 4AX
Tel: 01273 278575
Fax: 01273 416082
email: info@communicopia.co.uk
Website: www.communicopia.co.uk
Post production facility. Includes:

Fast 601 non-linear video post production suite. Broadcast quality MPEG2 601. GEM WK4 music workstation. Voice-over sound suite. Digital sound mixer. Track laying and audio mixing to picture. Broadcast standard, non-linear editing. 3D effect/DVE. Unlimited layering , all with colour correction, keying and DVE. High-speed background rendering . 36 Gigabytes of media storage. Huge picture library. Lightwave 5 graphics system. 3D full-featured animation system. CD ROM, CD Burner and CD Players. DAT player/recorder. VHS and S-VHS recorders. Music and sound effects library. Zip dives. ISDN

Complete
Slingsby Place
Off Long Acre
London WC2E 9AB
Tel: 020 7379 7739
Fax: 020 7497 9305
email: info@complete.co.uk
Richard Ireland, Lucy Pye, Sarah Morgan, Lisa Sweet and Holly Ryan Henry, Flame, Harriet. Digital editing. C-reality-Hires-Telecine. 3D Animation with Alias wave front and soft/maxDigital Ursa Diamond Telecine with Russell Square DI tape grading. Digital playouts and ISDN links. Award-winning creative team

Connections Communications Centre
Palingswick House
241 King Street
Hammersmith
London W6 9LP
Tel: 020 8741 1766
Fax: 020 8593 9134
email: info@cccmedia.co.uk
Website: www.cccmedia.co.uk
Denise Sample (Training)
Bill Hammond (Facilities)
Production Equipment
BETA SP, DV, DVCPRO, SVHS cameras. Wide range of lighting and sound including SQN stereo mixer and portable D.A.T.
Post Production Equipment
Avid Xpress Deluxe Non-Linear Edit system. BETA SP 3 machine suite with computerised edit controller SVHS on-line and off-line editing Final Cut Pro and AVID media composer Fully Wheelchair Accessible

Corinthian Television Facilities (CTV)
87 St John's Wood Terrace
London NW8 6PY
Tel: 020 7483 6000
Fax: 020 7483 4264
Website: www.ctv.co.uk
OBs: Multi-camera and multi-VTR vehicles. Post Production: 3 suites, 1 SP component, 2 multi-format with 1", D2, D3, Abekas A64, A72, Aston and colour caption camera. Studios: 2 fully equipped television studios (1 in St John's Wood, 1, in Piccadilly Circus), 1-5 camera, multi-format VTRs, BT lines, audience seating. Audio: SSL Scrrensound digital audio editing and mixing system

Dateline Productions
79 Dean Street
London W1V 5HA
Tel: 020 7437 4510
Fax: 020 7287 1072
email: miranda@dircon.com
Miranda Watts
Avid non-linear editing

De Lane Lea Sound Centre
75 Dean Street
London W1V 5HA

Tel: 020 7439 1721
Fax: 020 7437 0913
email: dll@delanelea.com
Website: www.delanelea.com
2 high speed 16/35mm Dolby stereo
dubbing theatres with Dolby SR; high
speed ADR and FX theatre (16/35mm
and NTSC/PAL video); Synclavier
digital FX suite; digital dubbing
theatre with Logic 2 console; 3 x
AudioFile preparation rooms; sound
rushes and transfers; video transfers
to VHS and U-Matic; Beta rushes
syncing. 24 cutting rooms/offices. See
also under studios

Denman Productions
60 Mallard Place
Strawberry Vale
Twickenham TW1 4SR
Tel: 020 8891 3461
Fax: 020 8891 6413
Video and film production, including
3D computer animation and web
design

Digital Audio Technology
134 Cricklewood Lane
London NW2 2DP
Tel: 020 8450 5665
Fax: 020 8208 1979

email: info@digitalauiotech.com
Website: digitalaudiotech.com
Ian Silvester
Providing a one-stop solution to all
your digital audio requirements for
music, film, television and DVD
productions

Diverse Production
6 Gorleston Street
London W14 8XS
Tel: 020 7603 4567
Fax: 020 7603 2148
Ray Nunney
TV post-production. Digital on-line
editing; off-line editing;
comprehensive graphic design
service; titles sequences, programme
graphics, generic packaging, sets and
printwork

Dolby Laboratories
Wootton Bassett
Wilts SN4 8QJ
Tel: 01793 842100
Fax: 01793 842101
email: info@dolby.co.uk
Website: www.dolby.com
Graham Edmondson
Cinema processors for replay of
Dolby Digital, Dolby Digital

Surround Ex and Dolby SR
(analogue) film soundtracks. Sound
consultancy relating to Dolby film
production, distribution and
exhibition. Signal processing
equipment for production and
broadcast of Dolby Surround, Dolby
Digital and Dolby E formats for TV,
DVD, and broadcast applications.
Audio noise reduction equipment

Dubbs
25-26 Poland Street
London W1F 8QN
Tel: 020 7629 0055
Fax: 020 7287 8796
email:
customer_services@dubbs.co.uk
Website: www.dubbs.co.uk
Contact: Bill Gamble, Customer
Services Director
Dubbs specialises in video
duplication, standards conversion,
disc authoring and replication,
providing a flexible, reliable, quality
service. Open 7 days a week, 24-
hours a day. Formats: D1; D2; D3;
D5; Digibeta; BetaSP; BetaSX; Digital-
S; M2; 1"C; DVCPRO; DVCAM; Mini
DV; Betacam; BVU/SP; U-matic; S-
VHS; VHS; Hi-8; Video-8; CD-ROM,

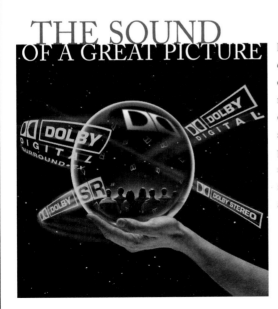

Audio CD and DVD Replication; ASF; AVI; Quicktime; MPEG-1 & MPEG-2 Encoding; Laser Disk; WAV files; DAT; DA-88; Mini Disc; Audio Cassette. Aspect Ratio Conversion. 5 x standards convertors inc. Alchemist Ph.C with Clean Cut, PAL, NTSC, SECAM V and H, PAL-M; PAL-N.

Edinburgh Film Productions
Traquair House
Innelleithen
Peeblessairl EH44 6PW
Tel: 01896 831188
Fax: 01896 831199

Edinburgh Film Workshop Trust
56 Albion Road
Edinburgh EH7 5QZ
Tel: 0131 656 9123
email: post@efwt.demon.co.uk
Website: www.efwt.demon.co.uk
David Halliday, Angus Ferguson
Beta SP production; 16mm Arri, 6-plates and rostrum, broadcst quality video animation and non-linear editing; off-line editing. Animation and video training, consultancy and project development. Specialists in enviornment, health and welfare

Edric Audio-visual Hire
34-36 Oak End Way
Gerrards Cross
Bucks SL9 8BR
Tel: 01753 884646
Fax: 01753 887163
Audiovisual and video production facilities

Elstree Light and Power
Millennium Studios
Elstree Way
Borehamwood
Herts WD6 1SF
Tel: 020 8236 1300
Fax: 020 8236 1333
Tony Slee
TV silent generators; Twin Sets HMI, MSR and Tungsten Heads. Distribution to BS 5550.Rigging Specialists

Eye Film and Television
The Guildhall
Church Street
Eye
Suffolk IP23 7BD
Tel: 01379 870083
Fax: 01379 870987
Betacam SP crews, Avid Non Linear offline & online systems available for wet & dry hire. Associated production services

Faction Films
26 Shacklewell Lane
London E8 2EZ
Tel: 020 7690 4446
Fax: 020 7690 4447
email: faction@factionfilms.co.uk
Website: www.factionfilms.co.uk
Susan Husband
Avid MC1000 composer; Sony VX1000 digi-cam; Sony Hi-8; HHB Portadat; Production office space

The Film Factory at VTR
64 Dean Street
London W1V 5HG
Tel: 020 7437 0026
Fax: 020 7494 0059
email: alan.church@filmfactory.com
Website: www.filmfactory.com
Alan Church, Simon Giles
The Film Factory is one of London's major feature film post-production facilities specialising in high-resolution digital effects. Credits include Deep Blue Sea, Tea With Mussolini, Lost in Space, The Wings of the Dove, Love is the Devil, Gormenghast and Seven Years in Tibet. Produce visual effects, digital opticals, titles, computer animation and visual effects and supervision. Title sequences include: The Adventures of Pinocchio, Best Laid Plans, Photographing Fairies, Bent, Saving Grace, Cousin Bette, Up 'n' Under, Tube Tales, I Want You and Pandaemonium. Company also has tape-to-film transfer service and full 35mm digital scanning and recording service

Film Work Group
Top Floor, Chelsea Reach
79-89 Lots Road
London SW10 0RN
Tel: 020 7352 0538
Fax: 020 7351 6479
Loren Squires, Nigel Perkins
Video and Film post-production facilities. AVID on-line (2:1) and off-line editing. 36 gigs storage, Digital Animation Workstations (draw, paint, image, modification, edit). 3 machine Hi-Band SP and mixed Beta SP/Hi-Band with DVE. 2 machine Lo-Band off-line with sound mixing. 6 plate Steenbeck. Special rates for grant aided, self-funded and non-profit projects

FinePoint Broadcast
Furze Hill
Kingswood
Surrey KT20 6EZ

Tel: 0800 970 2020
Fax: 0800 970 2030
email: hire@finepoint.co.uk
Website: www.finepoint.co.uk
Broadcast equipment hire. Cameras, lenses, control units, high speed cameras, disc recorder, cables, VTRs, edit controllers, digital video effects, vision mixers, monitors, sound kit

Fisher Productions Europe Ltd
Studio House
Rita Road
Vauxhall
London SW8 1JU
Tel: 020 7582 8750
Fax: 020 7793 0467
(See Cinebuild)

FrameStore
9 Noel Street
London W1F 8GH
Tel: 020 7208 2600
Fax: 020 7208 2626
email:
steph.bruning@framestore.co.uk
Website: www.framestore.co.uk
Full service digital video facility - Spirit Datacine, Ursa Diamond Telecine, 4 Inferno, 4 x Henry Infinity, Flame, Digital Editing, Avid, Softimage, Maya, After Effects, Commotion, Photoshop, Final Cut Pro, Premiere, Combustion

Mike Fraser
Unit 6
Silver Road
White City Industrial Park
London W12 7SG
Tel: 020 8749 6911
Fax: 020 8743 3144
email: mike@mfraser.demon.co.uk
Mike Fraser
Mike Fraser, Rod Wheeler
Telecine transfer 35mm, 16mm and S16; rushes syncing; c. reality high and scanning to HD TV, data files, disc as the start to the digital and lab process, non-linear edit suites; film video list management, post-production through OSC/R to negative cutting. Storage

Frontline Television Services
44 Earlham Street
Covent Garden
London WC2H 9LA
Tel: 020 7836 0411
Fax: 020 7379 5210
Charlie Sayle
Extensive edit, duplication, computer animation and multimedia facilities -

5 Avid Media Composers, Avid Symphony, DS, Linear Digital Betacam Suite. Low volume, low cost, quick turnaround duplication. 2D and 3D animation and graphics. Multimedia facilities including encoding.

FX Projects

Studio House
Rita Road
Vauxhall
London SW8 1JU
Tel: 020 7582 8750
Fax: 020 7793 0467
(See Cinebuild)

Goldcrest Post Production Facilities Ltd

Entrance 1 Lexington Street
36/44 Brewer Street
London W1F 9LX
Tel: 020 7439 7972
Fax: 020 7437 5402
email: mailbox@goldcrest-post.co.uk
Website: www.goldcrest.org
Alicja Syska, Raju Raymond
Theatre 1 with Otari Elite + console, Dolby SRD, Fairlight on fx3.48 DFWfilm + video projection; ADR & Effects recording, built in Foley surfaces and extensives props; Theatre 2 with Otari Elite + console, Dolby SRD, video projection, ADR & Effects recording, built in Foley surfaces & extensive props; Theatre 3 with Yamaha 02R console, ADR & Effects recording; All theatres equipped with ISDN link; Sound Transfer Bay for all film and video formats with Dolby SRD; Rank Cintel MKIIC Telecine enhanced 4:2:2, Pogle and secondary colour correction. Keycode and Aaton readers, noise reduction, video transfers to 1", Digibeta, Beta SP, U-Matics, VHS and D2, ADAC standards conversion. Non-linear editing on and off line Avids and Lightworks Turbo available. Cutting rooms, production offices, duplex apartments available

Hillside

Merry Hill Road
Bushey
Herts WD23 1DR
Tel: 020 8950 7919
Fax: 020 8421 8085
email: enquiries@hillside-studios.co.uk
Website: www.hillside-studios.co.uk
David Hillier

Production and Post-Production facilities to Broadcast standards. 1500 sq ft studio with 16 x 9 switchable cameras and Digital Mixer. Smaller studio and single camera location units available. Sounds Studios and Dubbing Suite, Non-Linear and Digital Editing. Graphics, Set Design and Construction. Offices, restaurant and parking

Holloway Film & TV

68-70 Wardour Street
London W1V 3HP
Tel: 020 7494 0777
Fax: 020 7494 0309
email: info@hollowayfilm-co.uk
Website: www.holloway.film.co.uk
James Greenwall
D5, D3, D2, Digital Betacam, 3 m/c Digital Betacam suite, AVID (AVRTT) on-line/Offline. Betacam SP, 1"C, BVU, Lo-Band Hi-8, Video-8, S-VHS, VHS, Standards Conversion, Audio Laybacks/Layoffs

Hull Time Based Arts

42 The High Street
Hull HU1 1PS
Tel: 01482 586340/216446
Fax: 01482 589952

email: timebase@htba.demon.co.uk
Website: www.timebase.org
Ammabel McCourt, Dan Van
Heeswyk
Avid Media Composer 9000XL non-linear editing suite with 1:1
compression, digital I/O and
Commotion 2.1 compositing
software, Avid Media Composer 1000
editing suite with 2:1 compression,
G4 with Final Cut Pro, ProTools
Audio Suite, Multimedia authoring,
DVC Pro, DVCam and DV cameras,
DAT recorder, Data projector and all
ancillary video equipment available.
Special rates for non commercial
projects

Humphries Video Services
Unit 2, The Willow Business Centre
17 Willow Lane
Mitcham
Surrey CR4 4NX
Tel: 020 8648 6111/0171 636 3636
Fax: 020 8648 5261
email: sales@hvs.bdx.co.uk
Website: www.hvs.co.uk
David Brown, Emma Lincoln
Video cassette duplication: all
formats, any standard. Standards
convertors. Macrovision anti-copy
process, labelling, shrink wrapping,
packaging and mail out services, free
collections and deliveries in central
London. Committed to industrial and
broadcast work

Interact Sound
160 Barlby Road
London W10 6BS
Tel: 020 8960 3115
Fax: 020 8964 3022
email: info@interact-sound.co.uk
Sandie Wirtz
Spacious digital and analogue
dubbing theatres. Dolby stereo, SR-D.
DTS compatable. Large screen film
and video projection. 5 digital audio
edit suites. Rooms available for
production offices. Mixers: Aad
Wirtz, Lee Taylor and John Falcini

ITN
200 Gray's Inn Road
London WC1X 8XZ
Tel: 020 7430 4134
Fax: 020 7430 4655
Martin Swain
Martin Swain, Jenny Mazzey
2400 sq ft studio; live or recorded
work; comprehensive outside source
ability; audience 65; crews; video
transfer; Westminster studio; graphics
design service using Flash Harry,

Paintbox etc; Training offered; Sound
and dubbing; tape recycling;
experienced staff

Lee Lighting
Wycombe Road
Wembley
Middlesex HAO 1QD
Tel: 020 8900 2900
Fax: 020 8902 5500
Website: www.lee.co.uk
Film/TV lighting equipment hire

Light House Media Centre
The Chubb Buildings
Fryer Street
Wolverhampton WV1 1HT
Tel: 01902 716044
Fax: 01902 717143
email: raj@light-house.co.uk
Website: www.light-house.co.uk
Contact: Technical department
Three machine U-Matic edit suite
(hi-band - BVE 900, lo-band BVE
600) VHS/U-Matic/Betacam/ENG
kits, also animation and chroma
keying

Lighthouse
9-12 Middle Street
Brighton BN1 1AL
Tel: 01273 384222
Fax: 01273 384233
email: info@lighthouse.org.uk
Website: www.lighthouse.org.uk
Technical Department
A training and production centre,
providing courses, facilities and
production advice. Avid off- and
online edit suites. Apple Mac graphics
and animation workstations. Digital
video capture & manipulation.
Output to/from Betacam SP. SVHS
offline edit suite. Post Production and
Digital Artists equipment bursaries
offered three times a year

The Lux Centre - Lux Production Facilities
The Lux Centre for Film, Video and
Digital Arts
2-4 Hoxton Square
London N1 6NU
Tel: 020 7684 0202
Fax: 020 7684 2222
email: lux@lux.org.uk
Website:www.lux.org.uk
Subsidised facilities for film, video
and digital media production. 8mm
& 16mm film cameras, digital video
cameras, film and multi-format video
editing, online and offline. Avids,
Telecine and video transter, digital
audio editing, multimedia and
Internet workstations, graphics,

animation and much more. LCD
video projectors, monitors and
playback equipment for exhibition
and events.
Optical Printer for gauge transfers,
colouring and all kinds of optical
manipulation of film: Macs with
Adobe Premiere for editing and
Macromedia Director for interactive
multimedia authoring: state of the art
Avid editing suite: 16mm black and
white film processing: Super 8, 16mm
and Super 16 camera kits; Lighting
including standard blonde and
redhead kits and the latest Dedolight
and Kino Flo Kits; Analogue editing
suites with Steenbecks, plus a rare
Super 8 Steenbeck; sound transfer
room; Rostrum Camera for
animation, titles and effects;
broadcast quality Telecine

MAC Sound Hire
1-2 Attenburys Park
Park Road
Altrincham
Cheshire WA14 5QE
Tel: 0161 969 8311
Fax: 0161 962 9423
email: info@macsound.co.uk
Website: www.macsound.co.uk
Professional sound equipment hire

The Machine Room
54-58 Wardour Street
London WIV 3HN
Tel: 020 7734 3433
Fax: 020 7287 3773
email: david.atkinson@
machineroom.co.uk
Website: www.themachineroom.co.uk
David Atkinson
2 wet/dry gate digital Telecine suites
Cintel and Shadow with DVNR. VT
viewing and sound layback suite.
Most digital and analogue video tape
formats in both PAL and NTSC.
Standards conversion with Alchemist
Phc and Vector Motion
Compensation (VMC). Programme
dubbing. VHS duplication.
Macrovision anti-piracy system, 2
edit suites. FACT accredited. Special
rates for archive film transferFull
range of film treatment services. See
also Film Treatment Centre under
Laboratories. Nitrate handling and
nitrate storage vaults. DVD
Authoring and encoding

Mersey Film and Video (MFV)
13 Hope Street
Liverpool L1 9BQ
Tel: 0151 708 5259

Fax: 0151 707 8595
email: mfv@hopestreet.u-net.com
Website: www.mfv.merseyside.org
Julie Lau (Resources Manager)
Patrick Hall (Resources Co-
Ordinator)
Production facilities for: BETA SP,
DVCPro, Hi8, MiniDV SVHS and
VHS – full shooting kits for all. Wide
range of grip and lighting equipment.
All format tape duplication and tape
stock. Guidance and help for funding,
finance, budgets production

Metro Broadcast
6-7 Great Chapel Street
London W1F 3FF
Tel: 020 7434 7700
Fax: 020 7434 7701
email: info@metrobroadcast.co.uk
Website: www.metrobroadcast.co.uk
Mark Cox
Broadcast Hire and Crewing:
Digital Beta, Beta SX, Beta SP, DVC
Pro, DV Cam, Mini DV, Hi-Def
CiniAlta
Avid: MCO, film Composers, 9000,
NT or MAC
Duplication: Alchemists standards
conversions from/to all formats.
Technical assessment. Format include:
D1, D2, D3, Digital Beta, Beta SX,
DVC Pro, DV Cam, Mini DV, CD
ROM, DVD

The Mill/Mill Film
40/41 Great Marlborough Street
London W1V 1DA
Tel: 020 7287 4041
Fax: 020 7287 8393
email: inb@mill.co.uk
Website: www.mill.co.uk
Emma Shield
Post Production for commercials and
feature films using Spirit, Ursa,
Inferno, Flame, Softimage, Henry,
Harry and digital editing

Millennium Studios
Elstree Way
Borehamwood
Herts WD6 1SF
Tel: 020 8236 1400
Fax: 020 8236 1444
Kate Tufano
Sound stage 80'x44'x24' with
6'x44'x11' balcony flying and cyc
grid. In house suppliers of: lighting;
generators; rigging; photography;
crew catering and fully licensed bar

Mister Lighting Studios Ltd
2 Dukes Road
Western Avenue
London W3 0SL

Tel: 020 8956 5600
Fax: 020 8956 5604
Steve Smith
Lighting equipment/studio hire

Molinare
34 Fouberts Place
London W1V 2BH
Tel: 020 7439 2244
Fax: 020 7734 6813
Video formats: Digital Betacam, D1,
D2, D3, 1", Beta SP, BVU, U-Matic,
VHS. NTSC: 1", Beta SP, U-Matic &
VHS. Editing: Editbox, three D1 serial
digital suite; two component multi-
format; one composite multi-format.
DVEs: two A57, four A53, DME, four
ADO, Encore. Storage: two A66, A64.
Caption Generators: Aston Motif,
A72, Aston Caption, Aston 3.
Graphics: Harry with V7 Paintbox,
Encore and D1. Harriet with V7
Paintbox, D1 and Beta SP. 3D
graphics with Silicon Graphics and
Softimage. Telecine: Ursa Gold with
Pogle + DCP, A57, Rank Cintel 111
with 4.2.2 digital links, wetgate, Pogle
and DCP controller and secondary
colour grading, 35mm, 16mm,
S16mm/S8. Audio: two digital studios,
two 24 track and AudioFile studios,
track-laying studio with DAWN, voice
record studios, transfer room, sound
Fx libraries. Duplication, standards
conversion, Matrix camera, BT
landlines, satellite downlink

Mosaic Pictures Ltd
8-12 Broadwick Street
London W1V 1FH
Tel: 020 7437 6514
Fax: 020 7494 0595
email: info@mosaicfilms.com
Website: www.mosaicfilms.com
Deborah Weavers, Facilities Manager
Avid Symphony, 6 Avid offline suites,
DV Camera Hire, Video Transfer
Suite, Final Cut Pro, DV Post-
Production expertise, Video encoding
for the Web, Digibeta/16mm Aaton
Cameramen, meeting room,
production offices

The Moving Picture Company
127 Wardour Street
London W1V 4AD
Tel: 020 7434 3100
Fax: 020 7437 3951/287 5187
Video formats: D1, D2, Digital
Betacam, Betacam SP, 1" C format,
hi-/lo-band.
Editing: 3xD1/Disk based edit suites,
Sony 9100 and Abekas A84 (8 layers)
A57 DVE, A64, A60 and A66 Disks;

A72 and Aston Motif caption
generator. Video Rostrum and Colour
Caption Camera
Non Linear Offline Editing: 1 x Avid
4000 with Betacam SP. 35/16mm
cutting room
Telecine: 2 URSA Gold 4 x 4 with
Pogle DCP/Russell Square Colour
Correction Jump Free, Low
Speed/Silk Scan Options, Matchbox
Stills Store, Key Code, noise
reduction
SFX: Discreet Logic 2 x Flame, 1 x
Flint and Quantel 2 x Henry
3D: Hardware: 7 x SGI systems (3 x
High Impacts and 4 x Indigo 2
Extremes). Software: Alias
Poweranimator, Custom
Programming and Procedural Effects,
Matador, 3D Studio Paint, Elastic
Reality and Pandemonium.
Rendering: SGI Challenge and Onyx
(x2). Digital Film: High resolution
35mm digital film post production,
comprising 7 x Kodak Cineon, 1 x
Discreet Logic Inferno and Matador.
Filmtel TM video tape to 35mm
transfer. Mac: Disk or ISDN input of
artwork. File transfer, Photoshop and
Illustrator and stills output to 35mm
or high resolution 5 x 4
transparencies
Studio: 47' x 30' with L cyc

Northern Light
35/41 Assembly Street
Leith
Edinburgh EH6 7RG
Tel: 0131 553 2383
Fax: 0131 553 3296
Gordon Blackburn
Stage lighting equipment hire. Mains
distribution, staging, PA equipment
hire. Sale of colour correction
pyrotechnics etc

Oasis Television
6-7 Great Pulteney Street
London W1V 3LF
Tel: 020 7434 4133
Fax: 020 7494 2843
Helen Leicester
14 online suites (including digital
linear, analogue linear, Jaleo Digital,
Non-linear, Avid Online). 2 fully
digital audiodubbing suites. 11 Avid
and Lightworkds offline services. 5
graphics suites C2D and 3D,
including illusion), standards
conversion. Full duplication facilities
multimedia

Ocean Post
5 Upper James Street
London W1R 3HF

Tel: 020 7287 2297
Fax: 020 7287 0296
email: bookings@oceanpost.co.uk
Editbox suite, Avid online suites, Avid offline suites

Omnititles
28 Manor Way
London SE3 9EF
Tel: 020 8297 7877
Fax: 020 8297 7877
email: Omnititles@compuserve.com
Spotting and subtitling services for film, TV, video, satellite and cable. Subtitling in most world languages

Oxford Film and Video Makers
The Stables
North Place
Headington
Oxford OX3 9HY
Tel: 01865 741682 or 01865 760074 (course enquiries)
Fax: 01865 742901
email: ofvm@ox39hy.demon.co.uk
Website: www.welcome.to/ofvm
Sue Evans, Office Administrator
Film and video equipment hire - including Beta SP and non-linear editing facility. FAST VM studio & Adobe Premier. Wide range of evening and weekend courses

Panavision Grips
5-11 Taunton Road
Metropolitan Centre
Greenford
Middx UB6 8UQ
Tel: 020 8578 2382
Fax: 020 8578 1536
email: pangrip.co.uk
Grip equipment and studio hire
The Greenford Studios
5-11 Taunton road
Metropolitan Centre
Greenford Middx UB6 8UQ
Tel: 0181 575 7300
Fax: 0181 839 1640

The Pierce Rooms
Pierce House
London Apollo Complex
Queen Caroline Street
London W6 9QU
Tel: 020 8563 1234
Fax: 020 8563 1337
email: meredith@pierce-entertainment.com
Website: www.pierce-entertainment.com
Meredith Leung, Studio Manager
Complete surround sound facilities: surround sound to picture recording. Foley and mixing. Large and accurate main control room - Neve VR 72-60

console with flying fader automation, recall and digital surround automation. Dynaudio M4-surround sound monitoring. Separate digital preproduction room. Permanent tie lines to Apollo theatre for studio quality live recordings. In house team of engineers and programmers; 24 hour maintenance; private parking

Pinewood Studios
Sound Dept
Pinewood Road
Iver Heath
Bucks SL0 0NH
Tel: 01753 656301
Fax: 01753 656014
email: graham_hartstone@pinewood-studios.co.uk
Website: www.pinewood-studios.co.uk
Graham Hartstone
Two large stereo dubbing theatres with automated consoles, all digital release formats. 35mm and Digital dubbing. Akai DD8 dubbers & recorders, ADR & Foley recording. Large ADR/Fx recording theatre, 35mm or AVID AUDIOVISION, removable drives, ISDN Dolbyfax with timecode in aux data. Digital dubbing theatres with AMS/NEVE Logic 2 and AudioFile Spectra 16. Preview theatre 115 seats. Formats 35/70mm Dolby SR.D, DTS and SDDS. Comprehensive transfer bay. Stereo Optical Negative transfer including Dolby SR.D, SDDS and DTS. Cutting rooms

PMPP Facilities
69 Dean Street
London W1V 5HB
Tel: 020 7437 0979
Fax: 020 7434 0386
Website: www.pmpp.dircon.co.uk
Off-line editing: BVW SP, lo-band and VHS. Non-linear editing: 5 custom built Avid suites either self drive or with editor. On-line editing: Digital Betacam, D3, D2, Beta SP, 1", BVU SP and Hi-8 formats. Three suites with Charisma effects Aston or A72 cap gen and GVG mixers. Graphics: Matisse Painting, Softimage 3D, Acrobat 3D, animation and T-Morph morphing on Silicon Graphics workstations. Sound dubbing on Avid Audiovision or AudioFile. Voiceover studio/A-DAT digital multi-track recording. Full transfer, duplication and standards conversion service. Pack shot studio

Post Box
8 Lower James Street
London W1R 3PL
Tel: 020 7439 0600
Fax: 020 7439 0700
Jo Smith
Jo Beddington, Jason Elliott, Alice Valdes-Scott
UK and international post production. Offline, online, editbox, Magnum and more - offering the whole package for broadcasters

Red Post Production
Hammersley House
London W1R 6JD
Tel: 020 7439 1449
Fax: 020 7439 1339
email: Red-Post@Demon.co.uk
email: Redfx@Demon.co.uk
Post production company specialising in design and technical special effects for commercials, video promos, broadcast titles and idents, feature film projects, broadcast projects utilising computer animation techniques. Motion capture, Flame, Henry, Flash Harry. Full technical supervision

Redapple
214 Epsom Road
Merrow
Guildford
Surrey GU1 2RA
Tel: 01483 455044
Fax: 01483 455022
email: redap@msn.com
Video formats: Beta SP, Beta Sx, NTSC/PAL. Cameras: Sony DNW 90WSP, 4:3016:9, IKEGAMI, V-55 Camcorders; Transport; VW Caravelle and Volvo Camera Cars, Twin Engine Aircraft

Redwood Studios Recording & Film Post Production
1-6 Falconberg Court
London W1V 5FG
Andre Jacquemin - Managing Director - Sound Designer
Post production for features including large f/x library and digital audio post work

Richmond Film Services
The Old School
Park Lane
Richmond
Surrey TW9 2RA
Tel: 020 8940 6077
Fax: 020 8948 8326
Sound equipment available for hire, sales of tape and batteries, and UK

agent for Ursta recordists' trolleys and Denecke timecode equipment

Salon Post-Productions

12 Swainson Road
London W3 7XB
Tel: 020 8746 7611
Fax: 020 8746 7613
email: hire@salonrentals.com
Website: www.salonrentals.com
Editing Equipment rental -
non linear systems including Avid
Film Composer & Lightworks, hard
disk storage, BetaSP and DAT etc
Film equipment - including 35mm
and 16mm Steenbecks and all editing
accessories and supplies. Edit suites in
Acton or delivered to any location.
Digital sound editing systems include
Audiovision, Protools

Sheffield Independent Film

5 Brown Street
Sheffield S1 2BS
Tel: 0114 272 0304
Fax: 0114 279 5225
email: admin.ympa@
workstation.org.uk
Colin Pons
Colin Pons, Gloria Ward,
Alan Robinson
Aaton XTR + (S16/St 16). Vision 12
tripod S16/St 16. 6-plate Steenbeck,
Picsync. Nagra IS. SQN 45 mixer.
Microphones: 416, 816, ECM 55s.
SVHS edit suite. Avid MSP edit suite
Sony DXC537. UVW100
Betakit/Betacam (PVE 2800)/Hi-band
SP (BVU 950)/Hi-8, 2 and 3 machine
edit suite. Three Chip cameras.
Lighting equipment. 1,200 ft studio.
Sony DVC Digital Camcorder

Shepperton Sound

Shepperton Studios
Studios road
Shepperton
Middx TW17 0QD
Tel: 01932 572676
Fax: 01932 572396
three Dubbing Theatres (16mm,
35mm, video) Post-sync, and
footsteps; effects, theatre, in-house
sound transfers

Shepperton Studios

Studios Road
Shepperton
Middx TW17 0QD
Tel: 01932 562611
Fax: 01932 568989
email: sheppertonstudios@
dial.pipex.com
Cutting rooms; 16mm, 35mm
viewing theatres

Soho Images

8-14 Meard Street
London W1V 3HR
Tel: 020 7437 0831
Fax: 020 7734 9471
email: sohogroup.com
Website: www.sohoimages.com
Zahida Bacchus
Kodak endorsed laboratory offers full
processing of 16/35mm film, 24
hours rushes, computerised in-house
negative cutting, cinema
commercials, broadcast and features
bulk prints, archive and restoration.
Facilities include: 8/16/35mm
Telecine transfers with Wet-Gate.
Spirit DataCine with POGAL
Platinum, URSA Gold with DCP,
Rank Cinitels' with up-grades. Sound
suite using Instant Sync, InDaw and
SADIE. Broadcast standards
conversions, aspect ration
conversions, edit suites, Avid
Symphony Universal with 24P, 3D
and Animation, Flame, Henry and
Edit Box

Studo Pur

c/o Gargoyle Graphics
16 Chart St
London N1 6UG
Tel: 020 7490 5177
Fax: 020 7490 5177
email: sbayly@ich.ucl.ac.uk
Website: www.ace.mdx.ac.uk
/hyperhomes/houses/pur/index.htm
Simon Bayly, Lucy Thane
Media 100 & After Effects, Pro Tools,
Sony DSR-200 DVCAM camcorder &
tripod, Tascam portable DAT, audio
effects processing, 500 lumens video
projector, multimedia workstation,
mics, lights & PA equipment

SVC

142 Wardour Street
London WIF 8ZO
Tel: 020 7734 1600
Fax: 020 7437 1854
Website: www.svc.co.uk
Catherine Langley
Video Post Production including the
following: Datacine, Inferno, Flame, 2
Infinitys; Henry, Computer
Animation and Motion Control

Tele-Cine

Video House
48 Charlotte Street
London W1P 1LX
Tel: 020 7208 2200
Fax: 020 7208 2250
email: telecine@telecine.co.uk
Website: www.telecine.co.uk

Wendy Bleazard
Digital linear and non linear editing;
telecine; audio post production; DVD
authoring; video compression; fibre
and satellite communications;
duplication

Terry Jones
PostProductions Ltd

The Hat Factory
16-18 Hollen Street
London W1V 3AD
Tel: 020 7434 1173
Fax: 020 7494 1893
Terry Jones
Paul Jones or Matt Nutley
Lightworks V.I.P. online and
Heavyworks editing suites. Plus
computerised Beta offline and 35mm
film editing facilities. Experiencd and
creative, award winning editors
handling commercials,
documentaries, features and
corporate work

The Video Lab

Back West Crescent
St Annes on Sea
Lancs FY8 1SU
Tel: 01253 725499/712011
Fax: 01253 713094
Cintel Telecine 9.5/8/Super
8/16/35mm, slides and stills. Video
formats: 2", 1"C, BVU, U-Matic, Beta
SP. Cameras: Sony. Duplication,
standards conversion. Specialists in
transfer from discontinued videotape
formats. Library of holiday videos
(Travelogue), corporate and TV
production, TV and cinema
commercial production

Tiny Epic Video Co

37 Dean Street
London W1V 5AP
Tel: 020 7437 2854
Fax: 020 7434 0211
Non-linear offlining on Avid, and
D/Vision. Tape offlining on Umatic &
VHS with and without shotlister.
Rushes dubbing. Tape transfers -
most formats including Hi-8 and
DAT. EDL Generation and
Translation

TVi

Film House
142 Wardour Street
London W1V 3AU
Tel: 020 7878 0000
Fax: 020 7878 7800
Website: www.tvi.co.uk
Mark Ottley
Mark Ottley, Joy Hancock
Post production; Telecine; sound

dubbing; copying and conversion. Extensive integrated services especially for film originated programmes. Full digital compo-nent environment. Wetgate digital Telecine with Aaton and ARRI and full range of gates including Super 16mm and 35mm wide aperture wetgate transfers. Full film rushes transfer service. Free film preparation service. Wide range of VTRs including Digital Betacam

TVMS, TV Media
420 Sauchiehall Street
Glasgow G2 3JD
Tel: 0141 331 1993
Fax: 0141 332 9040
Peter McNeill, Chas Chalmers
Media 100 off-line and on-line with Beta SP and Digital facilities for Broadcast, Commercials, and Corporate Productions

TVP Videodubbing Ltd
2 Golden Square
London W1R 3AD
Tel: 020 7439 7138
Fax: 020 7434 1907
Jaqui Winston
Telecine transfer from 35mm, Super 16mm, 16mm and Super 8mm to all video formats with full grading, blemish concealment and image restoration service. Video mastering, reformatting and duplication to and from any format; standards conversion service including motion compensation via the Alchemist Ph. C. digital converter. Also landlines for feeds to the BT Tower and commercials playouts. Laserdisc pre-mastering and full quality assessment. Packaging

Twickenham Film Studios
St Margaret's
Twickenham
Middx TW1 2AW
Tel: 020 8607 8888
Fax: 020 8607 8889
Gerry Humphreys,
ISDN: 0181 744 1415
Gerry Humphreys, Caroline Tipple
Two dubbing theatres; ADR/Foley theatre; 40 cutting rooms; Lightworks, Avid, 16/35mm

Vector Television
Battersea Road
Heaton Mersey
Stockport
Cheshire SK4 3EA
Tel: 0161 432 9000
Fax: 0161 443 1325

Martin Tetlow
Vector Graphics; Vector Digital Audio; Vector Digital editing; Vector Studios; 2D/3D design and visualisation consultancy

Video Film & Grip Company
23 Alliance Court
Alliance Road
London W3 0RB
Tel: 020 8993 8555
Fax: 020 8896 3941
Contact: G.Stubbings
Unit 9, Orchard Street Industrial Estate, Salford
Manchester M6 6FL
Tel: 0161 745 8146
Fax: 0161 745 8161
Cardiff Studios, Culverhouse Cross, Cardiff CF5 6XT
Tel: 01222 599777
Fax: 01222 597957
Suppliers of 35mm camera equipment. 16mm camera equipment for documentaries, Digital SP and Beta SP video equipment for broadcast, and extensive range of cranes, dollies and ancillary grip equipment

Videola (UK)
162-170 Wardour Street
London W1V 3TA
Tel: 020 7437 5413
Fax: 020 7734 5295
Video formats: 1", U-Matic, Beta SP. Camera: JVC KY35. Editing: three machine Beta SP. Computer rostrum camera. Lightworks offline

Videolondon Sound
16-18 Ramillies Street
London W1V 1DL
Tel: 020 7734 4811
Fax: 020 7494 2553
email: info@videolon.ftech.co.uk
Website: www.ftech.net/~videolon
Five sophisticated sound recording studios with overhead TV projection systems. 16mm, 35mm and video post-sync recording and mixing. Two Synclavier digital audio suites with four further Synclaviers, five AvidAudiovision, two StudioFrame and one AudioFile assignable to any of the studios. All sound facilities for film or video post-production including D3, DigiBetacam, Betacam SP, 1" PAL and Dolby Surround for TV with three Lightworks non-linear editing systems

Videosonics Cinema Sound
68a Delancey Street
London NW1 7RY

Tel: 020 7209 0209
Fax: 020 7419 4470
2 x All Digital THX Film Dubbing Theatres. Dolby Digital and SR 35 mm, 16mm and Super 16mm. All aspect ratios, all speeds. Video Projection if required Theatre I: AMS-Neve Logic II console (112 channels) with 24track Audiofile. Theatre II (Big Blue): AMS-Neve DFC console (224 channels) with 2 x 24 track Audio files. 3 x additional television Sound Dubbing Suites, 2 with AMS-Neve digital consoles, 1 x SSL console. 6 x Digital Audio Editing rooms, 35mm film editing, Facilities for Lightworks and Avid 2 x Foley and ADR Studios. A total of 14 AMS Audiofiles. Parking by arrangement. Wheelchair Access

VTR Ltd
64 Dean Street
London W1V 5HG
Tel: 020 7437 0026
Fax: 020 7439 9427
email: info@vtr.co.uk
Website: www.vtr.co.uk
Anthony Frend
VTR is one of London's major digital non-linear post production facilities specialising in commercials, corporates and promos. Facilities include: 2 x Spirit DataCines the world's first real-time high resolution film scanner for 35mm, 16mm and super 16mm; Ursa Gold telecines with Pogle Platinum and full range of Ursa optical effects incl. Kaleidoscope; Inferno and Flame for resolution independent special effects for TV and cinema. 3x Henry Infinity for non-linear digital editing and effects. 3D Computer Graphics and Animation with Maya Software; Flint RT, 3 x Macs; dubbing, ISDN and playout facilities. Domino (digital film effects) see under 'The Film Factory at VTR.'

Windmill Lane Pictures
4 Windmill Lane
Dublin 2
Ireland
Tel: (353) 1 6713444
Fax: (353) 1 6718413
Liz Murphy
Telecine, digital on-line, AVID off-line, Henry, Flame, Flint, EFP Crews and number 4 Audio Studio

World Wide Sound
21-25 St Anne's Court
London W1V 3AW
Tel: 020 7434 1121

Fax: 020 7734 0619
email: sound@worldwidegroup.ltd.uk
Website: worldwidegroup.ltd.uk
Richard King
16/35mm, digital and Dolby
recording, track laying facilities,
specialising in post sync foreign
dubbing. Mixing for film - television
incl. Dolby Surround

Worldwide Television News (WTN Facilities)

The Interchange
Oval Road
Camden Lock
London NW1
Tel: 020 7410 5410
Fax: 020 7410 5335
Anne Marie Phelan
2 TV studios (full cyc and component
key); Digital Betacam and Beta SP
editing (PAL and NTSC), Quantel
Newsbox Non-linear online editing;
Vistek VMC Digital standards
conversion; Soundstation Digital
Audio dubbing; UK and international
satellite delivery and crews

FESTIVALS

Listed below by country of origin are a selection of international film, television and video festivals with contact names and brief synopses

AUSTRALIA

Melbourne International Film Festival

- 18 July-5 August 2001
PO Box 2206, Fitzroy Mail Centre
Fitzroy 3065
Victoria
Tel: (61) 3 9417 2011
Fax: (61) 3 9417 3804
email: miff@vicnet.net.au
Website: melbournefilmfestival.com.au
Kate Marks
The Melbourne International Film Festival is a showcase for the latest developments in Australian and international filmmaking, offering audiences a wide range of features and shorts, encompassing fiction, documentaries, animation and experimental films with a programme of more than 350 films from over 40 countries

Sydney Film Festival

- June 2002
PO Box 950
Glebe NSW 2037
Tel: (61) 2 9660 3844
Fax: (61) 2 9692 8793
email: info@sydfilm-fest.com.au
Website: www.sydfilm-fest.com.au
A broad-based non-competitive Festival screening around 200 films not previously shown in Australia: features, documentaries, shorts, animation, video and experimental work. Competitive section for Australian short films only. Audience votes for best documentary, short and feature

AUSTRIA

Viennale - Vienna International Film Festival

- 19-31 October 2001
Siebensterngasse 2
A-1070
Vienna
Tel: (43) 1 526 5947
Fax: (43) 1 523 4172
email: office@viennale.at
Website: www.viennale.at
Andrea Glawogger
The non-competitive festival primary focal point is independent international cinema of every type and format - from avant-garde to controversial America genre films, from contemporary Asian cinema to essays films, documentaries and shorts. Homage to outstanding creative talent in form of special programs such as the Tributes. Extensive historical or thematic retrospective

BELGIUM

Brussels International Festival of Fantasy, Thriller and Science Fiction Films

- March 2002
8, rue de la Comtesse de Flandre
1020 Brussels
Tel: (32) 2 201 1713
Fax: (32) 2 201 1469
email: peymey@bifff.org
Website: www.bifff.org/
Georges Delmote
Competitive for features and shorts (less than 20 mins)

Brussels International Film Festival

- 16-26 January 2002
Leuvensesteenweg 30
B - 1210 Brussels
Tel: (32) 2 227 39 80
Fax: (32) 2 218 18 60
email: infoffb@netcity.be
Website: www.brusselsfilmfest.be
Christian Thomas, Director
This is a competitive festival for European general interest films, annually showing about 100 features and 120 shorts. European features and shorts eligible to compete for Golden and Silver Iris Awards. Belgian shorts eligible to compete for Golden Iris Awards. Sections include European Competition, Kaleidoscope of the World Cinema, Belgian Focus with a National Competition for shorts and documentaries, 2001: Focus on New German directors, Special Events and Tributes. Feature entries should be over 60 minutes

and shorts should be under 30 minutes. Formats accepted: 35mm, 16mm (Belgian films only). Deadline: 31st October. No entry fee

Flanders International Film Festival - Ghent

- 8-19 October 2002
1104 Kortrijksesteenweg
B-9051 Ghent
Tel: (32) 9 242 8060
Fax: (32) 9 221 9074
email: info@filmfestival.be
Website: www.filmfestival.be
Contact: Jacques Dubrulle, Secretary-general, Wim De Witte, Programme Executive
Marian Ponnet, Guest Officer.
Belgium's most prominent yearly film event. Competitive, showing 150 feature films and 80 shorts from around the world. Best film award $35,000. Deadline for entry forms mid August

BOSNIA

Sarajevo Film Festival

- 17-25 August 2001
Obala Kulina Bana 10
71000 Sarajevo
Bosnia and Herzegovina
Tel: (387) 7166 8186
Fax: (387) 7166 4547
email: sff@sff.ba
Website: www.sff.ba
Paula Gordon
A competitive festival screening features, shorts, documentaries and animation

BRAZIL

Festival Do Rio Br- Rio de Janeiro Film Festivals

- September
Rua Voluntários dá Pátria 97
Botalfogo - rio de Janeiro
Rio de Janeiro RJ 22270-000
Tel: (55) 21 5790352
Fax: (55) 21 5393580
email: films@festivaldoriobr.com.br
Website: www.festivaldoriobr.com.br
Ilda Santiago, Walkiria Barbosa
Non-competitive, feature films

Gramado International Film Festival - Latin and Brazilian Cinema

- August 2001
Rua Evaristo da Veiga 21/606
20031-040 Rio de Janeiro RJ
Tel: (55) 21 240-7804
Fax: (55) 21 537-2898
email: urano@ax.apc.org
Website: www.viadigital.com.br/gramado
For exhibition of audiovisual products from Latin language speaking countries

São Paulo International Film Festival

- 19 October-1 November 2000
Alameda Lorena 937, Cj 303
São Paulo SP 01424-001
Tel: (55) 11 3083 5137/3064 5819
Fax: (55) 11 3085 7936
email: info@mostra.org
Website: www.mostra.org
Renata de Almeida
Two sections, international selection (for features, shorts, documentary, animation.) and a competitive section for films of new directors (first, second or third feature), produced during two years preceding the festival

BURKINA FASO

Panafrican Film and TV Festival of Ouagadougou

- 22 February-1 March 2003
Secrétariat Général Permanent du FESPACO
01 BP 2505
Ouagadougou 01
Tel: (226) 30 75 38
Fax: (226) 31 25 09
email: sg@fespaco.bf
Website: www.fespaco.bf
Competitive, featuring African diaspora and African film-makers, whose work has been produced during the three years preceding the Festival, and not shown before at FESPACO

CANADA

Hot Docs Canadian International Documentary Festival

- April, May
517 College Street
Suite 420
Toronto
Ontario, M6G 4A2
Tel: (1) 416 203 2155

Fax: (1) 416 203 0446
email: info@hotdocs.ca
Website: www.hotdocs.ca
Founded in 1993 by the Canadian Independent Film Caucus, a national association of documentary producers and directors, and separately incorporated in 1996, Hot Docs has become North America's largest documentary festival. Hot Docs has built a reputation for showcasing the best of documentary cinema

The Atlantic Film Festival (Halifax)

- 14 - 22 September 2001
PO Box 36139
220-5600 Sackville Street
Halifax
Nova Scotia B3J 3S9
Tel: (1) 902 422 3456
Fax: (1) 902 422 4006
email: festival@atlanticfilm.com
Website: www.atlanticfilm.com
Gordon Whittaker - Executive Director
Lia Rinaldo - Program Director
Gregor Ash, Operations Manger
Entry Deadline: 9 June 2000
Located in coastal Halifax, Nova Scotia, the Atlantic Film Festival is a nine-day celebration of film known for its warm and festive atmosphere

Banff Television Festival

- 9-14 June 2002
1516 Railway Avenue
Canmore, Alberta, T1W 1P6
Tel: (1) 403 678 9260
Fax: (1) 403 678 92691
email: info@banfftvtest.com
Website: www.banff2001.com
W. Paterson Ferns - President + CEO
The Banff Television Festival takes place every June in Banff, Alberta. It is a special gathering place for television program producers and on-line content creators. The conference schedule features over 60 hours of workshops, plenary sessions, keynote speakers, master classes, market simulations and pitching opportunities. There is also the international Banff Rockie Awards program competition

Festival International de Nouveau Cinéma et des Nouveaux Médias de Montréal (FCMM)

- 11-21 October 2001
Boulevard Saint-Laurent 3530
Montreal

Quebec H2X 2V1
Tel: (1) 514 847 9272
Fax: (1) 514 847 0732
email: montrealfest@fcmm.com
Website: www.fcmm.com
Claude Chamberlan
Discovery and promotion of outstanding international films, video and new media creations produced during previous two years, which have not been previously screened in Canada. Non-competitive (although some prizes in cash are awarded)

Montreal World Film Festival (+ Market)

- 23 August - 3 September 2001
Boulevard Saint-Laurent 3530
Montreal
Quebec H2X 2V1
Tel: (1) 514 848 3883
Fax: (1) 514 848 0060
email: ffm@qc.aira.com
Website: www.ffm-montreal.org
Competitive festival recognized by the International Federation of Film Producers Associations. Categories: Official Competition; World Greats; World Cinema: Reflections of Our Time; Cinema of Tomorrow: New Trends; Latin American Cinema; Focus on Irish Cinema; Panorama Canada; Films for Television (documentaries and fiction films); Tributes

Ottawa International Animation Festival

- 19-24 September 2000
2 Daly Avenue
Ottawa
Ontario K1N 6E2
Tel: (1) 613 232 8769
Fax: (1) 613 232 6315
email: oiaf@ottawa.com
Website: www.awn.com/ottawa
Chris Robinson, Artistic Director
Competitive. Next festival in 2002

Toronto International Film Festival

- 6-15 September 2001
2 Carlton Street, Suite 1600
Toronto
Ontario M5B IJ3
Tel: (1) 416 967 7371
Fax: (1) 416 967 9477
email: tiffg@torfilmfest.ca
Website: www.bell.ca/filmfest
Nuria Bronfman
Non-competitive for feature films and shorts not previously shown in Canada. Also includes some American premieres, retrospectives and national cinema programmes.

Films must have been completed within the year prior to the Festival to be eligible

Vancouver International Film Festival

- 27 September-12 October 2001
Suite 410, 1008 Homer Street
Vancouver
British Columbia V6B 2X1
Tel: (1) 604 685 0260
Fax: (1) 604 688 8221
email: viff@viff.org
Website: Webstite: www.viff.org
Third largest festival in North America, with special emphasis on East Asian, Canadian and documentary films. Also British and European cinema and 'the Annual Film & Television Industry Trade Forum. Submission deadline mid-July

COLUMBIA

Cartagena Film Festival

- March 2002
Baluarte de San Francisco
Calle San Juan de Dios
A.A. 1834, Cartagena, Colombia
tel: (57-5) 660-0966
fax: (57-5) 660-0970
e-mail: spyder@escape.com
website: www.festicinecartagena.com
contact: Victor Nieto
A competitive festival screening mainly Latin American films, covering features, shorts and documentaries

CROATIA

World Festival of Animated Films-Zagreb

- 18-23 June 2002
Koncertna Direkcija Zagreb
Kneza Mislava 18
10000 Zagreb, Croatia
Tel: (385) 1 461 1808/461 1709
Fax: (385) 1 461 1807/1808
email: animafest@animafest.hr
Website: www.animafest.hr
Margit Antauer
Competitive for animated films (up to 30 mins). Categories: a) films from 30 secs-6 mins, b) films from 6-15 mins, c) 15 min-30mins. Awards: Grand Prix, First Prize in each category (ABC), Best First Production (Film Debut) Best Student Film, Five Special Distinctions. Films must have been completed in two years prior to the Festival and not have been awarded prizes. Biennial festival.

DENMARK

Dubrovnik Film and TV Festival (formerly Balticum Film and TV Festival)

- June
Art radionica Lazareti
Vesna Mitrovic
Pobijana 8
20000 Dubrovnik
Tel: 385 020 423 497
Fax: 385 020 421 114
email: art-lazareti@du.tel.hr
Website: www.filmfest.dk/dubrovnik/
Three competitive programmes:
South East Europe Documentaries
A competition programme with documentaries from each of the 13 participating SEE countries, regions and provinces:
Albania, Bosnia Herzegovina, Bulgaria, Croatia, FYR Macedonia, Greece, Hungary, Kosovo, Montenegro, Romania, Serbia, Slovenia and Turkey.
Entry deadline is 1 April, 2001.
Balticum Documentaries
A competition programme with documentaries from each of the 9 countries around the Baltic Sea:
Denmark, Estonia, Finland, Germany, Latvia, Lithuania, Poland, Russia and Sweden
Entry deadline 1 April 2001.
Film School Documentary Competition
A competition programme with documentaries from European film schools.
Deadline: April 1 2001

CUBA

International Festival of New Latin American Cinema

- December 2001
Calle 23
1155 Vedado
Havana 4
Tel: (53) 7 552 841/552 849
Fax: (53) 7 333 078/334 273
Competitive for films and videos

CZECH REPUBLIC

'Golden Prague' 39th International TV Festival

- May 5-9 (2001)
Czech Television
Kavci Hory
140 70 Prague 4
Tel: 004202 6113 4153/4133/4045
Fax: 004202 6121 2891
email: golden_prague@czech-tv.cz
Andrea Nahodilova, Administrative Manager, ITF Golden Prague/Int
The International Television Festival Golden Prague (ITF GP), by way of its competition, video library, workshops and public screenings, intends to promote programmes dedicated to music and dance.
Deadline: Entry forms by 28 February 2002, cassettes by 31 March 2002.
Fees: The competition entry fee is DEM 400. In case of additional entries the fee for the second and the third entry is to be DEM 250 each.
The entry fee for the non-competition section "cassetteria" is DEM 100.

Karlovy Vary International Film Festival

- 5-14 July 2001
Film Servis Festival Karlovy Vary
Panská 1
110 00 Prague 1
Tel: (420) -2 2423 5412
Fax: (420)-2 2423 3408
email: festival@iffkv.cz
Website: www.kviff.com
Jiri Bartoska, president
Non-specialised international competition of feature films; international competition of full-length and short documentary films; non-competitive informational film programmes, retrospectives, homage profiles and other accompanying events approved by the Film Servis Festival Board. Works produced after 1st January 1999 can be included in competitive sections. It is obligatory that these films have not been previously shown in the competition section of another international film festival

DENMARK

Copenhagen Film Festival

- October
FSI
Bulowsveg 50A
D-1870 Frederiks
1620 Copenhagen V
Tel: (45) 35 37 25 07
Fax: (45) 31 35 57 58
email: fside@datashopper.dk
Jonna Jensen
Festival for the public. Previews of American, European and Danish films, both by established filmmakers and those less well known. Around 120 films, plus seminars and exhibition

International Odense Film Festival

- 13-18 August 2001
Vindegade 18
5100 Odense C
Tel: (45) 6614 8814 x4044
Fax: (45) 6591 4318
email: off.ksf@odense.dk
Website: www.filmfestival.dk
Competitive for fairy-tale and experimental-imaginative films.
Deadline for entries 1 April

EGYPT

Cairo International Film Festival

- 9-20 October 2001
17 Kasr El Nil Street
Cairo
Tel: (20) 2 392 3962/3562
Fax: (20) 2 393 8979
email: info@cairofilmfest.com
Website: www.cairofilmfest.com
Hussein Fahmi, president
Competitive for feature films, plus a film, television and video market

Cairo International Film Festival for Children

17 Kasr el El Nil Street
Cairo
Tel: (20) 2 392 3562/3962/393 3832
Fax: (20) 2 393 8979
Competitive for children's films: features, shorts, documentaries, educative, cartoons, television films and programmes for children up to 14 years

FINLAND

Midnight Sun Film Festival

- 13-17 June 2001
Malminkatu 36
FIN-00100 Helsinki, Finland
Tel: (358) 9 685 2242
Fax: (358) 9 694-5560
email: office@msfilmfestival.fi
Website: www.msfilmfestival.fi
Non-competitive for feature films, held in Finnish Lapland

Tampere Film Festival

- 5-10 March 2002
Tullikamarinaukio 2
PO Box 305
33101 Tampere
Tel: (358) 3 213 0034
Fax: (358) 3 223 0121
email: office@tamperefilmfestival.fi
Website: www.tamperefilmfestival.fi
Antti Vuorio, Festival Director
Competitive for short films, max. 30 mins. Categories for animated, fiction and documentary short films, completed on or after 1st January 2000. Videos (VHS) required for selection, 16mm 35mm, Betacam, DVD and Digital Beta allowed as screening prints. Extensive special programme of short films from all over the world, film market.
Competition deadline 5 December 2001

FRANCE

20th Amiens International Film Festival

- 10-18 November 2001
MCA - 2 place Léon Gontier
F-8000 Amiens
Tel: (33) 3 2271 3570
Fax: (33) 3 2292 5304
Émail: contact@filmfestamiens.org
Jean-Pierre Garcia
Website: www.filmfestamiens.org
Films completed after 15 September 1998, and which make a contribution to the identity of people or an ethnic minority, are eligible for entry. They may be either full-length or short, fiction or documentary films

Annecy International Festival of Animation (+ Market)

- 3-9 June 2002
JICA/MIFA
6 avenues des Iles
BP 399
74013 Annecy Cédex
Tel: (33) 04 50 10 09 00
Fax: (33) 04 50 10 09 70
email: info@annecy.org
Website: www.annecy.org
Competitive for animated short films, feature-length films, TV films, commercials, produced in the previous 26 months

Cannes International Film Festival - Festival International du Film de Cannes 54 édition

- 9-20 May 2001
99 Boulevard Malesherbes
75008 Paris
Tel: (33) 1 45 61 66 00
Fax: (33) 1 45 61 97 60
email: festival@festival-cannes.fr
Website: www.festival-cannes.org
Gilles Jacob
Competitive section for feature films and shorts (up to 15 mins) produced in the previous year, which have not been screened outside country of origin nor been entered in other competitive festivals, plus non-competitive section: Un Certain Regard & Cinefondation. Other non-competitive events: Directors Fortnight (Quinzaine des Réalisateurs)
14, rue Alexandre Parodi
75010 Paris
Tel: (33) 1 44 89 99 99
Fax: (33) 1 44 89 99 60
Critic's Week (Semaine de la Critique)
52 rue Labrouste
75015 Paris
Tel: (33) 1 56 08 18 88
Fax: (33) 1 56 08 18 28

Cinéma du Réel, (International Festival of Visual Anthropology)

- 8 -17 March 2002
Bibliothèque Publique d'Information
25 rue du Renard
75197 Paris Cedex 04
Tel: (33) 1 44 78 44 21/45 16
Fax: (33) 1 44 78 12 24
email: cinereel@bpi.fr
Website: www.bpi.fr
Suzette Glenadel
Documentaries only (film or video). Competitive - must not have been released commercially or been awarded a prize at an international festival in France. Must have been made in the year prior to the Festival

Clermont-Ferrand Short Film Festival

- 1-9 February 2002
La Jetée
6 place Michel-de-l'Hospital
63058 Clermont-Ferrand
Cedex 1
Tel: (33) 4 73 91 65 73
Fax: (33) 4 73 92 11 93
email: info@clermont-filmfest.com
Website: www.clermont-filmfest.com
Christian Guinot
Short films, competitive

Cognac International Thriller Film Festival

- 4-7 April 2002
Le Public Systeme
36 rue Pierret
92200 Neuilly-sur-Seine
Tel: (33) 1 46 40 55 00
Fax: (33) 1 46 40 55 39
email: cognac@pobox.com
Website: www.cognac-France.com /polar
Competitive for thriller films, which have not been commercially shown in France or participated in festivals in

Europe (police movies, thrillers, 'film noirs', court movies, investigations etc)

Deauville Festival of American Film

- 31 August-9 September 2001
36 rue Pierret
92200 Neuilly-sur-Seine
Tel: (33) 1 46 40 55 00
Fax: (33) 1 46 40 55 39
email: info-deauville@deauville.org
Website: www.festival-deauville.com
Studio previews (non competitive)
Independent Films Competition and panorama. US productions only

Festival des Trois Continents

- 20-27 November 2001
19 A, Passage Pommeraye
BP 433002
44033 Nantes Cedex 1
Tel: (33) 2 40 69 74 14
Fax: (33) 2 40 73 55 22
email: festival@3continents.com
Website: www.3continents.com
Alain & Philippe Jalladeau
Feature-length fiction films from Africa, Asia, Latin and Black America. Competitive section, tributes to directors and actors, panoramas

Festival du Film Britannique de Dinard

- 4-7 October 2001
2, Boulevard Féart
35800 Dinard
Tel: (33) 0 99 88 19 04
Fax: (33) 0 99 46 67 15
email:
fest.film.britain.dinard@wanadoo.fr
Website: www.festivaldufilm-dinard.com
Competitive, plus retrospective and exhibition; tribute meeting between French and English producers

Festival International de Films de Femmes

- 15-24 March 2002
Maison des Arts
Place Salvador Allende
94000 Créteil
Tel: (33) 1 49 80 38 98
Fax: (33) 1 43 99 04 10
email: filmsfemme@wanadoo.fr
Website: www.filmsdefemmes.com
Jacki Buet
Competitive for feature films, documentaries, shorts, retrospectives directed by women and produced in the previous 23 months and not previously shown in France

FIFREC (International Film and Student Directors Festival)

FIFREC
BP 7144
30913, Nimes Cedex
Tel: (33) 66 84 47 40
Fax: (33) 72 02 20 36
Official film school selections (three per school) and open selection for directors from film schools, either students or recent graduates. Categories include fiction, documentaries and animation. Also best film school award. Films to be under 40 mins

Avignon French-American Film Workshop

- 24-29 June 2002
10 Montée de la Tour
30400 Villeneuve-les-Avignon
Tel: (33) 4 90 25 93 23
Fax: (33) 4 90 25 93 24
198 Avenue of the Americas
New York, NY 10013
Tel: (212) 343 2675
Fax: (212) 343 1849
email: JHR2001@AOL
Website: www.avignonfilmfest.com
Contact: Jerome Henry Rudes, General Director
The Workshop brings together independent filmmakers from the United States and France at the Avignon/New York Film Festival and Rencontres Cinématographiques Franco-Américaines d'Avignon (see below). French and American independent film is celebrated with new films, retrospectives, round-tables on pertinent issues and daily receptions
Avignon/New York Film Festival (April)
Alliance Française/French Institute, 22 East 60th Street, New York, NY-with 'the 21st Century Filmmaker Awards'
Rencontres Cinématographiques Franco-Américaines d'Avignon (June) Cinéma Vox, Place de l'Horloge, Avignon, France-with 'The Tournage Awards'

Gérardmer-Fantastic Arts International Fantasy Film Festival

- 16-20 January 2002
Le Public Systeme Cinema
40, rue Anatole France
92594 Levallois-Perret Cedex
France
Tel: (33) 1 41 34 20 33

Fax: (33) 1 41 34 20 77
email: jlasserre@le-systeme.fr
Website: www.gerardmer-fantasticart.com
Bruno Barde, Director
Competitive for international fantasy feature films (science-fiction, horror, supernatural etc)

MIP-TV

- 2-6 April 2001
Reed MIDEM Organisation
179 avenue Victor Hugo
75116 Paris
Tel: (33) 1 44 34 44 44
Fax: (33) 1 44 34 44 00
Website: miptv.com
International television programme market, held in Cannes

MIPCOM

- 8-12 October 2001
Reed MIDEM Organisation
179 avenue Victor Hugo
75116 Paris
Tel: (33) 1 44 34 44 44
Fax: (33) 1 44 34 44 00
Website: www.mipcom.com
International film and programme market for television, video, cable and satellite, held in Cannes

GERMANY

Berlin International Film Festival

- 6-17 February 2002
Internationale Filmfestspiele Berlin
Budapester Strasse 50
10787 Berlin
Tel: (49) 30 25 920 202
Fax: (49) 30 25 920 920
email: info@berlinale.de
Website: www.berlinale.de
Dieter Kosslick
Competitive for feature films and shorts (up to 10 mins), plus a separate competition for children's films-feature length and shorts-produced in the previous year and not entered for other festivals. Also has non-competitive programme consisting of forum of young cinema, panorama, film market and New German films

Feminale, 11th International Women's Film Festival

- October 2002
Feminale
Maybachstr, 111
50670 Cologne
Tel: (0049) 221 1300225
Fax: (0049) 221 1300281
email: info@feminale.de

Website: www.feminale.de
Veena Mund, Carla Despineux
Biannual festival for films and videos
by women directors only produced in
2001, all genres, formats, lengths

Femme Totale-International Women's Film Festival

- March 2002
c/o Kulturbüro der Stadt
Dortmund
Kleppingstr. 21-23
D – 44122 Dortmund
Tel: (49) 231 502 5162
Fax: (49) 231 502 5734
email: info@femmetotale.de
Website: www.femmetotale.de
Silke Johanna Räbiger
Held every two years. Women Film-
makers' Festival screens features,
short films, documentaries and
videos. Workshops and seminars.

Filmfest Hamburg

- September 2001
Postfach 500480
Friedensallee 44
22765 Hamburg
Tel: (49) 40 3982 6210
Fax: (49) 40 3982 6211
email: office@filmfesthamburg.de
Website: www.filmfesthamburg.de
Josef Wutz, Director
Non-competitive, international
features and shorts for cinema release
(fiction, documentaries), presentation
of one film country/continent,
premieres of Hamburg-funded films,
and other activities

International Festival of Animated Film Stuttgart

- April 2002
Festivalbüro
Teckstrasse 56 (Kulturpark Berg)
70190 Stuttgart
Tel: (49) 711 92 5460
Fax: (49) 711 925 4615
email: info@itfs.de
Website: www.itfs.de
Competitive for animated short films
of an artistic and experimental
nature, which have been produced in
the previous two years and not
exceeding 35 mins. Animation,
exhibitions and workshops. DM
139.000 worth of prizes

International Film Festival Mannheim-Heidelberg

- 8-17 November 2001
Collini-Center, Galerie
68161 Mannheim
Tel: (49) 621 102 943
Fax: (49) 621 291 564

email: ifmh@mannheim-
filmfestival.com
Website: www.mannheim-
filmfestival.com
Dr Michael Koetz, Director
Competition for young directors
from all over the world. (Deadline for
submission of films 25 August).
Former participants were Truffaut,
Fassbinder, Jarmusch, Egoyan,
Vinterberg. Additional parts of the
annual event are the "Co-Production
Meetings" for producers seeing co-
production opportunities/partners
(deadline for submission of projects:
31 July) and the "New Film Market"
for buyers

International FilmFest Emden

- May/June
An der Berufsschule 3
26721 Emden
Tel: (49) 4921 915 535
Fax: (49) 4921 915 591
email: filmfest@filmfest-emden.de
Website: www.filmfest-emden.de
Harald Tobermann, Thorsten Hecht
Established 1989. Germany's only fest
focussing on British films, including
a tribute to a British director.
Audience awarded prizes for best
feature film (DM20,0000) and best
short film/animation (DM8,000)
made in Northwest Europe and
German-speaking
countries, and trade union sponsored
jury award (DM7,500). British feature
submissions to: Harald Tobermann
Tel 0131 554 7391 email:
harald@britishfilms.cjb.net

Internationales Leipziger Fesztival für Dokumentar- und Animationsfilm

- 16-21 October 2001
Leipziger Dok-Filmwochen GmbH
Gro Re Fleischergasse 11
04109 Leipzig
Tel: (49) 341 980 3921
Fax: (49) 341 980 6141
email: dok-leipzig@t-online.de
Website: www.dokfetival-leipzig.de
Fred Gehler, Director
Competition, special programmes,
retrospective, international juries and
awards

Munich Film Festival

- 30 June-7 July 2001
Internationale Müenchner
Filmwochen
Sonnenstrasse 21
D-80331 Munich

Tel: (49) 89 3819 040
Fax: (49) 89 3819 0426
email: festivalleitung@filmfest-
muenchen.de
Website: filmfest-muenchen.de
Non-competitive for feature films
which have not previously been
shown in Germany

Munich International Documentary Festival

- 27 April -7 May 2001
Troger Strasse 46
Munich D-81675
Tel: (49) 89 470 3237
Fax: (49) 89 470 6611
email: filmstadt@t-online.de
Website:
www.artechock.de/dokfestival
Gudrun Geyer, Ulla Wessler

Nordic Film Days Lübeck

- 1-4 November 2001
Schildstrasse 6-8
23539 Lübeck
Tel: (49) 451 122 41 05
Fax: (49) 451 122 41 06
email: info@filmtage.luebeck.de
Website: www.filmtage.luebeck.de
Alexandra Brecht
Festival of Scandinavian and Baltic
films. Competitive for feature,
children's, documentary, and Nordic
countries' films

Oberhausen International Short Film Festival

- 2-7 May 2002
Grillostrasse 34
46045 Oberhausen
Tel: (49) 208 825 2652
Fax: (49) 208 825 5413
email: info@kurzfilmtage.de
Website: www.kurzfilmtage.de
Lars Henrik Gass, Director
Competitive for documentaries,
animation, experimental, short
features and videos (up to 35 mins),
produced in the previous 28 months;
international competition and
German competition; international
symposia

Prix Europa

- September/October
Sender Freies Berlin
D-14046 Berlin
Tel: (0049 30) 3031 1610
Fax: (004930) 3031 1619
email: prix-europa@t-online.de
Website: www.prix-europa.de
Susanne Hoffmann
Competitive for fiction, non-fiction,
current affairs, multicultural matters
(Prix Iris) in television; documentary,

drama, marketplace for your ears in radio. Open to all broadcasting organisations and producers in Europe

Prix Jeunesse International
- 5-11 June 2002
Bayerischer Rundfunk
80300 Munich
Tel: (49) 89 5900 2058
Fax: (49) 89 5900 3053
email: ubz@prixjeunesse.de
Website: www.prixjeunesse.de
Competitive for children's and youth television programmes (age groups up to 7, 7-12 and 12-17), in fiction and non-fiction, produced in the previous two years. (In odd years: seminars in children's and youth television)

GREECE

International Thessaloniki Film Festival
- 9-18 November 2001
40, Paparigopoulou Street
114 73 Athens
Tel: (30) 1 645 3669
Fax: (30) 1 644 8143
email: info@filmfestival.gr
Website: www.filmfestival.gr
Dedicated to the promotion of independent cinema from all over the world. International Competition for first or second features (Golden Alexander worth approx. $43,000, Silver Alexander $27,000). Official non competitive section for Greek films produced in 1998, informative section with the best independent films of the year, retrospectives (last year's retrospective dedicated to Claude Chabrol and Arturo Ripstein), exhibitions, special events etc

HONG KONG

Hong Kong International Film Festival
- April 2002
Film Programmes Office
Leisure & Cultural Services Dept
Level 7, Administration Building
Hong Kong Cultural Center
10 Salisbury Road, Tsim Sha Tsui
Kowloon, Hong Kong
Tel: (852) 28278786
Fax: (852) 28240585
email: hkiff@hkiff.org.hk
Website: www.hkiff.org.hk
Festival Director
Non-competitive for feature films, documentaries and invited short films, which have been produced in

the previous two years. Also a local short film and video competition, and a FIPRESCI Award for Young Asian cinema

HUNGARY

Hungarian Film Week
- February 2002
Magyar Filmunio
Varosligeti fasor 38
H-1068 Budapest
Tel: (361) 351 7759
Fax: (361) 351 8789
Erzsebet Toth, General Secretary
Competitive festival for Hungarian features, shorts and documentaries

INDIA

International Film Festival of India (IFFI)
- January 2002
Directorate of Film Festivals
Fourth Floor, Lok Nayak Bhavan
Khan Market,
New Delhi 110 003
Tel: (91) 11 4615953/4697167
Fax: (91) 11 4623430
Malti Sahai, Director
Organised from January 10-20, each year and recognised by FIAPF. It is held in different Indian Film Cities by rotation including New Delhi, Bangalore, Bombay, Calcutta, Hyderbad and Trivandrum. IFFI'98 was organised in New Delhi and featured a specialised competition section for Asian film makers

International Film Festival of Kerala
- March 2002
Kerala State Chalachitra Academy
TC 15/63, Elankom House
Elankom Gardens
Vellyambalam
Trivandrum 695 010
Kerala
Tel: (91) 471 310 323
Fax: (91) 471 310 322
email: chitram@md3.vsnl.net.in
Shaji N Karun, Director
Asian Cinema. Retrospectives of European, African and Japanese Cinema. International advertising films

Mumbai International Film Festival for Documentary, Short and Animation Films
- February 2002
Films Division, Ministry of Information and Broadcasting
Government of India

24-Dr G Deshmukh Marg
Bombay 400 026
Tel: (91) 22 386 4633/387 3655/386 1421/386 1461
Fax: (91) 22 386 0308/387 3655
email: filsd@bom4.vsnl.net.in
Website: www.filmsdivision.org
Ramaswamy Babu
Competitive for fiction, non-fiction and animation films, plus Golden/Silver Conch and cash awards and Information Section. Biennial

IRAN

Tehran International Market (TIM)
c/o CMI
53 Koohyari Street
Fereshteh Avenue, Tehran 19658
Tel: (98) 21 254 8032
Fax: (98) 21 255 1914
The fourth Tehran International Market is designed to provide major producers from the West a personalised arena to target regional program buyers and theatrical distributors in the lucrative Middle East market and surrounding areas. Buyers will also represent the Persian Gulf States, Asia and the Indian subcontinent, Central and Eastern Europe. More than 1,500 hours of programming was brought by Iranian TV alone during TIM'96

Tehran Internatinal Short Festival
- 23-28 October 2001
Iranian Young Cinema Society
Gandhi Ave, 19th St. No 20,
P.O. Box 15175
163 Tehran
Tel: (98)21 877 3114
Fax: (98) 21 879 5675
email: iycs@accir.com
Competitive short film festival

IRELAND

Cork International Film Festival
- 15-22 October 2001
10 Washington Street
Cork
Tel: (353) 21 427 1711
Fax: (353) 21 427 5945
email: info@corkfilmfest.org
Website: www.corkfilmfest.org
Mick Hannignan, Festival Director
Rory Concannon, General Manager
Angela Jones, Festival Administrator
Una Feely, Programmer
Robert Hamilton, Development

Officer
Non-competitive, screening a broad range of features, shorts and documentaries from over 40 countries. Films of every category welcomed for submission. Competitive: short films

Dublin Film Festival
- April 2002
1 Suffolk Street
Dublin 2
Tel: (353) 1 679 2937
Fax: (353) 1 679 2939
email: dff@iol.ie
Website: www.dublinfilmfestival.com

ISRAEL

Haifa International Film Festival
- 12-21 October 2001
142 Hanassi Avenue
Haifa 34633
Tel: (972) 4 835 3521/8353522
Fax: (972) 4 838 4327
email: haifaff@netvision.net.il
Website: www.haifaff.co.il
Pnina Blayer
The biggest annual meeting of professionals associated with the film industry in Israel. Competitions: 1. 'Golden Anchor' award $25,000 for mediterranean cinema. 2. Israeli Film Competition award $30,000

Jerusalem Film Festival
- 12 -21 July 2001
PO Box 8561, Wolfson Gardens
Hebron Road
91083 Jerusalem
Tel: (972) 2 672 4131
Fax: (972) 2 673 3076
email: jer-cin@jer-cin.org.il
Website: www.jer-cin.org.il
Lia Van Leer
Finest in recent international cinema, documentaries, animation, avant garde, retrospectives, special tributes and homages, Mediterranean and Israeli cinema, retrospectives, restored class Best Israeli Screenplay. Three international awards: Wim van Leer In Spirit of Freedom focus on human rights; Mediterranian Cinema; Jewish Theme Awards

ITALY

Da Sodoma a Hollywood - Turin Lesbian and Gay Film Festival
- 11-18 April 2001
Associazione Culturale L'Altra Communicazione

Piazza San Carlo 161
10123 Turin
Tel: (39) 11 534 888
Fax: (39) 11 534 796
email:glfilmfest@assioma.com
Specialist lesbian/gay themed festival. Competitive for features, shorts and documentaries. Also retrospectives and special showcases for both cinema and television work

Europa Cinema & TV Viareggio, Italy
- September
Lungotovere Flamionio 46
Pal. XXI, I-Rome 00196
Tel: (39) 6 320 8334
Fax: (39) 6 320 2765
Felice Laudadio
An international competition of European Films; a section of films regarding food; a retrospective section of films about 'The European Roots of American Cinema'; a retrospective of Radford's films; a section of Arte's (a European Cultural conference organised by ACE (Atelier du Cinéma Européen); a RAI première (opening day); screening of Ballando, Ballando by E.Scola (closing day)

Festival dei Popoli- International Review of Social Documentary Films
- 9-15 November 2001
Borgo Pinti 82r
50121 Firenze
Tel: (39) 55 244 778
Fax: (39) 55 241 364
email: fespopol@dada.it
Website: festivalpopoli.org
Mario Simondi, Director
Patricia Baroni (Assistant)
Paolo Fabbri (President)
Competitive and non-competitive sections for documentaries on sociological, historical, political, anthropological subjects, as well as music, art and cinema, produced during the year preceding the festival. The films for the competitive section should not have been screened in Italy before

Giffoni Film Festival
- 14 -21 July 2001
Piazza Umberto I
84095 Giffoni Valle Piana
Tel: (39) 0 89 868 544
Fax: (39) 0 89 866 111
email: giffonif@giffoniff.it
Website: www.giffoniff.it
Claudio Gubiosi

Competitive for full-length fiction for children 12-14 and 12-18 years. Entries must have been produced within two years preceding the festival

MIFED
- 29 October-2 November 2000
Largo Domodossola 1
20145 Milan
Tel: (39) 2 480 12912 -48012920
Fax: (39) 2 499 77020
email: mifed@fmd.it
Website: fmd.it/mifed
Euena Lloyd
International market for companies working in the film and television industries

Noir Film Festival
- 6-12 December 2001
Via Tirso 90
00198 Rome
Tel: 39 6 884 8030-8844672
Fax: 39 6 884 0450
email: noir@noirfest.com
Website: www.noirfest.com
Giorgio Gosetti
Competitive for thrillers between 30-180 mins length, which have been produced in the previous year and not released in Italy. Festival now takes place at Courmayeur (at the foot of Mount Blanc)

Pesaro Film Festival (Mostra Internazionale del Nuovo Cinema)
- 22-30 June 2001
Via Villafranca 20
00185 Rome
Tel: (39) 6 445 6643/491 156
Fax: (39) 6 491 163
email: pesarofmfest@mclink.it
Website: www.pesarofilmfest.it
Pedro Armocida, Secretary-General
Non-competitive. Particularly concerned with the work of new directors and emergent cinemas, with innovation at every level. In recent seasons the festival has been devoted to a specific country or culture

Pordenone Silent Film Festival (Le Giornate del Cinema Muto)
- 13-20 October 2001
c/o La Cineteca del Friuli
Via G. Bini, Palazzo Gurisatti
33013 Gemona (Udine)
Tel: (39) 0432 980458
Fax: (39) 0432 970542
email: info@cinetecadelfriuli.org
Website: www.cinetecadelfriuli.org/gcm

David Robinson, Director
The 2001 programme of the Giornate will include:
- Silent Japan (major retrospective of Japanese silent cinema)
- Oscar Micheaux and his circle: African-American Filmmaking and Race Cinema of the Silent Era
- The Griffith Project # 5 (Films produced in 1911)
- Save the Silents (American rarities preserved through the NFPF [National Film Preservation Foundation])
- Special closing event: Latest restoration of Abel Gance's NAPOLEON.
Plus FilmFair 2001
Film screenings will be hosted by the Teatro Zancanaro (except for NAPOLEON, that will be shown in Udine, at Teatro Nuovo Giovanni da Udine).

Pordenone Film Fair The-October

email:
filmfair.gcm@cinetecadelfriuli.org
An exhibition of books and journals, collectibles and ephemera presented by the Giornate del Cinema Muto. Authors attending the festival are invited to discuss their latest works

Prix Italia

- September
RAI Radiotelevisione Italiana
Via Monte Santo 52
00195 Rome
Tel: (39) 06 3728708
Fax: (39) 06 3723966
email: prixitalia@rai.it
Website: prixitalia.rai.it
Competitive for television and radio productions from national broadcasting organisations. Radio categories: music, single drama, drama serials and series, cultural documentaries, current affairs documentaries-maximum of four programmes. TV categories: performing arts (creative works of music, theatre, dance, figurative arts), single drama, drama serials and series, cultural documentaries, current affairs documentaries-maximum of three programmes

Taormina International Film Festival

- 29 June-7 July 2000
Palazzo Firenze
Via Pirandello 31
98039 Taormina
Sicily

Tel: (39) 942 21142
Fax: (39) 942 23348
Enrico Ghezzi
Website: www.taormina-arte.com
Competitive for features. Recognised by FIAPF, category B. Emphasis on new directors and cinema from developing countries

Torino Film Festival

- 15-23 November 2001
Via Monte di Pietà 1
10121 Torino
Tel: (39) 011 5623309
Fax: (39) 011 5629796
email: info@torinofilmfest.org
Website: www.torinofilmfest.org
Mara Signori
Competitive sections for feature and short films. Italian Space section (videos and films) open solely to Italian work. All works must be completed during 13 previous months, with no prior release in Italy

Venice Film Festival

- 29 August-8 September 2001
Mostra Internazionale d'Arte Cinematografica
La Biennale di Venezia
Ca' Giustinian
San Marco, 30124 Venice
Tel: (39) 41 521 8711
Fax: (39) 41 522 7539
email: das@labiennale.com
Website: www.labiennale.it
Competitive for feature films competitive for shorts (up to 30 mins); has competitive sections, perspectives, night and stars, Italian section; retrospective. Non-participation at other international festivals and/or screenings outside country of origin. Submission by 30 June

JAPAN

International Animation Festival in Japan, Hiroshima 2002 The 9th

- 22-26 August 2002
4-17 Kako-machi
Naka-ku
Hiroshima 730-0812
Tel: (81) 82 245 0245
Fax: (81) 82 245 0246
email: hiroanim@urban.ne.jp
Website: www.urban.ne.jp/home/hiroanim/
Sayoko Kinoshita, Festival Director
Competitive biennial festival. Also retrospective, symposium, exhibition etc. For competition, animated works under 30 mins, and completed during

preceding two years are eligible on either 16mm, 35mm, 3/4" videotape (NTSC, PAL, SECAM) or Betacam (only NTSC)

Tokyo International Film Festival

- 27 October-1 November 2001
Organising Committee
3F, Landic Ginza Bldg II
1-6-5 Ginza, Chuo-Ku
Tokyo 104-0061
Tel: (81) 3 3563 6305
Fax: (81) 3 3563 6310
Website: www.tokyo-filmfest.or.jp
Competitive for Young Cinema sections. Also special screenings, cinema prism, Nippon cinema now, symposium, no film market

Tokyo Video Festival

- 23 March 2002
c/o Victor Co of Japan Ltd
1-7-1 Shinbashi
Victor Bldg, Minato-ku
Tokyo 105
Tel: (81) 3 3289 2815
Fax: (81) 3 3289 2819
Website: www.jvc-victor.co.jp
Competitive for videos; compositions on any theme and in any style accepted, whether previously screened or not, but maximum tape playback time must not exceed 20 minutes

MALTA

Golden Knight International Amateur Film & Video Festival

- 29 November-1 December 2001
PO Box 450
Marsa CMR01
Tel: (356) 446617/412382/418387
Fax: (356) 372343/313113
email: macc@global.net.mt
Website: www.global.net/macc
Alfred Stagno Navarra
Three classes: amateur, student, professional-maximum 30 mins

MONACO

Monte Carlo Television Festival and Market

- 16-22 February 2001
4, boulevard du Jardin Exotique
Monte-Carlo 98000 Monaco
Tel: 337 93 10 40 60
Fax: 337 93 50 70 14
email: info@tvfestival.com
Website: tvfestival.com
Contact: David Tomatis
Annual festival and market, includes

awards for television films, mini-series and news categories. In 1996 joined with Imagina conference

THE NETHERLANDS

Cinekid
- October
Korte Leidesedwarsstraat 12
1017 RC Amsterdam
Tel: (31) 0 20 5317890
Fax: (31) 0 20 5317899
email: infro@cinekid.nl
Website: www.cinekid.nl
Director: Sannette Naeyé
International children's film and television festival. Winning film is guaranteed distribution in the Netherlands

Netherlands Film Festival
- 19-28 September 2001
Stichting Nederlands Film Festival
PO Box 1581
3500 BN Utrecht
Tel: (31) 30 232 2684
Fax: (31) 30 2313200
email: info@filmfestival.nl
Website: www.filmfestival.nl
Michiel Berkel, Director
Annual screening of a selection of new Dutch features, shorts, documentaries, animation and television drama. Retrospectives, seminars, talkshows, Cinema Militans Lecture, Holland Film Meeting, outdoor programme. Presentation of the Grand Prix of Dutch Film: the Golden Calf Awards

International Documentary Filmfestival Amsterdam
- 22 November-2 December 2001
Kleine-Gartmanplantsoen 10
1017 RR Amsterdam
Tel: (31) 20 627 3329
Fax: (31) 20 638 5388
email: idfa@xs4all.nl
Website: www.idfa.nl
Ally Derks
Competition programme: compet-itive for documentaries of any length, 35mm or 16mm, produced in 15 months prior to the festival; retrospectives; Joris Ivens award; Top 10 selected by well-known filmmaker; competitive video-programme; forum for international co-financing of European documentaries. Workshop, seminar and debates

International Film Festival Rotterdam
- 23 January-3 February 2002
PO Box 21696

3001 AR Rotterdam
Tel: (31) 10 890 9090
Fax: (31) 10 890 9091
email: tiger@iffrotterdam.nl
Website:
www.filmfestivalrotterdam.com
Sandra den Hamer, Director
Addition to Tiger Award competition: three premiums, each 10,000 Euro cash, as well as guaranteed theatrical distribution in The Netherlands, and a broadcasting commitment from Dutch public broadcaster VPRO

NEW ZEALAND

Auckland International Film Festival
- 6-22 July 2001
PO Box 9544
Te Aro
Wellington 6035
Tel: (64) 4 385 0162
Fax: (64) 4 801 7304
email: enzedff@actrix.gen.nz
Website: www.enzedff.co.nz
Bill Gosden, Director
Festival includes feature films, short films, documentaries, video and animation

Wellington Film Festival
- 13-29 July 2001
New Zealand Film Festival
PO Box 9544
Te Aro
Wellington
Tel: (64) 4 385 0162
Fax: (64) 4 801 7304
email: enzedff@actrix.gen.nz
Website: www.enzedff.co.nz
Bill Gosden, Director
Festival includes feature films, short films, documentaries, video and animation

NORWAY

Norwegian International Film Festival
- 25 August-1 September 2001
PO Box 145
5501 Haugesund
Tel: (47) 52 734 430
Fax: (47) 52 734 420
email: haugfest@online.no
Website: www.filmfestivalen.no
Gunnar J. Lovvik
Non-competitive film festival, highlighting a selection of films for the coming theatrical season. New Nordic films-a market presenting Nordic films with a potential outside the Nordic Countries (27-29 Aug)

POLAND

International and National Documentary and Short Film Festival in Kraków
- 24 – 28 May 2002
c/o Apollo-Film
ul. Pychowicka 7
30-364 Krakow
Tel: (48) 1033 12 267 13 55
Fax: (48) 1033 12 267 23 40
email: festiwal@apollo.pl
Website: www.shortfilm.apollo.pl
Krzysztof Gierat, Festival Director
Programme Director: Tadeusz Lubelski
Competitive for short film (up to 60 mins), including documentaries, fiction, animation, popular science and experimental subjects, produced in the previous 15 months.The deadline for submitting films to the selection is 31st January 2002

PORTUGAL

Cinanima (International Animated Film Festival)
- November
Apartado 743
Rua 62, 251
4501-901 Espinho Codex
Tel: (351) 22 734 4611/734 1621
Fax: (351) 22 734 6015
email: cinanima@mail.lelepac.pt
Website: www.cinanima.pt
Organising Committee
Competitive for animation short films, features, series, first films, didactic and educational, publicity, title sequences and information. Entries must have been completed after 1st January 2000

Encontros Internacionais de Cinema Documental
- November
Centro Cultural Malaposta
Rua Angola, Olival Basto
2675 Odivelas
Tel: (351) 9388570/407
Fax: (351) 9389347
email: amascultura@
mail.telepac.ptther
Director: Manuel Costa e Silva
Two categories: film and video (competition). Only event dedicated to documentary in Portugal, to increase awareness of the form and show work from other countries

Fantasporto 2002-22nd Oporto International Film Festival
- 15 February-4 March 2002

Rua Aníbal Cunha
84 -sala 1.6
4050-048 Porto
Tel: (351) 2 2207 6050
Fax: (351) 2 2207 6059
email: info@fantasporto.online.pt
Website: www.fantasporto.online.pt
Mário Dorminsky
The Oporto International Film
Festival is held annually in February
and goes now to its 22nd edition. The
first edition of FANTASPORTO, as
the festival is usually known, was held
in 1981 and was non-competitive. All
the following editions included a
Competitive Section. The Oporto
Festival was founded by the editors of
the film magazine Cinema Novo and
is sponsored by the Portuguese State
and private sponsors. It is an
independent film festival. The awards
granted yearly include feature and
short films presented to the
competitive Sections. The New
Directors Section includes first and
second feature films. The festival
receives entry forms from all over the
world, mostly from European
countries and the United States. The
Festival runs now in 6 screens (2.500
seats alltogether) and shows over 200
new feature films each year, in the
Official Competitive Section (Fantasy
films), Directors Week (non-fantasy
films), Directors Week (non-fantasy
films), Music Videos section and in
the Retrospective Sections (general)

International Film Festival of Troia XVI edition

- 1-10 June 2001
International Film Festival of Troia
Forum Luisa Todi
Av. Luisa Todi, 61-65
2900-461 Setúbal
Tel: (351) 265 525 908-534 059
Fax: (351) 265 525 681
email: fretroia@mail.teleweb.pt
Website: www.festroia.pt
Fernanda Silva, Director
Four categories: Official Section, First
Works, American Independents, Man
and The Official Section is devoted to
films coming from those countries
which havea limited production (less
than 21 features per year). films must
not have been screened previously in
Portugal and must have been
produced during 12 months
preceding the Festival. Also film
market, retrospectives in the
information section, Gay and Lesbian
section. Jury selection

RUSSIA

Moscow International Film Festival

- 21-30 July 2001
Interfest, General Management of
International Film Festivals
10 Khokholski Per
Moscow 109028
Tel: (7) 95 917 9154
Fax: (7) 95 916 0107
email: siv@cityline.ru
Website: miff.ru
Sergei Soloviev, Alexandr Abdulov
Competitive festival

St. Petersburg International Film Festival of Festivals

- 23-29 June 2002
10 Kamennoostrovsky Avenue
St Petersburg 19711101
Tel: (7) 812 237 0072
Fax: (7) 812 237 03 04
email: info@filmfest.ru
Website: www.filmfest.ru
Alexander Mamontov
Non-competitive, aimed at
promoting films from all over the
world that meet the highest artistic
criteria, and the distribution of non-
commercial cinema

SERBIA

Belgrade International Film Festival

- January 2002
Sava Centar
Milentija Popovica 9
11070 Novi Beograd
Tel: (38) 11 222 4961
Fax: (38) 11 222 1156
Non-competitive for features
refl-ecting high aesthetic and artistic
values and contemporary trends

SINGAPORE

Singapore International Film Festival

- April 2002
45A Keong Saik Road
Singapore 089149
Tel: (65) 73 87567
Fax: (65) 73 87578
email: filmfest@pacific.net.sg
Website: filmfest.org.sg
Philip Cheah, Director
Specialised competitive festival for Best
Asian Film. Non-competitive includes
panorama of international film. 8mm,
16mm, 35mm and video are accepted.
Films must not have been shown
commercially in Singapore

SLOVAKIA

International Film Festival Bratislava

- 30 November-8 December 2001
Fialkové údolie 5
811 01 Bratislava
Tel: (42) 7 5441 0673
Fax: (42) 7 5441 0674
email: iffbratislava@ba.sunnet.sk
Website: www.iffbratislava.sk
International competition for first
feature films at least 50 minutes long,
and made or first shown in the 16
months preceding the Festival

SOUTH AFRICA

Cape Town International Film Festival

- November 2001
University of Cape Town
Private Bag
Rondebosch 7700
Cape Town
Tel: (27) 21 423 8257
Fax: (27) 21 423 8257
email: filmfest@hiddingh.uct.ac.za
Trevor Steele Taylor, Director
Steve Drake, Programme Co-
ordinator
Oldest film festival in South Africa.
Screen Features, Documentaries and
Short Films on 35mm, 16mm or
Video. Emphasis on the independent,
the transgressive and the iconoclastic.
Major profile of South African
production

Durban International Film Festival

Centre for Creative Arts
University of Natal
4014 Durban
Tel: (27) 31 260 2506
Fax: (27) 31 260 3074
email: diff@nu.ac.za
Website: www.und.ac.za/und/carts
Peter Rorvik, Director
This longest-running South African
international film festival screens
over 50 films from around the world,
most of them premiere showings in
Durban. The festival also promotes
local films and offers workshops
featuring visiting directors,
screenwriters, actors etc to stimulate
developing filmmakers. The
programme includes screenings in
areas where cinemas are non-existent.
The Festival has a competition and
screens short films

SPAIN

Festiva Internacional de Cine Independente de Ourense/International Independent Film Festival

- 3-9 November 2001
Rua Arcediagos 3-2 dta
32005 Ourense
PO Box "Addo. 664m E-32080
Ourense (Spain)"
Tel: (34) 988 224127
Fax: (34) 988 249561
email: oufest@ourencine.com
Website: www.ourencine.com
Henrique Torreiro
Sixth international festival for independent cinema. Competitive sections for every independent short or long length film

Bilbao International Festival of Documentary & Short Films

- 23 November-1 December 2001
Colón de Larreátegui 37
4o drcha
48009 Bilbao
Tel: (34) 94 424 8698
Fax: (34) 94 424 5624
email: info@zinebi.com
Website: www.zinebi.com
Competitive for animation, fiction and documentary

Donostia-San Sebastian International Film Festival

Plaza Oquendo S/N
20004 San Sebastian
Tel: (34) 943 481 212
Fax: (34) 943 481 218
email: films@sansebastianfestival.com
Website: www.sansebastianfestival.ya.com/temporal/entrein/index.htm
Diego Galan
Competitive for feature films produced in the previous year and not released in Spain or shown in any other festivals. Also retrospective sections

International Film Festival For Young People

- 23-30 November 2001
Paseo de Begona, 24-Ent
33207 Gijón
Tel: (34) 98 534 3739
Fax: (34) 98 535 4152
email: festivalgijon@telecable.es
Website: www.gijonfilmfestival.com
Competitive for features and shorts. Must have been produced during 18 months preceding the festival and not awarded a prize at any other major international film festival

International Short Film Contest 'Ciudad de Huesca'

- 7-16 June 2001
C/Del Parque 1,2
(Circulo Oscense)
Huesca 22002
Tel: (34) 974 212 582
Fax: (34) 974 210 065
email: huescafest@tsai.es
Website: www.huesca-filmfestival.com
Jose Maria Escriche
Competitive for short films (up to 30 mins) on any theme except tourism and promotion

L'Alternativa-Independent Film Festival of Barcelona

November 2002
Centre de Cultura Contemporania de Barcelona
C/Montalegre 5
08001 Barcelona
Tel: (34) 93 306 4100
Fax: (34) 93 306 4104
email: alternativa@cccb.org
Website: alternativa.cccb.org
Contact: Tessa Renaudo
International competitive for shorts, animation, documentary and features. Accept films made on 35mm, 16mm, 8mm, Beta SP and DV with screening copy on 35mm, 16mm or Beta SP (PAL)

Mostra de Valencia/Cinema del Mediterrani

- October 2001
Pza del Arzobispo 2 bajo
46003 Valencia
Tel: (34) 6 392 1506
Fax: (34) 6 391 5156
email: festival@mostravalencia.com
Website: www.mostravalencia.com
Luis Fernandez, Director
Competitive official section. Informative section, special events section, 'mostra' for children, and International Congress of Film Music

Sitges International Film Festival of Catalonia

- 4-13 October 2001
Av Josep Tarradellas
135 ESC A, 3r. 2a.
08029 Barcelona
Tel: (34) 3 93 419 3635
Fax: (34) 3 93 439 7380
email:cinsit@sitgestur.com
Website: www.sitges.com/cinema
Roc Villas (Director)
Two official sections. One for fantasy films and another for all-genre films. Also shorts, retrospectives, animation, video, exhibitions, etc

Valladolid International Film Festival

- 26 October-3 November 2001
Teatro Calderón
C/Leopoldo Cano, s/n
47003 Valladolid
Tel: (34) 983 305 700
Fax: (34) 983 309 835
email: festvalladolid@seminci.com
Website: www.seminic.com
Fernando Lara, Director
Denise O'Keeffe, Coordinator
Competitive for 35mm features and shorts, plus documentaries, entries not to have been shown previously in Spain. Also film school tributes, retrospectives and selection of new Spanish productions

ST BARTH

Cinéma Caribéen-St Barth Film Festival

- 17-22 April 2001
B.P. 1017
St Jean 97012
St Barthelemy Cedex
French West Indies
Tel: (590) 27 80 11
Fax: (590) 29 74 70
email: jharrison@stbarthff.org
Website: www.stbarthff.org
Ellen Lampert-Gréaux, Joshua Paul Harrison
While covering a wide range of topics, fiction and non-fiction, film and video, the festival celebrates Caribbean culture and offers a meeting place for regional filmmakers to screen and discuss their work,

SWEDEN

Göteborg Film Festival

- 26 January-5 February 2001
Box 7079
402 32 Gothenburg
Tel: (46) 31 41 05 46
Fax: (46) 31 41 00 63
email:goteborg@filmfestivl.org
Website:
www.goteborg.filmfestival.org
Agneta Green, Program Coordinator
Non-competitive for features, documentaries and shorts not released in Sweden

Stockholm International Film Festival

- 8-18 November 2001
PO Box 3136

103 62 Stockholm
Tel: (46) 8 677 5000
Fax: (46) 8 20 0590
email: info@cinema.se
Website: www.filmfestivalen.se
Git Scheynius, Director
Competitive for innovative current
feature films, focus on American
Independents, a retrospective,
summary of Swedish films released
during the year, survey of world
cinema. Around 100 films have their
Swedish premiere during the festival.
FIPRESCI jury, FIAPF accredited.
'Northern Lights'-Critics Week

Umea International Film Festival
- 13-20 September 2001
PO Box 43
S 901 02
Umea
Tel: (46) 90 13 33 88
Fax: (46) 90 77 79 61
email: film.festival@ff.umea.com
Website: www.ff.umea.com
Thom Palmen
Non-competitive festival with focus
mainly on features but does except
shorts and documentaries. About 150
films are screened in several sections.
The festival also organises seminars

Uppsala International Short Film Festival
- 22-28 October 2001
Box 1746
S-751 47 Uppsala
Tel: (46) 18 120 025
Fax: (46) 18 121 350
email: uppsala@shortfilmfestival.com
Website: www.shortfilmfestival.com
Asa Garnert
Competitive for shorts (up to 60
mins), including fiction, animation,
experimental films, documentaries,
children's and young people's films.
16 and 35mm only

SWITZERLAND

Vevey International Comedy Film Festival
- July
La Grenette, Cp 325,
1800 Vevey
Tel: (41) 21 922 2077
Fax: (41) 21 922 202
Competitive for medium and short
films, hommage and retrospective

Biennale de l'image en mouvement/Biennial of Moving Images
- November odd years

Saint Gervais Gènève, Centre pour
l'image contemporaire
5 rue du Temple
1201 Geneva
Tel: (41) 22 908 20 60
Fax: (41) 22 908 20 01
email: cic@sgg.ch
Website: www.centreimage.ch/bim
Lysianne Léchot Hirt, PR
Competition with international
entries; seminars and conferences;
retrospectives; special programmes;
installations; Swiss and European art
schools programme

Festival International de Films de Fribourg
-10-17 March 2002
Rue de Locarno 8
CH -1700 Fribourg
Tel: (41) (26) 322 22 32
Fax: (41) (26) 322 79 50
email: info@fiff.ch
Website: www.fiff.ch
Martial Knaebel
Competitive for films from Africa,
Asia and Latin America (16/35mm,
video). Films (16/35mm) may be
circulated throughout Switzerland
after the Festival

Golden Rose of Montreux TV Festival
- April
Télévision Suisse Romande
PO Box 234
1211 Geneva 8
Tel: (41) 22 708 8599
Fax: (41) 22 781 5249
email: info@rosedor.com
Website: www.rosedor.com
Jacqueline Colle
Competitive for television
productions (20-60 mins) of light
entertainment, comedy, sitcoms,
variety, music and game shows, first
broadcast in the previous 14 months

VIPER-International Festival for Film, Video and New Media
- 24 -28 October 2001
PO Box
4002 Basil
Tel: (41) 61 283 27 00
Fax: (41) 61 283 27 05
email: info@viper.ch
Website: www.viper.ch
The festival presents new
international innovative,
experimental and artistic media
productions: Film, Video, CD-ROM,
internet-projects. Two competitions:
International competition for Film

and Video (award sum SFR 10.000)
and national competition for Film
and Video (award sum SFR 5.000
plus material assets). VIPER also
includes the "Videogallery", an
outstanding selection of film and
video work which is run by co-
operating European festivals

Locarno International Film Festival
- 2-12 August 2001
Via della Posta 6
CP 844
6601 Locarno
Tel: (41) 91 751 0232
Fax: (41) 91 751 7465
email: info@pardo.ch
Website: www.pardo.ch
Programme includes: a) Competition
reserved for fiction features
representative of Young Cinema (first
or second features) and New Cinema
(films by more established
filmmakers who are innovating in
film style and content and works by
directors from emerging film
industries). b) A (non-competitive)
selection of films with innovative
potential in style and content. c) A
retrospective designed to enlarge
perspectives on film history

Nyon International Documentary Film Festival - Visions du Réel
- April 2002
PO Box 593
CH -1260 Nyon
Tel: (41) 22 361 60 60
Fax: (41) 22 361 70 71
email: docnyon@iprolink.ch
Website: www.visionsdureel.ch
Jean Perret, Director
International competition screening
documentaries

Le Nombre d'Or, International Widescreen Festival, Amsterdam
- 14-18 September 2001
IBC Office
Aldwych House, 81 Aldwych
London WC2B 4EL
Tel: (44) 020 7611 7511
Fax: (44) 020 7611 7530
email: joconnell@ibc.org
Website: www.ibc.org
Jarlath O'Connel, Festival Director
Competitive television Festival
celebrating widescreen production in
all genres and held as part of IBC in
Amsterdam. Programmes must have
been broadcast or have a broadcast

date scheduled. The focus is on mainstream programming with documentaries, dramas and music programmes making up the bulk of the entries. Programmes must have been shot on widescreen video (including HD) or in Super 16 or 35mm. Around 35 programmes are screened before an International Jury over five days of screenings. Winning programmes are re-screened with Q&A sessions with the producers. IBC also includes Masterclasses, Panel Discussions and Workshops aimed at the production community. The recent Festival attracted 105 entries from 18 countries. Deadline for entries is lat May each year

TAIWAN

Taipai Golden Horse Film Festival

- 17-30 November 2001
T.F, 37, Kaifeng St.
Taipei 100, Taiwan, ROC
Tel: (886) 2 2388-3880
Fax: (886) 2370-1616/(886) 2 2388-3874
email: tghffctt@ms14.hinet.net
Website: www.goldenhorse.org.tw
Wei-jan Liu, Coordinator
Founded in 1964, TGHFF has two main sections: 1) Golden Horse Awards — Competition of Chinese-language films, including features, shorts, documentary and animation. 2) International Film Exhibition (started in 1979), a non-competitive showcase of a wide range of films from all over the world.

TUNISA

Carthage Film Festival

- October/November
The JCC Managing Committee
5 Avenue Ali Belahouane
2070 La Marsa
Tel: (216) 1 745 355
Fax: (216) 1 745 564
Official competition open to Arab and African short and feature films. Entries must have been made within two years prior to the festival, and not have been awarded first prize at any previous international festival in an African or Arab country. Also has an information section, an international film market (MIPAC) and a workshop

TURKEY

International Istanbul Film Festival

- April 2002

Istanbul Foundation for Culture and Arts
Istiklal Cad Luvr
Apt No: 146
80070 Beyoglu
Istanbul
Tel: (90) 212 293 3133
Fax: (90) 212 249 7771
email: film.fest@istfest-tr.org
Website: www.istfest.org
Hulya Ucansu, Director
Two competitive sections, international and national. The International Competition for feature films on art (literature, theatre, cinema, music, dance and plastic arts) is judged by an international jury and the 'Golden Tulip Award' is presented as the Grand Prix. Entry by invitation

UNITED KINGDOM

Animated Encounters Film Festival

April 2002
Watershed Media Centre
1 Canon's Road
Harbourside
Bristol BS1 5TX
United Kingdom
Tel: 0117 925 2455
Fax: 0117 91 358
email: info@animatedencounters.org.uk
Website:www.animated-encounters.org.uk
Rachel Caddick, Adminstrator
Non-competitive animation festival

Bath Film Festival

18 October-3 November 2002
7 Terrace Walk
Bath BA1 1LN
Tel: 01225 401149
Fax: 01225 401149
bff@appleonline.net
www.bathfilmfestival.org
Chris Baker, co-ordinator
Non-competitive, screening c30, preview, current, recent and classic features. 'Events Programme' of workshops, seminars, courses, film with other art forms especially music, screenings of the work of emergent filmmakers, and one or two 'keystone' events each year aimed at attracting national interest

Filmstock: Luton Film Festival

- 1 -15 June 2001
c/o Zero Balance Ltd
24 Guildford Street
Luton
Beds LU1 2NR

Tel: 01582 752908
Fax: 01582 423347
email: filmstock@grouchomarx.co.uk
Website: www.filmstock.co.uk
Justin Doherty, Neil Fox, Directors
The organisers write: "FILMSTOCK is more than a film festival. It is about cinema in its entirety and aims to fuse the joy of movie-going with the art of filmmaking in one simultaneous experience. It is not place or person specific but instead is aimed at anybody who watches or makes films, for whatever reason."

Birmingham Film and TV Festival

- 15-24 November 2001
9 Margaret Street
Birmingham, B3 3BS
Tel: 0121 212 0777
Fax: 0121 212 0666
email: info@film-tv-festival.org.uk
Website: www.film-tv-festival.org.uk
Barbara Chapman
Non-competitive for features and shorts, plus retrospective and tribute programmes. The Festival also produces events exploring debating topical issues in moving image production and exhibition

Bite the Mango

- 21-29 September 2001
National Museum of Photography, Film & Television
Bradford BD1 1NQ
Tel: 01274 203308/203311
Fax: 01274 394540
email: l.kavanagh@nmsi.ac.uk/i.ajeeb@nmsi.ac.uk
Website: www.bitethemango.org.uk
Lisa Kavanagh, Irfan Ajeeb
Europe's only annual festival for Black and Asian film and television. Entries accepted from Asian and Black film and video-makers. Provisional deadline for entries last Friday in June 2002

Bradford Animation Festival

- 16-18 November 2001
National Museum of Photography Film and Television
Bradford BD1 1NQ
Tel: 01274 203308
Fax: 01274 394540
email: l.kavanagh@nmsi.ac.uk
Website: www.baf.org.uk
Lisa Kavanagh
Competitive festival for animated shorts involving 8 categories: professional, commercial/promotional, series for

children, films for children, experimental, digital, non-professional and under 16

Bradford Film Festival

- 8-23 March 2002
National Museum of Photography, Film & Television
Pictureville
Bradford BD1 1NQ
Tel: 01274 203320/203308
Fax: 01274 770217
email: a.earnshaw@nmsi.ac.uk
Website: www.bradfordfilm
Non-competitive for feature films. Strands include widescreen with world's only Cinerama Screen and IMAX. Focus on national cinema of selected European countries. Provisional deadline November 2001

British Animation Awards

- 15 March 2002
c/o 219 Archway Rd
London N6 5BN
Tel: 020 8340 4563
email: jsp@easynet.co.uk and baa.002@virginnet
The next animation awards are planned for 2002. A bi-annual event

Brief Encounters - Bristol Short Film Festival

- 14-18 November 2001
Watershed Media Centre
1 Canon's Road
Harbourside
Bristol BS1 5TX
Tel: 0117 925 2455
Fax: 0117 921 3958
email: brief.encounters@genie.co.uk
Website: www.brief-encounters.org.uk
Competitive for short film in all categories (up to 30 mins). Thematic and specialised programmes and special events. Audience award.

Cambridge Film Festival

- 12-22 July 2001
Arts Picture House
38-39 St. Andrews Street
Cambridge CB2 3AR
Tel: 01223 578944
Fax: 01223 578956
email: festival@cambarts.co.uk
Non-competitive; new world cinema selected from international festivals. Also featuring director retrospectives, short film programmes, thematic seasons and revived classics. Conference for independent exhibitors and distributors. Public debates and post-screening discussions

Celtic Film and Television Festival

- 20-23 March 2002
249 West George Street
Glasgow G2 4QE
Tel: 0141 302 1737
Fax: 0141 302 1738
email: mail@celticfilm.co.uk
Website: www.celticfilm.co.uk
Frances Hendron
Competition for films whose subject matter has particular relevance to the Celtic nations. Being held in Quimper, Brittany in 2002

Chichester Film Festival

- 9-23 September 2001
Chichester Cinema at New Park
New Park Road
Chichester
West Sussex PO19 1XN
Tel: 01243 784881/786650
Fax: 01243 539853
email: Chifilm@newpart2000.fsnet.co.uk
Contact: Roger Gibson
This is a non-competitive festival that focuses on previews, retrospectives, with a special emphasis on UK and other European productions. There is also an International Short Film Competition with a first prize sponsored by Anita Roddick (deadline 31 May)

Cinemagic-World Screen Entertainment for Young People

- 30 November-10 December 2001
3rd Floor, Fountain House
17-21 Donegall Place
Belfast BT1 5AB
Tel: (028) 9031 1900
Fax: (028) 9031 9709
email: info@cinemagic.org.uk
Website: www.cinemagic.org.uk
Nicki Fulcher, Programmer
A competitive festival for international short and feature films and programmes for children and young people (ages 4-18). The festivals includes big movie premieres, competitions, practical workshops, director's discussions, masterclasses with industry professional and specialist events

Edinburgh International Film Festival

- 12-26 August 2001
Filmhouse
88 Lothian Road
Edinburgh EH3 9BZ
Tel: 0131 228 4051
Fax: 0131 229 5501
email: info@edfilmfest.org.uk
Website: www.edfilmfest.org.uk
Cathy Ferrett, Production Facilities Administrator
Patron: Sean Connery
Chairman: John McCormick
Director: Lizzie Francke
Producer: Ginnie Atkinson
Longest continually running film festival in the world. Unique showcase of new international cinema with a special focus on the British film sector. Programme sections: Focus on British Film; Retrospective; Gala (World, European, British premieres); Rosebud (first and second time directors); Director's Focus; Reel Life (illustrated lectures by filmmakers); Documentary; Mirrorball (music video); short films; animation. Industry office, inclduing British film market place. Awards for British feature, British director, British short film, British animation. Submissions deadline April

Festival of Fantastic Films

- 24-26 September 2001
33 Barrington Road
Altrincham
Cheshire WA14 1H2
Tel: 0161 929 1423
Fax: 0161 929 1067
email: 101341.3352@compuserve.com
Website: www.fantastic-films.com
Festival celebrates science fiction and fantasy film. Features guests of honour, interviews, signing panels, dealers, talks and over 30 film screenings

Foyle Film Festival

- 9-18 November2001
The Nerve Centre
7-8 Magazine St
Derry,
BT48 6HJ
Tel: 028 267432
Fax: 01504 371738
email: S.Kelpie@nerve-centre.org.uk
Shauna Kelpie (Festival Director)
Northern Ireland's major annual film event celebrated its 10th year in 1996. The central venue is the Orchard cinema in the heart of Derry city centre

French Film Festival UK

- November
12 Sunbury Place
Edinburgh EH4 3BY
Tel: 0131 225 6191

Fax: 0131 225 6971
email: fff@frenchfilmfestival.org.uk
Website: www.frenchfilmfestival.org.uk
Ilona Morison
As the only British festival devoted exclusively to le cinéma francais, the French Film Festival UK has, since 1991, earned an unrivalled and unique reputation as a showcase for contemporary and classic French cinema in the UK and abroad. Programme falls in two categories: Panorama, devoted to the best names in French Cinema and New Waves, showcasing first and second-time directors. Edcucational events also take place in all cities. Held yearly in Edinburgh, Glasgow, Aberdeen, Dundee and London during the last two weeks in November

Greenwich Film Festival

October 2001
Studio 2B1 London House
The Old Seager Distillery
Brookmill Road
London SE8 4JT
Tel: 020 8694 2218
Fax: 020 864 2971
email: info@greenwichfilmfestival.co.uk
Website: www.greenwichfilmfestival.co.uk
Megan Davis, Liza Brown
Covers a wide range of programming, focuses on specific themes and showcases local talent

Guardian Edinburgh International Television Festival The

- 24-27 August 2001
1st Floor
17-21 Emerald Street
London WC1N 3QN
Tel: 020 7430 1333
Fax: 020 7430 2299
email: info@tvyp.co.uk
Website: www.tvyp.co.uk
Komal Trivedi, Festival Administrator
The Guardian Edinburgh International Television Festival (GEIFT) is the key television industry forum where current creative practice is celebrated and assessed by all levels of the industry and where industry concerns can be debated collectively and objectively. Held over four days, GEITF uses debate and presentation to talk about the skill and business of television through a varied programme of sessions workshops, lectures, screenings, demonstrations and networking parties

Human Rights Watch Internation Film Festival

March 2002
The Ritzy Cinema
Brixton Oval, Coldharbour Lane
Bixton, London SW2 1JG
Tel: 020 7737 2121
Fax: 020 7733 8790
email: andersj@hrw.org
Website: www.hrw.org/iff
John Anderson
Non competitive festival featuring films with human rights themes

International Film Festival of Wales

- 22-29 November 2001
Market House
Market Road
Cardiff CF5 1QE
Dyfed SY23 3AH
Tel: 029 20 406220
Fax: 029 20 233751
email: enq@iffw.co.uk or
Website: www.iffw.co.uk
michelle.williams@iffw.co.uk
Michelle Williams
Non-competitive for international feature films and shorts, together with films from Wales in Welsh and English. Also short retrospectives, workshops and seminars. The DM Davies Award is the single largest short film prize in Europe. It is presented to the director who is of Welsh origin or a native of Wales for two or more years for the best short submitted to the competition.

Italian Film Festival

- April
82 Nicolson Street
Edinburgh EH8 9EW
Tel: 0131 668 2232
Fax: 0131 668 2777
email: italianinstitute@btconnect.com
Website: italcult.net/edimburgo
A unique UK event throwing an exclusive spotlight on il cinema italiano over ten days in Edinburgh (Filmhouse) Glasgow (Film Theatre); and London (Riverside). Visiting guests and directors, debates, first and second films, plus a broad range of current releases and special focuses on particular actors or directors

IVCA Awards

- March 2002
IVCA
Business Communication Centre
19 Pepper Street, Glengall Bridge
London E14 9RP
Tel: 020 7512 0571

Fax: 020 7512 0591
email: info@ivca.org
Website: www.ivca.org
Competitive for non-broadcast industrial/training films and videos, covering all aspects of the manufacturing and commercial world, plus categories for educational, business, leisure and communications subjects. Programme, Special and Production (Craft) Awards, and industry award for effective communication. Closing date for entries December

KinoFilm

- 20-28 October 2001
Manchester International Short Film and Video Festival
42 Edge Street
Manchester M4 1HN
Tel: 0161 288 2494
Fax: 0161 281 1374
email: Kino.info@good.co.uk
Website: www.kinofilm.org.uk
John Wojowski
Kinofilm is dedicated to short films and videos from every corner of the world. Emphasis is placed on short innovative, unusual and off-beat productions. Films on any subject or theme can be submitted providing they are no longer than 30 minutes and were produced within the last two years and have not been previously submitted. All sections of film/video making community are eligible. Particularly welcome are applications from young film-makers and all members of the community who have never had work shown at festivals. Special categories include: Gay and Lesbian, Black Cinema, New Irish Cinema, New American Underground, Eastern European Work, Super 8 Film. Closing date for submissions is June 16, with the final deadline being 30 June (by prior arrangement with the festival director only). Application forms can be downloaded from the Kino website. Competive strand was introduced for 1999

Leeds International Film Festival

- 27 September-12 October 2001
Town Hall
The Headrow
Leeds LS1 3AD
Tel: 0113 247 8389
Fax: 0113 247 8397
email: debbie.maturi@leeds.gov.uk
Website: www.leedsfilm.com

Chris Fell
Competitive for features by new directors, ('Leeds New Directors Awards') and Fiction and Animated Shorts (Louis le Prince International). Over 10 strands including 'evolution' (interactive and online), Eureka (European Films), Film Festival Fringe, Voices of Cinema and Fanomenon (Cult Films)

Leeds Children's Film Festival

March-April 2002
Town Hall
The Headrow
Leeds LS1 3AD
Tel: 0113 247 8398
Fax: 0113 247 8397
email: debbie.maturi@leeds.gov.uk
Website: www.leedsfilm.com
Debbie Maturi
Sister festival to the Leeds International Film Festival.
Competitive for features. Also presents short films, animation and workshops

London Latin American Film Festival

September
Metro Pictures
79 Wardour Street

London W1V 3TH
Tel: 020 7434 3357
Fax: 020 7287 2112
Non-competitive, bringing to London a line up of contemporary films from Latin America and surveying current trends

London Lesbian and Gay Film Festival

March 2002
Festivals Office
National Film Theatre
South Bank
London SE1 8XT
Tel: 020 7815 1323/1324
Fax: 020 7633 0786
email: carol.coombes@bfi.org
Website: llgff.org.uk
Carol Coombes
Non-competitive for film and videos of special interest to lesbian and gay audiences. Some entries travel to regional film theatres as part of a national tour from April to June

Raindance Ltd

- 17-26 October 2001
81 Berwick Street
London W1V 3PF
Tel: 020 7287 3833
Fax: 020 7439 2243

email: info@raindance.co.uk
Website: www.raindance.co.uk
Daniel Fellows
Britain's only film market for independently produced features, shorts and documentaries. Deadline 1 September

Regus London Film Festival

- 7-22 November 2001
National Film Theatre
South Bank
London SE1 8XT
Tel: 020 7815 1322/1323
Fax: 020 7633 0786
email: sarah.lutton@bfi.org.uk
Website: www.lff.org.uk
Sarah Lutton
Britain's premier film festival screening the best in new cinema from around the world including previews of international feature films, shorts and videos. Selected highlights from the Festival go on tour to regional film theatres from November to December

Sheffield International Documentary Festival

- 22-28 October 2001
The Workstation

15 Paternoster Row
Sheffield S1 2BX
Tel: 0114 276 5141
Fax: 0114 272 1849
email: info@sidf.co.uk
Website: www.sidf.co.uk
Kathy Loizou
The only UK festival dedicated to
excellence in documentary film and
television. The week long event is
both a public film festival and an
industry gathering with sessions,
screenings and discussions on all the
new developments in documentary.
The festival is non-competitive. A
selection of films from the festival
tours to cinemas in the UK from
November to February each year

Out Of Sight -International Film And Television Archive Festival

- April 2002
Broadway
14-18 Broad Street
Nottingham NG1 3AL
Tel: 0115 952 6600/6611
Fax: 0115 952 6622
email: info@broadway.org.uk
Laraine Porter
Festival dedicated to film archive
work.

Start Moving Image Festival

- 14-15 July 2001
P.O. Box 82
Plymouth PL4 8XY
email: start@sundog.co.uk
Website: http//start.at/start
Stuart Moore
Non competitative festival featuring
independent films and videos made
by artists/filmmakers living in the
Southwest region

Television and Young People (TVYP)

- August
1st Floor
17-21 Emerald Street
London WC1N 3QN
Tel: 020 7430 1333
Fax: 020 7430 2299
email: info@tvyp.co.uk
Website: www.typ.co.uk
Simon Harrison
Television and Young People (TVYP)
is the educational arm of the
Guardian Edinburgh International
Television Festival (GEITF) and the
UK's leading forum for young people
aspiring to work in television. Taking
place over five days, TVYP offers new
entrants a unique insight into the

television industry through a
programme of masterclasses,
workshops, screenings and career
surgeries. Successful delegates will
have the unique opportunity to meet,
work with and learn from the leading
creative talent in the industry. Each
year, 150 places are offered to young
people aged 18-21 from across the
UK-other than their travel to and
from Edinburgh, all expenses are
covered by TVYP

Video Positive

- March/April 2003
International Biennale of Video and
Electronic Media Art Foundation for
Art and Creative Technology (FACT)
Bluecoat Chambers
School Lane
Liverpool L1 3BX
Tel: 0151 709 2663
Fax: 0151 707 2150
email: fact@fact.co.uk
Non-competitive for video and
electronic media art produced
worldwide in the two years preceding
the festival. Includes community and
education programmes, screenings,
workshops and seminars. Some
commissions available

Wildscreen

- October
PO Box 366
Bristol BS99 2HD
Tel: 0117 915 7100
Fax: 0117 915 7105
email: info@wildscreen.org.uk
Website: www.wildscreen.org.uk
Sue Lion
International festival of moving
images from the natural world.
Competitive: Panda Awards include
Conservation, Revelation, Newcomer,
Children's, Outstanding Achievement,
Craft. Eligible productions completed
after 1 January 2000 and not entered
in Wildscreen 2000. Week long festival
includes screenings, discussions, video
kiosks, masterclasses and workshops

URUGUAY

Montevideo International Film Festival for Children and Young People

- 9-20 July 2001
Cinemateca Uruguaya
Lorenzo Carnelli 1311, Casilla de
Correo 1170
11200 Montevideo
Tel: (598) 2 409 5795
Fax: (598) 2 409 4572
email: cinemuy@chasque.apc.org

Website: www.cinemateca.org.uv
Competitive for fiction international
films, documentaries and animation
for children

Montevideo International Film Festival

- March 2002
Cinemateca Uruguaya
Lorenzo Carnelli 1311, Casilla de
Correo 1170
11200 Montevideo
Tel: (598) 2 408 2460
Fax: (598) 2 409 4572
email: cinemuy@chasque.apc.org
Website: www.cinemateca.org.uy
Manual Martinez Carril, director
Competitive for fiction and Latin
American videos

USA

AFI Fest: American Film Institute Los Angeles International Film Festival

- 1-11 November 2001
2021 N Western Avenue
Los Angeles
CA 90027
Tel: (1) 323 856 7707
Fax: (1) 323 462 4049
email: afifest@afionline.org
Website: www.afifest.com
Julianna Brannum, Festival Manager
Christian Gaines, Festival Director
Official competition, New Directions
(American Independents), European
Film Showcse, Latin Cinema Series,
Shorts, Documentaries. Final
deadline for entries 4 July.

AFM (American Film Market)

- 21-28 February 2001
9th Floor, 10850 Wilshire Blvd,
Los Angeles
CA 90024-4311
Tel: (1) 310 446 1000
Fax: (1) 310 446 1600
email: afm@afma.com
Website: www.afma.com
Annual market for film, television
and video

Asian American International Film Festival

- 19 -28 July 2001
c/o Asian CineVision
32 East Broadway, 4th Floor
New York, NY 10002
Tel: (1) 212 925 8685
Fax: (1) 212 925 8157
email: acvinnyc@aol.com
Website: www.asiancinevision.org
Non-competitive, all categories and

lengths. No video-to-film transfers accepted as entries. Films must be produced, directed and/or written by artists of Asian heritage

Chicago International Children's Film Festival

- 25 October-9 November 2001
Facets Multimedia
1517 West Fullerton Avenue
Chicago IL 60614
Tel: (1) 773 281 9075
Fax: (1) 773 929 5437 or 773 929 0266
email: kidsfest@facets.org
Website: www.cicf.org
Kathleen Beckman
Competitive for entertainment films, videotapes and television programmes for children. Deadline for entries 28 May 1999

Chicago International Film Festival

- 4-18 October 2001
32 West Randolph Street
Suite: 600, Chicago
Illinois 60601 USA
Tel: (1) 312 425 9400
Fax: (1) 312 425 0944
email: filmfest@wwa.com
Website: www.chicagofilmfestival. com
Contact: Michael Kutza
Founder & Artistic director
Competitive for feature films, documentaries, shorts, animation, student and First and Second Features

Cleveland International Film Festival

- March 2002
Cleveland Film Society
2510 Market Avenue
Cleveland, OH 44113
Tel: (1) 216 623 0400
Fax: (1) 216 623 0103
email: cfs@clevelandfilm.org
Website: www.clevelandfilm.org
William Frank Guentzler
Non-competitive for feature, narr-ative, documentary, animation and experimental films. Competitive for shorts, with $2,500 prize money

Columbus International Film and Video Festival (a.k.a. The Chris Awards)

- 23-25 October 2001
5701 High Street
Suite 200
Worthington
Ohio 43085
Tel/fax: (1) 614 841 1666
email: info@chrisawds.org
Website: www.chrisawds.org

The Chris Awards is one of the longest-running competitions of its kind in North America, specialising in honouring documentary, education, business and information films and videos, as well as categories for the arts and entertainment. Entrants compete within categories for the first place Chris statuette, second place Bronze plaque and third place Certificate of Honorable Mention Expanded public screenings. Entry deadline 1 July

Denver International Film Festival

- 11-20 October 2001
1430 Larimer Square, Suite 320
Denver
CO 80202
Tel: (1) 303 595 3456
Fax: (1) 303 595 0956
email: dfs@denverfilm.org
Website: www.denverfilm.org
Brit Withey, Program Director
Non-competitive. New international features, tributes to film artists, independent features, documentaries, shorts, animation, experimental works, videos and children's films

Florida Film Festival

- 8-17 June 2001
1300 South Orlando Avenue
Maitland
FL 32751
Tel: (1) 407 629 1088
Fax: (1) 407 629 6870
email: filmfest@enzian.org
Website: www.enzian.org
Matthew Curtis
A 10-day event involving over 100 films, several seminars and social events. Highlights include an Americn Independent Film Competition with three categories (Dramatic, Documentary and Shorts) a Kodak cinematography award, an International Showcase for features and shorts, Midnight Movies, "Spotlight Films", and special screenings and tributes

Fort Lauderdale International Film Festival

- 30 October-11 November 2001
1314 East Lasp;as B;vd 007
Fort Lauderdale
FL 33301
Tel: (1) 954 760 9898
Fax: (1) 954 760 9099
email: brofilm@aol.com
Website: www.fliff.com
Bonnie Adams
The festival typically features 40-50

full length features, plus documentaries, an art on film series, short subjects, as well as animation. Awards are presented for Best Film, Best Foreign Language Film, Documentary, Short, Director, Actor, Actress and an Audience Award. The Festival also features an international student film competition with $5,000 in product grants from Kodak

Hawaii International Film Festival

- 2-11 November 2001
1001 Bishop Street
Pacific Tower, Suite 745
Honolulu Hawaii 96813
Tel: (1) 808 528 3456
Fax: (1) 808 528 1410
email: hiffinfo@hiff.org
Website: www.hiff.org
Chuck Boller, Managing Director
HIFF is a competitive festival with awards for best feature, documentary, short and an audience award. The festival is committed to presenting artistic, political and commercial works from around the world with an emphasis on Pacific Rim filmmakers

Houston International Film Festival: Worldfest Houston

(+ Market) 5-14 April 2002
WorldFest-Houston
PO Box 56566
Houston
TX 77256-6566
Tel: (1) 713 965 9955
Fax: (1) 713 965 9960
email: worldfest@aol.com
Website: www.worldfest.org
Kathleen Haney
Competitive for features, shorts, documentary, television production and television commercials. Independent studios, experimental and video. Worldfest Discovery Programme where winners are introduced to organisers of top 200 international festivals. Screenplay category. Winning screenplays submitted to top 100 US creative agencies

Independent Feature Film Market

- September
12th Floor
104 West 29th Street
New York
NY 10001-5310
Tel: (1) 212 465 8200
Fax: (1) 212 465 8525
email: marketinfo@ifp.org
Website: Web site: www.ifp.org

The Independent Feature Film Market is the longest running market devoted to new, emerging American independent film talent seeking domestic and foreign distribution. It is the market for discovering projects in development, outstanding documentaries, and startling works of fiction

Miami Film Festival

- February 2002
Film Society of Miami
444 Brickell Avenue, Suite 229
Miami FL 33131
Tel: (1) 305 377 3456
Fax: (1) 303 577 9768
email: mff@gate.net
Website: www.miamifilmfestival.com
Non-competitive; screenings of 25-30 international films; all cate-gories considered, 35mm film only. Entry deadline 1 November

Mobius Advertising Awards Competition

- 7 February 2002
841 North Addison Avenue
Elmhurst, IL 60126-1291
Tel: (1) 630 834 7773
Fax: (1) 630 834 5565
email:mobiusinfo@mobiusawards.com
Website: www.mobiusawards.com
J.W. Anderson
International awards competition for television and radio commercials produced or released in the 12 months preceding the annual 1 October entry deadline. Awards early February each year. Founded in 1971

New York Film Festival

- 28 September-14 October 2001
Film Society of Lincoln Center
70 Lincoln Center Plaza, 4th Floor
New York NY 10023
Tel: (1) 212 875 5638
Fax: (1) 212 875 5636
Website: www.filmlinc.com
Sara Benson
Non-competitive for feature films, shorts, including drama, documentary, animation and experimental films. Films must have been produced one year prior to the Festival and must be New York premieres

Nortel Palm Springs International Film Festival

- January 2002
1700 E. Tahquitz Canyon, #3
Palm Springs, CA 92262
Tel: (1) 760 322 2930
Fax: (1) 760 322 4087

email: info@psfilmfest.org
Website: www.psfilmfest.org
Craig Prater, Director
At each festival world premieres mix with social functions, cultural events, industry seminars, student activities and directors workshops

Portland International Film Festival

- February 2002
Northwest Film Center
1219 SW Park Avenue
Portland, OR 97205
Tel: (1) 503 221 1156
Fax: (1) 503 294 0874
email: info@nwfilm.org
Website: www.nwfilm.org
Bill Foster
Invitational survey of New World cinema. Includes over 100 features, documentary and short films from more than two dozen countries. Numerous visiting artists. Attendance for the 23rd Festival is expected to be 35,000, drawn from throughout the North West of America

San Francisco International Film Festival

- March 2002
346 Ninth Street, 2nd Floor
San Francisco, CA 94103
Tel: (1) 415 863 0814
Fax: (1) 415 863 7428
email: festival@naatanet.org
Website: www.naatanet.org/festival
Brian Lau, Director
Feature films, by invitation, shown non-competitively. Shorts, documentaries, animation, experimental works and television productions eligible for Golden Gate Awards competition section. Deadline for Golden Gate Awards entries early December

San Francisco International Lesbian & Gay Film Festival

- 20-30 June 2002
Frameline
346 Ninth Street
San Francisco CA 94103
Tel: (1) 415 703 8650
Fax: (1) 415 861 1404
email: info@frameline.org
Website: www.frameline.org
Largest lesbian/gay film festival in the world. Features, documentary, experimental, short film and video. Deadline for entries 10 January 2002

Seattle International Film Festival

- May/June

911 Pine St, 6th Floor
Seattle
WA 98101
Tel: (1) 206 464 5830
Fax: (1) 206 264 7919
email: mail@seattle.com
Website: www.seattlefilm.com
Darryl Macdonald, Festival Director
Jury prize for new director and American independent award. Golden Space Needle awards voted by audience. Submissions accepted 1 December to 1 March

Sundance Film Festival

- January 2002
PO Box 16450
Salt Lake City
UT 84116
Tel: (1) 801 328 3456
Fax: (1) 801 575 5175
email: institute@sundance.org
Website: www.sundance.org
Competitive for American independent dramatic and documentary feature films. Also presents a number of international and American premieres and short films, as well as sidebars, special retrospectives and seminars

Telluride Film Festival

- 31 August-3 September 2001
379 State Street
Portsmouth, NH 03801
Tel: (1) 603 643 9202
Fax: (1) 603 643 9206
email: tellufilm@aol.com
Website: www.telluridefilmfestival.com
Non-competitive. World premieres, archival films and tributes. Entry deadline 15 July

US International Film & Video Festival

- June
841 North Addison Avenue
Elmhurst
IL 60126-1291
Tel: (1) 630 834 7773
Fax: (1) 630 834 5565
email: filmfestinfo@filmfestawards.com
Website: www.filmfestawards.com
J.W. Anderson
International awards competition for business, television, documentary, industrial and informational productions, produced or released in the 18 months preceding the annual 1 March entry deadline. Awards presentations early June each year. Founded 1968

FUNDING

ADAPT (Access for Disabled People to Arts Premises Today)
The ADAPT Trust
8 Hampton Terrace
Edinburgh EH12 5JD
Tel: 0131 346 1999
Fax: 0131 346 1991
email: adapt.trust@virgin.net
Website: www.adapttrust.co.uk
Director: Stewart Coulter
Charitable trust providing advice and challenge funding to arts venues - cinemas, concert halls, libraries, heritage and historic houses, theatres, museums and galleries - throughout Great Britain. ADAPT also provides a consultancy service and undertakes access audits and assessments. Grants and Awards for 2000 advertised as available

ADAPT (Northern Ireland)
185 Stranmillis Road
Belfast
BT2 7AF
Tel: 028 9023 1211
Fax: 028 9024 0878
email: cshiels.adaptni@dnet.co.uk
Website: www.adf.dnet.co.uk/adapt
The ADAPT Fund for Northern Ireland was granted independent status in June 1996 by the Inland Revenue. ADAPT aims to promote universal accessibility in arts, cultural and community venues in Northern Ireland by providing advice, training and support and to develop a programme of activities and events which will involve disabled and non-disabled people at all levels in a way which is relevant to the objectives of the organisation. ADAPT's remit covers arts and community centres, theatres, concert halls, libraries, museums and public galleries, community centres and other buildings where arts and social activities take place. ADAPT aims to improve accessibility in the future, not just in terms of the built environment but in the widest sense of access through projects, which encourage awareness, participation, integration and employment.

Arts Council of England
Visual Arts Department
14 Great Peter Street
London W1P 3NQ
Tel: 020 7333 0100
Fax: 020 7973 6581
email: gary.thomas@
artscouncil.org.uk
Website: www.artscouncil.org.uk
Gary Thomas
The Visual Arts Department works with national agencies for artists' film and video. The National Touring Programme offers opportunities for organisations to commission and tour work; guidelines can be requested on 020 7973 6517. Project funding, including production funding for individual artists, is primarily the responsibility of the regional arts boards (or media development agencies).
Animate!
A collaboration with Channel 4 to commission innovative and experimental animation for television from individual animators and artists (including those living in Northern Ireland, Scotland and Wales).
Deadline: January 2001

BBC 10x10
Bristol Television Features
Whiteladies Road
Bristol BS8 2LR
Tel: 0117 974 6746
Fax: 0117 974 7452
email: 10x10@BBC.co.uk
Series Producer: Jeremy Howe
Produces 10 ten-minute films per series, documentary or fiction films for broadcast on BBC2. It is an initiative to encourage and develop new and innovative filmmaking talent in all genres, through the provision of modest production finance combined with practical guidance. The scheme is open to any director with no commissioned broadcast UK Network directing credit. All applications must include a showreel with their proposals - which should be treatments for documentary, scripts for drama

British Council
11 Portland Place

London W1N 4EJ
Tel: 020 7389 3065
Fax: 020 7389 3041
Website: www.britfilms.com
Assists in the co-ordination and shipping of films to festivals, and in some cases can provide funds for the film-maker to attend when invited.

British Screen Finance Limited
(See the Film Council)

Channel 4/MOMI Animators
Professional Residencies
Museum of the Moving Image
South Bank
London SE1 8XT
Tel: 020 7815 1376
Louise Spraggon
Professional residencies are awarded to animators who have graduated within the last 5 years. Animators receive a fee, plus budget towards materials. At the end of the residencies projects will be considered for commission by Channel 4
British Animation Training Scheme
Museum of the Moving Image
Southbank
Waterloo
London SE1 8XT
Tel: 020 7815 1376
Contact: Louise Spraggon
The assisting in animation course for profesionals in animation offers comprehensive training in all aspects of assisting in drawn animation. The course is delivered by professional animators working in the industry. Vocational over 30 weeks

Cineworks
Glasgow Media Access Centre
3rd Floor
34 Albion Street
Glasgow G1 1LH
Tel: 0141 553 2620
Fax: 0141 553 2660
email: Cineworks9@aol.com
Website: www.g-mac.co.uk
Cordelia Stephens
Cineworks is a Scottish short film production scheme which produces original and innovative films from emergent talent in the disciplines of

drama, documentary and animation. It is run by the Glagow Medial Access Centre in partnership with the Film and Video access Centre, Edinburgh and in association with Scottish Screen. Cineworks develops 12 projects each year through script editing, producer training, workshops, masterclasses and mentoring and funds five projects on awards of £10,000 or £15,000. There are also £5,000 completion awards available. The five films are premiered at the Edinburgh International Film Festival and are distributed by Scottish Screen. BBC Scotland holds the options to broadcast the films

first take films

Anglia Television
Anglia House
Norwich
Norfolk NR1 3JG
Tel: 01603 756879
Fax: 01603 764665
email: cnorbury@angliatv.co.uk
Executive Producer: Caroline Norbury
Administrator: Annette Culverhouse
Marketing & Distribution: Kate Gerova
first take films is a joint initiative set up by Eastern Arts Board and Anglia Television. It is a regional cultural production agency whose principal function is to facilitate, encourage and promote the creative arts of film, video and moving image in the East of England. Its training and development initiative, called new voices, provides an opportunity for young people completely new to film making to train in production and make a programme which are screened on Anglia Television. first take films selects eight documentary ideas from new directors who then undertake intensive training in all aspects of production including research and camera skills. Four projects are then be selected for production and the director of each film works with a small professional crew and directs and shoots their own footage. Submissions are usually need to be submitted by February

The Glasgow Film Fund

249 West George Street
Glasgow G2 4RB
Tel: 0141 302 1757
Fax: 0141 302 1714
Contact: Judy Anderson
The Glasgow Film Fund (GFF) provides production funding for companies shooting films in the Glasgow area or produced by Glasgow-based production companies. Applications are accepted for films intended for theatrical release and with a budget of at least £500,000. The maximum investment made by the GFF in any one project is normally £150,000, however, where there is an exceptionally high level of economic benefit the GFF may consider raising its maximum investment to £250,000. GFF application forms, meeting dates, submission deadlines and further information are available from the GFF office. Production credits include, Shallow Grave, Small Faces, Carla's Song, Regeneration, Orphans, My Name Is Joe, The Acid House and House of Mirth

Kraszna-Krausz Foundation

122 Fawnbrake Avenue
London SE24 0BZ
Tel: 020 7738 6701
Fax: 020 7738 6701
email: info@k-k.org.uk
Website: www.k-k.org.uk
Andrea Livingstone, Administrator
The Foundation offers small grants to assist in the development of new or unfinished projects, work or literature where the subject specifically relates to the art, history, practice or technology of photography or the moving image (defined as film, television, video and related screen media)
Annual awards, with prizes for books on the moving image (film, television, video and related media), alternating with those for books on still photography. Books, to have been published in previous two years, can be submitted from publishers in any language. Prize money around £10,000, with awards in two categories. The 2001 awards are for books on the moving image

Moving Image Development Agency (MIDA)

109 Mount Pleasant
Liverpool L3 5TF
Tel: 0151 708 9858
Fax: 0151 708 9859
email: enquire@mida.demon.co.uk
The Moving Image Development Agency (MIDA) is a non-profit making agency limited by guarantee. It was established in Liverpool in 1992 with the intention of supporting and nurturing a sustainable independent film and television industry throughout the North West

Nicholl Fellowships in Screenwriting

Academy of Motion Picture Arts and Sciences
8949 Wilshire Boulevard
Beverly Hills, CA 90211
USA
Tel: (1) 310 247 3059
email: nicholl@oscars.org
Website: www.oscars.org/nicholl
Annual Screenwriting Fellowship Awards
Up to five fellowships of US$30,000 each to new screenwriters. Eligible are writers in English who have not earned more than $5,000 writing for commercial film or television. Collaborations and adaptations are not eligible. A completed entry includes a feature film screenplay approx 100-130 pages long, an application form and a US$30 entry fee. Deadline 1 May

The Prince's Trust

18 Park Square East
London NW1 4LH
Tel: 0800 842842
Fax: 020 7543 1200
email: info@princes-trust.org.uk
Website: www.princes-trust.or.uk
The Prince's Trust aims to help young people to succeed by providing opportunities which they would otherwise not have. This is achieved through a nationwide network which delivers training, personal development, support for business start ups, development awards and educational support.
Richard Mills Travel Fellowship
In association with the Gulbenkian Foundation and the Peter S Cadbury Trust, offers three grants of £1,000 for people working in community arts, in the areas of housing, minority arts, special needs, or arts for young people, especially the unemployed. The Fellowships are applicable to people under 35

Scottish Screen

Second Floor
249 West George Street
Glasgow G2 4QE
Tel: 0141 302 1700
Fax: 0141 302 1711
email: info@scottishscreen.com
Website: www.scottishscreen.com
Chief Executive: Steve McIntyre
Scottish Screen is responsible to the Scottish Parliament for developing all

aspects of screen industry and culture in Scotland through script and company development, short film production, distribution of National Lottery film production finance, training, education, exhibition funding, the Film Commission locations support and the Scottish Screen Archive.

Film Schemes

Tartan Shorts
A joint initiative with BBC Scotland. Three projects are awarded a maximum of £60,000 to produce a short drama of abut 15 mins duration.

New Found Land
A collaboration with the Scottish Media Group for new filmmakers. Six half-hour projects commissioned with budgets of around £48,000.

Short Film Factory
A drama based scheme to make four 8.5 minute films per year. An extensive training and development programme is attached.

Four Minute Wonders
A music production scheme. Each month around £5,000 can be won to develop and produce a video based on a new piece of music. The new track is then uploaded to the 4minutewonders.com website.

Digit
As part of Scottish Screen's commitment to New Media a new production and development scheme will be launched to support new talent working in the area of interactive media.

Other Funding
Outside of the various schemes, Scottish Screen occassionaly will invest in one-off short film projects.

Development
Advice and Finance for the development of feature films. (See entry for National Lottery)

MEDIA Plus
At Scottish Screen MEDIA Antenna Scotland can help you access MEDIA Plus and other European support programmes.

Sgrîn, Media Agency for Wales

The Bank, 10 Mount Stuart Square
Cardiff Bay
Cardiff CF10 5EE
Tel: 029 2033 3300
Fax: 029 2033 3320
email: sgrin@sgrin.co.uk
Website: www.sgrin.co.uk
Production coordinator: Gaynor

Messer Price
Sgrîn, Media Agency for Wales, is the primary organisation for film, television and new media in Wales. Sgrîn operates an independent film-makers' fund, offering grants for development, production and completion of short films. It also provides funding support for cinema venues, both public and private, cultural and interpretive printed and audiovisual material which complements and promotes exhibition programmes, and events. Guidelines and deadlines are available on request

National Lottery

Arts Council of Northern Ireland
Lottery Department
MacNeice House, 77 Malone road
Belfast BT9 6AQ
Tel: 028 9066 7000
Fax: 028 9066 4766
email: lottery@artscouncil-ni.org
Website: www.artscouncil-ni.org
Lottery Director: Tanya Greenfield

Arts Council of Wales
Lottery Unit
Holst House
9 Museum Place
Cardiff CF10 3NX
Tel: 029 20 376500
Fax: 029 20 395284
email: information@ccc-acw.org.uk
Website: www.ccc-acw.org.uk
Anneli Jones or Kath Davies, Lottery Unit

Film Council
10 Little Portland Street
London W1W 7JG
Tel: 020 7861 7861
Fax: 020 7861 7862
email: info@filmcouncil.org.uk

Websites: www.filmcouncil.org.uk
www.firstlightmovies.com
Contact: Tina McFarling/Ian Thomson
John Woodward, Chief Executive
The Film Council, the Government-backed film agency (not just film funding) is responsible for the creation of a sustainable film industry and developing education and film culture in the UK. On April 1 2000 the Film Council took responsibility for the British Film Commission, the Arts Council of England's Lottery Film Department, British Screen Finance and the British Film Institute's Production Department. The British Film Institute continues to run as an independent body funded by the Film Council. The Film Council channels £55 million a year of into the industry – a combination of Lottery and Government grant in aid funding. Three production funds have been set up with an overall budget of £20 million a year to spend on film production and development – the Premiere Fund (£10m), the New Cinema Fund (£5m) and the Development Fund (£5m). The Film Council also has a Training Fund (£ 1 million a year) expanding training for scriptwriters and producer/film-makers in partnership with Skillset, the National Training Organisation for the film industry. In addition, a grant-funded programme supported by £1 million of Lottery funds called "First Light" offering children and young people the opportunity to experience film-making and display their talents using low-cost technology has been launched.

As a strategic body the Film Council has created the £6 million a year Regional Investment Fund for England (RIFE) which is available to support cultural and industrial film initiatives in the English regions. The Film Council has also developed a joined-up UK-wide agenda with its sister organisations the national organisations Scottish Screen, Sgrin, and the Northern Ireland Film Commission. The Film Council also continues to administer Lottery funds to the film production franchises set up by the Arts Council of England in 1997 and awarded to The Film Consortium, Pathé Pictures and DNA Films.

Northern Ireland Film Commission

21 Ormeau Avenue
Belfast BT2 8HD
Tel: 028 9023 2444
Fax: 028 9023 9918
email: info@nifc.co.uk
Website: www.nifc.co.uk
The Northern Ireland Film
Commission offers loans to
production companies for the
development and production of
feature films or television drama
series or serials that are intended to
be produced primarily in Northern
Ireland. During 2000, the funding
came from a one off EU grant of
£500,000. The money allocated to
production has been used up, but
there still remains some funding for
development. On the 1 April 2000 the
NIFC will receive new and ongoing
funding from the National Lottery. A
process of consultation is presently
being carried out as to how the
money is to be available.

Scottish Screen

Second Floor
249 West George Street
Glasgow G2 4QE
Tel: 0141 302 1700
Fax: 0141 302 1711
email: info@scottishscreen.com
Website: www.scottishscreen.com
From 7 April 2000, Scottish Screen
assumed full responsibility for
allocating National Lottery funds for
all aspects of film production in
Scotland. There are currently seven
funding programmes:
1. Feature Film Production Funding
Funding is available up to £500,000
per project for feature films
(including feature length
documentaries) aimed at theatrical
distribution
2. Short Film Production Funding
Applications for under £25,000 are
accepted on a continuous basis, and
will be decided on by the appropriate
monthly officers' meeting
3. Project Development Funding
Funding up to £75,000 is available for
second-stage development of feature
films. This is aimed at projects
already at a relatively advanced stage.
It will support elements such as script
polish, preparation of schedule and
budget, casting, etc
4. Distribution and Exploitation
Support
Funding of up to £25,000 is available
for completed feature films to
support Print and Advertising costs.
5. Company Development
Programme
Finance of up to £75,000 is available
as working capital funding into
companies to support a slate of film,
television and multimedia.
6. Short Film Award Schemes
On an annual basis, Scottish Screen
will consider applications, of up to
£60,000, from outside bodies to
operate short film production
schemes.
7. Twenty First Films - Low Budget
Film Scheme
This scheme offers support for low
budget features (including feature
documentaries) with budgets up to
around £600,000.

Regional Arts Boards and Regional Schemes

Croydon Media Awards

Croydon Clocktower
Katharine Street
Croydon CR9 1ET
Tel: 020 8760 5400 ext 1048
email: paul-johnson@croydon.gov.uk
Co-ordinator: Paul Johnson
The Croydon Media Awards is an
ongoing production initiative co-
funded by the LFVDA and the
London Borough of Croydon. The
£10,000 scheme supports locally
produced film, video and new media
work, with completed productions
screened at the David Lean Cinema

East Midlands Arts Board

Mountfields House
Epinal Way
Loughborough
Leics LE11 0QE
Tel: 01509 218292
Fax: 01509 262214
email: info@em-arts.co.uk
Website: www.arts.org.uk
Suzanne Alizar, Film and Digital
Media Production Officer
New work and commissions, script
research and development awars,
production awards and distribution
awards

East England Arts

Eden House
48-49 Bateman Street
Cambridge CB2 1LR
Tel: 01223 454000
Fax: 0870 242171
email: info@eearts.co.uk
Website: www.eastenglandarts.org.uk
Cinema and Broadcasting Officer:
Martin Ayres
Media Assistant: Helen Dixon
Eastern Arts Board is the regional arts
development and funding agency for
the counties of Bedfordshire,
Cambridgeshire, Essex, Hertfordshire,
Norfolk and Suffolk, and the unitary
authorities of Luton, Peterborough,
Rochford and Thurrock. The new
East of England Regional Arts Lottery
Programme and Small Scale Capital
Scheme includes priority support for
film, video, cinema and multimedia
activity. EAB Open Access schemes
will offer support for individuals.
EAB assists a network of agencies and
venues, including first take (see entry
for first take) with Anglia Television.

Policy, information, development services and funding for Cinema & Broadcasting covers five interlocking areas: Collections, Education & Training, Exhibition, Production, and Artists Film & Video & Multimedia. From Autumn 1999 EAB specialist film and video production, scriptwriting, co-commissioning funding and development services will be delivered through first take (see entry for first take).
East of England Regional Production Fund
Launched in Autumn 1999, this fund seeks to assist innovative practice and creative experimentation in a range of genres, styles and formats. It offers seed funding for the realisation, development and production of one-off moving image projects

English Regional Arts Boards
5 City Road
Winchester
Hampshire SO23 8SD
Tel: 01962 851063
Fax: 01962 842033
email: info@erab.org.uk
Website: www.arts.org.uk
Carolyn Nixson, Administrator

London Arts
2 Pear Tree Court
London EC1R ODS
Tel: 020 7608 6100
Fax: 020 7608 4100
email: firstname.surname@lonab.co.uk
Website: www.arts.org.uk/londonarts
Chief Executive: Sue Robertson
The London Arts Board has no dedicated funds for Film and Video. However, it does offer awards to individual artists working in the medium of film and video and New Media. Write to LAB at the above address for funding guidelines. For all other film and video enquiries, call the London Film and Video Development Agency (qv)

London Film and Video Development Agency
114 Whitfield Street
London W1T 5EF
Tel: 020 7383 7766/7755
Fax: 020 7383 7745
email: lfvda@lfvda.demon.co.uk
Website: www.lfvda.demon.co.uk
Production Executive: Maggie Ellis
East London Media Initiative executive: Rebecca Maguire

London Film and Video Development Agency currently operates the following production schemes but check their website for up to date guidelines and deadlines.
London Production Fund supports film, video and television projects by independent film-makers living/working in the Greater London region. The Fund is financially supported by Carlton Television and the Film Council and has an annual production budget of approximately £120,000. LPF offers Production and Completion Awards up to £15,000 each for production or part-production costs. Awards are made on the basis of written proposals and applicants' previous work. The Fund is interested in supporting as diverse a range of work as possible.
Digital Tales: an initiative in partnership with Film Four Lab aimed at filmmakers with a background in artists' film and video, photography or digital media. The emphasis is on combining the creative use of technology with strong visuals and narrative. Budgets up to £6,000.
London Artists Film Fund: an annual awards scheme supported by London Arts enabling artists to produce short films and videos for cinema exhibition. Selected films will form part of a touring programme screening through the UK at regional film theatres. Budgets to £18,000.
East London Media Initiative: this new fund to be established in Autumn 2001 builds on the successful East London Film Fund and is primarily aimed at business support and project development for companies based in the East London region. There will be small awards available through local Borough production schemes. For further details contact ELMI at LFVDA

North West Arts Board
Manchester House
22 Bridge Street
Manchester M3 3AB
Tel: 0161 834 6644
Fax: 0161 834 6969
email: info@nwarte.co.uk
Website: www.arts.org.uk/nwab
Julie Leather, Administrator
Information
NWAB offers a range of funding schemes covering Production, Exhibition, Training and Media

Education for those resident in the NWAB region

Northern Arts
Ground Floor
Central Square
Forth Street
Tel: 0191 281 6334
Fax: 0191 230 5566
email: info@northernarts.org.uk
Website: www.arts.org.uk
Head of Film Media and Literature: Mark Robinson
Northern Production Fund (NPF)
The aim of NPF is to support the production of short and long form drama, for film, television and radio, animation, creative documentaries, and all forms of experimental film-making, including work for gallery exhibition. The foremost concern of NPF is for the quality of the production. NPF to support productions which are imaginative, innovative, thoughtful, courageous and powerful. NPF normally holds three meetings per year to consider applications under the small scale production, development and feature film development headings.
Production
Support of up to £30,000 for production or part-production costs or completion costs.
Development
Support of up to £5,000 to assist in the development of scripts, storyboards, full treatments, pilot production, etc. This includes research and development for feature films, short drama for film or radio, animation, documentary projects and innovative television drama.
Feature Film Developments
A maximum of £10,000 awards for feature film development will be available for projects each year. These awards will normally be made to production companies, working with a Northern-based writer, who are able to demonstrate their ability to match the Northern Arts contribution. Matching funding may include the cost of feature film development expertise and/or the contribution of another funding partner.
Company Support
Support for companies is available to assist in the development of a programme of work. Company support will normally be awarded to support several projects rather than production costs.
Broadcaster Partnership Schemes

The Northern Production Fund also works in partnership with broadcasters to offer production schemes for short drama and documentary production

South East Arts
Union House
Eridge Road
Tunbridge Wells
Kent TN4 8HF
Tel: 01892 507200
Fax: 01892 549383
email: info.sea@artsfb.org.uk
Website: www.arts.org.uk
Production Grants
Offers grants of up to £10,000 for full or part-funding of films or videos for more experienced filmmakers. Grants of up to £1,000 are available to newcomers or those with little production experience

South West Arts
Bradninch Place
Gandy Street
Exeter EX4 3LS
Tel: 01392 218188
Fax: 01392 229229
email: info@swa.co.uk
Website: www.swa.co.uk
John Prescott Thomas
Chief Executive: Nick Capaldi

South West Media Development Agency
Website:
www.swmediadevagency.co.uk
(For details about regional funding contact the Film Council)

Southern Arts Board
13 St Clement Street
Winchester
Hants SO23 9DQ
Tel: 01962 855099
Fax: 01962 861186
email: info@southernarts.co.uk
Website: www.arts.org.uk
Film and Video production grants available in two categories: production (up to £5,000) and completion (up to £3,000). Co-production funding is strongly encouraged. First Cut (with Central) and Taped Up (with Meridian) are both broadcast schemes to support filmmakers new to television to make short films for broadcast. The David Alsthul Award is a competitive award for creative achievement in film and video production available to those who live or work in the Southern region including students. Annual prize money of £1,000. Exhibition

Development Fund supports programming, marketing, training and research and includes support for artists working with digital technology and installation work. Media Education Development Fund supports strategic development of regional media education. Full details on all the above on application

West Midlands Arts Board
82 Granville Street
Birmingham B1 2HJ
Tel: 0121 631 3121
Fax: 0121 643 7239
email: info@west-midlands-arts.co.uk
Media Officer: Film and Video:
Laurie Hayward
email: laurie.hayward.@west-midlands-arts.co.uk
First Cut" Film and Video Production Scheme.
A broadcast initiative supported by West Midlands Arts, Birmingham City Council, the Media Development Agency for the West Midlands (MDAWM), Central Broadcasting, BBC Resources Midlands and East, and the Midland Media Training Consortium. The aim is to produce a range of diverse programmes for regional television. Recipients of the awrd work with a Production Co-ordinator based at (MDAWM) to develop a project through training, production support and access to the broadcast industry. A minimum of five awards are made with budgets of up to £7,500. The scheme results in the Central Television 'First Cut' programme which will be broadcast in the Autumn of 2000. Application deadline January 2000.
New Work and Commissions
Offer artist film and video makers an opportunity to produce new work in film, video and new technology. The scheme seeks proposals which demonstrate innovation and experimentation. Awards are made for pieces up to ten minutes with a maximum budget of £5,000. The scheme favours work for screening in conventional, sites specific and other contexts. Application deadlines February/September.
Research and Development Awards
Enables makers to develop their proposals for future productions. Research and Development Awards are expected to range between £200 to £1,000. Deadline February/September

European and Pan-European Sources

Eurimages

Council of Europe
Palais de l'Europe
67075 Strasbourg Cédex
France
Tel: (33) 3 88 41 26 40
Fax: (33) 3 88 41 27 60
Website:
www.culture.coe.fr/eurimages
Provides financial support for
feature-length fiction films,
documentaries, distribution and
exhibition. Applications from the UK
can only be accepted if a UK
producer is a fourth co-producer in a
tripartite co-production or the third
in a bipartite, provided his/her share
does not exceed 30 per cent of the co-
production

European Co-production Association

c/o France 2
7 Espanade Henri de France
75907 Paris
Cédex 15
France
Tel: (33) 1 56 22 42 42
Website: www.france2.fr
Secretariat: Claire Heinrich
A consortium of European public
service TV networks for the co-
production of TV fiction series. Can
offer complete finance. Development
funding is also possible. Proposals
should consist of full treatment,
financial plan and details of proposed
co-production partners. Projects are
proposed directly to Secretariat or to
member national broadcasters
(Channel 4 in UK)

FilmFörderung Hamburg

Friedensallee 14-16
22765 Hamburg
Germany
Tel: (49) 40 398 370
Fax: (49) 40 398 3710
email: filmfoerderung@ffhh.de
Website: www.ffhh.de
Eva Hubert
Producers of cinema films can apply
for a subsidy amounting to at most
50 per cent of the overall production
costs of the finished film. Foreign
producers can also apply for this
support. We recommend to co-
produce with a German partner. It is
necessary to spend at least 150 per
cent of the subsidy in Hamburg. Part
of the film should be shot in
Hamburg. Financial support
provided by the FilmFörderung
Hamburg can be used in
combination with other private or
public funding, including that of TV
networks

CARTOON (European Association of Animation Film)

418 Boulevard Lambermont
B-1030 Brussels
Belgium
Tel: (32) 2 245 12 00
Fax: (32) 2 245 46 89
email: cartoon@skynet.be
Website: www.cartoon-media.be
Contact: Corinne Jenart, Marc
Vandeweyer
CARTOON, based in Brussels, is a
European animation network which
organises the annual CARTOON
FORUM, co-ordinates the grouping
of European animation studios and
runs specialist training courses in
animation

Europa Cinemas

54, rue Beaubourg
F-75 003 Paris, France
Tel: (33) 1 42 71 53 70
Fax: (33) 1 42 71 47 55
email: europacinema@magic.fr
Website: www.europa-cinemas.org
Contact: Claude-Eric Poiroux, Fatima
Djoumer
This project encourages screenings
and promotion of European films in
a network of cinemas in European
cities. It offers a financial support for
screening European films, for
promotional activities and for special
events

MEDIA Programme

MEDIA Plus Programme

European Commission, Directorate
General X:
Information, Communication,
Culture, Audio-visual
rue de la Loi, 200
1040 Brussels, Belgium
Tel: (32) 2 299 11 11
Fax: (32) 2 299 92 14
Head of Programme: Jacques
Delmoly

The MEDIA Plus Programme (2001 -
2005) is an European Union
initiative that aims at strengthening
the competitiveness of the European
audiovisual industry with a series
support measures dealing with the
training of professionals,
development of production projects,
distribution and promotion of
cinematographic works and
audiovisual programmes. The
programme was introduced in
January 2001 as a follow up to the
old MEDIA 2 programme. MEDIA
Plus is managed by the Directorate
General for Education and Culture at
the European Commission in
Brussels. It is managed on a national
level by a network of 31 offices called
the MEDIA Desks, Antennae or
Service.

Programme Contents

MEDIA Training

- the programme offers funding for
pan-European training initiatives.
The Commission supports courses
covering subjects such as economic,
financial and commercial
management, use of new technologies
and scriptwriting techniques. These
courses are open to all EU nationals.
For details on how to participate on
these courses, your local Desk,
Antenna or Service, will supply you
with details.

MEDIA Development

- the programme offers financial
support to European independent
production companies to develop
new fiction, documentary, animation
or multimedia projects. Financial
support is offered to catalogues of
projects (through the "slate funding"
scheme) or to one project at a time.

The amounts awarded will not exceed 50% of development budgets. If the project co-financed by MEDIA Plus goes into production, the company has an obligation to reinvest the same amount in the development of one or more production projects. Companies may apply for funding at any time of the year.

MEDIA Distribution

- the programme supports the distribution and broadcasting of audiovisual works (fiction, documentary, animation, interactive programmes) and of European films in movie theaters, on video, on digital disc and on television. It also provides support to networks of cinemas for the promotion and marketing of European films. There are fixed deadlines for this funding.

MEDIA Promotion

- the programme offers financial support to encourage all kind of promotional activities designed to facilitate European producers and distributors' access and participate at major European and international events. There are fixed deadlines running throughout the year.

Contact Details:

Members of the UK MEDIA team listed below should be the first point of contact for UK companies or organisations seeking information and advice on the MEDIA Plus programme. Guidelines and application forms for all schemes are available from them or downloadable from their web-site: www.mediadesk.co.uk. However, all completed application forms should be sent directly to the MEDIA Programme office in Brussels, details of which you will find below.

MEDIA Desk UK,

C/o Film Council
10 Little Portland Street
London W1W 7JG
Tel: 020 7861 7507
Fax: 020 7861 7867
email: england@mediadesk.co.uk
Website: www.mediadesk.co.uk
Agnieszka Moody, Director
Will move to permanent office in Central London in
November 2001 – contact Film Council for new address

MEDIA Antenna Cardiff

C/o SGRÎN,
The Bank, 10 Mount Stuart Square,
CARDIFF
UK – CF 10 5EE
Tel.: 00 44 29 20 33 33 04
Fax : 00 44 2920 33 33 20
email : antenna@sgrin.co.uk
Website: www.mediadesk.co.uk
Gwawr Hughes,

MEDIA Antenne Glasgow,

249,West George Street,
Glasgow
UK-G2 4QE.
Tel.: 00 44 1 41 302.17.76
Fax : 00 44 1 41 302 17 78
email: media.scotland@scottishscreen.com
Website: www.mediadesk.co.uk
Emma Valentine

MEDIA Service for Northern Ireland

21, Ormeau Avenue,
Belfast, UK-BT2 8HD
Tel : 00 44 2890 23 24 44
Fax : 00 44 2890 23 99 18
email: media@nifc.co.uk
Heike Meyer Döring

MEDIA Plus Office in Brussels

MEDIA Plus Programme,
European Commission,
DG Education and Culture, C3,
100, Rue Belliard,
B-1040 Brussels,
Belgium
Tel: 00 322 295 84 06
Fax: 00 322 299 9214
Website:europa.eu.int/comm/avpolicy/media/index_fr.html
Head of Unit : Jacques Delmoly
Development : Jean Jauniaux
Training: Gisela Gauggel-Robinson
Distribution: Anne Boillot
Promotion/Festivals: Elena Braun

CARTOON

(European Association of Animation Film)
314 Boulevard Lambermont
B – 1030 Brussels
Belgium
Tel: 00 32 2 245 1200
Fax: 00 32 2 245 4689
email: cartoon@skynet.be
Website: www.cartoon-media.be
Contact: Corinne Jennart, Marc Vendeweyer
CARTOON, based in Brussels, is a European animation network which organises the annual CARTOON FORUM, co-ordinates the grouping of animation studios and runs specialist training courses in animation.

EUROPA CINEMAS

54 rue Beaubourg
F – 75 003 Paris
France
Tel: 00 33 1 42 71 53 70
Fax: 00 33 1 42 71 47 55
email: europacinema@magic.fr
Website: www.europa-cinemas.org
Contact: Claude-Eric Poiroux, Fatima Djoumer
The project encourages screenings and promotion of European films in a network of cinemas in European cities. It offers financial support for screening European films, for promotional activities and for special events.

MEDIA SALLES

Via Soperga, 2
I – 20 127 Milan
Tel: 00 39 02 6698 4405
Fax: 00 39 02 669 1574
email: infocinema@mediasalles.it
Website: www.mediasalles.it
Secretary General, Elisabetta Brunella
MEDIA SALLES with Euro Kids Network is an initiative aimed at consolidating the availability of 'cinema at the cinema' for children and young people in Europe, and at raising the visibility of European film to a younger audience

INTERNATIONAL SALES

Below is a selection of companies which acquire rights to audiovisual products for sale to foreign distributors in all media – see also Distributors (Non–Theatrical) and (Theatrical)

Action Time
Wrendal House
2 Whitworth Street West
West Manchester M1 5WX
Tel: 0161 236 8999
Fax: 0161 236 8845
Specialises in international format sales of game shows and light entertainment

Alibi Films International
35 Long Acre
London WC2E 9JT
Tel: 020 7845 0400
Fax: 020 7836 6919
email: info@alibifilms.co.uk
Website: www.alibifilms.co.uk
Gareth Jones
Alibi is active in the financing, international sales and distirbution of theatrical feature films and the production of feature film, television drama and children's programming. Titles include: One More Kiss (1999); One of the Hollywood Ten (2000)

All American Fremantle International
57 Jamestown Road
London NW1 7DB
Tel: 020 7284 0880
Fax: 020 7916 5511
London arm of NY-based Fremantle Int. Produces and distributes game shows and light entertainment programmes

APTN (Associated Press Television News)
The Interchange
Oval Road, Camden Lock
London NW1 7EP
Tel: 020 7482 7400
Fax: 020 7413 8327 (Library)
Website: www.aptn.com
N. Parsons, David Simmons
International TV news, features, sport, entertainment, documentary programmes and archive resources. Camera crews in major global

locations, plus in-house broadcasting and production facilities

Australian Film Commission
Level 4, 150 William Street
Woolloomooloo 201
Tel: (61) 2 9321 6444
Fax: (61) 2 9357 3631
email: marketing@afc.gov.au
Website: www.afc.gov.au
Sabina Finnern
Australian government-funded body set up to assist in development, production and promotion of Australian film, television, video and interactive product

BBC Worldwide
Woodlands
80 Wood Lane
London W12 0TT
Tel: 020 8433 3000
Fax: 020 8749 0538
Website: www.bbc.worldwide.com
Programme, Sales and Marketing - the sales and licensing of BBC programmes and international broadcasters, and the generation of co-production business; Channel Marketing - the development of new cable and satellite delivered television channels around the world

Beyond Films
3rd Floor
22 Newman Street
London W1V 3HB
Tel: 020 7636 9613
Fax: 020 7636 9614
email: dee-emerson@beyond.com.au
Website: www.Beyond.com
Dee Emerson
Films: *Strictly Ballroom, Love & Other Catastrophes, Love Serenade, Kiss or Kill, Heaven's Burning, SLC Punk, Orphans, Two Hands, Paperback Hero, Kick, Fresh Air, In a Savage Land, Cut*

bfi Sales
21 Stephen Street
London W1T 1LN
Tel: 020 7957 8909
Fax: 020 7580 5830
email: sales.films@bfi.org.uk
Website: www.bfi.org.uk
John Flahive, Film Sales Manager,

Laurel Warbrick-Keay, Film Sales Co-ordinator
Sales of BFI produced features, shorts and documentaries, archival and acquired titles including: early features by Peter Greenaway and Derek Jarman, Free Cinema, shorts by famous directors including Ridley Scott and Stephen Frears, shorts by new directors including Richard Kwietniowski, Sara Sugarman and Tinge Krishnan, and from the archives - *South* and *The Edge of the World*

 bfi Archival Footage Sales
21 Stephen Street
London W1T 1LN
Tel: 020 7957 8934
Fax: 020 7580 5830
email: footage.films@bfi.org.uk
Website: www.bfi.org.uk
Jan Faull or Simon Brown
Material from the largest collection of film footage in Britain - the National Film and Television Archive. Television, films, documentaries, newsreels and animation are all covered with over 350,000 titles to choose from, including material dating back to 1895. First stop for serious research on subjects that have shaped the 20th century. Research facilities available

Boudicca
75 East Road
London N1 6AH
Tel: 020 7490 1724
Fax: 020 7490 1764
email: sales@boudiccafilms.com
Website: www.boudiccafilms.com
Ray Brady
A new British independent Sales & Distribution Company set up by the Producer/Director Ray Brady attempting to produce, promote, sell and distribute its own and other British feature films

The Box Office
12 Ogle Street
London W1W 6HU
Tel. 020 7612 1701
Fax. 020 7612 1705
email: paul@box-office.demon.co.uk

International film and television consultancy

British Home Entertainment
5 Broadwater Road
Walton-on-Thames
Surrey KT12 5DB
Tel: 01932 228832
Fax: 01932 247759
email: clivew@bhe.prestel.co.uk
Clive Williamson
Video distribution/TV marketing. An Evening with the Royal Ballet, Othello, The Mikado, The Soldier's Tale, Uncle Vanya, King and Country, The Hollow Crown, The Merry Wives of Windsor

Bureau Sales
c/o The Short Film Bureau
47 Poland Street
London W1F 7NB
Tel: 020 7734 8708
Fax: 020 7734 2406
email: sales@shortfilmbureau.com
Dawn Sharpless
International sales agent for short films. Sells to traditional outlets such as terrestrial, cable and satellite television, as well as new media such as DVD, Broadband, narrowband and WAP

National Film Board of Canada
Canada House
Trafalgar Square
London SW1Y 5BJ
Tel: 020 7258 6484
Fax: 020 7258 6532
Helen Rawlins
European sales office for documentary, drama and animation productions from Canada's National Film Board

Capitol Films
23 Queensdae Place
London W11 4SQ
Tel: 020 7471 6000
Fax: 020 7471 6012
email: films@capitolfilms.com
Valencia Haynes
Recent productions include: Beautiful Joe, House of Mirth, Drowning Mona, Wilde and Among Giants

Carlton International Media
35-38 Portman Square
London W1H 0NU
Tel: 020 7224 3339
Fax: 020 7486 1707
email: enquiries@carltonint.co.uk
Website: www.carltonint.co.uk
Director of Sales: Louise Sexton

International TV programme and film sales agent, now representing Carlton Television, Central Television, HTV, ITN Productions and Meridian Broadcasting as well as a growing number of independent production companies. It holds the ITC Library which was aquired in 1999 by Carlton International. The library includes such celebrated films as *The Eagle has Landed, The Big Easy, The Boys from Brazil, On Golden Pond, Farewell My Lovely, Sophie's Choice* and *The Last Seduction*. It also features a huge array of classic series including *The Saint, The Prisoner, Randall and Hopkirk (Deceased)* and *Space 1999* and some of the most popular children's programmes including Gerry Anderson's *Thunderbirds, Joe 90 and Captain Scarlet.* Carlton also holds a number of other film collections including the Rohauer Library (classic silent films, the Korda Library (many classic British films of the 30s), the Romulus Library (films produced by John Woolf's company), and the Rank Library (major library of British films made from the 30s to 80s)

Cascade Worldwide Distribution
3 Waterhouse Square
138-142 Holborn
London EC1N 2NY
Tel: 020 7882 1000
Fax: 020 7882 1020
email: adrian.howells@scottishmediagroup.com
Adrian Howells, Head of Sales
Tim Mutimer, Anne-Marie Scholey, Julie Norman.
International distribution of STV, Grampian and Third Party programming in the following genres: Drama, factual, children's and animation. Titles include: *Taggart, Rebus, The Last Musketeer, McCallum, Harry and the Wrinklies, Celtic America*

Castle Target International
A29 Barwell Business Park
Leatherhead Road
Chessington
Surrey KT9 2NY
Tel: 020 8974 1021
Fax: 020 8974 3707
Brian Leafe
Buddy's Song, The Monk, That Summer of White Roses, Conspiracy

CBC International Sales
43-51 Great Titchfield Street

London W1P 8DD
Tel: 020 7412 9200
Fax: 020 7323 5658
Susan Hewitt, Michelle Payne, Janice Russell
The programme sales division of Canadian Broadcasting Corporation and Société Radio-Canada

Channel Four International
124 Horseferry Road
London SW1 2TX
Tel: 020 7396 4444
Fax: 020 7306 8363
Website: www.c4international.com
Paul Sowerbutts
Handles C4 television material

Chatsworth Television Distributors
97-99 Dean Street
London W1V 5RA
Tel: 020 7734 4302
Fax: 020 7437 3301

Circle Communications
see Southern Star Circle Communications

Columbia TriStar International Television
Sony Pictures, Europe House
25 Golden Square
London W1R 6LU
Tel: 020 7533 1000
Fax: 020 7533 1246
European TV production and network operations and international distribution of Columbia TriStar's feature films and TV product

CTVC
Hillside Studios
Merry Hill Road
Bushey
Watford WD2 1DR
Tel: 020 8950 4426
Fax: 020 8950 1437
email: ctvc@ctvc.co.uk
Website: www.ctvc.co.uk
Ann Harvey
International programme sales and co-productions in documentary, music, children's, drama and arts programmes

DLT Entertainment UK Ltd
10 Bedford Square
London WC1B 3RA
Tel: 020 7631 1184
Fax: 020 7636 4571
John Bartlett, John Reynolds
Specialising in comedy and drama programming. Recent titles include: *My Family* (2 series); *As Time Goes*

By, series Eight for BBC Television; *Bloomin' Marvellous*, eight-part comedy series for BBC Television

Documedia International Films Ltd

19 Widegate Street
London E1 7HP
Tel: 020 7625 6200
Fax: 020 7625 7887
Distributors of innovative and award winning drama specials, drama shorts, serials, tele-movies and feature films; documentary specials and series; for worldwide sales and co-production

Entertainment Rights

Colet Court
100 Hammersmith Road
London W6 7JP
Tel: 020 8762 6200
Fax: 020 8762 6299
Website: www.entertainmentrights.com
Craig Hemmings
Specialises in children's material and animation. Entertainment Rights was formed in November 1999 following the merger of SKD Media and Carrington Productions International. The company has the two top rated animation series, *Meeow* (Scottish TV/Siriol Prods) and *Lavender Castle*, produced by Gerry Anderson and Cosgrove Hall. Other titles in the ER catalogue include *Budgie the Little Helicopter*, *The Tidings* and *Dr Zitbag's Transylvania Pet Shop*

EVA Entertainment

Studio 8
125 Moore Park Road
London SW6 4PS
Tel: 020 7384 1002

FilmFour International

76-78 Charlotte Street
London W1P 2TX
Tel: 020 7868 7700
Fax: 020 7868 7769
Website: www.filmfour.com
Susan Bruce-Smith, Director of World-wide, Sales and Marketing
The international sales arm of C4's stand-alone film company FilmFour Ltd. Recent titles represented by FFI include *East is East*, *Sexy Beast*, *Gangster No 1*, *The Filth and The Fury*

Freemantle Media

1 Stephen Street
London W1P 1PJ
Tel: 020 7691 6000
Fax: 020 7691 6060

Website: www.pearsontv.com
Managing Director: Brian Harris
Executive Vice President: Joe Abrams
Pearson Television International is one of the world's premier developers and distributors of entertainment programming. Highlights of PTI's extensive catalogue include: 11 volumes of ACI television movies - most recently Robert B Parker's *Thin Air* starring Joe Mantegna, *The Golden Spiders* with Timothy Hutton, and *Stolen from the Heart* starring Tracey Gold and Barbara Mandrell. Sitcoms - *Mr Bean* to Simon Nye's *Beast* and *Men Behaving Badly* and Marks and Gran's *Birds of a Feather*. Serial drama - *Neighbours*, *Shortland Street* and *Family Affairs*. Drama - highlights include Francis Ford Coppola's sci-fi series *First Wave*, *Baywatch Hawaii*, *The Bill* and *Homicide: Life on the Street*. Documentaries - *Secrets of War*, *Destination Space*, *Fame and Fortune* and *Final Day*. Comedy legends including Benny Hill, Tommy Cooper and Morecombe and Wise

Gem

Shepherds Building Central
Charecroft Way
Shepherds Bush
London W14 0EE
Tel: 0870 333 1700
email: gemlinfo@endymoluk.com
Website: www.endymoluk.com

Goldcrest Films and Television

65/66 Dean Street
London W1V 4PL
Tel: 020 7437 8696
Fax: 020 7437 4448
Major feature film production, sales and finance company. Recent films include *Space Truckers*, *Clockwatchers*. *To End All Wars* starring Robert Carlyle. Library titles include *The Mission, the Killing Fields, Name of the Rose*

Grampian Television

Queen's Cross
Aberdeen AB15 4XJ
Tel: 01224 846846
Fax: 01224 846800
Alistair Gracie (Controller) Hilary I. Buchan (Head of Public Relations)
North Scotland ITV station producing a wide range of programming including documentaries, sport, children's, religion and extensive daily news and current affairs to serve ITV's largest region

Granada International

48 Leicester Square
London WC2H 7FB
Tel: 020 7491 1441
Fax: 020 7389 7845
email: int.info@granadamedia.com
Website: www.granadamedia.com/international
Nadine Nohr, Managing Director
Granada International is responsible for more than 15,000 hours of animation, reality, factual, drama, comedy, natural history, wildlife, entertainment and lifestyle programming. Granada International is part of Granada plc

Hollywood Classics

8 Cleveland Gardens
London W2 6HA
Tel: 020 7262 4646
Fax: 020 7262 3242
email: HollywoodClassicsUK@compuserve.com
Website: www.hollywoodclassics.com
Melanie Tebb
Hollywood Classics has offices in London and Los Angeles and sells back catalogue titles from major Hollywood studios for theatrical release in all territories outside North America. Also represents an increasing library of European and independent American titles and has all rights to catalogues from various independent producers.

IAC Film

Greencoat House
15 Francis Street
London SW1P 1DH
Tel: 020 7592 1620
Fax: 020 7592 1627
email: oliver@iachddings.co.uk
Website: www.iacfilm.co.uk
Oliver Rowe

Icon Entertainment International

The Quadrangle , 4th Floor
180 Wardour Street
London W1V 3AA
Tel: 020 7494 8100
Fax: 020 7494 8151
Ralph Kamp: Chief Executive
Jamie Carmichael: Head of Sales
Caroline Johnson: Marketing Manager

ITC Library

Tel: 020 7836 7701
(See Carlton International)

J & M Entertainment

2 Dorset Square

London NW1 6PX
Tel: 020 7723 6544
Fax: 020 7724 7541
Nigel Bremner
Specialise in sales of all media,
distribution and marketing of
independent feature films

Link Entertainment
Colet Court
100 Hammersmith Road
London W6 7JP
Tel: 020 8762 6200
Fax: 020 8762 6299
Website: www.entertainmentrights.
com
(now part of Entertainment Rights)
Specialists in children's programmes
for worldwide distribution and
character licensing. New properties
include: Chatterhappy Ponies; The
Forgotten Toys Series; Pirates Series
III; Caribou Kitchen Series III; The
First Snow of Winter

London Films
71 South Audley Street
London W1K 1JA
Tel: 020 7499 7800
Fax: 020 7499 7994
Website: www.londonfilms.com
Andrew Luff
Founded in 1932 by Alexander Korda,
London Films is renowned for the
production of classics. Co-
productions with the BBC include
Poldark and *I Claudius*. More recent
series include *Lady Chatterley*
directed by Ken Russell and *The
Scarlet Pimpernel* starring Richard
E.Grant

London Television Service
21-25 St Anne's Court
London W1V 3AW
Tel: 020 7434 1121
Fax: 020 7734 0619
email: lts@londontv.com
Website: www.londontv.com
John Ridley
LTS is a specialist production and
distribution organisation that handles
the promotion and marketing of
British documentary and magazine
programmes worldwide to television,
cable, satellite and non-broadcast
outlets. The flagship science and
technology series Perspective has sold
to television in over 100 countries

NBD Television
Unit 2, Royalty Studios
105 Lancaster Road
London W11 1QF
Tel: 020 7243 3646

Fax: 020 7243 3656
Nicky Davies Williams, Andrew
Winter, Sales Manager, Matt Cowley,
Sales Executive
Company specialising in music and
light entertainment

Orbit Media Ltd
80a Dean Street
London W1D 3SN
Tel: 020 7287 4264
Fax: 020 7287 0984
Website: www.orbitmedia.co.uk
Chris Ranger, Jordan Reynolds
Specialises in vintage product from
the first decade of American TV: The
Golden Years of Television and 65 x
30 mins Series NoireTV series

Paramount Television
49 Charles Street
London W1J 5EW
Tel: 020 7318 6400
Fax: 020 7491 2086
Website: www.paramount.com
Stephen Tague

Photoplay Productions
21 Princess Road
London NW1 8JR
Tel: 020 7722 2500
Fax: 020 7722 6662
Kevin Brownlow, Patrick Stanbury
TV production company. Resoration
and presentation of silent films.
Archive of silent era

Portman Entertainment Ltd
Portman Film
21-25 St. Anne's Court
London W1V 3AW
Tel: 020 7494 8024
Fax: 020 7494 8046
email: email
sales@portmanfilm.co.uk
Tristan Whalley
Portman Television
Hampton House
20 Albert Embankment
London SE1 7TJ
Tel: 020 7840 5030
Fax: 020 7840 5040
email: sales@sport-ent.co.uk
Contact: Clive Jordan

Primetime
see Southern Star

Reuters Television
85 Fleet Street
London EC4P 4AJ
Tel: 020 7250 1122
Fax: 020 7542 4995
Website: www.reuters.com
Alan Balwin (sport), Ralph Gowling
(news)

Distribution of international TV
news and sports material to
broadcasters around the world

RM Associates
46 Great Marlborough Street
London W1V 1DB
Tel: 020 7439 2637
Fax: 020 7439 2316
email: rma@rmassociates.co.uk
Neil Mundy: Director of Programmes
Sally Fairhead: Head of Publicity
In addition to handling the exclusive
distribution of programmes
produced/co-produced by RM Arts,
RM Associates works closely with
numerous broadcasters and
independent producers to bring
together a comprehensive catalogue
of music and arts programming

S4C International
50 Lambourne Crescent
Llanishen
Cardiff CF4 5DU
Tel: 029 20741440
Fax: 029 20754444
email: international@s4c.co.uk
Website: www.s4ci.com
Rhianydd Darwin, Head of
International Sales
Hugh Walters, Head of Co
Productions
Programme distribution, co-
productions, documentaries,
animation

Safir Films Ltd
49 Littleton Rd
Harrow
Middx HA1 3SY
Tel: 020 8423 0763
Fax: 020 8423 7963
email: safir@afma.com
Lawrence Safir
Hold rights to numerous Australian,
US and UK pictures, including Sam
Spiegel's Betrayal

The Sales Company
62 Shaftesbury Avenue
London W1D 6LT
(new address pending)
Tel: 020 7434 9061
Fax: 020 7494 3293
Aline Perry, Rebecca Kearey and Joy
Wong
The Sales Company is owned by The
Film Consortium (75 per cent) and
BBC Worldwide (25 per cent), and
handles international sales of
shareholder films for theatrical
distribution and all rights. The
Company often pics up independent
films for sales rights. Recent films

include: *Bread and Roses*, directed by Ken Loach; *Saltwater* directed by Conor McPherson; *Liam*, directed by Stephen Frears; *Last Resort* directed by Pawel Pawlikowski; *Dust* directed by Milcho Manchevski and *Gabriel and Me* directed by Udayan Prasad

Screen Ventures
49 Goodge Street
London W1T 1TE
Tel: 020 7580 7448
Fax: 020 7631 1265
email: info@screenventures.com
Website: www.screenventures.com
Christopher Mould
Specialise in international film, TV and video licensing of music, drama and arts featuring such artists as John Lennon, Bob Marley, Nirvana. Worldwide sales representation for international record companies and independent producers. Screen Ventures is also an independent producer of television documentaries and music programming

Smart Egg Pictures
11&12 Barnard Mews
Barnard Road
London SW11 1QU
Tel: 020 7350 4554
Fax: 020 7924 5650
email: sepsvs@cs.com
Tom Sjoberg, Judy Phang
Independent foreign sales company. Titles include *Spaced Invaders, Dinosaurs, Montenegro, The Coca-Cola Kid, Rave Dancing to a Different Beat, Phoenix and the Magic Carpet* and *Evil Ed*

Southern Star Circle Communications PLC
45-49 Mortimer Street
London W1N 7TD
Tel: 020 7636 9421
Fax: 020 7436 7426
email: cbirks@sstar.uk.com
Clare Birks
Circle is an international television rights group. Based in the UK, and trading in all the major territories of the world, Circle provides a range of services for producers and broadcasters. Circle comprises distinct businesses principally engaged in the creation, acquisition, marketing and licensing of visual entertainment rights. The companies within Circle Communications are:
Carnival (Films & Theatre)
Pavilion International
Delta Ventures
Production Finance &

Management
Independent Wildlife
Harlequin Films & Television
Oxford Scientific Films
La Plante International

Trans World International
TWI House
23 Eyot Gardens
London W6 9TR
Tel: 020 8233 5400
Fax: 020 8233 5401
Website: imgworld.com
Eric Drossart, Bill Sinrich, Buzz Hornett
The world's largest independent producer and distributor of sports programmes, TWI is owned by Mark McCormack's IMG Group and specialises in sports and arts programming. Titles include: *Trans World Sport, Futbol Mundial, PGA European Tour productions, ATP Tour highlights, West Indies Test Cricket, Oddballs, A-Z of Sport, Goal!, The Olympic Series, Century* and *The Whitbread Round The World Race*

Turner International Television Licensing
CNN House
19 Rathbone Place
London W1P 1DF
Tel: 020 7637 6900
Fax: 020 7637 6925
Ross Portugeis
US production and distribution company of films and programmes from Hanna-Barbera (animation), Castle Rock, New Line, Turner Pictures Worldwide, World Championship Wrestling, Turner Original Productions (non-fiction), plus a library of over 2,500 films, 1,500 hours of television programmes and 1,000 cartoons from the MGM (pre-1986) and Warner Bros (pre-1950) studios

Twentieth Century Fox Television
31-32 Soho Square
London W1V 6AP
Tel: 020 7437 7766
Fax: 020 7439 1806
Website: www.fox.co.uk
Stephen Cornish, Vice President
Randall Broman, Director of Sales
TV sales and distribution. A News Corporation company

VCI Programme Sales
VCI
76 Dean Street
London W1V 5HA

Tel: 020 7396 8888
email: vcipr@vci.co.uk
Website: vciplc.co.uk
Robert Callow
A wholly owned subsidiary of VCI PLC, responsible for all overseas activities. Distributes a wide variety of product including music, sport, children's, fitness, documentary, educational, special interest and features

Victor Film Company Ltd
4th Floor
1 Great Cumberland Street
London W1H 7AL
Tel: 020 7535 3380
Fax: 020 7535 3383
email: post@victor-film-co.uk
Website: www.victor-film-co.demon.co.uk
Alasdair Waddell
Vic Bateman
International sales agent for independent producers of commercial films. Recent titles include: *House! 24 Hours in London, Pasty Faces.* Forthcoming titles include: *Dog Soldiers, Father Figure, Chocolate Vanilla, Reckoning Day, Those Nagging Doubts*

Vine International Pictures
VIP House, Greenacres
New Road Hill
Downe, Opington
BR6 7JA
Tel: 01689 854123
Fax: 01689 850990
email: info@vineinternational.co.uk
Website: www.vine-international.co.uk
CEO: Marie Vine, MD: Barry Gill, Sales exec: Sarah Goodwin
Sale of feature films such as *Rainbow, The Pillow Book, The Ox and the Eye, Younger and Younger, The Prince of Jutland, Erik the Viking, Let Him Have It, Trouble in Mind*

The Walt Disney Television International
3 Queen Caroline Street
Hammersmith
London W6 9PA
Tel: 020 8222 1000
Fax: 020 8222 2795
MD: Etienne de Villiers
VP, Sales & Marketing: Keith Legoy
International television arm of a major US production company

Warner Bros International Television
98 Theobalds Road

London WC1X 8WB
Tel: 020 7494 3710
Fax: 020 7287 9086
Website: www.wbitv.com
Richard Milnes, Donna Brett, Tim
Horan, Ian Giles
TV sales, marketing and distribution.
A division of Warner Bros
Distributors Ltd, A Time Warner
Entertainment Company, LP

Winchester Entertainment plc

19 Heddon Street
London W1R 7LF
Tel: 020 7851 6500
Fax: 020 7851 6505
email: mail@winchesterent.co.uk
Website: www.winchesterent.com
Billy Hurman

LABORATORIES

Bucks Laboratories Ltd
714 Banbury Avenue
Slough
Berks SL1 4LR
Tel: 01753 501500
Fax: 01753 691762
Website: www.bucks.co.uk
Darren Fagg
Comprehensive lab services in Super
35mm and 35mm, Super 16mm and
16mm, starting Sunday night. West
End rushes pick up unit 10.30 pm.
Also day bath. Chromakopy: 35mm
low-cost overnight colour reversal
dubbing prints. Photogard: European
coating centre for negative and print
treatment. Chromascan: 35mm and
16mm video to film transfer

Colour Film Services Group
10 Wadsworth Road
Perivale
Middx UB6 7JX
Tel: 020 8998 2731
Fax: 020 8997 8738
email: ruthlawton@
colourfilmservices.co.uk
Website: www.colourfilmservices.
co.uk
Ruth Lawton
Film Laboratory: full 16mm and
35mm colour processing laboratory,
with Super 16mm to 35mm blow up
a speciality. Video Facility: broadcastt
standard wet gate telecines and full
digital edit suite. Video duplication,
CD mastering and archiving to
various formats. Superscan: unique
tape to film transfer system in both
Standard Resolution and High
Resolution. Sounds Studios: analogue
and digital dubbing, track laying,
synching, voice overs and optical
transfer bay
CFS in soho
26 Berwick Street
London W1F 8RG
Tel: 020 7734 4543
Fax: 020 7734 6600
email: cfsinsoho@
colurfilmservices.co.u
Website: www.colourfilmservices.co.uk
Contact: GrahamTolley

Colour-Technique
Cinematograph Film Laboratories

Finch Cottage, Finch Lane
Knotty Green
Beaconsfield HP9 2TL
Tel: 01494 672757
Specialists in 8mm, Super 8mm and
9.5mm blown up to 16mm with wet
gate printing. Stretch printing 16 and
18 Fps to 24, 32 and 48 Fps. 16mm to
16mm optical copies with wet gate
and stretch printing. World leader for
archival film copying for 8mm, Super
8mm, 9.5mm and 16mm with wet
gate printing from old shrunk films,
B/w dupe negs and colour internegs.
Also Super 8mm blown up to Super
16mm wet gate printing and stretch
printing. 16mm to Super 16mm wet
gate and stretch printing. Colour
internegs and B&W dupe negatives.
Super 8mm blown to 35 mm

**Deluxe Laboratories
Limited**
North Orbital Road
Denham, Uxbridge
Middlesex UB9 5HQ
Tel: 01895 832323
Fax: 01895 832446
Website: www.bydeluxe.com
David Dowler
Deluxe London, together with Deluxe
Hollywood, Deluxe Toronto and
Deluxe Italia are subsidaries of
Deluxe Entertainment Services
Division which forms part of The
Rank Group. Comprehensive world
wide laboratory services to the
Motion Picture, Commercial and
Television industries. London and
Toronto include video transfer suites.
Toronto has complete sound and
dubbing suites. Part of the London
operation is the well known special
effects and Optical house General
Screen Enterprises now with digital
Cineon and Optical Effects Unit at
Pinewood Studios

East Anglian Film Archive
University of East Anglia
Norwich NR4 7TJ
Tel: 01603 592664
Fax: 01603 458553
Specialises in blow-up printing of Std
8mm, Super 8mm, 9.5 mm, and
17.5mm b/w or colour, onto 16mm film

Film and Photo Ltd
13 Colville Road
South Acton Industrial Estate
London W3 8BL
Tel: 020 8992 0037
Fax: 020 8993 2409
email: info@film-photo.co.uk
Website: www.film-photo.co.uk
Managing Director: Tony Scott
Post production motion picture
laboratory. 16/35mm Colour & B/W
reversal dupes. 16/35mm b/w
neg/pos. 35mm E6 camera reversal
processing. Tape to film transfers.
Nitrate restoration/preservation

Film Lab North Ltd
Croydon House
Croydon Street
Leeds LS11 9RT
Tel: 0113 243 4842
Fax: 0113 2434323
email: fin@globalnet.co.uk
Full service in 16mm colour Negative
Processing, 16mm colour printing,
35mm colour printing video transfer.
Super 16mm a speciality - Plus 35mm
colour grading and printing

**Hendersons Film
Laboratories**
18-20 St Dunstan's Road
South Norwood
London SW25 6EU
Tel: 020 8653 2255
Fax: 020 8653 9773
Preserves nitrate film footage. A total
black and white Laboratory Service in
35mm and 16mm . Printing and
processing black and white stocks

The Lux Centre
2-4 Hoxton Square
London N1 6NU
Tel: 020 7684 0202
Fax: 020 7684 1111
email: production@lux.org.uk
Website: www.lux.org.uk
Production
Avid editing, linear video editing, film
editing, processing and printing,
cameras, film and video transfers,
sound, lights and exhibition equipment

Metrocolor London
91-95 Gillespie Road
Highbury

London N5 1LS
Tel: 020 7226 4422
Fax: 020 7359 2353
Len Brown, Terry Lansbury,
Alan Douglas
Offers complete service for features, commercials, television productions and pop promos for 16mm, Super 16mm, 35mm and Super 35mm. Day and night processing and printing colour, b/w and vnf. Overnight rushes and sound transfer. Overnight 'best-light' and 'gamma' Telecine rushes transfer and sync sound. Computerised logging and negative matching. Sound transfer to optical negative - Dolby stereo, Dolby SRD Digital stereo and DTS Timecode. Specialist Super 16mm services include: 35mm fully graded blow-up prints; 35mm fully graded blow-up immediates; fully graded prints re-formatted to standard 16mm retaining 1.66:1 aspect ratio

Soho Images

8-14 Meard Street
London W1V 3HR
Tel: 020 7437 0831
Fax: 020 7734 9471
email: sohogroup.com
Website: www.sohoimages.com
Soho Laboratories offer day and night printing and processing of 16mm (including Super 16mm) and 35mm colour or b/w film

Technicolor Film Services

Technicolor Ltd
Bath Road
West Drayton
Middx UB7 0DB
Tel: 020 8759 5432
Fax: 020 8759 6270
Chris Gacon
West End pick-up and delivery point:
F.M.F.
52 Berwick Street
London W1F 8SL
Tel: 020 7287 5596
Technicolor is a worldwide film and telecine operation, with laboratories in Hollywood, London, Rome, New York and Montreal. It offers a 24 hour service covering all film formats - 16mm, 35mm and 65mm large screen presentation. The extensive sound service operation complements customers' requirements by offering transfers to all digital formats. The newly created Technicolor Imaging is designed to service feature, commercial and 16mm drama/documentary markets. Five telecine suites accommodate two ITK Millennium telecines, URSA and two high grade Rank Cintel machines. Other services include feature mastering, drama finishing, sound laybacks, DVD video and audio pre-mastering all available under the same secure roof making Technicolor Europe's largest and most comprehensive film processing laboratory

Todd-AO UK

13 Hawley Crescent
London NW11 8NP
Tel: 020 7284 7900
Fax: 020 7284 1018
Roger Harlow
Complete 35mm, Super 16 and 16mm film processing laboratory and sound transfer service with full video post-production facility including Digital Wet Gate Telecines, D3, Digital Betacam, Betacam SP and other video formats. On-line editing, duplication and standards conversion. Sync sound and A+B roll negative to tape transfer, neg cutting service

LEGISLATION

This section of the Handbook has a twofold purpose, first to provide a brief history of the legislation relating to the film and television in the United Kingdom, and second to provide a short summary of the current principal instruments of legislation relating to film, television and video industries in the United Kingdom and in the European Community. Current legislation is separated into four categories: cinema and broadcasting; finance; copyright and European Union legislation.

Legislative History

Cinema

Legislation for the cinema industry in the United Kingdom goes back to 1909, when the Cinematograph Act was passed providing for the licensing of exhibition premises, and safety of audiences. The emphasis on safety has been maintained through the years in other enactments such as the Celluloid and Cinematograph Film Act 1922, Cinematograph Act 1952 and the Fire Precautions Act 1971, the two latter having been consolidated in the Cinemas Act 1985.

The Cinematograph Films (Animals Act) 1937 was passed to prevent the exhibition and distribution of films in which suffering may have been caused to animals. The Cinematograph (Amendment) Act 1982 applied certain licensing requirements to pornographic cinema clubs. Excluded from licensing were the activities of bona fide film societies and 'demonstrations' such as those used in shops, as well as exhibitions intended to provide information, education or instruction. Requirements for licensing were consolidated in the Cinemas Act 1985.

The Sunday Entertainments Act 1932 as amended by the Sunday Cinema Act 1972 and the Cinemas Act 1985 regulated the opening and use of cinema premises on Sundays.

The Sunday Entertainments Act 1932 also established a Sunday Cinematograph Fund for 'encouraging the use and development of cinematograph as a means of entertainment and instruction'. This was how the British Film Institute was originally funded.

Statutory controls were imposed by the Cinematograph Films Act 1927 in other areas of the film industry, such as the booking of films, quotas for the distribution and renting of British films and the registration of films exhibited to the public. This Act was modified by the Cinematograph Films Acts of 1938 and 1948 and the Film Acts 1960, 1966, 1970 and 1980 which were repealed by the Films Act 1985.

The financing of the British film industry has long been the subject of specific legislation. The National Film Finance Corporation was established by the Cinematograph Film Production (Special Loans) Act 1949. The Cinematograph Film Production (Special Loans) Act 1952 gave the National Film Finance Corporation the power to borrow from sources other than the Board of Trade. Other legislation dealing with film finance were the Cinematograph Film Production (Special Loans) Act 1954 and the Films Acts 1970 and 1980. The Cinematograph Films Council was established by the Cinematograph Films Act 1948, but like the National Film Finance Corporation, the Council was abolished by the Films Act 1985.

The Cinematograph Films Act 1957 established the British Film Fund Agency and put on a statutory footing the formerly voluntary levy on exhibitors known as the 'Eady levy'. Eady money was to be paid to the British Film Fund Agency, which in turn was responsible for making payments to British film-makers, the Children's Film Foundation, the National Film Finance Corporation, the British Film Institute and towards training film-makers. The Film Levy Finance Act 1981 consolidated the provisions relating to the Agency and the exhibitors' levy. The Agency was wound up in 1988 pursuant to a statutory order made under the Films Act 1985.

The British Film Institute used to obtain its funding from grants made by the Privy Council out of the Cinematograph Fund established under the Sunday Entertainments Act 1932 and also from the proceeds of subscriptions, sales and rentals of films. The British Film Institute Act 1949 allows for grants of money from Parliament to be made to the British Film Institute as the Lord President of the Privy Council thinks fit.

Broadcasting

The BBC first started as the British Broadcasting Company (representing the interests of some radio manufacturers) and was licensed in 1923 by the Postmaster General under the Wireless Telegraphy Act 1904 before being established by Royal Charter. The company was involved in television development from 1929 and in 1935 was licensed to provide a public television service.

The Independent Television Authority was established under the Television Act 1954 to provide additional television broadcasting services. Its existence was continued under the Television Act 1964 and under the Independent Broadcasting Act 1973, although its name had been changed to the Independent Broadcasting Authority by the Sound Broadcasting Act 1972 (which also permitted it to provide local sound broadcasting services).

The Broadcasting Act 1981 amended and consolidated certain provisions contained in previous legislation including the removal of the prohibition on certain specified people from broadcasting opinions expressed in proceedings of Parliament or local authorities, the extension of the IBA's functions to the provision of programmes for Channel 4 and the establishment of the Broadcasting Complaints Commission.

Cable programme services and satellite broadcasts were the subject of the Cable and Broadcasting Act 1984. This Act and the Broadcasting Act 1981 were repealed and consolidated by the Broadcasting Act 1990 which implemented proposals in the Government's White Paper Broadcasting in the 1990's: Competition Choice and Quality (Cm 517, November 1988). Earlier recommendations on the reform of the broadcasting industry had been made in the Report of the Committee on Financing the BBC (the Peacock Report) (Cmnd 9824, July 1986) and the Third Report of the Home Affairs Committee's inquiry into the Future of Broadcasting (HC Paper 262, Session 1987-88, June 1988).

Current UK/EU Legislation

BROADCASTING AND CINEMAS

Broadcasting Act 1996

The Broadcasting Act 1996 makes provision for digital terrestrial television broadcasting and contains provisions relating to the award of multiplex licences. It also provides for the introduction of radio multiplex services and regulates digital terrestrial sound broadcasting. In addition, the Act amends a number of provisions contained in the Broadcasting Act 1990 relating to the funding of Channel Four Television Corporation, the funding of Sianel Pedwar Cymru, and the operation of the Comataidh Craolidgh Gaialig (the Gaelic Broadcasting Committee). The Act also dissolves the Broadcasting Complaints Commission and Broadcasting Standards Council and replaces these with the Broadcasting Standards Commission. The Act also contains other provisions relating to the transmission network of the BBC and television coverage of listed events.

Broadcasting Act 1990

The Broadcasting Act 1990 established a new framework for the regulation of independent television and radio services, and for satellite television and cable television. Under the Act, the Independent Broadcasting Authority (IBA) and the Cable Authority were dissolved and replaced by the Independent Television Commission. The Radio Authority was established in respect of independent radio services. The Broadcasting Standards Council was made a statutory body and the Act also contains provisions relating to the Broadcasting Complaints Commission. Besides reorganising independent broadcasting, the Act provided for the formation of a separate company with responsibility for effecting the technical arrangements relating to independent television broadcasting - National Transcommunications Limited ñ as a first step towards the privatisation of the former IBA's transmission functions.

The Broadcasting Act 1990 repealed the Broadcasting Act 1981 and the Cable and Broadcasting Act 1984, amended the Wireless Telegraphy Act 1949, the Wireless Telegraphy Act 1967, the Marine [&c] Broadcasting (Offences) Act 1967, and the Copyright, Designs and Patents Act 1988, and also implements legislative provisions required pursuant to Directive 89/552 - see below.

The Broadcasting Act 1990 requires the British Broadcasting Corporation, all Channel 3 Licensees, the Channel Four Television Corporation, S4C (the Welsh Fourth Channel Authority) and the future Channel 5 Licensee to procure that not less than 25 per cent of the total amount of time allocated by those services to broadcasting "qualifying programming" is allocated to the broadcasting of a range and diversity of "independent productions". The expressions "qualifying programming" and "independent productions" are defined in the Broadcasting (Independent Productions) Order 1991.

Cinemas Act 1985

The Cinemas Act 1985 consolidated the Cinematographic Acts 1909 to 1952, the Cinematographic (Amendment) Act 1982 and related enactments. The Act deals with the exhibition of films and contains provisions for the grant, renewal and transfer of licences for film exhibition. There are special provisions for Greater London.

The Cinemas Act specifies the conditions of Sunday opening, and provides for exempted exhibition in private dwelling houses, and for non-commercial shows in premises used only occasionally.

Video Recordings Act 1984

The Video Recordings Act 1984 controls the distribution of video recordings with the aim of restricting the depiction or simulation of human sexual activity, gross violence, human genital organs or urinary or excretory functions. A system of classification and labelling is prescribed. The supply of recordings without a classification certificate, or the supply of classified recordings to persons under a certain age or in certain premises or in breach of labelling regulations, is prohibited subject to certain exemptions.

Classification certificates are issued by the British Board of Film

Classification. It is an offence to supply or offer to supply, or to have in possession for the purposes of supplying, an unclassified video recording. Supplying recordings in breach of classification, supplying certain classified recordings otherwise than in licensed sex shops, supplying recordings in breach of labelling requirements and supplying recordings with false indications as to classification, are all offences under the Act. The Video Recordings Act provides for powers of entry, search and seizure and for the forfeiture of video recordings by the court.

Telecommunications Act 1984

The Telecommunications Act 1984 prohibits the running of a telecommunications system within the United Kingdom subject to certain exceptions which include the running of a telecommunication system in certain circumstances by a broadcasting authority. A broadcasting authority means a person who is licensed under the Wireless Telegraphy Act 1949 (see below) to broadcast programmes for general reception. Telecommunications systems include, among other things, any system for the conveyance of speech, music, other sounds and visual images by electric, magnetic, electro-magnetic, electro-chemical or electro-mechanical energy.

Wireless Telegraphy Acts 1967 and 1949

The 1967 Act provides for the Secretary of State to obtain information as to the sale and hire of television receiving sets. The Act allows the Secretary of State to prohibit the manufacture or importation of certain wireless telegraphy apparatus and to control the installation of such apparatus in vehicles.

The 1949 Act provides for the licensing of wireless telegraphy and defines "wireless telegraphy" as the sending of electro-magnetic energy over paths not provided by a material substance constructed or arranged for that purpose. The requirements to hold a licence under the Wireless

Telegraphy Act 1949 or the Telecommunications Act 1984 are separate from the television and radio broadcast licensing provisions and cable programme source licensing provisions contained in the Broadcasting Act 1990.

Marine [&c] Broadcasting (Offences) Act 1967

The making of broadcasts by wireless telegraphy (as defined in the Wireless Telegraphy Act 1949) intended for general reception from ships, aircraft and certain marine structures is prohibited under this Act.

The Cinematograph Films (Animals) Act 1937

The Cinematograph Films (Animals) Act 1937 provides for the prevention of exhibiting or distributing films in which suffering may have been caused to animals.

Celluloid and Cinematograph Film Act 1922

This Act contains provisions which are aimed at the prevention of fire in premises where raw celluloid or cinematograph film is stored or used. Silver nitrate film which was in universal use until the 1950s and was still used in some parts of the world (notably the former USSR) until the 1970s, is highly inflammable and becomes unstable with age. The purpose of the legislation was to protect members of the public from fire risks.

FINANCE

Finance (No 2) Act 1997

Section 48 Finance (No 2) Act 1997 introduced new rules for writing-off production and acquisition expenditure of British qualifying films costing £15 million or less to make. The relief applies to expenditure incurred between 2 July 1997 and 1 July 2000. Section 48 allows 100 per cent write-off for production or acquisition costs when the film is completed.

A British qualifying film is one certified as such by the Department of Culture Media and Sport under the Films Act 1985. In order to be certified a number of criteria must be met. These include the requirement for the maker of the film to be a

UK/European Economic Area ("EEA") company and the requirement for a certain percentage of labour costs to be spent on UK/EEA nationals. The prohibition on using a foreign studio was relaxed in 1999.

The Inland Revenue made an announcement on 25 March 1998 that the Government intends to extend the time limit for relief under section 48 from 3 years to 5 years in a future Finance Bill. The relief will then apply to expenditure incurred between 2 July 1997 and 1 July 2002. The Film Review Group issued a report on 25 March 1998 which sets out an action plan for delivery by April 1999.

The Finance Act 1990, Capital Allowances Act 1990 and Finance (No 2) Act 1992

Section 80 and Schedule 12 to the Finance Act 1990 deals with the tax issues relating to the reorganisation of independent broadcasting provided for in the Broadcasting Act 1990.

Section 68 of the Capital Allowances Act 1990 replaces Section 72 of the Finance Act 1982 providing for certain expenditure in the production of a film, tape or disc to be treated as expenditure of a revenue nature.

Sections 41-43 of the Finance (No 2) Act 1992 amend the tax regime to provide accelerated relief for pre-production costs incurred after 10 March 1992 and production expenditure on films completed after that date. Section 69 of the Act makes certain consequential amendments to Section 68 of the Capital Allowances Act 1990.

Films Act 1985

The Films Act 1985 dissolved the British Film Fund Agency, ending the Eady levy system established in 1951. The Act also abolished the Cinematograph Film Council and dissolved the National Film Finance Corporation, transferring its assets to British Screen Finance Limited. The Act repealed the Films Acts 1960 - 1980 and also repealed certain provisions of the Finance Acts 1982 and 1984 and substituted new provisions for determining whether or not a film was 'British' film eligible for allowances. Under the Finance Acts 1997 (No 2), 1992 (No2) and 1990. These provisions have been further amended to relax the prohibition on using a foreign studio

National Film Finance Corporation Act 1981

The National Film Finance Corporation Act 1981 repealed the Cinematograph Film Production (Special Loans) Acts of 1949 and 1954 and made provisions in relation to the National Film Finance Corporation which has since been dissolved by the Films Act 1985. The National Film Finance Corporation Act 1981 is, however, still on the statute book.

Film Levy Finance Act 1981

Although the British Film Fund Agency was dissolved by the British Film Fund Agency (Dissolution) Order 1988, SI 1988/37, the Film Levy Act itself is still in place.

COPYRIGHT

Copyright, Designs and Patents Act 1988

This Act is the primary piece of legislation relating to copyright in the United Kingdom. The Act provides copyright protection for original literary, dramatic, musical and artistic works, for films, sound recordings, broadcasts and cable programmes, and for typographical arrangements of published editions.

The Act repeals the Copyright Act 1956 which in turn repealed the Copyright Act 1911, but the transitional provisions of the Copyright, Designs and Patents Act 1988 apply certain provisions of the earlier legislation for the purpose of determining ownership of copyright, type of protection and certain other matters. Because the term of copyright for original literary, dramatic and/or musical works is the life of the author plus 50 years, the earlier legislation will continue to be relevant until well into the next century. The provisions of the Act have been amended by EU harmonisation provisions contained in Directive 93/98 extending the term of copyright protection in relation to literary, dramatic, musical and artistic

works originating in countries within the European Economic Area or written by nationals of countries in the EEA, to the duration of the life of the author or last surviving co-author plus, 70 years calculated from 31 December in the relevant year of decrease.

The Act provides a period of copyright protection for films and sound recordings which expires 50 years from the end of the calendar year in which the film or sound recording is made, or if it is shown or played in public or broadcast or included in a cable programme service, 50 years from the end of the calendar year in which this occurred. The provisions of the Act have been amended by EU harmonisation provisions contained in Directive 93/98 extending the term of copyright protection for films, to a period equal to the duration to the lifetime of the last to die of the persons responsible for the making of the film, plus 70 years calculated from 31 December in the relevant year of decrease.

The Act introduced three new moral rights into United Kingdom legislation. In addition to the right not to have a work falsely attributed to him or her, an author (of a literary dramatic musical or artistic work) or director (of a film) has the right to be identified in relation to their work, and the right not to permit their work to suffer derogatory treatment. A derogatory treatment is any addition, deletion, alteration or adaptation of a work which amounts to a distortion or mutilation of the work, or is otherwise prejudicial to the honour or reputation of the author or director. A person who commissions films or photographs for private and domestic purposes enjoys a new right of privacy established by the Act.

Another new development is the creation of a statutory civil right for performers, giving them the right not to have recordings of their performances used without their consent. United Kingdom copyright legislation was amended following a decision in Rickless -v- United Artists Corporation ñ a case which was brought by the estate of Peter Sellars and involved The Trail of the Pink Panther. The legislation is

retrospective and protects performances given 50 years ago, not just in the United Kingdom, but in any country if the performers were "qualifying persons" within the meaning of the relevant Act. The performances which are covered include not only dramatic and musical performances, but readings of literary works, variety programmes and even mime.

Numerous other provisions are contained in the Copyright, Designs and Patents Act including sections which deal with the fraudulent reception of programmes, the manufacture and sale of devices designed to circumvent copy-protection, and patent and design law.

EUROPEAN COMMUNITY LEGISLATION

Directive 89/552 – on television without frontiers

The objective of the Directive is to eliminate the barriers which divide Europe with a view to permitting and assuring the transition from national programme markets to a common programme production and distribution market. It also aims to establish conditions of fair competition without prejudice to the public interest role which falls to be discharged by television broadcasting services in the EC.

The laws of all Member States relating to television broadcasting and cable operations contain disparities which may impede the free movement of broadcasts within the EC and may distort competition. All such restrictions are required to be abolished.

Member States are free to specify detailed criteria relating to language etc. Additionally, Member States are permitted to lay down different conditions relating to the insertion of advertising in programmes within the limits set out in the Directive. Member States are required to provide where practicable that broadcasters reserve a proportion of their transmission time to European works created by independent producers. The amount of advertising is not to exceed 15 per cent of daily transmission time and the support advertising within a given one hour period shall not exceed 20 per cent.

Directive 92/100 – on rental rights

Authors or performers have, pursuant to the Directive, an unwaiveable right to receive equitable remuneration. Member States are required to provide a right for performers in relation to the fixation of their performances, a right for phonogram and film producers in relation to their phonograms and first fixations of their films and a right for broadcasters in relation to the fixation of broadcasts and their broadcast and cable transmissions. Member States must also provide a 'reproduction right' giving performers, phonogram producers, film producers and broadcasting organisations the right to authorise or prohibit the direct or indirect reproduction of their copyright works. The Directive also requires Member States to provide for performers, film producers, phonogram producers and broadcasting organisations to have exclusive rights to make available their work by sale or otherwise ñ known as the 'distribution right'.

Directive 93/83 on Satellite Transmission and Cable Retransmission

This Directive is aimed at eliminating uncertainty and differences in national legislation governing when the act of communication of a programme takes place. It avoids the cumulative application of several national laws to one single act of broadcasting.

The Directive provides that communication by satellite occurs in the member state where the programming signals are introduced under the control of a broadcaster into an uninterrupted chain of communication, leading to the satellite and down towards earth. The Directive also examines protection for authors, performers and producers of phonograms and broadcasting organisations, and requires that copyright owners may grant or refuse authorisation for cable retransmissions of a broadcast only through a collecting society.

Directive 98/98 on harmonising the term of protection of copyright and certain related rights

This Directive is aimed at harmonising the periods of copyright throughout the European Union where different states provide different periods of protection. Although the minimum term established by the Berne Convention on Copyright is 50 years post mortem auctoris, a number of states have chosen to provide for longer periods. In Germany the period of literary dramatic musical and artistic works is 70 years pma, in Spain 60 years (or 80 years for copyrights protected under the Spanish law of 1879 until its reform in 1987). In France the period is 60 years pma or 70 years for musical compositions.

In addition to the differences in the term of rights post mortem auctoris, further discrepancies arise in protection accorded by different member states through wartime extensions. Belgium has provided a wartime extension of 10 years, Italy 12 years, France six and eight years respectively in relation to the First and Second World Wars. In France, a further period of 30 years is provided in the case of copyright works whose authors were killed in action - such as Antoine de Saint-ExupÈry.

The Directive also provides that rights of performers shall run from 50 years from the date of performance or if later, from the point at which the fixation of the performance is lawfully made available to the public for the first time, or if this has not occurred from the first assimilation of the performance. The rights of producers of phonograms run 50 years from first publication of the phonogram, but expire 50 years after the fixation was made if the phonogram, but expire 50 years after the fixation was made if the phonogram has not been published during that time. A similar provision applies to the rights of producers of the first fixations of cinematographic works and sequences of moving images, whether accompanied or not by sound. Rights of broadcasting organisations run from 50 years from the first transmission of the broadcast.

The Directive provides that the person who makes available to the public a previously unpublished work which is in the public domain, shall have the same rights of exploitation in relation to the work as would have fallen to the author for a term of 25 years from the time the work was first made available to the public. The Directive applies to all works which are protected by at least one member state on 1 July 1995 when the Directive came into effect. As a result of the differing terms in European states, many works which were treated as being in the 'public domain' in the United Kingdom will have their copyright revived. Works by Beatrix Potter, James Joyce and Rudyard Kipling are all works which will benefit from a revival of copyright. The provisions relating to the term of protection of cinematographic films are not required to be applied to films created before 1 July 1994. Each member state of the European Union's required to implement the Directive. The precise manner of implementation and the choice of transitional provisions, are matters which each state is free to determine.

Directive 93/98 was implemented in the United Kingdom by the Rights in Performances Regulations 1995/3297 which took effect from 1 January 1996. The term of copyright protection for literary dramatic musical or artistic works expires at the end of the period of 70 years from the last day of the calendar year in which the author dies. Copyright in a film expires 70 years from the end of the calendar year in which the death occurs of the last to die of the principal director, the author of the screenplay, the author of the dialogue or the composer of the music specially created for and used for the film. The period of copyright previously applying to films under the Copyright, Designs and Patents Act 1988 ended 50 years from the first showing or playing in public of a film, and the effect of the implementation of Directive 93/98 is to create a significant extension of the period in which a film copyright owner has the exclusive economic right to exploit a film. If, as anticipated, the United States of America also extends the duration of the copyright period applying to films, the value of intellectual property rights in audiovisual productions may increase significantly.

LIBRARIES

This section provides a directory of libraries which have collections of books, periodicals and papers covering film and television. It includes the libraries of colleges and universities with graduate and post-graduate degree courses in the media. Most of these collections are intended for student and teaching staff use: permission for access should always be sought from the Librarian. Where possible a breakdown of types of resources is provided

 bfi National Library
21 Stephen Street
London WIT 1LN
Tel: 020 7255 1444
        020 7436 0165 (Information)
Fax: 020 7436 2338
The *bfi*'s own library is extensive and holds the world's largest collection of documentation on film and television. It includes both published and unpublished material ranging from books and periodicals to news cuttings, press releases, scripts, theses, and files of festival material.
Reading Room opening hours
Monday   10.30am - 5.30pm
Tuesday   10.30am - 8.00pm
Wednesday   1.00pm - 8.00pm
Thursday   10.30am - 8.00pm
Friday   10.30am - 5.30pm
Institutional pass: £50.00
Library pass: £33.00
NFT Members pass: £25.00
Discount passes   £20.00*
Weekly pass   £15.00
Day pass   £ 6.00**
*Available to Senior Citizens, Registered Disabled and Unemployed upon proof of eligibility. Students may also apply for a discounted library pass.
**Available to anyone. Spaces may be reserved by giving 48 hours notice.
Enquiry Lines
The Enquiry Line is available for short enquiries. Frequent callers subscribe to an information service. The line is open from 10.00am to 5.00pm Monday to Friday - 020 7255 1444
Research Services:
For more detailed enquiries, users should contact Information Services by fax or mail

Key to Resources

A   Specialist sections
B   Film/TV journals
C   Film/TV/CD ROMS
D   Video loan service
E   Internet access
F   Special collections

Aberdeen

Aberdeen University Library
Queen Mother Library, Meston Walk, Aberdeen
Grampian AB24 3UE
Tel: 01224 272579
Fax: 01224 487048
email: library@abdn.ac.uk
Website: www.abdn.ac.uk/library/
Contact: University Librarian

Bangor

Normal College
Education Library
Bangor
Gwynedd LL57 2P
Tel: 01248 370171
Fax: 01248 370461
Contact: Librarian

Barnet

Middlesex University Cat Hill Library
Cat Hill, Barnet
Herts EN4 8HT
Tel: 020 8362 5042
Fax: 020 8440 9541
Contact: Art and Design Librarian

Bath

Bath University Library
Claverton Down
Bath BA2 7AY
Tel: 01225 826084
Fax: 01225 826229
Contact: University Librarian

Belfast

Belfast Central Library
Royal Avenue
Belfast
Co. Antrim BT1 1EA
Tel: 01232 332819
Fax: 01232 312886
Contact: Chief Librarian

Northern Ireland Film Commission
21 Ormeau Avenue
Belfast BT2 8HD
Tel: 01232 232444
Fax: 01232 239918
email: info@nifc.co.uk
Website: www.nifc.co.uk
Information Officer
Resources: B, D

Queen's Film Theatre
25 College Gardens
Belfast BT9 6BS
Tel: 01232 667687 ext. 33
Fax: 01232 663733
email:m.open@qub.ac.uk
Contact: Administrator/Programmer
Resources: B, C, E, F

Birmingham

BBC Pebble Mill
Information Research Library
Pebble Mill Road
Birmingham B5 7QQ
Tel: 0121 432 8922
Fax: 0121 432 9589
Contact: Information Research Librarian
Resources: B, C, E

Birmingham University Library
Edgbaston
Birmingham B15 2TT
Tel: 0121 414 5817
Fax: 0121 471 4691
email: library@bham.ac.uk
Website: www.is.bham.ac.uk
Contact: Librarian, Arts and Humanities

Information Services
Franchise Street
Perry Barr

Birmingham B42 2SU
Tel: 0121 331 5300
Fax: 0121 331 6543
Contact: Dean of Information
Services

University of Central England
Birmingham Institute of Art &
Design
Gosta Green
Birmingham B4 7DX
Tel: 0121 331 5860
Contact: Library staff

Vivid - Birmingham's Centre for Media Arts
Unit 311 The Big Peg
120 Vyse Street, Jewellery Quarter
Birmingham B18 6ND
Tel: 0121 233 4061
Fax: 0121 212 1784
email:info@vivid.org.uk
Website: www.vivid.org.uk
Marian Hall, Facilities Co-ordinator
Resources: A, B, D, E

Brighton

University of Brighton Faculty of Art, Design and Humanities
St Peter's House Library
16-18 Richmond Place
Brighton BN2 2NA
Tel: 01273 643221
Contact: Librarian

University of Sussex Library
Falmer
Brighton
East Sussex BN1 9QL
Tel: 01273 877097
Fax: 01273 678441
email: library@sussex.ac.uk
Website: www.sussex.ac.uk/library
Dheirdre Mitchell
Contact: Audio-Visual Section

Bristol

Bristol City Council
Leisure Services
Central Library, Reference Library,
College Green
Bristol BS1 5TL
Tel: 0117 927 6121
Fax: 0117 922 6775
Contact: Head of Reference &
Information Services

University of Bristol
University Library
Tyndall Avenue

Bristol BS8 1TJ
Tel: 0117 928 8017
Fax: 0117 925 5334
Website: www.bris.ac.uk
Contact: Librarian
Resources: A,B, C, E

University of Bristol Theatre Collection
Department of Drama
Cantocks Close
Bristol BS8 1UP
Tel: 0117 928 7836
Fax: 0117 928 7832
email: theatre-collection@bris.ac.uk
Website:
www.bristol.ac.uk/theatrecollection
Contact: Keeper

University of the West of England, Bristol
Library, Faculty of Art, Media &
Design
Bower Ashton Campus
Clanage Road
Bristol BS3 2JU
Tel: 0117 344 4750
Fax: 0117 344 4745
Website: www.uwe.ac.uk/library
Contact: Geoff Cole, Campus/Subject
Librarian, Art, Media and Design

Canterbury

Canterbury Christ Church College Library
North Holmes Road
Canterbury
Kent CT1 1QU
Tel: 01227 782354
Fax: 01227 767530
email: libl@cant.ac.uk
Website:
www.cant.ac.uk./depts/services/library/library1.html
Contact: Director of Library Services
Resources: A, B, C, D, E

Kent Institute of Art & Design at Canterbury
New Dover Road
Canterbury
Kent CT1 3AN
Tel: 01227 769371
Fax: 01227 817500
Website: www.kiad.ac.uk
Kathleen Godfrey: Campus Librarian

Templeman Library
University of Kent at Canterbury
Canterbury
Kent CT2 7NU
Tel: 01227 764000
Fax: 01227 459025
Contact: Librarian

Cardiff

Cardiff University
Bute Resource Centre
PO Box 430
Cardiff CF10 3XT
Tel: 029 20874611
Fax: 029 20874192
email: buteliby@cardiff.ac.uk
Website: www.cardiff.ac.uk
Contact: Librarian

Coleg Glan Hafren
Trowbridge Road
Rumney
Cardiff CF3 1XZ
Tel: 029 20 250250
Fax: 029 20 250339
Website: www.glan-hafren.ac.uk
Contact: Learning Resources
Development Manager

Carlisle

Cumbria College of Art and Design Library
Brampton Road
Carlisle
Cumbria CA3 9AY
Tel: 01228 400300 x 312
Fax: 01228 514491
Website: www.cumbria@ac.uk
Contact: Librarian

Chislehurst

Ravensbourne College of Design and Communication Library
Walden Road, Chislehurst
Kent BR7 5SN
Tel: 020 8289 4900
Fax: 020 8325 8320
email: library@rave.ac.uk
Website: www.rave.ac.uk
Contact: Librarian

Colchester

University of Essex
The Albert Sloman Library
Wivenhoe Park
Colchester CO4 3SQ
Tel: 01206 873333
Contact: Librarian

Coleraine

University of Ulster
Library
Coleraine
Northern Ireland BT52 1SA
Tel: 01265 32 4345

Fax: 01265 32 4928
Contact: Pro-Librarian
Resources: A, B, C, D

Coventry

Coventry City Library
Smithford Way
Coventry CV1 1FY
Tel: 01203 832314
Fax: 01203 832440
email: covinfo@discover.co.uk
Contact: Librarian - Karen Berry

Lanchester Library
Frederick Lanchester Building
Coventry University
Gosford Street
Coventry CV1 5DD
Tel: 024 7688 7543
Fax: 024 7688 7525
Website: www.library.coventry.ac.uk
Contact: Sub-Librarian, Arts, Design
and Media

Warwick University Library
Gibbet Hill Road
Coventry CV4 7AL
Tel: 01203 524103
Fax: 01203 524211
Contact: Librarian
Resources: A, B, C, D, E, F
 Collection of German film
programme from the 1930s

Derby

Derby University Library
Kedleston Rd
Derby DE3 1GB
Tel: 01332 622222 x 4061
Fax: 01332 622222 x 4059
Contact: Librarian

University of Derby
Library and Learning Resources
Derby DE1 !RX
Tel: 01332 622222 Ext 3001
Website: www.derby.ac.uk
Contact: Subject Adviser, Art &
Design
Resources: A, B, C, D, E

Doncaster

Nova Productions
11a Winholme
Armthorpe
Doncaster DN3 3AF
Tel: 01302 833422
Fax: 08701 257917
email: library@novaonline.co.uk
Website: www.novaonline.co.uk
Contact: The Administrator

Dorking

Surrey Performing Arts Library
Vaughan Williams House
West Street
Dorking, Surrey RH4 1BY
Tel: 01306 887509
Fax: 01306 875074
email: p.arts@dial.pipex.com
Website:
www.surreycc.gov.uk/libraries
Senior Librarian: G.Muncy
Contact: Librarian
Resources: A, B, C, D, E, F
Scripts

Douglas

Douglas Corporation
Douglas Public Library
Ridgeway Street
Douglas
Isle of Man
Tel: 01624 623021
Fax: 01624 662792
Contact: Borough Librarian

Dundee

Library Duncan of Jordanstone College
University of Dundee
13 Perth Road
Dundee DD1 4HT
Tel: 01382 345255
Fax: 01382 229283
Contact: College Librarian
Resources: A, B, C, D, E, F
Few scripts

Egham

Royal Holloway University of London Library
Egham Hill
Egham
Surrey TW20 OEX
Tel: 01784 443330
Fax: 01784 477670
Website: www.lb.rhbnc.ac.uk
Contact: Librarian
Resources: A, B, C, D, E,

Exeter

Exeter University Library
Stocker Road
Exeter
Devon EX4 4PT
Tel: 01392 263869
Fax: 01392 263871
Website: www.ex.ac.uk/
library/internet/film.html
Contact: Librarian
Resources: A, B, C, D, E, F
The Bill Douglas Centre for the
History of Cinema and Popular
Culture

Farnham

Surrey Institute of Art & Design, University College
Falkner Road
The Hart, Farnham
Surrey GU9 7DS
Tel: 01252 722441
Fax: 01252 892616
Contact: Institue Librarian
Resources: A, B, C, D, E
Registered users only

Gateshead

Gateshead Libraries and Arts Department
Central Library
Prince Consort Road
Gateshead
Tyne and Wear NE8 4LN
Tel: 0191 477 3478
Fax: 0191 477 7454
Contact: The Librarian

Glasgow

Glasgow Caledonian !Jniversity Library
Cowcaddens Road
Glasgow G4 0BA
Tel: 0141 331 3858
Fax: 0141 331 3005
Website: www.gcal.ac.uk
Contact: Assistant Academic Liaison
Librarian for Media, Language and
Leisure Mgt
Resources: A, B, C, D, E

Glasgow City Libraries
Mitchell Library
North Street
Glasgow G3 7DN
Tel: 0141 287 2933
Fax: 0141 287 2815
email: arts@gcl.glasgow.gov.uk
Website: www.mitchellibrary.org
Contact: Departmental Librarian,
Arts Department

Glasgow School of Art Library
167 Renfrew Street
Glasgow G3 6RQ
Tel: 0141 353 4551
Fax: 0141 353 4670

email: e.monteith@gsa.ac.uk
Contact: Principal Librarian

Scottish Council for Educational Technology
Dowanhill
74 Victoria Crescent Road
Glasgow G12 9JN
Tel: 0141 337 5000
Fax: 0141 337 5050
Website: www.sect.com
Contact: Librarian
Resources: D

Scottish Screen
Second Floor
249 West George Street
Glasgow G2 4QE
Tel: 0141 302 1700
Fax: 0141 302 1711
email: info@scottishscreen.com
Website: www.scottishscreen.com
Chief Executive: Steve McIntyre
Resources: D, F*
*Production/Information
Access to the Shiach Script library
with over 100 feature and short film
scripts. Video, publications resource.
Internet site, National Archive
collection of factual documentary
material reflecting Scotland's social
and cultural history. Available to
broadcasters, programme makers,
educational users and researchers.
Distribution of Scottish shorts with
back catalogue.

University of Glasgow
The Library
Hillhead Street
Glasgow G12 8QQ
Tel: 0141 330 6704/5
Fax: 0141 330 4952
Contact: Librarian

Gravesend

VLV - Voice of the Listener and Viewer
101 King's Drive
Gravesend
Kent DA12 5BQ
Tel: 01474 352835
Fax: 01474 351112
Contact: Information Officer
In addition to its own VLV holds
archives of the former independent
Broadcasting Research Unit (1980-
1991) and the former British Action
for Children's Television (BACTV)
(1988-1994) and makes these
available for a small fee together with
its own archives and library. VLV
represents the citizen and consumer

interest in broadcasting and is
working for quality independence
and diversity in British broadcasting
Resources: A, E, F

Huddersfield

Kirklees Cultural Services
Central Library
Princess Alexandra Walk
Huddersfield HD1 2SU
Tel: 01484 221967
Fax: 01484 221974
Contact: Reference Librarian
Resources: C, D, E

Hull

Hull University Brynmor Jones Library
Cottingham Road
Hull
HU6 7RX
Tel: 01482 466581
Fax: 01482 466205
email: ibhelp@acs.hull.ac.uk
Website: www.hull.ac.uk/lib
Contact: Library Manager

Humberside

Humberside University
School of Art, Architecture and
Design Learning Support Centre
Guildhall Road
Hull HU1 1HJ
Tel: 01482 440550
Fax: 01482 449627
Contact: Centre Manager

Keele

Keele Information Services
Keele University
Keele
Staffs ST5 5BG
Tel: 01782 583239
Fax: 01782 711553
Contact: Visual Arts Department
Resources: B, C, D, E

Kingston upon Thames

Kingston Museum & Heritage Service
North Kingston Centre
Richmond Road
Kingston upon Thames
Surrey KT2 5PE
Tel: 020 8547 6738 or 6755
Website: www.kingston.ac.uk

Contact: T. Everson, Local History
Officer
Resources: E, F
Eadweard Maybridge Collection

Kingston University Library Services
Art and Design Library
Knights Park
Kingston Upon Thames
Surrey KT1 2QJ
Tel: 020 747 2000 x 4031
Fax: 020 7547 8039
email: library@kingston.ac.uk
Website:
www.king.ac.uk/library_media/index.
html
Contact: Faculty Librarian (Design)

Kingston University Library Services
Library and Media Services
Penrhyn Road
Kingston Upon Thames
Surrey KT1 2EE
Tel: 020 8547 2000
Fax: 020 8547 7111
email: library@kingston.ac.uk
Website:
www.king.ac.uk/library_media/index.
html
Contact: Head of Library and Media
Services

Leeds

Leeds City Libraries
Central Library
Municipal Buildings
Calverley Street
Leeds, West Yorkshire LS1 3AB
Tel: 0113 247 8265
Fax: 0113 247 8268
Contact: Director of Library Services

Leeds Metropolitan University
City Campus Library
Calverley Street
Leeds, West Yorkshire LS1 3HE
Tel: 0113 283 2600 x3836
Fax: 0113 242 5733
Contact: Tutor Librarian, Art &
Design

Trinity and All Saints College Library
Brownberrie Lane
Horsforth
Leeds, West Yorkshire LS18 5HD
Tel: 0113 283 7100
Fax: 0113 283 7200
Website: www.tasc.ac.uk

Contact: Librarian
Resources: A, B, D, E

Leicester

Centre For Mass Communication Research
104 Regent Road
Leicester LE1 7LT
Tel: 0116 2523863
Fax: 0116 2523874
email: cmcr@le.ac.uk
Website: www.le.ac.uk/cmcr/
Contact: Director

De Montfort University Library
Kimberlin Library , The Gateway
Leicester LE1 9BH
Tel: 0116 255 1551
Fax: 0116 255 0307
Contact: Senior Assistant Librarian (Art and Design)

Leicester Central Lending Library
54 Belvoir Street
Leicester LE1 6QL
Tel: 0116 255 6699
Contact: Area Librarian
Resources: D, E,

Leicester University Library
PO Box 248
University Road
Leicester LE1 9QD
Tel: 0116 252 2042
Fax: 0116 252 2066
Website: www.le.ac.uk
Contact: Librarian
Resources: A, B, E

Liverpool

Aldham Robarts Learning Resource Centre
Liverpool John Moores University
Mount Pleasant
Liverpool L3 5UZ
Tel: 0151 231 3104
Contact: Senior Information Officer (Media, Critical and Creative Arts)

Liverpool City Libraries
William Brown Street
Liverpool L3 8EW
Tel: 0151 225 5429
Fax: 0151 207 1342
Contact: Librarian

Liverpool Hope University College
Hope Park
Liverpool L16 9LB

Tel: 0151 291 2000
Fax: 0151 291 2037
Website: www.hope.ac.uk
Contact: Director of Learning Resources
Resources: A, B, C, D, E

London

Barbican Library
Barbican Centre
Silk Street, London EC2Y 8DS
Tel: 020 7638 0569
Fax: 020 7638 2249
email: barbicanlib
Website: www.cityoflondon.gov.uk
John Lake
Contact: Librarian

BKSTS - The Moving Image Society
63-71 Victoria House ,
Vernon Place
London WC1B 4DA
Tel: 020 7242 8400
Fax: 020 7405 3560
email: movimage@bksts.demon.co.uk
Contact: John Graham

British Universities Film & Video Council Library
77 Wells Street
London W1T 3QJ
Tel: 020 7393 1500
Fax: 020 7393 1555
email: ask@bufvc.ac.uk
Website: www.bufvc.ac.uk
Luke McKernan, Head of Information
Resources: B, C, D, E, F
= Scientific Film Association papers, BKSTS book collection, Slade Film History Register, Reuters Television newsreel documents

Brunel University
Twickenham Campus
300 St Margarets Road
Twickenham TW1 1PT
Tel: 020 8891 0121
Fax: 020 8891 0240
Contact: Director of Library Services
Resources: A, B, C, E

Camberwell College of Arts Library
London Institute
Peckham Road
London SE5 8UF
Tel: 020 7514 6349
Fax: 020 7514 6324
Contact: College Librarian
Resources: A, B, E

Camden Public Libraries
Swiss Cottage Library
88 Avenue Road
London NW3 3HA
Tel: 020 7974 6522
Fax: 020 7974 6532
email: swisslib@camden.gov.uk
Website: www.camden.gov.uk
Contact: Librarian
Resources: A, B, D, E

Carlton Screen Advertising
127 Wardour Street
London W1V 4NL
Tel: 020 7439 9531
Fax: 020 7439 2395
Contact: Secretary

Cinema Theatre Association
44 Harrowdene Gardens
Teddington, Middlesex TW11 0DJ
Tel: 020 8977 2608
Website: www.cinema-theatre.org.uk
Contact: Secretary

Institute of Education Library (London)
20 Bedford Way
London WC1H OAL
Tel: 020 7612 6080
Fax: 020 7612 6093
email: lib.enquiries@ioe.ac.uk
Contact: Librarian

International Institute of Communications
Library and Information Service
3rd Floor, Westcott House
35 Portland Place
London W1N 3AG
Tel: 020 7323 9622
Fax: 020 7323 9623
email: enquiries@iicom.org
Website: www.iicom.org
Contact: Information & Library Manager

London Borough of Barnet Libraries
Hendon Library
The Burroughs
Hendon
London NW4 4BQ
Tel: 020 8359 2628
Fax: 020 8359 2885
Contact: Librarian

London College of Printing & Distributive Trades
Media School
Backhill
Clerkenwell EC1R 5EN
Tel: 020 7514 6500
Fax: 020 7514 6848
Contact: Head of Learning Resources

London Guildhall University
Academic Services,
Calcutta House,
Old Castle Street
London E1 7NT
Tel: 020 7320 1000
Fax: 020 7320 1177
email: kelso@lgu.ac.uk
Website: www.lgu.ac.uk
Ian Kelso
Contact: Head of TV Services

Middlesex University Library
Bounds Green Road
London N11 2NQ
Tel: 020 8362 5240
Contact: University Librarian

Royal College of Art
Kensington Gore
London SW7 2EU
Tel: 020 7590 4224
Fax: 020 7590 4500
email: library@rca.ac.uk
Website: www.rca.ac.uk
Contact: Library Desk

Royal Television Society, Library & Archive
Holborn Hall
100 Grays Inn Road
London WC1X 8AL
Tel: 020 7430 1000
Fax: 020 7430 0924
Contact: Archivist

Slade/Duveen Art Library
University College London
Gower Street
London WC1E 6BT
Tel: 020 7504 2594
Fax: 020 7380 7373
email: r.dar@ucl.ac.uk
Contact: Art Librarian: Ruth Dar
Resources: A, B, C, E
For UCL staff and students

Thames Valley University
St Mary's Road
Walpole House
Ealing
London W5 5RF
Tel: 020 8231 2248
Fax: 020 8231 2631
Website: www.tvu.ac.uk
Contact: Humanities Librarian

The College of North East London Learning Resource Centre
High Road
Tottenham
London N15 4RU
Tel: 020 8442 3013

Fax: 020 8442 3091
Contact: Head of Learning Resources

University of East London
Greengate House Library
School of Art & Design
89 Greengate Street
London E13 0BG
Tel: 020 8590 7000 x 3434
Contact: Site Librarian

University of London: Goldsmiths' College Library
Lewisham Way
London SE14 6NW
Tel: 020 7919 7168
Fax: 020 7919 7165
email: lbsølpm@gold.ac.uk
Website: www.gold.ac.uk
Contact: Subject Librarian: Media & Communications
Resources: A, B, C, D

University of North London
The Learning Centre
236-250 Holloway Road
London N7 6PP
Tel: 020 7607 2789 x 2720
Fax: 020 7753 5079
email: c.partridge@unl.ac.uk
Website: www.unl.ac.uk/library/aishums/films.html
Crispin Partridge
Resources: B, C, D, E

University of Surrey Roehampton
Information Services
Roehampton Institute London
Learning Resources Centre
Digby Stuart College
Roehampton Lane
London SW15 5SZ
Tel: 020 8392 3251
Fax: 020 8392 3259
Website: www.roehampton.ac.uk
Contact: Information Adviser (Performing Arts)
Resources: B, C, E

University of Westminster
Harrow Learning Resources Centre
Watford Road
Northwick Park
Harrow HA1 3TP
Tel: 020 7911 5885
Fax: 020 7911 5952
Website: www.wmin.ac.uk/harlib
Contact: Library Manager
Resources: A, B, C, E, F

Westminster Reference Library
35 St Martins Street
London WC2H 7HP

Tel: 020 7641 4636
Fax: 020 7641 4640
Contact: Margaret Girvan, Arts Librarian
Resources: A, B, C, E

Loughborough

Loughborough University Pilkington Library
Loughborough University
Loughborough LE11 3TU
Tel: 01509 222360
Fax: 01509 234806
Contact: Assistant Librarian

Luton

University of Luton Library
Park Square
Luton LU1 3JU
Tel: 01582 734111 Ext 2093
email: alan.bullimore@luton.ac.uk
Alan Bullimore
Contact: Humanities Academic Liaison Librarian

Maidstone

Kent Institute of Art & Design at Maidstone
Oakwood Park
Maidstone
Kent ME16 8AG
Tel: 01622 757286
Fax: 01622 692003
Contact: College Librarian

Manchester

John Rylands University Library
Oxford Road
Manchester M13 9PP
Tel: 0161 275 3751/3738
Fax: 0161 273 7488
Website: rylibweb.man.ac.uk
Contact: Head of Public Services

Manchester Arts Library
Central Library
St Peters Square
Manchester M2 5PD
Tel: 0161 234 1974
Fax: 0161 234 1963
email: arts@libraries.manchester.gov.uk
Website: www.manchester.gov.uk/libraries
Contact: Arts Librarian
Resources: A, B, D, E

Manchester Metropolitan University Library
All Saints Building

Grosvenor Square, Oxford Road
Manchester M15 6BH
Tel: 0161 247 6104
Fax: 0161 247 6349
Contact: Senior Subject Librarian

North West Film Archive
Manchester Metropolitan University
Minshull House
47-49 Chorlton Street
Manchester M1 3EU
Tel: 0161 247 3097
Fax: 0161 247 3098
email: n.w.filmarchive@mmu.ac.uk
Website: www.nwfa.mmu.ac.uk
Director: Maryann Gomes
Enquiries: Lisa Ridehalgh
Resources: D, E, F
Ephemera

Newcastle upon Tyne

Newcastle Upon Tyne University Robinson Library
Robinson Library
Newcastle Upon Tyne NE2 4HQ
Tel: 0191 222 7662
Fax: 0191 222 6235
Website: www.ncl.ac.uk/library
Contact: The Librarian
Resources: A, B, C, D, E

University of Northumbria at Newcastle Library Building
Ellison Place
Newcastle Upon Tyne NE1 8ST
Tel: 0191 227 4132
Fax: 0191 227 4563
Website: www.unn.ac.uk
Contact: Jane Shaw, Senior Officer, Information Services Department

Newport

University of Wales College, Newport
Library and Learning Resources,
Caerleon Campus
PO Box 179, Newport NP18 3YG
Tel: 01633 432294
Fax: 01633 432108
email: llr@newport.ac.uk
Website: www.library.newport.ac.uk
Contact: Art, Media and Design Librarian

Northumberland

Northumberland Central Library
The Willows

Morpeth
Northumberland NE61 1TA
Tel: 01670 534514
Fax: 01670 534521
Contact: The Adult Services Librarian
Resources: A, B, C, D, E

Norwich

East Anglian Film Archive
Centre for East Anglian Studies
University of East Anglia
Norwich NR4 7TJ
Tel: 01603 592664
Fax: 01603 458553
Contact: Assistant Archivist

University of East Anglia
University Library
Norwich NR4 7TJ
Tel: 01603 592421
Fax: 01603 259490
email: library@uea.ac.uk
Website: www.lib.uea.ac.uk
Film Studies Librarian

Nottingham

Nottingham Central Library
Angel Row
Nottingham NG1 6HP
Tel: 0115 941 2121
Fax: 0115 953 7001
Contact: Librarian

Nottingham Trent University Library
The Boots Library
Goldsmith Street
Nottingham NG1 5LS
Tel: 0115 848 2110
Fax: 0115 848 2286
Website: www.ntu.ac.uk
Contact: Faculty Liaison Officer (Art & Design)
Resources: A, B, C, D, E

University of Nottingham Library
Hallward Library
University Park
Nottingham NG7 2RD
Tel: 0115 951 4584
Fax: 0115 951 4558
Website: www.nottingham.ac.uk/library
Contact: Humanities Librarian
Recources: A, B, C, E

Plymouth

College of St Mark and St John Library
Derriford Road

Plymouth
Devon PL6 8BH
Tel: 01752 636700
Fax: 01752 636712
email: agress@majon.ac.uk
Website: www.marjon.ac.uk
Contact: Resources Librarian
Resources: B, C, E

Plymouth College of Art & Design Library
Tavistock Place
Plymouth
Devon PL4 8AT
Tel: 01752 203412
Fax: 01752 203444
Contact: Librarian
Resources: A, B, C, D, E

Pontypridd

University of Glamorgan
Learning Resources Centre
Pontypridd
Rhondda Cynon Taff CF37 1DL
Tel: 01443 482625
Fax: 01443 482629
email: pjatkins@glam.ac.uk
Website: www.itc.glam.ac.uk/lrc
Contact: Head of Learning Resource

Poole

Bournemouth & Poole College of Art & Design
Fern Barrow,
off Wallisdown Road, Poole
Dorset BH12 5HH
Tel: 01202 533011
Fax: 01202 537729
Contact: University Librarian

Bournemouth University Library
Dorset House
Talbot Campus
Fern Barrow
Poole
Dorset BH12 5BB
Tel: 01202 595011
Fax: 01202 595475
email: dbath@bournemouth.ac.uk
Website: www.bournemouth.ac.uk
David Ball
Contact: Librarian

Portsmouth

Highbury College Library
Cosham
Portsmouth
Hants PO6 2SA
Tel: 023 92313213
Fax: 023 92325551

email: email; library@highbury.ac.uk
Contact: College Librarian

Portsmouth University Library

Frewen Library
Cambridge Road
Portsmouth
Hampshire PO1 2ST
Tel: 023 92843222
Fax: 023 92843233
Website: www.libr.port.ac.uk
Contact: University Librarian
Resources: A, B, C, D, E

Preston

University of Central Lancashire Library

St Peter's Square
Preston
Lancashire PR1 2HE
Tel: 01772 201201 x 2266
Fax: 01772 892937
Contact: Senior Subject Librarian

Reading

Reading University Library

Woodlands Avenue
Reading RG6 1HY
Tel: 0118 931 8652
Fax: 0118 931 8651
Website:
www.rdg.ac.uk/libweb/lib/bulm/index
.html
Contact: Faculty Team Manager
(Education & Community Studies)

Rochdale

Rochdale Metropolitan Borough Libraries

Wheatsheaf Library
Wheatsheaf Centre
Baillie Street, Rochdale
Lancashire OL16 1AQ
Tel: 01706 864914
Fax: 01706 864992
Contact: Librarian

Salford

University of Salford, Academic Information Services (Library)

Adelphi Campus
Peru Street
Salford
Greater Manchester M3 6EQ
Tel: 0161 295 6183/6185
Fax: 0161 295 6083
Website: www.ais.salford.ac.uk
Contact: Sue Slade (Faculty co-

ordinator)
Contact: Andy Callen (Information
Officer, Music & Media Productions)
Resources: A, B, C, D, E, F
Scripts

Sheffield

Sheffield Hallam University Library

Psalter Lane Site
Sheffield
South Yorkshire S11 8UZ
Tel: 0114 225 2721
Fax: 0114 225 2717
email: c.abson@shu.ac.uk
Website:
www.shu.ac.uk/services/lc/people/psa
lter1.htm
Claire Abson, Information Specialist,
School of Cultural Studies
Resources: A, B, C, D, E

Sheffield Libraries & Information Services

Arts and Social Sciences Section
Central Library, Surrey Street
Tel: 0114 273 4747/8
Fax: 0114 273 5009
Contact: Librarian

Sheffield University Library

Main Library
University of Sheffield
Western Bank
Sheffield
South Yorkshire S10 2TN
Tel: 0114 222 7200/1
Fax: 0114 273 9826
Contact: Head of Reader Services

Solihull

Solihull College

Chelmsley Campus, Partridge Close
Chelmsley Wood
Solihull B37 6UG
Tel: 0121 770 5651
Contact: Librarian

Southampton

Periodical Office, Hartley Library

University of Southampton
University Road, Highfield
Southampton
Hants S017 1BJ
Tel: 01703 593521
Fax: 01703 593007
Contact: Assistant Librarian, Arts
Resources: B, D, E, F
Personal papers, pressbooks

Southampton Institute, Mountbatten Library

East Park Terrace
Southampton
Hampshire SO17 1BJ
Tel: 01703 319000
Fax: 01703 3576161
Website: www.solent.ac.uk/library/
Contact: Information Librarian
(Communications)
Resources: D, E
For existing Institute staff and
students

University of Southampton New College

The Avenue
Southampton SO17 1BG
Tel: 023 80597220
Fax: 023 80597339
email: nclib@soton.ac.uk
Website:
www.soton.ac.uk/~library/new
Gail McFarlane
Contact: Librarian

Stirling

University of Stirling Library

Stirling FK9 4LA
Tel: 01786 467 235
Fax: 01786 466 866
Website: www.stir.ac.uk
Contact: Librarian

Stoke-on-Trent

Staffordshire University Library and Information Service

College Road
Stoke-On-Trent
Staffordshire ST4 2DE
Tel: 01782 294770/294809
Fax: 01782 744035
Contact: Art & Design Librarian

Sunderland

City Library and Art Centre

Fawcett Street
Sunderland SR1 1RE
Tel: 0191-514 1235
Fax: 0191-514 8444
Contact: Librarian

Sunderland University Library

Langham Tower
Ryhope Road
Sunderland SR2 7EE

Tel: 0191 515 2900
Fax: 0191 515 2423
Contact: Librarian

Sutton

Sutton Central Library
Music and Arts Department
St Nicholas Way
Sutton
Surrey SM1 1EA
Tel: 020 8770 4764/5
Fax: 020 8770 4777
Contact: Information Manager
(Recreation)

Swansea

Swansea Institute of Higher Education Library
Townhill Road
Swansea SA2 OUT
Tel: 01792 481000
Fax: 01792 298017
email: enquiry@sihe.ac.uk
Website: www.sihe.ac.uk
Contact: Librarian
Resources: B, C, E

Warrington

Warrington Collegiate Institute
Faculty of Higher Education
The Library, Padgate Campus
Crab Lane, Warrington WA2 ODB
Tel: 01925 494284
email: l.crewe@warr.ac.uk
Website: www.warr.ac.uk
Lorna Crewe, Deputy College
Librarian

Winchester

King Alfred's College Library
Sparkford Road, Winchester
Hampshire SO22 4NR
Tel: 01962 827306
Fax: 01962 827443
Website: www.wkac.ac.uk/
Contact: Librarian

Winchester School of Art
Park Avenue, Winchester
Hampshire SO23 8DL
Tel: 02380 596941
Fax: 02380 596901
email: wsaenqs@soton.ac.uk
Website: www.soton.ac.uk/
Contact: Head of Library and
Information Services
Resources: B, E

Wolverhampton

Light House
Media Reference Library
The Chubb Buildings
Fryer Street
Wolverhampton WV1 1HT
Tel: 01902 716055
Fax: 01902 717143
email: info@light-house.co.uk
Website: www.light-house.co.uk
Contact Library: Librarian
Publicity and Information Officer:
Emma Baghan
Chief Executive: Frank Challenger
Resources: A, B, E, F
 Scripts, pressbooks

Wolverhampton Libraries and Information Services
Central Library
Snow Hill
Wolverhampton WV1 3AX
Tel: 01902 312 025
Fax: 01902 714 579
Contact: Librarian
Resources: B, D

Wolverhampton University
Art and Law Library
54 Stafford Street
Wolverhampton WV1 3AX
Tel: 01902 321597
Fax: 01902 322668
Contact: Art and Design Librarian

Wolverhampton University
Dudley Learning Centre
University of Wolverhampton
Castle View
Dudley
West Midlands DY1 3BQ
Tel: 01902 323 560
Fax: 01902 323 354
Website: www.wolverhampton.ac.uk
Learning Centre Manager
Resources: A, B, C, D, E

York

College of Ripon and York St John Library
Lord Mayors Walk
York YO3 7EX
Tel: 01904 616700
Fax: 01904 612512
email: library@ucrysj.ac.uk
Website: www.ucrysj.ac.uk/library
Contact: Librarian
Resources: B, C, D, E,

ORGANISATIONS

Listed below are the main trade/government organisations and bodies relevant to the film and television industries in the UK. This is followed by a separate list of Regional Film Commissions. Finally, a small selection of organisations from the US concludes this section

ABC (Association of Business Communicators)
1 West Ruislip Station
Ruislip
Middx HA4 7DW
Tel: 01895 622 401
Fax: 01895 631 219
Roger Saunders
Trade association of professionals providing the highest standards of audiovisual/video equipment/services for use in corporate communication

AC Nielsen EDI
Sixth Floor, Endeavour House
189 Shaftsbury Avenue
London WC2H 8TJ
Tel: 020 7170 5200
Fax: 020 7170 5201
Website: www.entdata.com

ACCS (Association for Cultural and Communication Studies)
Dept of Literature & Languages
Nottingham Trent University
Clifton Site
Nottingham NG11 8NS
Tel: 0115 941 8418 x3289
Fax: 0115 948 6632
Georgia Stone
Provides a professional forum for teachers and researchers in Media, Film, Television and Cultural Studies in both further and higher education

Advertising Association
Abford House
15 Wilton Road
London SW1V 1NJ
Tel: 020 7828 2771/828 4831
Fax: 020 7931 0376
email: aa@adassoc.org.uk
Website: www.adassoc.org.uk
Andrew Brown
A federation of 26 trade associations and professional bodies representing advertisers, agencies, the advertising media and support services. It is the central organisation for the UK advertising business, on British and European legislative proposals and other issues of common concern, both at national and international levels, and as such campaigns actively to maintain the freedom to advertise and to improve public attitudes to advertising. It publishes UK and European statistics on advertising expenditure, instigates research on advertising issues and organises seminars and courses for people in the communications business. Its Information Centre is one of the country's leading sources for advertising and associated subjects

Advertising Producers' Association (APA)
26 Noel Street
London W1V 3RD
Tel: 020 7434 2651
Fax: 020 7434 9002
email: info@a-p-a.net
Website: www.a-p-a.net
Stephen Davies, Chief Executive
The APA represents production companies making TV and cinema commercials. It regulates agreements with agencies and with crew and provides a telephone advice service on production and legal matters and other services for members

Advertising Standards Authority (ASA)
Brook House
2 Torrington Place
London WC1E 7HW
Tel: 020 7580 5555
Fax: 020 7631 3051
Website: www.asa.org.uk

AFMA Europe
49 Littleton Road
Harrow
Middx HA1 3SY
Tel: 020 8423 0763
Fax: Tel: 020 8423 7963
email: lsafir@afma.com
Website: www.afma.com
Chairman: Lawrence Safir

AIM (All Industry Marketing for Cinema)
22 Golden Square
London W1F 9JW
Tel: 020 7437 4383
Fax: 020 7734 0912
email: sfd@sfd.demon.co.uk
Peter Dobson
Unites distribution, exhibition and cinema advertising in promoting cinema and cinema-going. Funds Film Education, holds Cinema Days for regional journalists, markets cinema for sponsorship and promotional ventures and is a forum for cinema marketing ideas. In 2001, AIM and the Film Council jointly established the Cinema Marketing Agency with a remit to increase and broaden further the UK cinema audience

Amalgamated Engineering and Electrical Union (AEEU)
Hayes Court,
West Common Road,
Bromley,
Kent BR2 7AU
Tel: 020 8462 7755
Fax: 020 8462 4959
Website: www.aeeu.org.uk
Trade union representing - among others -people employed in film and TV lighting/electrical/electronic work

AMCCS (Association for Media, Cultural and Communication Studies)
Media and Cultural Studies
Middlesex University
Trent Park
Bramley Road
London N14 4XS
Tel: 020 8362 5065
Fax: 020 8362 5791

AMPS (Association of Motion Picture Sound)
28 Knox Street
London W1H 1FS
Tel: 020 7723 6727
Fax: 020 7723 6727
Website: www.amps.net
Brian Hickin
Promotes and encourages science, technology and creative application

of all aspects of motion picture sound recording and reproduction, and seeks to promote and enhance the status of those therein engaged

APRS - The Professional Recording Association

PO Box 22
Totnes
Devon TQ9 7YZ
Tel: 01803 868600
Fax: 01803 868444
email: info@aprs.co.uk
Website: www.aprs.co.uk
Peter Filleul, Acting Executive Director
Represents the interests of the professional sound recording industry, including radio, TV and audio studios and companies providing equipment and services in the field. The Recording Technology exhibition ran at the Business Design Centre in June 2000

Arts Council of England

14 Great Peter Street
London SW1P 3NQ
Tel: 020 7333 0100
Fax: 020 7973 6590
email: enquiries@artscouncil.org.uk
Website: www.artscouncil.org.uk
David Curtis, Gary Thomas
ACE has lead responsibility in England for artists' film and video and for large scale captial projects relating to film

Arts Council of Wales

9 Museum Place
Cardiff CF10 3NX
Tel: 029 20 376500
Fax: 029 20 395284
email: information@ccc-acw.org.uk
Website: www.ccc-acw.org.uk
Anneli Jones or Kath Davies, Lottery Unit

ASIFA

International Animated Film Association
94 Norton Gardens
London SW16 4TA
Tel: 020 8681 8988
Fax: 020 8688 1441
Pat Raine Webb
A worldwide association of individuals who work in, or make a contribution to, the animation industry, including students. Activities include involvement in UK and international events and festivals, an Employment Databank, Animation Archive, children's workshops. The UK group provides

an information service to members and a news magazine

Association for Media Education in Scotland (AMES)

c/o Scottish Screen
249 West George Street
Glasgow G2 4QE
Tel: 01224 481976
email: d@murphy47.freeserve.co.uk
Website: www.ames.org.uk
Robert Preece

Audio Visual Association

Herkomer House
156 High Street
Bushey
Herts WD2 3DD
Tel: 020 8950 5959
Fax: 020 8950 7560
email: multimedia@visual-arena.co.uk
Website: www.visual-arena.co.uk
Mike Simpson FBIPP
The Audio Visual Association is a Special Interest Group within the British Institute of Professional Photography. With the Institute's current thinking of lateral representation within all categories of imaging and imaging technology, the AVA represents those individuals involved in the various disciplines of audiovisual

Australian Film Commission (AFC)

Level 4, 150 William Street
Woolloomooloo 201
99-101 Regent Street
London W1R 7HB
Tel: (61) 2 9321 6444
Fax: (61) 2 9357 3631
email: marketing@afc.gov.au
Website: www.afc.gov.au/
Pressanna Vasudevan
The AFC is a statutory authority established in 1975 to assist the development, production and distribution of Australian films. The European marketing branch services producers and buyers, advises on co-productions and financing, and promotes the industry at markets and through festivals

Authors' Licensing & Collecting Society

Marlborough Court
14-18 Holborn
London EC1 N 2LE
Tel: 020 7395 0600
Fax: 020 7395 0660
email: alcs@alcs.co.uk

Website: www.alcs.co.uk
The ALCS is the British collecting society for all writers. Its principal purpose is to ensure that hard-to-collect revenues due to authors are efficiently collected and speedily distributed. These include the simultaneous cable retransmission of the UK's terrestrial and various international channels, educational off-air recording and BBC Prime. Contact the ALCS office for more information

BAFTA (British Academy of Film and Television Arts)

195 Piccadilly
London W1V OLN
Tel: 020 7734 0022
Fax: 020 7734 1792
Website: www.bafta.org
John Morrell
BAFTA was formed in 1947 by Britain's most eminent filmmakers as a non-profit making company. It occupies a pivotal, unique position in the industry with a clear aim to promote excellence in film, television and interactive entertainment. BAFTA is a diverse organisation: it is a charity and a members' club; it undertakes a number of educational and training activities (including scholarships and workshops) and has an active and successful trading arm. Membership is available to those who have a minimum of three years professional experience in the film, television or interactive entertainment industries (or any combination of these), who are able to demonstrate significant contribution to the industry. BAFTA has facilities for screenings, conferences, seminars and discussion meetings. Its awards for film and television are annual televised events. There are also awards for children's' programming and interactive entertainment. The Academy has branches in Manchester, Glasgow, Cardiff, Los Angeles and New York

BARB (Broadcasters' Audience Research Board)

2nd Floor
18 Dering Street
London W1R 9AF
Tel: 020 7529 5531
Fax: 020 7529 5530
Website: www.barb.co.uk
The main source of television audience research in the United Kingdom is supplied by BARB

(Broadcasters Audience Research Board Limited). The company represents the major UK broadcasters, the British Broadcasting Corporation (BBC), the Independent Television Association (ITVA), Channels 4 and 5, BSkyB and The Institute of Practitioners in Advertising (IPA). BARB was created in August 1980 when the BBC and ITV decided to have a mutually agreed source of television audience research. BARB became operational in August 1981

BECTU (Broadcasting Entertainment Cinematograph and Theatre Union)

111 Wardour Street
London W1V 4AY
Tel: 020 7437 8506
Fax: 020 7437 8268
email: info@bectu.org.uk
Website: www.bectu.org.uk
General Secretary: Roger Bolton
Press Officer: Janice Turner
BECTU is the UK trade union for workers in film, broadcasting and the arts. Formed in 1991 by the merger of the ACTT and BETA, the union is 30,000 strong and represents permanently employed and freelance staff in television, radio, film, cinema, theatre and entertainment. BECTU provides a comprehensive industrial relations service based on agreements with the BBC, ITV companies, Channel 4, PACT, AFVPA and MFVPA, Odeon, MGM, Apollo, Society of Film Distributors, National Screen Services, independent exhibitors and the BFI itself. Outside film and television, the union has agreements with the national producing theatres and with the Theatrical Management Association, the Society of London Theatres and others

BKSTS - The Moving Image Society

63-71 Victoria House
Vernon Place
London WC1B 4DF
Tel: 020 7242 8400
Fax: 020 7405 3560
email: movimage@bksts.demon.co.uk
Website: www.bksts.com
Executive Director: John Graham
Formed in 1931, the BKSTS is the technical society for film, television and associated industries. A wide range of training courses and

seminars are organised with special rates for members. The society produces many publications including a monthly journal Image Technology and a quarterly Cinema Technology both free to members. Corporate members must have sufficient qualifications and experience, however student and associate grades are also available. Biennial conference has become a platform for new products and developments from all over the world. The BKSTS also has a college accreditation scheme and currently accredits 9 courses within the HE + FE sector

BREMA (British Radio & Electronic Equipment Manufacturers' Association)

Landseer House
19 Charing Cross Road
London WC2H 0ES
Tel: 020 7930 3206
Fax: 020 7839 4613
Trade association for British consumer electronics industry

British Academy of Composers and Songwriters

2nd Floor
British Music House
26 Berners Street
London W1T 3KR
Tel: 020 7636 2929
Fax: 020 7636 2212
email: info@britishacademy.com
Website: www.britishacademy.com
Julian Lancaster
The Academy represents the interests of music writers across all genres, providing advice on professional and artistic matters. The Academy publishes a quarterly magazine and administers a number of major events including the Ivor Novello Awards

British Actors Equity Association

Guild House
Upper St Martin's Lane
London WC2H 9EG
Tel: 020 7379 6000
Fax: 020 7379 7001
email: info@equity.org.uk
Website: www.equity.org.uk
General Secretary: Ian McGarry
Equity was formed in 1930 by professional performers to achieve solutions to problems of casual

employment and short-term engagements. Equity has 40,000 members, and represents performers (other than musicians), stage managers, stage directors, stage designers and choreographers in all spheres of work in the entertainment industry. It negotiates agreements on behalf of its members with producers' associations and other employers. In some fields of work only artists with previous professional experience are normally eligible for work. Membership of Equity is treated as evidence of professional experience under these agreements. It publishes Equity Journal four times a year

British Amateur Television Club (BATC)

Grenehurst
Pinewood Road
High Wycombe
Bucks HP12 4DD
Tel: 01494 528899
email: memsec@batc.org.uk
Website: www.batc.org.uk
Non-profit making organisation run entirely by volunteers. BATC publish a quarterly technical publication CQ-TV which is available via subscription

British Board of Film Classification (BBFC)

3 Soho Square
London W1D 3HD
Tel: 020 7440 1570
Fax: 020 7287 0141
email: webmaster@bbfc.co.uk
Website: www.bbfc.co.uk
Under the 1909 Cinematograph Films Act, local authorities were made responsible for safety in cinemas and also for what was shown. In 1912, the British Board of Film Censors was set up by the film industry to establish uniformity in film classification across the UK. The British Board of Film Censors became the British Board of Film Classification in 1985. The Board classifies films on behalf of local authorities and films cannot be shown in public in the UK unless they have a BBFC certificate or the relevant local authorisation. Local Authorities can, and sometimes do, overrule BBFC classification decisions. The Video Recordings Act 1984 requires that videos and video games which come under the Act must carry a BBFC classification if they are sold or rented in the UK. The BBFC is funded entirely from the fees charged for classification.

The Board classifies works using a published set of Guidelines (available on the BBFC website) which are the result of extensive research and public consultation. In addition, the Board must have regard to relevant legislation. The Video Recordings Act requires the BBFC to have special regard to the likelihood of works being viewed in the home, and to any harm to those likely to view a video and any harm to society through the behaviour of those viewers afterwards.

The classification categories are as follows:

'U' - UNIVERSAL. Suitable for all.

'Uc'- UNIVERSAL. Videos which are particularly suitable for young children.

'PG' - PARENTAL GUIDANCE. Suitable for children of eight or over, but some scenes may be unsuitable for small children.

'12' - Suitable only for persons of 12 years and over (introduced on video 1st July 1994)

'15' - Suitable only for persons of 15 years and over.

'18' - Suitable only for persons of 18 years and over.

'R18' - FOR RESTRICTED DISTRIBUTION ONLY, Videos which are only available through licensed sex shops and available to persons of 18 and over

British Broadcasting Corporation (BBC)

Television Centre
Wood Lane
London W12 7RJ
Tel: 020 8743 8000
Website: www.bbc.co.uk

The BBC provides two national television networks, five national radio networks, as well as local radio and regional radio and television services. They are funded through the Licence Fee. The BBC is a public corporation, set up in 1927 by Royal Charter. Government proposals for the future of the BBC were published in a White Paper in July 1994. The BBC also broadcasts overseas through World Service Radio and Worldwide Television, but these are not funded through the Licence Fee

British Copyright Council

29-33 Berners Street
London W1P 4AA
Tel: 01986 788 122
Fax: 01986 788847

Janet Ibbotson

Provides liaison between societies which represent the interest of those who own copyright in literature, music, drama and works of art, making representation to Government on behalf of its member societies

The British Council

Films and Television Department
11 Portland Place
London W1B 1EJ
Tel: 020 7389 3065
Fax: 020 7389 3041
Website: www.britfilms.com

The British Council is an independent, non-political organisation with offices in 110 countries, operating in the fields of arts and culture, education, science and English teaching. The main purpose of the work in film and television is to broaden and build international audiences – particularly among young people – for new work from Britain. To do this there is a core team of sector specialists with critical skills, a wide knowledge of contemporary British cinema and personal relationships with a range of film industry professionals around the world. The British Council works closely with a large number of festivals, markets and showcase events and are a co-funder with the Film Council, Scottish Screen, PACT and others of the British Film Office in Los Angeles

British Design & Art Direction (D&AD)

9 Graphite Square
Vauxhall Walk
London SE11 5EE
Tel: 020 7840 1111
Fax: 020 7840 0840
email: info@dandad.co.uk
Website: www.dandad.org
Marcelle Johnson, Marketing Director

A professional association, registered as a charity, which publishes an annual of the best of British and international design, advertising, television commercials and videos, and organises travelling exhibitions. Professional awards, student awards, education programme, lectures. Membership details are available on request

British Educational Communications and Technology Agency (Becta)

Milburn Hill Road
Science Park

University of Warwick
Coventry CV4 7JJ
Tel: 024 7641 6994
Fax: 024 7641 1418
email: Becta@becta.org.uk
Website: www.becta.org.uk

The British Educational Communications and Technology Agency [Becta] is the Government's lead agency for ICT in education. Becta supports the UK Government and national organisations in the use and development of ICT in education to raise standards, widen access, improve skills and encourage effective management. Becta works in partnership to develop the National Grid for Learning strategy

British Federation of Film Societies (BFFS)

The Ritz Building
Mount Pleasant Campus
Swansea Institute of Higher Education
Swansea SA1 6ED
Tel: 01792 481170
email: info@bffs.org.uk
Website: www.bffs.co.uk

The BFFS exists to promote the work of some 300 film societies in the UK

British Film Commission

10 Little Portland Street
London W1W 7JG
Tel: 020 7861 7860
Fax: 020 7861 7864
email: info@bfc.co.uk
Website: www.bfc.co.uk

Originally established in 1991, The BFC is now a division of the Film Council, funded through the department of Culture, Media and Sport. Its remit is to attract inward investment by promoting the UK as an international production centre to the film and television industries and encouraging the use of Britain's locations, services, facilities and personnel. Working with the UK Screen Commission Network, the BFC also provides a bespoke information service to producers worldwide and assists those filming in the UK both before and during the shoot

British Film Designers Guild

24 St Anslem's Place
London W1Y 1FG
Tel: 020 7499 4336
Fax: 020 7499 4336

Promotes and encourages activities of all members of the art department. Full availability and information service open to all producers

British Film Institute
21 Stephen Street
London W1P 2LN
Tel: 020 7255 1444
Fax: 020 7436 7950
Website: www.bfi.org.uk
Jon Teckman, Director
Founded in 1933, the BFI was
incorporated by Royal Charter in
1983; it is the UK national agency with
responsibility for encouraging the arts
of film and television and conserving
them in the national interest

**British Institute of
Professional Photography**
Fox Talbot House
Amwell End , Ware
Herts SG12 9HN
Tel: 01920 464011
Fax: 01920 487056
Website: www.bipp.com
Company Secretary: Alex Mair
The qualifying body for professional
photography and photographic
processing. Members represent
specialisations in the fields of
photography, both stills and moving
images

**British Interactive
Multimedia Association Ltd**
5/6 Clipstone Street
London W1P 7EB
Tel: 020 7436 8250
Fax: 020 7436 8251
email: enquiries@bima.co.uk
Website: www.bima.co.uk
Janice Cable, Administrator

**The British Phonographic
Industry Ltd (BPI)**
25 Savile Row
London W1S 2ES
Tel: 020 7851 4000
Fax: 020 7851 4010
email: general@bpi.co.uk
Website: www.bpi.co.uk
Andrew Yeates, Director General
The BPI is the industry association
for record companies in the UK. It
represents over 240 record companies
from small independent labels to
multinational companies. It protects
rights, fights piracy and promotes
export opportunities. Brit Awards Ltd
(which stages the BRITAwards and
classical BRITS is a wholly owned
subsidiary of the BPI). Information
service available

**British Recording Media
Association**
Ambassador House

Brigstock Road
Thornton Heath CR7 7JG
Tel: 020 8665 5395
Fax: 020 8665 6447
email:rma@admin.co.uk
Trade association for the
manufacturers of blank audio and
videotape

**British Screen Advisory
Council (BSAC)**
19 Cavendish Square
London W1M 9AB
Tel: 020 7499 4177
Fax: 020 7306 0329
email:bsac@bsacouncil.co.uk
Director: Fiona Clarke-Hackston,
Chairman: David Elstein
Events & Communications Officer:
Anna Pottle
BSAC is an independent, advisory
body to government and policy
makers at national and European
level. It is a source of information
and research for the screen media
industries. BSAC provides a unique
forum for the audio visual industry
to discuss major issues which effect
the industry. Its membership
embraces senior management from
all aspects of television, film, and
video. BSAC regularly commissions
and oversees research on the audio
visual industry and uses this research
to underpin its policy documents. In
addition to regular monthly
meetings, BSAC organises
conferences, seminars, industry
briefings and an annual reception in
Brussels. BSAC is industry funded

**British Screen Development
(BSD)**
14-17 Wells Mews
London W1P 3FL
Tel: 020 7323 9080
Fax: 020 7323 0092
Head of Development: Jenny
Borgours
BSD makes loans for the
development of British and European
cinema feature films. Films such as
Photographing Fairies; Wilde; Before
the Rain; Antonia's Line; Land and
Freedom; Rob Roy; House of
America; The Tango Lesson; Jilting
Joe. It has a two-tier loan system:
screenplay loans for new writers;
development loans for production
companies to pay writers, and
ancillary costs. BSD also part-
finances, administers and oversees the
production of a variety of short films
around the country. In 1999 some 15

short films will be commissioned
with budgets of around £25,000. In
Europe, BSD supports and sponsors
candidates through the SOURCES,
ACE and ARISTA programmes

**British Society of
Cinematographers (BSC)**
11 Croft Road
Chalfont St Peter
Gerrards Cross
Bucks SL9 9AE
Tel: 01753 888052
Fax: 01753 891486
email: BritCinematographers@
compuserve.com
Website: www.bscine.com
Frances Russell
Promotes and encourages the pursuit
of the highest standards in the craft
of motion picture photography.
Publishes a Newsletter and the BSC
Directory

Broadcasting Press Guild
Tiverton
The Ridge
Woking
Surrey GU22 7EQ
Tel: 01483 764895 or 0208 624 9052
Fax: 01483 765882 or 0208 624 9096
email: torin.douglas@bbc.co.uk
Joint Secretary: Richard Last, Torin
Douglas
An association of journalists who
specialise in writing about the media
in the national, regional and trade
press. Membership by invitation.
Monthly lunches with leading
industry figures as guests. Annual
Television and Radio Awards voted
for by members

Broadcasting Research Unit
VLV Librarian
101 King's Drive
Gravesend
Kent DA12 5BQ
Tel: 01474 352835
Fax: 01474 351112
The Broadcasting Research Unit was
an independent Trust researching all
aspects of broadcasting, development
and technologies, which operated
from 1980-1991. Its publications and
research are now available from the
above address

**Broadcasting Standards
Commission**
7 The Sanctuary
London SW1P 3JS
Tel: 020 7808 1000
Fax: 020 7233 0397
email: bsc@bsc.org.uk

Website: www.bsc.org.uk
Donna Moinian, Communications
Director
Chairman: Lord Dubbs of Battersea
Deputy Chairs: Jane Leighton and
Lady Suzanne Warner
Director: Stephen Whittle
The Broadcasting Standards
Commission is the statutory body for
both standards and fairness in
broadcasting. It is the only
organisation within the regulatory
framework of UK broadcasting to
cover all television and radio. This
includes BBC and commercial
broadcasters as well as text, cable,
satellite and digital services. As an
independent organisation
representing the interests of the
consumer, the Broadcasting
Standards Commission considers the
portrayal of violence, sexual conduct
and matters of taste and decency. As
an alternative to a court of law, it
provides redress for people who
believe they have been unfairly
treated or subjected to unwarranted
infringement of privacy. The
Commission has three main tasks
which are set out in the 1996
Broadcasting Act: - produces codes of
practice relating to standards and
fairness; considers and adjudicates on
complaints; monitors, researches and
reports on standards and fairness in
broadcasting. The Commission does
not have the power to preview or to
censor broadcasting

BUFVC (British Universities Film and Video Council)
77 Wells Street
London W1T 3QJ
Tel: 020 7393 1500
Fax: 020 7393 1555
email: ask@bufvc.ac.uk
Website: www.bufvc.ac.uk
Luke McKernan, Head of
Information
The BUFVC exists to promote the
production, study and use of moving
images and related media for higher
and further education and research in
the UK. It maintains an information
service with a number of on-line
databases: AVANCE (audio-visual
programmes of use of higher and
further education in UK
distribution), Television Index
(selected British television
programmes since 1995 - this will be
replaced by the far more extensive
Television and
Radio Index for Learning and

Teaching in 2002), British Universities
Newsreel Project Database (data on
160,000 British cinema newsreel
stories), the Researcher's Guide
Online (moving image and sound
research collections in the UK and
Ireland) and the Moving Image
Gateway (websites relating to the use
of moving images and sound in
education). The BUFVC also
organises regular courses on the
issues relating to the use of moving
images and sound in learning and
teaching, conferences, and its unique
Off-Air Recording Back-up Service
(open to all member institutions with
an Educational Recording Agency
licence)

BVA (British Video Association)
167 Great Portland Street
London W1 5FD
Tel: 020 7436 0041
Fax: 020 7436 0043
email: general@bva.org.uk
Website: www.bva.org.uk/
Lavinia Carey
Represents, promotes and protects
the collective rights of its members
who produce and/or distribute video
cassettes for rental and sale to the
public

Cable Communications Association
5th Floor
Artillery House
Artillery Row
London SW1P 1RT
Tel: 020 7222 2900
Fax: 020 7799 1471
Chief Executive: Bob Frost
Represents the interests of cable
operators, installers, programme
providers and equipment suppliers.
For further information on cable, see
under Cable and Satellite

Campaign for Press and Broadcasting Freedom
8 Cynthia Street
London N1 9JF
Tel: 020 7278 4430
Fax: 020 7837 8868
email: cpbf@aritechs.com
Website: www.architechs.com/cpbf
A broad-based membership organisation campaigning for more diverse,
accessible and accountable media in
Britain, backed by the trade union
movement. The CPBF was established
in 1979. The mail order catalogue is
regularly updated and includes books

on all aspects of the media from
broadcasting policy to sexism; its bi-
monthly journal Free Press examines
current ethical, industrial and
political developments in media
policy and practice. CPBF acts as a
parliamentary lobby group on
censorship and media reform.

Celtic Film and Television Festival Company
1 Bowmont Gardens
Glasgow G12 9LR
Tel: 0141 342 4947
Fax: 0141 342 4948
email: mail@celticfilm.co.uk
Frances Hendron
Organises an annual competitive
festival/conference, itinerant
Scotland, Ireland, Cornwall, Wales
and Brittany in March/April.
Supports the development of
television and film in Celtic nations
and indigenous languages

Central Office of Information (COI)
Films and Video
Hercules Road
London SE1 7DU
Tel: 020 7261 8495
Fax: 020 7261 8877
Ian Hamilton
COI Films and Video is responsible for
government filmmaking on
informational themes. The COI
organises the production of a wide
range of TV commercials and trailers,
documentary films, video programmes
and CD ROMs. It uses staff producers,
and draws on the film and video
industry for production facilities

CFL Vision
PO Box 35
Wetherby
Yorks LS23 7EX
Tel: 01937 541010
Fax: 01937 541083
email: euroview@compuserve.com
CFL Vision is one of the oldest
established video library operations
in the UK. It is part of the Central
Office of Information and distributes
their video and CD ROM productios,
as well as programmes acquired from
both public and private sectors. Over
200 titles are available for loan or
purchase by small businesses,
industry, local authorities and
schoolsWebsite: www.euroview.co.uk

Chart Information Network
3rd Floor
Century House

100 Oxford Street
London W1N 9FB
Tel: 020 7436 3000
Fax: 020 7436 8000
Supplies BVA members with detailed sales information on the sell-through video market. Markets and licenses the Official Retail Video Charts for broadcasting and publishing around the world

Children's Film and Television Foundation (CFTF)

Elstree Film Studios
Borehamwood
Herts WD6 1JG
Tel: 020 8953 0844
Fax: 020 8953 1113
email: annahome@cftf.onyxnet.co.uk
Anna Home, Chief Executive
In 1944 Lord Rank founded the Children's Entertainment Film Division to make films specifically for children. In 1951 this resulted in the setting up of the Children's Film Foundation (now CFTF), a non-profit making organisation which, up to 1981, was funded by an annual grant from the BFFA (Eady money). The CFTF no longer makes films from its own resources but, for suitable children's/family cinema/television projects, is prepared to consider financing script development for eventual production by commercial companies. Films from the Foundation's library are available for hiring at nominal charge in 35mm, 16mm and video format

Church of England Communications Unit

Church House
Great Smith Street
London SW1P 3NZ
Tel: 020 7222 9011 x356/7
Fax: 020 7222 6672
Rev Jonathan Jennings
(Out of office hours: 0171 222 9233)
Responsible for liaison between the Church of England and the broadcasting and film industries. Advises the C of E on all matters relating to broadcasting

Cinema Advertising Association (CAA)

12 Golden Square
London W13 3AF
Tel: 020 7534 6363
Fax: 020 7534 6464
Website: www.adassoc.org.uk
Bruce Koster

The CAA is a trade association of cinema advertising contractors operating in the UK and Eire. First established as a separate organisation in 1953 as the Screen Advertising Association, its main purpose is to promote, monitor and maintain standards of cinema advertising exhibition including the pre-vetting of commercials. It also commissions and conducts research into cinema as an advertising medium, and is a prime sponsor of the CAVIAR annual surveys

Cinema and Television Veterans

Elanda House
9 The Weald
Ashford
Kent TN24 8RA
Tel: 01233 639967
An association open to all persons employed in the United Kingdom or by United Kingdom companies in the cinema and/or broadcast television industries in any capacity other than as an artiste, for a total of at least thirty years

Cinema Exhibitors' Association (CEA)

22 Golden Square
London W1R 3PA
Tel: 020 7734 9551
Fax: 020 7734 6147
email: cea@cinemauk.ftech.co.uk
John Wilkinson
The first branch of the CEA in the industry was formed in 1912 and consisted of cinema owners. Following a merger with the Association of Independent Cinemas (AIC) it became the only association representing cinema exhibition. CEA members account for the vast majority of UK commercial cinemas, including independents, Regional Film Theatres and cinemas in local authority ownership. The CEA represents members' interests - within the industry and to local, national and European Government. It is closely involved with legislation (current and proposed) emanating from the UK Government and the European Commission which affects exhibition

Cinema & Television Benevolent Fund (CTBF)

22 Golden Square
London W1F 9AD
Tel: 020 7437 6567
Fax: 020 7437 7186
email: infor@ctbf.co.uk

Website: www.ctbf.co.uk
Sandra Bradley
The CTBF is a trade fund which offers caring help, support and financial assistance, to all staff, at all levels, salaried, freelance or retired, with 2 years work 'behind the camera' in the British film, cinema, commercial television, cable, satellite or affiliated industries. Information pack is available on request

Cinema Marketing Agency

(See AIM and Film Council)
In 2001, AIM and the Film Council jointly established the Cinema Marketing Agency with a remit to increase and broaden further the UK cinema audience

Cinema Theatre Association

44 Harrowdene Gardens
Teddington
Middx TW11 0DJ
Tel: 020 8977 2608
Website: www.cinema-theatre.org.uk
Adam Unger
The Cinema Theatre Association was formed in 1967 to promote interest in Britain's cinema building legacy, in particular the magnificent movie palaces of the 1920s and 1930s. It is the only major organisation committed to cinema preservation in the UK. It campaigns for the protection of architecturally important cinemas and runs a comprehensive archive. The CTA publishes a bi-monthly bulletin and the magazine Picture House

Cinergy

Minema Cinema
45 Knightsbridge
London SW1X 7NL
Tel: 020 7235 4226
Fax: 020 7235 3426
Creative Director: Nick Walker
Co-ordinatior: Damian Spandley
Multimeidator: Nick Perry
Cinergy is a multimedia cabaret club with a special emphasis on short films. It is open to the public and welcomes submissions from filmmakers on all formats and with high, low or no budgets.

Comataidh Craolaidh Gaidhlig (Gaelic Broadcasting Committee)

4 Harbour View, Cromwell Street
Stornoway
Isle of Lewis HSI 2DF
Tel: 01851 705550
Fax: 01851 706432

email: admin@ccg.org.uk
Website: www.ccg.org.uk
John A. Mackay
The Gaelic Television Fund and
Comataidh Telebhisein Gaidhlig was
set up under the provisions of the
Broadcasting Act 1990. Funds made
available by the Government were to
be paid to the ITC for the credit of
the fund to be known as the Gaelic
Television Fund. The Fund was to be
managed by the body known as the
Gaelic Television Committee. Under
the Broadcasting Act 1996 the Gaelic
Television Fund was redesignated as
the Gaelic Broadcasting Fund and the
Gaelic Television Committee became
the Gaelic Broadcasting Committee

Commonwealth Broadcasting Association

17 Fleet Street
London EC4 1AA
Tel: 020 7583 5550
Fax: 020 7583 5549
email: cba@cba.org.uk
Website: www.cba.org.uk
Elizabeth Smith, Secretary General
An association of 93 public service
broadcasting organisations in 55
Commonwealth countries, supporting
quality broadcasting through training,
consultancies, conferences magazine
and the exchange of information

Critics' Circle

Critics' Circle
4 Alwyne Villas
London N1 2HQ
Tel: 020 7226 2726
Fax: 020 7354 2574
Chairman: Christopher Tookey
Vice-Chairman: John Marriott
Hon. Secretary: Tom Hutchinson
Hon. Treasurer: Peter Cargin
The film section of the Critics' Circle
brings together leading national
critics for meetings, functions and the
presentation of annual awards

Deaf Broadcasting Council

70 Blacketts Wood Drive
Chorleywood, Rickmansworth
Herts WD3 5QQ
Tel: 01923 284538
Fax: 01923 283127
email: rmyers@waitrose.com
Website: deafbroadcastcouncil.org.uk
Ruth Meyers
An umbrella organisation working to
ensure TV broadcasters are aware of
the needs of deaf and hard of hearing

Defence Press and Broadcasting Advisory Committee

Room 104
Ministry of Defence
Metropole Building
London WC2N 5BP
Tel: 020 7218 2206
Fax: 020 7218 5857
Website: www.dnotice.org.uk
Secretary: Rear Admiral Nick
Wilkinson
The Committee is made up of senior
officials from the Ministry of
Defence, the Home Office and the
Foreign & Commonwealth Office and
representatives of the media. It issues
guidance, in the form of DA Notices,
on the publication of information
which it regards as sensitive for
reasons of national security

Department for Culture, Media and Sport - Media Division (Films)

2-4 Cockspur Street
London SW1Y 5DH
Tel: 020 7721 6000
Fax: 020 7711 6249
Website: www.culture.gov.uk
Contacts:
For BFI, British Screen Finance
(BSF), European Co-production fund
(ECPF): Craig McFarlane
Tel:020 7211 6429
For Enquiries concerning film which
might be made under UK Co-
production Agreements: Diana
Brown
Tel: 020 7211 6433
For MEDIA Programme, British Film
Commission (BFC), National Film
and Television School (NFTS) and
Audiovisual Eureka (AVE): Peter
Doogan
Tel: 020 7211 6435
Statistics and Social Policy Unit
Tracy Dalby
Tel: 020 7211 6395
The Department for Culture Media
and Sport is responsible for
Government policy on film, relations
with the film industry and
Government funding for: the British
Film Institute, British Screen Finance,
the European Co-Production Fund
(administered by British Screen
Finance), the British Film
Commission and the National Film
and Television School. It is also
responsible for Government policy
on and contribution to, the EC Media
Programme and Audiovisual Eureka.

It also acts as the UK competent
authority for administering the UK's
seven bilateral co-production
agreements and the European Co-
production Convention

Department for Education and Employment (DFEE)

Sanctuary Buildings
Great Smith Street
London SW1P 3BT
Tel: 020 7925 5000
Fax: 020 7925 6000
email: info@dfee.gov.uk
Website: www.dfee.gov.uk
Public enquiries: 0171 925 5555
The DFE is responsible for policies
for education in England and the
Government's relations with
universities in England, Scotland and
Wales

The Directors' and Producers' Rights Society

15-19 Great Titchfield Street
London W1P 7FB
Tel: 020 7631 1077
Fax: 020 7631 1019
email: dprs@dial.pipex.com
Suzan Dormer
The Directors' and Producers' Rights
Society is a collecting society which
administers authorials rights
payments on behalf of British film
and television Directors

Directors' Guild of Great Britain

Acorn House
314-320 Gray's Inn Road
London WC1X 8DP
Tel: 020 77278 4343
Fax: 020 7278 4742
email: guild@dggb.co.uk
Website: www.dggb.co.uk
Sarah Wain
Represents interests and concerns of
directors in all media. Publishes
regular magazine DIRECT

European Captioning Institute

Thurston House
80 Lincoln Road
Peterborough PE1 2SN
Tel: 0207 323 4657
Fax: 0207 323 4658

Federation Against Copyright Theft (FACT)

7 Victory Business Centre
Worton Road
Isleworth
Middx TW7 6DB
Tel: 020 8568 6646

Fax: 020 8560 6364
R Dixon, Director General
DNL Lowe, Company Secretary
FACT, Federation Against Copyright Theft, is an investigative organisation funded by its members to combat counterfeiting, piracy and misuse of their products. The members of FACT are major companies in the British and American film, video and television industries. FACT is a non-profit making company limited by guarantee. FACT assists all statutory law enforcement authorities and will undertake private criminal prosecutions wherever possible

Federation of Entertainment Unions (FEU)

1 Highfield
Twyford
Nr Winchester
Hants SO21 1QR
Tel: 01962 713134
Fax: 01962 713134
email: harris@interalpha.co.uk
Steve Harris
The FEU represents 140,000 people looking across the media and entertainment industries in the UK. It is a lobbying and campaigning group and meets regularly with statutory bodies and pressure groups ranging from the BBC, the ITC, the Film Council and the British Film Commission through to the Parliamentary All Party Media Committee and the Voice of the Listener and Viewer. The Federation comprises British Actors' Equity Association, Broadcasting Entertainment Cinematograph and Theatre Union, Musicians' Union, National Union of Journalists, Writers' Guild of Great Britain and Amalgamated Engineering & Electrical Union (Electricians Section). It has three standing committees covering Film and Electronic Media, European Affairs and Training

The Feminist Library

5a Westminster Bridge Road
London SE1 7XW
Tel: 020 7928 7789
email: feministlibrary@beeb.net
Website:
www.gn.apg.org/womeninlondon
The Feminist Library provides information about women's studies, courses, and current events. It has a large collection of fiction and non-

fiction books, pamphlets, papers etc. It holds a wide selection of journals and newsletters from all over the world and produces its own quarterly newsletter. Social events are held and discussion groups meet every other Tuesday. The library is run entirely by volunteers. Membership library. Open Tuesday (11.00am-8.00pm) Wednesday (3.00pm -5.00pm) and Saturday (2.00-5.00pm)

Film Artistes' Association (FAA)

111 Wardour Street
London W1V 4AY
Tel: 020 7437 8506
Fax: 020 7437 1221
email: smacdonald@bectu.org.uk
Spencer MacDonald
The FAA represents extras, doubles, stand-ins. Under an agreement with PACT, it supplies all background artistes in the major film studios and within a 40 mile radius of Charing Cross on all locations

Film Complaints Panel

22 Golden Square
London W1R 3PA
Chief Administrator: Annette Bradford

Film Council

10 Little Portland Street
London W1W 7JG
Tel: 020 7861 7861
Fax: 020 7861 7862
email: info@filmcouncil.org.uk
Websites: www.filmcouncil.org.uk
www.firstlightmovies.com
Contact: Tina McFarling/Ian Thomson
John Woodard, Chief Executive
The Film Council, the Government-backed film agency (not just film funding) is responsible for the creation of a sustainable film industry and developing education and film culture in the UK. On April 1 2000 the Film Council took responsibility for the British Film Commission, the Arts Council of England's Lottery Film Department, British Screen Finance and the British Film Institute's Production Department. The British Film Institute continues to run as an independent body funded by the Film Council. The Film Council channels £55 million a year of into the industry – a combination of Lottery and Government grant in aid funding. Three production funds have been set up with an overall budget of £20

million a year to spend on film production and development – the Premiere Fund (£10m), the New Cinema Fund (£5m) and the Development Fund (£5m). The Film Council also has a Training Fund (£ 1 million a year) expanding training for scriptwriters and producer/film-makers in partnership with Skillset, the National Training Organisation for the film industry. In addition, a grant-funded programme supported by £1 million of Lottery funds called "First Light" offering children and young people the opportunity to experience film-making and display their talents using low-cost technology has been launched.
As a strategic body the Film Council has created the £6 million a year Regional Investment Fund for England (RIFE) which is available to support cultural and industrial film initiatives in the English regions. The Film Council has also developed a joined-up UK-wide agenda with its sister organisations the national organisations Scottish Screen, Sgrîn, and the Northern Ireland Film Commission. The Film Council also continues to administer Lottery funds to the film production franchises set up by the Arts Council of England in 1997 and awarded to The Film Consortium, Pathé Pictures and DNA Films.

Film Education

Alhambra House
27-31 Charing Cross Road
London WC2H 0AU
Tel: 020 7976 2291
Fax: 020 7839 5052
email: postbox@filmeducation.org
Website: www.filmeducation.org
Ian Wall
Film Education is a registered charity supported by the UK film industry and the bfi. For nearly a decade it has been at the forefront of the development of Film and Media Studies and the use of film across the curriclum in schools and colleges and now has more than 23,000 primary and secondary school teachers on its unique database. The main aims of Film Education are to develop the use of film in the school curriculum and to facilitate the use of cinemas by schools. To this end it publishes a variety of free teaching packs and guides, produces television programmes, organises INSET and workshops as well as special film

screenings for schools. All Film Education resources are carefully researched and written by teachers for teachers

Film Archive Forum
c/o British Universities Film & Video Council (BUFVC)
77 Wells Street
London W1T 3QJ
Tel: 020 7393 1500
Fax: 020 7393 1555
email: faf@bufvc.ac.uk
Website: www.bufvc.ac.uk
Luke McKernan, Chair
Represents all of the public sector film and television archives which care for the UK's moving image heritage. Members: BFI Collections (National Film and Television Archive), East Anglian Film Archive, Imperial War Museum Film & Video Archive, North West Film Archive, Scottish Screen Archive, South East Film & Video Archive, South West Film and Television Archive, Wales Film and Television Archive, Wessex Film and Sound Archive, Yorkshire Film Archive. Emerging Members: Media Archive for Central England, Northern Region Film and Television Archive

The Film Office
The Old Town Hall
Patriot Square
Bethnal Green
London E2 9NP
Tel: 020 8980 8771
Fax: 020 8981 2272
email: filmoffice@easynet.co.uk
Website: www.filmoffice.co.uk
Works in association with local authorities in London to assist with filming in London locations

Film & Television Commission
North West England
Pioneer Buildings
65-67 Dale Street
Liverpool L2 2NS
Tel: 0151 330 6666
Fax: 0151 330 6611
FTC north west is the official film commission for the north west of England, working in partnership with the film offices of Liverpool, Manchester, Lancashire, Isle of Man and Cheshire

Film Unit Drivers Guild
136 The Crossways
Heston
Middlesex TW5 OJR
Tel: 020 8569 5001
Fax: 020 8569 6001
email: letstalk@fudg.uk.com
Website: www.fudg.com
L. Newell
FUDG represents its freelance members in the Film and Television industry when they are not on a production. It supplies them with work, such as pick ups and drops to any destination the client wishes to travel. Guild members are made up of professional film unit drivers and will look after all transportation needs

First Film Foundation
9 Bourlet Close
London W1P 7PJ
Tel: 020 7580 2111
Fax: 020 7580 2116
email: info@firstfilm.demon.co.uk
Website: www.firstfilm.co.uk
First Film Foundation is a charity that exisits to help new British writers, producers and directors make their first feature film by providing a range of unique, educational and promotional programmes. FFF also provides impartial practical advice on how to develop a career in the film industry

FOCAL International Ltd (Federation of Commercial Audio-Visual Libraries)
Pentax House
South Hill Avenue
South Harrow
Middx HA2 ODU
Tel: 020 8423 5853
Fax: 020 8933 4826
email: info@focalint.org
Website: www. focalint.org
Commercial Manager: Anne Johnson
An international, non-profit making professional trade association representing commercial film/audiovisual libraries and interested individuals. Among other activities, it organises regular meetings, maximises copyright information, and produces a directory of libraries and quarterly journal

German Federal Film Board and Export Union of Germany Cinema
Top Floor
113-117 Charing Cross Road
London W2H ODT
Tel: 020 7437 2047
Fax: 020 7439 2947
Iris Kehr

UK representative of the German Federal Film Board (Filmförderungsanstalt), the government industry organisation, and the German Film Export Union (Export Union des Deutschen Films), the official trade association for the promotion of German films abroad. For full details see entries under Organisations (Europe)

Glasgow Film Fund
249 West George Street
Glasgow G2 4RB
Tel: 0141 302 1757
Fax: 0141 302 1714
Judy Anderson
The Glasgow Film Fund provides production funding for companies making feature films in the Glasgow area or produced by Glasgow-based production companies. Applications are accepted for films intended for theatrical release, with a budget of at £500,000. The maximum investment made by the Glasgow Film Fund in any one project will be £150,000, however, where there is an exceptionally high level of local economic benefit the GFF may consider raising its maximum investment to £250,000. Glasgow Film Fund application forms, meeting dates, submission deadlines and further details are available from the GFF office. Production credits include: Shallow Grave, The Near Room, Small Faces, Carla's Song, The Slab Boys, Regeneration, The Life of Stuff, Orphans, My Name is Joe, The Acid House and The Debt Collector

Grierson Memorial Trust
c/o Ivan Sopher & co
5 Elstree Gate
Elstree Way
Borehamwood
Herts WD6 1JD
Tel: 020 8207 0602
Fax: 020 8207 6758
email: accountants@ivansopher.co.uk
Website: www.editor.net/griersontrust
John Chittock, Chairman

Guild of British Camera Technicians
5-11 Taunton Road
Metropolitan Centre
Greenford
Middx UB6 8UQ
Tel: 020 8578 9243
Fax: 020 8575 5972
Office manager: Maureen O'Grady
Magazine Editors, Eyepiece: Charles

Hewitt and Kerry-Anne Burrows
The Guild exists to further the professional interests of technicians working with film or video motion picture cameras. Membership is restricted to those whose work brings them into direct contact with these cameras and who can demonstrate competence in their particular field of work. By setting certain minimum standards of skill for membership, the Guild seeks to encourage its members, especially newer entrants, to strive to improve their art. Through its publication, Eyepiece: disseminates information about both creative and technical developments, past and present, in the film and television industry

Guild of British Film Editors
Travair, Spurlands End Road
Great Kingshill , High Wycombe
Bucks HP15 6HY
Tel: 0149 712313
Fax: 0149 712313
email: cox.gbfe@btinternet.com
To ensure that the true value of film and sound editing is recognised as an important part of the creative and artistic aspects of film production

Guild of Stunt and Action Co-ordinators
72 Pembroke Road
London W8 6NX
Tel: 020 7602 8319
Sally Fisher
To promote the highest standards of safety and professionalism in film and television stunt work

Guild of Television Cameramen
1 Churchill Road
Whitchurch, Tavistock
Devon PL19 9BU
Tel: 01822 614405
Fax: 01822 615785
Sheila Lewis
The Guild was formed in 1972 'to ensure and preserve the professional status of the television cameramen and to establish, uphold and advance the standards of qualification and competence of cameramen'. The Guild is not a union and seeks to avoid political involvement

Guild of Vision Mixers
147 Ship Lane
Farnborough
Hants GU14 8BJ
Tel: 01252 514953
Fax: 01252 656756

Peter Turl
The Guild aims to represent the interests of vision mixers throughout the UK and Ireland, and seeks to maintain the highest professional standards in vision-mixing

IAC (Institute of Amateur Cinematographers)
24c West Street
Epsom
Surrey KT18 7RJ
Tel: 01372 739672
Fax: 01372 739672
email: iacfilmvideo@compuserve.com
Website: www.theiac.org.uk
Janet Smith, Admin Secretary
Encouraging amateurs interested in the art of making moving pictures and supporting them with a variety of services

Imperial War Museum Film and Video Archive
Lambeth Road
London SE1 6HZ
Tel: 020 7416 5299
Fax: 020 7416 5379
email: film@iwm.org.uk
Website: www.iwm.org.uk
See entry under Archives and Film Libraries

Incorporated Society of British Advertisers (ISBA)
44 Hertford Street
London W1Y 8AE
Tel: 020 7499 7502
Fax: 020 7629 5255
Website: www.isba.org.uk
Deborah Morris
The ISBA was founded in 1900 as an association for advertisers, both regional and national. Subscriptions are based on advertisers' expenditure and the main objective is the protection and advancement of the advertising interests of member firms. This involves organised representation, co-operation, action and exchange of information and experience, together with conferences, workshops and publications. ISBA offer a communications consultancy service for members on questions as varied as assessment of TV commercial production quotes to formulation of advertising agency agreements

Incorporated Society of Musicians (ISM)
10 Stratford Place
London W1N 9AE
Tel: 020 7629 4413
Fax: 020 7408 1538

email: membership@ism.org
Website: www.ism.org
Chief Executive: Neil Hoyle
Professional association for all musicians: teachers, performers and composers. The ISM produces various publications, including the monthly Music Journal, and gives advice to members on all professional issues

Independent Film Distributors' Association (IFDA)
10a Stephen Mews
London W1P 0AX
Tel: 020 7957 8957
Fax: 020 7957 8968
IFDA was formed in 1973, and its members are mainly specialised film distributors who deal in both 16mm and 35mm and every type of film from classic features to 'popular music.' Supply many users including universities, schools, hospitals, prisons, independent cinemas, hotels, film societies, ships etc

Independent Television Commission (ITC)
33 Foley Street
London W1P 7LB
Tel: 020 7255 3000
Fax: 020 7306 7800
email: Publicaffairs@itc.org.uk
The ITC is the public body responsible for licensing and regulating commercially funded television services. These include Channel 3 (ITV), Channel 4, Channel 5, public teletext and a range of cable, local delivery and satellite services and digital television services

Institute of Practitioners in Advertising (IPA)
44 Belgrave Square
London SW1X 8QS
Tel: 020 7235 7020
Fax: 020 7245 9904
The representative body for UK advertising agencies. Represents the collective views of its member agencies in negotiations with Government departments, the media and industry and consumer organisations

International Association of Broadcasting Manufacturers (IABM)
Broad Oaks
Parish Lane
Farnham Common

Slough SL2 3JW
Tel: 01753 645682
Fax: 01753 645682
email: info@iabm.org.uk
Website: www.iabm.org.uk
Secretariat: Brenda White
IABM aims to foster the interests of
manufacturers of broadcast
equipment from all countries. Areas
of membership include liaison with
broadcasters, standardisation, other
technical information, an annual
product Award for design and
innovation and exhibitions. All
companies active in the field of
broadcast equipment manufacturing
are encouraged to join

International Federation of the Phonographic Industry (IFPI)
IFPI Secretariat
54 Regent Street
London W1R 5PJ
Tel: 020 7878 7900
Fax: 020 7878 7950
Director General: Nicholas Garnett
An international association of 1,300
members in 71 countries,
representing the copyright interests of
the sound recording and music video
industries

International Institute of Communications
Tavistock House South
Tavistock Square
London WC1H 9LF
Tel: 020 7388 0671
Fax: 020 7380 0623
The IIC promotes the open debate of
issues in the communications field
worldwide. Its current interests cover
legal and policy, economic and public
interest issues. It does this via its: bi-
monthly journal Intermedia; through
its international communications
library; annual conference; sponsored
seminars and research forums

International Intelligence on Culture
4 Baden Place
Crosby Row
London SE1 1YW
Tel: 020 7403 6454
Fax: 020 7403 2009
email: enquiry@international-arts.org
Website: www.intelculture.org
Information Service
The International Intelligence on
Culture specialises in providing
information and advice on a range of
international arts issues, including

cultural policies, networks and
funding programmes from around
the world. It offers monthly one-to-
one funding advice 'surgeries'; a
range of publications including a bi-
monthly journal called International
Arts Navigator; it also runstraining
seminars on European policies,
structures and funding opportunities,
and undertakes research and
consultancy for national, regional and
local cultural agencies

ITV Network Ltd
200 Gray's Inn Road
London WC1X 8HF
Tel: 020 7843 8000
Fax: 020 7843 8158
email: dutyoffice@itv.co.uk
Website: www.itv.co.uk
Director of Programmes: David
Liddiment
A body wholly owned by the ITV
companies which independently
undertakes the commissioning and
scheduling of those television
programmes which are shown across
the ITV Network. It also provides a
range of services to the ITV
companies where a common
approach is required

IVCA (International Visual Communication Association)
Business CommunicationCentre
19 Pepper Street, Glengall Bridge
London E14 9RP
Tel: 020 7512 0571
email: info@ivca.org
Website: www.ivca.org
Chief Executive: Wayne Drew
The IVCA is the largest European
Association of its kind, representing a
wide range of organisations and
individuals working in the established
and developing technologies of visual
communication. With roots in video,
film and business events industries,
the Association has also developed
significant representation of the new
and fast growing technologies, notably
business television, multimedia,
interactive software and the internet.
It provides business services for its
members: legal help, internet service,
insurance, arbitration etc. and holds
events/seminars for training,
networking and for all industry
related topics

Kraszna-Krausz Foundation
122 Fawnbrake Avenue
London SE24 0BZ
Tel: 020 7738 6701

Fax: 020 7738 6701
email: info@k-k.org.uk
Website: www.k-k.org.uk
Andrea Livingstone, Administrator
The Foundation offers small grants of
up to £5,000 to assist in the
development of new or unfinished
projects, work or literature where the
subject specifically relates to the art,
history, practice or technology of
photography or the moving image
(defined as film, television, video and
related screen media) and sponsors
annual book awards for books on
photographyy and the moving image
(see Funding)

Learning On Screen
(The Society for Screen-Based
Learning)
9 Bridge Street
Tadcaster LS24 9AW
North Yorkshire
Tel: 01937 530520
Fax: 01937 530520
email: josie.key@learningonscreen.u-
net.com
Website:
www.learningonscreen.org.uk
Learning on Screen is the new
identity of the Educational Television
and Media Association (ETmA). The
Society for Screen-Based Learning is
an organisation providing all kinds of
support and assistance to those
involved in any form of screen-based
learning. this is part of the continuing
evlution of the Association from an
organisation set up in 1967 to
support those in the new technology
of closed-circuit television. Now
support is given to learning material
delivered via a screen. Annual
Production Awards: Deadline first
week of November for educational
videos and multimedia programmes
made in the previous 12 months.
Categories: Broadcast (Compulsory
and Non-Compulsory Education),
Multi-Media (On-Line and Off-line),
Wellcome Trust Award for Biology &
Medicine, Training & Instructional
Award, Student Production
(F.E.&H.E.) Premier Award and Best
Craft Awards. Membership details
from the Administrator

London Film Commission
20 Euston Centre
Regent's Place
London NW1 3JH
Tel: 020 7387 8787
Fax: 020 7387 8788
email: lfc@london-film.co.uk

Website: london-film.co.uk
Sue Hayes, Film Commissioner
Daniela Kirchner, Information
Manager
Anna Faithful, Office Manager
The London Film Commission
encourages and assists film and
television production in London and
holds databases of locations,
personnel and facilities. Funded by
Government, the film industry and
other private sector sponsors, it
works to promote London as a first
choice destination for overseas filmmakers. It collaborates with the Local
Authorities, the police and other
services to create a film friendly
atmosphere in the capital

Mechanical-Copyright Protection Society (MCPS)

29/33 Berner Street
London W1P 4AA
Tel: 020 8664 4400
Fax: 020 8769 8792
email: info@mcps.co.uk
Website: www.mcps.co.uk
Contact: Non-retail Licensing
Department
MCPS is an organisation of music
publishers and composers, which
issues licences for the recording of its
members' copyright musical works in
all areas of television, film and video
production. Free advice and further
information is available on request

Medialex - Legal & Business Training

15 Sandycombe Road
Kew
Richmond
Surrey TW9 2EP
Tel: 020 8940 7039
Fax: 020 8758 8647
email: info@medialex.co.uk
Industry approved Media Law
seminars designed for the film and
television industry including
copyright, contracts, industry
agreements, music copyright, internet
and new media

Mediawatch-uk

3 Willow House
Kennington Road
Ashford
Kent TN24 0NR
Tel: 01233 633936
Fax: 01233 633836
email: info@mediawatchuk.org
Website: www.mediawatchuk.org
Director: John C Beyer
Formerly the National Viewers' &
Listeners' Association (NVALA)

Founder & President Emeritus: Mary
Whitehouse CBE
Concerned with moral standards in
the media

Mental Health Media Council

356 Holloway Road
London N7 6PA
Tel: 020 7700 8171
Fax: 020 7686 0959
email: info@mhmedia.com
Website: www.mhmedia.com
An independent charity founded in
1965, MHMC provides information,
advice and consultancy on film/video
and multimedia production to
relevant to mental health and
learning difficulties. Resource lists on
audiovisual materials. Producers of
video and broadcast programmes

Metier

Glyde House
Glydegate
Bradford BD5 0BQ
Tel: 01274 738 800
Fax: 01274 391 566
Chief Exec: Duncan Sones
A National Training Organisation,
developing National and Scottish
Vocational Qualifications for
occupations in performing and visual
arts, arts administration, front-of-house,
arts development & interpretation and
technical support functions in the arts
and entertainment sector. It is
responsible for strategic action to
improve the quality, availability and
effectiveness of vocational training
within its industrial sector

Music Publishers Association Ltd

3rd Floor
18/20 York Buildings
London WC2N 6JU
Tel: 020 7389 0665
Fax: 020 7839 7776
email: pbrindley@mpaonline.org.uk
Website: www.mpaonline.org.uk
Alex Webb, Communications
Manager
The only trade association repre-
senting UK music publishers. List of
members available at £10.00

Music Video Producers' Association (MVPA)

26 Noel Street
London W1V 3RD
Tel: 020 7434 2651
Fax: 020 7434 9002
Stephen Davies
The MFVPA represents production

companies making music promos. It
advises on agreements and provides a
telephone advice service to members
on production and legal matters

Musicians' Union (MU)

60-62 Clapham Road
London SW9 0JJ
Tel: 020 7582 5566
Fax: 020 7793 9185
email: info@musiciansunion.org.uk
Media Department Contacts: Howard
Evans, Marilyn Stoddart
Represents the interests of virtually
all professional musicians in the UK.
The media department deals with all
music related issues involving film
and TV: day to day working and
interpretation of the MU/PACT
agreement, synchronisation of audio
recordings and advertisements and
film and rights clearances. Queries
regarding video, DVD, promotional
filming, EPK's, contractors,
musicians, composers and arrangers

National Association for Higher Education in Film and Video (NAHEFV)

c/o London International Film
School
24 Shelton Street
London WC2H 9HP
Tel: 020 7836 9642/240 0168
Fax: 020 7497 3718
The Association's main aims are to act
as a forum for debate on all aspects of
film, video and TV education and to
foster links with industry, the
professions and Government bodies. It
was established in 1983 to represent all
courses in the UK which offer a major
practical study in film, video or
television at the higher educational level

National Campaign for the Arts

Pegasus House
37-43 Sackville Street
London W1X 1DB
Tel: 020 7333 0375
Fax: 020 7333 0660
email: nca@ecna.org
Vandna Synghal
Director: Victoria Todd
Deputy Director: Anna Leatherdale
The NCA is the only independent
lobbying organisation that represents
all the arts. The campaign is funded
entirely by its members to ensure its
independence. It gives a voice for the
arts world in all its diversity. The
NCA meets, lobbies and influences
decision makers - ministers, shadow

ministers, officials, council leaders, peers, journalists and influential back benchers. It discusses policy and proposals in detail with major arts funders on a regular basis

National Film and Television School
Beaconsfield Studios
Station Road
Beaconsfield
Bucks HP9 1LG
Tel: 01494 671234
Fax: 01494 674042
email: admin@nftsfilm-tv.ac.uk
Website: www.nftsfilm-tv.ac.uk
Director Full Time Programme,
Roger Crittenden
Director: Stephen Bayly
The National Film and Television School provides advanced training and retraining in all major disciplines to professional standards. Graduates are entitled to BECTU membership on gaining employment. It is an autonomous non-profit making organisation funded by the Department for Culture, Media and Sport and the film and television industries. See also under Courses

National Film Trustee Company (NFTC)
14-17 Wells Mews
London W1P 3FL
Tel: 020 7580 6799
Fax: 020 7636 6711
An independent revenue collection and disbursement service for producers and financiers. The NFTC has been in business since 1971. It is a subsidiary of British Screen Finance

National Museum of Photography Film & Television
Bradford BD1 1NQ
Tel: 01274 202030
Fax: 01274 723155
Website: www.nmpft.org.uk
Bill Lawrence, Head of Film
The world's only museum devoted to still and moving pictures, their technology and history. Features Britain's first giant IMAX film system; the world's only public Cinerama; interactive galleries and 'TV Heaven', reference library of programmes and commercials

National Screen Service
Unit 1
Perivale Industrial Park
Horsenden Lane South
Greenford

Middlesex UB6 7RU
Tel: 020 8991 2121
Fax: 020 8991 5757
Pat Walton
Formed in 1926 as a subsidiary of a US corporation and purchased by its present British owner/directors in 1998. It distributes trailers, posters and other publicity material to UK cinemas and carries out related printing activity

National Union of Journalists
314 Gray's Inn Road
London WC1X 8DP
Tel: 020 7278 7916
Fax: 020 7837 8143
Deputy General Secretary: John Fray
Direct line to Broadcasting Office:
0171 843 3726
Represents nearly 5,000 journalists working in broadcasting in the areas of news, sport, current affairs and features. It has agreements with all the major broadcasting companies and the BBC. It also has agreements with the main broadcasting agencies, WTN, Reuters Television and PACT

NESTA (The National Endowment for Science, Technology and the Arts)
Fishmongers' Chambers,
110 Upper Thames Street
London, EC4R 3TW
Tel: Tel 0207 645 9500
Fax: Fax 0207 645 9501
email: nesta@nesta.org.uk
Website: www.nesta.org.uk
Chief Executive: Jeremy Newton
Chairman: Lord Puttnam
'NESTA - the National Endowment for Science, Technology and the Arts - was set up to find and nurture creative excellence throughout the UK, supporting innovative individuals and ideas that could benefit our economy and society. It also runs an education programme which seeks out new and imaginative ways of stimulating creativity in people of all ages and of increasing public understanding of science, technology and the arts

Networking
c/o Vera Media
30-38 Dock Street
Leeds LS10 1JF
Tel: 0113 2428646
Fax: 0113 2451238
email: networking@vera-media.demon.co.uk

Membership organisation for women working, seeking work or interested/involved in film, video or television, colleges, libraries, careers depts., production companies welcome to join. Members receive quarterly 20-page newsletter with events, production info., letters, reports, news and views; entry in NETWORKING index; individual advice and help; campaigning voice. £15 pa (UK), £18 (abroad)

New Producers Alliance (NPA)
9 Bourlet Close
London W1W 7BP
Tel: 020 7580 2480
Fax: 020 7580 2484
email: publications@npa.org.uk
Website: www.newproducer.co.uk
The NPA is the national membership and training organisation for independent new producers and filmmakers. It provides access to contacts, information and advice regarding film production to over 1,000 members, ranging from film students and first timers to highly experienced feature filmmakers, major production companies and industry affiliates. Members services include; specialised producer training programmes from entrance' to advanced' levels; ongoing events, masterclasses, seminars, networking evenings, practical workshops and preview screenings; free advice services including legal and tax & accountancy; monthly newsletter and online members' directory.

Northern Ireland Film Commission
21 Ormeau Avenue
Belfast BT2 8HD
Tel: 01232 232444
Fax: 01232 239918
email: info@nifc.co.uk
Website: www.nifc.co.uk
The Northern Ireland Film Commission promotes the growth of film and television culture and the industry in Northern Ireland

Office for National Statistics
1 Drummond Gate
London SW1V 2QQ
Tel: 020 7533 5725

Office of Fair Trading
Field House
15-25 Bream's Buildings
London EC4A 1PR

Tel: 020 7242 2858
Fax: 020 7269 8800
The Director General of Fair Trading has an interest in the supply of films for exhibition in cinemas. Following a report by the Monopolies and Mergers Commission (MMC) in 1994, the Director General has taken action to ensure that the adverse public interest findings of the MMC are remedied. Under the Broadcasting Act 1990, he also has two specific roles in relation to the television industry. In his report published in December 1992 he assessed the Channel 3 networking arrangement and from 1 January 1993 he had to monitor the BBC's progress towards a statutory requirement to source 25 per cent of its qualifying programming from independent producers

PACT (Producers Alliance for Cinema and Television)

45 Mortimer Street
London W1W 8HJ
Tel: 020 7331 6000
Fax: 0020 7331 6700
email: enquiries@pact.co.uk
Website: www.pact.co.uk
Chief Executive: John McVay
Scotland Office:
249 West George Street
Glasgow G2 4QE
Tel: 0141 302 7120
Fax: 0141 302 1721
Founded in 1991, PACT ˇ The Producers Alliance for Cinema and Television ˇ is the major trade association for the UK film and television production industries. It represents the commercial interests of over 1,000 independent television, feature film, animation and new media production companies. It also represents the interests of companies providing finance, distribution, facilities and other commercial services relating to production. PACT has established a reputation for successfully lobbying Government and regulators on its members' behalf. However, the bulk of its resources are devoted to providing a comprehensive range of services to its members. PACT provides a Business Affairs Advisory Service ; Legal Service; Copyright Registration Service are all available to PACT members. PACT publishes a monthly magazine, annual Directory of Independent Producers, an Annual Report and targeted publications directed at assisting film and television producers in all areas of activities.

PACT represents its members at international film and television markets worldwide such as MIPTV, the Cannes Film Festival, NAPTE, and the Toronto Film Festival. PACT represents the training interests of the independent film and television production sector. PACT organises a wide range of membership events on industry issues for film, television and new media in London and the nations and regions. Dedicated Industrial Relations Service - Negotiating agreements with the industry's trade unions, designing model contracts, providing advice in pre-production meetings, as well as individual back-up throughout production. For further information on PACT membership or services, contact David Alan Mills, Membership Officer

Pearl & Dean

3 Waterhouse Square
138-142 Holborn
London EC1N 2NY
Tel: 020 7882 1100
Fax: 020 7882 1111

Performing Right Society (PRS)

29-33 Berners Street
London W1P 4AA
Tel: 020 7580 5544
Fax: 020 7306 4455
Website: www.prs.co.uk
PRS is a non-profit making association of composers, authors and publishers of musical works. It collects and distributes royalties for the use, in public performances, broadcasts and cable programmes, of its members' copyright music and has links with other performing right societies throughout the world

Phonographic Performance (PPL)

1 Upper James Street
London W1R 3HG
Tel: 020 7534 1000
Fax: 020 7534 1111
Head of External Affairs:
Colleen Hue
Controls public performance and broadcasting rights in sound recordings on behalf of approximately 2,000 record companies in the UK. The users of sound recordings licensed by PPL range from BBC and independent TV and Radio, pan-European satellite services, night clubs and juke boxes, to pubs, shops, hotels etc

The Production Guild of Great Britain

Pinewood Studios
Pinewood Road
Iver Heath
Bucks SL0 0NH
Tel: 01753 651767
Fax: 01753 652803
email: admin@productionguild.com
Website: www.productionguild.com
Angela Pyle, General Manager
President: Michael O'Sullivan
Organisation for senior management employed within the British Film and Television industry. The guild strives to be the first port of call for both the studios and production companies looking for experienced management teams but more importantly and additionally, will become a meaningful point of consultation for Government and Industry bodies when planning new legislation etc

Production Managers Association (PMA)

Ealing Studios
Ealing Green
Ealing
London W5 5EP
Tel: 020 8758 8699
Fax: 020 8758 8658
email: pma@pma.org.uk
Website: www.pma.org.uk
C.Fleming
Represents over 140 broadcast production managers who all have at least three years experience and six broadcast credits. Provides a network of like-minded individuals

Radio, Electrical and Television Retailers' Association (RETRA)

Retra House
St John's Terrace
1 Ampthill Street
Bedford MK42 9EY
Tel: 01234 269110
Fax: 01234 269609
Fred Round
Founded in 1942, RETRA represents the interests of electrical retailers to all those who make decisions likely to affect the selling and servicing of electrical and electronic products

Reel Women

57 Holmewood Gardens
London SW2 3NB
Tel: 020 8678 7404
A networking organisation for all women in film, video and television. It places particular emphasis on the

creative interaction between women from the broadcast, non-broadcast and independent sectors and higher education, aiming to provide a forum for debate around issues affecting women in all areas of production and training, as well as around broader concerns about the representation and position of women in the industry and on screen. Seminars, screenings and workshops are held as well as regular 'nights out'

The Royal Photographic Society

Milsom Street
Bath, Avon BA1 1DN
Tel: 01225 462841
Fax: 01225 448688
email: rps@rps.org
Website: www.rps.org
A learned society founded for the promotion and enjoyment of all aspects of photography. Contains a specialist Film and Video Group, secretary John Tarby, FRPS, with a regular journal, meetings and the opportunity to submit productions for the George Sewell Trophy and the Hugh Baddeley Trophy; and an Audiovisual group, secretary Brian Jenkins, LRPS, offering an extensive programme of events, seminars and demonstrations, and the bi-monthly magazine AV News. Membership open to both amateur and professional photographers

Royal Television Society

Holborn Hall
100 Grays Inn Road
London WC1X 8AL
Tel: 020 7430 1000
Fax: 020 7430 0924
Dep. Exec. Director: Claire Price
The RTS, founded in 1927, has over 4,000 members in the UK and overseas, which are serviced by the Society's 17 regional centres. The Society aims to bring together all the disciplines of television by providing a forum for debate on the technical, cultural and social implications of the medium. This is achieved through the many lectures, conferences, symposia and workshops and master classes organised each year. The RTS does not run formal training courses. The RTS publishes a journal ten times a year Television. The RTS organises awards for journalism, sports, craft and design, education, general programmes and student television

Scottish Arts Council

12 Manor Place
Edinburgh EH3 7DD
Tel: 0131 226 6051
Fax: 0131 225 9833
Director: Seona Reid
See entry for Scottish Screen, the lead body for film in Scotland

Scottish Screen

Second Floor
249 West George Street
Glasgow G2 4QE
Tel: 0141 302 1700
Fax: 0141 302 1711
email: info@scottishscreen.com
Website: www.scottishscreen.com
Chief Executive: Steve McIntyre
Scottish Screen is responsible to the Scottish Parliament for developing all aspects of screen industry and culture in Scotland through script and company development, short film production, distribution of National Lottery film production finance, training, education, exhibition funding, the Film Commission locations support and the Scottish Screen Archive

Screenwriters' Workshop

Suffolk House
1-8 Whitfield Place
London W1T 5JU
Tel: 020 7387 5511
Fax: 020 7387 5511
email: screenoffice@cw.com.net
Website: www.lsw.org.uk
Katherine Way
Run by writers, for writers, the SW promotes contact between screenwriters and producers, agents, development executives and other film and TV professionals through a wide range of seminars. Practical workshops provide training in all aspects of the screenwriting process. Membership is open to anyone interested in writing for film and TV and to anyone working in these and related media. Registered Charity No: 1052455

The Script Factory

Linton House
24 Wells Street
London W1P 3FG
Tel: 020 7323 1414
Fax: 020 7323 9464
email: general@
scriptfactory.freeserve.co.uk
Website: www.scriptfactory.com
Nadia Ward

Sgrîn (Media Agency for Wales)

The Bank, 10 Mount Stuart Square
Cardiff Bay
Cardiff CF10 5EE
Tel: 029 2033 3300
Fax: 029 2033 3320
email: sgrin@sgrin.co.uk
Website: www.sgrin.co.uk
Chief Executive: J. Berwyn Rowlands
Sgrin is the primary organisation for film, television and new media in Wales. Sgrin promotes production, education and exhibition and is home to the Wales Film and Television Archive and Media Antenna Cymru Wales

The Short Film Bureau

47 Poland Street
London W1F 7NB
Tel: 020 7734 8708
Fax: 020 7734 2406
email: info@shortfilmbureau.com
Website: www.shortfilmbureau.com
Contact: Kim Leggatt
Patrons: Sir Sydney Samuelson OBE Steve Woolley, Brian Cox, Kenneth Branagh
The Bureau has two goals: To help new filmmakers find audiences for their work an dto raise the profile and acceptance of short films in general. This is done by offering advice and support on funding, production, marketing and distribution. The website offers proffessional and practical advice on all aspects of short film making. The Cinema Programme provides an opportunity for filmmakers to have their work assessed for potential theatrical release by UK distributors and exhibitiors.

SKILLSET

The National Training Organisation for Broadcast, Film, Video and Multimedia
103 Dean Street
London W1V 5RA
Tel: 020 7534 5300
Fax: 020 7534 5333
email: info@skillset.org
Website: www.skillset.org
Chief Executive: Dinah Caine
Director of Development: Kate O'Connor
Communications Director: Gary Townsend
Founded and managed by the key employers and unions within the industry, SKILLSET operates at a strategic level providing relevant

labour market and training information, encouraging higher levels of investment in training and developing and implementing occupational standards and the National and Scottish Vocation Qualifications based upon them. It seeks to influence national and international education and training policies to the industry's best advantage, strives to create greater and equal access to training opportunities and career development and assists in developing a healthier and safer workforce. SKILLSET is a UK-wide organisation

Society for the Study of Popular British Cinema
Department of Media and Cultural Production
Faculty of Humanities and Social Science
Gateway House
De Montfort University
Leicester LE1 9BH
Fax: 0116 2577199
Contact: Alan Burton, Secretary
Society which produces a newsletter and the Journal of Popular British Cinema and encourages an interest in British films

Society of Authors' Broadcasting Group
84 Drayton Gardens
London SW10 9SB
Tel: 020 7373 6642
Fax: 020 7373 5768
email: authorsoc@writers.org,uk
Specialities: Radio, television and film scriptwriters

Society of Cable Telecommunication Engineers (SCTE)
Fulton House Business Centre
Fulton Road, Wembley Park
Middlesex HA9 0TF
Tel: 020 8902 8998
Fax: 020 8903 8719
email: office@scte.org.uk
Website: www.scte.org.uk
Mrs Beverley K Allgood FSAE
Aims to raise the standard of cable telecommunication engineering to the highest technical level, and to elevate and improve the status and efficiency of those engaged in cable telecommunication engineering

Society of Film Distributors (SFD)
22 Golden Square

London W1F 9JW
Tel: 020 7437 4383
Fax: 020 7734 0912
email: sfd@sfd.demon.co.uk
Chief Executive: Mark Batey
The SFD is the trade association for film distributors in the UK. Founded in 1915 and membership includes all the major distribution companies and several independent companies. It promotes and protects its members' interests and co-operates with all other film organisations and Government agencies where distribution interests are involved

Society of Television Lighting Directors
4 The Orchard
Aberthin
Cowbridge
South Glamorgan CF7 7HU
The Society provides a forum for the exchange of ideas in all aspects of the TV profession including techniques and equipment. Meetings are organised throughout the UK and abroad. Technical information and news of members' activities are published in the Society's magazine

Sovexportfilm
11b Paveley Drive
Morgans Walk
London SW11 3TP
Tel: 020 7358 1226
Fax: 020 7358 1226
Exports Russian films to different countries and imports films to Russia. Provides facilities to foreign companies wishing to film in Russia. Co-production information for producers

TAC (Welsh Independent Producers)
Gronant
Caernarfon
Gwynedd LL55 1NS
Tel: 01286 671123
Fax: 01286 678890
email: email tac@taccyf.demon.co.uk
Website: www.taccyf.demon.co.uk
Dafydd Hughes
TAC is the trade association representing the 95 production companies working for Welsh broadcasters. It offers a full IR service and conducts negotiations on standard terms of trade with the broadcasters

Television Monitoring Services Ltd
74-76 London Street

Reading
Berkshire RG1 4SJ
Tel: 0118 956 7991
Fax: 0118 956 7992
email: info@MonitoringServices.com

Variety Club of Great Britain
Variety Club House
93 Bayham Street
London NW1 0AG
Tel: 020 7428 8100
Fax: 020 7428 8111
email: info@varietyclub.org.uk
Website: www.varietyclub.org.uk
Ginny Martin
Charity dedicated to helping disabled and disadvantaged children throughout Great Britain

The Video Standards Council
Kinetic Business Centre
Theobald Street
Borehamwood
Herts WD6 4PJ
Tel: 0208 387 4020
Fax: 0208 387 4004
Website: www.videostandards.org.uk
The VSC was established in 1989 as a non-profit making body set up to develop and oversee a Code of Practice and Code of Practice Rules designed to promote high standards within the video industry. The Code and Rules have subsequently been expanded to promote high standards within the computer and video games industry

Videola (UK)
Paramount House
162/170 Wardour Street
London W1V 3AT
Tel: 020 7437 2136
Fax: 020 7437 5413

VLV - Voice of the Listener and Viewer
101 King's Drive
Gravesend
Kent DA12 5BQ
Tel: 01474 352835
Fax: 01474 351112
email: vlv@btinternet.com
Website: www.vlv.org.uk
Linda Forbes
An independent non-profit making society which represents the citizen and consumer interest in broadcasting and which supports the principle of public service in broadcasting. Founded in 1983, by Jocelyn Hay, VLV is the only consumer body speaking for listeners

and viewers on the full range of broadcasting issues. VLV has 2,000 members, nearly 30 corporate members (most of which are registered charities) and over 50 colleges and university departments in academic membership. VLV is funded by its members and free from any sectarian, commercial or political links. Holds public lectures, conferences and seminars and arranges exclusive visits for its members to broadcasting centres in different parts of the country. Publishes a quarterly newsletter and briefings on broadcasting developments. Has responded to all parliamentary and public inquiries on broadcasting since 1984 and to consultations by the ITC, Radio Authority, BBC and Broadcasting Standards Council since 1990. Is in frequent touch with MPs, civil servants, the BBC and independent broadcasters, regulators, academics and relevant consumer bodies at UK and European level. Holds the archive of the former independent Broadcasting Research Unit and of the former British Action for Children's Television (BACTV) and makes these available for a small fee together with its own archives and library. Runs the VLV Forum for children's broadcasting which holds annual conferences on children's radio and television. Acts as secretariat for the European Alliance of Listensers' and Viewers' Associations which has member associations in seven of European Union countries

Women in Film and Television (UK)
6 Langley Street
London WC2H 9JA
Tel: 020 7240 4875
Fax: 020 7379 1625
email: info@wftv.org.uk
Director: Kate Norrish
Administrator: Donna Coyle
A membership organisation for women working in the film and television industries. WFTV aims to provide information and career support through a monthly programme of events that are free to members. In addition WFTV safeguards the interests of the members through its lobbying and campaigning. WFTV exists to protect and enhance the staus, interests and

diversity of women working at all levels in both film and television

Writers' Guild of Great Britain
430 Edgware Road
London W2 1EH
Tel: 020 7723 8074
Fax: 020 7706 2413
email: admin@writersguild.org.uk
Website: www.writers.org.uk/guild
Bernie Corbett, General Secretary
Anne Hogben, Assistant General Secretary
The Writers' Guild is the recognised TUC-affiliated trade union for writers working in film, television, radio, theatre and publishing

Regional film commissions and film offices

Bath Film Office
Trimbridge House
Trim Street
Bath BA1 2DP
Tel: 01225 477711
Fax: 01225 477221
email:
bath_filmoffice@bathnes.gov.uk
Website: www.visitbath.co.uk
Maggie Ainley, Film Commissioner
As a member of the UK Screen Commission Network, the Bath Film Office offers a free service for TV, film and commercials in Bath and North East Somerset. This covers a wide range of city and country locations, together with access to a comprehensive database of experienced local crew and facilities based in the region.

Central England Screen Commission
Unit 5, Holliday Wharf
Holliday Street
Birmingham B1 1TJ
Tel: 0121 643 9309
Fax: 0121 643 9064

East London Film Fund
(See London Film and Video Development Agency)

East Midlands Arts Board
Mountfields House
Epinal Way
Loughborough
Leicestershire LE11 0QE
Tel: 01509 218292
Fax: 01509 262214
email: info@em-arts.co.uk
Website: www.arts.org.uk
Chief Executive: Laura Dyer
Caroline Pick, Film, Video and Broadcasting Officer, Suzanne Alizart
- Officer (Film, Digital Arts and Broadcasting); Carol Clarke, Assistant Film Officer
Derbyshire (excluding High Peak District), Leicestershire, Northamptonshire, Nottinghamshire, Rutland, Lincolnshire

East Midlands Screen Commission
Broadway
14-18 Broad Street
Nottingham NG1 3AL
Tel: 0115 910 5564

Fax: 01159 105563
email: emsc@org.uk
Website: www.emsc.org.uk
Phil Nodding/Emily Lappin
Covers Nottinghamshire,
Northamptonshire, Derbyshire,
Leicestershire, Rutland and
Lincolnshire

East England Arts
Eden House
48-49 Bateman Street
Cambridge CB2 1LR
Tel: 01223 454000
Fax: 0870 242171
email: info@eearts.co.uk
Website: www.eastenglandarts.org.uk
Chief Executive: Andrea Stark
Arts Development Officer
(Broadcasting): Martin Ayres
Bedfordshire, Essex, Cambridgeshire,
Hertfordshire, Norfolk and Suffolk

Eastern Screen
Anglia TV
Norwich NR1 3JG
Tel: 01603 767077
Fax: 01603 767191
The Film Commission for the East of
England offering free help and advice
on locations, facilities companies
local services and crew to anyone
intending to film within the region

Edinburgh Film Focus
Castlecliff
25 Johnston Terrace
Edinburgh EH1 2NH
Tel: 0131 622 7337
Fax: 0131 622 7338
email: edinfilm@ednet.co.uk
George Carlaw, Ros Davis
The Film Commission for the City of
Edinburgh and the coastline,
countryside and counties of Lothian
and the Scottish Borders. Free advice
on locations, crews, facilities and
liasion with local authorities

English Regional Arts Boards
5 City Road
Winchester, Hants SO23 8SD
Tel: 01962 851063
Fax: 01962 842033
email: info@erab.org.uk
Website: www.arts.org.uk
Carolyn Nixson, Administrator
Liaison, lobbying, information and
support for Regional Arts Boards

Film & Television Commission North West England
Pioneer Buildings

65-67 Dale Street
Liverpool L2 2NS
Tel: 0151 330-6666
Fax: 0151 330-6611
email: ftc@nwengland.co.uk
Andrew Patrick: Chief Executive
Helen Bingham: Director of
Marketing & Information

Film Dundee
Dept of Economic Development
Dundee City Council
3 City Square
Dundee DD1 3BA
Tel: 01382 434 292
Fax: 01382 434 650
email:
filmdundee@dundeecity.gov.uk
Website: www.dundeecity.gov.uk

Film Link
South Way
Leavesden
Hertfordshire WD2 5LZ
Tel: 01923 495 051
Fax: 01923 333007
email: locations@filmlink.org.uk
Website: www.filmlink.org.uk
Roger Harrop

Glasgow Film Office
City Chambers
Glasgow G2 1DU
Tel: 0141 287 0424
Fax: 0141 287 0311
Website: www.glasgowfilm.org.uk

Isle of Man Film Commission
Illiam Dhone House
2 Circular Road
Douglas
Isle of Man 1M1 1PJ
Tel: 01624 685864
Fax: 01624 685454
email: filmcomm@dti.gov.im
Website: www.gov.im/dti/iomfilm
Hilary Dugdale, Project Manager
Nick Cain, Contracts Manager
Kim Fletcher, Film Officer

Lanarkshire Screen Locations
Dept of Planning & Environment
North Lanarkshire Council
Kildonan Street
Coatbridge ML5 3LN
Tel: 01236 812 387
Fax: 01236 431 068
email: lesliea@northlan.gov.uk
Alan J. Leslie
Covers North Lanarkshire, South
Lanarkshire

Lancashire Film and Television Office
Unit G14
Preston Technology Management
Centre
Marsh Lane
Preston
Lancashire PR1 8UD
Tel: 01772 889090
Fax: 01772 889091
email: lftvo@hotmail.com
David Nelson
Lynda Banister

Liverpool Film Office
Pioneer Buildings
67 Dale Street
Liverpool L2 2NS
Tel: 0151 291 9191
Fax: 0151 291 9199
email: lfo@liverpool.gov.uk
Website: filmliverpool.com
Lynn Saunders, Film Commissioner
Information and Liaison: Tracy Owen
Provides a free film liaison service,
and assistance to all productions
intending to use locations, resources,
services and skills in the Merseyside
area. Undertakes research and
location scouting, liaises with local
agencies and the community. Offers
access to the best range of locations
in the UK through its extensive
locations library. Twelve years
experience of providing a quality
one-stop shop service

London Arts
2 Pear Tree Court
London EC1R 0DS
Tel: 020 7608 6100
Fax: 020 7608 4100
email: Nicola.Reeves@lonab.co.uk
Website: www.arts.org.uk/londonarts
Nicola Reeves, Visual Arts
Administrator
The London Arts Board has no
dedicated funds for Film and Video.
However, it does offer awards to
individual artists working in the
medium of film and video and New
Media. Write to LAB at the above
address for funding guidelines. For all
other film and video enquiries, call
the London Film and Video
Development Agency (qv)

London Film and Video Development Agency (LFVDA)
114 Whitfield Street
London W1T 5EF
Tel: 020 7383 7755
Fax: 020 7383 7745

email: lfvda@lfvda.demon.co.uk
Website: www.lfvda.demon.co.uk
Chief Executive: Gill Henderson
The area of the 32 London Boroughs
and the City of London

Media Development Agency for the West Midlands incorporating Central England Screen Commission

Broad Street House
3rd Floor, 212 Broad Street
Birmingham B15 IAY
Tel: 0121 643 9309
Fax: 0121 643 9064
email: info@mda-wm.org.uk
Website: www.cesc-online.org.uk
Media Development Agency for the
West Midlands and Central England
Screen Commission, Directory &
Database of local production
facilities, crews and talents; location
finding and liaision: low budget
production funding including First
Cut Production scheme; information
resources and counselling service;
legal surgeries; seminars and
masterclasses; media business
development support; copyright
registration scheme

Mid Wales Film Commission

6G Science Park Cefn Llan,
Aberystwyth
Ceredigion SY23 3AH
Tel: 01970 617995
Fax: 01970 617942
email: info@midwalesfilm.com
Website: www.midwalesfilm.com
Mid Wales Film Commission seeks to
promote the use of Mid Wales
facilities and locations for the
production of films, television
programmes and commercial

The North Wales Film Commission

Mentee
Deiniol Road
Bangor
Gwynedd LL57 2UP
Tel: 01286 679685
Fax: 01286 673324
email: fil@gwynedd.gov.uk
Hugh Edwin Jones, Peter Lowther
Area film liaison office for
information on filming in the county
of Gwynedd and Anglesey.
Information provided on locations,
facilities and crew

North West Arts Board

Manchester House
22 Bridge Street
Manchester M3 3AB
Tel: 0161 834 6644
Fax: 0161 834 6969
email: info@nwarte.co.uk
Website: www.arts.org.uk/nwab
Julie Leather, Administrator
Information
Chief Executive: Michael Eakin
Howard Rifkin: Director of Visual
and Media Arts
Arts development organisation for
the North West - Cheshire, Greater
Manchester, Lancashire, Merseyside,
High Peak of Derbyshire

Northern Arts

Ground Floor
Central Square
Forth Street
Newcastle upon Tyne NE1 3PJ
Tel: 0191 255 8500
Fax: 0191 230 5566
email: info@northernarts.org.uk
Website: www.arts.org.uk
Chief Executive: Andrew Dixon
Head of Film, Media and Literature:
Mark Robinson
Teesside, Cumbria, Durham,
Northumberland, Tyne and Wear

Northern Screen Commission (NSC)

Bio Science Centre
International Centre For Life
Times Square
Newcastle upon Tyne NE1 4EP
Tel: 0191 233 9234
Fax: 0191 233 9233
email:nsc@filmhelp.demon.co.uk
Website: www.nsc.org.uk
Peter Spark
Seeking to attract film, video and
television production to the North of
England, NSC can provide a full
liaison service backed by a network of
local authority contacts and public
organisations. Available at no cost is a
locations library, a database on local
facilities and services as well as a full
list of local crew or talent

Scottish Highlands and Islands Film Commission

Comisean Fiolm na Gaidhealtachd's
nan Eilean Alba
Inverness Castle
Inverness 1V2 3EG
Tel: 01463 710221
Fax: 01463 710848
email: trish@scotfilm.org
Website: www.scotfilm.org

Trish Shorthouse, Gordon Ireland,
Anne Wilson
The Scottish Highlands and Islands
Film Commission provides a free,
comprehensive liaison service to the
film and television industry,
including information and advice on
locations, permissions, crew and
services etc. We cover Argyll and
Bute, Highland, Moray, Orkney,
Shetland and the Western Isles, and
have a network of local film liaison
officers able to provide quick and
expert local help, whatevern your
project

Scottish Screen

Second Floor
249 West George Street
Glasgow G2 4QE
Tel: 0141 302 1700
Fax: 0141 302 1711
email: info@scottishscreen.com
Website: www.scottishscreen.com
Chief Executive: Steve McIntyre
Scottish Screen promotes Scotland as
an international filming destination
and encourages incoming production
by co-ordinating locations enquiries.
Working in partnerhip with area
offices Scottish Screen provides
detailed support on locatins, crewing
and facilities and has a library of
35,000 stills covering 4,000 locations,
all on database.

South East Arts Board

Union House
Eridge Road
Tunbridge Wells
Kent TN4 8HF
Tel: 01892 507200
Fax: 01870 242 1259
email: info@seab.co.uk
Website: www.arts.org.uk/sea
Chief Executive: Felicity Harvest
East Sussex, Kent, Surrey and West
Sussex and the unitary authorities of
Brighton and Hove and Medway

South Wales Film Commission

The Media Centre
Culverhouse Cross
Cardiff Cf5 6XJ
Tel: (029) 2059 0240
Fax: (029) 2059 0511
email:
southwalesfilm@compuserve.com
Website: www.southwalesfilm.com
Yvonne Cheal, Commissioner
A member of the British Film
Commission and AFCI, providing
information on locations, media
facilities and services across south

Wales for film and television productions

South West Film Commission (South)
18 Belle Vue Road
Saltash
Cornwall PL12 6ES
Tel: 01752 841199
Fax: 01752 841254
email: infosouth@swfilm.co.uk
Website: www.swfilm.co.uk
Film Commissioner: Sue Dalziel
Offers professional assistance to productions shooting in Devon, Cornwall, Somerset, Dorset, Bristol City, Gloucestershire, Wiltshire
South West Film Commission (North)
59 Prince Street
Bristol B51 4QH
Tel: 0117 907 4315
Fax: 0117 907 4384
email: nfonorth@swfilm.co.uk

South West Media Development Agency
Website: swmediadevagency.co.uk
(For details about regional funding contact the Film Council)

Southern Arts Board
13 St Clement Street
Winchester
Hampshire SO23 9DQ
Tel: 01962 855099
Fax: 01962 861186
email: info@southernarts.co.uk
Website: www.arts.org.uk
Chief Executive: Robert Hutchison
Film, Video and Broadcasting Officer: Jane Gerson
Berkshire, Buckinghamshire, South East Dorset, Hampshire, Isle of Wight, Oxfordshire and Wiltshire

Southern Screen Commission
Town Hall
Bartholomew Square
Brighton BN1 1JA
Tel: 01273 384211
Fax: 01273 384211
email: southernscreen@pavilion.co.uk
Philippe Chandless
Southern Screen promotes and markets locations, personnel and services in the South East to the film and television industries

South West Scotland Screen Commission
Gracefield Arts Centre
28 Edinburgh Road
Dumfries DG1 1NW

Tel: 01387 263666
Fax: 01387 263666
email: screencom@dumgal.gov.uk
Selle Doyle
An unrivalled variety and wealth of locations to suit any style of shoot or budget, plus a free location finding and film liaison service for South West Scotland

West Midlands Arts Board
82 Granville Street
Birmingham B1 2LH
Tel: 0121 631 3121
Fax: 0121 643 7239
email: info@west-midlands-arts.co.uk
Website: www.west-midlands.arts.co.uk
Chief Executive: Sally Luton
Media Officer (Film & Video): Steve Chapman
Minicom/textphone: 0121 643 2815
Herefordshire, Worcestershire, Shropshire, the Wrekin and Telford, Staffordshire, Stoke on Trent, Warwickshire, and the Metropolitan Districts of the West Midlands

Yorkshire Arts Board
21 Bond Street
Dewsbury
West Yorks WF13 1AX
Tel: 01924 455555
Fax: 01924 466522
email: info@yarts.co.uk
Website: www.arts.org.uk
Chief Executive: Roger Lancaster

Yorkshire Screen Commission
The Workstation
15 Paternoster Row
Sheffield S1 2BX
Tel: 0114 279 9115
Fax: 0114 2798593
email: ysc@workstation.org.uk
Website: www.ysc.co.uk
Liz Rymer, Commissioner
Emma Waite – Crew & Facilties Manager
Kaye Elliott – Productions Officer
Stella Litou – Locations Administrator
YSC facilitates film and tv production in the Yorkshire and Humber region and operates a location-finding and crewing service in addition to negotiating location use and securing permissions

US Organisations

American Film Institute
P.O. Box 27999/ 2021
North Western Avenue
Los Angeles, CA 90027
Tel: (323) 856-7600
Fax: Fax (323) 467-4578
Website: www.afionline.org/
The John F. Kennedy Center for the Performing Arts
Washington, D.C. 20566
Tel: (202) 828-4000
Fax (202) 659-1970
Organisation dedicated to preserving the heritage of film and television

AMPAS (Academy of Motion Picture Arts & Sciences)
8949 Wilshire Boulevard
Beverly Hills
CA 90211
Tel: (1) 310 247 3000
Fax: (1) 310 859 9619
Organisation of producers, actors and others which is responsible for widely promoting and supporting the film industry, as well as awarding the annual Oscars

Hollywood Foreign Press Association
292 S.LaCienega Blvd, 316
Beverly Hills
CA 90211
Tel: (1) 310 657 1731
Fax: (1) 310 657 5576
Journalists reporting on the entertainment industry for non–US media. Annual event; Golden Globe Awards – awarding achievements in motion pictures and television

Museum of Television and Radio
25 West 52 Street
New York
NY 10019
Tel: (1) 212 621 6600/6800
Fax: (1) 212 621 6715
The Museum (formerly The Museum of Broadcasting) collects and preserves television and radio programmes and advertising commercials, and makes them available to the public. The collection, which now includes nearly 60,000 programmes, covers 70 years of news, public affairs programmes, documentaries, performing arts, children's programming, sports, and comedy. The Museum organises exhibitions, and screening and listening series

The following is a list of some of the main pan–European film and television organisations, entries for countries of the European Union and the various MEDIA II projects instigated by the European Commission

Pan-European Organisations

ACE (Ateliers du Cinéma Européen/European Film Studio)
68 rue de Rivoli
75004 Paris
France
Tel: (33) 1 44 61 88 30
Fax: (33) 1 44 61 88 40
email: jessica.ace@wanadoo.fr
Director: Sophie Bourdon
ACE is a year-long training-through-projects and development programme designed for independent European cinema producers who have already produced at least one feature film. The selected producers then remain part of the ACE Producers' Network

AGICOA (Association de Gestion Internationale Collective des Oeuvres Audio-Visuelles)
rue de St-Jean 26
1203 Geneva
Switzerland
Tel: (41) 22 340 32 00
Fax: (41) 22 340 34 32
email: info@agicoa.org
Website: www.agicoa.org Hein Endlich, Managing DirectorAGICOA ensures the protection of the rights of producers worldwide when their works are retransmitted by cable. By entering their works in the AGICOA Registers, producers can claim royalties collected for them.

Audio-Visual EUREKA
Permanent Secretariat
rue de la Bonté 5-7
1000 Brussels,
Belgium
Tel: (32) 2 543 76 60
Fax: (32) 2 538 04 39
email: secretariat@aveureka.be
Website: www.aveureka.be
Director: Sylivie Forbin
Audiovisual Eureka is a Pan-European Intergovernmental Organisation for the promotion of cooperation in the European Audiovisual Sector. Membership consists of the 35 members including the European Commission (member) and the Council of Europe (associate member). From 1996-1998 Audiovisual Eureka concentrated on Training (1996), Development (1997) and Distribution (1998). Currently Audiovisual Eureka is focussing on consolidation of the works undertaken so far and accomplishing an external evaluation of the actions and initiatives launched since 1996

Bureau de Liaison Européen du Cinéma
74 avenue Kléber
75016 Paris
Tel: (33) 1 56 90 33 00
Fax: (33) 1 56 90 33 01
email: film.paris@wanaduu.fr
Gilbert Grégoire
Umbrella grouping of cinema trade organisations in order to promote the cinema industry, including CICCE, FEITIS, FIAD, FIAPF, FIPFI and UNIC

Centre for Cultural Research
Dahlmannstr, 26
53113 Bonn
Germany
Tel: (49) 228 211058
Fax: (49) 228 217493
email: zentrum@kulturforsdung.de
Website: www.kulturforsdung.de
Prof Andreas Johannes Wiesand
Research, documentation, and advisory tasks in all fields of the arts and media, especially with 'European' perspectives. Participation in arts and media management courses at university level. Produces publications and supports the founding secretariat of the European Institute for Comparative Cultural Policy and the Arts (ERICArts) with members in 25 European countries (www.ericarts)

EURIMAGES
Council of Europe
Palais de l'Europe
avenue de l'Europe
67075 Strasbourg Cédex, France
Tel: (33) 88 41 26 40
Fax: (33) 88 41 27 60
Website:
www.culture.coe.fr/eurimages
Contact: Executive Secretary
Founded in 1988 by a group of Council of Europe member states. Its objective is to stimulate film and audio-visual production by partly financing the co-production, distribution and exhibition of European cinematographic and audio-visual works. Eurimages now includes 24 member states

Eurocréation Media
rue Debelleyme 3
75003 Paris, France
Tel: (33) 1 44 59 27 01
Fax: (33) 1 40 29 92 46
Jean-Pierre Niederhauser, Anne-Marie Autissier (Consultant)
Eurocr
ation Media develops consultation and expertise in the field of European audio-visual and cinema (research, support for the organisation and conception of European events, training activities)

European Academy for Film & Television
rue Verte 69
1210 Brussels, Belgium
Tel: (32) 2 218 66 07
Fax: (32) 2 217 55 72
Permanent Secretary: Dimitri Balachoff
The purpose of the Academy, a non-profit making association, is the research, development and disclosure of all matters relating to cinema and television chiefly in the European continent, and also in other continents, taking into account artistic, commercial, cultural, economic, financial, historical, institutional, pedagogical, trade union and technical aspects. Quarterly newsletter, ACANEWS

European Audio-visual Observatory

76 allée de la Robertsau
67000 Strasbourg, France
Tel: (33) 3 88 144400
Fax: (33) 3 88 144419
Website: www.obs.coe.int/
Executive Director: Wolfgang Cross.
A Pan-European institution working in the legal framework of the Council of Europe. The Observatory is a public service centre providing information on the European television, film and video industries, aimed at the audio-visual industry, and available in English, French and German. It provides legal, economic and market, and film and television funding related information and counselling, and is working with a network of partner organisations on the developing harmonisation of data covering the whole of Europe. The Observatory also publishes a monthly newsletter (IRIS) on legal development in all of its 33 member States, as well as an annual Statistical Yearbook on Film, Television, Video and New Media and a Legal Guide: Audiovisual Media in Europe. The internet site of the Observatory provides a substantial number of additional reports

European Broadcasting Union (EBU)

Ancienne Route 17a
1218 Grand-Saconnex
Geneva, Switzerland
Tel: (41) 22 717 2111
Fax: (41) 22 717 2200
Website: www.ebu.ch/
Jean-Pierre Julien
The EBU is a professional association of national broadcasters with 117 members in 79 countries. Principal activities: daily exchange of news, sports and cultural programmes for television (Eurovision) and radio (Euroradio); Tv coproductions; technical studies and legal action in the international broadcasting sphere

European Co-production Association

c/o France 2
22 avenue Montaigne
75387 Paris Cedex 08
France
Tel: (33) 1 4421 4126
Fax: (33) 1 4421 5179
A consortium of, at present, six European public service television networks for the co-production of television programmes. Can offer complete finance. Proposals should consist of full treatment, financial plan and details of proposed co-production partners. Projects are proposed to the ECA Secretariat or to member national broadcasters

European Coordination of Film Festivals

64 rue Philippe le Bon
1000 Bruxelles
Tel: (32) 2 280 13 76
Fax: (32) 2 230 91 41
email: cefc@skypro.be
Website: www.eurofilmfest.org
Marie José Carta
A network of 150 audio-visual festivals in Europe to promote the diversity of the European moving image through collaboration projects such as touring programmes, staff exchanges, reserach and conferences on the socio-economic impact of film festivals, electronic subtitling and sponsorship, the quarterly newsletter (EuroFilmFest). The Coordination is funded by MEDIA

European Film Academy (EFA)

Kurfurstendamm 225
D-10719 Berlin
Germany
Tel: (49) 30 88 71 67 - 0
Fax: (49) 30 88 71 67 77
email: efa@europeanfilmacademy.org
Website: www.europeanfilmacademy.org
Chairman: Nik Powell,
Director: Marion Döring
Promotes European cinema worldwide to strengthen its commercial and artistic position, to improve the knowledge and awareness of European cinema and to pass on the substantial experience of the Academy members to the younger generation of film professionals. The European Film Academy presents the annual European Film Awards

European Institute for the Media (EIM)

Kaistrasse 13
40221 Düsseldorf, Germany
Tel: (49) 211 90 10 40
Fax: (49) 211 90 10 456
Head of Research: Runar Woldt
Head of East-West: Dusoun Rejic
Acting Head of Library,
Documentation and Statistics Centre:
Helga Schmid
A forum for research and documentation in the field of media in Europe. Its activities include: research into the media in Europe with a political, economic and juridicial orientation; the organisation of conferences and seminars such as the annual European Television and Film Forum; East-West Co-operation Programme; the development of an advanced studies programme for students and media managers. Publication of the Bulletin in English/French/German, quarterly on European media development, and of the Ukrainian and Russian Bulletin as well as research reports. Officers in Kiev and Moscow. Organises the European Media Summer School, an annual course on media development for advanced students and professionals, and facilitates an information request service

EUTELSAT (European Telecommunications Satellite Organisation)

Tour Maine-Montparnasse
avenue du Maine 33
75755 Paris Cédex 15, France
Tel: (33) 1 45 38 47 47
Fax: (33) 1 45 38 37 00
Website: www.eutelsat.org/
Vanessa O'Connor
EUTELSAT operates a satellite system for intra-European communications of all kinds. Traffic carried includes Television and Radio channels, programme exchanges, satellite newsgathering, telephony and business communications

Fédération Européenne des Industries Techniques de l'Image et du Son (FEITIS)

avenue Marceau 50
75008 Paris
France
Tel: (33) 1 47 23 07 45
Fax: (33) 1 47 23 70 47
A federation of European professional organisations representing those working in film and video services and facilities in all audio-visual and cinematographic markets

Federation Internationale de la Press e Cinématographique (International Federation of Film Critics) (FIPRESCI)

Schleissheimer Str 83
D-80797 Munich
Tel: (49) 89 18 23 03
Fax: (49) 89 18 47 66

Klaus Eder, General Secretary

Fédération Internationale des Producteurs de Films Indépendants (FIPFI)

avenue Marceau 50
75008 Paris,
France
Tel: (33) 1 47 23 70 30
Fax: (33) 1 47 20 78 17
Federation of independent film producers, currently with members in 21 countries. It is open to all independent producers, either individual or groups, provided they are legally registered as such. FIPFI aims to promote the distribution of independent films, to increase possibilities for co-production, to share information between member countries and seeks to defend freedom of expression

FIAD (Fédération Internationale des Associations de Distributeurs de Films)

74 avenue Kléber
75016 Paris
Tel: (33) 1 56 90 33 00
Fax: (33) 1 56 90 33 01
email: film.paris@wanaduu.fr
Président: Gilbert Grégoire
Président d'honneur: Luc Hemelaer
Vice Président: Stephan Hutter,
Antonio Llorens Olive
Secrétaire Général: Antoine Virenque
Represents the interests of film distributors

FIAPF (Fédération Internationale des Associations de Producteurs de Films)

avenue des Champs-Elysées 33
75008 Paris, France
Tel: (33) 1 42 25 62 14
Fax: (33) 1 42 56 16 52
An international level gathering of national associations of film producers (23 member countries). It represents the general interests of film producers in worldwide forums (WIPO, UNESCO, WCO, GATT) and with European authorities (EC, Council of Europe, Audio-visual EUREKA), it lobbies for better international legal protection for film and audio-visual producers

FIAT/IFTA (International Federation of Television Archives)

NRK Norwegian Broadcasting Corp.

DAFA
N-0340 OSLO
Norway
Tel: (+47) 2304 9135
Fax: (+47) 2304 9320
email: Office@fiatifta.org
Website: www.fiatifta.org
Liv Sonstebo, Administrative Coordinator
Peter Dusek (President)
Tedd Johansen (General Secretary)
FIAT membership is mainly made up of the archive services of broadcasting organisations. However, it also encompasses national archives and other television-related bodies. It meets annually and publishes its proceedings and other recommendations concerning television archiving

IDATE (Institut de l'audio-visuel et des télécommunications en Europe)

BP 4167
34092 Montpelier Cédex 5
France
Tel: (33) 4 67 14 44 44
Fax: (33) 4 67 14 44 00
email: info@idate.fr
Website: www.idate.fr
Jean-Dominique Séval: Marketing and Commercial Director

Institut de Formation et d'Enseignement pour les Métiers de l'Image et du Son (FEMIS)

rue Francoeur 6
75018 Paris
France
Tel: (33) 1 42 62 20 00
Fax: (33) 1 42 62 21 00
High level technical training in the audio-visual field for French applicants and those from outside France with a working knowledge of French. Organises regular student exchanges with other European film schools

Institut de Journalisme Robert Schuman - European Media Studies

rue de l'Association 32-34
1000 Brussels
Belgium
Tel: (32) 2 217 2355
Fax: (32) 2 219 5764
Anne de Boeck
Postgraduate training in journalism. Drawing students from all over Europe, it offers nine months

intensive training in journalism for press, radio and television

International Cable Communications Council

boulevard Anspach 1, Box 34
1000 Brussels
Belgium
Tel: (32) 2 211 94 49
Fax: (32) 2 211 99 07
International body gathering European, Canadian, North American and Latin American cable television organisations

International Federation of Actors (FIA)

Guild House
Upper St Martin's Lane
London WC2H 9EG
Tel: 0171 379 0900
Fax: 0171 379 8260
Trade union federation founded in 1952 and embracing 60 performers' trade unions in 44 countries. It organises solidarity action when member unions are in dispute, researches and analyses problems affecting the rights and working conditions of film, television and theatre actors as well as singers, dancers, variety and circus artistes. It represents members in the international arena on issues such as cultural policy and copyright and publishes twice yearly newsheet FOCUS

ISETU/FISTAV

(International Secretariat for Arts, Mass Media and Entertainment Trade Unions/International Federation of Audio-Visual Workers)
IPC, boulevard Charlemagne 1
PO Box 5
1040 Brussels, Belgium
Tel: (32) 2 238 09 51
Fax: (32) 2 230 00 76
General Secretary: Jim Wilson
Caters to the special concerns of unions and similar associations whose members are engaged in mass media, entertainment and the arts. It is a clearing house for information regarding multi-national productions or movement of employees across national borders, and acts to exchange information about collective agreements, legal standards and practices at an international level. It organises conferences, has opened a campaign in support of public service broadcasting, and has begun initiatives ranging from defending screen writers to focusing on the concerns of special groups

The Prince's Trust Partners in Europe

8 Bedford Row
London WC1R 4BA
Tel: 0171 405 5799
Contact: Anne Engel
Offer 'Go and See' grants (max £500) towards partnership projects in Europe to people under 26 out of full time education.

Telefilm Canada/Europe

5 rue de Constantine
Paris 75007
Tel: (33) 1 44 18 35 30
Fax: (33) 1 4705 72 76
email: tfcsheila@attglobal.net
Website: www.telefilm.gc.ca
Director: Sheila de La Varende
Canadian government organisation financing film and television productions. European office provides link between Canada, UK and other European countries

UK EUREKA Unit

Department of Trade and Industry,
3rd Floor, Green Core
151 Buckingham Palace Road
London SW1W 9SS
Tel: 0171 215 1618
Fax: 0171 215 1700
For Advanced Broadcasting Technology: Brian Aldous
Tel: 0171 215 1737
A pan-European initiative to encourage industry-led, market-driven collaborative projects aimed at producing advanced technology products, processes and services

UNIC (Union Internationale des Cinémas)

15 Rue de Berri
75008 Paris
France
Tel: (33) 1 53 93 76 76
Fax: (33) 1 45 53 29 76
Defends the interests of cinema exhibitors worldwide, particularly in matters of law and economics. It publishes UNIC News and a Bulletin. Also provides statistical information and special studies concerning the exhibition sector, to members and others

URTI (Université Radiophonique et Télévisuelle Internationale)

General Secretariat
116, avenue du Président Kennedy
75786 Paris Cedex 16
France

Tel: (33) 1 42 30 39 98
Fax: (33) 1 40 50 89 99
President: Roland Faure
A non-governmental organisation recognised by UNESCO and founded in 1949, URTI is an association of professionals in the audio-visual field from all over the world. Promotes cultural programmes and organisation of projects including the International Grand Prix for Creative Documentaries, the Young Television Prize at the Monte Carlo International Television Festival, the Grand Prix for Radio (since 1989)

Austria

Animation Studio for Experimental Animated Films

University of Applied Arts
Vienna
A - 1010 Wien Salzgries 14
Tel: (43) 1 71133-4635
Fax: (43) 1 71133-4635
email: hubert.sielecki@uni-at.ac.at
Website: www.angewanolte.at
Hubert Sielecki

Association of Audio-visual and Film Industry

Wiedner Haupstrasse 63
1045 Wien
PO Box 327
Tel: (43) 1 50105/3010
Fax: (43) 1 50105/276
email: film@fafo.at
Dr Elmar Peterlunger

Austrian Film Commission

Stiftgasse 6
A-1070 Vienna
Tel: (43) 1 526 33 23-0
Fax: (43) 1 526 68 01
email: office@afc.at
Website: www.afc.at
The Austrian Film Commission is an export and promotion agency. The organisation, financed by public funds, offers a wide variety of services for Austrian producers and creative artists, it acts as consultant whenever its productions are presented in international festivals, and it provides members of the profession in all sectors with comprehensive information as to current activity in the Austrian film industry. It is the aim of all activities to enhance the perception of Austrian film-making abroad. In addition to the major festivals in Berlin, Cannes, Venice and

Toronto, the Austrian Film Commission currently provides support for more than 300 international film festivals and markets. The catalogue Austrian Films published annually, offers an overview, divided in sections, of current Austrian film-making. Others publications: the Austrian Film Guide designed to provide quick access to the Austrian film industry and the newsletter Austrian Film News

Austrian Film Institute

Spittelberggasse 3
A-1070 Wien
Tel: (43) 1 526 97 30
Fax: (43) 1 526 97 30/440
email: office@filminstitut.or.at
Website: www.filminstitut.or.at
Andreas Hruza
Film funding, Eurimages, MEDIA Plus (MEDIA Desk)

Filmakademie Wien

National Film School
Vienna Hochschule für Musik und darstellende Kunst
Metternichgasse 12
A-1030 Wien
Tel: (43) 1 713 52 12 0
Fax: (43) 1 713 52 12 23

Wiener Film Fonds (Vienna Film Fund)

Stiftgasse 6 /2/3
A -1070 Vienna
Tel: (43) 1 526 50 88
Fax: (43) 1 526 50 88
email: wff@wff.at
Website: www.wff.at/wff
Dr Peter Zawrel
The Vienna Film Fund supports professional film making in Vienna and is the key agency contributing to the growth of the national film industry which reflects Austrian society and culture. The Vienna Film Fund works with new and established film makers with a commitment to the film and culture and industry in Vienna. The principal funding categories are Development schemes, Production funding for audiovisual products of all genres and formats and Distribution and marketing schemes. Applicants agree to spend at least twice the investment made by the Vienna Film Fund in their production. Financial support takes either the form of an interest free loan, to be repaid of the net profits when the film is subsequently completed and distributed or the form of a non-repayable subsidy

Belgium

Cinémathèque Royale de Belgique/Royal Film Archive
Rue Ravenstein 23
1000 Brussels
Tel: (32) 2 507 83 70
Fax: (32) 2 513 12 72
email: filmarchive@ledoux.be
Gabrielle Claes
Film preservation. The collection can be consulted on the Archive's premises for research purposes. Edits the Belgian film annual

Commission de Sélection de Films
Ministère de la Culture et des Affaires Sociales
Direction de l'Audio-visuel
Boulevard Léopold II 40
1080 Brussels
Tel: (32) 2 413 22 39
Fax: (32) 2 413 22 42
Christiane Dano, Serge Meurant
Assistance given to the production of short and long features, as well as other audio-visual production by independent producers

Commission de Selection des Films
Ministère de la Communauté francaise de Belgique
Service général de l'Audiovisuel et des Multimèdias
Boulevard Léopold II 44
1080 Brussels
Tel: (32) 2 413 33 42
Fax: (32) 2 413 20 68
email: veronique.pacco@cfwb.be
Website: www.cfwb.be/av
Véronique Pacco
Assistance given to the production of documentaries, short and long features by independent producers

Film Museum Jacques Ledoux
Rue Baron Horta 9
1000 Brussels
Tel: (32) 2 507 83 70
Fax: (32) 2 513 12 72
email: filmmuseum@ledoux.be
Gabrielle Claes
Permanent exhibition of the prehistory of cinema. Five screenings per day - three sound, two silent. Organises one double festival a year: L'Age d'Or Prize and prizes for the distribution of quality films in Belgium

IDEM
227 Chaussee D'ixelles
1050 Brussels
Tel: (32) 2 640 77 31
Fax: (32) 2 640 98 56
Trade association for television producers

Radio-Télévision Belge de la Communauté Française (RTBF)
Blvd Auguste Reyers 52
1044 Brussels
Tel: (32) 2 737 21 11
Fax: (32) 2 737 25 56
Administrateur Général: Jean-Louis Stalport
Public broadcaster responsible for French language services

VRT
Auguste Reyerslaan 52
1043 Brussels
Tel: (32) 2 741 3111
Fax: (32) 2 734 9351
Managing Director: Bert De Graeve
Television: Piet Van Roe
Radio: Chris Cleeren
Public television and radio station serving Dutch speaking Flemish community in Belgium

Denmark

Danish Film Institute/Archive and Cinemateque
Gothersgade 55
DK - 1123 Copenhagen K
Tel: (45) 3374 3400
Fax: (45) 3374 3599
email: museum@dfi.dk
Website: www.dfi.dk
Dan Nissen, Director
The Archive and Cinematheque, founded in 1941, is one of the world's oldest film archives. It has a collection of 25,000 titles from almost every genre and country, and has daily screenings. There is also an extensive library of books and pamphlets, periodicals, clippings, posters and stills

Danmarks Radio (DR)
Morkhojvej 170
2860 Soborg
Tel: (45) 35 20 30 40
Fax: (45) 35 20 26 44
Public service television and radio network

DFI (Danish Film Institute)
Vognmagergade 10
DK - 1120 Copenhagen

Tel: (45) 33 74 34 00
Fax: (45) 33 74 34 01
An autonomous self-governing body under the auspices of the Ministry of Culture, financed through the state budget. Provides funding for the production of Danish feature films, shorts and documentaries, and also supports distribution and exhibition of feature films. Promotes Danish films abroad and finances two community access workshops. FurthermoreDFI purchases and rents out shorts and documentaries on 16mm and video to educational institutions/Libraries and private persons

Film-og TV
Arbejderforeningen
Danish Film and Television Workers Union
Kongens Nytorv 21
Baghuset 3. sal
1050 Copenhagen K
Tel: (45) 33 14 33 55
Fax: (45) 33 14 33 03
Trade union which organises film, video and television workers, and maintains the professional, social, economic and artistic interests of its members. Negotiates collective agreements for feature films, documentaries, commercials, negotiating contracts, copyright and authors' rights. Also protection of Danish film production

Producenterne
Kronprinsensgade 9B
1114 Copenhagen K
Tel: (45) 33 14 03 11
Fax: (45) 33 14 03 65
The Danish Producers' Association of Film, Television, Video and AV

Finland

AVEK - The Promotion Centre for Audio-visual Culture in Finland
Hietaniemenkatu 2
FIN - 00100 Helsinki
Tel: (358) 9 43152350
Fax: (358) 9 43152388
email: avek@avek.kopiosto.fi
Website: www.kopiostofi/avek
AVEK was established in 1987 to promote cinemas, video and television culture. It is responsible for the management of funds arising from authors' copyright entitlements and is used for authors' common purposes (the blank tape levy).

AVEK's support activities cover the entire field of audio-visual culture, emphasis being on the production support of short films, documentaries and media art. The other two activity sections are training of the professionals working in the audio-visual field and audiovisual culture in general

Finnish Film Archive/Suomen Elokuva-arkisto

Pursimiehenkatu 29-31 A
PO Box 177
FIN-00151
Helsinki
Tel: (358) 9 615 40 00
Fax: (358) 9 615 40 242
email: sea@sea.fi
Website: www.sea.fi
Matti Lukkarila
Stock: 10,000 feature film titles; 30,000 shorts and spots; 18,000 video cassettes; 20,000 books and scripts; 330,000 different stills, 110,000 posters; and 40,000 documentation files. The archive arranges regular screenings in Helsinki and other cities. Documentation, database, publications (Finnish national filmography). Publications

Finnish Film Foundation

Kanavakatu 12
Fin-00160 Helsinki
Tel: (358) 9 6220 300
Fax: (358) 9 6220 3050
email: ses@ses.fi
Website: www.ses.fi
Rauha Petähäniemi
Film funding for script, development and production of feature film and documentaries. Audio post production and auditorio services. Distribution and screening support. International activities (cultural export and promotion of Finnish Film)

France

Bibliothèque du Film (BIFI)

100 rue du Faubourg Saint-Antoine
75012 Paris
Tel: (33-1) 53 02 22 30
Fax: (33-1) 53 02 22 39
Website: www.bifi.fr
Contact: Laurent Billia
Documentation
Contact: Marc Vernet
Head Manager

Centre National de la Cinématographie (CNC)

rue de Lübeck 12
75016 Paris
Tel: (33) 1 45 05 1440
Fax: (33) 1 47 55 04 91
Website: www.cnc.fr/
Director-General: Dominique Wallon, Press, Public & Internal Relations: Patrick Ciercoles
A government institution, under the auspices of the Ministry of Culture. Its areas of concern are: the economics of cinema and the audio-visual industries; film regulation; the promotion of the cinema industries and the protection of cinema heritage. Offers financial assistance in all aspects of French cinema (production, exhibition, distribution etc). In 1986, the CNC was made responsible for the system of aid offered to the production of films made for television. These include fiction films, animated films and documentaries. The aim here corresponds to one of the principal objectives of public sector funding, where support is given to the French television industry while the development of a high standard of television is encouraged

Chambre Syndicale des Producteurs et Exportateurs de Films Francais

rue du Cirque 5
75008 Paris
Tel: (33) 1 53 89 01 30
Fax: (33) 1 42 25 94 27
email: cspeff@wanadoo.fr
Pascal Rogard, General Secretary
National federation of French cinema production

Cinémathèque Française - Musée du Cinéma

4, rue de Longchamp
75016 Paris
Tel: (33) 1 53 65 74 57
Fax: (33) 1 53 65 74 97
email: cinematec-jz@magic.jz
Website: www.cinematheque.tm.fr
Marianne de Fleury
Founded in 1936 by Henri Langlois, Georges Franju and Jean Mitry to save, conserve and show films. Now houses a cinema museum, screening theatres, library and stills and posters library

Fédération Nationale des Distributeurs de Films

74 avenue Kliber
75016 Paris
Tel: (33) 1 42 66 05 32
Fax: (33) 1 42 66 96 92
email: film.paris@wanaduu.fr
Antoine Virenque
President: Nicolas Seyilouse, Délégué général: Antoine Virenque
National federation of film distributors

Fédération Nationale des Industries Techniques duCinéma et de l'Audio-visuel

(FITCA)
avenue Marceau 50
75008 Paris
Tel: (33) 1 47 23 75 76
Fax: (33) 1 47 23 70 47
A federation of technical trade associations which acts as intermediary between its members and their market. Maintains a database on all technical aspects of production, and helps French and European companies find suitable partners for research and development or commercial ventures

Forum des images (ex Vidéothèque de Paris)

Forum des Halles
2, Grande Galerie
Porte Saint-Eustache
75001 Paris
Tel: 01 44 76 62 00
Website: www.vdp.fr/

France 2

avenue Montaigne 22
75008 Paris
Tel: (33) 1 44 21 42 42
Fax: (33) 1 44 21 51 45
France's main public service terrestrial television channel

Institut National de l'Audiovisuel (INA)

4, avenue de l'Europe
94366 Bry-sur-Marne Cédex
Tel: (33) 1 49 83 20 00
Fax: (33) 1 49 83 25 80
Website: www.ina.fr/
Television and radio archive; research into new technology; research and publications about broadcasting; production of over 130 first works for television and 15 major series and collections. INA initiates major documentaries and cultural series involving partners from Europe and the rest of the world

Les Archives du Film du Centre National de la Cinématographie

7 bis rue Alexandre Turpault

78390 Bois d'Arcy
Tel: (33) 1 30 14 80 00
Fax: (33) 1 34 60 52 25
email: michelle.aubert@cnc.fr
Website: www.cnc.fr
Michelle Aubert
The film collection includes some 64,000 titles, mostly French features, documentaries and shorts from 1895 to date through the new legal deposit for films which includes all categories of films shown in cinemas including foreign releases. Since 1991, a special pluriannual programme for copying early films, including nitrate film, has been set up. So far, some 1,000 titles have been restored including the whole of the Lumière brothers film production from 1895 to 1905 which covers 1,400 short titles. A detailed catalogue of the Lumiére production is available in print and CD-Rom. Enquiries and viewing facilities for film are available on demand

TF1

1 Quai du Point du Jour
92656 Boulogne, Cédex
Tel: (33) 1 41 41 12 34
Fax: (33) 1 41 41 29 10
Privatised national television channel

Germany

ARD (Arbeitsgemeinschaft der öffentlich rechtlichen Rundfunkanstalten der Bundesrepublik Deutschland)

Programme Directorate of Deutsches Fernsehen
Arnulfstrasse 42
Postfach 20 06 22
80335 Munich
Tel: (49) 89 5900 01
Fax: (49) 89 5900 32 49
email: info@das-erste.de
Website: www.das-erste.de
Christian Blankenburg
One of the two public service broadcasters in Germany, consisting of 10 independent broadcasting corporations

Beauftragter der Bundesregierung für Anglelengesheiten der Kultur und de Medien

Postfach 170290
53108 Bonn
Tel: (49) 1888 681 3594
Fax: (49) 1888 681 3885
email: FriedrichWilhelm.moog@

bkm.brni.bund400.de
Website: www.filmfoerderung-bkm.de
Friedrich-Wilhelm Moog
Awards prizes, grants funds for the production and distribution of German feature films, short films, films for children and young people and documentaries. Promotes film institutes, festivals and specific events. Supervisory body of the Federal Archive for national film production

BVDFP (Bundesverband Deutscher Fernseh - produzenten)

Widenmayerstrasse 32
80538 Munich
Tel: (49) 89 21 21 47 10
Fax: (49) 89 228 55 62
Trade association for independent television producers

Deutsches Filminstitut-DIF

Schaumainkai 41
60596 Frankfurt/Main
Tel: (49) 69 9612200
Fax: (49) 69 620 060
email: Deutsches.Filminstitut@em.uni-frankfurt.de
Website: www.filminstitut.de
Raimar Wiegand
The German Institute for Film Studies is a non-profit making organisation, and its remit includes amassing culturally significant films and publications and documents about film; to catalogue them and make them available for study and research. It also supports and puts on screenings of scientific, cultural and art films

Deutsches Filmmuseum

Schaumainkai 41
60596 Frankfurt/Main
Tel: (49) 69 21 23 88 30
Fax: (49) 69 21 23 78 81
email: info@deutsches-filmmuseum.de
Website: www.deutshces-filmmuseum.de
Prof. Walter Schobert, Director
Hands-Peter Reichmann, Exhibitions/Archives
Ulrike Stejelmayer, Filmtheatre
Thomas Worschech, Filmarchiv
Permanent and temporary exhibitions, incorporates the Cinema, the municipally administered cinémathéque. Film archive and collections of equipment, documentation, stills, posters and designs, music and sound. Library and videothéque

Export-Union des Deutschen Films (EXU)

Sonnenstr. 21
80331 München
Tel: (49) 89 599 787-0
Fax: (49) 89-599 787-30
email: export-union@german-cinema.de
Website: german-cinema.de
Board of Directors: Jochem Strate, Antonio Excoustos, Rolf Bahr, Michel Weber
Managing Director: Christian Dorsch
PR Manager: Susanne Reinker
The Export-Union des Deutschen Films (EXU) is the official trade association for the promotion of the export of German films, with overseas offices located in London, Paris, Rome, Madrid, Buenos Aires, Tokyo, Hongkong, New York and Los Angeles. The EXU maintains a presence at all major film and TV festivals (ie Berlin, Cannes, Montreal, Toronto, Locarno, Venice, MIP-TV, MIPCOM and MIFED). It has a switchboard function for German film companies working abroad as well as for foreign companies and buyers looking for media outlets and coproduction facilities in Germany

FFA (Filmförderungsanstalt)

Presse- und Öffentlichkeitsarbeit
Grosse Präsidentensrasse 9
10178 Berlin
Tel: 030 27 57 7 414/415
Fax: 030 27 57 7 444
email: presse@ffa.de
Website: ffa.de
Rolf Bahr, - Directors General
The German Federal Film Board (FFA), incorporated under public law, is the biggest film funding institution in the country. Its mandate is the all-round raising of standards of quality in German film and cinema and the improvement of the economic structure of the film industry. The annual budget of about 105 million Deutschmarks (53,7 million Eruo) is granted by a levy raised from all major German cinemas and video providers and money of TV-stations. The administrative council of 29 members is a representative cross section of the German film industry including members of the government's upper and lower house as well as public and private TV stations. Funding is offered in the following areas: full-length features, shorts, screenplays, marketing,

exhibition, additional prints and professional training. The Export-Union des Deutschen Films e.V. largely represents the FFA's interests abroad

Film Förderung
Hamburg GmbH
Friedensalle14-16
22765 Hamburg
Tel: (49) 40 39837-0
Fax: (49) 40 39837-10
email: filmfoerderung@ffhh.de
Website: www.ffhh.de
Managing director: Eva Hubert
Subsidies available for: script development; pre-production; co-production and distribution

Filmmuseum Berlin - Deutsche Kinemathek
Potsdamer Strasse 2
10785 Berlin
Tel: (49) 030 300 903
Fax: (49) 030 300 903-13
Hans Helmut Prinzler
German Film Archive with collection of German and foreign films, cine-historical documents and equipment (approx. 10,000 films, over a million photographs, around 20,000 posters, 15,000 set-design and costume sketches, projectors, camera and accessories from the early days of cinema to the 80s). Member of FIAF

FSK (Freiwillige Selbstkontrolle der Filmwirtschaft)
Kreuzberger Ring 56
65205 Wiesbaden
Tel: (49) 611 77 891 0
Fax: (49) 611 77 891 39
email: fsk@spio-fsk.de
Website: www.spio-fsk.de
Film industry voluntary self-regulatory body. Activities are: to examine together with official competent representatives which films can be shown to minors under 18 year olds and under; to discuss the examination of films with youth groups; to organise seminars on the study of film, videos and new media

Kunsthochschule für Medien Köln (Academy of Media Arts)
Peter-Welter-Platz 2
50676
Cologne
Tel: (49) 221 201890
Fax: (49) 221 2018917
The first academy of Arts in Germany to embrace all the audio-visual

media. It offers an Audio-visual Media graduate programme concentrating on the areas of Television/Film, Media Art, Media Design and Art and Media Science

ZDF (Zweites Deutsches Fernsehen)
ZDF-Strasse
PO Box 4040
55100 Mainz
Tel: (49) 6131 702060
Fax: (49) 6131 702052
A major public service broadcaster in Germany

Greece

ERT SA (Hellenic Broadcasting Corporation)
Messoghion 402
15342 Aghia Paraskevi
Athens
Tel: (30) 1 639 0772
Fax: (30) 1 639 0652
National public television and radio broadcaster, for information, education and entertainment

Greek Film Centre
10 Panepistimiou Avenue
10671 Athens
Tel: (30) 1 361 7633/363 4586
Fax: (30) 1 361 4336
Governmental organisation under the auspices of the Ministry of Culture. Grants subsidies for production, promotion and distribution

Ministry of Culture
Cinema Department
Boulinas Street 20
10682 Athens
Tel: (30) 1 322 4737

Ireland

An Chomhairle Ealaíon/The Arts Council
70 Merrion Square
Dublin 2
Tel: (353) 1 6180200
Fax: (353) 1 6761302
The Arts Council/An Chomhairle Ealaíon is the principal channel of Government funding for the arts in Ireland. In the area of film the Council focuses its support on the development of film as an art form and on the individual film-maker as artist. With a budget for film of £975,000 in 1998 the Council supports a national film centre and

archive, four film festivals and a number of film resource organisations. It administers an awards scheme for the production of short dramas, experimental films and community video. It also co-operates with the Irish Film Board and RTE Television in Frameworks, an animation awards scheme

Bord Scannán na hÉireann/Irish Film Board
Rockfort House
St. Augustine Street
Galway
Tel: (353) 91 561398
Fax: (353) 91 561405
email: info@filmboard.ie
Website: www.filmboard.ie
Chief Executive: Rod Stoneman
Business Manager: Andrew Lowe
Applications Officer: Lara de Roiste
Information Co-ordinator: Anna O'Sullivan
Bord Scannán na hÉireann promotes the creative and commercial elements of Irish film-making and film culture for a home and international audience. Each year it supports a number of film projects by providing development and production loans. Normally three submission deadlines annually. Dates and application procedures available from the office

Film Censor's Office
16 Harcourt Terrace
Dublin 2
Tel: (353) 1 676 1985
Fax: (353) 1 676 1898
Sheamus Smith
The Official Film Censor is appointed by the Irish Government to consider and classify all feature films and videos distributed in Ireland

Film Institute of Ireland
Irish Film Centre
6 Eustace Street, Temple Bar
Dublin 2
Tel: (353) 1 679 5744/677 8788
Fax: (353) 1 677 8755
email: info@ifc.ie
The Film Institute promotes film culture through a wide range of activities in film exhibition and distribution, film/media education, various training programmes and the Irish Film Archive. Its premises, the Irish Film Centre in Temple Bar, are also home to Film Base, MEDIA Desk, The Junior Dublin Film Festival, The Federation of Irish Film Societies, and Hubbard Casting. The Building has conference facilities, a

bar cafe and a shop as well as 2 cinemas seating 260 and 115

RTE (Radio Telefis Eireann)
Donnybrook
Dublin 4
Tel: (353) 1 208 3111
Fax: (353) 1 208 3080
Public service national broadcaster

Italy

ANICA (Associazione Nazionale Industrie Cinematografiche e Audiovisive)
Viale Regina Margherita 286
00198 Rome
Tel: (39) 6 442 31 480
Fax: (39) 6 442 31 296/6 440 41 28
Gino de Dominicis
Trade association for television and movie producers and distributors, representing technical industries (post productioncompanies/dubbing/studios/labs); home video producers and distributors; television and radio broadcasters

Fininvest Television
Viale Europa 48
20093 Cologno Monzese, Milan
Tel: (39) 2 251 41
Fax: (39) 2 251 47031
Adriano Galliani
Major competitor to RAI, running television channels Canale 5, Italia Uno and Rete Quattro

Fondazione Cineteca Italiana
Villa Reale, Via Palestro 16
20121 Milan
Tel: (39) 2 799224
Fax: (39) 2 798289
email: cinetecaitaliana@digibank.it
Website: www.cinetecamilano.it
Film Museum
Palazzo Dugnani
Via D Manin 2/b
Tel: (39) 2 6554977
Gianni Comencini
Film archive, film museum. Set up to promote the preservation of film as art and historical document, and to promote the development of cinema art and culture

Istituto Luce S.p.A
Via Tuscolana 1055
00173 Rome
Tel: (39) 6 722931/729921
Fax: (39) 6 7222493/7221127
Presiolente e Administratore

Delegato: Angelo Guglieluni Diretore
Ufficio Stampa e Pubblicità: Patrizia de Cesari
Diretiore Commerciale: Leonardo Tiberi
Created to spread culture and education through cinema. It invests in film, distributes films of cultural interest and holds Italy's largest archive

Museo Nazionale del Cinema
Via Montebello 15
10124 Turin
Tel: (39) 11 8154230
Fax: (39) 11 8122503
Giuliano Soria, Paolo Bertetto, Sergio Toffetti, Donata Pesenti Campagnoni, Luciana Spina. The museum represents photography, pre-cinema and cinema history. Its collections include films, books and periodicals, posters, photographs and cinema ephemera

RAI (Radiotelevisione Italiana)
Viale Mazzini 14
00195 Rome
Tel: (39) 6 361 3608
Fax: (39) 6 323 1010
Italian state broadcaster

Surproduction S.A.S
Via del Rosso Fiorentiono 2/b
50142 Firenze
Tel: (39) 055 712127
Fax: (39) 055 712127
email: contact@surproduction.com
Website: surproduction.com
Bruno Spinazzola

Luxembourg

Cinémathèque Municipale - Ville de Luxembourg
rue Eugène Ruppert 10
2453 Luxembourg
Tel: (352) 4796 2644
Fax: (352) 40 75 19
Official Luxembourg film archive, preserving international film heritage. Daily screenings every year 'Live Cinema' performances - silent films with music. Member of FIAF, (13,000 prints/35mm, 16mm, 70mm)

RTL Group
Blvd Pierre Frieden 45
1543 Luxembourg
Tel: (352) 42 1 42 1
Fax: (352) 42 1 42 2760
email: firstname.lastname@

Rtlgroup.com
Website: www.rtlgroup.com
Anette Rey, Head of Pr
Director of Corporate Communications: Roy Addison
Radio, television; productions and rights, internet

The Netherlands

Filmmuseum
PO Box 74782
1070 BT Amsterdam
Tel: (31) 20 589 1400
Fax: (31) 20 683 3401
email: filmmuseum@nfm.nl
Website: www.nfm.nl/filmmuseum
Film museum with three public screenings each day, permanent and temporary exhibitions, library, film café and film distribution

Ministry of Education, Culture and Science (OCW)
Film Department
PO Box 25.000
2700LZ Zoetermeer
Tel: (31) 79-3234368
Fax: (31) 79-3234959
Rob Docter, Séamus Cassidy
The film department of the Ministry is responsible for the development and maintenance of Dutch film policy. Various different organisations for production, distribution, promotion and conservation of film are subsidised by this department

Nederlandse Omroep Stichting (NOS)
Postbus 26444
1202 JJ Hilversum
Tel: (31) 35 6779 222
Fax: (31) 35 6773 586
Louis Heinsman
Public corporation co-ordinating three-channel public television

Vereniging van Onafhankelijke Televisie Producenten (OTP)
Sumatralaan 45
PO Box 27900
1202 KV Hilversum
Tel: (31) 35 6231166
Fax: (31) 6280051
Director: Andries M. Overste
Trade association for independent television producers (currently 14members)

Portugal

Cinemateca Portuguesa - Museu do Cinema (Portuguese Film Archive - Museum of Cinema)

Rua Barata Salgueiro, No 39
1200-059 Lisboa
Portugal
Tel: 351 21 359 62 00
Fax: 351 21 352 31 80
email: cinemateca@cpmc.pt
João Bénard da Costa, President
José Manuel Costa, Vice President,
Rui Santana Brito, Vice President
National film museum and archive,
preserving, restoring and showing
films. Includes a public documentation
centre, a stills and posters archive

Instituto Português da Arte Cinematográfica e Audiovisual (IPACA)

Rua S Pedro de Alcântara 45-1o
1250 Lisbon
Tel: (351) 1 346 66 34
Fax: (351) 1 347 27 77
President: Zita Seabra, Vice-
Presidents: Paulo Moreira, Salvato
Telles de Menezes
Assists with subsidies, improvement,
regulation and promotion of the
television and film industry

RTP (Radiotelevisão Portuguesa)

Avenida 5 de Outubro 197
1094 Lisbon Cedex
Tel: (351) 1 793 1774
Fax: (351) 1 793 1758
Maria Manuela Furtado
Public service television with two
channels: RTP1 - general, TV2 -
cultural and sports. One satellite
programme, RTP International,
covering Europe, USA, Africa, Macau

Spain

Academia de las Artes y de las Ciencias Cinematográficas de España

General Oraá 68
28006 Madrid
Tel: (34) 1 563 33 41
Fax: (34) 1 563 26 93

Filmoteca Española (Spanish National Film Archive)

Caalle Magdalena 10
28012
Madrid
Tel: 34 91 369 21 18
Fax: 34 91 3699 12 50
Website: www.mcu.es
Director: José Maria Prado; Deputy
Director: Catherine Gautier;
Documentation: Dolores Devesa
National Film Archive, member of
FIAF since 1958. Preserves 26,000
film titles including a large collection
of newsreels. Provides access to
researchers on its premises. The
library and stills departments are
open to the public. Publishes and co-
produces various books on film every
year. Five daily public screenings with
simultaneous translation or
electronic subtitles are held at the
restored Cine Doré, C/Santa Isabel 3,
in the city centre, where facilities
include a bookshop and cafeteria

ICAA (Instituto de la Cinematografia y de las Artes Audio-visuales)

Ministerio de Cultura
Plaza del Rey No1
28071 Madrid
Tel: (34) 1 532 74 39
Fax: (34) 1 531 92 12
Enrique Balmaseda Arias-Dávila
The promotion, protection and
diffusion of cinema and audiovisual
activities in production, distribution
and exhibition. Gives financial
support in these areas to Spanish
companies. Also involved in the
promotion of Spanish cinema and
audio-visual arts, and their influence
on the different communities within
Spain

RTVE (Radiotelevision Española)

Edificio Prado del Rey - 3a planta
Centro RTVE, Prado Del Rey, 22224
Madrid
Tel: (34) 1 5 81 70 00
Fax: (34) 1 5 81 77 57
Head of International Sales RTVE:
Teresa Moreno
National public service broadcaster,
film producer and distributor

Sweden

Oberoende Filmares Förbund (OFF)/Independent Film Producers Association

Box 27 121
102 52 Stockholm
Tel: (46) 8 665 12 21
Fax: (46) 8 663 66 55
email: kansliet@off.se
Website: www.off.se
OFF is a non-profit organisation,
founded 1984, with some 300
members. OFF promotes the special
interests of filmmakers and
independent Swedish producers of
documentaries, short and feature
films. Our purpose is twofold: to raise
the quality of Swedish audiovisual
production and to increase the
quantity of domestic production.
OFF works on many levels. The
organisation partakes in public
debate, organises seminars, publishes
a quarterly newsletter, does lobby-
work on a national level besides
nordic and international networking.
OFF aids its producers with legal
counsel as well as copyright,
economic and insurance policy
advisement

Statens biografbyrå

Box 7728
103 95 Stockholm
Tel: (46) 8 24 34 25
Fax: (46) 8 21 01 78
email:
registrator@statensbiografbyra.se
Website: www.statensbiografbyra.se
Gunnel Arrbäck, Director
The Swedish National Board of Film
Classification (Statens biografbyrå)
was founded in 1911. Films and
videos must be approved and
classified by the Board prior to
showing at a public gathering or
entertainment. For videos intended
for sale or hire, there is a voluntary
system of advance examination

Svenska Filminstitutet (Swedish Film Institute)

Box 27 126
Filmhuset
Borgvägen 1-5
S-10252 Stockholm
Tel: (46) 8 665 11 00
Fax: (46) 8 661 18 20
email: janerik.billinger@sfi.se
Jan-Erik Billinger: Head of the
Information Department
The Swedish Film Institute is the
central organisation for Swedish
cinema. Its activities are to: support
the production of Swedish films of
high merit; promote the distribution
and exhibition of quality films;
preserve films and materials of
interest to cinematic and cultural
history and promote Swedish

cinematic culture internationally

Sveriges Biografägareförbund

Box 1147
S 171 23 Solna
Tel: (946) 8 735 97 80
Fax: (946) 8 730 25 60
The Swedish Exhibitors Association is a joint association for Swedish cinema owners

Sveriges Filmuthyrareförening upa

Box 23021
S-10435 Stockholm
Tel: (946) 8 441 55 70
Fax: (946) 8 34 38 10
Kay Wall
The Swedish Film Distributors Association is a joint association for film distributors

Swedish Women's Film Association

Po Box 27182
S-10251 Stockholm
Visitors address: Filmhuset,
Borgvägen 5
Tel: (46) 8 665 1100/1293
Fax: (46) 8 666 3748
Anna Hallberg
Workshops, seminars, festivals and international exchange programme

MEDIA Programme

MEDIA Plus Programme

European Commission, Directorate General X:
Information, Communication, Culture, Audio-visual
rue de la Loi, 200
1040 Brussels, Belgium
Tel: (32) 2 299 11 11
Fax: (32) 2 299 92 14
Head of Programme: Jacques Delmoly

The MEDIA Plus Programme (2001 - 2005) is an European Union initiative that aims at strengthening the competitiveness of the European audiovisual industry with a series support measures dealing with the training of professionals, development of production projects, distribution and promotion of cinematographic works and audiovisual programmes. The programme was introduced in January 2001 as a follow up to the old MEDIA 2 programme. MEDIA Plus is managed by the Directorate General for Education and Culture at the European Commission in Brussels. It is managed on a national level by a network of 31 offices called the MEDIA Desks, Antennae or Service.

Programme Contents

MEDIA Training

- the programme offers funding for pan-European training initiatives. The Commission supports courses covering subjects such as economic, financial and commercial management, use of new technologies and scriptwriting techniques. These courses are open to all EU nationals. For details on how to participate on these courses, your local Desk, Antenna or Service, will supply you with details.

MEDIA Development

- the programme offers financial support to European independent production companies to develop new fiction, documentary, animation or multimedia projects. Financial support is offered to catalogues of projects (through the "slate funding" scheme) or to one project at a time.

The amounts awarded will not exceed 50% of development budgets. If the project co-financed by MEDIA Plus goes into production, the company has an obligation to reinvest the same amount in the development of one or more production projects.
Companies may apply for funding at any time of the year.

MEDIA Distribution

- the programme supports the distribution and broadcasting of audiovisual works (fiction, documentary, animation, interactive programmes) and of European films in movie theaters, on video, on digital disc and on television. It also provides support to networks of cinemas for the promotion and marketing of European films. There are fixed deadlines for this funding.

MEDIA Promotion

- the programme offers financial support to encourage all kind of promotional activities designed to facilitate European producers and distributors' access and participate at major European and international events. There are fixed deadlines running throughout the year.

Contact Details:

Members of the UK MEDIA team listed below should be the first point of contact for UK companies or organisations seeking information and advice on the MEDIA Plus programme. Guidelines and application forms for all schemes are available from them or downloadable from their web-site:
www.mediadesk.co.uk. However, all completed application forms should be sent directly to the MEDIA Programme office in Brussels, details of which you will find below.

MEDIA Desk UK,

C/o Film Council
10 Little Portland Street
London W1W 7JG
Tel: 020 7861 7507
Fax: 020 7861 7867
email: england@mediadesk.co.uk
Website: www.mediadesk.co.uk
Agnieszka Moody, Director
Will move to permanent office in Central London in
November 2001 – contact Film Council for new address

MEDIA Antenna Cardiff

C/o SGRÎN,
The Bank, 10 Mount Stuart Square,
CARDIFF
UK – CF 10 5EE
Tel.: 00 44 29 20 33 33 04
Fax : 00 44 2920 33 33 20
email : antenna@sgrin.co.uk
Website: www.mediadesk.co.uk
Gwawr Hughes,

MEDIA Antenne Glasgow,

249,West George Street,
Glasgow
UK-G2 4QE.
Tel.: 00 44 1 41 302.17.76
Fax : 00 44 1 41 302 17 78
email: media.scotland@
scottishscreen.com
Website: www.mediadesk.co.uk
Emma Valentine

MEDIA Service for Northern Ireland

21, Ormeau Avenue,
Belfast, UK-BT2 8HD
Tel : 00 44 2890 23 24 44
Fax : 00 44 2890 23 99 18
email: media@nifc.co.uk
Heike Meyer Döring

MEDIA Plus Office in Brussels

MEDIA Plus Programme,
European Commission,
DG Education and Culture, C3,
100, Rue Belliard,
B-1040 Brussels,
Belgium
Tel: 00 322 295 84 06
Fax: 00 322 299 9214
Website:europa.eu.int/comm/avpolicy
/media/index_fr.html
Head of Unit : Jacques Delmoly
Development : Jean Jauniaux
Training: Gisela Gauggel-Robinson
Distribution: Anne Boillot
Promotion/Festivals: Elena Braun

CARTOON

(European Association of Animation
Film)
314 Boulevard Lambermont
B – 1030 Brussels
Belgium
Tel: 00 32 2 245 1200
Fax: 00 32 2 245 4689
email: cartoon@skynet.be
Website: www.cartoon-media.be
Contact: Corinne Jennart, Marc
Vendeweyer
CARTOON, based in Brussels, is a
European animation network which
organises the annual CARTOON
FORUM, co-ordinates the grouping
of animation studios and runs
specialist training courses in
animation.

EUROPA CINEMAS

54 rue Beaubourg
F – 75 003 Paris
France
Tel: 00 33 1 42 71 53 70
Fax: 00 33 1 42 71 47 55
email: europacinema@magic.fr
Website: www.europa-cinemas.org
Contact: Claude-Eric Poiroux, Fatima
Djoumer
The project encourages screenings
and promotion of European films in
a network of cinemas in European
cities. It offers financial support for
screening European films, for
promotional activities and for special
events.

MEDIA SALLES

Via Soperga, 2
I – 20 127 Milan
Tel: 00 39 02 6698 4405
Fax: 00 39 02 669 1574
email: infocinema@mediasalles.it
Website: www.mediasalles.it
Secretary General, Elisabetta Brunella
MEDIA SALLES with Euro Kids
Network is an initiative aimed at
consolidating the availability of
'cinema at the cinema' for children
and young people in Europe, and at
raising the visibility of European film
to a younger audience.

bfi Publishing

bfi Publishing produce a wide range of books for a variety of
audiences, covering film theory, world cinema, film-makers,
television and media studies.

Our authors range from renowned academics and
novelists to film makers, industry specialists and critics,
all sharing their passion for the cinema.

Highlights from our recently published titles include
The British Cinema Book 2nd Edition, the most
comprehensive overview available of the major topics
in British cinema; the first two titles in our BFI
World Directors series, *Youssef Chahine* and
Jane Campion and a fascinating account of an
artist's thinking over three decades in
Experimental Cinema in the Digital Age by
Malcolm Le Grice.

We are also pleased to have published *The
Television Genre Book*, a uniquely ambitious
guide to a major area within television and media
studies, and *The Global Media Atlas*, a
graphically presented guide to the global
communications revolution.

And we continue to produce our indispensable,
annually updated media guides, *Media Courses UK*
and the *BFI Film and Television Handbook*.

Publishing

bfi

PR COMPANIES

The Associates
34 Clerkenwell Close
London EC1R OAU
Tel: 020 7608 2204
Fax: 020 7250 1756
Catherine Flynn, Alison Marsh

Avalon Public Relations
4a Exmoor Street
London W10 6BD
Tel: 020 7598 7222
Fax: 020 7598 7223
email: edt@avalonuk.com
Edward Thomson
Specialist entertainment based pr
agency providing services from pr
and unit publicity to transmission
publicity and media launches

Blue Dolphin PR and Marketing
40 Langham Street
London W1N 5RG
Tel: 020 7255 2494
Fax: 020 7580 7670
email: traceyhislop@
bluedolphinfilms.com
PR and marketing company that
specialises in key areas, such as film,
video, television and music

Byron Advertising, Marketing and PR
Byron House
Wallingford Road
Uxbridge
Middx UB8 2RW
Tel: 01895 252131
Fax: 01895 252137
Les Barnes

Jacquie Capri Enterprises
3rd Floor
46/47 Chancery Lane
London WC21 1JB
Tel: 020 7831 4545
Fax: 020 7831 2557

Emma Chapman Publicity
2nd Floor
18 Great Portland Street
London W1N 5AB
Tel: 020 7637 0990
Fax: 020 7637 0660
email: emma@ecpub.com
Contact: Emma Chapman

CJP Public Relations Ltd
Park House
8 Grove Ash
Mount Farm
Milton Keynes MK 1B2
Tel: 01908 275271
Fax: 01908 275 272
email: c.jardine@cjppr.co.uk
Website: www.cjppr.co.uk
Carolyn Jardine

Max Clifford Associates
109 New Bond Street
London W1Y 9AA
Tel: 020 7408 2350
Fax: 020 7409 2294
Max Clifford

Corbett and Keene
122 Wardour Street
London W1V 3LA
Tel: 020 7494 3478
Fax: 020 7734 2024
Ginger Corbett, Sara Keene, Charlotte
Tudor

Dennis Davidson Associates (DDA)
Royalty House
72-74 Dean Street
London W1V 5HB
Tel: 020 7439 6391
Fax: 020 7437 6358
email: info@ddapr.com
Dennis Davidson, Stacy Wood, Chris
Paton

FEREF Limited
14-17 Wells Mews
London W1A 1ET
Tel: 020 7580 6546
Fax: 020 7631 3156
email: timgarbutt@feref.co.uk
Website: www.feref.com
Peter Andrews, Robin Behling, Brian
Bysouth, Tim Garbutt, Chris Kinsella

Lynne Franks PR
327-329 Harrow Road
London W9 3RB
Tel: 020 7724 6777
Fax: 020 7724 8484
Julian Henry

HPS–PR Ltd
Park House
Desborough Park Road

High Wycombe
Bucks, HP 123 DJ
Tel: 01494 684353
Fax: 01494 440952
email: r.hodges@hps-pr.co.uk
Ms Ray Hodges, MCam MIPR

Sue Hyman Associates
70 Chalk Farm Road
London NW1 8AN
Tel: 020 7485 8489/5842
Fax: 020 7267 4715
email: sue.hyman.@btinternet.com
Sue Hyman

JAC Publicity
1st Floor, Playhouse Court
64 Southwark Bridge Road
London SE1 0AS
Tel: 020 7261 1211
Fax: 020 7261 1214
Claire Forbes

Richard Laver Publicity
3 Troy Court
Kensington High Street
London W8 7RA
Tel: 020 7937 7322
Fax: 020 7937 5976
email: richard@lavpub.u-net.com
Richard Laver

McDonald and Rutter
34 Bloomsbury Street
London WC1B 3QJ
Tel: 020 7637 2600
Fax: 020 7637 3690
email: info@mcdonaldrutter.com
Charles McDonald, Jonathan Rutter

Optimum Communications
34 Hanway Street
London W1P 9DE
Tel: 020 7580 5352
Fax: 020 7636 3945
Nigel Passingham

Porter Frith Publicity & Marketing
26 Danbury Street
London N1 8JU
Tel: 020 7359 3734
Fax: 020 7226 5897
Sue Porter, Liz Frith

S.S.A. Public Relations
Suite 323/324
The Linen Hall

162-168 Regent Street
London W1R 5TB
Tel: 020 7494 2755
Fax: 020 7494 2833
Website: www.ssapr.com
Andrew O'Driscoll
S.S.A Public Relations is a full service
public relations firm that provides
trade and consumer publicity for a
wide range of corporate and
entertainment clients. The company
specialises in key areas, representing
television and theatrical film
production and distribution companies

Soren Fischer

67 Parkway Drive
Queens Park
Bournemouth BH8 9JS
Tel: 01202 393033
Fax: 01202 301516
email: Sorenfischer@
Compuserve.com
Soren Fischer
PR co-ordinator and British
representative, Berlin Film Festival

Peter Thompson Associates

134 Great Portland Street
London W1N 5PH
Tel: 020 7436 5991/2
Fax: 020 7436 0509
Peter Thompson, Amanda Malpass

Town House Publicity

45 Islington Park Street
London N1 1QB
Tel: 020 7226 7450
Fax: 020 7359 6026
email: townhouse@lineone.net
Mary Fulton

UpFront Television Ltd

39-41 New Oxford Street
London WC1A 1BH
Tel: 020 7836 7702
Fax: 020 7836 7701
email: upfront@binternet.com
Claire Nye
Richard Brecker

Warren Cowan/Phil Symes Associates

35 Soho Square
London W1V 6AX
Tel: 020 7439 3535
Fax: 020 7439 3737
Phil Symes, Warren Cowan

Stella Wilson Publicity

130 Calabria Road
London N5 1HT
Tel: 020 7354 5672
Fax: 020 7354 2242
email: stella@starmaker.demon.co.uk
Stella Wilson

PRESS CONTACTS

6degrees.co.uk
39 King Street
London WC2E 8JS
Tel: 020 7420 6315
Fax: 020 7420 6314
email: publisher@6degrees.co.uk
Website: www.6degrees.co.uk
Publisher: Justin Bowyer
Editor: Nick Walker
6degrees is the online UK
independent film magazine, covering
independ, art house and world
cinema news, reviews and article -
plus free weekly newsletter

19
(Monthly)
IPC Magazines
King's Reach Tower
Stamford Street
London SE1 9LS
Tel: 020 7261 6410
Fax: 020 7261 7634
Film: Corrine Barraclough
Magazine for young women
Lead time: 8 weeks
Circulation: 187,740

Arena
(Bi-monthly)
Third Floor, Block A
Exmouth House
Pine Street
London EC1R 0JL
Tel: 020 7689 2266
Fax: 020 7689 0900
Magazine for men covering general
interest, film, literature, music and
fashion
Lead time: 6-8 weeks
Circulation: 100,000

Ariel
(Weekly, Tues)
Room 123, Henry Wood House
3 and 6 Langham Place
London W1A 1AA
Tel: 020 7765 3623
Fax: 020 7765 3646
Deputy Editors: Sally Hillier and
Cathy Loughran
BBC staff magazine
Lead time: Tuesday before
publication
Circulation: 24,000

Art Monthly
Britannia Art Publications,
Suite 17
26 Charing Cross Road
London WC2H 0DG
Tel: 020 7240 0389
Fax: 020 7497 0726
email: info@artmonthly.co.uk
Website: www.artmonthly.co.uk
Editor: Patricia Bickers
Aimed at artists, art dealers, teachers,
students, collectors, arts
administrators, and all those inter-
ested in contemporary visual art
Lead time: 4 weeks
Circulation: 4,000 plus

Asian Times
(Weekly, Tues)
138-148 Cambridge Heath Road
London E1 5QJ
Tel: 020 7702 8012
Fax: 020 7702 7937
Editor: Sanjay Gohil
National, weekly newspaper for
Britain's English-speaking, Asian
community
Press day: Thurs
Circulation: 30,000

BBC News Online
Rm 1560, White City Building
Wood Lane
London W12 7TS
Tel: 020 8752 5318
Fax: 020 8752 7667
Jackie Finlay

The Big Issue
(Weekly, Mon)
236-240 Pentonville Road
Kings Cross
London N1 9JY
Tel: 020 7418 0418
Fax: 020 7418 0427
email: london@bigissue.com
Website: www.bigissue.com
Editor: Becky Gardiner
Arts: Tina Jackson
Film editor: Xan Brooks
General interest magazine, with
emphasis on homelessness. Sold by
the homeless
Lead time: Tues, 3 weeks before
Circulation: ABC figure 142,937

British Film and TV Facilities Journal
Kildare House
102-104 Sheen Road
Richmond
Surrey TW9 1UF
Tel: 020 8334 1159
Fax: 020 8332 1161
email: editorial@dial.pipex.com
Editor: Colin Lenthall
Journal for those working in British
film, TV and video industry

Broadcast
(Weekly, Fri)
EMAP Media
33-39 Bowling Green Lane
London EC1R 0DA
Tel: 020 7505 8014
Fax: 020 7505 8050
Publisher/Editor: Jon Baker
Broadcasting industry news magazine
with coverage of TV, radio, cable and
satellite, corporate production and
international programming and
distribution   Press day: Wed. Lead
time: 2 weeks Circulation: 13,556

The Business of Film
(Monthly)
41-42 Berners Street
London W1P 3AA
Tel: 020 7372 9992
Fax: 020 7486 1969
Website: www.thebusinessoffilm.com
Publisher/executive editor: Elspeth
Tavares
Aimed at film industry professionals -
producers, distributors, exhibitors,
investors, financiers
Lead time: 2 weeks

Cable and Satellite Communications International
(Monthly)
104 City View
463 Bethnal Green Road
London E2 9QY
Tel: 020 7613 5553
Fax: 020 7729 7723
email: de81@dial.pipex.com
Editor: Joss Armitage
Business magazine for professionals in
the cable and satellite television industry
Circulation: 4,029

Caribbean Times

incorporating African Times
(Weekly, Mon)
138-148 Cambridge Heath Road
London E1 5QJ
Tel: 020 7702 8012
Fax: 020 7702 7937
Editor: Clive Morgan
Tabloid dealing with issues pertinent
to community it serves
Press day: Fri
Circulation: 25,000

City Life

(Fortnightly)
164 Deansgate
Manchester M60 2RD
Tel: 0161 832 7200
Fax: 0161 839 1488
email: editorial@citlife.co.uk
Website: www.citylife.co.uk
Editor: Luke Bainbridge
Film editor: Danny Moran
What's on in and around Greater
Manchester
Circulation: 20,000

Company

(Monthly)
National Magazine House
72 Broadwick Street
London W1V 2BP
Tel: 020 7439 5000
Fax: 020 7439 5117
Glossy magazine for women aged 18-
30
Lead time: 10 weeks
Circulation: 272,160

Cosmopolitan

(Monthly)
National Magazine House
72 Broadwick Street
London W1V 2BP
Tel: 020 7439 5000
Fax: 020 7439 5101
Editor: Mandi Norwood
Arts/General: Sarah Kennedy
For women aged 18-35
Lead time: 12 weeks
Circulation: 461,080

Creation

(Monthly)
Contentrepublic
3 St Peter's Street
Islington Green
London N1 8JD
Tel: 020 7704 3309
Fax: 020 7704 8760
Website: contentrepublic.com
Editor: Clare Mount
Film, television, new media
publication
Circulation: 8,000

Creative Review

(Monthly)
St. Giles House
50 Poland Street
London W1V 4AX
Tel: 020 7439 4222
Fax: 020 7734 6748
Editor: Lewis Blackwell
Publisher: Morag Arman-Addey
Trade paper for creative people
covering film, advertising and design.
Film reviews, profiles and technical
features
Lead time: 4 weeks
Circulation: 15,206

Daily Mail

Northcliffe House
2 Derry Street
London W8 5TT
Tel: 020 7938 6000
Fax: 020 7937 4463
Chief showbusiness writer: Baz
Bamigboye
Film: Christopher Tookey
TV: Peter Paterson
National daily newspaper
Circulation: 2,163,676

The Daily Star

Ludgate House
245 Blackfriars Road
London SE1 9UX
Tel: 020 7928 8000
Fax: 020 7922 7962
Film: Sandro Monetti
TV: Pat Codd
Video: Sandro Monetti and Pat Codd
National daily newspaper
Circulation: 654,866

Daily Telegraph

1 Canada Square
Canary Wharf
London E14 5DT
Tel: 020 7538 5000
Fax: 020 7538 6242
Film critic: Quentin Curtis
Arts Editor: Sarah Crompton
TV: Marsha Dunstan
National daily newspaper
Lead time: 1 week
Circulation: 1,117,439

Diva

(Monthly)
Ground Floor
Worldwide House
116-134 Bayham Street
London NW1 0BA
Tel: 020 7482 2576
Fax: 020 7284 0329
email: diva@gaytimes.co.uk
Website: www.gaytimes.co.uk
Editor: Gillian Rodgerson

Lesbian news and culture
Lead times: 4-6 weeks
Circulation: 35,000

Eclipse

(Monthly)
Phoenix Magazines Limited
PO Box 33, Liskeard
Cornwall PL14 4YX
Tel: 01579 344313
Fax: (01579) 344313
email: phoenixmgs@aol.com
Editor: Simon Clarke
Magazine covering the entire
spectrum of science fiction in books,
cinema, television and comics, along
with role playing and computer
games. News, reviews, interviews,
competitions, features, profiles, etc.
Lead time: six weeks
Circulation: 15,000

The Economist

(Weekly)
25 St James's Street
London SW1A 1HG
Tel: 020 7830 7000
Fax: 020 7839 2968
Website: www.economist.com
Film/video/television
(cultural): Tony Thomas;
(business): Frances Cairncross
International coverage of major
political, social and business
developments with arts section
Press day: Wed
Circulation: 327,689

Elle

(Monthly)
Endeavour House
189 Shaftesbury Avenue
London WC2H 8JG
Tel: 020 7208 3458
Fax: 020 7208 3599
Editor: Fiona McIntosh
Arts Ed: Jenny Dyson
Glossy magazine aimed at 18-35 year
old working women
Lead time: 3 months
Circulation: 205,623

Empire

(Monthly)
Elan Network
Endeavour House
189 Shaftesbury Avenue
London WC2H 8JG
Tel: 020 7437 9011
Fax: 020 7859 8613
email: empire@ecm.emap.com
Website: www.empireonline.co.uk
Quality film monthly incorporating
features, interviews and movie news
as well as reviews of all new movies

and videos
Lead time: 3 weeks
Circulation: 161,503

The European
(Weekly, Thurs)
200 Gray's Inn Road
London WC1X 8NE
Tel: 020 7418 7777
Fax: 020 7713 1840/1870
Arts Editor: Andrew Harvey
Editor in Chief: Andrew Neil
In-depth coverage of European news,
politics and culture
Press day: Thurs
Circulation: 160,511

Evening Standard
(Mon-Fri)
Northcliffe House
2 Derry Street
London W8 5EE
Tel: 020 7938 2648
Fax: 020 7937 3193
Film: Alexander Walker, Neil Norman
Media editor: Victor Sebestyen
London weekday evening paper
Circulation: 438,136

Everywoman
(Monthly)
9 St Alban's Place
London N1 0NX
Tel: 020 7704 8440
Fax: 020 7226 9448
Arts editor: Nina Rapi
Feminist magazine covering
mainstream issues
Lead time: 6 weeks
Circulation: 15,000

The Express on Sunday
Ludgate House
245 Blackfriars Road
London SE1 9UX
Tel:020 7928 8000
Fax: 020 7620 1656
Film: Chris Peachment
TV: Nigel Billen
National Sunday newspaper
Circulation: 1,159,759

The Express,
Ludgate House
245 Blackfriars Road
London SE1 9UX
Tel: 020 7928 8000
Fax: 020 7620 1654
Showbusiness editor: Annie Leask
Film: Jason Solomons
TV/Theatre critic: Robert GoeLangton
Showbusiness Correspondent: David
Wigg
National daily newspaper
Circulation: 1,227,971

The Face
(Monthly)
Second Floor, Block A
Exmouth House
Pine Street
London EC1R 0JL
Tel: 020 7689 9999
Fax: 020 7689 0300
Film: Charles Gant, Adam
Higginbotham
Visual-orientated youth culture
magazine: emphasis on music,
fashion and films
Lead time: 4 weeks
Circulation: 100,744

FHM
(Monthly)
Mappin House
London W1N 7AR
Tel: 020 7312 8707
Fax: 020 7312 8191
Editor: Anthony Noguera
Deputy Editor: Ed Halliwell
Assistant Editor: Richard Galpin
Men's lifestyle magazine
Lead time: 6 weeks
Circulation: 755,000

Film Review
(Monthly + 4 specials)
Visual Imagination
9 Blades Court, Deodar Road
London SW15 2NU
Tel: 020 8875 1520
Fax: 020 8875 1588
email: filmreview@visimag.com
Website: www.visimag.com/filmreview
Editor: Neil Corry
Reviews of films on cinema screen
and video; star interviews and
profiles; book and CD reviews
Lead time: 1 month
Circulation: 50,000

Film Waves
(Quarterly)
Obraz Productions Ltd
PO Box 420 Edgware HA8 0XA
Tel: 020 8951 1681
email: filmwaves@filmwaves.co.uk
Website: www.filmwaves.co.uk
Magazine for low/no-budget
filmmakers

Financial Times
1 Southwark Bridge
London SE1 9HL
Tel: 020 7873 3000
Fax: 020 7873 3076
Website: www.ft.com
Arts: Annalena McAfee
Film: Nigel Andrews
TV: Christopher Dunkley
National daily newspaper

Circulation: 316,578

Gay Times
(Monthly)
Ground Floor
Worldwide House
116-134 Bayham Street
London NW1 0BA
Tel: 020 7482 2576
Fax: 020 7284 0329
email: edit@gaytimes.co.uk
Arts editor: James Cary Parkes
Britain's leading lesbian and gay
magazine. Extensive film, television
and arts coverage. Round Britain
guide
Lead time: 6-8 weeks
Circulation: 65,000

The Guardian
119 Farringdon Road
London EC1R 3ER
Tel: 020 7278 2332
Fax: 020 7837 2114
Website: www.guardian.co.uk
Film: Derek Malcolm, Johnathan
Romney
TV critic: Nancy Banks-Smith
Media editor: John Mulholland
Arts editor: Claire Armitstead
Head of Press, PR & Corporate
Affairs: Camilla Nicholls
Weekend editor: Deborah Orr
National daily newspaper
Circulation: 407,870

Harpers & Queen
(Monthly)
National Magazine House
72 Broadwick Street
London W1V 2BP
Tel: 020 7439 5000
Fax: 020 7439 5506
Arts & Films: Anthony Quinn
Glossy magazine for women
Lead time: 12 weeks
Circulation: 93,186

Heat
4th Floor, Mappin House
4 Winsley Street
London W1N 7AR
Tel: 020 7436 1515
Fax: 020 7817 8847
email: heat@ecm.emap.com

The Herald
195 Albion Street
Glasgow G1 1QP
Grays Inn House
127 Clerkenwell Road
London EC1R 5DB
Tel: 020 7405 2121
Fax: 020 7405 1888
Film critic: William Russell (London

address)
TV editor: Ken Wright
Scottish daily newspaper
Circulation: 107,527

The Hollywood Reporter
(daily; weekly international, Tues)
50-51 Bedford Row
London WC1R 4LR
Tel: 020 7822 8301
Fax: 020 7420 6054
email: cdunkley@
hollywoodreporter.com
European bureau chief: Ray Bennett
Deputy bureau chief/European News
Editor: Cathy Dunkley
Showbusiness trade paper
Circulation: 39,000

Home Entertainment Week
(Weekly, Fri)
Bleeding Edge
2-6 Baches Street
London N1 6DL
Tel: 020 7839 7774
Fax: 020 7839 4393
Editor: John Ferguson
Video trade publication for rental
and retail
Lead time: Monday before
publication
Circulation: 7,613

i-D Magazine
(Monthly)
Universal House
251-255 Tottenham Court Road
London W1P 0AE
Tel: 020 7813 6170
Fax: 020 7813 6179
Film & TV: David Sandhu
Youth/fashion magazine with film
features
Lead time: 8 weeks
Circulation: 45,000

Illustrated London News
(2 pa)
20 Upper Ground
London SE1 9PF
Tel: 020 7805 5555
Fax: 020 7805 5911
Editor: Alison Booth
News, pictorial record and
commentary, and a guide to coming
events
Lead time: 8-10 weeks
Circulation: 30,000

In Camera
(Quarterly)
Kodak
Professional Motion Imaging
PO Box 66, Hemel Hempstead
Herts HP1 1JU

Tel: 01442 844875
Fax: 01442 844987
Editor: Josephine Ober
Business editor: Giosi Gallotli
Journal for motion picture industry,
primarily for cinematographers, but
also for other technicians and anyone
in the industry
Lead time: 4 weeks
Circulation: 45,000

The Independent on Sunday
Culture
Independent House
191 Marsh Wall
London E14 9RS
Tel: 020 7005 2362
Fax: 020 7005 2627
Film critic: Jonathan Romney,
Nicholas Barber
TV: Charlotte Edwards
National Sunday newspaper
Lead time: 2 weeks
Circulation: 275,000

The Independent
1 Canada Square
Canary Wharf
London E14 5DL
Tel: 020 7293 2000
Fax: 020 7293 2047
Film: Sam Taylor
TV: Tom Sutcliffe, Gerard Gilbert
Media: Rob Brown
National daily newspaper
Circulation: 257,594

International Connection
25 South Quay
Gt Yarmouth
Norfolk NR30 2RG
Tel: 01493 330565
Fax: 01493 331042
email: film@bnw.demon.co.uk
Website: www.filmtv.dir.co.uk
Susan Foster
Film and TV industry business
magazine

Interzone
(Monthly)
217 Preston Drove
Brighton BN1 6FL
Tel: 01273 504710
Editor: David Pringle
Film: Nick Lowe
Science-fiction magazine
Lead time: 8 weeks
Circulation: 10,000

Jewish Chronicle
(Weekly, Friday)
25 Furnival Street
London EC4A 1JT
Tel: 020 7405 9252

Editor: Edward J Temko
Film critic: Alan Montague
TV critic: Helen Jacobus
Lead time: 2 days
Press day: Wed
Circulation: 47,273

The List
(Fortnightly, Thur)
14 High Street
Edinburgh EH1 1TE
Tel: 0131 558 1191
Fax: 0131 557 8500
email: editor@List.co.uk
Website: www.list.co.uk
Editor: Mark Fisher
Film editor: Miles Fielder
TV: Brian Donaldson
Glasgow/Edinburgh events guide
Lead time: 1 week
Circulation: 18,000

Mail on Sunday
Northcliffe House
2 Derry Street
London W8 5TS
Tel: 020 7938 6000
Fax: 020 7937 3829
Film: Sebastian Faulks
TV critic: Jaci Stephen
National Sunday newspaper
Press day: Fri/Sat
Circulation: 2,325,618

Marie Claire
(Monthly)
2 Hatfields
London SE1 9PG
Tel: 020 7261 5240
Fax: 020 7261 5277
Film Critic: Demetrious Mattheo
Film Editor: Kerry Smith
Women's magazine
Lead time: 3 months
Circulation: 457,034

Media Week
(Weekly, Thur)
Quantum House
19 Scarbrook Road
Croydon CR9 1LX
Tel: 020 8565 4317
Fax: 020 8565 4394
email: mweeked@media.emap.co.uk
Editor: Susannah Richmond
News magazine aimed at the
advertising and media industries
Press day: Wed
Circulation: 13,209 ABC

Melody Maker
(Weekly, Weds)
26th Floor
King's Reach Tower
Stamford Street

London SE1 9LS
Tel: 020 7261 6229
Fax:020 7261 6706
Editor: Mark Sutherland
Film: Ben Knowles/Colin Kennedy
Pop/rock music newspaper
Press day: Fri
Circulation: 40,349

Midweek (Weekly, Thur/West End, Mon/City)
7-9 Rathbone Street
London W1P 1AF
Tel: 020 7636 6651
Fax: 020 7255 2352
Editor: Bill Williamson
Film editor: Derek Malcolm
General interest male/female London
living and arts oriented.
18-35 target age readership
Lead time: 2 weeks
Circulation: 100,000

The Mirror
1 Canada Square
Canary Wharf
London E14 5DP
Tel: 020 7293 3000
Fax: 020 7293 3409
Film: Simon Rose
TV : Tony Purnell
National daily newspaper with
daily/weekly film and television
column
Circulation: 2,355,285
incorporating The Daily Record
(Scottish daily newspaper)

Morning Star
1-3 Ardleigh Road
London N1 4HS
Tel: 020 7254 0033
Fax: 020 7254 5950
Film/TV: Mike Parker
The only national daily oned by its
readers as a co-operative. Weekly film
and TV reviews
Circulation: 9,000

Ms London
(Weekly, Mon)
7-9 Rathbone Street
London W1P 1AF
Tel: 020 7636 6651
Fax: 020 7255 2352
Films: Dee Pilgrim
Free magazine with drama, video,
film and general arts section
Lead time: 2 weeks
Press day: Thurs
Circulation: 94,100

New Musical Express
(Weekly, Wed)
25th Floor

King's Reach Tower
Stamford Street
London SE1 9LS
Tel: 020 7261 5723
Fax: 020 7261 5185
Website: www.nme.com
Film/TV editor: John Mulvey
Rock music newspaper
Lead time: Mon, 1 week before press
day
Circulation: 121,001

New Scientist
(Weekly, Sat avail Thur)
151 Wardour Street
London W1F 8WE
Tel: 020 7331 2701
Fax: 020 7331 2772
email: news@newscientist.com
Website: www.newscientist.com
Editor: Jeremy Webb
Contains articles and reports on the
progress of science and technology in
terms which the non-specialist can
understand
Press day: Mon
Circulation: 135,835

New Statesman and Society
(Weekly, Fri)
7th Floor,
Victoria Station House
191 Victoria Street
London SW1E 5NE
Tel: 020 7828 1232
Fax: 020 7828 1881
email: info@newstatesman.co.uk
Website: www.newstatesman.co.uk
Editor: Peter Wilby
Arts films: Frances Stonor Saunders
Independent radical journal of
political, social and cultural comment
Press day: Mon
Circulation: 26,000

News of the World
News International
1 Virginia Street
London E1 9XR
Tel: 020 7782 1000
Fax: 020 7583 9504
Editor: Phil Hall
Films: Johnathon Ross
TV critic: Charles Catchpole
National Sunday newspaper
Press day: Sat
Circulation: 4,434,856

Nine to Five
(Weekly, Mon)
7-9 Rathbone Street
London W1P 1AF
Tel: 020 7636 6651
Fax: 020 7255 2352

Film: Bill Williamson
Free London magazine
Press day: Wed
Circulation: 160,000

Observer Life Magazine
(Weekly, Sun)
119 Farringdon Road
London EC1R 3ER
Tel: 020 7278 2332
Fax: 020 7239 9837
Supplement to The Observer

The Observer
(Weekly, Sun)
119 Farringdon Road
London EC1R 3ER
Tel: 020 7278 2332
Fax: 020 7713 4250
Arts editor: Jane Ferguson
Film critic: Philip French
TV: Mike Bradley
National Sunday newspaper
Lead time: 1 week
Press day: Fri
Circulation: 450,831

Options
(Monthly)
King's Reach Tower
Stamford Street
London SE1 9LS
Tel: 020 7261 5000
Fax: 020 7261 7344
Film: Susy Feag
TV: Stuart Husband
Women's glossy magazine
Lead time: 3 months
Circulation: 146,692

The PACT Magazine
Producers Alliance for Cinema and
Television
published by MDI Ltd
30/31 Islington Green
London N1 8DU
Tel: 020 7226 8585
Fax: 020 7226 8586
Editor: Clare Mount
PACT members' monthly
Circulation:2,000

The People (Weekly, Sun)
1 Canada Square
Canary Wharf
London E14 5AP
Tel: 020 7510 3000
Fax: 020 7293 3810
Films: Jane Simon
TV: Rachel Lloyd
National Sunday newspaper
Press day: Sat
Circulation: 1,932,237

Picture House
(Annual)

Cinema Theatre Association
c/o Neville C Taylor
Flat 1, 128 Gloucester Terrace
London W2 6HP
Tel: 01444 246893
Documents the past and present
history of cinema buildings
Lead time: 8 weeks
Circulation: 2,000

Pink Paper The
(Weekly, Thur)
Cedar House
72 Holloway Road
London N7 8NZ
Tel: 020 7296 6210
Fax: 020 7957 0046
Editor: Alistair Pegg
Film/TV: Neil Edwards
Britain's national lesbian and gay
newspaper
Lead time: 14 days
Circulation: 53,780

PIX
c/o BFI Publishing
21 Stephen Street
London W1P 2LN
Tel: 020 7957 4789
Fax: 020 7636 2516
Ilona Halberstadt
A counterpoint of images and critical
texts, PIX brings together
experimental, independent and
commercial cinema from all over the
world and explores its relation to
other arts

Press Gazette
19 Scarbrook Road
Croydon
Surrey CR9 1LX
Tel: 020 8565 4200
Fax: 020 8565 4395
email: pged@app.co.uk
Website: www.pressgazette.co.uk
Editor: Philippa Kennedy
Weekly magazine covering all aspects
of the media industry: journalism;
advertising; broadcast; freelance
Press day: Thurs
Circulation: 8,500

Q
(Monthly)
1st Floor
Mappin House
4 Winsley Street
London W1N 7AR
Tel: 020 7312 8182
Fax: 020 7312 8247
Website: www.qonline.co.uk
Editor: Andy Pemberton
Specialist music magazine for 18-45
year olds. Includes reviews of new

albums, films and books
Lead time: 2 months
Circulation: 212,607

Radio Times
(Weekly, Tues)
BBC Worldwide
Woodlands
80 Wood Lane
London W12 0TT
Tel: 020 8576 3999
Fax: 020 8576 3160
Website: www.rtguide.beeb.com
Editor: Sue Robinson
Films: Barry Norman
Features: Kim Newson
Listings: Caroline Meyer
Weekly guide to UK television, radio
and satellite programmes
Lead time: 14 days
Circulation: 1,406,152

Regional Film & Video
(Monthly)
Flagship Publishing
164-165 North Street
Belfast BT1 IGF
Tel: 028 9031 9008
Fax: 028 9031 9101
Editor: Steve Preston
Film and Video Trade Newspaper
Circulation: 12,000

Satellite TV Europe
531-533 King's Road,
London SW10 0TZ
Tel: 020 7351 3612
Website: www.satellite-tv.co.uk/

Scotland on Sunday
108 Holyrood Road
Edinburgh EH8 8AS
Tel: 0131 620 8620
Fax: 0131 620 8615
email: spectrum_sos@scotsman.com
Film: Allan Hunter
Arts and Features: Fiona Lieth
TV: Eddie Gibb
Scottish Sunday newspaper
Lead time: 10 days
Circulation: 110,000

The Scotsman
108 Holyrood Road
Edinburgh EH8 8AS
Tel: 0131 620 8620
Fax: 0131 620 8620
email: online@scotsman.com
Website: www.scotsman.com
Arts Editor: Andrew Burnet
Film critic: Damien Love
Scottish daily newspaper
Circulation: 77,057

Screen Digest
(Monthly)
Lyme House Studios
38 Georgiana Street
London NW1 0EB
Tel: 020 7482 5842
Fax: 020 7580 0060
email:
screendigest@compuserve.com
Managing director: Allan Hardy
Editor: David Fisher
Executive editor: Ben Keen
Deputy editor: Mark Smith
International industry news digest
and research report covering film,
television, cable, satellite, video and
other multimedia information. Has a
centre page reference system every
month on subjects like law, statistics
or sales. Now also available on a
computer data base via fax at 0171
580 0060 under the name Screenfax
(see entry under Screenfax)

Screen Finance
(Fortnightly)
Informa Media
Mortimer House
37-41 Mortimer Street
London W1T 3O7
Tel: 020 7454 1185
Fax: 020 7490 1686
email: x 25@compuserve.com
Editor: Neil McCartney
Detailed analysis and news coverage
of the film and television industries
in the UK and Europe
Lead time: 1-3 days

Screen International
(Weekly, Thur)
EMAP Media
33-39 Bowling Green Lane
London EC1R 0DA
Tel: 020 7505 8056/8080
Fax: 020 7505 8117
email:
Leo.Barraclough@media.emap.co.uk
Website: screendaily.com
Managing Editor: Leo Barraclough
Features: Leo Barraclough
International trade magazine for the
film, television, video, cable and
satellite industries. Regular news,
features, production information
from around the world
Press day: Tue
Features lead time: 3 months
Circulation: 10,000

Screen
(Quarterly)
The Gilmorehill Centre
University of Glasgow

Glasgow G12 8QQ
Tel: 0141 330 5035
Fax: 0141 330 3515
email: screen@arts.gla.ac.uk
Website: www.screen.arts.gla.ac.uk
Caroline Beven
Journal of essays, reports, debates and
reviews on film and television
studies. Organises the annual Screen
Studies Conference
Circulation: 1,400

Screenfax
(Database)
Screen Digest
Lyme House Studios
38 Georgiana Street
London NW1 0EB
Fax: 020 7580 0060
Available on-line via Dialog, Profile,
Data-Star, MAID and most other on-
line databases, or by fax: 0171 580
0060. Provides customised print-outs
on all screen media subjects with
summaries of news developments,
market research. See entry under
Screen Digest

SFX
Future Publishing
30 Monouth Street
Bath BA1 2BW
Tel: 01225 442244
Fax: 01225 480696
email: sfx@futurenet.co.uk
Website: www.sfx.co.uk
Editor: Dave Golder

Shivers
(Monthly)
Visual Imagination
9 Blades Court
Deodar Road
London SW15 2NU
Tel: 020 8875 1520
Fax: 020 8875 1588
Editor: David Miller
Horror film reviews and features
Lead time: 1 month
Circulation: 30,000

Sight and Sound
(Monthly)
British Film Institute
21 Stephen Street
London W1P 2LN
Tel: 020 7255 1444
Fax: 020 7436 2327
Editor: Nick James
Incorporating 'Monthly Film
Bulletin'. Includes regular columns,
feature articles, a book review section
and review/synopsis/credits of every
feature film theatrically released, plus
a brief listing of every video

Copy date: 4th of each month
Circulation: 26,000

South Wales Argus
Cardiff Road
Newport
Gwent NP9 1QW
Tel: 01633 810000
Fax: 01633 462202
Film & TV editor: Lesley Williams
Regional evening newspaper
Lead time: 2 weeks
Circulation: 32,569

The Spectator
(Weekly, Thur)
56 Doughty Street
London WC1N 2LL
Tel: 020 7405 1706
Fax: 020 7242 0603
Arts editor: Elizabeth Anderson
Film: Mark Steyn
TV: James Delingpole and Simon
Hoggart
Independent review of politics,
current affairs, literature and the arts
Press day: Wed
Circulation: 56,313

Stage Screen & Radio
(10 issues a year)
BECTU
111 Wardour Street
London W1V 4AY
Tel: 020 7437 8506
Fax: 020 7437 8268
Editor: Janice Turner
Journal of the film, broadcasting,
theatre and entertainment union
BECTU. Reporting and analysis of
these industries and the union's
activities plus coverage of
technological developments
Lead time: 4 weeks
Circulation: 34,600

The Stage
(Weekly, Thurs)
Stage House
47 Bermondsey Street
London SE1 3XT
Tel: 020 7403 1818
Fax: 020 7357 9287
email: info@thestage.co.uk
Website: www.thestage.co.uk
Editor: Brian Attwood
Weekly trade paper covering all
aspects of entertainment
Circulation: 40,198 ABC

Starburst
*(Monthly + 4 Specials + German
language version)*
Visual Imagination
9 Blades Court

Deodar Road
London SW15 2NU
Tel: 020 8875 1520
Fax: 020 8875 1588
email: Star@cix.compulink.co.uk
Website: www.wisimag.com
Editor: Stephen Payne
Science fiction, fantasy and horror
films, television and video
Lead time: 1 month
Circulation: 45,000

Subway Magazine
The Attic
62 Kelvingrove Street
Glasgow G3 7SA
Tel: 0141 332 9088
Fax: 0141 331 1477
Editor: Gill Mill

The Sun
PO Box 481
1 Virginia Street
London E1 9XP
Tel: 020 7782 4000
Fax: 020 7488 3253
Films: Nick Fisher
Showbiz editor: Dominic Mohan
TV editor: Danny Buckland
TV News: Sarah Crosbie
National daily newspaper
Circulation: 3,875,329

Sunday Express Magazine
Ludgate House
245 Blackfriars Road
London SE1 9UX
Tel: 020 7922 7150
Fax: 020 7922 7599
Editor: Katy Bravery
Supplement to The Express on
Sunday
Lead time: 6 weeks

Sunday Magazine
1 Virginia Street
London E1 9BD
Tel: 020 7782 7000
Fax: 020 7782 7474
Editor: Judy McGuire
Deputy Editor: Jonathan Worsnop
Supplement to News of the World
Lead time: 6 weeks
Circulation: 4,701,879

Sunday Mirror
1 Canada Square
Canary Wharf
London E14 5AP
Tel: 020 7293 3000
Fax: 020 7293 3939
Film critic: Quentin Falk
TV: David Rowe, Pam Francis
National Sunday newspaper
Circulation: 2,268,263

Sunday Telegraph
1 Canada Square
Canary Wharf
London E14 5DT
Tel: 020 7538 7391
Fax: 020 7538 7872
email: starts@telegraph.co.uk
Arts: Susannah Herbert
Film: Jenny McCartney
TV: John Preston
National Sunday newspaper
Circulation: 886,377

Sunday Times
1 Virginia Street
London E1 9BD
Tel: 020 7782 5000
Fax: 020 7782 5731
Film: Tom Shone
TV reviews: A A Gill
Video: George Perry
National Sunday newspaper
Press day: Wed
Circulation: 1,314,576

Sunday Times Magazine
Admiral House
66-68 East Smithfield
London E11 9XW
Tel: 020 7782 7000
Fax: 020 7867 0410
Editor: Robin Morgan
Supplement to Sunday Times
Lead time: 4 weeks
Circulation: 1,314,576

Talking Pictures
34 Darwin Crescent
Laira
Plymouth PL3 6DX
Tel: 01752 347200
Fax: 01752 347200
email: nhwbw@netscapeonline.co.uk
Website: Weebsite:
www.talkingpix.co.uk
Editor: Nigel Watson
Online magazine (formerly Talking
Pictures) devoted to a serious yet
entertaining look at film, computer
entertainment, television and video/DVD

Tatler
(Monthly)
Vogue House
1 Hanover Square
London W1R 0AD
Tel: 020 7499 9080
Fax: 020 7409 0451
Website: www.tatler.co.uk
Editor: Jane Procter
Arts: Celia Lyttleton
Smart society magazine favouring
profiles, fashion and the arts
Lead time: 3 months
Circulation: 88,235

The Teacher
(8 p.a.)
National Union of Teachers
Hamilton House
Mabledon Place
London WC1H 9BD
Tel: 020 7380 4708
Fax: 020 7387 8458
Editor: Mitch Howard
Circulation: 250,000 mailed direct to
all NUT members and to educational
institutions

Telegraph Magazine
1 Canada Square
Canary Wharf
London E14 5AU
Tel: 020 7538 5000
Fax: 020 7513 2500
TV films: Jessamy Calkin
Supplement to Saturday edition of
the Daily Telegraph
Lead time: 6 weeks
Circulation: 1,300,000

Television
(10 p.a.)
Royal Television Society
Holborn Hall
100 Gray's Inn Road
London WC1X 8AL
Tel: 020 7430 1000
Fax: 020 7430 0924
email: info@rts.org.uk
Website: www.rts.org.uk
Editor: Peter Fiddick
Television trade magazine
Lead time: 2 weeks
Circulation: 4,000

Televisual
(Monthly)
St. Giles House
50 Poland Street
London W1V 4AX
Tel: 020 7970 6666
Fax: 020 7970 6733
Editor: Mundy Ellis
Assistant Editor; Keely Winstone
Monthly business magazine for
production professionals in the
business of moving pictures
News lead time: 1 month
Features lead time: 2 months
Circulation: 8,040

Time Out
(Weekly, Tues)
Universal House
251 Tottenham Court Road
London W1P 0AB
Tel: 020 7813 3000
Fax: 020 7813 6028
Website: www.timeout.co.uk
Film: Geoff Andrew, Tom Charity

Video: Derek Adams
TV: Alkarim Jivani
London listings magazine with
cinema and television sections
Listings lead time: 8 days
Features lead time: 1 week
Circulation: 100,000 plus

The Times Educational Supplement Scotland
(Weekly, Fri)
Scott House
10 South St Andrew Street
Edinburgh EH2 2AZ
Tel: 0131 557 1133
Fax: 0131 558 1155
email: scoted@tes.co.uk
Website: www.tes.co.uk/scotland
Editor: Willis Pickard
Press day: Wed
Circulation: 10,000

The Times Educational Supplement
(Weekly, Fri)
Admiral House
66-68 East Smithfield
London E1 9XY
Tel: 020 7782 3000
Fax: 020 7782 3199
Editor: Caroline St John-Brooks
Review editor, Friday magazine:
Geraldine Brennan
Press day: Tuesday
Lead time for reviews: copy 14-21 days
Circulation: 157,000

The Times Higher Educational Supplement
(Weekly, Fri)
Admiral House
66-68 East Smithfield
London E1 9XY
Tel: 020 7782 3000
Fax: 020 7782 3300
Film/TV editor: Sean Coughlan
Press day: Wed
Lead time for reviews: copy 10 days
before publication
Circulation: 26,666

The Times Literary Supplement
(Weekly, Fri)
Admiral House
66-68 East Smithfield
London E1W 1BX
Tel: 020 7782 3000
Fax: 020 7782 3100
email: lettersethe-tls.co.uk
Website: www.the-tls.co.uk
Arts editor: Will Eaves
Press day: Tues
Lead time: 2 weeks
Circulation: 35,000

The Times
1 Pennington Street
London E1 9XN
Tel: 020 7782 5000
Fax: 020 7488 3242
Website: www.the-times.co.uk
Film/video critic: Geoff Brown
Film writer: David Robinson
TV: Matthew Bond
National daily newspaper
Circulation: 747,054

Top Review
England House
25 South Quay
Gt Yarmouth
Norfolk NR30 2RG
Tel: 01493 330565
Fax: 01493 331042
email: edit@bnw.demon.co.uk
Website: www.review.uk.com
Lauren Courtney
Film, video, car, computer book,
travel and DIY reviews
Circulation: 60,000

Total Film
Future Publishing
99 Baker Street
London W1M 1FB
Tel: 020 7317 2600
Fax: 020 7317 1123
email: totalfilm@futurenet.co.uk
Website: www.futurenet.co.uk
Editor: Matt Mueller

Tribune
(Weekly, Fri)
6 Arkwright Road
London NW3 6AN
Tel: 020 7433 6410
Fax: 020 7833 0385
email: george@tribpub.demon.co.uk
Website: www.tribuneuk.co.uk
Editor: Max Seddon
Review editor: Caroline Rees
Political and cultural weekly
Lead time: 14 days
Circulation: 10,000

TV Quick
(Weekly, Mon)
25-27 Camden Road
London NW1 9LL
Tel: 020 7284 0909
Fax: 020 7284 0593
Editor: Jon Gower
Mass market television magazine
Lead time: 3 weeks
Circulation: 799,000

TV Times
(Weekly, Tues)
10th Floor
King's Reach Tower
Stamford Street
London SE1 9LS
Tel: 020 7261 7000
Fax: 020 7261 7777
Editor: Liz Murphy
Film editor: David Quinlan
Weekly magazine of listings and
features serving viewers of
independent TV, BBC TV, satellite
and radio
Lead time: 6 weeks
Circulation: 981,311

TV Zone
(Monthly + 4 specials)
Visual Imagination Limited
9 Blades Court
Deodar Road
London SW15 2NU
Tel: 020 8875 1520
Fax: 020 8875 1588
email: tvzone@visimag.com
Website: www.visimag.com/tvzone
Editor: Tom Spilsbury
Magazine of cult television, past,
present and future, with emphasis on
science fiction and fantasy
Lead time: 1 month
Circulation: 45,000

Uncut
IPC Magazines Ltd
King's Reach Tower
Stamford Street
London SE1 9LS
Tel: 020 7261 6992
Fax: 020 7261 5573
Website: www.uncut.net
Editor: Allan Jones

Variety
(Weekly, Mon) and Daily (Mon-Fri)
6 Bell Yard
London WC2A 2JR
Tel: 020 7520 5222
Fax: 020 7520 5220
email: adam.dawtrey@rbi.co.uk
Website: www.variety.com
Lionel O'Hara, International Sales
Director
European editor: Adam Dawtrey
International showbusiness
newspaper
Press day: Thurs
Circulation: 36,000

View
Oakwood House
422 Hackney Road
London E2 7SY
Tel: 020 7729 6881
Fax: 020 7729 0988
Editor: Branwell Johnson
A weekly trade magazine for the
video industry covering news relevant
to the business from a retail to
distributor level. It carries a complete
listing of the month's rental releases
and a highlighted sell through list.
Regular features include coverage
from the US and interviews with
leading industry figures
Circulation: 8,000

Viewfinder
(4 p.a.)
BUFVC
77 Wells Street
London W1T 3QJ
Tel: 020 7393 1511
Fax: 020 7393 1555
email: viewfinder@bufvc.ac.uk
Website: www.bufvc.ac.uk
Hetty Malcom-Smith, Editor
Periodical for people in higher
education and further education and
research, includes articles on the
production, study and use of film,
television and related media. Also
includes supplement Media Online
Focus Deadlines: 25 January, 24 April,
24 August, 25 October
Lead time: 6 weeks
Circulation: 5,000

Vision
Cinram UK Limited
2nd Floor
109-111 Hammersmith Road
Hammersmith
London W14 OQH
Tel: 020 7471 7800
Fax: 020 7471 7801
email: vision@cinram.com
Bob Thomson
Magazine which provides articles and
information on trends in media
manufacturing, distribution and
retail.

Vogue
(Monthly)
Vogue House
Hanover Square
London W1R 0AD
Tel: 020 7408 0559
Fax: 020 7493 1345
Website: www.vogue.co.uk
Editor: Alexandra Shulman
Films: Susie Forbes
Glossy magazine for women
Lead time: 12 weeks
Circulation: 201,187

The Voice
(Weekly, Monday)
370 Coldharbour Lane
London SW9 8PL
Tel: 020 7737 7377
Fax: 020 7274 8994

Editor in chief: Mike Best
Arts: Lee Pinkerton
Britain's leading black newspaper
with mainly 18-35 age group
readership. Regular film, television
and video coverage
Press day: Friday
Circulation: 52,000

The Web
Media House, Adlington Park
Macclesfield SK10 4NP
Tel: 01625 878888
Fax: 01625 879967
email: web@idg.co.uk
Editor: Mike Cowley
Focusing on lifestyle and culture on
the Net, film and television is
extensively covered with features,
leaders and listing
Lead time: 2 weeks

Western Mail
Thomson House
Cardiff CF1 1WR
Tel: 01222 223333
Fax: 01222 583652
Film: Carolyn Hitt
Daily newspaper
Circulation: 60,251

What DVD?
Future Publishing
Beauford Court
30 Monmouth Street
Bath BA1 2BW
Tel: 01225 442244
Fax: 01225 732282
Website: www.futurenet.com/

What's On In London
(Weekly, Tues)
180 Pentonville Road
London N1 9LB
Tel: 020 7278 4393
Fax: 020 7837 5838
Editor: Michael Darvell
Films & Video: David Clark
London based weekly covering
cinema, theatre, music, arts, books,
entertainment and video
Press day: Mon
Lead time: 10 days
Circulation: 42,000

What's On TV
(Weekly, Tues)
King's Reach Tower
London SE1 9LS
Tel: 020 7261 7769
Fax: 020 7261 7739
Editor: Mike Hollingsworth
TV listings magazine
Lead time: 3 weeks
Circulation: 1,676,000

Yorkshire Post
Wellington Street
Leeds
West Yorkshire LS1 1RF
Tel: 0113 238 8536
Fax: 0113 244 3430
TV editor: Angela Barnes
Regional daily morning newspaper
Deadline: 10.00 pm
Circulation: 100,126

BBC Radio

BBC
Broadcasting House
Portland Place
London W1A 1AA
Tel: 020 7580 4468
Fax: 020 7637 1630

BBC CWR (Coventry & Warwickshire)
25 Warwick Road
Coventry CV1 2WR
Tel: 01203 559911
Fax: 01203 520080

BBC Essex
198 New London Road
Chelmsford
Essex CM2 9XB
Tel: 01245 616000
Fax: 01245 492983
email: essex@bbc.co.uk
Website: www.bbc.co.uk/essex
Margaret Hyde, Station Manager

BBC GMR Talk
PO Box 951
Oxford Road
Manchester M60 1SD
Tel: 0161 200 2000
Fax: 0161 228 6110

BBC Hereford & Worcester
Hylton Road
Worcester WR2 5WW
Tel: 01905 748485
Fax: 01905 748006

BBC Radio Bristol
Broadcasting House
Whiteladies Road
Bristol BS8 2LR
Tel: 0117 974 1111
Fax: 0117 923 8323

BBC Radio Cambridgeshire
Broadway Court, Broadway
Peterborough PE1 1RP
Tel: 01733 312832
Fax: 01733 343768

BBC Radio Cleveland
PO Box 95FM
Broadcasting House
Newport Road
Middlesbrough TS1 5DG
Tel: 01642 225211
Fax: 01642 211356

BBC Radio Cornwall
Phoenix Wharf
Truro TR1 1UA
Tel: 01872 275421
Fax: 01872 240679

BBC Radio Cumbria
Hartington Street
Barrow-in-Furness
Cumbria LA14 5SC
Tel: 01228 835252
Fax: 01228 870008

BBC Radio Derby
PO Box 269
Derby DE1 3HL
Tel: 01332 361111
Fax: 01332 290794
email: radio.derby@bbc.co.uk
Website: bbc.co.uk/radioderby

BBC Radio Devon
PO Box 1034
Broadcasting House
Seymour Road
Mannamead
Plymouth PL3 5YQ
Tel: 01752 260323
Fax: 01752 234599
email: john.lilley@bbc.co.uk
Website: www.co.uk/devon
John Lilley, Editor

BBC Radio Foyle
8 Northland Road
Londonderry BT48 7JD
Tel: 01504 378 600
Fax: 01504 378666

BBC Radio Guernsey
Commerce House
Les Banques
St Peter Port
Guernsey GY1 2HS
Tel: 01481 728977
Fax: 01481 713557

BBC Radio Humberside
9 Chapel Street
Hull HU1 3NU
Tel: 01482 323232
Fax: 01482 226409

BBC Radio Jersey
18 Parade Road
St Helier
Jersey JE2 3PL
Tel: 01534 87000
Fax: 01534 32569

BBC Radio Lancashire
Darwen Street
Blackburn
Lancs BB2 2EA
Tel: 01254 262411
Fax: 01254 680821

BBC Radio Leeds
Broadcasting House
Woodhouse Lane
Leeds LS2 9PN
Tel: 0113 244 2131

Fax: 0113 242 0652

BBC Radio Leicester
Epic House
Charles Street
Leicester LE1 3SH
Tel: 0116 251 6688
Fax: 0116 251 1463

BBC Radio Lincolnshire
PO Box 219
Newport
Lincoln LN1 3XY
Tel: 01522 511411
Fax: 01522 511058

BBC Radio Merseyside
55 Paradise Street
Liverpool L1 3BP
Tel: 0151 708 5500
Fax: 0151 794 0909
Film and video reviewer: Ramsey
Campbell

BBC Radio Newcastle
Broadcasting Centre
Fenham
Newcastle Upon Tyne NE99 1RN
Tel: 0191 232 4141
Fax: 0191 232 5082

BBC Radio Norfolk
Norfolk Tower
Surrey Street
Norwich NR1 3PA
Tel: 01603 617411
Fax: 01603 633692

BBC Radio Northampton
Broadcasting House
Abington Street
Northampton NN1 2BH
Tel: 01604 239100
Fax: 01604 230709

BBC Radio Nottingham
PO York House
Mansfield Road
Nottingham NG1 3JB
Tel: 0115 955 0500
Fax: 0115 955 0501

BBC Radio Oxford
269 Banbury Road
Oxford OX2 7DW
Tel: 01865 311444
Fax: 01865 311996

BBC Radio Sheffield
Ashdell Grove
60 Westbourne Grove
Sheffield S10 2QU
Tel: 0114 268 6185
Fax: 0114 266 4375

BBC Radio Solent
Portfolio House

3 Princes Street
Dorchester
Dorset DT1 1TP
Tel: 01305 269654
Fax: 01305 250910
email: trevor.bevins@bbc.co.uk
Trevor Bevins

BBC Radio Stoke
Cheapside
Hanley
Stoke-on-Trent ST1 1JJ
Tel: 01782 208080
Fax: 01782 289115

BBC Radio Sussex & Surrey
Broadcasting House
Guildford
Surrey GU2 5AP
Tel: 01483 306306
Fax: 01483 304952

BBC Radio WM
PO Box 206
Birmingham B5 7SD
Tel: 0121 414 8484
Fax: 0121 414 8817

BBC Somerset Sound
14-16 Paul Street
Taunton TA1 3PF
Somerset
Tel: 01823 251641
Fax: 01823 332539

BBC Southern Counties
Broadcasting Centre
Guildford GU2 5AP
Tel: 01483 306306
Fax: 01483 304952

BBC Three Counties Radio
PO Box 3CR , Hastings Street
Luton
Bedfordshire LU1 5XL
Tel: 01582 441000
Fax: 01582 401467

BBC Wiltshire Sound
Broadcasting House
Prospect Place
Swindon SN1 3RN
Tel: 01793 513626
Fax: 01793 513650

BBC World Service
Bush House
Strand
London WC2B 4PH
Tel: 020 2757 2171
Fax: 020 7240 3938

Independent Radio

Classic FM
Academic House
24-28 Oval Road
London NW1 7DQ
Tel: 020 7284 3000
Fax: 020 7713 2630

Longwave Radio
Atlantic 252
74 Newman Street
London W1P 3LA
Tel: 020 7637 5252
Fax: 020 7637 3925
Trim, Co Meath, Ireland
Tel/Fax: 00353 463655

Virgin 1215 AM
1 Golden Square
London W1R 4DJ
Tel: 020 7434 1215
Fax: 020 7434 1197

Television

Anglia Television
Anglia House
Norwich NR1 3JG
Tel: 01603 615151
Fax: 01603 615032
Website: www.anglia.tv.co.uk

British Broadcasting Corporation
Television Centre
Wood Lane
London W12 7RJ
Tel: 020 8743 8000
Website: www.bbc.co.uk

Border Television
Television Centre
Carlisle CA1 3NT
Tel: 01228 525101
Fax: 01228 541384
Website: www.border-tv.com

Carlton Television
35-38 Portman Square
London W1H oNU
Tel: 020 7486 6688
Fax: 020 7486 1132

Central Independent Television (East)
Carlton Studios
Lenton Lane
Nottingham NG7 2NA
Tel: 0115 986 3322
Fax: 0115 964 5018

Central Independent Television (South)

9 Windrush Court
Abingdon Business Park
Abingdon
Oxon OX14 1SA
Tel: 01235 554123
Fax: 01235 524024

Channel Five Broadcasting
22 Long Acre
London WC2E 9LY
Tel: 020 7550 5555
Fax: 020 7550 5554

Channel Four Television
124 Horseferry Road
London SW1P 2TX
Tel: 020 7396 4444
Fax: 020 7306 8353

Channel Television
Television House
Bulwer Avenue
St Sampsons
Guernsey GY2 4LA
Tel: 01481 41888
Fax: 01481 41889
The Television Centre
La Pouquelaye
St Helier
Jersey JE1 3ZD
Tel: 01534 816816
Fax: 01534 816689

GMTV
London Television Centre
Upper Ground
London SE1 9TT
Tel: 020 7827 7000
Fax: 020 7827 7249
email: malcolm.douglas@gmtv.co.uk
Website: www.gmtv.co.uk

Grampian Television
Queen's Cross
Aberdeen AB15 4XJ
Tel: 01224 846846
Fax: 01224 846802/846800
North Tonight; Crossfire; News Programmes

Granada Television
Quay Street
Manchester M60 9EA
Tel: 0161 832 7211
Fax: 0161 827 2324
Albert Dock
Liverpool L3 4BA
Tel: 0151 709 9393
White Cross
Lancaster LA1 4XQ
Tel: 01524 606688
36 Golden Square
London W1R 4AH
Tel: 0171 734 8080

Bridgegate House
5 Bridge Place
Lower Bridge Street
Chester CH1 1SA
Tel: 01244 313966

HTV Wales
Television Centre
Culverhouse Cross
Cardiff CF5 6XJ
Tel: 01222 590590
Fax: 01222 590759

HTV West
Television Centre
Bath Road
Bristol BS4 3HG
Tel: 0117 9722722
Fax: 0117 972 3122
HTV News; The West This Week,
West Eye View

Independent Television News (ITN)
200 Gray's Inn Road
London WC1X 8XZ
Tel: 020 7833 3000

Meridian Broadcasting
TV Centre
Northam Road
Southampton SO14 0PZ
Tel: 023 8022 2555
Fax: 023 8033 5050
Website: www.meridiantv.com

S4C
Parc Ty Glas
Llanishen
Cardiff CF4 5DU
Tel: 01222 747444
Fax: 01222 754444
email: s4c@s4c.co.uk
Website: www.S4c.co.uk
Head of Press and Public Relations:
David Meredith

Scottish TV
Cowcaddens
Glasgow G2 3PR
Tel: 0141 300 3000
Fax: 0141 332 9274

Tyne Tees Television
The Television Centre
City Road
Newcastle upon Tyne NE1 2AL
Tel: 0191 261 0181
Fax: 0191 232 2302

Ulster Television
Havelock House
Ormeau Road
Belfast BT7 1EB
Tel: 01232 328122
Fax: 01232 246695

Westcountry Television
Western Wood Way
Language Science Park
Plymouth PL7 5BQ
Tel: 01752 333333
Fax: 01752 333033

Yorkshire Television
The Television Centre
Kirkstall Road
Leeds LS3 1JS
Tel: 0113 243 8283
Fax: 0113 243 3655

News and Photo Agencies

Associated Press
12 Norwich Street
London EC4A 1BP
Tel: 020 7353 1515
Fax: 020 7583 0196

Bridge News
78 Fleet Street
London EC4Y 1HY
Tel: 020 7842 4000
Fax: 020 7583 5032
Business Information Service

Central Office of Information
Hercules Road
London SE1 7DU
Tel: 020 7928 2345
Fax: 020 7928 5037

Central Press Features
20 Spectrum House
32-34 Gordon House Road
London NW5 1LP
Tel: 020 7284 1433
Fax: 020 7284 4494
Film/TV: Chris King

Fleet Street News Agency
68 Exmouth Market
London EC1R 4RA
Tel: 020 7278 5661
Fax: 020 7278 8480

London News Service
68 Exmouth Market
London EC1R 4RA
Tel: 020 7278 5661
Fax: 020 7278 8480

Press Association
292 Vauxhall Bridge Road
London Sw1V 1AE
Tel: 020 7963 7000
Fax: 020 7963 7192
email: www@padd.press.net
Website: www.pa.press.net/

Reuters Ltd
85 Fleet Street
London EC4P 4AJ
Tel: 020 7250 1122
Fax: 020 7542 7921
Website: www.reuters.com
Media: Mary Ellen-Barker

United Press International
408 The Strand
London WC2R 0NE
Tel: 020 7333 0990
Fax: 020 7333 1690

PREVIEW THEATRES

BAFTA
195 Piccadilly
London W1V 0LN
Tel: 020 7465 0277
Fax: 020 7734 1009
Website: www.bafta.org
Formats: Twin 35mm all aspect
ratios. Dolby A, SR, SRD, DTS sound.
35 Double head mono, twin/triple
track stereo plus Dolby Matrix. Twin
16mm and super 16mm, 16 double
head stereo plus Dolby Matrix.
BARCO 9200 Data Video Projector
VHS, Lo Band/Hi Band U-matic,
Beta, Beta SP, Digi Beta. Interfaces for
most PC outputs, SVGA, MAC etc.
35mm slides single, twin and disolve
multi-wau control, Audio, RGB Video
Tie Lines in Theatre. ISDN 2.
Catering by Roux Fine Dining. Seats:
Princess Anee Theatre, 213 Run Run
Shaw Theatre, 30 (not all formats
available), Function Room, up to 200

BUFVC
77 Wells Street
London W1T 3QJ
Tel: 020 7393 1500
Fax: 020 7393 1555
email: services@bufvc.ac.uk
Website: bufvc.ac.uk
Geoffrey O'Brien, Assistant Director
Formats: Viewing rooms equipped
with 16mm double-head, Betacam,
SVHS, VHS, lo-band and hi-band U-
Matic, Betamax, Phillips 1500
Seats: 20-30 max

British Film Institute
21 Stephen Street
London W1P 2LN
Tel: 020 7957 8976
Fax: 020 7436 7950
email: roger.young@bfi.org.uk
Website: www.bfi.org.uk
Roger Young
Picture Formats: All aspect ratios
Film Speeds: 16fps-30fps
Formats: 35mm: Mono/Dolby
A/SR/SRD+EX
16mm: Mono/Dolby A/SR
Video Projection: VHS/SVHS/U-
Matic/Beta SP/DVD/Laserdisc
Hospitality Room; Disabled Access
Seats: 1: 36, 2: 36

Century Preview Theatres
31-32 Soho Square
London W1V 6AP
Tel: 020 7753 7135
Fax: 020 7753 7138
email: projection@foxing.com
Nick Ross
Picture Formats: 1.1:37, 1.1:66,
1.1:85, Super 35, Scope
Sound Formats: (CP 500) Mono,
Dolby A, SR, SR-D+EX. DTS. Double
Head 6 TRK (Magnetic) 2000 ft. Also:
Spotlighting, microphones, lecturns,
for conventions. Most video formats
using DLP
Seating Capacity: 73

Chapter Cinema
Market Road
Canton
Cardiff CF5 1QE
Tel: 01222 311050
Fax: 01222 313431
email: chaptercinema@easynet.co.uk
Website: www.chapter.org.uk
Tony Whitehead, Cinema
Programmer
Formats: 35mm optical, 16mm
optical/sep mag, high quality video
projection, U-Matic/VHS - all
standards. Beta SP PAL2 Channel
infra-red audio
amplification/simultaneous
translation system in both screens.
Reception space, bars and restaurant
Seats: 1:194, 2:68

Columbia TriStar Films UK
Sony Pictures Europe House
25 Golden Square
London W1R 6LU
Tel: 020 7533 1095
Fax: 020 7533 1105
Formats: 35mm optical (SDDS,
Dolby "SR" + "A" type)/double head,
SVA Mag, 16mm optical (Mono),
Super 16 and Super 35. BETA SP,
BVU/U-Matic, VHS, High Definition
Video. Large reception area. Seats: 80

Computer Film Company
19-23 Wells Street
London W1P 3FB
Picture Formats: 1.1:33, 1.1:66,
1.1:85, Super 35, Scope. Variable
speeds, reverse projection if required.
Sound Formats: Mono, Dolby A, SR,
SRD. Video on request. Bar area
Seating: 64

The Curzon Minema
45 Knightsbridge
London SW1X 7NL
Tel: 020 7235 4226
Fax: 020 7235 3426
email:info@minema.com
Website: www.minema.com
Formats: 35mm and 16mm, video
and AV presentations

Curzon Soho
93-107 Shaftesbury Avenue
London W1D 5DY
Tel: 020 7734 9209
Fax: 020 7724 1977
email: joe.bateman@curzon.net
Joe Bateman
Picture Formats: 1.1:33, 1.1:66,
1.1:85, Scope. Kodak slide projection,
Video Projection: Beta SP, Digi-Beta,
Powerpoint Capable, Analogue
Projector, PA on request, all theatres
to THX standard
Sound Formats: Mono, Dolby, A+SR,
SRD, Double headed (magnetic) 3
and 6 Track. Six channel A type and
SR Reduction
Large lounge/reception area available
for hire. In-house Catering: breakfast,
canape and buffet menus available on
request. Full conferencing. Facilities
available
Seats: 1:249 2: 130 3: 110

De Lane Lea
75 Dean Street
London W1V 5HA
Tel: 020 7432 3800
Fax: 020 7432 3838
email: dll@delanelea.com
Website: www.delanelea.com
Picture Formats: 35mm. 1.1:33,
1.1:66, 1.1:85. Super 35, Scope
Sound Formats: Mono, Dolby, A + SR
with double-head capacity
(magnetic) 6,4,3 track stereo
Video: VHS, U-Matic, DVD, Beta sp.
Bar and catering available.
Seating Capacity: 37

Edinburgh Film & TV Studios
Nine Mile Burn
Penicuik EH26 9LT

Tel: 01968 672131
Fax: 01968 672685
(Closed for refurbishment during 2001). Formats: 16mm and 35mm double-head stereo, U-Matic, VHS
Seats: 100

Eon Theatre

Eon House
138 Piccadilly
London W1J 7NR
Tel: 020 7493 7953
Fax: 020 7408 1236
email: Nikki.Hunter@eon.co.uk
Nikki Hunter
Projection 35mm. Picture Formats: 1.1:33 & 1.1:85 Scope
Sound Formats: Mono, Dolby, A&S-R
Video Projection: Video, VHS, BETA SP, DVD, U-Matic & Laserdisc
Computer Projection Facility available for Powerpoint Presentations
Hospitality Suite
Seating: 22

FilmFour Ltd

77-78 Charlotte Street
London W1P 1X
Tel: 020 7868 7700
Fax: 020 7868 7767
Website: www.filmfour.com
Picture Formats: 35mm, 16mm, 16mm super. 1.1:33. 1.1:66, 1.1: 85, Scope
Sound Formats: Mono, Dolby, A+SR, SRD, Double headed (magnetic) (3 Track)
Seating Capacity: 30

Foresight Preview Theatre

Beaumont House
Kensington Village
Avonmore Road
London W14 8TS
Tel: 020 7348 1065
35mm Optical (Dolby A, SR, SRD), 35mm Sep Mag (Monon & Stereo) VHS, Umatic, Betacam, DVD Large Screen Television, Slides, OHP and Multimedia presentation
Seats: 55-70

ICA

12 Carlton House Terrace
London SW1Y 5AH
Tel: 020 7930 0493
Fax: 020 7873 0051
Formats:
Cinema 1: 185 seats 35mm com-opt, Dolby CP, 16mm com-opt, + Sep Mag; video projection Super 16mm
Cinema 2: 45 seats, 35mm com-opt, 16mm com-opt, Super 8, video projection all formats.

Both Cinmas available up to 4.30pm weekdays, 2pm at the weekend. Two regency reception rooms also available, level access to cinemas. Cafe bar available exclusively till noon

Imperial War Museum

(Corporate Hospitality)
Lambeth Road
London SE1 6HZ
Tel: 020 7416 5394
Fax: 020 7416 5392/0171 416 5374
email: film@iwm.org.uk
Website: www.iwm.org.uk
Formats: 35mm and 16mm; Betacam, U-Matic, SVHS and VHS. Catering by arrangement. Large Exhibit Hall, capacity: 1,000 Disabled access
Seats: Cinema: 200

King's Lynn Arts Centre

27/29 King Street
King's Lynn
Norfolk PE30 1HA
Tel: 01553 765565
Fax: 01553 762141
Formats: 16mm, 35mm
Seats: 349

The Lux Cinema

2-4 Hoxton Square
London N1 6NU
Tel: 020 7684 2855
Fax: 020 7684 2222
email: lux@lux.org.uk
The Lux Cinema opens onto Hoxton Square with a distinctive lobby dominated by a back-projection wall and video floor, available for promotional use. The cinema has a polished, semi-sprung wooden floor with stylish, upholstered and fully removable seating. It can be adapted from an auditorium to a 126 square meter shell for master-classes, live music, performance and studio production of film and video. All major projection formats are available, including data projection, with variable and fully programmable electronic screen, lighting and acoustic qualities. Full disabled access throughout, with lower level counter and induction loop
Seats 120

Mr Young's

14 D'Arblay Street
London W1V 3FP
Tel: 020 7437 1771
Fax: 020 7734 4520
Contact: Reuben/Andy/Derry
Formats: 35mm, Super 35mm, U-Matic, VHS, Betacam SP, Dolby stereo double-head optical and magnetic Dolby SR. Large screen video

projection. Bar area, catering by request. Theatres non-smoking
Seats: 1: 42, 2: 25, 3:45

Picture Production Company

19-20 Poland Street
London
W1F 8QF
Tel: 020 7439 4944
Fax: 020 7434 9140
email: sales@theppc.com
Website: www.theppc.com
Sales and Marketing Director: Steve O'Pray
Deluxe Screening Room, Twin 35 mm century projectors, Barco Video Projector, VHS triple standard, umatic triple standard, digibeta and beta sp, DVD and laser disc, Dolby CP500 Cinema Sound Processor, DTS Digital Soundtrack Capacity, Sony SDDS DFP-D3000 Sound Processor, Sondor 3 track magnetic soundhead follower, JBL Screen and Surround Speakers. Modern Catered bar, 40" Pioneer Plasma Screen, Functions, launches, Parties, Private Screenings.
Seats: 25

Pinewood Studios

Sound Department – Preview Theatres
Pinewood Road
Iver Heath
Bucks SL0 0NH
Tel: 01753 656296
Fax: 01753 656014
email: helen_wells@pinewood-studios.co.uk
Website: www.pinewood-studios.co.uk
Contact: Helen Wells
Formats: 35mm, 70mm, Dolby SR, SR.D, DTS, SDDS. Compot, Commag, Sepmag. Separate timecode digital sound screening by arrangement. Screen width 34ft. Disabled access. Lounge available.
Seats: 115 seats

Planet Hollywood

13 Coventry Street
London W1
Tel: 020 7437 7827
Fax: 020 7439 7827
Formats: 35mm, 70mm, SVHS/VHS, U-Matic, Laser Disc, Lucasfilm Ltd THX Sound Sytem, Dolby CP200 + SRD/DTS digital stereo. Super 35mm with separate magnetic tracks and remote volume control. Microphone facilities. Lifts for the

disabled available
Seats: Cinema: 75, Dining area: 85, 120 (standing)

Prominent Facilities THX
68a Delancey Street
London NW1 7RY
Tel: 020 7284 1020
Fax: 020 7284 1202
Formats: 35mm Dolby optical and magnetic, 2,000' double-head, rock 'n' roll. All aspect ratios, and Super 35, 24-25 30fps, triple-track, interlock, Dolby A + SR stereo, 16mm double-head married. Fully air conditioned, kitchen and reception area. Wheelchair access. Seats: 26

RSA
8 John Adam Street
London WC2N 6EZ
Tel: 020 7839 5049
Fax: 020 7321 0271
email: Conference@rsa-uk.demon.co.uk
Website: www.rsa.org.uk
The Great Room
Video Formats: SVHS, Beta SP. Other formats by arrangement.
Barcographics 8100 Projector for Video and Data Projection. Loop system for hard of hearing, disabled access to all rooms. Full catering available: Seats: 202
Durham House Street Auditorium
Video Formats: SVHS, Low band U-matic. Other formats by arrangement. Sony 1252 Projector for Video and Data Projection. Loop system for hard of hearing, disabled access to all rooms. Full catering available. Seats: 60

Screen West
John Brown Publishing
136-142 Bramley Road
London W10 6SR
Tel: 020 7565 3321
Fax: 020 7565 3077
email: projectionist@johnbrown.co.uk
Website: www.johnbrown.co.uk/swest.htm
Jess Tully
Enquiries: Sarah Alliston, Alex Fernades
State of the art preview theatre with luxury seating for 74 people. Formats: 35mm, 16mm, Super 35mm, Double Head, Beta, VHS, PC. Surround Sound: Optical, Magnetic, Digital (SRD and DTS). and full catering facilities in the adjoining function

The Screening Room
The Moving Picture Company
127 Wardour Street

London W1V 4NL
Tel: 020 7494 7879
Fax: 020 7287 9698
email: screening@moving-picture.co.uk
Website: www.moving-picture.co.uk
Matt Bristow, Chief Film Technician (AMPS)
Mark Wiseman, Senior Film Technician
Picture Formats: 35mm Projection, 1.1:37, 1.1:66, 1.1:85, Scope, Super 35. Speeds: 0-50 FPS Forwards/Reverse High Speed Shuttling @ 250 FPS Xenon Lamps with controlled colour temperature
Sound Formats: Optical; Mono, Dolby A, Dolby SR, Dolby Digital SRD, DTS. Magnetic; 6 track, 3 track, 1 track, with/without Reduction.
Video: High Quality 5GV Digital Projection. VHS (PAL, NTSC, SECAM), SVHS, U-Matic(High/Low Band), Digi-Beta, Betacam-SP, D1, DVD(All regions/5.1), VGA, SVGA, XGA. Powerpoint PA System: CD Cassette Stage with Lecturn Autocue(By Arrangement)
Self catering bar/reception area up to 75 people. Fully air conditioned, wheelchair accessible
Seating capacity: 75

Shepperton Studios
Studios Road
Shepperton
Middx TW17 0QD
Tel: 01932 562611/572350
Fax: 01932 568989
email: sheppertonstudios@dial.pipex.com
Formats: 35mm double-head and married, Dolby A + SR, Video U-Matic, NTSC, PAL, SECAM, VHS.
Seats: (35mm) 17

Total Film
99 Baker Street
London W1M 1FB
Tel: 020 7317 2600 or 07788 847190
Fax: 020 7317 1123
Graham Singleton
Fully air conditioned screening room facility with Crestron touch screen remote for computer generated presentations and adjacent boardroom facilities. Format: 35mm print, Betacam and VHS through an overhead CRT with line doubler. Ernemann 15-laser audio projector with both scope and flat lenses. Sony Betacam SP player and professional JVC HRH 507MS VCR with overhead CRT projector. Sound delivery by Sony Digital Camera System with Dolby SR set-up & installed by Dolby

Laboratories
Seats: 24

Twentieth Century Fox
31-32 Soho Square
London W1V 6AP
Tel: 020 7735 7135
Fax: 020 7735 7138
email: projection@foxinc.com
Peter Holland
Picture formats: 1.1:85, 1:1:66 Scope, Super 35
Sound formats (CP500) Mono, Dolby A, SR, SR-D-EX
Double Head (magnetic) 2000ft
Also microphones, most video formats using DLP
Seating: 37

Twickenham Film Studios
St Margaret's
Twickenham
Middx TW1 2AW
Tel: 020 8607 8888
Fax: 020 8607 8889
Formats: 16mm, 35mm.
Seats: 31

UIP International Theatre
UIP House
45 Beadon Road
Hammersmith
London
Tel: 020 8741 9041
email: george_frith@uip.com
George Frith, Chief Projectionist
Picture Formats: 1.1:33, 1.1:66, 1.1:85, Scope
Sound Formats: Mono, Dolby, A+SR, SRD +EX, DTS, SDDS, Double head (magnetic). Mono, SVA, 6 Track
Video: VHS, U-Matic, Beta SP
Seating capacity: 43

Warner Bros
98 Theobalds Road
London WC1X 8WB
Tel: 020 7984 5272

Watershed Media Centre
1 Canons Road
Bristol BS1 5TX
Tel: 0117 9276444
Fax: 0117 9213958
email: info@watershed.co.uk
Formats: Super 8mm, Super 16mm (C1) double-head, 35mm, 35mm double head (C1) (max run 40 mins), 3 Chip D.L.P Video and Computer Projection (C1). Video and data Projections C2 S-VHS U-Matic lo-band, Betacam SP, Dolby A + SR. Lift access, for wheelchair spaces each theatre (prior notification for C2 required)
Seats: 1: 200. 2: 55

A19 Film and Video
21 Foyle Street
Sunderland SR1 1LE
Tel: 0191 565 5709
Fax: 0191 565 6288
Documentary programmes for television. Education/training material for distribution. Low budget fiction work. Production support offered to local and regionally based film-makers, schools, community groups etc

Aardman Animations
Gas Ferry Road
Bristol BS1 6UN
Tel: 0117 984 8485
Fax: 0117 984 848mail
email: mail@aardman.com
Website: www.aardman.com
Award winning character led model animation studio producing films, commercials and television series. Aardman's first theatrical feature film, *Chicken Run*, was released last year. *Tortoise versus Hare* is currently in production

ABTV
From July 99 Agran Barton Television (ABTV) has operated under the name of Harbour Pictures. Harbour Pictures is a subsidiary of Agran Barton Television (ABTV)

Acacia Productions
80 Weston Park
London N8 9TB
Tel: 020 8341 9392
Fax: 020 8341 4879
email: acacia@dial.pipex.com
www.acaciaproductions.co.uk
Recent productions: *Macroeconomics: The Decision-Makers* - a series of (5x30 mins) educational videos for the IMF Institute and CcFiMS at SOAS; *Partnerships in Sustainable Forestry* (16 mins) for Just World. Partners programme for the Community Channel. *Last Plant Standing* , international series of programmes about the global conservation of plant genetic resources (4x50mins) *Seeds of Hope for Rwanda* (25 mins); *A Future for Forests* (25 mins); *The Wokabout Somil* (25 mins); *Spirit of Trees* (8 x

30 min, C4). Current project: *Under Mount Fuji* (2x50 mins on the future of Japanese Society)

Action Time
Wrendal House
2 Whitworth Street West
Manchester M1 5WX
Tel: 0161 236 8999
Fax: 0161 236 8845
email: enquiries@actiont.demon.co.uk
Website: action-time.com
Entertainment programme devisors and producers in UK and Europe. Recent productions: *Catchphrase* (ITV)

Addictive Television
The Old House
39a North Road
London N7 9DP
Tel: 020 7700 0333
Fax: 020 7700 0303
email: mail@addictive.com
Website: www.addictive.com
Nick Clarke, Jim Walters
Recent productions include: *The Web Review* - Internet review series. 52x30mins for ITV. *Transambient* - 6 part music series for C4. *The Short Show* - Short film showcase. 13x1hour for LWT. *Nightshift* - Series of interstitials for ITV.

Adventure Pictures
6 Blackbird Yard
Ravenscroft Street
London E2 7RP
Tel: 020 7613 2233
Fax: 020 7256 0842
email: mail@adventurepictures.co.uk
Produced Sally Potter's *The Man Who Cried*, *Orlando* and *The Tango Lesson* with other features in development. Television documentaries include: Death of a Runaway (RTS award nomination 1992); *Child's Eye* (RTS award nomination 1995); *Looking for Billy*; *Let Me See My Children*; *Our House*; *Searching for Susan*; *Home Alone*; *Stepfamilies*; *The Test*; *Men Who Pay For Sex*; *Footballer's Wives*; *The End is Nigh*; *The Fire Investigators*

After Image
32 Acre Lane

London SW2 5SG
Tel: 020 737 7300
Fax: 020 7326 1850
Website: www.after.arc.co.uk
Currently developing dramas. Recent Productions include Television *Songs of Seduction*, a music drama; *Pull*, a sculptural dance. 2 documentaries shot in Africa. 2 television operas called Camera and *The Empress* (C4) plus *The Score* (BBC2) a classical music magazine series and *The Life*, a dance drama

Agenda Television
Agenda Centre
Park Street
Llanelli FA15 3YE
Tel: 01554 880880
Fax: 01554 880881
email: agenda@agendatv.co.uk
Website: www.agendatv.co.uk
Wales' largest independent production company. Entertainment, drama, features for S4C, C4, BBC, corporate sector. Co-producer of Welsh-based feature films, like *TwinTown*

Alibi Productions
35 Long Acre
London WC2E 9JT
Tel: 020 7845 0420
Fax: 020 7379 7039
email: productions@alibifilms.co.uk
Website: www.alibifilms.co.uk
Linda James
Alibi is active in the financing, international sales and distirbution of theatrical feature films and the production of feature film, television drama and children's programming. Production titles include: *Another Life* (1999) - feature film. *Without Motive* (2000) - 6 part television drama. the *Safe House* (2001) 2 part television drama. *Dead* (2001) - 2 Part Television Comedy

Alive Productions
37 Harwood Road
London SW6 4QP
Tel: 020 7384 2243
Fax: 020 7384 2026
email: alive@chartshow.com
Website: www.alivetelevision.com
TV programme production company

included *Star Test* and *Star Chamber* (both for C4). The company is now producing The Chart Show and a range of animation projects

Allied Films
Kent House
Market Place
London W1N 8AR
Tel: 020 7323 5151
Fax: 020 7631 3568
(See Pathé Productions - Lottery Film Production Franchises)

Alomo Productions
1 Stephen Street
London W1T 1AL
Tel: 020 7691 6531
Fax: 020 7691 6081
Television comedy and drama: *Goodnight Sweetheart; Birds of a Feather; Love Hurts, Shine On Harvey Moon.* A Freemantle Media company

Amy International Productions
PO Box 17
Towcester
Northants NN12 8YJ
Tel: 01295 760256
Fax: 01295 760889
email: simon@ amyinternational.demon.co.uk
Development/pre production: *The Rolex Murder, Dick Francis, Relic Hunter*

Angel Eye Film & TV
Suite 119 29 Great Pulteney Street, London
W1F 9NN
Tel: 020 7437 0082
Fax: 020 7437 0084
email: office@angeleye.co.uk
Website: www.angeleye.co.uk
Having made documentaries for tv for a number of years, recent productions including Fashion *Cuts* (C4) and *The Estate Agents* (series for C4), the company produced their 1st feature *Beginners Luck*, a comedy with Julie Delpy and Steven Berkoff for release in 2001.

Angelic Pictures
21a Colebrooke Row
Angel
Islington
London N1 8AP
Tel: 020 7359 9514
Fax: 020 7359 9153
email: rslw1@hotmail.com
Website: www.angelicpictures.co.uk
Rebecca Wilson
Angelic Pictures supports a broad

range of individual productions - both broadcast and non-broadcast as well as multimedia. A young, dynamic independent whose recent commissions include *Planet Football* for Nickelodeon UK

Anglia Television Limited
Anglia House
Norwich NR1 3JG
Tel: 01603 615151
Fax: 01603 631032
Website: www.anglia.tv.co.uk

Anglo American Pictures
1st Floor, 47 Dean Street
Soho
London W1V 5HL
Tel: 07802 666693
Fax: 01489 894 768
email: inthecannes@hotmail.com
Website:
www.angloamericanpictures.com
Chris Barfoot, President
David Upton (Vice-president)
Productions in development: *Hellion* (The Jesus Gene). *Knights of Delirium*. Productions from this multi-award winning company include *Phoenix* (winner of the Platinum Remi for sci fi/ horror at the Houston Worldfest) and *Dead Clean* (winner of Gold Remi for comedy at the Houston Worldfest). Innovative trailer for *Hellion* picked up Platinum Remi for commercials at Houston

Anglo/Fortunato Films
170 Popes Lane
London W5 4NJ
Tel: 020 8932 7676
Fax: 020 8932 7491
Luciano Centellino
Feature film production company.

The Animation Station
Leisure and Tourism Department
Cherwell District Council
Bodicote House
Bodicote, Banbury
Oxon OX15 4AA
Tel: 01295 252535
Fax: 01295 263155
Suzanne Kennedy
Suzanne.kennedy@cherwell-dc.gov.uk
A specialist arts education producer, distributor and trainer. Works in collaboration with innovative artists and performers from across the world, selecting and commissioning a broad range of high quality work

Animha Productions
121 Roman Road

Linthorpe
Middlesbrough TS5 5QB
Tel: 01642 813 137
email: info@animha.com
Website: www.animha.com
Dave Brunskill

Animus Entertainments
67/71 Goswell Road
London EC1V 7EN
Tel: 020 7490 8234
Fax: 020 7490 8235
Ruth Beni

Antelope
29B Montague Street
London WC1B 5BW
Tel: 020 7209 0099
Fax: 020 7209 0098
email: antelope@antelope.co.uk
Website: antelope.co.uk
Mick Csaky
Dramas and documentaries for broadcast TV in UK, USA, Europe and Japan. Recent productions: *444 Days, A Very British Psycho, Kung Fu Business, Himalaya, Rebel Music* (Bob Marley profile), *People's Planet* (6 x 1 hr ecology series), *Geiko Girl, Russian Missileers, Mozart in Turkey*

Arcane Pictures
46 Wetherby Mansions
Earl Court Square
London SW5 9DI
Tel: 020 7244 6590
Fax: 020 7565 4495
email: info@arcanepictures.com
Philippa Green
Producers: Meg Thomson, George Duffield
Recent productions: *Milk*

Archer Street Ltd
Studio 5
10/11 Archer Street
London W1D 7AZ
Tel: 020 7439 0540
Fax: 020 7437 1182
email: films@archerstreet.com
Andy Paterson, Producer
Feature film production company owned by Frank Cottrell Boyce, Anand Tucker and Andy Paterson, the writer/director/producer team behind the Oscar-nominated *Hilary and Jackie*

Ariel Productions Ltd
Ealing Studios
Ealing Green
Ealing
London W5 5EP
Tel: 0208 567 6655
Otto Plaschkes

Production and development of outsider projects through the National Film Development Fund

Arlington Productions
Pinewood Studios
Iver Heath
Bucks SLO ONH
Tel: 01753 651700
Fax: 01753 656050
TV filmmaker (previously as Tyburn Productions Ltd): *The Masks of Death; Murder Elite; Peter Cushing: A One-Way Ticket to Hollywood*

Ashford Entertainment Corporation
182 Brighton Road
Coulsdon
Surrey CR5 2NF
Tel: 020 8645 0667
Fax: 020 8763 2558
email: info@ashford-entertainment.co.uk
Website: www.ashford-entertainment.co.uk
Georgina Huxstep
Ashford Entertainment is an international award-winning television production company working in the UK, USA and New Zealand. The company produces series, one-off dramas and documentaries on a commission or pre-sale basis only for major broadcasters but is always open to new ideas and submissions from both new and established writers

Assembly Film & Television
Riverside Studios
Crisp Road, Hammersmith
London W6 9RL
Tel: 020 8237 1075
Fax: 020 8237 1071
email: judithmurrell@riversidestudios.co.uk
Website: www.chrysalis.co.uk
William Burdett-Coutts
Television services and feature film development

Richard Attenborough Productions
Twickenham Studios
St Margaret's
Twickenham TW1 2AW
Tel: 020 8607 8873
Fax: 0208744 2766
Judy Wasdell
Recent productions: *Grey Owl*

Avalon Television
4a Exmoor Street
London W10 6BD

Tel: 020 7598 7280
Fax: 020 7598 7281
The Frank Skinner Show (BBC1); *Harry Hill* (Channel 4); *Quiz Ball* (BBC1)

Bark Films
14 Poland Street
London W1F 8QD
Tel: 020 7439 1333
Fax: 7439 1369
email: mail@barkfilms.co.uk
Website: www.barkfilms.co.uk
Paul Blake
Bark Films is an independent production company specializing in commercials and TV sponsorship credits. With extensive experience in all areas of production from live action to animation, clients include BT, Coca Cola, Cadburys, PepsiCo and News International.

Basilisk Communications
Suite 323
Kemp House
152-160 City Road
London EC1V 2NX
Tel 020 7566 4065
email: daybreak@prontomail.com
Jim Hickey

Peter Batty Productions
Claremont House
Renfrew Road
Kingston
Surrey KT2 7NT
Tel: 020 8942 6304
Fax: 020 8336 1661
email: peter@batty.freeserve.co.uk
Recent C4 productions: *Swastika Over British Soil; A Time for Remembrance; The Divided Union; Fonteyn and Nureyev; The Algerian War; Swindle; Il Poverello*. Independent productions: *The Story of Wine; Battle for Warsaw; Battle for Dien Bien Phu; Birth of the Bomb; Search for the Super; Battle for Cassino; Operation Barbarossa; Farouk: Last of the Pharaohs*

Bazal
Shepherds Building Central
Charecroft Way
Shepherds Bush
London W14 0EE
Tel: 0870 333 1700
email: bazalinfo@endymoluk.com
Website: www.endymoluk.com
Peter Bazalgette
Britain's largest non-broadcaster producer of factual entertainment and reality TV, its formats are sold all over the world. It is the creative force behind the UK versions of Endemol

Entertainment's international phenomenon, *Big Brother*. Bazal has pioneered a range of influential genres, including leisure entertainment shows such as *Changing Rooms* and *Ground Force*. Other ongoing peak time successes include *Celebrity Ready Steady Cook* and *Food & Drink*, now in its twentieth year on BBC 2. Bazal is also known for its popular stripped reality shows such as *Pet Rescue* (Channel 4) and *Brighton Rocks* for the Living Channel.

Beambright
Debnershe
The Street
Shalford
Surrey GU4 8BT
Tel: 01483 539343
Fax: 01483 539343
email: theresepickard@cs.com

The Big Group
91 Princedale Road
London W11 4HS
Tel: 020 7229 8827
Fax: 020 7243 146
email: ed.riseman@biggroup.co.uk
Website: www.biggroup.co.uk
Ed Riseman
Services for television and film (PR/Marketing)

Big Wave Productions
7 St. Pancras
Chichester
West Sussex
PO19 1SJ
Tel: 01243 532531
Fax: 01243 532153
email: info@bigwavetv.com
Website: www.bigwavetv.com
Sarah Cunliffe, Nick Stringer
This prize winning documentary company formed in 1995 specialises in human interest, nature and conservation films and is one of the worlds leading independents in this genre of programming. Recent programmes include: *They call him Chantek* (Survival Anglia/Animal Planet), *The Body Snatchers* (National Geographic Explorer), *Shark City* (One Prods), *The Real Dian Fossey* (C4/NGT/PBS) and *Meerkat Madness* (National Geographic Explorer / CNBC)

Black & White Pictures
Teddington Studios
Teddington TW11 9NT
Tel: 020 8614 2344
Fax: 020 8614 2500

email: production@
blackandwhitepictures.co.uk
Joy Mellins - Sean Blowers
(Producers)

Black Coral Productions
2nd Floor
241 High Road
London E17 7BH
Tel: 020 8520 2881
Fax: 020 8520 2358
email: bcp@coralmedia.co.uk
Website: www.black-coral.com
Lazell Daley, Managing Director,
Producer Marcia Miller, Production
Assistant Young indie, nurturing new
talent bringing original perspectives
to the screen in drama, documentary
and multimedia projects

Black Dog Films
42044 Beak Street
London W1F 9RH
Tel: 020 7430 0787
Fax: 020 7734 4978
Website: www.rsafilms.co.uk
Adrian Harrison
Music video company formed by Jake
Scott

Blast! Films
225a Brecknock Road
London N19 5AA
Tel: 020 7267 4260
Fax: 020 7485 2340
email: email:blast@blastfilms.co.uk
Website: www.blastfilms.co.uk
Since its formation in 1994 for the
production of high-profile, distinctive
documentaries about compelling
human stories, starting with *I'll Be
Your Mirror*, about the American
photographer Nan Goldin, Blast! has
completed a number of other
documentary projects including *Soap
Fiction, One Night Stand, The Real Er,
Life After Soap, Boogie Nights In
Suburbia, The Two Cultures, and
Secrets And Lines.* The arts series Vile
Bodies and Cutting Edge special Tina
Goes Shopping have both received
BAFTA nominations. The company
has also now moved into drama
production, which includes *Tales
From Pleasure Beach*, a darkly comic
three part drama series.

Roger Bolton Productions
6-9 Cynthia Street
London N1 9JF
Tel: 020 7713 6868
Fax: 020 7713 6999
email: info@rogerboltonco.uk

Braunarts
The Beehive
226a Gipsy Road
London SE27 9RB
Tel: 020 8670 9917
Fax: 020 8670 9917
email: terry@braunarts.com &
gabi@braunarts.com
Website: www.braunarts.com
Contact: Gabi Braun & Terry Braun
Braunarts (previously known as
Illuminations Interactive) works as
both broadcast television and
multimedia producers with a strong
emphasis on the production of digital
media. Braunarts focuses on three
interconnected areas of work:
* The Performing Arts
* Education
* Creative Consultancy
The common link across these areas
of interest is embodied in Braunarts
commitment to the commissioning
and production of new collaborations
in the Digital Arts and Media

Brighter Pictures
10th Floor, Blue Star House
234-244 Stockwell Road
London SW9 9SP
Tel: 7733 7333
Fax: 7733 6333
email: info@brighter.co.uk
Website: www.brighter.co.uk
Gavin Hay
Part of the Endemol Group
Set up in 1992, Brighter Pictures
produces distinct and original
programmes across different genres,
including 'factual entertainments',
investigative journalism and art films
- for terrestrial, cable and satellite
broadcasters. In the area of
documentaries, it makes popular and
entertaining films on a wide range of
subjects from Modern Obsessions to
Jamaica Girls - *Life with Bossy;
Looking Like Diana to Bright Lights
Big City*. Company recently acquired
by Endemol.

British Lion Film Corporation
Pinewood Studios
Iver Heath
Bucks SLO 0NH
Tel: 01753 651700
Fax: 01753 656391

Bronco Films
The Producer's Centre
61 Holland Street
Glasgow G2 4NJ
Tel: 0141 287 6817

Fax: 0141 287 6815
email: broncofilm@btinternet.com
Peter Broughan

Brook Lapping Productions
6 Anglers Lane
London NW5 3DG
Tel: 020 7482 3100
Fax: 020 7284 0626
Anne Lapping

Buena Vista Productions
Centre West
3 Queen Caroline Street
Hammersmith
London W4 9PE
Tel: 020 8222 1000
Fax: 020 8222 2795
International television production
arm of The Walt Disney Studios

John Burder Films
7 Saltcoats Road
London W4 1AR
Tel: 020 8995 0547
Fax: 020 8995 3376
email: jburder@aol.com
Website: www.johnburder.co.uk
Corporate and broadcast worldwide,
productions for many leading
sponsors. Including *The Common
Sense Guides,* and *ABC of Guides*

Buxton Raven Productions
102 Clarence Road
London E5 8HB
Tel: 020 8986 0063
Fax: 020 8986 2708
email: jb@buxtonraven.com
Website: buxtonraven.com
Jette Bonnevie, Jens Ravn
Founded in 1988, Buxton Raven
focuses on feature film development
and production

Capitol Films
23 Queensdae Place
London W11 4SQ
Tel: 020 7471 6000
Fax: 020 7471 6012
email: films@capitolfilms.com
Simon Radcliffe, Director of
Acquisitions and Development
Recent productions include: *Beautiful
Joe, House of Mirth, Drowning Mona,
Wilde* and *Among Giants*

Carlton Productions
35-38 Portman Square
London W1H ONU
Tel: 020 7486 6688
Fax: 020 7486 1132
Owned by Carlton Communications.
Includes: *Soldier Soldier; Peak
Practice*

14.
Carnival (Films and Theatre)
12 Raddington Road
Ladbroke Grove
London W10 5TG
Tel: 020 8968 1818
Fax: 020 8968 0155
email: info@carnival-films.co.uk
Website: www.carnival-films.co.uk
Recent productions: Films - *Firelight;
Up on the Roof; The Mill on the Floss;
Shadowlands; Under Suspicion;*
Television - *The Tenth Kingdom;
Agatha Christie's Poirot; Lucy Sullivan
is Getting Married; Every Woman
Knows A Secret; Oktober; BUGS;
Crime Traveller; Jeeves & Wooster;
Fragile Heart; Porterhouse Blue*

Cartwn Cymru
Ben Jenkins Court
19a High Street
Llandaf
Cardiff CF5 2DY
Tel: 02920 575999
Fax: 02920 575919
email: production@cartwn-
cymru.demon.co.uk
Animation production. Recent
productions: Testament: *The Bible in
Animation;* (S4C/BBC2). *The Miracle
Maker* (S4C/BBC/British
Screen/Icon); 90 minute theatrical
feature. *Faeries* (HIT Entertainment):
75 minute TV feature for Tx on CITV
Christmas '99. In production:
Otherworld/The Mabinogi (S4C/BBC);
animated feature of medieval epic;

Catalyst Television
Brook Green Studios
186 Shepherd's Bush Road
London W6 7LL
Tel: 020 7603 7030
Fax: 020 7603 9519
email: info@catalyst-films-tv.com
Website: www.catalyst-films-tv.com
Tony Laryea
Gardeners World (BBC); *Absolute
Beginners* (C5); *Gardening From
Scratch* (BBC), *Women Who Kill*

15.
Celador Productions
39 Long Acre
London WC2E 9JT
Tel: 020 7240 8101
Fax: 020 7836 1117
Paul Smith
Television: primarily entertainment
programming for all broadcast
channels. Includes *Who Wants to be a
Millionaire?* plus other game shows,
variety, with selected situation
comedy, drama and factual output

Celtic Films
Room 21, Ground Floor
Bromyard Avenue
London W3 7XH
Tel: 020 8740 6880
Fax: 020 8740 9755
email: celticfilm@compuserv.com
Muir Sutherland
Sharpe (Carlton UK Productions),
Red Fox (LWT), *Riszko* (ITV)

CF1 CYF
Uppercliff House
Uppercliff Close
Penarth CF64 1BE
Tel: 02920 400820
Fax: 02920 400821
email: CF1CYF@hotmail.com
Website: www.fearmovie.com

Chain Production
2 Clanricarde Gardens
London W2 4NA
Tel: 020 7229 4277
Fax: 020 7229 0861
email: films@chain.production.co.uk
Website: www.chain.production.
co.uk
Garwin Davison, Roberta Licurgo
Development and Co-Production
Feature Films, Previous
Coproduction with India, Italy and
USA

15.
Channel X
22 Stephenson Way
London NW1 2HD
Tel: 020 7387 3874
Fax: 020 7387 0738
email: mail@channelx.co.uk
*XYZ; Jo Brand Through the Cakehole;
The Smell of Reeves and Mortimer;
The Unpleasant World of Penn and
Teller; Funny Business, Phil Kay
Feels..., Food Fight, Barking . Turning
Trick with Paul Zenon, Families at
War, The Cooler, Bang, Bang It's
Reeves and Mortimer, Leftfield, All
Back to Mine* series 1 and series 2;
*Johnny Meets Madonna, Comedy Cafe,
Vic Reeves Explains, The Daven Saint
Show, Celebrities...The Truth*

Charisma Films
507 Riverbank House
1 Putney Bridge Approach
London SW6 3JD
Tel: 020 7610 6830
Fax: 020 7610 6836
email: charismafi@aol.com
Alan Balladur, Head of Development

Chatsworth Television
97-99 Dean Street
London W1D 3DE

Tel: 020 7734 4302
Fax: 020 7437 3301
email: television@chatsworth-tv.co.uk
Website: www.chatsworth-tv.co.uk
Malcolm Heyworth, Managing
Director
Sister company to Chatsworth
distribution and merchandising
companies. Producers of light
entertainment and drama. Best
known for the long running *Treasure
Hunt* and *The Crystal Maze* (C4),
Mortimer's Law (BBC)

Cheerleader Productions
43 Whitfield Street
London W1T 4HA
Tel: 020 7258 6800
Fax: 020 7258 6888
Bruce Lippold
Specialists in live and post-produced
sports programmes, documentaries,
leisure, entertainment

The Children's Film Unit
South Way
Leavesden
Herts WD2 7LZ
Tel: 01923 354656
Fax: 01923 354656
email: cfilmunit@aol.com
Website: www.btinternet.com/~cfu
Carol Rennie
A registered Educational Charity, the
CFU makes low-budget films for
television and PR on subjects of
concern to children and young
people. Crews and actors are trained
at regular weekly workshops at
Leavesden Studios. Work is in 16mm
and video, and membership is open
to children from 8-18. Latest films for
C4: *The Gingerbread House; Awayday;*
Administrator: Carol Rennie

Chrysalis Visual Entertainment
The Chrysalis Building
13 Bramley Road
London W10 6SP
Tel: 020 7221 2213
Fax: 020 7465 6159
email: visent@chrysalis.co.uk
Website: www.chrysalis.co.uk
Charlotte Boundy
The following are all part of Chrysalis
Visual Entertainment: Assembly Film
and Television; Bentley Productions;
Cactus TV, Chrysalis Television
(includes Chrysalis Sport, Chrysalis
Sport USA, Mach1, Chrysalis TV,
Chrysalis Television North, Chrysalis
Creative). Lucky Dog, Red Rooster,
Tandem Television,. Watchmaker
Production, Chrysalis Television

International, Chrysalis Distribution, IDTV (The Netherlands), South Pacific Pictures (New Zealand)

Cinema Verity Productions
11 Addison Avenue
London W11 4QS
Tel: 020 7460 2777
Fax: 020 7371 3329
Verity Lambert
Recent projects include *The Cazalets* made for the BBC.

Circus Films
Shepperton Studios
Shepperton
Middlesex TW17 OQD
Tel: 01932 572680/1
Fax: 01932 568989
Film Development Corporation Ltd
St Georges House
14-17 Wells Street
London W1P 3FP
Tel: 020 7323 6603
Fax: 020 7636 9350

Civilian Content plc
4th Floor
Portland House
4 Great Portland Street
London W1N
Tel: 020 7612 0030
Fax: 020 7612 0031
email: contact@civiliancontent.com
Website: www.civiliancontent.com
Richard Holmes, Managing Director
Civilian Content plc's core business is the financing, production, and exploitation of UK film and TV rights. The acquisition of The Film Consortium in April 2000 enabled the company to bring together the largest single commercial grouping of independent film and television producers in the UK. It now has close relationships with some ten film and television production houses either as subsidiaries or as close commercial partners

The Comedy House
6 Bayley Street
London WC1B 3HB
Tel: 020 7304 0047
Fax: 020 7304 0048
John Goldstone, Producer
Set up in 1990 to develop comedy films with British talent

The Comic Strip Ltd
Dean House
102 Dean Street
London W1V 5RA
Tel: 020 7734 1166
Fax: 020 7734 1105

Recent productions: *Four Men in a Car* - a one-off 30 minute comedy for C4

Company Pictures
2nd Floor
Suffolk House
1-8 Whitfield Place
London W1T 5JU
Tel: 020 7380 3900
Fax: 020 7380 1166
email: enquiries@companypictures.co.uk
George Faber, Charlie Pattinson

Connections Communications Centre
Palingswick House
241 King Street
Hammersmith
London W6 9LP
Tel: 020 8741 1767
Fax: 020 8563 1934
email: @cccmedia.co.uk
Website: www.cccmedia.co.uk
Jacqueline Davis
A registered charity producing promotional and educational videos for the voluntary and statutory sectors. Also able to provide training for such groups in video production. Fully wheelchair accessible

Contrast Films
311 Katherine Road
London E7 8PJ
Tel: 020 8472 5001
Fax: 020 8472 5001
Produce documentaries and feature films.Productions include: *Bangladesh 25: New Eastenders*(BBC Pebble Mill); *Rhythms* (C4); *Flame in my Heart* (C4), *That Beautiful Smile* in development - feature about gang warfare in the East End

Cosgrove Hall Films
8 Albany Road
Chorlton-cum-Hardy
Manchester M21 0AW
Tel: 0161 882 2500
Fax: 0161 882 2555
email: animation@chf.co.uk
Website: www.chd.uk.com
Susan Ennis, Head of Production
Award-winning animation company
Producer of drawn and model animation. Creators of: *Dangermouse; The Wind in the Willows; Count Duckula; The B.F.G.; Discworld, Foxbusters; Little Grey Rabbit; Rotten Ralph; Bill and Ben* and *Albie*

Cosgrove Hall Digital
8 Albany Road

Chorlton-cum-Hardy
Manchester M21 0AW
Tel: 0161 882 2500
Producing high quality CGI animation

Cowboy Films
11/29 Smiths Court
London W1V 7PF
Tel: 020 7287 3808
Fax: 020 7287 3785
Lisa Bryer

Dakota Films
12a Newburgh Street
London W1F 7RR
Tel: 020 7287 4329
Fax: 020 7287 2303
Previous productions: *Let Him Have It; Othello; Janice Beard 45wpm*
In development: *Fade to Black; Me Without You; Mother of Pearl; Garnethill, Me Without You* (dir: Sandra Goldbacher)

Dan Films Ltd
32 Maple Street
London W1T 6HB
Tel: 020 7916 4771
Fax: 020 7916 4773
email: office@danfilms.com
Website: www.danfilms.com
Cilla Ware (Director)
Julie Baines (Producer); Sarah Daniel (Producer); Carlos Lopez (Producer's Assistant); Jason Newmark (Head of Development);
Recent productions: *LA Without a Map* (feature); *The Rise & Fall of Studio 54* (documentary); *Hothouse* (single drama tv); *Butterfly Kiss* (feature); *Madagscar Skin* (feature)

De Warrenne Pictures Ltd.
St. Anne's House
Diadem Court
London W1D 3EF
Tel: 020 7734 7648
email: info@dewarrenne.com
Website: www.dewarrenne.com
Contact: Tom Waller
Feature film production and development company. Recent projects include *Monk Dawson*, based on the award winning novel by Piers Paul Read, and *Butterfly Man*, directed by Kaprice Kea. Projects in development include romantic comedies, action thrillers and historical dramas

Different Films
2 Searles Road
London SE1 4YU
Tel: 0845 4 58 57 90

Fax: 0845 4 58 57 91
email: info@differentfilms.co.uk
Website: www.differentfilms.co.uk
Douglas M Ray
Specialising in feature film and
television drama

Dirty Hands
2nd Floor
6-10 Lexington Street
London W1F OLB
Tel: 020 7287 7410
Fax: 020 7734 7131

Diverse Productions
6 Gorleston Street
London W14 8XS
Tel: 020 7603 4567
Fax: 020 7603 2148
Website: www.diverse.co.uk
Roy Ackerman, Narinder Minhas
Established in 1982, Diverse is one of
Britain's leading independent factual
programme makers, and has recently
expanded into Interactive media

DLT Entertainment UK
10 Bedford Square
London WC1B 3RA
Tel: 020 7631 1184
Fax: 020 7636 4571
John Reynolds; John Bartlett, Gary
Mitchell
Specialising in entertainment
programming

DNA Films
3rd Floor
75-77 Margaret Street
London W1N 8HB
Tel: 020 7291 8010
Fax: 020 7291 8020
email: info@dnafilms.com
Joanne Smith
(See DNA Film Ltd - Lottery Film
Production Franchises)
Projects include: *Beautiful Creatures,
Strictly Sinatra, The Final Curtain,
The Parole Officer*

Documedia International
Films Ltd
Production Office
19 Widegate Street
London E1 7HP
Tel: 020 7625 6200
Fax: 020 7625 7887
Producers and distributors of
documentary and drama
programming; corporate and Internet
adaptations

Domino Films
7 King Harry Lane
St Albans AL3 4AS

Tel: 01727 750153
Fax: 01727 750153
email: Jo@dominofilms.co.uk
Joanna Mack
Well-established company producing
wide range of factual programmes
which include: the award-winning
*Selling Murder; Secret World of Sex;
Lost Children of the Empire; Heil
Herbie*. Other productions include:
*Eve Strikes Back; Breadline Britain
1990s; Soviet Citizens; Take Three
Girls; Windows on the World; What's
the Evidence*

Double Exposure
Unit 22-23
63 Clerkenwell Road
London EC1M 5PS
Tel: 020 7490 2499
Fax: 020 7490 2556
email: admin@doublex.com
Website: www.doublex.com
Andrew Bethell, Sandy Balfour
Production and distribution of
broadcast and educational
documentaries in the UK and abroad

Downtown Pictures
4th Floor, Suite 2
St Georges House
14-17 Wells Street
London W1P 3FP
Tel: 020 7323 6604
Fax: 020 7636 8090

Dragon Pictures
23 Golden Square
London W1R 3PA
Tel: 020 7734 6303
Fax: 020 7734 6202
email: info@dragonpictures.net
Katie Goodson

The Drama House
Coach Road Cottages
Little Saxham
Bury St Edmunds 1P29 5LE
Tel: 020 7586 1000
Fax: 020 7586 1345
email: jack@dramahouse.co.uk
Website: www.dramahouse.co.uk
Jack Emery

Dramatis Personae
19 Regency Street
London SW1P 4BY
Tel: 020 7834 9300

Ecosse Films
12 Quayside Lodge
Watermeadow Lane
London SW6 2UZ
Tel: 020 7371 0290
Fax: 020 7736 3436
email: info@ecossefilms.com

Website: www.ecossefilms.com
Alexandra McIntosh
*McCready and Daughter, Charlotte
Gray, Mrs. Brown, The Ambassador,
Unsuitable Job for a Woman, Monarch
of the Glen*

Edinburgh Film & Video
Productions
Traquair House
Innelleithen
Peeblessairl EH44 6PW
Tel: 01896 831188
Fax: 01896 831198
Robin Crichton
Major Scottish production company
established in 1961

Edric Audio Visual
34-36 Oak End Way
Gerrards Cross
Buckinghamshire SL9 8BR
Tel: 01753 481416
Fax: 01753 887163
email: robin@edic-av.co.uk
Website: www.edric-av.co.uk
Robin Congdon, Managing Director
Feature films

Element Productions
66a Pembroke Road
Clifton
Bristol BS8 3DX
Tel: 0117 9738799
Fax: 0117 9730568
email: element.pa@netgates.co.uk
Website: netgates.co.uk/element
Richard Edwards
Element Productions is one of the
leading independent production
companies in the West Country and
Wales. Founded in 1989, the company
specialises in high quality, tightly
budgeted, series. We are currently in
the fifth year of supplying BBC Wales
with a 30 part rural/environmental
series Homeland, and the third series
of People and Pets is currently being
transmitted on HTV West.

Elmgate Productions
Shepperton Studios, Studios Road
Shepperton
Middx TW17 0QD
Tel: 01932 562611
Fax: 01932 569918
email: elmgate@dial.pipex.com
Chris Burt
Feature films, television films and
series

Endboard Productions
114a Poplar Road
Bearwood
Birmingham B66 4AP

Tel: 0121 429 9779
Fax: 0121 429 9008
email: endboard@btconnect.com
Website: www.endboard.com
Producers of television programmes.
Recently completed a True Stories for
Channel.4

Endemol Entertainment (UK)

Shepherds Building Central
Charecroft Way
Shepherds Bush
London
W14 0EE
Tel: 0870 333 1700
email: info@gmgendemol.com
Website: www.endemoluk.com
Tom Barncoat
Endemol Entertainment UK plc is the
largest non-broadcaster
entertainment producer in Britain. Its
three production brands - Bazal,
Initial and Brighter Pictures – are
behind some of the most successful
programmes to come out of the UK.
Gem is Endemol UK's commercial
exploitation arm and is responsible
for ancillary rights across all media.

Eon Productions

138 Piccadilly
London W1Z 9FH
Tel: 020 7493 7953
Fax: 020 7408 1236
Website: www.007.com
Producers of James Bond films

Equilibrium Films

28 Sheen Common Drive
Richmond TW10 5BN
Tel: 020 8898 0150/ 07980 622964
Fax: 020 8898 0150
Titles include: *The Tribe That Time
Forgot* - an Equilibrium Film
production in association withWGBH
Boston/Nova for PBS;
Jaguar People;*Yemen's Cultural Drug:
Dream or Nightmare;Yemen's Jambiya
Cult;Sudan's Slave Trade;
First Contact - Last Rites* - a Bare
Faced Production for BBC; *Egypt
Powerplays, Burma's Final Solution,
Conquering The Mountain of Fire,
Barefoot Among The Tame Tigers,*
Dispatches C4

Evolution Films

Red Hill House
Hope Street
Chester CH4 8BU
Tel: 01244 689699
Fax: 01244 68747

Extreme International

The Coach House
Ashford Lodge
Halstead
Essex C09 2RR
Tel: 01787 479000
Fax: 01787 479111
email: xdream@dream.co.uk
Website: www.extremeinternational.
com
Alistair Gosling
Specialises in the production and
distribution of extreme sports, travel,
technology, nature and wildlife and
children's programmes.
Extreme Sports Channel
A cable/satellite channel currently
broadcasting across Europe and
shortly going worldwide
email: al@extreme.com
Website: www.extreme.com
Extreme Interactive
International distribution and
production of Interactive Narrow and
Broadband Video Content and
Internet Broadcast Channels
email: xdream@xdream.co.uk
Website: www.extremeineractice.net

Eye to Eye Productions

63 Collier Street
Kings Cross
London N1 9BE
Tel: 020 7278 7666
Fax: 020 7278 8228
email: eyetoeyetv@aol.com
Website: www.eyetoeyetv.co.uk
Andrew Guy
Eye to Eye is a production company
offering you the very best in television,
video and interactive media services.
Established in 1988, Eye to Eye has
gained a reputation for quality,
reliability and innovation. Non-
broadcast clients include Friends of the
Earth, Shelter, MENCAP and WaterAid

Fasterfaster Films

180 Ladbroke Grove
London W10 5LZ
Tel: 020 7359 1323
Fax: 020 7359 1323
email: fasterfasterfilms@yahoo.co.uk
David Hayman, Fiona Stewart

Feasible Films

105 Golden House
29 Great Pultenay Street
London W1F 9NN
Tel: 020 7494 4422
Fax: 020 7494 4433
email: info@feasiblefilms.co.uk
Website: feasiblefilms.co.uk
Barney Reisz, Toby Reisz

Festival Film and Television

Festival House
Tranquil Passage
Blackheath Village
London SE3 OBJ
Tel: 020 8297 9999
Fax: 020 8297 1155
email: info@festivalfilm.com
Website: www.festivalfilm.com
Ray Marshall
The company concentrates mainly on
popular television drama and
continues production of its Catherine
Cookson mini-series for ITV. Recent
completed productions include: *The
Secret and A Dinner of Herbs.* Series in
development include *Decline and Fall*
by Evelyn Waugh, Mrs Pargeter, based
on the books by Simon Brett and
Sixsmith, a detective series based on
the books by Reginald Hill

Figment Films Ltd

3rd Floor
75-77 Margaret Street
London W1W 8BH
Tel: 020 7291 8030
Fax: 020 7291 8040
email: figment@globalnet.co.uk
Website: www.figmentfilms.com
Productions include: *Shallow Grave;
Trainspotting, Twin Town, A Life Less
Ordinary, The Beach*
(See DNA Film - Lottery Film
Production Franchises)

Film and General Productions

4 Bradbrook House
Studio Place
London SW1X 8EL
Tel: 020 7235 4495
Fax: 020 7245 9853
Clive Parsons, Davina Belling

The Film Consortium

6 Flitcroft Street
London WC28H 8DJ
Tel: 020 7691 4440
Fax: 020 7691 4445
Contact: Linda Gamble
Consists of: Greenpoint Films,
Parallax Pictures, Scala and Skreba
(See The Film Consortium - Lottery
Film Production Franchises)
(See also Civilian Content plc)

FilmFair Animation

Unit 8
Silver Road
White City Industrial Park
London W12 7SG
Tel: 020 8735 1888
Fax: 020 8743 9591
email: info@film.co.uk

Producers of model animation series, special effects and commercials. Productions include: *The Wombles; Paddington Bear; Huxley Pig; Gingerbread Man; Astro Farm ; The Dreamstone; Brown Bear's Wedding; White Bear's Secret; The Legend of Treasure Island*

Film Form Productions
64 Fitzjohn's Avenue
London NW3 5LT
Tel: 020 7794 6967
Fax: 020 7794 6967
Film/video production, drama and documentary for television and video distribution. Full crewing, writers, producers and directors

FilmFour Ltd
76-78 Charlotte Street
London W1P 1LX
Tel: 020 7868 7700
Fax: 020 7868 7769
Website: www.filmfour.com
Paul Webster, Chief Executive
Film Four Ltd is Channel 4 Television's wholly owned film company and operates in the areas of film development, production, sales and distribution. FilmFour Productions funds around 15-20 films a year, many of them with co-finance from other partners and some fully funded. The FilmFour Lab champions the spirit and practice of creative low-budget filmmaking and aims for a slate of around four films a year. Recent productions include *Lucky Break, Charlotte Gray, Buffalo Soldiers* and *Late Night Shopping*

Filmhouse
2 Wedgewood Mews
12-13 Greek Street
London W1F 8TP
Tel: 020 7813 4800
Fax: 020 7813 4808
email: info@filmhouse.co.uk
Website: www.filmhouse.co.uk
Michael Günther, Madeleine Lim
Best known for documentaries such as *The Silk Road, Hans Falk,* and *Earthquake in Turkey,* the company has recently produced the feature, *The Honeytrap.*

Filmworks
6 Amor Road
Hammersmith
London W6 OAN
Tel: 020 8741 5631
Fax: 020 8748 3198
Geraldine Easter

Fine Line Features
CNN House
19-22 Rathbone Place
London W1T 1HY
Tel: 020 7637 6700
Fax: 020 7307 6264
Website: www.newline.com
European film production
Sweet Hereafter, Deconstructing Harry

The First Film Company
38 Great Windmill Street
London W1D 7LU
Tel: 020 7439 1640
Fax: 020 7437 2062
email: firstfilm@bizonline.co.uk
Roger J Randall-Cutler, Rob Cheek
Feature film and television production. *Dance with a Stranger; Soursweet; The Commitments; The Railway Station Man; A Kind of Hush.* Among projects in development: *Flying Hero Class,* based on the novel by Thomas Keneally; *Django Reinhardt,* an original screenplay by Shelagh Delaney; *No Man's Land,* an original screenplay by John Forte. *The Bombard Story* based on the novel by Alain Bombard

Flashback Television
9-11 Bowling Green Lane
London EC1R OBG
Tel: 020 7490 8996
Fax: 020 7490 5610
email: mailbox@fflashbacktv.co.uk
Website: www.flashbacktv.com
Taylor Downing, David Edgar, Timothy Ball
Award-winning producers of a wide range of factual programming including *Battle Stations* (A&E), *Nigella Bites* (C4), *Hitler's Brides* (C4), *Don Roaming* (C4), *The Hot Seat* (Artsworld), and *Lost Gardens* (C4). Flashback re-versions programming for The History Channel, The Biography Channel, C4, and C5. Interactive projects include History Quest (4 Learning).

Flashlight Films
15-19 Great Titchfield Street
London W1W 8A2
Tel: 020 7908 7270
Fax: 020 7436 6980
email: kate@flashlightfilms.com
Kate Hagar, Aaron Simpson

Focus Films
The Rotunda Studios
Rear of 116-118 Finchley Road
London NW3 5HT
Tel: 020 7435 9004
Fax: 020 7431 3562

email: focus@pupix.demon.co.uk
David Pupkewitz
Marsha Levin, Lisa Nicholson, Malcolm Kohll, Lucinda Van Rie
Feature Film Production and Financing Company.: *The 51st State* directed by Ronny Yu (Cast: Samuel L.Jackson; Robert Carlyle; Emily Mortimer). Selected Credits: *Secret Society* directed by Imogen Kimmel (Cast: Charlotte Brittain; Lee Ross; Annette Badland). *Crimetime* directed by George Sluizer (Cast: Stephen Baldwin; Pete Postlethwaite; Sadie Frost). *Othello* directed by Janet Suzman In development: Sandmother / Barry / 90 Minutes / Triomf

Mark Forstater Productions
27 Lonsdale Road
London NW6 6RA
Tel: 020 7624 1123
Fax: 020 7624 1124
Recent productions: *Paper Marriage; The Touch; La Cuisine Polonaise; Grushko, BBC drama series; Between the Devil and the Deep Blue Sea; The Last Resort; The Glitterball*

Fox Searchlight Pictures
(see Twentieth Century-Fox Productions Ltd)
Twentieth Century-Fox Film Co Ltd
Twentieth Century House
31-32 Soho Square
London W1V 6AP
Tel: 020 7437 7766
Fax: 020 7734 3187
Website: www.fox.co.uk/
Recent productions: *Smilla's Feeling for Snow; Cousin Bette; Oscar and Lucinda*

Fragile Films
97-99 Dean Street
London W1D 3TE
Tel: 020 7287 6200
Fax: 020 7287 0069
email: fragile@fragilefilms.com
(See Pathé Productions - Lottery Film Production Franchises)
Barnaby Thompson, Uri Fruchtmann
An Ideal Husband

Freedom Pictures
10 Rylett Crescent
Shepherds Bush
London W12 9RL
Tel: 0468 855746
Fax: 020 8743 6981
email: timwhite@ freedompictures.co.uk
Tim White

Front Page Films
507 Riverbank House
1 Putney Bridge Approach
London SW6 3JD
Tel: 020 7736 4534
Fax: 020 7610 6836
email: charismafi@aol.com
Alan Balladur, Head of Development

Fugitive Films
2 1/2 Gate Street
London WC2A 3HP
Tel: 020 7242 6969
Fax: 020 7242 6970
email: john@fugitivemusic.f9.co.uk

Fulcrum TV
254 Goswell Road
London EC1V 7RE
Tel: 020 7253 0353
Fax: 020 7490 0206
email: info@FulcrumTV.com
Website: www.FulcrumTV.com
Richard Belfield, Producer/Director
Tracey Gardiner, Producer
Christopher Hird, Producer
Most recent productions include, for
Channel 4: *Can You Live Without,
God List, Crime List, Desperately
Seeking Dad, Beef Encounter, Power
2000, Pulp,* and *Your Voice Your Vote;*
for BBC Learning Zone: *Ready for
work* and *Training for Profit*

Gainsborough (Film & TV) Productions
The Groom Cottage
Pinewood Studios
Pinewood Lane
Iver Heath
Iver Bucks SLO ONH
Tel: 01753 651700
Fax: 01753 656844
John Hough
In development: *Dangerous Love;
Bewitched; A Heart in the Highlands*

Global Vision Network
Elstree Film Studios
Borehamwood
Hertfordshire WD6 1JG
Tel: 020 8324 2333
Fax: 020 8324 2700
email: info@gvn.co.uk
Website: www.gvn.co.uk

Goldcrest Films International
65-66 Dean Street
London W1V 4PL
Tel: 020 7437 8696
Fax: 020 7437 4448
email: mailbox@goldcrest-fiilms.com
Major feature film production, sales
and finance company. Recent

productions: *Space Truckers,
Clockwatchers*

Granada Film
4th Floor
48 Leicester Square
London WC2H 7FB
Tel: 020 7389 8555
Fax: 020 7930 8499
email: granada.film@
granadamedia.com
Jacky Fitt
Head of Film: Pippa Cross
Established in 1989 - a subsidiary of
the Granada Media Group. Feature
films: *Ghost World, The Hole, House of
Mirth, Longitude, Seeing Red, The
Heart; Up On the Roof; Some Kind of
Life; August; Jack & Sarah; The Field;
My Left Foot; The Fruit Machine;
Essex Boys; The Weekend; The
Misadventures of Margaret; Captain
Jack; Rogue Trader*

Granada Wild
The Television Centre
Bath Road
Bristol BS4 3HG
Tel: 0117 972 2507
Fax: 0117 971 4350
email: granadawild@
granadamedia.com
Phil Fairclough (Head of Granada
Wild), Andrew Buchanan (Head of
Development)
Makers of wildlife documentaries and
videos for television and educational
distribution. Recent productions
include: *The Secret of Sharks and the
Otters of Yellowstone* (BBC The
Natural World and PBS) *Deadly
Crocodiles and The Ten Deadliest
Snakes in the World* (ITV), *Forces of
the Wild* (Canal+ and PBS), *The
Human Sexes* (The Learning
Channel), *Amazing Animals* (Disney
Channel), *Animal Alphabet* (C4)

Greenpoint Films
27-29 Union Street
London SE1 1SD
Tel: 020 7357 9924
Fax: 020 7357 9920
Website: greenpointskreba@
compuserve.com
A loose association of ten filmmakers:
Simon Relph, Christopher Morahan,
Ann Scott, Richard Eyre, Stephen
Frears, Patrick Cassavetti, John
Mackenzie, Mike Newell, David Hare
and Christopher Hampton
(See The Film Consortium - Lottery
Film Production Franchises)

Gruber Films
1st Floor
74 Margaret Street
London W1N 7HA
Tel: 020 7436 3413
Fax: 020 7436 3402
email: gruber@civiliancontent.com
Neil Peplow
Recent productions: *Walking Ned,
Shooting Fish, Dead Babies*
In development: *Raving Beauties,
Snookered, Trilogy, The Abduction
Club*
(See also Civilian Content plc)

Gullane Entertainment PLC
Stoneham Gate
Stoneham Lane
Eastleigh S050 9NW
Tel: 023 8064 9200
Fax: 023 8064 9201
Website: www.gullane.com
Recent productions: *Thomas the Tank
Engine and Friends, Art Attack, Sooty,
Captain Pugwash, James the Cat,
Zzzap! It's a Mystery, Thomas and the
Magic Railroad* (movie)

Halas & Batchelor
The Halas & Batchelor Collection
67 Southwood Lane
London N6 5EG
Tel: 020 8348 9696
Fax: 020 8348 3470
email: vivien@haba.demon.co.uk
Animation films from 1940

Hammer Film Productions
92 New Cavendish Street
London W1M 7FA
Tel: 020 7637 2322
Fax: 020 7323 2307
Website: www.hammerfilms.com
Terry Ilott
The company responsible for many
classic British horror films

Harbour Pictures
The Yacht Club
Chelsea Harbour
London SW10 0XA
Tel: 020 7351 7070
Fax: 020 7352 3528
email: username@
harbourpictures.com
Website: www.harbourpictures.com
Nick Barton, Suzanne Mackie, Cathy
Haslam
Productions in development: *The
Next Big Thing* (BBC Films);
Calendar Girls (BVI); *Kinky Boots*
(Feature Film); *Sculpture*
(Documentary); *Genius*
(Documentary). Recent productions
as ABTV: *Great Excavations* (C4);

Righteous Babes (C4); *Brimful of Asia* (C4). Previous productions as ABTV: *The Vanishing Man* (ITV); *Byzantium - The Lost Empire* (TLC C4); *The Wimbledon Poisoner* (BBC); *Boswell and Johnson* (BBC); *Moving Story* (ITV); *Bye Bye Baby* (FilmFour).

Harcourt Films
58 Camden Square
London NW1 9XE
Tel: 020 7267 0882
Fax: 020 7267 1064
Producer of documentaries and arts programmes. Recent productions: 90 minute TV special *The Capeman* for HBO, One hour music docs

Harry Nash
32/33 Kingley Court
Kingly Street
London W1B 5PW
Tel: 020 7287 6800
Fax: 020 7287 680
email: reception@harrynash.co.uk
www.harrynash.co.uk

Hartswood Films
Twickenham Studios
The Barons
St Margarets
Twickenham
Middx TW1 2AW
Tel: 020 8607 8736
Fax: 020 8607 8744
Debbie Vertue
Recent productions: *The Savages* (6x30 min sitcom); *The War Behind the Wire* (2x60 min documentary); *Border Café* (8x 45 min drama); *Coupling* (6x30 min sitcom); *Wonderful You* (7X60min drama); *Men Behaving Badly* (6 series and 4 Christmas Specials, sitcom); *Is it Legal?* (3 series, sitcom); *In Love With Elizabeth* (1x60min, documentary); *Officers and Gentlemen* (1x60min, documentary); *The Red Baron* (1x60min, documentary); *Going to Chelsea* (1x60min, documentary); *My Good Friend* (2 series, comedy drama); *The English Wife* (drama); *A Woman's Guide to Adultery* (drama); *Code Name Kyril* (drama)

Hat Trick Productions
10 Livonia Street
London W1V 3PH
Tel: 020 7434 2451
Fax: 020 787 9791
Website: www.hattrick.com
Denise O'Donoghue
Jimmy Mulville, Hilary Strong
Specialising in comedy, light entertainment and drama.

Productions include: *Father Ted; Drop the Dead Donkey; Have I Got News For You; Confessions; Whatever You Want; Game On; The Peter Principle; If I Ruled the World; Clive Anderson All Talk; Room 101 and Whose Line is it Anyway?* The company's drama output includes: *A Very Open Prison; Boyz Unlimited; Eleven Men Against Eleven; Lord of Misrule; Crossing the Floor; Gobble* and *Underworld*

Jim Henson Productions
30 Oval Road, Camden
London NW1 7DE
Tel: 020 7428 4000
Fax: 020 7428 4001
Producers of high quality children's/family entertainment for television and feature films, usually with a puppetry or fantasy connection. Recent productions: *Muppet Treasure Island* - feature

Holmes Associates
37 Redington Road
London W13 QY
Tel: 020 7813 4333
Fax: 020 7435 7905
email: info@andrewholmes.com
Long-established UK independent production company for broadcast television

Michael Hurll Television
5th Floor
Avon House
Kensington Village
Avonmore Road
London W14 8TS
Tel: 020 7371 5354
Fax: 020 7371 5355
email: alices-s@uniquegroup.co.uk
Alex Hardcastle

Iambic Productions
89 Whiteladies Road
Bristol BS8 2NT
Tel: 0117 923 7 222
Fax: 0117 923 8343
email: team@
bristol.iambicproductions.com
Chris Hunt
All Iambic's documentaries from 1991 to 1998 have won or been nominated for major awards in the UK or US, including BAFTAs and an international Emmy

IBT Productions
3-7 Euston Centre
Regent's Place
London NW1 3JG
Tel: 020 7874 7650
Fax: 020 7874 7644

email: mail@ibt.org.uk
Website: www.ibt.org.uk
An independent, non-profit television production company and educational charity, specialising in making programmes on development, environment and human rights issues for UK and international broadcast. Recent productions include: a four-part series for BBC2 from young European directors on anti-racism and cultural diversity; a two-part fly-on-the-wall documentary series *inside the World Bank*, for Channel 4; a 30 minute documentary for Channel 4 following a VSO mental health worker to Zanzibar; a ten-part series on globalisation for BBC Education and a five-part series on globalisation for BBC Education and a five-part series on China for Channel 4 Schools Television

Icon Entertainment International
The Quadrangle, 4th Floor
180 Wardour Street
London W1V 3AA
Tel: 020 7494 8100
Fax: 020 7494 8151
Recent productions: *Hamlet; Immortal Beloved; Braveheart; Anna Karenina.* In development: *Farenheit 451*

Idealworld Productions
St George's Studios
93-97 St George's Road
Glasgow G3 6JA
Tel: 0141 353 3222
Fax: 0141 353 3221
email: mail@idealglasgow.com
Zad Rogers
Film and television production. *Deals On Wheels* (C4); *Tool Stories* (C4); *Equinox - Ekranoplan* (C4); *Beg To Differ* (C4); *Italian Cookbook* (C4); 1998 Transmissions Island Harvest (BBC Scotland)

Illuminated Pictures
115 Gunnersbury Lane
Acton W3 8HQ
Tel: 020 8896 1666
Fax: 020 8896 1669
email: iain@illuminated.com
Iain Harvey

Illuminations Films/Koninck
19-20 Rheidol Mews
Rheidol Terrace
London N1 8NU
Tel: 020 7288 8400
Fax: 020 7359 1151

email: griff@illumin.co.uk
Website: www.illumin.co.uk
Producers of fiction films for television and theatric release. Latest productions: *In Absentia* by The Brothers Quay; *Robinson in Space* by Patrick Keiller; *Otesanek* by Jan Svankmajer; *Dance of the Wind* by Rajan Khosa: *The Falconer's and Asylum* by Chris Petit & Iain Sinclair; *Deadpan* by Steve McQueen

Illuminations Interactive
(See entry for Braunarts)

Illuminations Television
19-20 Rheidol Mews
Rheidol Terrace
London N1 8NU
Tel: 020 7226 0266
Fax: 020 7359 1151
email: illuminations@illumin.co.uk
Website: www.illumin.co.uk
Producers of cultural programmes for C4, BBC and others. Recent productions: *Richard II*, Deborah Warner's acclaimed production starring Fiona Shaw for BBC2 Performance; Tx 3 (BBC2), arts series; *The Net 4* (BBC2), magazine series about computers and the digital world;

Illustra Television
13-14 Bateman Street
London W1V 6EB
Tel: 020 7437 9611
Fax: 020 7734 7143
Douglas Kentish

Imaginary Films
1st Floor, 15 Boss Business Village
7-11 Sugar House Lane
London E15 2QS
Tel: 020 8215 8009
Fax: 020 7215 8001
email: brady@imagfilm.demon.co.uk
Website: www.imagfilm.co.uk
Ray Brady
An independent feature film production company, films include *Boy Meets Girl* (94), *Little England* (96) *Kiss Kiss Bang Kiss* (99), *Love Life* (2001) all directed by Ray Brady. In pre-production and development are the features films *Day of the Sirens* (2000) thriller, *Fate* a psychological horror film, *Adrenaline* - black comedy/action.

Impact Pictures
12 Devonhirst Place
Heathfield Terrace
London W4 4JB
Tel: 020 734 9650

Fax: 020 7734 9652
email: impactpix.aol.com
Jeremy Bolt
Productions include: *Shopping*, directed by Paul Anderson and *Stiff Upper Lips*, directed by Gary Sinyor, *Mortal Kombat*, directed by Paul Anderson, *Event Horizon* also directed by Paul Anderson, *Vigo*, directed by Julien Temple with Nitrate Film/Channel 4, also *Soldier*, directed by Paul Anderson, with Gerry Weintraub. Most recently *There's Only One Jimmy Grimble* with Pathe, Shadows (for TV), with 20th Century Fox/BskyB and *The Hole*, with Pathe, *Death Race 3000*, to be directed by Paul Anderson, with Paramount and *Stonehenge* with Constantin Film.

InFilm Productions
23 Queensdale Place
London W11 4SQ
Tel: 020 7610 5157
Fax: 0207610 5179
email: infilm@infilmproductions.com
Website: www.infilmproductions.com
Dorothy Berwin, Paul Augarde
Recent production: *The Safety of Objects, Bedrooms and Hallways*

Initial
Shepherds Building Central
Charecroft Way
Shepherds Bush
London W14 0EE
Tel: 0870 333 1700
email: initialinfo@endymoluk.com
Website: endymoluk.com
Initial has developed an extensive slate of prime-time entertainment and reality TV for the international market. It is also building on its long established reputation as the UK's leading producer of music and live event programming. Series include *The Pepsi Chart* (Channel 5) and reality dating show Chained, which launched on E4 in early 2001. *Under Pressure* is a sports entertainment series for Channel 5 and *Bar Wars* is a new late-night entertainment series for Channel 4. Initial is also producing comedy series *Ed Stone Is Dead* for the BBC. The company is part of the Endemol Group

Intermedia
9-13 Grosvenor Street
London W1K 4QA
Tel: 020 7495 3322
Fax: 020 7495 3993
email: info@intermediafilm.co.uk
Website: www.intermediafilm.co.uk
Paul Davis

Jeremy Isaacs Productions
11 Bowlins Green Lane
London EC1R 0BG
Tel: 020 7253 8898
Fax: 020 7253 8098
email: jip@jip.co.uk
Gillian Widdicombe, Jeremy Isaacs

Jack Strong
143 Wardour Street
London W1F 8WA
Tel: 020 7437 8855
Fax: 020 7437 8866
email: jackstrong@dial.pipex.com
Peter Richardson

J&M Entertainment
2 Dorset Square
London NW1 6PX
Tel: 020 7723 6544
Fax: 020 7724 7541
email: sales@jment.com
Website: ww.jment.com
Julia Palau
Recent productions: *Forever Mine, The Guilty Complicity, A Texas Funeral, History is Made at Night, Bruno*

Jagged Films
Cheyne Walk
Chelsea
London SW3
Titles include: *Enigma*

Just Television
4 Northington Street
Londonn WC1N 2LG
Tel: 020 7916 6200
Fax: 020 7692 9080
email: info@justtv.co.uk
Website: justtv.co.uk
Olwyn Silvester
Just Television is an independent television production company making broadcast documentaries, current affairs and factual programmes primarily in the United Kingdom. Investigative journalism is one of the major strengths of the company. Successes include *Diana, The Mourning After* and an edition of Channel 4's *Dispatches* investigating the true state of the evidence against Louise Woodward. The company recently branched out into drama, with *Hungry* for Channel 4. Amongst the company's principal products is *the Trial and Error* series, dedicated to overturning miscarriages of justice.

Kai Film & TV Productions
1 Ravenslea Road
London SW12 8SA
Tel: 020 8673 4550

Fax: 020 8675 4760
email: mkwallington@cwcom.net
Recent productions: *The Unbearable Shiteness of Being; Leopoldville*

Bill Kenwright Films
BKL House
106 Harrow Road
London W2 1RR
Tel: 020 7446 6200
Fax: 020 7446 6222
email: info@kenwright.com
Website: www.kenwright.com
Bill Kenwright, Liz Holford
Recent productions: *Don't Go Breaking My Heart, Zoe*

Kinetic Pictures
Video and Broadcast Production
The Chubb Buildings
Fryer Street
Wolverhampton WV1 1HT
Tel: 01902 716055
Fax: 01902 717143
email: kinetic@waverider.co.uk
Contact: Paul Owens, Creative Director

King Rollo Films
Dolphin Court
High Street
Honiton
Devon EX14 1HT
Tel: 01404 45218
Fax: 01404 45328
email: admin@kingrollofilms.co.uk
Clive Juster
Produce top quality animated entertainment for children. Winners of BAFTA 2000 and British Animation 2000 for best pre-school animation for Matisy. Producers of the animated series: *Mr Benn; King Rollo; Victor and Maria; Towser; Watt the Devil; The Adventures of Spot; The Adventures of Ric; Anytime Tales; Art; Play It Again; It's Fun to Learn with Spot; Buddy and Pip, Spot's Magical Christmas, Little Mr Jakob; Philipp; Happy Birthday; Good Night, Sleep Tight; Spot and his Grandparents go to the Carnival, Maisy; Spot's Musical Adventures; Maisy's ABC; Maisy's Farm*

Kismet Film Company
25a Old Compton Street
London W1D 5JW
Tel: 020 7734 0099
Fax: 020 7734 1222
email: kismetfilms@dial.pipex.com
Erol Hunt
Titles include: *Photographing Fairies; This Year's Love; Wonderland; Born Romantic*

Landseer Film & Television Productions
140 Royal College Street
London NW1 0TA
Tel: 020 7485 7333
Fax: 020 7485 7573
email: mail@landseerfilms.com
Website: www.landseerfilms.com
Documentary, music arts, dance and children's programming. Recent prouductions: *Routes of Rock* (Carlton), *Death of a Legend - Frank Sinatra* (LWT), *Benjamin Zander - Living on One Buttock* (BBC), *Zeffirelli - South Bank Show* (LWT), *Bing Crosby - South Bank Show* (LWT), *See You in Court* (BBC), *Ballet Boyz* (Channel Four), *4Dance* (Channel 4), *The Magic Mountain* (Artsworld/BBC), *Bourne to Dance* (Channel 4)

Langham Productions
(A division of the Man Alive Group)
Westpoint
33-34 Warple Way
London W3 0RG
Tel: 020 8743 7431
Fax: 020 8740 7454
Michael Latham, Michael Johnstone

La Plante Productions
Paramount House
1620170 Wardour Street
London W1F 8ZX
Tel: 020 7734 6767
Fax: 020 7734 7878
email: admin@
laplanteproductions.com
Website: laplanteproductions.com
Since its launch in 1994 with *The Governor*, a hard-hitting drama series focusing on the tough realities of life for a female prison governor, La Plante Productions has had many hours of programming aired in the UK and around the world. Following *The Governor I & II*, the company produced *Supply & Demand*, a two-hour television series, and *Trial & Retribution*, a four-hour mini-series, both commissioned directly by the ITV Network Centre. Both series have subsequently been re-commissioned .

Large Door Productions
3 Shamrock Street
London SW4 6HF
Tel: 020 7627 4218
Fax: 020 7627 2469
email: email@ldoor.demon.co.uk
John Ellis
Founded in 1982 to specialise in documentaries about cinema and popular culture with an international emphasis. Now concerned with consultancy work

Leda Serene
31 Holberton Gardens
London NW10 6AY
Tel: 020 8969 7094/020 8346 4482
Fax: 020 8964 3044
email: Is@ledaserene.demon.co.uk
Frances-Anne Solomon, Rene Mohandas

Little Bird Co
9 Grafton Mews
London W1P 5LG
Tel: 020 7380 3980
Fax: 020 7380 3981
email: info@littlebird.co.uk
Website: www.littlebird.ie
James Mitchell, Jonathan Cavendish
Feature films: *Nothing Personal; December Bride; Into the West; All Our Fault; A Man of No Importance; My Mother's Courage, Ordinary Decent Criminal.* TV: *The Hanging Gale; Divine Magic, Relative Strangers, All For Love,* (Documentary: *Waiting for Harvey, In the Footsteps of Bruce Chatwin*)

Little Dancer
Avonway
Naseby Road
London SE19 3JJ
Tel: 020 8653 9343
Fax: 020 8653 9343
email: Littdan99@cs.com
Recent productions: *Wind, the Uninvited, the Cappuccino Years* in development: *Adios by Sue Townsend; Wilderness Years by Sue Townsend. R.E.M. a teen series; digital Drama, The House, The Great Silence*

Living Tape Productions
84 Newman Street
London W1T 3EU
Tel: 020 7299 1805
Fax: 020 7299 1818
email: mail@videotel.mail.com
Website: videotel.co.uk
Robin Jackson
Producers of documentary and educational programmes for television and video distribution

London Films
71 South Audley Street
London W1K 1JA
Tel: 020 7499 7800
Fax: 020 7499 7994
Website: www.londonfilms.com
Andrew Luff

Founded in 1932 by Alexander Korda. Many co-productions with the BBC, including *Scarlet Pimpernel* starring Richard E. Grant for BBC TV/A+E Network, *Lady Chatterley, Resort to Murder; I, Claudius, Poldark and Testament of Youth*. Produced The Country Girls for C4.

LWT & United Productions
London Television Centre
Upper Ground
London SE1 9LT
Tel: 020 7620 1630
Website: www.granadamedia.com
John Willis

Malachite Productions
East Kirkby House
Spilsby
Lincolnshire PE23 4BX
Tel: 01790 763538
Fax: 01790 763409
email:malachite @csi.com
London Office: 020 7487 5451
Charles Mapleston, Nancy Thomas, Nikki Crane
Producers of people-based documentary programmes on music, design, painting, photography, arts, anthropology and environmental issues for broadcast television. The company also produces dramatised documentary programmes, is developing micro-budget fiction films, and is experimenting with new technologies to communicate in new ways. Recent productions: *John Clare's Journey; Clarke's Penny Whistle; A Voyage with Nancy Blackett; Small Silver Screens; Sequins in my Dreams*

Malone Gill Productions
27 Campden Hill Road
London W8 7DX
Tel: 020 7937 0557
Fax: 0207 376 1727
email: malontgill@cs.com
Georgina Denison
Recent productions: *The Face of Russia* (PBS); *Vermeer* (ITV); *Highlanders* (ITV); *Storm Chasers* (C4/Arts and Entertainment Network); *Nature Perfected* (C4/NHK/ABC/Canal Plus/RTE); *The Feast of Christmas* (C4/SBS); *Nomads* (C4/ITEL)

Jo Manuel Productions
11 Keslake Road
London NW6 6DG
Tel: 020 8930 0777
Fax: 020 8933 5475
Recent productions: *The Boy From*

Mercury directed by Martin Duffy with Hugh O'Conor, Rita Tushingham and Tom Courtenay. *Widow's Peak* (Rank, Fineline, British Screen), directed by John Irvin with Mia Farrow, Joan Plowright, Natasha Richardson. In pre-production: *Mattie* starring Mia Farrow, Beyond the Meadow (to be directed by Richard Spense)

Maya Vision International
43 New Oxford Street
London WC1A 1BH
Tel: 020 7836 1113
Fax: 020 7836 5169
email: info@mayavisionint.com
Website: www.mayavisionint.com
John Cranmer

Media Legal (Originations)
Media Legal
West End House
83 Clarendon Road
Sevenoaks
Kent TN13 1ET
Tel: 01732 460592
Production arm of Media Legal developing legal projects for film and TV

The Media Trust
3-7 Euston Centre
Regent's Place
Off Euston Road
London NW1 3JG
Tel: 020 7874 7600
Fax: 020 7874 7644
email: info@mediatrust.org
Website: www.mediatrust.org
Simon Gallimore
The Media Trust helps other charities and voluntary organisations to understand and access the media

Meditel Productions
17 Ivy Ladge
122 Notting Hill Gate
London W11 3QS
Tel: 020 7727 6301
Fax: 020 7792 5059
email: meditel@compuserve.com
Provides medical, science-based and factual documentaries for television. Past productions: *AZT - Cause for Concern; The AIDS Catch; AIDS and Africa* (C4 Dispatches); *Impotence - One in Ten Men* (C4); *HRT - Pause for Thought* (Thames TV This Week)

Mentorn Barraclough Carey
43 Whitfield Street
London W1T 4HA
Tel: 020 7258 6800
Fax: 020 7258 6888

email: mbc@mentorn.co.uk
Website: www.mentorn.co.uk
Tom Gutteridge
Entertainment, drama, entertainment news, documentaries, news and current affairs, children's and features

Merchant Ivory Productions
46 Lexington Street
London W1R 3LH
Tel: 020 7437 1200/439 4335
Fax: 020 7734 1579
email: miplondon@ merchantivory.demon.co.uk
Website: www.merchantivory.com
Paul Bradley
Merchant Ivory Productions is the collaboration of Ismail Merchant, James Ivory and Ruth Prawer Jhabvala, the screenwriter. The company is the longest, most prolific filmmaking partnership in the world having made over 42 films over the last 30 years including: *Shakespeare Wallah, Savages, Roseland, The Europeans, Heat and Dust, A Room With a View, Maurice, Mr. and Mrs. Bridges, Jefferson in Paris, Howards End* and recently *Cotton Mary* with Greta Scaachi and Madhur Jaffrey and *The Golden Bowl* with Uma Thurman, Nick Nolte and Angelica Houston. *The Mystic Masseur* and Dan Leno and *The Limehouse Golem* are among forthcoming projects

The Mersey Television Company
Campus Manor
Childwall Abbey Road
Liverpool L16 0JP
Tel: 0151 722 9122
Fax: 0151 722 6839
email: admin@merseytv.com
Website: www.merseytv.com
Independent production company responsible for C4 thrice-weekly drama series, *Brookside* and *Hollyoaks*

Mike Mansfield TV
5th Floor
41-42 Berners Street
London W1T 3NB
Tel: 020 7580 2581
Fax: 020 7580 2582
email: mikemantv@aol.com

Millennium Pictures
Pinewood Studios
Iver Heath
Bucks SL0 0NH
Tel: 01753 651700
Fax: 01753 655025
email: daniel@figuero.freeserve.co.uk
Website: www.millennium-

pictures.co.uk
Daniel Figuero

Mirage Films
5 Wardour Mews
London W1V 3FF
Tel: 020 7734 3627
Fax: 020 7734 3735
email: miragefilms@compuserve.com
Ian Llande/Thomas Ritter

Momentum Productions
90 York Road
Teddington TW11 8SN
Tel: 020 8977 7333
Fax: 020 8977 6999
email: production@momentum.co.uk
Guy Meyer/Darren Cavanagh
Specialists in on-screen marketing
and promotion of feature films -
trailers, promos, commercials and CD
ROMs. Producers of corporate films
90 York Road
Teddington TW11 8SN
Tel: 020 8977 7333
Fax: 020 8977 6999
email: production@momentum.co.uk
Guy Meyer/Darren Cavanagh

Morningside Productions Inc
8 Ilchester Place
London W14 8AA
Tel: 020 7602 2382
Fax: 020 7602 1047

Mosaic Films
2nd Floor
8-12 Broadwick Street
London W1V 1FH
Tel: 020 7437 6514
Fax: 020 7494 0595
email: info@mosaicfilms.com
Website: www.mosaicfilms.com
Adam Alexander
The Old Butchers Shop
St Briavels
Glos GL15 6TA
Contact: Colin Luke
Recent productions: *Adult Lives*
(BBC2), *Wicked Weekend* (Channel 4)
Return to Wonderland - a series for
BBC2; *Think of England* for BBC
Modern Times; Unholy Land - a series
for C4; *Vyvan's Hotel* - for BBC
*Picture This; Patriarchs, Presidents and
Profits* - BBC Correspondent Special,
The Princess's People (BBC2)

MW Entertainments
48 Dean Street
Soho
London W1D 5BF
Tel: 020 7734 7707
Fax: 020 7734 7727

email: contact@michaelwhite.co.uk
Michael White
(See Pathé Productions - Lottery Film
Production Franchises)
Film and theatre productions

Noel Gay Television
Shepperton Studios
Studios Road
Shepperton
Middx TW17 OQD
Tel: 01932 562611
Fax: 01932 572172
Anne Mensah, Lesley McKirdy
TV Drama and TV entertainment.
Associate companies: Grant Naylor
Production. Noel Gay Motion
Picture Company, Noel Gay Scotland,
Rose Bay Film Productions, Pepper
Productions

North South Productions
60 King Street
Twickenham TW1 2SH
Tel: 020 8892 0022
Fax: 020 8892 7836
email: mail@northsouth.co.uk
Development, travel and other
international themes
Susan Keefe, Stephen Bottomore

Nova Productions
11a Winholme
Armthorpe
Doncaster DN3 3AF
Tel: 01302 833422
Fax: 08701 257917
email: info@novaonline.co.uk
Website: www.novaonline.co.uk
Andrew White, Maurice White,
Gareth Atherton
Film, television and graphics
production company, specialising in
documentary, entertainment, special
event and music promo production.
Producer of programmes released on
sell-through video on its own label
via subsidiary Nova Home
Entertainment and on other labels.
Game show format development and
graphic production. Also training,
promotional and multi-camera OB
production for broadcast and non-
broadcast. Recent productions:
*Sheffield Remembered - The Last
Trams*, West Yorkshire Rail, *The Steam
Years* - documentaries; Beat Box -
karaoke music quiz game show;
Remembrance Sunday - Multi-camers
OB; Idendt graphics for Harrogate
International Centre and OK Video

Nunhead Films plc
Pinewood Studios
Pinewood Road

Iver Heath
Bucks SL0 0NH
Tel: 01753 650075
Fax: 01753 655 700
email: info@nunheadfilms.com
Website: nunheadfilms.com
Carol Lemon, John Stewart
In distribution: *The Asylum*, a feature
film produced by Carol Lemon,
written and directed by John Stewart

Open Media
The Mews Studio
8 Addison Bridge Place
London W14 8XP
Tel: 020 7603 9029
Fax: 020 7603 9171
email: contact@openmedia.co.uk
Website: www.openmedia.com
Sebastian Cody
Best known for the Channel 4
discussion programme *After Dark*,
Open Media has produced around
400 hours of television for all the
main UK network broadcasters,
making entertainment series and
factual specials. Among its many
series are *The Secret Cabaret, Is This
Your Life?* and *James Randi: Psychic
Investigator*

Opus Television
60 Severrn Grove
Canton
Cardiff CF11 9EP
Tel: 029 2022 3456
Fax: 029 7434 9288
Roland Tonge

Orbit Media
80a Dean Street
London W1D 3SN
Tel: 020 7287 4264
Fax: 020 7287 0984
Website: www.orbitmedia.co.uk
Jordan Reynolds

Orlando TV Productions
Up-the-Steps
Little Tew
Chipping Norton
Oxon OX7 4JB
Tel: 01608 683218
Fax: 01608 683364
email: orlando.tv@btinternet.com
Website: www.miketomlinson.
btinternet.co.uk
Mike Tomlinson
Producers of TV documentaries:
Nova (WGBH-Boston); Horizon
(BBC); QED (BBC)

Oxford Film and Video Makers
The Stables

North Place
Headington
Oxford OX3 9HY
Tel: 01865 741682 or 01865 760074
(course enquiries)
Fax: 01865 742901
email: office@ofvm.co.uk
Website: www.ofvm.co.uk
Contact: Geron or Jim
Oxford Film and Video Makers supports a broad range of individual productions - both broadcast and non-broadcast - giving a voice to people normally under-represented in the media. Promoting experimental film and video art through 'Arteaters'. Supporting productions with campaigning groups through the CCD group. Production company facility now also available

Oxford Film Company

6 Erskine Road
London NW3 3AJ
Tel: 020 74383 3637
Fax: 020 7483 3567
email: mail@oftv.co.uk
Website: oftv.co.uk
Released Hilary and Jackie starring Emily Watson, directed by Anand Tucker and Restoration directed by Micahel Hoffman

Oxford Scientific Films

Lower Road
Long Hanborough
Oxford OX8 8LL
Tel: 01993 881881
Fax: 01993 882808
email: enquiries@osf.uk.com
Website: www.osf.uk.com
Film Library: Sandra Berry, Jane Mulleneux
Photo Library: Suzanne Aitzetmuller
Commercial Production: Nicholas Unsworth
Naturanl History Production: Sean Morris

Pacesetter Productions

The Gardner's Lodge
Cloisters Business Centre
8 Battersea Park Road
London SW8 4BH
Tel: 020 7720 4545
Fax: 020 7720 4949
email: info@pace-setter.co.uk

Pagoda Film & Television Corporation

Twentieth Century House
31-32 Soho Square
London W1V 6AP
Tel: 020 7534 3500
Fax: 020 7534 3501

email: pag@pagodafilm.co.uk
Head of Development
In development: *Mary Stuart; That Funny Old Thing; The Corsican Sisters; Blaz Getting Paid; Welcome to America; Hardcore Pornography*
(See also Civilian Content plc)

Paladin Pictures

22 Ashchurch Grove
London W12 9B7
Tel: 020 8740 1811
Fax: 020 8740 7220
Quality documentary, drama, music and arts programming. Recent productions include: *Wallis Simpson: The Demonised Duchess* (C4); *The People's Duchess* (C4); *Plague Wars* (BBC1 series/WGBH Frontline); *Purple Secret* (C4-Secret History); *The Last Flight of Zulu Delta 576* (C4-Cutting Edge); *A Death In Venice* (BBC2-The Works); *Brothers & Sisters* (C4 series); *The Shearing Touch* (ITV-South Bank Show). Current Productions: *Georgiana - Duchess of Devonshire* (C4 historical biography); *Blood Family - a history of the Spencers* (C4 series); *Travels With My Tutu, with Deborah Bull* (BBC2 series on ballet); *The Secret Life of Daphne du Maurier* (BBC); *The Assassin's Wife* (2hr Movie of the Week)

paradogs ltd

1st floor
17 - 25 Cremer St
London E2 8HD
Tel: 020 7613 3001
email: paradogs@pinkpink.demon.co.uk
Website: www.omsk.org.uk
Director/producer Steven Eastwood
Paradogs specialises in innovative documentary (in particular the subject of mental health) experimental fiction and artists film/video

Parallax Pictures

7 Denmark Street
London WC2H 8LS
Tel: 020 7836 1478
Fax: 020 7497 8062
email: info@parallaxpictures.co.uk
Website: www.parallaxpictures.co.uk
Sally Hibbin
Recent productions: Ken Loach's *My Name is Joe, Bread and Roses, The Navigators;* Les Blair's *Jump the Gun; Bad Behaviour, Bliss;* Philip Davis's *ID , Hold Back the Night* Christopher Monger's *The Englishman Who Went Up the Hill, But Came Down a Mountain,* (See The Film Consortium - Lottery Film Production Franchises)

Pathé Pictures

Kent House
Market Place
London W1N 8AR
Tel: 020 7323 5151
Fax: 020 7636 7594
Website: www.pathe.co.uk
Contact: Peter Scott
Consists of: Thin Man Films and Imagine Films, Allied Filmmakers and Allied Films , NFH, Pandora Productions, Sarah Radclyffe Productions, Fragile Films and MW Entertainment
(See Pathé Productions - Lottery Film Production Franchises)

Pearl Media

11 Holbein House
London SW1 W8NH
Tel: 020 7259
Fax: 020 7259 9278
email: info@pearlproductions.co.uk
Website: www.pearlproductions.co.uk
Camilla Doege-Kohle
Film production company. Also involved in the European Short Film Festival

Peninsula Films

Unit 230, Canalot Studios
22 Kensal Road
London W10 5BN
Tel: 020 8964 2304
email: julian@peninsula-films.demon.co.uk
Website: www.peninsula-films.demon.co.uk
Peninsula Films is a London based film and documentary production company. Documentaries include *The Gambler's Guide To Winning* (C4),*The Mystery of Anastasia* (C4), *Love Hurts* (ARTE) About the Manic Street Preachers pop group. Their first feature film *Weak at Denise* (www.weakatdenise.com) received a UK release

Penumbra Productions

80 Brondesbury Road
London NW6 6RX
Tel: 020 7328 4550
Fax: 020 7328 3844
Cinema and television productions, specialising in contemporary issues and in the relationship between 'North' and 'South'. Recent productions: *China Rocks; Repomen; Bombay and Jazz; Divided By Rape; Stories My Country Told Me*. In development: a cinema feature, *Sold*; several documentary series relating to history, the environment and the future

Persistent Vision Productions
299 Ivydale Road
London SE15 3DZ
Tel: 020 7639 5596
Carol Lemon, John Stewart
Crash; The Gaol; The Break-In

Photoplay Productions
21 Princess Road
London NW1 8JR
Tel: 020 7722 2500
Fax: 020 7722 6662
email: photoplay@compuserve.com
Kevin Brownlow, Patrick Stanbury
Producers of documentaries and
television versions of silent feature
films

Picture Palace Films
13 Egbert Street
London NW1 8LJ
Tel: 020 7586 8763
Fax: 020 7586 9048
email: info@picturepalace.com
Website: www.picturepalace.com
Malcolm Craddock
Specialise in feature film and TV
drama and documentary
Rebel Heart (4x1 hour TV drama,
BBC Northern Ireland, Irish Film
Board, Irish Screen), *Large* (feature
film for Film Four & The Film
Consortium), *Extremely Dangerous*
(4x1 hour series for ITV, with
Northwest One Films starring Sean
Bean), *The Acid House* (feature film
for FilmFour); *A Life for a Life - The
True Story of Stefan Kiszko* starring
Olympia Dukakis (1 x 2hr film, co-
production with Celtic Films), *Sharpe*
(5 series (14 x 2 hrs, Carlton),
starring Sean Bean set in the
Peninsular War. *Little Napoleons* (4 x
1 hr, C4)

Picture Production Company
19-20 Poland Street
London W1F 8QF
Tel: 020 7439 4944
Fax: 020 7434 9140
email: sales@theppc.com
Website: www.theppc.com
Sales and Marketing Director:
Steve O'Pray
Theatrical Trailers, TV Advertising
Campaigns, 3D Animation and
Graphics,
Television Programming, Radio
Commercials, Film Title Sequences,
ISDNTransfer, Interstitials, 35mm
Editing, Music Videos, On-line
Editing, Promos, Event Management,
Video Conferencing, Electronic Press
Kits, Point of Sale, Agency Reels

Pioneer Productions
Voyager House
32 Galena Road
London W6 0LT
Tel: 020 8748 0888
Fax: 020 8748 7888
email: pioneer@pioneertv.com
Website: www.pioneertv.com
An independent film and television
company specialising in science and
technology, Pioneer has gained an
unparalleled reputation for bringing
natural phenomena on the largest
scale to the television screen, by
means of spectacular time-lapse and
special effects cinematography.
Among its many programmes are:
*Universe, Black Holes, ET Please Phone
Earth, Extreme Machines* and *Raging
Planet*

Planet 24 Productions
The Planet Building, Thames Quay
195 Marsh Wall
London E14 9SG
Tel: 020 7345 2424/512 5000
Fax: 020 7345 9400
email: thebigbreakfast@channel4.com
Website: www.planet24.com
Mary Durkan
Recent productions: *The Big Breakfast*
(C4); *Hotel Babylon* (ITV); *Gaytime
TV* (BBC2); *Nothing But the Truth*
(C4); *The Word* (C4); *Delicious*
(ITV);*The Weekend Show* (BBC)

Portman Productions
21-25 St Anne's Court
London W1F 0BJ
Tel: 020 7494 8024
Fax: 020 7468 3499
Major producer in primetime drama
and feature films worldwide. Recent
productions include: *Nancherrow*
(2x2), *Savage Honeymoon* (feature),
Scarfies (feature), *Clandestine
Marriage* (feture),*Wrestling with
Alligators* (feature); *Coming Home*
(2x2); *Spanish Fly* (feature); *Rebecca*
(2x2); *September* (2x2); *An Awfully
Big Adventure* (feature); *Famous Five*,
series I & II; *Hostage* (feature); *Fall
From Grace* (4 x1); *Friday on my
Mind* (3x1); *Blackwater Trail*
(feature); *Little White Lies* (feature);
Seventh Floor (feature); *Crime Broker*
(feature); *A Woman of Substance*
(4x1); *Via Satellite* (feature)

Praxis Films
PO Box 290
Market Rasen
Lincs LN3 6BB
Tel: 01472 399976
Fax: 01472 399976
email: info@praxisfilms.com
Website: www.praxisfilms.com
Sue Waterfield
Internet, new media, film, tv
production company. Documentaries,
current affairs, educational
programming for UK and
international broadcasters. Extensive
archive of sea, fishing, rural material

Presence Films
66a Great Titchfield Street
London W1W 7QJ
Tel: 020 7636 8477
Fax: 020 7636 8722
email: alan@presencefilms.com
Alan Dewhurst
In production: *The Inharmonious
Dachshund* directed by Kirsten Kelly
(short animation for Channel 4). In
development: several large format
films, including *Around the World in
80 Days*, directed by Bibo Bergeron
(40 minutes animation) and Bertolt
Brecht's *War Primer* (television arts
feature)

Pretty Clever Pictures
Shepperton Studios
Shepperton
Middx TW17 0QD
Tel: 01932 572047
Fax: 01932 572454
email: pcpics@global~net.co.uk
Gelly Morgan, Managing Director
Film and TV production,
commericals, promos, corporate
videos, interactive and film titles

Prominent Features
34 Tavistock Street
London WC2E 7PB
Tel: 020 7497 1100
Fax: 020 7497 1133
Steve Abbott
Company owned by Steve Abbott,
John Cleese, Terry Gilliam, Anne
James, Terry Jones and Michael Palin
which has produced six feature films
to date

Prominent Television
34 Tavistock Street
London WC2E 7PB
Tel: 020 7497 1100
Fax: Fax; 020 7497 1133
Anne Jones
Company owned by Steve Abbott,
John Cleese, Terry Gilliam, Anne
James, Terry Jones and Michael Palin
which has produced three travel
documentary series to date

Sarah Radclyffe Productions

5th Floor
83-84 Berwick Street
London W1V 3PJ
Tel: 020 7437 3128
Fax: 020 7437 3129
email: srpltd@globalnet.co.uk
Sarah Radclyffe, Bill Godfrey
Sarah Radclyffe previously founded and was co-owner of Working Title Films and was responsible for, amongst others, *My Beautiful Laundrette, Wish You Were Here, and A World Apart*. Sarah Radclyffe Productions was formed in 1993 and productions to date are: *Second Best*, dir Chris Menges; *Sirens*, dir. John Duigan; *Cousin Bette*, dir. Des McAnuff; *Bent*, dir. Sean Mathias; *Les Misérables*, dir Bille August; *The War Zone*, dir Tim Roth *There's Only One Jimmy Grimble*, dir John Hay
(See Pathé Productions - Lottery Film Production Franchises)

Ragdoll Limited

Pinewood Studios
Pinewood Road
Iver Heath
Bucks SL0 0NH
Tel: 01753 631800
Fax: 01753 631831
email: pinewood@ragdoll.co.uk
Website: www.ragdoll.co.uk
Liz Queenan
Specialist children's television producer of live action and animation, producing long-running series *Tots TV, Rosie and Jim* (for ITV); *Teletubbies; Brum and Open A Door* (for BBC) and *Bad Jelly the Witch*

Rapido TV

14-17 Great Pulteney Street
London W1F 9ND
Tel: 020 7440 5700
Fax: 020 7439 4046
Website: www.rapido.co.uk
Isobel Oram, Peter Stuart, Mark Ford

Raw Charm

Ty Cefn
Rectory Road
Cardiff CF1 1QL
Tel: 029 20 641511
Fax: 029 20 668220
email: pam@rawcharm.co.uk
Website: www.rawcharm.co.uk
Pamela Hunt
Kate Jones-Davies
Documentary, contemporary and history. Recent productions: *New Generation* (HTV Wales), *Wings Over Wales* (HTV Wales)

Recorded Picture Co

24 Hanway Street
London W1P 9DD
Tel: 020 7636 2251
Fax: 020 7636 2261
email: rpc@recordedpicture.com
Jocelyn Jones
Chairman: Jeremy Thomas
Films produced include: *Brother* (1999 Dir Takeshi Kitano), *Sexy Beast* (1999 Dir Jonathan Glazer), *Gohatto* (1999 Exec Prod - Dir Nagisa Oshima), *The Cup* (1999 Exec Prod - Dir Khyentse Norbu) *All the Little Animals* (1997 Dir Jeremy Thomas), *The Brave* (1997 Exec Prod - Dir Johnny Depp), *Victory* (1997 Exec Prod - Dir Mark Peploe), *Blood and Wine* (1996 Dir - Bob Rafelson), *Crash* (1995 Exec Prod - Dir David Cronenberg)

Red Mullet

30 Percy Street
London W1
Tel: 020 7636 7870
Fax: 020 7636 7860
Mike Figgis

Redwave Films (UK)

31-32 Soho Square
London W1V 6AP
Tel: 020 7753 7200
Fax: 020 7753 7201
Uberto Pasolini, Polly Leys

The Reel Thing

182 Brighton Road
Coulsdon
Surrey CR5 2NF
Tel: 020 8668 8188
Fax: 020 8763 2558
email: info@reelthing.tv
Website: www.reelthing.tv
Chris Day
A full service non-broadcast production company specialising in corporate and business television supplying in all delivery media including video, DVD's and CD ROM's from its state of the art edit and post production facilities in South London. The Reel Thing also specialises in event and exhibition management

Reeltime Pictures

150 Venner Road
London SE26 5JQ
Tel: 020 8659 1717
Fax: 020 8695 1818
email: keith.barnfather@talk21.com

Formed in 1984, Reeltime specialises in the production of drama and documentaries connected with cult film and television for theatrical and non-theatrical release. The company also purchases and distributes sell-through video under its own label and aims to promote independent genre film and television production. Titles include *Myth Makers, Doctor Who's Return to Devils End* (doc); *Wartime, Downtime, PROBE* and *The Stranger* (drama)

Renaissance Films

34-35 Berwick Street
London W1V 3RF
Tel: 020 7287 5190
Fax: 020 7287 5191
email: info@renaissance-films.com
Website: www.renaissance-films.com
Angus Finney
Development, production, finance and sales company. Films include: *Wings of the Dove, The Luzhin Defence, Disco Pigs*

Renegade Films

1st Floor
92-93 Great Russell Street
London WC1B 3PS
Tel: 020 7691 3060
Fax: 020 7691 3070
email: renprism@dircon.co.uk
Website: renegadefilmsltd.co.uk
Robert Buckler, Amanda Mackenzie Stuart, Ildiko Kemeny
Productions include: *Brothers in Trouble, Pressure, The Last Place on Earth, Facts of Life, Midnight Expresso, The Star, The Sin Eater Hotel Splendide* and (as Prisma Communications) The Financial Times Business Toolkit. Development projects include: *The Go Kart, Room To Rent, Hotel Sordide, The Thought Gang*

Replay

20 Greek Street
London W1D 4DU
Tel: 020 7287 5334
email: solutions@replayfilms.co.uk
Website: www.replayfilms.co.uk
Production of broadcast and corporate documentaries and drama

Revolution Films

10 Little Turnstile
London WC1V 7DX
Tel: 020 7242 0372
Fax: 020 7242 0407
email: email@revolution-films.com
Michael Winterbottom, Andrew Eaton

Recent productions: *The Claim, 24 Hour Party People*

Richmond Light Horse Productions
3 Esmond Court
Thackeray Street
London W8
Tel: 020 7937 9315
Fax: 020 7938 4024
Euan Lloyd

Riverchild Films
2nd floor, 26 Goodge St
London W1T 2QG
Tel: 020 7636 1122
Fax: 020 7636 1133
email: riverchild@
riverchild.demon.co.uk
Features and short film production

Riverfront Pictures
Dock Cottages, Peartree Lane
Glamis Road
Wapping
London E1 9SR
Tel: 020 7481 2939
Fax: 020 7480 5520
Specialise in music, arts and drama-documentaries. Independent productions for television. Recent productions for C4 Cutting Edge and BBC Arts

RM Associates
46 Great Marlborough Street
London W1V 1DB
Tel: 020 7439 2637
Fax: 020 7439 2316
email: rma@rmassociates.co.uk
Neil Mundy (Director of Programmes)
Sally Fairhead (Head of Publicity)
RM Associates produces and distributes a broad range of music, arts and documentary programming for international television, videogram, and educational release, coproducing widely with major broadcasters and media companies world-wide, including BBC, LWT, ARD and ZDF, NOS, SVT, ABC Australia, PBS America, YLE Finland, ARTE and RAI

Roadshow Productions
11 Elvaston Place
London SW7 5QG
Tel: 020 7584 0542
Fax: 020 7584 1549
email: dzuhot@hotmail.com
Daniel Unger

Rocket Pictures
1 Blythe Road

London W14 OHG
Tel: 020 7603 9530
Fax: 020 7348 4830
Recent productions include: *Women Talking Dirty*

Rodney Read
45 Richmond Road
Twickenham
Middx TW1 3AW
Tel: 020 8891 2875
Fax: 020 8744 9603
email: Rodney_Read
@Compuserve.com
R.J.D. Read
Film and video production offering experience in factual and entertainment programming. Also provides a full range of back-up facilities for the feature and television industries, including 'making of' documentaries, promotional programme inserts, on air graphics and title sequences, sales promos, trailers and commercials. Active in production for UK cable and satellite

RSA Films
42-44 Beak Street
London W1F 9RH
Tel: 020 7437 7426
Fax: 020 7734 4978
email: info@rsafilms.com
Website: www.rsafilms.co.uk
Adrian Harrison
Founded by Ridley and Tony Scott in 1968, RSA is a multi-award winning commercials company with offices in London, NY and LA, whose clients include Philip Morris, Coca Cola, Kodak, Visa and Nokia.

RSPB Film
The Lodge, Sandy
Beds SG19 2DL
Tel: 01767 680551
Fax: 01767 683262
email: mark.percival@rspb.org.uk
Website: www.rspb.org.uk
Mark Percival
Producer of wildlife films. Over 100 titles including: *Ospray; Kingfisher; Skyobnrer; Flying For Gold*; and most recently: The undiscovered country. Also produces environmental and conservation films, shorts, promos and VNRs for RSPB publicity, education, training and corporate communications

Running Dog Films
8 Salvesen Crescent
Edinburgh EH4 5JN
Tel: 0131 538 6978
email: dog@runningdogfilms.co.uk

Website: www.bloodjunkies.com
Bruce Naughton

Samuelson Productions
13 Manette Street
London W1D 4AW
Tel: 020 7439 4900
Fax: 020 7439 4901
email: samuelsonp@aol.com
Marc Samuelson
Arlington Road dir Mark Pellington, starring Tim Robbins, Jeff Bridges, Joan Cusack and Hope Davis; *Wilde* dir Brian Gilbert, starring Stephen Fry, Jude Law, Vanessa Redgrave and Jennifer Ehle; *The Commissioner* starring John Hurt and Armin Mueller-Stahl; *Dog's Best Friend* starring Richard Milligan and Shirley Jones; Previously: *Tom and Viv*; *Playmaker*; and documentaries *Man, God and Africa; Vicars; The Babe Business, Ultimate Frisbee*

Sands Films
119 Rotherhithe Street
London SE16 4NF
Tel: 020 7231 2209
Fax: 020 7231 2119
email: ostockman@sandsfilms.co.uk
Website: www.sandsfilms.co.uk
Olivier Stockman
Recent productions: *The Butterfly Effect; As You Like It. Amahl and the Night Visitors. The Nutcracker Story, The Children's Midsummer Night's Dream* In preparation and development: *Nursery Rhymes, Cathedrals, Colla-Verdi*

Saracen Street Productions
88 Park Avenue South
London N8 8LS
Tel: 020 8341 9977
Fax: 020 8341 1900
Ruth Kenley-Letts

Scala Productions
15 Frith Street
London W1V 5TS
Tel: 020 7734 7060
Fax: 020 7437 3248
email: scalaprods@aol.com
Nik Powell, Amanda Posey, Rachel Wood, Finola Dwyer, Laurie Borg, Jonathan Karlsen
Recent productions: Shane Meadows' *Twentyfourseven* starring Bob Hoskins.
Mark Herman's *Little Voice* starring Michael Caine, Brenda Blethyn, Ewan McGregor, Jane Horrocks
Chris Menges' *The Lost Son* starring Daniel Auteuil and Nastassja Kinski
Kay Mellor's *Fanny & Elvis* starring

Kerry Fox and Ray Winstone
Deborah Warner's *The Last September* starring Maggie Smith and Michael Gambon
Julian Fariono's *The Last Yellow* starring Mark Addy; Charlie Creed-Miles and Samantha Morton
Tom Connolly's *Five Seconds to Spare* starring Max Beesley
Declan Lowney's *Wild About Harry* starring Brendan Gleeson and Amanda Donohoe
Projects in development
The Brian Jones Project, Single Shot Jonathan Wild, Last Order, Shang-A-Lang, Money

Scottish Television Enterprises

Cowcaddens
200 Renfield Street
Glasgow G2 3PR
Tel: 0141 300 3000
Fax: 0141 300 3030
Darrel James, Managing Director
Producers of: *Taggart* (drama), *Inspector Rebus* (drama), *Sherlock Holmes in the 22nd Century* (animation), *How 2* (teenage/education), *Fun House* (children's game show), *Get Wet* (children's gameshow), *The Last Musketeer* (drama)

Screen Production Associates

10 Courthope Road
London NW3 2LB
Tel: 020 7267 9953
Fax: 020 7267 9953
email: piersjackson@screenpro.co.uk
Website: www.screenpro.co.uk

Screen Ventures

49 Goodge Street
London W1P 1FB
Tel: 020 7580 7448
Fax: 020 7631 1265
email: infro@screenventures.com
Website: www.screenventures.com
Christopher Mould, Karen Haigh, Naima Mould, Daniel Haggett.
Recent projects: *Life and Limb* (3 part series for Discovery Health). In production: 'The Incredible String Band' (working title) a documentary about the Sixties band

September Films

Glen House
22 Glenthorne Road
London W6 ONG
Tel: 020 8563 9393
Fax: 020 8741 7214
email: september@

septemberfilms.com
David Green, Elaine Day, Sally Miles
TV Includes: *Hollywood Confidential, The Secret History of Hacking, Soap Secrets, Manhattan on the Beach, Eddie Irvine: The Inside Track*. Films includes: *Breathtaking, Solomon & Gaenor, House of America*

Siren Film and Video

5 Charlotte Square
Newcastle-upon-Tyne NE1 4XF
Tel: 0191 232 7900
Fax: 0191 261 6620
email: sirenfilms@aol.com
Film and television production company specialising in work for and about children

Siriol Productions

Phoenix Buildings
3 Mount Stuart Square
Butetown
Cardiff CF1 6RW
Tel: 02920 488400
Fax: 02920 485962
email: robin.lyons@siriol.co.uk
Robin Lyons, Managing Director
Formerly Siriol Animation. Producers of high quality animation for television and the cinema. Makers of: *SuperTed; The Princess and the Goblin; Under Milk Wood; Santa and the Tooth Fairies; Santa's First Christmas; Tales of the Tooth Fairies, The Hurricanes; Billy the Cat; The Blobs; Rowland the Reindeer*

Skreba

Union Hall
29 Union Street
London SE1 1SC
Tel: 020 7357 9924
Fax: 020 7357 9920
email: greenpointskreba@compuserve.com
Ann Skinner, Simon Relph
(See The Film Consortium - Lottery Film Production Franchises)

Sky Pictures

BSky B, 6 Centaurs Park
Grant Way, Syon Lane
Isleworth
Middlesex TW7 5QD
Tel: 020 7941 5588
Fax: 0207 941 5599
Titles include: *Milk; Saving Grace; Best; When the Sky Falls; Most Fertile Man in Ireland; On the Nose; Breathtaking; Paranoid; Kiss Kiss Bang Bang; Gypsy Woman; Fourth Angel; My Kingdom; The Escapist; Tube Tales; Is Harry on the Boat*

Skyline Films

PO Box 8210
London W4 1WH
Tel: 020 8354 2236
Fax: 020 8354 2219
email: skyline@ukonline.co.uk
Steve Clark-Hall, Mairi Bett
Recent productions: *The Winter Guest* (with Ed Pressmann), *Love and Death on Long Island, Small Faces, Margaret's Museum, Still Crazy* (for Margot Tandy)

Slice Films

35-37 William Road
London NW1 3ER
Tel: 020 7388 3387
Fax: 020 7383 0302
email: slice@addisonlee.com
Website: www.thebigfinish.co.uk
Lisa Emmett

Smoking Dogs Films

26 Shacklewell Lane
London E.8 2EZ
Tel: 020 7249 6644
Fax: 020 7249 6655
email: smart@smokingdogsfilms.com
John Akomfrah, Lina Gopaul, David Lawson
Independent production and distribution company. Recent titles include: *Digitopia* (Smoking Dogs/Sidus); *A Death in the Family* (Channel 4); *Riot* (Channel 4); *The Wonderful World of Louis Armstrong* (BBC); *Goldie – When Saturn Returnz* (Channel 4); *The Call of Mist* (BBC); *Speak Like a Child* (BBC/BFI); *Memory Room 451* (Arte); *Martin Luther King – Days of Hope The Mothership Connection* (Channel 4); *The Last Angel of History* (ZDF); *Beaton But Unbowed* (Channel 4); *Lush Life* (Granada); *The Darker Side of Black* (BBC Television); *A Touch of the Tar Brush* (BBC Television); *Who Needs a Heart* (Channel 4); *Black Cab* (Channel 4); *Seven Songs For Malcolm X* (Channel 4); *Mysteries of July* (Channel 4); *Testament* (Channel 4); *Twilight City* (Channel 4); *Handsworth Songs* (Indie)

Soho Communications

2 Percy Street
London W1P 9FA
Tel: 020 7637 5825
Fax: 020 7436 9740
email: istaton@dircon.co.uk
Website: sohocommunications.com
Jon Staton/Tony Coggans

Sony Pictures Europe UK

Sony Pictures Europe House
25 Golden Square
London W1R 6LU
Tel: 020 7533 1111
Fax: 020 7533 1105
Recent productions: *Virtual Sexuality*

Southern Star Primetime

Southern Star Sales (UK) Limited
45-49 Mortimer Street
London W1N 7TD
Tel: 020 7636 9431
Fax: 020 7436 7426
Simon Willock: General Manager,
Wild & Real
Victoria Ryan, Head of European
Sales, Southern Star Primetime
Catherine Neubauer: Head of
European Sales, Southern Star Kids
Production and Distribution
Productions includes: *Nicholas
Nickleby, Porgy & Bess, Great
Expectations, Othello, Neville's Island*
Distribution includes: *Bugs, Every
Woman Knows a Secret, Imogen's Face,
Home and Away, 99-1, In the Wild, Our
Friends in the North, Bodyguards,
Oklahoma, Famous Five, Eyes on the
World*

Specific Films

25 Rathbone Street
London W1T 1NQ
Tel: 020 7580 7476
Fax: 020 7494 2676
Michael Hamlyn
Recent productions: the *Last
Seduction 2*, dir Terry Marcel; *PAWS*
(exec. prod) dir Carl Zwicky; *The
Adventures of Priscilla, Queen of the
Desert*, directed by Stephan Elliott; *Mr
Reliable* dir by Nadia Tass. Developing
a number of feature film projects

Spice Factory

81 The Promenade
Peacehaven
Brighton
East Sussex BN10 8LS
Tel: 01273 585275
Fax: 01273 585304
email: sfactory@fastnet.co.uk
Michael L.Cowan
Films, Games & Television
Production Company. Productions:
Killer Tongue (1997), *Dying to Go
Home* (1997), *Ricky 6* (1998), *New
Blood* (1998), *Pilgrim* (1999),
(1999). In development: *Fry; Crush
Hour; The Void; Breaking the Code;
Our Game; Bat Out of Hell*. Television
project in development: Kremlin
Contact; Paramount/BBC/Bavaria

based on best selling book by Donald
James. In Production: *Heist and
Sambaland*

Stagescreen Productions

12 Upper St Martin's Lane
London WC2H 9DL
Tel: 020 7497 2510
Fax: 020 7497 2208
email: stgescreen@aol.com
Jeffrey Taylor
Film, television and theatre company
whose work includes: *A Handful of
Dust; Death of a Son* (BBC TV);
*Where Angels Fear to Tread; Foreign
Affairs* (TNT); *What's Cooking?*
(Lionsgate)

Stage to Screen

1st Floor
Boss House
11 Sugarhouse Lane
London E15 2QS
Tel: 020 8215 8010
Fax: 020 8215 8010
email: info@s2s.co.uk
Website: www.randallsflat.com
Charles Auty

Sterling Pictures

53 Great Portland Street
London W1W 7LG
Tel: 020 7323 6810
Fax: 020 7323 6811
email: admin@sterlingpictures.com
Website: www.sterlingpictures.com
Mike Riley

Talent Television

2nd Floor Regent House
235 Regent Street
London W1B 2EH
Tel: 020 7434 1677
Fax: 020 7434 1577
email: entertainment@talenttv.com
John Kaye Cooper, Managing
Director
Current productions: *The Villa* series
3 - reality/docu-soap, Sky One; *Next!*
- entertainment series, Sky One; *Bill
Bailey: Bewilderness* - comedy,
Channel 4; *It's Your Funeral* - talk-
show Channel 5, *Juggling* - sitcom,
ITV. Recent credits: *Making of Witches
of Eastwick* - documentary, ITV;
Smirnoff Fashion Awards -
documentary

Talisman Films Limited

5 Addison Place
London W11 4RJ
Tel: 020 7603 7474
Fax: 020 7602 7422
email: email@talismanfilms.com
Richard Jackson, Hans Baernhoft,

Caroline Oulton
Production of theatric features and
the whole range of television drama.
Recent productions: *Where There's
Smoke* (2x90 mins, ITV Network)
drama thriller starring Zara Turner;
Complicity (feature) starring Jonny
Lee Miller, Brian Cox and Keeley
Hawes; *The Secret Adventures Of Jules
Verne* (22x50 mins) drama series
starring Michael Praed and
Francesca Hunt; *Remember Me?*
(feature) starring Robert Lindsay,
Rik Mayall, Imelda Staunton, Brenda
Blethyn and James Fleet; *Rob Roy*
(feature for United Artists) starring
Liam Neeson, Jessica Lange, John
Hurt, Tim Roth, Eric Stoltz and
Brian Cox; *Just William* (series 1 & 2,
BBC) drama series based on Richmal
Crompton classic stories; *The
Rector's Wife* (4x50mins, Channel 4)
drama serial starring Lindsay
Duncan

TalkBack Productions

20-21 Newman Street
London W1T 1PG
Tel: 020 7861 8000
Fax: 020 7861 8001
email: recption@talkback.co.uk
Website: www.talkback.co.uk
Peter Fincham, Griff Rhys Jones, Mel
Smith
Productions include: *Smith and Jones*
(+ 5 previous series, BBC1); *They
Think It's All Over* (+3 previous
series, BBC1); *Never Mind The
Buzzcocks* (+ 1 previous series,
BBC2); *The Lying Game* (BBC1); *In
Search of Happiness* (BBC1); *Brass Eye*
(Channel 4); *Knowing Me Knowing
You... with Alan Partridge* (BBC2);
The Day Today (BBC2); *Murder Most
Horrid* (+ 2 previous series, BBC2)

Tall Stories

Studio 40
Clink Street Studios
1 Clink Street
London SE1 9DG
Tel: 020 7357 8050
Fax: 020 7357 0889
email: tallstories@compuserve.com
Dan Weldon, Bruce Woolford

Taylor Cartoon Films Richard

River View, Waterloo Drive
Clun, Craven Arms
Shropshire SY7 8JD
Tel: 01588 640 073
Production of all forms of drawn
animation

Telescope Pictures

Twickenham Film Studios
Saint Margarets
Twickenham
Middlesex TW1 2AW
Tel: 020 8607 8888
Fax: 020 8607 8889
Recent productions: *Princess Caraboo*,
dir Michael Austin. In development:
The Revengers' Comedies (dir
Malcolm Mowbray); In
development: *Red Right Hand, Slow
Train to Milan*

Teliesyn

Chapter Arts Centre
Market Road
Cardiff CF5 1QE
Tel: 029 2030 0876
Fax: 029 2030 0877
email: ebost:tv@teliesyn.demon.co.uk
Website: www.teliesyn.co.uk
Involved in feature film, television
drama and television documentary
/feature

Tell Tale Productions

Elstree Film Studios
Shenley Road
Borehamwood
Herts WD6 1JG
Tel: 020 8324 2308
Fax: 020 8324 2696

Tempest Films

33 Brookfield
Highgate West Hill
London N6 6AT
Tel: 020 8340 0877
Fax: 020 8340 9309
In development: *The York Mysteries*
with YTV. Stop Press - 6 part TV
series; *The Actresses* - 3 part mini-
series; *Mallory Short* and *the Very Big
Bass* - feature film

Testimony Films

12 Great George Street,
Bristol BS1 5RS
Tel: 0117 925 8589
Fax: 0117 925 7668
Steve Humphries
Specialists in social history
documentaries. Recent productions:
*Labour of Love: Bringing up Children
in Britain 1900-1950* (6 x 40 min,
BBC2); *Forbidden Britain: Our Secret
Past* (6 x 40 min, BBC2); *A Man's
World: The Experience of Masculinity*
(6 x 40 minutes, BBC2); *The Call of
the Sea: Memories of a Seafaring
Nation* (6 x 40 minutes, BBC2); *The
Roses of No Man's Land* (1 x 60
minutes C4); *Sex in a Cold Climate* (1
x 60 minutes C4); *Hooked: Britain in*

Pursuit of Pleasure (6 x 30 minutes
C4). *Veterans: The Last Survivors of
the Trench War* (2x50 mins BBC1);
*Far Out: The Dawning of New Age
Britain* (3x60 minutes C4); *Green and
Pleasant Land* (6x60 minutes C4);
Prisoners of the Kaiser (1x60 min C4);
Some Liked it Hot (2x60 mins ITV);
Pocketful of Posies (1x60 mins BBC2)

Thin Man Films

9 Greek Street
London W1D 4DJ
Tel: 020 7434 7372
Fax: 020 7287 5228
Simon Channing-Williams, Mike
Leigh
Recent productions: *Career Girls;
Secrets & Lies*
(See Pathé Productions - Lottery Film
Production Franchises)

Three Rivers

Room 10
26 Old Compton Street
London W1V 5PB
Tel: 020 7287 2567
Fax: 020 7287 3072
Olivia Stewart

Tiger Aspect Productions

5 Soho Square
London W1D 3QA
Tel: 020 7434 0672
Fax: 020 7287 1448
email: general@tigeraspect.co.uk
Website: www.tigeraspect.co.uk
Harry Enfield and Chums (2 series
BBC); *The Vicar of Dibley* (BBC1)
The Thin Blue Line (BBC1) *The
Village* (7 series for Meridian)
Howard Goodall's Organ Works
(Ch4) *Hospital* (Ch5) *Deacon Brodie*
(Screen One for BBC 1)

TKO Communications

PO Box 130, Hove
East Sussex BN3 6QU
Tel: 01273 550088
Fax: 01273 540969
email: jkruger02@aol.com
A division of the Kruger
Organisation, making music
programmes for television, satellite
and video release worldwide as well
as co-producing various series and
acquiring rights to full length feature
films for distribution. Co-production
with Tros TV Holland will result in a
new release "*Marvin Gaye Live in
Concert*". 39x30 minutes TV Specials
called "Masters of the Martial Arts"
starring John Saxon and featuring 4
world champions demonstrating all
aspects of the martial arts. A 30

minute special on Jerry Lee Lewis.
Launching a library archive footage of
stars including Glen Campbell, Vic
Damone, Frankie Laine, Johnny Cash,
Kris Kristofferson, Daniel O'Donnell,
Willie Nelson, Conway Twitty,
Dionne Warwick, George Burns, Jerry
Lewis, The Stylistics, Anne Murray
and many more. Distributing for TV
and Satellite and Video release of two
digitalised, animated full length
movie features, *Gallavants* and *The
Three Musketeers*

Toledo Pictures

3rd Floor
75-77 Margaret Street
London W1N 7HB
Tel: 020 7291 8050
Fax: 020 7291 8060
email: adam.tudhope@dnafilms.com
Adam Tudhope, Assistant to Duncan
Kenworthy
Duncan Kenworthy
(See DNA - Lottery Film
Production Franchises)

Topaz Productions

Manchester House
46 Wormholt Road
London W12 0LS
Tel: 020 8749 2619
Fax: 020 8749 0358
email:
prints@topazprods.freeserve.co.uk
In production: ongoing corporate
productions

Trademark Films

New Ambassoadors Theatre
West Street
London WC2H 9ND
Tel: 020 7240 5585
Fax: 020 7240 5586
email: mail@trademarkfilms.co.uk
Liz Barron, Karen Katz, Cleone
Clarke, David Parfitt

Trans World International

TWI House
23 Eyot Gardens
London W6 9TR
Tel: 020 8233 5400
Fax: 020 8233 5401
Television and video sports
production and rights representation
branch of Mark McCormack's
International Management Group,
TWI produces over 2,500 hours of
broadcast programming and
represents the rights to many leading
sports events including Wimbledon,
British Open, US Open, and World
Matchplay golf. Productions include:
Trans World Sport; Futbol Mundial;

PGA European Tour; ATP Tour Highlights; West Indies, Indian and Pakistan Test cricket; Oddballs; A-Z of Sport; High 5; The American Big Match and Blitz; The Olympic Collection and *The Whitbread Round The World Race*

Transatlantic Films
Building No 4
266 Chiswick High Road
London W4 5YA
Tel: 020 8735 0505
Fax: 020 8735 0605
Cabalva Studios
Whitney-on-Wye
Hereford
Herts HR3 6EX
Tel: 01497 831428
Fax: 01497 831677
email: mail@transatlanticfilms.com
Revel Guest, Justin Albert
Recent Programming: *Horse Tales* 13x30 mins stories about the special bond between people and horses, for *Animal Planet*; *Amazing Animal Adaptors* - 1x60 mins special for Discovery Channel; *History's Turning Point* - 26x30 mins about decisive moments in history, for Discovery Europe. *Trailblazers* - 13x60 mins, travel and adventure series for Discovery Europe, Travel Channel; *Three Gorges* - 2x60 mins, the building of the World's biggest dam in China, for Discovery Channel/TLC

Tribune Productions
22 Bentley Way
Stanmore
Middlesex HA7 3RP
Tel: 020 8420 7230
Fax: 020 8207 0860

Trijbits Productions
14 -16 Great Pulteney Street
London W1R 3DG
Tel: 020 7439 4343
Fax: 020 7434 4447
email: trijbits@globalnet.co.uk
Julia Caithness
Paul Trijbits' previous producer and executive producer credits include *Hardware, Dust Devil, The Young Americans, Boston Kickout, Roseanna's Grave, Milk, Paranoid* and *20:13 Thou Shalt Not Kill.* In production: *My Brother Rob,* funded by FilmFour Lab, The Film Council & British Screen & to be directed by Dom Rotheroe. In development: *Unnatural Murder* with BBC Films, John Duigan's *Salt of the Earth, Diamond Geezers, Is Harry on the Boat?* and *Happy Now* with Ruby

Films, *Frozen Summer* with Granada Films, *Porn* with Piers Thompson Productions, See Under Love with Greenpoint Films, Airside with Ijswater Films, Costa Brava with Clea de Koning CV and Allegra Huston's short, *Good Luck Mr Gorski*

Try Again Limited
Leigh Grove Farmhouse
Leigh Grove
Bradford on Avon
Wilts BA15 2RF
Tel: 01225 862 705
Fax: 01225 862 205
Michael Darlow, Rod Taylor, Chris Frederick
Produces drama, music, arts, documentary programmes. Recent productions include: *War Cries - Angels of Mercy?* C4 1 x 30 mins. *Martin Parr and the Ladies of the Valley* BBC 2 x 40 mins; 1:4; *The Lost Child - The Works* BBC 2 x 30 mins. *Something of a Different Pace - The Works* BBC 2 x 30 mins; *Under the Skin, Dennis Potter - Close Up* BBC2. 1 hour

Turn On TV
1st Floor
77 Leonard Street
London EC2A 4QS
Alison Higgins

TV Cartoons
39 Grafton Way
London W1P 5LA
Tel: 020 7388 2222
Fax: 020 7383 4192
John Coates, Norman Kauffman
Productions include: *The Snowman*, Academy Award nominated film and the feature film *When the Wind Blows*, both adaptations from books by Raymond Briggs; *Granpa*, a half hour television special for C4 and TVS; half hour special of Raymond Briggs' Father Christmas (C4); *The World of Peter Rabbit & Friends* (9 x 30 min), based on the books by Beatrix Potter, *The Wind in the Willows*, a TVC production for Carlton UK Television and Willows in Winter, Famous Fred Academy Award Nominated 1998 (C4&S4C). Latest productions are *The Bear* and *Oi Get off Our Train* which was the first film by Varga tvc

TV Choice
22 Charing Cross Road
London WC2H OHR
Tel: 020 7379 0873
Fax: 020 7379 0263

email: tvchoiceuk@aol.com
Chris Barnard, Norman Thomas
Producer and distributor of dramas and documentaries about business, technology and finance. TV Choice videos and learning packs are used in education and training in the UK and overseas. Co-producers of feature film Conspiracy with new features in development

TVF
375 City Road
London EC1 V 1NB
Tell: 020 7837 3000
Fax: 020 7833 2185
email: info@tvf.co.uk
Website: www.tvf.co.uk
Hilary Lawson
Over the last 15 years TVF has produced more than 500 hours of broadcast tv. Programming has spanned all areas of factual output, from science, arts and documentaries through to investigative current affairs along with feature and travel programmes. The company has made programmes for *Equinox, Horizon, Dispatches, The Money Programme* and *Everyman*. Recent productions include 4 part series on hallucinogenic plants for C4 called *Sacred Weeds, Bioterror*, a film on germ warfare for C4, and Learning Channel and *Living Dangerously* a film about risk for C4/Discovery

Twentieth Century-Fox Productions
20th Century House
31-31 Soho Square
London W1V 6AP
Tel: 020 7437 7766
Fax: 020 7734 3187
Recent productions: *The Full Monty, Braveheart, Stealing Beauty; Titanic*

Twenty Twenty Television
Suite 2, Grand Union House
20 Kentish Town Road
London NW1 9NX
Tel: 020 7284 2020
Fax: 020 7284 1810
email: mail@twentytwenty.tv
The company continues to produce programmes exclusively for broadcast television, specialising in worldwide investigative journalism, documentaries, productions, factually based drama, science and childrens programmes. Recent productions include: *The Big Story* (Carlton); *Secret Lives Walt Disney* (C4); *Un Blues* (C4) and *Cutting Edge* (C4)

Tyburn Film Productions
Pinewood Studios
Iver Heath
Bucks SLO ONH
Tel: 01753 651700
Fax: 01753 656050
Filmmaker: *The Creeping Flesh*;
Persecution; *The Ghoul*; *Legend of the Werewolf*

UBA (United British Artists)
21 Alderville Road
London SW6 3RL
Tel: 01984 623619
Fax: 01984 623733
Production company for cinema and
TV projects. Past productions include:
Keep the Aspidistra Flying for OFE;
Sweeney Todd for Showtime/
Hallmark; *Champions for Embassy*;
Ghost Hunter for Granada; *Windprints* for MCEG Virgin Vision; *Taffin*
for MGM; Castaway for Cannon; *The
Lonely Passion of Judith Hearne* for
HandMade Films; *Turtle Diary* for the
Samuel Goldwyn Company

Uden Associates
Chelsea Wharf
Lots Road
London SW10 0QJ
Tel: 020 7351 1255
Fax: 020 7376 3937
Website: www.uden.com
Michael Proudfoot
Film and television production
company for broadcast through C4,
BBC and corporate clients. Recent
productions: *Classic Trucks*, 6 x 30
min for C4 and various projects for
Equinox, *Cutting Edge* (Nurses, A is
for Accident) and *Short Stories*,
Classic Ships, 6 x 30 min for C4,
Autoerotic II, 3 x 30 min for C4, *Secret
Lives: The Young Freud*

Unicorn Organisation
Pottery Lane Studios
34a Pottery Lane
Holland Park
London W11 4LZ
Tel: 020 7229 5131
Fax: 020 7229 4999

Union Pictures
36 Marshall Street
London W1F 7EY
Tel: 020 7287 5110
Fax: 020 7287 3770
Recent productions include: T*he
Crow Road*; *Deadly Voyage*;
Masterchef; *Junior Masterchef*; *The
Roswell Incident*

Universal Pictures
1 Hamilton Mews
London W1V 9FF
Tel: 020 7491 4666
Fax: 020 7493 4702
Recent productions: *The Jackal*,
DragonHeart, Fierce Creatures

UpFront Television
39-41 New Oxford Street
London WC1A 1BH
Tel: 020 7836 7702
Fax: 020 7836 7701
email: upfront@binternet.com
Claire Nye
Richard Brecker

Vera Productions
3rd Floor
66/68 Margaret Street
London W1W 8SR
Tel: 020 7436 6116
Fax: 020 7436 6117/6016
Contact: Elaine Morris

Victor Film Company
4th Floor
1 Great Cumberland Street
London W1H 7AL
Tel: 020 7535 3380
Fax: 020 7535 3383
email: post@victor-film-co.uk
Website: www.victor-film-
co.demon.co.uk
Alasdair Waddell
Forthcoming titles include: *Dog
Soldiers, Father Figure, My Sister in
Law*

Videotel Productions
84 Newman Street
London W1T 3EU
Tel: 020 7299 1800
Fax: 020 7299 1818
Producers of educational and training
packages for television and video
distribution

Vine International Pictures
VIP House, Greenacres
New Road Hill
Downe, Opington
BR6 7JA
Tel: 01689 854123
Fax: 01689 850990
email: info@vineinternational.co.uk
Website: www.vine-international.
co.uk
CEO: Marie Vine, MD: Barry Gill
Sale of feature films such as *Rainbow,
The Pillow Book, The Ox and the Eye,
Younger and Younger, The Prince of
Jutland, Erik the Viking, Let Him Have
It, Trouble in Mind*

Vixen Films
13 Aubert Park
Highbury
London N5 1TL
Tel: 020 7359 7368
Fax: 020 7359 7368
email: tg@tgraham.demon.co.uk
Film/video production and
distribution, mainly feature
documentaries. Recent projects: *Gaea
Girls* - a film about Japanese women
wrestlers

Viz
4 Bank Street
Inverkeithing
Fife KY11 1LR
Tel: 01383 412811
Fax: 01383 418103
email: gregarfilm@aol.com
Murray Gregor

Wall To Wall Television
8-9 Spring Place
Kentish Town
London NW5 3ER
Tel: 020 7485 7424
Fax: 020 7267 5292
email: mail@walltowall.co.uk
Alex Graham
Producers of quality innovative
programming including, drama:
*Statement of Affairs; You Me and It;
Plotlands*. Natural history: *Baby It's
You*. Leisure: *Eat Your Greens; Sophie's
Meat Course; For Love or Money*.
Entertainment: *Big City; Heartland;
The Big Country*. Arts and culture:
Fantasy by Gaslight; Rwandan Stories

Walsh Bros
24 Redding House, Harlinger Street
King Henry's Wharf
London SE18 5SR
Tel: 020 8858 6870/020 8854 5557
Fax: 020 8858 6870
email: walshbros@lycosmail.com
John Walsh
Feature film and factual programme
company. Credits include: *Monarch* -
acclaimed feature on the death of
Henry VIII. Currently developing
feature film on the life and death of
Liberace. Documentary: *Trex 2*
13x30min (Channel Five); *Trex*
13x30min (Channel Five); *boyz &
girlz* 13x30mins (Channel Five) *Nu
Model Armi* (Channel Four); Ray
Harryhausen: *Movement Into Life*
profile of Oscar-winning animator;
Masque of Draperie in the presence of
HM The Queen; *The Comedy Store*;
Drama: *The Sleeper; The Sceptic and
the Psychic; A State of Mind*

Warner Bros. Productions

98 Theobalds Road
London WC1X 8WB
Tel: 020 7494 3710
Fax: 020 7287 9086
Recent productions: *Eyes Wide Shut,
The Avengers*

Warner Sisters Film & TV, Cine Sisters

The Cottage
Pall Mall Deposit
124 Barlby Road
London W10 6BL
Tel: 020 8960 3550
Fax: 020 8960 3880
email: sisters@warnercine.com
Directors: Lavinia Warner, Jane
Wellesley, Anne-Marie Casey and
Dorothy Viljoen
Founded 1984. Drama, Comedy. TV
and Feature Films. Output includes *A
Village Affair; Dangerous Lady;
Dressing for Breakfast; The Spy Who
Caught a Cold; Capital Sins; The Bite;
The Jump; Lady Audley's Secret* - and
feature film *Jilting Joe*. Developing a
wide range of TV and feature projects

Watermark Films

First Floor
62 Frith Street
London W1V 5TA
Tel: 020 7439 2274
Fax: 020 7439 2279
email: mail@watermarkfilms.com
Website: www.watermarkfilms.com
Nick Heyworth

The Wickes Company

Suite 5
169 Queens Gate
London SW7 5HE
Tel: 020 7225 1382
Fax: 020 7222 0822
email: wickesco@aol.com
David Wickes, Heide Wilsher

Winchester Entertainment

19-21 Heddon Street,
London,
W1R 7LF.
Tel: 020 7851 6500.
Fax: 020 7851 6505
Chief Executive: Gary Smith
Recent productions: *Shooting Fish;
Stiff Upper Lips; Divorcing Jack*

Dennis Woolf Productions

169 Didsbury Road
Stockport
Cheshire SK4 2AE
Tel: 0161 422 8175
Fax: 0161 442 8175

Working Title Films

Oxford House
76 Oxford Street
London W1N 9FD
Tel: 020 7307 3000
Fax: 020 7307 3001/2/3
Tim Bevan, Eric Fellner
Recent film productions: *The
Hudsucker Proxy; Four Weddings and
a Funeral; French Kiss; Loch Ness;
Moonlight and Valentino; Fargo; Dead
Man Walking*. In 2000, they produced
the major successes *Bridget Jones Diary*
and *Captain Corelli's Mandolin*

World Productions

Norman House
105-109 Strand
London WC2R 0AA
Tel: 020 7240 1444
Fax: 020 7240 3740
Tony Garnet, Sophie Balhatchet
Website: www.world-
productions.com

The Worldmark Production Company

7 Cornwall Crescent
London W11 1PH
Tel: 020 7792 9800
Fax: 020 7792 9801
David Wooster
Current productions: *Swimming with
Sharks* 1x52min for MNET *South
Africa; England 2006 - FIFA World Cup
Bid Film for the Football Association*.
Recent productions: *La Coupe de la
Glorie - 1998 FIFA World Cup Official
Film; Gary Lineker's Golden Boots* 8x30
min for BBC; *Living with Lions -
2x120 min for Sky Sports*

WTTV

77 Shaftesbury Avenue
London W1D 5DU
Tel: 020 7494 4001
Fax: 020 7255 8600
Simon Wright, Tim Bevan
Recent productions: *The Borrowers*
(series 1&2), *Tales of the City, Further
Tales of the City, Randall & Hopkirk
(Deceased)* (series 1&2), *Last of the
Blonde Bombshells, Lucky Jim, Come
Together*

Zenith Entertainment plc

43-45 Dorset Street
London W1H 4AB
Tel: 020 7224 2440
Fax: 020 7224 3194
email: general@zenith.tv.co.uk
Website: www.zenith-
entertainment.co.uk
Film and television production

company. Recent feature films: Todd
Haynes' *Velvet Goldmine*; Nicole
Holofcener's *Walking and Talking*; Hal
Hartley's *Amateur*. Recent television
drama: *The Uninvited* (ITV);
Bodyguards (Carlton); Hamish
Macbeth (3 series, BBC Scotland);
Rhodes (BBC1), *Bomber* (ITV)
SMTV:CDUK (ITV)

Zenith North

11th Floor
Cale Cross House
156 Pilgrim Street
Newcastle upon Tyne NE1 6SU
Tel: 0191 261 0077
Fax: 0191 222 0271
email: zenithnorth@dial.pipex.com
Ivan Rendall, Peter Mitchell
(Managing Director), John Coffey
Productions include: *Byker Grove*
(BBC1); *Blues and Twos*
(Carlton/ITV); *The Famous Five*
(ITV); *Animal Ark* (HTV); *Dear
Nobody* (BBC); *Pass the Buck* (BBC);
Network First (Carlton ITV); music
specials for S4C; variety of regional
productions for Tyne Tees TV

Zephyr Films

48a Goodge Street
London W1
Tel: 020 7255 3555
Fax: 020 7255 3777
email: chris@zephyrfilms.co.uk
Chris Curling, Philip Robertson,
Pippa Best

Zooid Pictures

66 Alexander Road
London N19 5PQ
Tel: 020 7281 2407
Fax: 020 7281 2404
email: pictures@zooid.co.uk
Website: www.zooid.co.uk
Producers of experimental and
television documentaries, various
shorts; documentaries; Anglo-
Brazilian-German co-productions

PRODUCTION STARTS

These are feature-length films intended for theatrical release with a significant British involvement (whether creative, financial or UK-based) which went into production between January and December 2000. The production start date and release information is given where known up to 12 September 2001. Films awaiting distribution deals are indicated with ADD. Single television dramas in production for the same period are indicated with *. Compiled by Linda Wood

Alone
8 October
CFI Evolution Films
Budget: £6.00m
Dir: Philip James Claydon
with John Shrapnel, Miriam Margolyes, Laurel Holloman, Isabel Brook, Claire Goose, Claudia Harrison, Caroline Carver
Distributor: ADD
UK

Al's Lads
12 November
Alchmey Pictures, Evolution Films
Budget: £3.50m
Dir: Richard Standeven
with Marc Warren, Stephen Lord, Ralf Little, Julian Littman, Richard Roundtree, Rick Tomlinson
Distributor: ADD
UK

The Biographer
3 April
First Biographer Films, Pipeline (Germany)
Budget: £4.66m
Dir: Philip Saville
with Paul McGann, Brian Cox, Faye Dunaway
Distributor: ADD
Germany

Born Romantic
7 February
Kismet Films, BBC Films, Redbus, Harvest Pictures

Budget: £3.20m
Dir: David Kane
with Craig Ferguson, Ian Hart, Jane Horrocks, Adrian Lester, Catherine McCormack, Jimi Mistry, David Morrissey, Kenneth Cranham
Distributor: Optimum Releasing
UK
Release date: 9 March 2001
Opening weekend: £198,388
Box office: £198,388
No of screens: 222
S&S reference: March 2001 p.40-41

Bridget Jones's Diary
16 May
Working Title, Universal Pictures International (US), Studio Canal+(France), Miramax
Budget: £14m
Dir: Sharon Maguire
with Renée Zellweger, Colin Firth, Hugh Grant, Jim Broadbent, Gemma Jones, Sally Phillips, Shirley Henderson, James Callis
Distributor: UIP
UK/US/France
Release date: 13 April 2001
Opening weekend: £5.72m
Box office: £41.692m
No of screens: 417
S&S reference: April 2001 p.36-37,39-40

Buffalo Soldiers
6 November
FilmFour, Gorilla Entertainment (Germany), Good Machine (US), Odeon Pictures (Germany), NFG (German regional film funding board), Grosvenor Park
Budget: £10.34m
Dir: Gregor Jordan
with Joaquin Phoenix, Ed Harris, Scott Glenn, Leon, Michael A Pena, Amani Gether, Anna Paquin, Elizabeth McGovern
Distributor: ADD
UK/US/Germany

The Bunker
31 July
Millennium Pictures
Budget: £1.92m
Dir: Rob Green
with Nicholas Hamnett, Charley Boorman, John Carlisle, Jack

Davenport, Christopher Fairbank, Jason Flemyng, Simon Kunz
Distributor: ADD
UK

Captain Corelli's Mandolin
18 May
Working Title for Universal Studios
Budget: £13.00m
Dir: John Madden
with Nicolas Cage, Penélope Cruz, John Hurt, Christian Bale, David Morrissey, Irene Papas, Gerasimos Skiadaresis
Distributor: UIP
UK/US/France
Release date: 4 May 2001
Opening weekend: £1.722m
Box office: £8.361m
No of screens: 379
S&S reference: May 2001 p.44-45

The Cat's Meow
14 November
Cat's Meow (Germany), Dan Films, KC Medien (Germany)
Budget: £4.30m
Dir: Peter Bogdanovich
with Jennifer Tilly, Eddie Izzard, Joanna Lumley, Kirsten Dunst, Edward Herrmann, Cary Elwes
Distributor: ADD
UK/Germany

Chocolat
2 May
David Brown, Miramax International (US), Miramax (UK)
Budget: £18m
Dir: Lasse Hallström
with Juliette Binoche, Judi Dench, Alfred Molina, Lena Olin, Johnny Depp, Carrie-Anne Moss
Distributor: Buena Vista
US
Release date: 2 March 2001
Opening weekend: £938,266
Box office: £6,813m
No of screens: 207
S&S reference: March 2001 p.42,44

Christmas Carol: The Movie
1 July
The Film Consortium, Scala, Illuminated Film Company, Medien Beteiligungs (Germany), Channel Four, Winchester Films, United

International Pictures (US), Arts
Council of England
Budget: £10.00m
Dir: Jimmy Teru Murakami
with Simon Callow, Kate Winslet,
Nicolas Cage, Jane Horrocks, Michael
Gambon, Juliet Stevenson, Rhys Ifans
(voices)
Distributor: ADD
UK/Germany/France

The Claim (Kingdom Come)

7 February
Pathe Pictures, Revolution Films,
United Artists Film (US), BBC Films,
Telemunchen (Germany), Alliance
Atlantis (Canada), The Film Council,
Le Studio Canal+
Budget: £12.50m
Dir: Michael Winterbottom
with Wes Bentley, Milla Jovovich,
Nastassja Kinski, Peter Mullan, Sarah
Polley, Ron Anderson, Marty
Antonini
Distributor: Pathé Distribution
UK/Canada/France
Release date: 2 February 2001
Opening weekend: £38,975
Box office: £627,849
No of screens: 24
S&S reference: March 2001, p.44-45

Club Le Monde

12 November
Screen Production Associates, 2M
Films
Budget: £0.63m
Dir: Simon Rumley
with Daniel Ainsleigh, Annette
Badland, Bruce Byron, Tom Connolly,
Tom Fisher, Tania Emery
Distributor: ADD
UK

Crush

19 June
Pipedream Pictures, Lee Thomas
Productions, FilmFour, FilmFour
International, Senator Films
(Germany), Film Council
Budget: £3.11m
Dir: John McKay
with Andie MacDowell, Imelda
Staunton, Anna Chancellor, Kenny
Doughty, Bill Paterson, Caroline
Holdaway, Joe Roberts, Josh Cole,
Gary Powell
Distributor: FilmFour Distributors
UK/Germany/US
Release date: 28 September 2001

Daddy

24 June
Imaginary Films
Budget: £1.50m

Dir: Ray Brady
with Des Backhouse-Brady, Galit
Hershkovitz, Surinder Duhra, Luk
Goss
Distributor: ADD
UK

Dead Creatures

24 January
Long Pig Productions
Budget: £0.10m
Dir: Andrew Parkinson
with Beverley Wilson, Antonia
Beamish, Brendan Gregory, Anna
Swift
Distributor: ADD
UK

Dead in the Water

3 December
Spice Factory, Redbarn, Enterprise
Films
Budget: £2.40m
Dir: Merlin Ward
with George Asprey, Michael Elphick,
Celia Imrie, Sophia Myles, Sophie
Ward
Distributor: ADD
UK

Disco Pigs

3 April
Temple Films (Ireland), Renaissance
Films, The Irish Film Board, Section
481
Budget: £3.08m
Dir: Kirsten Sheridan
with Elaine Cassidy, Cillian Murphy,
Charles Bark, Eleanor Methven,
Geraldine O'Rawe, Brían F O'Byrne,
Darren Healy
Distributor: ADD
Ireland/UK

Dog Eat Dog

5 June
Tiger Aspect Pictures Production,
Shona Productions, FilmFour,
FilmFour International, Senator
Films (Germany)
Budget: £1.60m
Dir: Moody Shoaibi
with Mark Tonderai, Nathan
Constance, David Oyelowo, Crunski,
Alan Davies, Melanie Blatt, Gary
Kemp
Distributor: Film Four Distributors-
not released as of 12 September 2001
UK/Germany

Dream

5 November
Final Cut, Scandinavian
Entertainment
Budget: £1.43m

Dir: Mikael Hylin
with Sinéad Cusack, Joe Absolom,
Brian Conley, Kelly Harrison, Stewart
Howson
Distributor: ADD
Sweden

Dust

4 April
Ena Films (Germany), Fandango
Productions (Italy), History Dreams,
Alta Films (Spain), Highlight
Communications (Germany),
Medusa (Italy), The Film Council,
European Co-production Fund,
Filmstiftung, NRW, The Film
Consortium, Shadow Dooel
(Macedonia)
Budget: £11.00m
Dir: Milcho Manchevski
with Joseph Fiennes, David Wenham,
Adrian Lester, Anne Brochet
Distributor: ADD
UK/Germany/Italy/

The Emperor's New Clothes

11 September
Redwave Films, FilmFour, FilmFour,
Senator Films (Germany), Alta Films
(Spain), Mikado Films (Italy)
Budget: £6.00m
Dir: Alan Taylor
with Ian Holm, Iben Hjejle, Tim
Mcinnerny, Trevor Cooper
Distributor: ADD
UK/Germany

End Game

23 October
Various Films, Evolution Films
Budget: £3.50m
Distributor: ADD
UK

Enigma

17 April
Codebreaker Productions, Senator
Films (Germany), Mees Pierson
Budget: £18.90m
Dir: Michael Apted
with Dougray Scott, Kate Winslet,
Saffron Burrows, Martin Glyn
Murray, Jeremy Northam, Tom
Hollander, Matthew Macfadyen,
Robert Pugh
Distributor: Buena Vista
International (UK)
UK/Netherlands/US/Germany
Release date: 28 September 2001

51st State

25 September
Momentum Pictures, Focus Films,
Alliance Atlantis (Canada),
Momentum Pictures, Film

Consortium, Artists Production
Group
Budget: £19.38m
Dir: Ronny Yu Yan-Tai
with Samuel L Jackson, Robert
Carlyle, Emily Mortimer, Rhys Ifans,
Ricky Tomlinson, Sean Pertwee,
Meatloaf, Eric Cantona
Distributor: ADD
US/UK

The Final Curtain
28 May
Young Crossbow/DNA Films,
Universal Pictures International
(US), Arts Council of England
Budget: £4.00m
Dir: Pat Harkins
with Peter O'Toole, Aidan Gillen,
Adrian Lester, Julia Sawalha, Patrick
Malahide, Henry Goodman
Distributor: ADD
UK

The Fourth Angel
14 August
Rafford Films, Norstar Filmed
Entertainment (Canada), Sky
Pictures
Budget: £9.69m
Dir: John Irvin
with Jeremy Irons, Forest Whitaker,
Charlotte Rampling, Elizabeth
McGovern, Jason Priestley, Kal Weber,
Lois Maxwell
Distributor: ADD
UK/Canada

Four Feathers
9 October
Belhaven Productions (US), High
Command Productions (US),
Paramount (US), Miramax (US)
Budget: £26.00m
Dir: Shekhar Kapur
with Heath Ledger, Wesley Bentley,
Djimon Hounsou, Michael Sheen,
Kristopher Marshall, Rupert Penry-
Jones, Alex Jennings
Distributor: ADD
US

Gabriel & Me (Jimmy Spud)
29 May
Samuelson Productions, Arts
Council of England, British Screen,
The Film Consortium, Isle of Man
Film Commission
Budget: £3.11m
Dir: Udayan Prasad
with Billy Connolly, Iain Glen, Rosie
Rowell, Sean Landless, Ian Cullen,
Sean Foley, Trevor Fox, Bridie Hales
Distributor: Pathé Distribution
UK

Global Heresy
26 October
GFT Entertainment (US), Ultimate
Pictures
Budget: £5.13m
Dir: Sidney J Furie
with Peter O'Toole, Joan Plowright,
Alicia Silverstone, Lochlyn Munro,
Martin Clunes, Matthew Lillard
Distributor: ADD
UK/Canada

Gypsy Woman
25 September
Sky Pictures, Starfield Productions,
Imagico Entertainment, Wave
Pictures, Isle of Man Film
Commission
Budget: £2.90m
Dir: Sheree Folkson
with Jack Davenport, Neve Mcintosh,
Julian Wadham, Nick Brimble, Corin
Redgrave
Distributor: ADD
UK

Happy Now
30 October
Ruby Films, Arts Council of Wales
Budget: £3.11m
Dir: Philippa Cousins
Distributor: ADD
UK/Germany/South Africa

Harry Potter and the Sorcerer's Stone
2 October
Heyday Films/Warner Brothers (US)
Budget: £90m
Dir: Chris Columbus
with Daniel Radcliffe, Emma Watson,
Rupert Grint, John Cleese, Robbie
Coltrane, Richard Griffiths, Richard
Harris, Ian Hart, Alan Rickman,
Fiona Shaw
Distributor: Warner Brothers
US

High Heels and Low Lifes
17 July
Fragile Films, Buenea Vista
International (US)
Budget: £6.50m
Dir: Mel Smith
with Minnie Driver, Mary
McCormack, Kevin McNally, Mark
Williams, Danny Dyer, Michael
Gambon, Darren Boyd
Distributor: Buena Vista
International (UK)
UK
Release date: 20 July 2001
Opening weekend: £434,989
Box office: £1.384m

No of screens: 271
S&S reference: July 2001, p.43

The Hole
2 July
Cowboy Films, Granada Film,
Impact Pictures, Pathé, Arts Council
of England
Budget: £4.16m
Dir: Nick Hamm
with Thora Birch, Desmond
Harrington, Daniel Brocklebank,
Laurence Fox, Keira Knightley, Steven
Waddington, Embeth Davidtz
Distributor: Pathe Distribution
UK/France
Release date: 20 April 2001
Opening weekend: £673,777
Box office: £2.229m
No of screens: 322
S&S reference: May 2001, p.52

The Honeytrap
2 November
Honeytrap Productions
Budget: £0.83m
Dir: Michael Günther
with Emily Lloyd, Valerie Edmond,
Stuart McQuarrie, Zoë Eeles, Natalie
Walter, James Clyde, Richard Hope,
Jonah Russell, Clive Rowe
Distributor: ADD
UK

Hot Gold
5 December
Little Wing Films, SDA Productions
Budget: £14.50m
Dir: Andrew Gillman
with Owen Teale, Daniela Nardini,
John Standing, Philip Davis, Honor
Blackman
Distributor: ADD
UK/Canada

Intimacy
19 January
Telema Productions (France),
Greenpoint, Le Studio Canal+,
Centre National de la
Cinematographie
Budget: £4.00m
Dir: Patrice Chéreau
with Mark Rylance, Kerry Fox,
Timothy Spall, Alastair Galbraith,
Philippe Calvario, Marianne Faithfull,
Susannah Harker
Distributor: Pathé Distribution
France/UK
Release date: 27 July 2001
Opening weekend:
Box office:
No of screens:
S&S reference: August 2001, p.47-48

Invincible
21 March
Werner Herzog Film Production (Germany), Tatfilm (Germany), Little Bird, FilmFour, Zephir Films (Germany), Fine Line (US), ARTE (France), WDR Cologne, BR (Germany)
Budget: £4.50m
Dir: Werner Herzog
with Jouko Ahola, Tim Roth, Udo Kier, Gustav-Peter Wöhler, Max Raabe, Renate Krössner, Anna Gourari
Distributor: Film Four Distributors
UK/US/Ireland/Germany

Is Harry on the Boat?
2 October
Sky Pictures, Ruby Films, Rapido Television
Budget: £1.00m
Dir: Menhaj Huda
with Danny Dyer, Davinia Taylor, Daniela Denby-Ashe, Ralph Little, William Mellor
Distributor: ADD
UK

Jesus the Curry King
15 August
Aylesbury Films
Budget: £0.01m
Dir: Marc John
Distributor: ADD
UK

Killing Me Softly
20 October
Montecito Pictures (US), MGM (US), Media Capital Partners
Budget: £16.50m
Dir: Kaige Chen
with Joseph Fiennes, Heather Graham, Natascha McElhone, Ulrich Thomsen, Ian Hart, Jason Hughes
Distributor: ADD
US

Kiss Kiss (Bang Bang)
27 March
Pagoda Films, Sky Pictures, M&M Productions (Scandanavia), Television Production Company
Budget: £4.30m
Dir: Stewart Sugg
with Stellan Skarsgård, Chris Penn, Paul Bettany, Jacqueline Mckenzie, Sienna Guillory, Martine McCutcheon
Distributor: ADD
UK/Germany/Italy

Lara Croft Tomb Raider
31 July

Paramount Pictures (US) and Mutual Film Company present a Lawrence Gordon Production in association with Eidos Interactive Ltd, produced in association with the BBC
Budget: £60.00m
Dir: Simon West
with Angelina Jolie, Jon Voight, Noah Taylor, Iain Glen, Daniel Craig, Christopher Barrie, Julian Rhind-Tutt, Leslie Phillips
Distributor: UIP
US/Japan/UK/Germany
Release date: 6 July 2001
Opening weekend: £3.846m
Box office: £12.597m
No of screens: 444
S&S reference: August 2001, p.50

Large
5 March
Picture Palace North, FilmFour International, The Film Consortium, Yorkshire Media Production Agency
Budget: £1.40m
Dir: Justin Edgar
with Luke de Woolfson, Melanie Gutteridge, Simon Lowe, Lee Oakes, Mirren Delaney, Emma Catherwood, Zita Sattar
Distributor: United International Pictures (UK) Ltd
UK
Release date: 5 October 2001

Last Orders
18 October
MBP (Germany), Scala Productions, Metrodome
Budget: £8.30m
Dir: Fred Schepisi
with Michael Caine, Tom Courtenay, David Hemmings, Bob Hoskins, Helen Mirren, Ray Winstone
Distributor: Metrodome
Germany/UK

Late Night Shopping
29 May
Ideal World Films, FilmFour, Senator Films (Germany), Glasgow Film Office, Scottish Screen
Budget: £1.60m
Dir: Saul Metzstein
with Luke de Woolfson, James Lance, Kate Ashfield, Enzo Cilenti, Heike Makatsch, Shauna Macdonald
Distributor: Film Four Distributors
UK/Germany
Release date: 22 June 2001
S&S reference: June 2001, p.47

Lawless Heart
30 November
Martin Pope Productions, The Isle of

Man Film Commission, British Screen, Film Council, October Productions
Budget: £1.50m
Dir:Tom Hunsinger
with Douglas Henshall, Tom Hollander, Sukie Smith, Bill Nighy, Ellie Haddington, Clémentine Célarié, Josephine Butler, Stuart Laing
Distributor: ADD
UK

Liam
29 April
Laim Films, BBC Films, Diaphana (France), Road Movies (Germany), BIM (Italy), ABC (Australia), MIDA
Budget: £1.60m
Dir: Stephen Frears
with Ian Hart, Claire Hackett, Anne Reid, Anthony Borrows, Megan Burns, David Hart, Russell Dixon
Distributor: Artificial Eye
UK/Germany/Italy
Release date: 23 February 2001
S&S reference: March 2001 p.54

Long Time Dead
26 July
WT2, Lola Productions, Universal Pictures (US)
Budget: £3.20m
Dir: Marcus Adams
with Alec Newman, Joe Absolom, Lukas Haas, James Hillier, Marsha Thomason, Lara Belmont
Distributor: United International Pictures (UK) Ltd
UK
Release date: 26 October 2001

Lucky Break
4 September
Fragile Films, FilmFour, Lucky Break Productions, Senator Films (Germany), Paramount (US), Miramax (US), FilmFour
Budget: £4.00m
Dir: Peter Cattaneo
with James Nesbitt, Olivia Williams, Christopher Plummer, Timothy Spall, Bill Nighy, Lennie James
Distributor: Film Four Distributors
UK/US/Germany
Release date: 31 August 2001
Opening weekend: £348,613
Box office: £1.11m
No of screens: 270
S&S reference: September 2001, p.49

Mad Dogs
31 July
Roaring Mice Films
Budget: £0.50m
Dir: Ahmed Alauddin Jamal

with Iain Fraser, Indira Varma, Clive Russell, Jonathan Pryce, Paul Barber, Saeed Jaffrey, Mike Leigh
Distributor: ADD
UK

The Martins
3 July
Tiger Aspect Productions, Isle of Man Commission
Budget: £3.00m
Dir: Tony Grounds
with Lee Evans, Kathy Burke, Linda Bassett, Eric Byrne, Terri Dumont, Frank Finlay, Lennie James, Jack Shepherd, Mark Strong, Lloyd Harvey
Distributor: Icon Film Distribution
UK
Release date: 14 September 2001
S&S reference: June 2001, p.48-49

Me Without You
22 November
Dakota Films, Road Movies (Germany), Momentum, The Isle of Man Film Commission, British Screen, Banque Luxembourg, Matrix Film Britannia
Budget: £3.70m
Dir: Sandra Goldbacher
with Anna Friel, Michelle Williams, Kyle Maclachlan, Oliver Milburn, Trudie Styler
Distributor: ADD
UK

The Meeksville Ghost (The Silver Winchester)
22 May
Peakviewing Productions
Budget: £2.34m
Dir: David Lister
with Judge Reinhold, Lesley-Anne Down, Andrew Kavovit, Tanja Reichert, Anne Curteis
Distributor: ADD
UK

Morality Play
16 October
Renaissance Films, Kanzaman (Spain), MDA Films
Budget: £9.62m
Dir: Paul McGuigan
with Willem Dafoe, Paul Bettany, Brian Cox, Gina McKee, Najwa Nimri, Jared Harris, Simon McBurney
Distributor: ADD
UK/Spain

Mrs Caldicot's Cabbage War
6 November

Cabbage Films, Evolution Films
Budget: £3.00m
Dir: Ian Sharp
with Pauline Collins, Peter Capaldi, Gwenllian Davies, Sheila Reid, Frank Mills, John Alderton, Paul Freeman
Distributor: ADD
UK

Mumbo Jumbo
14 February
Mumbo Jumbo Productions, Firelight (Germany), BV Films (Scaninavia), Apollo Media (Germany)
Budget: £2.84m
Dir: Stephen Cookson
with Jamie Walters, Joss Ackland, Brian Blessed, John Inman, Sylvester McCoy, Richard O'Brien, Melinda Messenger
Distributor: ADD
UK/Germany

The Mummy Returns
10 May
Universal Pictures (US), Alphaville Productions (US), UIP
Budget: £72.00m
Dir: Stephen Sommers
with Brendan Fraser, Rachel Weisz, John Hannah, Arnold Vosloo, Oded Fehr, Patricia Velasquez, Freddie Boath, Alun Armstrong
Distributor: UIP
US
Release date: 18 May 2001
Opening weekend: £5.929m
Box office: £201,707,096
No of screens: 454
S&S reference: July 2001, p.45-46

My Brother
17 July
BFI Productions, FilmFour Lab, FilmFour, British Screen, Film Council, Media II, Filmboard Berlin-Bradenburg
Budget: £1.00m
Dir: Dom Rotheroe
with Jenna Harrison, Ben Whishaw, Adrian Rawlins, Judith Scott, Richard Hope, Jonathan Hackett, Patrick Godfrey
Distributor: ADD
UK/Germany

My Kingdom
16 October
Close Grip Films, Primary Pictures, Sky Pictures, Key Films (Italy), Sky Pictures
Budget: £5.00m
Dir: Don Boyd
with Richard Harris, Paul McGann,

Jimi Mistry, Lorraine Pilkington, Colin Salmon, Lynn Redgrave, Reece Noi, Aidan Gillen
Distributor: ADD
UK/Italy/US

The Navigators
9 October
Parallax Pictures, Road Movies (Germany), Tornasol, Alta (Spain), Channel Four, Bim Distribuzione (Italy), Diaphana (France), Cineart (Belgium), Arts Council of England through The Film Consortium
Budget: £1.70m
Dir: Ken Loach
with Thomas Craig, Joe Duttine, Steve Huison
Distributor: ADD
UK/Spain/Italy/France

Off Key (Desafinado)
27 June
Lola Films (Spain), Lola Films (UK)
Budget: £6.37m
Dir: Manuel Gomez-Pereira
withDanny Aiello, Joe Mantegna, George Hamilton, Anna Galiena, Ariadna Gil, Claudia Guerini, Ashley Hamilton
Distributor: ADD
Spain

One of the Hollywood Ten
31 January
Morena (Spain), Alibi Films, BBC Wales, Canal Plus (Spain), Lucky
Budget: £4.00m
Dir: Karl Francis
with Jeff Goldblum, Greta Scacchi, Ángela Molina, Christopher Fulford, Antonio Valero, John Sessions
Distributor: ADD
Spain/US/UK

The Parole Officer
20 August
DNA Films, Figment Films, Toledo Pictures, Universal Pictures International (US), Arts Council of England
Budget: £5.99m
Dir: John Duigan
with Steve Coogan, Lena Headey, Om Puri, Steven Waddington, Ben Miller, Jenny Agutter, Emma Williams
Distributor: UIP
UK
Release date: 10 August 2001
Opening weekend: £902,028
Box office: £3.13m
No of screens: 288
S&S reference: 9 August 2001, p.54

Pasty Faces
31 January
Noel Gay Motion Pictures Company
Budget: £0.50m
Dir: David Baker
with David Paul Baker, Alan
McCafferty,
Gary Cross, Martin Mcgreechin, Cora
Bissett, Chloë Annett, Geoff
McKnight
Distributor: Metrodome
UK

Plato's Breaking Point
4 March
Robark Pictures,
Budget: £0.75m
Dir: Nigel Barker
with Joe Ferrera, William Halliday,
Delphine Lanson, Melodi Boreland,
Ashley Miller
Distributor: ADD
UK

Possession
30 August
Baltimore Spring Creek Productions
(US), Warner Bros. (US), USA Films
(US)
Budget: £20.39m
Dir: Neil LaBute
with Gwyneth Paltrow, Jeremy
Northam, Jennifer Ehle, Toby
Stephens, Anna Massey, Graham
Crowden, Trevor Eve, Tom Hollander,
Tom Hickey, Aaron Eckhart
Distributor: Warner Bros
Distributors (UK)
US

Princesa
8 February
Parallax Pictures BIM (Italy), Road
Movies (Germany),
Budget: £0.97m
Dir: Henrique Goldman
with Ingrid de Souza, Cesare Bocci,
Lulu Pecorari, Mauro Pirovano, Biba
Lerhue, Sonia Morgan
Distributor: ADD
UK/Italy/Germany

Proof of Life
28 February
Castle Rock Entertainment (US),
Warner Bros (US), Bel Air
Entertainment
Budget: £47.00m
Dir: Taylor Hackford
with Meg Ryan, Russell Crowe, David
Morse, Pamela Reed, David Caruso,
Anthony Heald
Distributor: Warner Bros
US
Release date: 2 March 2001

Opening weekend: £762,614
Box office: £2.607m
No of screens: 295
S&S reference: March 2001 p.57

Puckoon
6 November
Insight Ventures, Northern Ireland
Film Commission, Arts Council of
Northern Ireland, Section 481
Budget: £3.50m
Dir: Terence Ryan
with Sean Hughes, Elliott Gould,
Richard Attenborough, Daragh
O'Malley, John Lynch
Distributor: ADD
UK

Quicksand
4 December
Geoff Reeve Film, Cinesand (France),
Visionview, Cinerenta (Germany)
Budget: £6.33m
Dir: John MacKenzie
with Michael Caine, Michael Keaton,
Judith Godrèche, Rade Serbedzija
Distributor: ADD
UK

Randall's Flat
23 September
Stage to Screen
Budget: £1.50m
Dir: Chris Atkins
with Peter Broome, Andrew Hoggarth,
Abigail Good, John Moraitis, Kevin
Rundle, Zoe-Anne Phillips, Adam Smith
Distributor: ADD
UK

Revelation
29 October
Romulus Films
Budget: £4.13m
Dir: Stuart Urban
with Terence Stamp, Liam
Cunningham, James D'Arcy, Udo
Kier, Natasha Wightman, Derek
Jacobi, Heathcote Williams
Distributor: ADD
UK

The Safety of Objects
16 October
Infilm Productions (US), Killer Films
(US), Clear Blue Sky Productions
(US), Renaissance Films
Budget: £4.86m
Dir: Rose Troche
with Glenn Close, Dermot Mulroney,
Patricia Clarkson, Timothy Olyphant,
Mary Kay Place, Jessica Campbell,
Moira Kelly, Robert Kline
Distributor: ADD
US/Canada

The Search for John Gissing
1 July
Sunlight Productions (US)
Budget: £6.00m
Dir: Mike Binder
with Mike Binder, Janeane Garofalo,
Alan Rickman, Juliet Stevenson, Allan
Corduner
Distributor: ADD
US

Semana Santa
1 October
Schlemmer (Germany), Wandering
Star
Budget: £4.77m
Dir: Pepe Danquart
with Mira Sorvino, Olivier Martinez,
Féodor Atkine, Luis Tosar, Fermí
Reixach, Alida Valli,
Distributor: ADD
Germany/Switzerland/France

Shiner
16 January
Wisecroft Productions, IAC Films
Budget: £7.00m
Dir: John Irvin
with Michael Caine, Martin Landau,
Frances Barber, Claire Rushbrook,
Frank Harper, Andy Serkis, Kenneth
Cranham
Distributor: Momentum Pictures
UK
Release date: 14 September 2001

The Sleeping Dictionary
1 May
Fine Line Production (US)
Budget: £6.00m
Dir: Guy Jenkin
UK

The Sorcerer's Apprentice
14 August
Peakview Transatlantic
Budget: £2.35m
Dir: David Lister
with Robert Davi, Kelly LeBrock
Distributor: ADD
UK

Spy Game
5 November
Universal Pictures (US), Beacon
Pictures (US)
Budget: £55.00m
Dir: Tony Scott
with Robert Redford, Brad Pitt,
Catherine McCormack, Stephen
Dillane, David Frankel
Distributor: UIP
US

South West Nine

11 August
Fruit Salad Films, Irish Screen
Budget: £2.00m
Dir: Richard Parry
with Wil Johnson, Stuart Laing, Mark
Letheren, Amelia Curtis, Orlessa
Edwards, Nicola Stapleton, Frank
Harper, Zebida Gardener-Sharper,
Jenny Jules
Distributor: Fruit Salad Distribution
UK/Ireland
Release date: 9 October 2001

Superstition

3 October
MovieMasters (Netherlands),
Woodline Productions, DeLux
Productions (Luxembourg)
Budget: £4.50m
Dir: Kenneth Hope
with Sienna Guillory, Mark Strong,
Charlotte Rampling, Frances Barber,
Alice Krige, David Warner, Derek de
Lint
Distributor: ADD
Netherlands/UKß

Tabloid

4 December
Ultimate Pictures
Budget: £5.00m
Dir: David Blair
with Matthew Rhys, Mary Elizabeth
Mastrantonio, John Hurt
Distributor: ADD
UK

This Filthy Earth

28 August
FilmFour Lab, Tall Stories, BSkyB,
FilmFour
Budget: £1.10m
Dir: Andrew Kotting
with Rebecca R. Palmer, Shane
Attwooll, Demelza Randall, Xavier
Tchili, Dudley Sutton, Ina Clough,
Peter-Hugo Daly, Eve Steele, Ryan
Kelly
Distributor: ADD
UK

The Triumph of Love

4 September
Fiction (Italy), Recorded Picture
Company, Medusa (Italy), Odeon
Pictures (Germany)
Budget: £3.50m
Dir: Clare Peploe
with Mira Sorvino, Ben Kingsley,
Fiona Shaw, Rachael Stirling, Luis
Molteni, Ignazio Oliva
Distributor: ADD
UK/Italy/Germany

Unconditional Love

1 February
Avery Pix Inc (US), New Line
Cinema (US), Zucca (US)
Budget: £20.00m
Dir: P.J. Hogan
with Kathy Bates, Rupert Everett, Dan
Aykroyd, Jonathan Pryce, Jack
Noseworthy
Distributor: Entertainment Film
Distributors Ltd
US
Release date: 27 April 2001

Villa Des Roses

26 June
Favourite Films (Belgium), Isabella
Films (Netherlands), Samsa Films
(Luxembourg), Dan Films
Budget: £2.40m
Dir: Frank van Passel
with Julie Delpy, Tara Fitzgerald,
Shaun Dingwall, Shirley Henderson,
Harriet Walter, Timothy West
Distributor: ADD
UK/Belgium/Netherlands/
Luxembourg

The War Bride

26 April
Random Harvest Pictures, DB
Entertainment (Canada), A Channel
Drama Fund (Canada)
Budget: £3.70m
Dir: Lyndon Chubbuck
with Anna Friel, Brenda Fricker,
Molly Parker, Julie Cox
Distributor: ADD
UK/Canada

RELEASES

Listed here are feature-length films, both British and foreign which had a theatrical release in the UK between January and December 2000. Entries quote the title, distributor, UK release date, certificate, country of origin, director/s, leading players, production company/ies, duration, gauge (other than 35 mm) and the Sight and Sound reference. Compiled by Linda Wood

Films released in the UK in 2000

* denotes re-release

JANUARY

1	BLACKADDER BACK & FORTH
7	THE LOSS OF SEXUAL INNOCENCE
7	LES AMANTES DEL CÍRCULO POLAR, LOS/THE LOVERS OF THE ARCTIC CIRCLE
7	BRINGING OUT THE DEAD
7	LE TEMPS RETROUVÉ/ TIME REGAINED
14	ANGELA'S ASHES
14	SLEEPY HOLLOW
14	THREE SEASONS
14	THE DARKEST LIGHT
14	SUMMER OF SAM
14	WONDERLAND
14	THE BONE COLLECTOR
21	STIGMATA
21	STRANGE PLANET
21	BICENTENNIAL MAN
21	* SCARLET STREET
21	MUSIC OF THE HEART
21	LIMBO
28	AMERICAN BEAUTY
28	RANCID ALUMINIUM
26	SIMPATICO
28	DOUBLE JEOPARDY
28	FAST FOOD
28	STRONG LANGUAGE
28	THE WOOD

FEBRUARY

4	A ROOM FOR ROMEO BRASS
4	TOY STORY 2
4	* REAR WINDOW
4	THE BIG TEASE,
4	HOUSE ON HAUNTED HILL
11	THE END OF THE AFFAIR
11	THE BEACH
11	THE CHERRY ORCHARD/ VISINOKIPOS, O
11	XIAO WU
18	THE BACHELOR
18	BODY SHOTS
18	TOPSY-TURVY
18	APO TIN AKRI TIS POLIS/ FROM THE EDGE OF THE CITY
18	* YOU ONLY LIVE ONCE
25	THE GREEN MILE
25	THE TALENTED MR. RIPLEY
25	ABRE LOS OJOS/OPEN YOUR EYES

MARCH

3	FUCKING ÅMÅL/SHOW ME LOVE
3	THREE KINGS
3	AGNES BROWNE
3	TUMBLEWEEDS
10	SLC PUNK!
10	THE INSIDER,
10	WHATEVER HAPPENED TO HAROLD SMITH?
10	JEANNE D'ARC /JOAN OF ARC
10	NEXT FRIDAY
10	LOLA + BILIDIKID/LOLA AND BILLY THE KID
17	ORDINARY DECENT CRIMINAL
17	MAGNOLIA
17	BEING JOHN MALKOVICH
17	THE CIDER HOUSE RULES
17	RIEN SUR ROBERT
17	*A CLOCKWORK ORANGE,
17	NÁVRAT IDIOTA /THE IDIOT RETURNS
17	EN PLEIN COEUR/IN ALL INNOCENCE
24	BROKEN VESSELS
24	* MATTER OF LIFE AND DEATH, A
24	THE HURRICANE
24	GIRL, INTERRUPTED

24	BLEEDER
24	THE LAST BROADCAST
31	LOVE'S LABOUR'S LOST
31	HOLY SMOKE
31	ANY GIVEN SUNDAY
31	MANSFIELD PARK
31	LAKE PLACID
31	LES CONVOYEURS ATTENDENT /THE CARRIERS ARE WAITING,

APRIL

7	BOYS DON'T CRY
7	HURLYBURLY
7	ERIN BROCKOVICH
14	PIPPI LONGSTOCKING
14	THE TIGGER MOVIE
14	ASTERIX AND OBELIX TAKE ON CAESAR
14	MISSION TO MARS
14	POKÉMON THE FIRST MOVIE: MEWTWO STRIKES BACK
14	L'ENNUI
14	* ONCE UPON A TIME IN THE WEST
21	SEX THE ANNABEL CHONG STORY
21	CRADLE WILL ROCK
21	KEVIN AND PERRY GO LARGE
21	SNOW DAY
21	AMERICAN PSYCHO
21	THE STORY OF US
28	GHOST DOG: THE WAY OF THE SAMURAI
28	SCREAM 3
28	NAPFÉNY ÍZE, A/SUNSHINE
28	THE MILLION DOLLAR HOTEL,
28	ICON FILM DISTRIBUTION
28	GALAXY QUEST

MAY

1	BEST
5	HOUSE!
5	JANICE BEARD 45 WPM
5	* THE LONG GOOD FRIDAY,
5	THE LAST SEPTEMBER
5	TRICK
5	MAN ON THE MOON
12	CIRCUS
12	SNOW FALLING ON CEDARS
12	GLADIATOR

12 HANGING UP
12 THE FILTH AND THE FURY
19 THE WHOLE NINE YARDS
19 SAVING GRACE
19 DOWN TO YOU
19 FINAL DESTINATION
19 NORA
19 THE VIRGIN SUICIDES
19 THE ADVENTURES OF ELMO
IN GROUCHLAND
26 BOILER ROOM
26 FANTASIA 2000
26 STIR OF ECHOES
26 SIMON MAGUS
26 DEUCE BIGALOW: MALE
GIGOLO
26 HONEST

JUNE

2 BATTLEFIELD EARTH A SAGA
FOR THE YEAR 3000
2 MAYBE BABY
2 U-571
2 NEUVIÈME PORTE, LA/THE
NINTH GATE
9 GANGSTER NO. 1
9 SWEET AND LOWDOWN
9 [EYE] OF THE BEHOLDER
9 DRIVE ME CRAZY
16 SUPERNOVA
16 28 DAYS
16 FOR LOVE OF THE GAME
16 SMALL TIME OBSESSION
16 FREQUENCY
23 THE NEXT BEST THING
23 CHILL FACTOR
23 BIG MOMMA'S HOUSE
23 RELATIVE VALUES
26 WHEN THE SKY FALLS
30 REINDEER GAMES
30 BEYOND THE MAT
30 THREE TO TANGO
30 CHICKEN RUN

JULY

7 MISSION: IMPOSSIBLE II
7 AMERICAN MOVIE THE
MAKING OF NORTH
WESTERN
7 FLAMENCO
14 BREAKFAST OF CHAMPIONS
14 24 HOURS IN LONDON
14 THOMAS AND THE MAGIC
RAILROAD
14 THE PATRIOT
14 ESSEX BOYS
21 STUART LITTLE
21 FORTRESS 2: RE-ENTRY
21 HIGH FIDELITY
28 THE PERFECT STORM
28 LENGUA DE LAS

MARIPOSAS,
LA/BUTTERFLY'S TONGUE
28 THE FLINTSTONES IN VIVA
ROCK VEGAS
28 TITAN A.E.

AUGUST

4 THE ROAD TO EL DORADO,
4 GONE IN SIXTY SECONDS
4 VEUVE DE SAINT-PIERRE,
LA/THE WIDOW OF SAINT-
PIERRE
11 RULES OF ENGAGEMENT
11 THE WEDDING TACKLE
11 MY DOG SKIP
18 THE LITTLE VAMPIRE
18 RINGU/ RING,
18 THE X-MEN
18 THE JOLLY BOYS' LAST
STAND
21 THE LUZHIN DEFENCE
25 SOME VOICES
25 GOSSIP
25 SHANGHAI NOON
25 THERE'S ONLY ONE JIMMY
GRIMBLE
25 CHERRY FALLS

SEPTEMBER

1 SNATCH
1 MISS JULIE
1 NURSE BETTY
1 TITUS
8 THE CLOSER YOU GET
8 KEEPING THE FAITH
8 SCARY MOVIE
15 THE CELL
15 SHAFT
15 O BROTHER, WHERE ART
THOU?
15 DANCER IN THE DARK
22 ME, MYSELF & IRENE
22 SPACE COWBOYS
29 BILLY ELLIOT
29 HOLLOW MAN

OCTOBER

6 THE NUTTY PROFESSOR II
KLUMPS
6 GUN SHY
6 SORTED
13 ROMEO MUST DIE
13 THE HOUSE OF MIRTH
13 ROAD TRIP
13 DINOSAUR
20 COYOTE UGLY
20 BRING IT ON
20 WHAT LIES BENEATH
20 MEMENTO
27 IT WAS AN ACCIDENT

27 HUAYANG NIAHUA/IN THE
MOOD FOR LOVE
27 BOOK OF SHADOWS BLAIR
WITCH 2

NOVEMBER

3 LOSER
3 GREY OWL
3 WONDER BOYS
3 PURELY BELTER
3 THE GOLDEN BOWL,
5 MAN WHO CRIED, THE
6 HARRY, UN AMI QUI VOUS
VEUT DU BIEN/HARRY IS
HERE TO HELP
6 DISNEY'S THE KID
6 THE YARDS
6 PITCH BLACK
6 BEDAZZLED
17 WHERE THE HEART IS
17 THE WAY OF THE GUN
17 LITTLE NICKY
17 SECOND GENERATION
20 DONALD CAMMELL'S WILD
SIDE
24 POURQUOI PAS MOI?
24 CHOPPER
24 EST-OUEST/EAST-WEST
24 THE SKULLS
24 READY TO RUMBLE
24 CHARLIE'S ANGELS
24 FREEWAY II CONFESSIONS
OF A TRICKBABY

DECEMBER

1 DR. SEUSS' HOW THE
GRINCH STOLE CHRISTMAS
1 URBAN LEGENDS FINAL CUT
1 DUETS
1 RED PLANET
1 SMALL TIME CROOKS
8 LES DESTINÉES
SENTIMENTALES
8 THE ART OF WAR
8 102 DALMATIANS
8 CECIL B. DEMENTED
8 MAUVAISE PASSE
8 HAMLET
8 6TH DAY
8 MEET THE PARENTS
22 THE FAMILY MAN
22 POKÉMON: THE POWER OF
ONE
29 UNBREAKABLE

Abre los ojos

(1997)
aka: Open Your Eyes (UK)
Ouvre les yeux (France)
Apri gli occhi (Italy)
Redbus Film Distribution – 25
February
(15) Spain/France/Italy
Dir Alejandro Amenábar
with Eduardo Noriega, Penélope
Cruz, Chete Lera, Fele Martínez,
Najwa Nimri, Gérard Barray, Jorge de
Juan, Miguel Palenzuela, Pedro
Miguel Martinez, Ion Gabella
© Sociedad General de Cine, S.A./Las
Producciones del Escorpion, S.L./Les
Films Alain Sarde/Lucky Red SRL
A production of José Luis Cuerda for
Sogetel, Las Producciones del
Escorpion, Les Films Alain Sarde,
Lucky Red with the participation of
Sogepaq and the collaboration of
Canal+ España
Supported by Eurimages
119 mins 5 seconds
Subtitles
S&S March 2000 p. 50

The Adventures of Elmo in Grouchland

(1999)
Columbia TriStar Films (UK) – 19
May
(U) US/Germany
Dir Gary Halvorson
with Mandy Patinkin, Vanessa
Williams, Sonia Manzano, Roscoe
Orman, Alison Bartlett-O'Reilly, Ruth
Buzzi, Emilio Delgado, Loretta Long,
Bob McGrath, Kevin Clash
© 1999. Global Entertainment
Productions GmbH & Co. Medien
KG
Jim Henson Pictures presents a
Children's Television Workshop
production
73 mins
S&S July 2000 p.38

Agnes Browne

(1999)
United International Pictures (UK)
Ltd – 3 March
(15) Ireland
Dir Anjelica Huston
with Anjelica Huston, Marion
O'Dwyer, Ray Winstone, Arno
Chevrier, Gerard McSorley, Niall
O'Shea, Ciarán Owens, Roxanna
Williams, Carl Power, Mark Power
© 1999. October Films present a
Hell's Kitchen production
an Anjelica Huston film
Produced with the support of

investment incentives for the Irish
Film Industry
provided by the Government of
Ireland
Produced with the assistance of Bord
Scannán na hÉireann/The Irish Film
Board
91 mins 53 seconds
S&S March 2000 p.38

Los Amantes del Círculo Polar

aka: The Lovers of the Arctic Circle
(English title)
Les Amants du cercle polaire
(France)
The Lovers from the North Pole
(USA)
(1998)
Metro Tartan Distributors – 7
January
(15) Spain/France
Dir Julio Medem
with Najwa Nimri, Fele Martínez,
Nancho Novo, Maru Valdivielso, Peru
Medem, Sara Valiente, Victor Hugo
Oliveira, Kristel Díaz, Pep Munné,
Jaroslaw Bielski
© Sociedad General de Cine, S.A.
Alicia Produce and Bailando en la
Luna production for Sogetel
with the collaboration of Canal+ and
Sogepac with the participation of Le
Studio Canal+
105 mins
Subtitles
S&S February 2000 p.48-49.

American Beauty

(1999)
United International Pictures (UK)
Ltd – 28 January
(18) US
Dir Sam Mendes
with Kevin Spacey, Annette Bening,
Thora Birch, Wes Bentley, Mena
Suvari, Peter Gallagher, Allison
Janney, Scott Bakula, Sam Robards,
Chris Cooper
©1999. DreamWorks LLC
DreamWorks SKG
Dreamworks pictures presents
a Jinks/Cohen Company production
121 mins 53 seconds
S&S February 2000 p.40

American Movie The Making of Northwestern

(1999)
Columbia TriStar Films (UK) – 7
July
(15) US
Dir Chris Smith
with Mark Borchardt, Tom
Schimmels, Monica Borchardt, Alex

Borchardt, Chris Borchardt, Ken
Keen, Mike Schank, Matt Weisman,
Bill Borchardt, Cliff Borchardt
© 1999 Northwestern Movie
Company LLC
C-Hundred Film Corp and Bluemark
Film present
a film by Chris Smith, Sarah Price
104 mins 44 seconds
S&S July 2000 p.36-38

American Psycho

(2000)
Entertainment Film Distributors Ltd
– 21 April
(18) US/Canada
Dir Mary Harron
with Christian Bale, Willem Dafoe,
Jared Leto, Josh Lucas, Samantha
Mathis, Matt Ross, Bill Sage, Chloë
Sevigny, Cara Seymour, Justin
Theroux
© 2000. Am Psycho Productions, Inc.
Lions Gate Films presents an Edward
R. Pressman production in
association with
MUSE Productions and Christian
Halsey Solomon
a Mary Harron film
101 mins 26 seconds
S&S May 2000 p.42

Angela's Ashes

(1999)
United International Pictures (UK)
Ltd – 14 January
(15) US/UK
Dir Alan Parker
with Emily Watson, Robert Carlyle,
Joe Breen, Ciarán Owens, Michael
Legge, Ronnie Masterson, Pauline
McLynn, Liam Carney, Eanna
MacLiam, Andrew Bennett
© 1999. Universal/PolyGram
Holdings, Inc.
Universal/Paramount - a Viacom
company
Universal Pictures International and
Paramount Pictures present
a David Brown/Scott Rudin/Dirty
Hands production
an Alan Parker film
Produced with the support of
investment incentives for The Irish
FilmIndustry provided by The
Government of Ireland
145 mins 51 seconds
S&S January 2000 p.40-42

Any Given Sunday

(1999)
Warner Bros Distributors (UK) – 31
March
(15) US

Dir Oliver Stone
with Al Pacino, Cameron Diaz,
Dennis Quaid, James Woods, Jamie
Foxx, J LL Cool, Matthew Modine,
Charlton Heston, Ann-Margret,
Aaron Eckhart
© 1999 Warner Bros
Warner Bros presents
an Ixtlan/The Donners' Company
production
an Oliver Stone film
150 mins 23 seconds
S&S April 2000 p.38-40

Apo tin akri tis polis

(1998)
aka: From the Edge of the City (UK)
Millivres Multimedia – 18 February
(18) Greece
Dir Constantine Giannaris
with Stathis Papadopoulos, Kostas
Kotsianidis, Panagiotis
Chartomatsidis, Dimitris Papoulidis,
Theodora Tzimou, Anestis
Polychronidis, Nikos Kamontos,
Stelios Tsemboglidis, Giorgos
Mavridis, Panagiota Vlachosotirou
©1998 Mythos - Cultural Action
Mythos - Cultural Action in
association with Rosebud, Hot Shot
Productions,
Hellenic Film Centre presents
a film by Constantine Giannaris
93 mins 10 seconds
Subtitles
S&S March 2000 p.43-44

The Art of War

(2000)
Warner Bros Distributors (UK) – 8
December
(18) Canada/US
Dir Christian Duguay
with Wesley Snipes, Anne Archer,
Maury Chaykin, Marie Matiko, Cary-
Hiroyuki Tagawa, Michael Biehn,
Donald Sutherland, Liliana
Komorowska, James Hong, Paul
Hopkins
© 2000. Filmline International (Art)
Inc.
Morgan Creek Productions, Inc. and
Franchise Pictures and Amen Ra
Films
present a Filmline International
production
a film by Christian Duguay
with the participation of The
Canadian Film or Video Production
Tax Credit and
Quebec Film and Television Tax
Credit
a Filmline International production
117 mins 13 seconds

S&S January 2001 p.40-41

Astérix & Obélix contre César

(1999)
aka: Asterix and Obelix Take On
Caesar (English title)
Asterix & Obelix gegen Caesar
(Germany)
Asterix e Obelix contro Cesare
(Italy)
(1999)
Pathé Distribution – 14 April
(PG) France/Germany/Italy
Dir Claude Zidi
with Gérard Depardieu, Christian
Clavier, Roberto Benigni, Michel
Galabru, Claude Piéplu, Daniel
Prévost, Pierre Palmade, Laetitia
Casta, Arielle Dombasle, Sim
©1999 Katharina/Renn
Productions/TF1 Films
Production/Bavaria Film/Bavaria
Entertainment/Melampo
Cinematografica
Claude Berri presents
a French/German/Italian co-
production of
Katharina/Renn Productions/TF1
Films Production/Bavaria
Film/Bavaria
Entertainment/Melampo
Cinematografica
with the participation of Canal+
with the participation of Centre
National de la Cinématographie
This film was supported by FFF
FilmFernsehFonds Bayern/FFA
Filmförderungsanstalt Berlin and
Eurimages
a Katherine/Renn production
a Claude Zidi film
110 mins 18 seconds
S&S May 2000 p.43-44

The Bachelor

(1999)
Entertainment Film Distributors Ltd
– 18 February
(12) US
Dir Gary Sinyor
with Chris O'Donnell, Renée
Zellweger, Hal Holbrook, James
Cromwell, Artie Lange, Edward
Asner, Marley Shelton, Sarah
Silverman, Stacy Edwards, Rebecca
Cross
© 1999. New Line Productions, Inc.
New Line Cinema presents a Lloyd
Segan Company production in
association with
George Street Pictures
102 mins 1 sec
S&S April 2000 p.41

Battlefield Earth a Saga for the Year 3000

(2000)
Warner Bros Distributors (UK) –
2nd June
(12) US
Dir Roger Christian,
with John Travolta, Barry Pepper,
Forest Whitaker, Kim Coates, Richard
Tyson, Sabine Karsenti, Michael
Byrne, Christian Tessier, Sylvain
Landry, Christopher Freeman
© 2000 Battlefield Productions, LLC
Morgan Creek Productions, Inc and
Franchise Pictures present
a Franchise Pictures, Jonathan D.
Krane production, JTP Films
production
117 mins 32 seconds
S&S July 2000 p.40-41

The Beach

(2000)
20th Century Fox (UK) – 11
February
(15) US/UK/Thailand
Dir Danny Boyle
with Leonardo DiCaprio, Tilda
Swinton, Virginie Ledoyen,
Guillaume Canet, Robert Carlyle,
Paterson Joseph, Lars Arentz Hansen,
Daniel York, Patcharawan
Patarakijjanon, Somboon Phutaroth
© 2000. Twentieth Century Fox Film
Corporation
Twentieth Century Fox presents a
Figment film
118 mins 58 seconds
S&S March 2000 p.39-40

Beautiful Creatures

(2000)
United International Pictures (UK)
Ltd – 19 January 2001
(18) UK
Dir Bill Eagles
with Rachel Weisz, Susan Lynch, Iain
Glen, Maurice Roëves, Alex Norton,
Jake D'Arcy, Tom Mannion, Paul
Doonan, Robin Laing, Pauline Lynch
© 2000. DNA Films Limited.
DNA Films present
a Snakeman production for DNA
Films in association with Universal
Pictures International
supported by the National Lottery
through the Arts Council of England
87 mins 54 seconds
S&S February 2001 p.35

Bedazzled

(2000)
20th Century Fox (UK) – 10
November

(12) US/Germany
Dir Harold Ramis
with Brendan Fraser, Elizabeth
Hurley, Frances O'Connor, Miriam
Shor, Orlando Jones, Paul Adelstein,
Toby Huss
© 2000. Twentieth Century Fox Film
Corporation, Monarchy Enterprises
B.V. and
Regency Entertainment (USA) Inc.
Twentieth Century Fox and Regency
Enterprises present a Trevor Albert
production
a Harold Ramis Film
In association with Taurus Film
93 mins 3 seconds
S&S December 2000 p.40

Being John Malkovich
(1999)
United International Pictures (UK)
Ltd – 17 March
(15) US
Dir Spike Jonze
with John Cusack, Cameron Diaz,
Catherine Keener, Orson Bean, Mary
Kay Place, W. Earl Brown, Carlos
Jacott, Willie Garson, Byrne Piven,
Gregory Sporleder
© 1999. PolyGram Holdings, Inc.
Universal Gramercy Pictures
presents
a Propaganda Films/Single Cell
Pictures production
112 mins 35 seconds
S&S March 2000 p.40-41

Best
(2000)
Optimum Releasing – 1 May
(15) UK/Ireland
Dir Mary McGuckian
with John Lynch, Ian Bannen,
Jerome Flynn, Ian Hart, Patsy Kensit,
Cal Macaninch, Linus Roache, Adrian
Lester, David Hayman, James Ellis
© 1999 Best Films Ltd
IAC Film/Sky Pictures/The Isle of
Man Film Commission in association
with
Smoke & Mirrors Film Productions
and Pembridge Pictures present a
film by Mary McGuckian
106 mins 25 seconds
S&S June 2000 p.36

Beyond the Mat
(1999)
United International Pictures (UK)
Ltd – 30 June
(15) US
Dir Barry W. Blaustein
with the participation of Vince
McMahon, Darren Drozdov, Roland
Alexander, Tony Jones, Mike Modest,

Terry Funk, Vicki Funk, Stacey Funk,
Brandee Funk, Paul Heyman
©1999 Universal Studios
Imagine Entertainment
a Barry W. Blaustein film
©1999 Universal Studios
Imagine Entertainment
a Barry W. Blaustein film
103 mins 5 seconds
S&S September 2000 p.38

Bicentennial Man
(1999)
Columbia TriStar Films (UK) – 21
January
(PG) US
Dir Chris Columbus
with Robin Williams, Sam Neill,
Embeth Davidtz, Oliver Platt, Wendy
Crewson, Hallie Kate Eisenberg,
Stephen Root, Lynne Thigpen,
Bradley Whitford, Kiersten Warren
©Touchstone Pictures and Columbia
Pictures
Touchstone Pictures and Columbia
Pictures present
a 1492 Pictures production in
association with Laurence Marks
Productions and
Radiant Productions
130 mins 59 seconds
S&S March 2000 p.41-42

Big Momma's House
(2000)
20th Century Fox (UK) – 23 June
(12) US/Germany
Dir Raja Gosnell
with Martin Lawrence, Nia Long,
Paul Giamatti, Jascha Washington,
Terrence Howard, Anthony Anderson,
Ella Mitchell, Carl Wright, Phyllis
Applegate Starletta DuPois
©2000. Twentieth Century Fox Film
Corporation, Monarchy Enterprises
B.V. and
Regency Entertainment (USA), Inc.
Twentieth Century Fox and Regency
Enterprises present
a David T. Friendly/Runteldat
Entertainment production
In association with Taurus Film
98 mins 23 seconds
S&S August 2000 p.39-40

The Big Tease
(1999)
Warner Bros Distributors (UK) – 4
February
(15) US/UK
Dir Kevin Allen
with Craig Ferguson, Frances Fisher,
Mary McCormack, Donal Logue,
Larry Miller, Charles Napier, Michael
Paul Chan, Sara Gilbert, Ted

McGinley, Nina Siemaszko
© 1999. Warner Bros.
Warner Bros. presents a Crawford P.
Inc. production in association with
I Should Coco Films
a Kevin Allen film
86 mins 16 seconds
S&S January 2000 p.43-44

Billy Elliot
(2000)
United International Pictures (UK)
Ltd – 29 September
(15) UK
Dir Stephen Daldry
with Julie Walters, Gary Lewis, Jamie
Draven, Jean Heywood, Jamie Bell,
Adam Cooper, Stuart Wells, Mike
Elliot, Billy Fane, Nicola Blackwell
© 2000. Tiger Aspect Pictures Ltd.
Universal
Working Title Films and BBC Films
in association with the Arts Council
of England present
a Tiger Aspect Pictures production in
association with
WT2
Developed by BBC Films
Supported by the National Lottery
through The Arts Council of England
110 mins 9 seconds
S&S October 2000 p. 40

Blackadder Back & Forth
(1999)
Public Exhibition – 1 January
UK
Dir Paul Weiland
with Rowan Atkinson, Tony
Robinson, Stephen Fry, Hugh Laurie,
Tim McInnerny, Miranda
Richardson, Patsy Byrne, Rik Mayall,
Colin Firth, Kate Moss
© 1999. NME.
Blackadder Films in association with
Baldrick Catering Co. present
Tiger Aspect Productions for New
Millennium Experience Company
In association with Sky Television
35 mins
No S&S reference
Note: Projected in 70mm in BSkyB's
Skyscape at the Millennium 'baby'
dome from 1 January 2000. Special
one-off final episode.

Bleeder
(1999)
Metrodome Distribution Ltd – 24
March
(18) Denmark
Dir Nikolas Winding Refn
with Kim Bodnia, Mads Mikkelsen,
Rikke Louise Andersson, Liv
Corfixen, Levino Jensen, Zlatko

Buric, Claus Flüggare, Ole
Abildgaard, Gordana Radosavljevic,
Marko Zecewic
© 1999. Kamikaze ApS
Kamikaze presents
A Scanbox Entertainment release (in
Denmark) of a Kamikaze
production, in
association with Scanbox Denmark,
TV2 Denmark, Zentropa
Entertainment and
TempoMedia. (International sales:
Scanbox, Copenhagen.)
97 mins 28 seconds
Subtitles
S&S April 2000 p.42

Body Shots
(1999)
Entertainment Film Distributors Ltd
– 18 February
(18) US
Dir Michael Cristofer
with Sean Patrick Flanery, Jerry
O'Connell, Amanda Peet, Tara Reid,
Ron Livingston, Emily Procter, Brad
Rowe, Sybil Temchen, Joe Basile, Scott
Burkholder
© 1999. New Line Productions Inc.
New Line Cinema a Time Warner
company
New Line Cinema presents
a Colomby/Keaton production
105 mins 39 seconds
S&S April 2000 p.42-43

Boiler Room
(2000)
Entertainment Film Distributors Ltd
– 26 May
(15) US
Dir Ben Younger
with Giovanni Ribisi, Vin Diesel, Nia
Long, Nicky Katt, Scott Caan, Ron
Rifkin, Jamie Kennedy, Taylor
Nichols, Bill Sage, Tom Everett Scott
© 2000. New Line Productions, Inc.
New Line Cinema presents a Team
Todd production
119 mins 35 seconds
S&S June 2000 p.36-37

The Bone Collector
(1999)
Columbia TriStar Films (UK) – 14
January
(18) US
Dir Phillip Noyce
with Denzel Washington, Angelina
Jolie, Queen Latifah, Michael Rooker,
Mike McGlone, Luis Guzmán, Leland
Orser, John Benjamin Hickey, Ed
O'Neill, Bobby Cannavale
© 1999. Universal Studios and
Columbia Pictures Industries, Inc.

Columbia Pictures and Universal
Pictures present a Bregman
production
117 mins 47 seconds
S&S March 2000 p.42-43

Book of Shadows Blair Witch 2
(2000)
Momentum Pictures – 27 October
(15) US
Dir Joe Berlinger
with Kim Director, Jeffrey Donovan,
Erica Leerhsen, Tristen Skyler,
Stephen Barker Turner, Kurt Loder,
Chuck Scarborough, Bruce Reed, Joe
Berlinger, Sara Phillips
©2000. Artisan Film Investors Trust
Momentum Pictures/Artisan
Entertainment/Haxan Films
Artisan Entertainment presents
a Joe Berlinger film
90 mins 16 seconds
S&S December 2000 p.42

Boys Don't Cry
(1999)
20th Century Fox (UK) – 7 April
(18) US
Dir Kimberly Peirce
with Hilary Swank, Chloë Sevigny,
Peter Sarsgaard, Brendan Sexton III,
Alison Folland, Alicia Goranson,
Matt McGrath, Rob Campbell,
Jeannetta Arnette, Cheyenne Rushing
©1999 Twentieth Century Fox Film
Corporation
Fox Searchlight Pictures and The
Independent Film Channel
Productions present
a Killer Films/Hart-Sharp
Entertainment production
a Kimberly Peirce film
Developed with the assistance of the
Sundance Institute
118 mins 24 seconds
S&S April 2000 p.43-44

Breakfast of Champions
(1999)
Warner Bros Distributors (UK) – 14
July
(15) US
Dir Alan Rudolph
with Bruce Willis, Albert Finney, Nick
Nolte, Barbara Hershey, Glenne
Headly, Lukas Haas, Omar Epps,
Vicki Lewis, Buck Henry, Ken
Campbell,
© 1999. Sugar Creek Productions,
Incorporated
Hollywood Pictures/Summit
Entertainment and Flying Heart Films
an Alan Rudolph film

109 mins 45 seconds
S&S September 2000 p.38-39

Bringing Out the Dead
(1999)
Buena Vista International (UK) – 7
January
(18) USA
Dir Martin Scorsese
with Nicolas Cage, Patricia Arquette,
John Goodman, Ving Rhames, Tom
Sizemore, Marc Anthony, Mary Beth
Hurt, Cliff Curtis, Nestor Serrano,
Aida Turturro
© 1999. Paramount Pictures
Corporation and Touchstone
Pictures
Paramount Pictures/Touchstone
Pictures
Touchstone Pictures and Paramount
Pictures present
a Scott Rudin - Cappa/De Fina
production
a Martin Scorsese picture
120 mins 58 seconds
S&S January 2000 p.45-46.

Bring It On
(2000)
Entertainment Film Distributors Ltd
– 20 October
(12) US
Dir Peyton Reed
with Kirsten Dunst, Eliza Dushku,
Jesse Bradford, Gabrielle Union,
Sherry Hursey, Holmes Osborne,
Clare Kramer, Nicole Bilderback,
Tsianina Joelson, Shamari Fears
© 2000. Beacon Communications,
LLC
Universal Pictures and Beacon
Pictures present
98 mins 36 seconds
S&S November 2000 p.45-46

Broken Vessels
(1998)
Feature Film Company – 2nd June
(18) US
Dir Scott Ziehl
with Todd Field, Jason London,
Roxana Zal, Susan Traylor, James
Hong, Brent David Fraser, William
Smith, David Baer, Stephanie Feury,
Patrick Cranshaw
© 1999. Broken Vessels
Unapix and Zeitgeist Films present a
Ziehl and Zal production
a film by Scott Ziehl
91 mins 30 seconds
S&S April 2000 p.44, 46

Cecil B. Demented
(2000)
Momentum Pictures – 8 December

(18) US/France
Dir John Waters
with Melanie Griffith, Stephen Dorff,
Alicia Witt, Adrian Grenier, Larry
Gilliard Jr, Maggie Gyllenhaal, Jack
Noseworthy, Mink Stole, Ricki Lake,
Patricia Hearst
© 2000. Arctic Productions LLC
Artisan Entertainment
Artisan Entertainment presents in
association with Le Studio Canal +
a Polar Entertainment production
a John Waters film
88 mins 11 seconds
S&S January 2001 p.42-43

The Cell
(2000)
Entertainment Film Distributors Ltd
– 15 September
(18) US/Germany
Dir Tarsem Duamdwar
with Jennifer Lopez, Vince Vaughn,
Vincent D'Onofrio, Marianne Jean-
Baptiste, Jake Weber, Dylan Baker,
James Gammon, Tara Subkoff, Gerry
Becker, Dean Norris
©2000. Katira Production GmbH &
Co. KG
New Line Cinema presents
a Caro-McLeod/Radical Media
production in association with
Katira Productions GmbH & Co.
KG/New Line Production Inc.
109 mins 2 seconds
S&S November 2000 p.46-47

* C'era una volta il West
aka: Once Upon a Time in the West
(English title)
(1969)
BFI Collections – 14 April
(A) Italy/US
Dir Sergio Leone
with Claudia Cardinale, Henry
Fonda, Jason Robards, Charles
Bronson, Gabriele Ferzetti, Paolo
Stoppa, Woody Strode, Jack Elam,
Keenan Wynn, Frank Wolff
Rafran Cinematografica
San Marco Cinematografica
Euro International Films
Paramount Pictures Corporation
168 mins
Monthly Film Bulletin.v36. n428.
September 1969 p.187-8; Aigist 1982
p.162-163

Charlie's Angels
(2000)
Columbia TriStar Films (UK) – 24
November
(15) US/Germany
Dir McG

with Cameron Diaz, Drew
Barrymore, Lucy Liu, Bill Murray,
Sam Rockwell, Tim Curry, Kelly
Lynch, Crispin Glover, John Forsythe,
Matt LeBlanc
© 2000. Global Entertainment
Productions GmbH & Co. Movie KG
Columbia Pictures presents a
Leonard Goldberg/Flower Films/Tall
Trees production
98 mins 20 seconds
S&S January 2001 p.43-44

Cherry Falls
(2000)
Entertainment Film Distributors Ltd
- 25 August
(15) US
Dir Geoffrey Wright
with Brittany Murphy, Michael Biehn,
Gabriel Mann, Jesse Bradford,
Jay Mohr, Douglas Spain, Keram
Malicki-Sanchez, Natalie Ramsey,
Candy Clark, Amanda Anka
© 1999. October Films, Inc.
[al] USA Films / Rogue Pictures
Rogue Pictures presents an Industry
Entertainment and Fresh Produce
Company production
a Geoffrey Wright film
91 mins 33 secs
S&S October 2000 p.41

The Cherry Orchard
aka: Visinokipos, O (Greece)
aka: Cerisaie, La (France)
(1999)
Melanda Film Production –11
February
(PG) Greece/Cyprus/France
Dir Michael Cacoyannis
with Charlotte Rampling, Alan Bates,
Katrin Cartlidge, Owen Teale, Tushka
Bergen, Xander Berkeley, Gerald
Butler, Andrew Howard, Melanie
Lynskey, Ian McNeice
Melanda Film Productions present
a Michael Cacoyannis film
a Melanda Films production in
association with The Greek Film
Centre/Amanda Productions
(Cyprus)/Films de l'Astre (France)
with the participation of Canal+
Eurimages Counsel of Europe
141 minutes 18 seconds
S&S February 2000 p.42

Chicken Run
(2000)
Pathé Distribution – 30 June
(U) US/UK
Dir Peter Lord
with the voices of Phil Daniels, Lynn
Ferguson, Mel Gibson, Tony
Haygarth, Jane Horrocks, Miranda

Richardson, Julia Sawalha, Timothy
Spall, Imelda Staunton, Benjamin
Whitrow
© 2000 DreamWorks LLC/Aardman
Chicken Limited/Pathé Image
DreamnWorks Pictures in
association with Pathé presents
an Aardman production
84 mins 14 seconds
S&S August 2000 p.41-42

Chill Factor
(1999)
Warner Bros Distributors (UK) – 23
June
(15) US
Dir Hugh Johnson
with Cuba Gooding Jr, Skeet Ulrich,
Peter Firth, David Paymer, Hudson
Leick, Daniel Hugh Kelly, Kevin J.
O'Connor, Judson Mills, Jordan Mott,
Dwayne Macopson
© 1999. Morgan Creek Productions
James G. Robinson presents a
Morgan Creek production
101 mins 48 seconds
S&S August 2000 p.42

Chopper
(2000)
Metrodome Distribution Ltd – 24
November
(18) Australia
Dir Andrew Dominik
with Eric Bana, Simon Lyndon, David
Field, Dan Wyllie, Bill Young, Vince
Colosimo, Kenny Graham, Kate
Beahan, Renee Brack, Gregory Pitt
©2000. Australian Film Finance
Corporation Limited, Mushroom
Pictures Pty Ltd,
Pariah Films Pty Ltd
Beyond Films/Palace
Films/Mushroom Pictures
Australian Film Finance Corporation
and Mushroom Pictures present
a Pariah Film production
financed with the assistance of
Australian Film Finance Corporation
financed with the assistance of
Mushroom Pictures
development assistance and producer
attachment provided by Film
Victoria - a
division of Cinemedia
distributed in Australia & New
Zealand by Palace
international sales: Beyond Films
94 mins
S&S December 2000 p.43

The Cider House Rules
(1999)
Buena Vista International (UK) – 17
March

(12) US
Dir Lasse Hallström
with Tobey Maguire, Charlize
Theron, Delroy Lindo, Paul Rudd,
Michael Caine, Jane Alexander, Kathy
Baker, Kieran Culkin, Kate Nelligan,
Heavy D
© 1999. Miramax Film Corp.
Buena Vista International/Miramax
International/20th
Anniversary Miramax Films
Miramax Films presents a
FilmColony production
a film by Lasse Hallström
125 mins 33 seconds
S&S February 2000 p.42-43

Circus

(2000)
Columbia TriStar Films (UK) – 12
May
(18) US/UK
Dir Rob Walker
with John Hannah, Famke Janssen,
Peter Stormare, Brian Conley, Tiny
Lister, Amanda Donohoe, Fred Ward,
Eddie Izzard, Ian Burfield, Neil Stuke
© 2000 Columbia Pictures Industries
Inc Columbia Pictures presents
a Film Development Corporation
production
95 mins 28 seconds
S&S June 2000 p.37-38

*A Clockwork Orange

(1971)
Warner Bros Distributors (UK) – 17·
March
(18) UK
Dir Stanley Kubrick
with Malcolm McDowell, Patrick
Magee, Michael Bates, Warren Clarke,
John Clive, Adrienne Corri, Carl
Duering, Paul Farrell, Clive Francis,
Michael Gover
Warner Bros.
Polaris Productions
Hawk Films
136 mins
S&S May 2000 p.22-24; Monthly
Film Bulletin v39. n457. February
1972 p.28-29

The Closer You Get

(2000)
20th Century Fox (UK) – 8th
September
(12) US/UK/Ireland
Dir Aileen Ritchie
with Ian Hart, Sean McGinley, Niamh
Cusack, Ruth McCabe, Ewan Stewart,
Pat Shortt, Cathleen Bradley, Sean
McDonagh, Risteard Cooper,
Maureen O'Brien
©1999. Twentieth Century Fox Film

Corporation
Fox Searchlight Pictures presents a
Redwave production
Produced with the support of
investment incentives for the Irish
Film Industry
provided by the Government of
Ireland
92 mins
S&S July 2000 p.41

Les Convoyeurs attendent

aka: The Carriers Are Waiting,
(English title)
(1999)
Artificial Eye Film Company – 31
March
(15) France/Belgium/Switzerland
Dir Benoît Mariage
with Benoît Poelvoorde, Morgane
Simon, Bouli Lanners, Dominique
Baeyens, Philippe Grand'Henry, Jean-
Francois Devigne, Lisa Lacroix,
Philippe Nahon, Edith Le Merdy,
Patrick Audin
© K-Star/K2/RTBF/CAB
Productions/SSR
Dépôt légal. 1999
A production of K-Star, with the
participation of Canal+, with the
participation of Centre National de
la Cinématographie (France), K2,
RTBF (Télévision belge), with the aid
of Centre du Cinéma et de
l'audiovisuel de la Communauté
française de Belgique (Belgium),
CAB Productions, la Télévision
Suisse Romande (TSR), l'office
Fédéral de la Culture (Switzerland)
Supported by Eurimages
Dominique Janne presents
a film by Benoît Mariage
93 mins 18 seconds
Subtitles
S&S April p.46

Coyote Ugly

(2000)
Buena Vista International (UK) – 20
October
(12) US
Dir David McNally
with Piper Perabo, Adam Garcia,
John Goodman, Maria Bello, Izabella
Miko, Tyra Banks, Bridget Moynahan,
Melanie Lynskey, Del Pentecost,
Michael Weston
© 2000. Disney Enterprises, Inc.
©2000. Touchstone Pictures and
Jerry Bruckheimer, Inc.
Touchstone Pictures/Jerry
Bruckheimer Films
100 mins 47 seconds
S&S November 2000 p.49-50

Cradle Will Rock

(1999)
Buena Vista International (UK) – 21
April
(15) US
Dir Tim Robbins
with Hank Azaria, Rubén Blades,
Joan Cusack, John Cusack,
Cary Elwes, Philip Baker Hall,
Cherry Jones, Angus Macfadyen,
Bill Murray, Vanessa Redgrave
©1999 Touchstone Pictures
Touchstone Pictures presents
a Havoc production
Produced in association with
Krakower/Beacham Productions
134 mins 29 seconds
S&S May 2000 p.40-41, 45-46

Dancer in the Dark

(2000)
FilmFour Distributors – 15
September
(15) Denmark/France/Sweden/Italy/
Germany
Dir Lars von Trier
with Björk, Catherine Deneuve,
David Morse, Peter Stormare, Joel
Grey, Vincent Paterson, Cara
Seymour, Jean-Marc Barr, Vladica
Kostic, Siobhan Fallon
©2000 Zentropa Entertainments4
Aps/France 3 Cinéma/Arte France
Cinéma/Trust
Film Svenska/Liberator
Productions/Pain Unlimited
Presented by Zentropa
Entertainments 4, Trust Film
Svenska, Film i Väst and
Liberator Productions
In co-production with
Pain Unlimited GmbH
Filmproduktion, Cinematograph
A/S, What Else? B.V.,
Icelandic Film Corporation, Blind
Spot Pictures, France 3 Cinéma,
Danish Broadcasting Corporation,
Arte France Cinéma, SVT Drama,
Arte/WDR
In collaboration with
Angel Films A/S, Canal+, Film Four,
Fine Line Features, Filmek,
Constantin Film, Lantia Cinema &
Audiovisivi (Leo Pescarolo), TV
1000, VPRO Television (The
Netherlands), WDR, YLE TV1
with the support of
Danish Film Institute (Mikael
Olsen), Eurimages, Swedish Film
Institute (Mats Arehn), Norwegian
Film Institute (Harry Guttormsen),
Icelandic Film Fund
140 mins 16 seconds
S&S October 2000 p.41-42

The Darkest Light

(1999)
Pathé Distribution – 14 January
(12) UK/France
Dir Bille Elringham
with Stephen Dillane, Kerry Fox, Keri
Arnold, Kavita Sungha, Jason Walton,
Nisha K. Nayar, Nicholas Hope, Alvin
Blossom, Kathryn Hunt,
Isobel Raine
© 1999. Pathé Fund Limited
Pathé Pictures presents in association
with the Arts Council of England/Le
Studio Canal+ and BBC Films with
the support of the Yorkshire Media
Production Agency
A Footprint Films production
Developed with the assistance of
British Screen Finance Limited,
London, England
Supported by The National Lottery
through The Arts Council of England
Part funded by the European
Regional Development Fund
Developed in association with BBC
Scotland
93 mins 52 seconds
S&S February 2000 p.43-44

Les Destinées sentimentales

aka: Sentimental Destination
(English title)
(2000)
Pathé Distribution – 8 December
(12) France/Switzerland
Dir Olivier Assayas
with Emmanuelle Béart, Charles
Berling, Isabelle Huppert, Olivier
Perrier, Dominique Reymond, André
Marcon, Alexandra London, Louis-
Do de Lencquesaing, Valérie
Bonneton, Julie Depardieu
©Arena Films/TF1 Films
Production/CAB Productions
dépôt légal: 2000
visa d'exploitation: 97809
Arena Films presents a French/Swiss
co-production: Arena Films/TF1
Films Production/CAB Productions
with the participation of
Canal+/Cofimage 11/Eurimages
With the support of Centre National
de la Cinématographie/Conseil
Général de la Charente/L'Office
Fédéral de la Culture (Suisse) in co-
production with
Télévision Suisse Romande (TSR) -
une entreprise de la SSR/SRG ideé
Suisse
A French/Swiss co-production: Arena
Films/TF1 Films Production/CAB
Productions
with the participation of Canal+

/ Cofimage II/Arcade/Eurimages
With the support of Centre National
de la Cinématographie/ Procirep/
L'OfficeFédéral de la Culture (Suisse)
In co-production with Télévision
Suisse Romande (TSR) - une
entreprise de la SSR/SRG ideé Suisse
Developed with the support of the
MEDIA Programme de l'Union
Européenne/Conseil Général de la
Charente
180 mins 7 seconds
Subtitles
S&S January 2001 p.46-47

Deuce Bigalow: Male Gigolo

(1999)
Buena Vista International (UK) – 26
May
(15) US
Dir Mike Mitchell
with Rob Schneider, William
Forsythe, Eddie Griffin, Arija
Bareikis, Oded Fehr, Gail O'Grady,
Richard Riehle, Jacqueline Obradors,
Big Boy, Amy Poehler
© 2000. Touchstone Pictures
Touchstone Pictures presents a
Happy Madison production in
association with
Out of the Blue Entertainment
88 mins 27 seconds
S&S June 2000 p.38

Dinosaur

(2000)
Buena Vista International (UK) – 13
October
(PG) US
Dir Ralph Zondag
with the voices of D.B. Sweeney, Alfre
Woodard, Ossie Davis, Max Casella,
Hayden Panettiere, Samuel E. Wright,
Julianna Margulies, Peter Siragusa,
Joan Plowright, Della Reese
© 2000 Disney Enterprises, Inc.
Walt Disney Pictures presents
82 mins 2 seconds
S&S November 2000 p.50-51

Disney's The Kid

aka: Disney's The Kid
(2000)
Buena Vista International (UK) – 10
November
(PG) US
Dir Jon Turteltaub
with Bruce Willis, Spencer Breslin,
Emily Mortimer, Lily Tomlin, Chi
McBride, Jean Smart, Dana Ivey,
Daniel Von Bargen, Stanley
Anderson, Susan Dalian
© 2000. Disney Enterprises, Inc.
Walt Disney Pictures presents

a Junction Entertainment production
a Jon Turteltaub film
104 mins 13 seconds
S&S December 2000 p.44-45

Donald Cammell's Wild Side

(1995)
Metro Tartan Distributors – 30 June
2000
(18) US
Dir Donald Cammell
with Christopher Walken, Joan Chen,
Steven Bauer, Anne Heche, Allen
Garfield, Adam Novack, Zion,
Richard Palmer, Randy Crowder,
Marcus Aurelius
©1995 Wild Side Productions Inc
and Mondofin B.V.
Nu Image presents
a John Langley production
Donald Cammell's...
115 mins 18 seconds
S&S August 2000 p.59

Double Jeopardy

(1999)
United International Pictures (UK)
Ltd – 28 January
(15) US/Germany
Dir Bruce Beresford
with Tommy Lee Jones, Ashley Judd,
Bruce Greenwood, Annabeth Gish,
Benjamin Weir, Jay Brazeau, John
MacLaren, Edward Evanko, Bruce
Campbell, Brennan Elliott
© 1999. MFP Munich Film Partners
GmbH & Co. I. Produktions KG
Paramount Pictures presents a
Leonard Goldberg production
Produced in association with MFP
Munich Film Partners GmbH & Co.
I. Produktions KG
105 mins 18 seconds
S&S February 2000 p.44-45

Down to You

(2000)
FilmFour Distributors – 19 May
(12) US
Dir Kris Isacsson,
with Freddie Prinze Jr, Julia Stiles,
Selma Blair, Shawn Hatosy, Zak Orth,
Ashton Kutcher, Rosario Dawson,
Lucie Arnaz, Henry Winkler, Lauren
German
© 2000. Miramax Film Corp.
Miramax International presents an
Open City Films production
a Kris Isacsson picture
92 mins 10 seconds
S&S June 2000 p.40

Drive Me Crazy

(1999)

20th Century Fox (UK) – 9 June
(12) US
Dir John Schultz
with Melissa Joan Hart, Adrian
Grenier, Stephen Collins, Susan May
Pratt, Mark Webber, Kris Park,
Gabriel Carpenter, Ali Larter, Lourdes
Benedicto, Keri Lynn Pratt
© 1999. Twentieth Century Fox Film
Corporation
Twentieth Century Fox presents an
Amy Robinson production
91 mins 1 second
S&S July 2000 p.42

Dr. Seuss' How the Grinch Stole Christmas
(2000)
United International Pictures (UK)
Ltd – 1 December
(PG) US/Germany
Dir Ron Howard
with Jim Carrey, Jeffrey Tambor,
Christine Baranski, Bill Irwin, Molly
Shannon, Clint Howard, Taylor
Momsen, Anthony Hopkins, Kelley,
Jeremy Howard
© 2000. LUNI Productions GmbH &
Co. KG
Universal/Imagine Entertainment
Universal Pictures and Imagine
Entertainment present
a Brian Grazer production
a Ron Howard Film
105 mins 1 second
S&S January 2001 p.49-50

Duets
(2000)
Icon Film Distribution – 17
November
(15) US
Dir Bruce Paltrow
with Maria Bello, André Braugher,
Paul Giamatti, Huey Lewis, Gwyneth
Paltrow, Scott Speedman, Marian
Seldes, Kiersten Warren, Angie
Phillips, Angie Dickinson
© 2000. Buena Vista Pictures
Distribution
Hollywood Pictures presents in
association with Seven Arts Pictures
and Beacon Pictures
a Kevin Jones production
a Bruce Paltrow film
111 mins 48 seconds
S&S December 2000 p.45-46

The End of the Affair
(1999)
Columbia TriStar Films (UK) – 11
February
(18) US/Germany
Dir Neil Jordan
with Ralph Fiennes, Julianne Moore,

Stephen Rea, Ian Hart, Jason Isaacs,
James Bolam, Samuel Bould, Heather
Jay Jones, Cyril Shaps, Penny Morrell
©1999. Global Entertainment
Productions GmbH & Co. Movie KG
Columbia Pictures presents a
Stephen Woolley production
a film by Neil Jordan
101 mins 26 seconds
S&S February 2000 p.38-39, 46

L'Ennui
aka: Boredom (English title)
(1998)
Artificial Eye Film Company – 14
April
(18) France
Dir Cédric Kahn
with Charles Berling, Sophie
Guillermin, Arielle Dombasle, Robert
Kramer, Alice Grey, Maurice Antoni,
Tom Ouedraogo, Patrick
Arrachequesne, Mirtha Caputi
Medeiros, Pierre Chevalier
© 1998 Gemini Films
Paulo Branco presents
122 mins 6 seconds
Subtitles
S&S May 2000 p.46-47

En plein coeur
aka: In All Innocence (English title)
(1998)
Pathé Distribution – 17 March
(15) France
Dir Pierre Jolivet
with Gérard Lanvin, Virginie
Ledoyen, Carole Bouquet, Guillaume
Canet, Aurélie Vérillon, Jean-Pierre
Lorit, Denis Podalydès, Anne Le Ny,
Nadia Barentin, Mar Sodupe
© Légende Entreprises/France 3
Cinéma/Légende Productions
Dépot dégal 1998
Alain Goldman presents
a Légendes Entreprises-France 2
Cinéma production
With the participation of Canal+ and
soficas Sofigram 2 and Gimages
a film by Pierre Jolivet
101 mins 14 secs
Subtitles
S&S May 2000 p.52

Erin Brockovich
(2000)
Columbia TriStar Films (UK) – 7
April
(15) US
Dir Steven Soderbergh
with Julia Roberts, Albert Finney,
Aaron Eckhart, Marg Helgenberger,
Cherry Jones, Veanne Cox, Conchata
Ferrell, Tracey Walter, Peter Coyote,
Scotty Leavenworth

© 2000 Columbia Pictures Industries
Inc/Universal Studios
Columbia Pictures and Universal
Pictures present
a Jersey Films production
131 mins
S&S May 2000 p.47-48

Essex Boys
(2000)
Pathé Distribution – 14 July
(18) UK
Dir Terry Winsor
with Sean Bean, Alex Kingston,
Charlie Creed-Miles, Tom Wilkinson,
Larry Lamb, Gareth Milne, Amelia
Lowdell, Michael McKell, Holly
Davidson, Terence Rigby
© 1999. Granada Film limited
Granada presents a Granada Film
production
102 mins 7 seconds
S&S August 2000 p.44

Est-ouest
aka: East-West (English title)
(1999)
Gala Film Distributors – 24
November
(12) France/Russia/Belgium/Spain
Dir Régis Wargnier
with Sandrine Bonnaire, Oleg
Menchikov, Sergueï Bodrov Jr,
Catherine Deneuve, Tatiana
Doguileva, René Feret, Grigori
Manoukov, Atanass Atanassov,
Bogdan Stupka, Meglena
Karalambova
©1999. UGC YM/France 3
Cinéma/NTV Profit/Gala Films
Ltd/Mate Productions
visa d'exploitation: 92 496
[al] UFD - UGC Fox Distribution
UGC YM presents a Franco-Russo-
Bulgaro-Espagnole co-production of
UGC YM/France 3 Cinéma/NTV
Profit/Gala Films Ltd/Mate
Productions
this film was supported by the fund
Eurimages
with the participation of the sofica
Sofinergie 5
and of Canal+
with the support of Procirep
a film de Régis Wargnier
with the participation of Centre
National de la Cinématographie
124 mins 44 seconds
S&S December 2000 p.46

[Eye] of the Beholder
(1999)
Metrodome Distribution Ltd – 9
June
(18) Canada/UK/US/Australia

Dir Stephen Elliott
with Ewan McGregor, Ashley Judd,
Patrick Bergin, k.d. Lang, Jason
Priestley, Geneviève Bujold, Anne-
Marie Brown, Kaitlin Brown, David
Nerman, Steven McCarthy
©1998. Filmline International
(Beholder) Inc./Eye of the Beholder
Limited
[start - for UK/Ireland]
Behaviour Worldwide in association
with Village Roadshow-Ambridge
Film partnership present a Hit &
Run/Filmline International
production
With the participation of SODEC
Société de développement des
entreprises culturelles Quebec
Government (Tax Credit Program)
and The Canadian Film
or Video Production Tax Credit
[for Canada]
an official Canada/United Kingdom
co-production
a Filmline International/Hit & Run
production in association with Eye of
the Beholder Limited
[for the United Kingdom]
an official United Kingdom/Canada
co-production
a Hit & Run/Filmline International
production in association with Eye of
the Beholder Limited
[for the rest of the world]
an official Canada/United Kingdom
co-production
a Hit & Run/Filmline International
production in association with Eye of
the Beholder Limited
109 mins 38 seconds
S&S July 2000 p.42-43

The Family Man
(2000)
Entertainment Film Distributors Ltd
– 22 December
(12) US
Dir Brett Ratner
with Nicolas Cage, Téa Leoni, Jeremy
Piven, Josef Sommer, Saul Rubinek,
Don Cheadle, Mary Beth Hurt, Harve
Presnell, Tom McGowan, Lisa
Thornhill
© 2000 Beacon Communications,
LLC
Beacon Pictures presents
a Riche/Ludwig-Zvi Howard
Rosenman and Saturn production
a Brett Ratner film
125 mins 50 seconds
S&S February 2001 p.41-42

Fantasia 2000
(1999)
Buena Vista International (UK) – 26

May
(U) US
Dir Pixote Hunt
with Steve Martin, Itzhak Perlman,
Quincy Jones, Bette Midler,
James Earl Jones, Penn, Teller ,
James Levine, Angela Lansbury,
Wayne Allwine, Tony Anselmo, Russi
Taylor
© Disney Enterprises, Inc
Walt Disney Pictures
74 mins 32 seconds
S&S June 2000 p.41-42.
Note: 'Standard cinema version'
released 26th May 2000. IMAX
version released on 22nd December
1999

Fast Food
(1998)
Optimum Releasing – 28 January
(18) UK
Dir Stewart Sugg
with Douglas Henshall, Emily Woof,
Miles Anderson, Gerard Butler,
Stephen Lord, Danny Midwinter,
Robert Donovan, Graham Turner,
Sean Hughes, David Yip
© 1998. Fast Food Films Ltd.
Twin Pictures and Fast Food Films in
association with Vine International
Pictures present
99 mins 32 seconds
S&S February 2000 p.47

The Filth and the Fury
(2000)
FilmFour Distributors – 12 May
(15) UK/US
Dir Julien Temple
onscreen participants Paul Cook,
Steve Jones, Glen Matlock, John
Lydon, Sid Vicious, Nick Kent
© 1999. Sex Pistols Residuals
FilmFour presents in association
with The Sex Pistols a Jersey
Shore/Nitrate
Film production
a Julien Temple film
a Jersy Shore/Nitrate Film
production for Film Four Limited
107 mins 21 seconds
S&S June 2000 p.43

Final Destination
(2000)
Entertainment Film Distributors Ltd
– 19 May
(15) US
Dir James Wong
with Devon Sawa, Ali Larter, Kerr
Smith, Kristen Cloke, Seann
WilliamScott, Chad E. Donella,
Amanda Detmer, Daniel Roebuck,
Roger Guenveur Smith, Tony Todd

© 2000 New Line Productions Inc
Entertainment Film Distributors
New Line Cinema
New Line Cinema presents
a Warren Zide/Craig Perry
production
98 mins 2 seconds
S&S July 2000 p.43-44

Flamenco
(1995)
Metrodome Distribution Ltd – 7 July
(U) Spain
Dir Carlos Saura
with the particpation of La Paquera
de Jerez, Merche Esmeralda, Manolo
Sanlucar, Joaquín Cortés, Manuel
Moneo, Agujeta, Mario Maya, Paco
Toronjo, Antonio Toscano, Fernando
de Utrera
©1995. Juan Lebrón Producciones,
S.A.
a Juan Lebrón Producciones
production with the participation of
RTVA Radio
Televisión de Andalucía and with
collaboration of Sogepaq/Canal+
España/Junta de Andalucía/Sociedad
General de Autores y Editores
102 mins 19 seconds
With subtitles
S&S August 2000 p.44-45

The Flintstones in Viva Rock Vegas
(2000)
United International Pictures (UK)
Ltd – 28 July
(PG) US
Dir Brian Levant
with Mark Addy, Stephen Baldwin,
Kristen Johnston, Jane Krakowski,
Thomas Gibson, Alan Cumming,
Harvey Korman, Joan Collins, Alex
Meneses, John Taylor
© 2000 Universal Studios and
Amblin Entertainment, Inc
Universal Pictures presents
a Hanna-Barbera/Amblin
Entertainment production
a Brian Levant film
90 mins 55 seconds
S&S September 2000 p.41

For Love of the Game
(1999)
United International Pictures (UK)
Ltd – 16 June
(12) US
Dir Sam Raimi
with Kevin Costner, Kelly Preston,
John C. Reilly, Jena Malone, Brian
Cox, J.K. Simmons, Vin Scully, Steve
Lyons, Carmine D. Giovinazzo, Bill
Rogers

© 1999. Universal Studios
Universal Pictures presents a Beacon
Pictures/TIG Productions/Mirage
Enterprises production
138 mins 3 seconds
S&S July 2000 p.44-45

Fortress 2: Re-Entry

(1999)
Columbia TriStar Films (UK) – 21
July
(15) US/Luxembourg
Dir Geoff Murphy
with Christopher Lambert, Patrick
Malahide, Liz May Brice, Anthony C.
Hall, Willie Garson, Yuji Okumoto,
Fredric Lane, Nick Brimble, Beth
Toussaint, David Roberson
©1999 Gower Productions, Inc
Gower Productions presents
a John Flock production in
association with
The Carousel Picture Company
a film by Geoff Murphy
92 mins 33 seconds
S&S September 2000 p.42

Freeway II Confessions of a Trickbaby

(1999)
Metro Tartan Distributors – 24
November·
(18) US/France/Canada
Dir Matthew Bright
with Natasha Lyonne, Maria
Celedonio, Vincent Gallo, David Alan
Grier, Michael T. Weiss, John Landis,
Max Perlich, Bob Dawson, Jenn
Griffin, April Telek
© 1999. Kushner-Locke Company
Kushner-Locke Company
The Kushner-Locke Company and
Davis Film present
a Muse/Brad Wyman production
in association with Incognito
Entertainment
a Matthew Bright film
with the participation of The
Government of British Columbia
Production Services Tax Credit
97 mins 30 seconds
S&S January 2001 p.44-45

Frequency

(2000)
Entertainment Film Distributors Ltd
– 16 June
(15) US
Dir Gregory Hoblit
with Dennis Quaid, Jim Caviezel,
André Braugher, Elizabeth Mitchell,
Noah Emmerich, Shawn Doyle,
Jordan Bridges, Melissa Errico, Daniel
Henson, Stephen Joffe
© 2000 New Line Productions, Inc.

New Line Cinema - a Time Warner
company
New Line Cinema presents a Gregory
Hoblit film
118 mins 28 seconds
S&S August 2000 p.45-46

Fucking Åmål

aka: Show Me Love (English Title)
(1998)
Alliance Releasing (UK) – 3 March
(15) Sweden/Denmark
Dir Lukas Moodysson
with Alexandra Dahlström, Rebecca
Liljeberg, Mathias Rust, Erica
Carlson, Stefan Hörberg, Josefin
Nyberg, Ralph Carlsson, Maria
Hedborg, Axel Widegran, Jill Ung
©1998 Memfis Film
Produced by Memfis Film in co-
production with Zentropa
Productions/Film i
Väst/SVT Drama Göteborg
With support by
Svenska Filminstitutet (Charlotta
Denward)
Det Danske Filminstitutet (Mikael
Olsen)
Europeiska Unionen/Europeiska
Gemenskapens Strukturfonder
89 mins 15 seconds
Subtitles
S&S March 2000 p.52

Galaxy Quest

(1999)
United International Pictures (UK)
Ltd – 28 April
(PG) US
Dir Dean Parisot
with Tim Allen, Sigourney Weaver,
Alan Rickman, Tony Shalhoub, Sam
Rockwell, Daryl Mitchell, Enrico
Colantoni, Robin Sachs, Patrick
Breen, Missi Pyle
© 1999 DreamWorks LLC
DreamWorks Pictures presents
a Mark Johnson production
102 mins 20 seconds
S&S May 2000 p.48-49

Gangster No. 1

(2000)
FilmFour Distributors – 9 June
(18) UK/Germany/Ireland
Dir Paul McGuigan
with Malcolm McDowell, David
Thewlis, Paul Bettany, Saffron
Burrows, Kenneth Cranham, Jamie
Foreman, Razaaq Adoti, Doug Allen,
Eddie Marsan, David Kennedy
© 2000. No.1 Films Ltd & Road
Movies Filmproduktion GmbH
FilmFour presents a Pagoda Film &
Television Corporation production

in association with Road Movies
Filmproduktion
with the participation of British
Screen and BSkyB
a Paul McGuigan film
In association with NFH and
LittleBird Productions
a UK/German co-production
a Pagoda Film production in
association with Road Movies Film
Produktion GmbH
for FilmFour
with the support of Filmboard Berlin
Brandenburg
102 mins 35 seconds
S&S July 2000 p.45-46

Ghost Dog: The Way of the Samrai

aka: Ghost Dog - Der Weg des
Samurai (Germany)
Ghost Dog, la voie du samouraï
(France)
(1999)
Film Four Distributors – 28 April
(15) US/Japan/France/Germany
Dir Jim Jarmusch
with Forest Whitaker, John Tormey,
Cliff Gorman, Henry Silva, Isaach de
Bankolé, Tricia Vessey, Victor Argo,
Gene Ruffini, Richard Portnow,
Camille Winbush
FilmFour
© 1999. Plywood Productions, Inc.
JVC/Le Studio Canal+ and BAC
Films present in association with
Pandora
Film/ARD-Degeto Film
a Plywood production
a film by Jim Jarmusch
115 mins 46 seconds
S&S May 2000 p.49-50

Girl, Interrupted

(1999)
Columbia TriStar Films (UK) – 24
March
(15) US
Dir James Mangold
with Winona Ryder, Angelina Jolie,
Clea DuVall, Brittany Murphy,
Elisabeth Moss, Jared Leto, Jeffrey
Tambor, Travis Fine, Jillian
Armenante, Angela Bettis
©1999 Global Entertainment
Productions GmbH & Co. Movie KG
Columbia Pictures presents
a Red Wagon production
a film by James Mangold
127 mins 13 seconds
S&S April 2000 p.47   ·

Gladiator

(2000)
United International Pictures (UK)

Ltd – 12 May
(15) US
Dir Ridley Scott
with Russell Crowe, Joaquin Phoenix, Connie Nielsen, Oliver Reed, Richard Harris, Derek Jacobi, Djimon Hounsou, David Schofield, John Shrapnel, Tomas Arana
© 2000. DreamWorks LLC and Universal Studios
Universal Pictures and DreamWorks Pictures present
a Douglas Wick production in association with ScottFree
155 mins
S&S June 2000 p.34-35, 44-45

The Golden Bowl

(2000)
Buena Vista International (UK) – 3 November
(12) UK/France/US
Dir James Ivory
with Kate Beckinsale, James Fox, Anjelica Huston, Nick Nolte, Jeremy Northam, Madeleine Potter, Uma Thurman, Nicholas Day, Peter Eyre, Nickolas Grace
©2000. Golden Bowl Productions Ltd.
Merchant Ivory Productions and TF1 International present in association with
Miramax Films a Merchant Ivory film
134 mins
S&S November 2000 p.51-52

Gone in Sixty Seconds

(2000)
Buena Vista International (UK) – 4 August
(15) US
Dir Dominic Sena
with Nicolas Cage, Angelina Jolie, Giovanni Ribisi, Delroy Lindo, Will Patton, Christopher Eccleston, Chi McBride, Robert Duvall, Scott Caan, Timothy Olyphant
© 2000. Touchstone Pictures and Jerry Bruckheimer, Inc.
Touchstone Pictures and Jerry Bruckheimer Films presents
117 mins 55 seconds
S&S August 2000 p.46-47

Gossip

(2000)
Warner Bros Distributors (UK) – 25 August
(15) US/Australia
Dir Davis Guggenheim
with James Marsden, Lena Headey, Norman Reedus, Kate Hudson, Marisa Coughlan, Sharon Lawrence,

Eric Bogosian, Edward James Olmos, Joshua Jackson, Kwok-Wing Leung
© 2000. Warner Bros.
Warner Bros. presents in association with Village Roadshow Pictures and NPV Entertainment
an Outlaw production
90 mins 14 seconds
S&S October 2000 p.44-45

The Green Mile

(1999)
United International Pictures (UK) Ltd – 25 February
(18) US
Dir Frank Darabont
with Tom Hanks, David Morse, Bonnie Hunt, James Cromwell, Michael Clarke Duncan, Michael Jeter, Graham Greene, Sam Rockwell, Doug Hutchinson, Barry Pepper
© 1999. CR Films, LLC
Castle Rock Entertainment presents a Dark Woods production
Castle Rock Entertainment / Universal
188 mins 41 seconds
S&S March 2000 p.44-45

Grey Owl

(1999)
20th Century Fox (UK) – 3 November
(PG) UK/Canada
Dir Richard Attenborough
with Pierce Brosnan, Annie Galipeau, Renée Asherson, Stephanie Cole, Nathaniel Arcand, Stewart Bick, Chip Chuipka, John Dunn-Hill, David Fox, Saginaw Grant
©1998. Beaver Productions Ltd & Ajawaan Productions, Inc
Largo Entertainment presents in association with Transfilm and BeaverProductions
a Jake Eberts presentation
....in Richard Attenborough's film...
a United Kingdom-Canada co-production
Co-produced by Beaver Productions Ltd & Ajawaan Productions, Inc with the assistance/participation of the Canadian Film or Video Production Tax Credit and the assistance of the Government of Québec (Tax Credit Program)
118 mins 14 seconds
S&S December 2000 p.47-48

Hamlet

(2000)
FilmFour Distributors – 15 December
(12) US
Dir Michael Almereyda

with Ethan Hawke, Kyle MacLachlan, Diane Venora, Sam Shepard, Bill Murray, Liev Schreiber, Julia Stiles, Karl Geary, Paula Malcomson, Steve Zahn
© 2000. Hamlet Inc.
Miramax International presents a Double A Films production
111 mins 27 seconds
S&S January 2001 p.50,52

Hanging Up

(2000)
Columbia TriStar Films (UK) – 12 May
(15) US
Dir Diane Keaton
with Meg Ryan, Diane Keaton, Lisa Kudrow, Walter Matthau, Adam Arkin, Cloris Leachman, Jesse James, Edie McClurg, Duke Moosekian, Ann Bortollotti
© 2000. Global Entertainment Productions GmbH & Co. Movie KG
Columbia Pictures presents a Nora Ephron and Laurence Mark production
94 mins 33 seconds
S&S May 2000 p.50-51

Harry, un ami qui vous veut du bien

aka: Harry Is Here to Help
(2000)
Artificial Eye Film Company – 10 November
(15) France
Dir Dominik Moll
with Laurent Lucas, Sergi López, Mathilde Seigner, Sophie Guillemin, Liliane Rovère, Dominique Rozan, Michel Fau, Victoire de Koster, Laurie Caminita, Loréna Caminita
©2000. Diaphana Films/M6 Films/Diaphana Distribution
dépôt légal: 96 744
Diaphana Films presents a co-production of Diaphana Films/M6 Films
with the participation of Canal +/M6 with the participation of Centre National de la Cinématographie in association with the sofica Sofinergie 5
with the support of Procirep
a co-propduction of Diaphana Films/M6 Films/Diaphana Distribution
with the participation of Canal +/M6/Centre National de la Cinématographie/sofica Sofinergie 5
with the support of Procirep
116 mins 43 seconds
S&S December 2000 p.49-50

High Fidelity
(2000)
Buena Vista International (UK) – 21 July
(15) US/UK
Dir Stephen Frears
with John Cusack, Iben Hjejle, Todd Louiso, Jack Black, Lisa Bonet, Catherine Zeta-Jones, Joan Cusack, Tim Robbins, Chris Rehmann, Ben Carr
© 2000. Touchstone Pictures
Touchstone Pictures presents a Working Title Films production in association with Dogstar Films/New Crime
Productions
113 mins 39 seconds
S&S August 2000 p.36-37, 47-48

Hollow Man
(2000)
Columbia TriStar Films (UK) – 29 September
(18) US/Germany
Dir Paul Verhoeven
with Elisabeth Shue, Kevin Bacon, Josh Brolin, Kim Dickens, Greg Grunberg, Joey Slotnick, Mary Randle, William Devane, Rhona Mitra, Pablo Espinosa
© 2000. Global Entertainment Productions GmbH & Co. Movie KG.
Columbia Pictures presents a Douglas Wick production
a Paul Verhoeven film
112 mins 24 seconds
S&S October 2000 p.45

Holy Smoke
(1999)
FilmFour Distributors – 31 March
(18) US
Dir Jane Campion
with Kate Winslet, Harvey Keitel, Pam Grier, Julie Hamilton, Tim Robertson, Sophie Lee, Daniel Wylie, Paul Goddard, George Mangos, Kerry Walker
© 1999. Miramax Film Corp
FilmFour / Miramax International
Miramax Films presents
a Jan Chapman production
a film by Jane Campion
114 mins 35 seconds
S&S April 2000 p.48

Honest
(2000)
Pathé Distribution – 26 May
(18) UK/France
Dir David A. Stewart
with Nicole Appleton, Peter Facinelli, Natalie Appleton, Melanie Blatt,

James Cosmo, Jonathan Cake, Rick Warden, Annette Badland, Sean Gilder, Corin Redgrave
© 2000. Honest Productions Limited
Pathé Entertainment presents a Seven Dials Films production in association with Pandora
a David A. Stewart film
Developed with the support of the European Script Fund - an initiative of the MEDIA programme of the European Union
110 mins 3 seconds
S&S July 2000 p.46-47

House!
(2000)
Pathé Distribution – 5 May
(15) UK
Dir Julian Kemp
with Kelly Macdonald, Gwenllian Davies, Sue Hopkins, Eileen Edwards, Marlene Griffiths, Freddie Jones, Mossie Smith, Jason Hughes, Bruce Forsyth, Miriam Margolyes
©1999 House Film Ltd
Supported by the National Lottery through the Arts Council of England
89 mins 46 seconds
S&S April 2000 p.49

The House of Mirth
(2000)
FilmFour Distributors – 13 October
(PG) UK/US
Dir Terence Davies
with Gillian Anderson, Dan Aykroyd, Eleanor Bron, Terry Kinney, Anthony LaPaglia, Laura Linney, Jodhi May, Elizabeth McGovern, Eric Stoltz, Penny Downie
© 2000. Granada Film Limited and FilmFour Limited
Granada presents in association with The Arts Council of England/ FilmFour/ The Scottish Arts Council/ Showtime/ Glasgow Film Fund
a Three Rivers production
Developed with the support of the MEDIA Programme of the European Union
Supported by the National Lottery through The Arts Council of England and The Scottish Arts Council
Glasgow Film Fund is financed by the Glasgow Development Agency and the City of Glasgow Council
With the kind support of the Glasgow Film Office
a Three Rivers Production for Granada Film limited/The Arts Council of England/The Scottish Arts Council National Lottery Fund/Glasgow Film Fund/Showtime/ FilmFour

140 mins 24 seconds
S&S November 2000 p.53-54

House on Haunted Hill
(1999)
Warner Bros Distributors (UK) – 4 February
(18) US
Dir William Malone
with Geoffrey Rush, Famke Janssen, Taye Diggs, Ali Larter, Bridgette Wilson, Peter Gallagher, Chris Kattan, Max Perlich, Jeffrey Combs, Dick Beebe
© 1999 Warner Bros.
Warner Bros. presents a Dark Castle Entertainment production
92 mins 42 seconds
S&S March 2000 p.45-46

Huayang Nianhua
aka: In the Mood for Love
(2000)
Metro Tartan Distributors – 27 October
(PG) Hong Kong/France
Dir Kar-Wai Wong
with Maggie Man-Yuk Cheung, Tony Chiu Wai Leung, Rebecca Pan, Chun Lui, Ping-Lam Siu, Chi-Ang Chin, Man-Lui Chan, Kam-Wah Koo, Hsien Yu, Po-Chun Chow
© 2000. Block 2 Pictures Inc.
Fortissimo Sales presents
Block 2 Pictures/Paradis Films present a Jet Tone Films production
Subtitles
97 mins 52 seconds
S&S November 2000 p.55

Hurlyburly
(1998)
Metrodome Distribution Ltd – 7 April
(18) US
Dir Anthony Drazan
with Sean Penn, Kevin Spacey, Robin Wright Penn, Chazz Palminteri, Garry Shandling, Anna Paquin, Meg Ryan, Gianna Renaudo, David Fabrizio, Kenny Vance
© 1998 Carol Drive Productions Inc
Storm Entertainment presents
a film by Anthony Drazan
122 mins 33 seconds
S&S May 2000 p.51

The Hurricane
(1999)
Buena Vista International (UK) – 24 March
(15) US
Dir Norman Jewison
with Denzel Washington, Vicellous

Reon Shannon, Deborah Kara Unger, Liev Schreiber, John Hannah, Dan Hedaya, Clancy Brown, David Paymer, Debbi Morgan, Harris Yulin
© 1999. Beacon Communications, LLC
Beacon Pictures presents an Azoff Films/Rudy Langlais production
145 mins 26 seconds
S&S April 2000 p.49-50

The Insider
(1999)
Buena Vista International (UK) – 10 March
(15) US
Dir Michael Mann
with Al Pacino, Russell Crowe, Christopher Plummer, Diane Venora, Philip Baker Hall, Lindsay Crouse, Debi Mazar, Stephen Tobolowsky, Colm Feore, Bruce McGill
© 1999 Touchstone Pictures
Touchstone Pictures presents a Mann/Roth production
a Forward Pass picture
157 mins 59 seconds
S&S March 2000 p.46-47

It Was an Accident
(2000)
Pathé Distribution – 27 October
(18) UK/France
Dir Metin Hüseyin
with Chiwetel Ejiofor, Max Beesley, James Bolam, Nicola Stapleton, Neil Dudgeon, Hugh Quarshie, Thandie Newton, Jacqueline Williams, Sidh Solanki, Cavan Clerkin
© 2000 Pathé Fund Limited
Pathé Pictures presents
in association with the Arts Council of England and Le Studio Canal+
A Litmus production
Supported by the National Lottery through the Arts Council of England
100 mins 45 seconds
S&S November 2000 p.56

Janice Beard 45 WPM
(1999)
United International Pictures (UK) Ltd – 19 May
(15) UK
Dir Clare Kilner
with Rhys Ifans, Patsy Kensit, David O'Hara, Eileen Walsh, Sandra Voe, Frances Gray, Zita Sattar, Amelia Curtis, Mossie Smith, Sarah McVicar
©1999. The Film Consortium Limited
The Film Consortium presents in association with the Arts Council of England/

WAVE Pictures and Channel Four a Dakota film
Developed with the support of Judy Counihan Films Limited/Hungry Eye Films Limited & The Film Consortium Limited and the National Lottery through the Arts Council of England, London, England
81 mins 8 seconds
S&S January 2000 p.55

Jeanne d'Arc
aka: Joan of Arc (UK title)
(1999)
Columbia TriStar Films (UK) – 10 March
(15) France
Dir Luc Besson
with Milla Jovovich, John Malkovich, Faye Dunaway, Dustin Hoffman, Pascal Greggory, Vincent Cassel, Tchéky Karyo, Richard Ridings, Desmond Harrington, Timothy West
© 1999 Gaumont
Columbia Pictures and Gaumont present
a film by Luc Besson
a Gaumont production
157 mins 42 seconds
S&S February 2000 p.30-32

The Jolly Boys' Last Stand
(2000)
National Film Theatre – 18 August
(Not submitted) UK
Dir Christopher Payne
with Andy Serkis, Milo Twomey, Anton Saunders, Edward Woodall, Matt Wilkinson, Rupam Maxwell, Sacha Baron Cohen, Mark Frost, Sean Graham, Rebecca Craig
Copyright Christopher Payne & Jolly Productions, 1998
87 mins
No S&S reference

Keeping the Faith
(2000)
Buena Vista International (UK) – 15 September
(12) US
Dir Edward Norton
with Ben Stiller, Edward Norton, Jenna Elfman, Anne Bancroft, Eli Wallach, Ron Rifkin, Milos Forman, Holland Taylor, Lisa Edelstein, Rena Sofer
©2000. Spyglass Entertainment Group, LP
Touchstone Pictures and Spyglass Entertainment present
a Koch Co./Norton-Blumberg production
a Barber/Birnbaum production

129 mins 26 seconds
S&S October 2000 p.48-49

Kevin and Perry Go Large
(2000)
Icon Film Distribution – 21 April
(15) UK/US
Dir Ed Bye
with Harry Enfield, Kathy Burke, Rhys Ifans, Laura Fraser, James Fleet, Louisa Rix, Tabitha Wady, Paul Whitehouse, Natasha Little, Henry R. Enfield GCE
© 2000 Tiger Aspect Pictures Ltd
a Tiger Aspect Pictures production in association with
Icon Productions and Fragile Films an Icon Entertainment International presentation
83 mins 9 seconds
S&S May 2000 p.52-53

Die Kleine Vampir
aka: The Little Vampire
(2000)
Icon Film Distribution – 20 October
(U) Germany/Netherlands/UK/US
Dir Uli Edel
with Jonathan Lipnicki, Richard E. Grant, Jim Carter, Alice Krige, Pamela Gidley, Tommy Hinkley, Anna Popplewell, Dean Cook, Rollo Weeks, John Wood
© 2000. Vampire Productions BV
Cometstone Pictures presents....
in association with Comet Film/Avrora Media/Stonewood Communications
a Richard Claus production
a German/Dutch co-production of Comet Film GmbH and Stonewood Communications
BV in co-production with CV The Little Vampire in association with Avrora Media FGmbH and Propaganda Films
produced by Vampire Productions BV
95 mins 25 seconds
S&S November 2000 p.57-58

Lake Placid
(1999)
20th Century Fox (UK) – 31 March
(15) US
Dir Steve Miner
with Bill Pullman, Oliver Platt, Bridget Fonda, Brendan Gleeson, Betty White, David Lewis, Tim Dixon, Natassia Malthe, Mariska Hargitay, Meredith Salenger
© 1999. Phoenix Pictures Inc.
Fox 2000 Pictures presents from Phoenix Pictures a Rocking Chair production

a Steve Miner film
82 mins
S&S April 2000 p.51-52

The Last Broadcast
(1998)
Metrodome Distribution Ltd – 24
March
(18) US
Dir Stefan Avalos
with David Beard, James Seward,
Stefan Avalos, Lance Weiler, Rein
Clabbers, Michele Pulaski, Tom
Brunt, Mark Rublee, A.D. Roso, Dale
Worstall
© FFM Productions
Wavelength Releasing
86 minutes 17 seconds
S&S April 2000 p.52-53

The Last September
(1999)
Metro Tartan Distributors – 5 May
(15) UK/Ireland/France
Dir Deborah Warner
with Maggie Smith, Michael
Gambon, Jane Birkin, Fiona Shaw,
Lambert Wilson, David Tennant,
Richard Roxburgh, Keeley Hawes,
Tom Hickey, Gary Lydon
©1999. The Matrix Films 'Last
September' Partnership. Scala
Thunder Limited and
IMA Films SA
Metro Tartan
Matrix Films and Scala present
in association with Bord Scannán na
hÉireann/The Irish Film Board [and]
Radio Telefís Éireann
with the participation of BSkyB and
British Screen
in association with IMA Films and
Canal +
a Scala Thunder production
a film by Deborah Warner
103 mins 11 seconds
S&S June 2000 p.46

La Lengua de las mariposas
aka: Butterfly's Tongue (English title)
(1999)
Metrodome Distribution Ltd – 28
July
(15) Spain
Dir José Luis Cuerda
with Fernando Fernán-Gómez,
Manuel Lozano, Uxía Blanco,
Gonzálo Uriarte, Alexis de los Santos,
Tamar Novas, Guillermo Toledo,
Elena Fernández, Jesús Castejón,
Tatán
© Sociedad General de Cine, S.A./Las
producciones del Escorpión S.L.
depósito legal no. M-44660-1998
a Sogetel production

Las producciones del
Escorpión/Grupo Voz/with the
collaboration of Canal+ and
of T.V.G. with the participation of
T.V.E.
With the collaboration of La
Consellería de Cultura, Communica-
ción Social y Turismo Xunta
95 mins 34 seconds
Subtitles
S&S September 2000 p.39-40

Limbo
(1999)
Columbia TriStar Films (UK) – 21
January
(15) US/Germany
Dir John Sayles
with Mary Elizabeth Mastrantonio,
David Strathairn, Vanessa Martinez,
Kris Kristofferson, Casey Siemaszko,
Kathryn Grody, Rita Taggart, Leo
Burmester, Michael Laskin, Herminio
Ramos
© Global Entertainment Productions
GmbH & Co. Medien KG
Screen Gems presents
a Green/Renzi production
126 mins 47 seconds
S&S February 2000 p.47-48

Little Nicky
(2000)
Entertainment Film Distributors Ltd
– 17 November
(12) US
Dir Steven Brill
with Adam Sandler, Patricia Arquette,
Harvey Keitel, Rhys Ifans, Allen
Covert, Tommy 'Tiny' Lister Jr, Kevin
Nealon, Jon Lovitz, Michael McKean,
Quentin Tarantino
© 2000. New Line Productions, Inc.
New Line Cinema presents a Happy
Madison production in association
with RSC Media
90 mins 9 seconds
S&S January 2001 p.52-53

Lola + Bilidikid
aka: Lola and Billy the Kid (English
title)
(1999)
Millivres Multimedia – 10 March
(18) Germany
Dir Kutlug Ataman
with Baki Davrak, Gandi Mukli, Erdal
Yildiz, Michael Gerber, Murat Yilmaz,
Inge Keller, Hakan Tandogan,
Cihangir Gümsturkmen, Celal Perk,
Mesut Özdemir
©1998. Zero Film
[al] Millivres Multimedia
Zero Film presents
a film by Kutlug Ataman

with funding from Filmförderung in
Berlin-Brandenburg/Filmstiftüng
Nordhein-Westfalen
a co-production with WDR/ARTE
95 mins 2 seconds
Subtitles
S&S April 2000 p.53-54

* The Long Good Friday
(1980)
Metrodome Distribution Ltd – 5
May
(18) UK
Dir John MacKenzie
with Paul Freeman, Leo Dolan, Kevin
McNally, Patti Love, P.H. Moriarty,
Derek Thompson, Bryan Marshall,
Bob Hoskins, Helen Mirren, Ruby
Head
Black Lion Films
Calendar Productions
114 mins
Monthly Film Bulletin. v48. n566.
March 1981 p.51

Loser
(2000)
Columbia TriStar Films (UK) – 3
November
(12) US
Dir Amy Heckerling
with Jason Biggs, Mena Suvari, Zak
Orth, Tom Sadoski, Jimmi Simpson,
Greg Kinnear, Dan Aykroyd, Twink
Caplan, Bobby Slayton, Robert Miano
© 2000. Columbia Pictures
Industries, Inc.
Columbia Pictures presents an Amy
Heckerling film
95 mins 5 seconds
S&S December 2000 p.52-53

The Loss of Sexual Innocence
(1999)
Columbia TriStar Films – 7 January
(18) US/UK
Dir Mike Figgis
with Julian Sands, Saffron Burrows,
Stefano Dionisi, Kelly Macdonald,
Gina McKee, Jonathan Rhys-Meyers,
Bernard Hill, Rossy De Palma, John
Cowey, Nina McKay
© 1998. The Fred Mullet LP
Summit Entertainment in
association with Newmarket Capital
Group present
a Red Mullet production
105 mins 48 seconds
S&S December 1999 p.49-50.

Love's Labour's Lost
(1999)
Pathé Distribution – 31 March
(U) UK/France/US

Dir Kenneth Branagh
with Alicia Silverstone, Natascha
McElhone, Emily Mortimer, Carmen
Ejogo, Richard Clifford, Daniel Hill,
Alessandro Nivola, Kenneth Branagh,
Matthew Lillard, Adrian Lester
© 1999. Kenneth Branagh and
Intermedia Film Equities Ltd.
Miramax Films and Intermedia
Films present
in association with Pathé Pictures,
The Arts Council of England, Le
Studio Canal+
a Shakespeare Film Company
production
Supported by the National Lottery
through the Arts Council of England
93 minutes 34 seconds
S&S April 2000 p.54-55

The Luzhin Defence

(2000)
Entertainment Film Distributors Ltd
– 8 September
(12) UK/France/Italy/Hungary/US
Dir Marleen Gorris
with John Turturro, Emily Watson,
Geraldine James, Stuart Wilson,
Christopher Thompson, Fabio Sartor,
Peter Blythe, Orla Brady, Mark Tandy,
Kelly Hunter
© 2000 Renaissance
Films/ICE3/France 3 Cinéma/Lantia
Cinema & Audiovisivi/Magic Media
Renaissance Films and Clear Blue
Sky Productions present
a Renaissance/ICE3 production
in association with
Lantia Cinema and Magic Media and
France 3 Cinéma
a Marleen Gorris film
108 mins 57 seconds
S&S October 2000 p.50

Magnolia

(1999)
Entertainment Film Distributors Ltd
– 17 March
(18) US
Dir Paul Thomas Anderson
with Jeremy Blackman, Tom Cruise,
Melinda Dillon, April Grace, Luis
Guzmán, Philip Baker Hall, Philip
Seymour Hoffman, Ricky Jay,
Orlando Jones, William H.Macy
© 1999. New Line Productions, Inc.
New Line Cinema presents a Joanne
Sellar/Ghoulardi Film Company
production of
a P.T. Anderson picture
188 mins 25 seconds
S&S April 2000 p.56-57

Man on the Moon

(1999)

United International Pictures (UK)
Ltd – 5 May
(15) US
Dir Milos Forman
with Jim Carrey, Danny DeVito,
Courtney Love, Paul Giamatti, Tony
Clifton, Vincent Schiavelli, Peter
Bonerz, Jerry Lawler, Gerry Becker,
Greyson Pendry
©1999. Universal Studios
Mutual Film Company and Universal
Pictures present a Jersey
Films/Cinehaus
production in association with
Shapiro/West Productions
118 mins 47 seconds
S&S April 2000 p.57-58

The Man Who Cried

(2000)
United International Pictures (UK)
Ltd – 8 December
(12) UK/France
Dir Sally Potter
with Christina Ricci, Cate Blanchett,
John Turturro, Johnny Depp, Harry
Dean Stanton, Claudia Lander-Duke,
Oleg Yankowskiy, Danny
Scheinmann, Anna Tzelniker, Barry
Davis
© 2000. Gypsy Films Limited
Universal/Studio Canal - a Canal+
company
Studio Canal and Universal Pictures
present a Working Title production
in association with Adventure
Pictures
a Sally Potter film
Developed with the assistance of
British Screen Finance Limited,
London, England
a British-French co-production
99 mins 46 seconds
S&S January 2001 p.53-54

Mansfield Park

(1999)
Buena Vista International (UK) – 31
March
(15) US/UK
Dir Patricia Rozema
with Embeth Davidtz, Jonny Lee
Miller, Alessandro Nivola, Frances
O'Connor, Harold Pinter, Lindsay
Duncan, Sheila Gish, Victoria
Hamilton, James Purefoy, Hugh
Bonneville
© 1999. Miramax HAL Films Ltd.
Miramax International / HAL Films
Miramax Films and BBC Films
present in association with the Arts
Council of England
a Miramax HAL Films production
a Patricia Rozema film
English Heritage

supported by the National Lottery
through the Arts Council of England
112 mins 10 seconds
S&S April 2000 p.58-59

bfi * A Matter of Life and Death

(1946)
BFI Collections – 24 March
(U) UK
Dir Michael Powell
with David Niven, Roger Livesey,
Raymond Massey, Kim Hunter,
Marius Goring, Abraham Sofaer,
Robert Coote, Joan Maude, Kathleen
Byron, Bonar Colleano
Archers Film Productions
J. Arthur Rank Film Productions
A production of The Archers
104 mins
Monthly Film Bulletin. v13. n155.
November 1946 p.148

Mauvaise passe

(1999)
Pathé Distribution – 8 December
(18) France/UK
Dir Michel Blanc
with Daniel Auteuil, Stuart
Townsend, Liza Walker, Noah Taylor,
Frances Barber, Claire Skinner,
Béatrice Agenin, Keith Allen, Ben
Whishaw, Barbara Flynn
©1999. Renn Productions - Pathé
Productions Ltd - France 3 Cinéma
Claude Berri presents
a British-French co-production
Pathé Productions Ltd/Renn
Productions - France Cinéma
with the participation of Canal+
with the participation of Centre
National de la Cinématographie
a film by Michel Blanc
a British - French co-production
between Pathé Productions Ltd -
Renn
Productions SA - France 3 Cinéma
106 mins 4 seconds
S&S January 2001 p.48

Maybe Baby

(2000)
Redbus Film Distribution – 2 June
(15) UK/France
Dir Ben Elton
with Hugh Laurie, Joely Richardson,
Adrian Lester, James Purefoy, Tom
Hollander, Joanna Lumley, Rowan
Atkinson, Dawn French, Emma
Thompson, Rachael Stirling
©1999. Inconceivable Films
Ltd/Pandora Investment S.A.R.L.
Pandora/BBC Films
Pandora and BBC Films present a
Phil McIntyre production of a film

by Ben Elton
104 mins 46 seconds
S&S July 2000 p.50

Meet the Parents
(2000)
United International Pictures (UK)
Ltd – 15 December
(12) US
Dir Jay Roach
with Robert De Niro, Ben Stiller,
Blythe Danner, Teri Polo, James
Rebhorn, Jon Abrahams, Owen
Wilson, Nicole DeHuff, Thomas
McCarthy, Phyllis George
© 2000. Universal Studios and
DreamWorks LLC
DreamWorks Pictures and Universal
Pictures present a Nancy Tenenbaum
Films and
a Tribeca production
a Jay Roach film
107 mins 57 seconds
S&S January 2001 p.54-55

Memento
(2000)
Pathé Distribution – 20 October
(15) US
Dir Christopher Nolan
with Guy Pearce, Carrie-Anne Moss,
Joe Pantoliano, Mark Boone Junior,
Stephen Tobolowsky, Harriet Sansom
Harris, Callum Keith Rennie, Larry
Holden, Russ Fega, Jorja Fox
© 2000. I Remember Productions,
LLC
Newmarket presents in association
with Summit Entertainment a Team
Todd
production
a film by Christopher Nolan
113 mins 15 seconds
S&S November 2000 p.42-43, 58

Me, Myself & Irene
(2000)
20th Century Fox (UK) – 22
September
(15) US
Dir Bob Farrelly
with Jim Carrey, Renée Zellweger,
Chris Cooper, Robert Forster, Richard
Jenkins, Rob Moran, Traylor Howard,
Daniel Greene, Zen Gesner, Tony Cox
© 2000. Twentieth Century Fox Film
Corporation
Twentieth Century Fox presents a
Conundrum Entertainment
production
a Farrelly Brothers movie
Dolby Digital/DTS/SDDS
Colour by DuArt Film and Video
Prints by DeLuxe
produced and released by Twentieth

Century Fox
116 mins 26 seconds
S&S October 2000 p.50-51

The Million Dollar Hotel
(2000)
Icon Film Distribution – 28 April
(15) Germany/US
Dir Wim Wenders
with Milla Jovovich, Jeremy Davies,
Mel Gibson, Jimmy Smits, Peter
Stormare, Amanda Plummer, Gloria
Stuart, Tom Bower, Donal Logue, Bud
Cort
© 1999 Road Movies Filmproduktion
GmbH, Berlin
Icon Entertainment International
presents
a Road Movies production in
association with Icon Productions
and Kintop Pictures
a Wim Wenders film
121 mins 48 seconds
S&S May 2000 p.53-54

Mission: Impossible II
(2000)
United International Pictures (UK)
Ltd – 7 July
(15) US/Germany
Dir John Woo
with Tom Cruise, Dougray Scott,
Thandie Newton, Ving Rhames,
Richard Roxburgh, John Polson,
Brendan Gleeson, Radè Sherbedgia,
William Mapother, Dominic Purcell
©2000 MFP Munich Film Partners
GmbH Co. MI 2 Productions KG
Paramount Pictures presents
a Cruise-Wagner production
In association with MFP Munich
Film Partners GmbH Co. MI 2
Productions KG
Time 123 mins 38 seconds
S&S July 2000 p.51

Mission to Mars
(2000)
Buena Vista International (UK) – 14
April
(PG) US
Dir Brian De Palma
with Gary Sinise, Don Cheadle,
Connie Nielsen, Jerry O'Connell, Kim
Delaney, Tim Robbins, Peter
Outerbridge, Kavan Smith, Jill Teed,
Elise Neal
© 2000. Touchstone Pictures
Touchstone Pictures presents a
Jacobson Co. production
112 mins
S&S May 2000 p.54-56

Miss Julie
(1999)

Optimum Releasing – 1 September
(15) UK/US
Dir Mike Figgis
with Saffron Burrows, Peter Mullan,
Maria Doyle Kennedy, Tam Dean
Burn, Heathcote Williams, Eileen
Walsh, Sue Maund, Joanna Page,
Andrea Ollson, Sara Li Gustafsson
©1999. Daza Productions Ltd. and
Gallery Motion Pictures Ltd.
United Artists - an MGM company
Moonstone Entertainment presents
a Red Mullet production
Developed with the support of the
European Script Fund - an initiative
developed in association with Left
Handed Pictures Limited
100 mins 55 seconds
S&S October 2000 p.51-52

Music of the Heart
(1999)
Buena Vista International (UK) – 21
January
(PG) US
Dir Wes Craven
with Meryl Streep, Aidan Quinn,
Gloria Estefan, Angela Bassett, Jane
Leeves, Cloris Leachman, Kieran
Culkin, Charlie Hofheimer, Jay O
Sanders, Josh Pais
© 1999. Miramax Film Corp.
Miramax Films presents in
association with Craven/Maddalena
Films
a film by Wes Craven
124 mins 2 seconds
S&S February 2000 p.49-50

My Dog Skip
(2000)
Warner Bros Distributors (UK) – 11
August
(U) US
Dir Jay Russell
with Frankie Muniz, Diane Lane,
Luke Wilson, Kevin Bacon, Mark
Beech, Susan Carol Davis, David
Pickens, Bradley Coryell, Daylan
Honeycutt, Cody Linley
© 1999 MDS Productions, LLC
Alcon Entertainment presents
a Mark Johnson/John Lee Hancock
production
95 mins 9 seconds
S&S September 2000 p.44-45

A Napfény íze
Aka: Sunshine (English title)
Sunshine - Ein Hauch von
Sonnenschein (Germany)
(1999)
Alliance Releasing (UK) – 28 April
(15)
Hungary/Germany/Canada/Austria/

UK
Dir István Szabó
with Ralph Fiennes, Rosemary Harris,
Rachel Weisz, Jennifer Ehle, Deborah
Kara Unger, Molly Parker, James
Frain, David de Keyser,
© 1999 ISL Film Kft/Kinowelt
Filmproduction
GmbH/Screenventures XXXIX
Productions Ltd, an Alliance Atlantis
company/DOR Film
Produktiongesellschaft m.b.H.
Alliance Atlantis and Serendipity
Point Films in association with
Kinowelt present
a Robert Lantos production
a film by István Szabó
a Hungary-Germany-Canada-Austria
co-production
Made with the financial participation
of Film Four
Financially supported by the
Bavarian Film and TV Fund
(FilmFernsehFonds
Bayern) FFF
Supported by Eurimages
Produced with the participation of
TMN
Produced with the participation of
Telefilm Canada
179 mins 59 seconds
S&S May 2000 p.62-63

Návrat idiota
aka: Idiot Returns, The
(International: English title)
aka: Return of the Idiot
(1999)
Institute of Contemporary Arts – 17
March
(Not submitted) Czech Republic/
Germany
Dir Sasa Gedeon
with Pavel Liska, Anna Geislerová,
Tatiana Vilhelmova, Jirí Langmajer,
Jirí Machácek, Pavel Marek, Zdena
Hadrbolcová, Jitka Smuná
A CinemArt release (in Czech
Republic) of a Negativ Ltd./Czech
TV production, in association with
Cinemasound, Stillking Films and
ZDF (Germany)
99 mins
Subtitles
No S&S reference

La Neuvième porte
Aka: The Ninth Gate, (English title)
(1999)
United International Pictures (UK)
Ltd – 2 June
(15) France/Spain/US
Dir Roman Polanski
with Johnny Depp, Lena Olin, Frank
Langella, James Russo, Jack Taylor,

José López Rodero, Allen Garfield,
Barbara Jefford, Emmanuelle Seigner,
Tony Amoni
©1999 RP Productions
Artisan Entertainment presents
a Roman Polanski film
a French-Spanish co-production
RP Productions, Orly Films, TF1
Filmproduction with the
participation of
BAC Films and Canal+ and Kino
Visión, Origen Producciones
Cinematográficas
with the participation of Via Digital
133 mins
S&S September 2000 p.45-46

The Next Best Thing
(2000)
Buena Vista International (UK) – 23
June
(12) US
Dir John Schlesinger
with Madonna, Rupert Everett,
Benjamin Bratt, Michael Vartan, Josef
Sommer, Malcolm Stumpf, Lynn
Redgrave, Neil Patrick Harris, Mark
Valley, Suzanne Krull
© 2000. Lakeshore Entertainment
Corp. and Paramount Pictures
Paramount Pictures/Lakeshore
Entertainment
Lakeshore Entertainment and
Paramount Pictures present a
LakeshoreEntertainment production
a film by John Schlesinger
107 mins 52 seconds
S&S August 2000 p.53

Next Friday
(2000)
Entertainment Film Distributors Ltd
– 10 March
(15) US
Dir Steve Carr
with Ice Cube, Mike Epps, Justin
Pierce, John Witherspoon, Don 'D.C.'
Curry, Jacob Vargas, Tamala Jones,
Clifton Powell, Kirk Jones, Kym E.
Whitley
© 2000. New Line Productions, Inc
New Line Cinema presents a
Cubevision production
97 mins 57 seconds
S&S April 2000 p.60-61

Nora
(2000)
Alliance Releasing (UK) – 19 May
(15) UK/Ireland/Germany/Italy
Dir Pat Murphy
with Ewan McGregor, Susan Lynch,
Peter McDonald, Roberto Citran,
Andrew Scott, Vincent McCabe,
Veronica Duffy, Aedín Moloney,

Pauline McLynn, Neilí Conroy
© 2000
Natural Nylon Entertainment in
association with IAC Holdings
Volta Films/Road Movies Vierte
Produktionen/Gam
Film/Metropolitan Films
Supported by Bord Scannán na
hÉireann/Irish Film
Board/Eurimages/FilmFörderung
Hamburg GmbH/Ministero per I
Beni e le Attività Culturali -
dipartimento della Spettacolo/Radio
Telefís Éireann
Developed in association with Sally
Ann O'Reilly and Ben Barenholtz
106 mins 30 seconds
S&S June 2000 p.49

Nurse Betty
(2000)
Pathé Distribution – 1 September
(18) US
Dir Neil LaBute
with Morgan Freeman, Renée
Zellweger, Chris Rock, Greg Kinnear,
Aaron Eckhart, Tia Texada, Crispin
Glover, Pruitt Taylor Vince, Allison
Janney, Kathleen Wilhoite
A USA Films release of a Gramercy
Pictures presentation, in association
with
Pacifica Film Distribution, of a
Propaganda Films/ab'-strakt
pictures/IMF production.
109 mins 58 seconds
S&S October 2000 p.53

Nutty Professor II The Klumps
(2000)
United International Pictures (UK)
Ltd – 6 October
(12) US
Dir Peter Segal
with Eddie Murphy, Janet Jackson,
Larry Miller, John Ales, Richard Gant,
Anna Maria Horsford, Melinda
McGraw, Jamal Mixon
© 2000. Universal Studios
Universal Pictures and Imagine
Entertainment present a Brian
Grazer production
a Peter Segal film
106 mins 34 seconds
S&S November 2000 p.59-60

O Brother, Where Art Thou?
(2000)
Alliance Releasing (UK) – 15
September
(12) US/France/UK
Dir Joel Coen
with George Clooney, John Turturro,
Tim Blake Nelson, Charles Durning,

John Goodman, Michael Badalucco, Holly Hunter, Stephen Root, Chris Thomas King, Wayne Duvall
©2000 Touchstone Pictures/ Universal Studios
Touchstone Pictures and Universal Pictures present
in association with Studio Canal
a Working Title production
107 mins 2 seconds
S&S October 2000 p.38-39, 54

102 Dalmatians
(2000)
Buena Vista International (UK) – 8 December
(U) US
Dir Kevin Lima
with Glenn Close, Ioan Gruffudd, Alice Evans, Tim McInnerny, Ian Richardson, Gérard Depardieu, Ben Crompton, Carol MacReady, Jim Carter, Ron Cook
©2000. Disney Enterprises, Inc.
Walt Disney Pictures
Walt Disney Pictures presents an Edward S. Feldman production
100 mins 10 seconds
S&S January 2001 p.56

One More Kiss
(1999)
Metrodome Distribution Ltd – 18 February
(12) UK
Dir Vadim Jean
with Gerard Butler, James Cosmo, Valerie Edmond, Valerie Gogan, Carl Proctor, Danny Nussbaum, Dilys Miller, Ron Gutherie, Michael Murray, Oscar Fullane
© 1999. One More Kiss Ltd.
Mob Films presents in association with Jam Pictures and Freewheel International
Developed by Metrodome/The European Script Fund
102 mins 18 seconds
S&S February 2000 p.52

Ordinary Decent Criminal
(2000)
aka: Ganz gewöhnlicher Dieb, Ein (Germany)
Icon Film Distribution – 17 March
(15) Ireland/Germany/US/UK
Dir Thaddeus O'Sullivan
with Kevin Spacey, Linda Fiorentino, Peter Mullan, Stephen Dillane, Helen Baxendale, David Hayman, Patrick Malahide, Gerard McSorley, David Kelly, Gary Lydon
© 1999 Unicorn Distributors Limited
Icon Entertainment International presents

a film by Thaddeus O'Sullivan
a Little Bird production in association with Tatfilm and Trigger Street Productions
Produced in association with Miramax Films, Bord Scannán na hÉireann/The Irish Film Board, The Greenlight Fund, Filmstiftung NRW
Supported by The National Lottery through The Arts Council of England
Produced with the support of incentives for the Irish Film industry provided by the Government of Ireland
93 mins 57 seconds
S&S April 2000 p.61-62

The Patriot
(2000)
Columbia TriStar Films (UK) – 14 July
(15) US/Germany
Dir Roland Emmerich
with Mel Gibson, Heath Ledger, Joely Richardson, Jason Isaacs, Chris Cooper, Tchéky Karyo, René Auberjonois, Lisa Brenner, Donal Logue, Leon Rippy
© 2000. Global Entertainment Productions GmbH & Co. Movie KG
Columbia Pictures presents a Mutual Film Company production/a Centropolis Entertainment production
a Roland Emmerich film
164 mins 33 seconds
S&S September 2000 p.46-47

The Perfect Storm
(2000)
Warner Bros Distributors (UK) – 28 July
(12) US
Dir Wolfgang Petersen
with George Clooney, Mark Wahlberg, John C. Reilly, Diane Lane, William Fichtner, John Hawkes, Allen Payne, Karen Allen, Bob Gunton, Christopher McDonald
© 2000 Warner Bros.
Warner Bros. presents
a Baltimore Spring Creek Pictures production in association with Radiant Productions
a Wolfgang Petersen film
129 mins 46 seconds
S&S September 2000 p.47-48

Pippi Långstrump
aka: Pippi Longstocking (English title)
Pippi Langstrumpf (Germany)
(1997)
Optimum Releasing – 14 April
(U) Sweden/Germany/Canada

Dir Clive Smith
with the voices of Catherine O'Hara, Dave Thomas, Gordon Pinsent, Wayne Robson, Melissa Altro, Carole Pope, Richard Binsley, Rick Jones, Chris Wiggins
©1997 AB Svensk Filmindustri/Iduna Produktiongesellschaft GmbH & Co/TFC Trickompany Filmproduktion GmbH/Nelvana Limited
a co-production of AB Svensk Filmindustri, Iduna Film, TFC Trickompany and Nelvana
Produced with the participation of Telefilm Canada
a Canada-Germany-Sweden co-production
Produced with the participation of TELETOON and with the assistance of the Government of Canada - Canadian Film or Video Production
77 mins 41 seconds
S&S May 2000 p.58

Pitch Black
(2000)
United International Pictures (UK) Ltd – 10 November
(15) US/Australia
Dir David N. Twohy
with Vin Diesel, Radha Mitchell, Cole Hauser, Keith David, Lewis Fitz-Gerald, Claudia Black, Rhiana Griffith, John Moore, Simon Burke, Les Chantery
Gramercy Pictures presents an Interscope Communications production
With the assistance of Pacific Film and Television Commission
110 mins 8 seconds
S&S August 2000 p.54-55

Pokémon the First Movie: Mewtwo Strikes Back
aka: Gekijôban Poketto Monsutâ Miutsû No Gyakushû (Japanese title)
(1999)
Warner Bros Distributors (UK) – 14 April
(PG) Japan/US
Dir Kunihiko Yuyama
with the voices of Veronica Taylor, Philip Bartlett, Rachael Lillis, Eric Stuart, Addie Blaustein, Ikue Ôtani, Ed Paul
© Pikachu Project '98
Warner Bros. presents
a 4Kids Entertainment production
74 mins 57 seconds
S&S June 2000 p.50-51

Pokémon: The Power of One

aka: Poketto monsutaa Maboroshi no Pokemon Lugia bakudan (Japanese title)
(1999)
Warner Bros Distributors (UK) – 22 December
(PG) Japan/US
Dir Kunihiko Yuyama
with the voices of Veronica Taylor, Rachael Lillis, Eric Stuart, Addie Blaustein, Ed Paul, Ikue Ôtani, Michelle Goguen, Eric Rath
© 1999, 2000
Nintendo/Creatures/Game Freak/TV Tokyo/Shopro/JR Kikaku
©Pikachu '99
Warner Bros Kids presents
a 4Kids Entertainment production
80 mins 29 seconds
S&S February 2001 p.44

Pourquoi pas moi?

(1999)
Millivres Multimedia – 24 November
(15) France/Spain/Switzerland
Dir Stéphane Giusti
with Amira Casar, Julie Gayet, Bruno Putzulu, Alexandra London, Carmen Chaplin, Johnny Hallyday, Marie-France Pisier, Brigitte Roüan, SAssumpta Serna, Elli Medeiros
©1998. Elzevir Films/M6 Films/Glozel/Maestranza Films/Sogedasa/Alhena Films
[al] Millivres Multimedia
supported by Eurimages
a co-production of Elzevir Films/M6 Films/Glozel (P. Goter)/Maestranza Films (Seville)/Sogedasa (Barcelona)/Alhena Films
with the participation of the soficas Sofinergie 4 & Sofinergie 5
with the participation of Canal+ and of M6
un film de Stéphane Giusti
a French/Spanish/Swiss co-production of Elzevir Films/M6 Films/Glozel (P. Goter)/Maestranza Films (Seville)/Sogedasa (Barcelona)/Alhena Films
with the participation of Canal+/M6/Sofinergie 4 & 5
supported by Eurimages
94 mins 17 seconds
S&S December 2000 p.53

Purely Belter

(2000)
FilmFour Distributors – 3 November
(15) UK
Dir Mark Herman
with Charlie Hardwick, Tim Healy,
Roy Hudd, Kevin Whately, Chris Beattie, Greg McLane, Jody Baldwin, Kerry Ann Christiansen, Tracy Whitwell, Kate Garbutt
© 2000. FilmFour
FilmFour presents a Mumbo Jumbo production
a film by Mark Herman
98 mins 57 seconds
S&S November 2000 p.60-61

Rancid Aluminium

(2000)
Entertainment Film Distributors Ltd – 28 January
(18) UK
Dir Edward Thomas
with Rhys Ifans, Joseph Fiennes, Tara Fitzgerald, Sadie Frost, Steven Berkoff, Keith Allen, Dani Behr, Andrew Howard, Nick Moran, Olegario Fedoro
© 2000 Entertainment Film Distributors Limited
Entertainment Film Distributors present
a Mark Thomas/Fiction Factory production
91 mins 15 seconds
S&S March 2000 p.50-51

Ready to Rumble

(2000)
Warner Bros Distributors (UK) – 24 November
(15) US
Dir Brian Robbins
with David Arquette, Oliver Platt, Scott Caan, Bill Goldberg, Rose McGowan, Diamond Dallas Page, Joe Pantoliano, Martin Landau, Richard Lineback, Chris Owen
© 2000. Warner Bros. and Bel-Air Entertainment, LLC
Warner Bros. presents in association with Bel-Air Entertainment
an Outlaw production in association with Tollin/Robbins productions
106 mins 21 seconds
S&S January 2001 p.57-58

* Rear Window

(1954)
aka: Alfred Hitchcock's Rear Window
United International Pictures (UK) Ltd – 4 February
(PG) US
Dir Alfred Hitchcock
with James Stewart, Grace Kelly, Wendell Corey, Thelma Ritter, Raymond Burr, Judith Evelyn, Ross Bagdasarian, Georgine Darcy, Sara Berner, Frank Cady
© Patron Inc.
112 mins
Monthly Film Bulletin February 1984 p.34-36
Monthly Film Bulletin.v21.n248. September 1954 p.129

Red Planet

(2000)
Warner Bros Distributors (UK) – 1 December
(12) US/Australia
Dir Antony Hoffman
with Val Kilmer, Tom Sizemore, Carrie-Anne Moss, Benjamin Bratt, Simon Baker, Terence Stamp, Jessica Morton, Caroline Bossi, Bob Neill
©2000 Warner Bros. (US/Canada/Bahamas/Bermuda)
©2000 Village Roadshow Films (BVI) Limited (all other territories)
Warner Bros. Pictures presents in association with Village Roadshow Pictures and NPV Entertainment
a Mark Canton production
106 mins 23 seconds
S&S February 2001 p.46, 48

Reindeer Games

(2000)
Buena Vista International (UK) – 23 June
(15) US
Dir John Frankenheimer
with Ben Affleck, Gary Sinise, Charlize Theron, Dennis Farina, James Frain, Donal Logue, Clarence Williams III, Dana Stubblefield, Mark Acheson, Tom Heaton
© 2000. Miramax Film Corp.
Dimension Films presents
a Marty Katz production
a John Frankenheimer film
104 mins 20 seconds
S&S August 2000 p.43

Relative Values

(2000)
Alliance Releasing (UK) – 23 June
(PG) US/UK
Dir Eric Styles
with Julie Andrews, Edward Atterton, William Baldwin, Colin Firth, Stephen Fry, Sophie Thompson, Jeanne Tripplehorn, Stephanie Beacham, Gaye Brown, Anwen Carlisle
© 2000 Replyearth Limited
Midsummer Films and Overseas Film Group present in association with
The Isle of Man Film Commission
a Christopher Milburn production
an Eric Styles film
Developed in association with Hallelujah Productions
Isle of Man Film Commission

89 minutes 8 seconds
S&S July 2000 p.52

Rien sur Robert
(1999)
Millennium Film Distributors – 17
March
(18) France
Dir Pascal Bonitzer
with Fabrice Luchini, Sandrine
Kiberlain, Valentina Cervi, Michel
Piccoli, Bernadette Lafont, Laurent
Lucas, Denis Podalydès, Nathalie
Boutefeu, Micheline Boudet, Edouard
Baer
©1998 Rezo Films/Assise
Production/France 3 Cinéma
Rezo Films presents
a co-production of Rezo Films/Assise
Production/France 2 Cinéma
with the participation of Canal+,
sofica Sofinergie 4 and Sofinergie 5
and Centre National de la
Cinématographie
106 mins 37 secs
Subtitles
S&S May 2000 p.59

Ringu
aka: Ring, The (English title)
(1998)
Institute of Contemporary Arts – 18
August
(15) Japan
Dir Hideo Nakata
with Nanako Matsushima, Miki
Nakatani, Hiroyuki Sanada, Yûko
Takeuchi, Hitomi Sato, Yôichi
Numata, Yutaka Matsushige, Katsumi
Muramatsu, Rikiya Ôtaka, Masako
©1997. Omega Project
Ace Pictures / Asmik-Ace
Entertainment
Omega Project Inc. production
Kadokawa, Pony Canyon, Toho,
Imagica, Asmik-Ace & Omega
Project present
95 mins 21 seconds
Subtitles
S&S September 2000 p.48-49

The Road to El Dorado
(2000)
United International Pictures (UK)
Ltd – 4 August
(U) US
Dir Éric Bergeron
with the voices of Kevin Kline,
Kenneth Branagh, Rosie Perez,
Armand Assante, Edward James
Olmos, Jim Cummings, Frank
Welker, Tobin Bell, Duncan
Marjoribanks, Elijah Chiang
© 2000 DreamWorks LLC
DreamWorks Pictures presents

89 mins 45 seconds
S&S September 2000 p.49-50

Road Trip
(2000)
United International Pictures (UK)
Ltd – 13 October
(15) US
Dir Todd Phillips
with Breckin Meyer, Seann William
Scott, Amy Smart, Paulo Costanzo, DJ
Qualls, Rachel Blanchard, Anthony
Rapp, Fred Ward, Tom Green, Andy
Dick
© 2000. DreamWorks LLC
DreamWorks Pictures and The
Montecito Picture Company present
an Ivan Reitman production
a Todd Phillips film
93 mins 55 seconds
S&S November 2000 p.61

Romeo Must Die
(2000)
Warner Bros Distributors (UK) – 13
October
(15) US
Dir Andrzej Bartkowiak
with Jet Li, Aaliyah, Isaiah
Washington, Russell Wong, Henry O,
D.B. Woodside, Edoardo Ballerini,
Jon Kit Lee, Anthony Anderson,
DMX
© 2000. Warner Bros.
Warner Bros. Pictures - a Time
Warner Entertainment company
Warner Bros. presents
a Silver Pictures production
114 mins 26 seconds
S&S November 2000 p.62

A Room for Romeo Brass
(1999)
Alliance Releasing (UK) – 4 February
(15) UK/Canada
Dir Shane Meadows
with Bob Hoskins, Andrew Shim, Ben
Marshall, Paddy Considine, Frank
Harper, Julia Ford, James
Higgins,Vicky McClure, Ladene Hall,
Martin Arrowsmith
© 1999. Romeo Brass Limited
Alliance Atlantis
Alliance Atlantis and BBC Films
present in association with the Arts
Council of England
a Company Pictures/Big Arty
production
a Shane Meadows film
90 minutes 28 seconds
S&S February 2000 p.52-53

Rules of Engagement
(2000)
United International Pictures (UK)

Ltd – 11 August
(15) US/Germany
Dir William Friedkin
with Tommy Lee Jones, Samuel L.
Jackson, Guy Pearce, Bruce
Greenwood, Blair Underwood, Philip
Baker Hall, Anne Archer, Mark
Feuerstein, Ben Kingsley, Dale Dye
©2000. MFP Munich Film Partners
GmbH & Co. ROE Productions KG
Paramount Pictures presents in
association with Seven Arts Pictures
a Richard D. Zanuck/Scott Rudin
production
a William Friedkin film
in association with MFP Munich
Film Partners GmbH & Co. ROE
Productions KG
127 mins 28 seconds
S&S September 2000 p.50-51

Saving Grace
(2000)
20th Century Fox (UK) – 19 May
(15) UK
Dir Nigel Cole
with Brenda Blethyn, Craig Ferguson,
Martin Clunes, Tchéky Karyo, Jamie
Foreman, Bill Bailey, Valerie Edmond,
Tristan Sturrock, Clive Merrison,
Leslie Phillips
© 1999. Rich Pickings and British
Sky Broadcasting
Twentieth Century Fox and Sky
Pictures present in association with
Portman Entertainment and Wave
Pictures
a Homerun production
92 mins 32 seconds
S&S June 2000 p.53

 * Scarlet Street
(1945)
BFI Collections – 21 January
(PG) US
Dir Fritz Lang
with Edward G. Robinson, Joan
Bennett, Dan Duryea, Margaret
Lindsay, Rosalind Ivan, Jess Barker,
Charles Kemper, Anita Bolster,
Samuel S Hinds, Vladimir Sokoloff
© Universal Pictures Company Inc
Walter Wanger presents
a Fritz Lang production
a Diana production
101 mins
S&S Supplement n5. February 1946
p.14
Monthly Film Bulletin. v13 p.19

Scary Movie
(2000)
Buena Vista International (UK) – 8
September
(18) US

Dir Keenen Ivory Wayans
with Jon Abrahams, Carmen Electra, Elizabeth Shannon, Anna Faris, Kurt Fuller, Regina Hall, Lochlyn Munro, Cheri Oteri, Dave Sheridan, Marlon Wayans
© 2000. Miramax Film Corp
Miramax International/Dimension Films present
a Wayans Bros. Entertainment
Gold-Miller, Brad Grey Pictures
a film by Keenen Ivory Wayans
88 mins 14 seconds
S&S October 2000 p.55-56

Scream 3
(2000)
Buena Vista International (UK) – 28 April
(18) US
Dir Wes Craven
with David Arquette, Neve Campbell, Courteney Cox Arquette, Patrick Dempsey, Scott Foley, Lance Henriksen, Matt Keeslar, Jenny McCarthy, Emily Mortimer, Parker Posey
©2000. Miramax Film Corp
Dimension Films
a Konrad Pictures production in association with Craven/Maddalena Films
a Dimension Films presentation
a film by Wes Craven
116 mins 44 seconds
S&S May 2000 p.59-60

Second Generation
(2000)
Second Generation Films – 17 November
(15) UK
Dir Shane O'Sullivan
with Hanayo, Shigetomo Yutani, Nitin Chandra Ganatra, Adrian Pang, Kriss Dosanjh, Saeed Jaffrey, Shujul Miah, Ahmed Jaber, Andrew Cooper, Vince Johnson
©1999. Second Generation Films
Second Generation Films presents a Shane O'Sullivan film
This film was made in association with VET and was developed with the support
of the Moonstone Filmmakers' Lab
80 mins 27 seconds
S&S January 2001 p.59

Sex The Annabel Chong Story
(1999)
Metrodome Distribution Ltd – 21 April
(18) US/Canada
Dir Gough Lewis

with Grace Quek, Annabel Chong, John Bowen, Ed Powers, Dr Walter Williams, Charles Conn, Dick James, Monica Moran, Steve Austin, Jim South
© 1999 Coffee House Films/Omni International/Greycat Releasing
Omni International & Greycat Releasing present
a Coffee House Films production
a film by Gough Lewis
86 mins 46 seconds
S&S May 2000 p.60-61

Shaft
(2000)
United International Pictures (UK) Ltd – 15 September
(18) US/Germany
Dir John Singleton
with Samuel L. Jackson, Vanessa Williams, Jeffrey Wright, Christian Bale, Busta Rhymes, Dan Hedaya, Toni Collette, Richard Roundtree, Ruben Santiago-Hudson, Josef Sommer
©2000 MFP Munich Film Partners GmbH & Co. Shaft Productions KG
Paramout Pictures presents
a Scott Rudin/New Deal production
a John Singleton film
In association with MFP Munich Film Partners GmbH & Co. Shaft Productions KG
99 mins 22 seconds
S&S October 2000 p.57-58

Shanghai Noon
(2000)
Buena Vista International (UK) – 25 August
(12) US/Hong Kong
Dir Tom Dey
with Jackie Chan, Owen Wilson, Lucy Liu, Roger Yuan, Walton Goggins, Xander Berkeley, Jason Connery, Brandon Merrill, Rafael Baez, P. Adrien Dorval
© 2000. Spyglass Entertainment Group, L.P.
Buena Vista International/ Touchstone Pictures/Spyglass Entertainment
Touchstone Pictures and Spyglass Entertainment present a
Birnbaum/Barber
production in association with a Jackie Chan Films Limited production
110 mins 18 seconds
S&S October 2000 p.58-59

Simon Magus
(1999)
FilmFour Distributors – 26 May

(PG) UK/Germany/Italy/France
Dir Ben Hopkins
with Noah Taylor, Embeth Davidtz, Stuart Townsend, Sean McGinley, Terence Rigby, Amanda Ryan, Ian Holm, Rutger Hauer, David De Keyser, Toby Jones
© 1999 FilmFour Limited and The Arts Council of England
FilmFour, Lucky Red, ARP and Hollywood Partners in association with the Arts Council of England present
a Jones company production
a Jones company production for Film Four, Lucky Red, ARP, Hollywood Partners in association with The Arts Council of England
Developed with the support of British Screen Finance Limited and Miramax Films
Developed with the support of the MEDIA programme of the European Union
Supported by the National Lottery through the Arts Council of England
106 mins 26 seconds
S&S July 2000 p.53-54

Simpatico
(1999)
Alliance Releasing (UK) – 28 January
(15) US/France
Dir Matthew Warchus
with Nick Nolte, Jeff Bridges, Sharon Stone, Catherine Keener, Albert Finney, Shawn Hatosy, Kimberly Williams, Liam Waite, Whit Crawford, Bob Harter
©1999. Le Studio Canal+
Alliance Atlantis / Emotion Pictures
Emotion Pictures in association with Le Studio Canal+ presents
a Jean-François Fonlupt production in association with Kingsgate
a Matthew Warchus film
106 mins 21 seconds
S&S February 2000 p.53-54

6th Day
(2000)
Columbia TriStar Films (UK) – 15 December
(15) US
Dir Roger Spottiswoode
with Arnold Schwarzenegger, Tony Goldwyn, Michael Rapaport, Michael Rooker, Sarah Wynter, Wendy Crewson, Rod Rowland, Terry Crews, Ken Pogue, Colin Cunningham
© 2000 Phoenix Pictures, Inc.
Phoenix Pictures presents
a Jon Davison production
a Roger Spottiswood film
123 mins 24 seconds
S&S February 2001 p.51-52

The Skulls

(2000)
United International Pictures (UK)
Ltd – 24 November 2000
(15) US
Dir Rob Cohen
with Joshua Jackson, Paul Walker, Hill
Harper, Leslie Bibb, Christopher
McDonald, Steve Harris, William
Petersen, Craig T. Nelson, David
Asman, Scott Gibson
© 2000. Skulls Productions, LLC
Universal Pictures in association
with Original Film/Newmarket
Capital Group present
a Neal H. Moritz production
a Rob Cohen film
106 mins 51 seconds
S&S December 2000 p.55-56

SLC Punk!

(1999)
Columbia TriStar Films (UK) – 10
March
(15) US/Australia
Dir James Merendino
with Matthew Lillard, Michael
Goorjian, Annabeth Gish, Jennifer
Lien, Chris McDonald, Devon Sawa,
Jason Segel, James Duval, Summer
Phoenix, Adam Pascal
© 1998 Straight Edge Productions
LLC
Beyond Films presents
a Blue Tulip production of
a James Merendino film
97 mins 42 seconds
S&S May 2000 p.61

Sleepy Hollow

(1999)
Pathé Distribution – 14 January
(15) US/Germany
Dir Tim Burton
with Johnny Depp, Christina Ricci,
Miranda Richardson, Christopher
Walken, Michael Gambon, Caspar
Van Dien, Jeffrey Jones, Richard
Griffiths, Ian McDiarmid, Michael
Gough
© 1999. Paramount Pictures and
Mandalay Pictures LLC
Mandalay Pictures presents a Scott
Rudin/American Zoetrope
production in association with
Dieter Geissler film
a Tim Burton film
in association with Karol Film
Productions GmbH & Co. KG
105 mins 23 seconds
S&S February 2000 p.54-55

Small Time Crooks

(2000)

FilmFour Distributors – 1 December
(PG) US
Dir Woody Allen
with Woody Allen, Tony Darrow,
Hugh Grant, George Grizzard, Jon
Lovitz, Elaine May, Michael
Rapaport, Elaine Stritch, Tracey
Ullman, Carolyn Saxon
©2000. Magnolia Productions, Inc.
and Sweetland Films, B.V.
FilmFour/Sweetland Films
Sweetland Films present a Jean
Doumanian production
94 mins 43 seconds
S&S January 2001 p.59-60

Small Time Obsession

(2000)
Guerilla Films – 16 June
(15) UK
Dir Piotr Szkopiak
with Alex King, Juliette Caton, Jason
Merrells, Oliver Young, Richard
Banks, Kirsten Parker, Geoff Lawson,
Giles Ward, Jurek Jarosz, Teresa
Nowakowska
© 2000. Solo Films Ltd.
Guerilla Films presents
a Solo Films production in
association with the Seventh Twelfth
Collective
a film by Piotr Szkopiak
118 mins 52 seconds
S&S July 2000 p.54

Snatch

(2000)
Columbia TriStar Films (UK) – 1
September
(18) US/UK
Dir Guy Ritchie
with Benicio Del Toro, Dennis Farina,
Vinnie Jones, Brad Pitt, Rade
Sherbedgia, Jason Statham, Alan
Ford, Mike Reid, Robbie Gee, Lennie
James
© 2000. Columbia Pictures
Industries, Inc.
Columbia Pictures presents
in association with Ska Films
a Matthew Vaughn production
a film by Guy Ritchie
102 mins 37 secs
S&S October 2000 p.59-60

Snow Day

(2000)
United International Pictures (UK)
Ltd – 21 April
(PG) US/Germany
Dir Chris Koch
with Chris Elliot, Mark Webber, Jean
Smart, Schuyler Fisk, Iggy Pop, Pam
Grier, John Schneider, Chevy Chase,
Zena Grey, Josh Peck

© 2000. MFF Feature Film
Productions GmbH & Co. KG
Paramount Pictures and
Nickelodeon Movies present
in association with MFF Feature
Film Productions GmbH & Co. KG
89 mins 13 seconds
S&S July 2000 p.55

Snow Falling on Cedars

(1999)
United International Pictures (UK)
Ltd – 12 May
(15) US
Dir Scott Hicks
with Ethan Hawke, James Cromwell,
Richard Jenkins, James Rebhorn,
Sam Shepard, Max von Sydow, Youki
Kudoh, Rick Yune, Reeve Carney,
Anne Suzuki
© 1999 Universal Studios
Universal Pictures presents
a Harry J. Ufland/Ron Bass
production
a Kenney/Marshall production
a Scott Hicks film
127 mins 28 seconds
S&S June 2000 p.54

Some Voices

(2000)
FilmFour Distributors – 25 August
(15) UK
Dir Simon Cellan Jones
with Daniel Craig, David Morrissey,
Kelly Macdonald, Julie Graham, Peter
McDonald, Nicholas Palliser, Huss
Garbiya, Edward Tudor Pole, Ashley
Walters, Gem Durham
© 2000 FilmFour Ltd
FilmFour presents
a Dragon Pictures production
A Dragon Pictures production for
British Screen and FilmFour
101 mins 1 second
S&S September 2000 p.52-53

Sorted

(2000) - 6 October
Metrodome Distribution Ltd – 6
October
(18) UK
Dir Alex Jovy
with Matthew Rhys, Sienna Guillory,
Fay Masterson, Jason Donovan, Tim
Curry, Ben Moor, Claire Harman,
Mark Crowdy, Joseph Kpobie, Neil
Maskell
© 2000 Jovy Junior Enterprises Ltd
a Jovy Junior production
102 mins 22 seconds
S&S November 2000 p.62-63

Space Cowboys

(2000)

Warner Bros Distributors (UK) –
22 September
(PG) US/Australia
Dir Clint Eastwood
with Clint Eastwood, Tommy Lee
Jones, Donald Sutherland, James
Garner, James Cromwell, Marcia Gay
Harden, William Devane, Loren
Dean, Courtney B. Vance, Rade
Sherbedgia
© 2000. Warner Bros. (US, Canada,
Bahamas & Bermuda)
©2000. Village Roadshow Films
(BVI) Limited (all other territories)
Warner Bros. presents in association
with Village Roadshow
Pictures/Clipsal Films
a Malpaso production and Mad
Chance production
130 mins 21 seconds
S&S October 2000 p.60-61

Stigmata
(1999)
United International Pictures (UK)
Ltd – 21 January
(18) US
Dir Rupert Wainwright
with Patricia Arquette, Gabriel Byrne,
Jonathan Pryce, Nia Long, Enrico
Colantoni, Dick Latessa, Thomas
Kopache, Ann Cusack, Portia de
Rossi, Patrick Muldoon
©1999. Metro-Goldwyn-Mayer
Pictures Inc.
Metro-Goldwyn-Mayer Pictures
presents an FGM Entertainment
production
A Rupert Wainwright film
102 mins 14 seconds
S&S February 2000 p.55-56

Stir of Echoes
(1999)
20th Century Fox (UK) – 26 May
(15) US
Dir David Koepp
with Kevin Bacon, Kathryn Erbe,
Illeana Douglas, Liza Weil, Kevin
Dunn, Conor O'Farrell, Jenny
Morrison, Zachary David Cope, Luisa
Strus, Stephen Eugene Walker
© Artisan Pictures Inc
Artisan Entertainment present
a Hofflund/Polone production
99 mins 14 seconds
S&S June 2000 p.55

The Story of Us
(1999)
Warner Bros Distributors (UK) – 21
April
(15) US
Dir Rob Reiner
with Michelle Pfeiffer, Bruce Willis,

Rita Wilson, Julie Hagerty, Paul
Reiser, Tim Matheson, Colleen
Rennison, Jake Sandvig, Red Buttons,
Jayne Meadows
© 1999 CR Films, LLC
Warner Bros. presents
in association with Castle Rock
Entertainment
a Rob Reiner film
95 mins 32 seconds
S&S June 2000 p.55-56

Strange Planet
(1999)
Redbus Film Distribution – 21
January
(15) Australia
Dir Emma-Kate Croghan
with Claudia Karvan, Naomi Watts,
Alice Garner, Tom Long, Aaron
Jeffery, Felix Williamson, Hugo
Weaving, Rebecca Frith, Marshall
Napier, Loene Carmen
©1999. Australian Film Finance
Corporation Limited/New South
Wales Film and Television
Office/Premium Partnership and
Strange Planet Films Pty Ltd.
Beyond Films
Australian Film Finance Corporation
presents a Strange Planet production
in association with The Premium
Movie Partnership/Showtime
Australia & the New
South Wales Film & TV Office
Produced in association with The
Premium Movie Partnership for
Showtime Australia
Produced with assistance from the
New South Wales Film & TV Office,
Sydney, Australia This film was
produced with the financial
assistance of the Australian Film
Commission
96 mins 9 seconds
S&S February 2000 p.56-57

Strong Language
(1998)
National Film Theatre – 28 January
(Not certificated) UK
Dir Simon Rumley
with Ricci Harnet, Kelly Marcel, Tania
Emery, Julie Rice, Thomas Dyton,
Robyn Lewis, Stuart Laing, Shireen
Abdel–Moneim, Al Nedjari, Paul
Tonkinson
Rumleyvision Presents
a Simon Rumley Production
76 mins
No S&S reference

Stuart Little
(1999)
Columbia TriStar Films (UK) – 21

July
(U) US
Dir Rob Minkoff
with Geena Davis, Hugh Laurie,
Jonathan Lipnicki, (with the voices of
Michael J. Fox, Nathan Lane, Chazz
Palminteri, Steve Zahn, Jim Doughan,
David Alan Grier, Bruno Kirby)
© 1999 Global Entertainment
Productions GmbH & Co. Medien
KG
Columbia Pictures presents
a Douglas Wick and
Franklin/Waterman production
a film by Rob Minkoff
84 mins 26 seconds
S&S August 2000 p.55-56

Summer of Sam
(1999)
Downtown Pictures – 14 January
(18) US
Dir Spike Lee
with John Leguizamo, Adrien Brody,
Mira Sorvino, Jennifer Esposito,
Anthony LaPaglia, Bebe Neuwirth,
Patti LuPone, Ben Gazzara, John
Savage, Michael Badalucco
© 1999. Touchstone Pictures presents
a Forty Acres and a Mule Filmworks
production
a Spike Lee Joint
142 mins 7 seconds
S&S February 2000 p.57-58

Supernova
(2000)
United International Pictures (UK)
Ltd – 16 June
(15) US
Dir Walter Hill
with James Spader, Angela Bassett,
Robert Forster, Lou Diamond
Phillips, Peter Facinelli, Robin
Tunney, Wilson Cruz, Eddy Rice Jr,
Knox Grantham White, Kerrigan
Mahan
© 1999. Metro-Goldwyn-Mayer
Pictures Inc.
Metro-Goldwyn-Mayer Pictures
presents a Screenland
Pictures/Hammerhead production
90 mins 18 seconds
S&S August 2000 p.56

Sweet and Lowdown
(1999)
Columbia TriStar Films (UK) – 9
June
(PG) US
Dir Woody Allen
with Anthony LaPaglia, Brian
Markinson, Gretchen Mol, Samantha
Morton, Sean Penn, Uma Thurman,
James Urbaniak, John Waters, Tony

Darrow, Brad Garrett
©1999 Magnolia Productions,
Inc/Sweetland Films, B.V.
Jean Doumanian production
95 mins 23 seconds
S&S July 2000 p.55-56

The Talented Mr. Ripley
(1999)
Buena Vista International (UK) – 25
February
(15) US
Dir Anthony Minghella
with Matt Damon, Gwyneth Paltrow,
Jude Law, Cate Blanchett, Philip
Seymour Hoffman, Jack Davenport,
James Rebhorn, Sergio Rubini, Philip
Baker Hall, Celia Weston
© 1999 Paramount Pictures
Corporation/Miramax Films Corp.
Paramount Pictures and Miramax
Films present
a Mirage Enterprises/Timnick Films
production
139 mins 12 seconds
S&S March 2000 p.53-54

Le Temps retrouvé
(1999)
aka: Time Regained (English title) O
Tempo Reencontrado (Portugal) Il
Tempo ritrovato (Italy)
(1999)
Artificial Eye Film Company – 7
January
(18) France/Italy/Portugal
Dir Raúl Ruiz
with Catherine Deneuve,
Emmanuelle Béart, Vincent Perez,
Pascal Greggory, Marie-France Pisier,
Chiara Mastroianni, Arielle
Dombasle, Edith Scob, Elsa
Zylberstein, Christian Vadim
© Gemini Films/France 2
Cinéma/Blu Cinematografica
Gemini Films, France 2 Cinéma, Les
Films du Lendemain present
Paulo Branco presents
a Co-production of Gemini Films,
France 2 Cinéma, Les Films du
Lendemain, Blu
Cinematografica (Italy)
In association with Madragoa Filmes
with the support of Fonds Eurimages
with the participation of Canal+,
Centre National de la
Cinématographie
and the assistance of La Procirep
162 minutes 11 seconds
Subtitles
S&S January 2000 p.61

There's Only One Jimmy Grimble
(2000)

Pathé Distribution – 25 August
(12) UK/France
Dir John Hay
with Robert Carlyle, Ray Winstone,
Gina McKee, Lewis McKenzie, Jane
Lapotaire, Ben Miller, Wayne Galtrey,
Ciaran Griffiths, Bobby Power, Samia
Ghadie
© 2000. Pathé Fund Limited
Pathé Pictures presents
in association with the Arts Council
of England
and le Studio Canal+
a Sarah Radclyffe/Impact Films
production
supported by the National Lottery
through the Arts Council of England
105 mins 36 seconds
S&S September 2000 p.53-54

Thomas and the Magic Railroad
(2000)
Icon Film Distribution – 14 July
(U) US/UK
Dir Britt Allcroft
with Peter Fonda, Mara Wilson, Alec
Baldwin, Didi Conn, Michael E.
Rodgers, Cody McMains, Russell
Means, Jared Wall, Laura Bower,
Eddie Glen
© 2000. The Magic Railroad
Company Limited
Destination Films and Gullane
Pictures
Barry London/Brent Baum present
a Britt Allcroft film
presented in association with The
Isle of Man Film Commission
85 mins 45 seconds
S&S September 2000 p.54-55

Three Kings
(1999)
Warner Bros Distributors (UK) – 3
March
(15) US/Australia
Dir David O. Russell
with George Clooney, Mark
Wahlberg, Ice Cube, Nora Dunn,
Jamie Kennedy, Mykelti Williamson,
Cliff Curtis, Saïd Taghmaoui, Spike
Jonze, Holt McCallany
©1999 Warner Bros
(US/Canada/Bahamas/Bermuda)
©1999 Village Roadshow Films (BVI)
Limited (all other territories)
Warner Bros. presents
in assocation with Village Roadshow
Pictures/Village - A.M. Film
Partnership
a Coast Ridge/Atlas Entertainment
production
a David O. Russell film

114 mins 40 seconds
S&S March 2000 p.54-55

Three Seasons
(1999)
Pathé Distribution – 14 January
aka: Ba Mua
(12) US/Vietnam
Dir Tony Bui
Don Duong, Ngoc Hiep Nguyen,
Manh Cuong Tran, Zoë Bui, Huu
Duoc Nguyen, Thi Kim Trang Thach,
Harvey Keitel, Ngoc Minh, Phat Trieu
Hoang, Kieu Diem
© 1998. October Films, Inc.
October Films presents an Open City
production in association with
Goatsingers
and Giai Phong Film Studios
a film by Tony Bui
Developed with the assistance of the
Sundance Institute
108 mins 30 seconds
S&S February 2000 p.58-59

Three to Tango
(1999)
Warner Bros Distributors (UK) – 30
June
(12) US
Dir Damon Santostefano
with Matthew Perry, Neve Campbell,
Dylan McDermott, Oliver Platt, Cylk
Cozart, John C. McGinley, Bob
Balaban, Deborah Rush, Kelly Rowan,
Rick Gomez
©Village Roadshow Films (BVI)
Limited [all other territories]
Warner Bros. presents in association
with Village Roadshow Pictures and
Village-Hoyts Film Partnership an
Outlaw Production
98 mins 19 seconds
S&S August 2000 p.57

The Tigger Movie
(2000)
Buena Vista International (UK) – 14
April
(U) US
Dir Jun Falkenstein
with the voices of Jim Cummings,
Nikita Hopkins, Ken Sansom, John
Fielder, Peter Cullen, Andre Stojka,
Kath Soucie, Tom Attenborough,
Frank Welker
© 2000 Disney Enterprises, Inc
Walt Disney Pictures presents
Produced by Walt Disney Television
Animation
Animation production by Walt
Disney Animation (Japan) Inc
77 mins 8 seconds
S&S June 2000 p.56-57

Titan A.E.

(2000)
20th Century Fox (UK) – 28 July
(PG) US
Dir Don Bluth
with the voices of Matt Damon, Bill
Pullman, John Leguizamo, Nathan
Lane, Janeane Gerofalo, Drew
Barrymore, Ron Pearlman, Alex D.
Linz, Tone-Loc, Jim Breuer
©2000 Twentieth Century Fox Film
Corporation
Twentieth Century Fox Animation
presents
a Don Bluth film
a Gary Goldman production
in association with David Kirschner
Productions
94 mins 56 seconds
S&S August 2000 p.57-58

Titus

(1999)
Buena Vista International (UK) – 1
September
(18) US/UK
Dir Julie Taymor
with Anthony Hopkins, Jessica Lange,
Alan Cumming, Colm Feore, James
Frain, Laura Fraser, Harry Lennix,
Angus Macfadyen, Matthew Rhys,
Jonathan Rhys Meyers
© 1999 Clear Blue Sky Productions
Clear Blue Sky Productions presents
in association with Overseas
Filmgroup
a Urania Pictures and NDF
International production
a film by Julie Taymor
162 mins
S&S October 2000 p.61-62

Topsy-Turvy

(1999)
Pathé Distribution – 18 February
(12) UK/US
Dir Mike Leigh
with Jim Broadbent, Allan Corduner,
Timothy Spall, Lesley Manville, Ron
Cook, Wendy Nottingham, Kevin
McKidd, Shirley Henderson, Dorothy
Atkinson, Martin Savage
© 1999 Untitled 98 Limited
Thin Man Films Limited, The
Greenlight Fund, Newmarket Capital
Group present
a Simon Channing-Williams
production
a film by Mike Leigh
160 mins 22 seconds
S&S March 2000 p.36-37, 55

Toy Story 2

(1999)
Buena Vista International (UK) – 4
February
(U) US
Dir John Lasseter
with the voices Tom Hanks, Tim
Allen, Joan Cusack, Kelsey Grammar,
Don Rickles, Jim Varney, Wallace
Shawn, John Ratzenberger, Annie
Potts, Wayne Knight
© Disney Enterprises Inc/Pixar
Animation Studios
Walt Disney Pictures presents
a Pixar Animation Studios film
94 mins 45 seconds
S&S March 2000 p.56-57

Trick

(1999) - 5 May
Millivres Multimedia – 5 May
(15) US
Dir Jim Fall
with Christian Campbell, John Paul
Pitoc, Tori Spelling, Lorri Bagley,
Brad Beyer, Steve Hayes, Clinton
Leupp, Eric Bernat, Kevin
Chamberlin, Joey Dedio
©1999. Roadside Attractions, LLC
GM - Good machine International
a Roadside Attractions/Good
Machine production
a Jim Fall film
89 mins 1 second
S&S May 2000 p.63

Tumbleweeds

(1999)
Entertainment Film Distributors Ltd
– 3 March
(12) US
Dir Gavin O'Connor
with Janet McTeer, Jay O. Sanders,
Kimberly J. Brown, Gavin O'Connor,
Laurel Holloman, Lois Smith,
Michael J. Pollard, Ashley Buccille,
Cody McMains, Linda Porter
©ALH Entertainment, Inc
Spanky Pictures presents
a Solaris production in association
with River One Films
a Gavin O'Connor film
102 mins 27 seconds
S&S March 2000 p.57-58

28 Days

(2000)
Columbia TriStar Films (UK) – 16
June
(15) US
Dir Betty Thomas
with Sandra Bullock, Viggo
Mortensen, Dominic West, Diane
Ladd, Elizabeth Perkins, Steve
Buscemi, Alan Tudyk, Michael
O'Malley, Azura Skye, Reni Santoni
©2000 Columbia Pictures Industries,
Inc
Columbia Pictures presents
a Tall Trees production
A Betty Thomas Film
103 mins 52 seconds
S&S June 2000 p.57-58

24 Hours in London

(2000)
Blue Dolphin Film & Video – 14 July
(18) UK
Dir Alexander Finbow
with Gary Olsen, Anjela Lauren
Smith, Sara Stockbridge, John
Benfield, Amita Dhiri, Tony London,
David Sonnenthal, Luke Garrett,
Wendy Cooper, John Sharian
©1999. 24 Hours in London PLC
One World Films presents a film by
Alexander Finbow
90 mins 8 seconds
S&S August 2000 p.58-59

U-571

(2000)
Entertainment Film Distributors Ltd
– 2 June
(12) US
Dir Johathan Mostow
with Matthew McConaughey, Bill
Paxton, Harvey Keitel, Jon Bon Jovi,
Jake Weber, Dave Power, Derk
Cheetwood, Matthew Settle, Erik
Palladino, David Keith
©2000. Universal Studios
Studio Canal+
Universal Pictures present in
association with Dino De Laurentiis
a Jonathan Mostow film
116 mins 6 seconds
S&S July 2000 p.57-58

Unbreakable

(2000)
Buena Vista International (UK) –
29 December
(12) US
Dir M. Night Shyamalan
with Bruce Willis, Samuel L. Jackson,
Robin Wright Penn, Spencer Treat
Clark, Charlayne Woodard, Eamonn
Walker, Leslie Stefanson, William
Turner, Johnny Hiram Jamison,
Michaelia Carroll
© 2000. Touchstone Pictures
Touchstone Pictures presents a
Blinding Edge/Barry Mendel
production
an M. Night Shyamalan film
106 mins 31 seconds
S&S February 2001 p.54-55

Urban Legends Final Cut

(2000)
Columbia TriStar Films (UK) – 1

December
(15) US/France
Dir John Ottman
with Jennifer Morrison, Matthew
Davis, Hart Bochner, Joseph
Lawrence, Anson Mount, Anthony
Anderson, Eva Mendes, Michael
Bacall, Jessica Cauffiel, Marco
Hofschneider
© 2000. Phoenix Pictures Inc.
Phoenix Pictures presents a Neal H.
Moritz/Gina Matthews production
a John Ottman film
In association with Canal+ D.A.
98 mins 14 seconds
S&S January 2001 p.60-61

La Veuve de Saint-Pierre
aka: The Widow of Saint-Pierre,
(English title)
(2000)
FilmFour Distributors – 4 August
(15) France/Canada
Dir Patrice Leconte
with Juliette Binoche, Daniel Auteuil,
Emir Kusturica, Michel Duchaussoy,
Philippe Magnan, Christian
Charmetant, Philippe Du Janerand,
Reynald Bouchard, Ghyslain
Tremblay, Marc Béland
©2000. Epithète Films/France 3
Cinéma/France 2
Cinéma/Cinémaginaire Inc./
Production Veuve Saint-Pierre Inc.
Gilles Legrand & Frédéric Brillion
present a French/Canadian co-
production
Epithète Films, Cinémaginaire,
France 3 Cinéma, France 2 Cinéma
with the participation of Universal
Pictures (France)/Centre National de
la Cinématographie/Canal+/Téléfilm
Canada/SODEC Société
développement des entreprises
culturelles - Québec/Québec Crédit
d'impôt cinéma et télévision
with the collaboration of Radio
Canada
a film by Patrice Leconte
112 mins 15 seconds
Subtitles
S&S September 2000 p.56-57

The Virgin Suicides
(1999)
Pathé Distribution – 19 May
(15) US
Dir Sofia Coppola
with James Woods, Kathleen Turner,
Kirsten Dunst, Josh Hartnett, A.J.
Cook, Hanna Hall, Leslie Hayman,
Chelse Swain, Anthony DeSimone,
Lee Kagan
© 1999. Virgin Suicides, LLC
American Zoetrope presents a Muse

production in association with
Eternity Pictures
96 mins 55 seconds
S&S June 2000 p.59

The Way of the Gun
(2000)
Momentum Pictures – 17 November
(18) US
Dir Christopher McQuarrie
with Ryan Phillippe, Benicio Del
Toro, Juliette Lewis, Taye Diggs, Nicky
Katt, Geoffrey Lewis, Dylan Kussman,
Scott Wilson, Kristin Lehman, James
Caan
© 2000. Artisan Film Investors Trust
Artisan Entertainment presents a
Aqaba production
119 mins 15 seconds
S&S December 2000 p.56-57

The Wedding Tackle
(2000)
Ratpack Films Limited – 11 August
(15) UK
Dir Rami Dvir
with Adrian Dunbar, James Purefoy,
Tony Slattery, Neil Stuke, Leslie
Grantham, Victoria Smurfit, Susan
Vidler, Amanda Redman, Martin
Armstrong, Sara Stockbridge,
© 1999. Blackberry Ltd.
a Viking Films production
92 mins 54 seconds
S&S September 2000 p.57

Whatever Happened to
Harold Smith?
(1999)
United International Pictures (UK)
Ltd – 10 March
(15) UK
Dir Peter Hewitt
with Tom Courtenay, Michael Legge,
Laura Fraser, Stephen Fry, Charlotte
Roberts, Amanda Root, Lulu, David
Thewlis, Charlie Hunnam, Matthew
Rhys
©1999. Intermedia Film Equities
Limited
Arts Council of England
Yorkshire Media Production Agency
Part funded by the European
Regional Development Fund
95 mins 54 seconds
S&S March 2000 p.58-59

What Lies Beneath
(2000)
20th Century Fox (UK) – 20 October
(15) US
Dir Robert Zemeckis
with Harrison Ford, Michelle Pfeiffer,
Diana Scarwid, Victoria Bidewell, Joe
Morton, James Remar, Miranda Otto,

Amber Valletta, Katharine Towne,
Dennison Samaroo
© 2000. Twentieth Century Fox Film
Corporation and DreamWorks LLC
Twentieth Century Fox and
DreamWorks Pictures present an
Imagemovers production
129 mins 52 seconds
S&S November 2000 p.65

When the Sky Falls
(2000)
20th Century Fox (UK) – 16 June
(18) Ireland/US
Dir John MacKenzie
with Joan Allen, Patrick Bergin, Liam
Cunningham, Kevin McNally, Jimmy
Smallhorne, Gerard Flynn, Jason
Barry, Pete Postlethwaite, Des
McAleer, Owen Roe
© 1999 Irish Screen Pictures
Sky Pictures presents in association
with Irish Screen, Bord Scannán na
hÉireann/The Irish Film Board and
Redeemable Features
an Irish Screen production
a film by John Mackenzie
107 mins 4 seconds
S&S July 2000 p.58-59

Where the Heart Is
(2000)
20th Century Fox (UK) – 17
November
(12) US
Dir Matt Williams
with Natalie Portman, Ashley Judd,
Stockard Channing, Joan Cusack,
James Frain, Dylan Bruno, Keith
David, Sally Field, Richard Jones, Ray
Prewitt
© 2000. Twentieth Century Fox Film
Corporation
Twentieth Century Fox presents a
Wind Dancer production
119 mins 51 seconds
S&S December 2000 p.57-58

The Whole Nine Yards
(2000)
Warner Bros Distributors (UK) – 19
May
(15) US
Dir Jonathan Lynn
with Bruce Willis, Matthew Perry,
Rosanna Arquette, Michael Clarke
Duncan, Natasha Henstridge,
Amanda Peet, Kevin Pollack, Harland
Williams, Carmen Ferlan, Serge
Christianssens
© 2000 Nine Yards Productions, LLC
Morgan Creek Productions, Inc and
Franchise Pictures, LLC present
a Rational Packaging Films
production in association with

Lansdown Films
98 mins 53 seconds
S&S July 2000 p.59

Wonder Boys

(2000)
United International Pictures (UK)
Ltd – 3 November
(15) US/Germany/UK/Japan
Dir Chris Hanson
with Michael Douglas, Tobey
Maguire, Frances McDormand,
Robert Downey Jr, Katie Holmes, Rip
Torn, Richard Knox, Jane Adams,
Michael Cavadias, Richard Thomas
© 2000 MFF Feature Film
Productions GmbH & Co. KG
Mutual Film Company and
Paramount Pictures present
a Scott Rudin/Curtis Hanson
production
Produced in association with BBC,
Marubeni/Toho-Towa and Tele
München
In association with MFF Feature
Film Productions GmbH & Co. KG
111 mins 25 seconds
S&S December 2000 p.58-59

Wonderland

(1999)
United International Pictures (UK)
Ltd – 14 January
(15) UK
Dir Michael Winterbottom
with Shirley Henderson, Gina McKee,
Molly Parker, Ian Hart, John Simm,
Stuart Townsend, Kika Markham,
Jack Shepherd, Enzo Cilenti, Sarah-
Jane Potts
© 1999. PolyGram Films (UK)
Limited
Universal Pictures International and
BBC Films present a Kismet Film
Company
and Revolution Films production
Developed with the assistance of
British Screen Finance Limited,
London, England
a Kismet Film Company and
Revolution Films production for
PolyGram Filmed
Entertainment and BBC Films
108 mins 42 seconds
S&S January 2000 p.62

The Wood

(1999)
United International Pictures (UK)
Ltd – 28 January
(15) US
Dir Rick Famuyiwa
with Taye Diggs, Omar Epps, Richard
T. Jones, Sean Nelson, Trent
Cameron, Duane Finley, Malinda

Williams, DeAundre Bonds, Sanaa
Lathan, Lisa Raye
© 1999. Paramount Pictures
Corporation
Paramount Pictures presents an
MTV Films production in
association with Bona
Fide Productions
Developed in association with The
Sundance Institute
106 mins 40 seconds
S&S February 2000 p.59

Xiao Wu

(1997)
Institute of Contemporary Arts – 11
February
(not submitted) China/Japan
Dir Zhang-ke Jia
with Hongwei Wang, Hongjian Hao,
Baitao Zuo, Jinrei Ma, Junying Liu,
Yonghao Liang, Qunyan An,
Dongdong Jiang, Long Zhao, Reiren
Wang
©1997   Radiant Advertising
Beijng Film Academy
Hu Tong Communication & Radiant
Advertising
jointly present
presented by Wang Han Bing
produced by Li Kit Ming & Jia
Zhang Ke
a film by Jia Zhang Ke
distributed by Hu Tong
Communication
113 mins
S&S March 2000 p.59

X-Men

(2000)
20th Century Fox (UK) – 18 August
(12) US
Dir Bryan Singer
with Hugh Jackman, Patrick Stewart,
Ian McKellen, Famke Janssen, James
Marsden, Halle Berry, Anna Paquin,
Tyler Mane, Ray Park, Rebecca
Romijn-Stamos
© 2000. Twentieth Century Fox Film
Corporation
Twentieth Century Fox presents in
association with Marvel
Entertainment Group
The Donners' Company/Bad Hat
Harry production
a Bryan Singer film
104 mins 12 seconds
S&S September 2000 p.59

The Yards

(2000)
FilmFour Distributors – 10
November
(15) US
Dir James Gray

with Ellen Burstyn, Faye Dunaway,
Joaquin Phoenix, Charlize Theron,
Mark Wahlberg, James Caan, Victor
Argo, Victor Arnold, Steve Lawrence,
Tomas Milian
© 2000. Miramax Film Corp.
FilmFour/Miramax Films
Miramax Films presents
a James Gray film
a Paul Webster/Industry
Entertainment production
115 mins 41 seconds
S&S December 2000 p.59

bfi * You Only Live Once

(1937)
BFI Collections – 18 February
(15) US
Dir Fritz Lang
with Henry Fonda, Sylvia Sidney,
Barton MacLane, Jean Dixon, William
Gargan, Jerome Cowan, Chic Sale,
Margaret Hamilton, Warren Hymer,
Guinn Williams
United Artists
Walter Wanger Productions
87 mins
Monthly Film Bulletin v4. n39. March
1937 p.63

SPECIALISED GOODS AND SERVICES

This section has been divided into four parts. The first part features services specialising in actors, audiences and casting. The second lists costume, make-up and prop services. The third section is a general section of specialised goods and services for the film, television and video industries including such items as film stock suppliers, effects units and music services. The final section combines legal and business services for the industry

Actors, Audiences and Casting

Actors Inc
14 Dean Street
London W1
Tel: 020 7437 4417
Fax: 020 7 437 4221
Philip Ball

Avalon Publicity Limited
4a Exmoor Street
Lonodn W10 6BD
Tel: 020 7598 7222
Fax: 020 7598 7223
email: edt@avalonuk.com
Edward Thomson
Provides audiences for TV productions

Bromley Casting (Film & TV Extras Agency)
77 Widmore Road
Bromley BR1 3AA
Tel: 020 8466 8239
Fax: 020 8466 8239
email: admin@bromleycasting.tv
Website: www.showcall.co.uk
Website: www.bromleycasting.tv
Simon Allen
Providing quality background artists to the UK film and TV industry

Central Casting Inc
13-14 Dean Street
London W1
Tel: 020 7437 4211
Fax: 020 7 437 4221
M.Maco

Dolly Brook Casting Agency
52 Sandford Road
East Ham
London E6 3QS
Tel: 020 8472 2561/470 1287
Fax: 020 8552 0733
Russell Brook
Specialises in walk-ons, supporting artistes, extras and small parts for films, television, commercials, modelling, photographic, voice-overs, pop videos

Downes Agency
96 Broadway
Bexleyheath
Kent DA6 7DE
Tel: 020 8304 0541
Fax: 020 8301 5591
Agents representing presenters and actors experienced in the fields of presentations, documentaries, commentaries, narrations, television dramas, feature films, industrial videos, training films, voice-overs, conferences and commercials

Lip Service Casting
4 Kingly Street
London W1B 5PE
Tel: 020 7734 3393
Fax: 020 7734 3373
email: bookings@lipservice.co.uk
Website: www.lipserve.co.uk
Susan Mactavish
Voiceover agency for actors, and voiceover casting agency

Marcus Stone Casting
Georgian House
5 The Pavilions
Brighton BN2 1RA
Tel: 01273 670053
Fax: 01273 670053
Supplies television, film extras. Up to 1,000 extras available for crowd scenes

Costumes, Make-up and Props

Angels - The Costumiers
40 Camden Street
London NW1 OEN
Tel: 020 7 387 0999
Fax: 020 7 383 5603
email: angels@angels.uk.com
Website: www.angels.uk.com
Richard Green
Chairman: Tim Angel OBE
Contact: Jonathan Lipman
World's largest Costume Hire Company. Extensive ranges covering every historical period, including contemporary clothing, civil and military uniforms. Full in-house ladies and men's making service, millinery department, jewellry, glasses and watch hire. Branches also in Shaftesbury Avenue and Paris. Additional services:- experinced personal costumiers, designers office space, reference library and shipping department

Angels Wigs
40 Camden Street
London NW1 0EN
Tel: 020 7 387 0999
Fax: 020 7 383 5603
email: wigs@angels.uk.com
Ben Stanton
All types of styles of wigs and hairpieces in either human hair bespoke or synthetic ready-to-wear. Large stocks held, ready to dress, for hire including legal wigs. In house craftsmen to advise on style or period. Facial hair made to order for sale

Cabervans
Caberfeidh
Cloch Road
Gourock
Nr. Glasgow PA19 1BA
Tel: 01475 638775
Fax: 01475 638775
Make-up and wardrobe units, dining coaches, motorhomes, 3 & 4 bay American artistes Unit cars, minibuses and 77 seat coaches

Hirearchy Classic and Contemporary Costume

45 Palmerston Road
Boscombe
Bournemouth
Dorset BH1 4HW
Tel: 01202 394465
Website: www.hirearchy.co.uk
Specialising in the hire of ladies and gents costumes from medieval to present day. Also accessories, make-up, wigs, militaria jewellery, textiles and luggage

Hothouse Models & Effects

10 St Leonard's Road
Park Royal
London NW10 6SY
Tel: 020 8961 3666
Fax: 020 8961 3777
email: info@hothousefx.co.uk
Website: www.hothousefx.co.uk
Jez Clarke
All models, props and effects for film and television

The Image Co

Pinewood Studios
Iver Heath
Buckinghamshire SLO ONH
Tel: 01753 651700
John Prentice

Wardrobe costume badging service, prop and promotional clothing

Kevin Jones, Freelance Costume Assistant & Designer

32 Austen Walk
West Bromwich
West Midlands B71 1RD
Tel: (0121) 588 6801
Fax: (0121) 588 6801
email: kevinjones@onmail.co.uk
Mobile: 07775 623738
London Tel: 020 8977 6416
Costume Assistant, Designer, dresser for films television, commercials, pop videos, promotions, product launches, fashion shows, theatre

Neal Scanlan Studio

Elstree Film Studios
Borehamwood
Hertfordshire WD6 1JG
Tel: 0208 324 2620
Fax: 0208 324 2774
Animatronics and special makeup effects

Robert Hale Flowers

Interior and Flower Designers
8 Lovell Street
York YO123 1BO
Tel: 01904 613044

Contact: Robert Hale
Suppliers and designers of interior flower decoration

Ten Tenths

106 Gifford Street
London N1 0DF
Tel: 020 7607 4887
Fax: 020 7609 8124
email: mike@tentenths.co.uk
Website: www.tentenths.co.uk
Mike Hallows
Props service specialising in vehicles (cars, bikes, boats and planes) ranging from 1901 to present day - veteran, vintage, classic, modern - with complementary wardrobe facilities

Film Services

Aerial Cameras Systems Ltd
Shepperton Studios
Shepperton
Middx TW17 0QD
Tel: 01932 564885

Agfa-Gevaert
Motion Picture Division
27 Great West Road
Brentford
Middx TW8 9AX
Tel: 020 8231 4301
Fax: 020 8231 4315
Major suppliers to the Motion
Picture and Television Industries of
Polyester based Colour Print Film
and Optical Sound Recording Film

Any Effects
64 Weir Road
London SW19 8UG
Tel: 020 8944 0099
Fax: 020 8944 6989
email: jules@anyeffects.com
Website: www.anyeffects.com
Contact: Julianne Pellicci
Managing Director: Tom Harris
Mechanical (front of camera) special
effects. Pyrotechnics: simulated
explosions, bullet hits. Fine models for
close up camera work. Weather: rain,
snow, fog, wind. Breakaways: shatterglass,
windows, bottles, glasses, collapsing
furniture, walls, floors. Specialised
engineering rigs and propmaking service

Riky Ash Falling For You
c/o 65 Britania Avenue
Nottingham NG6 OEA
Tel: 0115 849 3470
Website: www.fallingforyou.co.uk
Television and Film Stuntman, Stunt
Coordinator, Action Sequence Director
with over 250 television and film
credits. Extensive work for TV, feature
films, commercials, non-broadcast
video, promotions and advertising

Audio Interactive Ltd
Pinewood Studios
Iver Heath
Buckinghamshire SLO ONH
Tel: 01753 651700
Dick Joseph
Sound for the Multimedia industry -
two fully soundproofed production
room, on-site composers and a
library of 30,000 sound effects

Charlie Bennett Underwater Productions
114 Addison Gardens
West Kensington
London W14 0DS
Tel: 020 7263 952
email: chazben@aol.com
Ifafa, Main Street
Ashby Parva
Leicestershire LE17 5HU
Tel: 01455 209 405
Mobile: 07702 263 952
Contact: Charlie Bennett
Underwater services to the film and
television industry, including
experienced qualified diving
personnel and equipment;
underwater film and video, stills
photography and scuba instruction.
Advice, logistics and support offered
on an international scale. Registered
HSE Diving contractor

Bionic Productions Ltd
Pinewood Studios
Iver Heath
Buckinghamshire SLO ONH
Tel: 01753 655885
Fax: 01753 656844
On-site computer playback, and
computer hire

Bonded Services
Aerodrome Way
Cranford Lane
Hounslow
Middx TW5 9QB
Tel: 020 8897 7973
Fax: 020 8897 7979
Inventory management, worldwide
freight, courier services, technical
facilities including film checking and
tape duplication, storage and
distribution

Boulton-Hawker Films
Hadleigh
near Ipswich
Suffolk IP7 5BG
Tel: 01473 822235
Fax: 01473 824519
Wide range of educational videos and
CD-ROMs. Subject catalogues on
request

C I Travel
Shepperton Studios
Shepperton, Studio 16
Middx TW17 0QD
Tel: 01932 572417
Fax: 01932 568989
email: steve@citravel.co.uk
Website: www.citravel.co.uk
Steve Garner
Transport and travel services

Camera Associates Ltd
Pinewood Studios
Iver Heath
Buckinghamshire SLO ONH
Tel: 01753 631007
Dave Cooper
Film video and grip hire service.
Workshop and repair service also
available on the Pinewood lot

celluloid dreams
6 Silver Place
London W1F OJS
Tel: 01273 729 115
Fax: 01273 729 115
email: celluloiddreams@hotmail.com
Website:
homepage.mac.com/celluloiddreams
Utilising a prodigious hoard of
archive treasures, celluloid dreams
provides bespoke replica publicity
posters for virtually any film. Also
specialise in recreating classic posters
to any new design specification from
postcard prints to quadras

Cinetron Desgin
Shepperton Studios
Shepperton
Middx TW17 0QD
Tel: 01932 572611
Fax: 01932 568989
Design

Concert Lights UK
c/o Elstree Film Studios
Borehamwood
Herts WD6 1JG
Tel: 020 8953 1600
Work on Who Wants to be a
Millionnaire for Celador Productions
and a number of TV shows

Connections Communications Centre Ltd
Palingswick House
241 King Street
Hammersmith
London W6 9LP
Tel: 020 8741 1767
Fax: 020 8563 1934
email: @cccmedia.co.uk
Website: www.cccmedia.co.uk
Jacqueline Davis
A registered charity producing
promotional and educational videos
for the voluntary sector. Currently in
production Travelling Forward a 25
minute documentary commissioned
by the Thalidomide Society

Cool Million
Mortimer House
46 Sheen Lane
London SW14 8LP
Tel: 020 8878 7887
Fax: 020 6878 8687
Dot O'Rourke

Promotional merchandising, launch
parties and roadshows

De Wolfe Music

Shropshire House
2nd Floor East
11/20 Capper Street
London WC13 6JA
Tel: 020 7631 3600
Fax: 020 7631 3700
email: dewolfe_Music@
Compuserve.com
Warren De Wolfe, Alan Howe
World's largest production music
library. Represents 40 composers for
commissions, television and film
scores. Offices worldwide, sound FX
department, 3 x 24-track recording
studies all with music to picture
facilities, also digital editing

Diverse Design

Gorleston Street
London W14 8XS
Tel: 020 7603 4567
Fax: 020 7603 2148
email: danielcr@diverse.co.uk
Website: www.diverse.co.uk
Daniel Creasey (Head of Design)
Graphic design for television
including titles, format and content
graphics. Recent work: The Knock,
Cor Blimey, Reach for the Moon,
Transworld Sport, Real Women 2,
Dispatches, Badger, Lawyers, Behind
the Crime, Hero of the Hour

Dynamic Mounts International

Shepperton Studios
Shepperton
Middx TW17 0QD
Tel: 01932 572348
Fax: 01932 568989
email: dmi@mega3.tv
Website: www.mega3.tv
Dan Gillham
Camera equipment

EOS Electronics AV

EOS House
Weston Square
Barry
South Glamorgan CF63 2YF
Tel: 01446 741212
Fax: 01446 746120
Specialist manufacturers of video
animation, video time laspsing and
video archiving equipment.
Products: Supertoon Low Cost
School Animation System, AC 580
Lo-band Controller, BAC900
Broadcast Animation Controller,
LCP3 Compact Disc, Listening Posts

ETH Screen Music

17 Pilrig Street
Edinburgh EH6 5AN
Tel: 0131 553 2721
Harald Tobermann
Producer and publisher of original
music for moving images. Complete
creative team - composers, arrangers,
musicians

Eureka Location Management

51 Tonsley Hill
London SW18 1BW
Tel: 020 8870 4569
Fax: 020 8871 2158
Suzannah Holt
Finds and manages locations for film
and television in Britain and abroad.
Offices in London and Toronto

The Film Stock Centre Blanx

68-70 Wardour Street
London W1F OTB
Tel: 020 7494 2244
Fax: 020 7287 2040
email: sales@fscblanx.co.uk
Rob Flood
A "Kodak @" reseller of motion picture
film stock and stills film, Sony and all
major brands of professional video

tape stock, film consumables,
professional audio products and data
media. Open weekdays 8.30am to 7pm.
Emergency callout service 0831 701407

Film Vault Search Service

Unit 7
The Boundary
Wheatley Road
Garsington
Oxford OX44 9EJ
Tel: 01865 361 000
Fax: 01865 361 555
email: mail@filmvault.co.uk
Website: www.filmvault.co.uk
Steve Cummings
The largest deleted video search
service in the country. No charges for
deposit or 'search fees'. Every video
sold is checked against faults and is
professionally cleaned, comes with
the correct copyright, BBFC
certificate and full guarantee.

Focus International Transport Ltd

Shepperton Studios
Shepperton
Middx TW17 0QD
Tel: 01932 572339
Fax: 01932 568989
Transport services

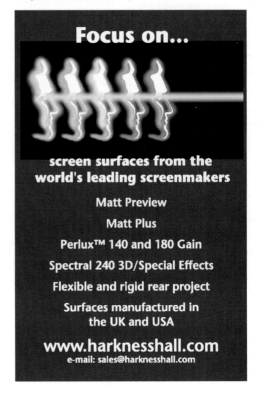

Harkness Hall Ltd

The Gate Studios
Station Road
Borehamwood
Herts WD6 1DQ
Tel: 020 8953 3611
Fax: 020 8207 3657
email: sales@harknesshall.com
Ian Sim, Robert Pickett
Projection screens and complete
screen systems, fixed and portable,
front or rear, flat, curved, flying, roller
etc. Curtain tracks, festoons,
cycloramas, raise and lower
equipment, stage equipment,
installation and maintenance

Heliphotos Aerial Photography

Elstree Aerodrome
Elstree
Hertfordshire
Tel: 0208 207 6042
Aerial photography

Kodak Limited

Entertainment Imaging
PO Box 66, Station Road
Hemel Hempstead
Herts HP1 1JU
Tel: 01442 845945
Fax: 01442 844458
Website: www.kodak.com/go/motion
Customer Service
Suppliers of the full range of Kodak
colour negative and print films,
including the new family of Vision
colour negative films

Little Cinema Company Limited

72 New Bond Street
London W1S 1RR
Tel: 020 7385 5521
Fax: 020 7385 5524
email: sales@littlecinema.co.uk
Joanne van Praagh
Suppliers and installers of digital
projection, sound, and control
systems for screening rooms and
private cinemas worldwide.

MBS Underwater Video Specialists

1 Orchard Cottages
Coombe Barton
Shobrooke, Crediton
Devon
Tel: 01363 775 278
Fax: 01363 775 278
email: mbscm@mail.eclipse.co.uk
Website: www.eclipse.co.uk.mbs
Contact: Colin Munro
MBS provides underwater stills

photography and videography
services, specialising in underwater
wildlife shots. We can provide full
HSE registered dive teams for UK
based work, and cover all aspects of
diving safety and support, vessel
servicing and specialist underwater
equipment supply

Media Education Agency

5A Queens Parade
Brownlow Road
London N11 2DN
Tel: 020 8888 4620
David Lusted
Consultancy, lectures and teacher in-
service education (INSET) in film,
television and media studies.
Contacts include academics,
educationists, broadcasters, writers
and actors

Midland Fire Protection Services

256 Foleshill Road
Coventry CV6 5AY
Tel: 024 7668 5252 (mobile) 07836
651408
Fax: 024 7663 7575
Robin Crane
Specialists in fire and rescue cover for
location, studio and stage work.
Special services, firefighters, action
vehicles, fully equipped fire and
rescue appliances, 5,000 gallons of
water storage systems available,
throughout the UK 24 hour service

Moving Image Touring Exhibition Service (MITES)

Foundation For Art & Creative
Technology (FACT)
Bluecoat Chambers
Liverpool L1 3BX
Tel: 0151 707 2881
Fax: 0151 707 2150
email: mites@fact.co.uk
Website: www.mites.org.uk
Simon Bradshaw
Extensive exhibition equipment
resource, DVD authoring and
production, archive and digital
mastering facility. Courses for artists,
gallery curators, technicians and
exhibitors concerned with the
commissioning and presentation of
moving image art works. Also
development, advice, consultation
services

Oxford Scientific Films (OSF)

Lower Road
Long Hanborough
Oxford OX29 8LL

Tel: 01993 881 881
Fax: 01993 882 808/883969
email: enquires@osf.uk.com
Website: www.osf.uk.com
Sean Morris
45-49 Mortimer Street
London W1N 7TD
Tel: 020 7323 0061
Fax: 020 7323 0161
Independent production company
specialising in blue-chip natural history
documentaries for broadcast. 30 years
of experience and innovation in
specialist camera techniques. Extensive
stills and stock footage libraries

Pirate Motion Control

St Leonards Road
London NW10 6ST
Tel: 020 8930 5000
Fax: 020 8930 5001
email: help@pirate.co.uk
Website: http://www.pirate.co.uk
Michael Ganss
Motion Control Studio for 16mm
film and video. 12 axis rig & 3
motion controlled lighting dimmer
circuits. Call for showreel

ProDigital Audio Services

3 George Street
West Bay
Dorset DT6 4EY
Tel: 01308 422 866
Sound equipment, service and
maintenance. Specialises in location
sound equipment for the film and
television industry - particularly DAT
recorders

Radcliffes Transport Services

3-9 Willow Lane
Willow Lane Industrial Estate
Mitcham
Surrey CR4 4NA
Tel: 020 8687 2344
Fax: 020 8687 0997
Ken Bull
Specialist transport specifically for
the film and television industry, both
nationally and internationally. Fleet
ranges from transit vans to 40' air
ride articulated vehicles with
experienced staff

The Screen Company

182 High Street
Cottenham
Cambridge CB4 8RX
Tel: 01954 250139
Fax: 01954 252005
Pat Turner
Manufacture, supply and installation
of all types of front and rear

projection screens for video, slide, film and OHP

Security Archives Ltd
1-8 Capitol Park
Capitol Way
London NW9 0EQ
Tel: 020 8205 5544
Fax: 020 8200 1130
Secure storage for film, video and audio tape in bomb-proof vaults with thermohydrographic controls and Halon fire suppression. 24hr collection and delivery, computerised, bar-coded management and tracking of clients' material

Snow-Bound
37 Oakwood Drive
Heaton
Bolton BL1 5EE
Tel: 01204 841285
Fax: 01204 841285
Suppliers of artificial snow and the machinery to apply it for the creation of snow/winter scenes. The product is life-like (not poly beads or cotton wool) adheres to any surface and is fire-retardent, non-toxic and safe in use, and eco-friendly

Stanley Productions
147 Wardour Street
London W1F 8WD
Tel: 020 7494 4545
Fax: 020 7437 2126
Richard Hennessy
Europe
s largest distributor of video tape and equipment. Full demonstration facilities with independent advice on suitable equipment always available

Studio Art
Elstree Film Studios
Boreham Wood
Hertfordshire WD6 1JG
Tel: 0208 324 2600
Fax: 0208 324 2601
Danny Rogers
Specialist manufacturers of signs, neon, props and graphics for features and television

Visionworks Internet Ltd
13 Chartfield Avenue
London SW15 6DT
Tel: 020 8789 4254
Fax: 020 8785 0520
Website:
www.visionworksinternet.com
Sandy Knight
Web design from basic level up to e-commerce

Woodbridge Productions Ltd
PO Box 123
Hounslow
London TW4 7EX
Tel: 020 8574 7778
Fax: 0208 574 7778
Covers all aspects of cosmetic and prosthetic make-up artistry

Wrap it up
116a Acton Lane,
Chiswick
London W4 5HH
Tel: 020 8995 3357 (Mobiles 0973 198154)
Fax: 020 82348 3030
Wrap it up provides production services which include transcription, post production scripts, voice scripts and logging of rushes for production companies. Recent work: September Films - Teenagers British lifestyles - Transcription and Post Production Scripts. Horizon BBC - Transcription. Dennis and Gnasher, Tony Collingwood Productions - Voice Scripts

Zooid Pictures Limited
66 Alexander Road
London N19 5PQ
Tel: 020 7281 2407
Fax: 020 7281 2404
email: pictures@zooid.co.uk
Website: www.zooid.co.uk
Richard Philpott
For over 20 years, Zooid has been a one-stop media resources supplier and researcher for all copyright materials including film/video, stills, illustration, animation and sound, from archives, libraries, agencies, private collections and museums worldwide, for use in film, television, book publishing, CD-Rom, multimedia, presentations and on-line services. Zooid manage all aspects from first briefing through to licensing. Zooid use advanced digital technologies and license their management system, Picture Desk, to leading international publishers

Legal and Business Services

Ashurst Morris Crisp
Broadwalk House
5 Appold Street
London EC2A 2HA
Tel: 0207 638 1111
Fax: 0207 972 7990
email: film.tv@ashursts.com
Website: www.ashursts.com
Tony Ghee, Tasha Stanford, Andrea Fessler, Charlotte Douglas, Vanessa Bertelli
Leading City law firm with a young and progressive media and telecommunications team. Advice is provided on all aspects of the film and television industry, including corporate, employment, property and tax issues. Clients include leading national broadcasters, cable network operators and a number of small independents

Barclays Bank Media Banking Centre
27 Soho Square
London W1A 4WA
Tel: 020 7445 5773
Fax: 020 7445 5802
email: geoff.l.salmon@barclayscorporate.com
Geoff Salmon
Large business centre providing a comprehensive range of banking services to all aspects of the film and television industry

Deloitte & Touche
Hill House
1 Little New Street
London EC4A 3TR
Tel: 020 7936 3000
Fax: 020 7583 8517
Website: www.deloitte.co.uk
Gavin Hamilton-Deeley
Advisors to film, television and broadcasting organisations. Business plans and financial models for companies, tax planning and business advice for individuals, and information on legal and regulatory developments affecting the sector

Film Finances
1-11 Hay Hill
Berkeley Square
London W1X 7LF
Tel: 020 7629 6557
Fax: 020 7491 7530
G J Easton, J Shirras, D Wilder, H Penallt Jones

Provide completion guarantees for the film and television industry

Henry Hepworth
Media Law Solicitors
5 John Street
London WC1N 2HH
Tel: 020 7242 7999
Fax: 020 7242 7988
A new specialist media and intellectual property practice with a distinctive high quality client base which is active across the entire spectrum of the copyright and intellectual property industries

The Media Law Partnership
187 Wardour Street
London W1V 3FA
Tel: 020 7479 7890
Fax: 020 7437 1558
email: mail@medialaw.uk.com
Adam Sutcliffe
Offers experience in all aspects of the negotiation and drafting of agreements for film production, film financing and international co-productions, with an emphasis on concise and effective documents, and a practical 'business affairs' approach to legal matters for all those involved in the film-making and distribution process

Nicholson Graham & Jones
110 Cannon Street
London EC4N 6AR
Tel: 020 7648 9000
Fax: 020 7648 9001
Selina Short, Communications
A City law firm and founder member of the international GlobaLex network in the UK, USA, Europe and the Far East. The Intellectual Property Group handles film and television production, financing and distribution, cable, satellite and telecommunications work, book and newspaper publishing, syndication, advertising, merchandising, sponsorship and sports law. Also advise on technology transfer, patent , trade mark, service mark, know-how arrangements and franchising as well as computer hardware and software agreements and all intellectual property copyright, moral and performers' right issues

Olswang
90 Long Acre
London WC2E 9TT
Tel: 020 7208 8888
Fax: 020 7208 8800
email: olsmail@olswang.co.uk

Website: www.olswang.co.uk
One of the UK's leading entertainment and media law firms. It provides specialist advice in all aspects of broadcasting, satellite, cable, multimedia, IT & telecommunications, media convergence and music law, to the European and US markets

Richards Butler
Beaufort House
15 St Botolph Street
London EC3A 7EE
Tel: 020 7247 6555
Fax: 020 7247 5091
email: law@richards-butler.com
Website: www.richardsbutler.com
Richard Philipps, Barry Smith, Stephen Edwards, Michael Maxtone-Smith
Richards Butler is an international law firm which has been associated with the media and entertainment industry for over 60 years

STUDIOS

BBC Television Centre Studios
Wood Lane
London W12 7RJ
Tel: 020 8700 100 883
email: bbcresources.co.uk
Website: bbcresources.com
National Call Centre
8 full-facility television studios
TC1 10,250 sq ft
TC3 8,000 sq ft
TC4 and TC8 8,000 sq ft (digital and widescreen capable)
TC6 8,000 sq ft (digital)
TC2, TC5 and TC7 3,500 sq ft

BBC South (Elstree)
BBC Elstree Centre
Clarendon Road
Borehanwood
Herts WD6 1JF
Tel: 020 8953 6100

Bray Studios
Down Place
Water Oakley
Windsor Road
Windsor SL4 5UG
Tel: 01628 622111
Fax: 01628 770381
Studio manager: Beryl Earl
STAGES
1 (sound) 955 sq metres
2 (sound) 948 sq metres
3 (sound) 238 sq metres
4 (sound) 167 sq metres
TELEVISION
Poirot 1999 - Dirty Tricks, Ruth Rendall, Unconditional Love, Shiner

Capital FX
20 Dering St
London W1S 1AJ
Tel: 020 7493 9998
Fax: 020 7493 9997
email: enquiries@capital.fx.co.uk
Website: www.capital.fx.co.uk
Graphic design and production, optical effects, film and laser subtitling

Capital Studios
Wandsworth Plain
London SW18 1ET
Tel: 020 8877 1234
Fax: 020 8877 0234
email: info@capitalstudios.co.uk

De Lane Lea Dean Street Studio
75 Dean Street
London W1V 5HA
Tel: 020 7439 1721/ 0171 432 3877
(direct line 24 hours)
Fax: 020 7437 0913
email: dll@delanelea.com
Website: www.delanelea.com
Studio manager: Dick Slade
1 86 sq metres
40x23x18 SYNC
lighting rig, film and TV make-up rooms, one wardrobe, one production office, full fitted kitchen

Ealing Studios
Ealing Studios
Ealing Green
London W5 5EP
Tel: 020 8567 6655
Fax: 020 8758 8658
email: ealingstudios@iname.com
Website: www.ealingstudios.co.uk
Bookings Office
Operations Department
STAGES
1 (silent) - bluescreen/motion control = area 232m2
2 (sound) - 864m2
3A (sound) 530m2
3B (sound) 530m2
3A/B 9combined) 1,080m2
4 (model stage silent) 390m2
5 (sound) 90m2
East is East
Mansfield Town
Notting Hill
Guest House Paradiso
TELEVISION
Bob Martin (Granada); *The Royle Family* (Granada); *Cor Blimey* (Company Pictures); *Perfect World* (Tiger Aspect); *Other People's Children* (BBC Drama), *High Heels and Low Life, Lucky Break*

Elstree Film and TV Studios
Shenley Road
Borehamwood
Hertfordshire WD6 1JG
Tel: 020 8953 1600
Fax: 020 8905 1135
email: info@elstreefilmtv.com
Website: www.elstreefilmtv.com
Director of studios: Neville Reid, Julie

Wicks
STAGES
1 (silent)
1 (sound) - 1465 sqm
2 (sound) - 1465 sqm
5 (silent) 503 sqm
6 (sound) - 357 sqm
7 (sound) - 462 sqm
8 (sound) - 700 sqm
9 (sound) - 700 sqm
tank 196 x 131 x 10
Alien Love Triangle, , Who Wants To Be A Millionaire, The Hoobs, The Tweenies

Granada Studios
Quay Street
Manchester M60 9EA
Tel: 0161 827 2020
Fax: 0161 832 8809

Halliford Studios
Manygate Lane
Shepperton
Middx TW17 9EG
Tel: 01932 226341
Fax: 01932 246336
email: sales@hallifordstudios.com
Website: hallifordfilmstudios..co.uk
Charlotte Goddard
STAGES
A 334 sq metres
B 223 sq metres

Holborn Studios
49/50 Eagle Wharf Road
London N1 7ED
Tel: 020 7490 4099
Fax: 020 7253 8120
email: reception@holborn-studios.co.uk
Website: www.holborn-studios.co.uk
Mike Hammond, Studio manager
STAGES
4 2,470 sq feet
6 2,940 sq feet
7 2,660 sq feet
18 roomsets 3,125 sq feet
Also eight fashion studios, set building, E6 lab, b/w labs, KJP in house, canal-side restaurant and bar.
Productions; National Lottery Stills; Advertisements for Scratch cards; Saatchis - photographer Dave Stewart

The Illustra Studio
14 Bateman Street
London W1V
Tel: 020 7437 9611
Fax: 020 7347 9611

Leavesden Studios
PO Box 3000
Leavesden
Herts WD2 7LT
Tel: 01923 685 060
Fax: 01923 685 061
email: info@Leavesden.com
Website: leavesdenstudios.com
Studio Manager: Daniel Dark
STAGES
A 32,076sq feet
B 28,116 sq feet
C 11,285 sq feet
D 11,808 sq feet
F 15,427 sq feet
G 14,036 sq feet
Flight Shed 1 35,776
Effects 15,367 sq feet
Back Lot 100 acres
180 degrees of clear and
uninterrupted horizon
Further 200,000 sq.ft of covered space
available
*GoldenEye, Mortal Kombat,
Annihilation; Sleepy Hollow, Star
Wars: Episode One - The Phantom
Menance, An Ideal Husband
Longitude, The Final Curtain, The
Beach, Harry Potter and the Sorcerer's
Stone*

London Studios
London Television Centre
Upper Ground
London SE1 9LT
Tel: 020 7620 1620
Fax: 020 7928 8405

The Maidstone Studios
Vinters Park
Maidstone
Kent ME14 5NZ
Tel: 01622 69111
Fax: 01622 684456
Janet Rayment
3 studios of varying size, the largest
being 6000 sq ft

Millennium Studios
Elstree Way
Herts WD6 1SF
Tel: 020 8236 1400
Fax: 020 8236 1444
email: joan@elstree-online.co.uk
Contact: Ronan Willson
'X' Stage: 327 sq metres sound stage
with flying grid and cyc. Camera
room, construction workshop,
wardrobe, dressing rooms, edit

rooms, hospitality suite and
production offices are also on site.
Recent productions: Carnival Films
'Bug' Series

Pinewood Studios
Pinewood Road
Iver Heath
Bucks SL0 0NH
Tel: 01753 651700
Fax: 01753 656844
Website: www.pinewood-
studios.co.uk
Managing Director: Steve Jaggs
STAGES
A 1,685 sq metres
(Tank: 12.2m x 9.2m x 2.5m)
B 827 sq metres
C 827 sq metres
D 1,685 sq metres
(Tank: 12.2m x 9.2m x 2.5m)
E 1,685 sq metres
(Tank: 12.2m x 9.2m x 2.5m)
F 698 sq metres
(Tank: 6.1m x 6.1m x 2.5m)
G 247 sq metres
H 300 sq metres
J 824 sq metres - dedicated TV Studio
K 824 sq metres
L 880 sq metres
M 880 sq metres
N/P 767 sq metres
R 1,780 sq metresß
S 1,789 sq metres
South Dock (silent)
1,547 sq metres
Albert R Broccoli 007 (silent) 4,223
sq metres (Tank: 90.5m x 22.3m x
2.7m Reservoir: 15.3m x 28.7m x
2.7m)
Large Process 454 sq metres
Exterior Lot 50 acres, comprising
formal gardens and lake, woods,
fields, concrete service roads and
squares
Exterior Tank 67.4m narrowing to
32m wide, 60.4 long, 1.06m deep.
Capacity 764,000 gallons. Inner Tank:
15.5m x 12.2m x 2.7m. Backing
73.2m x 18.3m
Largest outdoor tank in Europe
*Quills, Proof of Life, Tomb Raider,
Charlotte Gray, The Hours, Below, The
World is Not Enough, The Mummy
Returns, Enigma, Last Orders,
Revelation, Vertical Limit, My Wife Is
An Actress*
TELEVISION
*Dinotopia, Jack and the Beanstalk - the
Real Story, Hornblower, Thursday the
12th, Sam's Game, My Family, The
Merchant of Venice,
Hornblower II, One Foot In The Grave,
Wit, Queen Of Swords, The Play*

Riverside Studios
Crisp Road
Hammersmith
London W6 9RL
Tel: 020 8237 1000
Fax: 020 8237 1011
email: jonfawcett@
riversidestudios.co.uk
Website: www.riversidestudios.co.uk
Jon Fawcett
Studio One 529 sq metres
Studio Two 378 sq metres
Studio Three 130 sq metres
Plus preview cinema, various dressing
rooms, offices, café
TELEVISION
*T.F.I. Friday, 'Collins & McConies
Movie Club', Channel 4 Sitcom
Festival, 'This Morning with Richard
Not Judy', Top of the Pops* (2001)

Rotherhithe Studios
119 Rotherhithe Street
London SE16 4NF
Tel: 020 7231 2209
Fax: 020 7231 2119
Olivier Stockman, C Goodwin
STAGES
1 Rotherhithe 180 sq metres
Pre-production, construction, post-
production facilities, costume
making, props
The Nutcracker Story (IMAX 3D)
*The Children's Midsummer Night's
Dream*

Shepperton Studios
Studio Road
Shepperton
Middx TW17 0QD
Tel: 01932 562 611
Fax: 01932 568 989
email: admin@
sheppertonstudios.co.uk
Website: www.sheppertonstudios.
co.uk
Paul Olliver
STAGES
A 1,668 sq metres
B 1,115 sq metres
C 1,668 sq metres
D 1,115 sq metres
E 294 sq metres
F 294 sq metres
G 629 sq metres
H 2,660 sq metres
I 657 sq metres
J 1,394 sq metres
K 1,114 sq metres
L 604 sq metres
M 259 sq metres
T 261 sq metres
R 948 sq metres
S 929 sq metres

Shakespeare in Love; Elizabeth, Hilary & Jackie; Sliding Doors; Notting Hill; Love's Labour's Lost; End of the Affair, Possession, The Four Feathers, Ransom, Spy Game, Captain Corelli's Mandolin, Kavanagh Q.C.

Stonehills Studios
Shields Road
Gateshead
Tyne and Wear NE10 0HW
Tel: 0191 495 2244
Fax: 0191 495 2266
Studio Manager: Nick Walker
email: info@godnetwork.com
STAGES
1 1,433 sq feet
2   750 sq feet
The North's largest independent television facility comprising of Digital Betacam Edit Suite with the BVE 9100 Edit Controller, and Abekas ASWR 8100 mixer, A57 DVE and four machine editing, including two DVW 500s. Also three Avid off-line suites, 2D Matador and 3D Alias graphics and a Sound Studio comprising a Soundtracs 6800 24-track 32 channel desk and Soundscape 8-track digital editing machine
TELEVISION
Germ Genie, BBC 2; *The Spark*, Border; *Come Snow Come Blow*, Granada

Teddington Studios
Broom Road
Teddington
Middlesex TW11 9NT
Tel: 020 8977 3252
Fax: 020 8943 4050
email: sales@teddington.co.uk
Website: www.teddington.co.uk
Sales and Client Liaison
STUDIOS
1 653 sq metres
2 372 sq metres
3 120 sq metres
TELEVISION
This is Your Life; Des O'Connor Tonight; Harry Hill; Brian Conley Show; Alistair McGowan, My Hero, Beastly Behaviour, Coupling, The Brian Conley Show, Animal Magic, Black Books, This Is Your Life, Men Behaving Badly, Goodnight Sweetheart, Birds of a Feather, Heartburn Hotel, In Exile, Is It Legal?, Babes in the Wood, Barry Norman Movie Preview

Three Mills Island Studios
Three Mill Lane
London E3 3DU

Tel: 020 7363 0033
Fax: 020 7363 0034
email: threemills@compuserve
Website: www.threemills.com
Edwin Shirley
STAGES
1　31'x 28'x 18'
2　33'x 28'x 18'
3　14'x 28'x 18'
4　87'x 77'x 23'7"
5 143'x 74' x 22'
6　101'x 77' x 27'
7 212' x 77'x 33'5"
8　84' x 49' x 31'
9 104' x 84' x 31'
10 121' x 46' x 23'
11 106' x 89' x 33'
12 157' x 50' x 33'

Twickenham Film Studios
St Margaret's
Twickenham
Middx TW1 2AW
Tel: 020 8607 8888
Fax: 020 8607 8889
Website: www.twickenhamstudios.com
Gerry Humphreys, Caroline Tipple (Stages)
STAGES
1 702 sq metres
with tank 37 sq metres x 2.6m deep
2 186 sq metres
3 516 sq metres
2 x dubbing theatres; 1 x ADR/Foley theatre; 40 x cutting rooms; Lightworks, Avid 35/16mm

Westway Studios
8 Olaf Street
London W11 4BE
Tel: 020 7221 9041
Fax: 020 7221 9399
Steve/Kathy
STAGES
1 502 sq metres (Sound Stage)
2 475 sq metres
3 169 sq metres
4 261 sq metres

TELEVISION COMPANIES

Below are listed all British terrestrial television companies, with a selection of their key personnel, and in some cases programmes. A more comprehensive listing of programmes, producers and cast members can be found via the web pages of each company. Compiled by Linda Wood

BBC Television

British Broadcasting Corporation
Television Centre
Wood Lane
London W12 7RJ
Tel: 020 8743 8000
Website: www.bbc.co.uk
BBC Drama, Entertainment & Childrens
Centre House
56 Wood Lane
London W12 7SB
Tel: 020 8743 8000
BBC Broadcasting House
London W1A 1AA
Tel: 020 7580 4468
BBC Resources
BBC White City
201 Wood Lane
London W12 0TT
Tel: 020 8743 3200
BBC Worldwide
Woodlands
80 Wood LaneLondon W12 0TT
Tel: 020 8433 2000
Fax: 020 8749 0538
Website: bbcworldwide.com
Online Catalogue:
www.bbcworldwidetv.com
Chairman: Sir Christopher Bland
Director-General: Greg Dyke
Director, Drama, Entertainment & Childrens: Alan Yentob
Director, Television: Mark Thompson
Entertainment Commissioner: Danielle Lux
Digital Channels & Arts Commissioner: Roly Keating
Factual Commissioner: Nicola Moody
Controller, BBC1: Lorraine Heggessey

Controller, BBC2: Jane Root
Head of Programming:, BBC Choice: Stuart Murphy
Controller, Daytime: Jane Lush
Controller of Childrens: Nigel Pickard
Head of Entertainment & Features, Manchester: Wayne Garvie
Head of Fictionlab: Richard Fell
Head of Drama Series: Mal Young
Head of Film & Single Drama: David Thompson
Head of Drama Serials: Jane Tranter
Head of Comedy: Geoffrey Perkins
Head of Entertainment: Jon Plowman
Head of Light Entertainment: David Young
Chief Executive BBC Worldwide: Rupert Gavin
Deputy Chief Executive BBC Worldwide: Peter Teague
Chief Executive BBC Resources Ltd: Margaret Salmon
Director, World Service: Mark Byford
Director of Finance, Property and Business Affairs: John Smith
Director, Marketing & Communications: Andy Duncan
Director, BBC Sport: Peter Salmon
Director of Education: Michael Stevenson
Director, Radio and Music: Jenny Abramsky
Director, Distribution & Technology: Philip Langsdale
Director New Services and Deputy Director BBC Television: Richard Sambrook
Director, New Media: Ashley Highfield
Directors joint, Factual and Learning, Michael Stevenson, Glenwyn Benson
Director, Nations & Regions: Pat Loughrey
Director, Human Resources & Internal Communications: Gareth Jones
Director, Public Policy: Caroline Thomson

BBC Broadcast Programme Acquisition
Centre House
56 Wood Lane
London W12 7RJ
Tel: 020 8225 6721

Fax: 020 8749 0893
Controller, Programme Acquisition: Sophie Turner Laing
Senior Editor, Films: Steve Jenkins
Selects and presents BBC TV's output of feature films on all channels
Business Unit: Paul Egginton
Contact for commissioned material and acquisition of completed programmes, film material and sequences for all other programme departments
Business Development Executive: Paul Eggington
Contact for sub-licensing of material acquired by (but not produced by) the BBC

BBC East
St Catherine's Close
All Saint's Green
Norwich, Norfolk
Tel: 01603 619331
Fax: 01603 667865
email: look.east@bbc.co.uk
Head, Regional & Local Programmes: David Holdsworth

BBC East Midlands
East Midlands Broadcasting Centre,
London Road,
Nottingham NG2 4UU
Tel: 0115 955 0500
Fax:
email: enquiries.scot@bbc.co.uk
Head of Regional & Local Progs:
Liam McCarthy (Acting)

BBC London & South East
Elstree Centre
Clarendon Road
Borehamwood
Herts WD6 1JF
Tel: 020 8953 6100
Head of Regional & Local Programmes: Jane Mote

BBC North
BBC Broadcasting Centre
Woodhouse Lane
Leeds LS2 9PX
Tel: 0113 244 1188
Fax: 0113 243 9387
Head of Regional & Local Programmes: Ian Cundall

BBC North East & Cumbria
Broadcasting Centre

Barrack Rd
Newcastle upon Tyne NE99 2NE
Tel: 0191 232 1313
2210796
look.north.northeast.cumbria@bbc.
co.uk
Head of Regional & Local
Programmes: Olwyn Hocking

BBC North West
New Broadcasting House
Oxford Road
Manchester. M60 1SJ
Tel: 0161 200 2020
Head of Regional & Local
Programmes: Martin Brooks

BBC Northern Ireland
Broadcasting House
Ormeau Avenue
Belfast BT2 8HQ
Tel: 028 9033 8000
Fax: 028 9033 8800
email: ni@bbc.co.uk
Controller: Anna Carragher

BBC Scotland
Broadcasting House
Queen Margaret Drive
Glasgow G12 8DG
Tel: 0141 338 2000
Fax: 0141 334 0614
email: enquiries.scot@bbc.co.uk
Head: John McCormick
Broadcasting House
Queen Street
Edinburgh EH2 1JF
Tel: 0131 225 3131
Broadcasting House
Beechgrove Terrace
Aberdeen AB9 2ZT
Tel: 01224 625233

BBC South
Broadcasting House
Whiteladies Road
Bristol BS8 2LR
Tel: 0117 973 2211
Head of Regional & Local
Programmes: Andrew Wilson

BBC South West
Broadcasting House
Seymor Road
Mannamead
Plymouth PL3 5BD
Tel: 01752 229201
Fax: 01752 234595
email: spotlight@bbc.co.uk
Head, Regional & Local Programmes:
Leo Devine

BBC Wales
Broadcasting House
Llandaff
Cardiff CF5 2YQ

Tel: 029 2032 2000
Head: Menna Richards
Broadcasting House
Meirion Road
Bangor
Gwynedd LL57 2BY
Tel: 01248 370880
Fax: 01248 351443

BBC West Midlands
Pebble Mill
Birmingham B5 7QQ
Manchester. M60 1SJ
Tel: 0121 414 8888
Head, Regional & Local Progs: Laura
Dalgleis

Independent Television Companies

Anglia Television
Anglia House
Norwich NR1 3JG
Tel: 01603 615151
Fax: 01603 631032
Website: www.anglia.tv.co.uk
Regional Offices:
26 Newmarket Road
Cambridge CB5 8DT
Tel: 01223 467076
64-68 New London Road
Chelmsford CM2 0YU
Tel: 01245 357676
Hubbard House, Civic Drive
Ipswich
IP1 2QA
Tel: 01473 226157
16 Park Street
Luton LU1 2DP
Tel: 01582 729666
ADMAIL 3222
MIlton Keynes MK2 2NA
Tel: 01908 691660
77b Abingdon Street
Northampton NN1 2BH
Tel: 01604 24343
6 Bretton Green Village
Rightwell, Bretton
Peterborough PE3 8DY
Tel: 01733 269440
Chairman: David McCall
Managing Director: Graham
Creelman
Director of Programmes: Malcom
Allsop
Controller of Production: Neil
Thompson
Controller of News: Guy Adams
Part of the Granada Media Group
and covering the east of England,
during 2000, Anglia Television
produced/ commissioned 10 hrs. 15
mns of new programmes per week
for its own transmission. Anglia also
produces programmes for the ITV
Network and other broadcasters such
as Channel 4.
Programmes include:
Sunday Morning, religious magazine
Trisha, daytime talk show
Where the Heart Is, drama series
about two district nurses starring
Lesley Dunlop and Leslie Ash and
produced by Richard Broke
Get Packing (coproducted with
Meridian), travel series presented by
Amanda Redington
Air Ambulance (coproduced with

Meridian), series profiling the Essex and Kent amubance services
Whipsnade, series on well-known zoo
Town and Country, programme on the region hosted by colourful local historian Brian McNerny
Fair and Square, series covering consumers news
Cover Story, current affairs series
Day and Night, weekly listings magazine
Take It On, series of social action programmes covering topics as diverse as adoption, bullying and obesity
A Chance for Life, documentary series on the heart and lung transplant specialist unit at Papworth hospital, Cambridge
Go Fishing with John Wilson

Border Television
The Television Centre
Carlisle CA1 3NT
Tel: 01228 525101
Fax: 01228 541384
Website: www.border-tv.com
Chairman: James L. Graham
Acting Managing Director: Douglas Merrall
Director of Programmes: Neil Robinson
Head of News: Ian Proniewicz
Covering 288,000 homes in Cumbria, Border Television's broadcast coverage extends tfrom Peebles in the North, down to Seascale in the south and includes the Isle of Man., and viewers in the Border Television region watch more television than the national average. During 2000 Border Television produced/ commissioned 5 hrs. 34 mns of new programmes per week for its own transmission. It also producers material for the ITV Network, such as the award-winning series Innovators and other broadcasters including Channel 4.
Programmes include:
Food For Thought
Innovators, series of documentaries about science
Crucial, current affairs series which gave young people a platform to explore issues such as teenage pregnancy, smoking and drug abuse
Textile Tales, series on the history of the texile industry in the area
Blue Streak, documentary
Inside Sellafield, documentary
Windscale 1957, documentary
Dig That Plot, gardening competition series
TT Uncovered, series showing life

behind the scenes at the Isle of Man *TT Races*
Trailblazing
Home
Lookaround, regional news magazine
Coachtrippers, series following families from Cumbria on coach holidays to Spain
The Long Riders (coproduced with SMG), documentary about tradition ceremony in Selkirk deriving from protecting the town's common land
The Move, documentary on the closure of 3 Victorian hospitals with the opening of Cumberland Infirmary
A Day at The Dome, series about local school children spending a day at the London Dome

Carlton Television
101 St Martin's Lane
London WC2N 4AZ
Tel: 020 7240 4000
Fax: 020 7240 4171
Website: www.carlton.com
Chairman: Nigel Walmsley
Chief Executive: Clive Jones
Managing Director, Carloton Productions: Waheed Alli
Director of Programmes: Steve Hewlett
Chief Executive, Carlton Sales: Martin Bowley
Finance Director: Mike Green
Commercial Director: Tom Betts
Controller of Public Affairs: Hardeep Kalsi
Carlton Television holds 5 ITV franchises: Carlton London region (weekdays), Carlton Central region Carlton West Country, HTV Wales and HTV West. Most Carlton commissioning is now channeled through its subsidiary Carlton Productions - see below

Carlton Productions
35-38 Portman Square
London W1H ONU
Tel: 020 7486 6688
Fax: 020 7486 1132
Managing Director: Waheed Alli
Director of Programmes: Steve Hewlett
Managing Director, Action Time Productions: Trish Kinane
Managing Director, Planet 24 Productions: Anne Bulford
Managing Director of Content, Carlton Productions: Michael Foster
Controller, Business Affairs: Martin Baker
COMMISSIONERS FOR CARLTON PRODUCTIONS

Director of Drama & Co-production: Jonathan Powell
Controller of Children's & Young People's Programmes: Michael Forte
Deputy Controller Children & Young People's Programmes: David Mercer
Controller of Entertainment: Mark Wells
Controller of Comedy: Nick Symons
Controller, Factual Programmes: Sally Doganis
Deputy Controller, Factual Programmes: Nick Bullen
Controller Community Programmes: Peter Lowe

Carlton Broadcasting Central Region
West Midlands:
Central Court
Gas Street
Birmingham B1 2JP
Tel: 0121 643 9898
Fax: 0121 643 4897
East Midlands:
Carlton Studios,
Lenton Lane
Nottingham NG7 2NA
Tel: 0115 986 3322
Fax: 0115 964 5552
South Midlands:
Windrush Court
Abingdon Business Park
Abingdon OX1 1SA
Tel: 01235 554123
Fax: 01235 524024
Outside Broadcasting Facilities:
Carlton 021
12-13 Gravelly Hill Industrial Estate,
Gravelly Hill
Birmingham B24 8HZ
Tel: 0121 327 2021
Fax: 0121 327 7021
Managing Director, Carlton Broadcasting: Ian Squires
Head of Regional Programmes, Central: Duncan Rycroft
Director of Finance: Ian Hughes
Head of Aquisitions: John Broadbent
Head of Presentation: Wendy Chapman
Controller, News & Operations, Central: Laurie Upshon
Controller, Sports: Gary Newbon
Editor, Central News West: John Boileau
Editor, Central News East: Dan Barton
Editor, Central News South: Phil Carrodus
Head of Revional Affairs: Kevin Johnson
Managing Director Birmingham 021 Studios: Ed Everest

Covering the east, west and south Midlands, during 2000 Carlton Central Television produced/commissioned 16 hrs.51 mns of new programming per week for its own transmission. It also produces material for the ITV Network and other broadcasters.

Programmes for 2000 Include:

Peak Practice, drama series about a group of GPs in a small village, starring Gary Mavers and Gwynne Haydn

Family Fortunes, games show presented by Les Dennis

Drumbeat, a chat and music series

Simply Gardening (coproduction with Central London), gardening series

30 Minutes, current affairs series, series editor Andrew Fox

It's Your Shout, debates on local/national issues

Young Offenders, series on Stoke Heath detention Centre produced by Allister Craddock

The Night the Bombs Went Off, documentary about the Birmingham pub bombings 25 years ago, produced by Caroll Baker

Beryl Gets Younger by the Day, social action documentary about trying to get a great grandmother adopt a healthier lifestyle

Eye TV, arts series

First Cut, series of short films by new filmmakers

Barbara, situation comedy staromg Gwen Taylor

Carlton Broadcasting London Region

101 St Martin's Lane,
London WC2N 4AZ
Tel: 020 7240 4000
Fax: 020 7240 4171
London Television Centre
Upper Ground
London SE1 9LT
Tel: 020 7620 1620
Fax: 020 7827 7500
Head of Regional Programmes:
Emma Barker
Covering the London area weekdays, during 2000 Carlton Television London produced/commissioned 9hrs.03 mns of new programming per week for its own transmission. It also makes material for the ITV Network and other broadcasters.

Programmes include:

Pulling Power (coproduction with Central), motoring magazine

Dirty Tricks, drama series about an Oxford tutor who becomes a suspect for murder, starring Martin Clunes and directed by Paul Seed.

The Thing about Vince, comedy series about a builder going through a mid-life crisis, starring Timothy Spall and directed by Christopher King

The Vice, police drama series based on the vice unit of the Metropolitan Police, starring Ken Stott and David Harewood and executive produced by Rob Pursey

Britain at War in Colour, documentary series produced by Lucy Carter and Stewart Binns

London Tonight, news magazine

First Edition, current affairs series

Underground - The Story of the Tube, documentary series

Secret City, series about historical aspects of London presented by Adam Hart-Davis

The Wrong Side of the Rainbow, drama seriesabout homelessness, directed by Mike Mortimer and Fiona Oates

Legends, documentary series about the lives of actors and performers

Single Voices, short series of monologues on issues facing ethnic minorities, produced by Vir Parminder

Metroland, a showcase for new documentary directors

Carlton Broadcasting Westcountry Region

Western Wood Way
Langage Science Park
Plymouth PL7 5BG
Tel: 01752 333333
Fax: 01752 333444
Website: www.carlton.com/westcountry.co.uk
Managing Director: Mark Haskell
Director of Programmes: Jane McCloskey
Controller of News and Current Affairs: awaiting appointment
Controller of Features and Programme Development: Caroline Righton
Controller - Operations and Engineering : Mark Chaplin
Controller - Public Affairs: Mark Clare
Controller - Business Affairs: Peter Gregory
Owned by Carlton, Westcountry Television has a network of seven regional studios together with the main studio and headquarters in Plymouth and broadcasts to Cornwall and Devon and to much of Dorset and Somerset.The company transmits to 1.7 million people who live in one of the most diverse regions in the UK, and WT is strongly committed to reflecting this diversity in its regional coverage. During 2000, Westcountry Television produced/commissioned 11 hrs 18 mns of new programmes per week for its own transmission. The company also produces material for the ITV network and other broadcasters such as Channel 4

Programmes include:

Submarine (coproduction with Meridian), documentary series following twelve months in the life of the crew of Royal Navy hunter killer submarine HMS Superb. directed by Gary Johnston

Pulling Power (co-production with HTV) Motoring magazine prog

Camping it up, A light hearted series looking at the joys of caravanning and camping

Tales from the Snug, a series of stories from the past.

Hold the Front Page, series on the local regional newspaper

Westcountry Live at 1.00, midday news magazine

Westcountry Live, news magazine

The View from Here

Powergame

On the Hoof, series on horses

Wild West Country, natural history series

Moments, a series which sensitively covered a range of difficult topics such as child abuse and mental illness

Central Television

see Carlton Broadcasting Central Region

Channel 5 Television

22 Long Acre
London WC2E
Tel: 020 7550 5555
Duty Office 0845 7050505
Fax: 020 7550 5554
Website: www.channel5.co.uk
Chief Executive: Dawn Airey
Head of Press and Corporate affairs: Paul Leather
Deputy Chief Executive and Director of Sales: Nick Milligan
Director of Programmes: Kevin Lygo
Director of Finance: Grant Murray
Director of Legal and Business Affairs: Colin Campbell
Director of Marketing: tbc
Director of Broadcasting: Ashley Hill
Director of Acquisitions: Jeff Ford
Senior Programme Controller: Chris Shaw

Controller of Factual: Dan Chambers
Controller of Sport: Robert Charles
Controller of Drama: Corrine Hollingworth
Controller of Factual Entertainment: Sue Murphy
Controller of Entertainment: Andrew Newman
Controller of Special Events and Regions: Adam Perry
Controller of Interactive Programming: Sham Sandhu
Controller of Children's and Religion: Nick Wilson

Channel 5 launched on 30 March 1997, as the UK's fifth terrestrial broadcaster. Before broadcasting could begin, however, 5 was faced with the Herculean task of retuning 9 million homes across the UK. Coverage has now extended to 81% of homes with a share average for 2000 of 5.7%. Channel 5 is owned by two shareholders, RTL Group 65% and United Business Media 35%. Under its remit, 51% of programming must be original, 51% must be of European origin, 25% must be independent commissions, there must a minimum of 11 hours news programming; and 62 hours per week of programming must be subtitled. In 2000 Channel 5 made available a budget of £75 million for original commissions.

Programmes include:
5 News
Family Affairs, soap opera set in a London borough
The Nude
Floyd Around the Med, cook and bon viveur Keith Floyd, wanders around the Med and tries out various local dishes
The House Doctor, Ann Maurice gives advice on how to tart up homes to owners desperate to sell
Open House with Gloria Hunniford, afternoon magazine programme
The Miracles of Faith
The Third Reich in Colour, documentary using colour archival footage shot in Nazi Germany, directed by Georgia Harvey
Post Mortem, documentary series about the contribution forensic scientists can make to criminal investigations, directed by Clare Hudson
Too Much TV, computer generated youth magazine, produced by Peter Scott
Run for Your Life, documentary series about young athletes

Channel Four Television
124 Horseferry Road
London SW1P 2TX
Tel: 020 7396 4444
Fax: 020 7306 8353
Website: www.channel4.com
Executive Members
Chief Executive and Director of Programmes: Michael Jackson (leaving November 2001)
Managing Director: David Scott
Commercial Director: Andy Barnes
Director of Business Affairs: Janet Walker
Director of Strategy and Development: David Brook
Director of Programmes: Tim Gardam
Corporation Secretary: Andrew Brann
Non-Executive Members
Chairman: Vanni Treves
Deputy Chairman: Barry Cox
Deputy Director of Programmes: tbc
Controller of Acquisition: June Dromgoole
Head of Programme Planning & Strategy: Rosemary Newell
Head of Programme Finance: Maureen Semple-Piggott
Chief Engineer: Jim Hart
Head of Information Systems: Ian Dobb
Head of Business Affairs: Andrew Brann
Head of Legal Compliance: Jan Tomalin
Head of Corporate Relations: John Newbigin
Head of Press and Publicity: Matt Baker
Head of Commercial Marketing & Research: Hugh Johnson
Head of Presentation: Steve White
Head of Strategic Planning and Interactive Andy Anson
Head of Programmes (Nations and Regions): Stuart Cosgrove
Head of News, Current Affairs & Business: David Lloyd
Commissioning Editor, Current Affairs and News: Dorothy Byrne
Head of Drama: Tessa Ross
Commissioning Editors, Drama: Lucy Richer, Helen Gregory
Head of Entertainment: tbc
Head of Documentaries: Peter Dale
Commissioning Editor Documentaries: Hilary Bell
Commissioning Editor, Independent Film and Video: Adam Barker
Commissioning Editor, Nighttime: Jess Search
Head of History, Arts & Religion: Janet Hadlow
Commissioning Editor, History: Tim Kirby
Commissioning Editor, Religion: Elizabeth Clough
Commissioning Editor, Arts: Janet Lee
Commissioning Editor, Classical Music & Performance: Jan Younghusband
Commissioning Editor, Animation: Camilla Deakin
Head of Science and Education: Sara Ramsden
Commissioning Editors, Science: Charles Furneaux, Dan Chambers, Sarah Marris
Commissioning Editor, Education: Richard McKerrow
Head of Features:Janey Walker
Commissioning Editor, Daytime: Jo McGrath
Commissioning Editors, Multi-cultural Programmes: Yasmin Anwar, Narinder Minhas, Patrick Younge
Commissioning Editor, Ideas Lab: Liz Warner
Head of Entertainment: tbc
Head of Comedy: Caroline Leddy, Iain Morris
Commissioning Editors, Factual Entertainment: Steven Wright, Sue Murphy
Commissioning Editor, Entertainment: Robert Popper
Commissioning Editor, Big Breakfast: Sharon Powers
Commissioning Editor, Children and YP: Sarah Baynes
Commissioning Editor, E4: Andrew Newman
Commissioning Editor, Music and T4: Jo Wallace
Commissioning Editor, C4 Learning: John Richmond
Commissioning Editor, Sport: David Kerr
Managing Director, Digital and Pay TV(head of FilmFour and E4 Channels): Gerry Bastable
Head of Film Programming, Film Four Channel, Nick Jones
Director of 124 Facilities: David Mann
Managing Director 4Learning: tbc
Chief Executive FilmFour Ltd: Paul Webster
Managing Director Channel 4 International: Paul Sowerbutts

Channel 4 is a national service set up by Act of Parliament in 1982 as a non profit making corporation, funded principally by its revenue from advertising. Its remit is to: have a distinctive character of its own, and cater for interests not served by other channels; provide a diverse service including news, current affairs, education, religion and multicultural programming, all of which are to be an integral part of the peak-time programming strategy, reflect and respond to disability issues; place educational material at the heart of the schedule; play a central role in the UK film industry; and encourage a large and diverse independent production industry, within and outside London. With a handful of exceptions, C4 does not make programmes itself - it both commissions new material from production companies and buys in already completed programmes. In 2000, C4 66% of broadcast hours were made up of new programming, of which two thirds was supplied by independent producers, and C4 achieved 10.5 share of all viewing. As part of its strategy to turn C4 into a more commercially orientated organisation, 1999 saw a restructuring resulting in the film production, sales and facilities divisions being converted into stand-alone companies. Recent years have also seen C4 investing heavily in a range of spin-off activities, such as interactive services and the pay-for digital channels Film Four and EFour.

Programmes include:

Brookside, soap opera set in Liverpool
Hollyoaks, soap
Trigger Happy TV, Dominic Joly reinvents Candid Camera
Big Brother, Roman Games reinvented for the 20th Century and moved to Bromley-byBow
Longitude, drama starring Jeremy Irons and Michael Gambon, directed by Charles Sturridge
Never, Never, Tony Marchant's drama about loan sharking on a housing estate
Lock, Stock...
North Square, original dramaconcept about a group of yuppyish legal eagles sharing a house
Alt TV, series providing a showcase for a new generatioin of documentary filmmakers
Channel 4 News
T4, banner under which C4 puts out a range of youth programming
Chris Morris' The Jam
Time Team, series covering archaeological explorations
Slavery, documentary about the growth of the modern slave trade

Da Ali G Show, comedy series based on persona created by Sacha Baron Cohen
Black Books, sitcom
The Shock of the Old, series on the history of architecture presented by Piers Gough
Power Into Art
La Traviata, Verdi's opera staged over a weekend
Philosophy: A Guide To Happiness, Alain de Botton's novel take on philosophy
Why Weight
Elizabeth, David Starkey's documentary on EI
Victoria's Secrets, programme featuring Victoria Beckham
A Very British Murder, documentary series exploring contemporary British murder cases
White, Leo Regan takes up the story of a group of neo Nazis he'd previously filmed 10 years earlier
Generation Sex, sex education series
The Day the World Took Off, programme on the industrial revolution
Freak Out, factual entertainment series dealing with disability issues
Cutting Edge
True Stories
White Tribe, reflection by Darcus Howe on the English
Great Undertakings, about death
Saturday and Sunday, examination of attitudes to the weekend 'days of worship'
Witness, documentary series featuring ethical/religious issues
Marrying Out, series
Dispatches, current affairs series

Channel Television

Television Centre, La Pouquelaye
St Helier
Jersey JE1 3ZD
Tel: 01534 816816
Fax: 01534 816817
Television Centre, Bulwer Avenue
St Sampson
Guernsey GY2 4LA
Tel: 0481 41888
Fax: 0481 41866
email: broadcaast@channeltv.co.uk
Website: www.channeltv.co.uk
Chief Executive: Huw Davies
Managing Director: Michael Lucas
Directior of Productions: Phillipe Bassett
Head of Programmes: Karen Rankine
Head of Resource and Transmission: Tim Ringsdore

Finance Director: David Jenkins
Owned by Media Holdings and covering the Channel Islands, (principally the Islands of Jersey, Guernsey, Alderney, Herm and Sark), with a population of 150,000, Channel Television produced/commissioned 5 hrs 30 mins of new programming per week during 2000. The regional programme service iscentred around local events and current affairs and the station's main studios are based in Jersey with additional studios in Guernsey
Programmes for 2000 Include
Channel Report, regional news magazine
Stationary Ark, 60 minute documentary on Jersey zoo and Gerlad Durrell Wildlife Trust
Millennium Praise, outside broadcast of celebratory worship in the four main islands
Puffin's Pla(i)ce, a children's entertainment series featuring the character Oscar Puffin
Ant and Dec's Secret Camera Show

GMTV

London Television Centre
Upper Ground
London SE1 9TT
Tel: 020 7827 7000
Fax: 020 7827 7001
email: malcolm.douglas@gmtv.co.uk
Website: www.gmtv.co.uk
Chairman: Charles Allen
Managing Director: Christopher Stoddart
Director of Programmes: Peter McHugh
Managing Editor: John Scammell
Editor: Gerry Melling
Head of Press & PR: Sue Brealey
Presenters: Eamonn Holmes, Fiona Phillips, Lorraine Kelly, Penny Smith, Matthew Lorenzo
Owned by the Scottish Media Group and others, GMTV broadcasts nationally news and magazine programming, with features on life stle and showbusiness, on the ITV network from 6.00 am to 9.25 am

Grampian Television

Queen's Cross
Aberdeen AB15 4XJ
Tel: 01224 846846
Fax: 01224 846800
Website: www.grampiantv.co.uk
Managing director: Derrick Thomson
Chairman: Dr Calum A MacLeod CBE
Part of the Scottish Media Group and

covering the north of Scotland, including Aberdeen, Dundee and Inverness, during 2000, Grampian produced/commissioned 8 hrs.27 mns of new programming per week (including 54 minutes of material in Gaelic) for its own transmission. It also produces material for the ITV Network and other broadcasters such as Channel 4.
Programmes include:
North Tonight, local news and current affairs programme
The Week In Politics, a review of events in Parliament
Grampian Midweek, a weekly magazine covering social issues
The Big Beat, documentary series on policing in the area
New Found Land, series of shorts made by new filmmakers

Granada Television
Granada Television Centre
Quay Street
Manchester M60 9EA
Tel: 0161 832 7211
Website: www.granadamedia.com
4th Floor
48 Leicester Square
London WC2H 7FB
Tel: 020 7389 8555
Fax: 020 7930 8499
Granada News Centre
Albert Dock, Liverpool L3 4BA
Tel: 0151 709 9393
Fax: 0151 709 3389
Granada News Centre
Bridgegate House
5 Bridge Place
Lower Bridge Street
Chester CH1 1SA
Tel: 01244 313966
Fax: 01244 320599
Granada News Centre
White Cross, Lancaster LA1 4XQ
Tel: 01524 60688
Fax: 01524 67607
Granada News Centre
Daisyfield Business Centre
Appleby Street
Blackburn BB1 3BL
Tel: 01254 690099
Fax: 01254 699299
Chief Executive: Charles Allen
Joint Managing Director: Brenda Smith
Commercial Director: Katherine Stross
Director of Production and Resources: Max Graesser
Director of Broadcasting: Sue Woodward
Sales Director: Mick Desmond

Director of Production: Max Graesser
Director of Public Affairs: Chris Hopson
Technical Director: Roger Pickles
Finance Director Mike Fegan
Controller of Drama: Sally Head
Controller of Entertainment and Comedy: Andy Harris
Controller of Factual Programmes: Dianne Nelmes
Controller of Programme Services and Personnel: David Fraser
Head of Film: Pippa Cross
Head of Technical Operations: Chris Hearn
Head of Entertainment: Duncan Gray
Head of Features: James Hunt
Head of Factual Drama: Ian McBride
Head of Regional Affairs: Rob McLoughlin
Head of Planning and Marketing: Colin Marsden
Head of Production Services: Jim Richardson
Head of Music: Iain Rousham
Head of Regional Programmes: Mike Spencer
Head of Design and Post Production: Mike Taylor
Head of Current Affairs and Documentaries: Charles Tremayne
Head of Transmission Operations: Peter Williams
Granada has held the ITV franchise for the north of England since the start of commercial television in the UK in 1956. Its transmission area includes Manchester and Liverpool, and stretches from the Lake District to Shropshire, and from the North Wales coast to the Penines, serving a population of 6.2 million. During 2000, Granada produced/ commissioned 9 hrs.29 mns of new programming per week. for its own transmission. It also makes programmes for the ITV Network and other broadcasters such as Channel 4.
Programmes include:
The Beautiful North, art series made with Yorkshire TV, directed by Carl Hunter
Body Check, health education series produced by Christine Ruth and directed by Fay Gibson
Granada Tonight, regional news programme
Granby Street, documentary on multicultural school in Toxteth
Coronation Street, the UK's longest running soap
Frontline NHS, documentary on Salford Hospital

The Yeung Ones, series
Mean Streets, documentary series on crime in the North West, executive producer Vernon Antcliff
No Dream Impossible: The Russell Watson Story, documentary about popular tenor
The Club That Jack Built, documentary about Jack Walker former owner of Blackburn Rovers
Wired World, adult education series on developments in computer technology
For Arts Sake, series about art galleries
Riot! Strangeways 10 years, documentary on the causes of the riot
The Unknown Soldiers, documentary about the contribution of Asian troops during the Second World War directed by Jane Stanton

HTV Wales
The Television Centre
Culverhouse Cross
Cardiff CF5 6XJ
Tel: 02920 590 590
Fax: 02920 597 183
Website: www.htvwales.com
Carmarthen Office:
Top Floor
19-20 Lammas Street
Carmarthen SA31 3AL
Tel: 01267 236 806
Fax: 01267 238 228
email: smithg@htv-wales.co.uk
Colwyn Bay Office:
41 Conway Road
Colwyn Bay
Conwy LL28 5RB
Tel: 01492 533502
Fax: 01492 530720
email: cbay-news@htv-wales.co.uk
Swansea Office:
21 Walter Road
Swansea SA1 5NQ
Tel: 01792 459278
Fax: 01792 459 279
Mold Office:
The Harlech Building
County Civic Centre
Mold
Flintshire CH7 1YA
Tel: 01352 755 671
Fax: 01352 755 407
email: mewiesp@htv-wales.co.uk
Newtown Office:
St. David's House
Newtown
Powys SY16 1RB
Telephone: 01686 623381
Fax: 01686 624816
email: harta@htv-wales.co.uk
Wrexham Office:

HTV Wales
Crown Buildings
31 Chester Street
Wrexham
Tel: 01978 261 462
Chairman HTV Wales: Lord
Crickhowell
Managing Director: Jeremy Payne
Controller, Programming - HTV
Wales: Elis Owen
Manager, Business Affairs: Geraint
Curig
Head of Drama Development: Peter
Edwards
Group Controller of Corporate
Affairs: Iona Jones
Head of Features: Dafydd Llyr James
Head of Press and Public Relations:
Mansel Jones
Manager, Corporate and Community
Affairs: Mari Thomas
Head of News: John G Williams
Head of Human Resources: Julia
Cassley
Part of the Carlton group and
covering Wales, during 2000 HTV
Wales provided 11.25 of new
programming per week for its own
transmission. It also makes
programmes for the ITV Network
and other broadcasters and S4C. The
company is committed to producing
range of its programmes in the Welsh
language.
Progammes include:
The Ferret, consumer series
Wales This Week
The Front Row, series on Rugby
football presented by Ieuan Evans and
Stuart Davies
Sharp End, political series tackling
issues following the advent of a Welsh
Assembly
Waterfront
Soccer Sunday
Grass Roots, series about the Welsh
countryside
Opinion Zone
Pen Tennyn, dir Gareth Lloyd
Williams)
Nuts and Bolts, drama series focusing
on six families in the fictional town of
Ystrad, series producer Brian Roberts
Hot Pursuit, series on minority sports
Away Days, holiday series
Gyms and Arias, documentary series
about going on tour with Welsh
National Opera
A Mind To Kill, detective series
staring Philip Madoc, produced with
Channel 5
High Performance, art series produced
and presented by Nicola Heywood-
Thomas

HTV West
Television Centre
Bath Road
Bristol BS4 3HG
Tel: (0117) 972 2722
Fax: (0117) 971 7685
email: presspr@htv-west.co.uk
Website: www.htvwest.com
Managing Director: Jeremy Payne
Director of Regional Programmes:
Sandra Payne
Owned by Carlton and covering the
west of England, HTV
produced/commissioned 10 hrs 35
mns of new programmes per week
during 2000.
Programmes include:
Looking back at 2000
Going to the Dogs, documentary
about greyhound racing
From Hairs to Chairs, documentary
about clothmaking
The Picture House, profile about the
oldest cinema in Europe
Kageha's Story, documentary about
Kenjan woman adopted at birth by a
Bristol family
2bdiscovered.com, entertainment
series showcasing local bands
The Great Escape, holiday series

Independent Television News
200 Gray's Inn Road
London WC1X 8XZ
Tel: 020 7833 3000
Fax: 020 7430 4700
Website: www.itv.co.uk
ITN is the news provider nominated
by the Independent Television
Commission to supply news
programme for the ITV network.
Subject to review, this licence is for a
ten year period from 1993. ITN also
provides news for Channel 4,
Channel 5 and for the Independent
Radio News (IRN) network. ITN is
recognised as one of the world's
leading news organisation whose
programmes and reports are seen in
every corner of the globe. In addition
to its base in London, ITN has
permanent bureaux in Washington,
Moscow, South Africa, the Middle
East, Hong Kong, and Brussels as well
as at Westminster and eight other
locations around the UK.
News At Ten
Channel 4 News
Early Evening News
Lunchtime News
Morning and Afternoon Bulletins
Night-time Bulletins
Weekend Programmes

Five News
Five News Early
5.30am Morning News
Radio News
Travel News
The Big Breakfast News on Channel 4
ITN World News
House to House on Channel 4
First Edition on Channel 4
Special Programmes
News Archives
The Westminster Television Centre
ITN Productions

ITV Network Centre
200 Gray's Inn Road
London WC1X 8HF
Tel: 020 7843 8000
Fax: 020 7843 8160
Website: www.itv.co.uk
ITV is a federation of regional
broadcasters. National coverage is
achieved by 15 licensees, broadcasting
in 14 regional areas : Anglia, Border,
Carlton, Central, Channel,
Grampian, Granada, HTV, LWT ,
Meridian, STV, UTV, Westcountry,
Tyne Tees, Yorkshire. (London has
two licencees, one for the weekday -
Carlton and one for the weekend -
LWT)

LWT (London Weekend Television)
The London Television Centre
Upper Ground
London SE1 9LT
Tel: 020 7620 1620
Fax: 020 7261 1290
Website: www.lwt.co.uk
Chairman: Charles Allen
Managing Director: Liam Hamilton
Controller of Arts: Melvyn Bragg
Director of Programmes: Marcus
Plantin
Controller of Drama: Michelle Buck
Controller of Entertainment and
Comedy: Nigel Lythgoe
Controller of Factual Programmes:
Jim Allen
Director of Production: Tamara Howe
Part of the Granada Media Group,
LWT has the London Franchise for
the weekend, beginning 17.15 on
Fridays and ending 06.00 Mondays,
As LWT can be picked up well
beyond the London area, it serves a
population of around 11 million.
During 2000, the company
produced/commissioned 3.55 of new
programmes per week for its own
transmission. LWT is also a major
supplier of programmes to the ITV
Network and other broadcasters such

as Channel 4, Channel 5 and BSkyB.
Programmes include:
London's Burning, drama series set
around a fire station
The South Bank Show, arts series
produced and presented by Melvyn
Bragg
Blind Date, dating show introduced
by Cilla Black
London Tonight, local news
programme
Reach for the Moon, romantic drama
series about a teacher who remeets
his childhood sweetheart just as he is
about to get married, starring Lynda
Bellingham and Jonathan Kerrigan
and directed by Rob Evans
The Knock, drama series about the
Customs and Excise unit, executive
producer David Newcombe
The Big Stage, variety entertainment
show hosted by Bradley Walsh
The London Programme, award-
winning current affairs series
The Body Check, health series
The Real DIY Show
*Human Genome - Can We Now Play
God?*
*Michael Heseltine: a Life in the
Political Jungle*, political documentary
Love Bites, exploration of social issues
faced by local teenagers
Time Tales, series about school
children working on archeological
digs
Up Close Late, social action series
Cor Blimey!, drama about the Carry
On series directed by Terry Johnson
Britain's Most Wanted, series featuring
crime reconstructions
CD:UK, children's entertainment
programme

Meridian Broadcasting Ltd
Television Centre
Northam Road
Southampton SO14 0PZ
Tel: 023 8022 2555
Fax: 023 8033 5050
Website: www.meridiantv.com
Part of the Granada Media group of
companies and covers the South and
South East of England
Regional news centres:
West Point
New Hythe
Kent ME20 6XX
Tel: 01622 882244
Fax: 01622 714000
1-3 Brookway
Hambridge Lane
Newbury, Berks RG14 5UZ
Tel: 01635 522322
Fax: 01635 522620

Chairman: Charles Allen
Managing Director, Meridian: Mary
McAnally
Managing Director, Granada
Broadcasting: Stewart Butterfield
Director of Broadcasting: Mark
Southgate
Director of News: Andy Cooper
Director of Regional and Commercial
Affairs: Martin Morrall
Controller of Sport: Tony Baines
Controller of Network Factual: Trish
Powell
General Manager: Jan Beal
Controller of Personnel: Peter
Ashwood
Finance Controller: Steve Godwin
Part of the Granada Media Group,
Meridian covers the south and south
east of England, broadcasting to a
population of just under 6 million.
Meridian Broadcasting's main studio
complex is in Southampton with
additional studios at Maidstone,
Newbury and Brighton. During 2000,
the company produced/
commissioned 13 hrs. 40 mns of new
programmes per week for its own
transmission and also supplied
material to other networks including
Channel 4, Channel 5 and BBC.
Programmes include:
Freescreen, community access series
That's Esther, monthly magazine
presented by Esther Rantzen
Gay Dads, documentary
Meridian Tonight, local news
magazine
7 Days, series looking at political
issues
Meridian Focus, investigative
documentary series
Heritage Love it or Lose it, series on
architecture
The Frame, arts series on a wide range
of topics
The Battle Remembered, series about
the Battle of Britain, produced by Gill
Southcott
In the Past, programme about two
local film archives

S4C
Parc Ty Glas
Llanishen
Cardiff CF4 5DU
Tel: 01222 747444
Fax: 01222 754444
email: s4c@s4c.co.uk
Website: www.s4c.co.uk
Chairman: Elan Closs Stephens
Chief Executive: Huw Jones
Director of Productions: Huw Eirug
Director of S4C International: Wyn

Innes
S4C was established under the
Broadcasting Act, 1980 and is
responsible for providing a service of
Welsh and English programmes on
the Fourth Channel in Wales, with a
remit that the majority of
programmes shown between 18.30
and 22.00 should be in Welsh. It
broadcasts roughly 34 hours of Welsh
language promgramming per week
and the remainder of its output,
around 85 hours, is provided by
Channel 4 and is in English. 10 hours
per week of Welsh programmes are
provided by the BBC and the rest are
commissioned/purchased from
independent producers. Since 1993
S4C has been directly funded by the
Treasury and is responsible for selling
its own advertising. In 1998 S4C
Digital was launched, which only
transmits Welsh language
programmes and goes out from
midday to midnight.
Programmes include:
Pen Tennynt(HTV) recent politial
history, contemporary series dealing
with family tensions set in the
Cambrensis
llafur Cariad, (Teliesyn) portrays
political tensions in Wales during the
last 30 years
Porc Peis Bach, revolved round the
indiscretions of vicar's son Kenneth
set in the early sixties
Mae Gen I Gariad (Ffilmiau'r Nant)
the complexities of relationships and
a young married man's obsession
with Tony and Aloma
Yr Asembli (Al Frescro) comedy
about the assembly
The Animated Tales of the World
The Miracle Maker, portraying the life
of Jesus
Y Palmant Aur (Opus) sage of
Cardiganshire family and their dairy
business in London starring Delyth
Wyn
The Celts, documentary series
Dai Jones showed in Cefn Gwiad
Patagonia that the rural life in that
Welsh colony is surprisingly similar
to rural life in Wales
Experimental film *Diwrnod Hollol
Mindblowing Heddiw* directed by
Euros Lyn, country boy's discovery of
city pleasures

Scottish Television
200 Renfield Street
Glasgow G2 3PR
Tel: 0141 300 3000
Fax: 0141 300 3030

Website: www.smg.plc.uk
116 New Oxford Street
London WC1A 1HH
Tel: 020 7663 2300
Fax: 020 7663 2335
Chairman: Don Cruikshank
Chief Executive: Andrew Flanagan
Chief Executive TV Division: Donald
Emslie
Managing Director: Sandy Ross
Managing Director SMG Television
Productions: Jagdip Jagp
Head of Factual: Helen Alexander
Head of Youth: Elizabeth Partyka
Head of Features: Agnes Wilkie
Part of the Scottish Media Group,
Scottish TV has held the ITV licence
for Central Scotland since
commercial television started in 1957.
It remains the most watched station
in Scotland, broadcasting to 3.4
million viewe rs. During 2000
Scottish Television
produced/commissioned 17hrs. 23
mns (including approximately 4
hours in Gaelic) of new
programming per week for its own
transmission. In addition to
programmes for its own region, ST
also makes programmes for the ITV
Network and other broadcasters such
as Channel 4.
Programmes include:
Rebus, drama series adapted from the
Ian Rankin novels about an
Edinburgh detective John Rebus
starring John Hannah in the title role,
directed by Maurice Phillips
(Clerkenwell Films and Scottish
Television).
Harry and The Wrinklies, drama
about boy sent away to live with his
ageing aunts who discovers they're
robbing banks to support their
favourite cash-strapped causes.
directed by Andrew Morgan and
starring Nicholas Robinson, Mona
Bruce and Elsie Kelly
The Last Musketeer, a swashbuckling
adventure with Robson Green as a
man on the run who takes refuge in
an all-girls school, directed by Bill
Britten (Scottish Television and
Coastal Productions)
Wheel of Fortune, games show hosted
by John Leslie
Scotland Today, regional news
magazine
Loud TV, innovative late night
programme with various kinds of
content
Seven Days, current affairs/political
review programme
The Artery, eclectic arts series

Tyne Tees Television

The Television Centre
City Road
Newcastle Upon Tyne NE1 2AL
Tel: 0191 261 0181
Fax: 0191 261 2302
email: tyne.tees@granadamedia.com
Website: www.tynetees.tv
Chairman: Charles Allen
Managing Director: Margaret Fay
Director of Broadcasting: Graeme
Thompson
Director of Programmes: John
Whiston
Controller of Engineering: Dixon
Marshall
Head of Operations: Howard Beebe
Head of Regional Affairs: Norma
Hope
Head of Network Features: Mark
Robinson
Managing Editor - News: Graham
Marples
Editor - Current Affairs and Features:
Jane Bolesworth
Head of Sports: Roger Tames
Becoming part of the Granada Media
Group in 1997 and covering the
north east of England, TTTV has a
transmission area stretching from
Berwick in the North to Selby in the
South and across to Alston in the
West. During 2000 the company
produced/commissioned 10 hrs 04
mns of new programmes per week
for its own transmission. TTTV also
produces material for the ITV
network and other broadcasters such
as Channel 4.
Programmes include:
The 100 Greatest Kids TV Shows, for
Channel 4
The Secret, drama based on Catherine
Cookson novel, directed by Alan
Grint and starring Colin Buchanan
and Claire Higgens, for ITV
Dinner of Herbs, drama based on
Catherine Cookson novel, directed by
Alan Grint starring Billie Whitelaw
and Jonthan Kerrigan, for ITV
Blind Ambition, 2 hour drama
directed by Richard Standeven and
starring Robson Green and Imogen
Stubbs about a recently-blinded
athlete who is going for gold in the
800 metres at the Sydney
Paralympics, for ITV
After They Were Famous II,
entertainment feature, for ITV
North East Tonight with Mike Neville,
local news programme
Around the House, weekly political
round up with Gerry Foley
Grundy's Wonders, long running

series celebrating the North East
landscape
Party Nights, documentary series
about Northerners at play
Body Beautiful, series shot in north
east and America, looking at different
forms of body enhancement such as
tattoos, piercing and cosmetic surgery
Out of Town, Eric Robson and his
cantankerous border terrier, Raq, find
walks in the most unusual places.
Hoaxer II, documentary on the
Wearside man who derailed search
for the Yorkshire Ripper
Second Chance, documentary on a
young man coming to terms with life
in a wheelchair
Showreel UK, series featuring local
bands and singers
Cover Their Tracks, series on tribute
bands in the area
A Round with Rob, series with Rob
Andrew interviewing leading sports
figures during a round of golf
Slam XXL, award winning basketball
series
Dales Diary, Luke Casey uncovers the
beauty and characters of the northern
hill country
Red Hot Dance, series looking for the
five hottest, sexiest dancers in the
North East
First Cut, a series of six single half-
hour dramas showcasing directors
and writers new to television
Love in the City asks why five
attractive and vivacious women in
their thirties are still single, in the
middle of the world's top party City.
The Digital Age, Judie McCourt
unravels the technology and looks at
how the North East is leading the way
in this six part series.

Ulster Television

Havelock House
Ormeau Road
Belfast BT7 1EB
Tel: 028 90328122
Fax: 028 90 246695
email: info@utvplc.com
Website: www.utv.co.uk
Chairman: J B McGuckian
Managing Director: J McCann
Director of Programming: A Bremner
Head of Press and Public Relations:
Orla McKibbin
Head of News: Rob Morrison
Covering Northern Ireland, during
2000 UTV produced/commissioned
12 hrs 27 mins of local programmes
per week for its own transmission.
Programmes include:
UTV Live at Six – news programme

Insight – weekly current affairs programme
School Choir of the Year
UTV Life – popular mix of socially purposive programming and topical reports which reflects life in NI
The Family Show – weekly half hour programme on family issues
HOME – series of short films from new talent
Kelly – chat show
McKeever – comedy series
All Mixed Up – quiz programme with Eamonn Holmes
Cooking with Jenny - cookery series
Lesser Spotted Ulster
School Around the Corner
The Funeral of Joey Dunlop – outside broadcast special

Westcountry Television
see Carlton Broadcasting West Country Region

Yorkshire Television
The Television Centre
Leeds LS3 1JS
Tel: 0113 243 8283
Fax: 0113 244 5107
Website: www.yorkshire-tv.co.uk
Global House
96-108 Great Suffolk Street
London SE1 OBE
Tel: 020 7578 4304
Fax: 020 7578 4320
Charter Square
Sheffield S1 3EJ
Tel: 0114 272 3262
Fax: 0114 275 4134
23 Brook Street
The Prospect Centre
Hull HU2 8PN
Tel: 01482 24488
Fax: 01482 586028
88 Bailgate
Lincoln LN1 3AR
Tel: 01522 530738
Fax: 01522 514162
Alexandra Dock Business Centre
Fisherman's Wharf
Alexandra Dock
Grimsby NE Lincs
DN21 1UL
Tel: 01472 357026
Fax: 01472 341967
8 Coppergate
York YO1 1NR
Tel: 01904 610066
Fax: 01904 610067
Managing Director: Richard Gregory
Chairman: Charles Allen
Director of Broadcasting: Mike Best
Director of Programmes: John Whinston
Controller, Features: Bridget Boseley

Executive Producer Entertainment: Jim Brown
Controller of Factual Programmes: Chris Bryer
Director of Business Affairs Granada Content North: Filip Cieslik
Head of International Factual: Pauline Duffy
Head of Site Services: Peter Fox
Head of News & Current Affairs: Clare Morrow
Controller of Drama, YTV: Carolyn Reynolds
Controller of Comedy Drama and Drama Features: David Reynolds
Controller of Drama, YTTP: Keith Richardson
Deputy Controller of Children's, GMG: Patrick Titley
Controller of Factual Programmes: Helen Scott
Head of Media Relations North: Sallie Ryle
Head of Engineering: John Nichol
Head of Business Affairs: Justine Rhodes
Head of Sales and Planning: Jim Richardson
Director of Finance, Granada Content North: Ian Roe
General Manager: Peter Rogers
Head of Personnel: Sue Slee
Part of the Granada Media Group since 1997 and covering Yorkshire, Humberside and Lincolnshire, Yorkshire Television broadcasts to a population of 5.7 million Most of the 940 strong work force operate from studio complex in Leeds but the company maintains close links with its area through regional offices. During 2000 the company produced/commissioned 14 hrs 20 mns of new programmes per week for its own transmission. It also produces programmes for the ITV network and other channels, such as Channel 4.
Programmes include:
Emmerdale, soap set in farming community (Steve Frost, producer)
Heartbeat, drama series set in the 60s, centring round the local village police station (Keith Richardson, exec producer)
A Touch of Frost, award-winning series staring David Jason a a down at heel detective
Fat Friends, drama directed by David Wheatley and starring Alison Steadman and Ruth Jones
At Home with the Braithwaites, comedy drama series about a suburban family and the secrets they

keep from each other, directed by Robin Sheppard and starring Amanda Redman and Peter Davison
We Can Work It Out, series explaining consumers' rights
Bruce's Price is Right (Jim Brown, producer)
Calendar, local news/magazine programme
Q&A, current affairs series

VIDEO/DVD LABELS

These companies acquire the UK rights to all forms of audio-visual product and arrange for its distribution on videodisc, cassette or DVD at a retail level. Recent titles released on each label are also listed. A listing of all these available titles, and also those available for hire only, can be found in the trade catalogue *Videolog* (published by Trade Service Information) which is updated on a monthly basis. *Videolog* is used by most retailers - so check with your local store first - and may also be held by your local reference library. Compiled by Linda Wood

Academy Video
see Connoisseur/bfi video

Alliance Atlantis Communications
Alliance Video
2nd Floor, 184-192 Drummond St
London NW13HP
Tel: 020 7391 6900
Fax: 020 7383 0404

American Independence
68-70 Wardour Street
London W13 3HP
Tel: 020 7734 2266
Fax: 020 7494 0309

Arrow Film Distributors
18 Watford Road
Radlett
Herts WD7 8LE
Tel: 01923 858306
Fax: 01923 869673
Neil Agran
La Bonne Annee
Les Diaboliques
Europa Europa
Ginger and Fred
Montenegro
La Retour de Martin Guerre
Wages of Fear
Gulliver's Travels
Frank Sinatra: They Were Very Good Years
Leonardo DiCaprio: In His Own Words

Art House Productions
39-41 North Road
Islington
London N7 9DP
Tel: 020 7700 0068
Fax: 020 7609 2249
Richard Larcombe
Les Biches
Bicycle Thieves
Buffet Froid
Django
La Grande Bouffe
La Grande Illusion
The Harder They Come
Mephisto
Miranda
The Navigator
The Spirit of the Beehive
The Turning

Artificial Eye Video
14 King Street
London WC2E 8HR
Tel: 020 7240 5353
Fax: 020 7240 5242
email: video@artificial-eye.com
Website: www.artificial-eye.com
Robert Beeson, Steve Lewis
Beau Travail
Blackboards
Harry He's Here to Help
L'Humanité
Last Resort
Pola X
Three Colours Trilogy

BBC Worldwide Publishing
Woodlands
80 Wood Lane
London W12 0TT
Tel: 020 8576 2236
Fax: 020 8743 0393
Blackadder
Dr Who
Match of the Day series
One Foot in the Grave
Pole to Pole
Red Dwarf
Steptoe and Son

bfi Video
21 Stephen Street
London W1T 1LN
Tel: 020 7957 8957
Fax: 020 7957 8968
email: video.films@bfi.org.uk

Website: www.bfi.org.uk
bfi Video, incorporating Connoisseur and Academy, releases over 300 titles (including DVDs) covering every decade of cinema, from the 1890s to the present. Recent releases include Recent Connoisseur releases:
Salò (VHS and DVD)
People on Sunday
Thin Blue Line
Man Ray Films
British Transport Films
British Avant-Garde: Britain in the Twenties
British Avant-Garde: Britain in the Thirties
Hindle Waker
Lady Windemere's Fan
yojimbo (VHS and DVD)
Gallivant
Man with a Movie Camera (VHS and DVD)
Pink Narcissus

Blue Dolphin Film & Video
40 Langham Street
London W1N 5RG
Tel: 020 7255 2494
Fax: 020 7580 7670
Joseph D'Morais
Video releases to date:
A Great Day in Harlem
A Fistful of Fingers
Invaders from Mars
Destination Moon
Flight to Mars
Mister Frost
The Square Circle
Loaded
Different for Girls
American Perfekt
Mindwalk
Texas Chain Saw Massacre
The Ninth Configuration
Malcolm
Crystal Voyager

Blue Light
231 Portobello Road
London W11 1LT
Tel: 7792 9791
Fax: 7792 9871

Buena Vista Home Video
3 Queen Caroline Street
Hammersmith
London W6 9PE

Tel: 020 8222 1000
Fax: 020 8222 2795
Distribute and market Walt Disney,
Touchstone, Hollywood Pictures and
Henson product on video

BMG Music Programming
Bedford House
69-79 Fulham High Street
London SW6 3JW
Tel: 020 7384 7500
Fax: 020 7384 8010

Carlton Home Entertainment
The Waterfront
Elstree Road
Elstree
Herts WD6 3BS
Tel: 020 8207 6207
Fax: 020 8207 5789
Carlton Video releases sections from
Rank and Korda Collections. Also
features The Rohauer Collection,
Godzila - Japanese Originals
Up on the Roof, Made in Britain
Meantime, Prick Up Your Ears
Children's Programmes including:
Tots TV, Bananas in Pyjamas, The
World of Peter Rabbit and Friends, Old
Bear and Friends, Rudolph the Red-
Nosed Reindeer, Annabelle's Wish,
Dream Street, Big Garage, Jellikins,
Kingdom of Rhymes, The Fairies,
Extreme Dinosaurs, Timbuctoo,
Potamus Park
TV Programmes: *Inspector Morse,*
Soldier Soldier, The Vice, Sharpe,
Cadfael, Goodnight Mister Tom, The
Scarlet Pimpernel, Kavanagh QC,
Frenchman's Creek, Cider With Rosie,
A Rather English Marriage, The Jump

Century Media
12 Montague Road
London E8 2HW
Tel: 020 7254 9497
Fax: 020 7254 9497
New specialist micro-label. Video
production and distribution of visual
arts related titles. Include: *Bass on*
titles video about film titles design
presented by Saul Bass

Channel 5
Universal Pictures Video
1st Floor, 1 Sussex Place
Hammersmith
London W8 9XS
Tel: 020 8910 5000
Fax: 020 8910 5892

Cinema Club
78 Dean Street
London W1V 5HA

Tel: 020 7316 4488
Fax: 020 7316 4489

Classic Pictures Entertainment
Shepperton Film Studios
Studios Road
Shepperton TW17 0QD
Tel: 01932 572016
Fax: 01932 572046

Columbia TriStar Home Video
Sony Pictures Europe House
25 Golden Square
London W1R 6LU
Tel: 020 7533 1200
Fax: 020 7533 1172
Devil in a Blue Dress
First Knight
Higher Learning
It Could Happen to You
Legends of the Fall
Little Women
Mary Shelley's Frankenstein
Only You
The Quick and the Dead
Street Fighter

The Connoisseur Collection
2-3 Fitzroy Mews
London W1T 6DDF
Tel: 020 7383 7773
Fax: 020 7383 7724

Connoisseur Video
see *bfi* video

Contender Entertainment Group
48 Margaret Street
London W1N 7FD
Tel: 020 7907 3773
Fax: 020 7907 3777

Curzon Video
13 Soho Square
London W1V 5FB
Tel: 020 7437 2552
Fax: 020 7437 2992
Belle Epoque
Deadly Advice
Decadence
Fausto
The Hour of the Pig
How to be a Woman and Not Die in
the Attempt
In Custody

Disc Distribution
Unit 12
Brunswick Park Estate
Brunswick Way
New Southgate
London N11 1HX
Tel: 020 8362 8111
Fax: 020 8362 8118

DLT Entertainment
10 Bedford Square
London WC1B 3RA
Tel: 020 7631 1184
Fax: 020 7636 4571

Dreamworks Home Entertainment
UIP House
45 Beadon Road
London W6 OEG
Tel: 020 8563 4160
Fax: 020 8563 8486

DVD Direct
The Hub, Church Place
Swindon
Wilts SN1 5ED
Tel: 01793 603570
Fax: 01793 603521

Electric Pictures Video
see Universal Pictures Video
Angel Baby
Arizona Dream
The Baby of Macon
Before the Rain
Belle de Jour
Blood Simple
Butterfly Kiss
The Celluloid Closet
Cold Fever
The Cook, The Thief, His Wife and Her
Lover
Death and the Maiden
Delicatessen
La Dolce Vita
Drowning by Numbers
The Eighth Day
The Flower of my Secret
I Shot Andy Warhol
Kansas City
Ladybird, Ladybird
Love and Human Remains
Orlando
Priest
Prospero's Books
Raise the Red Lantern
Red Firecracker, Green Firecracker
Ridicule
The Runner
Shanghai Triad
The Story of Qiu Ju
Trees Lounge
The White Balloon
The Young Poisoner's Handbook
Walking and Talking

Electric Video
110 Park Street
London WD7 8ED
Tel: 020 7408 2121
Fax: 7409 1935

EMI Records
EMI House
43 Brook Green
Hammersmith
London W8 7EF
Tel: 020 7605 5000
Fax: 020 7605 5050
Blur: Showtime
Cliff Richard: The Hit List
David Bowie: The Video Collection
Iron Maiden: The First Ten Years
Kate Bush: The Line, The Cross and
The Curve
Peter Gabriel: Secret World Live
Pet Shop Boys: Videography
Pink Floyd: Pulse
Queen; Box of Flix
Tina Turner: Simply the Best

Entertainment in Video
108-110 Jermyn Street
London SW1Y 6HB
Tel: 020 7930 7766
Fax: 020 7730 9399
Kingpin
Last Man Standing
Leaving Las Vegas
Living in Oblivion
Twelfth Night
Up Close and Personal

The Entertainment Network
Rabans Lane
Aylesbury HP19 3BX
Tel: 01296 426151
Fax: 01296 565400

Eros International
Unit 26
Park Royal, Metro Centre
Britannia Way
Coronation Road
London NW10 7PR
Tel: 020 8963 8700
Fax: 020 8963 0154

First Independent Video
Sony Pictures Europe House
25 Golden Square
London W1R 6LU
Tel: 020 7533 1200
Fax: 020 7533 1172
Above the Rim
Automatic
Dumb and Dumber
The Lawnmower Man II
Little Odessa
Mortal Kombat
Nostradamus
Rainbow
Sleep With Me

4 Front Video
Universal Pictures Video
1st Floor, 1 Sussex Place

Hammersmith
London W6 9XS
Tel: 020 8910 5000
Fax: 020 8910 5362

Granada Media
Commercial Ventures
200 Grey's Inn Road
London WC1X 8XZ
Tel: 020 7396 6000
Fax: 020 7316 3222
Brideshead Revisited
Cracker - series 1 & 2
Gladiators
Hale & Pace - Greatest Hits
Jeeves & Wooster - series 1 & 2
Jewell in the Crown
London's Burning - series 1 & 6
Nicholas and Alexandra
Rik Mayhall Presents... - series 1 & 2

guerilla films
35 Thornbury Road
Iselworth
Middlesex TW7 4LQ
Tel: 020 7758 1716
Fax: 020 7758 9364
email: david@guerilla-films.com
Website: www.guerilla-films.com
David Nicholas Wilkinson
Includes films by Eric Rohmer, Barbet
Shroeder, Jacques Rivette, Monty Python

Helkon
17-18 Henrietta Street
London WC2 8OH
Tel: 020 7257 2000
Fax: 020 7257 2300
Website: www.films.helkon.co.uk

Icon Home Entertainment
The Quadrangle , 4th Floor
180 Wardour Street
London WV1 3AA
Tel: 020 7494 8100
Fax: 020 7494 8151

Le Channel Ltd
10 Frederick Place
Weymouth
Dorset DT4 8HT
Tel: 01305 780446
Fax: 01305 780446
Art videos about famous paintings of
the Western World. Palettes is a
collection of very high standard
videos about famous paintings of the
Western World. Adapted from the
French, the films have been
researched by leading art historians
and curators. Each Palette narrates
the creation of a painting, the story of
a painter, the progression of a Palette:
Claude; Leonardo; Monet Poussin,
Seurat, Vermeer

Made in Hong Kong
see Blue Light

Mainline Pictures
37 Museum Street
London WC1A 1LQ
Tel: 020 7242 5523
Fax: 020 7430 0170
email: tony.bloom@btinternet.com
Website: www.screencinemas.co.uk
Tony Bloom
Bandit Queen
The Diary of Lady M
A Flame in my Heart
Go Fish

Manga Entertainment
3MV, City Network House
81-83 Weston Street
London SE1 3RS
Tel: 020 7378 8866
Fax: 020 7378 8855

Medusa Communications & Marketing Ltd
Regal Chambers, 51 Bancroft
Hitchin
Herts SG5 1LL
Tel: 01462 421818
Fax: 01462 420393
email: steve@medusa.com.co.uk
Steve Rivers
Video and DVD distributors for:
Playboy; Hong Kong Legends;
Medusa Pictures; Osyssey; Adult
Channel; Eastern Heros

MGM Home Entertainment (Europe) Ltd
5 Kew Road
Richmond
London TW9 2PR
Tel: 020 8939 9300
Fax: 020 8939 9411

Millivres Multimedia
World Wide House
116-134 Bayham Street
London NW1 0BA
Tel: 020 7482 2576
Fax: 020 7284 0329

Momentum Pictures
2nd Floor
184-192 Drummond Street
London NW1 3HP
Tel: 020 7391 6900
Fax: 020 7383 0404

Nova Home Entertainment
11a Winholme
Armthorpe
Doncaster DN3 3AF
Tel: 01302 833422
Fax: 08701 257917

email: nhe@novaonline.co.uk
Website: www.novaonline.
co.uk/homevideo
Contact: Andrew White, Maurice
White, Gareth Atherton
Sell-through video distributor, a
subsidiary of Nova Productions, with
a catalogue based specialist and local
interest documentaries and nostalgia
programming. Recent titles include:
On Board, The Sounds of Trams,
Sheffield Remembered - The Last
Trams, Framing with Dave Woolass

Odyssey Video
Regal Chambers
51 Bancroft
Hitchin
Hertfordshire, SG5 1LL
Tel: 01462 421 818
Fax: 01462 420 393
email: adrian_munsey@msn.com
Adrian Munsey
Ambush in Waco
Beyond Control
Burden of Proof
Honour Thy Father & Mother
Lady Boss
Lucky/Chances
Out of Darkness
A Place for Annie
Remember
War & Remembrance

Orbit Media Ltd
7-11 Kensington High Street
London W8 5NP
Tel: 020 7221 5548
Fax: 020 7727 0515
Website: www.orbitmedia.co.uk
Chris Ranger
Jordan Reynolds
Screen classics label, feature films and
documentaries

Orion Home Video
Downtown Pictures
4th Floor, St Georges House
14-17 Wells Street
London W1P 3FP
Tel: 020 7323 6604
Fax: 020 7636 8090

Paramount Home Entertainment
180 Oxford St
London W1N 0DS
Tel: 020 7478 6866
Fax: 020 7478 6868

Pathé Distribution
Kent House
14-17 Market Place
Great Titchfield Street
London W1N 8AR

Tel: 020 7323 5151
Fax: 020 7631 3568
Website: www.pathe.co.uk

Picture Music International
see EMI Records

Pinnacle Vision
Electron House
Cray Avenue
St Mary's Cray
Orpington BR5 3PN
Tel: 01689 870622
Fax: 01689 836906

Pride Video
48 Independent Place
London E8 2HE
Tel: 020 7254 8005
Fax: 020 7409 1935

Quadrant Video
37a High Street
Carshalton
Surrey SM5 3BB
Tel: 020 8669 1114
Fax: 020 8669 8831
Sports video cassettes

Quantum Leap
7 Ermine Street
Huntingdon
Cambridgeshire PE18 7EX
Tel: 01480 450006
Fax: 01480 456686

Retro Video
Metro Tartan House
79 Wardour Street
London W1V 3TH
Tel: 020 7494 1400
Fax: 020 7439 1922
email: sdunn@metro-tartan.co.uk
Website: www.tartanvideo.co.uk
Sam Dunn
Cinema Paradiso
Man Bites Dog
Seventh Seal
The Umbrellas of Cherbourg
La Haine
The Dream Life of Angels
Kissed

Road Runner Video
10 Warple Way
Acton
London W3 OUL
Tel: 020 8749 2984
Fax: 020 8749 2523

Screen Edge
28-30 The Square
St Annes-on-Sea
Lancashire FY8 1RF
Tel: 01253 712453
Fax: 01253 712362

email: king@visicom.demon.co.uk
Website: www.visionary.co.uk
Rhythm Thief
Der Todesking
Pervirella

Select Music and Video
34 Holmethorpe Avenue
Redhill
Surrey RH12NN
Tel: 01737 760020
Fax: 01737 766316

S Gold & Sons
69 Flempton Road
Leyton
London E10 7EL
Tel: 020 8539 3600
Fax: 020 8539 2176

SIG Video Gems Ltd
The Coach House
The Old Vicarage
10 Church Street
Rickmansworth
Herts WD3 1BS
Tel: 01923 710599
Fax: 01923 710549
Black Beauty (TV series)
The Great Steam Trains
Minder
Moonlighting
Professionals
Return of the Incredible Hulk
Rumpole of the Bailey
Ruth Rendell
Sweeney
UK Gold Comdey Compilation
UK Gold Action/Drama Compilation

Sony Music Video
10 Great Marlborough Street
London W1V 2LP
Tel: 020 7911 8172
Fax: 020 7911 8813

Sony Classical
10 Great Marlborough Street
London W1V 2LP
Tel: 020 7911 8251
Fax: 020 7911 8537

Teldec Video (Warner Classics)
The Warner Building
28 Kensington Church Street
London W8 4EP
Tel: 020 7938 0167
Fax: 020 7938 3986

Telstar Video Entertainment
Prospect Studios
High Street
Barnes
London SW13 9LE
Tel: 020 8487 8002

Fax: 020 8741 5584
A sell-through video distributor of
music, sport, special interest, comedy,
children and film programmes
The Best Kept Secret in Golf
Foster & Allen: By Request
Harry Secombe Sings
Hollywood Women
John Denver: A Portrait
Michael Crawford: A Touch of
Music in the Night

Thames Video Home Entertainment
Freemantle Media
1 Stephen Street
London W1P 1PJ
Tel: 020 7691 6000
Fax: 020 7691 6079
Mr Bean; Tommy Cooper;
Wind in the Willows; World at War;
Men Behaving Badly; The Bill; The
Sweeney

THE (Total Home Entertainment)
National Distribution Centre
Rosevale Business Park
Newcastle under Lyme
Staffs ST5 7QT
Tel: 01782 566566
Fax: 01782 565400
email: jed.taylor@the.co.uk
Website: www.the.co.uk
Jed Taylor/Sue Nixon
Exclusive distributors for Visual
Corp, ILC, Quantum Leap, Mystique,
Prime Time, IMS, Wardvision,
Academy Media, Empire, RWP (over
6,000 titles)

Touchstone Home Video
3 Queen Caroline Street
Hammersmith
London W6 9PE
Tel: 020 8222 1000
Fax: 020 8222 1000

Trumedia Ltd
PO Box 374
Headington
Oxford OX3 7NT
Tel: 01865 763097
Fax: 01865 763097
email: sales@trumedia.co.uk
Website: www.trumedia.co.uk
Bill Cotten
Literary video and audio resources
and DVD. Other videos: History of
Art; Foreign Language; History

20th Century Fox Home Entertainment
Twentieth Century House
31-32 Soho Square

London W1V 6AP
Tel: 020 7753 8686
Fax: 020 7434 1625
Website: www.fox.co.uk
Airheads
Braveheart
Johnny Mnemonic
Judge Dredd
The Scout
The Shawshank Redemption
Stargate
Trapped in Paradise
Wes Craven's New Nightmare

Twentieth Century Video
Wembley Commercial Centre
East Lane
Wembley
Middlesex HA9 7UU
Tel: 020 8904 6271
Fax: 020 8904 0172

Universal Pictures Video/Universal TV
1 Sussex Place
Hamersmith
London W6 9XS
Tel: 020 8910 5000
Fax: 020 8910 5404

Video Collection International
76 Dean Street
London W1V 5HA
Tel: 020 7396 8888
Fax: 020 7396 8996

Virgin Records
Kensal House
553-579 Harrow Road
London W10 4RH
Tel: 020 8964 6000
Fax: 020 8964 6179

Visionary Communications
28-30 The Square
St Annes-on-Sea
Lancashire FY8 1RF
Tel: 01253 712453
Fax: 01253 712362
email: king@visicom.demon.co.uk
Website: www.visionary.co.uk
Scorpio Rising
The Pope of Utah
Three Films' Burroughs'/Gysin
Destroy All Rational Thought
Cyberpunk
Angelic Conversation
In the Shadow of the Sun
The Gun is Loaded
Freaks
Island of Lost Souls
Mystery of the Wax Museum

Visual Entertainment

Visual Online Partners
20 Albert Embankment
London SE1 7TJ
Tel: 020 7820 4410
Fax: 020 7582 9800

Walt Disney Video
see Buena Vista Home Video

WEBSITES

This section contains a small selection of useful websites which coincide with the sections in this book. For more detailed information visit the gateway film links section on the *bfi* website. www.bfi.org.uk/gateway

Archive and Film Libraries

National Film and TV Archive
http://www.bfi.org.uk/collections

ARKive
http://www.arkive.org.uk

British Association of Picture Libraries and Agencies (BAPLA)
http://www.bapla.org.uk

British Movietone News
http://movietone.com

British Universities Film and Video Council
http://www.bufvc.ac.uk/

Contemporary Films Archive
http://contemporaryfilms.com/archives/arc_set.htm

East Anglian Film Archive
http://www.uea.ac.uk/eafa/

FIAF: The International Federation of Film Archives
http://www.cinema.ucla.edu/FIAF/

FIAT: International Federation of Television Archives
http://camilla.nb.no/fiat

FOCAL
http://www.focalint.org

Footage.net
http://www.footage.net

France - La Vidéoteque de paris
http://www.vdp.fr/

Hulton Archive
http://www.archivefilms.com

Huntley Film Archives
http://www.huntleyarchives.com

Imperial War Museum Film and Video Archive
http://iwm.org.uk/lambeth/film.htm

National Museum of Photography Film & Television
http://www.nmsi.ac.uk/nmpft

North West Film Archive
http://www.nwfa.mmu.ac.uk

Scottish Film and Television Archive
http://www.scottishscreen.com

SEAPAVAA
http://members.nbci.com/archives/

South East Film and Video Archive
http://shs.surreycc.gov.uk/sefva.html

UK Film Archive Forum
www.bufvc.ac.uk/faf/faf.htm

Wales Film and Television Archive
Archif Ffilm a Theledu Cymru
http://www.sgrinwales.demon.co.uk/filmarchive.htm

Wessex Film and Sound Archive
http://www.hants.gov.uk/record-office/film.html

Awards

BAFTA
http://www.bafta.org/

Berlin
http://www.berlinale.de

Cannes
http://www.festival-cannes-fr

Edinburgh International Film Festival
http://www.edfilmfest.org.uk/

Emmys
http://www.emmys.org/

Emmys International
http://www.intlemmyawards.com/

European Film Awards
http://www.europeanfilmacademy.org

Golden Globes
http://www.hfpa.com

Golden Rose of Montreux
http://www.rosedor.ch

Golden Rasberry Awards
http://www.razzies.com/

Grierson Trust Awards
http://www.editor.net/griersontrustrman

Karlovy Vary
http://www.iffkv.cz/

Locarno
http://www.pardo.ch/

Oscars
http:// www.oscars.org/awards

Monte Carlo TV Festival
http://www.tvfestival.com/

Royal Television Society Awards
http://www.rts.org.uk/

Books

bfi Publishing
http://www.bfi.org.uk

Oxford University Press
http://www.oup.co.uk/

Routledge
http://www.routledge.com/

UKBookWorld
http://www.ukbookworld.com

Booksellers

Blackwell's
http://www.blackwell.co.uk/bookshops

Cinema Store
http://www.atlasdigital.com/cinemastore

Reel Posters
http://www.reelposter.com

Waterstones
http://www.waterstones.co.uk

Cable, Satellite and Digital

Cable/Satellite Guide
http://www.sceneone.co.uk/s1/TV

BSkyB
http://www.sky.co.uk

NTL
http://www.ntl.co.uk

ONDigital
http://www.ondigital.co.uk

SkyDigital
http://www.skydigital.co.uk

Telewest Communications
http://www.telewest.co.uk

Careers and Training

Film Education
http://www.filmeducation .org

Focal
http://www.focal.ch

Institut National de l'Audiovisual
http://www.ina.fr

National Film and Television School
http://www.nftsfilm-tv.ac.uk/

Skillset
http://www.skillset.org

Cinemas

Cinema Admissions
http://www.dodona.co.uk

Cinemas in the UK
http://www.aber.ac.uk/~jwp/cinemas

Apollo Cinemas
http://www.apollocinemas.co.uk

Caledonian Cinemas
http://www.caledoniancinemas.co.uk

Cineworld
http://www.cineworld.co.uk

Film Finder
http://www.yell.co.uk/yell/ff/

Fox Movies
http://www.foxmovies.com

Mainline
http://www.screencinemas.co.uk

Odeon
http://www.odeon.co.uk

Picturehouse
http://www.picturehouse-
cinemas.co.uk

Scoot
http://www.cinema.scoot.co.uk

Showcase Cinemas
http://showcasecinemas.co.uk

UCI (UK) Ltd
http://www.uci-cinemas.co.uk

Warner Village
http://warnervillage.co.uk

Courses

The American Intercontinental
University
http://www.aiulondon.ac.uk/

University of Bath
http://www.bath.ac.uk

Birkbeck College University of
London
http://www.birkbeck.ac.uk/

University of Birmingham
http://www.birmingham.ac.uk

Bournemouth University
http://www.bournemouth.ac.uk

University of Bradford
http://www.bradford.ac.uk

Bristol Animation Course
http://www.mediaworks.org.uk/anim
ate

University of Bristol
http://www.bristol.ac.uk

Brunel University
http://www.brunel.ac.uk

Canterbury Christ Church College
http://www.cant.ac.uk

Coventry University
http://www.alvis.coventry.ac.uk
Cyber Film School
http://www.cyberfilmschool.com

De Montfort University Bedford
http://www.dmu.ac.uk/Bedford

De Montfort University Leicester
http://www.dmu.ac.uk/Leicester

University of Derby
http://www.derby.ac.uk
University of East Anglia
http://www.uea.ac.uk

University of East London
http://www.bradford.ac.uk

University of Exeter
http://www.ex.ac.uk

University of Glasgow
http:// www.arts.gla.ac.uk/tfts/

Glasgow Caledonian University
http://www.gcal.ac.uk

Global Film School
http://www.globalfilmschool.com

Goldsmiths College
http://www.goldsmiths.ac.uk

Kent Institute of Art and Design
http://www.kiad.ac.uk

University of Kent
http://www.ukc.ac.uk

King Alfred's College Winchester
http://www.wkac.ac.uk

Kingston University
http://www.kingston.ac.uk

University of Leicester
http://www.le.ac.uk

University of Liverpool
http://www.liv.ac.uk

Liverpool John Moores University
http://www.livjm.ac.uk

London Guildhall University
http://www.lgu.ac.uk

London International Film School
http://www.lifs..org.uk

London School of Economics and
Political Science
http://www.lse.ac.uk

University of Manchester
http://www.man.ac.uk

Middlesex University
http://www.mddx.ac.uk

Napier University
http://www.napier.ac.uk

National Film and Television School
http://www.nftsfilm-tv.ac.uk

University of Newcastle upon Tyne
http://www.ncl.ac.uk/ncrif

Northern School of Film and
Television
http:// www.lmu.ac.uk

University of Northumbria at
Newcastle
http://www.unn.ac.uk

Nova Camcorder School
http:// www.novaonline.co.uk

University of Portsmouth
http://www.port.ac.uk

University of Reading
http://www.reading.ac.uk

College of Ripon and York St John
http://www.ucrysj.ac.uk

Roehampton Institute
http://www.roehampton.ac.uk

Royal College of Art
http://www.rca.ac.uk/Design

University of Salford
http://www.salford.ac.uk

University of Sheffield
http://www.sheffield.ac.uk

Sheffield Hallam University
http://www.shef.ac.uk

South Bank University
http://www.sbu.ac.uk

Staffordshire University
http://www.staffs.ac.uk

University of Stirling:Film and Media Studies Department
http://www-fms.stir.ac.uk

The University of Sunderland
http://www.sunderland.ac.uk

University of Sussex
http://www.sussex.ac.uk

Thames Valley University
http://www.tvu.ac.uk

Trinity and All Saints College
http:// www.tasc.ac.uk

University of Wales College, Newport
http://www.newport.ac.uk

University College Warrington
http://www.warr.ac.uk

University of Warwick
http://www.warwick.ac.uk

University of Westminster
http://www.wmin.ac.uk

University of Wolverhampton
http://www.wolverhampton.ac.uk

Databases/film reviews

625 Television Room
http://www.625.uk.com

All Movie Database
http://allmovie.com

Animation World Network
http://www.awn.com

Baseline
http://www.pkbaseline.com

Bib Online
http://www.bibnet.com

Box Office
http://www.entdata.com

Box Office Guru
http://www.boxofficeguru.com/

Castnet
http://castnet.com

Classic Movies
http://www.geocities.com/Hollywood/9766/

Classic TV
http://www.classic-tv.com

Cult TV
http://www.metronet.co.uk/cultv

European Cinema On-Line Database
http://www.mediasalles.it

FilmUnlimited
http://www.filmunlimited.co.uk

Hollywood Online
http://www.hollywood.com

InDevelopment
http://www.indevelopment.co.uk

Internet Movie Database
http://www.uk.imdb.com

The Knowledge
www.theknowledgeonline.com

The Location guide
http://www.thelocationguide.com

Media UK Internet Directory
http://www.mediauk.com/directory

Mandy's International Film and TV Production Directory
http://www.mandy.com

Moving Image Gateway
http://www.bufvc.ac.uk/gateway

Movie Map
http://www.visitbritain.com/moviemap/

Movie Page
http://www.movie-page.com

National Filmographies
http://www.rosland.freeserve.co.uk/filmbooks.htm

Popcorn
http://www.popcorn.co.uk

Production Base
http://www.productionbase.co.uk

Spotlight
http://www.spotlightcd.com
http://www.players-guide.com

TV Guide - Movies
http://www.tvguide.com/movies

UKTV
http://www.uktv.com

Distributors (Non-Theatrical)

Atom Films
http://www.alwaysindependentfilms.com

Central Office of Information
http:// www.coi.gov.uk/

CFL Vision
http://www.euroview.co.uk

Educational and Television Films
http://: www.etvltd.demon.co.uk

Vera Media
http://www.vera.media.co.uk

Distributors (Theatrical)

Alliance Releasing
http://www.alliance.

bfi
http://www.bfi.org.uk

Buena Vista
http://www.bvimovies.com

FilmFour
http://www.filmfour.com

Pathe Distribution´
http://www.pathe.co.uk

Twentieth Century Fox
http://www.fox.co.uk

UIP (United International Pictures)
http://www.uip.com

Universal Studios
http://universalstudios.com/

Warner Bros
http://www.warnerbros.com

Facilities

Abbey Road Studios
http://www.abbeyroad.co.uk/

Cinesite (Europe) Ltd
http://www.cinesite.com

Communicopia Ltd
http://www.communicopia.co.uk

Connections Communications Centre
http://www.cccmedia.demon.co.uk

Dubbs
http://www.dubbs.co.uk

Edinburgh Film Workshop Trust
http://www.efwt.demon.co.uk

The Film Factory at VTR
http://www.filmfactory.com

FrameStore
http://www.framestore.co.uk

Hillside Studios
http://www.ctvc.co.uk

Hull Time Based Arts
http://www.htba.demon.co.uk

Lee Lighting
http://www.lee.co.uk
PMPP Facilities
http://www.pmpp.dircon.co.uk

Salon Post-Productions
http://www.salon.ndirect.co.uk

Tele-Cine
http://www.telecine.co.uk

VTR Ltd
http://www.vtr.co.uk

Festivals

Film Festivals Servers
http://www.filmfestivals.com

Berlin
http://www.berlinale.de

Cannes
http://www.festival-cannes-fr

London Film Festival
http://www.lff.org.uk/

Film Societies

Film Societies
http://www.bffs.org.uk

Funding

Arts Council of England
http://www.artscouncil.org.uk/

Arts Council of Northern Ireland
http://www.artscouncil-ni.org/

Arts Council of Wales
http://www.ccc-acw.org.uk/

bfi
http://www.bfi.org.uk

British Council
http://www.britcoun.org/

The Film Council
http://www.filmcouncil.org.uk

Scottish Screen
http://www.scottishscreen.com

Sgrin, Media Agency for Wales
http://www.sgrinwales.demon.co.uk

UK Media
www.mediadesk.co.uk

Eastern Arts Board
http://www.eab.org.uk/

East Midlands Arts Board
http://www.arts.org.uk/directory/regi
ons/east_mid/

English Regional Arts Boards
http://www.arts.org.uk

London Arts Board
http://www.arts.org.uk/directory/regi
ons/london/

London Film and Video
Development Agency
http://www.lfvda.demon.co.uk/

Northern Arts Board
http://www.arts.org.uk/directory/regi
ons/northern/

Northern Ireland Film Commission
http://www.nifc.co.uk/

North West Arts Board
http://www.arts.org.uk/directory/regi
ons/north_west/

Scottish Arts Council
http://www.sac.org.uk/
Scottish Screen
http://www.scottishscreen.com/

Sgrîn
http://www.sgrinwales.demon.co.uk

Southern Arts Board
http://www.arts.org.uk/directory/regi
ons/southern/

South East Arts Board
http://www.arts.org.uk/directory/regi
ons/south_east/

South West Arts Board
http://www.swa.co.uk/

South West Media Development
Agency
http://www.swmediadevagency.co.uk/

West Midlands Arts Board
http://www.arts.org.uk/directory/regi
ons/west_mid/

Yorkshire Arts Board
http://www.arts.org.uk/directory/regi
ons/york/

International Sales

BBC Worldwide
http://www.bbc.worldwide.com

BRITE (British Independent
Television Enterprises)
http://www.brite.tv.co.uk

FilmFour International
http://www.filmfour.com

London Television Service
http://www.londontv.com

Pearson Television International
http://www.pearsontv.com

Twentieth Century Fox Television
http://www.fox.co.uk

Vine International Pictures
http://www.vineinternational.co.uk

Libraries

bfi National Library
http:// www.bfi.org.uk/library

British Library
http:// www.bl.uk/

COPAC
http://copac.ac.uk/copac/

Film Libraries - International
http://www.unesco.org/webworld/por
tal_bib/Library_Websites/Special/Fil
m_Libraries/

Library Association
http://www.la-hq.org.uk

Organisations

American Film Institute
http://www.afionline.org/

Arts Council of England
http://www.artscouncil.org.uk

BBC
http://www.bbc.co.uk

British Council - British films
http://www.britfilms.com

British Film Commission
http://www.britfilmcom.co.uk

British Film Institute
http://www.bfi.org.uk

BKSTS - The Moving Image Society
http://www.bksts.demon.co.uk

BUFVC(British Universities Film and
Video Council
http://www.bufvc.ac.uk

Department for Culture, Media and
Sport (DCMS)
http://www.culture.gov.uk/

Directors' Guild of Great Britain
http://www.dggb.co.uk

EDI
http://www.entdata.com

National Museum of Photography,
Film and Television
http://www.nmsi.ac.uk/nmpft/

New Producer's Alliance
http://www.npa.org.uk

PACT - Producers Alliance for
Cinema and Television
http://www.pact.co.uk

Scottish Screen
http://www.scottishscreen.com

Skillset
http://www.skillset.org

Organisations (Europe)

Association of European Film
Institutes
http://www.filmeurope.co.uk

Cordis
http://www.cordis.lu

European Association of Animation
Film
http://www.cartoon-media.be

European Audio-visual Observatory
http:// www.obs.coe.int

EURIMAGES
http://www.culture.coe.fr/eurimages

Europa
http://www.europa.eu.int

European Broadcasting Union (EBU)
http:// www.ebu.ch/

The European Coordination of Film
Festivals EEIG
http://www.eurofilmfest.org

European Documentary Network
http://www.edn.dk

European Film Academy
http://www.europeanfilmacademy.org

EUTELSAT (European
Telecommunications Satellite
Organisation)
http://www.eutelsat.org

Idea
http://www.europa.eu.int/idea

Belgium - The Flemish Film Institute
http://www.vfi-filminsituutbe

Denmark - Danish Film Institute
http://www.dfi.dk

Finland - AVEK - The Promotion
Centre for Audio-visual Culture in
Finland
http://www.kopiostofi/avek

Finnish Film Archive
http://www.sea.fi

The Finnish Film Foundation
http://www.ses.fi/ses

France - Bibliothèque du Film (BIFI)
http://www.bifi.fr
TV France International
http://www.tvfi.com

Germany - Filmf`rderungsanstalt
http://www.ffa.de

Iceland - Icelandic Film Fund
http://www.centrum.is/filmfund

Ireland - Bord Scann·n na
hÉ.ireann/Irish Film Board
http://www.iol.ie/filmboard

Film Institute of Ireland
http://www.iftn.ie/ifc

Poland - Polish Cinema Database
http://info.fuw.edu.pl/Filmy/

Portugal - Portuguese Film and
Audiovisual Institute
http://www.nfi.no/nfi.htm

Scottish Screen
http://www.scottishscreen.com

Press Contacts

6degrees.co.uk
http://www.6degrees.co.uk

Empire
http://www.empireonline.co.uk

Filmwaves
http://www.filmwaves.co.uk

Film Unlimited
http://filmunlimited.co.uk

Flicks
http://www.flicks.co.uk

Guardian online
http://www.guardian.co.uk/guardian

Inside Out
http://www.insideout.co.uk

Movie Club News
http://www.movieclubnews.co.uk

Premiere
http://www.premieremag.com

Radio Times
http://www.radiotimes.beeb.com

Screen
http://www.arts.gla.ac

Screendaily
http://screendaily.com

Screen Digest
http://www.screendigest.com

Sunday Times
http://www.sunday-times.co.uk

Talking Pictures
http://www.filmcentre.co.uk

Television
http://www.rts.org.uk

Time Out
http://www.timeout.co.uk/

Total Film
http://www.futurenet.co.uk

UK Government press releases
http://www.open.gov.uk/

Uncut
http:// www.uncut.net

Variety
http://www.variety.com

Visimag
http://visimag.com

Preview Theatres

BAFTA
http://www.bafta.org

The Curzon Minema
http://www.minema.com

RSA
http://www.rsa.org.uk

The Screening Room
http://www.moving-picture.co.uk

Production Companies

Aardman Animations
http://www.aardman.com

British Film Commission
http://www.britfilmcom.co.uk

British Films Catalogue
http://www.britfilms.com/

FilmFour Productions
http://www.filmfour.com

Fox Searchlight Pictures
http://www.fox.co.uk

guerilla films
http://www.guerilla.u-net.com

Hammer Film Productions Limited
http://www.hammerfilms.com

imaginary films
http://www.imagfilm.co.uk

Mosaic Films Limited
http://www.mosaicfilms.com

New Producers Alliance
http://www.npa.org.uk

PACT
http://www.pact.co.uk

Zooid Pictures Limited
http://www.zooid.co.uk

Specialised Goods and Services

Ashurst Morris Crisp
http://www.ashursts.com

Bromley Casting (Film & TV Extras
Agency)
http://www.showcall.co.uk

Hothouse Models & Effects
http://www.hothousefx.co.uk

MBS Underwater Video Specialists
http://www.eclipse.co.uk.mbs

Moving Image Touring Exhibition
Service (MITES)
http://www.mites.org.uk

Olswang
http://www.olswang.co.uk

Studios

Capital FX
http://www.capital.fx.co.uk

Elstree Film Studios
http://www.elstreefilmstudios.co.uk

Hillside Studios
http://www.ctvc.co.uk

Millennium Studios
http://www.elstree-online.co.uk

Television Companies

625 Television Room
http://www.625.uk.com

TV Commissions
http://www.tvcommissions.com

TV Guides
http://www.link-it.com/TV
http://www.sceneone.co.uk/s1/TV

Episode Guides Page
http://epguides.com/

Anglia Television
http://www.anglia.tv.co.uk/

BBC
http://www.bbc.co.uk/

Border Television
http://www.border-tv.com/

Carlton Television
http://www.carltontv.co.uk/

Channel Four
http://www.channel4.com

Channel 4
http://www.channel4.co.uk

Granada Television
http://www.granada.co.uk
HTV
http://www.htv.co.uk/

London Weekend Television (LWT)
http://www.lwt.co.uk/

Meridian Broadcasting Ltd
http://www.meridan.tv.co.uk/

S4C
http://www.s4c.co.uk/

Scottish Television
http://www.stv.co.uk/

Ulster Television
http://www.utvlive.com

Video Labels

British Videogram Association
http://www.bva.org.uk

Blockbuster Entertainment
http://www.blockbuster.com

DVD rental
http://www.movietrak.com

MovieMail
http://www.moviem.co.uk

Movies Unlimited
http://www.moviesunlimited.com

Videolog
http://www.videolog.co.uk

Websites

bfi Film and Television Handbook
http://www.bfi.org.uk/handbook

Workshops

City Eye
http://www.city-eye.co.uk

Edinburgh Film Workshop Trust
www.efwt.demon.co.uk

Hull Time Based Arts
http://www.htba.demon.co.uk

The Lux Centre
http://www.lux.org.uk

Pilton Video
http://www.piltonvideo.co.uk

The Place in the Park Studios
http://www.screenhero.demon.co.uk

Real Time Video
http://www.rtvideo.demon.co.uk

Vera Media
http://www.vera-media.co.uk

Vivid
http://www.wavespace.waverider.co.uk/~vivid/

WORKSHOPS

The selection of workshops listed below are generally non-profit distributing and subsidised organisations. Some workshops are also active in making audio-visual products for UK and international media markets

Amber Side Workshop
5-9 Side
Newcastle upon Tyne NE1 3JE
Tel: 0191 232 2000
Fax: 0191 230 3217
Murray Martin
Film/video production, distribution and exhibition. Most recent productions include: Letters to Katiya, 1 hour documentary; Eden Valley 90 minute feature film; The Scar 115 minute feature film. The Workshops National Archive is based at Amber. Large selection of workshop production on VHS, a substantial amount of written material and a database. Access by appointment

Belfast Film Workshop
37 Queen Street
Belfast BT1 6EA
Tel: 01232 648387
Fax: 01232 246657
Alastair Hrron, Kate McManus
Film co-operative offering film/video/animation production and exhibition. Offers both these facilities to others. Made Acceptable Levels (with Frontroom); Thunder Without Rain: Available Light; a series on six Northern Irish photographers, various youth animation pieces and a series of videos on traditional music

Black Coral Training
130 Lea Valley Techno Park
Ashley Road
London N17 9LN
Tel: 020 8880 4861
Fax: 020 8880 4113
Black Coral Training is a non-profit making organisation specialising in 1-4 day foundation and intermediate level courses in: Production Management; Producing for low budget features; business skills for freelancers; digtal sound editing; movie magic. Multi-skilling for

broadcast television; composing music for film & television; research for documentary; presenting and directing. Screenwriting courses include: Live script readings; script reading skills; TV script editing; developing comedy skills; writing a first short film; adapting a story into a short screenplay. All courses taught by industry professionals. Supported by Skillset, LFVDA and Middlesex University

Black Media Training Trust (BMTT)
Workstation
15 Paternoster Row
Sheffield S12 BX
Tel: 01142 492207
Fax: 01142 492207
Contact: Carl Baker
Film and video training. Commercial media productions facility and training resource within and for all Asian, African and African Caribbean communities for community development purposes. Also various commercial media consultancy and project services and facilities hire. Funded by National Lottery Single Regeneration Budget and church urban fund

Blaze the Trail Limited (Film & Television training)
2nd Floor
241 High Street
London E17 7BH
Tel: 020 8520 4569
Fax: 020 8520 2358
email: training@coralmedia.co.uk
Website: www.blaze-the-trail.com
Alex Rendell
Specializes in short-term training workshops in Film, TV and Broadcast media. Offering a variety of vocational driven courses ranging from entry level, intermediate and advanced. Tutors are active industry professionals who cover a wide range of areas including: Production training, Presentation Skills, Research, Budgeting & scheduling. Blaze the Trail provides practical development training for scriptwriters, script editors and script

readers via its Scriptcity programme. Blaze the Trail also offers individually structured programmes for corporate clients, details available on request.

Caravel Media Centre
The Great Barn Studios
Cippenham Lane
Slough SL1 5AU
Tel: 01753 534828
Fax: 01753 571383
email: caraveltv@aol.com
Website: caravelstudios.com
Anita See
Training, video production, distribution, exhibition and media education. Offers all these facilities to others. Runs national video courses for independent video-makers

The Children's Film Unit
South Way
Leavesden
Herts WD2 7LZ
Tel: 01923 354656
Fax: 01923 354656
email: cfilmunit@aol.com
Website: www.btinternet.com/~cfu
Carol Rennie, Adminstrator
A registered educational charity, the CFU makes low-budget films for television and PR on subjects of concern to children and young people. Crews and actors are trained at regular weekly workshops in Putney. Work is in 16mm and video and membership is open to children from 10 - 18. Latest films for Channel 4: Emily's Ghost; The Higher Mortals; Willies War; Nightshade; The Gingerbread House; Awayday. For the Samaritans: Time to Talk. For the Children's Film and Television Foundation: How's Business

City Eye
1st Floor, Northam Centre
Kent Street
Northam
Southampton SO14 5SP
Tel: 01703 634177
Fax: 01703 575717
email: info@city-eye.co.uk
Website: www.city-eye.co.uk
Richard McLaughlin
Film and video equipment hire. Educational projects. Production and

post-production and multimedia services. Screenings. Community arts media development. Training courses all year in varied aspects of video, film, photography and radio. Committed to providing opportunities for the disadvantaged/under-represented groups. 50 per cent discount on all non-profit/educational work

Connections Communications Centre
Palingswick House
241 King Street
Hammersmith
London W6 9LP
Tel: 020 8741 1766
Fax: 020 8563 9134
email: connections@
cccmedia.demon.co.uk
Website: www.cccmedia.demon.co.uk
Video production training for unemployed adults. NVQ assessment, 4 distinct mdules including Basic Video production, crewing on Live Events, Avid Editing, Production opportunities.
Introduction to Avid Editing for people in the multi-media industries who want to develop their digital editing skills. Fully wheelchair accessible

cre8 studios
Town Hall Studios
Regent Circus
Swindon SN1 1QF
Tel: 01793 463224
Fax: 01793 463223
Keith Phillips
Film & video production and training centre. Offers short courses and longer term media projects. First stop scheme offers funding for first time film/video makers. Also offers media education services, equipment hire, screenwriting advice and undertakes production commissions. Organises screenings and discussions

Cultural Partnerships
90 De Beauvoir Road
London N1 4EN
Tel: 020 7254 8217
Fax: 020 7254 7541
Heather McAdam, Lol Gellor, Inge Blackman
Arts, media and communications company. Offers various courses in digital sound training. Makes non-broadcast films, videos and radio programmes. Production-based training forms a vital part of the work. Studio facilities for dry/wet

hire: fully air-conditioned and purpose built, 8000 sq ft multi-purpose studio. Analogue and Digital audio studios. Live audio studio

Depot Studios
Bond Street
Coventry CV1 4AH
Tel: 024 76525074
Fax: 024 76634373
email: info@covdepot.demon.co.uk
Contact: Anne Forgan, Den Hands
A video and sound recording facility run by Coventry City Council, providing training, equipment hire, support and information. A full range of digital video and sound recording facilities available for hire, on a sliding scale. Projects and commissions also undertaken

Edinburgh Film Workshop Trust
56 Albion Road
Edinburgh EH7 5QZ
Tel: 0131 656 9123
email: post@efwt.demon.co.uk
Website: www.efwt.demon.co.uk
David Halliday
Scotland's only franchised workshop. Broadcast, non-broadcast and community integrated production. 24 years producing broadcast and non-broadcast film, video and animation

Exeter Phoenix
Media Centre
Bradninch Place
Gandy Street
Exeter
Devon EX4 3LS
Tel: 01392 667066
Fax: 01392 667596
email: media.admin@ukonline.co.uk
Jonas Hawkins/Christine Jowett
Video and multimedia training, access and activities. Betacam - SP, DV Cameras, G4 edit suite with Final Cut Pro Macintosh workstations, cinema, theatre and cafe

Film and Video Access Centre
25a SW Thistle Street Lane
Edinburgh EH2 1EW
Tel: 0131 220 0220 or 0131 477 4529
Fax: 0131 220 0017
email: fva-edinburgh@hotmail.com
Lara Celini
A membership-based association which provides resources and training for individuals and community groups to work with film and video. Courses are short and at basic or specialist level. Has VHS &

SVHS, MiniDV camcorders, Sony DVCam. Super 8 and 16mm production facilities, runs bi-monthly newsletter and information service. Also non-linear editing facilities on AVID

Film House/Ty Ffilm
Chapter Arts Centre
Market Road
Canton
Cardiff CF5 1QE
Tel: 01222 409990

Film Work Group
Top Floor
Chelsea Reach
79-89 Lots Road
London SW10 0RN
Tel: 0171 352 0538
Fax: 0171 351 6479
Loren Squires, Nigel Perkins
Video and film post-production facilities. Special rates for grant-aided, self-funded and non-profit projects.
Avid 'on line' (2:1) and 'off line' editing. 36 gigs storage. Digital Animation Workstations (draw, paint, image modification, edit).
3 machine Hi-Band SP and mixed Beta SP/Hi-Band with DVE
2 machine Lo-Band 'off line' with sound mixing.
6 plate Steenbeck.

First Take
Merseyside Innovation Centre
131 Mount Pleasant
Liverpool L3 5TF
Tel: 0151 708 5767
Fax: 0151 707 0230
email: all@first-take.demon.co.uk
Website: www.first-take.demon.co.uk
Mark Bareham, Lynne Harwood
First Take is an independent production and training organisation. It is the foremost provider of video training and production services to the volutary, community, arts, education and local authority sectors across the North West. Professional video training by BBC Assessors and broadcast quality productions

Four Corners Film Workshop
113 Roman Road
Bethnal Green
London E2 0QN
Tel: 020 8981 6111
Fax: 020 8983 4441
email: film@fourcorners.demon.co.uk
Website: www.fourcornersfilm.org
Lyn Turner

Originally established as a film collective in 1975, Four Corners supports the independent film sector by providing subsidised facilities (16mm/Super 16mm cameras, digital video, 2 Avid suites, 30 seat cinema, sound and lighting gear) and a range of training courses, including a 12-week ESF-funded course for ethnic minority women and short courses including digital video production, camera and lighting etc

Fradharc Ur
11 Scotland Street
Stornoway
Isle of Lewis PA87
Tel: 01851 703255
The first Gaelic film and video workshop, offering VHS and hi-band editing and shooting facilities. Production and training in Gaelic for community groups. Productions include: Under the Surface, Na Deilbh Bheo; The Weaver; A Wedding to Remember; As an Fhearran

Glasgow Media Access Centre
3rd Floor
34 Albion Street
Glasgow G1 1LH
Tel: 0141 553 2620
Fax: 0141 553 2660
email: admin@g-mac.co.uk
Website: www.g-mac.co.uk
Ian Reid, John Sackey, Blair Young, Stella Tobia, Cordelia Stephens
GMAC Ltd. is an open access training resource for film and video makers. Offers equipment hire and training courses at subsidised rates. Facilities include BETA SP, Mini DV, DVC Pro, S-VHS and VHS cameras and edits suites (including 2 Avids and a Steen Beck), a multimedia computer and Super 8mm and 16mm projectors. We also have studio space, a screening room and a duplication suite for hire. GMAC runs two short film schemes: Little Pictures for all members who have trained with us and Cineworks, funded by Scottish Screen and BBC Scotland. GMAC produces, distributes and exhibits corporate and community based projects.

Hull Time Based Arts
42 The High Street
Hull HU1 1PS
Tel: 01482 216446
Fax: 01482 589952
email: timebase@htba.demon.co.uk
Website: www.timebase.org
Annabel McCourt, Dan Van Heeswyk

HTBA promotes produces and commissions timebased art: film, video, performance, sound. The Lab is HTBA's timebased media production training and hire facilities. Equipment for hire includes two on-line Avid non-linear eding suites (Media Composer 9000 with uncompressed video also Media Composer 1000), output to DVCPro, Beta SP, DVCam. Pro Tools suite, DVCPro, DVCam cameras and production facilities, video projectors also for hire. Range of training courses

Intermedia Film and Video
19 Heathcote Street
Nottingham NG1 3AF
Tel: 0115 955 6909
Fax: 0115 955 9956
email: info@intermedianotts.co.uk
Website: intermedianotts.co.uk
Ken Hay, Director
Intermedia is the media production development agency for the East Midlands, providing a range of services to support media producers working at all levels of the industry. We provide facilities, training, production advice and support and manage EMMI, the East Midlands Media Initiative, which is able to make development awards to media producers and provide co-financing for media production activities.

Jubilee Arts Co Ltd
84 High Street
West Bromwich
West Midlands B70 6JW
Tel: 0121 553 6862
Fax: 0121 525 0640
email: @jubart.demon.co.uk
Jubilee Arts is a unique multi-media community arts team, formed in 1974. Skills include photography, video, drama, audio visual, music/sound, computers, training and graphic design. We work with communities, using the arts as a tool to create opportunities for positive ways for people to express themselves. Jubilee Arts works in partnership with a wide range of groups, agencies and voluntary and statutory bodies

Leeds Animation Workshop (A Women's Collective)
45 Bayswater Row
Leeds LS8 5LF
Tel: 0113 248 4997
Fax: 0113 248 4997
Jane Bradshaw, Terry Wragg, Stephanie Munro, Janis Goodman,

Milena Dragic
Production company making films on social issues and offer short training courses in basic animation Distributing over 20 short films including - Bridging the Gap; Tell it Like it is; Working with Care; A World of Difference; Waste Watchers; No Offence; Through the Glass Ceiling; Home Truths;

Lighthouse
9-12 Middle Street
Brighton BN1 1AL
Tel: 01273 384222
Fax: 01273 384233
email: info@lighthouse.org.uk
Website: www.lighthouse.org.uk
A training and production centre, providing courses, facilities and production advice for video and digital media. Avid off- and online edit suites. Apple Mac graphics and animation workstations. Digital video capture and manipulation. Output to/from Betacam SP. SVHS offline edit suite. Post Production and Digital Artists equipment bursaries offered three times a year

London Deaf Access Project
1-3 Worship Street
London EC2A 2AB
Tel: 0171 588 3522 (voice) Tel: 0171 588 3528 (text)
Fax: 0171 588 3526
email: lucyf@bda.org.uk
Website: www.bda.org.uk
Lucy Franklin, Production Coordinator
Translates information from English into British Sign Language (BSL) for Britain's deaf community, encourages others to do likewise and provides a consultancy/monitoring service for this purpose. Promotes the use of video amongst deaf people as an ideal medium for passing on information. Runs workshops and courses for deaf people in video production, taught by deaf people using BSL. Works with local authorities and government departments ensuring that public information is made accessible to sign language users. Titles include: School Leavers, Access to Women's Services, Health issues. Runs the yearly Deaf Film and TV Festival

The Lux Centre
Lux Building, 2-4 Hoxton Square
London N1 6NU
Tel: 0171 684 0101
Fax: 0171 684 1111
email: lux@lux.org.uk

Website: www.lux.org.uk
The Lux is dedicated to film, video and emerging technologies. Working closely with artists, they support the production and exhibition of work. The Lux seeks to provide a unique platform for innovative programming, exploration, discussion, insight and expertise. Offers a complete range of services including production based training, facility hire (production and post-production), distribution and exhibition

The Media Workshop

Peterborough Arts Centre
Media Department
Orton Goldhay
Peterborough PE2 0JQ
Tel: 01733 237073
Fax: 01733 235462
email: postmaster@p-arts.demon.co.uk
Video, multimedia and photography production, workshops and exhibitions. Offering DVCPRO, SVHS production/edit facilities and Media 100 non-linear editing. Also full multimedia authoring and design

Mersey Film and Video (MFV)

13-15 Hope Street
Liverpool L1 9BQ
Tel: 0151 708 5259
Fax: 0151 707 8595
email: mfv@hopestreet.u-net.com
Website: www.mfv.merseyside.org
Production facilities for: BETA SP, DVC PRO, MINI DV, multi-media stations, photoshop, Dolly and track, Jibarm, Lights, Mica, DAT etc. Post Production Avid, MC1000, SVHS, BBC FX & music library. Guidance and help for production, scripting, funding, budgets,

Migrant Media

90 De Beauvoir Road
London N1 4EN
Tel: 020 7254 9701
Fax: 020 7241 2387
Ken Fero, Ivan Ali Fawzi, Soulyman Garcia
Media production training and campaigning for migrants and refugees. Focus on African and Middle Eastern communities. Networks internationally on media/political issues. Broadcast credits include: After the Storm (BBC); Sweet France (C4), Tasting Freedom (C4), Justice For Joy (C4)

Moving Image Touring Exhibition Services (MITES)

Foundation For Art & Creative Technology (FACT)
Bluecoat Chambers
Liverpool L1 3BX
Tel: 0151 707 2881
Fax: 0151 707 2150
email: mites@fact.co.uk
Website: mites.org.uk
Simon Bradshaw
Courses for artists, gallery curators, technicians and exhibitors

Nerve Centre

7/8 Magazine Street
Derry BT48 6HJ
Northern Ireland
Tel: 02871 260562
Fax: 02871 371738
Website: www.nerve-centre.org.uk
Bernie McLaughlin, Aisling McGill

The Old Dairy Studios

156b Haxby Road
York YO3 7JN
Tel: 01904 641394
Fax: 01904 692052
Digital video production facilities inc. Fast video system, 32 Track digital recording studio, audio visual facilities with Adobe Photoshop, Radio Production and Midi Composition Studios are available. Courses in video production and editing, sound engineering, radio production, midi composition and digital imaging. Working with people with disabilities, unemployed people, people aged between 12 and 25 as well as with members of the community in general

Oxford Film and Video Makers

The Stables
North Place
Headington
Oxford OX3 9HY
Tel: 01865 741682 or 01865 760074 (course enquiries)
Fax: 01865 742901
email: ofvm@ox39hy.demon.co.uk
Website: www.welcome.to/ofvm
Accredited training in video, experimental film and 16mm film. Also offering courses in scriptwriting, directing and digital editing. Subsidised training for the unemployed and community groups. Production support through the OFVM millennium video project and regular screenings organised at local cinemas and the major summer

music festivals. Fast professional digital editing facility available for hire with or without editor

Panico London Ltd

PO Box 19054
London N7 0ZB
Tel: 020 7485 3533
Fax: 020 7485 3533
email: panico@panicofilms.com
Website: www.panicofilms.com
A training and production centre, providing courses facilities and production advice. Panico also hosts a club for individuals that want to work in the film industry. The club meets every thursday evening in Soho London. Through Club Panico you are able to make your own films, hire equipment and also have access to a unique list of opportunities/vacancies in the film industry. As well as social activities, surgeries are also regularly held, where members can raise technical, financial and career issues with knowledgeable professionals from the film industry

Picture This Moving Image

40 Sydney Row
Spike Island Studios
Bristol BS1 6UU
Bristol BS2 0QL
Tel: 0117 925 7010
Fax: 0117 925 7040
email: info@picturethis.demon.co.uk
Josephine Lanyon, Director
Picture This provides:
Training - a range of courses from beginner level to longer term training for under-represented groups. Short courses available in video, film and animation production and post production.
Awards and bursaries - opportunities for new work, with cash grants, advice and access to resources
Production and distribution - facilitate and commission productions for galleries, film festivals broadcasting agencies and cinemas
Membership scheme - support, information, and advice for individuals and groups
Facilities - access to film and video production and post production facilities ranging from 16mm film up to broadcast standard cameras and avid editing

Pilton Video

30 Ferry Road Avenue
Edinburgh EH4 4BA
Tel: 0131 343 1151

Fax: 0131 343 2820
email:
office@piltonvideo.freeserve.co.uk
Website: www.piltonvideo.co.uk
Hugh Farrell, Joel Venet, Eleanor Hill,
Graham Fitzpatrick
Training and production facilities in
the local community; documentary
and fiction for broadcast. 4 non-
linear edit suites

The Place in The Park Studios
Bell Vue Road
Wrexham
North Wales LL13 7NH
Tel: 01978 358522
email: knewmedia@
screenhero.demon.co.uk
Website: www.screenhero.
demon.co.uk
Richard Knew
Video/Film production access centre,
offering subsidised facilities hire.
Equipment includes Beta SP, Digital,
16mm and SVHS shooting and
editing kit. The Place in The Park acts
as a focal point/contact centre for
independent film and video makers
in the North Wales region and
beyond

Platform Films and Video
Unit 14, Pennybank Chambers
33-35 St Johns Square
London EC1M 4DS
Tel: 020 7336 7881 Mobile: 0973 278
956
Fax: 020 7278 8394
Chris Reeves
Film/video production and
distribution. Recent titles include:
SLP Election Broadcasts 2001; The
Cinema, a programme for English
and media studies students
commissioned by TV Choice, 2000;
Who Killed Mark Faulkner? three-
part forensic and social investigation
into the death and life of a young
homeless epileptic TX 4-6 Dec 2000
BBC2; Children and Disability, for
BBC2's Disability Programmes Unit,
2000; Pricecheck ˇ The Fight For
Union Rights, 2000; Old Hands-
British Labour Camps 1929-39, for
Writers Republic, 1999. Equipment:
BVW400 Beta SP shooting kit,
PD100P DV shooting kit, Avid
MC1000 off/on-line edit suite, AVRs
3-77, 126Gb, Beta SP/DVCam decks
etc, Sanyo 220 video projector.

Real Time Video
The Arts and Media Centre
21 South Street

Reading RG1 4QU
Tel: 0118 901 5205
Fax: 0118 901 5206
email: info@real-time.org.uk
Website: www.real-time.org.uk
Clive Robertson
Real Time is an educational charity
specialising in Participatory Video
and Digital media. Real Time
organises Participatory Video projects
and productions, workshops,
professional training in Participatory
Video, advice and consultancy,
production and post production
training. Digital non linear
(Media100) and tape based (DV,S-
VHS,VHS) edit facilities are available
with reduced rates for non profit
work.

Sankofa Film and Video
Spectrum House
Unit K
32-34 Gordon House Road
London NW5 1LP
Tel: 020 7692 0393
Fax: 020 7485 2869
Maureen Blackwood, Johann
Insanally,
Film production and 16mm editing
facilities, training in film production
and scriptwriting, screenings.
Productions include: The Passion of
Remembrance, Perfect Image;
Dreaming Rivers; Looking for
Langston; Young Soul Rebels; In
between; A Family Called Abrew;
Des'ree EPK; Home Away From
Home; Father Sons; Unholy Ghosts;
Is it the design on the Wrapper? +
Vacuum

Screenwriters' Workshop
Suffolk House
1-8 Whitfield Place
London W1T 5JU
Tel: 0171 387 5511
Fax: 020 7387 5511
email: screenoffice@cw.com.net
Website: www.lsw.org.uk
Katherine Way
Run by writers, for writers, the SW
promotes contact between
screenwriters and producers, agents,
development executives and other
film and TV professionals through a
wide range of
seminars. Practical workshops
provide training in all aspects of the
screenwriting process. Membership is
open to anyone interested in writing
for film and TV and to anyone
working in these and related media.
Registered Charity No: 1052455

Sheffield Independent Film
5 Brown Street
Sheffield S1 2BS
Tel: 0114 272 0304
Fax: 0114 279 5225
email: admin.sif@workstation.org.uk
Gloria Ward
A resource base for independent film
and video-makers in the Sheffield
region. Regular training workshops
and courses; access to a range of film
and video equipment; technical and
administrative backup; office space
and rent-a-desk; regular screenings of
independent film and video

Signals Media Arts
Victoria Chambers
St Runwald Street
Colchester CO1 1HF
Tel: 01206 560255
Fax: 01206 369086
email: admin@signals.org.uk
Website: signals.org.uk
Audrey Droisen
Film video and multimedia
production centre and facility.
Services in training, production,
media education and equipment hire.
Productions include: Three Hours in
High Heels is Heaven (C4), Coloured
(Anglia TV), Cutting Up (C4);
Garden of Eve (Anglia TV) and Fork
in the Road

Swingbridge Video
Norden House
41 Stowell Street
Newcastle upon Tyne NE1 4YB
Tel/Fax: 0191 232 3762
email: Swingvid@aol.com
Contact: Hugh Kelly
A producer of both broadcast and
non-broadcast programmes,
including drama and documentary
formats and specialising in socially
purposeful and educational subjects.
Offers training and consultancy
services to public sector, community
and voluntary organisations. Also
provides a tape distribution service.
Productions include: White Lies; An
English Estate; Happy Hour; Where
Shall We Go?; Sparks; Set You Free;
Mean Streets and many more

Trilith
Corner Cottage, Brickyard Lane
Bourton, Gillingham
Dorset SP8 5PJ
Tel: 01747 840750/840727
Trevor Bailey, John Holman
Specialises in rural television and
video on community action, rural

issues and the outlook and experiences of country born people. Also works with organisations concerned with physical and mental disability and with youth issues. Produces own series of tapes, undertakes broadcast and tape commissions and gathers archive film in order to make it publicly available on video. Distributes own work nationally. Recent work includes broadcast feature and work with farmers and others whose lives revolve around a threatened livestock market, and a production scripted and acted by people with disabilities. Another project enables young people to make programmes for local radio

Valley and Vale Community Arts Ltd

The Valley and Vale Media Centre, Heol Dew, Sant
Betws
Mid Glamorgan CF32 8SU
Tel: 01656 729246/871911
Fax: 01656 729185/870507
Video production, training, distribution and exhibition. Open access workshop offering training to community groups in production/post-production, Hi8, digital, Betacam SP and VHS formats, with linear and non-linear (media 100) editing facilities

Vera Media

30-38 Dock Street
Leeds LS10 1JF
Tel: 0113 2428646
Fax: 0113 242 8739
email: vera@vera-media.co.uk
Website: www.vera-media.co.uk
Al Garthwaite, Catherine Mitchell
Video production - documentary, education, arts equality, public sector, health. Training (ESF/other) for women/mixed. Screenings. Participatory productions. Information resource. Runs membership organisation (NETWORKING) for women in film, video and television

Vivid

Birmingham's Centre for Media Arts ltd
Unit 311
The Big Peg
120 Vyse Street, Jewellery Quarter
Birmingham B18 6ND
Tel: 0121 233 4061
Fax: 0121 212 1784
email: info@vivid.org.uk
Website: www.vivid.org.uk

Yasmeen Baig-Clifford
Marian Hall, Pat Courtney, Glynis Powell (Co-ordinators)
Training, resources and support for artists and media practitioners at all levels. Facilities include 16mm film production, Beta SX, DV Cam, Hi8 video production

Welfare State International (WSI)

The Ellers
Ulverston
Cumbria LA12 0AA
Tel: 01229 581127
Fax: 01229 581232
A consortium of artists, musicians, engineers and performers. Film/video production, hire and exhibition. Output includes community feature films King Real and the Hoodlums (script Adrian Mitchell) and work for television. Titles include: Piranha Pond (Border TV), RTS Special Creativity Award; Ulverston Town Map, community video; Community Celebration, Multinational Course leading to Lantern Procession (video) and Rites of Passage publications include: The Dead Good Funerals Book available from WSI. Recent Northern Arts Fellowships and exhibitions include Nick May, artist and filmmaker

West Yorkshire Media Services

Hall Place Studios
3 Queen Square
Leeds LS2 813U
Tel: 0113 283 1906
Fax: 0113 283 1906
email: m.spadafora@lmu.ac.uk
Website: www.hallplacestudios.com
Maria Spadafora
18 month Certificate in Film and Video Production courses accredited by Leeds Metropolitan University. A free course that welcomes applications from women and people people from minorities. Other courses and projects as per programme offers a thourough grounding in all aspects of film and video production.

WFA

Media and Cultural Centre
9 Lucy Street
Manchester M15 4BX
Tel: 0161 848 9785
Fax: 0161 848 9783
email: wfa@timewarp.co.uk
Website: www.wfamedia.co.uk

Lisa Whitehead
Main areas of work include media access and training, including City and Guilds 770 National Certificate, with a full range of production, post-production and exhibition equipment and facilities for community, semi-professional and professional standards. Video production unit (BECTU). Distribution and sale of 16mm films and videos, booking and advice service, video access library. Cultural work, mixed media events. Bookshop/outreach work

ABBREVIATIONS

ABC
Association of Business Communicators

ABSA
Association of Business Sponsorship of the Arts

ACCS
Association for Cultural and Communication Studies

ACE
Arts Council of England/Ateliers du Cinéma Européen

ADAPT
Access for Disabled People to Arts Premises today

AEEU
Amalgamated Engineering and Electrical Union

AETC
Arts and Entertainment Training Council

AFC
Australian Film Commission

AFCI
Association of Film Commissioners International

AFECT
Advancement of Film Education Charitable Trust

AFI
American Film Institute/Australian Film Institute

AFM
American Film Market

AFVPA
Advertising Film and Videotape Producers' Association

AGICOA
Association de Gestion Internationale Collective des Oeuvres Audiovisuelles

AIM
All Industry Marketing for Cinema

AMCCS
Association for Media, Cultural and Communications Studies

AME
Association for Media Education

AMFIT
Association for Media Film and Television Studies in Higher and Further Education

AMPAS
Adcademy of Motion Picture Arts and Sciences (USA)

AMPS
Association of Motion Picture Sound

APC
Association of Professional Composers

APRS
The Professional Recording Association

AVEK
The Promotion Centre for Audio Visual Culture in Finland

BAFTA
British Academy of Film and Television Arts

BARB
Broadcasters' Audience Research Board

BASCA
British Academy of Songwriters, Composers and Authors

BATC
British Amateur Television Club

BBC
British Broadcasting Corporation

BBFC
British Board of Film Classification

BCS
British Cable Services

BECTU
Broadcasting Entertainment Cinematograph and Theatre Union

BFB
Black Film Bulletin

BFC
British Film Commission

BFFS
British Federation of Film Societies

BFI
British Film Institute

BIEM
Bureau Internationale des Sociétés gérant les Droits d'Enregistrement

BIPP
British Institute of Professional Photography

BKSTS
British Kinematograph Sound and Television Society

BNFVC
British National Film and Video Catalogue

BPI
British Phonographic Industry

BREMA
British Radio and Electronic Equipment Manufacturers' Association

BSAC
British Screen Advisory Council

BSC
British Society of Cinematiographers

Broadcasting Standards Commission

BSD
British Screen Development

BSkyB
British Sky Broadcasting

BSS
Broadcasting Support Services

BTDA
British Television Distributors Association

BUFVC
British Universities Film and Video Council

BVA
British Video Association

CAA
Cinema Advertising Association

CARTOON
European Association of Animation Film

CAVIAR
Cinema and Video Industry Audience Research

CD
Compact Disc

CDI
Compact Disc Interactive

CD ROM
Compact Disc

Read Only Memory

CEA
Cinematograph Exhibitors' Association

CEPI
Co-ordination Européene des Producteurs Indépendantes

CFTF
Children's Film and Television
Foundation

CFU
Children's Film Unit

C4
Channel 4

CICCE
Comitédes Industries
Cinématographiques et
Audiovisuelles des Communautés
Européenes et de l'Europe
Extracommunautaire

CILECT
Centre Internationale de Liaison des
Ecoles de Cinéma et de Télévision

CNN
Cable News Network

COI
Central Office of Information

CPBF
Campaign for Press and Broadcasting
Freedom

CTA
Cable Television Association/

Cinema Theatre Association

CTBF
Cinema and Television Benevolent
Fund

DAT
Digital Audio Tape

DBC
Deaf Broadcasting Council

DCMS
Department for Culture Media and
Sport

DBS
Direct Broadcasting by Satellite

DFE
Department for Education

DFI
Danish Film Institute

DGGB
Directors' Guild of Great Britain

DTI
Department of Trade and Industry

DVI
Digital Video Interactive

DVD
Digital Versatile Disc

EAVE
European Audiovisual Entrepreneurs

EBU
European Broadcasting Union

ECF
European Co-Production Fund

EDI
Euopaaisches Dokumentarfilm
Institut/Entertainment Data
International

EFA
European Film Academy

EFCOM
European Film Commissioners

EFDO
European Film Distribution Office

EGAKU
European Committee of Trade
Unions in Arts, Mass Media and
Entertainment

EIM
European Institute for the Media

EITF
Edinburgh International Television
Festival

EMG
Euro Media Garanties

ENG
Electronic News Gathering

EU
European Union

EUTELSAT
European Telecommunications
Satellite Organisation

FAA
Film Artistes' Association

FACT
Federation Against Copyright Theft

FAME
Film Archive Management and
Entertainment

FBU
Federation of Broadcasting Unions

FEITIS
Fédération Européene des Industries
Techniques de l'Image et du Son

FEMIS
Institut de Formation et
d'Enseignement pour les Métiers de
l'Unage et du Son

FEPACI
Fédération Pan-Africain des Cinéastes

FESPACO
Festivale Pan-Africain des Cinémas de
Ougadougou

FEU
Federation of Entertainment Unions

FIA
International Federation of Actors

FIAD
Fédération Internationale des
Associations de Distributeurs de Films

FIAF

Fédération Internaionale des Archives
du Film

FIAPF
International Federation of Film
Producers Associations

FIAT
Fédération Internationale des
Archives de Télévision

FICC
Fédération Internationale des Ciné-
Clubs

FIFREC
International Film and Student
Directors Festival

FIPFI
Fédération Internationale des
Producteurs de Films Indépendants

FIPRESCI
Fédération Internationale de la Presse
Cinématographique

FOCAL
Federation of Commercial Audio
Visual Libraries

FTVLCA
Film and Television Lighting
Contractors Association

FX
Effects/special effects

HBO
Home Box Office

HDTV
High Definition Television

HTV
Harlech Television

HVC
Home Video Channel

IABM
International Association of
Broadcasting Manufacturers

IAC
Institute of Amateur
Cinematographers

ICA
Institue of Contemporary Arts

IDATE
Insitut de l'Audiovisuel et des
Télécommunications en Europe

IFDA
Independent Film Distributors'
Association

IFFS
International Federation of Film
Societies (aka FICC)

IFPI
International Federation of the
Phonographic Industry

IFTA

International Federation of Television Archives (aka FIAT)

IIC
International Institute of Communications

ILR
Independent Local Radio

INR
Independent National Radio

IPA
Institute of Practitioners in Advertising

ISBA
Incorporated Society of British Advertising

ISETV
International Secretariat for Arts, Mass Media and Entertainment Trade Unions

ISM
Incorporated Society of Musicians

ITC
Independent Television Commission

ITN
Independent Television News

ITV
Independent Television

ITVA
Independent Television Association

IVCA
International Visual Communications Association

IVLA
International Visual Literacy Association

JICTAR
Joint Industries' Committee for Television Audience Research

LAB
London Arts Board

LFF
London Film Festival

LFVDA
London Film and Video Development Agency

LSW
London Screenwriters' Workshop

LVA
London Video Access

LWT
London Weekend Television

MBS
Media Business School

MCPS
Mechanical Copyright Protection Society

MEDIA
Mesures pour Encourager le Développement de l'Industrie Audiovisuelle

MENU
Media Education News Update

MFVPA
Music, Film and Video Producers' Association

MGM
Metro Goldwyn Mayer

MHMC
Mental Health Media Council

MIDEM
MarchéInternational du Disque et de l'Edition Musicale

MIFED
Mercato Internazionale del TV, film e del Documentario

MIPCOM
MarchéInternaional des Films et des Programmes pour la TV, la Vidéo, le C,ble et le Satellite

MIP-TV
MarchéInternational de Programmes de Télévision

MOMI
Museum of the Moving Image

MPA
Motion Picture Association of America

MPEAA
Motion Picture Export Association of American

MU
Musicians' Union

NAHEFV
National Association for Higher Education in Film and Video

NAVAL
National Audio Visual Aids Library

NCA
National Campaign for the Arts

NCC
National Cinema Centre

NCET
National Council for Educational Technology

NCVQ
National Council for Vocational Qualifications

NFDF
National Film Development Fund

NFT
National Film Theatre

NFTC
National Film Trustee Company

NFTS
National Film and Television School

NFTVA
National Film and Television Archive

NHMF
National Heritage Memorial Fund

NIFC
Northern Ireland Film Council

NMPFT
National Museum of Photography, Film and Television

NoW
Network of Workshops

NPA
New Producers Alliance

NSC
Northern Screen Commission

NTSC
National Television Standards Committee

NUJ
National Union of Journalists

NUT
National Union of Teachers

NVALA
National Viewers' and Listeners'Association

PACT
Producers Alliance for Cinema and Television

PAL
Programme Array Logic/

Phase Alternation Line

PPL
Phonographic Performance

PRS
Performing Right Society

RAB
Regional Arts Board

RETRA
Radio, Electrical and Television Retailers' Association

RFT
Regional Film Theatre

RTBF
Radio Television Belge de la CommunantéFranÁaise

RTS
Royal Television Society

S4C
Siandel Pedwar Cymru

S&S
Sight and Sound

SAC
Scottish Arts Council

SBFT
Scottish Broadcast & Film Training

SCALE
Small Countries Improve their
Audio-visual Level in Europe

SCTE
Society of Cable Television Engineers

SECAM
Séquentiel couleur , mémoire

SFA
Short Film Agency

SFC
Scottish Film Council

SFD
Society of Film Distributors

SFPF
Scottish Film Production Fund

SFX
Special Effects

SIFT
Summary of Information on Film
and Television

SMATV
Satellite Mater Antenna Television

SOURCES
Stimulating Outstanding Resources
for Creative European Scriptwriting

TVRO
Television receive-only

UA
United Artists

UCI
United Cinemas International

UIP
United International Pictures

UNESCO
United Nations Educational,
Scientific and Cultural Organisation

UNIC
Union International des Cinémas

URTI
Université Radiophonique et
Télévisuelle Internationale

VCPS
Video Copyright Protection Society

VCR
Video Cassette Recorder

VHS
Video Home System

VLV
Voice of the Listener and Viewer

WGGB
Writers' Guild of Great Britain

WTN
Worldwide Television News

WTVA
Wider Television Access

YTV
Yorkshire Television

INDEX

C

Index of advertisers